CENTRAL TWO ZERO SEVEN NINE

Out!

By
Paul Canning

Grosvenor House
Publishing Limited

This book is published by
Grosvenor House Publishing Ltd
Link House
140 The Broadway, Tolworth, Surrey, KT6 7HT.
www.grosvenorhousepublishing.co.uk

A CIP record for this book
is available from the British Library

ISBN 978-1-83975-507-1

Front cover montage of two images:

Left hand image of me wearing glasses – photography by Peter Goadby-Watt, Hitchin, Herts., February 2019.

Right hand image of a younger me – photography by the late Ian Gordon Sellars, Bromley, Kent, Summer 1987.

Back cover image of me as a 5-year-old schoolboy, Wallington, London Borough of Sutton, Autumn 1968.

Dedication

To my awesome children, George and Lauren – you're the best! To my gorgeous wife, Wendy – thank you for 30 plus years of pure happiness. This one's for all of you.

Love you. X

Acknowledgements

I would like to thank the following for their unwavering help and support over the years, without whom, this book would not have become a reality:

My awesome wife, Wendy, for reading and amending the never ending drafts, together with my two children, George and Lauren who have always stood by me; my two oldest friends Aly Baines and Simon Wallis; Derek Cooke – the most loyal friend, guaranteed to make me laugh; my mate Pete (Peter Goadby-Watt) – without whose steer and strong friendship, I would never have become a qualified instructor; my former colleague Allan Ardon Bayle, one of the most highly regarded fingerprint experts and forensic practitioners in the world – for introducing me to Susan Sutovic and Erica Duggan – two remarkable women whose sons were taken so cruelly and at such a young age; last but by no means least – Mick Gardiner, the 'founding father' of Gardiner Associates Training and Research and undoubtedly, the 'Daddy' of UK fire investigation. Mick, you have helped me more than you will ever know!

My heartfelt thanks go to you all!

Central Two Zero Seven Nine: Out

Contents

Introduction

Vinegar and Farts! ... that's how a former Metropolitan Police Inspector (and old school chum of my sister Kate) described the smell of a rotting corpse.

I was reminded of that description when I arrived at a mind-blowingly depressing, rundown estate in Harlesden, North West London in late February 1991. I was there to take forensic photographs of an unknown male suspicious death scene. I'd undergone an intense period of training over many months prior to this memorable event, including attending a variety of crime scenes and what was known as puppy-walking or shadowing with established, experienced forensic photographers. It was now only my second day of working solo, helping to evidence the mayhem and destruction carried out by London's darker side and visually document the aftermath of violence, death and other felonious activity in all its lack of glory.

I'd phoned in to our duty office from Kensington (known then by the Met Police identifying code 'BD'), to be given the details of this particular suspicious death scene from a very chirpy Principal Photographer John Cook. John ran our HQ duty office in Amelia Street, Elephant and Castle on a daily basis like a slick operation and with military precision. I got on with him very well indeed and would often pull his leg. Many a morning, I'd ring into the duty office with notebook poised, a good ten minutes before the rush started, to be greeted with, "Have you wet the bed?", to which I cheekily retorted, "No, I just couldn't wait to hear the sound of your voice, John!" John Cook would inevitably come back with, "Ooh you saucy boy!" Other times, I'd be met with, "Early bird catches the worm", or his familiar sing song voice whilst John pondered which job to give me, "La, da di, la da di...". During quiet periods between jobs, you'd hear the inevitable, "Have a cup of tea!" (John's signature catch phrase), or if it was approaching that time in the middle of the day, it would be, "Have some luncheon dear boy". If you were required to help out on another area and perhaps initially drive from

Kensington to be geographically closer to a range of jobs, for example to Kentish Town (Station code, 'EK'), you might hear, "EK, givusaring, bye!" – all rattled off the tongue very quickly indeed. In the knowledge that John inevitably had three other callers on hold and talking time would be limited, on hearing John's voice I'd usually quickly identify myself with my last name, which would correspond to 'Canning' on a magnetic block sitting somewhere on one of two, large, white-coloured scenes of crime jobs boards ready to be moved next to one of many assignments for that day. Thus, I used to say, "Hello John, Canning at BD". If John was in a good mood I sometimes heard "Hello John Canning at BD", repeated slowly several times, or if I had to phone back to clarify something I'd say, "It's Canning again", to which John would retort "That's a funny name, 'Canning Again'". And so the light hearted banter would continue in the same vain.

On this particular morning, having been connected to our esteemed Duty Officer, it was the customary "Ah, hello young Canning at BD. I've got a nice little job for you up the road in Harlesden...". John gave me the address, officer and station dealing and the fact that it was a 'BIP' (body was in position). He stamped the piece of paper he was holding with the next crime number on the sequential, numbered stamping device, which he read out to me. John then left me hanging on the phone, picked up the other three telephones in quick succession saying "Photographic, can you hold please!", before picking up my receiver again and ending our conversation with his customary and quite abrupt "Thankyoubye". Abrupt, understandably, because the other three phones were in all probability incoming and urgent jobs – hence the need for John to get shot of me.

Satnav wasn't around in the early '90s so I looked up the Harlesden address in my standard issue, hard backed London A-Z street atlas. Having found the location with no difficulty (made easier as there were two, marked police vehicles parked outside the address!), I parked up and looked up at the two-storey network of flats. The moment I opened the van door, the stench hit me like a brace of muck spreaders chucking out concentrated, liquid excrement and worse – I could taste it as it first enveloped my uvula, before latching on limpet-like at the back of my throat...the potent combination of vinegar and farts, the unmistakable stench of a multiple day-old, rotting corpse – the smell of death.

I slung my weighty camera bag housing Pentax 6x7 gear over my shoulder, picked up my blue flash box (containing several Metz 45 flash guns, cluster batteries and Quantum flash power pack) in my left hand and sturdy Manfrotto tripod in my right hand and proceeded to climb a flight of external, concrete stairs – all the while, the disgusting smell getting stronger, indicating that I was very close to the scene. I stepped out onto a communal walkway and could see police cordon tape up ahead flapping in the breeze. A couple of burly, male, uniformed police constables stood guard outside the deceased's address. I popped all the gear down and produced my ID. On clocking my details, the older of the two coppers made a note of my arrival time and I duly did the same in my notebook. I was then informed that the scene was no longer considered suspicious. CID and pathologist had been and gone. Death had been certified and the scene was no longer a crime scene.

Nevertheless, it was still necessary to make a visual recording of the address for the Coroner. The middle-aged gentleman had died of natural causes and was lying on the floor in the doorway leading from the living room to the kitchen. The police officers exchanged glances and then smiled at me almost mockingly with a nod and a wink, in between covering up their noses with a handkerchief. I delved into my camera bag for some plastic, tripod feet covers and PPE (personal protective equipment). After donning a disposable, white, all in one forensic suit (no hood back then), shoe covers and gloves, I took a couple of images of the exterior, then ventured inside. The smell was so overpowering that I had to step back outside again almost immediately – my sensory cue to put a mask on! Leading off a small entrance hall, which was caked in visible dirt and dust and which looked like it hadn't seen a paint brush in years, was the only bedroom – untidy and equally minging. Next to this was a bathroom painted in a pukey yellow. The sink was filthy, the cracked lino floor was sticky under foot and the bath resembled a farmyard pig trough. The toilet had seen better days and I spied prominent, dark tram lines on the 'porcelain chariot' below water level and several, brown-coloured splatter marks up the sides of the loo.

Adjacent to the bathroom, there was quite a modest living room, off which, I could see behind the sofa, was the kitchen. The living room also didn't fail to disappoint – dirty cream walls and ceiling, which could have been white many moons ago, peeling wall paper, rickety TV and video recorder perched on a cheap looking unit opposite the sofa, mould-covered window area adorned with equally uninspiring curtains and a dingy, dark red carpet, stained with food, booze – or was it faeces? I couldn't be certain. Several magazines were scattered on the floor by the knackered grey sofa and there were some open magazines on the sofa itself. I took all this dismal scene in – all the while trying to dodge half a dozen or so blow flies – ugly buggers that had already laid their eggs, which had become maggots, now feasting on the corpse that I was soon to photograph. Even with all the windows open, the flies had yet to find their way out. I peered over the sofa from the front and just as I was swiping away a fly for the umpteenth time, I spied the deceased lying face up with his legs apart, his head and upper body slumped in the living room and his belly and legs occupying a significant chunk of kitchen space. He was totally naked and the body was a manky black colour, which post-mortem, had swelled considerably. Death had occurred many days prior to my visit. I stepped back into the relative comfort of the living room and I glanced down again to some of the open magazines on the sofa. It was then that the penny dropped. I found myself looking at images of bare-breasted young women. In fact, the photographs left nothing to the imagination. The models posing erotically for someone else's camera were totally naked and in very suggestive positions indeed with and without sex toys! All the magazines in the living room were of the pornographic variety and it transpired that the deceased, whilst having a 'J. Arthur' (J. Arthur Rank being cockney rhyming slang for masturbating) on the sofa, either pre or post ejaculation, had felt unwell and tried to make it to the kitchen for a glass of water and medication, but unfortunately had probably suffered a massive heart attack en route. Poor bastard.

This flat was in a shit state, but all thoughts of that had to be brushed aside as I planned my shots to tell the story of events. Having photographed the front entrance from the exterior looking into the hallway, I then covered the hallway, bedroom and bathroom with the wide-angle lens, before starting on the living room. Each image linked into the previous one by including an element that was shown in the last image, to enable the viewer to more easily relate to the scene. With shots depicting the deceased full length and in close up (face), then re-establishing the scene for the viewer by showing the view of the kitchen from the head of the body, all that was left for me to do was to photograph the kitchen from the other side of the body and to finish by looking from the kitchen back out into the living room, including the body with the feet closest to the camera.

There was just one problem. I needed to climb over the deceased, who was in effect totally blocking the doorway. With camera bag slung over my shoulder, I picked up the camera-mounted tripod, which was quite heavy and then proceeded to step over the head and torso and into the gap created by the man's legs. No sooner had my right foot made contact with the kitchen lino floor, I started to slide and temporarily let go of the tripod. I lunged for it, but in so doing continued to slide, so that now I was almost doing the splits over a corpse. I had slid in bodily secretions and it was now me who had come to rest in a very uncompromising position indeed – straddling a dead body with my crotch a pubic hair's width away from making contact with - and possibly bursting - the bloated belly. I had visions of being showered with a stinky mess! I had saved the camera from mortal damage, but now I needed saving as I just couldn't get up. I called out to the two coppers outside. After an agonising wait, the older one popped his head round the door and when he saw me, he just creased up laughing. He disappeared to get his mate and the two of them stood behind me clearly having a good old giggle at my expense. Thank God there were no 'selfies' back then. After what seemed to be ages, both coppers pulled me up and I was able to complete the last shots and thus the assignment. Leaving all my soiled PPE in a bag for the coppers to dispose of, I was clocked out of the scene with the two police officers still chuckling. "Bet you won't forget this one in a hurry", I heard the older copper shout after me as I left that address in search of cleaner air and a change of scenery. Thereafter followed hundreds of different forensic jobs, all with their own set of circumstances and all requiring the story of events to be documented with my faithful Asahi Pentax 6x7.

Friday 13th to many people conjures up images of evil - witchcraft, banshees, vampires, werewolves, monsters and matters satanic. The combination of day and date is supposed to be synonymous with the unlucky.

In the early hours on this very date in September 1963 a baby boy reputedly with an enormous head, burst into the world voicing his objections for all to hear. The mother collapsed exhausted, thankful that the labour and excruciating pain was now in the past - the pain must have been torment, agony, because the new-born's father had said 'no!' to any form of pain relief. Why? Because he commanded so. This man, the father of the new-born with the big head was the family patriarch and nobody dared to cross him or vie for his power. It would be a few years before this male progeny, fuelled by anger and mistrust, would dare challenge his father's authoritarian rule. For now, the nightmare that constituted the childhood years was already starting to unfold.

That baby fated to be born to a medical doctor and a housewife in a Croydon maternity home was to be christened Paul Stratford Canning. I was born a bastard. The 'B' word still has a sting attached to it for me, although the world has moved on somewhat and no-one really gives two hoots today about old-fashioned views. From an early age I became follicly challenged, so I guess I became a bald-headed bastard. In middle age, I piled the weight on, so I naturally became a fat bastard and ended up a fat, bald-headed bastard! That aside, it's good to laugh at yourself for as we know, laughter is the best medicine.

However, the journey from cradle to landing my first job, onwards to Cruise Ship Photographer, then to Metropolitan Police Forensic Photographic Instructor and onwards still to NHS Medical Photographer has been a difficult, rocky and at times unsettling one. How I have survived with relative sanity intact and confidence renewed is nothing short of a bloody miracle. This is my story.................

PART 1

The School and College Years

CHAPTER 1

South to North

Looking back on my childhood years, painful memories come flooding in that tease, play and often torment a philosophical, analytical mind. I was a melancholy kid who lived in trepidation of a dictatorial, Dickensian father. Come to think of it, that's the biggest understatement I've ever made - it's almost pleasant. For God's sake, I was petrified of my Dad and often thought that one day he'd kill me. I was brought up amidst an atmosphere of shouting, door slamming, physical abuse and then, a house shrouded in silence, whilst my father sulked with me for days on end - by far the worse punishment.

Earliest thoughts are of bed-wetting and then, "Agh, naughty, dirty boy!" And so, in a seemingly never ending vicious circle I would be walloped repeatedly. Of course, it doesn't need intelligence to work out that when a healthy little boy wets the bed with alarming regularity, it might just be due to something more than a weak bladder. When I lost control of my water works, I was terrified and shaking. I knew only of a world devoid of sunshine, warmth and security. It is true to say that laughter and happiness were in short supply, but when they fell into my lap, I lunged at them like a starved lion felling its prey and then I nurtured them, letting the feeling wash over me, desperately trying to heal and mend. No sooner had these joyous feelings arrived, they were quickly kiboshed by my father's explosive and uncontrollable rage.

There was, however, momentary weekly respite. Every Saturday morning, my older sister Vicky and I used to leave our house (29 Ashcombe Road, Carshalton, Surrey) and cross the spacious park opposite to Hubbards the sweet shop. We'd both have an old sixpence to spend on moreish, sugar rich confectionery. Back in the late 1960s, with that tiny silver coin (equivalent to two and a half new pence in today's coinage, which will buy you diddly squat) you could fill a party bag to the brim with Fruit Salads, Black Jacks, Parma Violets, sherbet fountains and liquorice allsorts and still have a little change. I'd stand, awe-struck, with wide, longing, hungry eyes at the numerous, colourful jars that were brimming with temptation. On the way home, we'd run by the stream in the park if the weather was kind or play hide and seek around the 'old dungeon', which I believe was still in existence until recent years, although somewhat dilapidated through vandalism. It was situated at the Ashcombe Road end of the park. In autumn, the horse chestnut trees that lined both sides of the stream inevitably dropped and scattered a cornucopia of ripened delights and I would scour the ground for these shiny, brown conkers, as if seeking out treasure. Collectively, they seemed to be a talisman, a representation of hope, however small, of something bright for a future that seemed a long way off. In a childhood dominated by crying, wetting and sometimes shitting myself with fear, it takes much soul searching to retrieve and then dwell on the few happy thoughts that lie hidden on the back burner of a scarred mind.

What pleasant memories, if any, can I conjure up about the annual family holiday to Rathmullan, in Ireland's County Donegal? Me, a 1970's Dick Whittington, combing the sands, post regatta, for carelessly discarded coins once the traders and punters had moved on and oh - Auntie Bridie's home-made scones and soda bread, which were to die for! Ice-creams at nearby Ramelton and Letterkenny and my favourite, playing on the beach with my older sister Vicky at Faughan, a deserted haven, where I did experience fleeting happiness and which, for me, has always held an ethereal quality. I half remember the caravanning sorties to Ireland's remotest and most beautiful corners. Kerrykeal was a regular haunt and I remember as a mere lad wandering off in search of adventure, I pretended to be one of Enid Blyton's Famous Five, clutching my old, black, woollen dog Peter Dougal. In my infantile mind, Peter Dougal and I would fight the Leviathan and return to the caravan victorious. In reality, all that I ever found was an ornate, rusty, donkeys-years-old key whilst trespassing in some ruins. However, to my young imagination, this tiny key was symbolic of pirate skulduggery and had been dropped in haste by a careless cut-throat, anxious to sequester his contraband and still make his escape on the skull and crossbones before the ebb of the tide.

There were endless visits to my father's cronies, frequenting the village hostelries like The White Harte, The Beachcomber and The Pier Hotel and watching inquisitively wondering why it was that my father talked louder with each slurp of golden liquid which he seemed to guzzle incessantly? To Dad, Rathmullan represented much more than his birthplace, he was obsessed with the place. Undoubtedly, his interest, or rather fascination, with this Donegal jewel went way beyond the boundaries of healthy nostalgia. No, each trip was a carte blanche excuse for him to get shit-faced drunk with his friends while showing off his wife and children to the locals. Pity - fatherly responsibilities and duties just kind of fell by the wayside.

It was here in Rathmullan that Dad's mother, my Grandmother Agnes Mary, (known by the family as 'Mama') ran the village shop. Domestically, she was the boss, a woman of incredible substance, of fearsome mien, who was by all accounts a 'cross me and you'll lose your bollocks' type of matriarch. My father was the youngest and the only boy amongst five older sisters: Bridget (Bridie), Mary, twins Kathleen and Sheila and Una. Reputedly, Mama ruled over her brood like Salem House's Mr Creakle, periodically flogging her 5 girls and wayward son with a big stick even when they weren't misbehaving - "that's in case you're about to be naughty" she would prematurely chastise. Hmm – maybe Mama Agnes Mary, God bless her soul, invented the department of pre-crime long before Tom Cruise's Minority Report was even conceptualised? For me, the tale of Mama chasing the six siblings around the kitchen table with a carving knife takes the biscuit. Mama may have had a leather-tough exterior, but I reckon she had a heart of gold.

Apparently, my paternal grandfather James Canning senior, was the complete contrast - laid back, quiet and gentle. When there was any trouble brewing, he would generally be found behind the sanctuary of his newspaper, smoking his pipe. He died in 1941 (22 years before I was born) during the Second World War and Mama Agnes Mary, the great Canning stalwart, passed away in September 1966, when I was barely three. How I would love to have known them both. When my father went to medical school in 1941 at University College Dublin (UCD), money was a sought-after commodity, often being rarer than an ice cube in the Sahara. It appears that Mama channelled what little funds were available to send her only son through medical school at the cost of the five sisters having an inferior quality education. In my opinion, this single action was the start of a lifetime of second-generation family enmity, the ripple effect of which has been far reaching. If Agnes Mary Canning had known what a tyrant her only son had become, she would turn in her grave, for speaking from bitter experience, Mama did indeed raise a blaggard!

I couldn't go back to Rathmullan, or indeed any part of Ireland, for many years because our infamous last family holiday in the summer of 1982 turned out to be a terrifying, traumatic event, unsurpassed. Dad was drunk and in a rage for the duration of the so called vacation. It was a complete nightmare that rocked all of us to the core, so much so, that it took me a quarter of a century to set foot on Irish soil again! I just didn't feel like I could write or even talk about those terrible three weeks that we all languished across the water, so many years ago. The long passage of time, however, has helped the mental healing and the 1982 Irish debacle will be mentioned a little later on.

The malaise that was so inherent throughout my salad days can be singularly attributed to my father. Why he acted in the way he did, rubbing everyone up the wrong way, slagging off the successful, is sometimes beyond me. Maybe he felt inadequate for making a complete balls up of his life and so chose to take it out on everyone else. I can see now that my wicked father's actions directly affected my childhood and adolescent behaviour. Whereas many of today's daredevils are into extreme sports, when I was little I was generally into extreme naughtiness! At five, I was playing with the next-door neighbour's umbrella and for whatever reason bounced up and down on it repeatedly and broke it. My father turned scarlet with fury, slapping me for what seemed like ages and shouting, so the entire neighbourhood could hear, "What do you say to Mr. Hopkins!!!?", to which I sobbed, "Sorry, Mr. Hopkins". Dad retorted, bellowing in characteristically maniacal style "Now gedubtabed!!" I didn't need to be told twice as I raced up to my room, cascading tears on the stairs as I went, like blood spurting from an adrenaline-charged stabbing victim, desperate to escape the clutches of their evil perpetrator.

Another time, I screwed up, scribbled on and subsequently ruined reams of my father's typing paper, for which I again remember bracing myself for another walloping. In a separate event, en route to Ireland one year, my father suddenly stopped in a lay-by, opened the rear car doors of his Wolseley 1660 automatic and produced a riding crop. He whipped my sister and me repeatedly and in a scene reminiscent of his own childhood with Mama, he shouted "that's in case you do anything naughty". Years later, I found that riding crop behind Dad's study door and in a fit of rage I took a hack saw to it and threw the bits of leather over the railway embankment for the weeds to smother.

In the rear garden of 29 Ashcombe Road I remember a mysterious air-raid shelter. This second world war relic had stone steps in the middle of the lawn leading to a reinforced room below ground. I used to love playing down there until my father had the bright idea of filling in the steps area with garden rubbish. In my disappointment, I wanted to fill him in! On one occasion, Mum and Dad were entertaining and I managed to blag a box of matches from the kitchen, sneak out to the garden and promptly set fire to the old shelter. Farcically, I tried to put the small blaze out with cups of water in my ensuing panic. Fortunately, Mum, who had heard me whimpering, came to the rescue and extinguished what, through the eyes of a small child, had been a conflagration. The postscript from that little 'adventurette' was that, unbelievably, I escaped without a beating - a rarity.

On Guy Fawkes night, back in November 1968, I was punished once again for doing something inexcusable that escapes me now, probably writing on my bedroom wallpaper. I remember that evening very clearly as a small, frightened, five-year old, because retribution was swift, severe and torturous. I was locked in my room and left home alone to wet the bed, whilst my mother, father and Vicky went to the bonfire party without me. I'll never forget the dark sky suddenly bursting into a spectrum of colour, an awe-inspiring panoply of shape and pattern. As I knelt up at the window, staring into the wonderful beyond, a tiny, innocent lad of five, I cried and cried, bawling huge sobs. Tears of rejection, tears of insecurity, tears of loneliness and tears of anger. From that moment onwards, I feared for my tomorrows. That one despicable act by my father has been etched in my mind forever and goes some way to summing up this nasty little man.

My father used to answer the telephone in an abrupt, strict style, stretching both his lips in to one thin line as he'd prepare to give whoever called, merry hell. "Wallington 1-4-9-8" my father cursed through his dentures, to which came the sing-song reply from an eight-year old boy in my sister's class "she loves you, yeah, yeah, yeah...". I'm glad that I wasn't on the receiving end of that call, as Dad dispatched the innocent little boy with typical, swift diplomacy – "bugger off!!!" On one occasion I was hastily summoned to the living room and told to bend over, while my father proceeded to mete out a ceremonious flogging. I felt like a chastised cabin boy on Bligh's 'Bounty'...horrible times. All the while, my mother sat opposite, in complete silence, as witness to this outrage. Halfway through this awful punishment, I got up and started to walk away as I'd clearly had enough, at which point my father glared at me and scowled, "come back, I haven't finished yet". I felt so much anger towards this vile man, who spent his entire life provoking discord and in the process, creating mayhem in the lives of others. Suffice to say that my youth was devoid of visible paternal love and hugs at a time when I so desperately craved the affection offered by normal fathers.

My first achievement that I can remember was as a five-year old, being presented at my nursery assembly with a pack of plasticine, a reward for coming first in a competition to make a steam train out of a toilet roll, card, drawing pins and cotton wool. My mother apparently did most of the work!

Several important events happened in 1969. My parents sent me to a strict, private school called 'Collingwood' situated in Wallington. My recollections of that school are, without exception, all bad. Back then it was an appalling place. Teaching and methodology were very much old school and corporal punishment was rife. In French classes we chanted out phonetically, parrot-fashion, numbers from one to ten: 'ern, der, twar, catra, sank, cease, sett, wheat, nerf and deace', tapping our regulation, black plimsolls on the polished wooden floor as we went. I was so chuffed that I could count in French, it was the pronunciation that was dire.

In the urinals, where you're supposed to aim straight, Brimelow (a classmate) urinated all over my leg for a dare. Naturally, I retaliated, only to get caught by a teacher and marched off to the head's study, for yes, you've guessed it, another leathering. In the film 'LA Confidential' a senior police officer who is riddled with corruption is seen by the new, young Lieutenant as the guy who always gets away with it and so the former is given a secret nickname 'Rollo Tomasi'. In my mind – that's my father! Ever since the urinal incident at Collingwood, all those years ago I've always believed myself to be the opposite, the guy who always gets caught, so have endeavoured never to be captured or compromised. Further, this probably in part explains why I always give 100% when I'm working, almost pushing it beyond the max.

School lunch was a compulsory affair with the choice of either fatty mince and vegetables or macaroni cheese, both of which had the appearance of pig swill, were an affront to the taste buds and reeked like vomit. You were ordered to eat your meal and you were watched, hawk-like, by venomous, hand-slapping, Flashmanesque prefects if you struggled. I always opted for the mince, but one lunchtime was offered up the macaroni by mistake. My protests fell on stony ground as I was made to eat that muck in between bouts of retching.

And like home, I sat there shaking, snivelling and willing the experience to go away.

In the May of 1969, my younger sister Kate was born. It was a joyous time for Vicky and me and one filled with nervous anticipation. I remember playing with Vicky by our favourite haunt, the dungeon, as we eagerly awaited the arrival of our new sibling. Then regimentally we were summoned indoors, where we all made such a fuss over this little baby. Even our cats Sirikit and Zarina (Siri and Zari for short), two gorgeous, pedigree, Seal point Siamese, jumped up onto the table, sniffing, meowing, peering into Kate's cot to give the happy, gurgling face the once over and the 'paws up', before standing as watchful sentinels over this precious new-born.

My parents met whilst my father was in medical general practice in Crusoe Road, Mitcham. My father was still married to Joan, his first wife and my mother was 18 at the time, a mere girl. The rest, as they say, is history and no bed of roses. From day one, my father weaved his wicked, manipulative spell and for most of her life with the blaggard, Mum was very much trodden on and treated like chattel.

Sadly, I felt that from the moment I came into this world, my father spurned and lost interest in me. I felt vilified for merely existing. Through my eyes, all his actions seemed repugnant and selfish - caring for no-one but himself. Could the man who provided the seed that fertilised the egg, which eventually grew into me, be so callous? From early on I guess that subconsciously I began my search for a surrogate father figure - someone who would be kind, strong and protective, but crucially someone I could love, respect and turn to in times of need.

Enter stage left...Henry Rickard Meyer, my maternal grandfather who was a kind, generous, witty and placid man. Born in Edward Street, Bath in 1906 he married my Grandma, Sylvia Lily, in 1935. My Grandad would turn his hand to most things, working in Parson's paint factory in Mitcham's Western Road and even cleaning aircraft at the old Croydon airport. When Grandad was called up in the early 1940s, he was posted to Blackheath, Abbey Wood and then the Orkneys, firing the big anti-aircraft guns to keep the 'Hun' at bay. At the close of the Second World War, my Grandad had fought for his King and country and rightly earned his Lance Bombardier stripe many times over, as well as the admiration of us all. On his 'Notification of Impending Release [from the Army]', dated 3rd January 1946, Grandad's superiors had written that his conduct was exemplary and he was, *"Reliable, conventional and trustworthy. Would prove invaluable in an administrative position, where his capacity for organisation could be used"*. I used to love the war stories which Grandma recalled with chilling and lucid accuracy. How you'd hold your breath when the bombs fell, counting in between the explosions and wondering if your number was up.

October 11th, 1940 saw yet another heavy bombing raid by the Germans. Along with many others across vulnerable target areas, the residents of Bruce Road, Mitcham took to their shelters. My Grandad, pre call-up, was 33 and my Grandma was 27 at the time and they quickly ushered my mum, then approaching 4 and my 9-month-old Uncle Graham into the Morrison shelter. Simultaneously, a few doors down, the Stringer family took to their air-raid shelter which was located in the cellar. By a cruel twist of fate, a bomb blew up not only the Stringer's house on the corner of Bruce Road and Inglemere Road, but also the water main, precipitating catastrophic consequences. The entire family, bar the old man who was down at 'the local' at the time, drowned and it was my brave grandad who helped to retrieve the bodies from that awful scene. It was particularly sad for my mum, who was only a few months younger than her best friend, little Shirley Stringer.

They were, like many others, killed needlessly and prematurely, so very young. They are now at peace and a poignant inscription beneath a large angel may be seen in the nearby London Road cemetery. Architecture of recent decades contrasts strongly with late nineteenth and early twentieth century buildings left intact, following the wave of Luftwaffe onslaughts. If you stop and look carefully, even today, you can see where the bombs fell all those years ago.

During the peace that followed, Grandad became a postman and continued his deliveries until his retirement early in 1972. He recalled two classic stories from his postman days. The first was when he told one lady "I've got some letters for you", to which she saucily replied in broad cockney "Oh that's alright love, just so long as they're not Frenchies". The second was from the First World War, circa 1916. An airman who had lost his bearings landed his bi plane on Mitcham's Figges Marsh. When a policeman ran up to the aircraft to check whether the pilot was friend or foe, the copper ended up giving the necessary directions and then helped to turn the plane around, so the cheeky pilot could affect his take-off. Grandad was a fascinated, nine-year-old onlooker at that time. To this day, I always think of my Grandad and that old plane landing on the marsh every time I'm in the vicinity of 'the ol' smoke' driving along London Road towards Grandma's humble dwelling, for old time's sake, or visiting their grave.

Grandad was the epitome of kindness, he exuded warmth and positivity. Jovial and humorous, he was a lovely, lovely man. I do miss him so much. God, I'd just like to give him a hug right now. My Grandad was typically equable and laid back but could equally be assertive. At six feet two, he was still striking, even in the winter of his life - he had real presence. Fondest images that float around my mind are of Grandad tending the fruit and vegetables in his nearby allotment, rolling his Boar's Head tobacco and reciting poetry. 'Harry' as my Grandad was called, had an enviable intellect and acuity. This was complemented by an engaging sense of humour. Recalling a few lines of verse, he would often change the odd word here and there to suit the occasion: -

"When the sun is sinking
And your mind from cares set free,
What a blessing, how refreshing
Is a cup of Sylvie's tea".

These lines I would later incorporate into my eulogy for my wonderful Grandma, Sylvie Meyer, following her passing in October 2006. Grandma made a great cup of tea right up until her death!

In August 1969, my father was offered the post of Medical Officer at the Department of Health and Social Security offices, Warbreck Hill, in Blackpool, just down the road from the famous local landmark, the water tower. We waved goodbye to Carshalton and ventured up north to George Formby country and settled in a four-bedroom dormer bungalow in Poulton-le-Fylde. It was a delightful village, not four miles from the famous tower and sea front and as it turned out, a couple of miles from one of George Formby's houses, 'Kirkstiles' on Singleton's Mains Lane.

Vicky and I joined the local Church of England primary, known locally as Sheaf Street School. I had just turned six in the mid-September and so joined Class 6 (year 1 in today's money) with Mrs. Gladys Etchells. Vicky, being two years and ten months my senior, was also three academic years ahead and so she started in Class 3. Kate, of course, was just a baby - not even four months old. Mum reckoned that within a week I had lost my southern accent, probably because I didn't want to stand out. Crucially, I couldn't read or write and was behind in most subjects. After an intensive remedial spell with Mrs. Wrightson, I soon caught up and that helping hand was very much down to the expertise of Mrs. Wrightson, Mrs. Etchells and headmaster, William Clarkson.

I loved my time at Poulton C. of E., my newfound friends, the teachers and the whole atmosphere. At Sheaf Street there was a strong sense of community belonging, which hitherto had been lacking in my life. For my seventh birthday, I received my first camera, a Kodak Instamatic, which Vicky still has in her possession. My year in Class 5 under the guidance of the somewhat austere Miss Cartwright, (I can still recall her in those hideous 1960's cat eye, winged spectacles) was memorable for two reasons. Firstly, my classmates and I made miniature Christmas trees out of 'Readers Digest' magazines. Secondly, I remember Steve S getting a right rollocking for forgetting his spelling book, to which he tearfully answered the teacher back with the immortal words "Spelling books don't walk, do they...No?!!!"

I moved into Class 4 (year 3 in today's terminology) with its wooden, Roman numeral clock, a prominent feature on one wall. Our new teacher was Vera Pilkington who had just joined the teaching staff following on from strict, white-haired, Mrs. Danson's retirement. Mrs. Pilkington was very patient, very disciplined and very jovial. She commanded instant respect and seemed to understand the antics of ebullient schoolchildren far better than Miss Cartwright, who was a strict, zero tolerance, old-fashioned spinster. Mrs. Pilkington's older daughter, Sandra, was also in our class. Sandra was a good friend back then. She'd come to my parties; she didn't seem to mind being the only girl and she reciprocated by inviting me to her parties at number one Staining Rise. I once wrote Sandra a letter saying that she could have my sixpence pocket money. When Mum found out, I was mildly chastised. It was a sweet thing to do and I'm quite sure Mrs. Pilkington was fine about it. I turned eight in the autumn of 1971 and it was about this time that I was persuaded to take up piano lessons with Mrs Barton of Brockway, Poulton. I studied for a couple of years and obtained Grade 4. I remember a smiling piano teacher, cup of tea in hand, listening to me play 'Greensleeves', whilst all the while my body hid my awful finger work as I tinkled away at the ivories. Mrs Barton never found out and I never quite mastered the finger work. I soon lost interest, but retained a love of playing church hymns well into my twenties. It was also about this time too that Dad took me to Farnborough air show in Hampshire. The event was exciting, but the trip there and back by train was arduous and I remember it so well because I was plagued with diarrhoea!

Class 4 saw the addition of a new pupil who had moved up from Sandwich situated on the River Stour, south of Ramsgate in Kent. Whether it had something to do with my southern roots, or just pure coincidence, I know not, but this new kid promptly parked himself next to me and although I didn't know it then, Simon Wallis was to become a close friend and confidante for life. I believe that true friends are a rarity but my friendship with Si has endured the ups and downs of nearly fifty turbulent years. Simon is now a much admired and respected head teacher at a Lancashire primary school, a diamond bloke and I feel proud and extremely fortunate to have him as a dear friend.

Class 2 teacher, Mrs. Margaret Saxton, used to deliver story-time to Class 4 once a week. More than four decades on and I still remember how enthralled we all were with 'The Enid Blyton Book of Brownies'- the adventures of the not so naughty Hop, Skip and Jump and the mischievous three's search for their 'goodness' and subsequent rescue of Princess Peronel from the wicked Witch Green-Eyes. A book that has been out of print for many years, it took much internet time for me to track down an intrinsically priceless, mint, 1967 copy, which came from the States of all places. Years later I couldn't wait to read the Book of Brownies to my son George. The happy memories from more than four decades ago came crowding in. Come to think of it, I think I was more excited than George, but it was weird playing Mrs. Saxton's role in front of my son. When it came to the end of each chapter, I'd close the book and say, "Well that's where we'll have to leave it, until next time". In my mind all thirty Class 4 children of yesteryear sighed their mutual objection. In the present, all that was audible was the solitary yawn from my son as he settled down to sleep.

To me Grandad was the replacement father. The problem was I never saw enough of him. My grandparents lived in London, a faraway place that was inaccessible to a mere child of nine. In the interim, I yearned for a father figure closer to home. Alan Pitchers' influence as my Class 3 teacher was major and prevails to this day. A kind, smiling, gentle, but disciplined teacher, he had the knack of making learning fun and stories come alive. Classics like Sir H. Rider

Haggard's King Solomon's Mines and the 1912 epic The Lost World by Sir Arthur Conan Doyle - Mr. Pitchers would recall them from memory, always leaving us spellbound. He was my favourite teacher at primary school. Just before Christmas 2013, I bumped into him while I was working at Blackpool Victoria Hospital and seeing his warm smile and shaking his hand, it took me right back. Top bloke! Class 3 was also the year of nationwide power cuts. As a family, we'd play cards under small bulb lighting, which my father rigged up to a spare 12-volt car battery and my mother would make tea, coffee and cook on a large, Calor gas stove. It was also in Class 3 that Sue K. threw up all over the end of year reports and Steve stunk the class out with diarrhoea. I have this very clear image of an embarrassed young Steve trying to clear up by pushing all the excrement off his little wooden chair, with the ubiquitous, regulation paper towels. Unfortunately, all he succeeded in doing was wafting the stink around. In both cases, caretaker Mr. Hardman donned his wellies and handled the clear up operation with inevitable finesse.

When it was time to say goodbye to Class 3 in the summer of '73, I was naturally gutted. There was, however, a consolation. Many long days of the holiday followed filled with exciting playtime and great television like Mission Impossible, Hawaii-Five-O and The Streets of San Francisco. My heroes were Greg Morris (playing gadgets man Barney in Mission Impossible), Jack Lord (Steve 'Book 'm Danno, Murder One' McGarrett) from Hawaii-Five-O and Karl Malden and Michael (buddy boy) Douglas from The Streets of San Francisco. I also enjoyed re-runs of fifties railroad western series Casey Jones, sixties series The Invaders starring Roy Thinnes as architect David Vincent and sixties series The Mysteries of Edgar Wallace. I also had a penchant for John Wayne and Jimmy Stewart westerns and of course Clint Eastwood films. Then there was The High Chaparral and The Beverly Hillbillies, 'Probe' aka 'Search (Control)' with Hugh O'Brian, Doug McClure and Tony Franciosa, Warship featuring Donald Burton and The Persuaders starring Roger Moore and Tony Curtis. They all made for compulsive viewing. Mum recalled with humour me saying at the time that Moore and Curtis were always 'loving ladies'. I remember the cars – for Lord Brett Sinclair, it was 'an Aston for an Aristocrat' (Aston Martin DBS) and for Danny Wilde, a Ferrari Dino 246 GT! I relished the Hanna-Barbera US series Banana Splits with characters Fleegle, Bingo, Drooper and Snorky and cartoons like The Wacky Races, Tom and Jerry, Top Cat and Scooby Doo. Re-runs of Laurel and Hardy always made me laugh. Then, of course, there were Gerry and Sylvia Anderson's Thunderbirds, UFO (I used to own a 'Shado' Interceptor), Tom Brown's Schooldays based on the 1857 Etonian novel by Thomas Hughes, Here Come The Double Deckers, On the Buses (with Blakey's catch phrase 'I 'ate you Butler'), John Pertwee's Dr. Who, Catweazle, Robinson Crusoe, The White Horses, The Adventures of Black Beauty and The Flaxton Boys. Record Breakers with Roy Castle, Norris and Ross McWhirter was another firm favourite and not forgetting Crackerjack with Michael Aspel, Animal Magic with Johnny Morris and Blue Peter with Valerie Singleton, Peter Purvis and John Noakes. The dogs, Patch and Petra and the gorgeous Seal Point Siamese tom called Jason were adorable and yes, I did have my very own Blue Peter badge. I also had a Blue Peter sweater that Mum had painstakingly and cleverly knitted for me. The summer holidays were over too quickly.

Mrs. Saxton's Class 2 beckoned and so did the 'merit card system'. One merit card was awarded for every good piece of work and three got you a silver star that was stuck on a chart. At the end of each term, the child with the most stars won a prize. Then there were the numerous songs we practised for school concerts and parent events, such as the old Jamaican folk song, 'Mango Walk':

'My brother did-a tell me that you go mango walk,
You go mango walk, you go mango walk,
My brother did-a tell me that you go mango walk
And steal all the number 'leven'.

We also had Christmas dances in class 2 (Year 5) and class 1 (Year 6) with the Gay Gordons booming out of the old record player, boys and girls partnering up...forwards, backwards, one, two three! Vicky, Kate and I grew strong on Mum's meals – a weekly feast of alternating recipes that included steak pie with all the veggies; corned beef and salad (where you opened the tin of corned beef with a little key); liver, bacon and onions; fish fingers, chips and peas; sardines on toast and Mum's signature Sunday roast, with all the trimmings that included Yorkshire pudding to die for, the centre piece of which was a joint of 'silverside' from Kevin Barry, the butcher on Hardhorn Road, supplied with lumps of fat for the cooking. Dessert would either be warm apple pie and custard or trifle, made by pouring melted, flavoured jelly over trifle sponges and once set in the fridge, alternate layers of sliced bananas and custard would be poured on top, finished with a sprinkle of hundreds and thousands and all served with a generous pouring of double cream – bloody delicious! It takes me back to a time when seemingly a few coppers could buy you loads of sweets and chocolate even post decimalisation. I still remember many of the adverts of the seventies and eighties: "A chew, chew Toffee Crisp for only two and a half" and "A finger of Fudge is just enough to give your kids a treat...". It was a time when chocolate bars were bigger and cheaper and crisp packets were full to the brim instead of two thirds empty and when 'Snickers' were Marathons (although weirdly in late 2019, I read that they're reverting back to Marathon again (yippee). Who remembers fruit Spangles and when Starburst used to be Opel Fruits ("made to make your mouth water") and Aztec bars in the purple wrapper were Cadbury's answer to the Mars ("A Mars a day helps you work, rest and play")? There was even a time when you could buy both a 9p and an 18p bar of Milk Tray ("And all because the lady loves...").

In 1973 we had two narrow boat holidays on the Leeds and Liverpool Canal, taking a hire craft on each occasion from Bank Newton and cruising around the Yorkshire Dales. Highlights of both trips included Mum pushing the boat off from the moorings and then falling into an icy canal, then my father getting the narrow boat stuck, broadside (completely blocking the canal) and negotiating the famous Foulridge tunnel and both the three and five-rise locks at Bingley. The lock keeper took us through the five-rise, but we were very much on our own for the three-rise. I raced along the towpath, an energetic youth, with lock key dangling around my neck and windlass in hand to fill the first of these three locks. Somehow, I cocked up the process of filling then emptying and ended up completely draining the middle lock - so much for water conservation! Trying to get to sleep at night was quite an ordeal as it was bitterly cold for both holidays. Nevertheless, we got the boating bug and early in 1974, my father bought a spacious, fibreglass dinghy for our enjoyment on the nearby Lancaster Canal. He called it 'Jay' and Jay was bloody heavy for a ten-year-old to help lift on and off the Wolsley 1660's roof rack. The air would always be filled with swearing and I would dread this operation. Jay had two outboard motors, an 'Ocean Super-4' and a small 'Evinrude' as a back up. When not in use, the two motors were stored in the garage at home, mounted on a sturdy workbench. Once, when my parents were out, I started the motors up, just for devilment and then panicked as the garage filled with noxious fumes. I quickly opened the garage doors and open they stayed until I was quite sure there were no tell-tale signs of exhaust present to betray my misdemeanour – no thought for the carbon footprint in those days!

My father and I were out one weekend, cruising down the canal at the official four miles per hour, when suddenly and quite bizarrely, the Ocean outboard snapped a thick piece of wood it was bolted on to and quite literally jumped off the back of the dinghy and disappeared down into the murky water. My father ordered me to go and get help, so I ran along the towpath and flagged down the first cruiser that came into view. Hitching a lift with these good samaritans, I sat on the bow of this luxurious craft and as we rounded a corner, a most peculiar sight greeted us. My father had stripped off to his 'Jockey's' and was bobbing up and down trying to see whether he could feel the lost engine on the canal bottom! Jesus, what a dick! The potential danger was so obvious to me, but of course, I kept schtum because I was too frightened to say anything. Divers were called in and the outboard motor was eventually found, some three hundred meters away. It had made its journey in a circular motion, sucking in silt and muck, before eventually conking out. Shortly afterwards, Dad sold Jay and the two outboards and bought a small cruiser called 'Lady Gayle', which had a permanent mooring at Galgate marina, near Lancaster. Our cruising days aboard Lady Gayle came to an abrupt end when my father made himself dangerously ill through a particularly heavy boozing session. He and I were alone on the boat, moored up in what seemed to be the middle of nowhere. My father had been drinking heavily and I had to walk miles to find a telephone box in order to quickly summon my mother. My father's actions not only stymied our fun but were both selfish and dangerously irresponsible. For any child to have to endure such an ordeal would be trauma enough, but there was to be more unpleasantness to come – oh, yes, much more.

Lady Gayle was sold to pay for my father's runaway drinking debts and so our boating days were done, but we still visited the Lancaster Canal for regular tow path walks. Although the cruiser was no more, we had retained the chandlery and one of my great pastimes (which was pure oxygen and very liberating) was to help inexperienced boaters down the series of locks on the Glasson section of the canal. With lock key around my neck and confident gesticulations with my windlass, these boating virgins saw me as the lock keeper's son. By that stage I was certainly no boating neophyte, holding parity with any keeper as I could fill and empty a lock with ease. Appreciated for a job well done, these holiday makers would tip me fifty pence, sometimes even a crisp pound note, which in the mid '70s was a small fortune to a pre-pubescent. I don't think it was Mama Agnes Mary's inherited business acumen thrust to the fore, as my father always made out, it had more to do with an inherent yearning, an overwhelming sense of being empowered and feelings of responsibility, honesty, trust, praise and of course, the central theme of wanting to please others. Being tipped for a quality service wasn't confined to the waterways. One of my other penchants was riding up and down lifts, my favourite being at Forton Service Station on the M6 (now called Lancaster Forton Services). However, it was in a hotel in Lancaster, whilst riding the floors, that I was mistaken as a lift boy by two old ladies and tipped handsomely.

By ten, I had rabbit teeth (horse gnashers in John Lydon's terminology). My two front teeth protruded, but orthodontic opinion of the day declared that my mouth was the wrong shape for a metal brace. There was also another problem. Due to overcrowding, all four of my back teeth had to be extracted. I was still ten when Mum took me to the Princess Avenue clinic in Poulton, adjacent to my school. I have this horrible memory of being led through to the dentist's chair. One moment, some woman was reassuring me that there was nothing to get upset about, then suddenly from nowhere she slapped this huge, black, rubber mask over my face. I remember struggling and fighting in a desperate bid to get this hideous thing away from my face and at the same time smelling that foul anaesthetic gas, to which I would inevitably succumb. The room, its contents and all the people present span violently - then nothing. Mum said afterwards that I shouted when I went under and that every mother nervously awaiting their child's turn, exchanged worried glances.

I'd reached my final year of Junior School and I still couldn't swim. Mum had heard that local husband and wife teachers, Harry and Mae Bates, were opening up a beginner's class for older children at their swim school in nearby Hambleton. Kate had started swimming almost before she could walk and under Mae Bates' expert instruction, I was quickly up to speed and swimming long distance. I recall one infamous occasion whilst waiting for my lesson to start. I was typically mucking about and splashing everyone else. This was followed by an overconfident dive under water, only to discover on reaching the surface of the pool a very stern looking Mae giving me the eyeball! I beamed at my teacher and said sweetly, cheekily and with gusto ‘Hello Mrs Bates’. ‘Hello Paul’ came back Mae Bates’ now somewhat more mellow reply, fully aware that I’d won her over!

My father always did have a natural ability for languages, learning Latin in addition to his native Gaelic at school. He had learned German on and off for many years and he thought that I should too. He used to stand over me menacingly and drill in the workbook ‘Kontakte’. “Jesus, for the fifth time Paul: einzelzimmer - single room, doppelzimmer – double room!” I found it a struggle, especially as it was meted out in bullying tones. It all got too much once and I just burst into tears at which my father turned to my mother in mock surprise. “Jesus dulling, he’s having a little weep”. He would never say darling, it was a combination of dalling and dulling, which I always found odd and extremely irritating.

My father possessed an electric lawnmower with open blades and every summer, one of my jobs was to help mow the lawn and empty the grass box. in addition to undertaking compulsory, back-breaking digging and weeding, which I detested and which almost certainly laid the foundations for my discs slipping in later years. To empty the grass box I’d wear huge, oversized gardening gloves and carefully pick any clumps of grass from the blades. Aware of the danger, I would always ensure that my father wasn’t touching the controls. I was still ten in the summer of ’74 and looking forward to joining the top Class 1 in the autumn. The birds were singing and the weather was glorious as we set to on the back lawn. I certainly had no premonition of what was about to unfold. My father was still holding on to the controls, while I crouched down with gloved hands to pick, or rather waft, the surplus grass from the blades. Then, without warning, the mower started up and the menacing blades spun round. I got my left hand clear immediately, but I couldn’t free my right. I tugged and tugged, but the blades were still spinning inexorably, luring me to impending disaster. Suddenly, my hand broke free, the glove fell off and I winced as the searing pain made connection. My hand was covered in blood and I was shaking, whimpering pathetically. My father whined at me repeatedly “stop that crying”, he told me to ssshh so no-one would hear, pretending to care, as he ran my gashed fingers under the cold tap in the outside washroom. Once a bandage had been attached, I sought out the garden bench facing the little steps in the rockery and the flowerbeds beyond. I slumped down, defeated and demoralised. My hand throbbed and as I sat there in slow recuperation, I suddenly went blind. It was a bright summer’s day, but for what seemed like ages,

I could see only blackness and stars. The birdsong was no longer joyous, more a lament.

Years later, I realised that the temporary blindness was attributable to severe shock. The blade had clipped the bone of my right middle finger and torn up some flesh on the adjacent forefinger - I was extremely fortunate. My hand could so easily have been severed. Strangely, I wasn't taken to hospital for an injury that should really have been stitched. I was left nursing a grotesque scab and bruised fingers, which took an eternity to heal. Shock gave way to anger. Why had that lawnmower started up when it did? In my mind, I've revisited the scenario so many times. At very best I believe that my father was downright careless and at worst, I think he was overcome with malevolence, planning and carrying out the wicked deed on purpose to derive pleasure from being the only witness to my writhing pain. I've never been able to forget that incident - I don't think I ever could. The physical scars, although now very subtle, of that dreadful day are permanent, but the mental scars have been tortuous and run deep.

Crying inside, screaming inwards for help and struggling with confusion, I periodically went off the rails. My extreme behaviour was sporadic and unpredictable, biting classmates' noses or shouting at them for no reason at school, in effect taking my anger for my father out on innocent bystanders. The kind of help I so desperately craved would not be forthcoming in my youth. Nobody, outside the immediate family, could ever have guessed that there were insurmountable problems at number 27 Victoria Road. Mum, my two sisters and I were locked in this bubble of despair and there just didn't seem to be any escape from this terrible situation. To the local community, my father was 'the good Doctor', the epitome of charm and humour. Behind closed domestic doors however, he ruled the roost with menace and stick beating violence. Make no mistake, that man was wicked and thoroughly unpleasant.

Between ten and eleven I was a kleptomaniac, another bi-product of an abusive and unhappy childhood. It began with loose change lying around. Undetectable, easy pickings. If it was visible, I'd have it away. I then graduated to stealing directly from my mother's purse and the missing amounts soon escalated. I narrowly escaped getting caught in the act by my father whilst stealing a five-pound note. When the missing fiver was realised, I was quizzed at length, especially by my mother. I vehemently denied everything and just lied and lied through my goofy teeth. I'd regularly spend the money on cream cakes from

Darlington's on the Breck and then undetected, I'd make my way to nearby St. Chad's Churchyard, hide behind a gravestone and then wolf the lot down, like a hungry pig. When a neighbour caught me with cream round my mouth, scoffing a sugary doughnut, I knew by her surprised expression that I'd be grassed up. Again, I lied my way out of trouble saying that I had simply spent accumulated pocket money. I sought solace in cakes, sweets and chocolate and the temporary sugar high experienced would just make me crave more. The stolen cash fed my habit. Instead of a flat stomach, photographs of me at ten and eleven show me as a slightly rotund kid with a wrinkled belly that at its worst, decades later expanded to a forty-three-inch waist with years of comfort eating. My thieving career culminated in my capture by an astute Mr. Harrison who owned the news agency on the Breck. I was caught putting a toy car in my pocket. After a severe bollocking, I dreaded my mother and father finding out. What the hell was I going to say to them? Unbelievably - and fortunately for me - Mr. Harrison kept the incident secret. Getting caught for stealing was enough to shake me to the core and as quickly as it had overwhelmed me, my kleptomania vanished.

Class 1 teacher, Mr. Hill, the deputy head and head of music guided me through my final year at Sheaf Street from September 1974 to July 1975. He was very much old school – strict, a shouter, consequently fearsome and a bit weird, with a droopy moustache, but he did possess a most engaging sense of humour. I decided from the outset that for my own survival I was going to have to get on with him or else! Members of the top class, as we were called, were each allocated a specific job. Gillian and Jennifer rang the school bell, whereas Simon was in charge of music stands and Adrian and the gang looked after the stacks of chairs in the hall. I remember the dinner ladies always gave them a little tip at Christmas, affectionately known as 'Chair Boys' pay'. Apart from getting Mr Hill's fags from Brimelows, the garage opposite (an act that would be completely illegal now), I can't remember what my specific job was.

Us Class 1 children, who were now ten going on eleven, also had the added responsibility of serving the lunchtime food to six younger children on our table. We all felt very important indeed. There was always a main course followed by dessert and whenever an unpopular dish was on the menu, mountains were left over. Mr. Clarkson would always rise from the staff dining table, following a tip-off from one of the dinner ladies (but somehow you all knew what was going to be said) and announce to the whole school "Now this is good food and it's not to be wasted!" Strangely Sheaf Street cabbage was always a favourite of mine. Everyone else, however, thought it was disgusting. My friend Roger Haslett (now an eminent Consultant Ophthalmic Surgeon) and I would regularly engage in cabbage eating competitions. These would only be conducted when the dessert was rice pudding, which nobody liked. If the sweet was Manchester tart, spotted dick or bananas and custard, then the cabbage would be eaten in moderation and the competition rain checked until the next time - for there was always a next time and cabbage, it seemed, was in plentiful supply. In addition to the great television programmes already mentioned, I enjoyed Dad's Army, Steptoe and Son, Some Mothers Do 'Ave 'Em, Are You Being Served?, It Ain't Half Hot Mum, re-runs of On The Buses, Planet of the Apes with Roddy McDowall and the 1973-4 series, The Magician, starring Bill Bixby as Anthony Blake. Bill Bixby went on to star as Dr David Banner in another TV favourite, the 1978-1982 series, The Incredible Hulk..." Don't make me angry Mr. McGee, you wouldn't like me when I'm angry!"

By coincidence, headmaster William Clarkson lived on our road, a few doors along. Occasionally, when the weather was inclement, he would give me a lift to school in his dark green, 1971 K-reg Ford Cortina with its olive-green upholstery. Mr. Clarkson had been born with only a stump for a right hand and it always used to amaze me how he'd drive that car normally, with no modifications to the controls. If you tendered a particularly good piece of work or performed well, Mr. Clarkson would give you a hug with his right arm and as an inquisitive child, you always noticed that peculiar right hand.

Under the terrible domestic regime, I was frightened, subdued and introverted. The anger I felt for my father was suppressed, which meant that occasionally there would be an eruption at school. As mentioned earlier, when I went through a phase of biting classmates' noses, nobody could possibly have suspected physical and mental cruelty at home as being the trigger for these defiant acts of bullying, which were in fact, a desperate cry for help. As I stood shaking with trepidation outside the headmaster's study, waiting for his return, I could think of only the impending punishment and my inherent unhappiness. Mr. Clarkson could not abide any form of bullying at his school. I trembled as he returned from lunch to his office, red faced and furious. I was made to bend over an armchair whilst he fetched a leather strap from one of the drawers in his desk. Suddenly, he told me to get up and, dangling the strap menacingly in front of my face, warned "this is what happens to bullies in my school" and promptly thrashed the now empty armchair. I started in fright. With one smack of the hand on my leg, it was all over quicker than a rat had time to scuttle up a drainpipe. Mr. Clarkson had shown great leniency that day. Why? Could he have intuitively felt that something was amiss or was it simply that in his eyes, a doctor's son should know better? I never did ask him. The strap was definitely a deterrent. Soon after my close shave, a young student teacher happened to be taking our class in Mr. Hill's absence, when in burst an irate headmaster wielding his instrument of punishment. Mr. Clarkson marched to the front and addressed a hushed class, firstly turning to a shocked teacher. "Now I'm sorry my dear if you find this upsetting, but someone in this room has been bullying!" We fidgeted in tremulous expectation and with that he brought the strap down so hard on the nearest empty desk that we all jumped in fright. Just when I was thinking, 'is it me he's after again?', Mr. Clarkson strode to the back of the class and yanked some poor lad up by the ear and out of the room and on to a certain thrashing.

Yes, corporal punishment existed, but it was only used rarely and when necessary. Mr. Clarkson was a very disciplined headmaster, but he was also kind, warm and funny. He was fundamentally passionate about his school, his staff and generations of young ones who ebbed and flowed through the gates of Hardhorn Road and Princess Avenue. He was totally committed to his profession and was well respected in the community. Above all, I admired him tremendously and remain convinced that I wouldn't have got where I am today without his expertise and guidance.

In Class 1, I sat my eleven plus exam for entrance to grammar school. Even to this day, I know that I ballsed the whole thing up, yet mysteriously I passed. Some years ago, Mum intimated that I was a borderline case, that I was expected to pass but the reality was that I probably didn't. I feel sure that Mr. Clarkson had a quiet word with the examiners and that as a result, my pass mark was expedited and I was 'helped through'. That single, unprovoked action sums up my old headmaster. Years later I so wanted to meet, thank and shake his left hand in appreciation for all that he did for not just me, but for so many children. Sadly, dear old William Clarkson, the epitome of the archetypal headmaster of yesterday, died before I got around to seeing him. Mr. Clarkson will always be remembered in my mind as a true Gent, an inspiration and for the positive impact he made on so many young people.

I happened upon my junior school reports recently. It was nostalgic looking at these tiny documents headed "Lancashire County Education Committee, C. of E. School, Poulton-Le-Fylde" Report Sheet. In July 1973 I obtained 'A's' in all subjects. The general comments ran as follows: 'Paul is a hardworking, determined boy. He applies himself diligently to all his work, performing equally satisfactorily in all subjects. Paul is a pleasant, well-mannered boy'. The report was signed by my teacher A.R. Pitchers and countersigned by W. Clarkson. The latter added the comment, 'A splendid report'. Mrs. Saxton wrote in July 1974 'Paul works hard and has obtained an excellent examination result. His year's work too has been very good and he makes some excellent contributions to oral lessons. He is a well-mannered boy and a pleasant, helpful member of the class. Well done, Paul!' Yeah, ha...my father had bullied, bellowed and thrashed good manners into me!

The good reports, however, shrouded the sadness within. I was so happy at Sheaf Street School and beside myself when it was time to move on in the summer of 1975. The grass seed had yet to spring up in the newly excavated and much extended school field. I would miss the autumn trips to St. Chad's Church, bearing Harvest Festival gifts for the sick and needy. And lovely Mrs. Medcalfe, the school secretary, who was a mother to us all. Never again would I play the football game 'three and in' with the likes of talented Pete Smith and Andy Lowe, or tease the girls whilst they lined up to take their turn on the big skipping rope, or playing ball games chanting:

"Queenie o' Coco, who's got the ball-o
See I haven't got it
See I haven't got it, it isn't in my pocket..."

Or the endless games of dodging the blue-coated dinner ladies, Mrs. Warsaw, Mrs. Bunce, Mrs. Speight, Mrs. Lucas, Mrs. Barlow and Mrs. Bickerdike. My pal Simon fondly likes to keep me reminded of the games of kiss chase we all played on the small school field. Somehow, I'd always end up with Heather 'milkmaid' or kicking Sue and Claire under the table in class.

On the eleventh day of July, I took my little blue autograph book in to school for teachers and pupils to sign. Reading some of the comments takes me back to innocent days, cherished memories of another time that will never fade. Stuart M. wrote 'YY UR, YYUB, IC UR, YY 4 ME'. The vicar's daughter, Felicity, wrote 'U R 2 Good 2

B 4 got 10'- kind sentiments. Maybe I wasn't such a naughty boy, as my father would have us believe after all. The chair boy king, Adrian, penned 'Top of the pops door man and part time Superman, thank you', whereas Wendy H. wrote '2 in a car, 2 little kisses, 2 weeks later, Mr. and Mrs', which I always thought was very daring. God only knows what some of today's ten- and eleven-year olds would write!

Just as my sister Vicky had done before me, I asked Mr. Clarkson if I could read the lesson for final assembly on the last day. After his address to the school, I would wait for Mr. Clarkson to turn to me and nod - the signal for me to start reading. It was a poignant moment and when I had finished my passage, the realisation hit me that I was leaving forever and that now it was indeed time to move on. I will always be indebted to Mr. Clarkson and all his staff for their guidance and teaching, for it was of the highest calibre. And of course, to my classmates, who not only helped to make my transition from the South to the North very quick and pain free, but they were all such wonderful friends. Where are they all now and what are they up to, I wonder? It would be great to see them all again.

CHAPTER 2

The Arnold School Years (1975-1982)

The former Arnold School (now Arnold King Edward Queen Mary School or AKS for short), was situated in Lytham Road and Arnold Avenue on the site of what is now the Armfield Academy (named after Blackpool and England soccer legend, the late Sir Jimmy Armfield), Blackpool. It was founded in 1896 and took its name from Dr. Thomas Arnold, the famous Rugby School headmaster. When I became a pupil in September 1975, it was an all boys' facility under the headship of the somewhat austere, but nevertheless gifted Scot, the late Cameron Cochrane.

I loathed any change, especially one as drastic as starting a new school. At Sheaf Street, I had a sense of belonging and importance in the top class which I didn't want to relinquish. On the first day of the autumn term, the start of the first year, I arrived nervous, lacking confidence and in a state of bereavement from missing my good times at junior school. It was all so very different and a complete shock. There was no getting away from it, the geography of the school environment, the overwhelming disposition, the teachers, the pupils, the routine and even the school uniform (white shirt with green and silver tie, black or dark grey trousers, black or dark grey socks and black shoes) - everything was so new and so much bigger.

I was told by a huge prefect (known as 'Tiny') who sported a black gown with red trim, to report to form 1-O, along the corridor and then take the stairs by room 'M'. No sooner had I taken my seat next to Simon and Andrew, who I'd been at Sheaf Street with, than in walked a stern looking man. Addressing us he shouted, "What do you do when a master enters the room?" Instantly all thirty odd boys scraped back their chairs, neatened their ties and new green blazers sporting the school crest and motto 'Honor Virtutis Premium' (honour is the reward of virtue) and stood up to attention. That was my introduction to Bill Roe - form master and biology teacher for the next five years. He was also a home brewer, fisherman, master of the catchphrase and someone whom I have always held in very high esteem. He was strict, but also very funny. When some lad had the temerity to burst in on one of his lessons without knocking Bill shouted, "Shut that door!", to which we all just cracked up laughing. Larry Grayson's saying from that era was legendary and we were quick on the uptake. Bill's response was equally funny "Ah yes, strictly hetero gentlemen, strictly hetero!" In my mind he was not only my mentor, but someone I looked up to and aspired to be like. He was a popular, wise, highly experienced and invaluable member of staff and by far had the most impact on me, which was positive, stabilising and lasts to this day.

However, we all dreaded Bill's biology tests and when one was due, he'd say "Right gentlemen, the next time I see you, I intend to find out what you know about the subject", which sent shivers down our spines. During the biology lesson in which the said test was due, loads of hands would shoot up in a vain effort to kill time and procrastinate the test. Bill Roe was no fool, he knew what we were up to and after five minutes of questions would come the inevitable, "Right gentlemen, exercise books - take this one down", at which point we all shat ourselves as simultaneously Terry, the lab technician, would emerge with Bill's mug of tea, containing two sugars. Having taken a satisfying sip of tea, this was followed by the immortal words "Ah yes, this'll sort the men from the boys". Other gems from the Bill Roe catch phrase anthology included:

- "Jesus wept"
- "Laddie, I once copped an essay entitled, 'The beauty of staring out of the window' - don't let history repeat itself"
- "You've got as much chance as doing [such and such] as a snowball has of trying to survive in hell"
- "Laddie, you've got a backbone, use it" (for a pupil leaning back on a chair)
- "What did your last nursemaid die of?"
- "Did it hell as like!"
- "Look at 'em, mugs alley - knowledge – ignorance" (sweeping a hand across the class) and if a bright pupil hadn't performed well
- "How the mighty hath fallen"
- Talking about plant toxins (e.g. foxglove, atropa belladonna aka 'Deadly Nightshade' and Giant Hogweed) if you accidentally ingested them "You would show your dislike of these by dying!"

- At exam time, questions about revision would always yield the advice "Start from the heading 'The Air' (the very first topic covered) and work your way forwards"

On that very first morning, Bill Roe took the register. We all had to state our full names. I was dreading my turn. "Paul Stratford Canning, sir", I said shakily. At the sound of Stratford, there were murmurings and giggles until Mr. Roe silenced the class once more. I had been given the middle name 'Stratford' after the brother of the eighteenth century English prime minister, George Canning and also after the actor, Stratford Johns. I had never liked it. Survival instincts kicked in and it became a priority to eliminate the source of ridicule. After that one humiliating incident, I had my middle name formally changed to James, my father's name, by deed poll and have regretted doing so ever since. My fellow classmates were just confirming what I already knew, that at the time 'Stratford' to 11-12 year old boys was a very odd name indeed.

I made friends slowly. Most of the lads each had two nicknames, a kind one and a derogatory, insulting one, designed to take the proverbial. The latter category included: 'Spring', 'Billy', 'Mr. Tungay', 'Custard', 'Bomber', 'Eddie Kidd', 'Veins', 'Big ears', 'Copper Knob', 'Cabbage fatty', 'Steed', 'Cannon', 'Plez', 'Os-Os', 'Weary' and 'Fat Nell'. Due to my buckteeth there was no shortage of nasty labels, which I had to endure. My names ranged from Rabbit, Goofy, Nyang- Nyang-Nyang and Lippy to Plug from The Beano comic. However, my kinder sobriquet was 'Cans', which stuck throughout Arnold. I was always getting into fights through over doing the piss-taking. I guess that I was asking to be whacked, repeatedly going up to a lad, invading his private space, holding eye contact for ages and then proceeding to mock him for his lisp. Bang - I was lucky to escape with a solitary smack in the face. Another lad's first and last names when reeled off the tongue quickly sounded like 'bollocks'. If I said it once, I wound him up a thousand times. Crack - another fist in the mouth and so it went on - one scrape over and then headlong into another one!

I wasn't happy at Arnold in the early years. I could just about cope with term time work, but when it came to some tests, I'd write out elaborate crib notes, balance them delicately on my shaking knees and cheat, because I had no confidence in my own ability. The February and summer exams were equally nightmarish. I couldn't retain the information and so my marks were consistently poor. I showed no flare for rugby or cricket and so was excluded from the rugger 'in crowd'. I believe that many teachers hated me, as I could often be disruptive in class and I sensed their disdain. Tony Clappison, my chemistry teacher, used to give Big Ears and me a lift to school every morning, during which we used to giggle inanely for the entire journey. Many teachers had their own desired form of corporal punishment, whether it be gym pump, ruler, or bare hand and so it was hardly surprising with our antics that we were gradually drifting towards a famous 'happy clappy hand sandwich' (you had to hold out your hand and he would bring his hand crashing down on top of yours) which hurt like hell. Lovely! The ultimate humiliation was for the punishment to be delivered publicly, in front of your peers. Looking back, even though I didn't like Clappison, I deserved a lot of what I got, acting foolishly the way I did. I'd wager the Canning factor was often the talk of the common room.

Puberty was hovering around the corner and the comparison of penis size inevitably occurred after games, whilst in the communal showers. We took the rip out of each other's sizes and the piss take at the time seemed incessant. Meanwhile, my ebullience and mood swings reflected the day to day domestic horror story - my increasing anger with my father, my unhappiness and my growing lack of confidence. I was heading off the rails and things were going from bad to worse. In the dinner queue one lunchtime, I cheekily shouted something at 'Tiny' the huge prefect, who had directed me to my form room on my first day. Thinking I'd got away with it, Tiny then strode up to me and smacked me in the face, instantly flooring me. All the other boys pointed and laughed at me, as I hastily picked myself up and got back in line. Tiny was an arsehole for gobbing me, but I guess that I asked for it.

Back in 1975, my dinner money was seventy-five pence a week, or fifteen pence a day. Most Mondays I'd blow half of it on 'mambos' and sweets from Earnie's milk float, which would emerge every morning break. The other half went during lunchtime at Ralph's ice cream van, where you'd hear the cockney Ralph shout, 'Get off me van, mind me wing mirror' and 'All out, all out, only smokey bacon flavour'. I'd often volunteer to go round and pick up all the discarded ice cream and lolly wrappers for Ralph, in return for a free ice cream at the end of lunch break because I was so hungry. On one occasion I was picked on by one of the older boys after being served by Ralph. This little shit walked up to me and firing a cap gun at point blank range, almost burst my eardrum. The pain was excruciating.

If I spent all my dinner money at the start of the week, I was faced with two choices - either starve at lunch time or borrow money from someone else. I normally opted for the latter and it was Wandsworth who was a couple of years my senior, whom I normally grovelled to when I was skint. The third former stipulated that payback with interest on the following Monday was a prerequisite. This meant that I was always in arrears. One Monday, I forgot to take that week's dinner money to school and tried to avoid a confrontation with Wandsworth, but he cornered me at morning break. When I told him that I didn't have his money, he kicked me with full force in the bollocks and I fell to the ground temporarily paralysed, clutching my genitalia in agony. Lesson learned, I never borrowed money at school again. The first year was like trying to win an already lost battle - one hurdle after the next in quick succession, knocking each one down in turn.

Dowding, May and Braxton were fifth formers. They were at that time also bullies. As I lined up for a maths lesson, they jostled me, threatened and then stabbed me in the shoulder with mathematical compasses. Badly shaken I was interviewed by Deputy Headmaster, Richard Rhodes and the next thing I knew, all three attackers had been marched up to the head's office and given 'six of the best' by Cameron Cochrane. Arthur Braxton reformed, took a leading role in school plays and with consummate performances under his belt, won back the respect of others, including myself. Tragically, some time after leaving school, he was killed in a climbing accident.

There were four 'houses': Pennington, Liston, Howarth and School. Most of the boarding pupils were members of School House. On a random selection, I became a member of Liston house, under the captaincy of swimming phenomenon and now successful solicitor John Taylor - a thoroughly decent guy. Arnold always offered a diverse range of sporting activities. The standard of tuition in most subjects was second to none, but I found one or two teachers wanting. A strong coaching influence came from rugby aces John Bevan and Sir Bill Beaumont, which boosted the school's already impressive credentials. If it wasn't competing on a north west or national platform, then the rugby team would be in Canada, New Zealand or elsewhere, winning trophies. There would also be regular inter-house competitions, which I tried my best to avoid. Whilst, by my own admission, I was crap at all sport except for cross-country running which I excelled at, I've always held a staunch belief that the more exposure children get to as many different sports as possible, then the better it will be for their all-round mental and physical development.

Halfway along the main corridor was a side corridor that led to the Memorial Hall. Generations of schoolchildren will remember singing the school hymn in there 'Now Thank We All Our God', or sitting their examinations with history head, the late, dear old Bernie Leather kicking off proceedings: "AEB maths, centre number two one four. Time – 09:30 begin". The numerous school plays and Gilbert and Sullivan musical productions under the skilful direction of Messrs Tomlinson (catch phrases: 'Button it boy!' and 'The organ is playing!') and Shenton (catch phrase: 'Altos, tenors and bases, 1.15pm, portacabin') were not only very popular and highly entertaining, but they were also pure quality.

Before you reached the hall, there was a laboratory just on the left. Back in the first year, now more than 4½ decades ago, I was in that room with the rest of my 1-O contemporaries on a Physics period with teacher Joe Holt. It was one of those lessons where the teacher is busy marking books and leaves the class to get on with set work. Predictably, I sat near the back, having a poor concentration span and my mind on anything but Physics. 'Veins' and I started mucking about with the taps, first twisting them and then folding them down onto the base of the sink. Inevitably, we turned on the water, with the objective of spraying the jacket of the unfortunate classmate who, sitting in front, made an ideal target. We took it in turns to turn the tap on a little more each time, alternating between this and pressing our hand over the tap, then suddenly letting go. With each attempt we managed to project the water spray a little further and all the time without Joe Holt even noticing. Veins held his hand tightly over the tap and I just thought, 'sod it' and went for it, turning the tap so far that it stuck in the open position. At that moment, Veins took his hand away and what happened next is indelibly etched into my memory. Things seemingly occurred in slow motion, everything just waiting for a catastrophe as we sat staring, opened mouthed. This enormous jet of water shot forwards and upwards with such force that it hit the ceiling above the front row of lads. We grappled with the tap frantically, but it wouldn't budge. The water jet was creeping further towards our Physics teacher. Suddenly Joe Holt leapt up and shouted "Oy!!" as water cascaded down on his open books, just as we managed to turn off the water supply. Joe Holt stormed out of class and fetched the gym pump. Fortunately, when he returned, he was in a calmer state and I believe the two of us managed to escape a beating as punishment was rapidly downgraded to a detention. For many years afterwards the water stain was still visible on the laboratory ceiling!

During some lunch hours, a group of us would play 'The Sweeney', a souped up version of hide and seek. Two lads would play Regan ('Shut it!') and Carter ('orwight guv?') and the rest of us would have a minute to get away and hide. The game was up when you got slapped on the shoulder with a resounding, "you're nicked!" The main aim was to avoid capture for the whole lunch period. One clever ploy was for two of us to hide in a toilet cubicle. Knowing that 'Regan' and 'Carter' would look underneath the bog doors, I pulled my strides down to make the whole thing look legit. Meanwhile, my partner in crime stood up, half crouching, half balancing on the bog lid behind me. Usually the stunt worked, if we didn't crack up laughing, and we'd survive being nicked.

I somehow managed to struggle through the trauma of first year blues. Games like 'The Sweeney' as a form of escapism certainly helped to temporarily alleviate my torment. Home life was dire, school life was unpalatable and I had a nasty feeling that things were coming to a head.

One of the lads in 1-O had a foreign penfriend with him in school for a time. For no apparent reason, one lunch hour another member of the form directed the penfriend and everybody's attention towards me. Pointing my way and speaking very slowly, so that the foreign visitor could understand, my devious classmate said, "he is a homosexual". Now lads of twelve are very impressionable and 1-O pupils collectively or individually were no exception. I was immediately ignored and frozen out of the group. It was a bastard card to play and the effect was devastating. I felt isolated, sickened inside, very unhappy, but overwhelmingly desperate - wondering just how the hell I was going to be re-accepted by my peers.

Within days of the homosexual incident, something magical happened. We were all hanging around outside the TV room (a tiered classroom resembling a miniature lecture theatre) shouting and generally misbehaving, waiting to go inside for another lesson. The door opened and a shortish, slightly rotund man in his 50s came out, temporarily abandoning his Latin students and peered at us disapprovingly over half-moon spectacles. Lieutenant Colonel Edward Jones, MBE, a hero of the World War 2 D-Day landings and then senior officer in charge of the school's Combined Cadet Force, stood there clearly incensed. "My two sixth form candidates are about to take their A-level, the most important examination of their lives and all you do is make an infernal din. Now please be quiet".

That little incident changed my life forever because Eddie Jones became the first of many impersonations that I would do of the Arnold School teachers and selected personalities. Although I frequently mimicked Colonel Jones, I always held him in very high regard and had the utmost respect for him. Men of such outstanding calibre are quite simply, a rarity. I tried out my 'Eddie Jones' on the class and it was a real hit. After that, I couldn't walk two paces without someone saying, "Ay Cans, give us an Eddie Jones". Overnight I had not only managed to unintentionally curry favour with the rest of 1-O, but by assuming the mask of another, I became for the duration of the impression, extroverted and the whole experience left me exuberant and inspired - feelings which had been hitherto alien to me. My confidence and self-esteem slowly began to increase. Perhaps more importantly, I was accepted at last as one of the lads. I was still, however, exceptionally immature, giggling through lessons, calling people names, shouting out as a dare and generally finding it difficult to curb my ebullience in class. On the Number 12 bus en route from school to Blackpool's Talbot Road bus station, I was being a complete dick pushing other lads around and generally being disruptive - actions that prompted my friend Simon's older brother, Tim, to casually get up from his seat, walk over to me and say, "if you do that again Canning, I'll hit you in the face".

On the television front, I became addicted to late night horror films from age 11. Christopher Lee's Dracula alongside Peter Cushing's Abraham Van Helsing or my two heroes reversing the good and bad roles in Frankenstein. I soaked it all up like a sponge. I began to emulate Vincent Price in such greats as:-

- The Abominable Dr. Phibes: "Nine murdered her, nine will die, nine eternities in doom!"
- In Cry of the Banshee: (Vincent Price as magistrate and maniacal witch hunter Lord Edward Whitman) "Margaret Donald, you were a kitchen maid in the house of the widow Rockby, who was burned as a witch this seven days. Heathen charms were found in your room, who gave them to you?"
- In Edgar Alan Poe's, The Pit and The Pendulum: (Price played the demented master of the torture chamber) "Isabella, why do you look so pale, does this place disturb you?"

- In Theatre of Blood: (Vincent Price as Edward Lionheart took revenge on the critics who doomed his acting career by subjecting each to a grisly Shakespearian death)

  From Troilus and Cressida…

  "Look Hector, how the sun begins to set;
  How ugly night comes breathing at his heels;
  Even with the vail and dark'ning of the sun,
  To close the day up, Hector's life is done".

The common denominator was the strong male characters occupying the lead roles. The central theme that I constantly identified with was power (which I yearned to have) and lack of power, or domination (reflecting my then situation as a child). Strangely, amidst an atmosphere of control and manipulation, I was allowed to stay up late and watch these films. The sinister character always represented my father and in my mind, films that portrayed the triumph of good over evil were important for me to focus on, so that I'd believe that my own situation wasn't totally hopeless, that there was a glimmer of light, however distant, however weak, after all. Horror films, which scared the shit out of me initially, also gave me my first taste of man's inhumanity to man (apart from my father), which of course I was to see in the '90s onwards, on a daily basis.

As the year wore on, I added one or two more teacher impersonations to my repertoire. I spent many hours reeling off Geography teacher Chas Ellis's 'The Fylde, physical and town' and 'blorn sand'.

Tall, very lean, dark haired and sporting tell-tale bow tie 'NPT' had joined the staff in September 1975 to teach Drama and English. The nickname of 'beanpole' seemed an obvious choice and catchphrases such as 'you stupid boy' and 'the organ is playing', made NPT fair game for mimicry. Another teacher, the late Ed Collins, taught Biology. He also had a nasty habit of giving pupils lines for the slightest misdemeanour. I was fortunate not to have him, for on the only occasion when he and I crossed paths, he came in to one of our lessons to invigilate in another's absence. I asked a classmate if I could borrow a ruler, when suddenly Ed Collins, sticking his chin out and pointing at me in characteristic pose shouted, "yoooo lad, you were talking - five sides of notes". "But Sir, I just…", "I saw your lips moving, therefore you were talking". What an injustice. There was no argument. However, the five sides of notes were downgraded to fifty lines - 'I must not talk in class'. Feeling cheeky and defiant, I drew fifty lines of varying lengths and set at different angles, almost pattern like across a sheet of paper and handed that to Collins instead. On submission, I was handed two hundred lines. I suppose that I was lucky to escape a Saturday morning detention. Mr. Groves, another senior member of the common room, had been given the nickname almost a generation before of comic strip caricature 'Billy Bean', so I homed in on his voice. Mr. Groves' wife, Gay, a lovely lady, reprimanded us one time whilst invigilating, but being so childish and disrespectful we just made fun of this poor woman. In that deep voice that I remember so well, I invented the following one-liner, "I gather you've been humiliating my wife, Gay Bean?". My 'Eddie Waring' ("Er rrugby league, up and under, three points for Kirklees but they've played their joker, so double it up to six") was another favourite on TV. 'It's a Knockout' was in its prime. Who could ever forget Jeux Sans Frontiers, the oversized costumes and of course Stuart Hall's laugh, which was pure quality. Nobody could have foreseen that years later Hall would tarnish all our childhood memories and be incarcerated for sexual crimes.

The first year at Arnold was at a close. Chris D. who had been knocked off his bicycle and seriously injured during the academic year, was thankfully making an excellent recovery. Now the heat wave of '76 beckoned. The long, hot summer of 1976 was just that, long and hot – sun and blue skies every day. That meant lots of great play time out on my bike, climbing every tree I could find and of course trespassing on the railway embankment in search of buried, old telegraph pole 'London Midland Scottish Railway (LMS)' red and white-coloured, porcelain insulator cups. I collected these by the dozen, they'd probably be worth something now. I also collected coins and 'PG Tips' playing cards.

In September 1976, the start of my second year, Arnold took girls for the first time in its history, with Shirley P literally being the initial senior school entrant and welcomed into the first year by headmaster Cameron Cochrane. The intakes were first formers and Lower Sixth. I became the lowest rung teenager that month and although puberty was just about upon me, the first-year girls at that time were just a mild irritation. However, along with the majority of boys in the school, I did have a crush on sixth former Karen Singleton who was a natural beauty. One could not fail to notice her. When

Nanette Newman's husband, Bryan Forbes, was filming International Velvet, starring Ryan O'Neal's daughter Tatum, the Arnold drama group were approached to form part of a crowd scene at Charnock Richard. Karen Singleton was part of that scene and when her photograph appeared in the Fylde newspaper The Evening Gazette, hundreds of lads' hearts instantly melted - mine included.

By the autumn of '76, I had been working illegally as a newspaper boy for almost two years. In the October, the news agency on The Breck was sold to Des Tweats, who arrived in a huge 1975 Citroen DS (the sort that used to rise up at the back when the car started up, thanks to its hydropneumatic self-levelling suspension) with his young family and Spencer, the old English sheep dog. Des was a very friendly, humorous and amenable guy and I not only loved my time working for him, but I liked and admired him. Of course, working as a paperboy, was an early form of escapism from my father's evil influence. I was to work with Des for the next seven and a half years.

The first three academic years, September 1975 to June 1978, passed by so painfully slowly. There were, however, one or two peaks which partly compensated for so many personal troughs and disasters. Second year English was brilliant because Arnold's sirdar, the great Eddie Jones, hero of the D-Day landings, holder of an MBE, Chevalier of the Order of Leopold 11 and the Croix de Guerre, taught us. The lessons were enjoyable and of course they also gave me the opportunity to study and perfect the Eddie Jones impersonation. On one occasion, Eddie was in mid-sentence reading Steinbeck's The Moon is Down to a hushed class, when suddenly from the other side of the door we heard an older boy shout at the top of his voice "Fat shit!". We sat there sniggering, but Colonel Jones, completely unflustered, was at the door in seconds. The lad had raced off down the corridor, but Eddie knowing who the culprit was anyway, summoned him back. In an infamous reprimand that must surely take pride of place in any book of schoolboy yarns and howlers, Eddie chastised, "Wandsworth - fat I may be, but shit I'm not!" Without batting an eyelid, the colonel then returned to the front of the class, picked up Steinbeck and just carried on reading. Eddie never lost his temper. He dealt with bad behaviour in a calm, firm, but measured way – perhaps as a result of making it through the Second World War, when many of his dear friends and comrades paid the ultimate sacrifice. I don't know about my contemporaries, but after that little incident, Colonel Jones won my respect for life - what a great man and one of life's 'salt of the earth' characters. I do so miss him. Wandsworth, in my view, had just been on the receiving end of poetic justice, not just for offending the great Colonel, but also for kicking me in the bollocks the previous year!

Denys Barber took us for French for the duration, as we made our transition from 1-O to 3-O. Short and slightly balding, he was affectionately nicknamed 'Pixie'. I look back with great fondness for a man who made French fun and comprehensible. Denys used to arrive in class sporting his trademark, brown, leather jacket and his opening catch phrase was always, "Bonjour mes eleves, asseyez vous". This would be followed by "Ooh Paul Canning, you've got nice hair, sign of a good upbringing - translate please, English to French". This would always make the class laugh and put us in a good mood for the day, so the atmosphere that Denys camped up and evoked was very conducive to student learning indeed. In the days before the techno revolution, we used to listen to old fashioned audio-visual tapes. I can still hear the introduction in my head…'Longmans Audio Visual French Stage 1 by Green and Company Limited.' Denys was invariably relaxed, kind, and praiseworthy. Above all, he was always smiling, jovial and extremely helpful. The hours spent under his tuition were of the highest quality and he did much to lift me out of frequent depression. His enthusiasm definitely rubbed off. Whilst he might have been a little short in stature, Denys stood head and shoulders above most teachers and I will always remember him as one of my all-time favourites. Little did I realise that, more than thirty years after leaving Arnold School, I'd run in to Denys and his wife Jean on a fairly regular basis, working in their award-winning voluntary capacity at Blackpool's Victoria Hospital. Both Denys and Jean are fantastic people and it's always great to meet them and catch up.

Sylvia Bamford (later, Parker) together with Gill Raby were in the early days placed in charge of the girls. On reading a modified school uniform list at the time, in addition to the standard green blazer, green blouses and green skirts, I noted with mild amusement that 'bottle green knickers' were de rigueur. I wondered whether impromptu checks were ever carried out by the above female staff and indeed if a punishment existed for non-conformists? Apparently, they were!

It was a miracle that I had not been expelled. I was in the third year and arguably the most immature pupil that Arnold had ever had the displeasure of teaching. NPT taught our form 3-O for English that year and I would do my best to duck and dive, weave and dodge his attention. Indeed, I was actually scared of him. NPT unsettled me.

He could be very authoritative and my worst nightmare was reading out loud to the class, as I had no self-confidence at all with large groups of people. I read out an essay once with shaking voice and the whole performance was met with scorn. Similarly, another essay - a marathon - was handed back with the following comments in red ink: 'This is the biggest load of cliché-ridden clap-trap that I have ever read in my life. Your mark is for quantity, not quality. 13/20.' Strangely, I both admired NPT and disliked him in equal measure back then. I was drawn to (and I guess a large part of me yearned for) the suave, self-assured, almost aristocratic image, which he portrayed in his consummate deliveries, but whenever I felt threatened by him I would mock him, big time, in a vain attempt to detract from my own inadequacies and miserable failings.

The era was dominated by Grease mania, bouffant hairdos, kipper ties, wide collars, flared trousers, (a hideous invention, as I'd always get oil from my bicycle chain on them – even wearing bicycle clips) high-heeled, wedge shoes, Abba and Bjorn Borg. Amongst this there existed a man who somehow didn't quite fit in to the prevailing fashion trend of the times. One of the school's cleaners had a most peculiar face indeed, right out of a fairy tale. This cleaner sported a mane of golden hair and always donned purple drainpipe trousers and an ill-fitting green jacket. Never wanting to pass by an impersonation opportunity, this poor cleaner became known as Rip Van Winkle or just simply 'Ripvan' for short. One lunchtime, I lay in wait for Ripvan. As he entered the television room (our form room) with broom in hand, I leapt out like a deranged criminal from behind the cover of the front bench and lunged at him, grabbing the brush from his hand. Putting a pair of bicycle clips around my flares to mimic the cleaner's drainpipes, I hurriedly wrapped myself up in one of the huge, green curtains that adorned the room and began pretending to sweep, chanting maniacally, "The man who swept for twenty years and his name was Rip Van Winkle!!". So cruel.

Our poor lab technician had one arm shorter than the other and for reasons that only a seriously mixed up child could explain, I cruelly nicknamed him 'Pig'. This great chap came in for so much stick. Similarly, I repeated the 'Ripvan' show in a brazen piss take with teacher 'Fez' Parker, who vaguely resembled the late Bruce Forsyth at the time. Pretending not to notice Fez, I went into full flow, singing 'The Generation Game' theme song. Fez was, understandably, not impressed and striding up to me, he yanked on one of my pubescent sideboards which really hurt. Why was I not surprised? The whole charade had been completely unnecessary, the resulting chastisement more than justified. It was, after all, just another bollocking amongst hundreds. All Fez and his contemporaries could see was a disruptive schoolboy. What they could not have known was that I was sobbing with unhappiness inside and that these sporadic shenanigans were a repeated plea for help, which the Arnold staff room could not possibly hear. Even if my domestic plight was common knowledge, staff were ill equipped to help me during this era.

The fear of paternal reprisals far outweighed any punishment the school could inflict, so I once more put up and shut up.

Simon and I used to catch the Ribble Bus Service number 85 together from Poulton to Blackpool and then change buses, picking up a number 12, which travelled along Lytham Road, via the promenade, stopping right outside the school. In the late '70s, Poulton Market Place was open to two-way traffic and Blackpool bound buses used to stop right outside St. Chad's Church. Well, every morning this rather obese lady would hoist herself on to the 85 and waddle to a seat. The temptation to say something was overwhelming. 'No don't Cans, please, ssh', Simon whispered to me. It was too late. Out it came, for everyone to hear. "I bet she likes her eggs and bacon!" The lady in question rightly scowled at me. I just sat there giggling, unrepentant. A short time later, things were hotting up and I took the piss out of my friend, Simon's dad, repeatedly. Sticking my finger in my mouth for a lollypop and flattening my hair back to create a sign of baldness, I jabbed at Si in Telly Savalas' Kojak style, "Who loves ya baby?" Simon, like so many of my contemporaries, was fed up with my incessant stupidity. I had, as the number 12 pulled into Talbot Road bus station, just over-stepped the mark. Gesticulating at my friend with the latest 'Commando' comic, I was on my umteenth 'Who loves ya baby?', when Si turned around and punched me in the face. The atmosphere instantly turned to one of hushed embarrassment. I was stunned more than hurt and shocked that my so-called friend could do such a thing. Who the hell was I kidding? Simon had been wound up until he could stand it no longer and had naturally snapped. I thoroughly deserved to be hit and looking back, I'm surprised he didn't hit me repeatedly right there on the bus station floor. I had been asking for it for ages. The joke of it was that Simon's father looked no more like Telly Savalas than I did.

Inevitably, the 'Kojak' incident resulted in us not talking to each other for a while and uncharacteristically, I used the time to take a stock of the situation. I think the mocking of fathers soon died a death, but seemingly lagging behind everyone else, I remained as ever, incredibly immature. In addition to my newspaper round and paid jobs for my father, I worked throughout the Queen's Jubilee summer of '77 in a local greenhouse, tomato picking. You'd crawl along on your hands and knees in the intense heat and humidity, eat one or two, mop the sweat off your brow, pick a couple and then eat some more. After a few hours, you'd have a break and help sort, grade and pack. This was good fun as it meant having quality interaction with the other lads. A laugh and plenty of jokes made the time, which in the greenhouse was so boring, fly by. After close of play each day, I'd cycle home to strange looks from passers by. They'd seen it in the UK a whole year before it aired on TV...The Incredible Hulk! I was covered from hair to feet in pungent, tomato plant dust, which always turned the bath water dark green and reeked the house out!

One August day that summer I was cycling around 'Mains 2' (the biggest paper round) when I stopped to pull out a tabloid for my first delivery and stared at the headline, stunned. 'The King is dead' was written in huge bold type on the front page. Surely not Prince Philip, but then he wasn't known as 'The King'. I read the small print only to discover that Elvis Aaron Presley had died 'The king of rock and roll', famed for his hip wiggling, shaky leg, stage presence and of course such mega hits as, Hound Dog, Suspicious Minds, Blue Suede Shoes, Love Me Tender and Are You Lonesome Tonight. He was only forty-two. I remember being very shocked at that time.

The only indirect contact I had with human death was as a nine-year old. Mr. Mellor, a lovely old boy who lived in the bungalow opposite had mysteriously parked his Triumph Toledo at an oblique angle, partially blocking our driveway. To expedite matters, my father went to investigate. When he returned, I eavesdropped on his conversation with Mum. Feeling unwell and in desperate need of his heart pills, poor Mr. Mellor had indeed parked in haste and fumbling for his house keys, had barely made it over the threshold of his abode, only to suffer a fatal coronary. "Oh, but he was very dead", said my blasé medical doctor father. Direct, almost daily contact with death in all its nastiness was to come for me much later.

By the end of the third year (year 9 in today's money) in the summer of 1978, we had to make 'our choices' for 'O' levels, which meant dropping some subjects. Looking back, nobody really advised me on the best subjects to take. Physics, Chemistry, Biology and Maths would form the core and everything else would slot in around them. Why? Because my father was pushing me down an avenue named medicine - shunting me towards a route that I was not interested in travelling, because I didn't want to be like him. So, just as like poles of a magnet repel, I felt repulsion.

September 1978 was the start of the fourth year. It was also the start of my academic 'annus horribilis'. Virtually everything bad happened in that year and this period of school life was when the train finally parted company with the rails. As a fifteen-year old, spotty, early adolescent, I went from having one crush on a girl to the next one, but without doing anything about it. There was Patricia, Angela and Sue, then Michelle and Philippa and so it went on - like Beautiful South's 'Song for Whoever'. In my mind I fancied them all, like crazy, 'from the bottom of my pencil case', but lacked sufficient courage to ask any of them out for fear of anger and ridicule in school and at home. In my father's eyes I was already useless (as he often told me) and the girls would probably have agreed with him and spurned me anyway. I just wasn't strong enough to stare yet more rejection in the face. To me, enforced celibacy was the only door open at that time. Cynics would probably have dismissed me as an out of control, emotional wreck, incapable of sustaining any kind of relationship. I just stood in the shadows, head bowed and miserable, letting the lads get on with it. Meanwhile, I felt the pangs of adolescent love almost suffocate me as strong feelings of desire eddied incessantly around my mind. I was rushing towards manhood, a complete dick head on the one hand and conversely, underneath, vulnerable and overly sensitive. I absolutely yearned for a girlfriend, but stood little chance of getting one under the prevailing climate. This period of my life was simply horrible.

During this fourth year, I fell into bad company and my schoolwork was sliding. I'd long endured the ascerbic criticism from one or two teachers on successive end of term reports, which made for uncomfortable reading. 'Winning on balance' seemed to be one of the kinder sentiments. Simon had left my form for another, 3B a year previously. That new class set up comprised, supposedly, all the weakest pupils in the old second year, namely 2-O, 2-M, 2-N and 2-L. I wished so very much that I had been part of 3B, because, knowing they had been given that label, everyone stuck two fingers up at the system, pulled together and went on to really achieve. It was the best move that Simon could have made - away from all the antics of 3-0.

On the last day of the Christmas term in 1978, just before assembly, a few of the lads sneaked over to the junior school for a clandestine drinking session down the 'Westover' cellars. I'd only just arrived and had downed barely a mouthful of Scotch, when guilt got the better of me and I decided that I'd better show my face at final assembly. The others stayed on. After assembly had finished, I made my way back to my form room to pick up my bag and en route suddenly froze. Striding down the corridor was the caretaker, who was frog-marching a clearly frightened Paul Willow to the deputy head's study. It was Willow who had enticed me to the illegal drink up. My heart beat faster as I wondered whether he'd talk. During the drink up, Billy, another participant, had not only combined scotch and vodka, but had consumed copious amounts, leaving him completely bladdered and incoherent. Unsure of what to do next, Willow panicked and instead of accompanying his classmate back home on the bus, Willow foolishly brought Billy back into the main school in a vain attempt at trying to sober up the highly intoxicated fourth former. With all staff and pupils supposedly present at final assembly, the body of the school resembled a Marie Celeste and so these two lads, one of whom was asleep, the other acting nervously, not to mention the stink of brewery about the place, must have stood out like the proverbial single, red poppy in a field of green to a suspicious caretaker. I had to find out whether or not I was in the clear. It transpired that Willow had cracked under the Deputy Head's interrogation, breaking the schoolboys' 'omerta'. Willow sang like a canary and in the process, grassed us all up. I went home shit scared, knowing that within days a letter from the headmaster would drop through the letterbox. I could intercept the post, but what good would that do? I had been found out, 'hoisted by my own petard' and would have to wait for the head's letter, detailing punishment.

Now it was headmaster Cameron Cochrane's way to make an individual stew for a while, prior to punishment. When his letter arrived, my parents went apeshit. The offence was certainly serious - I wagered that at best, punishment would either be four strokes of the cane or a week's suspension, or both. I dared not consider the worst option - expulsion. To his credit, my father was determined to get to the bottom of the matter immediately and not have this episode hanging over his family like the sword of Damocles. Cochrane's letter didn't mince words. I had been accused of being absent from final assembly and consuming a volume of alcohol on the school premises. Here was a glimmer of hope. There were witnesses - staff members who had not only seen me in the Memorial Hall, but who would testify that I was very much coherent. In particular, I knew that Denys

Barber had seen me during assembly and could vouch for my presence and sobriety. Before contacting Cochrane directly, my father phoned Denys, who confirmed seeing me that sinful morning. My wise old Junior School Head, William Clarkson, was also consulted for his esteemed opinion along with other members of the family. All agreed that my actions of popping across to the Junior School cellars during break for a couple of minutes and 'swallowing a small mouthful of scotch' (my own words at the time) amounted to nothing more than typical laddish behaviour - 'The little devil', William Clarkson chuckled. Although not my father's style, he was probably forced to eat a hefty slice of humble pie to Cochrane and apologise on my behalf for my misdemeanour as well as presenting the evidence. Whatever my father said to the Head did the trick, because Cochrane, probably in festive spirit, assured him that the culprits would merely receive a reprimand on the first day back after the holidays. With a history of heavy drinking under his belt, my father probably revelled in the momentary irony that his younger son, caught for a drinking offence, had taken the spotlight off himself. It was, however, only a moment and I was certainly no profligate son or chip off the old block. Fortunately, I've never been tempted down the road of incessant boozing...except for a while maybe, on cruise ships! More of that later.

The headmaster, true to his word, addressed us one by one on the first day of the new, 1979 spring term. Completely deflated, I stood before the Head, with my own head bowed, utterly ashamed. After the apologies were over, I vowed to myself that I would not be drawn into anything so stupid again. The realisation of how close I came to severe punishment hit me suddenly like a stroke of the cane that I was destined never to receive. My father's swift actions got us all off the hook. Not only would Billy and Willow have been expelled, but I would almost certainly have received my marching orders too!

Weeks later and in a fit of anger and depression, I decided to stay up late one night, shredding sheets of paper into hundreds of minute pieces. These then filled an entire carrier bag. Willow had done the same and together, one Friday, we smuggled our ammunition into school, waited until close of business and then made our way quickly and quietly to a first-floor classroom, which overlooked the sixth form centre and also looked down onto a small quadrangle. With no time to lose, Willow took up position at one end of the room and I did the same at the opposite end. Giggling, we both lifted up the sash windows and on a count of three, we simultaneously emptied our carrier bags full of paper on to the ground below. The sash windows were then hastily closed and the carrier bags stuffed into our pockets. Splitting up, we then dashed along the corridor, into the Physics labs and effected our escape.

Willow had completely vanished, but cheekily I exited school via the sixth form centre to survey our handiwork. The headmaster and a prefect were already gesticulating towards the new, recently carpeted, white paper courtyard. 'Goodbye sir, have a good weekend' I beamed at the Head. A clearly angry and scarlet-faced Mr. Cochrane briefly nodded my way in reply, before turning to the prefect and saying, 'I'll cane the person who's responsible for this mess'. I kept on going, not daring to look back, for like Lot's wife, I didn't fancy being turned into a pillar of salt, or indeed having to endure some other sufferance. Now you would have thought that I'd learned my lesson, but growing cockier by the day, Willow and I repeated the dare at the end of the following term, with hundreds of paper darts. Looking back on this episode, I shake my head in disbelief at the farcical, complete waste of time these pranks took up. But chucking paper out of windows or drinking whiskey down a cellar was positively mild compared with some of the shenanigans that others were doing – one poor lad was dangled upside down by his feet out of a first-floor window and another was shot in the arse with an air gun pellet, prompting a legendary lad's song, 'Who Shot Schuz?' Then, apparently, Willow allegedly sent a hearse round to the Headmaster's house via the 'Co-op' funeral service and had the effrontery to ask, "Do you do free stamps?" (in those days you could collect Co-op dividend stamps in a book and exchange the full books for vouchers to spend in store). And so it went on!

The February mock examinations held in 1979 were an early indicator of how well pupils were expected to do at 'O' level, which was to be in the summer of the following year and closing in rapidly. I went to pieces and scraped three passes out of the eight subjects. My ludicrous score of thirty odd percent for Chemistry was unacceptable. Pete 'Manny' Manson, one of the greatest teachers ever to walk this earth, called me in to the chemmy lab to tell me the bad news. "Paul" he said, "this result means that you're either thick or lazy, which is it?" I didn't like being called thick, so I told Manny that I had been lazy. I resat the exam a few days later, scraped a pass and vowed to myself that I was going to be successful at O-level – if only just to show Manny that I wasn't thick. Manny sat each thick pupil (of whom there were but a small handful) next to an intelligent one, so that the latter could gee up the former. Mark 'Mopps' was my coach. It was a great move from Manny. Mopps' enthusiasm was so infectious, I have to admit that some of it did spill over. Comments like 'tiddly pom', 'if I had a German test every day of my life, I'd be really pleased' and 'nice one' were all part of this studious, but genial classmate's character. The day Mopps' dad died, Mark came into school wearing a black tie. My hat was off to him for the dignified way he carried himself and the utter respect he publicly showed his late father. That took real guts – tremendous courage, especially from someone so young at what, barely fifteen? Good on you Mark!

Although I struggled like billio and by my own admission, I wasn't cut out to be a chemist, Manny Manson was very intelligent, a born wit, a consummate teacher and one of life's memorable characters. I can still see this learned, silver-grey haired man, donned in white lab coat in full flow, when abruptly the lesson was stopped, noticing that one or two of the lads had clearly not only zoned out but were staring out of the window. The object of the lads' gaze turned out to be a very pretty girl in figure-hugging white polo shirt and short, green gym skirt. As testosterone levels instantly exploded through the school roof, Manny declared to his class "Eyes left!" at which point we all ogled this poor girl, then just as quickly Manny said, "Eyes front!" as he picked up where he left off, somewhere in the middle of the periodic table. Can you imagine that happening today? Jesus – I shudder at the thought. Milliseconds later, Mopps farted loudly, the wooden benches seemingly amplifying his expelled wind, whereupon we all just cracked up laughing. Mopps, along with the rest of us, was still chuckling as Manny sent him out of class for the duration. Quality entertainment Mopps! Joking aside, as the memories come rushing in, I credit Mark with lifting my enthusiasm for chemistry – and ultimately for passing my chemistry 'O' level. Mark is now MD of his own civil engineering company based in east Lancashire – a top bloke indeed – Tiddly Pom!

There was a spate of mice appearing in school and dying prematurely. I was not involved at all - my cup was brimming over with problems and I didn't need to pop another paracetamol. Someone decided that these mice should be executed and via the grapevine I learned that one had already been reputedly gassed inside a pencil case in one of the labs. Another was flushed down the loo and its mate was put down the back of a piano, which was then played and the little creature was hammered to death. The biggest outrage, however, was an unconfirmed report that a mouse had been beheaded with a scalpel. As I tarried in my form room one lunchtime, I just knew that I would be questioned as in the eyes of many teachers, wherever Canning went trouble was fast on his heels. Sure enough, in marched NPT who immediately quizzed me accusatorily. "What do you know about this Canning?", as he reached inside the back of the piano and pulled out a recently, very much deceased mouse, by its tail. "Oh come, come Canning, what's this?", he said pointing at the dead mouse. "In the toilets too", he lamented "their poor little heads being flushed down the lavatory". It was NPT's staring face that did it. I just collapsed into laughter. He certainly did have a way with words, but over the mice incidents, I was innocent. NPT stormed out of the classroom to dispose of the dead mouse and report the matter to the Head. Later that afternoon, in marched a clearly irate Cameron Cochrane. A generation before, it would have actually been with cane in hand. After the lecture that was it - matter over. They never did find the guilty parties - but the lads, of course, knew.

Shortly after the February 1979 exams, I was sitting on my desk, staring aimlessly out into the corridor one lunchtime, idly swinging my legs to and fro and minding my own business. Classmate and hard case 'The Plez', (nicknamed due to his seemingly 'pleasant' nature.... or not?) suddenly squared up to me and said, "I hear you've been taking the piss out of my girlfriend". "What?" I replied incredulously. As I stared into his cold eyes, his right fist slammed into my mouth, Plez putting his full body weight behind the punch, sending me somersaulting backwards onto the floor. I didn't feel the other blows to my head and upper body, for the adrenaline rush had already kicked in. I had been wounded and the attack had been completely unprovoked. It was all lies. 'Cabbage fatty' had been shit-stirring and had just stitched me up big time. Plez, who was extremely sensitive to adverse comments about his girl, had been judge, jury and executioner. I had received The Plez' anger at its worst and as I cowered on the floor in a sad and sorry surrender waiting for my 'filling in' to end, I became aware of an agonising pain. Someone shouted, "Prefects are coming". Plez hurriedly left the room and as I picked myself up, I noticed the blood. I was covered in it! I had to get out of there fast, before any staff, or indeed the rapidly approaching prefects, arrived on scene. I retreated to a nearby toilet to clean up, survey the damage and take a stock of what had just happened. The left corner of my mouth had been cut open, but from what I could ascertain, all my teeth seemed to be intact. I couldn't possibly go back into class. I just didn't want the lads to see me. I was a pitiful sight and as I stared at my pathetic reflection in the toilet mirror, I realised that at that moment I had reached rock bottom. Surprisingly and perhaps perversely, I didn't blame the Plez at all – I actually really liked him. My outbursts in school had reached a crescendo and in many respects, Plez had silenced and knocked some sense into me (as well as the shit out of me), albeit for the wrong reasons. I was grateful to him for that. I took a back route up to Matron's office and made out that we had been larking around and that someone, unknown, had pushed me and that had caused me to lunge forward, biting into my lip. I was bundled into a taxi and when I arrived home, the doctor was called. I spun my family and the local GP the same story, which fortunately, they all swallowed. Coincidentally, that night I was struck down again, but this time it was by flu. I was off school for five days and as I fought the raging fever, a large scab formed over my mouth, forcing me to drink fluids via a straw. Back at school, the lads were nervous, including the Plez, convinced that severe damage had been inflicted and I was absent because of it. Everyone wondered what the final outcome would be. I never broke the schoolboy code of conduct by grassing up the Plez and so the staff never found out about the attack. It was because I was at an all-time low that I never confronted the little shit who put my face in line with Plez' fist. Cabbage Fatty should have considered himself very lucky not to have received the same fate - several retaliatory, full-force, smacks in the mouth, because by God, he deserved it!

My Sunday newspaper round, 'Mains 2', certainly offered a chance to escape the house and cycle for a couple of hours. My route took me out of Poulton along Garstang Road East and up to the traffic lights at Singleton, then down Poolfoot Lane and into Riverside and Wyre chalet parks, before returning back to the shop via Mains Lane and George Formby's old house. I still remember some of the house names - a Polish couple owned the aptly named 'Silesia', then there was 'Rookery Nook', 'The Moorings', 'Cooden' and 'The Nook'. Back in 1979, I could mark up the paper round from memory, I seldom needed the 'Huggler' (address book).

My father gave me his old cassette recorder and apart from Jim Croce with songs like 'New York's Not My Home', 'I'll Have to Say I'll Love You in a Song', 'Alabama Rain' and 'Lover's Cross', among the first music I ever bought was by Country and Western great, the late Don Williams. Classics such as 'You're my best friend', 'Living on Tulse time' and 'Rodeo Man', I'd hear over and over as the deep, dulcet tones played me lullabies and I'd escape the misery of the present. To me Don Williams represented a kind and loving father figure, the sort that every dejected, abused child yearned for. Don's music exuded such warmth and has always been a comfort to me. My Country and Western hero died on 8th September 2017 aged 77. Needless to say, it was a very sad day for me. In films, my all-time heroes were Clint Eastwood ('You don't listen, do-ya asshole?!') and Charles Bronson ("Only at the point of dyin'"). Their common denominator - tough and powerful!

From my home in Poulton-le-Fylde, you could easily reach the heart of the Lake District comfortably within the hour. I've been visiting this English gem for years, but truly fell in love with the place in my dross, fourth year. During the academic months, I actually did something positive. I joined the school's mountain club and quickly became hooked on the regular fell walks, which encompassed Lakeland's finest peaks. To escape the din of town life, to wander amidst awe-inspiring scenery, being surrounded by nature, has always been irresistible to me. I'm turned on by remote, picturesque scenery - mountains, lakes, tarns, cascading streams and 'a field or two of brighter green'. Cumbria has it all. From the time of my initial visit, I promised myself that someday I'd come back here. Standing on top of a mountain gazing at a beautiful vista below, gulping oodles of fresh air is sufficient to guarantee me an inspirational tonic and happiness. For me, to be at one with nature is to be at peace with myself - the whole experience is ethereal.

I've climbed all the well-known peaks, some more than once. My favourites have to be The Langdale Pikes (from west to east: Pike O'Stickle, Loft Crag, Harrison Stickle and Pavey Ark) ascending via the classic and very popular Dungeon Gyhll route, Pavey Ark (such a dominant feature with its characteristic diagonal traverse) Jack's Rake. Then there's the old Roman road at the top of High Street, ascending via Ill Bell and Thornthwaite Crag. Skiddaw, which retains a hawk eye on Keswick in the northern Lakes is another magnet. Scafell Pike, (England's highest mountain) Great Gable and Yewbarrow make for excellent hikes and stand at the head of Wastwater, England's deepest and arguably most inaccessible lake. Helvellyn, with it's infamous Striding Edge and Swirral Edge, and the neighbouring lower summit of Catstycam looking down on to Red Tarn are very enticing. Fairfield, Coniston Old Man and a cornucopia of smaller fells have an equal pull, but just to be there is a special and rewarding experience any visitor would feel compelled to repeat.

From an early age I have followed the careers of mountaineering phenomena Chris Bonington and Doug Scott, who became my climbing heroes, constantly pushing the envelope out further to the limits of their endurance to conquer most of the world's highest mountains. On November 21st 2018, my sister Vicky and I attended a lecture of theirs along with superb alpine climber Paul 'Tut' Braithwaite – three truly great icons of the mountaineering scene, at the Royal Geographical Society in Kensington. So many of their top climbing friends have been lost over the years - such greats as BBC cameraman Mick Burke, swept to his death during a snowstorm on Everest. Ian Clough, Dougal Haston, Joe Tasker, Peter Boardman and many more have fallen. Not one for heights, I have never rock climbed, but have stuck to rigorous fellwalking instead. However, these mountaineering icons have epitomised strength and courage and their exploits have helped lift and inspire me during the highs and lows of my chequered life.

Whilst I failed to kick arse academically during 'O' level years four and five, I did achieve on the outdoor front, gaining my Duke of Edinburgh bronze and silver awards (Gold came later). In addition to fellwalking, camping and cycling, I represented my school at cross-country running. The Arnold School cross-country course was a real tease as it involved running up and down a series of sand dunes before running past two rest homes (The Ormrod and Thursby on the outskirts of St. Annes-on-Sea) and then onto the beach for a level run back to the tram terminus at Starr Gate. If the dunes were dry, this was very bad news as you'd put one foot forward and slip two back!

Keen fell walker, skilled amateur photographer and Wadham College Oxford-educated, Andrew Bell, steered me successfully through Maths 'O' level. Equipped with slightly more than a hint of a northern accent, it was inevitable that Andrew would be added to my repertoire of staff impersonations – "Helloor…Or noor, you're here to wooerk - if you can't be prepared to wooerk, you can gedoutside now an' doo ya tie up!!" Equally, I had great respect for the late Ken 'Bubbles' Riding, who took me for Physics 'O'. My impersonation of him would always make reference to Ken's pet dislike: "If you've got red hair, write left-handed and play cricket - I'll kick your kneecaps in!"

When fourth form ended, I whistled through my teeth, relieved to see the back of a very bad year, during which, I had my face kicked in, failed exams left right and bloody centre and had come within an ace of being expelled. However, as a saving grace, I had joined the Naval section of the school's Combined Cadet Force in the third year. During my two-year stint I learned enough about balanced discipline, correct procedure and team work to set me up for life. Parading on a Friday afternoon was a prerequisite and I wore my uniform with pride. Pressed clothing, polished brass and shiny boots were a must. My blue shirt, navy tie and 'woolly-pully' were always immaculate. To reinforce the seven creases in my 'bell-bottoms' I ran a bar of dried soap along the lines inside of each trouser leg, weekly, ironing each crease with careful precision. My white belt was rigorously cleaned with liquid shoe polish and my beret, equally pristine, kept with regulation slant. CCF commanding officer Lt. Colonel Jones, my first impersonation, would make his address, "Parade, parade 'shun'!", after which there would be the familiar, "Standing easy everywhere, senior rates and N.C.O.'s carry on!"

I opted for several residential courses during my CCF years that were held at centres at opposite ends of the land, both steeped in Naval history. They included range firing at Barry Buddon camp near Rosyth and engineering on H.M.S. Rame Head in Portsmouth. The shooting course utilised GPMG's (general purpose machine guns), SLR's (self-loading rifles) and SMG's (sub machine guns). Targets were both inside and outdoors. The SLR was, however, the most commonly used and favoured firearm throughout the course. NCO (non-commissioned officer) 'Whiskey' had the unfortunate task of training around a score of reprobates who included yours truly. Donned in combat fatigues we were driven to the ranges, situated in the middle of bloody nowhere. On the first few mornings we'd been given all the health and safety lectures about fooling around with guns and correct procedure and had soon become adept at stripping, cleaning and reassembling the rifles.

Now as I assumed the prone position, rifle butt pressed well into the muscle of my right shoulder, ear defenders well down over my lugs, I was about to experience live fire. Everyone had taken their positions and as I waited for the command to shoot, I felt the adrenaline surge. Whiskey, nicknamed because of the colour of his hair, now stood behind and to my right at 4 o'clock. "A magazine of ten rounds - load!" I expertly attached the clip to the rifle. "A magazine of ten rounds, in your own time, fire!" At two hundred yards, the target was tiny, but I lined up the sight, squeezed the trigger and braced myself for the recoil, which my shoulder absorbed. Again and again I pulled the trigger and was just beginning to settle into things when Whiskey suddenly bellowed, "Cease firing now!" 'Shit', I thought, I'm sure I fired off only nine rounds. Surrounded by momentary silence, I squeezed the trigger one more time to get rid of the solitary round in the pipe. Bang! I was right - I had only fired the nine. Whiskey went apeshit. "Who the fuck was that?!", he bellowed. Still lying down, I turned gingerly towards the irate NCO and raised my hand. Whiskey marched up to me, barking "Keep that fucking rifle pointing down that fucking range!", as we had not yet made safe our weapons. I was crapping myself as Whiskey stared at me menacingly. "If ever you do that again, I'll get my fucking wife on you", was all that he said. It was legendary that Whiskey's other half was a fearsome twenty stone Mama, who had allegedly already squashed two regs (regular soldiers). Dying to laugh, I kept a straight face, but I knew I'd wallow in the piss take later, back at camp. My punishment for insubordination was a double two-hour shift, on the wrong side of midnight, patrolling the armoury. The downside was to be minimal shuteye that night. On the plus side, however, the NCOs had laid on fresh bread, a massive block of cheddar cheese and the most enormous catering sized pot of strawberry jam that I'd ever set eyes on. After all I was still only a boy. When I eventually crawled back to my pit at the ludicrous time of 4-30am, my bed had been completely stripped and my clothes and belongings hidden. I found the bed linen in the toilets and various items distributed throughout the mess. I made up the bed, zombie like and crawled in. No sooner had my head touched the pillow, there was a loud fracas and movement of bodies in the dark and my bed was suddenly upended. I was entombed - with a heavy wardrobe on either side, unable to move. I resigned myself to sleeping upside down, imprisoned until first light. I had learned another valuable lesson!

The language and terminology on these courses, as one might expect, was very colourful and so it didn't take me long to work out what a 'split arse' was! I loved the physical side of course work, especially the assault courses. The death slide (zip wire) was a winner as far as I was concerned. I'd tackle obstacle after obstacle and all the while some Geordie NCO would shout encouragingly, "Fuckin' c'morn lofty, orlmorst there, c'morn!" I loved the taste of independence away from my father's talons. The camaraderie and team spirit of every course was uplifting and like a drug fix,

I always went back for more. I looked up to my NCOs - they were real heroes. The mess food was of high quality. In Rosyth's canteen, I once discovered a huge, metal vat, which at the pull of a lever, seemingly dispensed an infinite supply of the most delicious custard I've ever tasted. Naturally, I'd be drawn back there for seconds and thirds.

One of my friends, Steve Mannion, twisted my arm to go on the engineering course in Portsmouth. With a mocking smile, Steve described the course venue to me, HMS Rame Head, as 'a floating crap 'eap'. The week was hard graft and at its conclusion, there was to be a written examination, with a pass mark of 50%. Bloody great, I thought, another exam! As fourth year pupils, we were two of the youngest in attendance. Many participants were in the throes of 'A' levels and already making their university choices. I was not looking forward to the course exam at all, but if I didn't stay up all night revising, failure, like the end result of most of my exams, would be guaranteed. I didn't care about the others - I was in competition with Steve, even though I knew I'd have no chance of even coming close to beating him. Steve was unquestionably gifted and arguably the most intelligent pupil in my year. Also good at sport, he excelled at karate and entered many tournaments. The sort of person who would have been successful at anything he turned his hand to, Steve is now a much in demand Consultant Orthopaedic Surgeon, who divides his time working at Blackpool Teaching Hospitals NHS Foundation Trust, Spire Fylde Coast Hospital and travelling to countries like Malawi, Laos and PNG, holding clinics, operating and teaching in extremely challenging conditions.

Effortlessly, Steve obtained something like 94%, which wasn't just the highest mark on the course, he'd beaten all those who were three years his academic senior. For someone who wrestled with anything academic, I was very content with my score of 78%, not just because I'd cleared yet another hurdle, but I had also unbelievably beaten one or two 'A' level students in the process myself. For me, this exam success was a taster of things to come. Rame Head was unexpectedly a complete surprise for me. I left Portsmouth on a high. As for my dissenters, they could stick that one in their pipes and smoke it!

My Combined Cadet Force experience at Arnold proved invaluable and without a doubt helped mould me into a better, more stable person. Taking the tiller of a modest sloop and cutting through the waters of the Firth of Forth with a vicious, Scottish wind in my face and sailing under the famous road and rail bridges, is a cherished memory. I'll also never forget the occasion when one of the nation's 'Four R' nuclear submarines - I forget which - (Renown, Revenge, Repulse and Revolution) docked in Rosyth for a refit, when I was on my second visit to the naval yard. The invitation of a guided tour was an opportunity of a lifetime and us lads relished it.

I was fourteen when I lit my first cigarette. My foray into smoking began on my first trip to Rosyth with a competition amongst the lads to see who would be first to smoke their ciggy down to the filter. Puffing away, I coughed and spluttered with each drag, which sent my head spinning. Naively, I inhaled too fast, shocked my system and broke out in a cold sweat. Consequently, I had to lie down for an hour to recover. I felt dire and vowed to myself that I'd never repeat the experience. However, my smoking career was to last for eleven years. In my early teens I'd raid my father's ashtrays, pinching his fag ends and when he switched to pipes, I'd take a packet of 'rizzlas', a box of matches and a small amount of discarded tobacco and hide in the bushes on the railway embankment at the bottom of the garden and enjoy a roll-up. I progressed to buying ten 'Number Six' on a fairly regular basis and remember how big and grown up it made me feel. I did enjoy the occasional cigar, but for whatever reason just decided to give up, thankfully, when I reached twenty-five.

Spotty, firing zits regularly at the bathroom mirror and staring sixteen in the face, I was still unattached and my parents kept pushing me towards this girl and that, but I kept resisting temptation and major aggravation. When finally I asked a girl out who went to Blackpool girls' school 'Elmslie' (long sinced demolished), my father immediately briefed me on courting etiquette. After his talk I felt silly and stupid about the forthcoming date. "Now when you escort her back home, don't forget to kiss her on the lips". I could have died. I was nervous enough already, embarrassed, completely lacking confidence and I didn't need the lecture. Nevertheless, I proceeded with the date. Blonde Gillian, who'd been in my class at junior school, was so very pretty, warm and exceptionally intelligent. She was just lovely - the date was good fun and when it was over, the knowledge that my first kiss was rapidly approaching made my heart pound with trepidation. The deed done, I had already decided that it was best to scuttle the romance before it reached the blossoming stage, due to my father's untimely interference. Many of the lads were going out with Elmslie girls at this time and so it was inevitable that both Gillian and I came in for some ribbing, much to our mutual chagrin. So sorry Gillian!

Homeward bound from school, I swapped from my usual 85 Knott End to the 92 Cleveleys bound bus service, knowing that I'd collide with a group of Elmslie girls who would tease me relentlessly about my all too brief flirtation with the fairer sex. This deliberate move was not born out of an inherent masochistic desire for public humiliation, but was due to the fact that my latest crush was to be regularly found amongst this gaggle of girlies. Dark haired, freckled, absolutely stunning and vivacious, Christine was unquestionably pre-possessing and I guess like most other adolescent guys who never came close, I pined for her. Alas, an almost suffocating crush on this beauty was all it was destined to be. To get close to Christine for me, meant unknown risk and almost certain ridicule if she ever guessed my intentions. Yet again I floundered on the fringes of the arena and admitting defeat to myself, I withdrew altogether, having to be content with the odd bashful smile tossed her way. I sighed and thought to myself, 'if only' and 'what it could have been'. The stink of it was that because of my nefarious father I not only lacked sufficient courage to ask Christine out, but I also just didn't permit myself even a chance and so fell at the first hurdle. This episode just fuelled my low self-esteem at the time and exacerbated my incessant psychological battering. On the upside, at least Mopps got to go out with her. Nice one Mark!

As a means of escape from my turbulent reality, there was no shortage of television series throughout the '70s, classics such as Peter Falk's Columbo, Telly Savalas' Kojak, Bill Bixby's The Incredible Hulk, Martin Landau in Space 1999, The Six Million Dollar Man starring Lee Majors, The Bionic Woman (God, I was so in love with Lindsay Wagner!), Charlie's Angels (I was even more in love with Jacqueline Smith!), Starsky and Hutch, starring David Soul and Paul Michael Glaser (er…I wasn't in love with David or Paul, but Huggy Bear was my favourite character!) and of course The Waltons (I was in love with Mary Ellen) (Goodnight John Boy, Goodnight Grandpa…) and Little House on the Prairie (oh my God, Mary Ingalls, played by Melissa Sue Anderson, was so pretty!). I was also keen on the globe-trotting travels of Alan Whicker in Whicker's World.

I wanted so much just to prove my worth. Growing up I was a closet actor. I'd harboured a secret ambition to perform on stage and I surprised myself when I plucked up monumental courage and approached NPT and Ken Shenton, drama and music directors respectively, who were holding auditions for the latest school play. After a very croaky voice test, which knocked me off balance, I ran and hid in the sixth form centre's reading room like a hunted fox, convinced I'd blown any chance of acting. I was trying to console myself whilst hiding behind the door when NPT suddenly burst in, causing me to start. How on earth had he found me? I can't recall what he said or indeed what the essence of my retort was, if any, I just remember his stern gaze, which was probably indicative of a bollocking. Whatever, I had indeed scuppered any thespian propensities that might have been festering within, at least for the time being. I was in disgrace - yet again.

In addition to being bad-tempered, unreasonable and generally nasty, my father had the proclivity to behave in a very odd manner. He would sit in his study and regularly soliloquise especially just prior to giving out at me or giving out to my mother about me – "Jesus, Dulling, he didn't just take one banana, he took two bananas...he's eating us out of fucking house and home!" Every time he'd decorate a room or buy something new, he would paint the date on an item of furniture – say on the back of a wardrobe and even worse – not paint behind the wardrobe! I discovered woodworm eating away at the base of one such wardrobe, a huge, old monstrosity on the landing that had been discarded by the previous owners. My parents were both out at the time so on a whim I took it on myself to get an axe to the thing and get rid of the wardrobe to prevent the spread of woodworm. Within an hour, I'd set fire to the infested planks and was surprised at how quickly the woodpile took to completely reduce to ashes. There was absolutely nothing left and filled with a sense of achievement for a job well done, I looked forward to telling my parents on their return. My mother was pleased but unexpectedly my father completely went off on one. Following the infamous melodramatic comment, "Ah Jesus, Mary and Joseph, Dulling – he's breaking up our home!" my father huffed with me for two whole days. I could never do anything right in my father's eyes and this little episode was no exception.

Once, Dad called the police to ascertain whether a solitary windowpane in my bedroom had been deliberately broken and if so, could it have been done internally – backing up his original claim that I was guilty as charged. I had of course denied breaking the window in a fit of frustration, as I didn't want to give the malevolent bastard the satisfaction. I remember a few very strange looks being exchanged between the constable and me. I'm convinced the copper had my father down as being a 'sandwich short of a picnic'. I'm very surprised that my father wasn't charged with wasting police time on a matter so amazingly banal.

Year after year my bedroom would become a seasonal dumping ground for my father's new plants and seedlings. This combined with condensation almost certainly triggered localised damp, which my father just left to fester and worsen. Fat pots containing nasturtium cuttings were crammed onto my windowsill and spilled over onto newspapers on the floor. Shrivelled leaves and crumbs of earth would serve to dirty my room and I took great objection to this annual ritual and longed to be rid of the clutter and the musty smell that purveyed around my bedroom like a damn greenhouse. Such was my fear of my father, I typically suffered in silent torment. I'd regularly wake up in the middle of the night with a full bladder and would have to muster every ounce of courage to force myself to creep downstairs to the only inside toilet, praying that I wouldn't wake up the ogre who slumbered on the other side of a door that was always kept ajar. On several occasions I woke the bastard up when the toilet was in mid-flush and after hastily washing my hands in a darkened bathroom, I would scurry back upstairs to the sounds of intermittent hog snores and "Who's making all that noise?!!" Fed up with regularly having to run this nocturnal gauntlet, fear eventually forced me to water my father's beloved plants by pissing all over them. Smelling quite pungent, one by one the plants mysteriously began to wilt and then die. My baffled father deduced that the climatic conditions in my bedroom were obviously not conducive to plant growth and suddenly decided to withdraw them all. I happened upon poetic justice by pure chance and by God it felt good!

At the end of summer 1979 the Provisional Irish Republican Army detonated a bomb, hidden on board a wooden fishing boat, Shadow V, in Mullaghmore, County Sligo in north-west Ireland. That explosion on 27th August killed the owner of the boat - the Duke of Edinburgh's uncle, 79-year-old Admiral of the Fleet, Lord Louis Mountbatten, (1st Earl Mountbatten of Burma), Lord Mountbatten's grandson (Nicholas), his son-in-law's mother (Doreen, Dowager Lady Brabourne), together with Paul, a young crew member. Lord Mountbatten's elder daughter, Patricia, (Lady Brabourne), her husband Lord Brabourne and their son Timothy Knatchbull (twin brother to Nicholas) survived the blast, but were seriously injured. On the same day, the IRA also ambushed and killed eighteen British soldiers at the gates of Narrow Water Castle, outside Warrenpoint in

County Down, Northern Ireland. These attacks sent shock waves around the nation. Lord Mountbatten, a mentor to Prince Charles, the Prince of Wales, was the last Viceroy of India in 1947 and the first governor-general of India, post-independence, from 1947 to 1948. During World War 2, Lord Mountbatten was Supreme Allied Commander, South East Asia Command between 1943 and 1946.

The crunch year five had arrived. Chemistry head, Manny Manson, had hinted that I lacked intelligence - I was determined to prove him and others wrong. My fourth year summer examination results certainly supported the hypothesis and to make matters worse Biology became more difficult when testing new concepts were introduced – I couldn't get to grips with them and started failing Bill Roe's tests. Come to think of it quite a few students began to struggle. I remember a clearly agitated Bill posing the question, "When the name of the game is biological genetics, gentlemen – what for crying out loud is going on?!" – loads of blank faces, mine included. Followed by, "Jesus wept, how the mighty hath fallen. You call yourselves an 'O' Level set?...I wouldn't even enter you as a committee for 'O' level!" I was inclined to agree with Bill Roe and that's when I really lost the plot in Biology. I really didn't know what was going on and prayed that there wouldn't be a big genetics question that would pull me down in our 'O' level summer paper.

Fuelled by anger though and a gut desire to succeed, I reconciled myself to winning through. I focused on the end goal - netting all eight 'O' levels. If I was to stand a sporting chance, I'd need to undertake hours upon hours of serious study, frequently burning the midnight oil. For Biology I read and re-read the mountain of handouts, constituting years 1 to 5, starting from the heading 'The Air', I perfected clearly labelled diagrams of, for example, the heart, digestive system, the kidney and bones of the skeleton, using reams of scrap paper. In Ken Riding's Physics, I swatted up on velocity and kinetic energy and looked at among other things the mechanics of different toilet flushing systems. In Chemistry I forced myself to memorise now long forgotten formulae. I devised a silly rhyme to make the first twenty elements of the periodic table stick in my mind. I still remember it to this day:

His (hydrogen = H) **heart** (helium = He) **lies** (lithium = Li) **beneath** (beryllium = Be) **blood** (boron = B) **coffins** (carbon = C). **Never** (nitrogen = N) **oxidise** (oxygen = O) **Friday** (flourine = F). **Nelly's** (neon = Ne) **Nan** (sodium = Na) **makes** (magnesium = Mg) **Alan's** (aluminium = Al) **sickly** (silicon = Si) **pink** (phosphorous = P)

socks (sulphur =S) **clot** (chlorine = Cl) **Arthur's** (argon = Ar) **kind** (potassium = K) **call** (calcium = Ca).

I was double entered to both GCE (O Level) and the lower standard CSE Mathematics exams, because it was predicted that I was borderline pass / fail for O Level. I forced myself to like maths, spending hours going over sums and calculations. In French, my teacher the late Phil Ford (catchphrase: 'Stop the yacking') had offered strong words of advice from the start "No vocab, no pass!" – so I swatted up on my French vocabulary. Overnight I was turned on to Geography and ploughed my way through revision notes covering such topics as glaciers, river processes and coastal erosion to energy, settlements, population, ecosystems, weather, climate, rocks and landscapes.

For English (language and literature), I used my tape recorder to real off notes, parrot fashion. Phil King, our English teacher, was renowned for his humour. He once pointed at the large, sash, classroom windows (the very ones I had tipped paper and darts out of barely two years before) during a spell of windy weather and commanded "Quiet windows", whereupon they suddenly stopped rattling, much to our amusement. Numerous quotations from English Literature I'd pour into the microphone - often mimicking a member of staff - in an effort to make the learning more interesting and for the knowledge to assimilate more quickly.

From star-crossed lovers 'Romeo and Juliet', my favourite quotes all emanate from kinsman Mercutio's lips: "*Ah, the immortal passado, the punto reverso, the hay!*" "*O calm, dishonourable, vile submission! Alla stoccata carries it away, Tybalt, you rat catcher, will you walk?*" After being stabbed – "*No, 'tis not so deep as a well, nor so wide as a church door. But 'tis enough; 'twill serve. Ask for me tomorrow, and you shall find me a grave man. Why the devil came you between us, I was hurt under your arm?*" and of course, "*A plague a both your houses!*"

I've always been inspired by, and have retained a strong love of poetry. I was eleven when I was first captivated by Alfred Noyes' The Highwayman, published in 1906. The poem tells the story of a highway robber who has fallen in love with a landlord's daughter, Bess. An ostler lad Tim, overcome with the green-eyed monster, grasses the couple up to King George's soldiers, but the highwayman narrowly escapes capture when his sweetheart sacrifices herself with a single gunshot to the chest, to warn him that soldiers are waiting to pounce, only for the highwayman to be gunned down himself on the lonely highway trying to effect his escape. The lovers are reunited in death, meeting up as ghosts on winter nights, as the last stanza dramatically plays out:

"...And the highwayman came riding –riding – riding...
...Over the cobbles he clatters and clangs in the dark inn-yard.
He taps with his whip on the shutters, but all is locked and barred.
He whistles a tune to the window, and who should be waiting there
But the landlord's black-eyed daughter,
Bess, the landlord's daughter,
Plaiting a dark red love-knot into her long black hair".

'The Highwayman' set in rural 18th Century England, feels as though you're in the wilds of Scotland and is famous for its strong, descriptive narrative – Noyes saying that the first line of the poem came to him one blustery night with the tempestuous sound of the wind, 'a torrent of darkness' whistling through the pines. The poem is filled with tension, mood, vivid imagery and pace. Phrase repetition is used to create the movement of horse and rider along a 'ribbon of moonlight' road and when you're wrapped up in the enthralling lines, you're right there on that lonely, dark night with the ill-fated couple, right there amidst the action as an invisible, utterly helpless bystander, with a strong feeling in your gut and a voice screaming at you inside your head that tells you, Shit! things aren't going to end at all well.

Our 'O' Level examination anthology, the poems of Thomas Hardy, I found eloquent, moving and quite poignant. The following selected lines are my personal favourites:

'...all mankind that haunted nigh
Had sought their household fires'
(from *The Darkling Thrush*)

'Rain came down drenchingly; but we unblenchingly
Trudged on beside them through mirk and through mire...'
(from *The Going of the Battery*) (A wives' Lament - November 1899)

'They throw in Drummer Hodge, to rest
Uncoffined - just as found...'
(from *Drummer Hodge*)

'I shot at him as he at me,
And killed him in his place..'
(from *The Man he Killed*)

'…when we walked where breakers dinned
It sported in the sun and wind…'
(from *On a Discovered Curl of Hair*)

'And many a skeleton shook his head.
'Instead of preaching forty year,'
My neighbour Parson Thirdly said,
'I wish I had stuck to pipes and beer'.
(From *Channel Firing*)

From Twentieth Century Short Stories, Joseph Conrad's The Secret Sharer brought home a powerful awareness of the alter ego. The Daughters of the Late Colonel by Katherine Mansfield is a farcical tale of two neurotic spinsters living together in the aftermath of their father's death. Having relied so completely on their strict patriarch, who effectively destroyed Josephine and Constantia's chances of experiencing real life, the two characters seem quite unable to make any sensible decisions at all. The sisters are completely paranoid and as the tale unfolds their preoccupation with absurdity becomes very evident. It is clear that these two are destined to lead a sad life, which is probably why I connected so strongly with them at the time - the story isn't just funny, it's simultaneously moving, powerful and consuming.

Whereas some people can scan read an article or a book very quickly and immediately grasp the gist of the plot, (life's clever bastards) my learning style has always favoured repetition and a studying environment devoid of distraction. After a year of slogging it out, enduring hundreds of hours of revising in my bedroom, wearing gun muffs to cut out the sound of the neighbour opposite oxyacetylene welding cars into countless late evenings - I sat my 'O' levels in the summer of 1980. Afterwards I went up to Skye for a week's hiking and youth hostelling with my two sisters. Skye in all its remoteness provided the perfect tonic. The tranquil scenery, punctuated only by the noise of wind and frothy burns the colour of a well-matured malt whiskey, enabled me to unwind sufficiently to experience actual enjoyment. It was a Moscow olympic summer and one of my sporting heroes, Sebastian 'Seb' Coe (now

Lord Coe) was triumphing on the track. There's a great shot of me outside Uig youth hostel doing my Seb Coe 1500 meters victory impersonation, side punching the air. After a great holiday and a week away from my father, which was always heaven, I returned to Lancashire for my 'O' level results. To my delight and others' astonishment I passed all eight subjects that no doubt sent shock waves reverberating around the Arnold school common room.

I had worked damn hard during the fifth year, with little respite. I set up the school's cycling club with the backing of German teacher Peter Helliwell and enjoyed many a Sunday outing to destinations such as Sunderland Point's Sambo's Grave and The Trough of Bowland fells in East Lancashire. At the end of the Christmas term, exactly a year after drinking down the junior school cellar, I went round to Steve Mannion's house to sample his home brew. On that occasion, I drank plenty and ended up completely bladdered. I have vague recollections of swinging from a bus shelter in Lytham Road, endeavouring to impersonate an ape. When I arrived home, my suspicious mother - as always the detective - challenged me. She had smelled the combination of Polo mints and brewery on my breath. 'Have you been drinking?' I slurred some reply. She poked me in the stomach and losing my balance, I fell back in a pathetic heap, like a wino, on to the sofa. My thoughts were bordering on the 'couldn't care less', when my mother, who wasn't laughing said, "Right, I'm telling your father about this when he comes home from work!". To which I quickly retorted, "Well, if you do that, our Christmas'll be ruined". Sometimes, emotional blackmail does pay dividends, perhaps more so when you're drunk. My mother knew that my utterance had made sense. My father would only capitalise on my drinking binge, blow the laddish event out of all proportion and all to deflect criticism away from his own alcoholic over-indulgences. I retreated to the kitchen and drank two pints of coffee, followed by two of water, spent the next half an hour in the loo and the next two days nursing my hangover – still, damn good home brew, Steve! Fortunately, my stratagem worked and I got away with it.

The euphoria of my 'O' level results over, I quickly had to make my choices for 'A' level. I was so mixed up, I hadn't got a bloody clue what I wanted to do with my life post Arnold and it vexed me that nobody really offered me any firm guidance as to what subjects to concentrate on. At this juncture, a career in photography was not on the agenda. Although I'd passed Chemistry, Physics and Biology, my grades weren't high enough for advanced level. My father had been pushing me towards medicine and I had rebelled. I just wasn't interested in becoming a doctor because in my mind, that meant becoming a clone of Dad. My mentor at Arnold, Bill Roe (who had taught me Biology for five years) told my mother and father at the last parents' evening held before 'O' levels that I wasn't suited to medicine, but whatever profession I took up, I'd always be involved with lots of people, as he saw my interpersonal skills as a strong point. How prophetic was his vision. I have a lot to thank that man for and I hope that one day I'll be able to meet him again, convey to him my gratitude over a beer or two and shake his hand warmly.

Left to my own choosing I opted for Politics (God knows why), Geography and Economics. My fourth 'A' level, General Studies, was compulsory. In hindsight, some of the subject matter was inappropriate. Having no set number of study books, Politics – a ghastly subject - was and still is a bottomless pit. Similarly, I found Economics difficult to understand and so inevitably I lagged behind. Geography (human and physical) was the only real area of interest. General studies for me, was a complete non-starter.

I was glad to leave years one to five behind. Lower and upper sixth, from September 1980 to June 1982 were to prove not only enjoyable but were undoubtedly my best and most profitable senior school years. Pushing seventeen, we were treated like and expected to behave as adults. Most teachers called us by our first names, although for some like NPT, this act seemed repugnant. I was and always will be, plain 'Canning'. The sixth form centre was out of bounds to the lower school pupils. Betty Chrichton was our secretary and one meeting with her was enough to convince me of just how immensely proud of her family she was. My chats with Betty were refreshing and inspirational, because she was always so positive about what was possible in life. This chirpy, vivacious Scot loved talking about the meteoric rise to fame of her showbiz daughter, Jacquie Scott, who incidentally studied at Cheethams and was once married to the late entertainer Keith Harris, of 'Orville' fame. Jacquie was stunningly attractive and whenever she visited her mother at Arnold, peculiarly, all the lads knew about it well in advance and we'd all be drooling on the crest of a testosterone high. The camaraderie of sixth form was second to none and some lasting friendships were forged.

November 1980 was a memorable month. I was shocked to hear of the death of one of my all-time favourite actors, Steve McQueen, who at the age of only fifty, had succumbed to mesothelioma (asbestos related) cancer. This was the month of my first ever visit to Oxford to see my elder sister, Vicky, who was studying Classics at Margaret Thatcher's old college, Somerville and McQueen's death at that time was headline news. Oxford is a quaint city steeped in history and ambience. Colleges are in abundance and the frenetic activity of student life is ever palpable. Two of my favourite eateries were the Nosebag café and Brown's restaurant. Outside of Beijing, I don't think I've ever seen so many bicycles per square mile. Ubiquitous is an adjective that immediately springs to mind.

A month and a day after the tragic passing of Steve McQueen, we were all assembled in the Arnold School lecture theatre when in walked Doctor Grimshaw ('Doc Grim'), our very personable and well-respected head of sixth form. Doc Grim's clearly shocked demeanour said it all as he announced to a hushed Upper and Lower Sixth that one of his idols, John Winston Ono Lennon MBE had been murdered, shot and killed by Mark Chapman outside the Dakota building in New York. Lennon had been taken at the tragically young age of 40. The world had lost a musical genius and like so many, I'll never forget that day.

Classic television series The Professionals, which ran from 1977 to 1983, was compulsive viewing and in full swing. Starring Gordon Jackson as CI5 head, 'George Cowley', Martin Shaw as 'Ray Doyle' and Lewis Collins as 'William Bodie', this was dynamite roughty-toughty boys' stuff. I couldn't get enough of it. I often dreamed of driving a Ford Capri and giving it some wellie. Bodie and Doyle were a great pairing. But I so wanted to be like Bodie. And so it was with great sadness that I read that Lewis lost his 5-year battle with cancer on 27th November 2013. He was just 67. What an actor, what a hero. RIP. Also in full swing and running from 1981 through to 1987 for 146 episodes, was Hill Street Blues, famed for Sergeant Phil Esterhaus' end of roll call catch phrase, "Let's be careful out there!"

Our Politics 'A' level set was quite a small group. Chris Harris not only imparted the knowledge, but he would deliver his catch phrases 'Morning men' and 'I would put it to you...', with characteristic and predictable Territorial Army authority. During an informal chat about siblings I happened to mention that my sister was an Oxford University undergraduate, to which Chris Harris replied, "So what happened to you?" The comment was light-hearted enough and at any other time I would have adopted a 'water off a duck's back' attitude, but unintentionally it sliced through my fragility with the ease of a surgeon's scalpel and its effect was cavernous and long lasting.

Prior to age seventeen, I was under a permanent curfew, which really pissed me off. Reg, Steve and the crew called round one Friday night, en route to the Illawala (a local country club). A major bender was on the cards that evening, everyone was turning out and so naturally I wanted to go out and play, but my father intervened in predictable style. Unprovoked, he yanked open our front door, glared at my assembled friends and bellowed at them. The words, 'Bugger off' could be heard down the whole street. I came within an ace of confronting my father for this outrage and with hindsight, I'm convinced that if I had been pushed just a tad more, I would have smacked him in the face and knowing my luck, precipitating disastrous consequences if I had done so. Instead, for the umpteenth time, I bit my lip hard, swallowed my pride and logged the incident for future reference. My immediate concern was damage limitation, how the lads had taken the insult and the inevitable piss take that would follow at school after the weekend. It didn't take me long to think of an explanation for my father's odd behaviour. On the Monday morning I ate a hefty slice of humble pie as I quickly apologised to all my mates. My father had always been a little mad and unpredictable, I said, but recently had been undergoing psychiatric treatment for a personality disorder. To my amazement, there seemed to be a general nod of the heads as the information was digested and the matter was instantly forgotten - but not by me. I swore blind to myself, that if ever my father dared to embarrass me again in front of my friends, then I'd offer him out!

I was made a house prefect early on in the Lower Sixth and became a full school prefect at Easter. Strangely, my new role involved my attending many school evening functions. To this end, I took my prefectorial duties very seriously indeed and used my commitments as a powerful lever with my father for getting out of the house at nights. The world of discos was a magical, huge magnetic arena, in which could be found a cornucopia of pretty, coquettish, young ladies, most of whom were out on 'the pull'. Too shy to get involved, I'd bop, boogie and generally get high on the adrenaline filled atmosphere, which invariably left me charged, ecstatic and always wanting to come back for more.

Traditionally the upper sixth always put on a prefects' concert that would be held on stage in the Memorial hall on the last day of the autumn term, prior to Christmas. A combination of satirical sketches and songs, the event would primarily be a send up of the teachers. My reputation for staff impersonations was school wide and I was flattered to be asked to perform in the bash of '80. The plan was for me to assume the guise of Colonel Jones and appear as one of four Mastermind quiz contestants. Rehearsals went well and head of Drama, NPT, who vetted all sketches for any possible inappropriate material, seemed pleased. When the big day finally arrived, I was unsurprisingly exceptionally nervous. I would be performing in front of the entire school, my contemporaries and full common room contingent. Therefore, in my mind, it was crucial that my sketch was not only consummate, but also that my act made everyone laugh. I was to be the last contestant in the pecking order and as I waited in the wings, my debut stage performance grew ever closer. The butterflies were rock and rolling in the pit of my stomach and I was just beginning to regret not having visited the toilet, when I was given the signal to enter the limelight.

The previous contestant, an ape dressed in a purple tracksuit (the late Dave Morley lookalike), exited the stage to rapturous applause and laughter. The giggling gave way to silence and then over the PA, 'Could we have our last contestant please'. Dressed in army fatigues, cap and boots, a pillow had been unceremoniously stuffed up my jumper to pad me out, I sauntered out in full view, with military baton tucked under my arm. I looked at 'Magnus Magnuson' and then turned to the audience and in classic Eddie Jones style, I beamed at everyone and said, 'Hello'. The applause and laughter for that one word seemed to last for ages and gave me a surge of confidence. The audience was on my side and my nerves were now under control. More importantly, I was beginning to enjoy myself. I took the hot seat and faced 'Polly' Beighton, who as quiz-master Magnus Magnuson, was famed for his Jack the lad sense of humour. It was obvious that Polly was dying to laugh and we did our best not to make too much eye contact. "Your name please". "Colonel Edward Jones, M.B.E., W.E.E.". The whole school erupted in spontaneous laughter. I glanced at Polly who was starting to crack up. He regained his composure. "Your chosen subject?" "Army manoeuvres". Again, I waited for the laughter to abate. Polly then said, "Colonel Jones, you have two minutes on army manoeuvres starting now". And so the well-rehearsed questions were put to me. Making reference to a famous Eddie Jones incident at Combined Cadet Force camp venue, 'Proteus', Polly asked, "How many schools were using showers and toilets and where were they?" "There were three schools using ablutions in my rear", came my quick word for word quoted retort.

The school clearly loved every minute of this sketch and once again, we had to wait a while for the laughter to die down, before we could continue. Without warning a beeb beeb beeb was clearly audible over the PA, signalling that my time was up. Someone had recorded the famous Mastermind bleep. Ad libbing, I slowly turned to the sea of pupils and teachers, lowered my half-moon spectacles and said, "Whoever made that stupid noise..." The school instantly erupted and at that moment I caught sight of the great Colonel, my first ever impression, standing at the back of the hall. He was wearing a wry smile! When all was relatively quiet, I continued. "Whoever made that stupid noise, can come and see me in my CCF office". Polly thanked me, I got up, saluted my audience and sidled off stage to yet further applause.

My performance, and indeed the whole prefects' concert, had gone down extremely well. I'd nailed it. I felt important. Hell, no, I felt like a Hollywood star for goodness sake – I was absolutely on fire with the adrenaline rush, almost 'ripped' as I walked, nay, floated off stage elated, as I simultaneously felt the hair on the back of my neck stand up. Staff and pupils alike came up to me and congratulated me and said how much they had enjoyed the show. Then suddenly, Plez, who I had really been avoiding since he cut my mouth open eighteen months previously, approached me and I had a weird sense of déjà vu. Should I duck and dive? Ready myself for a 'counter-parry'? Fortunately, on this occasion he slapped me warmly on the back. I could have hugged him as I thought all's well that ends well. That Christmas 1980 show was indeed my éclat, my finest hour to date. I had felt the affection and warmth of an entire school wash over me. It was indeed an overwhelming experience. The realisation that I might now just be a tad popular was somewhat difficult to handle as hitherto I had rejected such feelings. As I left school for the Christmas break, I punched the air defiantly and with jubilation. The fight back with my father had begun. My self-confidence, although still appallingly low, was at its highest level yet and for once, I didn't hate myself. Maybe, just maybe I thought, I'd do ok in life after all.

Well, that euphoric feeling was short lived when the February 1981 exams spelled another disaster and everything effectively went to ratshit - solace being found in the Geography field trip to Holland. We had a laugh on the ferry going over and there was a ready supply of 'lemonades'. After studying the polders and new town geography there was time to relax in the beautiful city of Amsterdam. A motor launch took us on a tour of the waterways, passing the Anne Frank museum and a houseboat seemingly overrun with cats. By far the highlight of the trip was of course, Canal Strasse in Amsterdam's infamous red-light district. I gawped with innocent wonder at all the topless hookers sitting in the windows doing their knitting whilst waiting for another punter. As we were all egging each other on to pay one of the prostitutes a visit, Howard pondered whether he might get a discount due to the size of his tackle. We all cracked up laughing, much to the prostitutes' chagrin, who thought that we were sniggering at them.

The day I hit seventeen, I had my first driving lesson with a company of national repute. Everyone remembers the car they learned to drive in. Mine was a V registration (August 1979) Triumph Dolomite, followed by Sir Michael Edwardes' new BL (British Leyland) Metro, launched as part of the LC10 project. Although I had a grumpy old bugger for my test, it didn't put me off and I was fortunate to pass first time and went straight back into school to wind up all the gang, letting them believe I'd failed. At that stage, my father was between cars (or that's what he told us ... later I believed he'd probably lost his licence for drinking and driving). His only form of transport was a bicycle and he routinely cycled to and from DHSS Warbreck Hill, his place of work, in all weathers. Then, towards the end of the Lower Sixth he splashed out on a nearly new, light metallic blue, Volvo 244 GL, complete with automatic gearbox. The Volvo, registration KFR 46W, had been purchased from Terry Joyce, a Blackpool second-hand car dealer for the grand sum of £7250. This gleaming almost new car was a real head turner and when I was granted occasional permission to take the car to school, I was naturally excited. 'Fanny Head', who owned a battered old Volvo, habitually parked in the same place in the sixth form centre car park every day, without fail. At the first opportunity, I couldn't resist the wind up and so I stole his space, waited for this teacher to arrive and then grin as he'd eye up this new Volvo with disgust.

'Lorna' was our year's beauty. She had a gorgeous figure and dark, wavy hair that fell over a pretty face. She was also highly intelligent, had an endearing personality, and I longed to go out with her. There were, however, two not so little obstacles to overcome. Firstly, all the other lads had their beady eyes on Lorna and secondly, I was still too shy to make any move. Alas, she picked the 'rugger' team. After briefly dating Chris, who had been knocked off his bike in the first year, Lorna was destined to go out with Richard ('Bammo boy'), a rugby player and budding thespian, who once commented that he wanted someone to come up from The Old Vic to discover him. After an exciting literary career, Richard was sadly taken by cancer in Melbourne at the tragically young age of 47 in March 2011.

When Lorna invited me to her eighteenth birthday party, I was in a quandary. Embarrassingly, I had to seek my mother's counsel as to what this eighteen-year old girl might like for a present. I was advised to purchase an exquisite make of soap - very English and awfully expensive! Can you imagine in today's world buying soap for an 18 year old!!! Fortunately, Lorna was delighted with the offering. She greeted all her guests with a kiss on the lips. 'Oh Jesus', I thought, as I waited nervously for my turn. What if it goes wrong and I kiss her chin or slobber all over her or something? My heart pounded as outwardly I smiled and puckered up. I kissed her quickly, our lips barely touching. To my shocked surprise, Lorna said, "That wasn't much of a kiss Paul" and then proceeded to throw her arms around me and give me a huge smackeroonie, which seemed to last forever (great!) and in full view of all the partygoers (not so great!). Lorna is now a very successful home counties GP, whom I haven't seen since leaving Arnold.

Although the embrace was momentary and embarrassing, crucially, I enjoyed being close to a girl. Afterwards, with a pint of my favourite brew 'Boddies' tucked securely into my left shoulder, I subconsciously analysed this brief flirtation. Although celibate, which of course was not of my choosing, I yearned for my own girlfriend all the more and I was overwhelmingly pleased that this encounter had confirmed to me what I already knew in my own mind - that I was irrevocably heterosexual. I was so mixed up throughout the emotionally charged vicissitudes of puberty and adolescence that I guess periodically, I lost touch with my own identity and at times, intuition.

At Easter 1981, it was time for the Upper Sixth (6A) to relinquish their prefectorial responsibilities and hand over their obligation to us in the Lower Sixth (6B), thereby devoting all available time to studying in the run up to A-levels. Richard Rhodes, who had served as Cameron Cochrane's deputy, was the governors' unanimous choice for headmaster, upon Mr. Cochrane's departure to Edinburgh's Fettes College. The resident incumbent had almost completed his second year as head and proved a popular choice. 'Dickie' Rhodes was a fair disciplinarian and had, in my opinion, what Cochrane lacked, approachability and charisma. Richard Rhodes was also an exceptionally good judge of character, for he must have seen some positive qualities in me when, to my delight, he made me a school prefect that Easter. That one single action by Dickie gave my confidence and self-esteem a tremendous boost. I owe a great deal to my old headmaster for giving me a chance to prove myself, following my down and out years of one to five.

Joining an elite band of contemporaries, I wore my distinctive black and silver striped tie with pride. At school functions, I also donned a red-trimmed black gown. I was allowed to dish out detentions to pupils in the lower school and make disruptive individuals stand in the corner. Occasionally, I could be a real bastard and make a pupil stand on tiptoes, their noses centralised inside a chalked circle on the wall opposite the chemmy lab. Anthony Lord, later destined to be my children's deputy headmaster at Preesall's St. Aidan's School, was one such unfortunate lad – sorry Ant! The downside of being a school prefect was that you were required to periodically read the lesson in assembly in front of the whole school. Head boy, Dave Brennand, stitched me up to be first in line. I can't remember the passage from the Bible that was to be my maiden reading, but I took nothing to chance. I smelled a possible wind up and I'd heard horror stories of prefects going up on stage to read the lesson, only to find that the Bible had been pinched from the lectern. Well, that just wasn't going to happen to me. I had a small Bible sequestered in my inside jacket pocket with the relevant page marked with elastic bands, so that it could not possibly open at the wrong page. Additionally, I hid another Bible in the wings that I could easily grab on my way up to take my seat on stage, should the lectern be bare. The third and final Bible was of course housed on the lectern itself and on the morning of the reading, I'd do the last-minute checks to make sure no sabotage had occurred.

The night before the dreaded task, I was burning the midnight oil going over and over the selected passage, for it had to be right. I had little sleep because I was so very nervous. I won't forget that night in a hurry. I felt uncomfortable and insecure, but despite all this, I never once doubted that I could pull this off. On the said morning, I arrived at school extra early and vacated my bowels not once, but three times within the space of an hour. I'd catered for every eventuality - for unbeknown to anyone, I'd even brought a spare pair of underpants and trousers with me, but prayed I wouldn't have need of them. The moment had arrived and the headmaster's entourage had gathered outside at the rear of the Memorial Hall, which itself was packed. I swallowed hard and after a few seconds of banter, the organ started to play - the signal for us to make our way down a side corridor to the wings and thence to the stage seating.

Suddenly I was there, standing in front of a sea of green blazers and faces that seemed to be all staring at me. We went straight in to 'All things Bright and Beautiful'. The last verse was my cue to move to the lectern and I was very relieved to notice that the Bible had not been touched. The school was now singing the final line and my heartbeat quickened. The organ was silent, everyone sat down and I waited a few seconds before starting. I read clearly and slowly, projecting my voice to the back of the hall, just as NPT had instructed and coached me. I was now completely calm and the reading was faultless. I finished my delivery with the words "Here endeth this morning's lesson" and then sat down. Here lay an advantage to the reader because now the head said, "Let us pray" and so I knew that nobody would be staring at me and this brief interlude offered me vital seconds to recompose myself. I felt elated with my maiden reading and was congratulated by the headmaster, when we all moved off stage at the end of assembly. The late Mike Butterworth, a well-respected, popular and gifted economics teacher also gave me a verbal pat on the back that morning during his economics period, so I knew that my performance had been sound. After that initial shock, reading the lesson became enjoyable and I readily volunteered. However, reading a passage in front of a thousand people was a walk in the park compared to giving any form of interactive presentation, which filled me with trepidation. Consequently, I avoided public speaking until fate had other ideas, many years later!

The sixth form studies are no more, sadly demolished along with many of the original Arnold School buildings. They once fronted Lytham Road with their distinctive, angled, black and white facades, standing for all the world like a range of infantry and with all the pride of a military inspection. Designed to house four students, I shared mine, the top middle study, with seven others! We moved in towards the end of the Lower Sixth. Relieved to get the summer examinations out of the way, which were another disaster, I looked forward to my Snowdonia walking holiday that August. The halfway stage in sixth form saw my Duke of Edinburgh Gold award almost three quarters complete. For the service part of my award, I worked part time throughout the academic year in the psychiatric wing of

Blackpool's Victoria Hospital. This essentially involved helping to organise, and then having full involvement with, patients' recreational activities. Engrossed in sculpting a small, wooden horse, David, a patient with schizophrenia, suddenly dropped his file. He stared menacingly at me and said, "You don't like me, do you?" I was just thinking, Oh shit, what the hell do I do now?, when before I could answer, a male nurse, who had been standing within earshot, whisked me away to another patient (Jesus, that was a close call). Later that same day I held a door open for Bruce (also with schizophrenia) and to my shocked surprise, the patient turned to me and landed a right hook on my cheek. I fell to the floor, completely stunned. Bruce, I soon learned, liked to do everything himself and any offer of help was greeted with disdain. Can you imagine if that happened today, a load of incident forms would have to be completed and people investigated as to why a young volunteer was left in that situation! Two bad experiences in one day was more than enough excitement and I was somewhat relieved when my stint at the hospital reached a successful conclusion. Little did I realise then, that I'd end up working at this same hospital full time, more than thirty years later!

For the residential section of the award, I chose canal conservation. The venue was Stratford-On-Avon and I would travel by coach. The week-long project for The National Trust was challenging as it involved long hours of graft, undertaken in the baking July sun. The bulk of the seven days focused on a large, wooded expanse and undergrowth that threatened to engulf a whole section of canal, rendering it unnavigable. What greeted my eleven other team members and me upon arrival, was a complete wilderness and the sighs were definitely audible. However, to tackle this leviathan job, a huge gardening arsenal was at our disposal. Tooled up with some serious gear (chain saws, scythes and long-handled secateurs) in-roads had already been made after the first hour. Even wearing heavy duty gloves, we still got scratched to bits by the myriad brambles, which got into and under most of our garments. When one of the party pissed off thousands of wasps, we nearly all managed to get stung. The uncovered nest was hastily zapped.

The end of the first day hailed a major success. Physically exhausted and nursing our war wounds (scratches and insect bites) we returned to the sanctuary of a nearby junior school where we were billeted for the next week. After a hearty meal, washed down with a few 'lemonades', there wasn't much left to do but retreat to our pits. As I don't remember getting into my sleeping bag, I guess

I fell asleep very quickly that night. So, the daily pattern of clearance continued. After five, full days on that one section, our work was complete. An uncontrollable wilderness had been replaced by a severely pruned, neat woodland. We were the forerunner of Groundforce! Crucially, the job had been accomplished on schedule and the boating contingent could now pass unhindered. In celebration of our achievements we jumped into the canal, as you do. Those who didn't jump were pushed or dragged and then pushed, which prompted one girl to scream in a toffish voice, "I'm wearing contact lenses!" This was followed by a sniggering voice to my rear, "so bloody well what?" Alas, it was too late. Nobody escaped a soaking and excuses fell on deaf ears. In postscript, I do believe that the girl in question survived her ordeal with contacts intact.

The remaining two days were taken up with tow path clearance and creosoting lock gates. At the end of my residential course, I felt knackered, but filled with a sense of enormous pride for what had proved a gutsy undertaking. One thing was for certain, I wasn't afraid of hard work, in fact I relished it. I returned to Blackpool by coach on July 29th, just in time to catch the aftermath of The Prince of Wales' marriage to Lady Diana Spencer on TV.

My walking holiday in Snowdonia with my sisters Vicky and Kate a few weeks later was marred by my sickness. During the daytime treks we would feast on raisins and nuts and then, on arrival at each respective youth hostel, the priority would be to quickly get a brew on whilst concocting a hot evening meal. At Idwal Cottage Hostel, having climbed Snowdon, our bean feast smelled and tasted delicious. Ravenous, I wolfed a pig-sized portion down in seconds and barely half an hour later, I turned white and felt quite unwell. My diary entry at the time was coded 'Four times bean feast / up she comes'. Some memories never fade and on that fateful night, I showed my dislike of bean feast by violently throwing up, not once, but four times. The typical pre-warning of impending sickness was a build-up of saliva. Surrounded by other walkers, I legged it outside for the solitude I suddenly craved. The instant evacuation of my stomach left me feeling much improved, but there was more to come. Twice more and I thought surely by now there was nothing left. Feeling tired and lethargic, I sought out the comfort of my sheet sleeping bag at around 9pm. But by lights out, an hour later, I wanted to throw up again for a fourth time. Now, being a typical, organised Virgo, I'd blagged an old wastepaper basket and bag-lined it with a triple layer to cater just for this eventuality. Sitting bolt upright, I fumbled for my torch and makeshift receptacle and proceeded to heave repeatedly. This was followed by characteristic moaning sounds, then silence. Just when I thought I'd got away with it, a little boy piped up from somewhere in the depths of this darkened dormitory. This shy lad whispered somewhat loudly to his father "Daddy, Daddy, someone's being sick". The father was quick with the reply "Ssh, go to sleep!" Fortunately, I'd managed some serious shuteye and woke before dawn and everyone else. This premature awakening offered me some privacy to dispose of the vomit, so remaining undetected.

I really wasn't up to walking one step, let alone several miles to the next hostel that day. Fatigued, dehydrated, with an inevitable loss of vital body salts, I teetered on, inevitably lagging behind my two energetic sisters. I had little in the tank and periodically felt delirious but sucking on glucose-rich sweets and sipping copious amounts of water, the nausea ebbed and I began to recover. Walking amidst serenity, trying my best not to think of food and feeling simply awful, I had a flashback to a time when I was about to leave home one evening, for cubs, aged about 8. Looking smart in grey shorts, dark green jersey adorned with different badges, neckerchief and woggle, I sat in the breakfast room, waiting to depart. Suddenly, my sister Vicky grabbed my cap and tossed it around the room in what was no more than a few minutes of brother-sister tomfoolery. My father, on witnessing our joy, went apeshit. He ran out of the house and into the tool shed, grabbed a long-handled pair of secateurs and cut a three-foot stick from the nearest tree. Having crudely pruned his weapon, he darted back into the house shouting maniacally as we had quickly scarpered like frightened animals. As I stared in disbelief, my father grabbed hold of Vicky and proceeded to mete out an incessant flogging. With each stroke, my sister screamed and cried, begging my father to stop, but oblivious to her pleas, he just carried on regardless. When finally the bully stopped, my evil father rounded on me, bringing the stick crashing down on my knee, bruising and cutting the skin enveloping my patella. Even at this young age, I could see neither logic nor justification for this harsh beating. The punishment was way, way over the top. I surmised that perversely, either he was jealous because he had been excluded from our enjoyment and / or he derived considerable pleasure from acting out a deranged fantasy. Sitting on a rock in the present, surrounded by a peaceful Welsh countryside, shrouded in mist, I realised just how much I despised this nasty little man who had inflicted so much pain on to my family. I longed for the day that my father received his comeuppance.

Now in the September of 6A, the Upper Sixth, in the home straight push to 'A' levels, I was keeping my fingers well and truly crossed that there wouldn't be any final stings in the tail of this last academic school year.

My father decided that he wanted to further his driving skills and roped me in as well. Following an intensive course of 'guidance drives' with an ex-policeman and advanced driver, both my father and I took the advanced test on the same day. My father went first and an hour and a half after setting off from Lytham, he returned and announced jubilantly that he had passed. (Bloody typical – smug bastard, I thought). Now it was my turn. I'd just had my eighteenth birthday and had owned a full driving license for barely six months, so I wasn't holding out much hope of passing this challenging test. I'd probably fail just for sporting too much bum fluff and looking too young. In the front passenger seat of the Volvo was a police sergeant who was to be my examiner. The first thing I noticed about him was that he was devoid of pen and clipboard. He must have an excellent retentive memory, I thought to myself. Two minutes into the test and I was negotiating twisting lanes. Without warning, a Mini carrying four toe rags, hurtled round the corner from the opposite direction, slightly lost it on the bend and narrowly missed me by what seemed like inches. I executed a textbook emergency stop, the sergeant spun round and with a pen that had materialised from nowhere, promptly noted the Mini's registration on his hand. "I don't know about you, but that looked pretty close from where I'm sitting". I just nodded and said, "Yes, it was, er, very". I took a deep breath and continued with the examination, which took in town, country, motorway driving and an array of manoeuvres. Integral to the test was an obligatory ten-minute running commentary, which seemed to go fine as I'd practised it so many times. On arrival back in Lytham, I was pleasantly surprised to learn that I'd passed. My driving skills and knowledge of the 'Highway Code' and advanced driving manual had been tested to the full. "Well done, that was excellent. All you need now is experience" my examiner told me on completion.

My Duke of Edinburgh Gold award was very nearly complete. My trip down to St. James's Palace now hinged on the expedition. I fitted the planning and organising of a cycling/camping expedition around a Geography field trip to Castleton in Derbyshire. I was cycling with four friends on my old Peugeot ten-speed with dropped handlebars, full panniers and an array of equipment, over 170 miles of difficult, undulating terrain. The assessed expedition was successfully undertaken around the Yorkshire Dales, at the end of which I had to write up a complete report of events. We had encountered all manner of weather conditions, from sun, rain and wind to snow, frost and hailstorms - all throughout the October half term. Memorable moments of the trip included my puncture, barely a mile from the finish and a bottle of milk left outside one of the tents all night at the campsite in Gargrave. It was completely frozen over.

Christmas 1981 was just around the corner, which meant planning for the Prefects' concert. In what was to prove another hit, one of my ideas was to read the lesson while changing to a different teacher's voice for every verse. It went down a treat. In another sketch, I wanted to pay tribute to my Biology teacher and so I had a couple of pupils come on stage with different flowers to examine. When the last pupil, a studious student, gave me his offering, I launched into a detailed examination of the flower with typical Bill Roe enthusiasm. "Ah yes lad, a perfect specimen. Here we can identify sepals, petals and stamen - anther and stigma clearly visible and what do you call this, lad?" A rather timid voice retorted "A wallflower, sir?" On cue, I then let rip, shouting "Jesus wept laddie, you call this a wallflower, how the mighty hath fallen!" With a sweeping hand across the whole school, I then shouted, "Look at 'em, Mugs' alley - knowledge..." and then gesticulating towards the Arnold school staff, "Ignorance!" I left the stage amidst thunderous applause and laughter.

One of my favourite sketches of this final prefects' concert was the opening sequence where Sean and the gang, dressed up as the cleaners, sidled up on to stage. They set about cleaning, whistling with brooms and mops in hand and seemingly oblivious to everyone. This charade had lasted but for a few seconds when suddenly, over the loudspeakers came Diana Ross and The Supremes with 'Ooh o ooh o baby love, my baby love...'. The audience was hysterical with laughter as cleaners' outfits swished rhythmically and mops and brushes became guitars or microphones on stands, as the crew sashayed, boogied, and gyrated around their platform. When just as quickly, the song reached its end and the music faded, the gang stopped dancing and immediately returned to cleaning mode. That sketch was brilliantly conceived and remains one of the funniest that I've ever seen. The audience loved it and the atmosphere was electric, but we were just getting warmed up.

In my opinion, the prize for best sketch of all time must surely go to my friend, Simon Wallis, who came mincing on to the stage, dressed up in an authentic pixie outfit that even included green tights. He then sat provocatively on the front of the headmaster's table, fore and middle fingers resting on his right cheek, fourth finger curled up on his lips, legs swinging to and fro and camping it up. He proceeded to give the school a French test in classic 'Pixie' style ... "Bonjour mes eleves". With the same two fingers still resting on his cheek in characteristic pose – "Number down one to ten, English to French - number one, 'bulwark', number two, 'buxom". So the risqué humour continued in the same vein, as we all cringed with laughter. Half way through Simon said, "Number six, bulge" then like lightening and with a mock pout "Ooh, that one's a bit below the belt!". The audience were in stitches and when the concert finished, everyone agreed that it had been a runaway success.

I was about to break up from School for the Christmas 1981 holidays when news came in on 19th December of the Penlee lifeboat disaster in Cornwall. The vessel 'Union Star' had run into difficulty in high seas off the south coast of Cornwall after its engines failed. By the time the wooden 47-foot lifeboat Solomon Browne, dispatched from Penlee Lifeboat Station near Mousehole at 8.12pm, reached the stricken vessel, hurricane force winds of around 100 miles per hour were gusting. Rescue conditions bordered on the impossible and were nothing short of treacherous. Waves were estimated to be 60 feet high. Nevertheless, Coxswain Trevelyan Richards and his brave volunteer crew (Stephen Madron, Nigel Brockman, John Blewett, Charlie Greenhaugh, Kevin Smith, Barrie Torrie and Gary Wallis) through 'persistent and heroic endeavours' initially managed to rescue four people from the Union Star after several attempts to draw alongside the doomed vessel. Trevelyan radioed in "We've got four off", but sadly that was the last transmission from the lifeboat. Shockingly, all eight lifeboatmen along with eight crew and passengers from the Union Star were taken by the rough seas that night – six days before Christmas. Nigel Brockman's son Neil had originally arrived at Penlee Lifeboat station on time to join the crew, but Trevelyan turned him down as he was reluctant to take two members of the same family out in rough seas that night. All the lost crew were posthumously awarded RNLI medals.

The disaster shook the nation and the beautiful county of Cornwall at a time of celebration, prompting a huge public appeal to help the village of Mousehole. Funds raised topped £3 million and barely 24 hours after the tragedy, enough people had volunteered to form a new lifeboat crew. The old Penlee lifeboat station located at Penlee Point today stands empty, but is now a memorial to the brave Solomon Browne crew. It was fitting that Neil Brockman later became coxswain of Penlee's new, larger, faster lifeboat, which could be kept moored in the harbour. Less than two years after the sea tragedy, the new Penlee lifeboat station was opened, located around the coast at Newlyn. Charlie Greenhaugh, one of the lifeboatmen who perished on 19 December, was the landlord of the Ship Inn on Mousehole's quay and two evenings prior to the disaster, had turned on the festive lights in the village. Every Christmas Mousehole is lit up and on the anniversary of the disaster, the lights are switched off for an hour out of respect and in memoria. Since my time as a sixth-former when this awful tragedy occurred, I've always remembered this selfless act of valour by Trevelyan Richards and his friends and colleagues, the crew of the Solomon Browne. Such brave men. Lest we forget.

The Christmas term was all complete, save for the carol service at South Shore's Holy Trinity Church, scene of my confirmation a few months previously. It was bitterly cold that December day and snow had been forecast. However, even if it did snow, nobody really thought that much would fall. To expedite my return trip from home to school, my father said that I could borrow the Volvo. Headmaster Richard Rhodes held a small drinks reception back at the school immediately following the annual carol service. By the time I pulled in to the sixth form car park, the sky, full of ominously dark clouds, let rip. The initial flutters very quickly turned in to a heavy snowstorm. Although safely ensconced in the warmth of the school, I was worried as my predicament deepened.

The journey was approximately six miles and normally would have taken about twenty minutes to complete. Decision time was rapidly approaching. The sensible approach was to telephone my father, explain the situation and tell him that I had been snowed in and would therefore have to take up the headmaster's suggestion that we bed down at the school until the storm abated and the road conditions returned to something approaching normality again. I phoned home and predictably my father was curt and furious at the prospect of not having his precious car back in the garage for a few days. He didn't once enquire as to my welfare. "You're to bring the car back immediately!" he snapped and with that he abruptly put the phone down on me. It transpired that he hadn't even bothered to look out of the window, for if he had indeed got off his lazy arse and ventured outside, the impossible situation that faced me would have been lucid, beyond doubt.

My headmaster certainly wasn't happy with me driving in such inclement and extreme weather, but what could he do? The snow had already started to drift and pile up around the car, so following a small clearance operation I started up the Volvo and put the automatic gear selector in to first and gently depressed the accelerator. Nothing happened. I revved the engine a little harder and could now hear the rear wheels spinning. A couple of the lads then managed to push me out of my space and I was soon rolling. I turned right out of the sixth form car park and on to Lytham Road. Nothing moved. The only sounds that I was aware of were those of the engine, fan heater and the windscreen wipers, which swept rhythmically across the screen. The area of windscreen not covered by the wipers was already caked in snow. There were no other cars around and no signs of pedestrians, which was hardly surprising as everything around me was a complete whiteout. It was late afternoon and already getting dark as I edged my way cautiously through the snow, which was coming down fast in large, thick flakes. Gripping the steering wheel I dared not stop for fear of getting stranded, so as I approached what appeared to be traffic lights, I cautiously looked in both directions and just carried on - not that I could see the individual lights, as they too, like everything else around, had become one large, grotesque, white mass. My mind kept playing tricks on me as periodically I swore that I could see huge snowman ghosts, lurking in doorways. In reality, I reasoned that it was simply the play of light and shade.

At one set of lights a car had been abandoned having wheel spun broadside on, completely blocking the road, so I was forced to drive on the wrong side of the road to avoid the obstruction. As I approached the junction of Lytham Road and the Promenade, there were more abandoned cars littering my route home and as I steered around this obstacle course, it crossed my mind that perhaps this was too great an undertaking and I too would succumb to the terrible conditions and not make it home that night. I headed north along the prom, passed Central Pier and Louis Tussaud's waxworks and on towards the tower, which I couldn't even discern, the ambient conditions were so appalling. As I worked my way onwards to North Pier, I thought to myself 'so far so good', but here amidst utter isolation, it wasn't the time for complacency. I allowed myself a quick sigh of relief upon reaching Talbot Road and passing Yates' Wine

Lodge, I edged the car slowly on towards the bus station. The repeated sight of abandoned motor vehicles, precariously placed in snow, was alien and surreal to me. Stage one had been completed and now filled with renewed vigour I made my way towards Poulton, via Layton for stage two.

My knuckles were white as I clung on vice-like to the steering wheel. My face was by now very warm and sweaty with concentration and as a by-product from the hot interior conditions as the fan heater, switched to its highest setting, directed hot air at full blast on to the windscreen. As I drove downhill along Westcliffe Drive, I prayed that I'd be able to stop and not collide with anything and that furthermore I'd then be able to negotiate St. Walburga's Road roundabout, which was rapidly approaching, without coming to grief. I was in luck and with no problems encountered, I just kept pushing on.

Entering the home straight, I had just gone past the junction with Blackpool Old Road when my heart skipped a beat. In front of me a tanker had jack-knifed opposite Collegiate High School playing fields, completely blocking the way ahead. Two or three cars had stopped and had become stuck as the sound of wheel spinning could once more clearly be heard. I quickly checked my rear-view mirror, glanced over my right shoulder and in a completely reckless, but gutsy manoeuvre, part executed a U-turn. However, with a little too much accelerator, the car spun round and my back wheels ended up spinning pathetically in the gutter. As luck would have it a couple of good Samaritans, realising that I was in distress, appeared out of nowhere and managed to get the Volvo free. After that close shave, I retraced my route back up Garstang Road and turned right into Blackpool Old Road. The car was now beginning to slide with alarming frequency, but completely focused on the task in hand, I tenaciously carried on. I passed Cottam Hall playing fields, which was home to the annual summer gala, and knowing that I was now so desperately close to home that I could have walked, I ticked off the side roads in my mind, even though I couldn't read them - Mossbourne Road on the right, then Raybourne Avenue on the left, followed by Wyresdale Avenue on the right and so it continued.

I was in Poulton at last, which was completely shrouded in snow and virtually cut off. Barely a stone's throw away from home, the task now was to see just how much further I could drive. I pressed on past the Teanlowe Centre and Market Place along Queen's Square and thence up Chapel Street. I drove carefully along the Breck, past the railway station and indicated right to turn in to Victoria Road.

Our house was situated towards the bottom of this road and I could virtually see it. Smiling triumphantly, but as it transpired, a tad prematurely, I suddenly lost control of the car midway through the right turn. The back end spun around violently, finally coming to rest in the gutter. I tried and tried to free the Volvo but to no avail. The wheels just kept spinning on ice. The car was heavy and I was disadvantaged with it being rear wheel drive, fighting against the camber. A couple of people emerged from a nearby house and tried in vain to push me out of my difficulty. After about twenty minutes, we managed to get the car parked parallel to the kerb, where I resigned myself that it would remain until the snow melted. For the first time, I suddenly caught sight of the temperature indicator, which was at the very top end of the red. The radiator grill had been completely clogged with snow, blocking all intakes. I was indeed lucky to have got this far, because the car could so easily have overheated at any stage, leaving me marooned.

I thanked the second lot of good Samaritans, locked up the car, donned my coat and trudged through the heavy snow until I reached our house. The snow, which was about five feet thick, had drifted up the driveway and had virtually engulfed the garage doors, so I took some comfort that I had got the car quite literally as far as I could in the prevailing conditions. There was no way that the Volvo could get into the garage without us first digging out the drive and even then, there was no guarantee that the car would make the incline, without sliding uncontrollably and quite possibly slamming into the adjacent brick wall. As I stood there surveying a truly amazing sight, alone with my thoughts in the snow, cold, tired and hungry, I braced myself as to how I was going to break the news to my father - that his precious car was not tucked up safely for the night, where it belonged.

I found my father lolling in his greasy back armchair watching television in the dining room. "I got the car to the end of the road" I said triumphantly. My father then predictably went off on one. Glaring at me he jabbed, "Ah Jesus, Mary and Joseph, where exactly is the car?" He got his coat and stormed out of the house to retrieve his most prized possession. Typically, he managed to get the car outside the house and this irked me. He then ordered Vicky and me to help him dig out the drive. After a couple of fruitless attempts and numerous kettles of hot water, we put some old curtains down so that the car could gain traction. It worked and darling Volvo was finally back in the garage. I received neither thanks nor apology from my father, just the cold shoulder - which was very much in character and what I'd come to expect. The vibes emanating from him convinced me that in his eyes I was simply an annoying irritation, utterly useless and 'eating us out of house and home, Dulling'. My father couldn't give a toss about me and I disliked him intently. His abhorrent personality often tested my nerves to the limit, for on many occasions I would love to have just smacked him one.

My interest in photography can be traced back to childhood when I was given my first Kodak Instamatic at the age of 7. At 14, I was still using it loaded with 126 cartridge Kodachrome 64 transparency, a film favoured for its colour saturation and resolution. Almost fifty years later and my sister, Vicky, still has my original Instamatic in her possession. In my mid teens, I had use of my father's 'Diaxette', a German 35mm with leaf shutter and used it in conjunction with an old Weston Euromaster light meter. I shot transparency almost exclusively until the old camera's shutter broke, prompting my father's infamous quote "Jesus, Dulling - everything he touches he buggers". The Diaxette in brown leather case was consigned to the knacker's yard and with accumulated savings, I brought a Fujica GER compact 35mm, followed by a Yashica 35mm with interchangeable lens capability.

My father's interest in photography rubbed off on me and when I was about ten, he rigged up a small black and white darkroom in one of the landing's side attics. In my opinion, you can't beat the traditional method of dish 'devving' (developing). I'll never forget the first images to magically appear whilst sloshing the developer backwards and forwards in rhythmical agitation. My colour photographs taken in the early years were extremely amateurish and with the passage of time have been whittled down to those which will always be retained within the family for intrinsic, nostalgic reasons. Having initially entered the sixth form without even a notion as to what I wanted to do in life, one day just after the start of spring term in the January of 1982 and with the end of sixth form and seven years of Arnold on a sixth month horizon, a friend, totally out of the blue, suggested that I contacted Blackpool and Fylde College. As it transpired, the ideal three-year course was available on my doorstep, an HND in professional photography coupled with the British Institute of Professional Photography's PQE (Professional Qualifying Examination). My successful application to the Palatine Road campus was conditional upon my gaining two 'A' level passes. Having spent a year meandering academically and thinking I'd end up a banker, I now had a professional goal.

1982 was also notable as Argentina invaded the 'Malvinas'. Britain declared that this was an act of war and dispatched a task force south to reclaim and reinstate British sovereignty of the Falkland Islands. It was the run up to 'A' levels and I followed the daily news accounts avidly with everyone else. We were informed about the battles, there was Goose Green, Darwin, the eventual retaking of Port Stanley, the sinking of the General Belgrano and the loss of HMS Sheffield following an Exocet missile strike and the subsequent loss of HMS Coventry. We were told about Special Forces involvement – although no precise details of course until much later and the casualties on both sides (649 Argentinian and 258 British losses). Two posthumous Victoria Crosses were awarded to Lt. Colonel 'H' Jones and Sergeant Ian McKay. Major General Jeremy Moore accepted the Argentinian surrender from Brigade General Mario Menendez on 14th June, ending a ten- week conflict that had started on 2nd April.

I remember feeling very patriotic. Simon Weston, OBE, a twenty-year old soldier at the time, was horrifically burned on RFA Sir Galahad during the hostilities (hauntingly, from the news reports of the day, I can still hear his painful cries of 'Leave, leave, leave, leave', as he was stretchered off). He almost became synonymous as one of the faces of the conflict. Under heavily restricted Ministry of Defence reporting guidelines, the late BBC correspondent Brian Hanrahan reassured a tense nation, when he observed Harrier jump jets taking off from HMS Hermes to begin the initial air attack on Port Stanley. In a very personal account, the skilful reporter informed us that he wasn't allowed to state specific numbers, but "I counted them all out, and I counted them all back". The Falklands conflict, now an important part of British history, seems like yesterday and I lived through it as a young eighteen-year-old, well, via the compelling news reports anyway. Margaret Thatcher provided steadfast leadership during the crisis and a year later the Conservatives won a landslide general election victory, taking 397 seats to Labour's 209.

All too quickly 'A' levels were upon me, following months of revision. Geography and Economics I felt had gone well. I waffled my way through General Studies and felt that I'd presented too biased a case for my Politics papers. I had a nerve-wracking wait until results day in mid-August. Before then, there was a three-week family 'holiday' to Ireland to get through. The sadness I felt at leaving such a fine institution as Arnold School, coupled with the certain knowledge that I might never see many of my contemporaries again, was profound.

I can't for the life of me remember the inevitable school leaving do, but there must have been one – maybe even several. In a way having A Level exams spread out made the leaving process easier. My last exam would have been in June 1982 and so it was that I went into the memorial hall for that exam and when I was finished, I simply left and didn't come back – well, not for many years anyway.

Looking back, whilst I underachieved academically, Arnold brought out and nurtured my love of the outdoors – the Combined Cadet Force, the Mountain and Cycling Clubs, the Duke of Edinburgh's Bronze, Silver and Gold Awards, as well as keeping fit with cross-country running (finishing my school days as cross-country captain). I am thankful to the many gifted teachers who guided me through the minefield of challenging subject matter. Such greats as Biology teacher, Bill Roe, by far my favourite teacher and for whom I had the utmost respect. Then there was Colonel Eddie Jones, Latin and English Master, head of the Combined Cadet Force, hero of the D-Day landings in World War 2 and of course, my first impersonation. Eddie was quite simply a great man and a wonderful character. They don't make them like that anymore! His pedestal was very high indeed – I can still see him peering at me inquisitively over his half-moon spectacles, before declaring, "Canning, stop making those stupid quacking noises!" Denys Barber was another firm favourite. His French lessons were fun and entertaining. The late Ken 'Bubbles' Riding, another character of the Arnold common room, I credit with getting me through the hurdle called Physics O Level. Then there was maths genius Andrew Bell, who essentially was the reason why I passed my crucial maths O Level. I enjoyed Andrew's maths lessons and time spent with him on many a school mountain club walk in the Lake District. He was a very likeable and good-humoured man. So too were my Geography teachers, the late Chas Ellis, Kendle Lee, John Ashcroft and Ian Winterflood.

Who could forget the character who is Max Kirkham - chemist, raconteur, rugby player and keep fit enthusiast. Max is a great guy, intelligent, witty and has always been very popular with the fairer sex! I have fond memories of Aly and me, weight training with Max down at Fylde Rugby Club, wearing our t-shirts emblazoned with the wording 'Smile, it's only pain'! as well as teaching him photography! As with any school, there were of course one or two duds who will remain in my memory forever as utterly useless teachers – one such teacher had a penchant for standing at the front of class with head bowed in silence for ages. Too many pregnant pauses – zero quality teaching – lack of interest for subject matter. That wouldn't be tolerated today, you wouldn't have lasted half a term mate! Then there was a certain teacher who I found very uninspiring indeed. Their whole demeanour grated on me. Married almost as many times as Henry V111, they had an attitude to match and always 'had a face on them'. Alas, I think this teacher had it in for me from day one. Suffice to say, when we parted company I didn't weep into my pillow at night! Fortunately, the duds numbered but a few. 'Pin 'ead', 'Wide ball' and 'Outcha come Clarkey, outcha come', whilst poor teachers, nevertheless provided me with more material for my impersonations and I'm glad to say that they suffered mercilessly at my hands!

But what about the teachers, the characters of the Arnold common room who never taught me, but who I inevitably stumbled across when they invigilated exams or sat in class during a colleague's absence? 'Billy Bean' (aka John Groves), Bernie Leather, Peter 'Basher' Bentley, Fred Liston, John Oram and Paddy McMahon were the teachers I yearned to have. They were all outstanding teachers and characters in their own right, but nobody came close in terms of memorable character status than the late, great Dave Miller. Multi-linguist, scholar, musical genius, fantastic teacher – Dave was a born entertainer. He should have been on stage. God love him, Dave had a penchant for the 'sherbets' and could often be found in the pub, the Winmarith, opposite sixth form, holding court. I think it's fair to say that Dave Miller almost enjoyed cult status amongst the guys and gals in school. Dave is probably making everyone laugh in his very own pub in the sky. He was one of life's gems and is very sadly missed.

I had the utmost respect for my head, Richard Rhodes, who was truly a head of his time. A Justice of the Peace from a very young age, Mr Rhodes went on to become Headmaster of his old school, Rossall, before retiring. A much in demand after dinner speaker, Richard Rhodes was the first Police Crime Commissioner of Cumbria up until mid-2016. What an enviable career – what a Gent!

Looking back on my seven years at Arnold, the lower and upper sixth forms were great, whereas years 1-5 were a continual car crash academically. However, I excelled on the outdoor pursuits side of things and this, coupled with my numerous piss-takes and impersonations of staff members, helped to balance up the scales. I decided to wind up NPT on one occasion, whose job it was to round up the upper sixth after morning break and ensure that we were all promptly seated in the lecture theatre in readiness for the guest speaker to arrive. A good ten minutes before the end of break, I hid behind one of the sixth form study doors and bellowed at the top of my voice in characteristic, well spoken, NPT style "6A forum, lecture theatre!!" (which roughly translated meant 'Get your arses to the lecture theatre, sharpish!'). To my surprise, the wind-up worked – everyone filed out of their studies like sheep, earlier than usual and the entire year was seated and quiet for a full five minutes when suddenly in walked the lean figure of a clearly astonished NPT, nevertheless looking immaculate in his suit, neatly combed jet-black hair and pristine bow tie. His totally perplexed demeanour was a picture. NPT couldn't understand why we were already seated and he wasn't for once forced to shout the immortal words of round up. Oh, yes, that was down to me!

Given my time again, I'd definitely work harder, but would have dropped 2 A Level subjects. I was privileged to be part of the massive techno revolution that saw the invention of the computer chip. I remember 'space invaders', the first 'Commodore' calculator, the first digital watches with red-coloured L.E.D. display. My year was the first to be allowed to use calculators in exams – before that it was logarithm tables. There wasn't a single computer in school because the desktop hadn't been invented. Mobile phones, iPads and Apps were science fiction. Land line telephones could not be unplugged and everyone used red telephone boxes, when the standard charge was 2 pence for a local call. Having a Wii/wee meant nipping to the bogs for a slash. Bjorn Borg and Abba dominated our lives...and then we had punk rock! (I can remember my sore neck from over pogoing in discos). I lived through the era of the 3-day week and power cuts, drainpipes, flares, kipper ties, high-heeled wedge shoes and long hair – now I don't have any! I had no girlfriend at school, because my father destroyed my confidence in that department, but I had friends and by God they were good friends. Friends such as Aly, Andy, Simon, Steve, Mark, Reg and Andy B, who was sadly destined to leave us quite quickly. Quite a short guy and nicknamed 'Errol', I can remember Andy B arriving at school with this massive bag slung over his shoulder and I'd shout out of the study window "Alright Errol!" I can see his face grinning at me like a Cheshire cat. Andy B was a whizz at economics and the stock exchange, who died suddenly following a berry aneurysm. He wasn't much over 30 and so very young. I still remember him snogging the vicar's daughter on the back of the 92 bus and playing Elvis Costello's 'Oliver's Army' on his cassette recorder on the way home. He was a lovely bloke – intelligent, hard-working and with a diamond sense of humour. He's so missed.

CHAPTER 3

The Summer of 1982

In the summer of '82 I was just a handful of months away from my 19th birthday. In addition to the obligatory gardening jobs and household chores to top up my spending money, I still delivered newspapers potentially seven mornings a week. On Saturday afternoons I would work in the news agency on the Breck for the owners, Des and Isla Tweats. Des spent most Saturdays refereeing football matches all over the North-West and Isla would normally go off shopping with her friend Katie, leaving me in charge. Saturday afternoons were great. They were normally steady to busy in the run up to the 'earlies' (early edition Evening Gazette newspaper) arriving mid-afternoon. Once the rush for the earlies had died down, Isla would return and this meant that I could take a break, popping next door to the lovely Anna Pawson's café for a bite to eat. My ritual was sitting in the window people watching, whilst enjoying a couple of toasted teacakes and a mug of coffee. When I returned, Isla would either go out again or the two of us would serve behind the counter until the next rush, the Gazette main edition, followed some time later by the Gazette 'Greens' (football results). I'd usually finish between 6 and 6.30pm.

I was in love with two local girls simultaneously at that time - Samantha and Janice. Sam, who was dark-haired and stunningly attractive worked with her Mum at the ladies' boutique on the corner. Janice, who was blonde, bustier, and just as pretty as Sam, worked in Blackpool, but lived a few minutes' walk away. Both girls would always come into the paper shop at some point during Saturday afternoons. Suffice to say that my heart always skipped a beat or two when these girls came in and funnily enough, it brightened up the whole day! Alas, I was destined to go out with neither girl.

Once, whilst counting out change in the shop, I was asked out by Peter, a middle-aged gay chap, whom I politely turned down. Thinking that this was the end of the matter, that very evening the same man turned up at my house in his best suit, having found out where I lived. Thankfully my younger sister answered the door to deliver the news to him that I was out with my girlfriend. Fortunately, Peter finally got the message and never bothered me again. Fast forward three and a half decades to 2017 and I was so shocked and upset to be photographing an aged Peter, who was now a desperately ill patient in Blackpool's Victoria Hospital. There was no hint of recognition in his eyes as he lay in his bed, silent, dejected, weak and forlorn, whilst I spoke to him softly and sympathetically about what I was photographing and how the images would be used by the medical team. Two days later when I returned to the same ward, surprised to see a different patient occupying Peter's bed, on enquiring to sister, I was shocked again to learn that Peter had sadly passed away, that very day – just hours after I'd photographed him. RIP Peter.

And so ... to our infamous last 'family holiday' in August 1982. Destination: Republic of Ireland. Route: by road to the port of Holyhead in Anglesey and then ferry to Dun Laoghaire (pronounced 'Dunleerie') south east of Dublin on Eire's east coast. Dad had meticulously planned this trip to take account of what he wanted to do for what we all thought was going to be, at best, a completely boring trip. That meant visiting as many relatives and friends as he could think of. However, there was to be a little respite. Incredibly Dad had given my two sisters and me permission for the three of us to go off for a week's walking and youth hostelling mid-way through the trip.

The Volvo was packed to the brim and what wasn't in the boot was crammed onto the roof rack. I don't remember anything of the trip to Holyhead, except that Dad started as he meant to go on – in a foul mood. Having disembarked the ferry at Dun Laoghaire, there was no let-up in his behaviour and I remember barely having left the ferry ramp before Dad let rip. He started rowing first with Mum and then snapping at the three of us, for no apparent reason. But this was very much in keeping with his character. A falsely posed photograph of a family group taken with tripod-mounted camera and self-timer during this holiday, desperately trying to look happy, but failing miserably, speaks volumes. The tone of the 'holiday' had been set and was there to stay. I believe we travelled firstly south to see one of Dad's university pals, Dr. Martin Rahill in Greystones, before heading south to Wicklow Head to visit an elderly cousin Vincent. From the Wicklow area, it was about turn, back up to fashionable Ard Na

Mara in Malahide, a suburb north east of Dublin, to visit another friend, Patrick MacMahon, who was head of the Irish Revenue.

The spreads were unbelievable and seemed to expand into feast like proportions with each visit. Dad, a native Irishman, had somehow forgotten to dial extremely kind and generous Irish hospitality into the equation and this was the third of four visits this first day. This call to the MacMahon family was memorable for two reasons – firstly, because I was so full I couldn't eat any more of the food repeatedly offered to me and secondly, when Patrick introduced me to his daughter Monica, who was three years my senior I was in love! The phrase 'drop dead gorgeous' didn't even come close. Dark-haired Monica was a true Irish beauty and then some – curvaceous, gorgeous figure, long legs, full, ruby lips and come to bed eyes and I couldn't take my own eyes off her. When it was time to say goodbye, if anyone had suggested at that very moment that I might like to stay for a few days, there would have been no complaints from my department! Alas, we had to leave and I was never to see Monica again. But the impression she made on me was long-lasting and helped carry me through some turbulent times that were now close at hand. From Malahide it was north again to Drogheda, skirting around Dublin in the process. Our final and fourth stop on this first day was to visit one of Dad's five sisters, my Auntie Una. It didn't seem to take us long from Malahide, but then Dad was in the driving seat...and driving like a complete and utter wanker. Drogheda, southernmost town in County Louth, straddles the River Boyne, scene of the historic Battle of the Boyne during Ireland's Williamite war in 1690. I remember commenting that the Boyne looked very muddy, dirty even, to which Dad insinuated that it was awash with human excrement!

Feeling quite stuffed after the four visits and unable to eat another morsel of food, we left Auntie Una's after a few hours and stayed at Tubbertoby Farmhouse, located between Termonfeckin and Clogherhead. The next day we travelled north west towards Dad's birthplace Rathmullan, in County Donegal, where we were based for the remainder of the holiday. Although Rathmullan is in the Irish Republic, the most direct route meant inevitably crossing into Northern Ireland. In the summer of 1982, the troubles were still on the boil with signs of enmity everywhere you looked. So, we had to pass the inevitable check points at strategic border crossings at Aughnacloy then onwards to Omagh in the County of Tyrone and thence to Strabane in the west of the same county. I remember feeling quite nervous driving through Northern Ireland at that time. You could feel the tension in the air travelling through Omagh, which had seen its fair share of sectarian violence. Sixteen years after our visit, Omagh was of course to witness a bomb which had particularly devastating consequences. An explosive device planted by the Real IRA killed 29 people and maimed and injured hundreds more when it was detonated on 15th August 1998. But it was driving through Strabane that really got me. The town had a depressed, eerie feel to it and looked like a war zone. So many bombed out buildings. Between the 1970's and the 1990's bombings and shootings were rife and Strabane once had the dubious honour of being the most bombed town in Northern Ireland.

The River Mourne runs through the centre of Strabane and eventually joins the River Finn, north west of the town to form the River Foyle. Give or take the odd mile, Strabane is approximately equidistant from Omagh, Derry and Letterkenny. I remember as a very small boy of five, playing with Vicky on the disused steam trains that littered the derelict Strabane sidings. Rusting boilers, giant hulks of scrap metal, miles of track buried beneath ubiquitous weeds - half-forgotten reminders that in their heyday these once smart locomotives had been an integral part of the old Londonderry and Enniskillen (L & ER) Railway, which reached Strabane in 1847.

And so it was with great relief that we made it through the Strabane check point, crossing the Lifford Bridge into the town of Lifford located over the border in the Irish Republic. Once at Lifford, it's normally a relatively simple matter of driving north-west to Letterkenny, a very scenic and enjoyable 45-minute journey, if the weather is kind, but not if the weather's shit and you have a father who drives like a dick. Having crossed over the River Swilly at Letterkenny, Dad insisted on an impromptu stop at some hotel whereupon he downed 2 double whiskies, one after the other in quick succession – God only knows why. With Dad now over the drink-drive limit and insisting on getting behind the wheel, we headed north along the R245 to Ramelton, a tiny village which is almost impossible not to stop at for ice cream. Grandfather James Canning was born here in Ramelton. At Ramelton the road splits and we followed the R247 in a north-easterly direction as the road hugged the western shores of Lough Swilly, a huge glacial fjord, the mouth of which opens into the North Atlantic at its northern end. Suddenly we were there, parking up at the old post office on Main Street - the home of Miss B Canning (aka Auntie Bridie and Dad's oldest sister, who was 16 years his senior). We could finally turn off the cassette tape that had been playing 'The Pretty Little Girl From Omagh' far too many times during the weary journey. When we were small children Dad bullied us into singing Irish songs like 'Mush-Mush-Mush Tural-i-addy' ('*.....If you're in for a row or a ruction, just tread on the tail of me Mush, Mush, Mush tural-i-addy, Singin' Mush, Mush, Mush tural-i-ay. If you're in for a row or a ruction, just tread on the tail of me coat.),* 'The maid of the Sweet Brown Owl' and John McCormack's 'The Garden where the Praties Grow' and hum songs like 'Dance at Fiona's Wedding'. Just prior to this trip he became obsessed with putting one of his sister Una's poems ('Teelin's Smiling Bay') to music and got us to learn it. His aim was to show off in front of his sisters. Whatever ... Dad had returned home. His watering holes The Beachcomber, The White Harte and The Pier Hotel were all in very close proximity and beckoned him as surely as a fly to shit. As it transpired all three pubs were soon to be frequented by him on a daily basis, as though he had issued himself a special decree to get drunk for the entire duration.

Would we be staying at the prestigious Rathmullan House Hotel, which was located right on the doorstep, or the equally refined Fort Royal? Not likely. Dad had rented a cold, cramped chalet, which smelled of mould for the three week stay. It was situated five miles further north in an area called Lehardan. Dad had us pronouncing this place name weeks before we came over the water, because he didn't want us to embarrass him in front of his sisters and friends with incorrect pronunciation. "Ah Jesus, five times, it's LYAR-HA-DEN!" he would whine. Now, as it turned out, Dad had it all wrong and to our delight the Canning stalwart, Auntie Bridie, who was in effect a replacement Mama Canning, corrected Dad in front of everyone. "No, no James, it's 'Le-her-den'" (rolled off the tongue very quickly).

Retribution was immediate and prolonged. Dad was in a foul mood, snapping and shouting at us and rowing with Mum. During the day, we would go for walks along the Swilly beaches or wander around Rathmullan's ancient Carmelite Friary ruins. Known locally as 'the Abbey', the picturesque ruins are covered in ivy and have a commanding view of Lough Swilly. Other walks would take in the old catholic cemetery just outside Rathmullan at Killygarven. It is at Killygarven that James Canning senior (my paternal Grandfather) was laid to rest in 1941. Mama Agnes Mary Canning, who died in 1966, is buried in Rathmullan Cemetery, opposite St. Joseph's

Church. My Auntie Bridie is also buried in the same plot and my father's ashes were later to be scattered on top of this grave. Whilst we enjoyed the tranquil scenery, Dad just ignored us and instead pitched up with friends like Eddie Toomey or Sammy Hussey in the White Harte where I somehow knew that Dad wouldn't be cradling just a pineapple juice and lemonade. At a pre-determined time, which I always dreaded, I would have to drive down from the chalet and pick Dad up, who I'd find somewhat unsurprisingly, pissed as a fart.

After a week of putting up with Dad binge drinking and the inevitable angry mood swings precipitated by his hangovers, Vicky, Kate and I breathed a sigh of relief as we escaped alone for a full seven nights of walking and youth-hostelling in beautiful Donegal countryside.

The youth hostelling break was over far too quickly and we were all dreading Dad picking us up. When his blue Volvo 244 came into sight however, something about the car looked a tad out of place. Then my attention was drawn to the front of the vehicle, which was all dented. It transpired that Mum and Dad had been in an accident. As Dad was driving uphill on a narrow stretch of road, close to the scenic Atlantic Drive, they met a local drinks lorry packed with huge, steel beer kegs coming down the hill. One suddenly broke loose, flew through the air and smacked into the front offside of Dad's car. The impact exploded the front offside tyre to the extent that my parents thought that a bomb had been detonated, cracked the bumper, dented the wing and bonnet, smashed the headlamp compartment and wrecked the power-assisted steering. Dad's pride and joy looked a sorry mess. There must have been a roll of gaffer tape holding everything in place. If Mum and Dad had been travelling in a smaller car, the accident could well have claimed their lives. In the protracted compensation that followed, Dad's greed got the better of him and he instructed Mum to turn on the tears in an effort to put across the fact that she had been completely traumatised by the crash. This was a falsehood and Dad's plan back fired. The pay-out was a paltry sum.

The accident did nothing to lighten Dad's mood. Already annoyed at having to break away from his cronies at the Pier Hotel in picking us up, the accident had sent him into a rage. This coupled with yet another hangover probably meant that Dad felt like death and in no fit state to drive. Thankfully, he gave me permission to drive the damaged car and all of us to Omagh, back over the border in Northern Ireland, where the nearest accident repair specialist was based. With the power assisted steering knackered, I drove the car like a cautious Colin, for if you took your hands off the wheel for one tiny moment, the steering, which had been knocked out of alignment by the force of the beer keg hitting the car, made the Volvo veer to the left! I was equally nervous as a soldier, rifle in hands, strolled up to my window, obviously attracted to the car by the scale of damage. I told him briefly what had happened and he inquired as to our destination. Smiling in sympathy he said in a broad Northern Irish accent "Good luck and aweeyago!" I smiled back in acknowledgement and breathed yet another sigh of relief as I moved the automatic gear selector from 'P' to 'D' and drove slowly away from the check point.

Having deposited the damaged Volvo at the garage in Omagh, I got us back to Rathmullan in the loan car - a smaller, pale metallic green, Volvo 343 GL manual, which was great to drive as it had some poke! En route to the chalet, I dropped Dad off at The White Harte under strict instructions to come back and pick him up at 6pm, which I duly did. As I drew up, I tensed as I saw him swaying from side to side and then as he made to grab the front passenger door handle, Dad vanished from view. One moment he was at the car, the next he was gone. My inebriated father had only gone and fallen in the gutter! Well, what the hell was I supposed to do? I'd be buggered if I was going to get out of the car and go around and pick him up. So I just sat there waiting to see what would happen. After what seemed like ages, this decrepit sixty-year old man's red face appeared at the passenger window once more. It took another eternity for him to open the door and get in. What happened next was farcical. As I looked over at my pathetic, clearly drunk father, I saw him trying to locate his seat belt in its fastener. Dad, whose vision (among other things) was impaired, was dancing around with the seat belt in his hand, continually missing the fastener and not even comprehending what was happening. After a few minutes, I got fed up, snatched the belt and fastened it for him.

Thinking that Dad would drop off on our way back to the chalet in Lehardan, not a mile out of Rathmullan, he suddenly seemed to come to and growled "Stop the car" to which I dutifully obeyed. Fortunately, there was a convenient lay-by up ahead. With no explanation, Dad then climbed out of the car, staggered round to the front offside and to my horror then unzipped his trousers, pulled out his todger and just stood there for ages having what must have been the longest piss in history! It was still daylight and cars were passing in both directions at regular intervals and would have clearly seen

Dad and his exposed penis. I just shrunk down in the driver's seat, incredulous and sickened. Once Dad had finished urinating in broad daylight and in full view of passers by, he calmly got back into the Volvo and we continued on our way back to the chalet. I was really shocked.

The following morning, I awoke unusually early and tip-toed to the bathroom, checking first to see whether I could hear Dad awake. On hearing his loud snores, I continued to the bathroom and quietly shut the bathroom door. When I'd finished, I opened the bathroom door once more and to my dismay Dad was in the living room glaring at me, holding his head. "You went to the bathroom before me!" a clearly angry Dad chastised. "I needed the toilet" I declared. "Don't answer back" he snapped. Vicky then came to my rescue and Dad about turned and went back to his bedroom, leaving me fuming at yet another drunken outburst. Dad then blamed me when he fell down, hit his head on the bedroom chest of drawers and hurt himself on hearing me go to the bathroom. It was my fault entirely, Dad jabbed at me.... because I had dared to disrupt his morning routine!

It was another beautiful day outside and I found myself needing to get out of the chalet quickly to cool off. The 'red mist' was descending and I just wanted to smack my father one. As I was sitting on the front lawn talking to Vicky and Kate, we heard Mum and Dad's top bedroom window suddenly being opened. We all looked round and to our astonishment saw this hand reach out and throw an empty bottle of whiskey onto the grass – no doubt to try and hide it from Mum. We all felt angry, dejected and utterly disgusted with the man that called himself our father. Even at Auntie Bridie's later that day, our mood hadn't brightened when we tucked into her delicious home-made scones. That was after Bridie Canning's hawk eyes had spotted the outline of a small bottle of whiskey in Dad's back pocket and wanted to know what it was. We all sat there as Dad bullshitted his way out of yet another awkward situation. The deflection, typically, was aimed at me. I was mid-way through my second scone topped with jam and cream, when Dad looked at me, sniffed, did his embarrassing "la-da-di" sing song and said to everyone "Paul's on his second scone already!" Auntie Bridie quickly retorted, "Well, you're not doing so badly yourself, James". I would have ordinarily punched the air in defiance, but because I felt so depressed, I barely noticed. But notice, nevertheless, we all did. Dad was not only drinking daily in all three of the local pubs and during evening meals, but now it was blatantly obvious he was sneakily drinking when we weren't looking as well. That meant all day and well into the evening.

It seemed like a life sentence, those three weeks that we all languished over the water, but just as quickly as it had come around, it was time to leave Rathmullan and head back to the ferry port at Dun Laoghaire. I remember nothing of the return journey in Ireland, only of our nightmare journey from Holyhead back to Poulton-le-Fylde. Thankfully, I drove the car off the ferry at Holyhead and I was blessed with having Vicky as a born natural organiser and an excellent navigator, who had maps already unfolded on her knees in the back of the car. Mum and Kate were also in the back and Dad was in the front. We were approaching a major junction when I asked Vicky a simple question. "Is it right or left here, Vicky?" Dad's afterburners had just been ignited as he bellowed, making us all jump in fright "Paul, stop the fucking car!!!" With Dad in this state, I should have refused, but he just repeated his outburst. Dad made me sit in the back and he shot off at breakneck speed as we all held on for dear life. That last section of the journey completely stressed us out. On top of everything that had already happened, we were also dog tired. Trying to stay awake, I kept drooping periodically as suddenly I was aware that we were on the M55 motorway near Kirkham with Dad driving on the hard shoulder. There was no reason for this – no diversion signs or accident – nothing. The way was clear. Dad had lost the plot. When he came off the motorway, too fast, at junction 3 Dad veered towards a dead end and not towards the A585 turn off, to which we all shouted, "LOOK OUT!". By some miracle we all arrived back home in the early hours of that mid-August morning, alive, with all our body parts intact, albeit very tired and shaken. Dad was cursing as he couldn't remember where he'd hidden all the keys to the internal doors. It took about ten minutes to find them, which at the time seemed like hours and even though it was late summer, the house was bloody freezing. Vicky, Kate and I just set about unpacking the car (when all we wanted to do was to go to bed), but we knew that we'd get a bollocking if we didn't help out. After the umpteenth trip out to the car, I went into the breakfast room to find Dad lying on the floor trying to light the boiler.

"Do you want a hand Dad?" I said simply. What happened next has been etched into my memory for life. My father picked himself up off the floor and with torch in hand glared at me. I was standing in the doorway from the hall looking into the breakfast room at his wicked face. Then to my utter horror Dad's eyes narrowed and he shouted at me in what constituted an unprovoked, vituperative outburst "Ahgg, you useless shit!!!!". He started to follow this bellicose insult with another expletive, but adrenaline had already kicked in and I didn't give the bastard the opportunity to finish as I bellowed at my father with all I had "Fuck off ya fat fart!!" Dad looked momentarily horrified that anyone, let alone me, should dare to stand up to him and what followed was a few seconds of tense stand-off, similar to a duel, pre-draw, in a western film gunfight.

I kept my eye on the big box torch my father had in his left hand as I was convinced he was going to try and deck me with it. My right fist curled tight as I readied myself to punch him. Dad then tried to counter by telling me where to go, but I kept repeatedly shouting over him. Simultaneously, Kate laughed nervously and then Dad rounded on Mum. "Look" he jabbed at each of us, "you've turned all these against me!" (referring to us as things and not children). I shouted back "No, your actions over the years have turned all of us against you". Still telling me in turn to foxtrot oscar and me repeatedly telling my father the same expletive, to my amazement, Dad backed down and disappeared out of the kitchen door to one of the outhouses. We all felt completely drained after that and went to bed. As I lay down on my bed in the early hours of that August morning, I cooled off and waited for sleep to come. The realisation of how close I had come to belting my father in the face, possibly inflicting severe injury on him, or worse, suddenly hit me. But Dad had long had it coming to him. He just went on and on and on at me until in the end, I just couldn't stand it any longer.

It had taken almost nineteen years to stand up to my father, but I didn't feel good about it at all. There was no 'yes' moment, no shaking my fist triumphantly in the air for a battle won. I was indifferent to the whole thing. As it turned out, my father huffed with me for three whole days, during which time he was obviously plotting and scheming how he was going to rebuild his power base. At the end of the third day I was summoned to the dining room. My father sat in his usual grease-stained chair. I sat to his left and Vicky sat on his right. Dad cleared his throat and addressed the room looking straight ahead. "Does Paul know the meaning of the word remorse?" I remained silent as the question had not been directed at me. Vicky leaned forward and looked enquiringly at me "Well, do you?" she said. I was pissed off when I replied "Yes". Dad continued, now directed at me, slowly and deliberately and with melodramatic false hurt mixed with warning in his voice. "What you said the other day,

I will probably take with me to my grave". After that, I just switched off. I wasn't expecting an apology, but some acknowledgement of his wrongdoing throughout the entire three-week Irish holiday. Being drunk everyday. His foul moods. The rows with Mum and generally making our lives hell. Not to mention driving whilst intoxicated. I got zilch of course, but make no mistake, Dad had in an instant re-established himself as the family patriarch and God help anyone who vied for his power.

Because we had such an awful experience in Ireland during the summer of 1982, it would be 25 years before I could return over the water and it only happened once Dad had died. It has also taken me more than 30 years to actually put pen to paper and write about those dreadful three weeks.

As far as my relationship with my father was concerned, to coin one of Dad's dramatic phrases when talking about his own relationship with Mum "it was hanging by the tiniest of threads". But deep down I knew there was no father son bond, no fatherly love. I used to shudder when shaking his hand for God's sake. Dad had in effect destroyed our relationship when he crossed the line - the day he labelled me a "useless shit." He clearly saw my very existence as a huge thorn in his side and by the same token, I had no love or respect for him either. Dad's behaviour was extreme to put it mildly and unforgivable, eventually leading to a permanent rift between us in 1999, which was to last until his death in February 2006.

Dad might have been academically clever as a medical doctor and charming to those outside the family, but make no mistake, that man was nasty to the core. My father was pernicious, self-centred, greedy, arrogant and an egregious boaster. He ate, drank and smoked to excess, had a vile temper, huffed like a kid and was an adulterer to boot. He absolutely loved himself, in my opinion had narcissism and narcissistic personality disorder and no doubt saw himself as the acme of fashionable masculinity. Over the top opprobrium? I think not. Dad was a smug libertine and he was morally diseased. His philanderings were well documented - he was very much the archetypal lothario.

When I was just a baby, instead of being a loving, attentive father, Dad was an adulterous love rat, in flagrante and screwing his way through teenage student lodgers and then rubbing Mum's nose in it – that is of course, when he wasn't performing botched-up illegal abortions in return for payment between the sheets.

Dad was a habitual pervert. He read scores of sordid novels and magazines, horded them all in the side attic and fantasised in his diaries about women. As one of Dad's milder, but lascivious entries documented "She had a bum sewn into tight black cords". My father was sexist and openly degraded women, especially professional ladies, by whom he felt threatened. Dad was also racist and homophobic - the gay community suffering mercilessly at his hands. My father's comments were vile, highly inappropriate and made me want to vomit. It was obvious that Dad had a huge inferiority complex which went way beyond 'little man syndrome'. He slagged off men and women in equal measure, whenever he saw fit. Everyone we knew had an unkind name or description, for example there was 'Roland Rat', 'Miss World', 'Mr and Mrs Beautiful' and of course 'Vic the Prick'. Even a young, local lass didn't escape when Dad described her as being "six-foot-tall and no shape". Jesus - and we had to live with this man.

We hadn't been home from Ireland long and the atmosphere was crap. My father had behaved abominably, we were all down and I was in a shit state. Now it was 'A' level results day and it was late summer 1982. Could my life get any worse? I had to travel into Arnold to find out my fate, which meant getting two separate buses to my South Shore school. The results were posted up on boards for all to see. Politics: Fail, Geography: Fail with an 'O' level pass, General Studies: Fail. Shit and derision! My mouth was dry. Economics – pass with a 'D' grade. One A Level. Bloody great. My results spelled 'F OF'. I needed two A Level passes Grade E or above to secure my place at Blackpool and Fylde College to study Photography. The realisation that this now wouldn't be happening hit me as quickly as one of Dad's insults. I'd fucked up and I'd fucked up royal! In terms of personal disasters this one was pretty damn bad.

Ordinarily, the thought of breaking this awful news to my parents would have been a big deal, but I was more concerned with the bigger picture i.e. what was I now going to do, I had no plan B? I felt completely empty, completely disconsolate and completely unfocused. In the wake of my results, I was summoned for an interview at Blackpool and Fylde College, but I didn't hold out much hope of getting through what was then a sort of local college 'clearing'. More days passed by in a haze when suddenly a letter postmarked Blackpool and Fylde College dropped through the letterbox. Convinced that the sheaf of correspondence would begin 'Dear Mr Canning, we regret to advise you…', unbelievably I couldn't have been more wrong as I read the accompanying letter in disbelief. I had been accepted, unconditionally onto the three-year photography course of study!

CHAPTER 4

Photography studies (The Blackpool & Fylde College Years) September 1982 – June 1985

In an instant, my poor performance at A Level was consigned to my mind's folder labelled 'Shit Memories' as I had just been dealt this unexpected friendly card. Someone upstairs was looking after me. God, I must have made a good impression at interview. Once again, similar to scraping through my 11 plus exam seven years earlier, I had won through on a wing and a prayer. I now had focus in my life and its name was photography.

In the beginning, college was a weird affair. It was weird because my fellow photography students hailed from all over the UK. I was the only one living with my parents and living quite literally on the doorstep of college. Well ok, it was a cycle ride to and from the Palatine Road campus and Poulton and it was good exercise on my light-blue, metallic, 10 speed Peugeot racing bike. The students were a mixed bag of talent, ranging from out of this world to the inevitable time wasters, with the majority like me, being simply average. Leading the field, Dominic and Gary were by far the best students, excelling in their craft and often collaborating on carefully worked out projects over one or two late night lemonades. They were, and still are, light years ahead of the rest of us in terms of their extraordinary creative thinking. It was pure joy to see their finished work and inspiring to see the shots in the making. But students like Guy, Craig, Paul I and Adrian couldn't so easily be ignored and were also very talented. Ladies' man Paul was a superb fashion photographer, whereas Adrian quickly made his mark in the commercial and industrial arena.

There were, as I intimated, quite a few students who shouldn't have been on the photography course and who did nothing to enhance or further the good reputation that Blackpool had back then in the early '80s. One such student was Ian Mallard, who could be found hiding behind his newspaper every morning in the studio. You'd greet him with "Morning Ian, what are you up to?" whereupon the paper would be lowered slightly to reveal the silver rimmed glasses followed by the enormous Cheshire cat grin. The paper was then brought back up again and the face once more disappeared. This told me everything I needed to know about this particular time waster. But there were others like 'Scrubber Munney', 'Ginger Simon' and 'Heather Peruski' who existed as an irritation.

My first-year tutor was Geoff Clarke (catchphrase: 'Right me ol' son'), who I found difficult to follow only due to the fact that his plane of thinking was much, much higher than mine. Nevertheless, my first-year theoretical course work was sound and I was readily aided by experienced, helpful tutors like Roger 'Mac' McDonald, who taught processing theory and practicals. In his spare time, Roger Mac used to do up old vintage cars and you'd often see him driving around the Fylde in an open top, wearing his driving goggles. I warmed to him instantly, not just because of his kind and friendly demeanour, but because whether wearing his driving apparel or not, he reminded me of the father figure 'Caractacus Potts' in the film Chitty Chitty Bang Bang, a childhood favourite. Ted Gray, who took us for technology theory taught us everything from dissecting the workings of different format cameras to the physics involved. Hours were spent getting to grips with concepts such as 'angle of reflection', 'depth of field', 'exposure', 'Scheimpflug rotation' (camera movements) and 'pin registration'. Ted was also a gifted retoucher and taught us how to mix retouching paints, stippling with different grades of brush and ultimately how to painstakingly retouch both negatives and prints. Now of course, with software such as Photoshop you can do the retouching job in a fraction of the time that it took with water and retouching paint. Similarly, the modern equivalent of pin registering a number of pieces of film exactly, is Photoshop's layers, which makes the whole task effortless. In the good old days, if you ballsed up pin registration and a piece of film wasn't an exact fit, it was a major embuggerance, whereas if you make a mistake in Photoshop, you can simply delete that layer. Ted had a vast amount of knowledge, which he was always ready to impart. However, I do remember him being just a tad cautious when lending out one of college's latest acquisitions, the Nikon F3! The camera in question was a 'beut' and Nikon's third pro SLR. It was brought to the market in 1980 and astonishingly, although superseded by the F4 in

1988 and then the F5 eight years later, the F3 remained in production until 2001. The F3, the first of many F-series cameras to have the trademark red stripe feature on its handgrip, was a manual and aperture priority semi-automatic camera.

Brian Cutler was another charming gent. With a world of professional experience under his belt, Brian was a very experienced portrait and wedding photographer who taught us portraiture in that first year. Under Brian's skilful guidance, we learned all about how to slim down a slightly rotund face or conversely fatten a thin face with narrow and broad lighting; what butterfly and flat lighting is, how to add measured fill-in light, high and low key portraits; the use of reflectors and also the addition of a hair light – all this whilst practising on each other. We'd normally use 35mm black and white film or if we were lucky the 'Blad' (Hasselblad medium format roll film camera) would be available. Films were then processed, printed and critiqued.

There were other tutors who had a lesser input. One grey haired chap, whose name I forget, took us for marketing. He was memorable for his bushy eyebrows and catch phrase "I would like to start this morning's proceedings by taking some sort of register!". His seminars were bearable, but crucially he helped mould my first ever personal profile. His definition of a good CV has stuck in my mind for eternity "your CV is the finest example of the best piece of written work of which you are capable".

That first semester, the autumn term of 1982, was a heady mix of new ideas, new planes of thinking and a new way of being – but the practical side remained an enigma. My creative juices just wouldn't flow. I was producing technically correct imagery, but it was piss boring compared to the likes of Dominic, Garry, Craig, Paul and Adrian, who had it sussed from the start. My frustration continued into the second and third semesters and was only lifted by two happy events. Firstly, my old school Arnold had awarded me the Community Service prize, which involved me attending the school's speech day at Blackpool's Winter Gardens in Church Street that October. Throughout the sixth form, I had been involved with community service projects with my mate Andy G. We'd pop round to old folks' houses and do their shopping, cleaning and tidying for them. One little old lady called Olive was such a sweetie. Into her 90s, Olive was very deaf, but we'd joke with her, make her chuckle and she'd always have a smile for us. "Do you know?", she'd point at us with a bony finger and a twinkle in her eyes, chuckling. I was very fond of her. So imagine my anger when I heard that social services had made an impromptu call to see Olive the day before we were due to call round one week in the closing stages of upper sixth, made a quick assessment of Olive and her surroundings and concluded that this old lady couldn't manage at home by herself. The next I heard was that Olive had been put into a rest home. Desperately unhappy and with her livelihood swept from underneath her, dear old Olive died barely two weeks later. It took me a long time to get over that one and the grief was still raw as I stepped up on stage to collect my community service award. I received the 1981 publication 'Lichfield on Photography' by my portrait hero and the Queen's cousin, Patrick Lichfield (aka Thomas Patrick John Anson, 5th Earl of Lichfield). Lord Lichfield suffered a major stroke and sadly died on Remembrance Day 2005.

Secondly, in March 1983, I travelled to St. James's Palace in London with Mum to receive my Gold Duke of Edinburgh's award. Prince Phillip did his usual round of talking to the various award recipients and as he approached my group, I was determined to speak with him. After HRH's usual "How long have you been waiting here?" Prince Philip seemed very interested to hear about my cycling expedition around the Yorkshire Dales. I was really chuffed that he'd singled me out. Then that was it, the great man was gone, whisked along to another group of award recipients. Once the Duke of Edinburgh had left the huge state room, it was down to individual celebrities to actually present each award. Breakfast television was the latest phenomenon, having only been on air a couple of months and its presenters, Frank Bough, Nick Ross and Selina Scott were the invited celebrities. There were six groups of ten recipients, which meant that each celebrity would be assigned two groups. Selina Scott, on whom I had a crush at that time, did the honours and presented me with my Gold award. I was all smitten and was more nervous talking to Selina Scott than talking with the Duke of Edinburgh! To make matters worse, I then 'pursued her' (my mother's words) afterwards for her autograph, to which she replied "Ah, Paul again!" Hmm – another embarrassing recollection from yours truly!

Moving swiftly on. I was given a maintenance grant from the local council as I was living at home. This derisory sum barely covered the cost of books and film, so it was with some measure of relief that I learned that at the end of the Palatine Road campus, the hairdressing students needed models of both sexes to practise on. The charge to us models was only 20 pence. The downside was it took over an hour. Still, I ended up with a professional looking haircut at next to no cost, which didn't dent my meagre student budget. My mate Aly's aunt used to be a hairdressing tutor at that salon and I popped in one time for my usual trim, only for my attention to be drawn to this comical figure cowering in a salon chair, obviously trying to hide from me. Wearing a translucent rubber hat full of holes, each with strands of hair poking through, it transpired that Aly was in having his hair streaked. He looked a picture and his face said it all. And the one time I didn't have a camera!

At the end of the first year, I'd saved up enough money through part-time work to go on a 10-day holiday with adventure company 'Trek Europa' (part of the Trek America company). The experience involved camping around Europe with people you'd never met before – 11 of you plus the driver / trek leader in a luxury mini-bus. We all shared the chores from cooking, washing up, erecting tents to cleaning the minibus, but it was great fun with everyone mucking in. Among the trek's highlights were Venice, Paris, the Jungfrau, the fairy tale Neuschwanstein castle (near Füssen in Bavaria), Amsterdam and knocking back the steins in Munich. In Heidelberg we ended up in some dodgy bar nervously cradling an 'Oettinger', whilst the DJ announced in English, but with a heavy German accent "Tonight's the night in Suzzie's Show Bar!" The holiday was overall a great experience and my first solo vacation. I had the travel bug.

Second year at College came around all too quickly and we had a new head of year tutor – Londoner Gordon Read. This affable pipe-smoker reminded me of a jovial cabby that I'd seen on television down in the metropolis. Second year was different to first year, there were fewer lectures and more practical time. Nevertheless, we still had Ted Gray's technical theory, marketing and processing. Techy back-up was initially provided by a wonderful Polish character, Stanislaw Josef Kruche Schuster, affectionately called Stan. His untimely death, at a relatively young age if I recall, shocked students and staff alike, as Stan was immensely popular.

I studied all the television adverts of the day and analysed what made them successful. I even studied various artists, looking at composition, use of light and shade, contrast, tone and colour – all the visual elements. One such painting which had a profound impact on me was 'The Triumph of Death' by sixteenth century Dutch artist Pieter Bruegel the Elder. A vast army of skeletons are seen wreaking mayhem across a scorched, barren earth. Distant fires burn and as one de-fleshed character maniacally tolls the death knell, men and women are hanged, crushed, stabbed and beheaded indiscriminately. Rotting fish and decaying cadavers lie strewn around the edges of a pond. Whilst the humans fight in vain, the skeletons parody the doomed survivors as the cull continues inexorably to the inevitable outcome. Leave aside that the whole painting is a bit disturbing, it comprises a myriad of unpleasant mini scenes. Two of my favourites are a skeleton mocking human happiness by playing a hurdy-gurdy, whilst simultaneously crushing a man with the wheels of his cart. And in another equally disturbing and totally bizarre scene, a fool plays the lute, whilst a skeleton behind him mockingly plays his. Everywhere you look there is iniquity. Even the skeleton deriving obvious pleasure from emptying the wine onto the floor is wicked. Discord very much prevails, yet although depressing, the whole painting is pure genius. Paintings depicting skeletons fine – real skeletons I would be acquainted with in later years!

Gordon was typically laid back and good humoured, but unfortunately, I didn't rate him as a tutor. It was more his funny stories I remember him for. In his cockney twang he would often regale us. One such tale involved a mate of his, renowned commercial photographer, Len Dance. On gaining the contract to photograph London's newly erected Nat West tower, which at the time of completion in 1980, was the UK's tallest building, Len had to think of a way to outsmart the competition and come up with a unique angle, in effect an exclusive. Len took an amazing shot with his fisheye lens from the driver's cab at the top of a huge crane, which gave him the perfect vantage point looking down and over the roof of the tower. Timing as always was crucial. Len's beautiful photograph shows the nearly complete Nat West tower with the London vista all around, far below. But what about other photographers trying to capture the same or similar view? Gordon went on "Well, Len got his shots in the nick of time, because the crane was dismantled as the weather quickly closed in. No suitable aircraft were available because of the low flying limit and Len bloody flogged it to 'em!!" Len Dance's iconic image of Tower 42, as it is now called, still ranks as one of my favourite photographs.

Second year's big hurdle was weekly 'print crit'. Each student would bring a printed photograph and display it for all to critique. The sessions were nerve-wracking because all three tutors were in attendance – Geoff (1st year), Gordon (2nd year) and Roger Goodwill (3rd year tutor and head of photography). Whilst some images were well received and others got balanced feedback, some got absolutely slated. As luck would have it, my first brief of second year was the 'building services brief', an open remit to photograph a person or people working in the building-related trades. I'd become good friends with Adrian, whose skill and expertise had rubbed off on me. We used to work together on assignments. I'd go as his assistant on his assignments and we'd then role reverse for my jobs. Inevitably, there would be talk about best shooting angle, moving this light a tad, models posing and so on. This had the effect that I got really enthused about the practical side of commercial and industrial photography. Two people working well together means double the learning, twice the creative thinking – it was a winning formula and just as the potent force of Dominic and Garry partnered up, I found my creative zeal with Adrian. I just wanted to get stuck in. If I was in overalls and hard hat and crawling around some huge, industrial complex, covered in grease and dirt in search of a good picture taking opportunity, then I was as happy as a pig in shit!

Adrian agreed to model for me and after we recced the Palatine Road boiler room, I soon hatched a plan – the bare bones of the brief were coming together. As with any brief there was much preparation. Date and time to be fixed, location to risk assess and arrange, camera, lenses, film, lighting and stands to book out with Peter in stores – getting in there quick before other students beat you to it and blagged the gear that you needed for your shoot (a real pain in the bum when that happened) plus of course clothing and accessories. I had Adrian kitted out in a blue boiler suit and protective eyeglasses. The pre-visualised image would see him buried amongst lots of big fat pipes all criss-crossing one another. As an accessory, I had Adrian leaning over one of these pipes, drill in hand with wire brush attachment going tooth and nail. On the day of the shoot, I'd hidden a couple of 'red-heads' (high powered tungsten lamps) behind Adrian to provide suitable back lighting and separation. A third red head was bounced off the wall behind and to the left of camera to provide frontal lighting. The addition of a white board reflector, kicking light back up into Adrian's face completed the lighting set. I'd been fortunate enough to get my hands on the Blad and loaded the 120 back with Kodak Vericolor Professional tungsten balance roll film (VPL 11 100). Although, the film's ASA / ISO was 100 speed, I rated it at 80 ISO to give the negatives a bit more punch, following C41 processing. The biggest coup, however, wasn't just that I'd got hold of a superb work horse that was the Hasselblad SWC, but I'd managed somehow to book out a Zeiss 50mm Distagon (wide angle lens) – a high quality, precision set of optics, which made you want to drool before you'd even handled it. The Distagon was the dog's bollocks!

After the inevitable faffing about, I quickly found the best camera angle. Although the Blad was tripod-mounted, the camera was virtually hugging the dirt on the floor, looking up and tilted at an angle to the right. This massively distorted perspective, sending converging verticals out of the window and creating a powerful, dynamic and exciting image, so much so that my hands almost trembled as I cupped them around the ground glass screen, before finally replacing the focusing hood. Having pre-metered, I put the back lighting a good stop and a half up on the front lighting and just went for it, bracketing the exposure in half stops and shooting off all twelve 2¼" square frames.

At Print Crit, the 20"x16" glossy image was really well received by all three tutors and fellow students. Composition, camera angle and use of lighting all scored highly. On the negative side, Adrian would have benefited by wearing a hard hat and gloves and one or two reflections on the pipework were too bleached out and therefore a tad distracting. Overall, this image was a winner and it also represented a pivotal point in my creativity, which took a massive upturn.

All my images prior to the building services brief were crap, in my opinion. I still cringe when I recall the 'Pear brief' – another open-ended assignment that meant getting creative with a piece of fruit. The hours I wasted building and painting an elaborate papier mache over wire frame volcano in the shape of an inverted pear, only to have the finished 'image' slated at print crit still haunt me. Compare this to Dominic and Garry's photo of a surprised, red-cheeked Dominic (of a photo within a photo) looking embarrassed as a beautiful model's (Garry's then girlfriend) hand enters the frame on the right-hand side delicately holding a pair of red, sexy, skimpy, lace knickers between forefinger and thumb. You took all the elements in – Dominic, his expression, the model's red-painted, glossy fingernails, the sexy, slightly erotic theme tempered with the humorous and you had a winning image if you just left it at that. And then you noticed what was in the background – a wall-mounted thermometer and my God, what was happening?...The temperature had shot off the scale, the red-stained alcohol had exploded out of the top and best of all, the alcohol bulb was, of course – pear shaped! I still remember that shot, 35 years plus after its inception.

Of equal brilliance was Garry and Dominic's dynamic, painted room set image, in which a pear-shaped mouse could be seen appearing out of a skirting board hole nibbling some cheese. Both images were shot using 5"x4" and 10"x8" cameras and involved different processes such as multiple exposure techniques, hand tinting and pin registration. Their effect on me has lasted to this day. Two totally different final photographs, cleverly conceived, carefully thought through and professionally executed. Pure genius!

Adrian and I enjoyed a good working relationship through second and third years. His visual communication skills were second to none. His skilful use of lighting, exposure control, use of models, coloured gels and camera angle to often turn the ordinary and mundane into an aesthetically exciting front cover or double page spread, he achieves with consummate professionalism. One must not forget Adrian's excellent rapport with the customer, for behind that friendly, relaxed demeanour and ready smile is a highly motivated and pin-sharp focused mind. As you might expect, Adrian is highly regarded in the commercial and industrial photography sector. Success hasn't come to him on a plate, cutting his teeth firstly in Liverpool and then for Aramco in Saudi Arabia, prior to setting up his own business. I congratulate him on all his achievements!

But my photography was taking off too. Around late 1983 / early 1984, I started working for what was then Imperial Chemical Industries Plc (ICI). Later in the early 1990's parts of ICI were sold off to 'Norsk Hydro', 'DuPont' and what was later to emerge as 'AstraZeneca'. I was doing bits of freelance work mainly in conjunction with 'Draeger Safety', producing photographs of breathing equipment and safety suits. On a maintenance grant, one needed extra 'reddies' to cash out for this and that. On one Draeger shoot at ICI's old Hillhouse site in Thornton-Cleveleys, with safety chief Charlie Tracey, I was wrapping up a final shot of a yellow suited guy clad in full breathing apparatus holding a giant wrench on a narrow gang plank with pipes and steam in the background – all this against a polarised blue sky, which sat well on the ground glass, let alone on the final 'trannies' (colour transparency film). I noticed a brand new petrol tanker draw up in the foreground. The driver climbed down from the cab and approached me. Shaking hands warmly, the driver told me that his managing director was looking for a really good photograph to depict his fleet of tankers – could I perhaps take a shot of this tanker? I didn't need to be asked twice!

The tripod-mounted 'RB' (Mamiya RB 6x7cm camera) was about two feet off the ground. I'd studied the background and directed the driver to carefully manoeuvre his gleaming silver-coloured tanker into position, which ran in a sort of arc across my landscape frame, the richness of the scarlet coloured cab being accentuated by each tweak of my polarising filter. I shot on fine grain, Fujichrome RDP 50 transparency, which I favoured for its colour saturation and sharpness, as well as for reproduction purposes. Back then 'repro' houses tended to favour trannies over negs and as I had two interchangeable film backs with me, I loaded the other back with Kodak VPS colour negative film. With contact details exchanged, I packed all the kit away in my father's Volvo and headed towards Blackpool town Centre. I made a beeline for Tom and Richard at 'Abbey Photographic' who ran this conveniently located photography shop, frequented on a regular basis by Blackpool and Fylde College photography students. An advanced order for fifty 10"x8" colour prints had been placed, but I needed 2 packs of paper (50 sheets in each) to cover test strips and test prints for the tanker shoot. From the centre of town, I drove the short distance to college, C41 processed the film and dropped my transparency films in for 'E6' slide processing (the techy would do a daily E6 process and in addition you could process your own slide film, which was a tricky, temperature and time-sensitive process). I hand printed the fifty 10"x8"s and had them in the post by close of play the same day. I spoke to the MD of the petrol tanker company the next day, who was so made up with his photographs, he broke official payment procedure and wrote me a cheque there and then for £300, which was gratefully received a day later by one hard up, not yet qualified photographer – not bad I thought for a 10 minute shoot, an hour's worth of processing, hand printing and admin.! More shoots followed and the monies earned helped to buoy up my coffers and see me financially into the black during and post college.

In addition to commercial and industrial photography, I had developed a predilection for landscapes. Rather than Bruegel's 'Triumph of Death', I like to think it was the stunning vistas of my hero Ansel Adams that helped mould my interest in imaging topography. I used to fantasise that if I had been born a generation or two earlier and in North America, I would be a main player in the infamous 'F64' club, along with Ansel Adams, Imogen Cunningham, Edward Weston et al, trekking through California's Yosemite National Park and capturing such stunning scenes as 'Moon and Half Dome', 'Half Dome, Merced River, Winter' and 'El Capitan, Merced River'. I'd say that Adams' photography (along with the work of war photographer Don McCullin of course) has had the most profound effect on me. 1984, amazingly the best part of four decades ago, was a significant year in many ways. In April 1984 I was mid-way through my 3-year photography course when Ansel Adams died. His legacy has been long lasting. He established 'the zone system' as a way of determining accurate camera exposure and the flexibility of tweaking the contrast of the final print. The depth and clarity of his predominantly black and white, cherished plates are truly awe inspiring.

As Ansel Adams once said:

"When words become unclear, I shall focus with photographs. When images become inadequate, I shall be content with silence...A great photograph is one that fully expresses what one feels, in the deepest sense, about what is being photographed".

On a bracing winter's day early in March 1984, I again managed to commandeer my father's Volvo. On such occasions I'd drop him off at work at Warbreck Hill, drive like Billy Buggery to the shoot location and then pick him up when he finished work. On this day, I headed up to my beloved Lake District with 35mm and 6x7 kit in the boot. It was a typical winter's day, deep blue sky and snow on the mountains and extremely cold, but I didn't give a stuff. The foolish, cocky bravado of youth told this young maverick that I could make it up a snow and ice strewn Hardknott Pass with a heavy, rear-wheeled drive car. In reality, I needed a 4x4 with lots of poke and fitted snow chains. In hindsight, the ascent of the pass was dangerous and I shouldn't have gone. With 90 degree, 1:3 bends, Hardknott Pass is comparable with Rosedale Chimney Bank on the North Yorkshire Moors for the joint steepest in England. Either way, if you've never driven up Hardknott, it's not for the Gladys and Toms of this world in their little deux cheveaux – it's best done giving the car some welly and with a clear run of course as you don't want to be meeting another motorist half way up. It's not to be undertaken in sub-zero temperatures in the middle of bloody winter!

Just to get to Hardknott Pass, you have to drive west from Ambleside over 15 miles of undulating terrain, a seemingly never-ending trail of twisty-turny road that takes you through Little Langdale and over Wrynose Pass. At the top is the historic Three Shire Stone, which marks the old meeting point of the counties of Westmorland, Cumberland and Lancashire. Then it's on along the Duddon Valley before finally the steep ascent of Hardknott can begin. You could of course approach Hardknott Pass from Eskdale to the West, but it's the longer way around.

After negotiating a series of these steep bends, there is a final, short, straightish stretch of road, which is nevertheless on quite an incline. Having passed snow and ice lower down, the Volvo's back wheels hit ice and immediately started to spin, sending the back end of the car skewing left and right. It was no use – the car just wouldn't make it to the top. I was gripping the steering wheel uselessly for dear life, praying that nothing would come the other way. Being an automatic, my foot was on the footbrake and I had to take my left hand off the steering wheel to yank the handbrake on. This just about held the car on the road. Behind me was a steep drop. What the hell was I going to do now? In desperation, I let the car roll back a few feet, thinking that I'd clear the patch of ice that the car was sliding on, paused for a few seconds and then once more, went for it hell for leather. Gear selector to '1' and foot down hard on the accelerator. The wheels started to grip, but the car was still sliding. This time I had sufficient welly to get the car to the summit of the pass. Phew – that was close. My dangerous encounter was quickly forgotten, however, when I stared in wonder at the scene stretched out before me. The second century Roman ruins of Hardknott Fort, known in ancient times as Mediobogdum (meaning situated in the middle of a curve), were clearly visible in the middle ground, with the Eskdale valley leading the viewer's eye towards the Cumbrian west coast in the distance.

The weather was perfect – blue sky, interspersed with fluffy white clouds. It was early morning and visibility was amazing, crystal clear. All around me were mountains, hills and moorland. I could barely detect a breeze. The scene was stunning. The pre-visualised image was already etched in my mind as, without really thinking, I'd quickly parked the Volvo half on and half off the road, making it difficult for other vehicles to pass. I only had my old Slik 88 tripod, which was really just designed for light weight 35mm camera usage. Now I required the Slik to support an RB 6x7 – it was a bit of a big ask! So, for maximum stability, I pulled the Slik's legs out nice and wide and then attached the RB. Two cable releases were then attached to this big beast of a camera, one to the camera body to trigger the mirror-up facility and the other to the 90mm standard lens. This meant I could operate the lens' leaf shutter once the vibrations of the mirror flipping up had stopped, thereby ensuring no blurred imagery through camera shake. The Cokin P polarising filter was then attached to the front of the lens and I made the final adjustments to the camera height and angle after looking at the image alternately on the ground glass and through the magnifying hood.

Having metered the scene, I then shot several frames on tranny, bracketing the exposure from normal to half a stop and then to 1 stop under. I also had to dial in an exposure compensation factor of about 1⅔ stops because of the light reduction caused by the polariser. This was always a bit of a cowsun to remember. With the transparency film's lack of tolerance to exposure errors (over more than under and bearing in mind I needed these trannies rich and punchy) this meant slightly underexposing them. With the colour negative film's longer tonal range, I gave the exposure an extra ½ stop. The job was in the bag and the equipment back in the car boot within 10 minutes and thankfully no car came along in that time. The resulting image was sold to the Cumbrian Tourist Board, made into a 40"x30" canvas framed print for my sister's wedding present in 1986 and was published in my first book 'Historic Lakeland' in the summer of 1989.

The Hardknott images barely had time to finish off in the drying cabinet at college, when I needed to make a very painful decision. I had been working at Des Tweats' newspaper shop on the Breck in Poulton from age eleven, grafting every morning before school as an illegal worker (the legal age was 13). I had worked my way up to managing the shop on Saturday afternoons when Des was off football refereeing. I worked with Des' Mum, Kath, on a Sunday morning marking up all the papers for the various rounds, which I knew off by heart as I'd have to go out delivering them if anyone called in sick. There was Lockwood, Victoria, Station Road, Moorland, Vicarage, Hardhorn, Highcross, Chester, Mains 1 and Mains 2, all named after the dominant road for each round. I'd had so many adventures working at the shop. One winter's Saturday teatime, I returned to the shop from Mains 2, frozen to the core with mini icicles hanging from my eyebrows. I was of course met with much laughter and a warm brew! On another notorious visit up Mains 2, Des, on hearing that the weather had closed in, came out to rescue me. I had just finished the round, so he put my bike in the back of his Citroen and drove back slowly in snow and ice the 2½ miles or so to Poulton. We got to the end of Vicarage Road, about to turn right onto the Breck, when we hit ice. Des looked at me and announced, "we're now sliding – no hass!" We both fell about laughing – it was just one of many funny moments.

Another time, it was very early one Summer's Sunday morning and I was marking up papers at the counter with Kath, when in walked a strange looking man who I guesstimated to be in his early 50s, with long, shaggy, unkempt, dark hair and silver rimmed spectacles. With both his hands initially tucked in his pockets, 'strange man' was looking about him nervously, but made straight for the magazines. He was so obviously eyeing up the array that adorned the top shelf. We both stopped to stare at him as out of his pocket came his right hand to reach out first to a copy of 'Mayfair', then to a copy of 'Oui', before finally resting on his magazine of choice 'Penthouse'. The hand had barely touched the magazine when it happened ... the entire top shelf full of magazines tumbled to the floor, ending up in a confused mess of upside-down bosoms, bums and nipples. Kath calmly approached 'strange man' and looked at him inquisitively, then down at the pile of porno mags. "You are going to pick them up, aren't you?" she said (it was a command, not a question). 'Strange Man' whose cheeks were now hued a rich scarlet, turned and scuttled like a rat out of the shop. Funny, but we never saw him again. It was left to me, being the taller of us, to return all the magazines from whence they came.

The following Sunday in walked 'even stranger man' with his guitar and long, unkempt and clearly unwashed hair. "Hello" he announced grinning. "I'm Jesus!" Just as I was wondering how to get rid of him, Kath beamed at 'even stranger man' and quickly retorted "Well, pleased to meet you Jesus!" After a couple of minutes of bible bashing, Jesus picked his guitar up and exited his stage, whereupon Kath and I fell about in raptures of laughter. It was almost a sigh of relief, therefore, to see the next customer roll in. Sunday morning regular Jack, was a retiree. Jack donned a shirt with rolled up sleeves and braces even in the middle of winter. Now this character with a lovely, strong and deep east Lancashire/West Yorkshire accent was at the counter. "Mornin! Newsatworld, Shundaypeople and Shundayporsht". The majority of customers were warm, friendly and made my time working at the newsagents memorable and worthwhile, there were just a few oddballs.

I was now 20 and sadly it was time to move on from the paper shop. Des' reaction took me by surprise when I broke the news to him that I had to leave. He was momentarily narked, probably because of the lack of notice putting him in an awkward position. But he quickly came around. I look back at my time working with Des as a truly great experience. As well as the newspaper rounds, Des trusted me to run the shop and I accrued invaluable customer relations skills along the way. He had a great sense of humour, we'd always be laughing as he'd announce on a Saturday, around 6.30pm with the shop closed, that he was just off to The Thatched pub for early doors and 'choir practise' (drinking) with Marshall, Robert and other local businessmen. Or when Des went on holiday, leaving his Mum in charge, Kath would turn a page in the shop diary only to find a large note scribbled from Des which would read 'admit defeat, contact the hotel such and such for assistance' to which Kath would say "Cheeky bugger!" Kath was also salt of the earth and always had me in stitches. Above all though, I admired and respected Des Tweats tremendously as a man who I aspired to be like.

I had been fortunate in securing a new Saturday position as assistant to local commercial, portrait and wedding photographer Chris Astbury at the nearby 'The Studio of Peter Astbury' in Poulton's Chapel Street. Chris, a former Blackpool and Fylde College student himself, ran this successful photography business with his then wife, Ruth and his mother Kitty. My joining this family business as a part-timer came only a few months after the tragic death of Chris' Dad, Peter, who was only in his late 50s at the time. Peter was a consummate, much admired photographer, of that there was no question. Before I actually worked there, I would often accompany Peter and Chris on commercial shoots, helping to lug the equipment, whilst watching, learning and absorbing. One such assignment was photographing the exterior of Blackpool's Winter Gardens at night. Peter had the Linhof Technika 5"x4" folding base board camera mounted on a Linhof tripod. This enviable equipment was set up on Abingdon Street near the old post office, but on the opposite side of the road. Typically, it was raining, so my job was to hold the big golf umbrella over the camera sufficiently high enough so as not to dip into the wide angle lens' field of view. This technique would serve me well years later as a Crime Scene photographer in London. One had to be especially careful as there was a fair bit of 'rising front' on the lens, so any drop of that umbrella would have buggered up the shots.

Chris, meanwhile, on the second walky-talky, had taken a stash of PF100's (Edison screw expendable flash bulbs) and was now inside the glass dome roof. During the perfectly synched timed exposure of around 30 seconds, Chris let rip with the PF100s creating a Hiroshima effect of white light, which illuminated the inside of this glass structure. He repeated the effect twice more as Peter shot both 5"x4" tranny and neg and, just as quickly as the father and son team had set up, the job was in the bag and it was time to dismantle the kit. I, meanwhile, was awestruck. If I wasn't hooked on photography up until this juncture, I was now! It was towards the end of Peter's life, that I bought one of his Mamiya RB 6x7 cameras off him as Chris was upgrading to the recently introduced RZ67. For a few hundred pounds of hard-earned cash, I got a Mamiya RB body with magnifying hood, an automatic and a semi-automatic roll film back, plus Sekor 127mm 1:3.8 and 90mm 1:3.8 lenses – a real advantage for a rookie photographer. However, I had no lighting equipment and no decent tripod sturdy enough to accommodate medium format. Hardknott Pass was shot on the old Astbury, now my faithful RB. The Mamiya would go on to pay for itself over and over again. Serviced only once in my 35 plus years of second-hand ownership, when the two roll film backs started to deteriorate, the RB was finally taken out of service in 2011 and now awaits the time when I can display it lovingly in a cabinet along with other treasured photography memorabilia.

The success of the Hardknott Pass image was followed by St. Chad's Church, Poulton-le-Fylde at Crocus Time. It was taken from a low church yard wall in Chapel Street at the rear of the Thatched House pub looking west towards the 1868 apse with the 17th century tower beyond. The morning March light was perfect, spilling amongst thousands of early spring crocuses that had only just flowered into a beautiful carpet of purple, white and saffron. Shot on roll film transparency and negative, I sold a framed copy to the Royal Bank of Scotland in Poulton and St. Chad's Church was also keen to purchase the image for post card use. A treasured souvenir which was still on sale until only very recently 30 years after that 'decisive moment' was created.

Saturdays at The Studio of Peter Astbury were a great learning curve (it was formerly called 'Cameragraphic' and then later to be known as The Astbury Studio). Occasionally there would be customer orders, but mostly the work was undertaken in the attic conversion, picture framing, canvas bonding prints and black and white dish printing, along with the inevitable tidying and sweeping. Chris would invariably be out photographing a wedding during the middle of the day and during the height of the wedding season, there would often be two events to attend, back to back. With attendance at the bride's home beforehand, the church or registry office and then reception venue, this all made for a long day. Chris shot on 120 colour neg, using his Mamiya RZ 67 and all his images were stunning. Chris taught me about natural light with reflector fill-in for outdoor portraiture and, studying his images, I started to get to grips with composition and posing required for weddings and portraiture. This all complimented Brian's excellent portraiture classes at college. My first attempts were a tad shaky. I photographed a local, retired architect with his bushy grey beard and pipe being the main areas of focus in quite a tight facial composition, the sitter staring out of frame at 45 degrees. I shot on the RB, but with a single, portable electronic flash unit as the main light source. There was no fill-in and the sitter's characteristic facial features blended with the dark background. Chris was great at providing constructive feedback. He liked the pose and close-up composition, but I should have used a reflector fill-in as well as background lighting. College print crit slated the image. I had lots of failures back then, lots of 'oh if only you had used such and such technique' but the pants images didn't deter me. I just picked myself up and kept on going.

Weddings and portraiture constituted one half of the Astbury business. The other half was Chris' commercial work, which included everything from 'pack shots' to room set interiors with or without models. Chris would shoot on 5"x4" and for each room set view, he would use one double dark slide loaded with tranny, the exposure the same for both sheets of film. Depending on how the lab's E6 process tolerance level was on the day, one sheet of tranny would be sent off for processing and one held back at the studio, should the latter tranny need a little 'pushing' in the developer. A third exposure would also be made on colour neg. Back then, as I intimated earlier, transparencies had the quality required for publications, whereas colour neg, with its longer tonal range, was ideally suited for straight prints.

Setting up the 5"x4" for interiors and working out your composition and angle of view was one thing but lighting the room set was a skilled job in itself. Sometimes Chris would use Bowens electronic studio flash heads, with a number of smaller Metz units for localised fill-in, on other jobs he would shoot solely tungsten. On many occasions, however, he would ingeniously employ mixed lighting, using both tungsten and daylight-balanced electronic flash – this concept had hitherto been completely alien to me, but I quickly got my head round it and found the regular challenge of mixed lighting, exciting and stimulating. Chris had a small set of tungsten bulbs called 'Lowell lights', each with a very long power lead which plugged into a central power console. Each one of the six lights could be switched on and off independently. This meant that during a single room set exposure, the house lights and Lowell lights could be switched off part way through a timed exposure based on his main lighting set up – each light being carefully metered. It wasn't unknown for someone to be responsible for the room lights, ready to kill them on Chris' command, me on the Lowell lights and Chris on camera. This method was frequently used with and without multiple exposures, which on the 5"x4", meant carefully re-cocking the lens' leaf shutter and capping then re-capping the lens. Lowell lights were small, so they were very handy for lighting particular features within a large room set. We used to light up small corners, hide them behind sofas, stick them up chimney breasts to light fireplaces and ingeniously use them to light sinks, positioning them in kitchen cupboards to shine up through the plug hole. Lowell lights could be hooked on a door or clipped to a work surface and angled in any chosen direction – all in all a nifty piece of kit.

As you might expect, Chris Astbury was a master photographer. Yes, he undoubtedly learned much from his father Peter, but Chris was a genius in his own right. People wanted an Astbury photograph because, like any sought-after gift, it was unique in its design and exuded superior quality. Chris's work was very saleable indeed and it was quite something to have an Astbury canvas adorning one of your walls with the idiosyncratic gold leaf, embossed signature 'Christopher' subtly placed in one of the bottom corners.

In addition to working Saturdays at the studio, I would assist Chris on commercial shoots during college practical periods. We'd just returned from a kitchen shoot in Farnworth having persuaded a really pretty girl in the admin office to model for some of the photos. Back at the studio in Poulton, I was busy offloading the gear to take it back into the studio when I was suddenly distracted by someone walking past. My heart skipped a beat. This wasn't just someone. This young lady was stunningly prepossessing. She had short brown hair, the most exquisite face, big brown eyes and a lovely figure - but it was this mystery girl's expression when our eyes locked momentarily that I remember. On hearing the clicking of her black court shoe heels on the pavement, I looked up from the back of Chris' Opel estate and this beautiful girl quickly glanced towards me, tossing me a beguiling smile. I instantly melted on Chapel Street that afternoon, back in late spring 1984. She didn't stop, but then why should she. We didn't know each other. In fact, I'd never seen this girl before, I didn't have a clue who she was. I was still gawping at this beauty when I smacked full face into a concrete lamp post, which hurt like hell. Thankfully this lovely vision didn't turn around to witness my stupidity! God, who was this girl? Where did she live? Was she a Poulton girl? Did she work locally? So many unanswered questions. In the interim another girl caught my eye – tall with short, light brown hair and looking very fetching in her long coat and heels, 'the yellow chevvy girl' I observed from my bedroom window a few times. So called, because she used to park her yellow Vauxhall Chevette along our road and collect it after business hours. However, just as quickly as she had provided eye candy, the yellow chevvy girl seemed to vanish into thin air.

About a week later, it was a tad past office closing hours and Chris and I were changing the display of photographs in the studio window, fronting Chapel Street, when to my delight along walked the same brunette who had caused me to walk into a lamp post seemingly a life time ago, but in actual fact was only a few days before. Again, my heart skipped a beat and even Chris, in declaring that she was 'double tasty', urged me to ask the girl out. The following day, I saw her emerging from an insurance brokers further down Chapel Street and deduced that she worked there, when she returned to the same place, not five minutes later. Coincidentally, I also found out on this same day that this beauty had a name – Jeanette.

It was now early May 1984 and that same night I saw Jeanette walk right past our house, with the tiniest of dogs. By the time I'd got my shoes on, my heart was racing. However, when I turned out of our drive Victoria Road was devoid of people. The elusive Jeanette had vanished again. Undeterred, I proceeded to go walk about into Poulton in an effort to find her. I just got to the top of Victoria Road and had turned left to go up Breck Road, when I almost ran into her with her dog, coming back towards me...and all I could do was smile nervously at her. I started beating myself up for not foreseeing this and throwing away an opportunity. I couldn't bring myself to turn around and go back after her. I simply kept going into Poulton, through the church yard, past the stocks, along Queen's Square, back round into Chapel Street, all the while trying to calm down and gather my thoughts. Then to my amazement, I saw her again just up ahead, still with her dog on its lead, looking in a shop window. She must have walked back round Vicarage Road and done a left down Chapel Street. This is it, I thought. Do not cock this up, the voice in my head kept telling me. Deep breath. Here goes. "Hi Jeanette, how are you doing?" Jeanette smiled at me coquettishly and said "Hi", back. She looked even more beautiful close-up in a pink skirt, white top and sandals. I then introduced myself and told Jeanette what I was doing and where I worked, as it suddenly occurred to me that she didn't know me from Adam – or maybe she did? Then with all the courage I could muster, I went for it and politely asked Jeanette out. This gorgeous girl tossed me the most wonderful, bashful smile, which was to die for and simply said "No, I'm sorry". And then she offered me a Malteser, which I declined. I then said "Maybe another time. See you around". Of course, Jeanette was going to turn me down. She was such a stunner that she was bound to have at least one boyfriend already. Still, in my mind, I had gone through with it. I hadn't lost my nerve. I hadn't made a complete balls up of the whole thing. Maybe I shouldn't have given up? Maybe I should have persisted in the days that followed? It was to prove the nicest 'turn down' I've ever had and was consigned to a folder in my mind, marked 'life's great memories'. Back then, Jeanette was by far the prettiest girl I'd ever met and she was never far from my mind.

May gave way to a warm June and I was still single. I popped into our local supermarket Booths and operating the checkout where I was queuing was a Saturday girl who I recognised as being a few years my junior at Arnold School. Still thinking about Jeanette, but in brazen mood, I thought 'What the hell, I've got nothing to lose'. The worst that can happen is I get another rejection, so now at the checkout and exchanging pleasantries, I asked this long-haired brunette out for a drink. Fully expecting the customary, "No, sorry", I was completely wrong-footed when the girl sitting at the checkout smiled back at me and said "Yes". This pretty, young girl of seventeen was of course, Lara Dee Mallinson.

We went to the old ABC cinema in Blackpool on the first date and all had gone well, that is until Lara dropped an almighty bollock on the way home. She already had a boyfriend! Shit! I'm not having much luck here. Knowing that Lara had in effect delivered me an early coup de grace, I shrugged my shoulders and thought I could at least go back to thinking about asking Jeanette out again. I dropped Lara back home, made my excuses to her parents as to why I wouldn't come in, thanked Lara for a pleasant evening and said goodnight in what I thought was to be a final farewell. The next thing I knew was that Lara was on the phone wanting us to go out on another date. Like a typical young fool hungry for his oats, I agreed quickly not wanting to dwell on the confusion, but yet not having the remotest idea as to what I was letting myself in for.

Approaching Singleton traffic lights on Garstang Road, I was nearing Lara's home on fashionable Poolfoot Lane after the end of our second date and saw Lara glance over at a car coming in the opposite direction. Lara then turned back to me and she was crying. The tears wouldn't stop. I immediately thought 'What the hell have I done – forgot the flowers, the chocolates and maybe insufficient compliments that night?' Had the whole evening gone down the wrong way? No, I wasn't even close. It transpired that the driver in the other car was Lara's boyfriend, who, due to the intervention of her parents disapproving for whatever reason of this 'boy next door', had just been relegated to the status of Lara's ex-boyfriend. I was now the man. I was Lara's new boyfriend. Lara was in effect going out with me directly on the rebound and muggins here took all the flack and fall-out. Rightly or wrongly, I stuck by this girl. I don't know if it was the kudos of having a pretty girl on my arm, or some other reason. Either way, I endured the vicissitudes of Lara's mood swings for many weeks into our relationship. It didn't help that we kept running into her 'ex' on a regular basis. If it wasn't 'The Buccaneer' pub or 'Illawalla' (an historic Edwardian building used as a night club, before it was demolished in 1996) in Thornton, it would be some other hostelry. And each time, as if rubbing my nose in it, Lara would leave me holding the drinks whilst she went off to flirt with her insurance broker ex-beau. If the truth be known, Lara was probably sweet on him throughout our relationship. I think Lara and I were both at fault. She shouldn't have strung me along whilst on the rebound and I should have told her to 'sling her hook' and shouldn't have put up with her antics and mood swings.

I had been with Lara for only a few weeks and it was now the end of second year at college. Two thirds of my photography course were now complete and my HND was passed with distinction. Best mate Aly and I had booked a lads' holiday together. One week in Athens, just the two of us, turned out to be great fun. Plenty of sight-seeing, sunbathing and alcoholic beverages and of course, lots of photographs. I took a fantastic image 'Athenian night-time cityscape' from our bedroom window. This shot, a timed exposure, was subsequently published and praised in 'Amateur Photographer' magazine.

Aly and I had plenty of laughs on that trip in the summer of '84, none more so than when it came to hiring a moped as the cheapest form of transportation to get us to Sounion. Prior to our vacation I had read of this magical place at Cape Sounion, famed for its sunsets. In fact, Cape Sounion juts out into the Aegean Sea as a promontory and the imposing c440 BC ruins of the Temple of Poseidon perch on top of the headland. Poseidon, in classical Greek mythology, is of course God of the sea, protector of all waters and brother of Zeus. Getting to Sounion for sunset and by student-affordable means, involved riding 40+ miles south-east out of Athens towards the southernmost point of the Attica peninsula. The man at the moped hire shop in Glyfada Square almost screamed at Aly "You not have bike, you not have bike". Aly was basically turned down flat because he couldn't ride a moped, but then stitched me up by saying to the man in slow English and pointing to me "he has done it before", which of course I hadn't. After about thirty seconds of very basic instruction, I got on and somehow made the moped go with ease, much to Aly's surprise and mutual relief. Foolishly, we both turned down the offer of crash helmets.

With my camera bag, tripod and water clipped to the back, Aly jumped on behind me and I throttled up, setting off on our journey on that late Athenian afternoon. For the second time in my life, I didn't dare to look back for fear that I would be turned into a pillar of salt, or in this case have the moped taken off me! I just rode out of that hire place like I had been riding all of my short life. Looking back, Aly and I were dressed naively and simply – t-shirts, shorts and trainers – no crash helmets or caps, no suntan lotion and no protection whatsoever. The ignorance of youth! Stuff it, it was all so liberating. Riding down to Poseidon in the right-hand lane meant we were hugging the Aegean all the way and I remember how great the warm air felt on my face and legs as it bounced off the sea. We arrived in good time, locking up the moped and making our way up to the temple ruins.

My two faithful workhorses were an Olympus OM-1N and an Olympus OM-2N, both clad in black and chrome. I liked the completely manual OM-1N, it was small, but rugged and a quality build, even the shutter blinds were precision and made of rubberised silk. The OM-1N's match needle metering system was easy to understand. The OM-1N was also completely mechanical in its operation, which was a huge plus if the battery (the now banned 1.35V mercury oxide (E)PX625, which only powered the light meter) suddenly died as you could still use the camera, which I did frequently in conjunction with my Weston meter. However, the OM-1N had no hot shoe, just a PC sync socket for flash, which was a bit of a pain. The OM-2N came with a prism-mounted hot shoe, was an aperture priority automatic SLR, but with full manual override and I used this bad boy as a back up to the OM-1N. I had been taught and had grown up in a photographic environment in which the cameras and metering were all manual and this is what I was used to. I had two or three Zuiko lenses, which included a medium zoom and a beautiful 21mm ultra wide angle. I shot exclusively transparency and my film of choice was 'Kodachrome 64', favoured for its fine grain, superb colour rendition and high quality.

The sunset at Sounion didn't disappoint. The early evening lighting had presented ideal shooting conditions and there was plenty of time to capture the Temple of Poseidon in all its glory. Polarising the rich, cloudless sky and bolting the wide angle onto the OM-1N, I shot from close to the ground on many views and produced such memorable images as 'Poseidon Columns' and 'Sounion Poseidon'. Once I'd filled my boots with the temple shots, it was time to pitch up for the sunset views. The colour of the sky changed dramatically over the minutes, prior to the sun going down. I shot a couple of rolls of tranny in no time at all and when the sun finally dipped below the horizon, disappearing from view, the calm and tranquillity were broken with spontaneous applause from the many tourists now gathered gazing at this awe-inspiring natural phenomenon. Aly and I had never seen this before and with both cameras safely tucked up in the bag, we both clapped along. It was a truly joyous moment.

The journey back was hair-raising as the darkness quickly started to lap at our feet, threatening to completely engulf us. The moped's headlight was about as useful as a chocolate fireguard and this wasn't the UK – there were no cat's eyes in this part of the world. Visibility was down to a few meters and I was all over the road. Then we ran out of petrol, fortunately approaching a village, but still some way from Glyfada. Working out where the petrol cap was located took us a few long minutes of head scratching. Of course, you had to lift the seat up to reveal the petrol tank – not easy when you're not told and you don't know the arse end of a moped from the front and you don't think to ask! By some miracle we got the moped back to the hirer by the allotted time. I think we were both glad to see the back of that machine and to get back to our hotel in one piece that night. We were both nursing quite bad sun burn and slept fitfully. Other notable highlights of this Greek trip included visiting the Parthenon, sitting proudly on the Acropolis and completed in 438BC. This dedication to the goddess Athena commands majestic views over the Hellenic capital. During a boat trip around part of the Saronic Gulf from the port of Athens, which took in the islands of Hydra, Poros and Aegina, I was rewarded with a whole bevvy of beautiful images, whilst documenting the exquisite temple, built circa 500BC and dedicated to the goddess Aphaia.

The week-long trip to Athens was a good tonic, but now Blighty beckoned. Aly and I were both looking forward to getting home and enjoying the rest of the summer break with our respective girlfriends. Life seemed sweet. I was enjoying my time working with Chris Astbury, I supplemented this cash with jobs for my Dad, anything not to be actually physically in his presence, and my girlfriend Lara was on my arm. The previous year, as part of his uni architecture project, Aly had asked me to do the interior and exterior photographs of the eye-catching Fleetwood pagoda known as 'The Mount', a Grade 2 listed building erected in 1902. Now, a year later, Aly's study turned to Lord and Lady Cavendish' family home, Holker Hall in Cark-in-Cartmel, Grange Over Sands. Once again, I was asked to do the photography of the magnificent Victorian, self-supporting, cantilever oak staircase. Booking out three red-head tungsten lights from college proved a stretch. I shot on 5"x4" because I needed rising front to keep the verticals straight and a touch of scheimpflug rotation to keep depth of field in check, as the plane of focus wasn't running just a straightforward front to back, it was slightly angled. Even viewing the image from under the dark cloth, upside down and laterally reversed on the camera's ground glass screen, I didn't need to be told that really the shot would have benefited from additional lighting under the stairs and on the top floor to light the upper stairs. What I should have done was multi-exposed. The first exposure would have been for the general scene, lit with the three tungsten heads and house lights. I should then have recapped the lens and re-arranged my three red heads, directing light under the stairs and from the top floor in a second exposure. All that would have been required following re-metering and recocking the shutter, would have been to kill the house lights and uncap the lens again, with of course a very steady hand, so as not to move the camera – voila! Today, using digital with its inbuilt 'polaroid' (ability to view the image after taking the shot) and with over three and a half decades of accrued professional experience, the job would be vastly easier. I would handle the lighting totally differently, employing a timed-exposure and more than likely, in the absence of a Bowens kit with cumbersome trailing wires, paint the whole shot with a couple of Metz or Nikon SB flash guns, having worked out beforehand, angles of reflection and number and direction of flashes (a combination of bounced and direct would have done it). Even so, I was still chuffed with my 5"x4" tranny (albeit a little 'thin' in places), Aly seemed pleased with the photo for his architectural project and further, Holker Hall purchased my image for £50, so I was made up!

1984 was an eventful year for many reasons. The Conservative government under Margaret Thatcher had been in power for five years and the Miners' strike, led by Arthur Scargill kicked off and spilled into the following year. Ronald Wilson Reagan was President of the USA and for a year, Konstantin Chernenko was leader of Russia. Two of my favourite comedians died, the much-loved Tommy Cooper and Eric Morecambe, their loss saddened the nation. If we weren't seeing friends at the Buccaneer pub, having a quiet drink at Wardleys in Hambleton, or boogying on down at the nearby Illawala country club, Lara and I were at the cinema, which seemed to be the date of choice and heavy on my wallet. Blockbuster films of 1984 included Beverly Hills Cop, Ghostbusters (I ain't afraid of no ghosts!) and Amadeus directed by Milos Forman. The classic dystopian film '1984' was also the last film of another of my favourite actors, Richard Burton. Burton, who had a powerful screen presence, sadly died two months before the British premier. He was only 58.

We had some great TV back in 1984 as the satirical puppet show Spitting Image became compulsive viewing. The Two Ronnies was also airing. The pop charts supplied us with a good variety of hits that included:

Frankie goes to Hollywood – *Relax, Two Tribes & The Power of Love*
Ray Parker Jnr - *Ghostbusters*
Phil Collins - *Against all Odds*
Paul McCartney - *No More Lonely Nights*
Queen - *I Want to Break Free & Radio Ga Ga*
Wham - *Last Christmas & Everything She Wants*
Madonna - *Like a Virgin*
The Cars – *Drive*
Alison Moyet - *All Cried Out & Love Resurrection*
Status Quo - *The Wanderer & Marguerita Time*
Howard Jones - *What is Love*
Band Aid - *Do They Know Its Christmas*

My favourite groups were Dire Straits and Genesis, but Sting, Elton John, Billy Joel, Queen, ELO, R.E.M., Pink Floyd, Vangelis, The Alan Parsons Project and the angelic voice of Karen Carpenter have always been special.

During the tail end of winter, around about the beginning of March 1984, I persuaded my father to let me landscape our back garden. There was a small area laid to lawn with an 'n' shaped path around its border, at the top of which were three steps leading up to a network of crazy paving and old rose beds. A battered old trellis separated the rose beds from the apple and pear orchard and rubbish tip beyond. In the bottom left-hand corner was a rusting old relic from the second world war – an Anderson air raid shelter. A privet hedge marked the garden's boundary, beyond which was the railway embankment where I used to trespass and also enjoy clandestine, illegal roll-ups when I was younger. At the foot of this slope was Poulton-le-Fylde railway station. You had to be cunning with my father. He usually agreed to the square root of sweet damn all if it wasn't his idea. After all, this was the man who accused me of 'breaking up our home' when I set fire to an old woodworm-riddled wardrobe on the landing, so I had to be careful. My angle was that I would probably soon be leaving home and the garden would be too much for my father to manage and "we wouldn't want to see it grow into an uncontrollable wilderness full of weeds would we?" My plan was simple but daring – to hire a series of mini skips over two successive weekends and then single-handedly dig up all the weeds, roots, trellis posts, crazing paving and apple trees (which were half dead anyway), then level the ground just using a spade, a fork and a rake. We would then grass seed the entire area, which would be a lot easier to manage through mowing. To my surprise, my father agreed to the plan. What I didn't tell him was that my ulterior motive in setting out this top area of garden to lawn, was that I was sick to my back teeth of weeding this vast expanse, which I'd been doing religiously since I was a small boy. I'd basically had enough. The job proved to be a herculean, dirty task. Dressed in old clothes and wellies, I'd barrow load all the rubbish into the skip and as each container became full, I telephoned the hire company and they duly came round, took away the full skip and deposited an empty one. After four long days, eighteen mini skips and numerous achy muscles later, I'd levelled the entire area. One of the hardest jobs was breaking up the clods of earth with a rake into fine pieces of soil and pulling out so many roots and bits of stone. My two sisters, Vicky and Kate then took over, doing a superb job grass seeding the neatly raked garden. With the job completed, I let nature take over, waiting for the grass seed to spring up. By April, the new garden was a lovely carpet of rich green. By early May, the virgin lawn was ready to mow. Save for a few undulations here and there, my new lawn turned out to be the success I'd envisaged. Amazing!

In September 1984, I turned 21 and opted for a romantic meal with Lara at the River House restaurant along Skippool Creek, a venue favoured by at least one former Prime Minister (Edward Heath) during Blackpool's political conference week. September was also the start of my third year at college. With an HND already under my belt, this final year focused on projects for the Professional Qualifying Examination (PQE) of the British Institute of Photography (BIPP). I needed to produce a number of images under the themes of advertising, commercial, industrial, portraiture, landscape and PR, each with an accompanying write up. Additionally, there was a major project which I undertook with fellow student Simon, which was a guide to selected historical places of interest within the English Lake District. In the same year, on 12th October, the IRA exploded a delayed time bomb at the Grand Hotel in Brighton, killing five and injuring thirty-one. Among the injured was Wyre MP, Sir Walter Clegg, who served the constituency from 1983-7. Prime Minister Thatcher narrowly escaped injury. One of the most shocking images on the news at that time was seeing an injured Lord Tebbit, covered in rubble dust and clearly in pain, being stretchered out of the hotel.

Just before Christmas it was Lara's 18th and she opted for a small party and gathering of friends. Prior to Lara's 18th, her stepfather Jeremy invited me to accompany Lara to a masonic 'Ladies Night' evening meal. He was a local solicitor and highly respected freemason in his local lodge 'Meliora Sequamur' (roughly translated 'let us follow better things'). This meant having to hire a tuxedo, formal shirt and bow tie as I didn't own any evening attire. I found the event fascinating. There were numerous toasts throughout the various courses and plenty of photographs taken. My fellow guests were charming. The highlight of this lovely evening was meeting the Grand Master and his wife. I felt utterly privileged to attend such a wonderful function.

As this eventful year gave way to 1985, I was accruing more experience both at college and working all the spare time I had with Chris Astbury. At college, I was regularly booking equipment out of stores with Peter, who wasn't one to get on the wrong side of. If you didn't have the stores manager on side, you were buggered. Quite simply, you wouldn't be loaned the kit you needed and therefore you would be snookered with your College brief commitments. I'd booked a 'Broncolor' flash pack out of stores for another industrial shoot and remember saying to Adrian, I'll just quickly test it. Plugging it into one of the corridor double sockets outside stores, I then got one of the flash heads and connected its multi-pin connector to the female socket on the power pack. I then flicked the 'on' switch, whereupon there was an almighty bang, which reverberated around the corridor for a few seconds, followed immediately by a smell of burning. Instantly, every door along the corridor opened and a concerned face stared out of each one. The whole thing was reminiscent of a comedy sketch. Peter in stores was very dischuffed and wasn't laughing, but somehow I managed to wangle a replacement Broncolor pack out of him – God knows how.

By March, things with Lara and me were starting to slide. Lara had her nice side, but it took me a while for the penny to drop that she was a gold digger. She never offered to pay when we went out and it was costing me a small fortune. I felt irked by this and my misery was reaching a crescendo. I decided that it was time to break off our relationship. This went down like a lead balloon with Lara, who called round at our house that evening and rang the doorbell for what must have been 10 minutes solidly. Fortunately, Mum and Dad were out and I stayed in the back dining room. There was no way that I was going to answer the door with Lara clearly in a state. After a while she gave up and Kate (who was with me) and I heard the letter box opening and something dropping to the porch floor. Lara had posted me a little squeaky elephant originally intended as a gift to celebrate our 9-month anniversary! With it was a note which read "was to have been for nine months – didn't realise it would be a keepsake!" After that incident, I knew that I'd have to front Lara out and tell her how it was. She met me at the Astbury studio the following Saturday lunchtime. We went down to Tiggywinkles on the corner of Chapel Street for a bite to eat and after a short discussion, rightly or wrongly, we got back together! What followed was to be an intense period all round – in our relationship and at college - for it was the final push to PQE and the end of my three-year course. I had fulfilled all the briefs. Some lovely outdoor portraits of Lara completed the portraiture brief and everything was laminated and board-mounted ready for the end of year display. My joint project with Simon on a selection of six historical Lakeland sites as part of some future book feature, had also been laid out on display board for the assessors, with the typing cut and pasted into position. After a nervous wait for my projects to be marked, I was thrilled to pass my PQE with distinction. Three years of college done and dusted.

I phoned Lara who congratulated me. In celebratory mood I then said "where do you fancy going tonight?" to which she replied "I'm busy". "Oh, er, ok, what about tomorrow night?" "I'm busy then as well" came back the quick reply. Slightly alarmed, I then said "So, if I was to phone you next week, would you also be 'busy'?" "Yes, I would" came her simple retort. And that was that, I had been ceremoniously dumped at a point of her choosing. A year after asking her out, Lara and I were now history. Although a bit miffed with the timing, strangely, I wasn't cut up. I wasn't in bits. There was no running to Mummy and weeping into her apron. No melancholy episodes. Nothing. It was just over. We'd had our good times, but Lara had proved to be heavy maintenance during the twelve months, draining my coffers bare and I also felt emotionally spent. So, I was actually relieved and strangely liberated having parted company, enjoying being single and my own boss once again. I immediately shaved off the ridiculous cluster of bum fluff that constituted the moustache that Lara had made me grow earlier that year, putting 20 years on me! Lara was a clever girl, academically a high-flier, who narrowly missed being accepted into Oxbridge. However, she was emotionally immature and very possessive and it had taken our breakup for me to be able to see that clearly. A part of me thought that she got rid of me as a punishment for me trying to do the same to her three months previously. Whatever.... bygones. It was now time to move on to better things.

Thinking that I was taking the break-up in my stride, my confidence actually seemed to have taken a knock. At the Astbury studio there was a ton and a half of black and white hand prints to get through along with loads of framing and I just seemed to go into hyper checking mode, slowing the working pace right down and generally feeling unsure about everything. This hadn't gone unnoticed. Simultaneously, I had approached Chris about the possibility of a pay rise. That night Chris and his first wife Ruth came round to our house with an envelope. Inside that envelope was a short note. To my utter horror, just like Lara, Chris and Ruth had given me my marching orders! I had just been sacked. The note went on "...We are more than happy to pay the going wage...but the snail's pace of your work of late, has left us in no doubt..." I dropped the note in shocked disbelief and embarrassment. I was actually shaking. In my mind here was tangible proof that other people, not just my father, thought that I was 'a useless shit.' This was my only sacking and from my perspective it was unjustified. The Astburys didn't sit down and talk to me to see whether there were any underlying causes for my workflow to suddenly decrease. Just like Manny Manson had done years before at school, when I had failed my fourth year February chemistry exam declaring "this result means you're either thick or you're lazy, which is it?" Both were instant and unfair judgements. I couldn't have predicted that my employment with the Astbury Studio would end badly. In both cases, there were reasons – my father's cruel and unusual behaviour affecting my schoolwork and the break-up with Lara, which had obviously affected my ability at the photography studio. Also, in both cases, undiagnosed executive functioning disorder also played a hand in bad recall for exams and intermittent, slow and ponderous work output.

Although I was cross at the time with the way the Astburys handled my sacking, I didn't hold it against Chris. It just went pear shaped for me at the end. I feel indebted to him for all he taught me about room set lighting techniques, weddings and portraiture among other things. He was my mentor and chief critic during my college years. I valued his opinion and assimilated his feedback. I aspired to become like Chris, who was a naturally gifted lensman. His wedding and portrait photographs were beautifully created and his commercial and industrial work was of an equally high calibre. He was approachable, relaxed and friendly and had a natural, inherent ability to establish an instant rapport with his clients. Chris also had an engaging sense of humour and we'd always be laughing. His catch phrase 'Right then' I remember well, when it was time to knuckle down. I kept meaning to pop round and look him up again to thank him for all he'd done for me when I heard the shocking news that Chris had died in hospital of pulmonary fibrosis on 30th April 2013. He was only 61. The BIPP had lost one of its master photographers, Poulton had lost a legendary cameraman. His photographic talent was handed down to at least one of his daughters and his legacy prevails across Fylde homes and north west businesses. His memory will live on and he will never be forgotten. Farewell then Christopher Astbury, you were a much-admired photographer and a consummate professional.

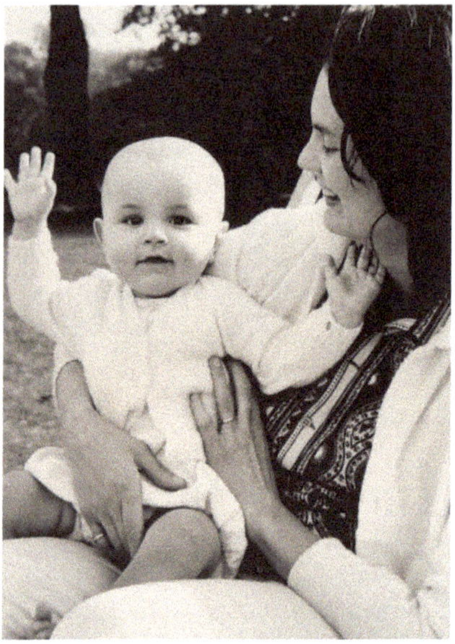

Me and Mum, 1964.

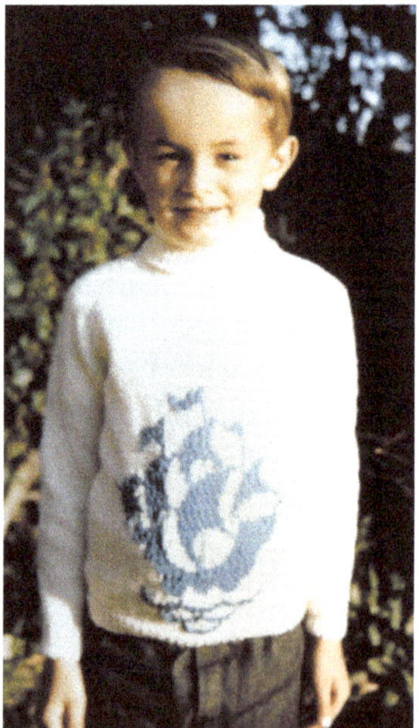

Me in Blue Peter sweater knitted by Mum, circa 1970, aged 7.

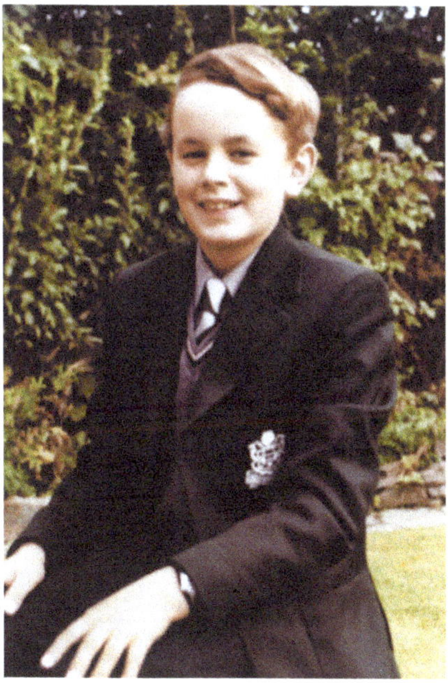

Me aged 12 in Arnold School uniform, September 1975.

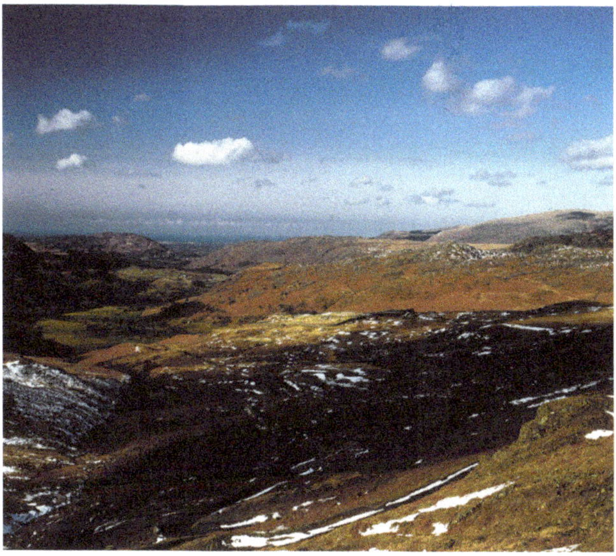

From the top of Hardknott Pass looking west towards Hardknott Roman Fort and along Eskdale to the Cumbrian coast, March 1984.

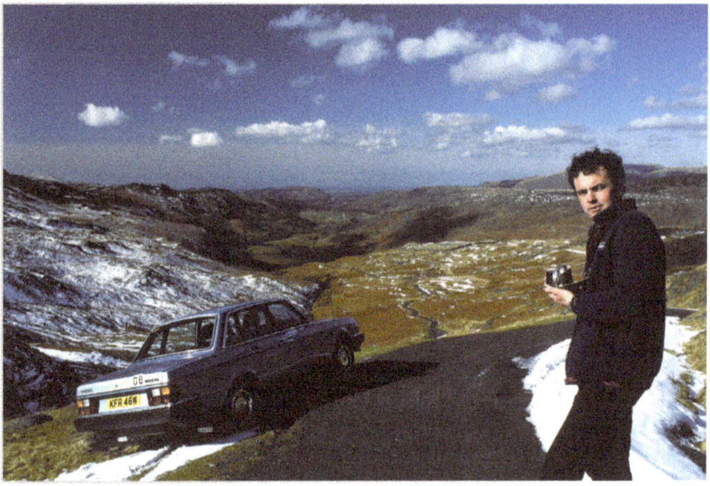

Me as a 20-year-old Blackpool & The Fylde College second year photography student, having just photographed Hardknott Fort & Eskdale, Cumbria, March 1984.

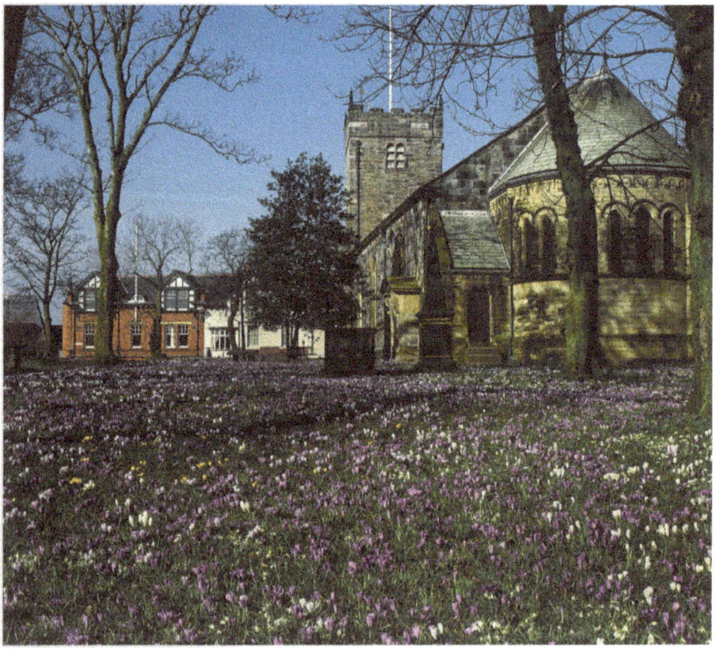

St. Chad's Church, Poulton-le-Fylde, Lancashire, at Crocus Time, March 1984.

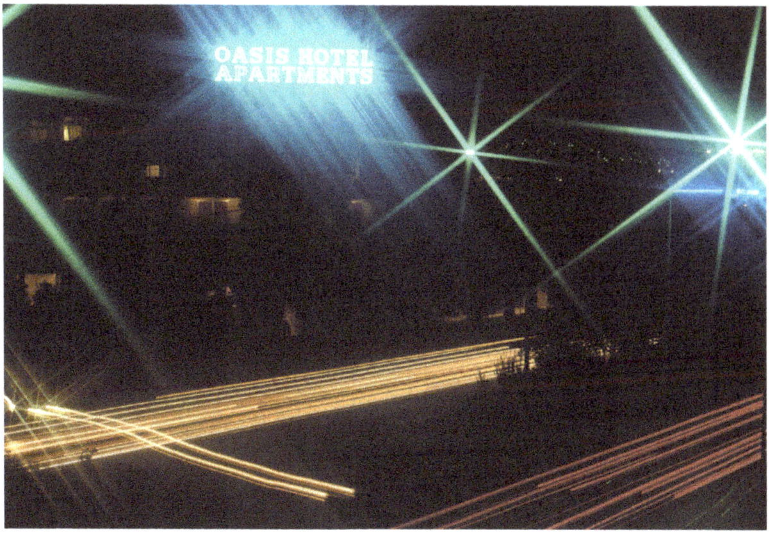

Athenian night-time cityscape, July 1984. This timed exposure image was highly commended in 'Amateur Photographer' magazine.

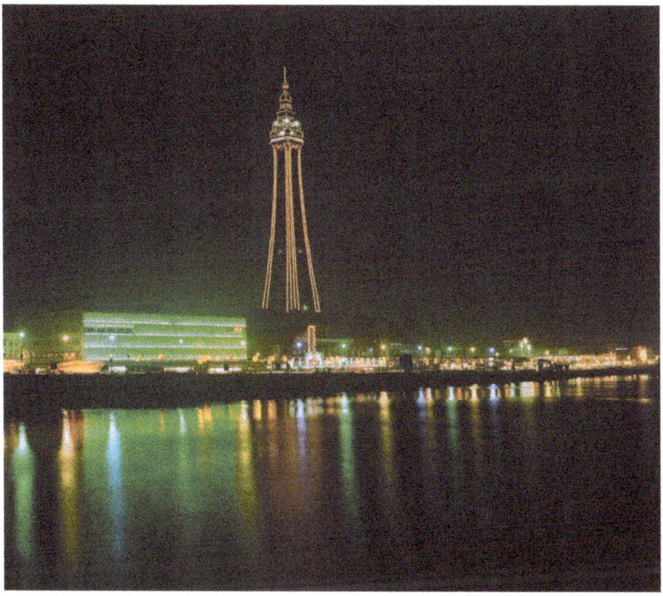

Blackpool Tower and Illuminations, October 1985. This image was sold to Blackpool Tourism and Leisure for a nationwide poster campaign with the strap line, 'Blackpool - Come up and see us some time'.

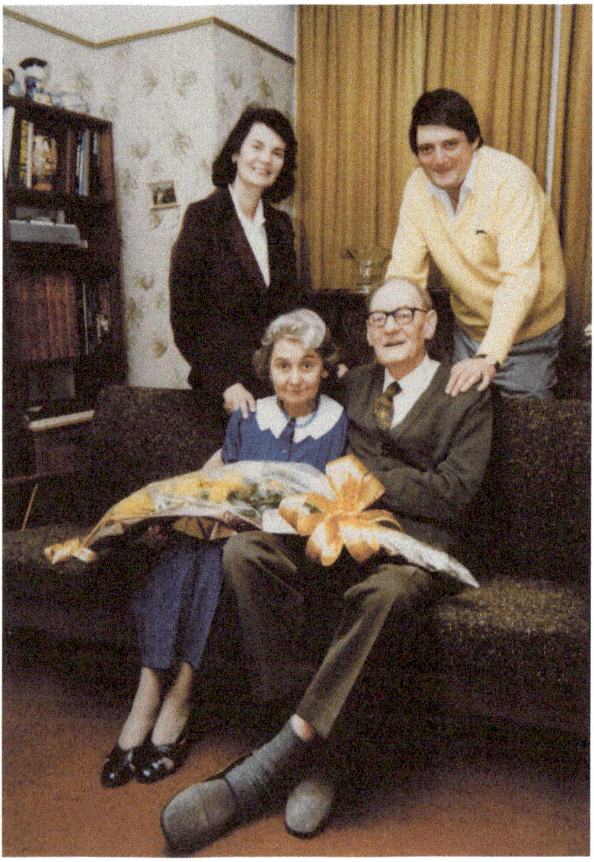

Four lovely people – Grandma and Grandad (sitting), Mum and Uncle Graham (standing), on the occasion of my Grandparents' Golden Wedding Anniversary, Bruce Road, Mitcham, Surrey, October 1985.

PART 2

First Book, First Job to a Life on the Ocean Wave

CHAPTER 5

My First Book

Three years at college studying professional photography had been successful, but I had no full-time job to go to. The college tutors were particularly poor at getting students lined up with definite offers of jobs. "Why not give Len Dance a ring or drop a line to such and such studios?" This was completely fruitless. Three and a half decades after leaving Blackpool & The Fylde College, I'm back in Blackpool, still working as a professional photographer, immersed and engaged in what I love doing – taking images. 35 years is a sod of a long time, people move on, technology changes. For me, the time since the mid '80s has been well spent, accruing valuable skills, experience and life lessons to impart to those joining the profession as fledgling photographers or those toying with the idea of a career in photography. My HND with PQE is now a BA degree awarded by Lancaster University. As you might expect, all my tutors have long since retired, but it is nice to know that my old college is alive and well and flying the flag for our profession.

To prepare students to hit the floor running and to be industry ready, they must first accrue vital technical, creative skills and marketing skills during their three years of studying. It's inspiring to discover that first year students are being taught to use 5"x4" cameras in conjunction with traditional large format film. Students get a better understanding of how the camera functions, which they might not necessarily get from using digital. They also learn traditional dark room skills as well as lighting skills and business skills. They're encouraged to build networks in the profession, which are of pivotal importance in supporting students' ongoing employing and professional practice. Many students want to specialise in a particular field, an area that they feel their strengths and passions are aligned to, whether it is architectural, advertising, fashion or commercial/industrial for example, but the secret is to be versatile and not put all your eggs in one basket – make yourself employable by working for a range of clients offering myriad products and services.

In 1985, in a pre-digital era, it was slowly sinking in that I had trained to become part of a fiercely competitive industry in which there was no guarantee whatsoever of a job amidst this dog eat dog quagmire. Looking back, my fundamental error was focusing too closely on nurturing my smattering of connections, whilst losing sight of the bigger picture. What few contacts I did have, by no means constituted a network capable of sustaining my professional practice long term. I'd scour the advertisements in professional magazines, but jobs were in short supply. I got sporadic interviews for lowly paid jobs, firstly with Rowntree Mackintosh in York, which proved unsuccessful. Then there was Castle Gardens Photography Studios in Manchester, where coincidentally Adrian also attended for interview at the same time going for the same job. When the MD of Castle informed me that the pay would be £3000 per annum (effectively nothing), I burst out laughing in front of him and said "It seems that I've wasted my time coming here. The salary is a joke!" much to the consternation of the MD. Adrian felt the same way. Over a pint, we chatted about the exploitative nature of our new profession after both of our interviews had concluded and quickly agreed that working for companies like Castle Gardens was a non-starter and these people, knowing that newbie photographers were desperate for work and experience and in some cases worked for free, virtually employed slave labour.

During the summer of 1985, I approached several publishing houses with the research and photography that I had completed on several historical Lake District sites as part of my final college year examination. My aim was twofold: firstly, to prove that a complete 'unknown' could get a book published and secondly to make some money. Admittedly I went through the phase of suffering delusions of grandeur … book signing sessions, turning up to bookshops up and down the country with camera flashes firing in my face everywhere I went, beautiful girls lining up for my autograph.....hmm...well I was a bit of a dreamer back then. I went to umpteen different publishers and each time the response was the same. I was turned down flat. Nobody wanted to know.

I was on the point of calling it a day, when I visited publishers Ian Allan at their Surrey base in Shepperton. They are renowned publishers of train, flight and travel books and magazines. I remember my first meeting over coffee and biscuits with Simon Forty and Andy

Farrow, who both showed a keen interest right from the start. Ian Allan had a gap in the market for a softback travel book and my idea to produce a guide to selected historical Lake District sites, in effect expanding on the work I'd done at College, was well received. By early September, Ian Allan gave me the green light.

The book, containing detailed information and cross referencing, maps, gazetteer and photographs would be split into roughly four geographic areas, each focusing on a selection of places of interest within the Lake District National Park. It would include Levens Hall and Sizergh Castle in the South East, Holker Hall and Muncaster Castle in the South West through to Hardknott Fort and Wordsworth House in the North West and finally Dalemain and Brougham Castle in the North East. To save on production costs, I was told that I would have to author the book as well as photograph. The subsequent planning for my first book represented a huge task. Hours would be spent at my local library researching the entire Lake District and deciding which sites to concentrate on, then there would be visits to site owners and custodians, meetings with representatives from the Lake District National Park, English Heritage, South Lakeland District Council, The Lake District Special Planning Board / National Park Authority and the National Trust, to name a few. Maps would also need to be drawn. To this end, I approached my best mate Aly Baines, already a highly respected north-west architect, who was happy to oblige. Then of course, I would have to timetable photographic shoots. With the exterior images, seasons, weather conditions, direction facing and lighting angle would all have to be taken into account. The majority of interiors would need to be undertaken on dull, overcast days (the darker the better) to lower the contrast between window light and interior lighting. This all translated into an average of two to three visits per site: one trip to recce and touch base with site owners/ custodians and subsequent trips for exterior and interior shoots. I would use a range of camera formats from 5"x4", 120 to 35mm and shoot low ISO rated transparency and black and white film.

Mid-way through October 1985, in a pre-home computer environment, I finally sat down and with a deep breath, hand wrote my first words for the 'Introduction' to what would become my first book ...Historic Lakeland.

"The sanctuary of beautiful Lakeland has long enticed the many in search of the tranquillity of this scenic mountain environment... Indeed, the great bard William Wordsworth was lured to Grasmere 'On nature's invitation'".

"I was first drawn to this delightful place during my schooldays and every time I return, not only are old memories of mountain club walks rekindled, but there are always new experiences for the mind to treasure. On one recent occasion I stood alone with my camera on the shores of Wastwater. It had been raining heavily, but the scene was clearing and as I watched the passage of sun behind several ominous, but broken clouds, I waited with tremulous excitement for it to emerge. Suddenly, light and shade played on the scene, the whole coming together like some incantation...it was then that I pressed the shutter. Awestruck, I knew that I had to return again soon".

Whilst waiting for my first full time job, there were oddments of freelance work – shots for ICI here, a graduation portrait there, images for my book, coupled with the inevitable jobs for my father which were a necessary evil. Forced to live at home, life was for the large part miserable, but I saved my pennies and at least I didn't have a gold digger girlfriend bleeding me dry. In October, I shot the illuminations in Blackpool and sold the trannies to Blackpool Tourism and Leisure. We travelled to Mitcham in south London for my dear grandparents' Golden wedding anniversary get together. Held in their tiny flat in Bruce Road, which holds so many precious memories for me, the 50th anniversary celebration was a lovely do and yours truly took all the photographs. In the November, I was awarded Licentiateship of the British Institute of Professional Photography and could use the letters L.B.I.P.P. after my name. But still I had no full-time job. Christmas came and went and I remained jobless. A bleak 1985 gave way to 1986 and being out of work, no, not even having started work yet, was getting me down. When anyone asked, I told them that I was freelance and working on my first book, which effectively meant that I was carrying an Unemployment Benefit attendance card Four Zero!

CHAPTER 6

My first full time job: Wedding & Portrait Photographer, South-East London

May 1986 – January 1988

In 1986 UK home computer usage was still more than a decade away. An iPad meant an eye dressing and my laptop was generally where my Siamese cats curled up! So, with no 'world wide web', job research was undertaken at the local library. I'd somehow got it into my head that I would write 100 speculative letters to potential employers all over the UK, each envelope also containing a stamped address envelope, in the desperate hope that I would receive a few dozen replies. I even wrote to the late Antony Armstrong-Jones, first Earl of Snowdon, who to his credit hand wrote a lovely card back to me, wishing me well in my search for gainful employment. 100 carefully hand-written letters and only 15 replies! Of those, 13 were standard 'regret to advise you' affairs and only two offered an interview. The first offer was to be for a Bristol-based PR company, whose studio was prestigiously located in the shadow of Brunel's SS Great Britain. However, it transpired that my getting the job as staff photographer all hinged on the present incumbent being stuck on for drink driving. The person in question somehow kept his driving license and Bristol, sadly, wasn't meant to be.

So, I turned to the second offer. Colin White had read "with great interest" my letter, which had arrived coincidentally as a vacancy had arisen for a staff photographer. He was the Managing Director of John F. White Studios, a long-established south-east London based firm of wedding and portrait photographers. The reply went on "…I would like you to attend interview on…" YES!!! In my mind, I'd already got the job. I'd waited for so long with nothing forthcoming. It was now the third week in April, and I was on a train bound for London and then to Catford, wherever the hell that was. I hadn't even entertained the possibility that I wouldn't be offered the job. I didn't stop to think that others would be going for the job or that I might not like the job specification or indeed the whole idea of living in a London suburb. I was just completely focused on getting this first job. The route from Euston was straightforward enough – Victoria line to Victoria then over ground train to Catford Bridge. Once at the railway station in Catford, it was left onto Catford Road, effectively onto the South Circ, then I kept left as the road became Rushey Green and just kept going. I crossed Rosenthal Road and there it was – the white awning of the studio with the wording 'The John F. White Studios' emblazoned across the middle. I stopped to look at the wedding and portrait photographs on display in the window, taking in composition, colour, tone, lighting and pose. Oddly, I found the door locked, so I rang the bell. I had timed it with 5 minutes to spare.

After a few seconds, the figure of a middle-aged man emerged from the darkness at the back of the premises. The door opened and the man smiled at me as I introduced myself. With thinning grey-brown hair, aquiline nose and black rimmed spectacles, the man who shook hands was the MD, Colin White. Colin seemed very pleasant. Dressed in shirt and tie, brown jacket and olive-green trousers, he was quietly spoken with a piercing stare. This didn't put me off as he led me along a narrow passageway through to a back room, which was obviously a workshop-type area and offered me a cup of tea. With the pleasantries dispensed with, it was down to business. Colin had my letter and CV in front of him and told me that he was very impressed with both. The vacancy was for an immediate (or soon as possible) start, for a staff photographer whose main responsibility would be for colour printing all the wedding 'proofs', mainly undertaken every Saturday and to then print all the wedding and studio portrait orders. There were nine wedding photographers who worked Saturdays. It transpired that eight were keen amateurs with only one being a full time professional, who was also a Director at John F Whites. Colin then gave me a tour of the studios, a ground floor house conversion. The shop was, as you might expect, in the front room. We had come along the passageway to the finishing area, which contained a work bench underneath a huge semi-glazed sash window, tea making facilities, a sink, a printing paper glazing machine and in one corner a little dark room which housed an automated C41, 'dip and dunk' colour processing machine. Opposite the work bench, I noticed two shelves crammed with brown A5 envelopes. Colin told me that each one of what appeared to be at least forty such envelopes stuffed full of wedding 'proofs' was a wedding order, awaiting printing. The staff member creating this vacancy had left a week ago and already the wedding order printing was behind and inexorably growing bigger. This would be my main responsibility if I got the job.

At the back of the work area was the door to another room, which housed the colour printing machine. The smell of chemistry told me all I needed to know – this print processor was in constant use. To one side of this machine was a small green door, through which was a tiny darkroom. This housed a Durst enlarger, baseboard, and a light-tight printing box, equipped with an automatic feed and advance. The bottom of the box, Colin told me, contained a roll of 8" wide colour printing paper on the left-hand side and take up spool on the right-hand side. The dark room wall had one or two sheets of paper with figures scribbled on and a shelf containing several large, square coloured filters. Next to this green door was the loo and at the back of the colour printing machine room was a final darkroom, housing a colour hand enlarger. All the enlargements greater than 8"x6" were undertaken here by Ian, the Director. Walking back along the passageway, a door to the left opened into the studio - a converted, spacious sitting room. At one end of this carpeted room, there were a number of coloured paper roll backgrounds, different size posing stools together with a gold coloured chaise longue. There were four Bowens studio electronic flash units, complete with reflective umbrellas and bowl reflectors. A couple of tripods had been left erected at the opposite end of the studio, just behind some very big, dark curtains. Behind these curtains, was a glass panelled door which led through to a tiny conservatory, containing another workbench. This is where Ian undertook all the print-to-board mounting, canvas bonding and picture framing. The day of the interview was Thursday, which was closing day. The new post required staff to work on Saturdays, so Thursday was given off in lieu.

Colin led me back to the working area where we had originally begun the interview and poured another cup of tea for us both. We were both stirring our brews at the same time when Colin looked at me and asked me what I thought. Answering with a young man's over enthusiasm, I told Colin that I was very impressed with the set up and I admired the variety of photographs that I had seen. "Hmm, yes, well, erm if you'd like it, the job is yours. I won't be interviewing anyone else". He smiled at me as the words sunk in. My face must have lit up like a Christmas tree. I could have hugged him. I accepted the offer of full-time employment immediately. With a start date of the first Monday in May, that gave me about ten days to wrap things up at Mum and Dad's and find accommodation in London. Colin had been very good. He asked me if I had any holiday booked. I dropped the bombshell towards the end of the interview that I had recently won an all-expenses paid holiday with adventure company 'Trek America' and that the trip was booked for the July. Colin pondered this a while and pondered some more when I also told him that my older sister Vicky was getting married on a Saturday in mid-August. He then told me that ordinarily I would only be allowed to take one week off in the summer during the peak weddings season and a week off during winter, but he was prepared to make an exception. My starting salary would be £7000 per annum, paid weekly in cash in a traditional, sealed paper pay packet. After tax and national insurance this meant that my weekly pay packet would contain about £98, out of which I would need to pay for accommodation, bills, food and clothing. Although the salary was low, it was about the going rate at that time for newbie photographers. Suffice to say, I didn't turn my nose up, for I had been offered this opportunity almost on a silver platter. It meant so many things, but crucially it was the chance of independence and escape from my nefarious father's talons.

I had barely been back in the north a handful of days when the nuclear disaster at Chernobyl struck. The power plant located in Pripyat, part of the former Ukrainian Soviet Socialist Republic blew up on 26th April, the exploding reactor and fire scattering radiation over much of western USSR and Europe. The news headlines made depressing reading. Could we be affected in Britain? What would be the impact in terms of radiation poisoning and resulting cancers? In going down to London, would I be any nearer the nuclear fall-out than living up in the north-west? Indeed, was there any point in continuing my journey – full stop? I pondered these and other grim questions as, with suitcase and rucksack in hand, I began my now slightly indeterminate road to freedom and the start of a new chapter in my life.

The immediate aftermath of Chernobyl rapidly downgraded the danger level for the UK and as time went on, sadly Chernobyl like so much other bad news, was consigned to history. Now back in London, I had booked a week's accommodation at a bed and breakfast in Lewisham, which was located a mile from my new place of work. I had arrived in the capital on the first Sunday in May and in the morning, dressed in grey jacket, smart black trousers, black shoes, shirt and tie, I left the B&B and headed for White's studios. As my working hours would be 9am until 5pm, I arrived 5 minutes early, only to find the studio door closed and locked. I looked around for signs of Colin and peered in a few times but couldn't see any movement.

Suddenly, a distinguished looking man in his middle 50s approached me with a key in his hand. Eyeing me suspiciously, he put the key in the lock, turned to me and said "Ah, you must be young Paul, the new photographer". He picked the milk off the doorstep and I followed him inside, where we shook hands. "I'm Ian Sellars" the middle-aged man said, smiling through his moustache, "Glad you're joining us". That was my very memorable introduction to Ian Gordon Sellars, professional wedding and portrait photographer, trusted mentor, former work colleague and gentleman. Ian reminded me of an RAF officer from world war two films, minus the posh accent. From day one I liked and respected Ian. He was generally friendly and placid by nature, but could quickly get irritated if people mucked him about.

We had only been in the studio's work area for a minute or two, when the front door chimed as it opened and an immaculately dressed trim lady with reddish hair and a friendly face bustled in. "Hello, I'm Jean" she said smiling, with her hand outstretched. I quickly learned that Jean was the 'glue' that held the business together. If Jean wasn't greeting customers, she was taking bookings, sorting out wedding orders, putting albums together and goodness knows what else. Jean seemingly did everything and like Ian, I warmed to her immediately.

As a Company Director, I learned that Ian was the main man. Colin had unfortunately suffered a mild heart attack in recent months and was obviously forced to look after his health, meaning that we only saw him once or twice a week and always at the end of the week on pay day. Ian was the lead photographer and if he wasn't out photographing a wedding or in the studio taking a group portrait, he could either be found out the back, in the dark room printing an enlargement, or in the little conservatory annexed to the back of the studio, canvas bonding or picture framing. Although I'd had a very informative tour from Colin, Ian nevertheless showed me round in more detail. My main area of responsibility was to print the wedding proof prints on Saturday nights and for any weekday weddings and also to print wedding and studio portrait orders. I would need to mix up chemistry for the print processor on an as and when basis and keep the machinery clean and functioning. As second staff photographer, I would also take studio portraits and be called on to photograph a wedding, should anyone call in sick. Ian showed me my new home – my darkroom, which housed the Durst enlarger, at which I was destined to produce many thousands of colour prints during my time at White's.

With both of us locked in the darkroom and in pitch darkness, Ian reached down, opened the fold down door to the paper transporter box and popped what was left of the roll inside a light tight bag, which he then put safely up on the shelf. Now with the lights on and having previously ripped a two metre length of now fogged paper off from the roll, Ian proceeded to show me how the paper roll transport mechanism worked, the complete function of the enlarger and crucially how the closing of metal flaps on the baseboard advanced your exposed piece of printing paper, in readiness for the next print exposure to be made. The colour enlarger could work very efficiently for maybe a week, but then due to fluctuations in the processing chemistry and perhaps a change in printing paper batch, or even a change of enlarger bulb, the colour could be thrown way out. This required a series of colour tests to be printed, in effect using a correctly exposed negative, an over and an underexposed negative from a standard set of Kodak grey scale and colour charts.

By morning break, I was up and running with the enlarger and printing system and Ian had left me to work my way through a mountain of printing orders. I was half way through a portrait, 3 shots of a black Labrador, when there was a knock on the darkroom door and Ian's voice called out "Tea up, Paul!" I emerged into the light and took a seat in the finishing room to see Ian pouring the tea. Jean handed me the biscuit tin and I politely took two digestives. Ian Sellars came a close second to my Grandma in making the best brew. Similar to Grandma, Ian used tea leaves and a strainer and my tea would always be with one sugar back then! There was always plenty of tea and of course time for a second cuppa within the fifteen-minute allotted tea break. Then it was back into the darkroom for more printing. I got into a system of strip-testing three or four orders, running that through the processor, colour assessing the test strips, colour and density correcting, then going for final printing. One of the little gimmicks of the time for wedding orders was for the happy couple to be printed inside a wine glass. This was quite tricky as it was a two-part exposure. The first exposure was made for a standard negative depicting the glass. One had then to quickly switch the paper transport off and close the light tight metal plates or flaps. The negative of the glass was taken out of the enlarger's neg carrier and replaced with that of the newlyweds. I then had to project the image of the couple through a wine glass shaped cut out in a piece of black card, which was attached to a clip and adjustable stand. The skill was in getting the projected image to just the right size. Too big and the couple would bleed over the edge of the glass, looking shoddy and unprofessional. Too small and the couple would look ridiculous inside a gigantic wine glass that dwarfed them. With practise and plenty of cockups under my belt, I eventually got it spot on.

Lunchtime at Whites was from noon until 1pm. On my first day, Ian asked what I was doing for lunch. I hadn't even thought about it, so Ian suggested I join him at a local café which did a tasty roast dinner, bread and butter, dessert and cup of tea for a reasonable price. Tony, a Turkish Cypriot, and his wife Joan owned the 'Sangley Café', a five-minute walk from the studio on Sangley Road. I liked them the moment we shook hands. Tony's cooking was excellent. Having my main meal during the day meant that I'd only need a snack in the evening and of course, breakfast was provided at the B&B in Lewisham. Joan was a lovely lady, very bubbly and always smiling. I remember her saying to me one time "I bet you miss your Mum's cooking, Paul?" to which I tactfully replied that Tony's roasts came a very close second.

The following day Colin came in and I met his wife Rita, who seemed very friendly. Colin was keen to hear that I was settling in well. He then disappeared upstairs to his office and I returned to the dark room. During tea break that afternoon Colin introduced me to his Dad, John F. White, the founding father of the studio bearing his name. In his late 80s and balding, stooped over and walking slowly but determinedly with the aid of two sticks, John F. White was a great character. Although he was a tad deaf, he had a razor-sharp recollection of events both in the distant and more recent past and I was fascinated with his stories of the early years. He seemed very interested in my background and education, he was a lovely man and I had the utmost respect for him.

Thursday was my day off. The studio was closed and I had already earmarked a couple of properties to visit that morning advertising house shares in the local Lewisham newspaper. The first one was in Lewisham itself, close to the B&B. One look inside and

I could see instantly that it was a dive. Bad vibes coupled with peeling wallpaper, the smell of damp and an even stronger smell of dog shit coming from close by, convinced me that property number one was a nogoer. The second house was located at the back of a hospital in Hither Green. My A to Z told me that I needed to walk from Lewisham to Catford and then head through Mountsfield Park. My meeting was for 11am and I rounded the corner with three minutes to spare, went up to the front door and donged the bell. There were colourful flowers in the front garden, which gave the property a cared for appearance. The door was answered by an attractive young lady with shoulder-length blonde hair, a tanned complexion and wearing a white polo top, gym skirt and training shoes. I guess she was a few years older than me. Wendi, a PE teacher, introduced herself, smiling warmly. She gave me a tour of the house. The most important feature, she said, was the alarm under the stairs. The lounge on the right was out of bounds, as it was Wendi's 'retreat'. Then it was on to a small kitchen, which seemed well equipped and a dining room beyond that. Outside the kitchen door was a small area where the washing machine was housed. This was covered by a sloping glass roof. Upstairs there were three bedrooms. Opposite the top of the stairs was Scott's room. Scott was a chef who worked for the health food chain Cranks. Turning sharp right, the bathroom was on the left.

Wendi then showed me the next room, which was the one she was letting. As the door opened, my heart sank. The whole room was decked out in pink. Very girly and so not me. Wendi smiled and apologised that she hadn't had time to decorate this room. The room next to this and overlooking the street was of course, Wendi's bedroom. We then went downstairs and she told me the weekly rent including bills, which was about average for the time. "So, what do you think?" Wendi said, nodding in approval at my two references. Here was a friendly, professional lady with a spotlessly clean house and with the added bonus of an alarm system. The semi-detached house was also situated on a corner plot, which meant not having strange people (or noises) coming from the other side of my bedroom wall. The only downside that I could see was the pink décor in my would-be room. "I'll take it" I said eagerly. Common sense told me that I was the only one that had to put up with the loud colour scheme. Nobody else had to see it. The place offered me somewhere to stay for my time at White's Studios. The timing was perfect. My last night in the B&B was to be that Saturday and Wendi suggested that I move in on the Sunday morning. I felt pleased with myself. Walking back into Catford, I decided to celebrate and get the bus into Bromley for a bite to eat.

My first Saturday at the studio was a real eye opener. Ian was out all day photographing not one, but two weddings and I spent the day either printing in the darkroom or in the studio taking portraits. Shortly before 5pm, Ian returned and he immediately locked himself in the C41 room and loaded his roll films onto the processor. A few minutes later he was out putting the kettle on. As soon as his films had cleared the drying cabinet, Ian gave them a quick visual inspection. Every neg was spot on exposure, lighting and composition wise. I had about eight rolls to proof print and that was just from Ian's weddings. Another eight photographers were yet to pitch up with their films. Ian, like the other photographers, was shooting 2 ¼ square, which meant twelve frames per roll. With ninety-six negs to print and the promise of more to follow, I disappeared back into my darkroom quicker than the speed of light. About 20 minutes later, I re-emerged from my little room having already loaded Ian's proof prints onto the paper processor. I opened the door to the work area to be met by Colin and several new faces, who I learned were other photographers employed by Whites on a Saturday basis. One such photographer was John Wylie, Jean's other half. John was a part-time university lecturer, model railway enthusiast and author. With thick greying hair, John was a friendly, jovial character who was always laughing and joking. Like Ian, I warmed to him immediately. The other photographers, although a nice bunch of guys, weren't professional, trained photographers. Despite having had countless tips from Ian on composition and exposure for example, their images were very amateurish. Compared with Ian and John's work, which was always a joy to print, I always had great difficulty printing the other photographers' work. If their negs weren't two stops overexposed, then composition left much to be desired. The 2 ¼ square frame was often taken too literally and the image would be framed as such. The trouble was, you needed to frame your composition with either a landscape or portrait crop in mind with the end result being printed to 8"x6".

After quick introductions, I grabbed another wodge of films and disappeared back into my little room. And so it went on. A photographer would return, give his films to Ian, who would load up the C41 processor and then once through the drying cycle, the wedding negs would then be handed to me for proofing. That first

Saturday, I lost count of the number of negs or films I proof printed, or indeed the number of times that I heard Ian stamp the middle of each print with the words 'Proof only', but incredibly we finished around 8.30pm. I felt knackered. Caked in dried sweat, I was longing for a bath and some serious shuteye. I'd only walked a few yards along Rushey Green when I stopped and sniffed the air - I suddenly transformed into Beatrix Potter's Samuel Whiskers, about to ask Anna Maria to 'make me a kitten dumpling roly-poly pudding' for my supper. I could smell garlic bread and pizzas cooking and just then I was instantly famished. The Hawaiian thin crust was promptly washed down with one or two 'lemonades' and this really hit the spot. Thereafter, I frequented the local pizzeria virtually every Saturday night after work.

The move from the Lewisham B&B went smoothly. After all, I only had a suitcase and a holdall, which I bundled onto the first bus bound for Hither Green. Wendi showed me the alarm system and I was even allocated a shelf in one of the kitchen cupboards for my food. Wendi then made me a mug of coffee and we sat in the dining room. Whilst she went over the house rules, I learned that Wendi taught PE at nearby independent school, Farringtons in Chislehurst. Just then, I heard someone plod downstairs and into the kitchen. It was a young man in his early 20s, similar in age to me. He had immaculate swept back, semi-permed, jet black hair and an aquiline nose. The young man had a strong air of suaveness about him and was almost as laid back as Dillon from the Magic Roundabout as he shook hands. That was my introduction to Scott, who was yawning now, having had a Sunday morning lie-in after working a busy Saturday night at Cranks in Covent Garden. From that initial introduction, I never really warmed to Scott. I couldn't quite put my finger on why I didn't particularly like him – maybe he was too overtly suave on occasions and it got under my skin. Maybe it was his supreme confidence as a chef and his culinary skills in Wendi's kitchen, which put me to shame. Maybe it was just his sanguine disposition, I don't know, but something niggled me about him and I never felt relaxed when Scott was around. I put up with him, because I liked living at 28 Woodlands Street and so I didn't kick up any fuss.

At Whites, Ian was a great mentor. On occasions I would be lucky enough to accompany him on a wedding or two. He was a natural and gifted photographer, who could pose the bride and groom or wedding group in seconds and with few verbal commands. With outstretched arms, Ian would cup each hand, indicating to the person at each end of a group to turn in slightly and then turn their heads back to the camera. With this movement, Ian avoided a group set up in a straight line, which always looks boring. Men would inevitably have their hands cupped over their 'family jewels' and Ian would make some quip, which immediately had everyone in stitches. It was then I heard the shutter fire. It never failed and Ian always got the shots in the bag. Shooting the couple at the altar inside a gloomy church represented another challenge. Ian tripod-mounted the 'Blad', composed the shot and waited for the all-important moment. I grinned when I heard the slow shutter speed. He's bound to have the couple blurred due to movement on that neg I thought to myself. "So, what was the exposure for the couple at the altar, Paul?" Ian asked me. "Sounded like a slow shutter speed" I replied. "A quarter at 4!" Ian grinned at me. Ian shot this at a quarter of a second at wide aperture (F4), with no pre-metering. The neg was clean, crisp and perfectly exposed. Most of all, it was pin sharp with no movement from the couple. 'A quarter at 4' was another Ian Sellars trademark and I loved to repeat this mantra to him regularly, when looking through his shots. Ian would always chuckle to me with a proud glint in his eyes and repeat "A quarter at 4".

If I had to go out and shoot a wedding, Colin would let me use his spare car, an old Datsun Sunny. I really cut my teeth at Whites and learned practical wedding photography the hard way – by getting stuck in and making mistakes. A misfire here, closed eyes on the bridegroom there, stupid expressions etc. But I stuck to it and learned, whether the assignment venue was at a registry office or church, involved attending the bride getting ready at home beforehand and or entailed taking shots at the reception, Ian would always critique my proofs and I made mental notes on his feedback about the do's and don'ts and continual ways to improve. Many a time, I'd have to pose wedding groups where the main players had drunk one too many! Whilst they all thought it was hilarious, staggering around larruped and pulling stupid faces at the camera, it made my job very difficult. Outwardly I'd laugh along with them just to get the shots, but inside I hated it – the fact they were drunk and mocking me. Colin used to send me to all these weddings and I don't think it was on purpose. What this period in my life represented however, was a steep learning curve and liquid gold experience.

Pressure wise, the photography of a wedding ranked high up there on the heart attack scale. I had been at Whites for a while when Colin asked me whether I could photograph a Greek wedding. He would pay overtime as the job would take most of Sunday and involve attending the bride's home beforehand, then the service at St. Mary's Greek Orthodox Cathedral in Camberwell, followed by attendance at the reception venue – Vauxhall's 'Podium' in Nine Elms Lane. I went over the shopping list of photographs with Ian and I had my checklist in my pocket. Both camera backs were loaded with roll film colour neg, I checked that I had plenty of spare film, spare flash batteries for the Sunpak gun and I also checked my Weston light meter and tripod.

On the morning of the wedding I had my A to Z with me and felt confident as I drove towards the bride's home, which was only a mile and a half from the Greek cathedral. The service was at 12 noon and I was booked to attend the bride's home for 10.30am. Turning up fashionably early ten minutes beforehand, I was somewhat startled to meet the bride, who greeted me at the front door with her hair in curlers, wearing jeans, a skimpy t-shirt and quite clearly, no bra. The bride, a raven-haired beauty showed me into the lounge and offered me a cup of coffee. It quickly transpired that this bride was operating on Greek time and had barely started to get ready. This stressed me out immediately and I kept looking at my watch nervously. Finally, an hour after arriving and with heart now pounding, I was summoned upstairs to take shots of the bride's hairdo, looking in the mirror shots and with bridesmaids. I left the house at 11.55 in the knowledge that the service was due to start five minutes later. I barely had time to complete the bride at home photographs. I raced down to the Greek Cathedral, parked up in a side street and quickly reloaded both camera backs.

As I approached the entrance to the cathedral, my heart sank. There were loads of people milling about and I didn't have a clue who was the groom for my wedding. I asked a couple of people, who just shrugged their shoulders and said, "we not know". It started to dawn on me what I was seeing. Due to the fact that everything was running late in typical Greek style, the guests of the previous wedding were mingling with those from my wedding and also with the following wedding. No chance of getting any groom and best man shots here then. I was just pondering this predicament when I heard clapping behind me and suddenly realised that a horse drawn carriage was approaching. Sure enough my bride and her father were arriving. I then went into urgent mode and took control. I was determined to get the 'bride arriving' shots. I bagged a superb shot of the carriage approaching and lovely images of the bride and her father sitting together in the carriage. The bride then gave her father a kiss, which proved to be a special moment. The Blad's shutter was clicking away through challenging lighting conditions. The early summer sun was top lighting my subjects, which meant that I needed a decent squirt of fill-in flash to lift those drop shadows. A quick check of the Sunpak flash told me that I needed to tweak the manual setting up a tad. The beautiful bride and her father looked resplendent in their respective outfits. I then photographed the father carefully helping his precious daughter down from the carriage. I'll remember his captured expression forever. His face was filled with pride. It was at that moment that I told myself, no matter how difficult this wedding was to photograph, I was going to do a great coverage of the day for this family. They deserved nothing less.

Racing in front of the bride and her father, I happened on a piece of luck. I ran into one of the bride's brothers. I relayed my predicament to him, of three weddings merging into one and although the bride's brother was laughing, he could see from my professional and non-Greek's perspective that I was very concerned that I capture all the important photographs. He suggested two things. Firstly, that I don't attempt to get any group shots outside the cathedral, rather, do these at the reception. Secondly, that he would not only tell me where to pitch up inside the cathedral to get a commanding view of the proceedings, this saviour would stand behind me and tap me on the shoulder moments before an important point in the ceremony needed to be photographed. I found this greatly reassuring. The cathedral interior was very atmospheric. Ornate carvings stared back at me everywhere I looked and the rich, aromatic blend of frankincense and myrrh hung heavily in the air. To add to this feeling of authenticity, a number of priests emerged all donned in traditional vestments and in the middle of this holy grouping, stood an Archbishop Makarios lookalike. At first, I thought the bride's brother had forgotten to tap me on the shoulder, but then as the ceremony got under way, the taps came thick and fast, threatening to overwhelm me. For some odd reason I had packed loads of film. Nobody had suggested how many rolls I should take, just as nobody had given me an indication of how many shots to take. I just kept taking photographs and reloading the Blad camera backs. I quickly lost count of how many photographs I'd taken inside the cathedral, but as the long ceremony drew to a close, my thoughts quickly turned to the reception venue and the majority of the traditional photographs that I'd yet to take – bride and groom full length, three quarters and close-ups, the cake-cutting, the kiss, best man and groom, all the key group shots. I checked my list of photographs and was alarmed by the fact that I hadn't got any of the main images yet. I resolved to myself that come what may, all these would be taken at the Podium in Vauxhall.

From what I remember, there was quite a delay in the wedding party leaving the cathedral and arriving at the Podium. When eventually the happy couple arrived at the reception, I was on a mission. I almost lunged at them as they waltzed in. Bride full length, ¾ and close up done. This was followed by the groom on his own, full length, ¾ and close up shots of the couple, the pretend cutting of the cake and the groom and best man together. I was just getting into full flow, when I was approached by an older man in his 60s who was frowning at me. "The bride and groom are required for the first dance" he said. Narked, I just had to hang about, as I still had all the group shots to do. Another hour went by during which time I had taken no photographs and I was getting seriously pissed off, so much so that I marched up to the father of the bride to let him know that I still needed to photograph the key group shots. Thankfully, he made an announcement and the relevant people made their way towards me and the area of the Podium I'd commandeered for photography, all in their own time. Slowly but surely, I ticked off the groups, building them up from the basic bride, groom, best man and bridesmaids, through to the couple with their respective parents, then adding brothers and sisters, followed by cousins and special requests, for example great Uncle Theo with the bride and groom.

I glanced at my watch. Incredibly, it was 8.40pm and I hadn't got a clue where the time had gone. I rechecked the list of photographs to take, crossing them off again one by one in my mind. I'd got them. I'd got them all, but God it had been a challenge. I was thinking it was time for the off, when the bride and groom reading my mind, rushed up to me and insisted that I stay not only for the speeches, but also for something to eat. With the key speeches covered, the last thing on my mind was food. I was too hyped up on adrenaline and once again found myself caked in dried sweat. It was now approaching 10pm and I had well and truly had enough. The job was in the bag, but it had been one hard slog. More than once, the whole day threatened to degenerate into one mother of a ridiculous fiasco. Memories of my attendance at this marathon event were brought crowding into my mind years later when I watched Nia Vardalos' 2002 Academy Award-nominated film, 'My Big Fat Greek Wedding'. It was exactly like the film – lots of people called Nick, Nicky and Nikos, lots of noise, seemingly lots of confusion, lots of food and lots of stress, but not a bottle of 'Windex' in sight!

When I brought all the films in to work the following morning, Colin was not pleased at all. Unusually, he'd come in on a Monday and he was seldom in at the beginning of the week. Far from congratulating me on all my hard work, he frowned and shook his head at the sheer number of films I had taken, which in his opinion, was very excessive. I also had the proof printing to do, which would take me away from printing other wedding orders. A few weeks later, my Greek wedding couple returned from honeymoon to place their order. The bride and groom ordered several albums and quite a few enlargements to boot. Jean told me that they were delighted with my photographs and the order total was well over £2,000. I was chuffed to bits on hearing this bit of news, but got not a single word of thanks from Colin. I've photographed many weddings in my time and all, without exception, have involved varying levels of stress, but this, my first and last Greek wedding took the biscuit!

In July 1986, Colin had given me a special dispensation to go on a three-week holiday to the USA. Unbeknown to me, I had won an all-expenses paid trip with adventure company 'Trek America' when sister company 'Trek Europa' had entered some of my images into an internal competition. I persuaded Aly to join me as I knew we'd have a laugh. Travelling from New York, west across the northern American States together with twelve other like-minded 18 to 38-year olds (including the trek leader) in a luxury, air conditioned mini-bus, proved very comfortable. We set up a rota for cooking, washing up, cleaning the van and loading the huge roof rack – all our luggage went on top of the mini-bus and was then covered by a huge, blue tarpaulin. There were to be so many highlights of this three-week vacation. In New York, having photographed the Empire State Building, the 1973 World Trade Centre twin towers beckoned. The views of New York City from the 110th floor observation deck of 2WTC (South Tower) were breath-taking. I took photographs from each side. I had photographs taken of me against the city skyline and when Aly and I had taken in the view, I wanted to photograph both north and south towers together from street level looking up. These towers were so monumentally huge, I remember not just having to look up but to really put my head right back as far as I could just to see the tops of these incredible structures. I hatched a plan, whereby I would lie on the 'sidewalk' and point my Olympus OM1-N and

21mm wide angle lens skyward, with Aly watching not just my back, but my whole body! The iconic resultant image taken all those years ago remains in my portfolio as one of my all-time favourite images. Little did I realise how poignant my WTC images would become just over fifteen years later, when both towers and surrounding buildings were completely destroyed in one of the most devastating international terrorist attacks of our time.

The three waterfalls that comprise Niagara Falls straddle the Canadian and United States borders, located between Ontario province and New York State. The magnificent falls are situated on the Niagara River, which drains into Lakes Erie and Ontario. Lying some 17 miles north west of Buffalo, New York State and approximately 75 miles South south east of Toronto, the falls are juxtaposed between the twin cities of Niagara Falls, Ontario and Niagara Falls, New York. We walked across to Canada from the USA and seemingly within touching distance of the top of the falls. I took images of the 'Maid of the Mist' boat taking tourists to the very base of the falls and then it was our turn to don the blue macs and get absolutely satched by the spray from above. That was a great experience.

The 'windy city' of Chicago was next, Chicago being the third most populous city in the United States after New York and Los Angeles. The 1973 Sears Tower (renamed Willis Tower in 2009) offered superb views of the city and surrounds. In the summer of '86 during my visit, Sears Tower ranked the tallest building in the world, this colossal skyscraper towering 1,451 feet (442 meters) above Chicago.

We were 5 hours out of the windy city, almost equidistant between Chicago and Minneapolis on a thrill-seeking white-water rafting adventure when we almost lost Aly. We were in a large inflatable, negotiating the sometimes treacherous rapids of the challenging Menominee River in northern most Michigan state, which hugs the Wisconsin border. Fourteen young souls helmeted and donned in life jackets, our craft tossing and turning, lunging and rolling, catapulting us through the fast current. My best mate was sitting confidently on the bow one minute and the next, a wave completely engulfed the front of the inflatable and swept him overboard. Without thinking, several members of the trek and myself let go of the safety ropes and leaned into the fast-moving waters to grab Aly and yank him back on board. I'll never forget his ashen, 'skull-like' face when he emerged from his river dunking, which was a mixture of horror and relief. We could so easily have lost him that day.

Continuing westwards, the landscape of Badlands National Park in south western South Dakota was surreal, offering awe-inspiring vistas which comprised mini plateau-like eroded buttes, pinnacles and spires in this, the largest, undisturbed wilderness of mixed grass prairie in the entire United States of America. Like the sights beforehand and those that were to follow, I felt privileged to be there.

I'd seen photographs of the presidents carved out of rock before, but actually being at Mount Rushmore was something else. Located near Keystone, South Dakota, the four presidents representing the first 150 years of American history have been carved out of the granite face. From left to right as you face this monument are George Washington, Thomas Jefferson, Theodore Roosevelt and Abraham Lincoln.

Just when I thought that I couldn't be impressed any more, we came to the Bear Lodge Mountains' Devils Tower in Black Hills, Crook County, Wyoming. This awe-inspiring 1,558-meter-high igneous intrusion or laccolith represented one hell of a photo opportunity. The weather was fabulous and I managed to get some pleasing images of this climbing magnet and phenomenal natural structure. The breath-taking scenery kept coming in the form of Grand Teton National Park and Jackson Hole, Yellowstone National Park, famed for the Old Faithful Geyser and then Sierra Nevada's huge freshwater Lake Tahoe, all of which, were picture-postcard pretty.

And then it was onwards, first to Yosemite and then to San Francisco, which I'd wanted to visit since my boyhood years, being an avid fan of Karl Malden and Michael Douglas in 'The Streets of San Francisco'. I was very satisfied with my images of the red-coloured Golden Gate Bridge and just to walk across from one side to another, stopping to take photographs every few minutes, was fantastic. Construction took just over four years to complete and the bridge was finished in April 1937. This paragon of structural excellence is 2,737 meters long, 227 meters high and just under 27.5 meters wide and links San Francisco with Marin County.

The trek across America had taken exactly three weeks, but we had allowed some extra time to visit my half-brother, his wife and one of my first cousins in Ventura, California as well as visiting Washington D.C., taking in sights such as 1600 Pennsylvania Avenue (aka the White House) and also the Lincoln Memorial. There were so many adventures and so many highlights of this month-long trip. Alcatraz prison was very atmospheric and I wanted to be photographed where Clint Eastwood had sat outside on the steps in the 1979 Don Siegel film 'Escape from Alcatraz', although I didn't have a hope in hell of recreating the often electrifying atmosphere of the film – a quick snap on Kodachrome 64 would have to suffice. Riding the cable cars along Powell, Hyde and Market Streets was great fun. San Francisco's steep road, Lombard Street, comprising eight 'switchback' hairpin bends and Fisherman's Wharf were equally fascinating. The chuckwagon dinners were memorable as was having my photograph taken with my arm around a black Doberman Pinscher, a breed of dog renowned for its potential aggression towards strangers. Visiting Hollywood was an eye-opener and I also had my photo taken in the Captain's seat of the 747 jumbo jet that Aly and I flew out to the States on. Since the massive clampdown in security post '9/11', you'd probably be hard pressed to get that kind of image nowadays. My overriding memory though is of the absolutely stunning scenery of Yosemite National Park – linking hands around a giant sequoia tree and in particular, gazing in awe and wonder at Half Dome. This giant, granite dome stands some 2.694 meters in height amidst the Sierra Nevada mountain range in Yosemite, California. Just to be there amidst that wonderful scenery and in the knowledge that I was treading in the footsteps of my landscape photographic hero, Ansel Adams, made Yosemite, for me a spiritual homage and was a very special moment. Knowing that not 60 years before Adams had immortalised Half Dome in such iconic, treasured black and white plates such as 'Monolith, The Face of Half Dome', 'Moon Over Half Dome' and 'Half Dome, Merced River, Winter, Yosemite, 1938'. What a remarkable holiday and what an experience!

I returned from the USA on a massive high as you can imagine. What's more, I discovered that every London tube station was displaying my image of Blackpool tower during the illuminations, portrayed on huge billboards. The tranny that I had sold the previous year, now had the strap line… 'Come up and see us some time'. This gave me one hell of a rush as I kept thinking – yeah, I took that. Then it was back down to earth with a big bump as I returned to White's. I summarised the entire month-long vacation into our 15-minute morning tea break for Ian and Jean who were fascinated. In my absence, Ian had printed the odd urgent wedding order here and there, but he had his own work to attend to and the shelf in the work room had grown to monumental proportions, crammed edge to edge with orders awaiting printing. Colin was quick to point out the need to eat into this backlog when he popped in later on during that first Monday back. The chemistry in the paper processor had started to go off and there was a significant colour shift in my first set of test prints, not helped by the fact that I was printing with a new batch of paper. This was a bastard to get the printing back on track and took me the whole of that first day. As fast as I tried to print the wedding orders, Jean would top them up from the other end of the shelf. This was soul destroying as the process felt very much like running up dry sand dunes, putting one foot forward, but then slipping two feet back.

I had only been back in Catford a couple of weeks, when my older sister's big day arrived. Vicky's wedding to Mark was on 16th August 1986 and this meant me taking yet another Saturday off work, which Colin had agreed to when he hired me. The setting for the day's nuptials was one of my favourite places, Oxford, where both Vicky and Mark had studied at university – Vicky at Somerville College and Mark at Brasenose College. The marriage ceremony was held in the beautiful Brasenose College chapel, which is steeped in history and which made the perfect setting for what proved a very grand affair indeed. Ian Sellars would have described this as a top-drawer wedding. Everyone looked immaculate - the men in morning dress and the ladies suitably attired in expensive dresses, hats, shoes and jewellery, but there was one notable exception. Grandad, who due to illness, couldn't make the wedding. One of Vicky and Mark's friends, a chaplain who was also a fellow Oxford graduate, conducted the service. My younger sister Kate, along with Mark's sister Claire, were bridesmaids. The reception was at the Randolph Hotel and photography was undertaken by a highly reputable local firm, complemented of course, by images from yours truly! The only spoiler to what proved a really enjoyable day was Dad's presence, made worse by a protracted wedding speech, which didn't keep to the agreed content or length, much to Vicky's chagrin.

I often wondered why the old saying 'never work with children and animals' had come into existence, but after working at John F. White Studios, I knew exactly why and had no doubt whatsoever of its meaning. In the studio, I was accruing plenty of experience taking family, group, individual and pet portraits. I experimented with back and hair lighting and soon got a sitting down to a fine art. Portraits were priced in groups of three shots, which meant three different poses, so if Jean called out "portrait six shots", you knew that the impending job was going to be quite big. Older couples would come in for their golden wedding shots, family christening groups would need to be posed, a mix of standing, sitting, kneeling and lying down with varying head height. The intention was to create an interesting composition and not have one boring line of misfits with their hands cupped over their private parts. New-borns and young tots required oodles of patience for the perfect moment, 21st birthday portraits were a delight to capture, graduations meant careful positioning of the parchment scroll and attention to detail with gown and mortarboard. Animals sometimes had a mind of their own – whether it was two Alsatians together, cats or pet rats, you name it, I did it. I also got to photograph some very attractive young ladies - an added bonus. Simplicity was the name of the game and I preferred minimal make up coupled with the use of Vaseline to accentuate the lips rather than lip gloss, which had a tendency to be a tad garish and didn't look quite as natural. Back in the mid to late '80s, portrait vignetting and misty effects were very popular, but I never overused them, preferring not to use filters and opting for the four-studio light set up – main light, fill-in, back light and hair light with the occasional addition of either white board, silver or gold-coloured reflector fill-in.

Getting out to cover a Saturday wedding meant that I could put all Ian's useful tips into practise: the best man and groom slightly turned in, shaking hands and with perhaps a tighter crop and emphasis on showing the ring and the now well clichéd image of the groom nervously checking his watch; tweaking the composition and fill-in for the bridesmaids, watching the position of the bride's hand resting gently on the open door as she's about to exit the car; Ian's famous ¼ at 4 church shot; the bride signing the register with the proud groom looking on; the couple back-lit and framed in the church doorway; the first kiss; the bride shots; the couple together and then the group shots, building them up from parents and family, to the entire wedding party, using an elevated viewpoint – I got to practise, practise it again and then practise it some more to get it right and to please my mentor. When I eventually got it right, Ian gave me a simple nod of approval and I detected a slight upturn movement of his moustache, but that's all I needed, because I knew he was pleased. I could also photograph weddings mid-week, especially if Ian was on holiday. Small wedding parties at Lewisham Registry Office were a weekly occurrence and this not only added to the job variety, but it was always a delight to see John, the Chief Registrar, who'd utter in an effected South London accent the immortal line "that's the first declaration over with", which would inevitably be coupled with an exaggerated, nervous laugh. Years later this could easily have been a Paul Whitehouse and Harry Enfield comedy sketch.

On one occasion, Jean called me out of the dark room for a 'portrait 3 shots' and I came face to face with four huge, black guys who really towered above me, making me instantly nervous. I quickly ushered them into the studio and I turned on all the lights. Talking to these guys, who were all brothers, I asked who was the eldest and a plan formulated in my head. With the eldest brother lying down on his side, propped up on one elbow, the other three brothers knelt down arced around the back of him, each with a supportive hand on their oldest brother. Instantly I got a rapport going with these guys, who were dressed in very trendy clothes. The eldest brother 'the main man', also wore a hat. All the jewellery added to the atmosphere and mood of the shot. I also decided to shoot against a black background, which was quite a bold statement. This required quite a bit of back lighting to get the necessary separation between skin and background colour. I shot on the Blad in colour and black and white, but gave the brothers the black and white version. They were made up with the portrait and all four shook my hand warmly, promptly ordering a 20"x16" enlargement on canvas as well as a variety of smaller print sizes. From being initially intimidated by these guys, I quickly got them on side by being myself, chatting and joking with them and in the process, established a good rapport and proceeded to get the shots in the bag and a big sale for the studio. They were lovely blokes – if only I'd kept the shot.... Aaaagh!

On my days off (Thursdays and Sundays) I'd get my washing and ironing done, pop to the gym in East Street, Bromley, nip over to Grandma and Grandad's in Mitcham for Sunday lunch and a catch up, or generally explore London. One of my favourite haunts was Greenwich, a lovely part of the capital steeped in maritime history. My frequent walks in the park would inevitably culminate at the Royal Observatory, which dates back to 1675. The observatory is the home of 'longitude zero degrees' (the world's Prime Meridian') and of course Greenwich Mean Time. I used to spend an entire day, quite content to wander around the maritime museum, the Old Royal Naval College and of course the 1869 tea clipper The Cutty Sark, which I had first seen as a small boy.

Sharing Wendi's house in Hither Green suited me fine. It was clean, tidy and warm and with the alarm also offered security. I soon got used to the pink décor in my bedroom. With a few posters up here and there, I never used to notice it. The three of us - Wendi, Scott and me - were rarely at home at the same time, so we didn't have chance to get under each other's skin. That is until the day Caroline, Scott's Spanish girlfriend-soon-to-be fiancée arrived. I can't remember exactly when Caroline came to stay at Woodlands Street, but it was for a significant time period. From the moment she arrived, Caroline irritated me and it was usually because she was in the bathroom when I wanted to go in. Either I was busting for a gypsy's kiss or worse – a tom tit and when I finally got to use the bathroom, all the water had run cold and I had to wait ages for it to warm up.

Wendi also had the occasional mouse around the house, which inevitably meant setting the odd trap here and there. On one occasion I came down to breakfast, turned off the alarm and went to the kitchen cupboard to get my muesli. I had bought the large bag of breakfast cereal only two days before. After opening, it had been sealed by my rolling the top down a few times and wedging it sideways against one edge of the cupboard shelf. Popping the muesli on to the kitchen work top next to a breakfast bowl and spoon, I unravelled the bag to reveal the corner that I'd cut. No sooner had I done that, a tiny mouse face popped out, causing me to start momentarily. The cheeky mouse stared at me for a split second and before I had time to grab it, this little animal leaped into the air and vanished. I was left still staring at the open bag. The real bummer was two-fold. Firstly, I had no breakfast that morning as the entire bag of cereal had to be thrown out and, secondly, with money being tight, it was typical that the bag of cereal was a new bag. I've had the ridiculous notion over the years of a team of 'crack' mice unravelling the bag inside the cupboard, one mouse jumping inside and then the others ravelling the cereal bag back up again, before scarpering, but the truth is just how that little rodent come to be hiding in my muesli with its ravelled down closed top, remains to this day, a complete mystery!

1986, the year that saw the start of my first full time job was over. It had been an eventful year. I was in gainful employment. I had spent nearly a month in America and my older sister had been married. On the UK front, unemployment reached a post-war high of a staggering 3,204,900 on 31 January. July witnessed a royal wedding – HRH The Duke of York to Sarah Ferguson at Westminster Abbey. In October, the first edition of The Independent Newspaper was published and on 29th of that month, the Prime Minister, Margaret Thatcher, opened London's orbital motorway the M25. The world's first heart, lung and liver transplant was undertaken at Cambridgeshire's Papworth Hospital in December and before the year was finally out, the man who's leadership of the nation was nearing its end just as I came into the world back in 1963, Harold Macmillan, the First Earl of Stockton, died aged 92 on 29th December.

1987 continued jobwise in the same vein as the previous year. I returned from the Christmas break to see a stack of wedding orders awaiting printing. However, the advantage of the winter months was that generally the big Saturday weddings were few and far between, being out of season. This meant that I could catch up with the backlog of orders. 1987 was to prove another eventful year. In January, the Archbishop of Canterbury Robert Runcie's special envoy in Lebanon, Terry Waite, disappeared and was subsequently held hostage in Beirut until 1991, whilst negotiating the release of hostages who included journalist John McCarthy. Barely two months later, on 6th March, 193 passengers and crew were killed when the 'RoRo' ferry, MS Herald of Free Enterprise, capsized whilst leaving Zeebrugge harbour in Belgium. At the end of July, the Queen opened Great Britain's first driver-less railway in London, Docklands Light Railway (DLR). Also in July, Ian Sellars photographed me outdoors for the back cover of my book 'Historic Lakeland'. Tragedy struck again on 19th August – this time in Berkshire, when gunman Michael Ryan killed 14 people in what became known as the 'Hungerford massacre'. Sixteen people were also injured and a few days after the shooting spree which saw Ryan take his own life, two further victims succumbed to their injuries in hospital. On 1st October Swedish retail company Ikea opened its first UK store in Warrington, Cheshire, which I so love to visit (not!).

Meteorologist Michael Fish' gave his infamous weather forecast informing the nation that there was no need to worry, a hurricane was not in fact on its way. Of course, later that same day, 15th October and into the following day, the great storm did in fact arrive with hurricane force winds battering the South East and in the process, killing 23 people. I remember the evening vividly. I just couldn't get to sleep as the wind was howling and whining continually like a banshee outside. I then drifted off, to be woken by an almighty crash. I popped my dressing gown on, grabbed a torch, only to be met by Wendi and Scott, similarly clad wafting their torches around in the darkness. The power was off – that much was evident. The crashing noise turned out to be a large roof tile which had become dislodged by the hurricane and had been hurled through the glass roof of the mini conservatory. All we could do was put a bucket on the floor to catch the rain drops and Sellotape a few black bin bags over the hole as a makeshift and very temporary repair. We then all returned to bed. By light of day, the destruction and sheer force of the hurricane revealed itself. As I walked through Mountsfield Park en route to Catford I looked around gobsmacked. Huge trees had been completed uprooted and were lying on their sides. Everywhere there were branches and leaves, bins and rubbish strewn indiscriminately. My journey to work wasn't straightforward as I was forever avoiding this tree or that branch. A while later power was restored and work continued. What I should have done, was grab a camera and record this historical event, even wagging off work for a bit – but it didn't once cross my mind to do so – even when I walked through Greenwich Park a few days later to witness all the prematurely felled trees there. Only later did it dawn on me that I was lucky to survive the hurricane of 1987 in the knowledge that quite a few people hadn't been so fortunate. The big storm caused a massive amount of damage all over England, downing some 15 million trees, including six of the seven famous oak trees in Sevenoaks, Kent.

On Guy Fawkes day, London City airport opened. A few days later, more upset ensued. The Provisional Irish Republican Army detonated a bomb at a remembrance service in Enniskillen, killing eleven people. The year had already witnessed a belly full of tragedy and as if this wasn't enough, disaster struck again on the London underground. The resulting Kings Cross fire of 18th November 1987, which started on an old, wooden Piccadilly line escalator, claimed the lives of 31 people.

My 24th birthday came and went, the temperature started to slide, leaves cascaded to the ground and once more autumn beckoned. It was October 1987 and I had been at the John F. White Studios for seventeen months. 'Itchy beard' had begun to set in as my thoughts turned to moving on. I was pondering this when Colin called in to the studio and asked Ian to pop upstairs for a chat. I thought nothing more of this, but at morning tea break, the calm and unflappable face of Ian Sellars looked like a thundering tempest. "You know what he's gone and done?" a clearly irate Ian announced to Jean and me. "He's just made me redundant". I just stared inanely at Ian, open mouthed, not knowing what to say. I knew that Ian didn't see eye to eye with Colin. 'Mutual dislike' would be a more accurate and probably kinder description of Ian and Colin's relationship, but the two tolerated each other professionally in the interests of the business. Ian had been a huge part of White's for thirty odd years and a two-year old could have told you that Ian was clearly shattered by this redundancy shock. Ian would be leaving the John F. White Studios at Christmas, never to return.

Five minutes after this bombshell news, it suddenly dawned on me that it could have been me heading out of the door as the business required cutbacks. I wasn't yet history because I was cheaper to keep on. I was numb for a while, a feeling which was compounded when Jean announced that she had had enough and would also be leaving with Ian in what was only a few weeks away. Ian and Jean were my life. The three of us ran the studio like a well-oiled machine. The thought of this coming to an end brought on bereavement-like symptoms in waves and shook my confidence. I'd return after the Christmas break to an empty studio, forced to run things by myself and be severely overloaded with work. My predecessor Alan (who apparently also didn't get on with the White family) was working with his colleague Tony in a rival wedding and portrait studio a few miles up the road in Downham and on hearing the news of Ian's redundancy, offered Ian almost full-time hours there and then, a tribute to the great man who was Ian Sellars. This was fantastic news – my mentor was sorted. Jean, if I recall was going to do some part time work for her husband John, which just left little old me to get employment elsewhere. I had all but finished 'Historic Lakeland' as I turned my attention to once more, scouring the employment pages of newspapers and professional magazines. My job hunting had started in earnest. I wanted out too. The count-down to Ian and Jean leaving was awful and a very sad time in my life. I remember Ian having to ask Colin, almost cap in hand, if Colin would allow him to take this photo or that canvas with him. Ian looked like a broken man, Jean had her sights on other things and my heart wasn't in it anymore. I suggested taking a studio portrait of the three of us as a memento and Ian and Jean loved the idea. Ian and I worked like a couple of old pros on this last job together, adjusting the lighting, laughing like old times, setting up the Blad and making sure the shot was just right. This nostalgic image was taken by Ian, who cradled a long cable release in his left hand, just out of shot, the other end of which, was attached to the shutter release button. Jean was positioned in the middle and Ian and I sat either side of her.

And then it was time to say a melancholy goodbye. I hugged Jean, shook hands warmly with Ian and then made my way back up to my parents in Poulton-Le-Fylde, Lancashire for the Christmas break. Ian and Jean were very kind to me and I had thoroughly enjoyed working with such lovely people. When I started my employment at Whites, I never ever thought that it would all end like this. What the hell was I going to do without them?

CHAPTER 7

Life as a ship's photographer: The Cruiseship Picture Years (1988-1989)

Predictably, when I returned to White's studios early in the new year of 1988, the atmosphere was awful. Colin and his wife Rita were in every day, but I was clearly on my own, very much doing all the practical stuff myself on a day to day basis, but it wasn't the same without Ian and Jean. The heart had gone out of the studio, like something had died there. I longed to be free of the place. I had to find something and fast. One or two applications were sent off with no joy and then an advert caught my eye in the BJP (British Journal of Photography) looking for cruise ship photographers. Travel abroad. Get to see the world. Flight and transfer to ship paid for. Fast promotion. Potential to earn big money. I liked what I was reading, so I duly applied to the Cruiseship Picture Company whose head office was based in Esher, a place I'd never heard of at that time. Barely a few days after sending my CV and accompanying letter to the Cruiseship Picture Company, I received a letter inviting me to Esher for an interview. My excitement grew.

I spun a yarn to Colin about a sick relative to explain away the emergency day off on a Monday that I'd need for my interview. I was greeted at the Esher offices of the Cruiseship Picture Company by a very friendly lady, Trisha Cottam who ushered me in to the Managing Director's office. Here I was introduced to two people, the MD himself Richard Dawson and Head of Operations, Tom Long. Richard was a very tall, solidly built man, over six foot, with dark hair and a similar complexion. He was immaculately dressed in a dark blue suit, white shirt and navy tie. My first impression was that he had presence. Tom, on the other hand, was much, much shorter and altogether seemed very laid back and affable. As you'd expect, the office was adorned with images of cruise liners taken against stunning backdrops, worldwide. The relaxed interview lasted about half an hour and in establishing my work ethic, I was asked how I'd cope with working long hours, working as part of a close-knit team and what I thought my priorities were for the company (making them loads of dosh whilst undertaking my duties in a thoroughly professional manner). I was also asked about my availability and how much notice I'd have to give my present employer. I had also brought a portfolio of photographs with me, which Richard and Tom perused with interest. If I was successful, I would need to purchase a tuxedo for formal nights on board ship. Outward flight, working visa, medical insurance, transfers and hotel accommodation prior to joining ship and a uniform would be provided.

I came out of the interview quietly confident that I had made a good impression. Richard and Tom could see that I wasn't afraid of hard work, that I wouldn't be calling Mummy at the first opportunity and pining for home. They could see that I had a friendly and outgoing personality, that I was courteous, tactful and flexible, that I was a good communicator, with the ability to establish an instant rapport with anyone I met, that I possessed a positive mental attitude and above all that I was young, energetic, highly motivated and focused on making the company money. My work at White's Studios had stood me in good stead.

The following day I was fantasising - still buzzing with excitement at the prospect of going to some far-flung corner of the earth, sipping exquisite cocktails on tropical paradise islands, an arm around not one, but two beautiful, busty girls. I was still daydreaming when suddenly the phone rang in the back work room, which returned me instantly to the here and now. I instinctively lunged for the receiver, simultaneously kicking a pale green door to the processing room closed, which had definitely seen better days, in order to quell the sound of the paper processor, chugging away.

"Good morning, John F. White Studios, Paul speaking", I said. The voice on the other end of the phone came back, "Richard Dawson, Cruise ship Pictures – can you talk freely?" "Er, not really" I replied a little anxiously, as my boss Colin hovered in the background, eager to talk to me. Richard continued, "Listen very carefully, I want to fly you out to Miami next week to join the team on board the SS Norway, the world's largest cruise liner. Contact my secretary, Trisha, and she will make all the necessary arrangements". "Thank you" was all I said as I replaced the receiver with a big grin on my face. Yes! Yes! Bloody Yes!! I had got the job. "Who was that?" Colin asked. "Just a portrait enquiry" I lied.

I'll remember that moment forever. Being given the opportunity of a lifetime by the head of Cruiseship Pictures – the chance to travel, to see exotic places and meet different people, make new friends and I guess, to 'sew my wild oats' – that life-changing telephone call was a complete one off special. That night I spent ages carefully deliberating over my letter of resignation that I would hand to Colin the following morning. I also told my landlady, Wendi, of my news and that I would be vacating my room the following week.

I went in to work on that Wednesday in January smiling because I knew I was leaving White's for good. It might have been the middle of winter, but I had spring in my steps as I purposely got into work extra early to put a celebratory brew on and have a cuppa before the White family arrived. Shortly after 9am, the front door opened and in walked Colin White, alone. I practically ran to meet him and before the poor fellow had had chance to take his coat off or warm up, I virtually thrust my envelope containing my resignation letter into his hand. "What's this?" Colin asked with a surprised look. "It's my letter of resignation. I've been offered a new job and I'll be leaving next week", I replied with over-the-top enthusiasm. "Oh, no, no, no" Colin said. "Oh, yes, yes, yes" I replied cockily, with an almost supercilious grin on my face. Colin looked wounded, nay defeated as if I was about to deliver the coup de grace - a military 'double-tap' to the back of the head from my phantom, unholstered Glock, as instead, I turned and walked away, feeling triumphant. I was very cross and hurt over the White family's treatment of Ian and had vowed to leave the business as quickly as possible following Ian and Jean's Christmas departure – I just didn't think that it would be so soon afterwards. At tea break, when Colin had had time to get over the shock that I was leaving, we had a calm chat. Naturally, Colin wanted me to work extra hours and concentrate on printing as many wedding orders to clear the backlog in my final week. I would certainly not be working extra hours and told Colin this. My final week was for once going to involve zero pressure. I took my foot off the gas and just plodded. I came into work, did what I had to do and then went back to my digs.

I had lunch with Ian on the Thursday and I'd never seen him look so well. He was very happy for me, as were Jean and her husband John when I phoned them with my good news. Over the weekend, I went over to Grandma and Grandad's for Sunday lunch. Grandad hadn't been well for a while. Several hospital stays and a series of mini strokes didn't bode well. When it was time to say goodbye, I remember shaking Grandad's hand warmly and my grandfather nodding and smiling back at me, which was absolutely characteristic of him. I was left wondering whether I'd ever see him again.

On the Tuesday, I finished work at the John F. White Studios in Catford for good. I don't remember anything of that last day there – only that I was glad to leave and it felt right to move on. In my mind, the White family owned the business, but Ian, Jean and I had run it. I had learned much from Ian and Jean and I felt indebted to them. John F. White, I had the utmost respect for – he was a lovely old man. As for the rest of the White family, suffice to say that I wasn't sorry to see the back of them!

With suitcase in hand and rucksack on my back, I headed back up to Lancashire. I only had a day's turn around. Having purchased a tuxedo from a formal wear retailer of national repute and with a repacked suitcase, I headed down to London once more and onwards to Esher and a local hotel for that night. My flight from Heathrow bound for Miami was on the Friday morning. At the time it all seemed like a dream. White's Studios was in the past and as the 747's wheels cleared the tarmac, I looked out over a grey, wintery 'Blighty', not actually knowing when I'd return. I was filled with excitement, anticipation and the realisation that at that very moment, I didn't actually care. I was young, free and single, away from my father's talons and I was bound for the United States of America, the port of Miami, Dade County, in the sunshine state of Florida.

After a multi hour flight I was in Miami. Customs officials gave me a bit of a roasting, before I was allowed my onwards travel to my hotel. Suddenly I found myself a tad jetlagged in the Florida sun. The mercury was touching the 90s Fahrenheit. The sky was a deep blue, the air smelled different, the buildings and cars were different – everything was different. I had arrived and my new adventure was about to unravel. At 10am the following morning, Saturday 30th January 1988, a taxi dropped me off at the port of Miami. As I stood alone with my luggage at the bottom of a short crew gangway waiting to be met by my new colleagues, I stared up and along the length of this leviathan blue and white painted cruise ship. This was to be my home and workplace for the next five months plus – Norwegian Cruise Line's SS Norway.

The Norway started life as 'The France' having been constructed in 1960 and put into service two years later. Norwegian Cruise Line (NCL) purchased The France in 1979 and following significant modifications, this huge ship was renamed SS Norway. I was going to be working on the longest cruise ship in the world. In fact, the Norway was to hold this record until the 1,131-foot RMS Queen Mary 2 was built in 2004. The Norway was 1,035 feet long and I would soon be getting a measure of that distance by regular daily walks from bow to stern. When I joined the 875 strong crew on board this majestic ship in the late '80s, Norway's gross tonnage recorded at 70,202. However, in an effort to compete with up and coming cruise ships, two additional decks were added in 1990 which were fitted with luxury suites and cabins. This extra weight increased the ship's gross tonnage to 76,049. Cruising speed reached an average of 30 knots (circa 35 mph). The Norway could carry 1,944 passengers and after her 1990 additions and refit, capacity increased to 2565 passengers. However, the death knell sounded for The Norway following a boiler explosion in May 2003, whilst the ship was docked in Miami. This incident claimed the lives of eight crew and in the process seventeen crew were injured. With bigger, modern and even more luxurious cruise liners providing serious competition, the SS Norway struggled to keep up and was eventually sold for scrap in 2006 by her NCL owners. The SS Norway was finally dismantled in Alang, India in 2008.

At the time of my joining the crew at the end of January 1988, the Norway's itinerary was a 7-day sail, departing on Saturday afternoon from Miami to the Caribbean. It was stopping off at St. Maarten, St. John (US Virgin Islands), St. Thomas and NCL's private island, Great Stirrup Cay in the Bahamas.

I was taking all this in when two guys, looking chilled and relaxed in t-shirts, shorts and sandals came down the crew gangway. The first guy was quite short with receding wavy blonde hair and a cheeky smile. "You must be our new photog. They call me 'Granville' or just 'Granners'", he said. The guy behind was much taller and solidly built. "Hi, I'm Doug". We all shook hands and Granville and Doug told me that they were the 'number 3' and 'number 4' photographers respectively out of a team of 6. As the new starter, I would naturally be the number 6, affectionately called 'Shagger'. Granville told me not to take it personally as all new ships' photographers were known as Shagger. I followed Granville and Doug on to the ship, where I was introduced to security, then to a very pretty chief purser and duly signed in, given my pass and welcomed aboard. I was shown to my cabin in the stern, which comprised bunk beds (I would be sharing with the number 5 photographer), two wardrobes with drawers, a bed side table and a shower, toilet and wash basin. The cabin was small, but functional. The number 5 had already bagged the top bunk, so I quickly unpacked my stuff and changed into sailing uniform of grey trousers, black shoes and open neck, short-sleeve, pale-grey shirt. Doug then gave me a guided tour of the Norway. We visited the darkroom, situated deep in the ship's bow, the photo gallery where I met the number 5 (Mal) and number 2 (Gary) photographers, then I was shown the crew bar, the restaurants, lounges – it went on for ever. Doug gave me a useful tip regarding orientation. Whilst walking from the stern to the bow along a passenger corridor, the carpet suddenly changed colour from salmon pink to green patterned. The join was approximately the centre of the ship. When the guided tour was over, we ended back at the gallery, where the rest of the team were busy stripping the walls down of the remaining prints left unsold from the previous cruise.

Mid-afternoon I followed Granville to the darkroom to get the camera bag ready for my first embarkation shoot. Two Leica cameras were loaded with 35mm colour negative film and Granville popped around twenty additional rolls of film in the bag. Granville saw me staring at the number of rolls of film and just grinned at me. We made our way up to the forward embarkation point where Granville picked up an A1 sized embarkation board with the words 'SS Norway, Welcome aboard' and set it to one side of the very long gangway. A black line had been taped on the floor. This, Granville informed me, was to get the 'coneheads' (passengers) to stand on. Granville and I were manning the forward embarkation while the aft embarkation was manned by Mal, the number 5 photographer. It was the Number 5 and 6's job to cover embarkation every Saturday afternoon.

Granville said that he would start off and then hand the camera over to me. We were all set up. Suddenly at 3pm a tidal wave – around a thousand passengers - surged towards us. An ultra confident Granville, ignoring me, stepped forward blocking the way. "Hi there folks. I'm Granville, one of your ship's photographers. And the first charming couple right up on the line. Arms around each other. Big smiles (click / flash) and thank you ... and the next lovely couple right up on the line – fantastic smiles (click / flash) ... welcome aboard Sir and Madam, look as if you know one another – champion! (click / flash / giggle) great stuff ... and the next family – group of four right up on the line. Big smiles everyone (click / flash). Fantastic! (quick laugh and giggle) ... and the next lovely couple step up on to the line. We came, we saw, we conquered! (cheeky smile, quick giggle) ...". And so it went on. Granville was an expert smudger (the art of quickly building a rapport by talking sensible bollocks, winning over the unsuspecting passenger and getting the shot firmly in the bag all within a matter of seconds).

No sooner had he started smudging, Granville was out of film. I handed him the other Leica and he bolted it on to the Sunpak flash in seconds, before he was off again. At the end of the roll of film, Granville was still smudging the next family, Leica rig slung over his arm whilst simultaneously rewinding the exposed roll of film, unclipping the Leica's base plate, loading a new roll and then finally bolting the Sunpak to the camera again. This all took no more than about fifteen or twenty seconds before Granville continued, still smudging the family he'd held up. I stood there watching and getting increasingly nervous by the second and thinking "Jesus, I'll never be able to do that" when Granville turned around and said, "Right Paul, over to you". I grabbed the Leica from Granville and stepped forward. "Er...right there. Hello...er....my name's Paul. I'm new to the ship......thank you. Er.... sir...er Madam, a little closer.....er... right...er...um...". I looked at Granville who was shaking his head in disbelief. "Faster Shagger, faster!" he said, a painful look of exasperation etched all over his face. In seconds, I was dripping with sweat in the 90 degree plus heat and humidity and Granville, on loading another Leica stepped back in and took over, much to my relief. We had close on a thousand people to smudge and I had to learn this game fast otherwise I'd be out and sent home. I've never felt so much pressure in all my life. The Greek wedding for White's Studios was literally a Sunday outing by comparison! When I took over from Granville again things were a little better, but not much. I didn't have the flow, speed and patter that Granville exuded effortlessly.

Things tailed off after an hour. Once we'd smudged the stragglers, we packed up and it was down to the dark room to process the films, then back to my cabin for a lightning shower before returning to the darkroom again for a quick pre-sailing chat by the Chief Photographer, Archie Osbaldeston, a fair-haired Geordie with slightly bulging eyes. Archie had been ashore in Miami all day. "Alreet ya bonnie lads listen in. For seerlin' I want Paul smudgin' with Doug and Granville with Mal. Gary, you work both sides – smudge any stragglers. They look a canny bunch of 'cooans' (cone heads), so we should get the rolls (of film) in. Watch ya fill in flash. Last seerlin' shots were abagashite – ya oover flashed 'em. Whey aye ya buggers. I want us to push 38K this cruise – let's make it a goodun. Paul, we'll have a bevvie leerter after introrsʺ. On first impressions, the number 1 photog, who was a year my junior, seemed ok. Archie may have been younger, but he acted years older than the other photogs and it was obvious who was the boss!

I was still reeling from the shock of 'embies' and now it was time to do it all again. This time it was for 'sailing' – shots of couples with Miami and Miami beach in the background as the SS Norway glided out of port. I found this less pressurised than embies and crucially sailing shots offered me the chance to get to grips with the art of smudging. The passengers who were mostly American, seemed very friendly and warmed to the English accent. On hearing my voice, one elderly American lady pointed out to her rotund husband in a southern American drawl, "Did you hear what he said, he called us 'Sir' and 'Meerdam'?!" Focusing the Leica was ultra quick as this rangefinder device had its focus lever on the lens, which you toggled back and forth until two pale yellow squares aligned in the viewfinder. There was no metering. Lighting was constant so exposures seldom changed from week to week. F16 at 1/125 second with fill in flash a stop and a bit under, seemed to be the norm. I felt quite sad leaving Miami for the first time, bound for the Caribbean, but as I practised smudging in gorgeous Florida sunshine I looked forward to the day when I was as good as Granville. By the time all five photogs had their sailing shots in the bag, the buildings that comprised the Miami skyline could only just be seen.

The processing room was off the main darkroom, the latter housing the printer nicknamed the 'Wanko'. Mal took me through the rudiments of processing, which was all manual tank processing with manual chemical agitation. It was like a sauna in there, so loading individual films into their spirals (each of which would then be loaded into a film basket and then subsequently processed) was generally conducted in a semi-naked state i.e. in shorts and a pair of flip flops. When loading the films onto the metal spirals prior to processing you had to be careful that you didn't put any kinks in the films otherwise this would wreck a frame or two. Agitation ('agi') involved lifting the basket of films halfway out of the bath of chemicals, leaning it over to one side and then giving the basket a couple of shakes, before resubmerging the whole thing in the chemicals once again. Making a balls up of the agi usually meant putting irreversible streaks across most of the images, so great care had to be taken to get the agitation method right. Automatic agi would have been so much more efficient. As soon as the films were ready for printing, another photographer would take them out of the drying cabinet and print them on the Wanko. Archie had already printed embies and now Gary printed our sailing shots. Having showered again and changed, all the photographers then met in the gallery to display the printed embies and sailing photographs. These 5"x7" images were sold to the customer inside a presentation folder with the SS Norway logo adorning the front for $4.95. Passengers could either have their total spend charged to their cabin, or they could pay cash. All passengers were required to settle up their bills on the penultimate day, after which the ship reverted to taking cash only. This ensured that there were no outstanding bills to pay.

With the gallery now tidy and with photographs displayed on the walls, Gary raised the shutters and let the first passengers in to peruse and hopefully purchase. Meanwhile, I accompanied Archie and the rest of the photogs to the Cruise introduction evening, known as 'Intros', where the Cruise Director would officially welcome aboard all the passengers, give them a load of blurb about their cruise including health and safety and fire drill information. He would then have representatives from every department (ranging from hairdressing and dancers to casino and photographers) take the microphone and introduce themselves. Five photographers were welcomed on to the platform and one by one we introduced ourselves. A tad nervously, I beamed and said, "Hi everyone, my name's Paul and I'm from London, England". Everyone applauded us. Granville took the piss afterwards saying that he thought I sounded very camp indeed. In the immortal words of my old biology teacher, Bill Roe, I assured Granners that I was strictly hetero. At this stage I hadn't been officially introduced to Neil, the Australian Cruise Director. My involvement with the Cruise Director thereafter was minimal – I generally only saw him at intro evenings and in the bar afterwards. My later involvement with the Cruise Director's secretary Patty, a blue-eyed blonde however, was … er … an 'involvement'. I was very sweet on her for a while. She wasn't just stunningly beautiful, she was such a lovely girl with it.

Following a stint in the gallery, I couldn't believe the time was now gone 10pm. The night was still young as the photographers headed for the crew bar, where I met loads of staff who worked in a variety of different areas. The Chief Photographer got the first round in and officially welcomed me to his team. Archie acknowledged that it was hard work, but was quick to point out that the rewards were good. He left out the bit about the rewards being not so good as a Shagger number 6, that I would be screwed left right and centre, but if I worked hard promotion would follow and I would see more money coming my way. Archie's watery, bulging eyes, betraying his penchant for snorting cocaine, seemed to be sizing me up. Even Archie's girlfriend, Jeany, seemed to be studying my face for any signs of weakness or possible rebellion. As the new boy, I was eager to please and so gave nothing away. For now, though, I was the dogsbody. I could be nothing but subservient. I would work damn hard, take the crap and just get the job done. I knew that promotion could come after a handful of weeks, as one photographer left to go on vacation, the inevitable rejuggling of the team would follow. Besides, I'd already heard on the grapevine that the Chief Photographer and his best mate, the former super confident number 2, the curly-haired, suave, Lorne Truthman, had made so much money on these Caribbean cruises, that they had each purchased a four-bedroomed, detached house and a brand new, gleaming black Porsche 911 Turbo in cash, all seemingly in a record number of weekly cruises and all from money accrued from working on the Norway! So, if there was money to be made, I wanted a slice of the action, which meant keeping my head down and not rocking the boat so to speak.

I put the thought from my mind as I saw the jovial figure of Granville bringing over a tray of sambuca shots. "Down the hatch, Shagger!", Granners shouted. I tipped the potent aniseed-flavoured liqueur down my throat and everyone cheered as I coughed with the sudden after burn. The empty glasses were quickly replaced with another round of shots, which vanished just as quickly as their predecessors. This was my initiation. The aim was to get me completely wasted. Well, this just wasn't going to happen for unbeknown to anyone, I'd lined my stomach with a large chocolate milkshake drink and some chocolate bars beforehand. I decided that my limit would be six Sambuca shots, on top of the four or five bottles of beer already consumed. Although I felt quite merry, I'd had enough and didn't relish the thought of throwing up, my cabin spinning as I simultaneously orbited into space clinging white-knuckled in vain to my bunk bed, whilst longing for sleep to take me. No, I needed to feign inebriation. I started to sing and wave my arms around like a bloody idiot. I got up to go to the loo, but promptly made myself fall over like a drunken bum, to much laughter. I was still giggling and now mumbling incoherently as Mal and Doug picked me up and with an arm round their shoulders, I was half carried and half dragged to my cabin and less than gently deposited on my bunk bed. Mal and Doug were still laughing in the corridor outside as they left, but it was me who had the last laugh! I had survived my initiation as a cruise ship photographer. Yes, I had cut and run, cheated a little, but only to self-protect as I didn't relish the thought of having to work the next day with a Sambuca hangover and a headache from hell.

The following day, Sunday, was a day at sea and involved long periods working in the photo gallery serving passengers. However, we did rotate and managed a few hours off in the middle of the day, which was normally spent working out in the gym, then sunbathing. In the evening was the first of two formal events, the Captain's Cocktail Party. This was a huge money earner for cruise ship photographers as there were several different smudges throughout the evening. Dressed in best bib and tucker, passengers would form an orderly queue along the promenade deck to shake hands with the Captain at the lounge door, after which they'd have pre-dinner cocktails. Similar to the rest of the lads, I wore a tuxedo, black bow tie and matching cummerbund for the occasion. Later, I purchased an array of colourful bow tie and cummerbund sets, which I'd regularly alternate. It was only the second time in my life that I had donned this formal attire. There were of course to be plenty more occasions thereafter. That first Sunday, Archie once again teamed me up with Granville. It was our job to get primarily full-length shots of couples, singles, families and groups whilst said passengers were queuing along the promenade deck waiting to meet the Captain.

This smudge was known as 'Street' and Granville worked the line expertly – he was a born natural. The cone heads warmed to his English accent, cheeky banter and grin. It was a pleasure to see him work. His rapport forming was instant and seemed effortless, but I had to remind myself that even Granners started life as a Shagger. Then it was my turn. Photography seemed to be better than the disaster which had constituted embies and I was acutely aware that we couldn't hang about and hold the line up. The last thing I wanted was to have the Captain, who was God on the ship, breathing down my neck! Granville was very encouraging, "Much better than embies Shagger, a bit faster next time and work on the patter". Little did I realise, that in only a handful of weeks, Granville would be handing this over to me and 'Street' would effectively become my smudge. All the cones looked immaculately dressed, the men mostly in black tuxedos, patent leather, black, shiny shoes, white formal shirts and sporting an array of coloured bow ties with matching cummerbunds. The ladies wore expensive dresses and shoes, equally expensive jewellery and it was obvious that the hairdressing salons and beauticians had done a roaring trade that afternoon. The young ladies looked stunning and didn't fail to catch my eye. It was the job of the Street smudger to report back to the other photographers on the tarts of interest. Girls were known simply as 'tarts', it wasn't designed to be a derogatory term, merely a cruise ship photog term of endearment.

At the start of this queue or 'line' as the Americans call it, was of course the Captain at the door to the lounge waiting to greet his passengers. Standing opposite was the Chief Photographer, Archie Osbaldeston, snapping away on a Leica with a Sunpak flash gun bolted on the side, capturing every handshake. As there was no time for Archie to reload his camera, Mal, the number 5 hovered at Archie's 7 o'clock, waiting to swap over Leica and Sunpak flash rigs. As soon as Archie came to the end of a roll of film, he quickly handed the camera and flash rig to the number 5 who just as quickly handed Archie an identical camera rig loaded with a fresh roll of film and wound on a few frames so that it was ready for immediate use. This way the line kept moving and there were no hold ups. Whilst Archie was smudging 'handshakes', Mal was rewinding the previous roll of film and loading a new roll, in effect prepping that rig in readiness for the camera handover again on Archie's command. It was a slick operation, held up only by the occasional film jam and the quite frequent lingering, brain dead cone who'd greet the Captain with "Hey, Cap'n, if you're down here...who's drivin' the Goddamn boat?!" or, "God, Cap'n, who's drivin' this sucker?" The crassest comment to the Captain I ever heard was some weeks later whilst assisting Archie with 'handshakes'. Step up one very fat, obviously filthy rich American dressed in a white suit and what appeared to be cowboy boots. "Cap'n, my wife and I think you're doin' a mighty fine job of drivin' this here boat, so we'd like to give you a token of our appreciation – a brand new five-dollar bill. Keep up the good work son!" The rotund, middle aged Texan, much to everyone's shocked embarrassment, thrust the five-dollar note into the Captain's breast pocket and then promptly slapped the Captain hard on the back, causing said Captain to wince. Archie was grinning as he turned to me and said, “You’ve seen it here Ugly.” For some odd reason, Archie had decided to nickname me ‘ugly’ instead of Shagger. If it was a thousand dollars, maybe, but a measly five dollars? I don’t know what was more cringeworthy, the brazen act itself or the paltry sum given?

Once the cones had met the Captain, they relaxed in the comfortable surroundings of the spacious lounge sipping exotic cocktails. Here Gary and Doug photographed the cocktail drinkers in a smudge that was simply known as ‘lounge’. The moment Gary and Doug had finished lounge, they left their rolls of film with Mal for processing and hot-footed it to the foyers outside the ship’s two dining rooms, the ‘Winward’ and the ‘Leeward’. Here, a simple portrait set-up had been erected at each location, which consisted of a couple of posing stools, a brown or blue-painted background and two Bowens electronic flash units, each mounted onto a suction pole that was wedged floor to ceiling. It was Gary and Doug’s job to smudge portraits before and after dinner. At $10 a pop for a high quality 10”x8” print mounted in a presentation folder, these were an excellent money earner. Gary and Doug used a hand-held Blad, with one of the electronic flashes synced via a long cable into the camera. The other Bowens flash was fired simultaneously by slave cell. There would always be queues for portrait sittings.

Following street, handshakes and lounge, Archie approached me. “Ugly, go and process”. The realisation of what the Chief Photographer had just said wrong footed me. I was to go solo after Mal had only shown me the set up once. I didn’t feel confident at all and I started to object. “But I’ve only….” I thought Archie was going to explode, when, with bulging, cocaine eyes, finger jabbing in the direction of the dark room and with a slightly raised voice he said, “You’re goin’ to turn around now, you’re goin’ to go down and process those films!” Such was the pressure of work on board ship, there was no time to nurse maid anyone. So, I took all the rolls of film that collectively constituted street, handshakes and lounge along with the Leica rigs and went down to the darkroom as instructed. It was roasting, so I quickly took off my formal shirt, bow tie and trousers so I would effectively be processing in my undies!

I counted all the rolls of film and worked out that they would completely fill a film basket, bar one. I then set the corresponding number of 35mm film spirals neatly out on the bench, which was set at right angles to the C41 processing baths. Placing the film basket next to the spirals, I checked that I knew where everything was.

I closed and locked the door to the processing room and looked round at the C41 baths, then finally checked everything. I stood close to the work bench and in front of me was a neat pile of films. Next to these films were the same number in spirals and next to the spirals was the empty film basket. I took a deep breath, checked the door was firmly shut and locked, then went for it. With a flick of the light switch, I was plunged into darkness. I was completely focused on the task at hand. There was no time to think that if I cocked this up I would be sent home and would be out of a job, or even to contemplate that, what if I suffer from claustrophobia and turn the light on in a panic, having just loaded all the films onto the spirals? I would fog all the films, ruin all the images and again find myself on a one-way ticket out of Miami on a plane bound for England with a 'UB40' handed to me by a pretty hostess masquerading as a 'smiling assassin'.

I was loading the rolls quickly but carefully, ensuring that the films were being taken up on the spirals smoothly, to avoid any kinks. As I got to the end of each film, I would rip it off its spindle and throw the spindle and empty film canister into a bin, located between my feet. With all films loaded into the film basket, I felt my way over to the C41 processing baths and then to the first developing bath lid. Holding the basket of films in my left hand, I took the lid off the developer with my right hand and then checked the previously set timer on the wall for the developer duration. The clock timer, which had luminous hands, was started and simultaneously I lowered the film basket into the warm, pungent developer. At regular intervals, I had to manually agitate, lifting the basket of films out of the developer bath halfway, tilting to a 45-degree angle, alternating left and right, then shaking the basket a couple of times, before lowering the films back in the developer once more. This agi was to ensure that a continuous supply of fresh developer reached the films.

The purpose of this first crucial developer bath is to produce a silver image in the film emulsion layers from the latent image produced when the film is exposed in camera. The colour developer develops silver within the film's three (from bottom to top: red, green and blue) emulsion layers which have been coated onto an acetate film base. In addition to light-sensitive components, each emulsion layer contains chemicals known as dye couplers, which produce cyan, magenta and yellow dyes when developed. The quantity of dye produced is proportional to the amount of silver image produced. As the silver develops, oxidised developer reacts with these dye couplers to form dyes.

Following the developer, a bleach bath then converts the metallic silver image, generated by the development process, back into fixer-soluble silver halide. After bleaching, a third bath containing fixer dissolves the now bleached silver image, together with the unexposed and therefore undeveloped silver halide that was originally present in the film, which can then be carried away by the washing bath process that follows. Once the films have cleared the bleach bath and are safely in the fix, the room lights can be turned on and the rest of the process can be conducted in the light. Washing will remove all processing chemicals from the film emulsion. Correct wash water rate and temperature are important to ensure the stability of the film dyes in the long term. A final stabiliser and rinse bath that contains a wetting agent to aid uniform drying (and decrease the prospect of getting drying marks) of the film and long-term stability, completes the C41 colour film process. C41 developer is temperature and agitation critical if accurate and consistent results are to be achieved. If the temperature is incorrect, severe colour shifts or under or overdevelopment of the film can result. Incorrect agitation can result in dark streaks running down the image, where exhausted developer hasn't been replaced by fresh developer. Aggressive or over-agitation can result in contrasty negatives.

Once my full basket of films was safely in the fixer bath, I went over to the door and felt in the dark for the room light. I also unlocked and opened the door to the darkroom, before returning to the C41 process. At the end of the stabiliser process, I sat the film basket to one side and nervously took the first film off its spiral and held it up to the light. Phew – all the images on there looked consistent. The orangey coloured negatives were punchy and crucially there were no agitation or drying marks. I examined the rest of the rolls, before carefully hanging them up in the drying cabinet. They were all fine and the success of this solo C41 process gave me a tremendous confidence boost. When I looked round, the Number One was waiting to examine the films and start printing. "That's great Ugly", a now much calmer Archie said to me, as he took a wodge of now dry 35mm films from the cabinet over to the Wanko. I would be processing again later, when the 120 roll films came down containing all the precious portraits. It was much easier to kink a 120-roll film when loading it on to the spiral due to the bigger surface area of the film, so I had to be very careful. Once again, the second solo process went well with only two small film kinks, which I managed to get away with as there were duplicate negs in each case.

Once all the film processing, chemical replenishment and tidying was finished, it was back to my cabin for a much-needed shower, before helping display the now printed street, handshakes and lounge pictures in the photo gallery.

Processing in my underpants and in the dark inevitably meant slopping developer over myself and on my tummy during agitation. After only a couple of weeks, nasty rashes appeared on my hands, feet and stomach. Doctors confirmed it was contact dermatitis. Dermy creams quickly cleared up the rashes and I ensured my feet were covered. I also invested in a pair of elbow length calf-delivering, rubber gloves to undertake the processing from then on. Lesson learned!

I was shocked to realise that the time was gone 11pm. Doug had just started to print portraits and we all knew that he'd be burning the midnight oil, eventually crawling into his bed very late indeed. I suddenly felt hungry, which was not surprising as none of us had eaten since breakfast in the crew dining room. Having been on the go all day, there was no time for 'chuffing'. One of the perks as crew members was that we were allowed to eat free at the passengers' midnight buffet, a sumptuous feast of savoury and sweet delights. However, if we were working beyond midnight and missed the buffet, we could always catch a noodle soup topped with an egg in the Korean Room off Slime Alley (the crew passageway that ran the length of the ship), which always hit the mark. You would normally find the Korean Room a hive of activity until around 2am. Mal, Granners, Gary and I were approaching the delightful setting of the outdoor midnight buffet on deck. We'd just waved to Petula Clarke who was performing on board (as we did the previous week with the late Lou Rawls) when an elderly American couple approached us. Addressing no-one in particular, the female cone piped up in an annoying, whiny drawl, "What time's the midnight buffet?" We all looked at each other very confused as Granners stepped forward. Scratching his chin, frowning and looking first at the floor, then at the heavens, before looking at the couple he said, "Let me see, er, I think it might be midnight". The couple thanked us profusely – they were serious. Granville's veiled quintessential English sarcasm had been totally lost on them. We just cracked up laughing, Granville wearing an enormous Cheshire cat grin which I'll never forget. The midnight buffet lived up to its excellent reputation. We all filled our boots and when we had finished, it was time to hit Dazzles, the legendary disco and dance floor, where you could see people swimming through portholes in one corner of the room. The rear swimming pool actually abutted the disco. In its day Dazzles was the place to be and though it's hard to believe now, I danced, boogied and gyrated around that famous dance floor, having the time of my life in the company of a great many, seriously good-looking girls!

One such young lady was Paula, a strikingly attractive brunette from Lexington, Kentucky, of whom I was very fond. I saw her every spare minute I had of every day. We were both passionate about each other and I was just beginning to think that our relationship might be going somewhere, when, on the tail end of yet another lingering embrace, Paula suddenly revealed that she was already 'penned' (spoken for) with a chap back home, so that was well and truly that. A Hillbilly-themed cruise saw a very strange bunch of people come aboard the Norway. During that particular week, I somehow met a young, nineteen-year old Hillbilly girl, whom I had an intense fling with. This petite brunette was very sweet, but somehow seemed to be a tad spaced out. Suffice to say that once I had 'swung my partner round and round' a few times, this romance too, came to an abrupt end. Memories of another liaison with a young lady come crowding in. This time, the late evening romance was with Anna, a pretty twenty-four-year old, blue-eyed, freckle-faced brunette, who hailed from Greenbay, Wisconsin on the western shores of Lake Michigan. Up on deck, enjoying each other's company on a late Caribbean evening, I had to pinch myself again to think that this was the stuff that dreams are made of and I was acting this out for real. A romance in paradise, what could be better?

On another occasion, a stunning brunette from Raleigh, North Carolina's capital city, invited me back for drinks in her cabin and as we were enjoying each other's company, I heard a continual chugging noise on the other side of the cabin wall…it was the noise of the print trimmer, punctuated by a photographer occasionally coughing and swearing when the print trimmer kept stopping – I had ended up in this girl's cabin (a disciplinary offence if you were caught), which was right next door to the darkroom! On a different cruise and after a testing, gruelling day's work, I remember arriving back at my cabin with two things on my mind – a shower and sleep, in that order. Having showered and in the process, squashing the umpteenth cockroach (devious buggers that would run and hide under the furniture, but would generally come out and buzz when you were in the shower with soap in your eyes, almost mockingly) I climbed into my bunk and just lay there exhausted. I was just on the point of dropping off, when a noise jolted me into full consciousness.

Promoted after a month in the job, I was now number 5 photographer and Alan the new Shagger, was asleep on the top bunk. I stared at the cabin door handle which started to move inexorably downwards. This was followed by the door slowly opening. My heart was racing as I clenched my fists ready to lash out at this intruder. The cabin door was now wide open and a dark shape just stood in the doorway silhouetted by the corridor lights. Who the bloody hell was this person and what did they want? Were they after cash and possessions or something else? "Who are you?" I ventured with as macho and menacing a voice as I could muster. There was no reply. The person, whom I naturally assumed to be a male aggressor, just stood there in silence, then after what seemed to be ages, moved slowly towards me, leaving the door slightly ajar. Ah, Jesus, I thought, I'm done for. Still puzzled, I couldn't detect any knife or gun, or other weapon, but now 'fight or flight' was upon me. Since I was trapped with nowhere to run, I prepared to do battle. I was about to bring my right fist up to my intruder's face when they spoke softly. 'He' was a 'she'! And at that moment as she came closer, I recognised the pretty girl standing a few feet away from me. Brooke was a beautiful, curvaceous brunette from Pittsburgh, Pennsylvania, whom I had spoken to and kissed only once, a few days previously. Somehow, she had found her way into the crew quarters, which was no doddle as my cabin was located in the bowels of the ship off Slime Alley and amidst a labyrinth of corridors, never mind being strictly out of bounds to passengers.

"Hi, Paul", was all she said with a big smile, as a now less than scantily clad Brooke, having already deposited a full bottle of very expensive looking peach schnapps on my bedside table, snuggled up next to me on my bunk bed. The rest, as they say, is consigned to a distant, but extremely pleasant memory. Just as quickly as she came into my life, Brooke vanished, for when I woke early the next morning, she had upped and gone and I never heard from her again. Such was the way and the world of cruise ship life!

The American girls loved to hear the English accent, which always proved to be an icebreaker as well as a bit of a relationship magnet I suppose. Working aboard ship for me, as you've probably gathered, was a single, young man's dream. There were pretty girls everywhere you looked. On one themed 'cheerleaders' cruise, the Norway was so overrun with attractive women, it beggared belief. I was working sixteen hours or more, day in and day out. If I finished work very late, I would often race back to my cabin, shower and change, just to catch the last ten minutes of disco vibe, for the work switch off and release that all the crew identified with and craved. You made friends quickly on-board ship because there was nowhere else to go. We were like a close-knit family. The ship almost became a prison of sorts when you were at sea, because you became confined. You couldn't just get off whenever the hell you felt like it. As a result, relationships were very intense and talk amongst staff generally revolved around vacation time – how long since your last vacation, how long it would be until your next vacation, where you'd be going and for how long and where you went on your last vacation?

I worked with some lovely people on the Norway from barmen to hairdressers and from cruise staff to dancers – there were some real characters. Spanish speaking cruise staff girl Elizabeth and 'Fit with Fun' girl Marissa were good friends (I was also sweet on both girls), as was cruise staff member Mark Hamilton from Bermuda. The photographers were always good friends with the hairdressers. We'd photograph the 'hairies' in their posh frocks on formal nights and supply them with an array of printed images and in return, the hairdressers would give us free haircuts. This gratis mutual arrangement suited us fine. My intense romance with Dade County girl Anne, the Chief Purser (whom I spotted on my very first day when I was welcomed aboard), lasted but a handful of weeks until she disembarked one Saturday whilst back in her home of Miami, destined never to return. The downer that followed was twofold. Firstly, I missed Anne lots and secondly this wasn't helped by the fact that Anne's replacement, Charlie, a blue-eyed blonde, herself a natural beauty from Fort Lauderdale, took an instant dislike to me… or so I thought. She was also one of Anne's friends. The face on her, a cross between a sour puss and a bag of spanners, every time we ran into each other. The other lads wagered that Charlie, who I ducked and dived to try and avoid, had the hump with me big time because she had the hots for me and desperately wanted us to get together. I was reminded of the 1973 Clint Eastwood film 'High Plains Drifter' when his character 'The Stranger' said to Callie Travers (played by Marianna Hill) after she purposely bumped into him, "If you wanted to get acquainted, why didn't you just say so?"

Monday was spent either in the gallery selling formal portraits, street, lounge and handshakes from the previous night or smudging the outdoor fitness activities and games, known affectionately as 'the Olympics'. I used to enjoy the Olympics as, donned in navy blue shorts and a white t-shirt with 'Norway, Olympics' embroidered on the front, I'd photograph individual participants. If Mark Hamilton was running the show, there would be lots of jokes throughout and the customary wind up. "Hey folks, I've spotted whales off the port side!", whereupon the games would suddenly be suspended, everyone would rush over to the left side of the ship and peer out to sea to try and be the first at glimpsing the elusive whales, only for a cheeky Mark to announce through his microphone that it was just a joke. Mark would then hand the mike to me and I'd announce in a slow, mock American drawl, "Hey, folks, we're havin' a whale of a time here!" Everyone would return to the games to sounds of "Gedoudahere!" The Olympics was an enjoyable ½ hour smudge. It got me out on deck in the fresh air. I was in good company with Mark and fellow cruise staff and the images always sold well. For those not taking part in the Olympics, there would always be an array of other activities such as swimming, running around the ship's perimeter, working out in the gym, quoits, outdoor board games or if the mood took you, trap shooting on Oslo deck aft. All this whilst bar tenders materialised at your side, supplying seemingly endless culinary delights, alcoholic and non-alcoholic beverages.

If you didn't want to do anything at all, there was of course lots of time to sunbathe. Calm blue seas, cloudless, rich blue skies, endless sunshine and balmy temperatures day after day, were the norm. I often had to pinch myself to check that it was real and keep myself reminded that cones paid thousands of dollars to come on these cruises and yes, I was working hard, but everything except laundry and bar bill were free to me. However, it was no mean feat to up sticks, leave your family and friends and then bugger off halfway round the world entrusting your own life to an unknown employer waving a carrot of potential earnings that exceeded 1,100 dollars per weekly cruise. I was working the equivalent of two working weeks in one. Why? Partly driven by the will to succeed, partly drawn by the promise and rumour of big earnings, coupled with seeing the world and meeting different people from myriad backgrounds and cultures – to work these equivalent crazy hours back at home would be deemed illegal and dangerous. All said and done however, this was indeed a golden opportunity, while it lasted.

Having processed Olympics, changed and now back in the gallery, sales were swift and it soon became apparent that we were well on the way to reaching the Chief Photographer's goal of $38,000 in photography takings for this, my first weekly cruise. Photographers were kings of the wind-up merchants and we all loved to take the piss out of the cones. A desk with sales slips would be placed in the middle of the gallery, the idea being that passengers would spot the photos of themselves displayed on the walls, take and fill out a sales slip, then take everything to the counter to have their photo purchases rung through the till. Well, the sales desk had a door beneath it, just large enough for a cheeky photographer to crawl inside and hide. A couple of unsuspecting, spaced out, elderly cone ladies would then be wandering around the gallery holding a wodge of photos, whereupon a ghost like voice would emit from seemingly nowhere "Proceed to the sales desk, fill out a sales slip...go to the counter to pay!" Simultaneously, two photographers behind the cash desk would be cracking up laughing as the confused cones would be staring at the ceiling and the floor, before looking at each other wondering what an earth was going on and indeed, where the voice had emanated from. Another blatantly cheeky cone wind up would be to say to a passenger in an alarmed tone "Quick, quick it's under your foot!" Said cone would be totally confused prompting us to repeat the statement several times. When eventually they started to examine the underside of each shoe, before admitting defeat with exasperated pleading, "What's under my foot, what's under my foot?" one of us would simply say, "The carpet". This usually went straight over the heads of the bemused American cones, who, not understanding the English sense of humour, would just repeat the question or mutter to one another "What did he say?" This just made the absurd situation even funnier. Oh, what cruel photographers!

Monday evenings presented the photographic team with another huge money earner – table group and couple shots in both 'Leeward' and 'Winward' dining rooms over two separate sittings. This pivotal smudge was known simply as 'rezzies' (restaurant shots). Three photographers would swoop down on one restaurant and two would work the second dining area. The first photographer to finish in the group of three would then hurry over to help his two colleagues mop up in the other dining room. Rezzies could often be quite a challenge. With rectangular tables seating six or eight, the end two people would be pulled out a little whilst you had to ensure that the people seated furthest away leant in far enough so you could see everyone's faces. Round tables were more awkward, as the shot worked best if you got two or three people nearest to you to stand up next to the people furthest away, rather than relying on these nearest people straining their necks to turn round. If there were eight people on a table, eight copies of that image would be printed. One photograph of a single table could generate a minimum of almost forty dollars. Americans loved photographs of themselves and when they bought, they bought big time.

Either way, you had to work each table very quickly to cause minimum disruption. Most passengers were ok with us as long as we were quick. Some rezzie refusals were commonplace on every cruise, as with all smudges. Occasionally, cones could be belligerent. On one cruise, I thought I'd fallen into a hornet's nest as I approached a corner table. "Good evening ladies and gent...." I didn't get to finish my patter, as one of the table of New York Jewish gentlemen glared at me and in a raised voice, replied "Na, fuck off, gedoudahere asshole, we're all pictured out!" I was quick with my retort, which was delivered with a smile in an exaggerated posh English accent. "How perfectly charming, sir, do have a lovely evening", whereupon I instantly pirouetted on one heel and turned to smudge the adjacent table. There was no call for downright rudeness in my book. The New Yorker was bang out of order. A simple 'no thank you' would have sufficed. Rezzies were hard work, made more testing by the fact that I had to process in between the two meal sittings and then race back and smudge the dining rooms all over again. And I thought rezzies would get easier as the weekly cruises progressed! With Leica rigs prepared and rolls of film lining our pockets, the photographers' ritual would be to hit the bar a quarter of an hour before people started filing, sheep like, into the dining rooms. This would give us time to have a few nifty lemonades. In my case, a couple of double scotches on the rocks always did the trick. I could float round the dining rooms very quickly, the alcohol bolstering my confidence and still get great saleable images. I also found that once the alcohol had taken affect, it helped deflect some of the abusive comments. Rightly or wrongly, I found that I couldn't smudge rezzies without that crutch they call booze. To smudge those huge dining rooms sober, perish the thought, would at the time I feel have been a challenge too far!

With second sitting rezzies processed, it was back towards my cabin along the only crew corridor which ran almost the entire length of the Norway. Affectionately known as Slime Alley, it took almost 2½ minutes to walk along the alley from the darkroom to my cabin. Many a time, after a late process and another marathon day's work, I'd be walking along the green painted metal deck, almost rushing to get to my bed. I'd visualise the white sheets, the pillow, the bottom bunk and my cabin – all I wanted to do was to sleep, when as so often was the case I would happen upon a corridor party, or rather a cabin party that had spilled out onto Slime Alley. Then I'd hear, "Hey Paul, buddy, good to see you", a cold beer would be thrust into my hand and that was that. I would miss that night's sleep, leave the party some time after dawn, nip back to my cabin for a shower, change and have breakfast and be ready to take the first tender ashore, usually with three of the other photographers to the first port of call, the island of St. Maarten in the U.S. Virgin Islands. After two days at sea, setting foot on terra firma was a Godsend. We'd have all day free to ourselves and be back aboard ship well before the Norway set sail at teatime.

St. Maarten island, with an area of roughly 34 square miles and a population of nearly 80,000, is located in the northeast Caribbean. The southern part of the island is Dutch owned, part of the Kingdom of the Netherlands and the northern part is French, a land division dating back to 1648. St. Maarten is approximately 190 miles east of Puerto Rico. The island's main cities are Philipsburg on the Dutch side and Marigot on the French side. Its main industry is tourism and it's famed for its Princess Juliana International airport runway. Here, landing aircraft come perilously close to Maho Beach and tourists cling to the perimeter fencing, getting an adrenaline rush from the engine backdraft of aeroplanes taking off. The main draw for Americans is that St. Maarten has many shops and boutiques in this duty-free haven, which offer massive discounts on a range of products. Apart from designer and leather goods, local art and craft, exotic foods, alcohol and cigarettes, there are also numerous jewellery shops and it was these that the other photogs always made a beeline for and enticed me into.

It was the big thing back then, a status symbol amongst photogs, to own a Rolex watch. These world renowned, extremely precise chronometers are characterised by on board self-winding movements giving rise to the second hand's characteristic smooth perpetual motion. Archie owned one. Former number 2, Lorne Truthman, ensured that he purchased one prior to leaving ships. Gary, the current number 2, owned a real beauty with gold-coloured bracelet, figures and hands, but it was the watch face that really caught your eye. To complement all this gold coloured craftsmanship, Gary's watch face was a rich mix of carmine, chestnut and rosso corsa. It was the dog's bollocks and set Gaz back a cool four thousand dollars! Granners also owned one and the other photogs were well on their way to making their purchases too. I gazed in awe at the array of magnificent watches that these shops had on display, but as a Shagger number six on a chickenshit wage, I wouldn't be getting one just yet. It was a month later when I was number 5 photographer that I came very close indeed to buying a beautiful gold coloured Rolex, similar in design to Gary's to celebrate my promotion. I was in the capital, Philipsberg, with Doug, Granners, Gary and Alan (the new number 6) staring at this thing for ages whilst continually fingering the wodge of four thousand hard earned dollars bulking out my pocket. I came that close to buying it, but itchy beard got the better of me and rightly or wrongly I ended up wiring all my money back to England.

If we weren't shopping in the capital, going on photo safari to Le Privilege, an awe inspiring secluded haven in the hills overlooking the protected white sandy beaches and turquoise waters of Marcel Cove, or exploring the rest of St. Maarten, we'd hire a catamaran with several crates of beer on board and take an excursion to Saint Barthelemy (known as St. Barts). This was an overseas collectivity of France lying about 22 miles south-east of St. Maarten and 150 miles to the west of Puerto Rico. After spending a blissful few hours swimming and sunbathing, the catamaran would return us to St. Maarten once more. Here the waiting tender would take us back to the Norway. On one memorable Tuesday I forewent a St. Barts trip and stayed behind on board the Norway as Ian Allan Publishers had posted out the final draft of my first book 'Historic Lakeland' for me to check through. I remember being terribly excited looking through what constituted hundreds of hours of work in photographs and words. I retreated to the lovely surroundings of the Club International Lounge to examine the draft. Excitement gradually turned to alarm as the draft was riddled with typos and printing errors. After I meticulously checked the draft, I packaged it up together with a few pages of suggestions and alterations and took a tender across to Philipsburg to get my precious package posted back to the publishers. Incredibly, it would be another year before 'Historic Lakeland' reached the UK bookshelves.

Tuesday evening following the St. Maarten visit was spent in the gallery, after which we'd hit the inevitable bars and of course Dazzles. Wednesdays were my favourite and like Tuesdays, we also had the bulk of the day to ourselves. Just after breakfast, the Norway called briefly at the island of St. John in the U.S. Virgin Islands, dropping off about forty or so passengers, before making its way to nearby St. Thomas where it would drop anchor. I'd always volunteer for the St. John crack of dawn smudge. As the Norway itself couldn't get close to St. John, let alone dock there as there are no docking facilities, one of the Norway's two tenders (called 'Little Norway 1' and 'Little Norway 2') would drop the cones and me off in St John around 8.30am. Armed with a Leica rig and a couple of rolls of film, I'd run on ahead and smudge passengers with the sand, sea and palm tree vista behind them. There is no airport on the island, so St. John is only reachable by boat. This popular American honeymoon venue is a beautiful Caribbean paradise, situated about four miles east of St. Thomas, the Norway's second port of call. I liked the St. John smudge because it was quick – only about 10 or 15 minutes. I could take two or three rolls of film in the knowledge that virtually every image was guaranteed to sell. Then, if I hadn't also volunteered to cover a couple's wedding photography (for which we got paid extra by the bride and groom), I usually curled up under a palm tree, clutching the camera bag, and got some serious shut eye for a couple of hours! I'd usually be woken by one of the other photographers prodding me and four of us, armed with our own cameras and equipment, would hire a jeep for a few hours and take off exploring this lovely island, almost two thirds of which has national park status.

St. John, having a current population of just over 4000, is almost 20 square miles in area and to say this haven is picture postcard pretty wouldn't be doing the place justice enough. The St. John vistas never failed to impress - views of Coral and Cinnamon Bays, or an elevated view looking down to the turquoise Caribbean across the Caneel Bay plantation, or views of famous Trunk Bay with its gorgeous, white sandy beach and coconut palms (renowned for being one of the top ten beaches in the whole world) - we photogs sought them all out. I had a soft spot for Peace Hill Windmill ruins, a reminder of St. John's sugar mill past. The site offers spectacular views of the north coast including Hawksnest Bay. From the ruins a short trail runs down to Denis Bay, which is just as appealing. Whether photographing the views or snorkelling in Trunk Bay amidst a variety of different coloured fish, I always came away from St. John feeling enriched, inspired, refreshed and with a deep sense of longing – to return, which of course I did, every Wednesday!

After our morning photographic safari, we'd drop the jeep back and catch the hourly ferry from Cruz Bay to St. Thomas, where the Big Blue Pig (as we affectionately called the SS Norway) would be anchored a little way out to sea from the port and island capital of Charlotte Amalie. It was always just the most perfect ferry crossing – temperatures in the high 80s to low 90s Fahrenheit, the sun, wind and salty sea spray in your face as you sat on the bow topping up your tan. St. Thomas, which has a population of around 52,000 is a U.S. Virgin Island with a land area of some 31 square miles. A post on this island was established by the Dutch West India Company in 1657. Nine years later, the Danish captured and controlled St. Thomas. Like St. John, the land of St. Thomas was farmed for sugar cane and also like St. John, the use of slave labour and slave trading was commonplace in centuries gone by.

If we weren't shopping and lunching in Charlotte Amalie, we'd hire a jeep and drive to the white sandy beach of Magens Bay, located on the North Atlantic side of St. Thomas, just to get away from the cones. Here we'd swim, drink and sunbathe. Then after catching the rays, we'd return to Charlotte Amalie, take the tender back to the Norway and graft another evening in the gallery, following processing and printing of the St. John smudge images.

Thursday was yet another day spent at sea. Following the inevitable stint in the photo gallery selling pics and winding up the cones, it was time for formal night preparations again with a repeat of Sunday evening's smudges, a change in outfits for the cones and a change in outrageous bow tie and cummerbund combo for us photogs.

Friday morning was the final smudge of the cruise. 'Beach' involved photographing passengers as they disembarked the tenders to come ashore onto NCL's private island, the Bahamian Great Stirrup Cay, purchased by Norwegian Cruise Line in 1977. This island paradise (well a paradise without two thousand cones on it), is located 125 miles from Miami. The smudge, employing two photographers (usually numbers 5 and 6 photogs) was generally wrapped up within 30-45 minutes and I'd take the rolls of film back for processing. Gaz quickly printed them. The other photogs had been busy setting up the gallery with the formal night photos in readiness for the big sell at teatime. The beach smudge photos would also be displayed in the gallery. We'd then get the tender ashore and have our customary run around the island before swimming and sunbathing.

Passengers were obliged to settle all their on-board accounts by Thursday evening, meaning that all purchases in the many departments on board ship had to be made in cash. The Friday teatime big sell was just that. Passengers flocked to the photo gallery in droves – seeing was believing. Trade was so brisk that there would be a rotation of three photographers behind the till. Archie would take the cash, whilst two other photogs would bag up purchases. After a few hours, the team rotated. When the gallery finally closed around 10pm, numbers 2 to 6 photogs collectively stripped down the photo gallery of remaining unsold prints and generally tidied up, whilst the Chief Photographer took the summary of takings till receipt, dollar notes and coins into the back room. After the big cash up some time later, Archie emerged jubilant. We had taken $42,000 over the week. As Shagger I was of course on the lowest commission at just one per cent of takings. In my first week I earned a mere $420 (circa £210) for working in effect two working weeks in one. Nevertheless, I was grateful to be earning and after barely a month Mal, the number 5 went on vacation and I was promoted to the number 5 position which in effect doubled my salary. When you combined this with commission for the odd St. John wedding photography, the pay started to look half reasonable.

After Archie had paid all the photographers, it was off to party or rather hit the bar, the disco and then numerous parties that were being held off Slime Alley. The only time I felt homesick was late on a Friday night, seeing all the passengers' suitcases outside the cabins awaiting collection in readiness for disembarkation the following morning back in Miami. Several times I felt seriously overwhelmed with the amount of work and started to have doubts about what I'd let myself in for. The other photogs were great. They had all had similar feelings and assured me it would get better as I grew accustomed to the work and environment. Doug was particularly good with me. Sometimes in the gallery and often in front of cones we'd pretend to crack up and cry that we couldn't stand it any longer. On one occasion I assumed the guise of a spoiled rich kid and shouted out "I wanna go 'ome, had enough, wanna go now". When we couldn't keep up the pretence any longer, Doug and I would crease up laughing about the situation, much to the bemusement of the cones. This anarchic, ebullient behaviour was our way of dealing with the stress of long working hours. The gallery shift could be very tedious and taking the piss out of the cones proved great entertainment. Things only got genuinely very bad on one occasion, prompting me to write home, almost as a pathetic cry for help. This caused some alarm back in Blighty with my sister Vicky writing to me and persuading me not to give up my job. I quickly got over that little wobble and the photogs would regularly wind each other up pretending that they'd gone over the edge, were shot-away and wanted out.

Following my promotion after only a handful of weeks, we all eagerly awaited the arrival of the new number 6. Alan was a fresh face - very young, happy go lucky and had an engaging smile. He fitted in instantly from the day I met him, coming up the gangway with his guitar in his hand. Above all he was friendly and always made me laugh. His catchphrase for when a cone had just done or said something well... er... cone-like was, "I think we've got something here", all said in a sing-song voice and with comically timed precision. Alan took the top bunk in our cabin that Mal had just vacated. It was Alan who got me into a whole variety of new music from Bunny Wailer and Morrissey and The Smiths to Aztec Camera's 'Walk out to Winter'. For Alan's initiation, I came up with a brilliant wind up. Following rezzies, I would switch the films for the same number of duff, fogged films and get Alan to process the duff films. I'd hide the good films ready to be processed immediately afterwards. And so, the scene was all set, I even volunteered to help Alan load up the films on to the spirals and stay with and help him. When processing had finished I said to Alan, "I'll just take a quick look at the first few rolls to make sure there's no agi marks on any of them".

As planned, I unravelled the first roll and in mock horror I turned to look at a bemused Alan. "There's nothing on this roll, it's all black ... looks like it's been fogged ... oh, no, this one's the same", I said with an increasingly alarmed tone. "You check that one, Alan". The new Shagger unravelled another of my pre-fogged films and then another. Of course, every film was the same – all fogged and not so much as a chink of an image on any frame. Alan was aghast. "Jesus, Alan, what did you do? I mean all that money down the drain. Everyone's going to be furious". I opened the door of the processing room and on cue the other photographers had already assembled, pretending to sort all the gear out. "Alan's fogged all the films...he's fucked up big time", I blurted out. The other photogs played along and looked horrified, shaking their heads in disgust. Poor Alan just stood there stunned, unable to work out what the hell had just happened. I stepped forward and looked at a dejected Alan. "I hate to have to tell you this Alan, but this whole thing's a complete wind-up. You've just been had!" whereupon we all cracked up laughing and I explained to Alan, the colour now returning to his cheeks, what I had done. "Bastards, all of you" Alan said, but with a smile on his face. After that, I returned to the processing room and helped Alan process all the correct rezzie films. I waited until it was safe to pop the light on and then I left Alan to finish off the process. “See you up in the crew bar”, I said smiling, leaving a now much more relaxed, as well as relieved, Number Six.

Part two of the wind-up had commenced. The films Alan was processing were all fine – that wasn’t the problem. Alan was processing in his boxer shorts and had left all his clothes in the darkroom and his cabin key was in his trouser pocket. We took all Alan’s clothes up to the crew bar and got the first round of beers in. Alan was left with no option but to make his way through a busy crew bar in nothing but his boxers to retrieve his belongings. We’d barely finished the first round when in walked a scantily clad Alan. The whole crew bar erupted into cheers and wolf whistles, after which we toasted his good health. The double wind-up had worked perfectly and Alan had proved to be a great sport. He was well and truly an archetypal Shagger. Alan had arrived!

Some time later, I had been working very late and feeling absolutely cream crackered, so headed back to my cabin with nothing but sleep on the brain. As I approached the cabin door, I stopped dead in my tracks and stared. Suspended from the door handle, almost mockingly, was a coat hanger! Now, this was an agreed signal that if one of us had a young lady in the room, the other had to keep away – even if that meant being up all night with no sleep. “Bastard” I muttered under my breath. But in that moment a plan was hatching. I went up to the crew bar to fetch the other photogs. Picking up a Leica rig each from the darkroom, we then made our way along Slime Alley to my cabin. With cameras prepped and ready and on the count of three, we barged in through the unlocked cabin door and subjected Alan and his lady friend to a barrage of flash photography. Laughing, we turned the light on and I remember Alan’s smiling face, as once more he found himself on the other side of a wind up. As for the girl in question, there was no sign of her. Embarrassment had buried her so deep beneath the sheets, I was worried she might suffocate!

I quickly developed a bit of a reputation as a wind-up merchant. I had been on the receiving end of much leg-pulling and shenanigans myself, including very nearly copping the bill for ‘D&P’. Naively, I had photographic ‘developing and printing’ on the brain when, on one occasion, the Norway casino manager suggested that the D&P be charged to my account. This was only just within earshot, but when I saw the barman carrying a magnum of Dom Perignon over to our corner of the bar, the penny dropped immediately. I turned from funny mimicry into Mr Serious in less than a millisecond. At well over a few hundred dollars, I wasn't about to pay for this particular D&P – no wuckin fay! I guess that all my wind ups stemmed from secondary school ebullience, impersonating half of the teachers. Well, as soon as I heard Aussie Cruise Director Neil's patter on 'Intros' night, there was only one thing for me to do, take the microphone and pretend to be Neil during photog intros. "G'day, my name's Paul and I come from Sydney, down under (chuckles from the photogs behind me). Just remember, when you see all those little boats bobbin' up and down (a reference to smaller cruise ships), you can hang your heads high, 'cause remember, you're on the Norway!" Everyone cheered. The other photogs were in stitches and Neil just about managed a sardonic smile through his moustache, but it took a lot of effort. Deep down I thought he was going to bollock me or even throw me off the ship, but strangely Neil never referred to the wind up at all after that night.

On one particular day, we all had to dress smartly as the boss was coming on board to get a 'sitrep' from Archie and to inspect his troops. The Norway at that time was Cruise Ship Pictures' flag ship and biggest earner. Well of course when Richard Dawson strode into the photo gallery, it was hilarious. My Richard Dawson impersonation was already a hit with the photogs and now we were seeing it enacted for real. Richard was immaculately dressed in shirt, tie, navy suit and pristine, black brogues, which all complemented his dark hair and tanned complexion. As Richard went along the line, it did feel very much like I was back in the combined cadet force at school being inspected by a senior officer. Suddenly Richard's mobile phone, which he had been continually waving around for show, rang. Richard almost dropped this brick like piece of technology with its bulbous antenna on his foot, as he strode around the gallery trying to get a good reception. It was Richard's business partner, Roy. "Hello Roy, yes, yes…I'm on the Norway … can't quite hear you ... going on deck to get a better signal" whereupon Richard did just that. With a few struts he was gone. We burst out laughing, the whole thing was like a Fawlty Towers comedy sketch and it was priceless.

Saturday mornings, we always arrived back in the port of Miami before breakfast. On one memorable return Caribbean cruise, I skipped sleep, spending the entire last night up on deck with the most delectable brunette, the beautiful, pale blue-eyed, freckle-faced Ashley, a 24-year old Californian stunner. Looking back, I sometimes have to pinch myself that such magical liaisons were actually real and happened.... They were and they did! With this particular young lady, we rounded off a starlit evening, night and early hours with a bottle of Moet – the champers being drained just as sunrise ushered in the most perfect Florida dawn. The Big Blue Pig gliding passed the southern tip of Miami Beach, to starboard, with the lure of downtown Miami to the west in the distance and the Port of Miami and our mooring, beckoning, up ahead. One last lingering embrace and the lovely Ashley like all the other girls, was gone.

Prior to a few precious hours of free time, there were one or two Saturday morning chores to undertake. Duties usually included bringing stores aboard such as processing chemicals, films, printing paper and presentation folders. After this, if we weren't going shopping in the beautiful malls of downtown Miami, we'd take a taxi southwest, to the suburb of Coconut Grove, get a posh haircut and seek out an English bar that served up the meanest fish and chips this side of the North Atlantic. I was now close to living the dream that I'd hankered after for so long. The chilled south Florida vistas depicted in my favourite television series of that era, 'Miami Vice' and I was now living and working amongst the stylish Sonny Crockett, Rico Tubbs, Martin Castillo, Gina Calabrese, Trudy Joplin and Stan Switek (aka the Miami Vice team). The relaxed vibe was ubiquitous and so palpable. I wore the expensive, fashionable, Vuarnet sunglasses, the white jacket and pants, the evocative Jan Hammer music was playing in my head, so much an integral part of the Miami Vice experience (I fantasised that I was driving a brand new, white, Ferrari Testarossa) and best of all my favourite TV series was still being filmed whilst I was out there, based in the Sunshine State...Cool runnin'!

Then it was back to the Big Blue Pig to do it all over again - for embies and sailing shots and another week-long Caribbean cruise. As time wore on, I settled into cruise ship life. After a couple of months on the Norway, I reckon I was part of the furniture, knowing the ship and my job from arse end to topside. We worked damn hard, but by the same token we played damn hard as well. I can't put my finger on precisely when it happened, but all five photographers started to get hacked off with the Chief Photographer's attitude towards us, which had become abrupt of late. This coincided with Archie cocking up the formal night Captain's table photograph, where the lighting was very uneven. The Hotel Director had summoned Archie to ask him "Why Captain's table looked so shitty?" I don't know what happened, but it seemed to exacerbate the way we all felt about Archie – that he was getting on our nerves. Archie snapped at Gaz one time "Gary, get the Blad!" On another occasion, one of the other photogs would be picked on and so it went on. I tried to keep out of Archie's way. It was pretty obvious that things were strained, because the five of us generally did things together and Archie was seldom with us, save for the odd catamaran trip to St. Barts. In the crew bar one night, us photographers jokingly hatched a plot to throw Archie overboard in the dead of night! Still, to give him his dues, there were chief photographers and managers at that time who had a reputation for being much, much worse. They were utter bastards to the poor photogs beneath them. Saul Frith was one such manager. He had a fearsome reputation as a bully. I only met him once on the Norway and fortunately he was in a jovial mood so I somehow managed to escape his 'Flashmanesque' grasp. Those photographers who didn't perform well or got into trouble were demoted and/or sent to a notorious punishment ship that was overrun with cockroaches called the 'Victoria', an old Greek cruise liner run by 'Chandris'. I'd heard enough horror stories about this ship and its substandard living conditions to make me determined not to end up there.

Sunday 10th April 1988 started off fine with the usual long stint in the gallery selling embies and sailing shots, smudged the previous day. Doug and I had just finished our shift and Granners and Alan took over from us. I returned to my cabin to change into shorts and t-shirt, as I had planned two hours of sunbathing up in the 'reserved for crew only' section between the Norway's twin funnels. I was just on the point of grabbing my towel, suntan lotion and sunglasses when there was a knock on my cabin door. It was a radio operator and I knew by the perturbed look on his face that something was amiss. "Please come to the radio room now, as there is an important message waiting for you", the young Filipino radio operator said. My first thought was that following his recent visit, senior manager Saul Frith had done my legs after all and I was to transfer immediately to the 'Victoria' without delay, but then if I was indeed destined for this punishment ship, surely Archie Osbaldeston, my current Chief Photographer, would have informed me?

As I followed a stony-faced radio operator from my cabin to the radio room, which was situated near to the bridge, it suddenly dawned on me – Grandad. I was greeted by an even more sombre radio controller who handed me a printed telex with the words, "Not very good news, I'm afraid". I opened up the folded piece of paper and read. It was from Mum. "Regret to inform you that Grandad died yesterday (9th April 1988). Please do not come home for the funeral…". (Mum was worried that I'd lose my job on the Norway, if I suddenly upped and flew back to England). I stared at the note, quickly assimilated the contents and thanked the radio operator who simply said, "Sorry for your bad news".

I was on auto pilot, nonchalantly returning to my cabin to pick up my sunbathing paraphernalia and then making my way up to the crew sunbathing area – for all intents and purposes looking to the whole world like a callous bastard, as if nothing had happened. That was me on the outside. Me on the inside told a different story. I was cut to pieces and racked with pain. Up on deck, there were beautiful, bikini-clad girls everywhere, the sun was hot, the sky was a polarised blue and the sea, an even darker blend of midnight and navy blues, was serenely calm. I sat down on my towel and surveyed the scene and then it hit me – a huge wall of grief that made me suddenly catch my breath. In my mind I saw myself shaking hands with Grandad for the last time a few days before flying to Miami back in January. I looked back and remembered that kind face. I saw Grandad on his allotment digging up vegetables and of the two of us picking his prized loganberries that he'd pot as jam and that Grandma would serve up later in an unsurpassed pie with custard. Grandad's London Road, Mitcham allotment was used as a location for the 1979 ITV television series, 'Danger UXB', starring Anthony Andrews and Judy Geeson. The series chronicled the exploits of a fictional Second World War Royal Engineers, bomb disposal unit. My Grandad gave out his fruit and veg to the cast and crew during takes and breaks and recalled with humour how filming had to stop every time an aircraft flew overhead and how one crew member was seen, cigarette hanging out of the corner of his mouth, with a huge, fake, bomb on his shoulder!

As a teenager, I saw Grandad in a yesteryear custom, moving to the outside of the pavement 'to protect' and then doffing his hat to a passing lady, as I ran up to meet him on a trip down to their Mitcham flat. I saw my Grandad peering out and waving at me as the inbound London Euston to Blackpool North train slowly rolled in to a once long Poulton-le-Fylde platform (before someone had the bright idea to lop it in half) and I remembered how excited I would be every summer just to see my Grandparents. I saw Grandad sitting in his armchair recounting a funny yarn as he puffed away at an aromatic 'Boar's Head' 'Golden Virginia' combo rollup, only to be scolded by my Grandma as some carelessly discarded ash had fallen on his new shirt and burnt a hole in it – Grandad said nothing, but just chuckled. Harry, loving husband to Sylvie for more than fifty-two years, my replacement father, my role model and a textbook grandfather, was gone. I'd never again see the kind, witty, clever and loving Grandad that I was so blessed and privileged to have known for more than 24 years.

Right there and then, I wanted so much just to burst out crying, but knowing that I couldn't bawl I simply sat there, enveloped in melancholic sadness looking out to sea through my Vuarnets, whilst tears defocused the scene, stung my eyes and their droplets rolled down my cheeks. I had lost my dear grandfather and my grief was immediate and long lasting. I remember thinking how odd the paradox was - what a contrast it seemed to be on this ocean of tranquillity surrounded by beautiful, bosomy, bronzed women, who were completely oblivious to my plight, in a setting that one would pay thousands for. People had pitched up everywhere I looked, keen to soak up the rays and cherish these idyllic moments. I was surrounded by happiness, but yet found no solace here for myself, because for me this was simply just a bastard day in paradise.

And then after he'd endured ten long months aboard the Big Blue Pig it was time to say goodbye to Granville. The number 3 had taken me under his wing from day one and effectively taught me the art of smudging from scratch, from that first sweat-drenched nightmare of a day photographing a thousand cones at embies on my maiden cruise through to rezzies and working the line that would become my smudge of choice – 'Street'. Granners taught me so much and I was indebted to him. But by his own admission, Granville felt 'shot away', completely knackered and in need of a vacation. I suggested that as a laugh for Granners' last beach smudge at Great Stirrup Cay, Granville, Doug, Alan and I would photograph the cones with us donning straw hats, tuxedos, formal shirts, bow ties….and shorts of course. It went down a hit and we sold masses of prints that night. Following the smudge and obligatory funny group photo, we took all the formal wear back to the ship and returned with beers, which we downed in copious amounts, whilst relaxing in the shallows of this Bahamian jewel. I had a great time in Granville's company. We had so many laughs, I can't remember them all, but on one occasion we were enjoying a beer or four in Granville and Doug's cabin and Granners had managed to get hold of the Billy Connolly video 'Billy and Albert – Live at the Royal Albert Hall', recorded the previous year in 1987. I've long since been a fan of Billy's crude sense of humour, observational comedy and personalised, outlook on life, so imagine the scene, when Billy's describing being alone in a hotel bedroom, unable to get to sleep when the couple in an adjoining room start up..." Yes!" "Yes!" "Yes!", "Yes!" and when Billy with exasperated pleading finally shouts out "Stop asking the fucking question!!" we all pissed our pants laughing. I was laughing so much, I really was clinging on to my sides. But that was just one of so many quality times in the company of my smudging mentor. A last wave and a cheeky smile walking down the crew gangway on the port of Miami the following morning with suitcase in hand and that was that. Granville was gone. A new number 3 took his place, who fitted in just fine. So, the team dynamics changed again – but it would never be the same without Granville – the patter, the Cheshire cat grin, the banter. One of life's memorable characters. Top bloke and to think I've not seen him since in more than 30 years.

Once Granville had left the Norway, the routine carried on, but life somehow wasn't as good. He had left big shoes to fill. Granners had worked long and hard on the Big Blue Pig – 10 months seemed an eternity at that time. I had just done 5 months when suddenly itchy beard set in and I started to sound off about going on vacation. Word got back to Esher and Auntie Trisha in the office and the next thing I heard of was that my leave had been approved. Others had stayed the course for much longer, but we all had different burn out rates and I just thought it was time to go whilst the going was good. I ensured my final week-long cruise was a good one – I worked hard, played harder and wound up the cones at every opportunity. In the Caribbean I visited all my old haunts that I'd grown to love. We hired jeeps on St. Maarten, St. Thomas and St John and I did the rounds one last time. I relished all the smudges from my last Norway embies and sailing through to Olympics and formal portraits. I thoroughly enjoyed Street, going overboard on my impersonations and patter to win over the cones...and the young ladies of course! I was pissed as a fart smudging rezzies, much to the amusement of the other photogs – come to think of it, I was inebriated most of that last week as I breezed from one party to the next. One photograph shows Alan and me, arms round each other, scantily clad in white boxers and me wearing John Lennon sunglasses, a bowler hat and gesticulating with a toilet plunger, looking very worse for wear!

After my last smudge, Beach, we had a run round 'private island' and then sat in the warm Bahamian waters lapping at the shores of Great Stirrup Cay sipping cold beer and telling jokes. It was a truly great time. Typically, I got no sleep that last night as I was partying hard. I'd packed during the afternoon and also settled up my modest laundry account and not so modest bar bill. My flight home to London didn't leave until early Saturday evening, which meant that I could enjoy a last meal and beers at our favourite Coconut Grove haunt with the rest of the lads. Then it was back to the Norway to collect my gear and say goodbye to my fellow photogs. I hung around on Miami dock to watch the SS Norway set sail late afternoon. As I admired and photographed this leviathan ship slowly gliding out of port, to the early '80s sound of Asia's 'Only time will tell' playing in my head ('You're leaving now, it's in your eyes, there's no disguising it...'), followed immediately by Peter Cetera's 1986 release, 'The Glory of Love', it was with mixed feelings that I waved her goodbye. It had been bloody hard work, but this had been tempered with the accumulation of a pot of cash and loads of great experiences. I had seen and photographed some beautiful places, met and had 'liaisons' with loads of drop-dead gorgeous girls, but above all, I had made some wonderful friends.

When the Big Blue Pig was a mere speck on the South Florida horizon and the previously bustling port now resembled a Mary Celeste, I turned and hailed a yellow cab to take me through the streets of Dade County to Miami International Airport.

It was mid July 1988 and I was eager to get back on English soil after months away. I had planned a four-week vacation and the initial homecoming was exciting, despite my father's inauspicious presence and deluded omnipotence. Once I had done the rounds of family and friends and of course had seen my dear grandmother and paid my respects at my grandfather's graveside, within a few days I had withdrawal symptoms and the cruise ship 'drug' called me back. I phoned Auntie Trisha in Cruiseship Pictures' Esher office to inform her that I wanted to cut my four-week vacation down and return to sea much earlier than planned – what could she offer me? A complete contrast was to be the answer – number 2 photographer on a 2-man ship called 'The Ocean Princess' which I was to join in the charming Danish capital of Copenhagen. In effect, I was to become a Shagger again, albeit on a much smaller scale.

I arrived in an overcast Copenhagen in early August with time to kill before boarding my new ship, so I photographed the waterfront and Edvard Eriksen's iconic statue 'Den lille havfrue' (The Little Mermaid) which is displayed on a rock by the water's edge at the Langelinie promenade. The famous statue, which has been vandalised many times over the years, is much smaller in real life, at about 1¼ meters in height.

Then it was time to wander back to the Ocean Princess, more the size of a luxury yacht than a cruise liner, with its distinctive yellow funnel set astern to rendezvous with the Chief Photographer. As soon as I rolled up to the crew gangway, the Number 1 came down to greet me. Loakey, who for all intents and purposes looked like a male model, was an inch taller than me, sported a good head of black, wavy hair and shook hands immediately. His reputation had preceded him. He was on Miami based ships before me and he was one of life's grafters. Loakey was friendly, albeit a touch reserved which meant that inevitably he came in for some ribbing. Archie Osbaldeston had nicknamed Loakey 'Dolly Dimples' no doubt as a reference to Loakey's thick, wavy 'barnet'.

Everything was so different to the Norway, with the exception of a Norwegian Captain and first officer. The working environment was different, much smaller. The passengers were different, mainly European and as I was to find out, tight spenders. The only American crew member happened to be the Cruise Director. There was a bigger contingent of British staff on board who included hairdressers, dancers, casino staff and of course photographers. The ship boasted two multi-lingual tour guides, both of whom were Dutch. Tall, slim and dark-haired Dorothy was sweetness personified. Elegant and attractive, she was very friendly and always smiling. Wilhelmina (Willy) wasn't nearly as tall as her colleague and sported short, honey blonde hair. Willy was quite pretty and she definitely liked herself. Often flirtatious, I didn't warm to her at all. Dorothy on the other hand was something else and Loakey and I had a soft spot for her. Both girls each spoke five languages fluently and they obviously performed an invaluable role. Paulette, a pretty, friendly brunette, was casino manager and it was towards the end of my time on the Princess that I briefly got together with her. I wished then that I had made the effort to get to know Paulette at the start of my Princess days as she was lovely – really lovely. I remember kicking myself at the time for not reading the signals and subsequently wasting an opportunity. Not for the first time in my life, I thought 'Slick Cans, mate, really slick!' Prior to that we all got on well as friends. I only had one other romantic liaison whilst on the Princess. Lucy, a British passenger, hailed from Croydon in Surrey and our mutual birthplace got our tryst off to an amazing start. Lucy, a City-based accountant, who was three years my senior, was a brown-eyed brunette who had long, wavy hair and an incredible figure to match. She was stunningly attractive and her looks were complemented with a beautiful personality. Lucy was very much an outdoor girl – into her skiing, horse riding, netball and running. She was so engaging, vivacious, caring and good humoured and I absolutely loved being in her company. Sadly, however, this was another romance destined to crash and burn, once Lucy disembarked at the end of her cruise. Quick sigh, as I park that one and refile it back into one of my mind's folders – you know, the one marked 'Extremely Pleasant Memories'.

Loakey and I shared our cabin with a scouse casino staff member, whose name now escapes me, but I can see his face as he was back then – balding, moustached, with a saucy smile and always telling jokes in that lovely, thick Liverpudlian accent – he was another of life's characters, friendly and jovial and we quickly became a tight-knit group.

Sandy haired, Austrian born singer and musician, Manfred Moser, looked like he'd been plucked right out of the Tyrol. All that was missing was his lederhosen and alpine horn. He was a consummate trumpet player with a rich baritone voice and when not performing, Manfred would often regale you with a tale or two. At times he could come across as being a tad boastful, but I found this an endearing quality. The Cruise Director, however, did not see eye to eye with Manfred and was frequently disparaging. The former would often repeat Manfred's catch phrase with a mocking sneer – "I play you beautiful, nice music". The ship's most notorious character just had to be 'Granville', a lovely Jamaican bar man with a skin as rich as ebony. Always friendly, forever smiling, Granville was quite saucy with the ladies. He was a very popular guy all round and wound me up on more than one occasion, saying that the 'duppy man' would get me if I wasn't good. In Jamaican folklore a duppy is a malevolent spirit! Whenever I'd ask Granville if he was ok, he'd reply, "Every little ting cool an' ireet!" When Granville asked how I was I'd joke "Duppy man cool and ireet", to which Granville would chuckle mischievously. I do so miss my time with Granville. I can see him now, replenishing my double Stoli on the rocks, both of us giggling, mid-way through a joke – he was such a marvellous character and I felt so enriched for having known him.

Once unpacked, I had quickly changed into standard uniform – short sleeve light grey shirt with epaulettes, grey trousers, dark socks and black shoes. Embies was a real eye opener. Smudging was very hard work. Unlike the Americans, who love having their photograph taken, the mostly European passengers declined to have their picture taken. I managed a couple of rolls and in fairness Loakey had warned me that it would be difficult. The smudges continued in the same vein. We did sell but on a much smaller scale compared with what I'd been used to. This inevitably had a knock-on effect on my commission. I'd gone from quite modest earnings to about $100 per cruise – tantamount to the cube root of sweet damn all! I wasn't happy, financially, but resolved to keep my head down and do a couple of months on this ship, photographing all the places of interest and gleaning everything out of this new experience that I could. On formal nights, once smudging had finished, we were encouraged to mingle with the passengers and make polite conversation. The upside of this was free canapés and champagne. Prior to my time on the Ocean Princess, I'd sampled bubbly on a handful of occasions, but now it was on tap and it was thrust in front of me, I developed a real taste for the stuff.

Loakey and I got on well, although he was different from the other photographers I'd come across. He could be a little quiet and yes, I found him quite reserved, but I think most of us have the capacity to be a tad introverted on occasions. I quickly established that Loakey hailed from an extremely wealthy family. Several times during conversation, Loakey referred to his butler as undertaking this task and that. I thought he was taking the piss and almost put my foot in it when I was about to wind him up and suddenly realised that Loakey was deadly serious. Loakey didn't need to work, but rather than sponge off his opulent parents and flit from one Chelsea bash to the next polo match, Loakey went off and grafted his way to success. I admired him for that.

As it turned out, I spent a very interesting two months visiting Amsterdam, parts of Scandinavia and Russia. The Princess visited all the Scandinavian capitals - Copenhagen, Stockholm, Helsinki and Oslo. It was in Stockholm that Paulette, Dorothy, Willy, Loakey and I, together with an English dancing couple, celebrated my 25th birthday, at the end of which I was challenged to eat a huge nut sundae. I fulfilled the challenge...but only just, coming within an ace of throwing up. Other highlights of my time aboard the Princess included the cruise up the 15km Geirangerfjord in western Norway. I remember being surrounded by imposing, steep cliffs as the Princess glided up this long, narrow inlet from the sea, one of many that had been formed by the submergence of a glaciated valley. At its widest point Geirangerfjord measures 1½ kilometres and is also famous for waterfalls such as the 'Seven Sisters', the 'Suitor' and the 'Bridal Veil'. Loakey and I hired bikes to explore Visby on the picturesque island of Gotland, lying slap bang in the middle of the Baltic Sea, culminating in a photo shoot by a pretty windmill.

My favourite highlight of my Ocean Princess experience was the visits to St. Petersburg, particularly the palace and park at Peterhof, which is also known as Petrodvorets. This majestic palace is very 'Versaille-esque' on first impressions. I spent hours wandering around this huge estate, gazing in awe at sculptures and rows of trim set flower beds. But by far the most impressive sight was the famous collection of fountains – some 64 in total, together with more than 200 bronze statues and bas-reliefs, which comprise the Grand Cascade. The centre piece is Rastrelli's awe-inspiring statue of Samson, who is depicted wrestling the jaws of a lion. The whole vista of the fountains set against a vast palace backdrop, the brainchild of Peter the Great, was truly breath-taking and was inevitably captured on Kodachrome 64 and like the rest of my precious images, destined to be high res scanned onto digital during the early years of the twenty first century.

Even though the Soviet Union, under the then eighth and last leader Mikhail Gorbachev, had undergone Perestroika and Glasnost (restructuring and publicity / increased openness, respectively), entering St. Petersburg reminded me of old, immediate post-cold war images I had seen in the media – drab, grey, uninspiring buildings, people standing on street corners staring at you suspiciously. You'd think that Loakey and I would want to have avoided all this, but oh no, what did we do? We sought out illegal back street traders for their Russian dolls and ornately painted lacquer boxes, even haggled with them to get the best US dollar prices for each (dollars as opposed to Russian roubles were much in demand and were the backstreet currency of choice) and then with the deal complete, we'd audaciously march through Russian port security each with a bag of booty hidden inside our coats which were slung over our shoulders. We were never caught. Instead we confidently smiled at Russian check point personnel and each time we visited, we were waved through to our ship by these bored, but intimidating looking security officers. Selling Russian dolls and lacquer boxes on board ship supplemented our meagre salaries. It wasn't enough for lacquer boxes to have the ornate gold coloured braiding running around the perimeter – it could still be a fake. I learned that authenticity was only guaranteed if the artist's signature was clearly discernible towards the front, bottom right hand corner of the box. I made sure that I brought home a fine lacquer box just for Mum, however I shudder when I remember my brazen cheek back then with both the illegal traders and Russian security – Jesus, to think we could have ended up in a Siberian prison camp!

Returning from St. Petersburg, having just visited for the last time, the Ocean Princess ran into a real tempest. The seas were without doubt the roughest I've ever sailed in. Whilst trying to sell photographs (and...er...other items) in the gallery, the ship was tossing and turning and all the while there were sounds of people retching and vomiting all over the ship. It was a bizarre sight – everywhere I looked there were forlorn, white faced people who, having puked so many times, had collapsed on the floor dehydrated and were propped up on pillows. At one stage, I ventured out on a small deck astern and caught sight of an oil tanker some distance behind us. Suddenly it disappeared and it was a full five seconds before it reappeared again. And then it dawned on me – if that tanker's being tossed around like that...we're doing the same. God, it was wild out there, violent winds and lashing rain. Needless to say, I was only out in it for about 30 seconds.

I think everyone was relieved when we eventually hit calmer seas and it was a very emotional experience to be in English waters again. Two tugs pulled the Ocean Princess slowly in reverse up the River Thames to finally moor up alongside HMS Belfast, in the vicinity of Tower Bridge, which not only signified the end of the current cruise itinerary, but also marked my disembarkation. I'd been on the Princess for two months and it was now the end of September. Saying 'Goodbye' to the beautiful Paulette at that time was the hardest thing for me. However, I'd received the joyous news from Auntie Trisha that I was to transfer to a new ship. Not only that, but I was being given a choice of ships: Chief Photographer aboard a ship cruising South America, or Chief Photographer aboard the Ocean Princess' sister ship the Ocean Pearl cruising the Far East. I took the latter opportunity and with barely four days in England to see family and friends, I was to take charge of the photography concession on my third ship on October 4th. Promotion, for me, had been rapid indeed.

My memories of the long-haul flight out to Hong Kong's old Kai Tak International airport are largely non-existent. My memories of the approach and landing, however, are very vivid indeed. Surrounded by mountains and skyscrapers, my 747 suddenly banked so sharply

I swear we were about to clip the buildings, which from my window seat looked to be perilously within touching distance. The jumbo jet made its final approach to the airport's only runway, which protruded out into Victoria Harbour. The feeling of relief amongst my fellow passengers was palpable. This hair-raising, spare underpants experience had momentarily scared the shit out of me!

Having checked in to my hotel, which I'd describe as being on the seedy side of awful, I decided to do the sensible thing and go out exploring ... by myself! As a young and thrusting upshot, personal safety back in the late '80s wasn't even on my radar. So there I was, immersing myself in this newfound culture, the heat, the humidity, the dialect, the people, the ubiquitous neon signs – I gazed in awe and drunk it all in as I pounded the streets of a pre-handover, downtown Hong Kong.

With breakfast done, the following morning a taxi took me and my worldly goods portside to rendezvous with the Ocean Princess' sister ship, the Ocean Pearl. Typically, the Pearl was painted white with the characteristic yellow Ocean Cruise Lines logo on her funnel. I had just missed seeing and getting a sit-rep from the Pearl's outgoing chief photographer, Alan Bream, but the Cruise Ship Pictures veteran had been good enough to leave me a few notes, which constituted handy tips and advice – the rest I would glean from my number 2 photographer Matt Doyle. Whilst I had been cruising the Baltic, Matt had been on the Pearl grafting alongside Alan Bream for some months beforehand. Matt was three years younger and also a good deal shorter than me. Sporting a generous head of wavy brown hair, boyish good looks and a winning Steve McQueen smile, Matt was unsurprisingly popular with both sexes and a very well-liked crew member. However, I was soon to learn that he was going steady with one of the casino girls, a pretty Welsh lass of similar age to Matt. Like the Princess and Norway before, I shared a cabin with my number 2, which would have been fine anyway, but Matt hardly ever used it as of course he kipped with his girl. On joining the Pearl, I was very much single, unattached and loving it – and that was fine by me.

The Pearl was similar in size, passenger and crew complement to the Ocean Princess. The Captain, First Officer and Staff Captain were Norwegian, whereas in contrast, the Hotel Director, Fabrizio Caveglione and Restaurant Manager, Giancarlo Roccatagliata, were Italian. The accountants were Malaysian, photographers, hairdressers, beauticians, gift shop and casino staff were English and the entertainers like the ship's pursers, were a mix of English and

American, although the latter boasted some Filipinos of both sexes. Bar staff and bus boys were also Filipino. The Pearl's DJ was a young Filipino girl called Jermaine, who I was convinced was a regular snorter as she always looked and sounded high on 'jingle-jangle', as they say in the hit CW series Riverdale. I remember she came in for quite a bit of flak from her fellow Filipino crew members because she was an American Filipino and according to them, not a true blood Filipino. Although frequently high, she was pleasant enough. Alan Scott, our Cruise Director was a charming American in his late 40s, who sported silver hair and matching beard and moustache. Nicky and Adam Derek were equally lovely – a young, vivacious married couple from the West Midlands. We shared a great laugh together regularly mimicking Jasper Carrott's football sketch 'They've got no cowin' Bovril' all said in broad, Brummy accent. Back then they were talented entertainers and dancers, now they run a highly successful, Staffordshire based theatre school. Adam also has a job as Cruise Director aboard a variety of cruise liners worldwide. Nicky and Adam soon became good friends. I got on well with everyone on board except perhaps the gift shop manageress and the casino girls, who were not a patch on their counterparts, Paulette and her staff from the Princess. Whether my number 2 bedding one of the Pearl's casino girls had something to do with the fact that I just didn't have an affinity with this new clutch of casino girls, or whether it was simply a case of mutual dislike, I'm not sure. The bottom line was that I thought the Pearl's casino girls were a let-down and they obviously sensed my disdain.

In old maritime law the Master-at-Arms, a position that still exists today, would be responsible for discipline. Punishments such as 'kissing the gunner's daughter' (flogging) and keelhauling have given way over the centuries to fines, verbal and written warnings and dismissal. On cruise ships, the Staff Captain is responsible for ensuring discipline. Blue-eyed Klaus, with his generous coiffed, Scandinavian blonde hair and similarly coloured floppy moustache, was renowned on board the Pearl for his harsh verbal warnings. If you received a summons to the Staff Captain's office, you could be assured of a suitable bollocking as you buttock-shifted nervously in the chair opposite him. I'd heard about 'the chair' and Klaus' legendary chastisements almost the moment I joined the Ocean Pearl and was determined that my posterior would never make contact with that dreaded seat. However, fate was to dictate differently as I will reveal a little later!

The Pearl's tiny photo sales kiosk made the Norway's gallery look like a grand hotel reception by comparison. Similar to the Ocean Princess, smudges were a much smaller and more chilled affair and hence salary was also a much smaller affair. The on board 'stock' smudges such as rezzies, lounge, handshakes, portraits and Olympics sold but a tiny fraction of the American based cruiseliners' smudges. The standard of photography was high, it's just that passengers weren't as keen on purchasing photographs. This meant that end of cruise photography takings were always low, adversely affecting salary, which was commission only. However, on the plus side, the Pearl had a far more colourful itinerary and many more excursions and this meant opportunities to smudge the cones amidst famous historic sites such as the Great Wall of China. I also needed to put this low salary malarkey into perspective by reminding myself that the average cone would have paid many thousands of pounds to be out in the Far East, whereas I was visiting the same sites, on more than one occasion – free. Anything of interest that caught my eye was captured on Kodachrome 64, of which I fortunately had a seemingly inexhaustible supply (bought on the cheap in the States!).

During October 1988, the Pearl would undertake around 4 back-to-back, identical cruises starting and finishing in Hong Kong, that would each take in the Chinese capital of Beijing, the Terracotta Soldiers in Lintong, Xi'an in China's Shaanxi Province and also the southernmost city in North East China, Dalian, with a final port of call being Pusan (now Busan) in South Korea.

From Hong Kong, my maiden Ocean Pearl cruise set sail in a north-easterly, then northerly direction to the port of Qinhuangdao. From there, a train took our group comprising cruise staff and of course cone heads some 300 kilometres west to the Chinese capital – Beijing, a journey of several hours. The Beijing tour was a two-day trip with an overnighter in some average, unremarkable, downtown hotel. Highlights of this first visit included photographing the locals, especially the children who were so photogenic; Tiananmen Square, the Forbidden City; the Temple of Heaven and of course, the Great Wall – albeit full of tourists!

Internationally recognised, Beijing's Tiananmen, meaning 'Gate of Heavenly Peace', lies to the north of Tiananmen Square and was first built during the Ming Dynasty in 1420. To reach the gate, above which hangs the famous portrait of Chairman Mao Zedong, one must walk through the square and cross Chang'an Avenue. Having endured an extremely uninteresting smudge with Matt, undertaken at breakneck speed, grabbing what cones we could who'd agree to have their photo taken with a giant image of Mao Zedong behind them (not many), I took some time to absorb the atmosphere of this great place. 1988 was the Chinese year of the dragon and everywhere I looked, interspersed with the ubiquitous lantern and bicycle, there were so many of these mythical fire-spewing monsters. All marvellously decorated, colourful effigies symbolising formidable and propitious powers associated with water and the heavens. Chinese dragons epitomise power and strength and good luck for those worthy of it!

Little did I realise, however, as I hastily changed camera lenses on this chilly October morning that the very spot that I was standing on would be transformed barely eight months later into a battlefield. Scenes of violence erupted on June 4th 1989, the culmination of mass dissent that had been building up in a series of spring demonstrations. A stunned world looked on as the student pro-democracy movement was stamped on by the will of the Communist heavy weights. Many innocent people were killed (and apparently not just in the capital) during a massive military mobilisation in Beijing in what became known as the Tiananmen Square massacre. I will never forget journalist Kate Adie's reports and the shocking video footage depicting, among other things, a solitary student frantically trying in vain to block the path of an advancing tank. This wasn't the first time that I had visited a place only to hear some time afterwards, that the particular location visited was scene to some disaster or other. 'There but for the grace of God, go I'.

So, leaving the portrait of Chairman Mao behind, I walked through The Gate of Heavenly Peace and stepped back in time as I found myself in the Forbidden City, a series of some 980 ornate buildings spread over 180 acres, dating from the early fifteenth century. The Forbidden City, which featured so prominently in the 1987 film The Last Emperor, was the Chinese imperial palace during both Ming and Qing dynasties. Also, in 1987, the Forbidden City became a World Heritage Site. I marvelled at what I was seeing – the traditional Chinese palatial architecture was stunning, but when I looked more closely, I was awestruck by the elaborately carved figures on the roofs, none more so than those adorning the roof ridge of the Hall of Supreme Harmony, which completely blew me away. Determined to do justice to these beautiful old buildings and ornate, wooden sculptures, I attached my polarising filter to the front of my zoom lens, rotating it to ensure deep colour saturation on my

Kodachrome transparencies. I soon realised that to fully appreciate the Forbidden City, you need a hell of a lot more time than the couple of hours I spent there. On my first visit, I skimmed it, almost racing from building to building, just because there was so much to see in such limited time. In fact, what I was seeing in a snapshot represents the world's largest collection of preserved, wooden buildings from a bygone era. The Forbidden City is a real treat. The visitor soon realises that there are many highlights within this one big Beijing highlight, such as The Meridian Gate, The Hall of Preserving Harmony, The Hall of Central Harmony and the Palace of Heavenly Purity. And then of course there are the majestic, gold-coloured lion statues guarding the front of the Palace of Tranquil Longevity, which make an equally imposing sight.

I'd shot almost three 36 exposure rolls of tranny just on Tiananmen Square and the Forbidden City, which also included building details as well as images of the locals - photographs such as 'Man and Bike', 'Emotional Content' (group meditation), 'Seller, Forbidden City (to cries of, "one, dollar, one dollar", that indicated the purchase price of the hat the man was willing me to buy) and 'Old Chinese Man, Sitting with Blue Bag'. Suddenly my attention was drawn to a little boy dressed all in red, wearing the infamous, characteristic, open crotch trousers, so called split pants, apparently to make urination easier.

This little fellow was so photogenic, I quickly clicked off a frame and it was only when I'd done so that I noticed what the kid was holding. I couldn't believe it – a small, toy camera. I gesticulated towards my camera and then pointed back to the child's toy camera, simultaneously raising and lowering my camera and pretending to take another photograph. The little boy just stared at me curiously, but I persevered. Just when it looked like he wouldn't play ball, the little boy suddenly raised the toy camera to his eye and took an imaginary picture of me. It was a truly magical moment and I only had one frame, literally, to get what acclaimed photographer Henri Cartier-Bresson aptly called the 'decisive moment'. I felt sure that I'd got it, but when I tried to advance the film to the next frame, the wind on lever stuck halfway, indicating the end of the film. I would have to wait until the end of January, once the slides had been processed by Kodak at their UK Hemel Hempstead facility, to be really certain. I was lucky – I did get the whole frame and not just half an image as frequently used to happen at the end of a roll of film. I was elated and could have hugged the little boy, but when I looked up from examining my camera's frame counter and rewinding the fully exposed film, both the child and his mother had disappeared into the crowd. 'Chinese Kid with Toy Camera' remains to this day, one of my favourite photographs of all time. This small, oriental infant and I may have originated from different parts of the world, been a generation apart and spoke in different tongues, but in that split-second a powerful, mutual connection was made in the realisation that I had communicated with him and he with me.

Following the Forbidden City, it was time to board coaches to take us to what would be (10 years after my visits) a further UNESCO World Heritage Site, another early fifteenth century marvel, The Temple of Heaven, which actually comprises three main groups of buildings. What the visitor generally refers to as the Temple of Heaven, is actually a truly remarkable, triple-gabled, all wooden, circular construction, some 38 metres in height by 36 metres in diameter called the Hall of Prayer for Good Harvests. Located due south and resembling this magnificent temple, but on a much smaller scale is The Imperial Vault of Heaven, which in turn is connected to the Hall of Prayer for Good Harvests by the Vermilion Steps.

Our tour of Beijing was rounded off with a visit to a huge expanse of palaces, gardens and lakes set out in 2.9 square kilometres, collectively known as The Summer Palace. Like the Temple of Heaven and Forbidden City, I found the palace and surrounds to be an awe-inspiring photographer's dream. Highlights included: The Tower of Buddhist Incense (the highest building standing atop the 60 metre Longevity Hill); The Great Opera Hall; The 728 metre Long Corridor, decorated with more than 14,000 paintings; The lakeside pavilion affectionately called The Marble Boat (aka 'The Boat of Purity and Ease'); The 17-Arch Bridge connecting the eastern shore with South lake Island and of course the vast man-made Kunming Lake itself. That first visit really was a whistle stop tour and I couldn't wait for our next cruise and a repeat visit.

There are many sections of the Great Wall to visit, some restored, some wild, remote and dangerous and others completely unrestored, yet equally alluring. Perhaps the easiest section to reach and of course the most popular, lying 76 km north of Beijing, is the Badaling section in Yanqing County. Opened to the public in 1957, the downside of Badaling is it is always crammed to bursting with tourists, of whom I was one! First impressions were disappointing. Following a complete abortion of a smudge (very few cones in my group wanted their photo taken), I set up my own camera on a small tripod and took a self-portrait using the self-timer function (how selfies used to be done in the good old days) of yours truly sitting on the Great Wall with thousands of 'ants' (people) behind me in the distance, climbing this famous structure just to prove how unbelievably busy it was. I wanted so much simply to photograph the Great Wall completely devoid of people, but with limited time before the coach departed I had as much chance of achieving this as I had of rocking up at Buckingham Palace and asking to photograph Her Majesty The Queen!

Alas, it was time to get the train back to Qinhuangdao, where the Ocean Pearl would be waiting for us. I left Beijing on that first visit, full of mixed emotions. Elated at the sights I'd captured with my lens, inspired by the thought of three more trips to Beijing during forthcoming cruises, providing even more time to capture shots that I'd perhaps missed on this lightning first visit, yet tempered with disillusionment because I didn't get the illusive shot of the Great Wall that I so wanted.

I was straddling the strange porcelain contraption at floor level which constituted a toilet on board the train back to the ship, one foot on each pedal astride the throne, so to speak, trying to work out how on earth anyone managed to do a comfortable number 1, let alone a number 2 without soiling their undergarments – when bizarrely two ideas hit me simultaneously!

Firstly, I nipped back to my seat on the train…er…after I had thoroughly washed my hands and quickly assembled a Leica rig, before returning to the same toilet. I shot a couple of frames of the porcelain chariot sunken into the floor, complete with silver coloured pedals either side. I thought this might go down well as a memorable souvenir amongst the cones. As it turned out, my hunch was right. 'Chinese Toilet' proved a massive hit with the passengers and as word spread through the ship, everyone wanted to visit the photo gallery to purchase their copy. Their whispers and nudges turned to giggles, as one American couple on spotting my toilet image proudly on display turned to one another and said, "Oh my God, the Photographer's taken a photo of that rest room, Chucky, I've just godda have myself a copy of that. The kids just won't believe it!" I initially printed forty of the damn things, but soon realised that I'd need loads more. At $4.95 a pop, sales were swift. And with each 'k-ching' of the till my Cheshire cat grin grew wider as the sales mounted. The passenger's inane comments fell on deaf ears, for as long as I was making money I didn't care.

Secondly, the desire to photograph an empty, desolate Great Wall became all consuming. I was talking this over with my entertainer friends, Nicky and Adam, when we hatched a plan together for Adam and me to hire a taxi from our Beijing Hotel on our next excursion, leaving at the ungodly hour of 4.30 in the morning to make the journey to Badaling and be in position ready for the sunrise. If all went to plan, Adam and I would get some breath-taking shots before the coaches arrived with the hordes of tourists. Weather wise, we had three more trips to Beijing and then that would be it. No more chances. The Ocean Pearl's itinerary was set to change in November to Manila based cruises. I kept my fingers firmly crossed that the weather would be favourable on our next visit to the Chinese capital. I'd missed out last time on the Xian visit to see the terracotta soldiers as there were not enough takers. My number 2, Matt and I ended up both going to Beijing. This also helped me out as Matt was able to prep me for all the smudges, location and timings wise. On this next trip to Qinhuangdao, it was agreed that Matt would accompany the cone group visiting Xian, whilst I would journey back to Beijing.

As the Pearl docked in Hong Kong once more, my first cruise with this sister ship of the Ocean Princess successfully under my belt, I was tidying things up in the darkroom, when I heard a loud knocking at the darkroom door. Standing in the entrance was a slender, bespectacled Chinaman in his early 40s, no taller than 5'4", who looked immaculate in pinstripe dark blue suit and conservative matching blue tie. I barely had time to say "Good morning" when said Chinaman had already brushed past me into my darkroom, removed the tape measure that was dangling proudly and with more prominence around his neck than a doctor's stethoscope and was already taking my vital measurements. Whilst totting up my inside leg stats, this kindly little man looked up at my somewhat bemused expression and said politely, "I make you good suits and some shirts, please". I was so bowled over with the tailor's gall and that I allowed myself to be completely taken in and smudged by him that before I knew it, I had ordered two, three piece suits – one dark blue and one black and four shirts, two white and two blue, all for next to nothing...well, ok, for a few hundred dollars, which was peanuts compared to what it would cost back home! So, with a quick handshake, he bade me farewell and promised to have everything ready when the Pearl docked in Hong Kong at the end of the next trip. "You pay me then" the little tailor said as he bustled away. I hadn't parted with any cash and as I suddenly came back down to earth after this quite bizarre experience, I didn't think for one moment, the tailor and I would ever cross paths again.

Weather reports for our second excursion from Qinhuangdao to Beijing were very auspicious indeed. I grew very excited at the prospect of Adam and I taxiing to Badaling. On the train journey from Qinhuangdao coastal port to the Chinese capital, we had plenty to eat and drink. Will Berg, a native American fluent in Chinese, was another valued member of the Pearl's cruise staff, employed as a tour guide for the China leg of the Pearl's itinerary. Prior to visiting Beijing, Will had been teaching us key words and useful phrases, not expecting for one moment that any fellow cruise staff member, let alone conehead, would remember anything taught on board ship. Knowing that Will was sitting within earshot, I seized my opportunity to show off as a young waiter drew near, managing to remain effortlessly upright on a train that constantly swayed and jolted, carrying a tray of very welcome, steaming hot tea, along the aisle. I waved to the waiter and as he approached I said, "Nin hǎo" (more polite form of hello) ..." Yībēi chá, qǐng" (a cup of tea please). Then, with a mouth full of prawn cracker, I couldn't say Xièxiè (thank you), so I knocked three times on the table – a sign that means thank you when you're unable to speak it, for example when you're in the middle of eating. On hearing me, Mr Berg looked up astonished and said "hey, Paul, was that you?" I nodded coolly at Will, who replied "that was awesome, Paul". I could tell he was impressed that I had made the effort and as a result, I felt chuffed to bits.

I didn't think the taxi would show. Adam and I were up at 4.00am and ready for the off half an hour later. We took it in turns to keep a look out for the taxi, which would take us to the Badaling section of the Great Wall. We were both yawning our heads off as true to his word, our driver walked into the hotel lobby at a fraction past 4.30. The journey took just over an hour and as we approached Badaling, I pulled a wodge of the local currency Renminbi out of my pocket and paid the driver. The plan was to walk along a completely deserted wall to a predetermined spot and wait until sunrise, then capture the Great Wall in all its glory under a rapidly changing early morning light, immediately post sunrise. It was still dark around 5.45am when we arrived at Badaling and we had time to read an informative plaque about this magnificent, ancient structure.

Initial construction, we were informed, was undertaken during the Zhou dynasty (770-221 BC), the Great Wall being the greatest military defence system in ancient China. Formerly, walls were built by various rival kingdoms along the borders at strategic points to protect their territories. In the third century BC after Qin Shi Huang, the first Emperor, unified China. He linked up the various sections of the wall and had them extended into Wang Li Chang Cheng (10,000 Li Long Wall aka The Great Wall, where a 'Li' means ½ a kilometre, so times this figure by 10,000 and this means that the wall was approximately 5,000 kilometres or 3,100 miles long in the Qin dynasty). In order to meet the needs of military defence, reinforcements and renovations were undertaken during many dynasties, with the wall being damaged throughout history. The wall that survives today mostly stems from the Ming dynasty. The wall rises up from the Yalujiang River in the East and falls in the Jiayuguan Pass in the West. The Great Wall twists and turns for almost 6000 kms and traverses 5 Provinces (Li Aoning, Hebei, Shanxi - meaning west of the mountains - Shaanxi and Gansu), two autonomous regions of Ning Xia and Inner Mongolia as well as two municipalities: Beijing and TianJin. The Badaling section of the Great Wall that Adam and I had come to photograph is the beginning of Juyonguan Pass of the Great Wall. The wall is more than seven meters high and five meters wide. Fortresses and beacon towers were constructed at the turns and at strategic points along the wall. Badaling is one of the best-preserved sections of the Great Wall and understandably, the most popular with tourists.

I had brought a Leica rig to smudge the coneheads hours later, but also my own faithful Olympus OM1N and OM2N, both loaded with Kodachrome 64 transparency film to shoot the sunrise. As Adam and I climbed up to our pre-determined spot, the wall stretched as far as one could see, snaking away beyond the horizon and bathed in a lovely pre-dawn glow. It was around 6am. Twenty-five minutes, give or take, to sunrise and we both had about four layers on as it was bitterly cold. I worked fast to set the equipment up, camera attached to my battered 'Slik 88' tripod and then to frame the initial shot. I checked focus and exposure and then kept re-setting the exposure as the light level was changing constantly. I clicked off a few pre-sunrise shots, as did Adam, and then we both waited eagerly for the big moment. The sky was clear, which meant only one thing – we would be rewarded with some great images.

I had previsualised 'Great Wall at Sunrise' for so long and now this superb picture taking opportunity was close at hand, I found myself naturally slipping into the zone, totally oblivious to the outside world, waiting patiently, hunter like, continually watching, tweaking the exposure, finger hovering over the shutter release, barely breathing, right thumb poised to the side of the advance lever, occasionally checking the tension of the film. Oh Jesus...and then it happened. Suddenly, the sun rose up, side-lighting the wall and instantly throwing this snaking structure into light and shade. I gasped. It was a beautiful and magical sight and the more the sun rose, the more the angle of light and shade shifted, the more breath-taking and magnificent the vista appeared. I had shot off a 36-exposure roll of tranny in no time, swapped cameras, took a few frames with the Leica rig to sell on board ship, then re-loaded my empty Olympus with tranny. By the time I'd finished photographing, I'd shot off about three rolls of tranny utilising both Olympus cameras, as I knew that there was a very good chance that I'd never be back here under these conditions to photograph what is rightly regarded as one of the seven wonders of the world. With the job well and truly in the bag, it was now a matter of waiting a few hours before the coaches arrived bringing the first of many cones to the wall and so heralding the start of the Badaling smudge. Although I had the negs to print for sale on board ship, it would be a good few months before I'd enjoy drooling over the processed transparencies. That early morning trip was so worth all the effort and lack of sleep. Some things in life you're destined to do only once and it's so important to cherish these memorable experiences and get as much out of them as you can. The little early morning sortie to the Great Wall of China is right up there with my all-time top experiences of a lifetime. Unforgettable!

From the port of Qinhuangdao, the Ocean Pearl cruised the Bohai Sea (part of the Yellow Sea) in a south easterly direction to Dalian, the southernmost city in north-east China. Dalian is a major seaport and city located in the south of Liaoning Province and at the tip of Liaodong Peninsula. Famed for its many beaches, mild climate and manufacturing industries among others, the highlight of our lightning stop over was hundreds of local, flag-waving school children cheering us ashore.

After Dalian, it was time to head south-eastwards to Pusan (now Busan), South Korea's second most populated city after Seoul. Over the years Busan developed into the economic, cultural and educational nerve centre of south east Korea. Busan's location is only about 120 miles from Japanese territory – the islands of Kyushu and Honshu. From Busan, the Ocean Pearl cruised both East and South China Seas, sailing past Taiwan and back to Hong Kong for the final time.

I met up with my tailor and was relieved to find that he hadn't betrayed me. The suits and shirts that I had been measured for some weeks previously fitted like a glove. I was very pleased with the finished garments.

I was sad to leave Hong Kong. I haven't been back in more than three decades and I'm quite sure I wouldn't recognise it now if I did. Having picked up vital supplies, it was onwards in a south, south easterly direction to the capital of the Republic of the Philippines, Manila, where passengers would disembark and a new series of cruises would begin.

The Philippines, a large south-east Asian country, is located in the western Pacific Ocean, bounded by the South China Sea to the west, the Philippine Sea to the east and the Celebes Sea to the south west. The Philippines is an archipelago comprising some 7,641 islands, with Quezon City being the most populated. The country has a population in excess of 100 million and it is the twelfth most populated country in the world. It's close to the equator, is located on the Pacific Ring of Fire and as such, makes it geologically and climatically volatile, susceptible to typhoons, volcanic eruptions and earthquakes. This is partially offset by the country's rich biodiversity and abundance of natural resources.

Once we'd docked in Manila, a group of us headed to a local fish restaurant which in effect was a mud shack and simply asked for the local fish. When said fish arrived, it came whole with some simple green salad type leaves, overlapping the tin plate, which was roughly the size of an English dinner plate. This whopping, great big dead fisheye stared at me as I simultaneously lost my appetite. However, I did persevere and after delicately unpicking the silvery skin, I was astonished to discover the most delicious, tender, white meat underneath. What a pleasant surprise. Ironically that local fish, whatever it was, turned out to be the nicest fish I've ever tasted! Following a quick hour or so wandering around the markets taking photographs, it was back to the ship.

Matt had disembarked the Pearl in Hong Kong along with other crew members and I was delighted to welcome aboard my new number 2, Alan, who had been Shagger on the Norway with me. Whilst Alan smudged embies, I unpacked all the stores. One of the first things I noticed was the number of new Filipino faces amongst the crew, one of whom, Maria, caught my eye on the reception desk. The Pearl, meanwhile, set sail for Borneo to the south west with the promise of a jungle wildlife excursion. Malaysian Borneo comprises two states, Sarawek with its capital of Kuching to its south west and Sabah at its northern end. We would be docking at the port of Sabah's capital, Kota Kinabalu, or KK for short. The two Borneo states are separated by Brunei. KK, renowned for its bustling markets, boardwalk, many beaches and prominent waterfront mosque, is a coastal city fronting the South China Sea and is partly surrounded by rainforest. KK also provides the gateway to Kinabalu National Park which houses the 4,095 peak, Mount Kinabalu, the highest mountain in Malaysia.

With regular lifeboat drills and scores of other non-photographic duties, Alan and I were kept busy. No sooner had we left KK, it seemed we were arriving at Brunei's capital, Bandar Seri Begawan, 185 kilometres to the south west. Every port we stopped at, it was a quick disembarkation, race around to the tourist site of choice, smudge said tourists and then fill your boots with your own photo opportunities. The Sultanate of Brunei, a tiny nation on the north western side of the island of Borneo, is officially governed as a municipality. The default smudge for Alan and I would be the ostentatious Sultan's Mosque with its chandeliers, Italian marble and stained glass. Situated just to the northwest is the Jame'Asr Hassanil Bolkiah Mosque with its striking twenty-nine golden domes. This turned out to be a really successful smudge and I was quite surprised that our photographs were actually selling. My overwhelming memory of Borneo is how humid it was. It was a 'four showers a day' existence. Just standing next to the mosques with a Leica rig held up to eye level and I could feel the sweat trickling down every avenue.

Leaving sticky Borneo behind, the Pearl headed south west to the global commerce, finance and transport centre that is the Republic of Singapore, a sovereign city-state located off southern Malaysia, South-east Asia. It has a tropical climate and a multicultural population. It is only 85 miles or so and one degree north of the equator. Singapore's territory consists of one main island together with 62 separate islets. In 1819, Sir Stamford Raffles founded colonial Singapore and helped establish it as a trading post for the British East India Trading Company. The year I was born, 1963, saw Singapore gain independence from the UK, separating from Malaysia in 1965 to become a sovereign nation.

From Singapore, the Pearl would undertake several return cruises south east to Bali, via Indonesia, before heading north to Penang and Phuket in Thailand. This involved 'Crossing the Line' or rather crossing the equator. Historically, this is a traditional maritime initiation ceremony, a rite of passage commemorating a sailor's first equator crossing. The ceremony, typically featuring King Neptune, lots of costumes and a ritual dowsing in baked beans, slop or other gooey mess is very big on cruise ships and provided us with a great smudging opportunity. It's very jovial, often raucous and just because yours truly was hiding behind a Leica rig smudging coneheads, this was no guarantee that I wouldn't be chucked in the outdoor pool and similarly dowsed! It was, looking back, great fun to be a part of it all.

We were now well into November. Just after leaving Manila, there was a crew party below deck and I met Maria, the beautiful Filipino, who I had spotted on reception. Maria turned out to be one of the Philippines' top multi-lingual tour guides and after the crew party, she and I became very closely romantically involved. In fact, barely a week after we got together, restaurant manager Giancarlo Roccatagliata was to say to Maria in a heavy Italian accent, "you canna replace him with 'asnapadifinger'". Charming I thought. I knew that there were other suitors lurking in the shadows, but I was to see the funny side in my impersonation of this suave Italian! After we had been spotted canoodling up on deck one calm, clear night by one of these green-eyed monsters, I wasn't surprised to receive a summons to the Staff Captain's office the following morning. The door opened and an ashen-faced Maria walked out. A mop of blonde hair then appeared and blue-eyed, moustachioed Klaus beckoned me to come in. I took a deep breath in preparation for the bollocking that was to come, then took my turn in the dreaded 'chair', determined that I wouldn't fidget and buttock shift. I clasped my hands and stared at the Staff Captain as he leaned forward and said with a marked Scandinavian twang, "Were the stars shining brightly last night?", to which I grinned and cheekily retorted that I wasn't paying the night sky and constellations much attention. After being told to 'tone it down' a little, we both ended up smiling and that was that. I got off quite lightly. I had survived 'the chair' – phew!

From Singapore, the Pearl headed south to the world's largest island country, the Republic of Indonesia, with some thirteen thousand volcanic islands situated between the Indian Ocean to the south and the Pacific Ocean to the north. In terms of land area, Indonesia is the world's fourteenth largest country. It has a population of over 261 million people, which makes it the world's 4th most populated country – Java being the world's most populated island, comprising half the Indonesian population. Java is also home to the capital and largest city, Jakarta, sitting on its north west coast. With a population in excess of ten million, Jakarta is the hub of Indonesian economics, culture and politics. The capital is a rich mix of Javanese, Malay, Chinese, Arab, Indian and European cultures. Kota Tua is the old town and is well known for its Dutch colonial architecture. Sunda Kelapa is the old port where the visitor will find traditional wooden schooners docked. Indonesia itself, located on the Pacific Ring of Fire is known for its volcanoes. I remember watching the 1969 film with the slightly misleading title of 'Krakatoa, East of Java', when I was young – misleading because Krakatoa (Krakatau in Indonesian) is actually west of Java! It's also known for its Komodo dragons, orangutans, elephants, tigers, beaches, traditional puppetry and percussive Gamelan music.

From Jakarta it was on to the port of Yogyakarta on the south Javan coast to look at the displays of traditional crafts, listen to the local music and watch some Javanese dancing. I managed to get plenty of photographs of locals in costume dress and also the children, who were especially photogenic. Then it was on to Borobudur temple, a remarkable, 9th century restored Mahayana Buddhist temple, located in Magelang in the centre of Java. The candi (Buddhist temple) at Borobudur comprises six square and three circular stacked platforms, on top of which a central dome is neatly perched. The entire structure is decorated with 2,672 relief panels and there are no fewer than 504 Buddha statues. After quite a strenuous climb to the top, Alan and I marvelled at the central dome, itself surrounded by 72 Buddha statues, each of which is seated inside a stupa (an upturned mound or bell-like, hemispherical structure perforated with square shaped holes). I ensured that I took one or two record photographs, but it was quite overcast and the task was made difficult by the fact the place was swarming with tourists.

From the port at Yogyakarta, the Ocean Pearl then headed east to the Indonesian tourist haven, the island and province of Bali. With tourism accounting for around eighty per cent of the Balinese economy, this lush island with a rich biodiversity is located at the western end of the Lesser Sunda Islands (also known as Kepulauan Nusa Tenggara) with the island of Java to the west and Lombok to the east. Bali has approximately four and a half million inhabitants and is home to most of Indonesia's Hindu minority. The Balinese capital, Denpasar, is located on the southern 'leg' of the island. We had a wonderful Balinese welcome when the crew of the Ocean Pearl came ashore and were treated to traditional and modern dancing by young, local girls clad in vibrant costumes and jewellery. Stalls displayed sculpture, paintings, metal work and leather goods, which had all been skilfully handcrafted. My abiding impression of Bali was just how beautiful it was. The grass was so tall and lush, I thought that I'd stepped into 'land of the giants'. One of the other highlights of Bali are the rice terraces. Tegalalang, located north of Ubud Bali, a twenty-five kilometre or so drive north of Denpasar, is probably the most famous, but unfortunately this means loads of tourists. As an alternative, Jatiluwih rice terraces, located in central Bali near Ganung Batukaru, (circa 50 kilometres / 1½ hour drive from the capital) are well worth a visit. Mostly devoid of people, lush and very green, these irrigated fields are like magical steps, climbing gracefully up the hillside into the sky. They are quite simply, stunning.

North-westwards with a return trip to Jakarta and then a few days at sea, brought the Ocean Pearl sailing back into Singapore. On one particular passage, the sea got a tad choppy, precipitating quite a lot of sickness on board. I remember smudging handshakes on one of the formal, Captain's cocktail evenings and even the Captain and I had to steady ourselves at one point for fear of falling over. There would be a few couples waiting in line to meet the Captain, but these would be interspersed with 'singles', because the partner had been felled with sea sickness. This prompted some crass comments from the American passengers: "Hey Cap'n, when are you gonna calm things down, eh?" and "Cap'n, my wife's very poorly, please stop this Godamn boat rockin'". Meanwhile for the crew, if Alan and I weren't smudging, one of us would be in the gallery selling prints and the other would be in the darkroom printing. On our down time, I'd be in the crew mess, watching videos like the 1986 Tom Cruise' Top Gun film, or I'd be bopping in the disco to songs like Kylie Minogue's Turn it into Love, with DJ Jermaine spinning the vinyl. And of course, there was always a party to be had, below decks.

There were a few more Singapore to Bali cruises to enjoy before the Pearl changed course for the west Malaysian coast and Thailand in December 1988. Although we enjoyed a lightning overnighter in the Kingdom of Thailand's capital, Bangkok, I cannot remember sailing directly from Singapore, although we must have done, sailing northwards through the Gulf of Thailand to get there. As the crow flies, the distance is in excess of 1,800 kilometres, so it would be more than this by sea. I don't recall any other stops en route.

Formerly known as Siam, Thailand is of course where the predecessors of my family's Seal and Chocolate point pedigree

Siamese cats, Siri, Zari, Scherri and Min, originated from. Bangkok has a hustle and bustle of vibrant street life like no other. The Thai Capital is renowned for its ornate shrines. The Chao Phraya River with its ubiquitous boats and the many water taxis, feeds the network of canals. Among the myriad sights are the luxurious Grand Palace and sacred Wat Phra Kaew temple and also the famous reclining Buddha in Wat Pho Temple, located in the Rattanakosin royal district. I was very much reminded of the 1984 Chess movie soundtrack by Murray Head 'One Night in Bangkok'. I couldn't get the song out of my brain and there were constant reminders:

"Bangkok, Oriental setting, and the city don't know that the city is getting...One night in Bangkok and the world's your oyster, the bars are temples but the pearls ain't free...Tea, girls, warm, sweet, whose every move's among the purest...This grips me more than would a muddy old river or reclining Buddha...so you better go back to your bars, your temples, your massage parlours... You'll find a god in every golden cloister, A little flesh, a little history, I can feel an angel sliding up to me...".

That song really summed up Bangkok for me. I remember taking my two cameras around the markets serving everything from rice to seasoned monkey brains! I was enveloped by abject poverty and felt the need to capture it on film to tell the story visually for the folks back home. The smells were a mixture of dirt and an array of spicy, cooked foods. Bangkok's floating market boat kitchens served tropical fruit and vegetables, tasty coconut juice and freshly cooked local delicacies.

Thailand's Go-Go culture all started in the famous red-light district of Patpong, long since usurped. Two parallel side streets located between Silom and Surawongse roads were packed with peep shows, strip bars, pole-dancers and girls by the dozen offering a plethora of naughtiness. Patpong's reputation preceded itself, so I had to see it for myself ... as a tourist of course, not as a punter! My abiding memory though, whilst taking photographs in Bangkok, is constantly being hassled by pretty, overly flirtatious young girls who couldn't have been much older than eighteen or twenty, tugging at my sleeve, relentlessly pleading with me to step inside, desperation etched into their young faces as they shouted in my ear, "Mister, mister, nofuckylongtime!" and all just to scrape a handful of Baht.

Sailing out of the Singapore Strait, the Pearl called first at the port of the Malaysian capital Port Klang, which took passengers on a forty-mile excursion into the capital itself, Kuala Lumpur or KL for short. KL is known for its colonial buildings and shopping. Ten years after my visit, the twin glass clad skyscrapers, the Petronas Towers, became the tallest buildings in the world from 1998 to 2004, standing at just under 452 metres. Malaysia, whose population stands at over 30 million, is known as a federal constitutional monarchy and comprises thirteen states and three federal territories. This south east Asian country is divided into two regions by the South China Sea – Peninsular Malaysia and Malaysian Borneo. Mainland Peninsular Malaysia is bounded by Singapore to the south and Thailand to the north. Cambodia and Vietnam are located to the north east. Indonesian Sumatra is to the west. Malaysian Borneo borders Brunei and Indonesia. Due to its position, near to the equator, Malaysia's climate is known as equatorial – hot and humid year-round. The average temperature is a sticky 27 degrees centigrade.

As we prepared to dock for KL, a stark printed message from the Captain was posted all over the crew quarters. It simply read:

'To: All officers, staff and crew on board
Re: KL call
Please note that trafficking of illegal drugs and possession of drugs is a serious offence in Malaysia.
The penalty for such offence is death.
Master'

This warning was clear and made me shudder. There had been rumours circulating that two Filipino crew had been caught in possession of illegal drugs on board the Pearl and were being severely dealt with.

Following the KL tour, it was then onwards and upwards, or rather north westerly, through the Malacca Straight to the Malaysian state of Penang, situated on Peninsular Malaysia's north west coast. Penang comprises two areas – Penang Island which is home to the state capital of George Town, famous among others for the colonial Fort Cornwallis and the narrow hinterland / city of Seberang Perai, located on the mainland Malay Peninsula.

Whilst I was out of the country cruising the Far East, December 1988 brought double tragedy to the UK. At 8.13 on the morning of 12th December faulty wiring and signalling caused a three-train crash south of Britain's busiest railway station, Clapham Junction. 35 people lost their lives and close to 500 were injured. Then just four days from Christmas a terrorist bomb exploded on board Pan Am Flight 103 bound for New York from London, destroying the 747 aircraft as it was flying over the Scottish town of Lockerbie. In what is referred to as the Lockerbie bombing - the worst terrorist attack in UK history, all 243 passengers, 16 crew and 11 people on the ground perished that fateful day.

During Christmas week, the Ocean Pearl left Penang and the Malacca Straight and we cruised on further in a north westerly direction into the Andaman Sea, eventually arriving at the southern Thai province of Phuket Island, which is surrounded by thirty-two smaller islands dotted around its coast. Phuket, connected to the mainland by the Sarasin Bridge to Phang Nga Province in the north, is located to the south west of Thailand. It is a mountainous, rain forested island with popular beaches, mostly located on its western shoreline. Phuket city, the island's capital is renowned for its bustling markets and shophouses, with Patong being the island's main resort town. My abiding memory of Phuket is spending many hours jet skiing along Phuket's western coastline and sunbathing under cloudless skies.

It was Christmas Day 1988 and I had only ever experienced Christmas in cold conditions back in the UK. I was a very happy man indeed. The 25th December was topped off with the most amazing feast back on board the Ocean Pearl. By the time my ship cruised back into Singapore and to dry dock for a re-fit and repairs in mid-January 1989, it was time for me to say a long good-bye to Maria, before flying home westwards to England once more. On the Singapore to Dubai leg of the journey I had an unexpected upgrade to first class, courtesy of our national airline, so I was feeling in buoyant mood – helped even more by the constant alcoholic beverages being given to me by very glamorous air stewardesses. My tour of the Far East had enriched me, surpassing all my expectations. Many of my rewarding experiences, like watching the sunrise over the Great Wall of China, were one-off, unrepeatable moments. I got so much out of my time on the Ocean Pearl. I had such an amazing, unforgettable few months.

My big mistake was being in too much of a hurry to get back to the UK in mid-January 1989. I had enough money accrued to do more far east touring or visit Australia. I've always regretted that decision, as I'd only been back in a freezing cold UK for two days when once again, itchy beard got the better of me and I phoned Auntie Trisha at Cruiseship Pictures' Esher Office to cut my vacation time down and return to cruise ships. On offer this time was firstly a two-week stint back on the Big Blue Pig, the Norway, with the promise of joining NCL's 'Seaward' after the fortnight. So it was that I found myself back on the Norway as joint number 4 photographer, under the infamous Chief Photographer, Andy Mac. His number 2, a slimy git called Ian tried to wind me up by sending me out on deck to smudge sailing shots in a torrential downpour – with a Nikonos underwater camera - but I was having none of it. I told Ian to bugger off. I'd done my time as Shagger.

It was weird being back on board the Norway, albeit for two cruises. I'd been away from this huge ship and the big money for six months and so it took a bit of adjustment doing familiar tasks on a massive scale. Never mind the photographic staff, most of the crew were all different and so the atmosphere wasn't how I remembered it from my first stint on board. Knowing that I'd only be on the Norway for two cruises, I was determined to milk the experience for all that it was worth. This meant visiting all my old Caribbean haunts again – twice – idyllic Saint John, St. Thomas, St. Martin and St. Barts (by catamaran). Although Andy Mac liked his lemonades and I guess, his 'snorty stuff', he had a very endearing personality. He was a legend amongst the cruise ship photographers and had served more years and been on more ships than I'd had sunburn. He loved winding us up and frequently telling a joke or two. Andy and I were in hysterics every time we did a joint Richard Dawson impersonation together and he frequently regaled us with his cruise ship antics that included the famous night he stumbled back to his cabin, worse for wear, sat naked on the edge of his bed and accidentally dropped a full glass bottle of Perrier water on his knob, resulting in very bruised and somewhat enlarged genitalia! Ouch!

The fortnight on the Big Blue Pig rocketed by and I'd had a blast. I disembarked in the port of Miami during the first week in February 1989 only to walk along to the next ship that had moored up, the 'Seaward', painted all in white. Due to the predominance of senior photographers, especially those working out of Florida and the Caribbean, I joined Seaward as number four photographer (not as joint 4 as originally thought), delighted to learn that the Chief Photographer would be Gaz and the number three would be Doug, both of whom I had worked with during my first stint on the Norway. The Number 2 was a quietly spoken chap, who was nice enough, but whose name escapes me. Photographers 5 and 6 were American girls – number 5 was Sandra and the Seaward's Shagger was Anna-Marie.

At the welcome and introduction to new staff members, we were all issued with a token condom, which received the usual round of embarrassed giggles and there were now condom machines placed in the crew area. I guess NCL was having a 'safe sex' drive.

The weekly cruises had a packed itinerary. Seaward would firstly sail south east to St. Thomas and Saint John, then westwards traversing the Caribbean Sea to Ocho Rios in Jamaica. From Ocho Rios, the Seaward cruised north west to Grand Cayman and then further northwest to Cozumel ('Coz') Mexico. From Coz the Seaward headed north east, through the Gulf of Mexico, completing the circular circuit and heading back to Miami. The island country of Jamaica, whose capital is Kingston, is the fourth largest Caribbean island country and is located approximately 90 miles south of Cuba. Jamaica is known for its reef-lined beaches, rainforests, mountains, colonial architecture around Montego Bay and of course was the birthplace of reggae music – the most famous singer-songwriter being among my favourites, Robert Nesta Marley (Bob Marley). The port town of Ocho Rios (which means eight rivers in Spanish), a former fishing village and for many years, a cruise ship magnet, can be found on Jamaica's north coast, east of the famous Montego Bay. The smudge at Ocho Rios involved photographing cones against a backdrop of the breath-taking, 180-metre high Dunn's River waterfall, a picture postcard, terraced, cascading water feature complete with lagoons and the whole area surrounded by rainforest.

When I first stepped off the Seaward onto Jamaican soil, or rather sand, in the parish of Saint Ann, I discovered what the word 'shit' really meant. I was faced with a middle-aged Rastafarian gentleman, who greeted me with a warm smile and the words "Hey marn, I give you good shit". He simultaneously took off his rasta cap or 'tam' and unravelled what appeared to be a miniature white scroll tucked into one of his dreadlocks. The scroll turned out to be quite a sizeable 'spliff'. Needless to say, I politely declined, much to the Rastafarian's mock chagrin.

The British Overseas Caribbean Territory and tax haven of Grand Cayman is the largest of the three Cayman Islands and from the capital George Town, is located approximately 75 miles south west of Little Cayman and 90 miles southwest of Cayman Brac. Grand Cayman, with a population of 53,000 plus, is approximately 22 miles long, 8 miles in width at its widest point and is famous for its white beaches and colourful coral reefs. The highest point of the island is only 60 feet above sea level. The most famous of Grand Cayman's beaches is Seven

Mile Beach, located on the island's west coast, north of George Town. I was only on the Seaward for 2½ months and found that I really enjoyed it. The only run in with a cone, was whilst smudging the after show 'doors', where one obstinate man actually physically pushed me out of the way. In front of everyone, I raced after this insolent man and told him in no uncertain terms "The correct response is NO THANK YOU!!" The cone man who was in his late 70s just put his head down and carried on walking out of embarrassment. My fellow photogs just cracked up laughing which helped further diffuse my anger.

From Grand Cayman, Seaward cruised north west to its last port of call, Cozumel, an island municipality which is part of the Mexican state of Quintana Roo, situated in the Caribbean Sea and along the east side of the Yucatán Peninsula opposite Playa del Carmen. Cozumel, the island of swallows, is 30 miles long, just under ten miles wide and lies approximately 51 miles south of Cancún and 12 miles from mainland Mexico. 'Coz' is Mexico's largest Caribbean island. It's covered in mangrove trees, is relatively flat and the highest point is around 49 feet above sea level. Most of the island's population (circa 80,000) live in San Miguel, on the west of Coz. There are many endemic animal species on the island such as the coati, raccoon and the black spiny tailed iguana. Six months previously, Chief photographer Gaz had been exploring Coz by moped when an iguana ran across the road and into the spokes of Gaz' machine, killing the animal and throwing Gaz off the moped. Gaz was subsequently airlifted to hospital, thankfully making a complete recovery, but with war wounds – scars on his head and chin - a reminder of that fateful day. One of my greatest memories isn't so much seeing the iguanas, as playing pool and drinking beer with the local guys. On one particular occasion, whilst playing a variation of 8-ball pool (two photogs would play 2 local lads), Gaz and I had just pocketed our numbered balls (1-7), the so called 'solids'. It was the best of ten games and it all hinged on me pocketing the last, 8-ball. I remember firstly downing a slug of my Corona, then coolly stepping up to visit the table and ramming the cue ball into the 8, sending it straight into a corner pocket – pure fluke of course, but no-one else knew that. Gaz and I both fist-punched the air as the Mexican lads conceded, but this was followed immediately with warm handshakes and hugs...and crucially with the Mexicans getting the rest of that day's beers in!

Gaz was so much better, more laid back and much more suited to being a Chief Photographer than Archie Osbaldeston. Teaming up with both Gaz and Doug again was a real bonus and utterly refreshing (where are you now, guys – a reunion is years overdue?). In fact, the whole Seaward photog team got on really well. Highlights of my Seaward stint included smudging the cones climbing up Ocho Rios waterfalls and then climbing it again hand in hand with fellow crew members; weekly breakfast and sunbathing on 7 Mile Beach in Grand Cayman and sinking beers and playing pool with the locals in Cozumel. Oh and let's not forget the time when the Seaward broke her moorings in Miami during the tail end of a hurricane. Amidst a violent thunder and lightning storm, Seaward's bow swung out to port and tugs had to push her back in to the quay side.

The end of my time on the Seaward came around far too quickly. Similar to my first time round on the Norway, I worked hard, savoured every last smudge and partied to excess, for in my bones, I knew that my cruising days were done. My time as a cruise ship photographer was now at an end. In as little as fifteen months I'd become a confident, fully fledged, 'kick ass' smudger. I'd made some really great friends in my fellow photogs and wider cruise staff, met loads of beautiful, stunningly attractive girls, travelled half way around the world, immersed myself in local culture, took hundreds of Kodachrome slides and felt better and more enriched as a person because of these magical experiences. Although I've since regretted my decision to leave the cruise ship photography game so abruptly (I could have earned a shed load more money), in my heart of hearts, at the time, I knew that I had to make a clean break.

That clean break turned out to be not that 'clean'. With final hugs and goodbyes now in the past, I turned my back on the Seaward, on Richard Dawson and on Auntie Trisha and all that Cruiseship Pictures meant to me, as my yellow cab drove me out of Biscayne Boulevard to spend a solitary last night in a Dade County hotel, before flying out of Miami to see my girlfriend, Maria Aquino. My destination was the Philippines and a love-struck yours truly couldn't get to this beautiful country fast enough. In my head I was hearing those famous lines 'Go west young man, go west', which meant me travelling west across the north Pacific and some twenty-one hours of flying time. When I arrived at Manila airport and saw Maria, whom I hadn't seen in 3 ½ months, my jetlag and tiredness instantly melted into nothingness. As one of only five, multi-lingual tour guides for the whole of the Philippines, I couldn't have asked for a more suited and better qualified person to show me the sights if I tried. I was to spend the best part of a month in Maria's country travelling through the north, by the traditional and ubiquitous kitsch decorated jeepney (a symbol of Philippine art and culture), car, bus and shanks' pony. It was to prove an amazing experience. Maria and I would be staying in cheap B&Bs, spartan shacks and the odd posh hotel. As a top tour guide, Maria was able to negotiate favourable discounts on everything, making travel and accommodation very affordable indeed.

The Philippines, with its rich biodiversity, beaches, mountains, forests, caves and multiculture, is a vast archipelagic country of many thousands of islands. It's located in the western Pacific, south of Taiwan, south east of Hong Kong, East of Vietnam and north of Indonesia. There are many active volcanoes on the Philippines, including Taal, Mayon and of course Mount Pinatubo, the latter located circa 90 plus miles north west of Manila on Luzon. We drove past Mount Pinatubo twice during my visit and I remember clearly seeing it smoking in the distance. The eruption of Mount Pinatubo in 1991 proved to be the world's second largest volcanic eruption of the twentieth century, surpassed only by Novarupta, Alaska, in 1912. I was visiting the Philippines during its warmest month, May. It was hot and humid but cooler air, a welcome relief, was to be found in the mountains and in the northern city of Baguio, Maria's birthplace and home. Three seasons characterise Philippine weather – a hot, dry three months from March to May, the rainy season (incorporating the south west monsoon, which of course I purposely avoided) from June to November and a cool, dry season from November through to January, the coolest month. February was the transition to the hot weather. Typical temperatures range from 21 to 32 degrees centigrade plus or minus depending on the season.

Even in a month, I only saw a tiny part of the Philippines, confining my tour to the north of the country, to mountainous Luzon, by far the Philippines' largest and most populated island. It's a tourist mecca, which isn't surprising as the Capital, Manila is also located on Luzon. During a bus tour of Manila in which I was the only western person in the party, (everyone was native Filipino and all could speak English) I was asked by the male tour guide if I knew any words in Tagalog, the native Filipino language. I turned to my girlfriend and replied cheekily "Maganda Dalaga Masarap", followed by the contrasting "Pangit Unggoy". Roughly translated this means 'pretty girl very tasty' and 'ugly monkey' respectively! The entire bus, including the tour guide, burst out laughing. I guess they just weren't expecting that!

Manila, famed for its waterfront promenade, is full of Spanish colonial landmarks and monuments, has many museums and a very old china town known as Binondo. South of the Pasig River is Intramuros, which was in ancient times a walled city and is located in the heart of Manila. 333 years under Spanish colonial rule, almost 50 years under the United States of America and harsh occupation by the Japanese during the Second World War have really moulded the nation, shaped the Philippines' political culture and way of thinking, turning its mindset into one of westernisation, yet its people are still Asian. In 1565, the first Hispanic settlers from Mexico arrived in Cebu to the South, with the explorer Ferdinand Magellan claiming the Philippines for Spain in 1521.

Maria's birthplace and home, the Philippines' summer capital, Baguio city is a cool mountain resort located approximately a 5-6 hour / 245-kilometre drive north of Manila in northern Luzon. Baguio is cool because it stands more than 5,000 feet above sea level, enveloped by tropical pine forests. When I visited more than thirty years ago, it was still very underdeveloped with signs of poverty everywhere, muddy roads, children in dirt-stained, rag clothing. Three decades later and Baguio has come on leaps and bounds. However, the city wasn't without its struggles. Just over a year after I returned home to the UK, on the afternoon of Monday 16th July 1990, a devasting earthquake of Richter scale 7.7 in magnitude hit Luzon with this massive seismographic activity precipitating the deaths of more than 1,600 people. Worst affected were the indigenous Cordillera mountain people and Baguio city itself. Baguio was cut off and its infrastructure completely fragmented. Water, electricity and communications were all but destroyed with arterial roads shut down because of landslides. Some twenty-eight buildings collapsed that included homes, shops, hotels, schools, university and government buildings. The poor people of Luzon were on their knees. I had just started my role as forensic photographer with the Met Police in London, when Maria sent me a chilling newspaper cutting showing amongst other devastation, the remains of the flattened 12 storey 'Hyatt Terraces' hotel in Baguio where Maria and I had stayed. The terraced front wing had collapsed into the lobby claiming the lives of more than fifty people. A little arrow pointing towards several large slabs of angled concrete said simply "this is where we stayed". The devastation in Baguio and surrounding Luzon was awful news and sickened and shocked me to the core.

From Baguio Maria and I journeyed 145 kilometres further north up into the Cordillera mountains of Northern Luzon, a 5-6-hour drive, to the peaceful, spiritual town of Segada. Here I saw the bizarre tradition of burial – the hanging coffins nailed to the mountainside, picture postcard cascading waterfalls and streams, lush green, tranquil rice terraces, magical caves and the Igorot culture and people. The native Igorot people, comprising several Austronesian ethnic groups, inhabit the provinces of the mountains of northern Luzon. They are also referred to as Cordillerans. Living on the banks of the Chico River in the Luzon's central Cordilleran province, one of these ethnic groups are former feared head-hunters, the Bontoc people who were marked with idiosyncratic body tattoos. Fortunately, head hunting is a thing of the past and today the Bontocs are a peaceful people who take their agriculture seriously and who, despite contact with the other ethnic groups, have remarkably retained a lot of their traditional culture. Whilst visiting, I photographed the traditional Bontoc home, a triangular structure with thatch type roof and thick log borders.

The Ifugao people inhabit the Cordilleran province of Ifugao. The word Ifugao means 'earth people' and it also means 'from the hill'. My visit to the famous Banaue Rice Terraces was slap bang in the middle of Ifugao country, to the south east of Segada. I'll never forget their traditional friendly greeting. Two craggy and characteristically line-faced elders put on a show for me with their spears at the ready. They were dressed in vibrant costumes, a brace of white-coloured bead and shell necklaces sitting proudly on their upper chests like a row of military medals, loin cloths and head gear complete with birds' beaks and white feathers, sporting hunting knives at their hips. This was all set against a backdrop of the beautiful rice terraces, which the Ifugao had been farming in the Cordilleras for over two thousand years. They were very happy to pose for photographs. The women were a little more reticent, but back then it probably wasn't very often that they had a tall, young, hairy-arsed white man trudging through their rice fields. I did feel so privileged to be there amongst the Ifugao and without a single, solitary other westerner for miles around.

Soon it was time to journey back to Baguio, where I went to Maria's parents' home, which was nothing more than a couple of tumble-down rooms with sheets of corrugated metal for roofing. They were welcoming, friendly people who were extremely poor and it was obvious that Maria, along with her brothers, helped provide for them. It also became obvious during our meeting that I was being prepped as Maria's future husband. I remember during our conversations suddenly being overwhelmed with a sense of panic, that not only was I being viewed seriously as husband material, but that I would be expected to live in the Philippines, specifically on Luzon. Maria had hidden all this from me, but it was obvious from her clingy hugs and tears when we parted that she was lining herself up as a would-be bride. She was 32 and I was only 25. Never mind getting hitched, settling down abroad wasn't on my agenda at all in the summer of '89. Nevertheless, it was very sad to say our goodbyes and I was quite relieved to escape and make it to Manila airport, where a couple of bottles of 'San Miguel' washed down with a few whiskey chasers, steadied my nerves!

Leaving Philippine air space, I flew first to Narita international airport in Tokyo and then east across the International Date Line, in effect losing a day, to LAX and there to spend three or four days with my half-brother Michael, his wife Patty and one of my first cousins Maire in Ventura, California. I touched down on English soil right at the end of May 1989 and straight into another amazing experience, the publication of 'Historic Lakeland'! I hadn't been home two days before Maria phoned wanting to know when we'd see each other again. Then, it was phone calls every week and Maria was becoming more possessive as time passed. I knew that there was no future for the relationship, besides which, I didn't even have a job. When Maria called for the last time, Mum answered the phone. She was very polite, but I knew she was keen for me to end things. I'll never forget Mum relaying Maria's conversation to Kate and me, saying disapprovingly that Maria said, "Hello Mummy" at which, Mum then said to us as she was recounting the story, among other things "Not yet, I'm bloody not!" That was typical of Mum though. She was only trying to be protective, but I only saw the funny side years later. Rightly or wrongly, I wrote to Maria to end the relationship thinking that the best way to tell her would be to say that I'd met another girl. Well, I got a letter back a week or so later full of chastisement. The saying 'Hell hath no fury as a woman scorned' didn't even come close. Maria had shown her true colours and bollocked me to kingdom come, like a possessive limpet, threatening to kill me if ever I set foot in the Philippines again!

Suffice to say, I've not been back to this wonderful country – I don't think I ever could. Although our relationship all went to ratshit at the end, Maria was a lovely person. We enjoyed some good times together on and off cruise ships and she showed me her home country. I got off the beaten track into villages whose inhabitants had clearly seldom or never seen a white face – I ended up being stared at, which was a very odd, slightly uncomfortable feeling, but I took some prized images of locals – some like the Ifugao people of Northern Luzon, in vibrant, traditional dress, others like children in rural, remote villages, just dressed in old, dirty t-shirts, ripped and riddled with holes and wandering around with dirty knees and feet. My pockets were full of pesos cent coins which I doled out to these photogenic little ones as a thank-you for me taking their picture. I'd travelled for miles, walked and climbed until my feet ached, took primitive showers throwing water from a tin over myself as well as washing in mountain streams. I'd seen waterfalls a plenty, mountain cave burial sites (ancient stone sarcophagi as well as the hanging coffins), volcanic gasses venting from the crater of Mount Pinatubo, colonial architecture, indigenous peoples and picture postcard, lush, green rice terraces carved by their hundreds into the tranquil Cordilleran mountains. I'd even seen a fiesta, a very traditional Philippine festival and way of affirming life and of celebrating family and food. I had been totally wrapped up in a carnival spirit and danced and partied with locals in the street.

In the Philippines, I hungered for adventure, I yearned for excitement. I was reaching out for something totally new and in this archipelagic, ring of fire country I sought and found a completely immersive cultural experience. I'd walked through doors as a stranger, but was always welcomed like a long-lost friend. I'd shared food and drink with locals as if I was bonded like one of their own. My gratitude to the wonderful, friendly Filipino people who showed me such kindness and gave me such an amazing experience can be summed up as follows: Maraming salamat po. Mabuhay! Thank you very much. Live!

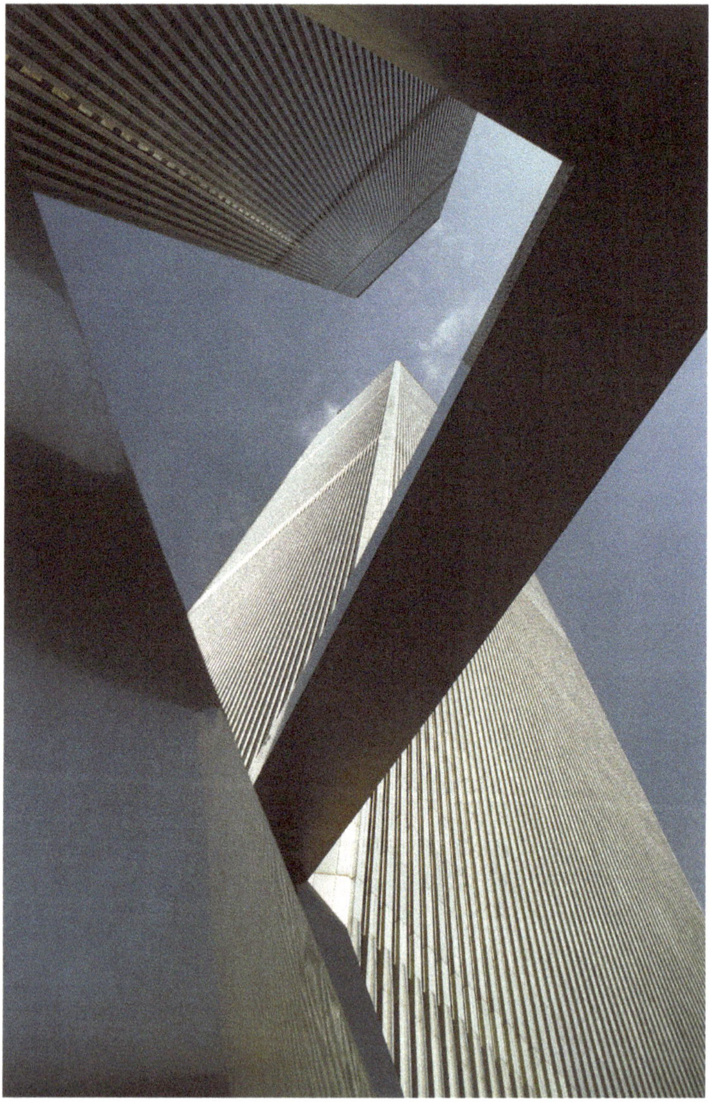

The 1973 World Trade Centre Twin Towers seen here in July 1986, prior to my Trek America holiday with my best man, Aly Baines.

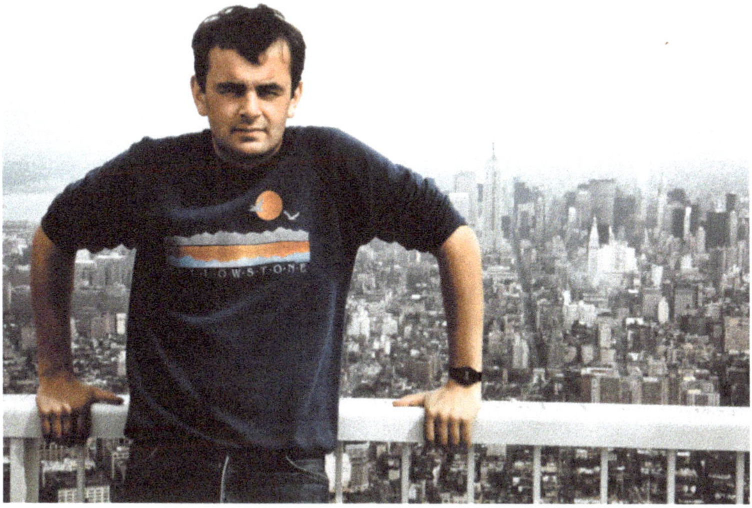

On the north World Trade Centre Tower looking towards
the Empire State Building, New York, July 1986.
Photograph by Alistair E.P. Baines

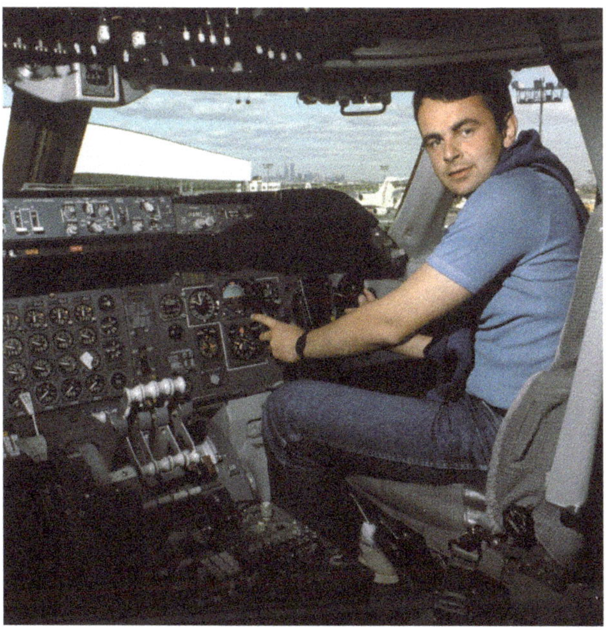

At the controls of a 747 Jumbo Jet, JFK International Airport, New York, USA, prior to my Trek America holiday with Aly Baines, July 1986. Photograph by Alistair E. P. Baines.

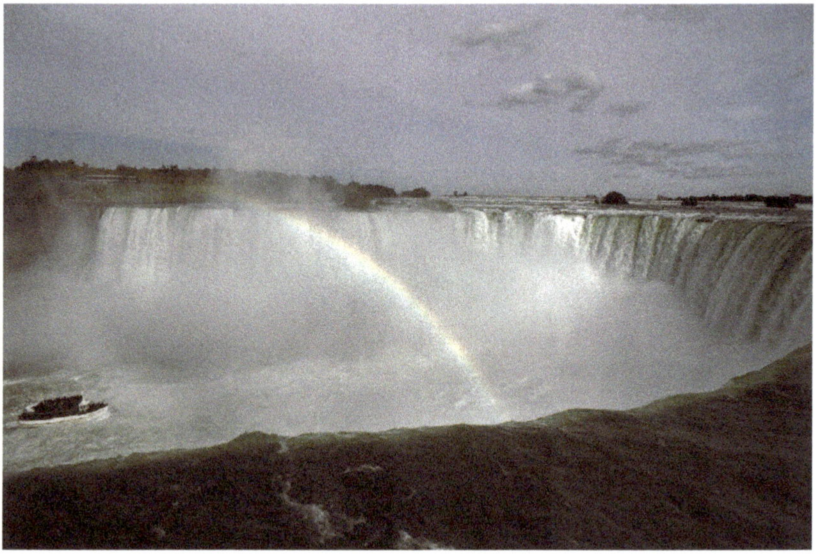

Maid of the Mist boat, Niagara Falls. Taken from the Ontario, Canada side during my Trek America holiday with Aly Baines, July 1986.

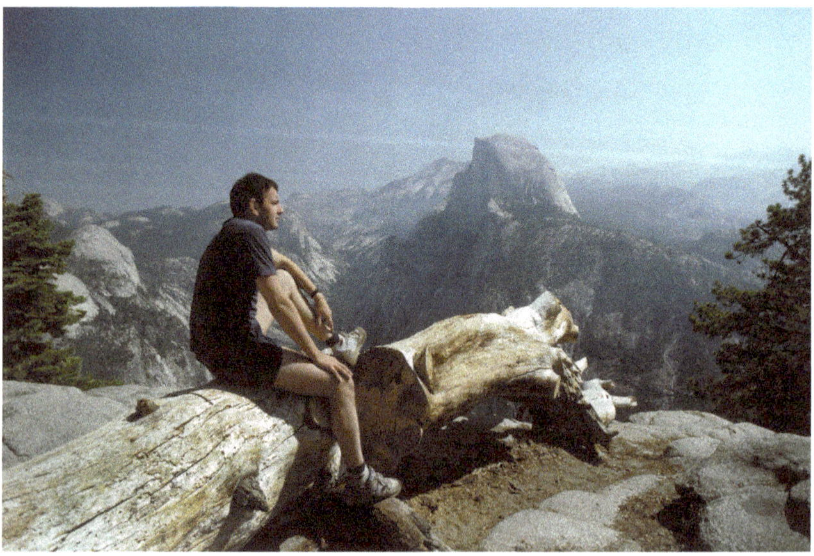

Admiring the view across to Half Dome, Yosemite National Park, California, USA, July 1986. Photograph by Alistair E. P. Baines.

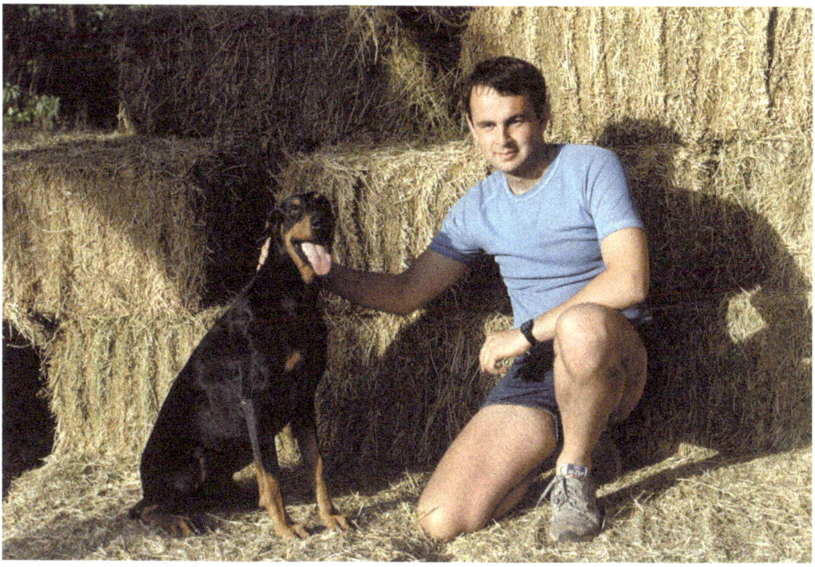

With a Doberman Pinscher, Ventura County, California, USA following the Trek America holiday, July 1986. Photograph by Alistair E. P. Baines.

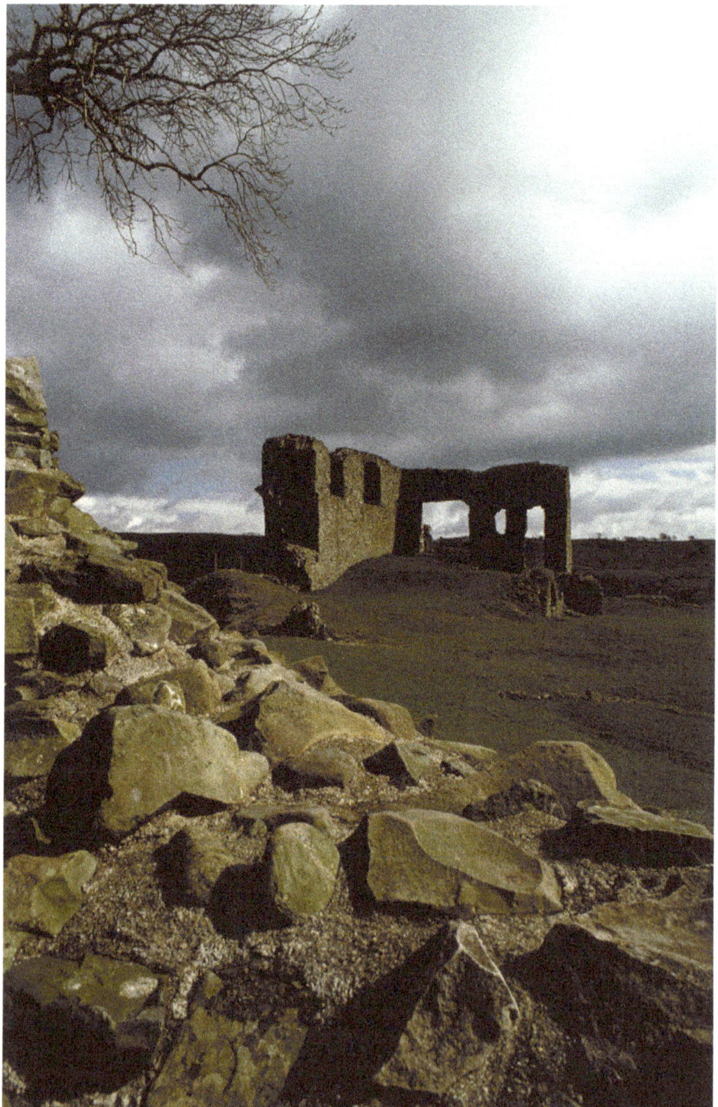

Kendal Castle 1985, one of many images for my first book, 'Historic Lakeland' published by Ian Allan in 1989.

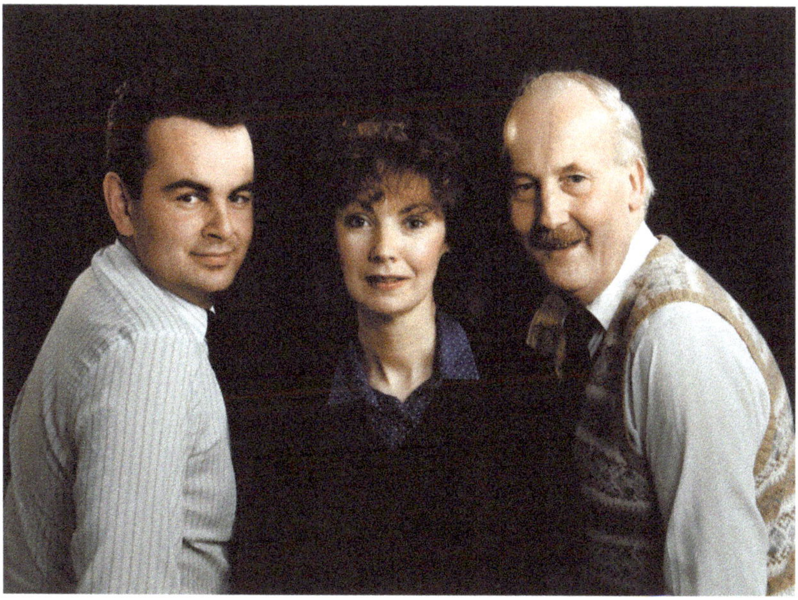

Me with colleagues Jean Wylie and Ian Gordon Sellars at John F White Studios, Catford, London SE6, December 1987.

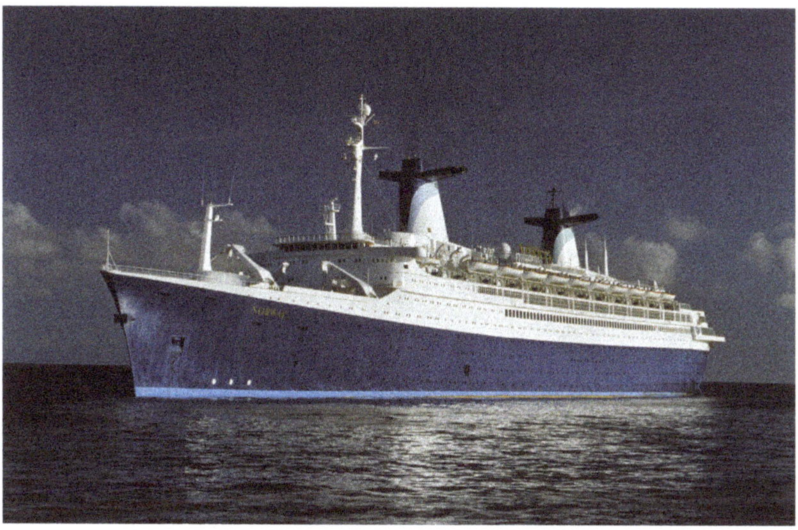

Norwegian Cruise Lines' SS Norway, constructed as 'The France' in 1960, was once the world's longest cruise liner at 1,035 feet and with a gross tonnage of 70,202. Seen here in 1988.

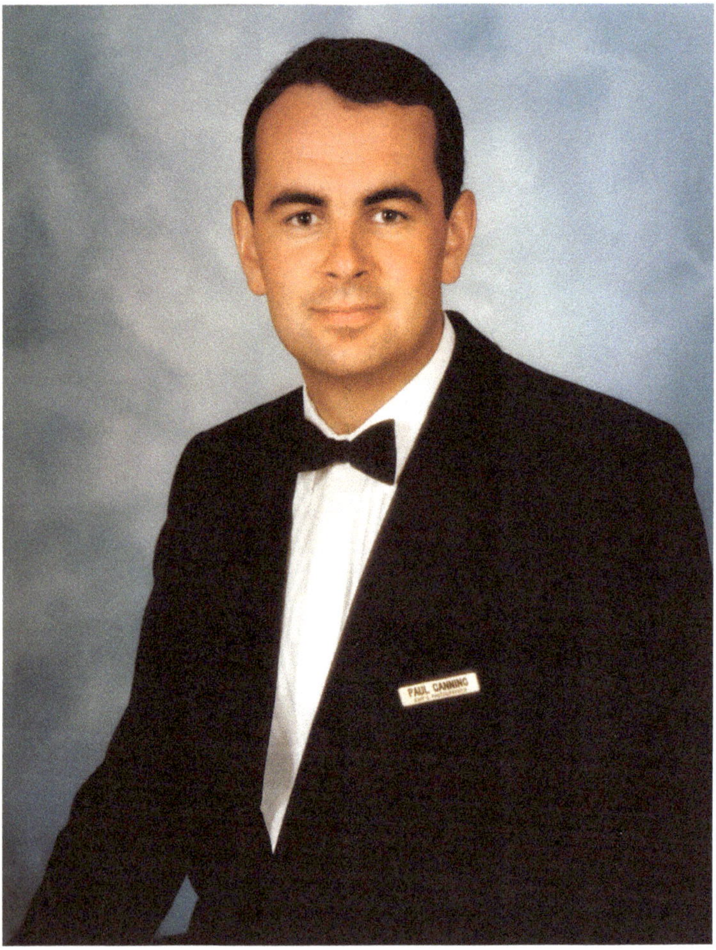

On one of many formal nights aboard the SS Norway, Caribbean, March 1988.

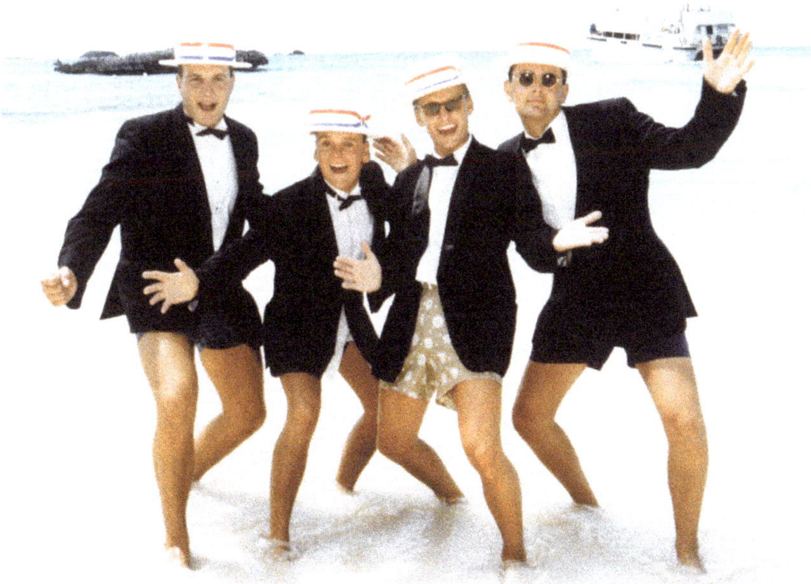

Doug, Granners, Alan & Me as NCL's SS Norway ship's photographers following 'Beach' smudge, Great Stirrup Cay, Bahamas, February 1988.

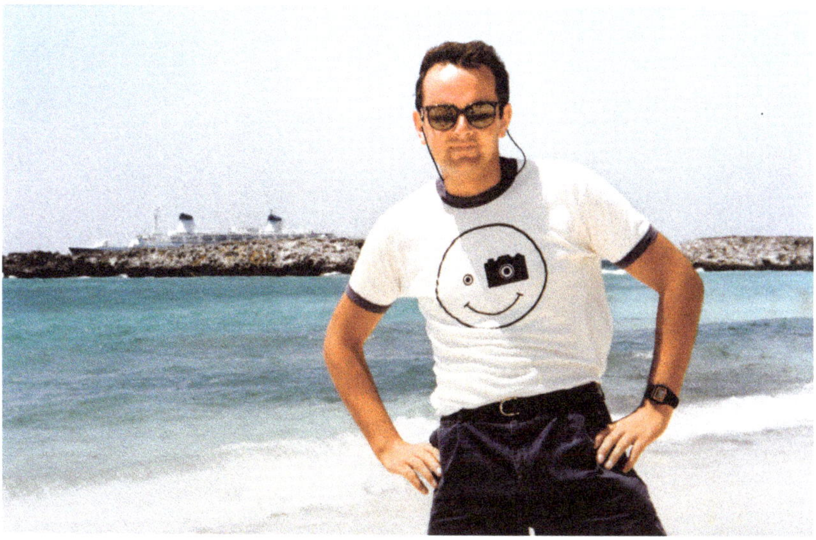

Ever the cruise ship photographer, in 'beach' smudging attire, with the SS Norway in the background, Bahamas, April 1988.

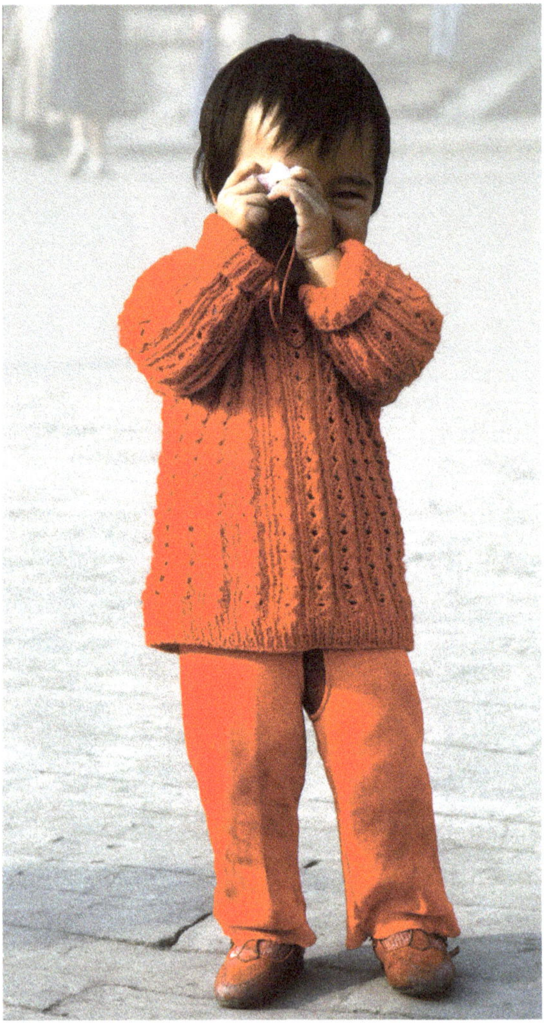

Chinese Kid with Toy Camera, Forbidden City, Beijing, China, October 1988.
Taken whilst Chief Photographer on board the MS Ocean Pearl.

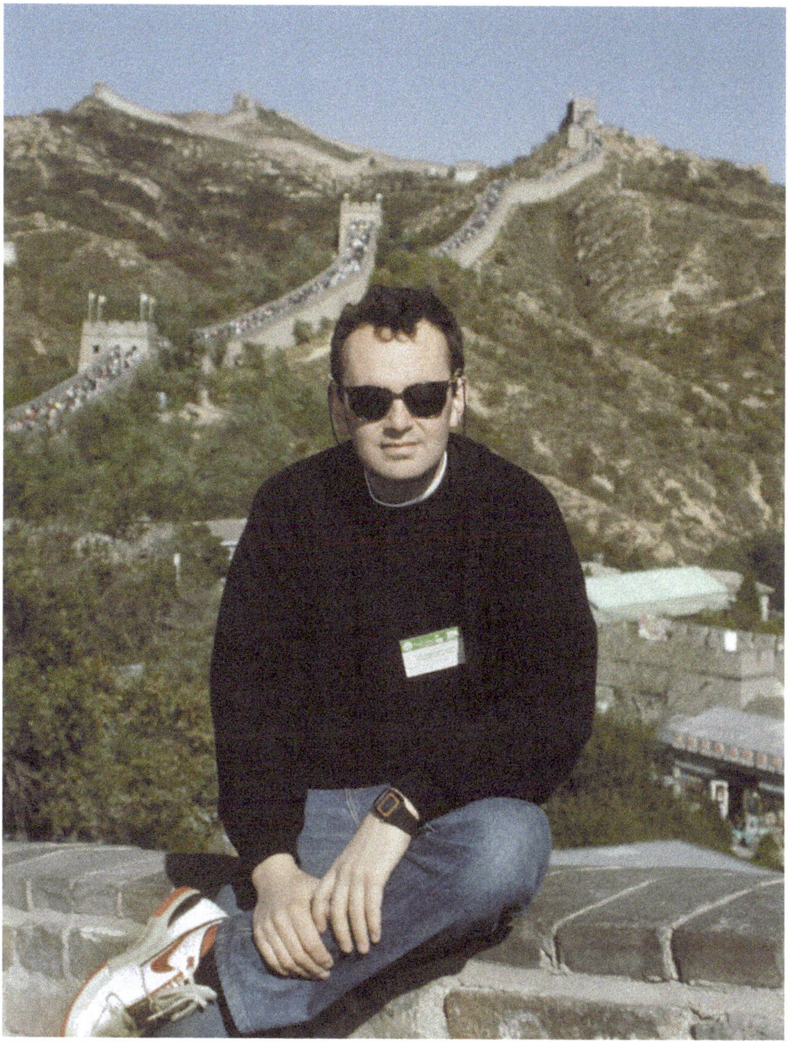

Sitting on the Badaling section of the Great Wall of China, October 1988.

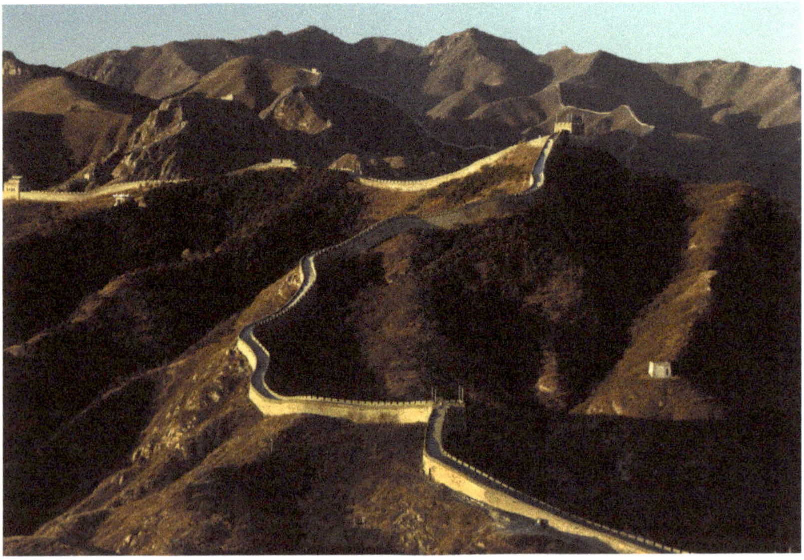

The Great Wall of China at Badaling, a truly awesome and inspiring sight, November 1988. Taken whilst cruising the Far East on board the MS Ocean Pearl.

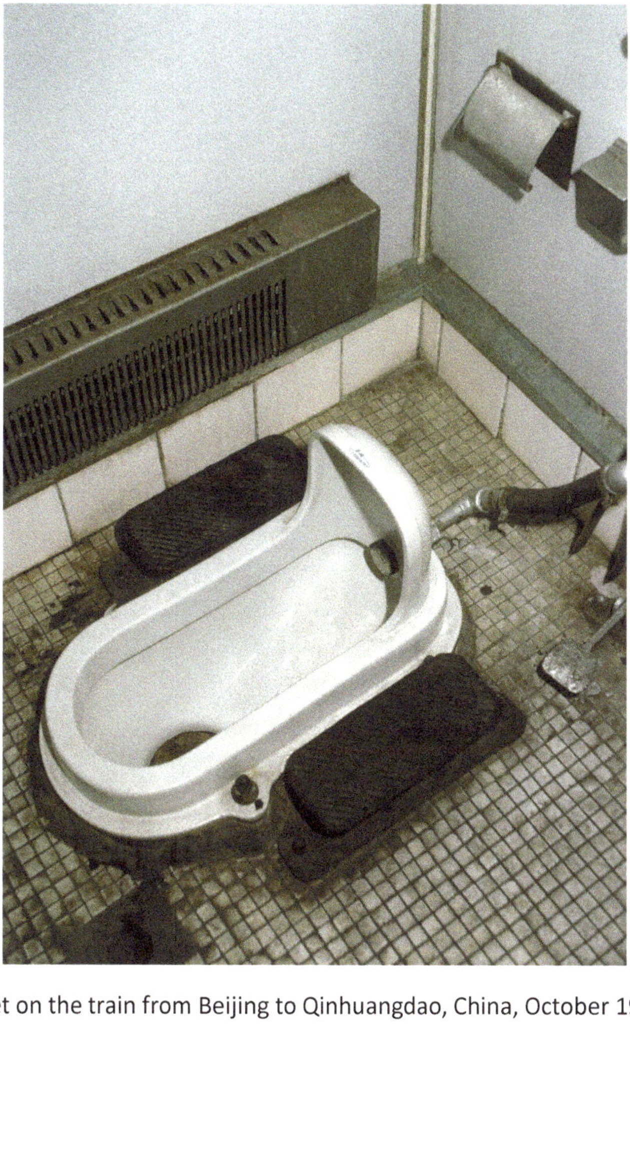

Toilet on the train from Beijing to Qinhuangdao, China, October 1988.

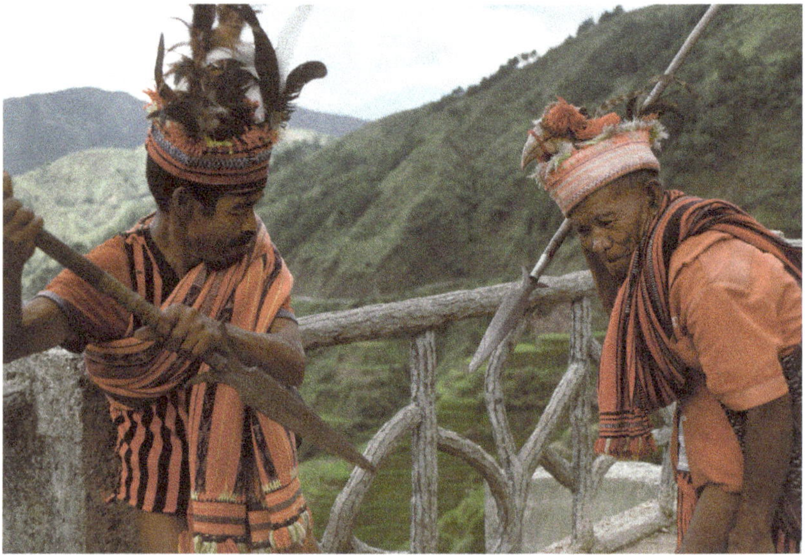

Ifugao elders putting on a display just for me, Banaue Rice Terraces, Cordillera Region, Northern Philippines, May 1989.

PART 3

Settling Down: The Metropolitan Police Forensic Photography Years

CHAPTER 8

Forensic photographer, Metropolitan Police Service, London

Landing the Dream Job and Settling Down

The Early 1990's

On 15th April 1989 during the FA semi-cup final between Liverpool and Nottingham Forest, 96 football supporters were crushed to death and hundreds more were injured when an influx of spectators led to an overcrowding and then a fatal crush in the central standing only pens at Sheffield's Hillsborough Stadium. On the back of this dreadful news my bittersweet return to the UK the following month via California, having just toured the Caribbean and the Philippines, was made infinitely more bearable with the publication of 'Historic Lakeland', which adorned the shelves of major bookshops up and down the country from virtually the moment I stepped back on English soil.

Seeing hundreds of hours of hard work come to fruition in a published book was a thrilling and very memorable experience. Mum, who accompanied me on many 'book seeking' tours (are they or aren't they stocking it – if not why the hell not?) in Lancashire and Cumbria was especially pleased. I'll always remember how proud and excited she looked when she spotted a stack of my books on some shop shelf. She squealed with excitement, like a little girl with a new toy! I had a massive reality check in early summer of '89 once the euphoria of my publication hitting the shelves had worn off and the withdrawal symptoms of missing foreign travelling, and I guess even my ex-Filipino girlfriend, had kicked in. It suddenly dawned on me that whilst all the travelling was very glamorous, it was by no means a secure lifestyle. I also had a growing feeling of wanting to settle down back in England. The thought of living under the same roof as Dad again was as about as exciting as inhaling the fumes from a toilet cubicle full of someone's mass clear out! I needed, nay craved, my independence, so I worked 9-5, Mondays-Fridays as a colour printer for Blackpool based Mowbray Colab. The pay was piss poor, minimum wage and all that, but I viewed it as a 'mither-free' means to an end, a stop-gap, a bit of a breather, just to keep it sweet, whilst scouring the jobs ads pages (in particularly the British Journal of Photography) for a more permanent position.

Tragedy struck in London in the early hours of 20th August 1989, when a party boat, 'Marchioness' carrying 130 people collided with the dredger 'Bowbelle' and quickly sank, with the loss of 51 people - the shocking incident occurring between Cannon Street railway bridge and Southwark Bridge.

Winter beckoned. My mood dampened. It was either freezing cold or chucking it down with rain most days. To cap it all, I was living in a small holiday flat a few miles from work, feeding the electricity meter every hour or so, praying that a good job would come along soon. Money had now become tighter than a duck's arse. I was even using Mum's Peugeot 10 speed to get me to and from Mowbray Colab just to save a quid here and fifty pence there. The contrast between my lucrative, champagne-fuelled cruise ship days and life in the back streets of Blackpool's South Shore couldn't have been greater. I felt at the time that I was just a few steps away from living on a park bench, a fact I was dreaming about, when I was woken from a deep sleep one Sunday morning to the sound of urgent banging on my flat door. Tasting night breath, hair all over the place, feeling groggy as hell, I stumbled towards the door, still managing to open it carefully, only to see the look of shock drain from my two best friends' (Simon and Aly) faces. They turned to one another in relief that I wasn't in fact suffering with a cardiac tamponade. "Thank God you're OK Cans, we thought you were dead!"

I was supposed to be ready and breakfasted an hour beforehand as we were going up to the Lake District fell walking. Mr Reliable here, the guy who's never late, had overslept by an hour and my friends had become concerned for my safety when they got no joy from repeatedly knocking on my door and from phoning "Poolton double eight four seven eight two" (Dad's standard telephone answering voice). Dad told Simon and Aly that he hadn't heard from me, nor did he seem to be in the remotest bit concerned.

Work at the lab was ok. The business was co-owned by 'Big Mike' who could always be found, cigarette in mouth, a gnat's step away from a major coronary, darting around the shop floor with gazelle-like agility, fixing this machine and that. He was a quietly spoken workaholic and I liked and admired him a lot. The other partner was Jeff, a married father, rumoured to be having carnal knowledge with Karen, one of the office staff. Karen was also very nosy with a face on her, who prided herself on knowing everyone's business. Remarking on Mum's Peugeot, she beckoned me over one morning to ask in a broad Lancashire accent "Is that your bike?" I worked alongside 'Mini-Mike', a really sound bloke. This fifty-year-old might have been small in stature, but he was kind, reliable, hard-working and possessed a great sense of humour. Mini-Mike and I would print standing up, side-by side at our respective colour printers, both of which had rear doors that opened up into a big darkroom, to enable printing paper loading and retrieval. I remember on one occasion sneaking into the darkroom, quietly opening up the doors to Mini-Mike's printer and suddenly letting rip with my 'Christie' impersonation. This was a string of quotes based on the late Lord 'Dickie' Attenborough's portrayal in the film '10 Rillington Place', of the notorious war time Notting Hill murderer John Reginald Halliday Christie: "Come in do!", "Now then, now then!", "D'you want to be hung, is that what you want?", "It's a whiff of gas, just like you get at the dentist", "I went to my doctor who prescribed some pills to alleviate the pain" and my invented line to his wife who had sussed out her nefarious husband, 'Well if that's your attitude, don't expect to survive the night!' All I could hear was Mini-Mike chuckling on the other side of his printer. I'd then emerge from the darkness and Mini Mike and I would still be laughing – my shenanigans helped pass the time. However, the weeks soon became months. I turned 26 in September and they'd just started to make Baywatch, the lifeguard television series during 1989. It starred David Hasselhoff and was to run for the next ten years (prior to this, David Hasselhoff's 'Knight Rider' ran from 1982 to 1986). Christmas 1989 came and went with nothing concrete on the job front. We exchanged Christmas cards at work and I inadvertently got into trouble with one of the office girls, a pretty brunette from bonny Scotland. My crime was to omit the word 'love' before signing my name, when I had put 'love' on all my other cards doled out to the rest of the girls. I still remember to this day, a clearly hurt young lady tossing her hair back as she waltzed up to me to give me a piece of her mind, "Och, ya dinny poot na love on my carrrd!" (Ooops!).

Suddenly we'd entered the last decade of the twentieth century, but in January 1990 there was still nothing, jobwise. The following month I was made redundant from Mowbray Colab and faced the unpalatable prospect of moving back to Mum and Dad's house. Looking back, the immortal words of LOTR's King Théoden in the 2002 masterpiece 'Lord of The Rings: The Two Towers' spring to mind. Bernard Hill's Théoden laments from the mountain fortress Hornburg, how utterly alone against Saruman's army of Orcs the 'Rohirrim' stand (Middle Earth's Rohan people) just before the Battle of Helm's Deep:

"Where now are the horse and the rider?
Where is the horn that was blowing?
They have past like rain on the mountain, like a wind in the meadow;
The days have gone down in the west, behind the hills into shadow.
How did it come to this?"

I felt similarly down, desperate and completely isolated. And at that moment, a single Orc could have taken me, never mind ten thousand of the ugly bastards! But yet, like Théoden, I was to rally. Odds and sods of photography freelance work came my way and coupled with work for Dad doing the usual gardening and other shitty jobs brought the sheckles in. In March, two adverts caught my eye within the pages of the unemployed photog's lifeline, the British Journal of Photography. 'Trainee Scenes of Crime Officer (SOCO) with Lancashire Constabulary' and 'Forensic Photographer with the Metropolitan Police Service in London'. I applied for both positions, but ensured that my CV was up to date first. I didn't really fancy working in London again. It had been more than two years since leaving White's Studios in 'SE6' and I had no burning desire to return to the 'old smoke' so soon. But then beggars can't be choosers and by my own admission, both vacancies seemed like great career opportunities. Easter 1990 saw me working at Blackpool's 'Coral Island', printing and selling photo t-shirts – again, this was a means to an end – the money came in and that's all that mattered. I'd just finished up on bank holiday Monday, printing my last cheesy t-shirt, when the business owner Diamuid Blaney, a short, rotund, middle-aged Irishman from County Wicklow, paid me my wages and asked me whether I could work regular shifts, starting the following week and for the entire summer holiday season. Smudging on a cruise ship in the Caribbean is one thing, but flogging cheap t-shirts to some unsavoury tourists in Blackpool was quite another. Outwardly, I smiled and told Diamuid that I'd let him know in the morning.

Well that very next morning, an official looking letter addressed to me and date stamped with the Metropolitan Police Service Crest, dropped through the letterbox and I soon learned that I'd been given an interview. I remember not being overly excited, as I hankered after the Lancashire Constabulary position. However, there was still no news on that front. Rightly or wrongly I gave Diamuid the 'heave ho', as I couldn't stomach printing another photo t-shirt and opted instead to do jobs for Dad, whilst actively looking for a permanent position. The Met Police I learned, employed scores of professional photographers who attended crime scenes, undertook surveillance and public order duties, photographed fatal road traffic accidents, victims of crime, stolen property and public relations. In fact, without pigeon-holing crime into different categories, the variety of work completely took me aback.

So now as I sat in front of a 2-man interview panel on the first floor of what to me appeared like a collection of unassuming, rust coloured, pre-fabricated buildings that constituted 'MPS SO3 (2) Photographic Branch', I was suddenly turned on to the idea of becoming a Met Police forensic photographer. In fact, I was already excited at the prospect of working in the Met during an informative guided tour by head of the colour printing department, Principle Photographer the late Keith Clarke – a kind and very friendly man. Photographic Branch had a reception and admin office on the ground floor, which led through to an open plan colour printing and album making room. Photographic stores were also located here and conveniently positioned close to the loading bay. The ground floor also housed Audio Visual (AV) that produced slides for inclusion in presentations, Video Production, who made high quality training films for the MPS, Operational Video Services, who undertook video at serious crime scenes and video film identification of suspects and prisoners. The fingerprint / black and white printing area and 'C41' and minilab processing were also here. There was a small cinema, small portrait studio and larger drive-in studio also on the same floor. The first floor housed the canteen, laboratory, offices and the Head of Photography's office. The more I saw, the more I yearned to be a part of this operation. To say that I was impressed was an understatement.

Keith's guided tour lasted about twenty minutes, then came the interview.

I was ushered into a modest sized meeting room, the walls of which, were adorned with PR crime related images. Two middle aged men, both Chief Photographer grades, stood up and offered their hands – Keith Maughan and Ernie Whatmore. Having got through the feeling of 'entering the Headmaster's study for six of the best', I shook hands warmly and sat down. I felt instantly at home. Keith and Ernie were very friendly and seemed interested in what I had to say. When I was asked to outline my career and relevant experience to date, I caught them exchanging subtle nods of approval. I thought the interview was going well and both my interviewers seemed to like my portfolio, which comprised commercial, industrial, portraiture and landscape work. Then I took out a mint copy of Historic Lakeland and handed it to both men. The image of Keith and Ernie thumbing through my first book is so memorable, they seemed to be impressed! Ernie peered over his glasses and said with a grin "Took you a long time, this?", to which I replied, "many months".

And that was that, the interview process was concluded, we shook hands and I thanked Keith and Ernie for their time. I left Met Police Photographic HQ and wandered back to the Elephant and Castle tube station, my head in a complete daze. I had come to London on a bit of a whim, not really hankering after working in the Met and if the truth be known, not overly enthusiastic at all about the prospect of seeing dead bodies, blood, guts and gore almost on a daily basis - a question that Keith had put to me at interview, "How do you think you'll handle seeing the death and destruction side of what we do?" I'd obviously thought about this pre-interview, but still gave a bit of a weak answer. "I think I'll be fine – it'll just take a bit of getting used to". Now, though, as I made my way back to the Elephant, I so wanted this job, to the extent that the CSI vacancy with Lancashire Constabulary almost fell by the wayside. A week later, a white envelope dropped through the letterbox at 27 Victoria Road and I pounced on it, having spied the MPS crest stamped on the front. I raced up to my bedroom and carefully tore open the letter, my heart pounding.

"Dear Mr. Canning, We are pleased to inform you…". Yes, yes, YES! I'd done it, I was in. Forensic Photographer, Metropolitan Police Service was in the bag. I was euphoric. I could now see a career path, prospects, promotion, satisfaction, overtime, staff benefits and all that went with an exciting new job. My start date was to be 18th

June 1990 and my accommodation, until I could find my own place, was to be the heavily subsidised police section house above Kensington Police Station, situated at the top end of the Earls Court Road and close to the junction with Kensington High Street. My journey to London on 16th June signified me leaving home for good and at long last escaping the talons of my evil father's grasp! I still hadn't heard from Lancashire Constabulary, but was eventually offered an interview, which of course I gracefully turned down. Just less than two and a half years after leaving White's Studio in Catford bound for a life on the ocean wave, I was back working in London for what would pan out to be just over fourteen quality years of amazing crime scene, teaching and life experience.

I arrived at Kensington section house with all my worldly goods – a large suitcase and a rucksack - to be greeted by the section house warden, Jack, a very friendly ex- army man approaching retirement. You'd often find a couple of off duty police officers, mugs of coffee in hand, sitting in Jack's office listening to him regaling some of his army day howlers. "Who's ya dodgy character, mate?", was this loveable cockney's catchphrase. Jack was always immaculately turned out. From his close-cropped hair and the press of his short-sleeved, white shirt to the mirror shine on his black Doc Martin shoes, the army had indeed left its mark. There were other wardens of course, some more friendly than others, but I had a soft spot for Jack and I spent quality time in his company – more often than not, sobering up with a coffee or two after a night on the lash, or following some nurse's party where I had somehow failed to score, or a West End art dealer's mind-blowingly uninteresting soiree – Christ knows why I was there?! Wherever I'd been, I inevitably ended up in Jack's office solving the problems of the world at some ungodly hour. So Jack was now going over section house rules with me. Following this, he showed me to my new home, room 312 up on the third floor of a five-storey, all male, police officer and police civilian accommodation block.

My room comprised a single bed, wardrobe and sink. The window looked out across Earls Court Road to Abingdon Villas. Having unpacked my case and backpack, I finished chatting to some of the guys on either side of me. Nick, a very jovial six foot five, solidly built copper and Vic, an equally friendly, Northern Irishman who I swear was about half of Nick's height. Nick's penchant for the ladies translated into an almost nightly cacophony of rhythmical headboard banging and bed spring creaking. Vic, by contrast, had a long-term girlfriend back home over the water and kept his sex life private. Vic was a warm, kind and generous man – he leant me his car on at least one occasion. How many people do that for goodness sake? Vic transferred to the Royal Ulster Constabulary after a few months (now 'The Police Service of Northern Ireland' having been reformed and renamed in 2001) and I sadly lost contact with him. I decided to go for a long walk in the warm London sunshine, first through Holland Park and then along Kensington High Street, taking in the shops, tube station and onwards along the A315 to the Royal Albert Hall – my new stomping ground!

I don't remember much about my first day as a probationary unestablished forensic photographer, save for meeting some of the experienced photographers and then in the ensuing weeks, the rest of my intake,10 staff, all new starters like me. As the new kids on the block we became pretty good friends, getting to know each other over numerous social events after work. I became particularly good friends with Nancy and Pete, meeting before work at 'Danny's Castle' at the 'Elephant' for a takeaway tea. Pete was destined years later to become my line manager at the Crime Academy Forensic Faculty. The new intake was split up and each of us undertook a two-week stint in the colour room, the black and white room, audio visual (AV), studio and video production which would give us an overview of each area. At the end of each two-week stint, we simply rotated and joined another team. Once we'd completed all the two-week stints, we were each allocated an internal department (either the colour room or fingerprint room) where we'd be based for quite a few months.

I joined the colour room and was thrown together with Pete, this young, friendly, happy-go-lucky guy, who I liked immediately mainly because he was my complete opposite – quite loud, outspoken, an ideas man and in terms of learning style, an activist. The department had six large Polielettronica (affectionately known as a 'Polly') automatic feed colour printers, four of which were allocated to crime scene photographers. After possibly a week out and about in London, photographers would come into Amelia Street to cut up and sort their processed colour negatives and sit at a Polly, printing a whole wodge of images. Italian manufactured, the Polly was a good workhorse and it was on the Pollies that Pete and I started working in earnest.

It transpired that there was a massive backlog of negatives that needed to be printed from Operation Carnaby, an ongoing police criminal investigation into what was described at the time in London as 'the worst riots seen in this city for a century'. One hundred and thirteen people were injured, of whom forty-five were police officers. Twenty police horses also sustained injuries. Disorder and chaos erupted late afternoon on Saturday 31st March 1990 during the public demonstration (one of many in British towns and cities) against the then Prime Minister Margaret Thatcher's hugely unpopular Poll Tax Policy. People were incensed about the poll tax because it was a levy on individuals and didn't take account of means. What had started from Kennington Park as a circa 200,000 strong relatively peaceful march to Whitehall, descended into mayhem with violent clashes between police, protesters and activists, followed by rampaging and looting in the West End, that continued until the early hours of the next morning. It had kicked off big time with protesters throwing bricks, cans, wood and stones. This precipitated some 500 arrests for public order offences. The anti-Poll Tax demonstrations up and down Britain, which culminated in the London demo and subsequent disorder, was a major contributing factor to Mrs Thatcher's downfall in November 1990. Pete's enthusiasm for wanting to get stuck into printing the Operation Carnaby pictures was infectious. We were young mavericks back then, embarking on an exciting new career and like Pete and the rest of the newbies, I just wanted to kick arse too! We soon got to grips with the Pollies and what followed was hours and days of solid colour printing and of course weekend overtime a plenty, which we grabbed with both hands!

After a few months in the colour room under the late Principal Photographer Keith Clark, I was moved into the black and white room under Principal Photographer Tony Rider. Here I was involved in photographing finger marks on myriad items of property using a variety of light sources, marks on ninhydrin-treated documents and lifted marks from crime scenes. I also undertook black and white film processing and printing using different enlargers. I feel indebted to Graham Chilton, who taught me everything I needed to know during a very enjoyable few months with the black and white team. At work Graham was quiet and unassuming, but in the pub, he could drink the best of us under the table. Apparently, Graham's claim to fame was the longest projectile vomit ever recorded in the history of Met Police Photographic! Graham was a gentle soul, who like the rest of us listened to the politics and gossip, but unlike the rest of us, never seemed to get phased by any of it. You'd never hear a bad word about Graham and we all loved him. So it was with great shock and sadness that I learned of his death in late February 2017. One of life's nice guys – a friendly, approachable and good-humoured colleague, who you could always turn to and rely upon absolutely. Graham is much missed. R.I.P. Graham Chilton.

Then by the autumn of 1990 it was back to the colour room again. All this internal training was necessary to gear us up for going out on scenes of crime. I used to think cruise ship photographers were the kings of wind ups until I joined Met Police Photographic. Some of the pranks erred on the cruel side, but most were plain outrageous. I think I'd been in the colour room for barely 2 days, when one of the more experienced photographers thrust a box under my nose, full of 10x8 inch colour prints. This was the famous 'gory box' shown to all initiates as an unofficial test to see whether we'd have the stomach for crime scene work. The box left nothing to the imagination – decapitations, heads torn apart by shotgun blast, slit throats, twisted limbs, mutilated and squashed bodies, blown up corpses, blood and brains, shit and gore, car crashes, post mortems, people shot, knifed, punched, glassed, hanged, run over by trains – every conceivable, high shock value image. You name it, the gory box had it. And look through it I did, because I had to. It was an unwritten prerequisite. It was part of my MPS baptism. It was what I was training to do. If I was going to puke, piss or shit myself, now was the time to do it. Better now than faint onto a bloodied body, or contaminate a scene by being sick all over it. I felt that the established photographers derived pleasure from seeing our reactions to the contents of the gory box, a hurdle which of course they all had to overcome.

I almost fell for one particular wind up when I took a call from the office of the then head of the anti-terrorist branch, the late Commander George Churchill-Coleman. A very irate 'bag man' was demanding to know why his Guv'nor hadn't received some urgent prints – somehow Commander Churchill-Coleman had been given my name? I shuddered when I heard the words "Commander Churchill-Coleman's going apeshit...!" I would be held fully responsible, no, I would lose my job if the requested photographs were not at NSY (New Scotland Yard / former Metropolitan Police Service Headquarters located at 10 Broadway, in Victoria, SW1) and in the Commander's hands within the hour! "Yes, sir, I'll see to it immediately, sir", I replied with more than a tremble in my voice. I was still holding the phone receiver when the line went dead and I was abruptly cut off.

I felt my whole world had suddenly collapsed. I'd only been in post a few months and now I was being told that I could lose my job.

Shit and derision. I felt like a sack of horse shit, the whole weight of the world crushing my twenty-six-year-old frame. But as I replaced the phone on the handset, I was aware of movement in my peripheral vision and glanced over to my left. I just caught sight of Chris Batt, keen horseman, expert wedding photographer and also one of the more experienced forensic photographers, moving quickly behind one of the Pollies at the back of the colour room...with a grin on his face. The penny dropped immediately as I raced to the other end of the colour room. "You bastard!" I said to Chris. Oh and what was this? The entire colour team and fingerprint team hiding up there as well! We all cracked up laughing. Fair dues. Good wind-up. However, I never did ask Chris how long he was going to leave it until he put me out of my misery by revealing the prank. I was to get my answer the following week when ginger-haired Rob, a newbie like me, picked up another urgent 'call', wanted by M'lud himself! Rob was required immediately to give evidence in number one court at the Old Bailey, London's Central Criminal Court and the most famous court in the world! "What's wrong Rob, you look like one of these dead bodies?" I asked, showing him one of the prints on my Polly. Rob could barely answer as mysteriously and almost instantaneously a 'driver' materialised saying that he had come to collect a Rob Naylor, wanted at the Central Criminal Court without delay. Poor Rob didn't have a clue about the prints that were required, he had no notes, no briefing, had never seen the inside of a pretend court, never mind the most formidable legal surroundings on the planet and here the poor soul was about to be whisked off for a public interrogation at the personal request of an eminent crown court judge! I do believe they drove Rob to the entrance of the Old Bailey, before finally coming clean. Again, bastards, but ace wind-up!

Other pranks included periodic lunchtime water fights – colour room versus the black and white team / fingerprint room – a full on, high powered water pistol war, at the end of which, all the floors would be mopped and dried before the Guvnors had taken their last bite of Pizza or had downed their final cup of tea at Mari's on the Wally (Walworth) Road. There were regular dunkings in the colour room's high-powered chemical shower, fellow photographers would scare you shitless by hiding out in the darkrooms - all they needed to do was to put a hand on your shoulder and you'd leap ten feet in the air. God forbid if you were having a birthday bash, you could end up with your pubes shaved lying on a pool table, blind-folded, driven miles out of town and stripped bollock naked and plasti-cuffed to a lamp post on a motorway fly-over! And so it went on, but it was all (relatively) harmless, laddish fun and I look back with fondness at the great camaraderie we all had then.

A short stint in the black and white room (later to become the Evidence Recovery Unit or ERU) followed, during which time I photographed hundreds of 'nins' (ninhydrin treated documents), finger marks on property, shoe marks and lifted marks on acetate ('lifts'). If I wasn't photographing, then I was processing and printing in the dark room. Larry Miles and Neil Banks, two experienced Senior Photographers, ran the black and white room on a day to day basis. I didn't warm to Larry at all. This stocky, dark-haired guy was a few years my senior and tended to be quite opinionated. Neil, in contrast, must have been at least 6 feet two, with curly blonde hair and possessed a wicked sense of humour. I liked him from day one. King of the wind ups – if there was even the remotest whiff of a prank going down, Neil would be there. It was towards the end of my time in the black and white room that Larry took me to one side for a private word. It was late November 1990 and Larry had got wind of some 'hot off the press' gossip that had come directly from the first floor. From the recent intake, Chief Photographers Ernie and Keith were apparently looking to promote me first!

This, if rumour control was to be believed, was exciting news indeed. After all, this is what I'd joined for – to be out and about all over London photographing scenes of crime, victims of crime, road traffic accidents and perhaps with a few prisoners and PR jobs thrown into the mix as well. My social life was excellent, surpassed only by my cruise ship days and consisted of a seemingly endless round of parties and after work piss-ups. But I hankered after more. I realised that this wasn't the be all and end all of life. I had secured not just any old job, but one with prospects, promotion possibilities, yearly salary rise, the chance to earn more money through overtime and on-call duties – but there was something missing, or rather, someone. A partner and a wife, someone who I could share life with. So I set out to look for not just a girlfriend, but a girlfriend who was wife material. The world cup summer of 1990 had focused on me settling in, acclimatising and learning the internal side of crime scene photography, but during the autumn it was time to look for a girlfriend. Going to rowdy parties wasn't really conducive to meeting someone special, so I enlisted the help of my CID friend, Paul, who with a wave of his police warrant card could gain us entry into some of Kensington's more refined party locations. I fondly remember Paul and I, bottles of Corona in hand, critiquing this young lady and that and Paul casting his eye over this particular Saturday night's target rich environment. I danced and dated a few girls, from Tara and Lucinda to Ophelia and Arabella, they were all very attractive and sweet, but so 'frightfully, frightfully champers Yar' and alas, we really didn't have anything in common. I quickly despaired as this strategy wasn't working either. So, it was back to the drawing board, or rather, the inevitable post-mortem of the night's events with policeman Paul, the two of us sitting on the roof of Kensington Police station, you know – care free with our legs dangling over the edge, enjoying a cheeky beer and half a juicy melon!

Shortly after Arabella 'Oh gosh darling' (such a shame, because I really liked her) was consigned to history and on one of my many evening walks in Kensington, I came across a smart office frontage, not a few streets away from my digs at Kensington Police Station section house. When I looked up to read the sign above the door, my heart started to race – 'Dateline'. On impulse, I went inside and was greeted by a young, well-dressed, pretty, brunette, who I deduced was a few years my junior. Freya was the office manager and after a brief chat, she gave me some printed literature and I left my contact details, which back in 1990, comprised an address only. Mobile phones of the half brick variety were fashionable for the affluent but cost prohibitive for the likes of l'il ol' me and there was no internet or email. I thought I might ask Freya out, but then suddenly I noticed a flash, a sparkle of something on her left hand catching the light – a diamond engagement ring. I tried not to let my disappointment show, but Freya caught me looking and tossed me a smile. I was instantly embarrassed as she seemed to read my thoughts. I thanked Freya for her time and said that I would get back in contact once I'd read through the literature that she'd given to me. Back in my room, I tuned out the noise of traffic and the police sirens on the Earls Court Road below and read with interest the Dateline literature. Today of course, online dating is commonplace, but back in 1990 it wasn't! You set out your 'WLTM' - likes, dislikes and preferences – blondes, brunettes, or both, height range, age range, hobbies etc. and together with your fee, entitled you to so many compatible girls' contact details. I think I was given six names and I had to hand write similar letters to all six. After two weeks I'd heard nothing and it was November, with winter virtually upon us, so I popped back in to Dateline and a member of Freya's team generated another six girl's names from their computer database. So, undeterred, I wrote another half dozen letters and hoped I'd at least get a response second time around, which to my delight, I did about a week later. I received 2 letters on the same day. The first was from Lynsey, who described herself as 5' 4", long dark brown hair, brown eyes, slim build, worked in PR and was a keen horsewoman, hockey player, lover of the outdoors and socialite. Lynsey said she'd love to meet up, but was in Liverpool for another week on business. Then I read the second letter from Wendy was also 5' 4", with short brown hair and blue eyes, enjoyed nights out as well as cosy nights in and like me, loved the outdoors. She was currently Office Manager at Regus Business Centre in Trafalgar Square. I was also interested to read that Wendy had grown up in Cornwall, a county that I'd heard so much about, but had never visited. We arranged to meet up at Muswells on the Strand, opposite Charing Cross Station for a 'no strings attached date' as I had put in my letter, after work one Friday evening.

That infamous Friday evening, 29th November 1990, I pitched up at Muswell's characteristically early having dressed quite smartly in grey trousers, black shoes and white shirt and I would be carrying my trademark black briefcase. Trendy, unfortunately, I was not. As was pointed out later, I had committed the cardinal sin of wearing white socks with black shoes! So there I was, checking my watch every ten seconds in characteristic Canning style, heartbeat quickening as the meeting time approached, waiting and wondering with slightly nervous anticipation and praying that my date didn't have a face like a camel's bum / bag of spanners combo with a personality to match! For this was high risk. This wasn't just a date, it was a blind date. Nothing prepared me for the moment when Wendy arrived. Being ever the gentleman, I shook hands and my date smiled warmly as we went down into the basement bar and ordered some drinks. Wendy was stunningly attractive, so much so, that I quickly forgot my nerves and settled easily into conversation and I couldn't take my eyes off her. By the end of the evening, we had both talked so much, we had forgotten to eat. I figured that if Wendy hadn't enjoyed her date, she would have made her excuses and left early. But it was late and after a kiss on the cheek, I had come away securing that vital and telling second date – same place, same time, the following Friday, for a meal. I couldn't wait for our second date, which went even better than our first one.

After that we became an item in breakneck time. Christmas 1990 was spent with our respective families in Lancashire and Cornwall, but Wendy and I brought 1991 in together in London. It was a magical time. In early February, Wendy took me to Cornwall to meet her delightful parents, Val and Laurie, during an idyllic mini break at their Wadebridge sanctuary, Pennard Cottage. We returned in March and on a cold, windswept, late afternoon on 23rd of that month, I proposed to Wendy overlooking the magical sea stack vista that is Bedruthen Steps. Fortunately, and to my relief Wendy said 'yes' immediately. However, my whole plan was close to being kiboshed because it was blowing a mini hooley on the cliffs and Wendy was cold. Next, being a traditional sort of fellow, I sought Wendy's father's permission for her hand in marriage, comically following him around the house for ages in a bid to get him on his own. When eventually I asked the great man's permission for his daughter's hand, finally confronting him in his workshop, I wagered for a moment that Laurie was going to give me a king sized bollocking. He looked down at the ground nodding, as I recall so vividly, as if surveying the sawdust and offcuts disapprovingly that adorned his ample mancave. When Laurie raised his head, pushing his glasses back into position on the bridge of his nose, he looked at me straight in the eye with those intelligent and wise eyes, twinkling and with a wry smile, said 'yes' with little or no hesitation. I could have hugged him in addition to shaking his hand. Then we left the workshop and went into the kitchen, where Val was preparing a roast dinner and Laurie promptly declared that "Paul has decided to make an honest woman of Wendy". All I remember is Val shrieking with delight in what was an all-embracing buoyant atmosphere and then Wendy's brother, Simon, swiftly went out to buy a bottle of champagne to celebrate.

Then it was off to a local jeweller to purchase the engagement ring. An ornate, gold affair with an amethyst stone (Wendy's birth stone), which my fiancée wore with a plaster until it could be altered, as the chosen ring was too big! The engagement was to be for eighteen months and our very small wedding at St. Breock Church, Wadebridge, was planned for 12th September 1992, the day before my 29th birthday. Our courting and engagement days were a truly magical time. We were both very heady with excitement and I guess from that first date at Muswells, I knew that Wendy would be my 'Mrs'. One look at my ironing skills, slowly and painstakingly smoothing out every micro crease and Wendy insisted that she take over all my ironing, including ironing my Grandma's pink sheets! I have very fond memories of looking out over the Earls Court Road to what was Henry J Beans, (a Sunday morning breakfast favourite haunt) and seeing my future wife park up her metallic blue Mini Mayfair, emerging with a wardrobe full of ironed shirts and trousers – looking for all the world like she ran a 'Pressed to Impress' business. Then there were the romantic walks through Central London's main parks, also Holland Park and along Ken High Street with its designer boutiques and top-drawer shops; we enjoyed candle lit meals at Palms and Bill Wyman's Sticky Fingers restaurants as well as nights in watching 'Challenge Anneka' over a Pizza Express special and garlic bread and just simply being together.

I for one was in clover. My happiness knew no bounds. I had secured the job of a lifetime and now the girl of my dreams. As colleague Dave Tyler so aptly put it, clutching his near empty pint in Holborn's 'Shakespeare's Head' public house, eying me through silver framed spectacles with more than a hint of the green-eyed monster - "You've got it all!" Indeed I had, but it was a long time coming and especially nice after a very unhappy childhood. Things were looking up after what I call the wilderness years of meandering from job to job, not really having the remotest clue about what I wanted to do in life or indeed what I wanted out of life. I seemed to fall into weddings and portraits, then move on to the cruise ship life almost with an unquestioning acceptance, a shrug of the shoulders sort of thing. Before Wendy, I only really had focus when I was photographing, I hadn't really looked beyond work at the bigger picture. But with my girl by my side, I felt elated, complete and inspired to do great things – the world was indeed my oyster.

A month before our engagement, in February 1991, I found myself transferred from the Colour room at Amelia Street to the Scenes of Crime Photography Department and God I was so excited, although a tad nervous as to how I'd react on seeing my first dead body! Immediately prior to scenes of crime, I was driven by Ian Scott, a veteran crime photographer and wonderful colleague, out to the Met Police vehicle compound at Chalk Farm, where, it transpired, I was to be dumped on my own for the next two days! During this time, I had a shopping list of about twenty vehicles to document, comprising different makes and models, photographing front three-quarter views, VIN plates, stamped in chassis frame numbers, window etchings and engine numbers for each. This herculean task called on a variety of personal, photographic and lighting skills and although all was left unsaid, it dawned on me that this was a test by management to assess my suitability for the scenes of crime team. As Ian dropped me off, he looked at me with a wry smile, as if to say, 'you poor bastard, I hope you don't fuck this up', but actually offering the kinder sentiment "are you sure you'll be alright?" I nodded and Ian headed back to Amelia Street.

I was more than alright – I was very confident. I was on fire! I first sought out the list of vehicles and drew a plan of where each was located and on which floor, whether a particular vehicle was blocked in, requiring the one car in front to be moved out, locating the keys for each car and ascertaining the exact position of each stamped in number or plate as the location of course was completely different for each vehicle. I methodically worked out a logical order, floor by floor, of how I would work, visually documenting each car on my list until the task was complete. Problems encountered included locked doors, inaccessibility of engine numbers and seeking help in the moving of other vehicles, but all this proved no barrier to me completing this huge assignment in the designated time (two days) and processing and printing the images myself. I then had a meeting with the two Chief Photographers, Keith and Ernie, who would look through the thick album of all my Chalk Farm images. Suffice to say the two Guv'nors seemed very impressed, with Ernie Whatmore peering at me over his glasses in characteristic style, for not the first or last time, beaming and saying "Yes, they're good, very good album of photographs".

The very next day, I joined scenes of crime. I was the first of our intake to become a crime scene photographer, having gained 'established photographer' status very quickly indeed. However, whilst I was confident and sure of my abilities, probably wrongly exuding an air of cockiness, I was by no means the most talented, for the likes of Pete, Nancy, Jock, Jackie, Paul Cowley and Paul H were all hot on my heels and all of whom were inherently much better photographers than me!

I managed to live in Kensington's police section house until Wendy and I bought our first place together, a first-floor flat in New Malden, Surrey. It was on Duty Officer John Cook's recommendation that we ended up looking for a property in the Wimbledon, Kingston, New Malden and Worcester Park areas of South West London. That was back in February 1992. A few months prior to that, on 24th November 1991, the simply awful news broke that Queen front man, lead vocalist, songwriter and record producer, Freddie Mercury (AKA Farrokh Bulsara) had died of complications due to AIDS. He was just 45 – no age at all. Famous for his four-octave vocal range, protruding teeth and on-stage flamboyance,

Freddie and Queen had hits such as 'Bohemian Rhapsody', 'We are the Champions', 'Killer Queen', 'Another One Bites the Dust', 'Bicycle Race', 'Flash's Theme' from the 1980 movie Flash Gordon, 'Under Pressure' and 'Don't Stop me Now'. Freddie also enjoyed a solo career, as well as performing with other artists. Freddie Mercury with guitarist Brian May and drummer Roger Taylor ranked one of my favourite pop artists / bands of all time. I had grown up with them as a kid and now Freddie was gone. This meant that I was compelled to go and pay my respects. The candle-lit vigil outside Freddie's house in Kensington was not even a couple of minutes' walk from the section house. The atmosphere was quiet and very moving, a complete contrast to how Freddie was in life. Even to this day Freddie Mercury is consistently voted one of the greatest singers of all time in the history of pop music. His untimely death, like so many other pop stars, was sorely felt. Even now, when I hear the replays of Brian May's excellent 'Who Wants to Live Forever' from the 1986 album 'A Kind of Magic' and recorded for the film 'Highlander', with Freddie following Brian and belting those lyrics out, it still makes the hair on my neck stand up. R.I.P. Freddie Mercury. You were so, so good and we all loved you!

My first two weeks on scenes of crime involved 'strapping' (accompanying) with experienced forensic photographers. I would journey into Amelia Street each morning and then go out with a different photographer each day. No photog worked exactly the same way. Each employed their own techniques, so I watched, I absorbed, I asked questions, I took notes and I learned, pulling on the best techniques that I'd witnessed. Some photographers were worryingly quick in their approach, others a little slap-dash and laid back – but all were accomplished and experienced. The late Morgan Helps, a veteran of the department, had been there and got the t-shirt countless times and his affable, slick approach to his craft took my breath away. They used to call him 'One shot Morgan', because he only took one image of each view instead of the customary minimum two photographs, such was his phenomenal experience. I yearned to be that good and so relaxed about everything. Gavin, in contrast, was a master with interiors, having provided many of the contingency planning images for all the London royal residencies, government, embassies and other high-profile buildings that could be potential terrorist targets. Gavin's photographs were excellent and I longed to tap into his expertise. Additionally, Gavin was our man in the sky having almost sole responsibility for aerial photography, accompanying the 'India 99' Met Police helicopter crew on its daily assignments from Lippitt's Hill.

Steve Patterson was not just an outstanding forensic photographer, but a highly gifted wedding photographer as well. He was blessed with a friendly, easy going personality and a wicked sense of humour. When Steve was around, you'd be guaranteed inspirational company and a bloody good laugh. But he was also a good listener and he'd always offer sound advice. I do miss his company as I miss Nick Hosegood, who was equally a sound colleague with whom you'd be guaranteed to have a laugh and a joke. Nick used to take the rip out of me on air, using the force radio, all harmless fun. I'd end up giggling to myself in my job van and of course reciprocating. For my part, I once phoned Nick up during his Christmas meal in the guise of a shrieking witch, threatening to turn him into a speckly toad…as you do!

Nigel had been in the job a good few years. Married to a doctor and with two young children, Nigel was friendly, good humoured and seemed about as laid back as Morgan. He explained the job in a no nonsense, easy to understand way and I got on with him very well. Steve Flain and Peter Finch were also friendly, steadfast colleagues. Julie just oozed confidence, was very friendly and keen to help me learn the tricks of the trade, including how to claim expenses for just about every occasion. There were other characters with whom I got along just fine, some I warmed to and others I just tolerated. Either way, I learned off each and every one of them and I'm grateful to this day for the knowledge these crime scene photographers imparted and the help they gave me.

I had only been with the crime scene team a few days and already I'd seen a number of assault victims, attended a shooting scene, a burglary scene (photographing a shoe mark with the camera and 90mm standard lens perpendicular to the mark, located on a kitchen work top. The image included scale rulers on both sides of the mark and also an identifying label) and an armed robbery scene and now I found myself shadowing Julie. We were just finishing off a mid-morning cup of tea at Ealing Police Station, with Julie going through the fundamentals of job paperwork, when her tone pager sounded abruptly, making me start. She picked up her notebook and pen and sidled over to pick up the canteen phone to dial the duty office. When Julie returned, she was smiling and I knew why. I was about to see my very first dead body – an unidentified, middle aged, male deceased, who up until a few hours ago had been residing in Ealing Hospital Mortuary's fridge room.

The deceased was already unclothed, so in addition to front and back views, facial images were required to help with identification. The man's body had been brought out of the fridge, placed on a white sheet draped over a metal tray on the mortuary floor in preparation for full length photographs. Close-ups would be undertaken with the body on the mortuary table. I felt quite apprehensive as I popped my plastic apron and overshoes on, a jittery post-mortem virgin, taking my initial, tentative steps out onto the mortuary floor for the very first time. I couldn't see the body at first as Julie was in front of me obscuring the view – or rather I was hiding behind Julie. When I eventually did set eyes on the deceased, it was a bit of an anti-climax. Yes, the body looked waxy, lifeless and pale, but I wasn't shocked, as I thought I might be. There was no blood, there were no visible marks or tell-tale signs of external injuries on the body, nor was the deceased malodorous. If anything, the mortuary ambience and the clinical aroma was more off-putting, together with the occasional buzzing sound, as yet another blow fly was dispatched by the wall-mounted zapper – the aptly named 'insectocutor'.

Julie talked me through the different photographs as she covered the assignment with breakneck speed and efficiency, at one stage standing on her flash box, Metz 45 flash guns outstretched in each hand, one synced to the camera, the other fired automatically by slave, and looking every inch the pro. With full face, side and three-quarter profile images in the bag, it was time to get changed and do the paperwork for this job, before ringing John Cook in the duty office once more. Blow me down with a feather, the very next job was a suspicious death scene. An old man had just been pulled out of a nearby canal, down the road in Greenford, West London. By the time we arrived on scene and had donned our PPE, the scene had been downgraded to non-suspicious. A bottle of what appeared to be whiskey was still tucked into the deceased's inside jacket pocket. This poor chap was a known alcoholic and probably worse for wear had fallen into the Grand Union canal and drowned. Once the full length and facial photos had been taken, including images of the right ear (which appeared to have been nibbled by rodents), the body was turned and examined by the late Bruce Hoskyns, the Laboratory Liaison Sergeant, for any signs of injury on the back. Like the mortuary job that had preceded this one, there was no decaying body smell, just the whiff of dirty canal water!

A few more days passed, a few fatal road traffic scenes covered, along with a copious amount of burglary shoe, finger and tool marks to record and I found myself partnered up with Chris, another very amenable and steadfast colleague. Chris was friendly and cheerful and an extremely competent photographer. Chris tended to cover South West London, but if other areas were busy with jobs, the duty officer would often pull photographers across to help out.

Chris and I had just photographed an assault victim, who resided in a very plush apartment overlooking the Thames in Richmond, when Chris's tone pager bleeped loudly. He asked the middle-aged man we'd just captured on camera whether he could use his house phone to call Amelia Street, explaining that it wouldn't cost anything as he would be using a free phone number. I watched Chris as he opened up his notebook and began scribbling away. I was aware of myself tensing up at the letters 'PM' and then 'Ealing Hospital Mortuary'. This was to be my third dead body sighting in just over a week and my second outing to this particular mortuary.

Having photographed clothed and unclothed views of a young, deceased male in his early 20s, with the body positioned on the mortuary floor, the deceased was then placed on the mortuary table and Chris and I waited to one side of the mortuary, with Manfrotto mounted Pentax 6x7cm poised for any additional images, as directed by the forensic pathologist Dr Richard Shepherd. I watched with morbid curiosity as Dr Shepherd expertly slit open the body with his scalpel from lower neck to groin. I'd heard about what the Americans refer to as a Y-incision and had seen other photogs' images, but I'd never seen this live before and was almost transfixed – it was bizarre. I turned back to look at Chris who was grinning like a Cheshire cat, so obviously relishing my nervousness and inexperience. Simultaneously, the stench of alcohol and body innards hit my nostrils and worse, I could taste this unpleasant combo at the back of my throat. Chris, mortuary humour getting the better of him, was still grinning at me as I suddenly felt faint, simultaneously went partially blind, began seeing twinkling stars and felt nauseous. The shock was overwhelming and engulfed my entire 6-foot frame within milliseconds.

"Are you ok, Paul, you don't look very well?" a seemingly unconcerned and still grinning Chris said. "Where's the door, I need to get out?" I remember saying. He pointed to the way out and I just about managed to stagger out of the mortuary and sit down. Someone handed me a drink of water and I fumbled in my pocket for a couple of extra strong mints (affectionately nicknamed 'mortuary mints'). Two minutes later, my sight returned to normal, I no longer felt faint or nauseous and was able to step back onto the mortuary floor to watch the rest of the PM. And the worst part, the lifting out of the main organs from the body cavity, the slicing and dicing of specimens for analysis and the dramatic, careful, stryker saw removal of firstly, the bony skull cap and then the outer protective brain lining, the 'dura mater' and subsequent inner 'meninges'. It's not easy to forget the smell of burning cranial bone dust, which clung to the mortuary air long after the skull had been 'de-brained'. It was all fascinating stuff, but I had come within an ace of fainting and throwing up in the mortuary and it was a truly awful feeling. And bugger me if Chris wasn't still grinning at me – what a bastard! However, I realised all too quickly that this had been a necessary part of my initiation to the crime scene team. I was able to use this experience when I became an instructor at Hendon some years later as part of a health and safety lecture to help train others. I'd learned a valuable lesson - that I should never take it for granted that I wouldn't feel unwell again when attending either post-mortems or scenes of death and mayhem and also to be on the lookout for my colleagues around me, experiencing similar feelings and symptoms.

Indeed, I remember attending a very long murder post-mortem at the infamous Westminster mortuary in the heart of London, hosted by the equally infamous forensic pathologist, the late Dr Iain West, where I witnessed a hardened Detective Inspector of thirty years plus service with the Met Police, pass out cold. From the elevated viewpoint of standing on my flash box, I looked up from the body cavity, wound my Pentax 6x7 onto the next frame and saw this poor fellow slide down the door and collapse in a crumpled heap on the mortuary floor. He was very embarrassed when he came round and shouldn't have been, because it stands as proof that we're all human and sudden shock and illness can quite literally happen to any of us. I wrongly stereotyped the hardened copper as being able to deal with it. I never made that mistake again!

CHAPTER 9

Joining the Scenes of Crime Team – February 1991

After a handful of weeks with a cross section of the crime scenes team, word was passed to the Amelia Street chiefs that I was competent to go it alone. I had been in the job for barely a pregnancy term. What followed was day in day out attendance and coverage of a multitude of crime scenes, victims, post mortems and fatal and serious personal injury road traffic accidents. I was working 8am to 4pm, Monday to Friday, with a 1 in 4 weekend on-call interspersed with a Monday to Thursday weekday night on call rota thrown into the mix. If you were lucky, you'd have at least 3 other photographers working with you on call. However, staff sickness or other absence would mean that you'd be guaranteed a thrashing, travelling all over the capital day and night with very little sleep for an entire weekend or weekday night on call stint. I'd be doing well if I managed to get a couple of hours of quality shut eye before the phone's piercing ring tone roused me from unconscious to barely awake within seconds. Being woken from a deep sleep by the on-call duty officer mumbling in your ear wasn't just a regular occurrence, it was an unpleasant experience, especially on a bitterly cold winter's night and I was usually so disorientated that I had to lay my shirt, trousers, underpants and socks out in order on the floor, so that I could find them easily to quickly get dressed and then down a coffee before leaving the house. Wendy would momentarily wake up too, turn over to find out what the job was and when I said the immortal words "double murder", she sighed, rolled over and was soon fast asleep. Lucky girl. I wanted so much to just put the phone down and go back to sleep too, but inevitably the urgency of the job always forced me out of the house and down to the nick to pick up my logbook and keys. The glove compartment of my police issue van would be stocked with comfort food - crisps and chocolate bars - and I always carried water and a flask. There were weekly opportunities to volunteer for additional weekend and weekday on-calls. Overtime was in plentiful supply back then and we photogs were raking it in.

Pre sat nav, my faithful A4 hard-backed London A-Z got me around and the chatter on my force radio kept me company. I was assigned the MPS call sign 'Central 2-0-7-9' with Central 2-0-2-0 being the Amelia Street Duty office. Channel 5 was the main working channel, with Channel 12 being the main 'Oscar' Traffic Division working channel. Control at NSY were in charge of base to car and car to car calls, so if you were out and about during the daytime and Amelia Street wanted to direct you to an urgent job, the radio conversation might have gone something like this:

Amelia Street Duty Office (John Cook): "Hello MP from Central 2-0-2-0. Could I have car to car with Central 2-0-7-9, working Channel Five, Central 2-0-2-0 over"

MP: "Thank you Central 2-0-2-0, standby all cars. Central 2-0-7-9, Central 2-0-7-9, are you receiving MP, over?

Me: "Central 2-0-7-9, Go ahead MP, seven nine, over"

MP: "Central 2-0-2-0, go ahead with your car to car now, MP over..."

Amelia Street Duty Office (John Cook): "Thank you MP. Central 2-0-7-9, you have 'two in position' Exhibition Road, junction with Imperial College Road, South West 7, 2-0-2-0 over."

Me: "On my way Central 2-0-2-0, thank you MP, Central 2-0-7-9, out."

Amelia Street Duty Office (John Cook): "Thank you MP, Central 2-0-2-0, out"

MP: "Thank you Central 2-0-2-0, All cars, MP out."

The 'two in position' was code for a two vehicle, fatal or serious personal injury accident, which you didn't want to spell out in case of listening press scanning the airwaves!

If I received my direction from the duty office via channel 5 about anything related to a road traffic accident, I'd then switch to traffic channel 12 and notify 'Oscar' traffic control at NSY of my ETA. Usually, I'd get to within a mile of the scene and traffic everywhere would be gridlocked. I'd then be forced to turn to Oscar for help to facilitate me getting to the scene as my white van was unmarked and I had no blues and twos. Police were keen to get me to the scene quickly so they could re-open the roads and get traffic moving again, so they would invariably send a motorcycle police officer (nicknamed a 'black rat') to get me to the RTA. On one such occasion, I'd been informed of a 'vehicles in position' on the A4 in Kensington. I was south of the Thames at the time, so I crossed over Albert Bridge onto Chelsea Embankment and no sooner had I turned left, I was brought to a complete halt. Traffic on the A3212 was going nowhere, so I was forced to contact Oscar on my radio. Unbelievably, within a minute, a black rat piped up over the airwaves, requesting Central 2-0-7-9 to put his hand out of his driver's window so that he could identify the photographer driving the unmarked, white Astramax van. Simultaneously, I looked in my mirror and the police motorcycle was next to me. A rather stern looking black rat with no time for niceties said, "Right, headlights on, follow me and keep close!" What happened next was a parting of the red sea. The black rat was Moses and his motorcycle blues and twos were his staff. Me, well naturally I was his solitary Israelite, but with no Egyptians in hot pursuit ... although there were one or two piss takers who thought they'd follow behind me only to be given a massive bollocking by the black rat, who'd clocked what had happened in his offside mirror. I'd never seen anything like it, cars on both sides of the road mounted pavements as we sped through like a cross country rally and headed north, crossing first the King's Road, then Fulham Road followed by Old Brompton Road, before turning right and north east along the A4 Cromwell Road to the junction of the south bound A3220, Earl's Court Road. The accident was located at that main junction on the A4 town bound. Although the black rat had vanished before I'd had time to thank him, this was a classic example of an efficient use of resources, borne out of necessity.

So, what is forensic photography?

'Forensic' and 'Photography' are two powerful words that form a potent combination. Together as one entity it is a key component in the daily fight against crime. The dictionary defines forensic as 'of or used in connection with courts of law'. 'Photography' is derived from the Greek words 'phōs' meaning 'light' and 'graphé' which means 'drawing'. Therefore, photography literally translated means 'drawing with light'. Forensic Photography - being specialised imaging used for legal purposes.

Photography in police work has long been a powerful visual tool for evidence recording. Police photographers world-wide perform a pivotal role, using the camera to document the story of events at a crime scene, where possible in chronological order, not just for the investigating officer but also for inevitable use at court. It is often said that a picture paints a thousand words and in the courtroom arena, the players and protagonists are very often devoid of ready access to the crime scene. Crime scene 'stills' photographs, along with video, communicate an accurate visual account of a scene and serve to re-create it, bringing the reality of the crime, with all that it entails, into the courtroom.

Police photographers must be unbiased and honest in the undertaking of their duties and must be confident in a court of law when justifying not only the taking of their photographs and all relevant actions, but also when having their integrity called in to question, a common defence counsel tactic. Photographs could be the vital factor, which could in turn make or break a case or indeed, refute a point made by the defence, so it is imperative that they serve as a true representation.

People have often said to me 'Why on earth be a police photographer - all those dead bodies, how do you cope?' or 'How do you become a police photographer?' Back in 1990, when I was given the opportunity to join the Metropolitan Police Service Photographic Branch in London, they were reputedly the best in Europe and among the finest Police Photographic Units in the world. They not only served the entire police force of some 26,000 employees, but also the whole of London (comprising then, some eight million inhabitants). In addition, they also had a pan UK and overseas responsibility with the Anti-Terrorist Branch and an international remit with the United Nations War Crimes Commission.

So why did I join? Well to me, a young newbie forensic photographer, having worked in industry, commerce and the private sector, the forthcoming challenges and opportunities sounded exciting and irresistible. I once confided in an aghast friend that I preferred 'still-life' photography, opting to photograph the most gruesome and arduous murder post-mortem, over trying to 'smudge' a drunken wedding party any day. At least my subject would not move or answer me back! Coping? Well the adverse side of the job affected all police photographers from time to time, being only human.

I think that hiding behind the camera made the gory sights easier to bear, together with becoming so focused on the urgency and importance of getting the photographs in the bag (there were no second chances) and always being professional in winning through and achieving the end result. I almost became de-sensitised to the horrors of what I saw and imaged, often becoming more shocked on seeing the printed photographs.

Photographers are artistes and tend to concentrate on a particular area of the marketplace, be that portraiture, industrial or fashion etc. and by nature we are somewhat opinionated. Operational Police Photographers have an awesome responsibility. They can be likened to field operatives - born survivors who are often labelled mavericks by other disciplines for their sheer gut determination in delivering the goods. Crime Scene Photographers very often operate under gruelling, challenging, dangerous and extreme circumstances. Freezing cold, wet, long hours, unsafe location, or just physically exhausting and mentally taxing conditions. Simultaneously they must be able to take high quality images that not only tell the story of events with each image linking to the next, but also take images that are sharp, scaled, well composed, evenly lit and exposed. They must always be ready to photograph everything and anything conceivably police/crime related, ensuring all procedures are complied with; written documentation is thorough and precise – all the while being able to stay awake long enough to drive home safely and do it all again the next day – one hell of a responsibility!

As a forensic photographer I was expected to undertake the following assignments, which by no means constitutes a definitive list. They include: major incidents including terrorism, murder, suspicious deaths, post mortems, racial incidents, serious road traffic accidents and traffic offences, rape/other sexual offences, kidnapping, arson and fatal fires, assault victims and victims of domestic violence, child abuse/neglect (care and protection), contingency plans, criminal damage, searches/raids, sieges, fraud/deception/counterfeiting/forgery, blackmail, firearms offences, licensing offences, drugs offences, armed robbery, burglary, theft, motor vehicle crime, health and safety and accident claims, complaints against police, surveillance, public order and identification parades with perhaps a little public relations photography thrown in for good measure.

Police Photographers are highly skilled and resourceful. Armed with at least one photography qualification (degree or equivalent), they are thoroughly dedicated to the task at hand, adopting a disciplined, analytical, yet flexible approach to their work. They must be assertive, but sympathetic and exercise good control, direction and common sense. As an expert in this very exacting science, one has to be a Jack of all trades. Later, when I became a forensic photographic instructor in the late '90s, I always told my students that being able to take police related photographs constituted only a small part of their job. It is also necessary to understand why you are taking a photograph and what purpose it will serve. As stated, essentially you are telling a story about what happened, presented as an album of printed photographs, a folder of digital images and/or a video film setting out the events, in order, as told by the officer in the case. You must also be confident when questioned by prosecution and defence over your album of photographs or video film in the courtroom.

The experienced police photographer, armed with both stills and video capability and so often employing specialist light sources, is usually one of the first on scene. He or she also acts as an additional pair of eyes, skilled in searching and detection, ever mindful of crime scene etiquette, scene and forensic awareness, health and safety issues and always cognisant of the correct protective clothing and equipment to employ. A knowledge and understanding of the law regarding photography and Community and Race Relations/Diversity are also a must. Working equally well alone or as part of a team, the photographer is integral and is absolutely vital to the successful investigation of many a crime. In addition, Police Photographers must have excellent inter-personal skills, being able to strike up an immediate rapport with people from all walks of life, communicating with ease and lucidity. A strong, cast iron stomach goes with the territory! However, it is a prerequisite for the Forensic Photographer to possess a completely wacky sense of humour to carry you through the day! In my case, it was my impersonations that lightened an otherwise sombre mood. Professionalism combined with regular laughter were key ingredients in my daily life at work.

To recount every job that I'd ever attended would be impossible, as well as mind-blowingly uninteresting for the reader. So, here's a breakdown of my MPS career over 14 years and 2 ½ months: -

1) June 1990 to February 1991 - Photographic Headquarters, Amelia Street, SE17 undergoing internal training
2) February 1991 to September 1993 - operational crime scene photographer

3) September 1993 to December 1995 - part of a specialist, 8-man team who video recorded every suspicious death, murder and video film identification in London. We were known as Operational Video Services, 4 'boys', each with his own manager and working as four, 2-man teams
4) January 1996 to 1998 - the MPS was restructured from 8 areas (if memory serves) down to 5 areas (North West, North East, South West, South East and Central). I was operational crime scenes photography working central London, with a shared office at Westminster (code CW), now the current headquarters of New Scotland Yard.
5) Late 1998, I slipped two discs in my lower back and was off work for a few weeks and was transferred to light duties back in the colour room at Amelia Street, processing and printing
6) May 1999 to mid-August 2004 - qualified as an instructor and became Forensic Training and Development Manager at the MPS Crime Academy Forensic Facility (formerly the 'Scientific Support College'), Rowan House, Peel Centre, Hendon.
7) I finished my Met Police career as Head of Photography Training.

Photographing survivors, victims of attempted murder and assault, were particularly challenging to deal with as the frightening feelings of attack were still very fresh in the victims' minds. The strong emotional undercurrent was always palpable whenever I documented victims' injuries. In February 1992, I had been covering crime scenes for a year and had photographed every gory sight imaginable. Then, one morning, I was directed to a police safe house to photograph the appalling injuries to 27-year-old Merlyn Nuttall. On her way to Brixton underground station first thing and thence to work, Merlyn was stopped by an agitated man apparently seeking help for his girlfriend. On following the man, Merlyn suddenly found herself being forced at knifepoint into a run-down, empty end of terrace house. What followed was a terrifying, frenzied, 45-minute rape and multiple assault ordeal, which left Merlyn bleeding from cheese wire wounds to the front and sides of her neck, leaving her windpipe exposed and broken bottle injuries to the back of her neck. In the struggle that ensued, Merlyn's thumb was almost severed. Courageously, she feigned death as her only way to survive and her attacker callously then set fire to the room where she had been held. In a cruel and calculated action, he removed the handle from the inside of the door to prevent her escape. The man was Anthony

Ferrira, an odious pimp, who was high on crack cocaine and out seeking a thrill. The attack on an innocent, defenceless young woman was barbaric, heinous and degrading. Somehow Merlyn, close to death, incredibly and with such bravery, managed to escape when a squatter opened the door from the outside and Merlyn then stumbled down several flights of stairs leaving the dingy room behind where Ferrira had repeatedly cut and violated her. Miraculously, she made it to the outside and attracted help from passers-by. She was burned and drenched in her own blood.

Following Merlyn's considerable time spent in hospital, I now found myself at the safehouse. I was led upstairs by a female police liaison officer to a clean, cosy living room where two other ladies (Merlyn's sisters) waited. I was offered tea or coffee, but politely declined. I had only been in the living room for a minute or so, when I saw the figure of a young, attractive woman coming upstairs. She wore a white Alice band to keep her air up and away from the angry, prominent neck injuries and to make it easier for me to photograph. The expression on her face was haunting, the whites of her eyes completely red and blood shot - her head remained perfectly motionless. She could have passed as one of Dracula's brides in a Christopher Lee Hammer horror, but the serene lady before me was in fact Merlyn Nuttall, who even courageously managed a smile when I introduced myself to her. It took me at least 20 minutes to photograph all of her injuries – her neck, her thumb and her burns. What I saw almost three decades ago, had such an effect on me then, that my visual documentation of Merlyn's awful injuries has stayed with me to this day.

Merlyn was born to be a survivor. She went on to help other victims of crime, appearing on television many times. Five years after her dreadful ordeal, Merlyn published an account of her attack, hospital treatment, recuperation, court and compensation battle in her book 'It Could Have Been You'. On buying a copy, I was pleased to notice that some of my forensic photographs had been used inside, but it was because that particular job had so affected me that I wanted to meet Merlyn again. I asked her to sign my copy of her book - perhaps I selfishly hoped this would bring me some personal closure. Finding Merlyn wasn't easy. I first had to go through her police liaison officer, who in turn contacted Merlyn for permission. Merlyn thankfully agreed. I met her in town where she was working and she happily signed my copy of her book. In our brief meeting, I shook hands with her and wished her all the very best. She thanked me for taking her police photographs and in turn I told her that I was glad to have helped in some small way. When I left her, Merlyn smiled. She looked radiant, happy, confident and full of life – just the way it should be. I came away so pleased for this particular survivor and relieved that life eventually turned out OK for Merlyn Nuttall!

Photography of assault victims took place either at their home or work address, a relative or friend's address, police safe house, police station, or hospital. In the poorer areas of London, many dwellings were filthy and smelly, so much so that often the soles of your feet would be sticky with mess. However, it was generally the poorer members of society who'd offer you a cup of tea, whereas there was generally nothing offered from the well to do! You'd have to almost beg for a glass of water!

In my first year out on crime scenes, I was sent to photograph a 23-year old girl who was recovering at home from a knife attack. Details from the duty office were minimal: name of victim, address, name of police officer and station dealing, crime number and that the victim was at home waiting for me to pop round. The address was in Balham, SW12. I was only down the road at Whiskey Delta (Tooting Police Station), W division's main HQ station, so this next job was convenient as it was close by. I found the address with no problems and approached the glossy, black-painted front door with my camera bag over my shoulder and Manfrotto tripod in my right hand. I pressed the doorbell and could see the shadow of someone approaching through the central frosted glass panel. The door opened and on showing my police pass, I was greeted with a smile from a very attractive brunette with shoulder length wavy hair, who confirmed that she was the victim I'd come to photograph.

The girl showed me into the front living room as I plonked my heavy camera bag down on the floor. "I'll be with you in just a minute. I'm just setting up my camera and flash guns", I said without turning around. I had just made a potentially life-threatening mistake – turning my back on a victim. She could have become violent and plunged a knife into me. When I stood up and turned around, Pentax 6x7 in hand, loaded with a new roll of film, I was shocked to see this young girl standing before me. My victim was totally naked, breasts, genitals and pubic hair on full view! I felt my cheeks flush red with embarrassment as my victim smiled and then asked me coquettishly "How do you want me?" To make matters worse, I pointed at the stitched injury on her left breast and said, "Is that all you've got?" I know, you don't have to say it, but you will anyway...Dick!

Ok, deep breath. So let's just take a moment and ponder that one for a second. What I should have done was to risk assess at the outset, take a female police officer as chaperone with me, immediately take control of the situation on entering the house, getting the victim seated and comfortable, then check the location of the victim's injury and direct the victim just to reveal that part of the breast where the injury could be seen i.e. covering up the rest of her body. There was no need for her to get undressed. Furthermore, by asking the victim "Is that all you've got?" is a rookie error, I should have clarified by asking her "Is it the one injury, or do you have any others? Also, I found that some victims were quite proud of their injuries and my comments could well have been perceived as belittling and derogatory. And I certainly should not have turned my back on her. I used this scenario as part of health and safety training for my students at Hendon years later, much to everyone's amusement. The fact that I could have been assaulted, or on leaving the victim's house, the girl could have reported me for indecent assault or worse, makes me shudder even to this day. Lessons learned, I never made these mistakes again.

Having photographed hundreds of victims throughout the '90s, it wasn't until I became an instructor at Hendon's Crime Academy Forensic Faculty in early summer of 1999, that I realised the teaching of assault victim photography required a hell of a lot more research and subsequent instructor input on 'communication' than simply teaching the practical elements. For example, posing a 6-foot five victim with a cut at the top of the head would require the victim to sit down and tilt the head forward or backward and to part their hair with their hands to reveal the injury if required. The general rule was always to start at the top of the body and work your way down. Add to the mix composition, lighting, when to handhold the camera versus tripod-mounted camera work, using scale tape if necessary, showing all visible injuries, thinking about the background (which should be white preferably or a plain coloured wall). Alongside all this, accurate notes on all crime scene assignments had to be taken. For facial photographs, the victim would be sitting down against a background (I used to carry a Lastolite grey background to solve the problem of clutter at an address). Bruised and bloodshot eyes often required several images, showing eyes closed to reveal the bruising on the upper lids and then open to reveal any bloodshot. In addition, whilst keeping their head still, the victim might have to move their eyes in multiple directions to reveal areas of bloodshot.

Looking into the mouth, it was often necessary to ask the victim to expose an internal injury by holding their lips up or down. Bite marks were scaled on all sides of the bite, all planes were photographed at ninety degrees perpendicular to the mark(s), for this ensured that a perpetrator's dental records could be examined and an accurate analysis could be made. Severe swelling photographs were usually photographed in profile, but it was often more powerful, when applicable, to compare the swollen area of the body to an uninjured area, for example, the hands, knees and feet. Arms and legs were generally shot in portrait (upright) format, with the victim standing and the arm(s) either down by the side or outstretched, against a plain background, using scale tape. If photographing the lower legs and feet, the victim would either put their legs up on a chair or similar (I'd use a plain sheet as a floor background), lie down, or even stand on a chair against a wall (if it was safe) so as to reduce the angle of photography and to exclude the floor from the photograph. Again, scale tape would be used. It would often be necessary to locate the injury by photographing in relation to a recognisable part of the body, for example, the belly button, prior to taking an image in close-up.

Photographing intimate injuries often proved very traumatic for victims and so it was a prerequisite to put the victim at ease and to provide constant reassurance that the photographs were for police and courtroom eyes only. The protection of the victim's dignity was essential, which is what I failed to do in the embarrassing case already highlighted, when presented with a young, female victim, who stood before a scarlet-faced yours truly, completely naked. Only the relevant area of the body must be exposed to show the injury and the photographer must come across as confident and utterly professional. When photographing a victim of the opposite sex, it was necessary to have a police officer, family member or friend with you, who was the same gender as the victim. When photographing victims in hospital, staff required permission from the victim before you were allowed access to them. Photographing lively babies and small children who often wouldn't keep still for very long usually required the Pentax to be handheld with a side-mounted Metz 45 flash gun. It was always necessary to have a relative or appropriate adult present to not only assist me, but also to witness the photography.

Invariably, I found that there was a delay incurred from the time of the assault to the time of photographing the injuries. This was beyond my control. We used to leave bruising injuries for at least

24 hours anyway, to allow the bruising to develop and show more clearly. People of course are all different and the time taken for the bruising to show up, the colour, scale, severity and the duration the bruise remained visible, also varied with every victim. Occasionally, I actually couldn't see any visible injuries, quite possibly because they had healed. We were advised then that taking a photograph for the sake of it showing no injury could actually have a detrimental effect on the case. In such circumstances, the doctor or Forensic Medical Examiner's (FME) report sufficed and it was necessary to communicate this fact to the victim.

As with any job, upper most in my mind was health and safety. I'd risk assess for physical, biological and chemical hazards before, during and on leaving the victim's location. My initial risk assessment of the victim centred around ascertaining just how safe it was going to be to visit the victim's home or work address. I had to consider numerous questions simultaneously such as: What is the location like? How safe is this particular estate? Can I park my vehicle safely nearby? How accessible is the location? Are the lifts up to the 20th floor working and reliable? Are my portable communications (radio, mobile phone and pager) likely to fail at the location – what's the signal like? Do I need a Police Officer to accompany me? (also to help me carry my equipment.) How long am I going to need the services of that police officer for? Am I going to photograph the scene as well? What is the age, gender and mental state of the victim? Do I need a chaperone? (essential if the victim is of the opposite sex and if the injuries are of an intimate nature.) Will a relative or friend be present? Is the victim a child/juvenile? (if so, an appropriate adult will have to give their consent to photographs being taken and be present during photography.) How mobile is the victim?', 'Does the victim have a disability or medical condition? (for example, are they blind, deaf with / without speech, or are they a wheelchair user?) Is the victim a prisoner? (in which case written consent was required in the custody record or the Superintendent's authority would have to be gained prior to photography being undertaken and one had to be mindful that the prisoner wasn't allowed to be restrained.) Will there be a language difficulty? (if there is, will my NVCs (non-verbal communications) suffice, or will the services of a recognised interpreter be required? Are there any cultural or religious factors to consider? (will the planned day of photography conflict with a religious event, for example? If so, I could be denied permission to photograph a female victim altogether.) Is the victim compos mentis?

(are they drunk, do they sound punch drunk, under the influence of drugs? Is there a history of violence?).

Following an assault, a victim may well be in shock, the effects of which are very diverse. They range from being visibly upset, extremely distressed, fearful, angry, shaking, fainting, feeling nauseous, to being quiet and withdrawn, or even over-friendly or hyperactive. The vibes that I got from the victim and their surroundings, coupled with my own intuition, told me within seconds of meeting them whether or not it was safe for me to enter their home. If I was ever unsure, I'd make my excuses and leave immediately. Even if a victim appeared friendly and calm, I'd always have to be on guard and ready for the possibility that they'd suddenly turn violent. In fact, I would be constantly analysing the victim and the location from start to finish. For the paperwork, I'd always check the victim's name and address details, before leaving, getting them to write in capitals their first, middle and last names if necessary.

I lost count of the number of assault victims that I photographed over the years. Offences included attempted murder, ABH (assault occasioning actual bodily harm), the more serious GBH (grievous bodily harm), rape, robbery and armed robbery. I photographed one young lady in her early 20s in hospital in the company of a female nurse and a female police officer chaperone. This poor girl, who had been subjected to a vicious rape only a handful of hours earlier, was still crying and trembling. Several times I had to stop photographing because she was too upset or wanted to be sick. Her back alone was riddled with injuries. There were friction burns and scratches where she'd been dragged along the ground and through rose bushes. There were also scratches and bruises on both shoulders and behind both ears. I remember repeatedly asking the victim if she was ok to continue, courageously she nodded 'yes'.

She was dressed only in a pair of black knickers with her hospital gown around her front. She had to lean against a wall with her left hand for support, while at the same time holding her long, dark-brown hair up out of the way with her right hand, so that I could see the injuries to the back of her neck, ears, shoulders and back. This was very powerful as a stand-alone image. However, there was a catalogue of other images that I had somehow managed to take of her bruised face, black eyes, arms, hands, bruises on her breasts, around her vagina, inner thighs, and legs. Just as I had taken my second shot of the back, shoulders, neck and ears, the victim started to sway and moan. Suddenly, the nurse and police officer lunged at the poor girl, grabbing her to break her fall as she fainted. Fortunately, I had just completed my visual documentation, but the whole experience had been extremely intense, distressing and unsettling and left me emotionally spent.

Early in January 1993, I attended Kingston Hospital, just down the road from where I was living in New Malden, to photograph yet another harrowing case. A young lad in his late teens had been kidnapped, beaten up, gang buggered and then had green-coloured, oil-based paint thrown in his face and over his body. As with any victim, it was imperative that I established an immediate rapport, beginning with a friendly, professional introduction and the showing of my official police identification, without which, photography could not have taken place. The victim's trust was often gained during photography. One's own inter-personal skills were crucial to the success of such assignments. I needed to be friendly, sympathetic, reassuring and a good listener, but simultaneously, assertive and confident, exercising good control and offering clear direction, providing explanations for what I was doing when asked.

I found that I had to be mindful of my own feelings and emotions, not just the victim's. It was important not to use any inappropriate terminology or body language, especially when dealing with graphic injuries, so as not to cause the victim to have an adverse reaction. My facial expressions and mannerisms never betrayed my inner feelings ... except in the case of the young lady, already discussed, who stripped off!

This Kingston victim had been left with bruised and bloodshot eyes and multiple injuries: - cuts inside his mouth, a knife wound to the left temple area, knife slash wounds to his left chest, upper right thigh and right buttock, cuts around his pubic area, bruises to his arms, back and legs, bleeding to his rectum and the remains of green-coloured oil based paint on his face, arms, legs and bottom. It was a particularly vindictive, inhumane and unusual assault, but after careful, methodical photography, I managed to successfully obtain all the images. What I'll never forget is the haunting way this poor, naked lad sat and stared, with his watery, bloodshot eyes into my camera lens – a resigned, vulnerable, lamentable look, having quite literally had his dignity stripped away from him.

Now wrapped up at Kingston Hospital, I'd barely got out of A&E, having turned off Galsworthy Road and onto the A238 Coombe Lane West, when I noticed flashing blue lights in my offside wing mirror, followed by headlights flashing me to stop.

I sat in my Astramax van, not having a clue why I'd been pulled over, wound my window down and waited for one of the male police officers to approach. "Good afternoon sir, does this vehicle belong to you?" the rather stern looking constable addressed me with more than a hint of an accusatory tone in his voice. At this juncture I couldn't resist the urge to be just a little bit cheeky, so I replied with mock confusion, "No, officer, it belongs to our boss". The officer stared at me frowning as I picked up the van's police logbook from the passenger seat and very nearly thrust it in his face. The officer's mood lightened and not for the first time the immortal words "piss-taker" were mouthed in my direction, as said officer about turned back to his marked car. It transpired that a van matching the description of the one I was driving had been involved in a number of burglaries in the local Kingston, Surbiton, New Malden, Tolworth and Raynes Park areas. I was left wondering why the officers had decided to pull me over first, before doing a PNC (Police National Computer) check on my Astramax van, for it would indeed have come back as being registered to 'The Commissioner of Police of the Metropolis'! The only other occasion that I was briefly pulled over in my job van, was in the middle of the night, having left an outdoor stabbing scene somewhere in Streatham, where the unfortunate young male victim had been dispatched with a shiv to the gut. The street was so brightly lit that I forgot to put my vehicle lights on – doh!

A few months after the Kingston job, I was called to Charing Cross New Hospital on Fulham Palace Road in Hammersmith to photograph a nineteen-year old female GBH victim in her hospital bed. She had been beaten black and blue, with her arms and legs covered in angry, purply-yellow bruises. With the victim's permission, together with that of the investigating officer and with the help of nursing staff, I photographed the victim full length as she lay slightly over on her left side, her modesty covered by a blanket, to show the awful extent of this poor young woman's injuries. I was to learn later that the image, together with the rest of the photographs in the album, had a powerful, dramatic effect, causing the jury at Number One Court of the Old Bailey to gasp simultaneously in horror.

A week later I drove to Hounslow in West London to photograph a ninety-two-year-old lady who had been raped and punched in the right eye. She had also sustained nasty bruising and cuts to her lower legs. I was left wondering whether the warped mind of the evil perpetrator at large could stoop any lower. As I was focusing up on her facial image, the victim looked into the camera with the saddest of eyes and managed a half smile. Ah, bless her, I could have cried and hugged her, she felt she needed to smile for the camera. This was a despicable crime carried out on a defenceless, lovely, old lady who reminded me so much of my dear Grandma, it was degrading and utterly heart-breaking.

CHAPTER 10

Attending Scenes of Murder, Suspicious Death and Post Mortems

Over the course of a working week, it wasn't uncommon to cover several murder assignments, nor was it uncommon to spend several hours at a murder scene, only to go directly to the mortuary afterwards for the post-mortem examination, spending additional hours there. Fortunately, the gruesome images in my mind from most of these scenes have not been retained.

Unfortunately, the images of the murder of a little lad from Hounslow who had been out playing but never returned home have never left me. Two boys discovered a body in an old, World War Two army pillbox, situated on the edge of Hounslow Heath. When I arrived on scene, I was first briefed by the Laboratory Liaison Sergeant, prior to me 'booting and suiting' in personal protective clothing (disposable forensic suit, gloves, mask and disposable shoe covers). It was also necessary to cover my tripod legs with disposable feet covers (affectionately nicknamed 'tripod condoms'). I noticed that a team of six police dog handlers were also conducting a briefing, just off to my left. Their six Alsatians were sitting down on the grass in a circle, leads dangling down, all with their tongues hanging out panting gently, but thankfully shaded by a canopy of trees on the edge of the golf course. At the head of the circle made by the dogs and furthest from me, their handlers formed a smaller circle. Some guys stood, some crouched, but all were studying intently a large map of the area. Having photographed half of Hounslow Heath Golf Course, I finished off my exterior coverage with approach images to the pillbox and then exterior shots from all sides of the pillbox itself, by which time the police dogs and their handlers had disappeared off to conduct their searches.

The pillbox entrance was very small and I had to get down on my hands and knees to partly crawl, partly shuffle inside. Having been given the location of the deceased inside the pillbox, it was so dark that I needed my 'boat lamp' (seek and search torch) on to see what I was doing and to be careful that I didn't stumble over and disturb the position of the body. Bruce Hoskyns, the Police Laboratory Liaison Sergeant, carefully handed me my camera bag, followed by my tripod. I laid a clean forensic suit on the floor, on which I laid my camera bag to prevent contamination. This was situated on the opposite side of the body, behind a central stone pillar. The space inside the pillbox was very cramped and I could barely stand up. It was necessary to compose the full-length shots of the deceased using my boat lamp to focus the camera. I then set the aperture to F16, locked open the camera's shutter and fired several flashes towards the deceased, altering the angle of each flash prior to firing. With the shutter still open and the scene still in pitch darkness, I shuffled around the central stone pillar and fired a few more flashes towards the deceased, again the flashes being fired from different angles – a technique known in the profession as 'a timed exposure with painting with light'. I then repeated the procedure at an aperture of F11 for my back-up photograph.

It was very macabre, because every time a flash fired, the deceased's face and body lit up for a fraction of a second. The body was naked and dirty from head to foot. The pillbox floor was also dirty and dusty. There was no sign of the deceased's clothing. I bolted the telephoto lens on to the front of the Pentax 6x7, following the wide-angle shots of the interior of the pillbox and deceased full-length. It was now important to document the head and noticeable ligature marks from different angles i.e. from either side of the pillbox central column, once again employing the same timed exposure / painting with light technique. Once I was satisfied that I had photographed the interior of the pillbox and the deceased completely, I shouted out to Bruce, who took my camera bag from me, followed by my tripod and forensic suit that had been used as a cover to rest my camera bag on. I was so glad to crawl out of that dark, dusty, claustrophobic pillbox. Although a local man was arrested and charged at the time, he was later acquitted at the Central Criminal Court. Sadly, to this day, the murder remains unsolved.

Whilst working on crime scenes, it was normal practice to accrue about 6 days photographing all manner of scenes and victims. Then I'd pop into Photographic HQ at Amelia Street, firstly to the general office to deliver all my case sheets / album indexes for Peggy the admin, to type up. I would frequently end up correcting Peggy's many typos and would then have to steel myself to resubmit my case sheets with a cheeky, less than subtle, "only fourteen mistakes this time Peggy", whereupon you were usually met with a ratty Peggy who'd whine at you with, "Well it wasn't my fault". Then you'd meet the cleaner, 'Mrs O' in the corridor, who always looked like she carried the problems of the world on her shoulders, muttering to herself and giving out about someone. A few paces further on and the PA fired into life. It was one of the Estates team, George: "Attention all staff, attention all staff, there will be a fire alarm test until further notice, a fire alarm test until further notice". Sometimes fellow photogs would wind Liz up on reception, phoning her up to put a cheeky announcement out on the tannoy: "DI Sir, DI Sir, please come to reception" (the next time it would be DC Ten). Then inevitably, the same cockney twang would announce, "Mike Hunt, Mike Hunt, please come to reception", to much hilarity from us photogs.

Next I'd drop off all my colour roll films (120s) and any black and white films containing shoe, finger and tool marks for 'C41' and black and white processing, respectively. Over the coming few days, I'd be in at Amelia Street cutting up and sorting out my negatives ready for colour printing to 10"x8" size, using one of the Polly printers. For any shoe, finger, or tool marks, I'd pop into the black and white room and use one of the many enlargers to print these. Having been out working solo on crime scenes and then driving into Amelia Street, meant that you could catch up with your colleagues, talk about jobs and air your feelings all over a big boy's breakfast either in the upstairs canteen, served by Rose, or down the 'Wally Road' at Mari's café, a very popular haunt!

Mortuary humour was a vital part of the job. Being able to talk and laugh about the horrendous sights with like-minded people, who understood the stresses and strains, gave you a sense that you were not alone and it helped you deal with it and get it out of your system. Laughing wasn't being disrespectful, it was just a way of letting off steam, without which you'd crack up. A group of us were having breakfast at Mari's on one memorable occasion and the conversation revolved around the number of murders each of us had attended that week. This then developed into who had photographed the most bodies at an individual murder scene. For most of us that week, it was one. In my case it was two bodies. Then Lee, a TVR enthusiast and also another great colleague, piped up with a grin "Well, I had six bodies last Tuesday and all in the same room!" And of course, we all leaned in, cradling our mugs of tea, whilst Lee regaled us with his 'tales from the crypt'.

I seemed to cop the unsolved murder cases and the slaying of a young teenage girl was no exception. It was barely the start of new year 1998, when she went missing. This poor girl's body was discovered partly hidden in undergrowth in a West London suburb in an apparently motiveless murder. The post-mortem that I attended immediately after photographing the murder scene, sickeningly revealed that this young victim had been stabbed repeatedly in her face and neck – in fact no fewer than twenty times.

When I arrived at the RVP (rendez-vous point) in the car park prior to photographing the scene, I was immediately briefed by police Lab Liaison. It was a bitterly cold winter's day, the sort of cold that penetrates to the bone. I was wearing multiple layers including thermal vest and leggings, fleece and woolly hat and yet I could still feel the cold. The area of woodland and the approaches to where the body lay were all cordoned off with police tape. This, for the duration of photography, was now my scene and I quickly took control. There were too many police personnel milling about, so they all needed to Foxtrot Oscar out of the way – and sharpish!

Using the classic scene documentation modus operandi, starting from afar with wide angle shots, then gradually working my way in to the main scene, I documented the entire area and all the possible views of routes leading up to where the body lay. After about half an hour, I had finally worked my way into the inner cordon and hence to the body – or what I could see of it. I remember only seeing the victim's upper body and back of her head. The majority of her body was hidden in undergrowth. I didn't know at this time that she had been stabbed repeatedly. I photographed the little that was visible and I recall trying to photograph the tiny part of the face that could be seen from a very low angle. My Pentax 6x7 was sitting on the Manfrotto, barely a foot off the ground – not an easy shot to do. Finally, after a couple of hours I was finished at the scene. I packed my camera and flash kit into my camera bag and folded up my Manfrotto.

I then made my way back downhill to the car park and my van, where a nice surprise was waiting for me. 'Teapot 1' (the affectionate nickname for the MPS mobile catering wagon) had arrived on scene and was already serving much needed, steaming hot cups of tea and bacon butties to police personnel. I packed my gear away into the Astramax van and made my way over to Teapot 1. A couple of plain clothes detectives were busy talking and munching on their bacon rolls, when one of them turned around, eyed me conspiratorially, before saying sarcastically to the caterer, "I suppose photog's gonna want a Rosie and Reg!" (roughly translated, Rosie Lee = cup of tea and Reg Varnie = Sarnie. Cockney rhyming slang abbreviated to confuse the hell out of, well, those of us not born within the sound of Bow Bells!). I was too cold to say anything and too thankful just to be offered a hot tea, never mind a bacon roll as well. They certainly hit the spot, but I was still famished and cold when I pitched up at Ealing Hospital Mortuary half an hour later. It would be another hour before the PM started, when I ran into the Coroner Dr John Burton, who was carrying a massive silver platter of assorted sandwiches down to the office adjacent to the mortuary. What a nice thought. I loaded some sandwiches onto a plate and as the office was already crammed full with standing room only, I leant against a mortuary table and filled my boots. Looking back, I can't believe I actually ate sandwiches in a mortuary!

As hinted at earlier, post-mortem photography isn't for the faint hearted. Working in the good old 120 roll film days with my faithful Pentax 6x7, I tended to frequent Westminster and Fulham mortuaries in the centre of town, especially for Home Office suspicious death and murder investigations – the so called 'special post-mortems' (or 'special' for short). I would occasionally get to Kingston, St George's (Tooting) or Ealing Hospital mortuaries, any number of other London borough mortuaries like Greenwich and Hackney, or even the old Kings Cross St Pancras mortuary, where I was first introduced to the infamous, toothless and aptly named mortuary technician 'Gummy Dave'. Gummy Dave not only scared me shitless the first time he peered round the front door at me, but I swear he wouldn't have looked out of place in a horror film. The mention of Kingston Hospital mortuary too, brings to mind yet another bizarre event. It was the third week in April 1992 and I had been dispatched by our esteemed Duty Officer, John Cook, to said mortuary to take facial mapping images of an unidentified, male deceased. I accompanied the mortuary technician to the fridge room, whereupon one of the many doors was opened, as my unidentified body was duly located. The technician then pointed to a big toe belonging to the adjacent dead person. It and the body it was attached to belonged to one Alfred Hawthorne Hill, who had died in Teddington just a day or so before on 20th April 1992. The gentleman in question had been famous in life. He was better known to the UK public as comedian and actor,

Benny Hill, perhaps best remembered for his burlesque, slapstick, slightly risqué television series, 'The Benny Hill Show'.

Post-mortems can be short – a quick photograph, full-length, front and back of the deceased - or multi-hour affairs in the case of complex murder investigations. The examination of the deceased involves a number of processes that include the collection of clothing and physical exhibits / personal items before the examination of the unclothed deceased can commence. Every stage of the examination, from clothed to unclothed, is documented with the camera, which will involve different camera angles, lenses and lighting techniques. Sometimes it is necessary to use a flash unit remote from the camera on a sync lead or even triggered wirelessly with the flash settings adjustable via the camera's menu, for example when taking photographs of the deceased full length and when capturing an image within a recess such as the body cavity or skull. Such angled or oblique lighting enables the photographer to reduce hotspots and reflections on areas of the body where moisture is present and also to reduce flare. An aperture of at least f16 is generally used to ensure good depth of field and hence, image sharpness. When photographing latent or hidden evidence, such as faded writing or marks on the skin, specialist lighting equipment such as ultraviolet flash guns, Crimescope and Crime Lites may be employed. As with every assignment, a minimum of two images would always be taken for every view. This recommendation started in the film era and has continued as best practise today with the digital age. The photographer must never delete in camera until the master images are safely stored and evidential and working copies have been produced. Using Nikon equipment, the general guidance varies a little between those who shoot with the camera set to take 'Raw plus a fine jpeg' image simultaneously, to those who just take fine jpeg images. In medical photography I take a Raw and a jpeg simultaneously so that I can post process the higher res file – using the jpegs as a reference tool.

Health and safety, as with any assignment, plays a huge part in post-mortem photography. A dynamic risk assessment would always be carried out and no actions would be undertaken without the appropriate safety measures and support in place. One always had to comply with strict protocols regarding PPE. Due to the risk of infection, any open cuts, wounds, grazes, or abrasions had to be covered with waterproof dressings prior to stepping out onto the mortuary floor. Protective clothing back then was a tad primitive and comprised little more than disposable plastic apron, overshoes and tripod condoms. Today, you'd be donning full disposable paper suit, gloves, mask, goggles / visor, overshoes or mortuary wellies. The minefield of hazards to negotiate include physical hazards (saws, cutting equipment, trolleys and tables), the entire contents of the fridge room, slips and trips and of course, feeling unwell. Biological hazards include blood and bodily fluids, bone dust, meningitis, AIDS and hepatitis. Chemical hazards include the ever-present embalming agents, formaldehyde, glutaraldehyde and ethanol. Finally, there are ergonomic hazards to consider such as manual handling, lifting, carrying, twisting and bending down.

Working in very close proximity to the deceased with the forensic pathologist, it is often necessary to get them to place scale on, or adjacent to, an area of the body or body part. Touching the deceased is always to be avoided. Immediately following the post-mortem, and in order to remove any bio-hazard contamination, all camera equipment needs to be thoroughly cleaned with a high-powered disinfectant. After that, a shower is recommended.

Nobody really knows what the accumulative effect of regularly witnessing harrowing and disturbing scenes (such as corpses being sliced and diced) will have on the mind of the forensic photographer. As I've mentioned elsewhere, I used to offload to my colleagues and they to me – often employing so called 'mortuary humour' to deal with all the distressing sights that I'd come across. My colleagues would handle their 'shit' in their own way. I never used to bottle my feelings, I'd always talk to someone and counselling was of course, readily available, although something of a rare commodity when I first started!

Wherever possible, and using a wide-angle lens zoom setting, front and back shots are taken first (full length clothed and unclothed) with the deceased on the floor, lying on a white sheet covering a metallic tray, or within an open body bag. Any visible injuries, tattoos, piercings, scarring, clothing, other identifying features and property recovered from the deceased, can also be taken with the deceased on the floor, without and then with scale. For standard images of injuries, the 50mm zoom setting is employed on zoom lenses for full frame digital cameras. Wherever possible, photographing square on (at ninety degrees perpendicular) is recommended. Often it is necessary to use a set of stepladders in order to gain the necessary height to look over the deceased. Facial mapping i.e. full face, side face, three quarter and both profile aspects of the head can also be undertaken with the deceased on the mortuary floor. After this, the tray on which the deceased is lying is raised and placed on the examination table. One must be mindful of the background, employing a white sheet, paper towel, or similar held by the mortuary technician, to declutter an otherwise distracting background behind body parts such as arms held out. Any external injuries, without and then with scale, not photographed with the deceased at floor level, can also be photographed with the deceased now at table height, together with any other identifying features. With very small injuries such as needle puncture marks and petechial haemorrhaging, which often indicate that death has been caused by manual strangulation, hanging, or smothering, a 60mm or 105mm macro lens is used and at least one locating shot is necessary to orientate the position of the mark(s).

Following the external assessment, the internal examination commences and images are taken of specific internal injuries, or indeed to show a lack of internal injuries. The pathologist may ask for a range of images to be taken in relation to any injuries present. Dissected organs may need to be photographed, which are placed on a surgical mat or plain sheeting. The camera is usually set to manual mode, with an ISO sensor sensitivity of around 400. Exposure is inevitably made with flash only, so it is important to check the maximum flash sync speed of the equipment in use to prevent shutter blind cut off. Alternatively, it is of course possible with some modern camera / flashgun combinations (e.g. Nikon) to use 'focal plane high speed sync', enabling flash synchronisation with very fast shutter speeds, e.g. up to 1/4000 second. Flash guns are usually fitted with wide angle diffusers. Polarising filters are fitted to the lens and over the flash guns, which cuts out light polarised at ninety degrees to the axis of the filter. These serve to saturate the image further, reduce unwanted reflections on the skin and enhance faded or old bruising that can be discerned with the naked eye. Using polarisers seems to work better on darker skin. Also, a polariser will cut down the transmitted light by approximately 2 f stops, so flash exposure compensation will be required. Photographing an x-ray sheet is undertaken with the camera perpendicular to the x-ray being mounted on a light box and therefore back lit. This will call for an ambient light exposure, which may need to be modified. White balance tends to be set to auto, but if working in close proximity to fluorescent tubes, for example, a modification to colour temperature may have to be made. Wherever possible, for mortuary photography, the camera is tripod-mounted for ease of framing and to free up the hands for flash gun holding. As with all assignments, accurate notes are always made, differentiating between left and right and employing correct medical terminology. Contact details are exchanged, the name of the pathologist, the name of the deceased and other relevant parties are recorded.

To aid electronic court presentation of images, the photographic documentation must always include location views to help orientate the position of the injury, together with detailed close-ups depicted without and then with scale included in the photograph. Just as I've found as a Medical Photographer in the case of a surgeon operating, it's often the case that a pathologist needs to be told of possible additional images that they would find beneficial to the investigation. Back then I had become so used to the clinical smell of the mortuary combined with the smell of the deceased, that I didn't wear a mask, but I did used to inhale Vicks and suck the odd 'mortuary mint' to try and disguise the stench.

It was at the old Hammersmith Mortuary of all places, when I was enjoying a welcome brew, courtesy of the mortuary technician, that I spotted the following version of an amusing poem entitled 'The Ages of Man' by 'Amen and Druse' attached to the office pinboard:

'From 20 to 30, if a man lives right
It's once in the morning and twice at night
From 30 to 40 , if he still lives right
He misses the morning and maybe a night
From 40 to 50, it's just now and then
From 50 to 60, it's Gods know when!
From 60 to 70, if he's still inclined
But don't let him kid you, it's just in his mind.
His sporting days are over, his little light is out
What used to be his sex appeal, is now his water spout
It used to be embarrassing, to make the thing behave
For nearly every morning, it stood and watched him shave
But now that it's getting older, it sure gives him the blues
To have it dangling down his leg and watch him clean his shoes!'

There were of course, many murder scenes I attended where there was no deceased in situ. The unfortunate victim had either died in the ambulance or later in hospital. The shocking murder of Nicholas John Hanscomb was a case in point. Dr Hanscomb was a brilliant genetic scientist who was involved with the development of the DNA genetic fingerprint test.

Dr Hanscomb was making his way home with some friends, towards the end of the Notting Hill Carnival on Bank Holiday Monday, 26th August 1991, when he ran into this group of youths on the edge of the carnival route. An argument ensued and one of the youths stabbed Dr Hanscomb in the upper thigh / groin with what witnesses described as a Rambo style blade. He managed to stagger some distance before collapsing into the arms of a policeman. Unfortunately, the knife attack had severed a major artery and Dr Hanscomb died in hospital three hours later. He was originally from Bolton in Greater Manchester, but had lived in Highgate at the time of his death and had been researching the ear condition tinnitus. This murder scene was particularly memorable for me as a) there was no body in situ and b) there was a considerable amount of blood dispersed along a protracted route. It was certainly one of the longest blood trails, if not the longest, that I've ever photographed. The stabbing scene itself necessitated taking views from all angles, including eye witness viewpoints, whilst the blood trail involved taking a series of images along a route, pausing at areas where there was a pool of blood - indicating where Dr Hanscomb had stopped momentarily on his quest to seek help. All the while it was necessary to ensure that the current image linked into the previous one, using clearly identifiable markers, i.e. street signs, cars, houses, in fact anything that the viewer could readily identify with. The senseless murder of Nicholas Hanscomb cut short a fine mind and a gifted scientist with an exciting career ahead of him.

Industrial and work-related accidental death scenes were part and parcel of forensic photography daily life. I attended multiple scenes from the large industrial complexes where victims had died as a result of slips, trips, falls, biohazards, sharps, items falling, crushing injuries and fire. The bizarre list of how victims came to meet their demise seems endless, but two particular jobs come to mind from the early '90s. The first of which was in Hammersmith, where a poor workman lost his life when he drilled through a live, underground electric cable in the pavement. The heat and sparks generated not only killed the victim, but melted a huge hole in the plastic awning of a kitchen appliances shop, located immediately behind the drilling site. A series of flimsy, red coloured, barriers enclosed this compact scene. A wheelbarrow full of debris was parked neatly next to the man-made hole in the pavement. A large sledgehammer and a pneumatic drill attached to a yellow cable, lay as lifeless in the road as the deceased would have been, close to a faded continuous yellow line, which was not quite abutting the kerb. The roadworks company sign, together with a couple of long handled shovels, completed the picture.

The second job also involved electrocution. Maintenance work in the form of rewiring was being carried out at the Royal Albert Hall in Kensington Gore, SW7. A metal, spiral staircase rail became live during a rewire and the resulting current proved lethal to another, unlucky victim. This job was memorable because there was so little room to work in. To do most of the shots on the staircase, my body was invariably contorted and I had to handhold my Pentax 6x7, whilst placing my flash guns on different stairs. It was cramped and because the power was off, very dark. Every shot had to be painstakingly set up and focused using my faithful, orange boat lamp.

On the subject of electricity, I attended one particular suicide in West London, again during my 1991-1993 initial stint on scenes of crime. A young chap had unfortunately decided to end it all by jumping off a bridge into the path of a high-speed train. Of course, I attended plenty of other suicide scenes, where the victim had jumped to their death from a building, bridge or other structure. Suffice to say, this particular railway job was nasty and for that reason, I don't intend to go into too much graphic detail. Although no trains were running and the power to the live rail had been switched off, I walked along the side of the track in my protective clothing carrying my camera bag, Manfrotto tripod and an ample supply of 120 roll film, albeit somewhat nervously. Even before I had begun my journey, I could smell charred human flesh in the air. It transpired that the victim had suffered traumatic amputation of both legs, one of which had got lodged in between the third live rail and one of the two track rails. The other leg was hanging precariously from a small overhanging branch nearby. If I hadn't realised by now that death had been instantaneous, I was left in no doubt when I spotted the mangled torso a little further on and to my shocked surprise it then dawned on me that the victim had been decapitated. Momentum had carried the head in question quite a way along the track, where it was being guarded by an ashen faced, young, female British Transport Police Officer. She nodded at me when I pitched up, managing a half smile, but couldn't speak to me for the duration. The haunted look on her pale, dry-mouthed face said it all and it was that look of horror, really, that I found particularly shocking and disturbing, more so than the peaceful expression on the grotesque face of the lifeless head that I was about to photograph. Not a pleasant type of job to do at all, but a classic example of how I dealt with such a situation. I got so wrapped up with the urgency of getting all the photographs firmly in the bag that I found that I was able to detach myself emotionally from the scene. The shots had to be sharply focused, well exposed and composed, evenly lit and scaled when necessary and they all had to link together to tell the story of events. I was simply there to make a visual document, to portray an authentic record of events and so bridge, track, torso, limbs and decapitated head became items to photograph, link together and portray an accurate story of what happened, nothing more. As I hinted at previously, it was far more shocking studying the printed photographs, (which incidentally made the 'gory box') some time later back at Amelia Street. At gruesome scenes such as this suicide assignment, I never allowed myself to ponder events for very long. I was much better at hiding behind my camera like a protective shield.

Every death we attended with a 'BIP' (body in position) was treated as suspicious until proven otherwise and like my colleagues I saw literally hundreds of dead bodies in myriad locations, from the mundane and accessible to the bizarre and ultra difficult to get to. Each would leave an impression on me, every death mask and facial expression indelibly etched, branded onto my subconscious. Even seemingly obvious suicide cases were suspicious deaths until the investigative team said to the contrary. In the early '90s, I went to Hampstead Heath in NW London to photograph a man hanging from a tree. It was suspicious from the outset because the deceased had been blindfolded tightly with a scarf, was partly kneeling down with his blue-coloured suit trousers undone and pulled halfway down to reveal white-coloured thermal leggings. The series of knots in what appeared to be lighting flex, in addition to the amount of surplus flex used to hang the deceased, was very intricate. An upturned briefcase had been left in the shape of a tent, with its contents scattered, close to the deceased. There was also a black duffel coat slung on the ground on the other side of the tree from the deceased and a single black glove was located at some distance from the hanging tree. The post-mortem that followed proved conclusively that the deceased had not committed suicide by hanging – he had been murdered elsewhere and at least two people had carried his body to the scene and partly strung up the body to make it look like a suicide. Having photographed the scarf and knots at various stages of being undone, the pathologist proved that the deceased could not have tied the knots himself.

Suicides, sorry, suspicious death scenes that turned out to be suicides were, sadly, a very common occurrence in the Capital and the method used to end one's life varied greatly. I started with the 'jumper' above and then there were those victims who'd put a plastic bag over their heads, had taken an overdose of pills, or had poisoned themselves. By their mere disturbing and very sad nature, several suicide assignments stick in my mind. I lost count of the number of hanging scenes I attended, be they indoors or outside. Hanging is defined as the suspension of a person using a noose or ligature around the neck using either the suspension method or the much rarer drop method. With the former method death usually occurs from strangulation and asphyxia. With the drop method, death can occur from cervical spine fracture with or without accompanying tracheal, larynx, pharynx and carotid artery injury.

In the summer of 1992, I was called to photograph a hanging scene in fields near Greenford and in an area not immediately visible to public gaze was a very sad sight indeed. A young, black, teenage lad was hanging from a tree branch from a rope noose, suspended with his feet about a foot off the ground. Characteristically, the victim's tongue was partially protruding and his head lolled to one side. The boy had been found by an older man out walking his dog, who by all accounts was still in shock. The job is memorable because the victim was wearing a bright red t-shirt, which against a backdrop of green foliage, served to immediately draw the viewer's eye into the photographs. This helped link the images and create a powerful visual documentation for the police and ultimately the Coroner. As with all hanging scenes, where the deceased was in situ, it was imperative that the knot or series of knots in the ligature were photographed in close-up, as this would either prove or disprove suicide. The beer cellar of an old pub in Barnes, SW13, provided the location of another suspension hanging scene, memorable because I was down in the basement room full of beer kegs, alone with the deceased, which gave me the willies and also because it was pitch dark down there. The male victim had died suspended, but partly kneeling with his feet making contact with the floor. Similar to the Hounslow Heath pill box murder, I used the timed exposure in conjunction with painting with light technique and as before, every time I fired a flash to light part of the scene, I would see the death mask of the victim's face lit up for a split second. Jesus, I worked like Billy buggery on that one – I couldn't wait to get out of the place.

During the tail end of my early '90s crime scene attachment, I photographed a few suicides by drowning and on one occasion, during a weekend on call, a very early Saturday wake-up summoned me to an area of the Thames just east of Tower bridge. An elderly gentleman who had grown weary of this mortal life, decided to end it all. By the time I arrived on scene, Thames Division (now the Marine Policing Unit) had already fished the body out of the river and it had been placed onto a white, plastic sheet to be photographed, prior to bagging up and removal to the mortuary. As I made my way down the uneven boat slipway, which was wet and covered in slippery green algae, I noticed a group of plain clothes detectives chatting with uniform officers around the body. Having cleared everyone away from the deceased, I took views of the dead man looking to the Thames beyond, full length shots of the deceased and close up photographs of the face to help the Coroner / police with identification. Views looking NW and SE along the River Thames were taken at the outset. My abiding memory of this job is the foul smell. The deceased had been in the water for some time and this combined with the dirty river water packed a punch on the putrefaction scale!

Firearms used as a method to commit suicide were again commonplace. Two jobs come to mind, both from the early '90s. I attended a house in Ealing, W5 where a middle-aged man had shot himself. As with most of the jobs I undertook, information relayed was minimal and I tended to join the dots once on scene. The house in question was a small bungalow, open plan on the ground floor, but when you walked in the front door, you realised that the house had undergone modifications. There was an open plan loft conversion, which was just that – open, so when you looked up, you saw the bannister rail of what was the deceased's office. Having been time checked into the scene (as with all scenes) by the officer outside and already donned in PPE, I then set about photographing the ground floor rooms - entrance vestibule, kitchen, bathroom and single bedroom - having ascertained that the deceased had shot himself with his own gun, whilst sitting at his desk. "Whereabouts is the deceased?" I asked a rotund, forty something, moustached detective. "Up there" he gesticulated, pointing up the stairs in the corner with a completely blank facial expression that gave nothing away. With my coverage of the ground floor complete, there were now quite a few detectives milling around. I approached the stairs and had barely got my right foot onto the first step when I froze. As I looked up, I found myself staring straight into the mouth of a double-barrelled shot gun! "Jesus!" I said in sudden horror, which was obviously audible as everyone stopped talking and turned to look at me, simultaneously, completely unconcerned. It had transpired that no-one had thought of the obvious health and safety risk – that there might well be a live cartridge in the pipe. The double-barreled shotgun, complete with a two-trigger mechanism, had been pointing directly at anyone coming upstairs and had not been made safe by a firearms team. I tactfully suggested that as time was tight, everyone was busy and the firearms team were tucked up, that a set of ladders be brought in, which surprisingly materialised within only a few minutes. This meant that I could safely gain access to the office via the ladders and climb over the horizontal, bannister rail. Crucially it meant that I would be working upstairs all the time with the firearm pointed away from me.

Once at the top of the ladders, I peered over the bannister and caught my first glimpse of the deceased. Dressed in a white polo shirt and jeans, the dead man had put his shotgun to his chest and pulled one of the triggers. He ended up half slumped over his desk and there was blood everywhere. There was even a significant pool on the floor by the deceased with blood splatter and body tissue spread over a wide, but localised area, including the ceiling, not to mention that the body was drenched in the stuff. Looking at the volume of blood and the firearm on the floor, it wasn't difficult to deduce cause of death. The shotgun had been placed low down with its stock on the floor, barrels pointing upwards towards the seated victim and cocked. Once the victim had made the decision to end his life, he reached down and squeezed the trigger. The recoil had made the firearm jump and land on the floor to the deceased's left, pointing downstairs, as I had discovered earlier. So, at the top of the stairs, on entering the office, the desk was end on facing the stairs. There were a few filing cabinets next to a stand-alone cupboard opposite the horizontal bannister and on the opposite side of the office to the desk was a couch, two armchairs and a coffee table, on top of which, was the latest copy of 'Country Life' magazine, adjacent to a number of other magazines. To complete the visual documentation of the scene, I took wide angle photographs from each corner of the office, blood splatter marks on the ceiling and walls, the deceased, pool of blood on the floor and surrounds, what little I could see of the deceased's face, the proximity of the firearm in situ to the dead man and of course the deceased's deleterious weapon of choice – the shotgun itself.

The postscript from that assignment was my hunch about there being a live cartridge in the other chamber turned out to be correct – primed and ready to fire. To think I had just stared down the business end of a double-barreled shotgun, which thankfully didn't go off in the split second that we had eyeballed each other! And so, I lived to see another day. However, that wasn't my only close shave, there were a few more courtships with danger to come before I handed my faithful 6x7 kit back into stores and finally waved goodbye to the Metropolitan Police Service.

When I first joined Scenes of Crime, I used to work SW London or '5 area' as it used to be known. However, if it was unusually quiet, John our beloved Duty Officer would pull you across to help out on other areas, so conceivably you could be working anywhere in London. On one particular morning I phoned John from Victor November (New Malden) and he sent me to a suspicious death scene at a business address in Edmonton, which at the time, embarrassingly, I'd never heard of! In fact, I stopped short of exclaiming to John that he was going to send me to Edmonton in Canada! North London in the early '90s was way out of my comfort zone. I would drive to a location, writing directions on post-it notes, like crib notes and frequently have to pull in to make sure I was on the right road. Then when I was within a mile or two of my destination, I would memorise the remaining route using left and right turns, e.g. L, L, L, R, R, L, L and surprisingly that usually worked. My system got me to the scene location, but I wouldn't have a clue about the proximity of other locations. At that time, for example, I didn't even realise that the famous football ground at White Hart Lane, home to Tottenham Hotspur, was literally, just down the road. It transpired that I was to drive north of the river to Edmonton N18 in the borough of Enfield. This was located about 8½ miles from the Strand in the centre of town and accessible from Junction 25 of the M25 and then south on the A10, or alternatively, using the good old North Circ. route. The M25 was a non-starter due to the mileage and rush hour congestion. The latter option, taking me first along the South Circ. to Hanger Lane Gyratory and then northwards via Wembley and Brent Cross, was by far the more sensible route.

The Edmonton sus death scene was located on a small industrial estate. The three-storey building was white in colour – a clean white, looking like it had recently been re-painted. The business itself specialised in selling second-hand computers. Incredibly, I was still a novice with the keyboard back then. As usual, there was a marked police car parked out front, which instantly confirmed to me that I had arrived at the correct address. I checked in at reception and was directed to the third floor. I took the lift up with the gear, and saw a middle aged, uniformed PC standing outside a door along the hallway to the left of the lift doors. The police officer, in noting my name and clocking my time of arrival, informed me that an employee of the company had taken his own life using a sawn-off shotgun. The deceased was a young male in his mid-20s, who had recently been made redundant. Depression had set in and the downwards spiral resulted in the unfortunate scene that I was about to photograph. The pathologist and detectives had been and gone and they were satisfied that the death itself was no longer suspicious. My photographs would now be used primarily by the Coroner. The PC had the decency to forewarn me that 'it's not a pretty sight in there'. The look he gave me was similar to my colleague Ian Scott when he dropped me off at Chalk Farm to photograph that famous shopping list of cars i.e. 'You poor bastard'! At least the warning gave me time to mentally prepare myself.

Leaving the PC outside, I pushed open the door to the scene and found myself in a spacious, light, white-coloured painted room. It was the third floor Gents' toilet. To my right were the urinals. In front of me were three toilet cubicles and opposite these and immediately on my right were the wash hand basins, with a mirror above each. The grizzly scene hit me immediately. The first toilet door was the only one of the three cubicle doors wide open and slumped, half sitting on the trap, half leaning on the tiled wall, was the deceased – or to put it more accurately, the deceased, minus most of his head. The dead man was clad in a pale blue pair of jeans, cheap, black trainers and a white t-shirt. His jeans and belt were both fastened and this coupled with the fact that he was sitting on a closed toilet seat lid, sadly indicated that he had intentions about as far removed from doing a 'Tom Tit' as you can get.

The business end of the sawn off looked to have been placed into the deceased's mouth and tilted upwards. The desired end result was catastrophic. Where there was once a nose and left eye, there was now nothing but fleshy innards and claret everywhere. The poor chap was devoid of a brain, as most of it was plastered on the cubicle tiles, high and to the deceased's left. What wasn't slapped on the walls, had collected into a congealing mass of splodgey, bluey-grey, red mess around the dead man's trainers. Unlike my previous encounter, the firearm had in fact been rendered safe by SO19 prior to my arrival and placed back approximately where it had come to rest. I surveyed the scene, taking in every detail. Having already photographed the communal hallway, views encompassing all three cubicles, urinals and wash hand basins, I now focused my lens on the left-hand cubicle and the deceased himself.

The wide-angle lens was used to cover the general shot of the deceased, which really set the scene in the left-hand cubicle. This was then followed by a wide-angle image showing the deceased's lower legs, floor area around the toilet bowl, blood and brain matter and location of the firearm. Images of the firearm itself and close ups of the deceased's upper body depicting traumatic shotgun blast damage to the head were then taken. A re-establishing photograph was taken showing the deceased's head at the bottom of frame, linking the top of the body to the blood and brain matter on the toilet ceiling. Just before pressing the shutter release at this stage, I had a sudden thought – what if some of that brain matter falls on my head whilst I'm photographing? I'd freak out! So, I went back to my camera bag, which was sitting on the floor near the door and pulled out a white, plastic, stretchy overshoe. I then proceeded to put this on my head for protection, as the original paper, disposable forensic examination all in ones had no built-in hood. In a scene reminiscent of the 1974 Clint Eastwood and Jeff Bridges film 'Thunderbolt and Lightfoot', I stared at my reflection in the toilet mirror for a few seconds. I realised how weird I looked with an overshoe on my head, so to lighten the mood, I pouted, blew my reflection a kiss and said in a low, husky voice, "Ooh, you sexy bitch!" In all seriousness, as crime scene photographers we often had to improvise and that overshoe literally saved the day and prevented blood and brain matter coming into contact with my scalp, for as surely as a dog returning to its vomit, it was whilst taking the last image of the dead man that I felt it......a splodge on my head! The overshoe was of course left at the scene as hazardous waste to be disposed of by thankfully someone other than me. I may well have looked a prat, but I had the last laugh!

The taking of one's own life using a knife, razor or other bladed instrument is by its nature, a very messy and unpleasant affair. My former colleagues and I attended a great many such scenes. Two particular jobs come to mind. The first was in early summer 1992. Duty Officer John Cook sent me to the affluent London suburb of Harrow on the Hill, located about 15 miles by road, north west of Charing Cross Station where, in a leafy street somewhere off the main A404 Kenton Road and within striking distance of the famous

Harrow School, was parked a blue, Ford Transit flatbed close to the kerb. The flat bed contained a few bags of what appeared to be rubble and a set of ladders. Nothing unusual there. Police tape had been used to cordon off the area and once I had been clocked into the scene, I set about building my story of events. Following images looking up and down the road, which both included the flat bed, I took a front ¾ photograph of the vehicle and shots showing the driver's door. When seen from the front at ninety degrees, give or take, the angle of the windscreen reflected houses and sky and this obscured the view of the deceased at the wheel. You virtually had to be up close to the driver's door to get the shock of your life, which is how a young Mum taking her daughter to school happened upon this dead body.

The dead man was in his late 50s, with curly grey hair, an aquiline nose and a couple of days' stubble growth. He wore a navy polo shirt, blue jeans and dark trainers and was sitting in the driver's seat with his head bowed and arms flopped down on his inner thighs, angled towards the footwell. Like so many of the suicide scenes I attended, I never got to hear the whys and wherefores leading up to the deceased's decision to end their life. Suffice to say, the instrument of choice was a Stanley knife blade, which the poor man had taken in his right hand and used to saw firmly and with purpose in many places on his left forearm. Undoubtedly, it would have been very painful and taken a while for the man to bleed out, lose consciousness and ultimately die. A large volume of claret had collected in the driver's footwell and resting in this blood, midway between the clutch and brake pedals, was the Stanley knife blade. Obviously, all photographs showing the deceased needed to be done with the driver's door open. I photographed firstly the closed door, then with the door open, looking straight in and across the deceased and gear stick to the passenger side, then an overlapping shot tilted down showing the legs of the deceased towards the footwell, I followed this with intermediate shots of the footwell and a close-up of the blade. I then took a re-establishing shot encompassing part of the footwell and the multiple injuries to the deceased's left forearm and of course a close-up shot of the slashed forearm. Finally, I took a reverse angle shot of the deceased from the open passenger door side. The job was memorable due to the confined space within which I had to work, the multitude of deep cuts on the forearm and of course the amount of blood that had collected in the footwell. However, despite the gruesomeness of the scene, nothing surpassed the moment when

I first set eyes on the shiny, Stanley knife blade and the sudden realisation of what it had just been used for. A very sad case indeed.

Equally upsetting was the suicide of a young, attractive brunette, who used a serated kitchen knife to slash her left wrist and stab herself in the chest, in the summer of 1992. When I arrived at the address in Twickenham, south west London, there were a number of marked police vehicles parked outside. The Laboratory Liaison Sergeant, the late Bruce Hoskyns, was standing outside talking to a middle-aged, balding, CID bloke, who had a face that was not only as hard as nails, but which was acutely pot marked, betraying the fact that this Detective Constable had suffered with severe acne in adolescence. The house in question had actually been converted into two separate flats and the deceased lived on the ground floor. Once I had put all my PPE on, I made a bee line for Bruce who briefed me on what was known so far. A 26-year old female had been found by her older sister, who had grown concerned that she was getting no response by telephone. The two sisters were very close and used to talk on the phone every few evenings. Images of the outside of the property were a real bastard, as, like so many jobs, I needed to get police vehicles and personnel shifted. The scene was suspicious because in addition to drips and splodges of blood seemingly all over the hall, there was a trail of bloody foot prints on the cream coloured carpet that seemed to lead to the bathroom and another set that seemed to lead from the bathroom to the front door.

Close-up photographs of the footprints were taken firstly without and then with scale. I then re-established the last bloody footprints on the hall carpet with the continuation of the footprints on the patterned, off-white lino floor covering in the bathroom. Although I had seen many dead bodies in a relatively short time period (just over a year), it was still momentarily shocking to first set eyes on a deceased person. This job was memorable because the deceased was clothed and lying half propped up in an empty bath. Once I had documented the bathroom with wide angle shots, I could concentrate on the deceased. And it was a very sorry sight. I noticed that her pale face, drained of blood, was smeared with copious amounts of the stuff. I noticed too, that her hair, short, straggly and brown, was swept back, loose, to reveal quite a high forehead. In death, her eyes were closed. Her forehead, chin, nose and outer cheeks were all smeared with blood, but her inner cheeks displayed less blood. The deceased's head was turned to her left and towards me, which meant that her left ear wasn't visible. Her right ear displayed what appeared to be a diamond stud. She wore a pale green and white casual check shirt with sleeves that came to just below the elbows. Her top had been rucked up to expose a bare abdomen and navel and her dark blue jeans had been unbuttoned and were gaping open, but didn't appear to have been pulled down. The dead girl's forearms were covered in blood. Her right hand, slightly curled, rested on her lower abdomen, where the top of her jeans were open. Her left hand was resting diagonally over her right upper chest, but tucked partially inside her heavily bloodied shirt. The top two buttons were undone. The white enamel bath was covered with smeared blood.

The bloodied, serrated kitchen knife could be seen on the bathroom floor, near to the deceased's bare feet. The blade, I estimated was a good eight inches long. This was confirmed when I photographed the knife in close-up without and then with a scale measure. These shots were linked to the deceased in the bath using my 45mm wide angle lens. There were bloodied marks and smeared blood on the pale blue-green tiles immediately above the height of the bath as well as blood spray patterns. The bathroom itself was quite compact, comprising the bath, which was immediately opposite the door, toilet to the right, behind the door and wash hand basin in between toilet and bath. The basin was smeared with blood, whereas the toilet had several blood drips on it. I couldn't see any blood spray at all on the white artex painted ceiling. It transpired that this young lady had first slashed her left wrist and then stabbed herself in the upper chest. I couldn't see the slash marks as the underside of her left wrist was facing down. At some stage during the proceedings, for reasons unknown, probably delirious and confused, she had staggered towards the front door and then back again into the bathroom, whereupon she flopped into the bath and writhed around in agony, all the while bleeding out and depositing blood smears, spray and drops around the room. By the time I had finished my visual documentation of the bathroom, CID were becoming more satisfied regarding their enquiries, with what was at first deemed to be a highly suspicious death scene and was now looking more like a suicide. The single bedroom on the left off the hallway and kitchen-diner further along on the left and opposite were all clean, neat and tidy. Nothing was out of place. There were no signs of any blood in these rooms, nor, tellingly, any signs of forced entry or struggle. The PM fell to one of my colleagues to cover and sadly the outcome was that the deceased had indeed killed herself.

As I have mentioned, it was very important to possess a mortuary sense of humour, to laugh at sick jokes, to share with your colleagues, otherwise you'd become totally 'FUBAR' ('Fucked Up Beyond All Recognition', from the 1998 film 'Saving Private Ryan'). As distasteful as it sounds to the uninitiated, there were plenty of jobs I went to where officers were having a laugh, even with the deceased still in situ! One suicide of a young lady in the mid 1990's was noteworthy, not just because she was totally naked lying on her chaise long, but because of a comment whispered in my ear, by a former colleague who was in training as a crime scene examiner and was just setting up his stall outside. With a wry smile and more than a mischievous twinkle in his eyes, Lew Packard whispered in my ear, just loud enough for me to hear one word "shaved". On entering this particular living room and seeing the twenty something naked deceased, the penny suddenly dropped – the dead girl was devoid of pubic hair. She was indeed, as Lew had indicated so succinctly "shaved".

Bryn Jones was a bespectacled and respected line manager who enjoyed a cigarette or three. He was also virtually bald and had a wicked sense of humour. Once, when I was in at Amelia Street sorting out my crime scene films, I noticed that one of my colleagues had stuck a 10"x8" of a deceased's head, taken at a post-mortem, up on one of the partitions dividing the sorting bays. With the deceased's brain removed, the scalp skin just flopped back over the void in the skull. The image bore an uncanny resemblance to Bryn Jones. To complete the likeness, someone had drawn a pair of glasses on the photo and stuck a part smoked cigarette, as if it was hanging out of the right corner of the deceased's mouth, bringing the whole creation to life. The resulting caricature was clever and simple in its conception and paradoxically, very funny indeed. However, even though he possessed a brilliant sense of humour, I'm not entirely sure that Bryn found the 'artwork' all that amusing! Remember, this was our way of dealing with stressful situations – it probably wouldn't be allowed today.

The death scenes that stick in my mind are all memorable because of the way the deceased was found, what they looked like, or what they were wearing. Or it may just be that I had a witty conversation with a colleague at the scene or perhaps that something unusual or funny (dare I say) happened at the scene. The common denominator is that there is something or someone in or at a scene that has enabled me to store that visual in an unlocked filing cabinet in my mind and recall the details multiple times over the years, as if on a film loop. Thankfully, when I conjure up images of death, I'm very calm, almost tranquil. They crop up almost daily. It doesn't bother me. I don't have nightmares – the images are just there. When I see the faces of dead people in a calm way, I like to think it's the spirits of the dead come to comfort me when I'm going through trying times. In some strange way, I've often felt that it's the deceased's way of thanking me for the small part I've played in documenting their case for the investigative teams and in many cases, helping the police to bring the perpetrators of heinous crimes to justice. Sounds a load of bollocks maybe, but it works for me and I've never left a scene disturbed or stressed out for longer than a few minutes or seconds and as far as I know, I haven't suffered from post-traumatic stress. Being calm and feeling comforted isn't what most people would envisage feeling after visiting the most terrible scenes of violence and carnage for hours at a time. I think I'm very lucky, for I know of two former colleagues, both of whom were experienced forensic photographers of many years standing and both of whom suffered with post-traumatic stress disorder (PTSD). One, a very dear friend of mine, whose PTSD manifests itself in acute, cluster headaches, the severity of which often causes him to continually head-but his bedroom wall in an effort to dull the pain. Both former colleagues, in my opinion, were treated appallingly by the Job's Occy Health department, prior to both being medically retired.

A couple of death scenes spring to mind that I've selected from the file in my mind, marked 'funny experiences'. Still in the early '90s, whilst on call one evening, I was sent to the old Wimbledon Odeon cinema, long since demolished, to photograph a middle-aged man who had committed suicide by fastening one end of a ligature around a pipe, located quite high up on a toilet cubicle wall, and the other end around his neck. When I arrived on scene, I checked that I didn't need to wear a disposable forensic suit, before photographs were firstly taken of the cinema entrance and vestibule, followed by linking shots to the Gents' toilet, and interior images documenting the urinals, wash basins and cubicles. There were several cubicles and the deceased was located in the end cubicle behind the closed toilet door. The cubicles in turn were opposite the urinals. Having photographed everything leading up to the deceased's cubicle, a specialist team was standing by to move in and dismantle the door from the outside as the deceased was wedged immediately behind the door, preventing entry. The dead man had been found by the first uniformed police officer on scene, peering firstly under the affected cubicle door to be greeted with the bottom of a pair of trousers and the back of a man's shoes – then secondly, standing on the toilet lid of the adjacent loo and peering over the top into the deceased's cubicle. Once the cubicle door had been removed, the hanged man could be photographed more or less, still in situ, with him facing the toilet and away from me, albeit with allowances made and duly documented of any small disturbance of the body's final resting place, having been made by the door coming off.

Prior to photographing the knots in the ligature in close-up, I set up photographing the deceased. Due to the close proximity of the cubicle door opening and deceased to the urinals, I was unable to photograph him and the attached ligature full length, so having re-established the door-less cubicle with the urinals, I then had to sit in a urinal to get the angle and give myself enough space for me to take an overlapping wide angle shot, I took this firstly from the feet to the head and then secondly, from half way up the body angled up towards the ligature tied to the wall-mounted pipe. It was whilst focusing up for the latter overlapping shot that the urinal automatic flushing system decided to activate and as I was hemmed into the urinal by my heavy Manfrotto tripod and of course sitting on the damn thing, I couldn't get out of the way quickly enough. I felt the cold water penetrate my 'shreddies' and I had to complete the assignment with a saturated derrière! Needless to say, I didn't tell a soul.... until now. The entire experience sort of gives a whole new meaning to the phrase 'taking the piss' or even 'pissed wet through'!

Equally humorous looking back, although not remotely funny at the time, was the sudden death of a Spanish diplomat's son in Notting Hill. Access to the modest, second floor flat was by a private entrance door with a frosted glass partition, which on opening, led up a flight of stairs to the deceased's living room. A young, uniformed policeman stood guard outside this door and on seeing me and examining my police pass, made a note of my details and arrival time. Bruce Hoskyns, the Lab Liaison Sergeant, had been in and surveyed the scene from the top of the stairs, which offered a good view of the living room and deceased on the floor. Bruce hadn't entered the accommodation to avoid contamination. Once I'd got changed, Bruce was happy for me to begin my visual documentation of the scene. I realised immediately why the scene was suspicious as soon as I got to the top of the stairs. In front of me was a desk, on which was a large VDU screen, with a computer floppy disk and hard drive underneath. The deceased, a computer whizz in life had been blessed with macho good looks and an enviable head of wavy black hair. He was lying on the floor in front of the desk in a fetal position, totally naked bar his underpants and surrounded by hundreds of floppy disks. And I do mean hundreds. There were disks everywhere, papers scattered liberally, chairs up turned, clothes strewn. The scene was as about as suspicious as it gets – unexplained, scantily clad, male deceased surrounded by computer disks, items upturned, stuff all over the place. This all amounted to major signs of a disturbance. Understatement of the year, the place was a bloody mess, it was completely trashed. What the hell had gone on here? Was the dead man murdered for secret information contained on a computer disc, now missing from the scene, or was the murderer leading us to believe this was the case to throw the investigative team off the scent, when really there was an unconnected motive? Whatever – it wasn't my job to do the detective work, my task at hand was to undertake an accurate, visual documentation, which I duly did. Interestingly, there were no signs of injury on the dead man, nor a drop of blood to be found either on the deceased or surrounding area, or in any of the other rooms. Once I had finished photography in the living room, I needed to link the deceased to the rest of the flat, as I still had the bathroom, single bedroom and small kitchen to document. Satisfied with this re-establishing shot, I then carefully tip-toed around the deceased's feet and set up an intermediate wide angle shot slightly closer and looking towards the open bedroom door.

So, imagine the scenario. I'm all alone in this death scene. I have the body perilously close on the floor behind me and I'm slightly stooped over, peering through the viewfinder framing up the next shot, focusing my tripod-mounted Pentax 6x7 and just pondering the lighting situation. Then I freeze in momentary terror......the deceased lets out a loud, deep, guttural groan!! A new definition of shitting your pants had just been invented as I legged it out of the flat to the constable at the bottom of the stairs. Said police officer refused to accompany me back inside (bastard!) but thankfully, a smiling Bruce Hoskyns agreed to come back with me. I was somewhat surprised, but thankful to find the deceased in exactly the same position that I'd left him. At that moment Bruce couldn't contain his laughter any longer and explained to me that contrary to my belief, the deceased hadn't come back to life. It was in fact the intestinal tract gases forming during decomposition that were escaping through the deceased's mouth and nose, causing the vocal cords to vibrate, that had caused the eerie sound. Having never come across this phenomenon before and nobody having explained it, understandably I was freaked out. I suppose I should have counted my blessings that the scary noise emitted wasn't a death fart, which would have been even more bizarre!

Bruce began his examination of the dead man and surrounding scene, whilst in a somewhat more relaxed state I finished my photography of the remaining rooms, which I found to be unremarkable, relatively tidy with no signs of disturbance. A colleague covered the post-mortem and I was to learn the following day, that cause of death was hypothermia i.e. natural causes! The Spaniard had flu before he died, which rapidly developed into hypothermia. Emergency help should have been summoned as hypothermia occurs when the body loses heat at a faster rate than it can produce it, precipitating a dangerously low body core temperature, failure of the heart, respiratory system and eventually death as in this case. The Diplomat's son, by all accounts a workaholic, probably tried to ignore the shivering as he slaved away for prolonged periods in a very cold room. The associated confused thinking, the loss of rationality as nerves get damaged, preventing self-awareness probably accounted for the deceased feeling irrationally overheated and consumed with a desire to cool off, whilst literally freezing to death, in all probability led to the hasty removal of all his clothes (referred to as paradoxical undressing) and accounted for him trashing his own living room and workspace.

Many suspicious death scenes where the deceased was in situ, as I've intimated, stand out for different reasons. The obese, middle-aged lady who I photographed in Teddington, was memorable because she was a hoarder – the entire house was crammed floor to ceiling with rubbish and cardboard boxes. My abiding memory is photographing this enormous woman lying on her bed surrounded by hundreds of cardboard boxes full of old books and junk. It was as if she had drowned in cardboard boxes. Images of a young Indian wife, stabbed by a controlling husband with a short fuse, come crowding in. The attractive lady, dressed in a short, navy blue skirt and white blouse, had died in her Chiswick home on her white tiled, blood spattered kitchen floor, having sustained several knife wounds to her stomach. I remember snippets of this job, because the victim had died open-mouthed, revealing an impeccable set of white teeth and with her eyes open staring skywards, still wearing a look of horror on her face.

Following a particularly heavy boozing session at a Fulham pub one summer's night in the early '90s, a fight had broken out on Fulham Road and an unfortunate middle-aged man ended up very much dead on the pavement due to one of his ex' two inch stiletto heels penetrating the front of his skull, right between his eyes at the top of his nasal ridge. Nasty! The job is memorable for two reasons. Firstly, the body, which was located at the junction of Fulham Road, Fulham Palace Road and Fulham High Street, was left in situ for my photographic coverage (there were no disposable crime scene examination tents then), but only because the police were able to close all the roads off. I used the body as a locator for all the main approach shots. This created a powerful link between each image. Secondly, one of my colleagues, the late Morgan Helps, once told me when I was 'strapping' with him, that if ever I got called to a murder scene in the middle of the night, then, "Whatever you do, don't rush. By the time all the troops turn up on scene it will take several hours". "If you rush", Morgan had said, "you'll be waiting around twiddling your thumbs". So, what was the first thing I did in the early hours of that fateful morning? I promptly forgot Morgan's sound advice and legged it to the scene, only to be the first person there and then I had to wait around for bloody ages. As impressionist Mike Yarwood's Lord Healey once said, "Who's a silly-billy…?"

Then there was the poor old Harlesden man, several years in rent arrears, who hadn't been seen for months. When police were notified by the council to gain access to his second floor flat, knocking over a mountain of unopened mail that had accumulated behind the front door in the process, it was quite apparent that this old man who lived all alone, had died all alone and had in fact been dead for at least two years! The deceased was lying on the living room floor, just clear of the doorway to the hall, wearing a vest and stripy, faded, brown-coloured, pyjama bottoms – and oh my God, he was totally skeletonised! I stared in disbelief because I'd never seen anything like this before. There was no smell. Blow flies attracted to the cadaver like a magnet, had been and gone, laid thousands of eggs and the hatched larvae or maggots had grown fat from burrowing into the deceased and during a feeding frenzy lasting between four and ten days, had filled their boots on the decaying corpse. Having undergone several stages of larvae moulting, the resulting pupae would have then developed into young flies, the whole cycle taking about two weeks. There were no signs of any living flies in this flat. One would have thought that residents living directly underneath would have detected a very unpleasant odour as decomposition sent gooey liquid seeping into the floorboards. Apparently not in this case. (I did attend a separate suspicious death scene where the deceased was found only after a couple noticed a foul-smelling brown liquid dripping down from their kitchen ceiling and alerted the council, who in turn contacted the police). The space between this second storey boarding and the ceiling of the first floor flat obviously contained everything. The most interesting aspect of this case was the deceased's hair, which had completely fallen out onto the floor and collected into a neat arc around the skull. The saddest fact was that this old man, who had no-one to call on him, had died about two years previously and because there were no relatives or visitors, the body had lain undiscovered for that length of time.

Outbuildings in a typical suburban semi-detached Roehampton street were the setting for a very peculiar case indeed, one summer's day in the early '90s. A foul smell emanating from a utility room and adjacent garage had been reported to police. On arrival police had discovered what looked suspiciously like parts of a rotting corpse that had been chopped up and left to fester in several large, white-coloured, plastic containers. When I arrived on scene, half the street had been cordoned off, a small inquisitive crowd had assembled with members of the press, rumour-mongering had shot into overdrive, CID and uniformed police were in abundance and the pathologist, Dr Rufus Crompton had just been clocked into the scene to examine the fetid remains and to give his opinion. I was waiting with my camera gear prepped ready to take detailed images of the street, premises and remains of the deceased in situ. Dr Crompton emerged from the outhouses after only a minute or so and with a slight grin told the assembled gathering that the deceased was in fact 'venison', the deer undoubtedly poached from nearby Richmond Park. There were sighs of relief and big smiles all round as what started as a potential murder scene was hurriedly downgraded! I worked with all the main Home Office Pathologists during my operational scenes of crime years, but I saw Dr Iain West, his wife Dr Vesna Djorovic, Dr Richard Shepherd, Dr Rob Chapman and Dr Rufus Crompton on an almost daily basis. My favourite forensic pathologist without a doubt was Dr Richard Shepherd, a learned, friendly, calm, but forceful presence in many a London mortuary. He was a great man to work with. Dick Shepherd introduced me to parts of the human body, I never thought existed! It was obvious Dick Shepherd was enthusiastic about his craft and that enthusiasm inevitably spilled over into the mortuary. Ever the teacher, he was always keen to point out 'bits and bobs' to those who expressed an interest and I always expressed an interest peering into hundreds of body cavities and staring at so many dead body parts with him. Top bloke! I also have visions of Dr Crompton wearing his plastic, green apron and white wellies, silver hair curled up at the back, walking carefully across Tooting's St. George's Hospital mortuary to the scales with somebody's brain in his cupped hands! I remembered thinking how utterly bizarre that image was then – thank God, not many of us get to witness such a sight.

CHAPTER 11

Bomb Standby On Call Rota and Drug Dealing to Care and Protection and Brothel Raids

From time to time I had occasion to be concerned for my own safety. This usually occurred when I found myself on a dodgy estate, for example, in Peckham or Stoke Newington at night, or when up several floors photographing perhaps, an arson scene and imagining being thrown out of an open window by a gang of burly toe rags! In the early '90s, with the Irish Republican Army active both on the UK mainland and over the water on the Irish mainland, SO3 (2) Photographic Branch as we were known, set up a bomb standby rota. In effect, an additional, separate photography on call to cover terrorist events.

I was duly summoned from my bed in the early hours of one summer's morning with the bare minimum of job details for security reasons – it seemed that maybe even Bomb standby Photogs weren't to be entirely trusted! The address was Ikea, Wembley, but I had to RV at 6am on Drury Way, some distance from the Swedish furniture giant's car park. The journey there was no hassle and meant driving first on the South Circ and then, once passed Hanger Lane Gyratory, the North Circ. I arrived with 10 minutes in hand and as instructed, I contacted MP on Channel 5, who relayed a message to covert officers on scene. Barely a minute after completing my radio message, a dark blue Astra emerged from nowhere and pulled up alongside me. I was to follow the covert officers and park up when they signalled for me to do so. I then followed the two officers, who were both of a similar age to me, to an OP (Observation Post) that had been set up on the second floor of Ikea. Even behind semi closed window blinds, I deduced that the OP had a great view of Ikea car park. Surveillance stills and video cameras were set up in the darkened room, pointing to a vehicle somewhere in the car park and this equipment was manned by dark clad UC's (Under Cover officers). I was given a quick briefing by a middle-aged, unshaven, balding DS, who, judging by the generous apron of belly overhanging the top of his jeans, had indulged in far too many well-oiled ruby murrays over the years!

The vehicle of interest to SO13 (Met Police Anti-Terrorist Squad) was in fact a trailer, minus the lorry cab, believed to contain around 15, steel beer kegs full of ammonium nitrate fertiliser explosives! My job was straightforward enough – plot up behind an armed police convoy, follow said convoy into the car park and take close-up photographs of this trailer unit from the front and from the rear. What could be simpler to the discerning forensic photographer? However, the seriousness and potential danger of the situation hit me like a thunderbolt, when I returned to my job Astramax van. I quickly wondered what it would be like to be blown up by a bomb and just as quickly, put the diabolical thought out of my mind. I was summoned over to another dark Astra and a nearside rear window was promptly wound down. A guy with dark brown hair and sporting several days' worth of stubble looked at me in a macho, no nonsense sort of way. "Follow us, stay close. Any sightings, we get out of there immediately, OK?" I nodded. I wasn't about to do anything to upset the apple cart, for who was I to argue? All four guys in this vehicle alone, not only looked as hard as nails, but they were also seriously tooled up. Although their side arms were concealed, I couldn't fail to see the H&K's (Heckler & Koch MP5, 9mm, sub-machine guns) resting on their laps – and there were multiple vehicles in the convoy!

No sooner had I jumped into my Astramax, the convoy was off. As instructed, I stuck close to the guys in front and concentrated on the task at hand. We parked up reasonably close to the lorry trailer and I wasted no time getting out immediately and marching round to the back of the van to get my equipment, whilst the convoy looked on. They were watching my every move as well as the rest of the car park (along with their surveillance officer colleagues). I strode over to a point that I'd eyed up on the way in and set up on a front three quarters shot. I quickly mounted the Pentax 6x7 on top of my Manfrotto and had the shot composed, focused and metered for the available light in next to no time. I then delved into my camera bag and set my two Metz 45 flash guns up, which would be used as fill-in light – one Metz wired into the camera and held in my left hand against a long bulb air cable release, the other Metz fired by slave unit. One shot at F16, the second at F11 and then I popped the flashes back in my camera bag, slung the bag over my shoulder, picked the tripod-mounted camera up and strode around to the back to set up on the rear three quarters shot. I employed the same procedure as for the front.

I had literally just taken the second image and thought 'Great, the job's in the bag', when I heard a police radio crackle into life "possible sighting, possible sighting, everyone out, everyone out!" I instantly thought that it had suddenly gone tits up. Shit, possible terrorists were in the vicinity and what was this? The convoy was already moving, potentially leaving me on my own! With no time to take the camera off the tripod, let alone collapse the Manfrotto tripod's legs, I flung open the van doors and literally threw all the kit in the back. I'd worry about whether the gear was still intact later. I slammed the doors sharpish, before running around to the driver's side. Amazingly, the convoy, although some way ahead, was still in sight. With heart beating fast, I turned the key in the ignition, flooring the Astramax' accelerator the moment the engine fired up. With a massive front wheel spin and a slewing of my job van from side to side, I was out of there quicker than a toupee lost in a hurricane! Fortunately, we were given the all clear soon afterwards and following a lightning de-brief, I was on my way southbound, back to Victor November, whistling between my teeth at the close call that was now behind me....and that the equipment survived intact!

The postscript from that little assignment came to light the following morning, when I learned that the IRA had got wise to police photographing suspect vehicles using flash as a fill-in light and had started to booby-trap cars and lorries containing explosive devices. The flash slave, working on the same frequency as the booby trap, would explode the bomb. Jesus! That was scary biscuits. The realisation of how close I came (within touching distance of that lorry trailer) to being vaporised into nothingness, hit me like Wandsworth's school days kick in the bollocks, all those years before. From that moment on, we were instructed not to use flash when photographing potential terrorist vehicles and devices. Talk about stable door, bolting, horse disappearing and all that! My colleagues shrugged off the news as if this was a minor embuggerance, whereas my friend and colleague, Derek, went one better. Wearing a huge grin on his stubbly face he turned to me and said, "Well Paul, just think, if you had been blown up, I would've been straight on the phone to your Missus, asking for all your Nikon gear!"

On one particularly memorable Thursday evening on call, Photographic Duty Officer Don Westhead (aka The Grim Reaper) sent me to Notting Hill Police Station. The brief from Solicitors' Branch (the legal team dealing with prosecutions), seemed very straightforward. I was required to photograph the exterior of a particular house in St. Luke's Road at 7pm. Apparently, there had been a serious assault outside the location at this exact time on this particular date precisely a year before. The Reaper had earned his nickname because he always came across as very pessimistic. Whenever there was a whiff of bad news, inevitably it would be the Reaper who'd deliver it to the Photographic masses. Famously, when the MPS underwent Market Testing, followed by restructuring and the outlook seemed a tad uncertain, it would be the Reaper who'd send the headless chicken brigade into overdrive, scurrying around stirring the shitty stick. In the midst of all this negativity, a few of us took a break from printing our crime scene negs and decided to pop down to Mari's on the Wally Road for a much needed, big boy's breakfast. Before we made it to the pedestrian entrance, we bumped into the Reaper having a cigarette in the car park. With a long drag on his ciggy and a disbelieving shake of his head, Don looked at us and said between pursed lips "I hope you've all got fucking protected mortgages!" Thanks for spoiling my breakfast Reaper. Photographic Branch survived Market Testing and restructuring and all the worrying at the time was over nothing. After that, I quickly learned to adopt a 'water off a duck's back' attitude whenever the Reaper prophesised.

This teatime, however, the Reaper was all for offering some sound advice. "Whatever you do, don't go to the address alone, call into BH first and get a police escort to the scene". The drive to Notting Hill Police Station took me from New Malden up the A3, north along Roehampton Lane to the junction with the South Circ at Barnes, then along Rocks Lane and Castelnau to Hammersmith Bridge, onwards to Shepherd's Bush and then to BH via Holland Park Avenue and Ladbroke Grove. On arrival at BH in Ladbroke Road, I popped into the control room, only to be told that a TSG (Territorial Support Group) carrier had been assigned to me, but unfortunately had just been re-assigned on an urgent 'shout'. They could offer me a beat Bobby. The only information I had been given was that I needed a police escort. God only knew why TSG had been assigned to me. It seemed a little OTT. I mulled over the job in my mind – it was very close to the 'nick' in terms of driving time and I'd already planned the images in my mind: three views, from opposite looking towards the address and views along St. Lukes Road in both directions that would include the address in shot. At that moment, the young beat constable popped his head round the control room door. About 5 feet seven in his DM's, the young officer didn't look a day over eighteen. I was half expecting his 'puppy walker' to materialise behind him and what was that – a shadow under his nose, or was it 'bum fluff', I couldn't be certain? Youngster or not, I would be taking a police officer with me and I was keen to get the job done and in the bag before another more protracted job, like a murder or fatacc (fatal road traffic accident) came my way. I kept asking myself, why on earth would I want a whole TSG carrier full of officers? It was anybody's guess, but this fact niggled me on my way to the scene.

It was only a few minutes' drive to St Lukes Road and the young constable pointed out the address in question. I parked on the opposite side of the road, the equivalent of half a dozen doors along. The two of us got out of the Astramax and I had a good look up and down the road and across to the house that I was to photograph. The place was like the Mary Celeste - eerily quiet, no cars, nobody else in sight and the address was in darkness. The PC stood by my van on the pavement, whilst I bolted the Pentax 6x7 onto the Manfrotto's quick release tripod head. A timed exposure of around 30 seconds at F8 would be needed for the view looking towards the house. A shorter timed exposure would be required for the views along the road, as the scene here was brighter. The semi-detached address, old paint peeling off its front façade, looked neglected, dingy and unloved and I was just pondering what sort of people might live here, whilst pointing my camera towards the address and focusing up, when suddenly, to my complete shock, all hell broke loose. The front door of the address was flung open, the noise punctuating the quiet, reverberating back and forth. A very tall and solidly built, black male in his mid-to late 30s came bounding over ranting a barrage of expletives. His high decibel, verbal diarrhoea and threatening body language very quickly told me that this guy hadn't come over for a bit of male bonding, fist-bumping and mutual backslapping, or to invite us in for a few cheeky beers!

"What the f***in' 'ell you doin' marn with that f***in' camera takin' f***in' pictures of my house? You f***in' c**t, you f***in' Babylon, I'll f***in' breakya f***'in' camera...". Weirdly, throughout this protracted tirade I was calm enough to take in the guy's demeanour and facial features. This Rastafarian had some of the longest dreadlocks I've ever seen – a few pock marks here and there and at least two gold teeth. I noticed that the whites of his eyes were watery and bloodshot and quickly deduced that he was taking something a little bit stronger than wacky-backy! I just about managed to get a word in and replied slowly that I had been asked by the police to take these photographs, but the angry Rastafarian was having none of it. "I'll break that f***'in' camera" he continued and suddenly lunged for it. "Don't touch that!", I countered, as I wrapped a protective arm around my camera kit. I simultaneously looked over my shoulder having noticed movement in my peripheral vision. I got the fright of my life, for at that moment, the young PC and I were completely surrounded by around eight, equally tall, young, black males all finger-pointing, jostling, at times invading my private space and all in all, being very intimidating. I heard strange sucking noises accompanied with, "Babylon" (local slang, of Jamaican origin, for the police) muttered several times. I looked anxiously at the PC, who, to give him credit, was already talking into his radio. "Assistance required, assistance required, non-urgent, repeat, non-urgent, over...". But the young copper was looking worried and I for one was beginning to feel very unsafe. I remember raising my voice, "What do you mean, non-urgent, it is bloody urgent!" The PC didn't need to be told twice as he corrected his previous radio call to urgent assistance required.

I heard one more cry of "Babylon", and within seconds the black guys seemed to vanish into thin air, just as two TSG carriers screeched to a halt. From the lead vehicle, a bald, moustached, middle-aged sergeant, whose appearance and deportment would have screamed ex-military to a two-year old, got out of the passenger side and marched around the front of the carrier glaring at me menacingly. Standing taller than me at around 6 feet two in his trademark standard issue MPS boots, the Sergeant's generous moustache twitched and then he let me have it – "What the bloody hell are you doing here?!" My instant relief on the 'fight or flight' scenario being narrowly avoided, turned to sudden anger. "Good evening to you as well Sergeant", I countered with more than a hint of daring sarcasm in my voice. "I've been asked to photograph the exterior of these premises for Solicitor's Branch". The Sergeant was now much more relaxed as he said, "Best you get yourself back to the station, sharpish". I nodded as it suddenly dawned on me that the TSG arrival in the nick of time had just prevented the fireworks from exploding.

I quickly dismantled the gear and put everything back into the Astramax. I gave the young PC a lift back to BH and I popped my head round the door of the control room. “Close call photog!” came a voice from somewhere to my left. A plain clothes detective in his early 50s smiled sympathetically and asked for me to follow him to a portacabin, located in the station yard. I opened the door and just stood there transfixed, gawping, lost for words. My eyes wandered over hundreds of images of the address I had just failed to photograph. There were aerial photos and surveillance images taken from every conceivable angle, pictures taken up and down St Lukes Road and towards the target address as well as photographs taken of people coming and going from the address. The CID guy studied me intently, before letting me have the good news. The address that I’d just come from was at that time the major centre for drug dealing in Notting Hill...Shit and bloody derision!

Just how close I had come to being seriously harmed or worse, hit me suddenly as I was driving back to New Malden over Hammersmith Bridge following my aborted assignment. The TSG had saved my life, for with all the jostling and taunting from that gang of huge blokes in what amounted to a few short, testosterone-fuelled moments, the truth of the matter was that I really didn’t have a clue what I had got myself into or what I was going to do to get myself out of it. The reality was that extreme danger was close at hand. Nobody had my back. Come to think of it, nobody was watching my front and sides either and it occurred to me in all the confusion, moments before the TSG arrived on scene, that it would have been so desperately easy for one of those Rastafarians to plunge a knife into me and slip away, stealthily into the Notting Hill ether, whilst guaranteeing yours truly a tray for my body to bunk down on that night...... in Westminster Mortuary’s fridge room!

I was really narked when I got home. My pen was scorching before I’d scribbled the first line of an emphatic letter of complaint that didn’t hold back. I handed it in to the Reaper first thing the following morning. Naturally, it fell on deaf ears because nobody gave a shit. Everything was quickly forgotten. Thankfully, I can count on the fingers of one hand, the times when I felt threatened and in danger, whilst working on crime scenes. The banter with colleagues and funny or bizarre situations you’d find yourself in far outweighed the few times I feared for my safety. Whilst writing this, I am suddenly reminded of the occasion when I was summoned to Buckingham Palace to photograph the rear of Her Majesty’s abode...because a guard had accidentally discharged a round from his rifle, which had punctured a neat hole through one of the large sash windows! I had visions of HRH Prince Philip, Duke of Edinburgh striding up to me, mid assignment and bollocking me to kingdom come, with an opening volley of, "What the bloody hell are you doing here – get orf Her Majesty's land?!"

As forensic photographers, we also got to cover 'care and protection' assignments, where children, unable to be adequately looked after, were found literally living destitute, surrounded by mess. In such impecunious circumstances, social services would have children taken into care. In the case of residing adults, social services usually deemed that they were unable to look after themselves through, for example, disability or protracted illness. Here we would be asked to evidence the squalor for Social Services' reports– visible dirt such as days old unwashed plates, filthy kitchen, evidence of faecal deposits on the floor and surfaces (both human as well as animal), dirty condition of the bathroom, living room and bedrooms. It was usual to meet police officers outside the address as they normally carried the front door key. On one such occasion during an evening call out to an address in Fulham, I was informed that four young children under the age of ten had been taken into care as the mother was an alcoholic. Just before opening the front door, the tired looking, plain clothes police officer, who I estimated to be in his mid-40s, turned to me and said, "It stinks in there, the place is a shit hole!" I had already donned my protective attire and having photographed the grotty hallway and minging living room of this ground floor flat, I worked my way into the kitchen. What a mess! There were dirty pots, pans and plates piled high and covered in mould and encrusted, decaying food in the kitchen sink and on the draining board that looked like they'd been there for weeks. The officer wasn't joking – the place smelled of ripe shit, pungent, stale piss and smegma, dust and decay. The dark brown lino floor looked for the whole world as if it had never seen a mop and every time I took a step my overshoes made a squelching sound as I cautiously traversed this sticky jungle.

Everywhere I looked, there was clutter and rot. I almost stepped in a runny turd, located on the floor immediately below the sink, which looked more human than dog, but I wasn't about to find out. I just ensured the excrement was visually documented. Pleased to get out of the kitchen finally, I was under no illusions regarding the adjacent bathroom, which didn't fail to disappoint. A single, low wattage, shade-less bulb hung down from grimy, yellow electrical flex, barely attached to the ceiling. The off-white bath was gross. The loo was disgustingly filthy. There was no seat, the toilet water was dirty, the sides of the loo had smears of faecal remnants, not to mention two large, mid-brown coloured, 'log' floaters half submerged in the toilet bowl. I spied another turd under the sink. The porcelain cistern lid had a chunk missing from its left side and I shuddered at the thought of little ones running around as I photographed the exposed sharp edge - a health and safety concern on its own, never mind the rest of the place! Even the bare floorboards were dirty. The once pristine, cream walls and white ceiling were now peeling and were a mix of grey and aged magnolia. With only two bedrooms to photograph, I was now keen to get out of the place. The first bedroom had two manky, soiled mattresses on the floor, which were surrounded by rubbish, plastic bags and old papers. A quick couple of images from the doorway was all that was required to show the general state of the room and sleeping conditions, devoid of bedding.

The second bedroom I glimpsed through the open doorway, off the hallway, revealed a single bed, amazingly perched on top of a frame. It was telling that this bed had been used to store boxes and junk on top of it. The light wasn't working, but even as the dingy hallway lighting spilled into this final room, I could see that the décor here was in a similar shit state to the rest of the flat. I would light the initial photo looking into this bedroom with flash and then look at taking another couple of images from inside the room, painting with light. With Pentax 6x7 framed for composition and focused on the scene, I checked my first Metz flash was wired into camera. I held this against the bulb cable release. I then angled my second slave flash as fill-in.

No sooner had the exposure been taken and the flashes fired, there was a sudden movement amongst the boxes, accompanied by a deep groaning noise. I stared in shocked disbelief as this white haired, dishevelled figure slowly sat up squinting and blinking in quick succession and turned his dirty, stubbly face towards mine. The guy, who was completely hammered, gesticulated wildly at me with a large bottle of Teachers Scotch Whiskey. The golden liquid about a quarter full, was slopping about precariously inside with every incoherent grunt and moan. All this gave me quite a start, as my adrenaline levels rocketed. I raced out of the address to the waiting police, who quickly ushered the vagrant squatter out of the flat. Satisfied that there were no more hidden surprises, I finished off the shoot, left my filthy PPE outside the scene and hot footed it out of there. Again – it took me a while to see the funny side to this assignment with that dark figure suddenly rising from the bed giving me an awful fright.

Working as a police photographer, you really did get to see all sorts. An early summer's evening on call assignment in 1992 took me to a sudden death scene in Overstone Road, W6 and a very clean and tidy ground floor Hammersmith flat. Wide angle establishing photographs were used to cover the hallway, bedroom, bathroom and lounge / diner, as the scene itself was all contained in the modest kitchen. An early to mid-30s, bald, male deceased was lying face up on the kitchen floor, completely naked apart from a light brown, thick, silver-studded dog collar sitting snuggly around his neck. The collar was attached to a lead of similar colour, the latter lying limp on the dark blue lino floor and stretched out to the deceased's right side. The arrival of the pathologist had made the story thus far much clearer. The deceased was engaged in probably both anal and oral sex with his boyfriend in the deceased's kitchen. To heighten pleasure in the moments preceding ejaculation, the deceased in all probability, bit down on an amyl nitrate capsule, at the same time as leaning back to tighten the collar around his neck, the other end of the looped lead had been hooked over the inside kitchen door handle. At this point, the deceased was either having a 'J Arthur', or being J Arthured by his partner. Unfortunately, at the moment of ejaculation, the tightened dog collar had strangled the deceased, causing the boyfriend to run off in a state of panic. This was the first case of potential auto erotic asphyxiation that I had encountered.

The overlapping establishing shots of the kitchen encompassed the kitchen units, cupboards and worktops and also the full length of the deceased. There appeared to be no visible signs of residual ejaculate either on or in the vicinity of the deceased's circumcised, detumescent penis. An intermediate shot was then taken to show the dog collar around the deceased's neck and lead. Close up images showed the deceased's face and dog collar. A re-establishing shot was then taken looking towards the kitchen worktops from the kitchen doorway, which included the deceased's head at the bottom of the picture. I then focused the camera on the kitchen worktop items. My eyes scanned multiple sex toys. I counted six dildos of varying sizes and colours, four cock rings, an opened pack of twelve Durex Featherlite condoms with an adjacent, discarded condom wrapper (a used condom was found in the kitchen bin), a pair of silver coloured handcuffs, one black PVC, one black rubber and one dark brown leather, full head and face masks, two leather riding crops, one leather 'flogger' (like a mini cat of nine tails...apparently!), two malacca canes of different thicknesses, several knotted gags, two identical, black rubber over metal, engraved butt plugs and a couple of other things that puzzled me. I turned to ask the middle-aged detective behind me, who was busy taking notes. I pointed inquisitively to the items, which looked for all the world like a cross between giant bulldog clips and the gizmo you usually pulled out of the kitchen drawer at Christmas to crack walnuts. "Ball crushers" the DC said, as he winked at me with a wicked grin! We both mentally crossed our legs at the agonising thought!

Brothel raids were a regular assignment – the offence? Owning and running a brothel and living off immoral earnings. Two Soho jobs immediately spring to mind. Firstly, a spacious basement flat in Rupert Street, W1, owned by a very wealthy 'Tom' (prostitute) comprised two double bedrooms, kitchen / diner and bathroom, all of which were immaculately clean and tidy. Having photographed all the rooms, that included a goldfish bowl containing assorted condoms in each bedroom, together with that many sex toys, I lost count and other paraphernalia, I turned to what I naturally thought was the lounge and opened the door. I stood there open mouthed. The décor of this spacious room was all black, including the floor and ceiling. To clarify, most of the ceiling was actually a giant mirror with a black coloured painted border. The centre piece was a double bed with red silk sheets. The big headboard had manacles and chains attached and a tad to the right, several sets of handcuffs were dangling from hooks. The right-hand wall was home to a variety of different sized whips, crops, canes, paddles and belts, whereas on the opposite wall were various masks that ranged from pvc to leather and from simple eye, masquerade style to full head and face coverings. Abutting the wall opposite the bed was a rail containing uniforms of every description. At the end of the bed was a gymnasium vaulting horse, although I wagered that very little vaulting had occurred over it – at least, not whilst it was located in this room. On the right-hand bedside table, I spied the all too familiar goldfish bowl containing assorted condoms. For my notebook and album index, I didn't really want to describe this room as the lounge or front room, so I turned to the DC behind me and said, "What shall I call this room?" The DC shrugged his shoulders and when I said, "The whipping room", we both creased up laughing!

The location of the second brothel raid in Tisbury Court, was just around the corner from the previous Rupert Street job, although there was a time difference of a few months. With the first job, the 'Tom' in question had already been arrested and I attended the scene with the officer from CID. This next job, however, necessitated me attending a pre-raid CID briefing at local Vine Street Police Station for 6pm prior to a 7pm raid, where the Madam along with her Toms would be arrested. Once the premises had been raided, arrests made and the place clear of bods, I was then to photograph the layout and interior rooms. There were about fifteen people in the first-floor office and the hardened, fifty something Detective Inspector running the operation, acknowledged my arrival with a quick nod of the head. The DI had visible war wounds - facial scarring from what appeared to be a three-inch knife wound to his left cheek and a smaller scar on his chin. He had a Jack Regan-esque air about him, which told the room very clearly not only who was boss, but also that he accepted shit from no-one!

The briefing commenced with a surveillance update detailing recent movements and that relevant parties were currently believed to be at the address. The DI then went from one officer to the next checking that he or she was clear of their role for that evening. This was followed by questions, which is when I piped up. "Anything in particular you'd like me to photograph, Guv?" "Well, you know what you're doing Photog, the usual layout, and the menu of course...". Without thinking, I stared at the DI and said, "Oh, why, do they serve food there?" With that, the whole briefing room collapsed into uncontrollable laughter and I just sat there grinning back at the DI, wondering what was so funny and then chuckling along with the rest of the guys, because I thought I should. The DI just eyeballed me and mouthed, "piss-taker" in my direction. After the laughter had died down, the moment came to plot up and hot foot it by van to the brothel concerned, which was less than half a mile to the north-east.

With all the arrests in the bag, it was time for me to do my bit. Having photographed the hallway, lounge, kitchen and bathroom, I photographed the first of four bedrooms. With the shots from the doorway looking across the black silk-sheeted double bed, I entered the room and set up at the foot of the bed to do the reverse angle shot that encompassed the headboard, bedside tables and doorway. It was then that I spied, what appeared to be a menu perched on the bedside table nearest to the door. It was also at that moment when the penny dropped, as I read the list of 'food' items on the menu, for example:

- Full Strip - £20
- Vibrator and oral – £25
- Spanking and hand – £25
- All position sex – £35
- Lisa's Extra Special – £45

Additional items included:

- Uniforms available £5 extra
- Something Else!! See Me!! In P.V.C
- Live out your fantasies from £30

The Menu ended with the wording spelled out in capitals, 'SUGGESTIONS WELCOME'! In fact, the only real food in the whole place was a few small packets of salted peanuts in one of the bedrooms, offering a convenient post-coital snack perhaps?

CHAPTER 12

Fatal and Serious Personal Injury Road Traffic Accidents

It was a Friday night on a mild October evening and I was on call. A fatal road traffic accident took me to Lambeth Bridge south side, where unfortunately a male in his early 30s had been knocked down and killed by a black cab whilst crossing the north bound carriageway. The victim, who had died on impact, had already been taken away. When I arrived on scene, I parked up on the left, having just turned into Lambeth Bridge Road from Albert Embankment. The entire north bound lane had been completely closed to traffic and blocked off by a police vehicle. Another police car on the north side of the Thames at the junction with Millbank was redirecting all vehicles south, with the exception of buses, along Millbank to Vauxhall Bridge. Back at the scene, I was briefed by the Accident Investigator and had worked out the images I needed to take to document the story of events. Two approach shots looking towards the black cab (still in situ) a reverse angle shot showing the scene looking approximately south, a front three-quarter view of the taxi and a close-up of the frontal impact damage (bumper, radiator and cracked windscreen).

Having tripod mounted the Pentax 6x7cm camera, my first approach shot towards the rear of the cab would be taken from adjacent to the police car blocking off northbound traffic, i.e. from the roundabout junction at the A3036, Albert Embankment. I would be taking two identical images at different exposures, F11 / F16 at around 1 to 1 ½ minutes. As soon as I had levelled the camera on both planes, composed, focused and set the aperture and then the shutter to between X sync and 1/000 second (the timed exposure setting), I signalled to one of the traffic officers behind me to radio to his colleague on the north side to stop buses and taxis coming across. Once the south bound lane was clear, I could take my photographs.

For the second of the approach images, I needed to move about thirty meters further north. I thought the traffic police would let some of the buses waiting on the north side to pass across Lambeth Bridge in between shots, but they obviously decided to let me crack on with my shots so I wouldn't get too disrupted. I went through the set-up procedure as per the previous shot, although this time I was somewhat closer to the back of the black taxi.

I checked focus and composition again to satisfy myself that all was well and was just about to trigger the shutter with my bulb cable release, when I noticed four men in their late 20s walking very quickly towards me, but on the opposite pavement. I was a little puzzled as I thought that pedestrian traffic had also been redirected away from Lambeth Bridge. As they drew nearer, one of the guys who seemed to be periodically covering his 'family jewels' looked familiar. Just as I was thinking that it looked like one of my colleagues, Neil Banks, sure enough I saw the familiar blonde wavy barnet, the tall, six foot two plus, athletic frame come bounding over to me. "Evening Paul", Neil said with a semi Cheshire cat grin, "So it's you that's holding half of London up. We've been stuck on a bus on the north side of the river going nowhere for ages, busting for a piss! In the end we just gave up and made a run for it". After a quick laugh and a mock apology offered from yours truly, Neil and his mates hurried off leaving me to finish documenting the rest of the scene.

The photography of fatal and serious personal injury road traffic accidents, known in the job as an 'RTA' or a 'fatacc', often constituted a very challenging assignment indeed. If they involved a police vehicle, the term 'PolAcc' would be used to denote 'Police Accident'. The forensic photographer's modus operandi followed a stringent set of guidelines for these particular types of scenes. Day or night, once mobile, you'd generally be on your vehicle's police radio to give an estimated time of arrival on scene. This would be particularly important to traffic control at New Scotland Yard, trying to calculate how long a road would take to re-open. Health and Safety as with all scenes is very important. I'd always don my fluorescent yellow hi visibility jacket before doing anything else. I'd have to be cognisant of my surroundings – bystanders not just ignoring and ducking under police cordons, but with a little too much interest, watching my camera gear and seeing money for drugs in their minds' eye. Or worse, a driver failing to stop, hell bent on getting from A to B and driving straight through a police cordon and right on through a fatal accident scene. This actually happened to one of my colleagues on a busy London arterial road. Traffic had been stopped and Matthew John left his tripod mounted Pentax in the middle of an empty A40 to go back to his van parked on the side of the road for another roll of film. Suddenly there was an almighty crash – a vehicle had driven straight through the police cordon and into the camera equipment, sending the Manfrotto and Pentax clattering to the ground. The driver, transfixed on getting home, had no idea what he'd just done, until of course he was stopped further along the A40 and rightly 'stuck on' by a waiting traffic unit!

Then there are always physical, chemical and biological hazards such as broken glass, jagged metal, vehicle debris, petrol, diesel, oil, brake fluid, blood and body parts, as well as unsafe structures to consider – when I'd always wear my hard hat and overalls. If I was called out at night, I had my own tiredness to consider. It always took me a while to get from asleep to fully awake every time the phone rang at some ungodly hour, no matter what the job was and I usually needed a caffeine injection before I left the house, but still – I was always extra careful driving at night. After every job, especially murders, sus deaths, post-mortems and fatal road traffic accidents, I'd always have to spray my equipment down with Trigene, a strong disinfectant.

Upon arrival at an RTA scene and having checked in with the Accident Investigator (A.I.), it was important to get my orientation before taking any images to get my exact location. Nowadays of course GPS and geotagging can form part of each digital image's metadata to pinpoint location. As with any assignment, the contact details of the officer dealing and the story of events would be obtained to enable me to plan which photos would be taken. Accurate notes, disclosable in court, would be made throughout to ensure the final album was presented in chronological order. The following types of images required the use of the Pentax 6x7cm 90mm lens as it approximated to the human eye viewpoint when looking straight ahead with minimal perspective distortion (with today's full frame DSLR cameras, a 50mm lens would be used):

Approach and witness viewpoints. I'd always liaise with the AI as to the position of the camera in relation to the driver / witness viewpoint. I would employ landmarks such as road names, junctions, lamp post numbers, house numbers, shops and business names to show my location. When none of these were available, for example, on a country lane in the middle of nowhere, the AI would employ their measuring wheel to determine distances from and to. Features such as road signs and markings would often need to be depicted in photographs and similarly, road surface features such as camber, potholes and whether the surface was wet or dry, would also need to be documented as well as lighting and weather conditions. A high viewpoint was often required by the AI, for example, from a bridge, rooftop, or other elevated vantage point, to obtain a complete overview of the scene. Nowadays, police officers have the added advantage of using drone imagery. Prior to drones, of course, it was Polecam for a short while and not forgetting 360-degree immersive imaging. Whether stills or video, a 360-degree platform or drone - all these devices are just tools for recording the scene efficiently and it's all about selecting the best tool(s) for documenting each job.

Any marks on the road, kerb, verge or property, including skid, drag or scuff marks would always be recorded. Some of these marks would be photographed first if there was a danger of the road surface drying out and the marks literally disappearing. Inevitably, some marks would be located underneath the crashed vehicles and had to be photographed last once the vehicles had been moved.

Front three-quarter, side, front, rear and roof views of all vehicles incorporating close-ups of any damage, possibly from multiple angles, would then need to be taken along with marks and damage to any tyres. At least one image showing the front interior of each vehicle (if practicable) would also be taken, for which a wide-angle lens would be used to get as much detail in the image composition as possible.

Special requests from the AI included photographing the view seen from the driver's seat, wing or rear-view mirror, speedometer dial, lorry tachograph, footwells, metal fatigue, unstable or heavy loads, views underneath vehicles (for example, to show hair fibres and of course, dead bodies in situ).

Photographing during daylight hours presented numerous challenges such as the sun creating too much contrast and flare in the lens. I'd regularly have to flag the lens in addition to using a lens hood and fill in flash to help lower contrast. Photographing into the sun, a real bastard, was sometimes necessary if recreating the driver's view. Then, there was always the problem of getting my shadow, or myself and my equipment in shot, or reflected in windows and vehicles. We had to photograph in all weather conditions – rain, wind, fog, snow and ice - each bringing with them their own problems. I used to carry a large golf umbrella and several clear plastic bags to protect the equipment, not myself! If it was ever windy, I'd suspend my heavy camera bag from the Manfrotto tripod's central column and use police vehicles and or personnel on either side of the camera as wind breaks. Using flash in foggy conditions had the same effect as using a vehicle's main beam – the light bounces off the fog creating flare, so it was never used.

Other problems to contend with included stopping the traffic. The inevitable wait whilst emergency vehicles left the scene or simply getting emergency vehicles to move if they were in shot. Flashing blue lights had to be switched off, they were not only distracting, but they'd annoyingly trigger my slave flash guns. Moving people out of shot, including the police and rubbernecking bystanders, as well as stopping people walking through my shot proved a regular cowson! Generally, people standing still gawping at the scene would register on the photographs, whereas people wearing dark clothing walking through a scene at night would not register. This was because I employed a timed exposure (see below) of a minute or longer to record the image fully in camera.

Photographing an RTA at night, brought with it additional health and safety as well as photographic considerations on top of those already mentioned for daylight photography. When called out from your bed whilst in a deep sleep, a hazard in itself, one always had to be mindful of driving whilst tired. On scene, the high vis jacket's reflective properties made it an essential item of clothing. You have to really hone your senses in the darkness and develop an acute awareness of your surroundings and potential physical, chemical and biological hazards.

The main photographic problem was the difficulty of focusing the camera in darkness. Once I'd framed and composed the shot, I'd shine my big, orange boat lamp approximately a third of the way into the scene, or if this wasn't possible, I'd place the lamp in the scene and focus on that, then remove the lamp and take the shot. For approach shots lit with average street lighting, a timed exposure would be used of approximately 1 minute / 1 ½ minutes at F16, adjustable depending on the intensity of streetlighting. Again, for my approach shots, if there were no streetlights such as on country lanes, and as an emergency only, I'd sometimes use police vehicle headlights, alternating dipped and main beam to try and lower the contrast a tad and make the lighting more even. The timed exposure would then be used in conjunction with a flash technique called painting with light that involved firing the flash multiple times and at different locations and angles for the duration of the timed camera exposure, for vehicles and property. The camera exposure would have to be adjusted for light, dark and red coloured vehicles. I also used my boat lamp to determine reflections, some of which could potentially ruin a shot. Just by standing a few feet to one side and / or lighting the subject from a different angle, it was possible to control unwanted reflections. You'd also still have to be mindful of getting the shadow of yourself and your camera equipment in shot, sometimes caused by streetlighting behind you. Then of course you'd have the added problem of oncoming headlights and taillights registering as distracting streaks on your image. The solution here was that during approach shots, all traffic would be stopped from driving past the scene in both directions (as you might be working with one or more lanes open) and the first few oncoming cars stopped in the distance would then be told to turn off their headlights for the duration of the camera timed exposure. When photographing traffic lights during a timed exposure in darkness, one would have to consider that all three lights may well register on the timed exposure, unless of course, it was a particularly long phase. The traffic lights would also affect the exposure if they were in close proximity to the camera.

If I was required to photograph underneath a vehicle, I'd always check the condition of the road surface beneath the vehicle, together with the underside of the vehicle and consider using a sheet to lie on and a cover for my head – in case of oil, grease, blood, etc. Wherever possible, I'd enlist the help of police officers if an extra pair of hands was needed. At the end of every RTA scene, as with any job, I'd run through the list of photographs taken with the investigating officer, as recorded in my notebook, to ensure that I had a complete visual documentation of the scene.

Fatal and serious personal injury road traffic accidents varied enormously in terms of type, i.e. you could be faced with car versus pedestrian, car versus car, lorry versus cyclist, motorcycle versus car, or multiple vehicles etc. In addition, the scene wasn't always compact. You could turn up in the dead of night to find one vehicle in someone's garden, another 100 yards down the road and another on its roof in a field. You'd have to photograph them all and link all the vehicles together, presenting your visual documentation in chronological order wherever possible, which was no mean feat, especially if it was lashing down with freezing cold rain blowing horizontally in strong winds!

Undoubtedly one of the worst fatal road accidents that I've ever been called to occurred early one summer on a stretch of triple carriageway, not a million miles from my home. I was awoken from a deep sleep just after 1 a.m. and given the location details of the assignment. Suffice to say, the job was so close to my house that it was further to drive to my local police station to pick up my job van, than it was to then drive to the scene about a mile away. This job proved to be one of only two fataccs where I didn't need to contact traffic control on my radio to give them an eta at the scene, purely because I was so close – there was no point. The entire north and southbound carriageways had been closed to traffic following the accident and as I approached a cordon on a slip road that would give me access to the triple carriageway, a confused traffic officer sidled up to my driver's window with a look on his face that said, "You can't come through here, mate, the road's closed". I waved my police logbook at the officer with the magical 'open sesame' word "Photographic" and I was greeted with "Blimey, that was quick!" The amenable police officer backed up a little to let me pass and I waved to him by way of a thank you. I saw the first set of flashing blue lights about a hundred meters along the road, the moment I joined the main carriageway from the slip road. I drew level with the police vehicle and waved my logbook at the officer, who beckoned me through. Another hundred meters or so further on, I could see a whole barrage of flashing blue lights and I realised that all three emergency services were in attendance.

I parked on the left some way behind a fire tender and went to the rear of my van to pop my hi vis jacket on over a navy-blue job mac. At this stage I couldn't see the fatacc scene because there were so many emergency vehicles parked in all three lanes, so obscuring my view. I saw Tony, the AI, emerge to greet me. "Nasty one this, Paul, triple fatal. The bodies are still in position and I could do with you photographing them all for the Coroner. Witness accounts say matey, who was on his mobile phone, was doing about a ton in lane three. He then clipped the kerb back there (Tony pointed to a chalked mark in the road and on the kerb, some way behind us), lost control of the vehicle, overcorrected the steering, whereupon the BMW swerved violently into lane one, where the car on hitting the kerb again, became airborne. The car flew through the air on its side and crashed into this steel pedestrian walkway, where it virtually disintegrated."

I had my boat lamp with me and Tony with his equivalent seek and search torch, took me into the inner scene for a recce. The BMW itself looked like some giant hand had scrunched the middle of the car. On impact with several of the walkway's steel support girders, the car had literally buckled in the middle sending the engine into the rear seating and killing all three occupants instantly. Although twisted and mangled, the main chassis was all in one piece – just. The rear half of the car was on its side and the front completely contorted section was bent back on itself so that the front wheels, just about intact, were facing the opposite direction towards the rear wheels. The remains of the male driver who had been squashed, were visible partly underneath the front section of the vehicle, buried in muddy foliage, like some gigantic hammer had whacked him into the ground. The upper part of a male passenger, whose legs were missing, could be seen hanging out of the concertinaed rear compartment with his arms outstretched and hands in the dirt, like he was bracing himself for a fall – but in reality, that's just how his body had ended up, post impact. His upper torso was twisted as if he had been burdened with scoliosis in life and his pale blue shirt had been rucked up to his neck exposing a trim, bare abdomen and upper buttocks. The view of the vehicle on its side, showing the two deceased men and part of the pedestrian walkway, would be a technical challenge and then some. I would need to paint the foreground scene with a shed load of flash during a timed exposure of at least a minute, maybe even two minutes, which would in turn overexpose the carriageway lights in the background. I would not only have to paint with light, but I'd need the Metz 60 flash and power pack due to the number of flashes required. The cluster batteries for this job would be as useful as a hog roast at a vegan wedding and would drain in next to no time, but nevertheless, I was in no doubt that I would need to call on them. Also, with plenty of metal in the scene, I'd have to watch lighting angles and control reflections.

The whole scene was a health and safety nightmare. There was jagged metal, broken glass, bodies, body parts, blood, fuel, oil and brake fluid to contend with, never mind the fact that I'd had less than two hours' sleep, which played havoc with my body's circadian rhythms! I'd need to be very careful indeed. On the opposite side of the wreckage, but more parallel to the road than the two, male deceased, Tony showed me the body of the third victim, who was a young, black female in her early 20s. Similar to the male passenger, this unfortunate girl had also suffered traumatic amputation of both legs on impact. She was lying on her back, with her face turned away from the road towards the underside of the rear of the vehicle, which as I've said was on its side. Her short, curly, brown hair clung to her muddied face, but it was still evident in death that she had been pretty in life. The white shirt she had been wearing had been forced up to her neck on impact. Her arms had come to rest above her head and I noticed a gash to her right elbow had stained her white sleeve crimson. She was also wearing a small, black, leather waistcoat, which had been ripped to bits and was barely attached. This young girl was wearing light blue jeans and around her waist I saw a broad, brown-coloured belt. She had lost her left leg below the knee and her right leg was missing, give or take, at the groin.

From the kerbside, the image encompassing the deceased girl looked as though the rear nearside tyre and wheel assembly was about to bare down on top of her. I clearly remember this young girl's fingernails, the tell-tail signs of a pre-night out manicure, all her nails still glossy red, her nail varnish still very much intact. Four or five flashes on manual half power in conjunction with a timed exposure would be quite adequate I surmised. Tony took me to the front of the wreckage, which was so dark we were waving our seek and search torches around in the blackness examining the damage. I crouched down and planned out another shot in my head, depicting the whole side of the vehicle (the opposite side to the two deceased men). Again, multiple flashes during a timed exposure would be required, with half a dozen manual full power flashes around the other side, fired as backlighting. I was still in a crouching position, as the angle was quite low to the ground, working out how many flashes and from which angle I'd fire them, when I heard Tony say, "Careful Paul, watch out!" Simultaneously, the A.I. grabbed my arm to stop me losing my balance and putting my outstretched hand onto one of the female deceased's severed legs, which bizarrely looked like part of a department store mannequin that had been discarded in the grass.

To photograph the entire vehicle and all three deceased in situ, took me a good hour as I first had to get emergency vehicles and personnel to Foxtrot Oscar out of shot. The painting with light involved numerous criss-crossed flashes for each view, which of course was doubled up (for the back-up negative). I drained a Metz 60 battery, a Quantum power pack and four cluster batteries in the process, but fortunately, being a bit of a cautious Colin, I had a reserve Metz 60 and Quantum pack on board the van. Once I was satisfied that the main scene had been fully documented, I indicated to the A.I. that the deceased could be safely removed. This process took at least half an hour, during which time I retreated back some way, waiting and watching with my tripod mounted Pentax 6x7 and camera bag at the kerbside. I felt quite knackered after this initial photography coverage. It had been emotionally and physically draining.

It wasn't even the early hours of the morning and I guess that momentarily I zoned out. When I came to, a young, pensive, female LAS paramedic was standing close to me at my three o'clock. I turned to look at her and she smiled and said, "I was watching you work just now and was wondering how on earth you do your job?" I smiled back and retorted "Well, I was just wondering how you do yours!" We both smiled again as we simultaneously realised that each other's answer was the same – you just get used to it. We all do. Those who don't, fall by the wayside or move into something less gruesome, less awful, maybe less stressful. Our professional respect for one another was mutual. When I resumed photography again, the road was devoid of the majority of emergency vehicles. Three or four approach shots were taken and intermediate and close up shots were also taken of the initial impact on lane three's kerb and also lane one's kerb, prior to the BMW becoming airborne. When at last I had finished documenting what turned out to be the worst and most herculean, challenging, fatal road traffic accident that I'd ever covered, I had been on scene for more than five hours. Whether driving a bad boy's Beemer or a humble Deux Chevaux, this fatacc left me with a strong sense that at such a high impact speed, you might just as well have been driving a cardboard cut-out car. The only upside apart from the fact that it hadn't been raining, was of course that my house was only a mile away. I had time to get home, put all the batteries on charge, shower, have breakfast, a brew and shut my eyes for an hour on our luxurious 'John Lewis' sofa (that was so comfortable, it could have been custom designed for forensic photography on call power napping). I was just able to gather my thoughts, before the phone summoned me and it was off out for an entire day and evening, non-stop, to do it all over again.

A few weeks later, I found myself volunteering for a weekend on call that was up for grabs, as a colleague had phoned in sick. It was a late May Saturday evening and the fatacc that I'd just been sent to by the duty officer, Benjy McPhee, was on the same stretch of triple carriageway but southbound instead of northbound. Yet again I found myself working a stone's throw away from home and yet again, officers dealing with the fatacc expressed their incredulous surprise at how quickly I materialised on scene. On a 70 mph stretch of road, this young, three series 'Beemer' driver had suddenly jammed the anchors on for reasons unknown, lost control of the vehicle, clipped the inside lane kerb, where once again the vehicle became airborne, took out several trees and came to rest on its roof in undergrowth, with the rear of the BMW nearest the kerb. The driver and his male front seat passenger had been taken to hospital with broken legs and bruised ribs, but unfortunately, the young female passenger, who was sitting in the back, had been catapulted out of the vehicle on impact and had subsequently died at the scene. Her body had been taken away to the local hospital mortuary.

It had been raining at the time of the accident and Paul Croft, the AI, was keen for me to photograph the long skid marks on the road before they dried out and disappeared. As soon as I had donned my hi-vis and had arranged for police vehicles to be moved out of shot, I got to work, first photographing from the start of the skid marks looking towards the scene, then from the end of the marks looking back (the reverse angle shot), then from half way along the marks in the direction of travel and finally at ninety degrees perpendicular to a set of tyre marks that had been chalked around by the AI to show detail. Once the marks had been documented, I needed another two approach views, which would take in the road scene and marks from a distance, before I could photograph the path cut through the trees by the airborne vehicle (for which I used my Metz 60 to light up all the trees and undergrowth) and finally a rear three quarter view of the BMW itself. Three of the wheels were visible on the upturned car, with the exception of the front nearside, which had foliage covering its entirety. The rear three quarter view required a timed exposure of at least a minute at F11 and based on the 'Inverse Square Law' (light fall off), four times the amount of flash hitting the front of the vehicle compared to the rear, which of course was closest to camera. Once again, I drew on my faithful Metz 60 because of the number of flashes required at manual full power. This job was memorable due to its close proximity to the triple fatacc on the opposite carriageway, the urgency of photographing the long skid marks and the BMW on its roof that needed careful, balanced lighting to even out the quantity of flash hitting the front compared with that fired at the rear of the vehicle.

At a fatal or serious personal injury accident, it was routine for the AI to try and reproduce a set of skid marks at the scene by using the vehicle (s) involved. If this just wasn't possible because the vehicles involved were too badly damaged in the accident, they would use a police vehicle (and if necessary, take a similar vehicle to a road-testing laboratory at a later date) and skid it to a halt from a known speed. To obtain a reasonably precise measure of the length of skid marks and therefore obtain a check on how fast the vehicle in the crash was travelling, a chalk gun was fitted to the car, front door mounted and aimed at the ground with the other end attached to the brake pedal. The chalk gun then fired a piece of chalk at the tarmac the moment the brakes were jammed on. I'd often stick around at the end of having photographed a fatacc to see the AI take a vehicle some distance away, turn it around, accelerate towards the scene, then at a predetermined point (the start of the original skid marks), hit the brakes hard. You'd hear a loud bang as the gun fired the chalk into the road surface. This would be coupled with the inevitable sound of skidding and the acrid smell of burning rubber.

One of the most spectacular chalk gun tests that I witnessed, involved a double decker bus that had previously knocked down and killed a pedestrian trying to cross the M4 would you believe? The bus was travelling east in a town bound direction on the M4 Harlington area of West London, located approximately between junctions four and three and just north of Heathrow airport. As the entire motorway had been closed in both directions, I stood at a safe distance on the opposite side of the crash barrier, in lane two of the west bound M4 to watch the bus, now being driven by Tony, the AI. The big red bus came hurtling along in lane one towards the scene of the impact. The AI jammed on the brakes, the familiar bang rang out as the chalk gun dispatched a piece of chalk into the road and the bus first skidded and then slewed to the offside, finally coming to rest in lane 2.

Another fatacc occurred again in mid-summer, in the early hours of a Saturday morning. It took me from my garaging station at Kensington, through Wandsworth and out along the A3 to an unlit country lane, seemingly in the middle of nowhere, but actually two miles from Cobham in Surrey. I hadn't got a clue how to get from Kensington to Cobham back then, so I relied almost entirely on my London A-Z (no sat navs available then!). In time, my route of choice was to head south on the A3220, hang a right off Edith Grove onto the King's Road (A308) and then a left at Eel Brook Common onto Wandsworth Bridge Road. Once over Wandsworth bridge, it would be a simple matter (well late at night anyway) of negotiating

Wandsworth and then heading out along the A3. Like so many serious accidents, speed had turned out to be the driver's undoing at this particular incident. It had been raining and it was still raining heavily when I arrived on scene. The driver had lost control of the vehicle on a bend, braked hard, mounted the pavement and hit a sizeable oak tree. The Mini Clubman, having lost the confrontation between itself and the big oak, had crumpled on impact and bounced off the tree, coming to rest in a ditch on its offside and at a forty-five-degree angle, adjacent to a two-plank fence. Both male occupants had died instantly.

Night fataccs are extremely challenging technically. When you dial tiredness and the inclement weather conditions into the equation, this particular assignment proved to be a tease and a half. Two approach shots covered the skid marks on the road and pavement and two shots of the vehicle, rear and front three-quarter views, completed the photographic coverage. Although the album comprised just four photographs, it was getting them that was the challenge. A traffic officer held my golf umbrella over the tripod-mounted Pentax 6x7, to keep the rain off the lens. When I ran around the scene firing flash off from my two Metz 45's, seemingly in all directions during the camera's timed exposure of about a minute and a half, I'd have to keep checking that the officer holding the brolly, hadn't lowered it because his arms were aching! This would of course have ruined the photographs. I remember this job well because the rotund oak tree enabled me to hide behind it and light the front of the Mini, in effect pointing the flash in the direction of the camera. I was chuffed to bits with how well the painting with light had worked under such testing conditions. I ended up lighting up the oak tree's overhanging branches and all of the fence and hedge behind the crashed Mini, achieving very pleasing separation between main subject and background. Without the painting with light, the black Mini risked being under lit and you just wouldn't have seen any detail in the front of the vehicle, let alone achieved anything like decent subject / background separation. I tended to favour using the Metz 45 flash guns on these compact jobs, but on larger scale assignments the more powerful Metz 60 with its beefy power pack complete with shoulder strap, would be a prerequisite.

Fragments of other vaguely remembered fataccs come to mind – several along London's shopping mecca that is Oxford Street. Pedestrians and cyclists knocked down by buses and taxis and the difficulty of taking the approach photographs without shoppers walking across your scene. I rocked up at one accident scene and the only thing that I remember is that it was pitch dark, it was an evening call out from home and the ambulance doors were open when I got out of my van. As I looked back, my eyes were drawn to that ambulance for inside I could clearly see a pair of deathly pale feet, protruding out from under the bottom of a white sheet that shrouded the deceased. I've never been able to erase the image of that poor dead man's feet from my memory, not ever. As for where the accident was located, the vehicles involved, the scene itself and even the AI dealing, I remember nothing at all!

Then there was a fatacc somewhere out in the sticks, near Green Street Green, south of Orpington, one chilly autumn weekday on call. Two lads, no doubt egging each other on, were tanking down a country lane in a classic 1983 Ford Escort Mark 111 XR3i. The driver lost control of the vehicle and on impact with a tree, a branch took the roof of the vehicle off and along with it, the heads of the driver and his front seat passenger. I remember how bizarre the headless corpses looked and even more macabre, how the two young lads' severed heads appeared like bloodied footballs carelessly tossed on the back seat.

Crystal Palace Park, located in London's SE19 postal district is a Victorian park and a venue for many cultural and sporting events. In the early '90s, it was memorable for me as I was called out again in the autumn on one dark, weekday evening to photograph a fatal RTA. The deceased had been racing his car inside the park, lost control of his vehicle and crashed into a tree. With the tyre skid marks being so long, I was left with no option but to use police vehicle headlights to light up the marks.

A different incident was in Victoria, where a businessman had correctly followed his green cross code before crossing the road, but unfortunately this poor fellow hadn't dialled into the equation that he was crossing a contra-flow bus lane and ended up under the wheels of a double decker bus, his face flattened into the tarmac. The contorted face and body was engulfed by a gallon of claret still trickling into a nearby gutter. I could still hear it tinkling as it hit the sub-surface drain and I can still hear it tinkling now as I write this (which probably in part explains why dripping taps still make me feel uneasy). It's etched into my mind, as is the black leather brief case that momentum had violently tossed further down the road.

Then there was the occasion on a wet evening call out, somewhere in the City. A lorry had knocked down and squashed a little old lady's head. Bits of brain matter and body tissue were stuck to the rear nearside mud flap and tyre. In addition to approach images and both rear and front three quarter views in the pouring rain, Mick, the AI, wanted detailed photos of this mud flap and tyre. I set to by placing a disposable plastic sheet on the road, underneath the lorry and then not only booting and suiting, but putting a disposable overshoe on my head, as I would be working centimetres from the oily drive shaft, which was also typically soiled with blood and brain matter. I needed a second pair of hands, so I had Mick cosy up to me holding firstly the boat lamp so that I could see to focus the camera (there being only just about enough room to get my eye to the viewfinder) but also so that Mick could hold the flashes still. There was no other way to get these shots. Tripod mounting was out of the question due to the limited height clearance between tarmac and underside of the lorry. The technique worked just fine. I remember Mick taking the piss out of me for wearing an overshoe on my head. He was very much your stereotypical man's man and he predictably declined the offer of an overshoe for a head covering, looking at me for all the world like I was totally FUBAR! Looking stupid or not, of overriding importance was that I nailed the shots with health and safety always at the forefront of my mind. Photographing underneath that enormous vehicle may well have proved a challenge, but at least it was dry and I had an extra pair of hands to help me!

With the majority of fatal and serious personal injury accidents that I attended, the victims had either been taken to hospital by ambulance or helicopter – or had been delivered to the mortuary. If the deceased were still in situ, it was not only because they were confirmed dead by emergency services upon their arrival on scene, but because the AI wanted the position of the deceased recording for the Coroner or in a criminal case, Criminal Investigation Department (CID). I've already mentioned the triple fatal above and the Ford Escort headless duo, but others are etched in my mind. I found myself just a tad south west of the start of the M1 in Neasden on the A4088, close to the junction with the North Circular. It was a normal working day, overcast, mid-morning when I pulled up on scene shortly after 10am. A young male pedestrian in his early 20s had been knocked down by a black-coloured Ford Granada 2.8 GL and had been dragged under the vehicle. The victim had sustained massive trauma to his head. LAS had just 'called it' (time of death) having worked in vain for ages to try and save the poor chap. The AI suggested that it would be good to get a quick full length shot of the deceased and close up of the head and face for the Coroner, prior to the body being taken away. My image depicted a naked deceased lying on a sheet that was almost as deathly pale in colour as the poor victim. Part of a light blue sheet covered the victim's genitalia. The deceased's arms were resting by his side. His face and generous head of black hair were smeared in blood and there was a considerable volume of claret on the ground immediately to the right of the deceased's head. Elsewhere there were superficial cuts and bruises to both arms and legs. LAS by necessity had cut away the victim's clothing and this could be seen bunched up on either side of the torso. The young man's white and black trainers with their distinctive turquoise inner lining visible on the quarter aspect, had almost been placed neatly and symbolically as a mark of respect, by the right foot. There was still evidence of LAS paraphernalia on scene – a red blanket by the left foot, a metal stretcher parked parallel with the deceased, not a meter away, plastic syringe caps and packaging for dressings here and there. The victim was also still wearing a neck brace. I had to work so fast that in my finished image, you could still see the bottom of a paramedic's legs as he walked quickly back to the ambulance. Tellingly, the rear of the Granada 2.8 GL was also visible at the top of the photograph. As with most of my assignments, I found looking at the finished photograph more disturbing than actually being on scene and viewing the sad, horrible sight for real. There was a short intermission whilst the deceased was removed, during which I planned out, in conjunction with the AI, two approach shots, a reverse angle approach shot depicting the front of the Granada from about thirty meters away, a front three quarter nearside view of the vehicle, close up bumper damage and an approximate victim's viewpoint from the edge of the pavement, as he looked right along the A4088, prior to crossing to his doom.

During a particularly busy summertime weekend on call in which photogs were thin on the ground (there were only three instead of the normal four), I found myself being dragged all over London on a variety of jobs – an armed robbery scene here, a stabbing scene there. Typically, it was one job after the next in quick succession. Having already photographed two fatal road traffic accidents, I was just topping and tailing my third fatacc, early afternoon, in West Drayton's Station Road, when the call came over police radios for Central 2-0-7-9's photographic presence required up in Ponders End, North London. Having packed my gear away and checked my notes from this third fatacc were all completed, I sat in the van with the A to Z open on my lap and worked out a route. If I dropped south to the M4, I could head town bound on the motorway to Junction 1, then pick up the North Circ at Gunnersbury / Chiswick. From there, I'd follow part of this 25½ mile long road, via Hanger Lane Gyratory, Neasden, M1 and A1 intersections and New Southgate, before eventually joining the A10. The traffic officers on scene in Ponders End knew that I'd be a while, but for peace of mind, once I had the route memorised, I got straight on the air to let Oscar know that I was leaving West Drayton. The tail end of my conversation with Oscar control at New Scotland Yard went something like this:

Me: "Oscar from Central 2-0-7-9, my ETA will be travelling time to the one you've got running at Ponders. Travelling via the M4, North Circular and A10, 7-9 over".

Oscar: "Central 2-0-7-9, thank you...". Then, making a sympathetic but tinged with mortuary humoured reference to being clobbered with fatacc assignments, "We're lining them up for you Central 2-0-7-9, we're lining them up". To which I retorted, "Much appreciated, Oscar, much appreciated, 7-9 out".

Nothing could be further from the truth. I was getting hammered and the last thing I wanted was yet another fatacc. However, after a deep sigh I put all bad thoughts to the back of my mind and set off for the scene, just east of Ponders End.

The uniformed guys and girls were lovely and full of sympathy when I eventually arrived at their north London location. One of the Traffic Officers gave me a bottle of Coke and a Mars bar to help me recharge my batteries. I could have hugged him as I had long since drained my water and food supply. Witnesses had described how an elderly male cyclist, on riding over a cat's eye located close to the nearside kerb, had wobbled into the path of a car speeding up behind him. Both victim and bicycle had gone under the vehicle, a Peugeot, and unfortunately the old man had died on scene from his injuries. This job was memorable for several reasons, firstly because it was the fourth fatacc in a busy day, secondly, for the sympathy and hospitality shown to me and thirdly because of a particular image that was required in addition to the usual shopping list of shots. On this assignment, the A.I. wanted a shot to try and depict how raised this particular cat's eye was. The only way to take the photograph was to pre-focus on the cat's eye in question from a set position close to the road then gently place the camera on the road, as I wouldn't be able to see through the viewfinder once the camera was set down that low on the tarmac. Taking the pentaprism off the camera and viewing the image on the ground glass screen was out of the question as there was too much bright, stray light bouncing around and I wouldn't have seen the image clearly. I wanted as much depth of field as possible. I knew that the cat's eye would be pin sharp, but by stopping the aperture down to about F22 from the usual F11, although out of focus, the viewer would still be able to discern detail in the rear of the Peugeot further up the road. This was important so I could show the proximity of the cat's eye to the rear of the vehicle involved in the collision. I had already attached my bulb cable release to take each shot, having triggered the mirror up first. Back then, more than twenty-five years ago, using relatively primitive kit in comparison to modern hi-tech gizmos, the Pentax 6x7's standard lens still ended up sitting several inches from the tarmac, when I could really have done with the camera sitting subsurface in a convenient pothole perhaps! Nowadays, you'd employ a small, high resolution digital device, that would get you closer to the tarmac.

Ask any forensic photographer if they've ever cocked up a job and I'm sure you'd get a few raised hands. I'd been on the scenes of crime team for close to two years and the only disasters that I'd suffered were on two occasions when the C41 colour negative processor broke down mid process and I lost two armed robberies and a stabbing scene. The Reaper, who was my line manager at the time, was straight on the phone on both occasions to the officers in the respective cases to inform them that the images had been ruined and that they wouldn't be getting any albums of prints. They were not best pleased, but it was an act of God. What could you do, blame it on dodgy film splicing? A bit harsh I'd say. Other colleagues suffered similarly – it was just one of those things that fortunately happened very rarely. In all my time on scenes of crime I only mucked up one job at the taking stage, but one was enough.

On a night-time call out to a fatacc scene on the M3 town bound, I drove, yawning my head off, from New Malden to Kingston Upon Thames, then out to Hampton Court and along the A308 Staines Road East to Sunbury. As the entire motorway had been shut in both directions, Oscar had advised me that I could approach the scene, located a couple of miles from Junction 1 on all three town bound lanes, via the slip road that in effect takes traffic coming from the south west off the M3 to the roundabout at the A308 junction. Weirdly I found myself driving down a slip road the wrong way and then along Lane 2 also the wrong way. Officers guided me around two dark coloured vehicles that were complete write offs, but amazingly were both upright. So, I ended up parking some distance behind the scene with all the other police vehicles. I did a u turn in the middle of all three lanes, so that my Astramax would be facing the right way for my departure, once photography was complete.

I was delighted to see Paul Croft again, a friendly, very experienced AI and police officer, whom I'd had the pleasure of working with on many previous occasions. I can't remember the cause of the accident or the makes / models of the vehicles, but what I do recall is that the weather was dry and the accident scene was located on an unlit section of the motorway. This presented a big problem in that the two approach shots showing all three lanes with the crashed vehicles in the background would require two police vehicles side by side lighting the motorway with their headlamps, alternating between dipped and main beam to try and even out the lighting. This was not ideal, but I just didn't have the flash power to light such a massive section of motorway. Even if I did, the job would have taken so long it wouldn't have been practical. As the vehicles had ended up close together, not quite end to end and straddling lanes 2 and 3, Paul then asked for views from all four sides depicting the final position of the vehicles and all the damage. Straightforward enough – if not time consuming due to the shear amount of painting with flash required for each view. Two negatives were taken for each view, which meant that I had to light eight shots. I had a final check with Paul that I had the location of the approach shots correct. They were taken opposite a set driver location motorway marker post for the first view and for the second, closer view, Paul measured out the distance from my tripod mounted camera to the scene with his yellow measuring wheel and we both duly noted that measurement. I made sure that my notes on the scene, from which the album index would later be compiled, were correct, before retracing my steps, driving around the scene on the hard shoulder and heading back to New Malden.

About three days later, having dropped a load of my films in for processing the day before, I popped into photographic HQ at Amelia Street again to pick up, sort out and print my wodge of processed 120 roll films. As was the practise, you'd find a large light box table in the colour room, lay your rolls of processed film out, put them in order of taking, by cross-referencing with the jobs taken in order in your notebook. Then you'd carefully cut up individual negatives, pop each into a transparent 120 sleeve for printing, whilst any misfires and spare duplicate negs would be collected into a pile and kept in a separate envelope pertaining to those jobs and filed.

The rolls of film laid out before me represented about six days' worth of work. There were victims' injuries, armed robberies, murder scenes, post-mortems – in fact a complete cross section of crime types that I had photographed over the last week. All looked good. Everything was well exposed, evenly lit and in sharp focus. I was just thinking that a Mari's breakfast would go down well, when I came to the M3 fatacc scene. I froze in horror! All the negatives were so thin and underexposed that I needed a magnifier to see any detail at all. With the exception of the approach views lit with vehicle headlights, all the three-quarter views of the damaged vehicles were seriously underexposed by at least 2 stops. To put this into context, the most important shots were unusable. They were more than just 'a wee bit ropey', as my former colleague Patrick would have said - they were all ruined. I felt the blood draining from my face and my mouth become dry as simultaneously, breakfast was the last thing on my mind. I searched for answers, for reasons why such a catastrophe had occurred. There were none, the fault was down to camera operator error. Me and me alone. There were no excuses, I'd quite simply cocked up big time. I'd gone into auto pilot when setting the crucial aperture for the vehicle shots. Simplifying the scene in lighting terms, I had two dark coloured vehicles set against a jet-black background (the night). My painting with light coverage – the more challenging aspect of the exposure set up, would have been lovely.... had I not inadvertently stopped the Takumar f2.8 90mm, standard lens down to F22! What I should have done was to double check that the aperture was opened up to a good F8 to compensate for the absorption factor of light by these dark vehicles. There was no use 'crying over spilled milk'. There was nothing for it but to get straight on the phone to Paul at Hampton Accident Investigation. Tired and run down from a busy week on scenes of crime didn't really cut it. Although he understood my explanation, to put it mildly, Paul was annoyed at this inconvenience, as he was relying on my images for this particular accident report and I was upset and angry with myself not just for cocking up, but for letting down someone for whom I had the utmost respect. That single cock-up during my whole time spent with the MPS has stayed in my mind all these years. However, every time I think of that fatacc, I'm reminded of what Joss Ackland said, playing the part of South African baddy Arjen Rudd in the film 'Lethal Weapon 2', ... "Don't worry my boy, these things 'appen!"

One of the strangest jobs that I ever attended also happened to be a serious personal injury accident scene in Sunbury in the early hours of one summer's Sunday morning. A dark red BMW 635 CSi clearly travelling way over the 30-mph speed limit, had just shot past a police van parked up at the side of the road. By the time the officers in the van had caught up with the BMW, they were met with an incredibly horrific sight. The BMW had hit a brick wall, taken out a concrete lamp post and had not only disintegrated, but the car had been cut into two. Debris was scattered over a hundred metres along a road that looked for all the world like an air crash site. Worse - there was no sign of the Beemer driver! Had he also disintegrated?

When I arrived on scene, the devastation was indeed incredible. The driver had been on the wrong side of the road when skidding and had impacted firstly with a brick wall encompassing a research station. Then the vehicle had uprooted a concrete streetlamp, which was seen further along the pavement on its side. One section of the BMW with its rear logoed BMW 635 CSI spoiler could be seen lying opposite the collapsed wall in the wrong lane, completely wrecked and looked like the car had been scrunched into a ball. A tyre could be seen on the pavement resting against a garden wall. In the middle ground most of the exhaust system could be seen, together with a whole wheel and its assembly interspersed with myriad debris. In the distance, close to a set of traffic lights, was the other half of the vehicle containing the mangled engine compartment, driver's seat, steering wheel and precious little else, pointing back towards the initial point of impact. The automatic gear selector looked as if some unseen hand had twisted it at a thirty-degree angle to the left. Even the handbrake was lying skew-whiff to the left. Lying on the road immediately in front of this section of the vehicle, was part of the streetlamp assembly. Apart from a small amount of smeared blood lying just below the gear selector, the driver's side was devoid of claret.

The officers driving the police van spent a while scouring the scene and adjoining front gardens, bracing themselves for the unenviable task of collecting body parts here and there. The fact that they could find no sign of the driver was perplexing, until that is, they heard someone singing and murmuring. On closer investigation, the driver was found crawling around on his hands and knees in someone's front garden, completely bladdered and incoherent, being worse for wear with alcohol. It was probably due to the fact that he didn't tense up on impact that the driver miraculously survived. He escaped with little more than a slight gash on his forehead. Back at Hampton garage, my images were the talk of the Accident Investigators, they'd never seen anything this bad, with a vehicle so utterly wrecked, where the driver had literally walked or in this case crawled away. My album of twenty or so images was subsequently taken halfway around the world for numerous talks and presentations to UK and International police forces.

As already stated, I used a timed camera exposure in combination with painting with light extensively on night-time fataccs, but I also used this trusted technique in any low light or pitch dark interior or exterior setting. Stabbing scenes at Leicester Square's Zoo Bar and the long since vanished 'Le Palais' (with Waldo Peppers bar) night club in Hammersmith, were both very dimly lit and leant themselves to being painted with light. Both venues had a number of wide pillars to hide behind, which meant that with the camera shutter open under very low ambient lighting, I could run into shot, conceal myself behind these pillars and fire flash into the scene and from different angles and all without myself registering on film. In being physically closer to the background, this helped even up the image lighting and overcome the problem of light fall off, which would have been the result if flash had only been fired from the camera position.

CHAPTER 13

The Photography of Fire Scenes

Of all the thousands of photographic assignments that I've covered, whether they were forensic, medical, commercial, industrial, public relations, weddings, portraiture or landscape and travel, the visual documentation of fire scenes ranks as the most challenging. Accidental fires, arson and fatal fire scenes (including vehicle fires) were a regular undertaking for me and they ranged from the contained 'letterbox job' (where an accelerant had been poured through a letterbox and ignited) through to multiple burnt out vehicles, where the perpetrators had tried to use fire to destroy forensic evidence associated with crimes such as rape and murder, perhaps committed elsewhere, or large industrial sites encompassing multiple floors that had either been partly or totally damaged by fire and smoke damage. Assignments were rarely more challenging when you were called out in the middle of the night to a multi-room, multiple fatalities with deceased in situ and working in dirty, smelly, hazardous conditions, in total darkness, whilst feeling knackered on very little sleep!

In this scenario, you'd be reliant on your boat lamp to help you to compose and focus each shot and to work out your lighting angles. Sometimes, you could use the fire service's portable lighting, but such lighting didn't always produce an even result and being tungsten halogen would produce a yellowy orange colour cast on the daylight balanced film we were using. I used to carry blue correction filters that would clip on to the front of my Metz 45's in conjunction with a blue filter taped over the lens, so I could use the flash as fill in, but this involved a lot of farting about and inevitably, the fire service would get another shout and have to take down their portable lights. It was quicker to work in darkness and paint the scene with light, but you'd have to be careful that the tripod feet were on stable ground and not resting on wobbly floorboards, as this had the potential to ruin a shot. In total darkness and with the camera shutter locked open, if you fired a couple of flashes off into the scene and then accidentally knocked the camera or moved position, the fact that the camera had moved during the lighting exposure would have the effect of creating a multi-image, similar to blurring. If you even suspected that this had happened, you'd need to wind on to the next frame and start again.

When faced with a fire and smoke damaged scene in daylight conditions, the nightmare scenario would be taking the all-important shot from the doorway into the scene, but looking directly at the sun shining in through a window opposite. Here you could tilt the camera down and around to a different angle, but in addition to a lens hood, you'd need to flag the lens to cut down on the flare created and use a flash gun to fill in the shadows (the burnt scene). If that shot from the doorway absolutely had to be taken, I tended do it later, out of sync, by which time the sun had moved round lessening the problem. The trouble is, the human eye has an amazing capacity for seeing detail in the whitest white and the blackest black within a scene, whereas the film's (sensor's) latitude by comparison, is somewhat restricted. The shot from the doorway would still be problematic even on an overcast day, as the contrast (the difference between the lighting level outside and inside or the difference between the whitest white and blackest black, as above) would be too high. With digital cameras, the problem of contrast is exacerbated due to their more restricted 'subject brightness range'. Whilst it is possible on some digital cameras to use the HDR facility (high dynamic range - where a number of exposures are taken of the same view in quick succession) then all the images that have taken account of the very light to the very darkest parts of the scene are combined into a final image. The disadvantage of this technique is that a loss of quality through image compression will result in an unnaturally sharp look to the image. HDR is often used by landscape photographers, but a downside is that the technique can be overused, making the results appear gimmicky.

When you're taking evidential photographs, it's important to get it right in camera using a single exposure, taking another shot as a back-up if necessary, not least because you might find yourself having to explain complicated techniques in court if you start using HDR! When I was on scenes of crime, we were still using film of course, so we had to get it right in camera. There was no HDR or photoshop back then. You generally took one shot at f16 and your back up spare duplicate negative was at f11. As stated, with the window generally being the lightest part of the fire scene, I'd usually tilt the tripod mounted Pentax down and around to one side and just include a tiny part of the windowsill to locate it in the scene. Automatically, you've won back control of a tricky lighting situation. You then take a light meter reading for the room, ensuring that the small part of the window sill doesn't over expose too much (you do this by making a compromise in the room exposure compared with the sill exposure) and then you fill in the shadows with a measured quantity of flash from one or more flash guns. If the window frame in this scenario was important because it showed buckling and or depicted an area of burnt frame together with an area of unburnt frame, then by physically taking the camera closer to the window / subject matter for the next shot, you're in a much better position to control the lighting contrast of exterior daylight to interior fill in flash, simply because your flash gun is more powerful being closer to the subject.

Away from the window light problem, general fire scene photography often presented other problems, as you'd have large expanses of black and then as if to throw a curve ball, you'd have an unburnt area of white or light-coloured material. It might also be crucial to show the open pages of a book to depict the contrast between undamaged and damaged areas. This involved a balancing act of how much flash you fired at the subject and where you pointed the flash gun. Additionally, I'd often find myself photographing a white coloured door, the top quarter of which, had been smoke stained a dirty black colour, or a floor burn pattern, where half the floor in the background was black and the other foreground half was white and unburnt. With both scenarios, the flash gun would be angled more to the black areas (as black absorbs light) and less towards the white or light-coloured areas, which reflect light. Angling the flash, acting as a fill-in towards the white or light areas, would result in those light areas over-exposing and possibly ruining the shot.

Reflections, the return of light rays to the camera lens from shiny, smooth or polished surfaces, are a pain in the bum with any scene. I would often be found waving my boat lamp from side to side (the eye will pick up a moving reflection better than a static one) to pinpoint unwanted reflections, much to the amazement of all and sundry on scene, who thought that I'd lost the plot completely! Reflections created by broken window glass, mirrors and television sets meant that I'd often have to change my shooting angle as well as my lighting angle.

As with any scene, my visual documentation started wherever possible from the outside and I would work my way methodically to the inside. By the same token I'd photograph from the unburnt to the most heavily burnt areas. I couldn't do any of this of course until the scene had been risk assessed. On the smaller, contained 'letterbox' fires, I'd undertake my own risk assessment. However, on the large building and industrial fires, access would only be gained once the borough surveyor and fire service had deemed it safe for me to enter. If it wasn't safe to go in, initial evidential photography was limited to daylight exterior images only. The scale and nature of the job would affect my choice of PPE. I'd always use disposable feet covers for my tripod. I could well be wearing: a hard hat (date-stamped with expiry date!), overalls or disposable forensic suit, plastic stretchy shoe covers or wellington boots with a reinforced metal plate running through the sole of the foot. If the scene flooring was dirty, I'd sacrifice a disposable forensic suit to put my camera bag on. This would ensure the base of the bag would be kept clean. I'd end up wiping all the gear down anyway after every job with strong, 'trigene' disinfectant spray. If the venue for my next job was an assault victim's home address, I didn't want to be pitching up and plonking a dirty camera bag and tripod down on their white-coloured lounge carpet.... and the MPS then being sued!

In addition to the general exterior shots to depict location utilising street signs, addresses and landmarks (showing all building sides and corners to really pinpoint orientation) and interior images showing all four walls and including the layout of furniture, depicting fire and smoke damage, my photographic documentation also included all or some of the following, but this is by no means an exhaustive list:

- the origin or seat(s) of fire; in situ furniture and other items within the area of origin before and after reconstruction; evidential items that may subsequently have been re-photographed back at the lab if more detailed views were required; structural failures such as windows, walls, ceilings and floors that can change the route a fire travels; significant ventilation points accessed or created by the fire; relevant cupboard / container exterior and interiors; both sides of doors in the immediate vicinity of the scene; smoke, heat and burn patterns (and the patterns created as a result of door and window position during a fire); gas and electrical utilities (entry points into a structure) and appliances, wiring, plugs, sockets, meters, fuse boxes / circuit breakers, heat producing equipment etc. (both inside and outside); the position of any controls on gas and electrical appliances; interior fire protection devices (detectors, sprinklers, extinguishers used, door closers); clocks that might have indicated the time power was discontinued to them or the time in which fire or heat physically stopped their movement; accelerant containers; evidence of accelerant use; I often had to photograph the cleared, as well as the reconstructed scene (following sweeping and removal of debris / evidence); with fatal fires, where it was possible, the deceased, or protected areas where the deceased was located were photographed; witness viewpoints, low viewpoints and elevated viewpoints were also considered. Today, drone and other aerial photography along with satellite imagery also need to be considered.

As I've intimated, my former colleagues and I attended many fire scenes and I don't remember them all, but one or two are etched in my mind forever. Half remembered snapshots of the middle-aged male suicide, who turned on all four gas cooker rings to high and in addition, brought into the hallway two large butane and propane gas camping stoves, then waiting a while before sealing his fate with a tossed match. Suffice to say that the victim's blackened and well-cooked remains made for grim visual documentation. The smell is one thing but actually tasting charred human flesh on the back of your throat is quite another matter and not easy to forget.

Then there was the call out in the middle of the night to a triple fatal fire in a third storey flat on a Peckham estate. Unfortunately, LFB (London Fire Brigade) were packing up as I was arriving, which meant them taking down their portable lighting, which would have been a handy visual aid. The fire was suspicious as the fatalities were all little ones in situ, with no sign of parents or guardians on scene. This meant that lab liaison and CID were present, who were able to brief me as to what needed photographing. The fire, amazingly, had been contained within this third floor flat. The fire had started in the kitchen and had quickly spread out to the hallway. The living room and adjacent bathroom, furthest away from the fire had been partly burned, but more smoke damaged. Walking along the hallway towards the kitchen, but on the opposite side to the living room and bathroom, were firstly the children's bedroom which had been badly fire and smoke damaged and secondly the master bedroom, which had all but totally been destroyed by fire. Wide angle general scene setting shots of the hallway and all the rooms were taken first. Everything in the kitchen including the ceiling, or what was left of it, was photographed and of course, what was believed to be the seat of fire, the gas cooker, now a burnt out and blackened version of its former self, was photographed in detail. This included the position of the control knobs, the front two of which, had been turned to the highest setting.

Then it was time to photograph the childrens' bedroom. I stood in total darkness in the open doorway, wearing my reinforced wellies, green fire scene overalls and hard hat, shining my boat lamp into the scene. Opposite where I stood, a charred window frame with most of its glass missing, greeted me. When I shone the torch down to the sill, the body of a small child was suddenly illuminated. Closer examination revealed that the child had tried to escape out of the window and had died leaning against the sill with its arms outstretched to the side and these and the rest of his upper body had partly melted into the window frame structure. It was a very pitiful sight, but there was more to come. I slowly swung my boat lamp across to the right-hand side of the room where I saw the remains of another small child lying on their front on the lower of two bunk beds. The body was blackened and charred and the feet had burned away into nothingness. Like the child by the window, it was impossible to say whether the victim was male or female. Having checked out the blackened ceiling, I returned to the bunk bed and then tracked the boat lamp across the charred floor, which in places exposed the joists.

Continuing further across to the left, I spied a small, single bed abutting the wall, upon which, the body of a third deceased child lay. The child was a male about seven or eight and he was lying in the recovery position facing into the room. He was naked apart from a pair of dark blue underpants. From what I could see, the little lad's back and right thigh were blackened. His face was intact, but his nose and right corner of his mouth were burnt. Both of his feet were blackened. The child's right arm was resting on the edge of the bed and his right hand had been severely burnt, exposing bone, causing the hand to lock into a clawing position. A small patch of duvet underneath this damaged hand was also burnt. Further towards the deceased's head, the burning had stopped just short of the chin. The side of the duvet and bed facing into the room was so badly burned that some of the mattress springs were visible with no residual damaged material in close proximity to these exposed springs. The end of the bed told the same story. The majority of the duvet, upon which the deceased child lay, although partly blackened, had not been touched by fire.

Although LFB had entered this room, due to the questionable integrity of the flooring, I had to take all my shots from just inside the doorway. Two, wide angle overlapping shots encompassed all three deceased, with a third and then a fourth wide angle shot documenting the damage to the floor and ceiling, respectively. The 90mm standard lens was needed to separately capture, all three victims. All the images presented a challenge as not only did I need a timed exposure with painting with light (x2 for each view), but the flooring was also unstable. As with all the other images taken in this flat, I first had to use my boat lamp to compose each shot and focus up the camera, then with that particular image etched in my mind, I could then lock open the shutter and paint the scene with flash. I ensured that I wasn't touching the camera or tripod and crucially that I didn't move my body whilst firing off all that flash, as it was highly likely that I could have ruined the shot with double imaging, mentioned above – another reason why we used to take a backup photograph. When I examined the processed negatives days later under a magnifying glass, I was relieved to learn that my camera had in fact remained still throughout. This job had a profound effect on me, but like most jobs it didn't hit me until I saw my printed 10"x8" photographs a few days later, which were far more shocking than actually being at the scene. This delayed shock – seeing the printed album, coupled with the everlasting memories of those poor little children, who I had first visualised when the beam from my boat lamp wafted over them - lifeless, little charred figurines who had died in all probability, alone, terrified and in agony. Their whole lives ahead of them full of excitement and adventure, now so cruelly and prematurely at an abrupt end. That gets me every time and will never leave me, how innocent and how very young they all were ...

There's an expression that's been used a few times throughout these pages - 'a picture paints a thousand words'. If ever I was to select just one of the many crime scene images I took, where just a single image completely summed up the story of events, it was an assignment in West London's Hammersmith. As was par for the course, I was given scant details, namely the address, officer dealing and that the job was a fatal fire with BIP (body in position). On arrival at the scene, I learned that LFB had only just left and there was a solitary, uniformed, male police officer standing outside. The scene was not suspicious, but photographs were needed for the Coroner. The ground floor one bedroomed flat was owned by an elderly gentleman who had lived alone. Away from the fire scene, the flat smelled old and musty. Leading off the hallway, there was a small kitchen, bathroom and bedroom – all reasonably tidy. The bed was made and a couple of coats lay on top. This gave me the impression that this bed hadn't been slept in for a while. When I stood in the doorway leading to the front room, it all made perfect sense. Like many elderly people living alone, this old man was no exception. He was using the living room as a bedroom as well, staying predominantly in one room. On the right-hand side of the room was a single 'put you up' bed with a brown coloured velvet studded headboard. The deceased was lying on top of the bed with his mouth wide open gazing up at the heavens. He was wearing what appeared to be a grey t-shirt, blue and white patterned cardigan, which was unbuttoned and light blue trousers. A pale, red-coloured bed spread partly covered the deceased's lower legs and I also noticed that the deceased was lying on the mattress with no mattress cover or sheet.

A framed landscape painting hung on the wall above the deceased. Next to the corpse, near to the head of the bed, there was a wooden trolley on castors comprising two shelves. On the top shelf, there was a blue flask, together with a book, a large box of matches and a packet of cigarettes and on the shelf underneath, I saw a pair of unfolded spectacles, next to two mugs. The three-quarter length carmine-coloured curtains were open. They revealed a net curtain behind and the state of west London's weather that morning, which was bright and sunny. There were a couple of rugs on the floor, but in places you could see a brown tiled flooring. To the right of the window was a tall shelving unit containing dusty nick knacks – trinkets, cups and saucers, old curiosities from a bygone era adorning every shelf. I noticed a smaller unit located in the top right-hand corner positioned at right angles to this larger shelving unit, upon which I could see a sizeable, old red book and a torch. On the opposite wall to the deceased, so on my left-hand side as I looked into the room, there was a large sideboard, above which, were wall-mounted cupboards. On top of the sideboard were scattered an array of papers and palliatives. Towards one end of the sideboard, nearest the door, was a zimmer frame. Opposite this and close to the other end of the sideboard was the old gentleman's high back chair, with the remains of a large cushion set at a forty-five-degree angle. This had been severely fire-damaged, together with a small stool in between the chair and sideboard. The carpet under and in front of the chair was also badly burnt, but the fire had been contained as LFB had arrived on scene very quickly following a prompt emergency call from neighbours. The seat of fire was the carpet immediately in front of the chair.

On the floor, in front of the bedside trolley, I could see two walking sticks. A dark brown stick lay on top of a much lighter sandy brown cane, at right angles. The rubber protection on the end of this cane was clean and intact, but when I looked at the base of the dark brown stick, I noticed that it was charred and blackened. This was a very sad story indeed, because what transpired was that the deceased gentleman, a life-long smoker, had been sitting in his chair. He undoubtedly nodded off, dropped his lit cigarette on the rug beneath his feet and came to, when the carpet started to burn. In his panic, he picked up the dark brown walking stick and tried to prod the flames to quell the fire, which was now spreading towards his recently vacated armchair. All to no avail. With the fire taking hold of the armchair, and the deceased now feeling very unwell, he probably had a heart attack as he lay down in bed, hoping that everything would just go away, half pulling the bedspread over his legs and dropping the charred walking stick on the floor in the process.

The one wide angle photograph taken from the doorway encompassed the entire story. On the left-hand side was the seat of fire and damaged property. On the right-hand side of the image was the deceased in bed and on the floor, the viewer could discern the charred walking stick. This remains one of the most powerful forensic images that I've ever taken. In postscript, I was recalling this scene to one of my good friends Mick Gardiner, from 'Gardiner Associates Training and Research' in 2007, some fifteen years after the event. It transpired that Mick, who was an operational fire officer at the time was actually in charge of the 'pump' (fire engine) that attended the scene and put out that very same fire. What a small world indeed!

CHAPTER 14

Theft and Attempted Theft, Criminal Damage, Armed Robbery, Fraud and Drugs Offences

In between all the big jobs, we'd be attending police station yards, photographing stolen motor vehicles. You were lucky if the vehicle in question was on its own in some corner and easy to access. However, usually, the vehicle that required photography was normally hemmed in by other vehicles and it sometimes required a few police personnel to shift other cars out of the way. Again, if luck was on your side, a front three-quarter view would be sufficient. Usually, you'd end up photographing the VIN plate, stamped in chassis frame number and engine number, as well as the tax disc or position of tax disc if this had been removed. You'd find that engine numbers had been ground out or acid erased to remove the original vehicle's identifying number. And of course, the position of these numbers varied depending on the make of vehicle. Identifying numbers could be found etched on windows and the best way of photographing these was to place either a piece of white or black paper (depending on what showed the number up best) inside the vehicle, behind the number and then to light the number with a flash held obliquely. The angle of flash would sometimes require a little experimentation. If a stamped in chassis frame number was located under the carpet down by the driver's door, once or twice I found that this had been acid erased. I used to photograph the damage with the vehicle door open, looking down more or less perpendicular to the area of damage and then, placing a mirror underneath the car, (which could reveal some of the destruction caused by the acid) photograph the reflection of the damage to the body work.

Criminal damage to property was another seemingly daily occurrence. Shop windows might need photographing or empty and furnished offices (some on several floors could be completely trashed, with ceiling lights ripped out and partitions sledgehammered to death). Graffiti is also classed as criminal damage and at its worst, could be spray painted in multiple rooms and stairwells, covering several floors. This very much lent itself to being video recorded, where you could start on the ground floor with a 'walk through' technique and cover all the graffiti and damage much quicker than the time it would take to photograph the whole scene.

Banks, building societies, safe deposit locations, jewellers, off licences and shops were all subjected to armed robberies on an alarmingly frequent basis. Exterior and interior of premises would be photographed, together with all damage, the safe and any money or jewellery dropped at the scene. If there were victims, they would be photographed either in hospital, at the police station, or at their home or work address. Anything connected with the scene such as blood, discarded property, masks and gloves, weapons, ammunition, crow bars, shoe, finger and tool marks as well as any vehicle associated with an armed robbery would also be photographed. An attempted armed robbery in Lewisham in August 1992 was thwarted when police boxed in a getaway vehicle and armed police recovered a Smith and Wesson' revolver with six bullets in the barrel. The weapon was immediately made safe by firearms officers and placed on the passenger seat with its empty barrel in the swung-out position. Armed police had propped the gun up in approximately the position it was found, together with the six bullets that they had removed. I photographed this as I found it – i.e. pointing away from me with a piece of six-inch, sticky scale tape on the seat above and just behind, to show the size of the pistol.

In June 1991 'Waterside Point' in Battersea was a newly opened set of decadent, exclusive apartments overlooking the Thames. A well to do middle aged lady had apparently committed fraud by embezzling charitable funds and I was called in to photograph her property and motor vehicles, which police would subsequently be seizing as part of their enquiry. Photography commenced in the basement car park, which was all strictly security controlled as you can imagine. Everywhere I looked, my eyes feasted on the most luxurious cars imaginable. Top end Mercs, Beemers, then cars for the playboys – Lamborghini's, Ferrari's and Maserati's. I wasn't required to photograph any of these (unfortunately!). I had been directed to the two vehicles in a space marked in yellow paint with the number '15' on the ground. There was a very sporty looking white Mercedes cabriolet, which was parked in front of a gleaming new, metallic, dark green Bentley, boasting a registration of '12 R'. Once finished in the garage, officers escorted me up to the penthouse suite, where oh my God, I was in for a treat. Everything screamed 'no expense spared'. Marble flooring, gold taps and fittings, the finest upholstery, lamps and ornaments that certainly wouldn't have looked out of place in Harrods or a boutique shop fronting Chelsea's Brompton Road or Kings Road. The master bedroom had a red theme going on – red curtains, red walls, red bedside lamp holders, red patterned rug overlaid on a pale grey coloured carpet and red and gold duvet with under sash. Even the ceiling, which had been designed in the shape of a giant flower and coving, was a deep red. A tasteful water colour of a bowl of fruit sat within at least a four-inch cream overlay. The whole thing being encompassed by a two-inch, gold-coloured mounting, which hung above the middle of the gold bed head. The matching foot of the bed was also gold coloured in the shape of two interlocking stretched loops. From where I initially stood towards the foot of the double bed, a large, gold-coloured ornately framed mirror adorned the opposite wall and in it I could see the reflection of part of the head of the bed, bedside table lamps and wall-mounted art. The sheets and pillowcases were all black satin. At the time I wouldn't mind betting that I could have comfortably retired on the sale of the contents of the master bedroom alone – never mind what was contained in the rest of this lavish apartment. Every room had been decorated to a similar exacting standard and it was a real pleasure to undertake such an interesting assignment.

Only a month before, an audacious plan to rob the National Gallery in Trafalgar Square of some of its precious artworks was thankfully foiled when a suspicious traffic warden spotted a van, which happened to be full of masked villains, parked up on double yellow lines at the back of the gallery. The quick-thinking warden alerted police, who swooped in to make all the arrests. As a result, the police asked me to photograph the entire layout of the gallery, comprising the corridors and rooms containing all the works of art, whilst Derek and Liam recorded the same on video. Police were especially interested in me photographing one particular, very famous collection indeed, which I understood to be priceless. Having been on scene for a good few hours my last photograph was the infamous, unmistakable 'Chair', a 92 cm by 73 cm oil on canvas original painted in 1888 by Vincent van Gogh. At the time, this famous piece of art was recessed in a bevelled, brown-coloured frame. Exhibiting predominantly yellow hues, an old wooden chair with its woven straw seat dominates the composition. The chair, upon which one can see a pipe and an unravelled pouch of pipe tobacco, sits on a tiled floor. Behind the chair, towards the top left corner of the composition is a box of onions on the front of which, the artist has signed his name, the instantly recognisable 'Vincent'. Prior to photographing van Gogh's 'Chair', I had also photographed 'Sunflowers', one of four original versions of the painting that the famous artist had crafted at the time he was working briefly in the south of France in the autumn of 1888 with Paul Gauguin.

To photograph 'Chair' recessed, as it was in this brown frame, firstly required all the house lights to be turned off in that part of the National Gallery. In semi darkness and with the camera's shutter locked open, I then fired two flashes, each from about a thirty-degree angle either side of the camera and from a distance of around six feet. This was to ensure that I didn't get any unwanted reflections from either the oil painting or the frame, which I undoubtedly would have done if I had blasted a flash off from anywhere near the camera angle.

To think that I came within touching distance of numerous, priceless paintings and that I could have comfortably retired on a slither of the value of just one of the many masterpieces! As I was packing up my gear, I couldn't resist asking the curator who had been accompanying me around the gallery during this assignment, just how much Van Gogh's original 'Chair' painting was actually worth. "All I know is that it's extremely valuable" he replied. I said, "But is it possible to put a price on such a treasure?" "Put it this way" the curator said, smiling, "You wouldn't get much change out of fifty million pounds!" My lower jaw dropped – and that was the best part of three decades ago. Goodness only knows what it and similar works of art would be worth now?

Where theft of property was concerned, I soon realised that no matter whether it was a worthless piece of tat or a prized oil painting – if you could lift the item and it had value, then it could be exchanged for money. It was therefore nickable! A mid-week assignment in normal working hours took me to a three-storey property, located somewhere off the A4 Cromwell Road, not a stones's throw away from Gloucester Road tube, which lay empty prior to sale. When I said empty, it was completely empty, including carpets, curtains and light fittings – there was nothing whatsoever in that property that could be stolen, short of taking off the doors I suppose.... or so I thought? When I attended this address however, one look into each bare room told me why this assignment was under the heading of 'theft'. Every room I popped my head around on all three floors had a whopping big dirty hole, where once there was a fireplace. But no ordinary fireplace of course. A team, dressed as builders had chiselled out every one of the property's expensive antique, Victorian fireplaces and loaded them with brazen assurance, onto a big truck, all in broad daylight with not so much as a ubiquitous metropolitan rat, or even an MPS 'Black rat' paying them a blind bit of attention. My mission was to photograph each dirty hiatus in the wall, where once a grandiose fireplace had stood.

Drugs offences were almost as commonplace as theft of property. I lost count of the number of drugs raids that I accompanied police officers to and of sizeable packages of heroin, cocaine, or other illegal narcotics along with wodges of bank notes seized, that I photographed under floorboards or sequestered in vehicle door panels. Drugs making paraphernalia, such as burners, lighters, foil, silver spoons, needles, syringes, razor blades and small mirrors etc. were also captured by my lenses. Cannabis factories ranged from the small, concealed attic conversion, to plants at different stages of cultivation occupying every room of an average London three bed semi right through to large scale professional operations utilising industrial greenhouses full of six foot plus tall plants, which were definitely not for personal use! Following general exterior and interior views to show the layout of the scene, any specialist equipment such as heating, illumination on tracking devices, timers, electrical supply and hydroponics would all require photography, together with a sample image of one or more cannabis plants full length without and then with scale and then a close-up view of a sample of leaves. Cannabis plants have a distinct, characteristically pungent aroma. I used to joke and call them tomato plants, whose leaves also have quite a musty odour. When photographing in the winter months, I used to warm the camera and lenses up on the van's heater beforehand, as it was normally so hot and humid in these cannabis growing areas that if you dared enter with a cold camera, you'd end up with condensation on your equipment, which would render photography temporarily useless.

In February 1992, Wendy and I purchased our first home together – a first floor, two-bedroomed maisonette at Number 1 Chestnut Grove in New Malden, Surrey. The flat was barely a year old, carpeted throughout and was immaculately decorated. It even came with its own parking space around the back. The loft was also spacious, which came in very handy for storage and was the cleanest attic I've ever seen. Having moved in from our respective digs (Kensington Police Section House for me and Claverton Street, Pimlico for Wendy), we were to spend 5½ happy years there. We used to go for regular walks in Richmond Park, shopping trips to Wimbledon and Kingston as well as trips into London.

The 15th July 1992 was just another blissful day as far as I was concerned. On the happiness front, I was in clover. Wendy and I had been engaged for more than fifteen months and now we were on the countdown to our September wedding day, which was less than two months away. Anything remotely negative I saw or experienced in the Met Police, I let my unshakable happiness just repel, as I looked forward with excitement to our big day. So it was that on this summer's morning, I found myself working in Earlsfield in south west London, having just photographed a young, female victim at her home address. When I had completed this job, I used the victim's home phone with our 0800 free phone number to contact the Amelia Street Duty office (no mobile phone then!). John Cook, on giving me the details for my next assignment, dispatched me on my merry way quicker than a turbo charged Reliant Robin. With his characteristic style (a combination of brusqueness and joviality), John had inevitably hung up on me before I'd had chance to say, "Thanks John, bye." My next job would take me to Elmwood Road, Mitcham and to the home address of yet another assault victim. The route from Earlsfield was simple – down the road to Tooting Broadway, on towards divisional HQ police station 'Whiskey Delta' at Tooting, passed Figge's Marsh on the left of London Road and then the cemetery opposite the marsh, where my dear Grandfather (and now my Grandmother) are buried (within spitting distance of Grandma's flat on Bruce Road) and on into Mitcham.

It was probably during my travelling time from Earlsfield to Mitcham that one of the most infamous and heinous murders in UK history was simultaneously being carried out, not a million miles from my current location and less than four miles from my house. 23-year-old Rachel Jane Nickell, a former model, was seemingly enjoying a nice summer's morning out walking her dog Molly, with her two-year-old son Alexander on Wimbledon Common. Suddenly a man who was a complete stranger, appeared from nowhere and launched an unprovoked, sustained, vicious, violent and frenzied rape and knife attack on Rachel, pushing the little toddler to the ground in the process. Sickeningly, Rachel's trousers and underwear were pulled down to her ankles and she was stabbed no fewer than forty-nine times. Her throat was slit and among the many injuries she sustained were defence wounds to her hands, indicating that she had tried to ward off her attacker during the maniacal onslaught of knife blows. This crime was utterly shocking in itself, but particularly heart-breaking as Rachel had been murdered in front of her little boy. He was found by horrified passers-by clinging to the blood-soaked body of his mother 'trying to tell Mummy to wake up' and sticking a piece of paper like 'a sticking plaster' onto her lifeless form 'to try and make Mummy better'. Little Alexander was later to recount that the murderer calmly walked away and washed his knife in a nearby stream.

Although there were reported to be some five hundred people on Wimbledon Common that morning, incredibly, not one person heard Rachel's screams. In the highly publicised and controversial investigation that followed, in the region of thirty-two men were questioned, including one of my colleagues (who simply bore a resemblance to the suspect). The spotlight soon fell on an innocent local Roehampton man, Colin Stagg, who was wrongly arrested by the police in August 1993 following an infamous honey-trap operation using an undercover female police officer. Colin Stagg subsequently spent more than a year in prison on remand until he was acquitted in September 1994 by an Old Bailey Judge, due to the use of wrongful entrapment evidence by the police. In 2004, with advances in forensic techniques, police were able to link Robert Napper, a sex offender, to the murder of Rachel. This followed Napper's conviction for the killing of Samantha Bisset and her four-year-old daughter in November 1993. These two murders were committed by Napper sixteen months after Rachel had been killed. It wasn't until December 2008, that Broadmoor inmate Napper, who following the judge's ruling that he was to be incarcerated indefinitely, confessed to the killing of Rachel Nickell on the grounds of diminished responsibility. This was sixteen years after this vile crime. Finally, justice had been allowed to prevail.

When I had finished photographing the assault victim in Mitcham, Duty Officer John Cook told me that it had been a toss-up between my colleague 'Billy the Fish' and me as to who would be sent to Wimbledon Common to cover the Rachell Nickel murder scene. We were both geographically equidistant at the time police phoned in the urgent request for forensic photographic attendance, Billy had apparently phoned the duty office a handful of minutes before me and so was given the important, but grim, task of hot footing it to the common. I had the pleasure of working with a really talented bunch of guys and gals in SO3(2) Photographic. In September 1993 I joined 'Operational Video Services' and subsequently spent so much time with this specialised team filming in Wimbledon for ongoing enquiries into the Rachel Nickell murder, I got to know the common like the back of my hand.

CHAPTER 15

A Cornwall Wedding, a USA Honeymoon and back to Scenes of Crime, September 1992+

As for my stag do, I was very nervous that I'd be kidnapped, stripped naked and driven to a motorway bridge, there to be handcuffed to the railings, pubic hair shaved and left to be arrested, as had been the case with at least one of my colleagues previously. I tried to control my event as much as possible by opting for a seemingly low key, well-oiled, sit down Indian meal on my home turf in New Malden. Also, I figured that if my mate Pete stayed over at our flat, he could keep an eye on proceedings and make sure they didn't result in the police being called.

The meal and drinks went well and just when I thought the lads were dispersing and making their way home – and I'd got away with it - I was jumped on from behind, dragged into some bushes and unceremoniously declothed. I do recall seeing both of my shoes flying through the air! The next thing I remember is being frog marched down the street, bare chested and made to sit down in front of some railings right opposite a pub and close to New Malden railway station. My arms were brought behind my back and my hands were plasticuffed to the metal bars. Next my trousers were unbuttoned and rolled down to my ankles. Now I quite literally was exposed to the elements. The lads were having a great time. I just remember lots of laughter, flash being fired as the 'evidence' was captured and then two attractive young ladies with the most concerned look on their faces, crouching down trying to release me and imploring the lads to let me go – all to no avail. Then suddenly, my Met Police colleagues scarpered up the road, never to return. Thankfully, Pete remained with me and produced a penknife. After some time, he was able to carefully saw through the cuffs and release me. He had also retrieved my shirt, shoes and socks. The biggest coup was not being arrested that night. We do have a copy of 'that' photograph somewhere. It's more embarrassing seeing the photo of me sitting virtually bollock naked, tanked up without a care in the world, whilst those two Samaritan young ladies are looking on trying to help. Thankfully, Wendy spared my blushes by drawing an extremely large fig leaf on said photo, to hide my family jewels from people in the future when thumbing through the albums.

I enjoyed a second, more civilised stag do with my two closest friends, Aly and Simon, in late August 1992 with a great fell walk in the Lake District filled with reminiscing and plenty of laughter. The walk culminated in the three of us completely stripping off, diving into a rock pool in a part of the River Esk situated below Hardknott Fort, for the best spot of skinny dipping ever. There we were, photographer, architect and teacher – the naked trio - inhibitions laid bare, so to speak, our mutual naturist bent out of the closet and thrust to the fore. And we loved it. I seem to recall Simon stripping off for his stag do, also Lakeland based, in 1994. Not to mention his own father who was once caught in Simon's headlights, doing a spot of late-night naked gardening, clad in little more than a pair of wellies and a sun hat...but maybe that's a story for another time! As I think of the stag dos, further memories come crowding in of hilarity, fun times and daredevil antics of my youth. Weight training at Fylde Rugby Club with Aly and Max Kirkham, former chemistry teacher at Arnold school, followed by beers and chatting up girls at the Talbot and County hostelries in Lytham. Max would spot a young lady and introduce Aly and me as his sons and that would be his in, we wouldn't see him for the rest of the evening. Aly and I, also 'out on the pull' but having failed miserably, would then console ourselves with a KFC and joke telling on the promenade. On another occasion, Aly and I were driving side by side doing 'a ton' in our parents' cars on the back road to Cockerham (not recommended), or driving from Staining windmill to Hardhorn Road, Poulton, 'quite' fast, when a rabbit bolted out in front of my Dad's Volvo. It caused me to jam on the anchors and almost sent Aly, driving behind, straight into the back of me! That would have taken some explaining to our parents. The overriding memories I have of being in the company of my friends is of inspirational conversation and so much belly laughter – cherished memories of such fantastic times, lads!

Having taken nearly a month off work for our wedding and honeymoon, we hired a Ford Fiesta to drive down to Cornwall from our New Malden flat a couple of days before the big day, deciding not to take Wendy's beloved Mini Mayfair due to its small size. We were to be married on Saturday 12th September 1992 by Father Peter Twistleton at the picturesque church of St Breock, which lies seemingly in the middle of nowhere, but is actually just over a mile to the south west of Wadebridge and immediately south of the Royal Cornwall Showground. The bustling town of Wadebridge, where Wendy and her brother Simon were raised, developed from the parishes of Egloshayle and St Breock. Dating from the thirteenth century, St Breock Church is dedicated to St Briocus, it has an imposing tower containing a set of five bells and was largely rebuilt in 1677.

The afternoon before the wedding, Simon and I left the hire car parked at the Crantock Bay Hotel outside Newquay (our wedding reception venue). This would be our getaway car following the reception. The hotel enjoyed stunning views out over Crantock Bay and we'd often pop in for afternoon tea there following a walk along the beach. The hotel itself had been owned jointly by the Ship and Eyles families for years. Sadly, the hotel closed before Christmas 2011 and has now been transformed into a luxury spa and self-catering apartments, still owned I believe by the Eyles family.

Following a rehearsal at the church the day before, we kept to tradition as much as possible with Wendy and our bridesmaid Julie staying with Val and Laurie at Pennard Cottage, while I was booked into a B&B just up the road in Whitecross. So, I spent my last evening as a single man enjoying one or two beers at the Molesworth Arms in Wadebridge with my brother-in-law to be and my closest friends. I still managed to get back to the B&B at a reasonable hour, but I couldn't sleep for two reasons. Firstly, I was pacing up and down my room going over my wedding speech for what must have been the umpteenth time and secondly, just when my head eventually did touch the pillow and silence began to envelope me, a couple in the room immediately above my head started up. The noises emanating from the ceiling bore all the hallmarks of the clichés associated with carnal knowledge, building up into a crescendo with increased pace and getting progressively faster and more audible as the inevitable climax (pun fully intended) was reached. I had no ear plugs to lessen this cacophony of love making, but I figured that when I eventually got to sleep it must have been well after one in the morning.

Following a sumptuous, traditional English breakfast on the morning of the wedding with some of my friends, I found out who'd kept me awake with their love-making above my head the night before (sorry, not telling...it's a secret! Suffice to say there were embarrassed giggles all round). There was nothing more to do than to change in to my navy blue suit, white shirt and patterned dark turquoise green tie and pin (which Aly also wore) and be deposited at St Breock Church by my best man Aly and his wife, Sarah. Wendy's brother, Simon, was on hand to dole out white carnations for the best man, ushers, the two fathers and to me. These were pinned in the left lapel. Wendy and I had purposely kept guest numbers to a minimum. An intimate gathering had the advantage of us being able to spend valuable time with everyone present, most of whom had travelled a long distance to be with us. The disadvantage of having a small wedding was the difficult decision of not inviting some people. Hindsight's a good thing, but even my sister Kate couldn't be with us as she was living in America at the time and was unable to leave.

Gradually, family and friends began to arrive at the church and it was lovely to see them all. Everyone looked resplendent, none more so than my dear Grandma in her cerise dress and dark blue hat and our two mothers, Val and Denise, one dressed in navy and white, the other dressed in black and white with complementary hats. Looking back at the time of writing this, it's very sad that most of the senior generation are of course, no longer with us. Both sets of parents, the absolute legend who was my lovely Grandma Sylvia Lily, Auntie Norah and Uncle Ron on my Grandfather's side, Joyce and Plummer on Wendy's Mum's side and even the kind, wise, selfless and magnanimous Uncle Nigel. Nigel was a keen amateur videographer (who provided an edited video of our wedding and reception) and was held in such high esteem. They've all now journeyed on to new adventures in the sky.

So, with everyone seated, my best man Aly, 'Lord and Keeper of the rings' and right-hand man took his place with me in the front right-hand pew as I grew anxious to see my bride. When the organ piped up to signal that Wendy and her father were poised at the back of the church, we were on our feet like soldiers. I couldn't resist a peek at my beloved and when I turned around it was a truly wow moment. Wendy looked stunning in an ivory silk dress and veil all complemented by a head dress of white and pale-yellow flowers and a white themed bouquet, containing a splash of purple and a hint of yellow. Her dress had been lovingly made by the wonderful mother of Wendy's best friend Jules, a dressmaker in her day. Wendy's Dad Laurie, a wonderful man, quite rightly looked so very proud as he walked his daughter slowly down the aisle. He had only recently been discharged from a spell in hospital. The short service went without a hitch, save for one or two discordant notes struck by the organist (a pity we'd pre-paid the fees, as I was thinking of negotiating a discount!). Hymns were sung, vows were exchanged, prayers were said in thanks to God and the register was duly signed. Then came the walk down the aisle as a married couple to the halt in the church doorway and the inevitable kiss. We both felt elated! All the formal wedding photographs, including those of Wendy and her family at the house beforehand, couples and group shots outside the church, cutting of the heart-shaped, two-tier, white patterned and iced fruit cake and further images of Wendy and me at the reception venue, were captured by local Wadebridge professional, Janet Young.

A quaint, little cherry-red-coloured, 1936 Austin Seven brought Wendy and her father to St Breock and was on hand to take us newlyweds to the wedding reception at the Crantock Bay Hotel, near Newquay. We were fortunate to enjoy perfect September weather, it was sunny and pleasantly warm. Trying to leave the church and negotiate the very narrow country lane leading up to the main A39 proved a little challenging. The majority of guests didn't know the route and felt that the wisest course of action was to tag on behind the wedding car. The route to the reception venue took us south past Winnard's Perch and St Columb Major, then west along the A392 via White Cross and Quintrell Downs, by-passing Newquay with its famous surfing mecca, Fistral Beach, to the south. A final right-hand turn along Halwyn Road brought us to our destination at West Pentire. The nineteen-mile journey in the little Austin Seven from church to reception was simply perfect (despite the convoy of cars behind us!) and we talked excitedly non-stop. Everyone waved and passers-by hooted at us, which made us even more euphoric. Our joy knew no bounds.

The inevitable speeches, video recorded by Uncle Nigel Schollick for posterity, followed final formal photographs by Janet Young, the meet and greet and a sumptuous wedding buffet. For someone who had a morbid fear of public speaking at that time, I was relieved that after months of preparation, my speech was devoid of nerves and seemed to be well received. Laurie's speech was excellent, so too was Aly's. All three speeches were littered with witticisms and amusing quips that all added to the upbeat nature of the day. We had lots of time to do the rounds and chat to every single family member and friend present, as we'd hoped. A room had been put aside for us to change into our honeymoon attire. Wendy, who always looks good in whatever she wears, wore a white coloured, short sleeved blouse and floral pastel skirt, whereas yours truly, forever the joker, wore a white shirt and tie, cream slacks and navy-blue blazer...and a fluorescent baseball cap complete with pony tail....as you do! After a seemingly endless round of thank yous, hugs, kisses and good-byes, it was time to leave everyone behind at the Crantock Bay Hotel and head off on honeymoon.

Bastards! As we went outside to get in the hire car, a quick pang of horror turned to one of uncontrollable giggling. True to wedding tradition, Aly and Si, my two closest friends had hi-jacked our hire car and 'decorated' the little red Fiesta in shaving foam, balloons and the obligatory inflated condoms. One sheath was stretched suggestively like a tumescent todger over the gear stick and another was flapping around with an orange coloured balloon outside, both of which, had been strung from the radio aerial on the roof. The entire car had been covered in some of my many impersonations, with the wording 'FB 4 Wend' taking centre stage on the front windscreen. FB was a reminder that I used to be known affectionately as 'Fat Bum'. And that was it – a final wave to everyone as I started the engine, squirting washer fluid frantically onto the windscreen to clear it, and we were off with the attached tin cans clattering along behind us. It had been a wonderful, magical day full of happiness and laughter and we were still chuckling as I drove us out of the car park.

We arrived back at an empty Pennard Cottage less than half an hour later, as we needed to change into more casual attire and gather up our pre-packed suitcases for the honeymoon ahead. We had to drive to Gatwick and leave the hire car there, so the car needed washing and tidying up before we could set off! On cue, it started to rain as I quickly went over the hire car washing it, having first tidied up the interior. After a quick shower, we were ready to leave Cornwall around 7.30pm for the four and a half hour, 250 odd mile journey from Wadebridge to Gatwick (LGW) Airport's Copthorne Tara Hotel, where we would be spending the rest of the night prior to a very early morning flight to the USA. The room had been booked as a present from our wonderful bridesmaid Julie (Oolie) and her brother Peter Little, they'd treated us to an executive suite of four-star luxury. That single act goes a long way to telling you just how lucky we are in having these kind, generous and warm-hearted Australians as our dear friends. Our route took us via Exeter and the A30, the A303 via Yeovil and Salisbury, the M3 via Farnborough, then the M25 south to the M23 and on to LGW. It was around midnight when we got to our hotel, completely shattered after the day's proceedings. Even though we only had a handful of hours before we needed to be up at the ungodly time of 3.30am, I for one was absolutely determined to use the jacuzzi bath!

The following morning, I celebrated my 29th birthday, a beaming and proud newlywed, embarking on a Stateside honeymoon with the girl of my dreams. Everyone had been so kind and generous to us, but there was more to come. Wendy's father had secretly been in touch with an old pal who worked with NorthWest Airlines (later to be absorbed into Delta Airlines in 2008), the carrier taking us from LGW to Minneapolis-St Paul (MSP) in Minnesota. On arrival at check in, we had another lovely surprise when we were informed by airline staff that we had been upgraded to business class in the upper tier of our 747's 'bubble'. Part way through the flight, an announcement over the public address system congratulated Wendy and me on our marriage. This was followed by a flight attendant bringing us a bottle of champagne, balloons and a box of chocolates to our seats. I felt more euphoria, especially when all our fellow passengers burst into spontaneous applause.

Following a couple of hours in the airport at MSP, the final leg of our journey brought us to the start of our honeymoon – San Francisco. My yearning to visit this picturesque Californian city began when I was kid growing up watching Karl Malden and Michael Douglas in Quinn Martin's 'The Streets of San Francisco'. Although I'd visited with Aly for the first time with Trek America in 1986, I longed to go back. Feeling tired and jetlagged on arrival at our downtown hotel, we arranged to meet up with my sister Kate the following morning.

San Francisco, known affectionately as 'Frisco' and 'SF' (among others), officially the city and County of San Francisco is a hilly city in the north of the Golden State located on the tip of a peninsula, surrounded by the Pacific Ocean and the bay area of San Francisco. The picturesque city is famous for many things, but amongst others are: its switchback, and in places, steep roads such as Lombard Street; Twin Peaks and Nob Hill; the cable cars ascending and descending Powell, Market, Hyde and Van Ness Avenue; the iconic Golden Gate Bridge; Fisherman's Wharf, Pier 39 and China Town; Alcatraz island (home to infamous former prisoners such as Al Capone, George 'Machine Gun' Kelly and Robert Franklin Stroud, the 'Birdman of Alcatraz'); an eclectic blend of architecture including colourful Victorian houses and year-round fog. San Francisco is the thirteenth most populated city in the USA and the fourth most populated in the Golden State. Frisco covers an area of just under 47 square miles and is the cultural, commercial and financial centre of Northern California. In 2017, the population stood at just under 900,000. San Francisco is also famous geologically, for sitting in close proximity to the Hayward fault and perhaps more famously the San Andreas Fault – the latter being the boundary between the Pacific and North American tectonic plates. Several earthquakes have occurred along this fault line over the decades, but none more devastating than the earthquake and fire that destroyed much of the city, very early in the morning of April 18th, 1906.

I think we had two days in SF and packed as much in as we could, before hiring a car that would take us out of the city and southbound along the breath-taking sea view route that is California State Route 1 (known more commonly as Highway 1). The picturesque, pacific coastal route is more than 655 miles long and runs from Route 101 north of SF near Leggett in Mendocino County to Interstate 5 near Dana Point in Orange County, just south of Los Angeles. Highlights of the drive included: the Half Moon Bay vista; Santa Cruz with its beach boardwalk; Monterey Bay; the scenic '17-mile drive' and of course Carmel. We had to wander through this pretty seaside village, with its twee shops, cafes and restaurants, where the film actor / director Clint Eastwood had famously once been Mayor. South of Carmel, we hit Big Sur – amazing! Travelling first over the 714-foot-long Bixby Bridge, reputedly one of the highest single span concrete bridges in the world at 280 feet, I don't think we've ever stopped so many times along a comparatively short stretch of road. Everywhere I looked there were photo opportunities: Pfeiffer Beach and Ragged Point were just two of the many highlights – so I think it's fair to say that I... er... took the opportunity around every corner!

Further south, we arrived at San Simeon and visited Hearst Castle on 'La Cuesta Encantada' (the Enchanted Hill). It was designed by architect Julia Morgan and built between 1919 and 1947 for the newspaper baron William Randolph Hearst. It took us a good few hours wending our way through the cottages, kitchens, suites and rooms that comprise this 250,000 acre wonderland – the gothic study, considerable collection of art and antiques, breath-taking libraries, refectory room, billiard room and theatre, Neptune and Roman pools, constituting just a fraction of the highlights.

Continuing our drive, we had an overnighter in Cambria village, courtesy of my half-brother Michael and his then wife Patty.

Champagne and flowers greeted us at our lodge and we had our own swimming pool. And very nice it was too. Moving southwards past Santa Maria and Santa Barbara, we eventually arrived in Ventura, where a big welcome meal was planned for us with one of my first cousins, Maire, her family, Michael and Patty. From Michael and Patty's, we had a pretty scary drive into Universal Studios, Hollywood, on 22nd September – multiple lanes with vehicles overtaking you on both sides. On the morning of 25th September, we bid the relatives good-bye and headed north east to Las Vegas via the uncompromisingly hot Mojave Desert, through southern California, southern Nevada, southwestern Arizona and southern Utah. I remember on that road trip, stopping for fuel and stepping out of our air-conditioned car and suddenly sucking in dry 90 degree plus Fahrenheit sandy air! You drive for miles and then suddenly the Las Vegas strip with all its buildings and casinos come into view – seemingly in the middle of nowhere. We were staying at the Mirage just for one night. Even though we were exhausted, we wandered the strip taking photos and ate out. My one abiding memory was in one of the casinos. Lots of little old ladies and little old men aimlessly popping a coin in the slot and continuously pulling the handles of the slot machines with no let up. I caught sight of one such lady, sitting in front of her machine feeding the slot with a bag full of coins held in her left hand and pulling the lever with her right. Time and time again, nothing would happen and then suddenly a whole deluge of money spewed out and Wendy and I almost leapt for joy. In contrast, such was her 'resting bitch face', the bored and resigned look on this woman, that she didn't even bat an eyelid. She simply picked up coins mechanically, as if on autopilot and fed them into the slot machine. We gave ourselves a limit of five dollars each (big spenders!) as we were terrified of getting hooked and then blew the lot in under ten minutes! Still, at least we can say we gambled in Vegas.

The following morning it was up early and off out to drive into Arizona to the Grand Canyon Lodge on the remote, less visited north rim of the Grand Canyon where we were to spend two nights and where Wendy passed on the clam chowder! This was followed by three nights on the south rim at Coconino County's Grand Canyon Village (GCV). This involved almost a day's drive firstly retracing our route back on Route 67 to then pick up 89A East at Jacob Lake, then on to Marble Canyon, before heading south on the 89 to Cameron and then north west on the 64 and thence to GCV to get from north rim to south rim. When you see the Canyon for the first time it's so vast that you can't comprehend its size at all. By some strange notion, I mistakenly got it into my head that I'd be able to see both ends and across to the other side. With the light changing constantly around sunrise and sunset, the vistas that I set my Mamiya RB67 to capture were awesome, the whole landscape being a photographer's seventh heaven. I can't believe that I'd brought my faithful RB67 roll film camera with me and two interchangeable film backs, one loaded with transparency film, the other with colour negative. I also had a Weston light meter. I took a risk relying on my Slik 88 tripod to support a beast such as the RB, but the 90mm's front shutter facility meant that I could engage the mirror up first with a cable release, wait a few seconds for the vibrations to die down, then carefully trigger the front shutter with a second screw-in cable release. I had sufficient rolls of both types of film. For 35mm, I used a black bodied Nikon FM2 with 24mm and standard to 200mm zoom, both manual focusing lenses. I quickly realised that I had married a very tolerant wife, who soon got used to me saying "Yeah just another five minutes more", when actually the shoot inevitably turned out to be at least another two hours. I remember being in my element capturing these canyon vistas and periodically checking on Wendy who had (and still has) the patience of a saint. She'd be sitting on a rock behind me, smiling through her sunglasses and soaking up the atmosphere, but perhaps underneath thinking, 'Dear God, how much longer is he going to be?'

The helicopter ride into the Canyon itself took us right down almost to floor level to view the Colorado River. Only by helicopter did we get a sense of how steep the sides of the canyon are and how deep it is at over a mile. The whole canyon is some 277 miles in length and between 4 and 18 miles wide. It's gargantuan!

Following five amazing days at the Grand Canyon and a honeymoon totalling just over two and a half weeks, it was time to say goodbye to the USA. We drove south from GCV on the AZ-64S, then Route 40 east and finally the 1-17 south to Phoenix (now known as Sky Harbor) International Airport to drop the car off, a journey of approximately 3¾ hours and some 230 miles. Then it was the flight back to England. The honeymoon had taken in San Francisco, Los Angeles, Californian Pacific Highway 1, Las Vegas and both north and south rims of the Grand Canyon. As a bonus we got to see my sister Kate, my half-brother and his wife along with my first cousin and their families and friends. It was one hell of a memorable holiday with many lovely highlights and hundreds of photographs taken. On the one hand, I suppose it was bloody selfish of me to take all my pro photographic gear out on our honeymoon. However, on looking at the images and with hindsight, I think that the decision to bring all this gear could be viewed more favourably as perhaps a judicious investment! The following weekend, on arrival back in the UK, I think we picked a hire car up from Kingston and drove straight down to Cornwall to stay with Val and Laurie and to visit Janet Young to select the images that would form the final selection for our wedding album. Having celebrated our silver wedding anniversary in 2017, this nostalgic album - a cross section of treasured plates from our special day and now more than a quarter of a century ago - is still in immaculate condition!

Wendy and I settled into married life and returned to our respective jobs. For me, scenes of crime was far from 'same old same old'. There was always variety and you never knew quite what you'd be photographing from one day to the next. The Irish Republican Army were very active on the UK mainland throughout the '90s and kept Photographic very busy indeed. My colleague, Jules Angel, had already covered the mortar attack on 10 Downing Street the previous year, on 7th February 1991 (which Wendy heard from her office at Number 1 Northumberland Avenue). The mortar launch that injured four, was an attempt on the lives of incumbent Prime Minister John Major and his Conservative cabinet. One mortar landed in the garden of Number 10. Later that same month, one man was killed and some thirty-eight people were injured when a bomb detonated at Victoria Station. More bombings were to follow - St. Albans in November 1991, London Bridge Station on 28th February 1992 and a large truck bomb on 10th April 1992 outside the Baltic Exchange building which killed three and caused around £800 million in damage. In June 1992, a wanted IRA member shot two unarmed police officers in North Yorkshire, one of whom died, and in the August before our wedding, the IRA planted three firebombs in Shrewsbury.

I think most crime scene photographers at some stage in their careers get to photograph a bomb scene or two. On December 14th, 1991, I was dispatched to photograph the aftermath of four incendiary devices that had exploded in two stores at Brent Cross shopping centre in North London during a firebomb campaign. In what was probably designed to cause more economic disruption, a clothes stand was burnt and sprinkler systems were activated. Luckily there were no injuries.

On 10th January 1992 at 9.10am, the IRA exploded a briefcase bomb that had been placed in between two parked cars in Whitehall Place, perilously close to the heart of Government. Bearing in mind how busy our great capital city is, miraculously there were no deaths or even major trauma injuries, although some people sustained cuts due to flying glass as buildings shook and windows were blown out by the blast. The explosion was heard by a number of senior officials including Prime Minister Major. I found myself being assigned to that scene. Although debris was spread over quite a wide area as was usually the case, most of the mess was broken window glass. The scene itself was quite compact. If memory serves, one of the vehicles was a white-coloured Rover, the front of which, taking most of the blast impact, was totally wrecked with its bonnet blackened and sitting open at a thirty-degree angle. Sizeable chunks of bumper were split, broken and hanging down. The windscreen was 'totalled', but not caved in. Side windows were missing and the metallic bodywork was rippled and distorted by the shock waves from the blast. The circular crater in front of this vehicle was approximately a few feet in diameter and a good few inches in depth. The vehicle was, as you might expect, a write off, but in contrast the parking meter right next to this vehicle was left still standing tall and upright, seemingly unscathed.

On 10th June 1992 a small bomb was detonated that was hidden in a litter bin near the Army and Navy department store in Wilcox Place off Victoria Street. I recall most of the damage again being shattered window glass. Fortunately, there were no injuries with this incident.

I'd been back from the States no more than a few weeks, when yet another terrorist device was detonated. This time the target was the Sussex Public House in Long Acre, a stone's throw from the heart of Covent Garden. The bomb, which had been planted in a Gents' toilet behind the bar on the ground floor, exploded at 1.22pm on Monday 12th October, killing one man who was closest to the blast and injuring four other people. Thankfully the pub, which was normally packed, was only half full at the time of the explosion, otherwise there would undoubtedly have been more casualties. My mate Pete and I covered the Sussex Pub bomb scene together, donned in green overalls, hard hats and reinforced wellies. Such was the force of the blast that my main photograph showed the ground floor bar pushed out into the lounge and seating area and the wall behind the bar, backing on to the toilet, destroyed. In contrast, some tables and chairs in the path of the blast I found to be upright. By the same token, pint beer glasses and bottles strewn on the floor were also intact. The biggest contrast was the champagne menu and price list hanging on a chalk board at one end of the bar, which was completely undamaged. It detailed Moet and Chandon at £19.95, Lambert X Dry at £17.00, Mercier at £18.90 and Bollinger at £29.50. Once we had completed the exterior and ground interior coverage, we popped downstairs into the basement. Here was an Aladdin's cave of beer, lager, wine, spirit and other assorted alcoholic and non-alcoholic drinks stocks. Although undamaged, it was important to undertake complete coverage to show the contrast between what had, and had not, been affected by the bomb. Just as I was taking the last wide angle shot on my Pentax 6x7, I said to Pete, "Shit, what if there's a secondary device down here?" It was an eerie feeling and we were both quiet for a second or two, the silence only being broken by my fellow forensic photographer, who cheekily sat atop a large metal beer keg and cracked open a bottle of Grolsch. Mortuary humour then got the better of us and we both had a good old belly laugh. I guess Pete thought that if we were both about to be blown sky high, he may as well enjoy one for the road!

On the home front, for our first anniversary, I thought it would be great if we could take up a new hobby, something that we could enjoy together. As a surprise for Wendy, I booked a course of weekly horse-riding lessons on Wimbledon Common, just a stone's throw away from our home. These were very enjoyable, as perched up high you got to see the world around you from a completely different perspective. However, on one trek, once the horses had been saddled up, I heard a few whispers about my horse 'Dusty', who had been a bit on edge and a tad frisky on the previous hack. Nevertheless, I was assured that Dusty was ok to ride. We all set out from the stables on to the common. All was well until we were halfway round when, approaching a crossroads of pathways a small chihuahua appeared from nowhere barking, causing Dusty to rear up suddenly. Horse, rider and crop parted company! In a split second I saw myself sailing through the air with the ground rapidly coming up to meet me. With a dull thud, I landed heavily on my left side, lying on the grass momentarily dazed as I looked up to see the shocked faces of the other riders staring down at me and Dusty, who had now morphed into a bucking bronco, galloping off into the distance. I got to my feet with help from one of the instructors, brushed down my jodhpurs and was relieved to find that there were no broken bones. I had escaped with just a bruise. It took an hour to round up and calm down a clearly spooked Dusty, who had dangerously shot out in front of Wimbledon Common traffic at least twice. I completed the trek back to the stables on Shanks's pony. When Wendy and I challenged the riding school over Dusty's behaviour, they were adamant that their horse was safe to ride. Suffice to say that we never went back after that episode and ignoring best advice, I never did get straight back into the saddle and haven't been near a horse since.

And so, the IRA campaign continued. In November 1992, a device failed to detonate at Canary Wharf, then in early December two car bombs exploded in Manchester city centre injuring 65 people.

With the aim of causing economic disruption and instability, the IRA targeted the Winwick Road Gas works, lying a couple of miles to the north of Warrington, Cheshire. As SO13 (the Met's Anti-Terrorist unit), had the remit to cover all UK terrorist incidents, Pete and I found ourselves travelling in convoy, northwards on a bitterly cold 26th February morning in 1993. The gas site was huge and spread out over a number of acres, at the back of which, was the West Coast Main railway line. Police deduced that the terrorists had entered the gas works from the railway in the dead of night and had planted devices on all the gasometers, with the aim of destroying the entire plant. Several of these gas holders had detonated around 4.10am, sending fireballs a thousand feet into the night sky. The intense fires, having burnt off, precipitated a flattened, disfigured and discarded metal outer casing like some twisted left over. Twenty minutes after the blasts, a hundred residents in nearby Orford were evacuated to St. Ann's C. of E. Primary School in Lathom Avenue. Following this incident and discussions with safety advisors and British Gas, the way that gas was stored changed and above ground gas storage all but disappeared.

Fifteen minutes before midnight, a male police officer in his mid-20s stopped a Mazda van in the centre of Warrington. As he was conducting his questioning, the constable was shot twice in the leg and again in the small of his back. Then at around 12.50am, three men hijacked a Ford Escort at gunpoint, locking the driver in the boot and speeding off towards Lymm. Ten minutes later, the car was spotted in Manchester and police gave chase in the direction of Liverpool. During the pursuit, shots were fired and two police vehicles were hit. Two men were subsequently arrested on the M62 near Croft, located north east of Warrington and one decamped, never to be caught. After a terrifying ordeal, the vehicle owner was released from the boot.

Pete was very keen to undertake all the aerial photography from Cheshire Constabulary's air support helicopter, leaving me to cover the visual documentation of the entire Winwick Road site from ground level. My part of the photographic coverage took several hours to complete – a job hampered by the freezing cold temperatures. The third gasometer in from the railway line had remarkably been left intact. However, officers informed me that the bomb had in fact partly detonated, sending a small rocket-like missile skywards, which ended up piercing a hole through the steel walkway, halfway up the gas tower. Having photographed all the evidence from ground level, I was left with no option but to climb up the tower and walk around until I could photograph the damage from the walkway itself. Once I was up on the walkway, I was happy as Larry, but I didn't like the actual climb up at all, which was very exposed. We spent the night with SO13 officers in a Warrington town centre hotel, along with the talented Ken Creer and his team from Lambeth's Forensic Science Laboratory. It was over a beer that night that Pete told me that he was lucky to be alive. For the aerial shots, he was half hanging out of the police helicopter and it wasn't until the job had been completed and the aerial support unit had landed, that Pete realised that he hadn't been buckled in securely. We both shuddered at the thought. Unfortunately, Pete was to have one or two more brushes with death during the time that I knew and worked with him in the MPS ... and indeed one or two more after that!

Before the long journey back to London the following afternoon, we had to photograph the Mazda Van and hijacked Ford Escort along with a sheltered wooded area at the bottom of a field outside the town centre, where it was believed the terrorists were camping out.

Less than a month later, the IRA hit Warrington again on 20th March 1993. The two small devices planted in rubbish bins outside shops in the town centre's Bridge Street were to have a devastating effect. The explosions killed three-year old Johnathan Ball, twelve-year old Tim Parry and injured more than fifty people.

Saturday 24th April 1993 witnessed the infamous Bishopsgate bombing – the explosion of a one tonne, ammonium nitrate, fuel oil bomb that had been hidden beneath a layer of tarmac in the back of a stolen Iveco tipper truck. The IRA detonated this device at 10.27am, the truck having been parked outside the former Hong Kong and Shanghai Bank at 99 Bishopsgate, close to the junction with the

A1211, Wormwood and Camomile Streets and right in the heart of the financial district in the City of London. The bombing killed a news photographer and injured more than forty people. The destructive force of the blast sent a mushroom cloud into the air, which could be seen across the Capital and damaged buildings 500 meters away. The NatWest Tower was badly affected and St. Ethelburga's Church (a Grade 1 listed building located extremely close to the bomb) was virtually levelled. It's since been fully restored, but the cost of the damage to the entire area was approximately £350 million.

Pete phoned me early on that morning at home to let me know that he had already volunteered his services. Unfortunately, I had plans that I couldn't cancel, otherwise I would have volunteered without hesitation. Several photogs attended the scene as the complete visual coverage was a leviathan undertaking. With shards of glass and debris still falling from office buildings, if not hanging precariously, the scene was also still dangerous and this made the wearing of hard hats and reinforced boots, compulsory. Pete's images were of course excellent. Inherently artistic and naturally gifted with a photographer's eye, his Bishopsgate 10"x8" s made for a sobering close inspection. The crater caused by the explosion, which measured more than four and a half metres in width, was particularly shocking.

Thursday 10th June 1993 saw me at Amelia Street. I had a one-to-one with the Grim Reaper, my then line manager. We were a few doors down the first-floor corridor from the Scenes of Crime Duty Office and ten minutes into our meeting, when we were both disturbed by a man shouting outside. "Where the bloody hell's Canning?!!" The Reaper got up and popped his head round the door. A clearly narked John Cook had come looking for me and with good reason. He was short staffed that day and he needed a photog immediately. The Reaper quickly smoothed things over as now a more sedate John turned to me. "You've got five minutes to get your gear ready. SO13 are en route to pick you up here as we speak. A bomb's gone off at an oil refinery in Newcastle and you'll be flying up from Gatwick". We'd now made our way back into the duty office, where I noticed all four phones were off the hook, receivers down on the desks. It had obviously just gone pear shaped for him. With that, John handed me an A5 piece of paper, which constituted the job, promptly stamped it with the next crime scene number and immediately gave me his back whilst he worked his way through the callers waiting.

With all thoughts of my meeting with The Grim Reaper and John Cook now forgotten, I raced downstairs to stores and booked a pack of 1000 ASA roll film out. Our roll film of choice for the Bronicas and Pentax cameras was Agfa 400 and I figured that I just might need that extra stop and a bit if I was required to shoot any aerial images. Then it was out to my van to pick up my camera bag containing my Pentax 6x7, spare camera body, lenses, accessories, PPE, plenty of film, my flash box containing two Metz 45 Flashguns, slaves, cluster batteries, Quantum battery pack and leads and of course - my Manfrotto tripod. Both camera bodies already had a quick release Manfrotto tripod plate attached to their undersides. I grabbed my scenes of crime coat as well.

Having assembled all my kit I returned my van's key to its logbook housed in the logbook rack, behind where our lovely, friendly receptionist, the late Kathy Kettle, a truly wonderful lady, was sitting. I'd quite literally been in Photographic reception for about thirty seconds when the entrance door opened and I found myself shaking hands with a clean shaven, dark-haired, middle aged police officer, who I instinctively knew to be Anti-terrorist squad. He helped me out with my equipment to the unmarked SO13 vehicle that had its blue lights flashing, parked in the middle of the yard and once I'd loaded everything into the boot, the detective sat up front with his response driver and I buckled up in the back. As soon as we were clear of Amelia Street's car park gates, the sirens were turned on and the driver accelerated. We headed south through Brixton, Streatham, Croydon and Purley on the A23, then joined the M23 and thence to Gatwick Airport. However, just south of Purley, the SO13 officer received a phone call to say that the scheduled flight to Newcastle, which had been held up for us, could no longer wait and so we missed our flight.

Plan B involved 'India 98', one of the Met's helicopters, flying from its base at Lippitts Hill, High Beach in Epping Forrest, down to Gatwick to pick us up and take us directly up to Newcastle. What an adventure this was turning out to be! I just about had time to make a call on the detective's mobile phone to let Wendy know that I was simply en route to Newcastle Upon Tyne and that in all probability I would be home very late, if not the following morning. Goodness knows what she thought with the din of the sirens drowning out much of our conversation, but she told me later that it all sounded very exciting. With all my gear loaded in the back of the helicopter, I shook hands with the pilot and India 98's Observer helped me on with my helmet, made sure that my comms were functioning and checked that I was buckled up in the back. On the way to LGW the SO13 man briefed me about what New Scotland Yard knew so far – or rather the précis version that I was required to know! A couple of devices had exploded late the previous night at the Esso oil terminal in North Shields, located east of Newcastle and close to the mouth of the River Tyne, which spills out into the North Sea. The IRA had previously attacked the same terminal a few months before. This current bombing came on the back of another attack on a gas storage tank in Gateshead. Fortunately, this tank was only half full, but nevertheless, a small hole was ripped in the side of the tank, which enabled gas to seep out and subsequently ignite.

If memory serves, I think we flew into Newcastle Airport, where local constabulary collected us and drove us firstly to the Gateshead site for photographs and then to the Esso oil terminal. It had been threatening rain since we arrived and so I knew I had to work pretty quickly. The visual documentation for both sites was covered at ground level with supplementary images being taken from elevated viewpoints around the terminal. It reminded me very much of the Warrington Winwick Road bomb scene that I had undertaken more than three months before. It was probably late afternoon when I finished my photographic coverage at ground level. The local guys and girls from Northumbria Police were very kind with all the local travel arrangements. They also laid on much appreciated refreshments.

My last part of the assignment was to take aerial shots of the entire Esso refinery. My main camera with 90mm standard lens attached and spare body were both set to 1/500 second to counteract the vibration of the helicopter, I pre-loaded both cameras with 1000 ASA, 120 colour roll film. This was fortuitous, because the weather conditions were shit! The sky was dark grey and the ambient lighting level had dropped considerably, which meant that I was left with no option but to shoot on open aperture for everything, which was far from ideal – even then, I was pushing it to get a half decent result. The pilot was great though. He flew slowly, three or four times around the circumference of the Esso terminal until I had all my shots in the bag.

The flight back from Newcastle to 'Lippitts' in the Bell 222 precipitated a headache from hell, brought about with the intense concentration of the day's proceedings, undoubtedly not drinking sufficient water and feeling the vibrations from the aircraft. Wearing the flight helmet was also claustrophobic for that length of time. The headache was exacerbated when the helicopter kept banking from one side to the other due to the volume of light aircraft in the London area that night and the pilot, employing skilled use of the cyclic, the collective, throttle and anti-torque pedals, continually having to take evasive action. We all became observers during that final approach to Epping Forrest. When we at last touched back down at Lippitts, it was gone midnight and I'd yet to get home. The helicopter base in north east London was just south of Junction 26 of the M25 and diagonally opposite where I needed to be, sixty-four miles away, from my bed in New Malden, Surrey!

As luck would have it, an articulated lorry loaded with helicopter rota blades requiring maintenance and repairs at Lambeth, was leaving for Lambeth in the next ten minutes. I was able to hitch a ride with a very friendly lorry driver and so began another 'first' experience, riding high above the road in one of the passenger seats, which was very comfortable indeed. Lambeth control had already been notified of my arrival and after thanking the lorry driver profusely, I offloaded all my gear and put it into an unmarked Astramax, where a Lambeth 'pool' driver took me home. I considered myself lucky to get in just after two in the morning on what was now Friday 11th June. One of my SW area crime scene colleagues gave me a lift back into Amelia Street mid-morning so that I could reunite my gear with my job van and of course drop all my films off for processing. I was very thankful that I wasn't on call that weekend as I felt knackered and just wanted to get my head down at the earliest opportunity. Whilst Pete, with Bishopsgate, had unquestionably photographed the mayhem caused by one of the largest and most powerful bomb scenes the British mainland had ever witnessed since the second world war, I think it's fair to say that I had arguably photographed one of the smallest!

I photographed many prisoners all over London from Belmarsh to Wormwood Scrubs and Wandsworth to Pentonville and also the now closed Holloway Women's prison. I even visited Feltham Young Offenders Institute on several occasions and I photographed in a variety of police stations throughout the Met. Photographing an IRA terrorist suspect, however, was a different ballgame altogether. Undertaken within the confines of the top security police station, Paddington Green, the photography of terrorist suspects had its own strict procedure. I treated suspect 'X' like any other person I was photographing, undertaking full length, side, rear and close-up facial views and all the time being courteous and professional. Throughout photography, subject 'X' was fully co-operative. Dressed in a white forensic paper suit, he wore a blank facial expression that gave nothing away and kept completely schtum, which I was warned about, but still found a tad unnerving. All the while, I could see the IRA man take on board everything that I was doing and clocking all the equipment that I was using.

1993 saw the introduction of the Ford Sierra as a replacement to the Mondeo. UK unemployment in June was around the 2.9 million mark. In the February the country witnessed the sickening abduction (in Bootle) and then murder (in Walton), of two-year-old James Bulger, by two ten-year olds, Jon Venables and Robert Thompson. In early April, Vauxhall launched its Corsa in the UK to replace the Nova. On 22nd April, black teenager Stephen Lawrence was stabbed to death at a bus shelter in Eltham, South East London - a disgusting, evil crime on a defenceless young man with a very bright future ahead of him. This was to have huge ramifications for the investigating police force, The Metropolitan Police Service, who were later to be accused by the Sir William Macpherson report published on 24th February 1999 as being 'Institutionally racist'. Among the many famous people who we lost that year included the actress Audrey Hepburn, the footballer Bobby Moore and the comedian Les Dawson. Les was a lovely, intelligent, friendly man, who I remember meeting and speaking with on several occasions at my old Arnold School in the early '80s, where he was just one of the proud Dads coming to pick his children up. In the same year, the Queen announced that Buckingham Palace would open its doors to the public for the first time.

Pop hits included Whitney Houston's 'I Will Always Love You', Take That's 'Pray', the amazing (and one of my all-time favourite pop singers) Freddie Mercury who had a posthumous number one hit with the remixed 'Living on My Own', Ace of Base with 'All that She Wants' and of course Meatloaf's 'I'd Do Anything for Love". On television, fictional police series 'The Bill' made for compulsive weeknight viewing. I can still remember the dramatic episode aired on 26th March in which DC Viv Martella, played by actress Nula Conwell, was shot and killed by a gunman after she approached his car. Nicholas Lyndhurst starred in 'Goodnight Sweetheart', a time travelling comedy series. 1993 was also the 30th anniversary of Doctor Who's first broadcast in the UK. The cinema brought us (among others), 'In the Name of the Father', 'Shadowlands', 'Jurassic Park', 'Schindler's List', 'The Firm', 'Sleepless in Seattle', 'Cliffhanger', 'The Pelican Brief', 'Indecent Proposal' and of course the much-loved and talented, the late Robin Williams as 'Mrs Doubtfire'.

CHAPTER 16

Videographer, Metropolitan Police Service SO3(2) Photographic, London September 1993 – December 1995

Wendy and I enjoyed a lovely summer break in 1993 on the Greek island of Skiathos in the north west Aegean, with mule rides into the hills, walks by the harbour and plenty of candle lit meals. When I returned to Scenes of Crime following this holiday, rumours were abound that the operational video team, who were responsible for covering all the murders and suspicious deaths throughout London, were looking to recruit another Photographic Officer into their ranks. When I first joined the scenes of crime team, I was known as Senior Photographer, but the ranking structure and pay grades were rejigged and with this came the new title of Photographic Officer, abbreviated to 'Pho'. Many of us objected to this as we lost the title 'Senior' which added a bit of clout to our standing. The video team comprised 4 Higher Photographic Officers (HPho's) and at the end of August 1993, 3 Pho's, one of whom was my mate Pete, who'd joined the video team in the July. There were 4 teams. Each HPho was partnered up with a Pho and each team was assigned an area of London to work as a rough guide, but of course flexibility meant that there could be, and often was, crossover. Liam and Derek worked north east and part of south east, Bill and Pete worked north west, David and Matthew worked west and part of south west and Bob, then on his own, worked part of south west and south east. Each team had their own Ford Transit van, or equivalent, complete with sliding door access to a middle, video copying section.

Seven members in the team with one person working on their own. It quickly became apparent that Bob Pickles was looking for a Pho to work with him and even up the team numbers. Having popped a batch of films in for processing at Amelia Street one late August morning, the Grim Reaper summoned me over to one corner of the colour room for a quiet word. It all seemed very hush hush as moments later I was then asked to go to the 'cinema', a small viewing area, close to both small and large studios, for a meeting with Bob Pickles and Liam Tadd. So, I opened the door to the cinema and I could feel an atmosphere the moment I walked in. Although there were smiles all round, it was as if I had jumped into part of a conspiracy story. Bob and Liam stopped talking as soon as I entered the room and throughout what I quickly assumed to be my 'interview', I was eyed conspiratorially, no doubt for my suitability, by Bob Pickles, the undisputed head of the team. Bob had joined the MPS in 1967 as a teenage assistant photographer at NSY and so had many years' experience under his belt. Shorter than me and in his early 40s, Bob had been blessed with a full head of thick, wavy black hair, which was in contrast to my 'slap head'. Bob also had much bigger hands than me and had an authoritative air about him that meant business. We exchanged pleasantries during which I expressed a strong desire to join this team and learn new skills. Then, out of the blue I was offered the post there and then! I was really made up. I had a few days to top and tail my assignments for the scenes of crime team, before joining what was known as 'Operational Video Services' (OVS) in the first week of September. The geographical location was one of the important factors in my selection to the team and it transpired that Bob garaged the video van at East Molesey Police Station, which of course was in close proximity to where I lived in New Malden.

Having surrendered my Astramax van back to the scenes of crime team, Bob picked me up on that first Monday morning and we travelled into Amelia Street to meet the rest of OVS, which had its own office along from the cinema, where I had my impromptu interview. Bob introduced me to everyone, before popping out to a meeting. Dark haired Shirley was lovely and looked after us all. She provided our admin support. Pete of course I already knew, as we joined the MPS more or less at the same time. Pete worked with his line manager, Bill Harper, who I warmed to immediately. Bill was a no nonsense, but happy go lucky, friendly and approachable Lancastrian. It transpired that he hailed from Fleetwood (Alfie Boe's hometown), a former fishing port at the mouth of the River Wyre and not six miles from where I was raised in Poulton-le-Fylde. Bill was also very humorous and I enjoyed his company tremendously. David was also very friendly and approachable with a great sense of humour. He had a sharp mind and in addition to scenes of crime, he had a wealth of surveillance experience. David lived up near Wendy's brother in Ruislip and his Pho was Matthew John, who resided in Staines and had been in the job a good four years longer than me. Liam Tadd was very pally with Bob, an impression I formed from day one. The two guys had formed OVS after all, so along with a common interest in computers and gadgets, they were going to have that connection anyway. Moustached Liam was a gnat's taller than me and good deal stockier. He had been a night club bouncer in his time, so I made a mental note not to get on the wrong side of him. As it turned out I got on with Liam very well, working with him on quite a few occasions.

Last but by no means least was Derek, Liam's Pho. Sitting on the edge of Shirley's desk, this six foot, muscly, forty year old legend of SO3(2) Photographic, (whose catchphrases included 'the van's full of jollop', 'press the tit' (for press the shutter release), 'it's a little bit winky-wanky' and 'scary biscuits') sported a good head of dishevelled, wavy, brown hair and three days of stubble. He wore an open neck, short sleeved red check shirt, scruffy jeans and a pair of old white trainers with at least two holes a piece and looked every bit a no bullshit man's man. Looking as if he was debating whether to punch my lights out, Derek stared at me with a semi 'resting bitch face' and announced to me and the rest of the office that, "I'm ignoring you for a whole month, during which time I'm gonna find out whether you're a wanker or not!" "Charming", was all I said before turning to the others who were grinning. However, they say you shouldn't judge a book by its cover and not only did this whole month ignoring thing only last a few days, but Derek, a keen Nikon camera enthusiast and photography book collector, turned out to be the most kind, generous and loyal person, one could ever hope to meet. Derek is quite simply one of life's great characters and I feel very fortunate and proud to call him my friend. The 4 Pho's, known by Pickles and Tadd as 'boys' (which we objected to), quickly became quite pally and we'd often be on the phone to each other.

September 1993 also heralded the start of The X-Files on television, starring David Duchovny as Fox Mulder and Gillian Anderson as Dana Scully. The series had cult status and became compulsive viewing stoking the ideas about conspiracy theories, extra-terrestrials and the supernatural. In my opinion, the main bad guy, CSM (Cigarette Smoking Man) was the true hero of the X-Files and my favourite character. He was portrayed by the talented Bill Davis (William B. Davis). Such was our obsession with the series, we'd have regular analysis chats over the weekly episodes and Derek even had an A1 size poster up on the wall in the OVS office depicting Mulder and Scully with the inevitable caption 'The Truth Is Out There.'

The two main functions of OVS were covering murders, sus deaths, raids, routes, marches and demonstrations on the one hand and Video Film Identification (VFI) on the other. Before you'd start any video recording, you'd always check the functionality of the kit, the camera controls and the cleanliness of the lens front element. With any scene work, you'd be reliant on your information retrieval and scene analysis to then tell the story of events in a logical order of carefully pre-planned shots, which you would map out in your head, two or three shots ahead. You'd then practise that shot, for example, a pan followed towards the end of the shot by a slow zoom in towards a murder weapon. Once you were happy with the practise, you'd call out "we are recording" (or between ourselves "Turning over / Camera speed") to notify police officers not to walk into shot and not to speak. Then you'd hit the record button and lay the shot down on tape. You'd always allow five seconds of settlement time recording at the start and end of every sequence, especially important when that involved a camera movement such as a pan, a zoom, or a walking shot. This enabled the viewer's eye to settle on and create familiarisation with the scene, before the camera moved away to a different view. Without this settlement time, you risked confusing the viewer. At the end of each recorded view the camera operator would hit the record button again and call out "tape stopped".

Constructing a video of a crime scene, sequence by sequence, so that the whole recording was slow, smooth, linked together and told the story of events, took me a lot of practise, initially undertaken in Amelia Street's cinema set up as a mock crime scene. For scenes of crime video recordings, editing the tape in camera was prohibited for continuity purposes as it could be alleged in court that you recorded something evidential and then rewound the tape and erased the material. So once you had laid the first video sequence to tape, if you wobbled the camera, if a pan wasn't smooth, if a zoom was jerky, or if someone walked into shot or uttered an expletive – it was tough shit, the error(s) had to remain on tape. This then proved to the court that, whilst you had made a mistake, you were being honest and open.

Video had its advantages over 'stills' images. It was easier to link one part of a scene with another, it was quicker, especially when multiple rooms were involved. Audio could be used on demonstrations and raids and for witness reconstruction routes for example. Video also enabled easier linkage and storytelling and could be used for briefings or in court to enable the viewer to gain a better understanding of the crime scene. This was especially useful having video recorded at a murder scene, for example. We'd make a VHS copy in the middle section of the van parked outside the scene, and then hand that labelled tape to an officer in the case, who would then have the tape for the murder investigation team to view – all prepared in a very timely manner indeed.

Focusing the camera was pretty quick as well. Provided that you had pre-checked and set the lens' back focus, you'd generally zoom into the middle of a scene, focus the lens and then zoom out again to recompose the initial shot. This was especially important if you were going to start off with a pan and then end up zooming in on a close-up. You needed to make sure that when you zoomed in, the shot didn't suddenly go out of focus – all because you had forgotten to check focus at the start. If a still shot was required, generally the maximum acceptable recording time was around twelve seconds, although there were occasionally exceptions.

A crime scene would be covered with a series of establishing shots, close-ups and re-establishing shots and would typically use a series of pans, zooms and 'cutaways' (still shots). Sometimes, walking with the camera would also be employed. You'd zoom in to emphasise a subject and zoom out to reveal that subject in its surroundings. The general rule with all video camera movements was that they were to be used when necessary and not to be overused. 'Hose piping' involved zooming in and out, often repeatedly, within one video sequence. It was a classic novice error, looked awful and therefore was to be avoided. You'd pan the camera in a single direction and avoid panning back in the same sequence like the motion of windscreen wipers, which constituted another no no. A 'jump cut', which occurred when you finished a shot and then started on the same view, with the same or similar lens magnification and angle of view, was also to be avoided. Another classic video error was to follow a view looking one way immediately with a reverse angle view, known as 'crossing the line'. This completely wrong-footed and confused the viewer. The solutions involved either filming a 360-degree sequence, filming a series of tracking shots, or using several linked cutaway shots to get you to the point where you were looking back the other way. For scenes such as murders and suspicious death, these were filmed without audio. It was essential to know beforehand whether audio was going to be required. The audit trail of copies involved producing two VHS tapes (one exhibit copy for court and one spare. Initially a U-Matic format tape was produced as the exhibit copy), exhibit labels, statement for court and the numbered and logged master M11 tape, being stored at Amelia Street's secure tape store.

From the start, I needed to learn the Panasonic camera from scratch. With a powerful Canon zoom lens bolted on to the front end, this thirty-odd pound 'bad boy' encased in a dark blue Portabrace equipment protector, was a broadcast quality M11 (M-two). It was essentially split into three component parts: detachable lens, camera housing the chip or CCD (Charged Coupled Device), which changed the visual images into electrical signals, which were then recorded to tape. The middle of the camera housed various controls, for example to change the white balance and chip sensitivity (gain) and the tape recorder mechanism was located at the back end. The tape deck accepted Panasonic twenty minute, M11 metal tapes, M11 having been developed by Panasonic back in 1986 as competition for Sony's 'Betacam SP'. M11 was technically similar to Betacam SP and used component video – splitting the video signal into separate channels. 20 minutes of recording time was more than ample for the majority of scenes, but multiple tapes were required for raids and demonstrations etc.. The middle section of each video van housed a Panasonic location recorder, which could accommodate the larger 90-minute M11 tapes as well as the 20-minute ones. The location recorder was generally linked to a small colour monitor and VHS recorder for tape copying purposes. The camera was powered by a beefy 'Pag' battery which clipped on to the underside of the camera at the back. If you were shooting a subject in close proximity under low light conditions, a handy 'Paglight' (a powerful tungsten halogen bulb complete with blue dichroic filter for use as a fill-in under daylight) clipped onto a hot shoe mounting. A long wire from this then plugged into a 'Pag belt' for power, which was worn by the operator. The Pagbelt had two batteries, one clipped on each side of the hip area. All in all, the entire kit was very heavy indeed. You could undertake basic weight training just by arm curling a single battery and if you were filming for hours on end during a raid or demonstration, you certainly knew about it. Suffice to say that OVS wasn't for the meek and mild!

The other function undertaken within OVS was Video Film Identification (V.F.I.), which was challenging technically and involved a high degree of skill and expertise. The end product was an edited film containing the suspect along with a minimum of eight similar looking participants to assist with the identification of the suspect by any number of witnesses. Code D of the Police and Criminal Evidence Act (PACE) permitted this procedure, but it was controlled by strict guidelines. A suspect had first to be offered the chance to appear on a formal ID parade or group ID parade. A group ID parade was normally held at a public place, such as the top of an escalator in a tube station, where the suspect 'suddenly' appeared with members of the public and the witness had to try and identify the suspect in the process. If a suspect refused to stand on a formal ID parade, or take part in a group ID parade, they were then given the option of agreeing to be filmed. In this case, the suspect would appear with similar looking volunteer participants with the purpose of producing an ID parade on video tape. If the suspect still refused to play ball, under PACE, the OVS team had the authority to film them covertly and still produce an edited video using the volunteer participants. One of the problems to overcome, however, with more professional criminals (those in the know), was that Code D required the suspect to be informed of the police's covert filming ability, before any covert video footage could take place and therefore used. This information was given verbally to the suspect by the identification officer and was contained on the 'Notice to Suspect', which was served when ID procedures were explained by the Identification Officer. The moment the suspect learned of this, there was usually an attempt made to hide the face, look down and generally make it difficult to obtain usable covert footage. However, this only constituted a small problem and back then, VFI was the most successful form of identification.

The initial request would be made from an authorised Video Identification Officer (VIO), a uniformed Police Inspector, having first satisfied themselves that the offence was not a minor one and that there was a reasonable chance of obtaining a positive identification. The VIO then required a Superintendent's authority to proceed, to prevent resources being wasted on a frivolous request. The VIO also had to ensure that all reasonable attempts had been made to hold a conventional ID or Group ID parade, or that the procedure was being requested for another permitted reason, mainly that the witness was unable or unwilling to attend an ID parade. The suspect was then filmed either with their consent or covertly.

Whether with consent or under covert conditions, once the suspect had been filmed, detailed measurements would be noted of camera (including correct time code) and tripod positioning and camera and lens settings. All room light settings were documented, even down to the fact that a bulb might be missing or not working, curtain or window blind positions and the camera white balance target. Filming a suspect with their consent was easier as you didn't have to hide the equipment. They were generally filmed with the camera's tungsten halogen Pag light illuminating them, standing in front of a portable background and after about 15 seconds, the suspect would be asked to turn their head to one side and remain still for another 10 seconds. The distance of the background to subject would be noted, together with the distance of the suspect to the camera and the type, wattage and zoom setting of the lamp. The lighting would be powered from the mains to ensure consistency in colour as near exhausted batteries were prone to changing the colour of the lighting. All this rigorous procedure and notetaking was designed to ensure that the set up could be replicated at a later date when filming the minimum of eight similar looking participants, undertaking similar actions (if applicable).

By far the best VFI I ever saw was shot by Dave and Matthew. I think they only managed to obtain a couple of seconds of their extremely cautious and switched on suspect, side on, whilst he was getting changed out of his prison attire. Dave and Matthew slow mo'd the footage down to gain more playing time and via skilful direction, got all the participants to do the same complicated actions. This included looking round to the left, then right, then round to the left again, whilst at the same time, pulling and zipping up their trousers – it was a genius VFI and I do believe the witness picked the suspect out from amongst all the participants on the edited tape. Great result guys!

Prior to recording the eight or more participants, it was often necessary to prepare a scene / action matching tape. A first preview edit tape would be prepared and the tape duplicated. A number of witness viewing edit tapes with tape duplication would then be made, with the suspect appearing in a different position on each tape. Sometimes the actual witness viewing procedure was also filmed with audio. This happened as a prerequisite when defence counsel declared that they were not co-operating with the VFI procedure. For this set up, knowing that we would need to record continuously for longer than 20 minutes (the length of a standard M11 tape), we would need the location M11 recorder from the van as it was capable of recording for 90 minutes. In the event of a positive identification being made, a statement would be prepared detailing all the photographer's actions in chronological order and additional working tape copies would be produced for court.

The audit trail for one's statement would start with brief photographer details: -

- the suspect recording and tape labelling details
- the set-up edit stage (a copy of the master suspect tape with reference number, to help you reproduce the participants as close to the suspect recording conditions as possible)
- the participant recording stage with allocated reference number
- the first edit (compilation tape) to show to the suspect and their solicitor with reference number
- subsequent edited tapes for witness viewing (with the suspect appearing in different positions on each tape) with reference numbers that were prepared from the original master suspect tape and original master participant's tape.

Two unedited VHS copies of each of these tapes (depicting suspect and witnesses) would then be made and labelled. Finally, if you were required to film the witness viewing stage, you'd have to detail how many separate video recordings you made (depending on how many witnesses were viewing each tape). Each M11 tape would need a reference number as well as its own VHS copy, which in turn would have its own reference number as well. Details of bag sealing and seal numbers would also need to be disclosed on the statement, as well as details as to where the master and edit tapes were stored.

It all seemed very complicated, but the whole process including all paperwork and tape labelling needed to be watertight, to prevent allegations of lack of continuity by defence.

Although I had an interest in video filming, prior to joining OVS I knew absolutely zilch about this exciting medium. I had to learn the Panasonic M11 from scratch, how to wire multiple pieces of equipment in together and also how to use the OVS edit suite, primarily to prepare video identification films for initial suspect with solicitor viewing and then subsequent witness viewing. I'd also never used a home computer before September 1993. We didn't buy our first one until early summer 1997 (we used the proceeds of a pay-out of damages after a truck drove into Wendy while she was driving with George in the back of the car). It helped immensely that Bob was also a bit of a computer anorak. If he wasn't filming or editing, he was tapping away at the keyboard. We needed an office computer for data entries and to produce our statements on word documents. I hovered at Bob's shoulder, listened, absorbed and learned. I owe all my early computer skills to Bob Pickles. The first time I sat in the edit suite next to my new line manager, it all looked very daunting. There were multiple consoles, with different coloured levers and buttons. One was labelled, 'mark in' and another 'mark out', others were 'set in' and 'set out'. There were caption generators, switches and sliders. On the upside I had been paired with an outstanding videographer. Bob had a vast amount of experience and he was a very patient teacher. He was very friendly and gave me invaluable tuition and feedback, especially useful when a crime scene video hadn't worked out the way I'd intended. In the early days, especially, I got on with him very well indeed and got to know how he worked, his likes and dislikes and I think that following a lengthy baptism of fire into video, we worked well as a team.

However, it wasn't all a bed of roses. When we were out together on scenes of crime and having watched the skilful way Bob operated, continually analysing his video technique, which I longed to emulate, I kept saying to Bob, "Please could I film this suspicious death?". To which Bob would inevitably reply "maybe the next one". I was eager to get in the driving seat, to be on camera and maybe this was Bob's way of slapping me down, flexing his muscles and reminding me who was boss. It just seemed to go on for ages until one day, out of the blue, having set up to record what had just been downgraded to a non-suspicious death, Bob handed me the video camera rig with a smug grin on his face. Having planned out my shots, I put the heavy beast on my right shoulder and Bob acted as my assistant, holding the supplementary Pag light in what was not quite a role reversal. The resulting video was far from perfect, with wobbles and jarring and the horizon, on occasions, was skew-whiff. What I needed was more practise at 'live' scenes, not being fobbed off with being told to practise in the cinema at Amelia Street. I'd done that and it just wasn't the same.

On about day two of me learning the edit suite, I popped back into the OVS office after copying some VFI edits only to run into Derek who cheekily asked me whether I'd got my notebook with me. It transpired that Bob had told the others that I took notes during my training sessions. I thought that was very odd, almost like telling tales. For my part, I needed to write stuff down as there was so much to learn. "Paul takes notes!" Wow, Jesus – I didn't see that one coming. Had I committed a crime, or was someone paranoid that I was taking notes about the department? Either way, shortly after the 'notebook' episode, I was sitting in the edit suite with Bob getting to grips with a particular sequence of function keys. I said light heartedly "So, Bob, what would happen if I was to hit that button by mistake?", knowing that this particular move might completely cock the job up. I was fully expecting Bob to come back with a retort along the lines of "Well, you don't want to be doing that as you'll have to do the whole thing again". So, I couldn't believe it when Bob turned to me with a sly, mischievous look in his eyes and with an audible sniff and a deliberate reclining of his head said, "If you do that, we'll talk about you like we do Bill!" I had no answer to that. Bob was deadly serious and it was no secret that he didn't like Bill. I guess from day one in OVS I wasn't the only one who was being 'talked about'. I suppose that it didn't help that conspiracy theories were abound with our weekly instalments of the X-Files. I for one was determined not to get paranoid and just brushed this episode off as Bob being a bit south of quirky.

Two teams worked on call in any given week and the other half of OVS undertook the pre-booked jobs such as VFIs, reconstruction routes, demonstrations and raids. It was a standing joke in our household that I seemed to be busier when I wasn't on call. I guess that Wendy was comparing my OVS hours to my on call with the scenes of crime team.

One such pre-booked video assignment was very much ongoing. In the old Kings Cross police station, located on the east side of Kings Cross Road, opposite the junction of Frederick Street, London WC1, the painstaking task of re-interviewing the many witnesses caught up in the 'Blakelock Enquiry' was undertaken over many months. Set against a backdrop of social unrest, tension and mistrust between police and black communities in several English cities during the '80s, violence erupted in Tottenham on 6th October 1985, the day after the search at the home address and subsequent death from a heart attack, of a local woman, Cynthia Jarrett. Forty-year old Met Police constable Keith Blakelock was set upon by an angry, hysterical mob and was murdered during the infamous Broadwater Farm riot. PC Blakelock suffered multiple, horrific machete and knife injuries and in an act of pure evil against 'one of our finest', Keith was also found with a knife in his neck that had been buried right up to the very hilt.

That one sinful deed alone speaks volumes about the definition of the word 'hatred'. The murder enquiry had been re-opened in 1992, following unsuccessful convictions. A room at Kings Cross Police station had already been set aside and kitted out to film witness interviews, with a tripod mounted camera front end, 'umbilicaled' out to video recording equipment in another room. Usually one of us OVS 'boys' would be dropped off at the station for a morning or even a whole day, with an M11 location recorder and a wodge of M11, 90-minute tapes. Here we would monitor proceedings, changing tapes for each witness interview when necessary.

It was in September 1993, during my initial few weeks with OVS, that I bought my first mobile phone, a 'Mercury' connected to the newly established 'One2One' network. It was more of a gimmick, rather than a necessity. Although the size of mobile phones had shrunk considerably since my cruise ship days and boss Richard Dawson striding into the photo gallery on board the 'Norway' back in 1988, carrying a great brick of a thing. The cost of phones and packages had also reduced and were now within easier reach of the masses. Liam Tadd, however, still cradled a big boy Vodaphone that sported a giant aerial.

The Rachel Nickel murder enquiry was also still ongoing and my manager, Bob Pickles and I were tasked with filming witness reconstruction routes, which took us the length and breadth of Wimbledon Common.

During the OVS years of 1993-5 and with mobile phones cheaper and more readily available to the masses, a new type of crime, 'theft of mobile phones from motor vehicles', was on the increase. As part of the police response, we undertook many hours of video surveillance in vulnerable target areas using a dummy mobile phone placed in a parked motor vehicle in full view of passers-by. This was designed as a magnet to lure the perpetrators to the scene. Surveillance was undertaken in supermarket car parks, overlooking business premises and on leafy suburban streets, from either fixed observation posts (OPs), or from a mobile OP, for example, the back of an unmarked van with blacked out windows. You could often be waiting for hours on end, always in a heightened state of alert and could go a whole day without so much as a single bite. If the two of us had pitched up in a fixed OP, at least Bob and I could take it in turns on camera. However, if you were cooped up in an 'obbo' van for ages, you had to train yourself not to go to the toilet. In emergencies, we did of course carry a suitable receptacle on board!

Bob was invariably on camera when any of the action went down and he did capture some fantastic footage. It seemed though that the more the adrenaline rushed, the less enthusiastic Bob was of letting me film, but during one surveillance assignment when a few hours had gone by with nothing to show on tape, Bob needed the loo and I took over on camera. We were in a fixed OP overlooking a supermarket of national repute and no sooner had Bob slipped off to the Gents, all hell broke loose. Radios crackled into life with, "Target sighted, target sighted, slim built, IC1 male, late teens, short brown hair, dark blue hooded top, blue denim jeans and black trainers riding a dark blue bicycle, taking a good look at all the vehicles". Then from the OIC (Officer in charge) – "All units stand by, stand by...". I had already zoomed into the suspect, focused, hit the record button and had captured a good few seconds of decent facial footage, before zooming out a tad wider and following the suspect as he made his approach to our vehicle with the mobile phone planted inside. "He's having a good look, yep he's definitely clocked it", one of the surveillance guys on the ground said over the radios. At that moment Pickles strode back in, got a measure of the situation immediately and went straight into directing mode, as he studied the colour monitor 'BNC'd' (Bayonet Neill-Concelman quick release coaxial video cable) from the camera with the live feed. "Come out a little wider Paul, stay with him. You are recording?" "Yep", I answered, as I sensed Bob doubly checking that the tape was whirring round. After cycling up and down a few more times to recce his intended booty, the suspect approached our target vehicle and with lightning speed produced a centre punch device seemingly from nowhere, smashed the driver's window, elbowed the broken glass to make a wider hole, whereupon the little scroat reached in and snatched the phone. "All units go, go, go!!", I heard, as simultaneously, four plain clothed surveillance officers materialised from my peripheral vision, jumped on 'chummy', made the arrest and had him in handcuffs quicker than you could say "You're nicked!" The team were delighted with the result and thanked Bob and me. It gave me an adrenaline high and even Pickles, who hadn't been on camera at the time of the collar, wore the smuggest grin I'd seen in a long time.

Occasionally I got to do video surveillance on my lonesome, which was great as I was free from Pickles' talons. On a chilly November morning, I found myself in the back of an obbo van with another surveillance officer, parked on a nondescript street in Forest Hill. The unmarked job van was parked opposite a crossroads, which, looking out of the darkened back windows, gave the video camera line of sight along the pavement to our silver Beemer with mobile phone placed in full view next to the automatic gear selector. The camera front end, mounted on a small tripod, was connected into the location recorder and powered by one of many Pag batteries I had with me. I'd taken the liberty of going to the loo just before we arrived at our location, but we had a couple of deep plastic containers just in case. Fortunately, I didn't need to resort to 'going in the van', which was a miracle considering that we were plotted up for the best part of five hours!

I experienced early problems trying to fire up the location recorder, which wouldn't work at all because of the humidity and condensation inside the vehicle. I got on the phone to Pickles, who told me that it was time to 'cuddle up to the recorder'! Having unplugged the damn thing, I had to stuff it up my jumper so my body heat would warm up the cold recorder, knock the 'dew' warning light off and, hopefully, fire the piece of kit back into life. If anything went down during this time, I would have missed it, much to the team's annoyance. Still, there was nothing more to do than to suck it up and cuddle up, as starting the engine to fire up the vehicle heaters was a definite no-no and would have compromised our position and worse, the whole operation. Amazingly this worked and I was very grateful to my former manager and colleague for this invaluable piece of advice. To give myself something to do and to kill the boredom, I'd periodically run the location recorder and film the street scene just to ensure that it was working ok. Each hour seemed to creep by and I think the team were resigning themselves to no result, when after four and a half hours of zero activity, the radios crackled into life with a suspect sighting. A skinny little IC1 who appeared to be no more than sixteen tops suddenly appeared in the distance. He was sporting an array of zits on his face and some strategically placed bum fluff on his top lip and chin. Donned in grey hoody, dark track suit bottoms with similar coloured trainers, he was giving it some wellie on a black cycle. Our suspect was on the pavement and approaching the Beemer at speed. I, meanwhile, was 'turning over' and recording Chummy's actions on M11 for posterity. The suspect definitely slowed to clock the phone when he drew parallel to the BMW, but then turned left at the crossroads junction and disappeared from view. I had been on enough obbos now to realise that what we had just witnessed was a recce and that there was a strong chance that the suspect would return. I was now in a high state of alert and having only paused recording for a few seconds, the radios announced the inevitable, that Chummy had cycled round the block and was now coming around for a second look, possibly more!

Although Pickles wasn't with me, his presence was palpable. I could almost hear him in my ear "Are you recording Paul?", "Check focus, don't zoom in too tight". I had it all under control. Just as the team thought Chummy was going to go for it, he stopped on the pavement parallel to our Beemer, no doubt checking for 'Old Bill', turned, cycled slowly in the opposite direction for about ten houses, turned round again, cycled gently and then when I heard, "stand by, stand by", everything seemed to happen in slow motion, but in reality, breathtakingly fast. Chummy was at the driver's window with his centre punch, I noticed glass flying as it caught the light, cascading to the pavement edge. This was followed by the inevitable reach in and mobile phone grab. Milliseconds later, plain clothes officers had the suspect off his bike, on the ground and handcuffed. Chummy, a serial offender, had no chance. The security 'box' around the Beemer saw police officers swooping down from all four sides, one of whom was hiding behind a half open wooden garden gate, right next to the BMW in question! Chummy was read the riot act and then led away handcuffed, bum fluff twitching and with head bowed so low, he was almost kissing the pile of dog shit that he narrowly missed treading in en route back to a waiting marked van that would chauffeur him back to the custody suite on Dartmouth Road SE26, aka Sydenham Police Station. At exactly the same time in our obbo van, I uttered the immortal words, "....and tape stopped", which was music to my own ears after a very long day.

London W12 formed the backdrop to another video surveillance obbo. There had been a rise in young women having their handbags stolen in the Shepherds Bush Green area during the spring of 1994, so I found myself six floors up a residential tower block in an OP with Bob Pickles, looking down the long lens onto an area close to where these thefts had been occurring. The modus operandi had thus far been to snatch, grab and then either run or cycle away like billy buggery. The handbags would generally be found discarded some distance away, devoid of cash, cards and other valuables. Well the police and the young lady victims had had quite enough of these violations, which were escalating with every day that passed. 'Jenny' and 'Carole', two plain clothes police officers were used as decoys, taking it in turns to saunter along our field of view. Both officers carried their black, leather handbags over their right shoulders and walked nonchalantly as if they hadn't a care in the world, confidant that their police colleagues were watching them from every angle ready to pounce at a moment's notice. After at least two hours of going to and fro, the radios crackled into life for the umpteenth time. "Recip, recip, Jenny's on the recip" indicating that Jenny, whose turn it was to do the walk through, had turned around at a pre-determined spot and was walking back the way she came. Once again I was on camera and recording, having taken over from Pickles when the radio announcement of Jenny's recip was followed immediately with "Suspect sighting, all units stand by, stand by". Then in my left ear I heard a clearly hyped up Pickles say, "You are recording Paul", as he simultaneously checked that the M11 tape was whirring round. I could detect him watching the action on the monitor's live feed and I almost had visions of him physically yanking me off camera and filming this bit himself! The adrenaline rush kicked in. Jenny suddenly appeared in my field of view, walking with her back to the camera and away from us. To her right was a low wall on top of which, were grey coloured railings. On Pickles' instructions, I zoomed out a tad wider and as I did so, an IC1 male, dark haired teenager clad in scruffy, black-coloured clothing also appeared in view, walking a few metres behind Jenny but up on the wall. I touched the zoom rocker forward to go tighter on the undercover police officer and suspect, allowing enough room for any action to happen. "That's fine, Paul, leave it there. Stay with them", Pickles told me. The suspect had closed the gap considerably, but still Jenny walked on as if she hadn't even noticed the suspect. Then it happened. The suspect jumped down onto Jenny and instead of making off with her handbag, he grabbed her right breast as she turned around. Police swarmed, the place was instantly surrounded by plain clothes officers and the toe rag was arrested for indecent assault. It was a good result, a great day's filming and damn good experience on camera.

I enjoyed video surveillance, it was quite a different discipline, camouflaging camera kit, making sure you and your equipment couldn't be seen, becoming totally au fait with the OP and your surroundings and getting into the mindset of obbo work. Where it was possible to do so and once we'd fully camouflaged the OP, Pickles would often wander out and walk past the OP to see whether he could spot the camera or officers inside. Whilst this was an invaluable exercise, I would find it quite comical, as he looked so suspicious pretending not to glance towards the OP. On one job, I remember being sneaked into an OP under cover of darkness. The first floor obbo was above a pub in an area of Stoke Newington where drug dealing was rife. The OP overlooked a dirty, paint-peeled front door of a very run-down house where there was a steady stream of undesirable characters coming and going. Our brief was to obtain good facial images over a period of a couple of weeks, which we did as a team, alternating crews.

Working in the capital offered a diverse range of assignments. We filmed demonstrations, marches and other public order events almost on a weekly basis. Memories of covering the M11 link road (now known as the A12 Hackney to M11 link road, connecting to the North Circular Road), come flooding in. These assignments generally involved a silly o'clock start in the morning. You'd attend an operational feeding centre to fill your boots with a big boy's breakfast, because you'd probably skip lunch (even though it was provided). Then a convoy of police carriers would plot up and drive to the latest trouble spot where UK road protesters had pitched up in droves to stall the road builders from moving in. The protesters were squatting in derelict houses earmarked for demolition, camping on rough ground, or were living in crude tree houses. Operational Video Services were on scene to film the orderly removal of protesters and to capture any violence if it all kicked off.

We made several visits to the Redbridge area of east London during 1994 and 1995. A few skirmishes inevitably did break out, but my abiding memory is on one particular visit, Pickles was on camera (of course) and I was watching his back, as well as lugging the spare batteries and Pag lighting kit around. Suddenly a scantily clad, very bohemian looking man in his early 20s, jumped down from a tree and came prancing over to us like a chirruping minstrel, who for all the world looked as if he'd leapt forward in time and come straight from the court of Henry V111. He then proceeded to sing and dance around us, obviously camping it up for the camera. Pickles' face was a picture. He was extremely serious in what was a very comedic situation. If the truth be known, I'd have wagered that the minstrel had got under Pickles' skin. The more Pickles pointed the camera at him and filmed, the more this seemed to play into the hands of the minstrel, who was becoming more ebullient by the minute with his puerile serenading. Before police led Chummy away, the minstrel broke into song, "You can't kill the spirit, you can't kill the spirit, you can't kill the spirit of the trees" – er, yeah, righteoh mate!

Notting Hill Carnival runs over August Bank Holiday every year and necessitates a huge police operation. Back in the mid '90s, that police presence included me as part of OVS. The carnival in London dates back to 1966, is attended by around a million people and is led by members of Britain's West Indian community. Carnival is noted for its sound systems, fantastic Caribbean music (which I love so much as it reminds me of my cruise ship days), excellent variety of food and drink, numerous floats, amazing dancing, beautiful, vibrant costumes and colourful feather headdresses, face masks and an electric, inspiring, traditional party atmosphere.

Operational Video Services normally pitched up on the roof of a pub or on the A40 Westway overlooking Ladboke Grove to film any crime. This would inevitably be drug dealing and steaming gangs. The latter violation normally involved a team of around four, who you could spot from a height, snaking through the masses. The front gang member would do the steal – a handbag or wallet - and immediately pass the booty to the second gang member behind and so on. If the lead gang member was challenged by a man bereft of his wallet, for example, of course they'd plead ignorance as they'd have nothing incriminating on them. I covered the Notting Hill Carnival using video in 1994 and 1995. In 1994 I was partnered up with Matthew John overlooking the carnival route from the Westway. Matthew had come equipped with a disposable barbeque and after hours of taking it in turns on camera, we enjoyed a sumptuous grilled feast with trout, sausages and beef burgers. There were, however, repercussions post carnival as it filtered back to Photographic that police personnel had fired up a barbecue on the Westway, as smoke had been spotted rising from our OP by India 99 (the police helicopter). I guess we were lucky to get away with that one! For the 1995 carnival coverage, I attended all three days (Saturday to Monday) by myself and pitched up at a different OP each day. Back then, I seem to remember Saturday as being Childrens day, which is held prior to the main carnival getting under way. I filmed several drug deals along with quite a few steaming gangs. They were long old days, but as a consolation I caned the overtime. Time and a half Saturday and double bubble for both Sunday and bank holiday Monday was there for the taking.

I lost count of the number of public order events I attended on OVS. Our role was to provide video coverage of any disorder, from a reasonably safe distance. However, when the Kurds decided to hold a sit-down protest in Victoria following a relatively peaceful march,

I knew in my waters that it was all going to go pear shaped. It had only been half a dozen years if that since former Iraqi dictator, Saddam Hussein, had ordered the mustard gas / nerve agent poisoning of thousands of Kurdish men, women and children in the Kurdish city of Halabja located in Northern Iraq. This was barely 260 kilometres south east of Erbil, Kurdistan's capital where I was later privileged to visit in 2012. The two men directly responsible for this outrageous attack, Saddam Hussein and his cousin, Ali Hassan al-Majid, (known as 'Chemical Ali') were hanged in 2006 and 2010 respectively. Additionally, the Kurdish insurgency had all been rumbling on since the 1970's and periodically the Kurds would hold demos in various cities, London being one of them, to bring their suffering to the attention of other countries and the World's media.

The two-man OVS team consisting of Bob Pickles and myself had been walking with the march through the centre of town, Pickles on camera as usual and yours truly as the humble bag man, to its sit-down conclusion protest in Victoria. I detected the vibe in the air and it was tense. The chants of "Viva, viva, Kurdistan" had notched up a few decibels and when I caught sight of something flying through the air, it was the signal for the red mist to descend and it very quickly all kicked off like the sudden boom from an inferno's backdraft. With the Panasonic M11 right shoulder mounted, your right side was completely blinded so I was watching Pickles like a hawk. "Paul, how's the tape?!" Pickles shouted to me above the din. I checked and said it was fine. We were both dressed in jeans, shirts and trainers – no protective clothing whatsoever, which looking back, was utterly ludicrous. All I had to protect the two of us was a weighty camera bag full of charged camera Pag batteries, which I quickly deployed as a protective shield, batting off relentless incoming sticks and other missiles hurled our way and all the while thinking, shit – this whole thing's going down the wrong way. A stick hit me on the back of my right shoulder, which stung momentarily and served just to piss me off rather than scaring me. I was left nursing a small bruise, which hardly constituted a war wound. Instead of retreating, Pickles edged nearer and stood within spitting distance of the troublemakers, filming defiantly. Having intercepted yet another missile, I was getting more narked that Pickles wasn't withdrawing. As a police TSG serial waded into the crowd with shields and truncheons at the ready, I shouted above the din to Pickles "We need to pull back, Bob, now!" "NO!!" came the over assertive reply, shouted from my manager. "Fuck's sake!" I muttered, but then five to ten minutes after the TSG had waded in, the violence abated as quickly as it had started, the demo dispersed and our job was done for the day. However, I still had the hump that Pickles hadn't backed off to a safer distance.

Searches of premises could often be a real bastard to cover, especially if an arrest had been made. Police officers would tend to start in one room, conduct the search in the presence of the handcuffed suspect and all the while you'd be on camera filming with audio for twenty minutes at a time – continuous recording. You'd then change tapes and carry on. The weight of that Panasonic camera on your right shoulder for several hours was an ordeal and a half. I remember many a time I'd be standing there, camera on shoulder, keeping the equipment rock steady with sweat trickling down my cheeks and willing the search to be wrapped up.

Searches of premises were often preceded by an 'in through the door' raid, which was always an adrenaline rush if you were on camera and immediately behind the officer with the red coloured ram raider, a nifty piece of kit. Following one or two swings with the ram raider, wood and glass would shatter, you'd be in through the door faster than a Tom could pull down her knickers, there'd generally be a lot of shouting and you'd see people running all over the place, often in a confused state.

One particular raid on a massage parlour in North London springs to mind, because it was a very cold October mid evening and we had plotted up around the corner. Knowing that the place had saunas and steam rooms (among other things!), I knew that if I didn't warm the camera up beforehand, the lens would steam up as soon as we gained entry and I would get no suitable footage. Twenty minutes before I went inside, I had my Pag belt on, I'd set a white balance on camera for the tungsten halogen lighting I would be using and had the camera itself sitting by my feet being blasted with hot air. As soon as I received the signal that we'd be entering the premises in five minutes, I locked up the van and followed officers quietly around the corner.

I took my place behind the ram raider and the arresting officer, announced in hushed tones that "I am recording", then bang!, bang!, bang!, the front door swung back, half broken. The ram raider peeled off and I followed right behind the arresting officer, who kicked down the first door. I was greeted with a totally naked middle age punter lying on his back on a white, towel-covered couch, with his head nearest to the camera and a young, scantily clad Thai girl, sporting enormous 'bristols', who was caught on camera in mid flow, rhythmically gobbling the punter's throbbing tumescence! Then it was straight into the next room. Same routine. The door was kicked open and whoa! What was this? Another middle-aged male punter, again lying on his back totally starkers. This time, another naked, young Thai girl, who had even bigger breasts than her friend next door, was busy caressing and sucking the punter's toes, whilst said punter J Arthured himself. I guess that's what you call 'having a toe job'! The girl looked up to camera like the proverbial rabbit in the headlights for a split second, before crouching down on the floor, farcically trying to hide. And at that precise moment, the lens totally steamed up and I couldn't get any more footage – shit and derision!

With drugs raids, we could be filming seized blocks of heroin, cocaine and cash under floorboards one minute and industrial greenhouses filled with row upon row of cannabis plants the next. Some of the raids were carried out in pubs where it was known that dealing was occurring, snorting was prevalent and substances a tad stronger than wacky backy were being smoked, snorted, injected and God knows what else, by multiple users. Pickles and I could often be on scene for an hour or more, filming the arrests and any evidence. The air was thick with the smell of drugs and it took a while for me to realise that the banging headache I used to get on these jobs was due to the fact that I had actually got high on the smoke inside and the rush of cold air outside had precipitated a rapid downer! Come to think of it, I'd often get a headache when photographing or filming shebeens (illegal drinking dens) – common denominator – drugs in the air!

I had only been on the OVS team for barely two months when, on 20th October 1993, Pickles and I got called to a shooting scene in Cato Road, Clapham, South West London. Police Constable Patrick Dunne, a forty-four-year-old local community officer, was in the middle of enquiries relating to a minor disturbance across the street at number 28, when he was interrupted by the sound of gunfire. PC Dunne went outside into the street to investigate, where he received a fatal gunshot wound to the chest. Witnesses saw three black men leaving the scene laughing triumphantly and firing gunshots into the air defiantly, as if they were celebrating. The scene itself, filmed early evening, was street related, with a suspect's address in Cato Road filmed as a secondary scene.

One of the most disturbing scenes I ever attended on OVS was the murder of an older couple and their daughter in Hounslow, West

London. By the time Pickles and I had put on our protective forensic suits and overshoes, Pag belts clipped on and spare Pag light at the ready, Crime Scene Photographer, Jackie Bishop had already covered most of the scene with 'stills'. Jackie had just emerged onto a communal walkway and was leaning over a parapet, Manfrotto tripod and camera bag by her side, halfway through taking long and deliberate drags of her cigarette. Jackie looked round at us and warned us that it was a horrible sight in there. She looked visibly drained and disconnected. When Pickles and I entered the scene, we learned why. The daughter had been raped and killed in one of the bedrooms and in the living room, lying on the floor, were the bodies of her parents, a few metres apart from one another. The male deceased's genitalia had been severed and stuffed down the poor guy's throat. This was a disgusting, despicable act which was so shocking, it left me angry and wishing that the death penalty was reinstated. I was reminded of Jackie's haunted look as she dragged hard on her cigarette. Fortunately, most of the horrible details of that scene have faded from the gory box in my mind. Suffice to say, that particular scene shocked at least two hardened forensic photographers that night.

On 7th February 1994, OVS were once again summoned on call to what came in as a 'possible murder of an M.P.' The venue was a pretty, terraced town house in Black Lion Lane, Chiswick and the deceased gentleman in question was none other than 45-year-old Stephen David Wyatt Milligan, Member of Parliament for Eastleigh, Hampshire and rising star of the Tory party, tipped to be a future Prime Minister.

When Pickles and I arrived at the location in darkness early that evening, we parked up on the left a few doors down from the scene. Opposite Mr Milligan's house was a huge barrage of press, comprising TV cameras, journalists and photographers. Red lights above their 'Betacam SP' TV cameras indicated that they were filming and probably broadcasting live. Periodically camera flashes fired and once Bob and I had locked the van, we carried the camera, lighting and spare Pag batteries to the front door of Mr Milligan's home. As soon as we stepped out from behind the van, loads of flashes fired and I just knew that somehow we'd make the evening news and the morning papers. Pickles, predictably, was on camera and I carried the camera bag and additional tungsten halogen lighting, dutifully. Once we had been checked into the scene and had been briefed by the Lab Liaison Sergeant, the first thing that struck me was how neat and tidy the place was. The front door was intact, there were no signs of forced entry, no signs of a struggle in the front living room, where I had been bracing myself to see the deceased. Once we'd covered the living room, we moved towards the kitchen, where I almost had to take a step back to take in what I was now seeing. On the circular kitchen-dining room table was the body of who we now know was Mr Milligan. He was lying on his back in an unclothed state with a black bin liner covering his head. His legs were dangling over the edge of the table and at ninety degrees to his torso. The M.P.'s feet were covered by another black bin liner and a length of what appeared to be electrical flex, ran from his feet, up his right side to around his neck. He was also donned in ladies' stockings. In an apparent act of 'autoerotic asphyxiation', sadly Mr Milligan, tightened the noose around his neck to a point where he strangled himself. It all seemed very odd, very mysterious and very bizarre, made all the more anomalous at the post-mortem, when an orange segment was apparently found in the M.P.'s mouth. Pickles and I obviously didn't see this at the scene as the black bin liner covered the deceased's face and mouth. The kitchen-diner mirrored the rest of the house for being immaculately clean and tidy - the scene being confined to the kitchen table and the deceased lying on top of it.

In post script, a few days after attending the scene of Stephen Milligan's death, The Met Commissioner at the time, Sir Paul (now Lord) Condon ordered an investigation by Police Complaints into all police personnel involved with the case and who had attended the scene to see if anyone had somehow insensitively leaked information surrounding the M.P.'s death to the press, before Mr. Milligan's family had been contacted. This meant that Pickles and I had to provide written and signed statements to say that we had not talked to anyone about the details of Mr Milligan's death. Sir Paul was rightly dotting the i's and crossing the t's, duty bound to explore all avenues of enquiry. It is possible of course, that a member of Mr Milligan's staff, on discovering the body of their employer, had, in all innocence, raised the alarm to the House of Commons?

The former Conservative politician's death in the mid '90s in such terrible, bizarre, sensitive and embarrassing circumstances was explosive news and unfortunately helped fuel the sleaze scandal at the time, which spelled eventual disaster for the Major government.

It has already been stated that the Irish Republican Army were very active on the British mainland during the 1990's. During the late evening of 9th March 1994, Pickles and I were called to the Excelsior

Hotel car park at Heathrow Airport (LHR), where the IRA had launched four mortar bombs. These missiles had subsequently landed on or near the northern runway. Two days later another four mortars landed close to an aircraft parking area in the vicinity of Terminal Four. On 13th March, five additional mortars were fired and landed close to Terminal Four. None of these exploded and there was little or no damage. However, the economic cost was huge with widespread travel disruption, thousands of inconvenienced passengers and areas of London's main airport closed over the period of attacks. I remember looking with trepidation and shuddering with the cold, down the barrels of the four mortar launch tubes that had been mounted in the back of a car which was now completely destroyed. Once we had filmed the car and mortar tubes, we were escorted onto the runway to film the missiles themselves. No prizes for guessing who was on camera? However, as a consolation, Pickles let me film a 'cutaway' of one of the mortars on the ground, which I first back-lit with the spare lighting rig and then used fill-in light from the Panasonic M11, which was sitting on the runway itself. There were large periods of bollocking about the airport - just waiting in the van whilst other areas were searched. The whole operation dragged on all night. We eventually wrapped up at LHR as dawn was breaking. We were due at Putney police station at 9am for crime reporting 'CRIS' software training, but all I wanted to do was go home and get some shut eye. Pickles was having none of it, not wanting to re-arrange the whole day of CRIS training, he persuaded me that it would be a good idea to journey over to Putney canteen, have a big boy's breakfast and hang around for the training as it wasn't worth going home. All I can say is that I disagreed and trying to learn this CRIS system over 7-8 hours in a very warm room without sleep was arduous and a real bastard!

The early part of 1994 was dominated by the Fred West murders. However, towards the end of March, the amazingly talented Steven Spielberg was triumphant at the Academy Awards by winning 7 Oscars for his Holocaust epic 'Schindler's List'. Easter fell over the weekend of 1-3 April in 1994 and it was a joyous time for Wendy and me. We had just learned that Wendy was pregnant and we were expecting our first child, a boy! We were over the moon and decided to celebrate by flying from London to Inverness over that Easter week, hiring a car and exploring the Highlands at leisure, ending up on the Isle of Skye. Shortly after we returned, there was more bad news on April 7th when the Rwandan genocide started in Kigali.

At the beginning of May, motor racing ace, three-times Formula One world champion, the much admired, Ayrton Senna was tragically killed in an accident during the San Marino Grand Prix in Imola, Italy. Following seven years of arduous graft, the Channel Tunnel opened on May 6th between England and France, which enabled people to travel to the continent in little more than half an hour. Four days later, Nelson Mandela became South Africa's first black President. In mid-June the animated film 'The Lion King' was released by Walt Disney Pictures. The phenomenally successful TV show 'Friends' starring Jennifer Aniston, Matt LeBlanc, David Schwimmer, Courtney Cox, Lisa Kudrow, Matthew Perry et al came to our screens in that year and on the pop song front Elton John had hits with 'Can You Feel the Love Tonight' and 'Circle of life'. Other chart hits included Madonna's 'Secrets', REM's 'What's the Frequency Kenneth', 'Cornflake Girl' by Tori Amos and Mariah Carey's 'All I Want for Christmas is You'.

The latter half of 1994 was spent making baby arrival preparations. The spare room in our New Malden flat was fully kitted out to receive the new addition to the Canning family. In July I had itchy beard when a sudden thought occurred to me. Once our baby had arrived, I wouldn't be able to spend so liberally on personal camera gear - so I went out on a clandestine shopping spree and came back with a brand-new Nikon F90-X SLR camera, Manfrotto tripod with pan and tilt head, lenses and various accessories! Needless to say, I didn't let on to 'the Wife' what the total spend came to. All I said was that I had made a few small purchases as I wouldn't be able to cash out on camera gear once we had kids. Ha, small purchases my arse – the total spend came to more than a 'bag of sand'!

Sadly, I hadn't been working with Pickles for a year and already he was starting to get under my skin. The only real time I got on camera, where I felt relaxed, was when he went on holiday and I had the video van for the whole duration. It was great and I got plenty of filming experience and loads of time to perfect every camera movement. The video van had been designed and kitted out well at MPS Main Repair Depot (MRD) in Northolt and was split into three sections: front, middle and rear. The front section was obviously the cockpit, the driver's and passengers' section, which also had Pag battery chargers mounted behind the driver's and passengers' seats. The middle section housed the recording equipment together with more battery chargers and was also handy as you could hide yourself away in here with the camera lens poking through a set of black curtains during a surveillance obbo. The rear section housed the camera, lenses, tripod and shelving full of accessories and lighting. The rear section also had a handy portable generator for, among other things, powering portable tungsten halogen lighting at night scenes. This area was also equipped with an 'Eeberspächer' heater. On top of each van were a set of spotlights and it was also possible to stand on top of the van and film, when a higher viewpoint was required. From time to time the vans would rotate going into to MRD for further tweaks and modifications. During my first few weeks on OVS, I had to undertake two tests, firstly a driving test for the automatic van, followed by a similar test for the outgoing old manual van. I passed both tests, which of course involved driving all over the capital, but I just recall the steering on the old manual van as being a real bastard in that it was very heavy when manoeuvring slowly and reversing.

Occasionally I'd work with the other managers and with my fellow 'boys' and got on just fine with all of them. However, Pickles with all his sayings, his hogging of the video camera, started to grate on me. I inevitably began to draw parallels with my Dickensian father. Sometimes I'd be in mid conversation with Pickles, we'd be on our way home after yet another very long day and he'd suddenly be scanning the airwaves. The scanner would crackle into life and he'd silence me with a "SSHH!!" chastising me like a naughty schoolboy. One of Pickles' other sayings was "SSH, the van may be bugged" and to Pete during an anti-British National Party rally "Possible BNP three o'clock, DON'T LOOK!!" On one occasion, whilst waiting in a police station vehicle yard, Pickles was fine tuning his little dashboard-mounted box of tricks, when a police colleague strolled up to the driver's window and pointed curiously at the illegal-to-use, square shaped device. "Isn't that a scanner, Bob?", to which Pickles smugly grinned at the officer, breathed in deeply and said, "It might be!"

It had taken me a good twelve months and plenty of experience before I felt confidant with the filming and VFI side to OVS. I reckon this time could have been halved if Pickles had let me on camera sooner and with more regularity. Looking back, I believe that Pickles mistook my enthusiasm for video as a threat to his position as top dog and overall leader of OVS. I also believe that Pickles' bullying tactics, depriving me of using the video camera and talking about me behind my back was paranoia on his part and a definite attempt to keep me on a short leash. What didn't help the situation was that the scenes of crime photographers were questioning the OVS boys' role.

All they could see was in effect two additional photographers turn up to a scene, one of whom would be on camera and the other, usually the boy if it was me, holding a light, seemingly surplus to requirements. We'd film it, give the VHS copy to the officer and then bugger off, before they'd even started. They very much resented our role, so much so that the OVS boys became known as 'lamp stands' amongst the scenes of crime photogs. This really annoyed me and I thought, the grass is always greener. They hadn't got a clue what we did, especially when it came to VFI and the in-depth knowledge of PACE Code D all of us in OVS possessed. All the 'stills' photogs could see was that we supposedly held an extra light at murder scenes and earned more than them. Er, yes, we did, but then we worked our arses off for the privilege.

During the tail end of 1994, Pickles was really starting to get to me. The other lads were great and we'd regularly take the piss and mimic Pickles, which I found eased my anxiety somewhat. One night I took the video van back to New Malden Police Station, because Pickles was on annual leave for a few days. I accidentally left the middle section light on and the following morning when I came to start the engine, I discovered that I'd flattened the battery. When I looked, I could see the light switch in the on position. Typically, I had no jump leads on me and was left with no alternative but to call Pickles at home. Before Bob arrived, I made sure that the middle section light switch was in the off position and pretended to look as perplexed as he did, when he surveyed the video van. I just shrugged my shoulders. Pickles jump started the battery from the onboard spare battery also housed in the engine compartment in next to no time. If I had been on better terms with Pickles, I might have owned up at the outset to my silly mistake, but knowing what he was like, I didn't want to give him ammunition to 'talk about me' some more. Shortly after that, I opened the door to our OVS office to see him, still donned for the outdoors in Gortex jacket with his van keys in his hand talking across to Liam Tadd who was entering tapes onto the computer behind the door. "Oh, Bill" I caught Pickles lamenting as I walked in. It had transpired that Bill had accidentally left a multi-thousand-pound Panasonic M11 broadcast quality camera on the ground and then somehow reversed back over it! Oops! Pickles was not at all happy with poor Bill. He and Pete were without a video camera for a while. Suffice to say that Bill was 'talked about' for a long time after the squashed camera incident.

As it approached Christmas 1994, my bad mood with Pickles improved considerably and all feelings of anxiety with him went on the back burner as the birth of our son was now close at hand. The baby had been a lively thing in the womb, regularly kicking when we spoke to him. I remember the joy of seeing the three-month scan pictures and staring and marvelling at them for ages. Leading up to the birth, our baby boy had decided that he wasn't going to turn and remained in the breech position. I definitely wanted to be with Wendy for the birth and having donned theatre scrubs, theatre hat and clogs, I took my place on a stool, seated next to Wendy's head and behind the Obs and Gynae surgeon's screen as our son was delivered by caesarean section (I'll openly admit here to watching much of the operation as well!). I stood up the moment our boy was lifted out of his Mum's tum and felt elated as I heard him cry. "Good set of lungs" on him I said to Wendy. We were ecstatically happy. George Patrick Canning, weighing in at eight pounds exactly, entered the world at 10.25am on Wednesday 21st December at Kingston upon Thames Hospital in Surrey. I quickly announced that Mother, son…and Father … were all doing well. I captured some images for the family album on my new Nikon F90-X. Mum popped in to meet her new grandson and then my mate Pete, from work, also visited. Santa also paid a special visit to the maternity ward on Christmas Eve. Wendy stayed in hospital for four days and on Christmas day we brought George home with us, where we were greeted by a lounge full of presents and decorations. We'd had no time to prepare special meals, so we had beans on toast on Christmas Day and it was fab! I remember that we lay George down on a blue and white patchwork quilt on our living room floor and just stared at him for ages. He was perfect. Early in January 1995, Wendy's Mum, Val (Gran) travelled up from her home in Cornwall to see her first grandchild. Wendy's Dad, Laurie wasn't at all well and her brother Simon needed to be in Cornwall to look after Laurie to enable Val to journey up to New Malden. The video I shot of Gran and baby George on their first meeting is priceless and, looking back, I'm so pleased that I captured these precious moments for posterity.

After the euphoria of George's birth, it was straight back into the thick of things for me working all hours God sent on crime jobs as well as video film identification. My relationship with Pickles was strained and in my mind his bullying tactics just seemed to be getting worse. It got to the stage where I was becoming so angry with him that I was taking out my frustration at my local Gym – pounding the weights and working out ways to punch his lights out, whilst running full pelt on the tread mill and pummelling the punch bag to near exhaustion!

Graffiti over multiple floors was best done on video as we could record continuously and walk the stairwells from the ground floor upwards. Linking and storytelling were seamless. We also got called in to film large scale recovered property, requiring several trips to Met Police property stores, which were more like warehouses. Then there were the Operation Bumblebee roadshows to display recovered stolen items of property. I usually teamed up with Derek for the day and we'd always have a good laugh and a piss take down at Charlton Property Store. We rigged up a makeshift studio with a huge light grey sheet as a background and had a team of 'movers and placers', popping each item into shot for us. These would then be photographed on stills and videoed to show potential 'losers' (owners who'd lost property) prior to the roadshows and hopefully, precipitating a rightful return of this lost or stolen property to the owners. We'd often work with antiques experts and usually it was the stuff we labelled as tat that turned out to be priceless and the seemingly valuable exhibits, to our untrained eyes, were the tat items. The roadshows were held throughout the MPS and well-advertised. I remember filming all the exhibits in glass cabinets down at Fairfield Halls in Croydon, my beloved birthplace, prior to the public coming in and viewing.

Some of the scenes where these high price stolen artefacts were recovered, took the OVS team out of town to picturesque Bath, where once again, identified items would be painstakingly photographed prior to being filmed. With these jobs, it always seemed to be Pickles using the video camera and yours truly taking the stills. It was as though Pickles had an aversion, nay, a morbid fear of picking up a Pentax 6x7 or Bronica stills camera. My theory was that he had been such a competent video operator for so long, that his 'stills' skills had got rusty, which would have inevitably led to a lack of confidence in this area, a fact that Bob seemed to confirm when I asked him one time. Variations of this job included raids and searches of premises in Chinatown, looking for evidence that parts of rare, endangered animals were being sold as delicacies, most notably tiger penis, used in very expensive soups. Tiger penis is said to contain therapeutic properties in traditional Chinese Medicine. However, the demand for Tiger parts, condemned by many countries and environmentalists, plays into the hands of poachers by exacerbating the tiger's endangered status.

We occasionally got called to police kennels located throughout the MPS to film under the 'Dangerous Dogs Act 1991'. The act essentially made it a criminal offence for owners to allow their dogs to be dangerously out of control in a public area, or an area where they were not permitted to be. If injuries were caused, the dog could be seized by the police, taken to kennels and subsequently destroyed, unless the owner could persuade the court that the animal was not a danger to the public. The Act also banned specific breeds such as the Pit Bull Terrier and the Japanese Tosa, which were subject to a mandatory destruction order. Sometimes tensions would be running high, with the owners on site and possibly animal rights protesters. We would normally film a dog's behaviour with audio. The officer in the case would get the dog to walk up and down for gait analysis and to show its breed, temperament and characteristics. If the dog was deemed too dangerous, we'd obviously be filming through a cage!

Pickles and I had attended a kennels somewhere in the heart of South East London, I forget where, and Pickles as usual was on camera. The dangerous dog in question was described as a Pit Bull Cross and the officer just wanted about thirty seconds of filming to show the animal's gait. For some odd reason, the officer requested that we film without audio, to which both Pickles and I pointed out that this may well be challenged in court. The officer remained insistent. I wasn't overly concerned as I felt comfortable in the knowledge that if we were called to court to give evidence, it would be Pickles as camera operator having to justify why sound was omitted from the recording – and certainly not me! A few months later, sure as hell, the job went to court and OVS were required to attend and give evidence. Typically, Pickles was on annual leave for two weeks so he couldn't attend. Worse – Sod's law, Defence insisted that I attend court in Pickles' place! Dave's 'boy' Matthew John was also on leave and Dave kindly offered to run me to Epsom Magistrates Court (which was later to close in 2011) for my appearance. I wasn't in the least bit worried. This was a Magistrate's court for God's sake, not Number One court of the Old Bailey. I envisaged that I'd be in the dock for a couple of minutes tops, I'd then be dismissed and Dave and I would go for a big boy's late breakfast, prior to any jobs coming in. How wrong I was.

There was no hanging around, as the moment I arrived I found myself at the front of the court, giving my oath and introductions. The surroundings of the court were certainly not as imposing as the Old Bailey and I felt quite relaxed. I saw Dave sitting opposite me next to the Officer in the case. Apart from Magistrate, Prosecution, Defence, stenographer, dog owner and ushers, I don't remember many other people in that court room. Prosecution's questions were over very quickly and then Defence counsel stood up. The lady in question was, I guessed, a similar age to me in her early 30s, about 5' 6" tall, with long dark brown hair tied back in a ponytail and silver rimmed spectacles perched on the bridge of her nose. There was a brief, courteous, professional smile tossed my way before her opening question ...

Defence: "Mr Canning, you say you have been filming dogs under the 'Dangerous Dog Act 1991' since September 1993, is that correct?"

Me: "Yes, that is correct".

Defence: "Specifically, how many jobs have you filmed?"

Me: "I really don't know, without looking the figures up on our office computer".

Defence: "Is it fifty, thirty, ten...", she said in a staccato manner, really throwing me off guard. I suddenly felt uncomfortable.

Me: "Oh, it's more than ten".

Defence: "But you said, not a few moments ago that you were unsure, now you seem to be sure that it's more than ten!"

Me: "Yes, but...." I had fallen straight into her trap and was starting to get flustered.

Defence: "More than twenty?"

Me: "Probably less than twenty".

Defence: "Eighteen...fifteen...twelve", she said in very quick succession.

Me: "I really can't be sure".

Defence: "Surely, you must have some idea?", she said with mock exasperated pleading.

Defence had really started to unnerve me. My mouth was dry and I tried to remain on point and focus on the questions directed at me.

Me: "I would need time to get the figures from our computer". Better answer. Suddenly Defence dropped that line of questioning and moved on.

Defence: "How many jobs of this nature do you film with the sound on?" Oh, shit, I thought, here it comes....

Me: "I really don't know without looking the entries up on our office computer".

Defence: "How many jobs of this nature do you film with the sound switched off?"

Me: "Again, I really don't know without looking the entries up on our office computer".

Defence: "Is it normal, when filming this type of assignment to deliberately switch the sound off?" I could feel my heart thumping louder, as I concentrated on steadying my nerves and providing a clear answer. I could see both the Officer in the case and Dave, boring their eyes into me, waiting in anticipation for what I was going to say next.

Me: "It depends on whether sound is required or not. If we are filming a dog's gait, there's no need to have sound on. However, if a dog is barking or whining for example, we'd record with audio on".

Defence: "Who decides whether sound is required or not?"

Me: "We talk to the Officer in the case at the outset and establish what they are trying to show".

Defence: "Who's decision was it, specifically, in this case to film deliberately without the sound switched on?" There it was, the crunch question. I was under oath and certainly had no intention of perjuring myself.

Me: "The Officer in the case told us that he did not want us filming with audio". I looked at the officer in the case whose head, at that moment, was in his lap. Dave sat there, clearly pissed off with me, nodding his head from side to side in disbelief.

Defence: "Thank you Mr Canning, no further questions".

Following my dismissal from court, Dave wasn't backward about coming forward with the way he felt about my performance. "You stitched the poor officer in the case up really good, Gord, Blimey". To cap it all, it transpired that the OIC just happened to be a close friend of Dave's. I was really narked at Dave and became all defensive "I told the truth Dave, what was I supposed to do, perjure myself?" Dave didn't reply. His silence was deafening and spoke volumes. There was no telling him, because in his eyes, I'd just dropped his mate in the stinky brown stuff. I had enjoyed a good working relationship with Matthew John's manager, but this little episode really annoyed me. I vowed never again to be complacent when attending any court. My Epsom Magistrates Court appearance in the spring of 1995 completely wrong footed me. My performance was barely passable at best and bordered on a bollocks up, at worst. I waltzed into the courtroom feeling almost suave and overconfident and emerged from an unsurpassed ordeal having been in effect, torn up for arse paper by an extremely astute Defence Counsel. Jesus... lesson learned!

My working relationship with Pickles wasn't getting any better. I opened the OVS office door one time to see him and Tadd at the computer. Pickles carried on his conversation. "Aagh, thank heavens for Norton!", he said to Tadd, as if talking in code. Without thinking, I piped up "Oh you mean, Norton Utilities? We got computer problems?" Pickles just glared at me. It was obvious that he didn't like the fact that I had not only heard of Norton, but I knew what Norton was used for. So bloody well what. There were more of these little episodes and Pickles was grating on me as much as I seemed to be grating on him. The 'divisions' between some of the managers and the 'boys' was, by mid-1995 quite marked. Derek didn't like Liam Tadd, Matthew John had his ups and downs with Dave. I was nearing my wit's end with Pickles. Only Pete and Bill seemed to enjoy a mutually beneficial working relationship.

By the summer of 1995, I'd been with OVS for the best part of two years and the dichotomy between the 'boys' and the OVS leadership – Pickles and Tadd, was there for all to see. We were working all hours – earning loads of money yes, but we were all in agreement that we needed to cut the hours down to something more manageable, as we were all feeling knackered. So, a meeting was called in the cinema at Amelia Street between us boys and the HPO's (our managers). Generally, the meeting allowed us to vent our feelings, to say what was bugging us. Derek, as 'senior boy' immediately kicked off proceedings and said that he had got the hump, big time, with not only being called 'boy', but also being treated like one. We all agreed. 'Boy' within OVS was derogatory and inappropriate terminology. The terms 'lamp stand' and 'lacky' were also thrown into the pot. It was clear that we weren't happy. Then we moved on to the subject of overtime and all four of us boys put our thoughts forward. When it came to my turn, I leaned forward and said, "I'd be happy with any system that gave me more time with my family." I noticed Pickles' face when I'd finished speaking. His arms were folded across his body and he was glaring at me, giving me a death stare from hell, as if I had murdered a member of his family!

The meeting broke up, not really having resolved anything except that we wouldn't be called 'boys' anymore (whoopy do!). Pickles and I had to leave straight away to film a VFI suspect at Brixton Police Station Identification Suite. The atmosphere between us was palpable as we undertook the VFI in near silence together. It was late when we packed the gear away and I jumped up into the passenger seat. Before Pickles turned the key in the ignition, I decided there and then to have it out with him. I turned to my manager and said, "Look Bob, regarding that meeting, it wasn't as if I was trying to take over your job or anything like that." Pickles glared at me and then between in takes of breath and with a slightly raised voice, he declared his hand, "You won't take over my job, I won't let you!!" Jesus, I thought, there it was – verbal confirmation from the man himself that he not only regarded our earlier meeting as an attempted coup, but had singled me out as a direct threat to his position. There was no point in continuing the conversation after that and I sat in awkward silence, with the right old hump, thoroughly pissed off, all the way home. That night the boys were on the phone to each other.

Rightly or wrongly, Dave's boy threw in the towel, much to our chagrin. Matthew John was more concerned with the overtime he'd potentially lose and sided with Pickles, which meant that we were back to square one – with nothing achieved.

Wendy and I had booked our summer leave for the second week in August. We drove down to Wadebridge with a not quite eight-month old George strapped into his car seat. After the four-hour plus journey, we stepped inside the Laight family home, Pennard Cottage. We expected to see Val come running to greet us, with Laurie not far behind with a glass of sherry at the ready. We were surprised that the place looked a bit like the Mary Celeste. Wendy called out and after a while, Val shouted down from upstairs saying she'd be with us soon. After what seemed ages, Val emerged to greet us. I for one was really shocked. A normally immaculate looking Val appeared tired, unkempt and with bedraggled hair. It quickly transpired that Laurie had not been at all well for the last few weeks and was pretty much bed bound. Val, always one for putting her family first, had let herself go whilst looking after Wendy's Dad. Val then returned upstairs and left us to our own devices, before returning to us again some time later and indicating that it would be ok for us to go up and say hello to Laurie. Whilst Val kept an eye on George, Wendy and I went upstairs to see Laurie. I was completely shocked when I saw him and instinctively knew that he didn't have much time left to live. He managed a few words and a smile, but he was clearly seriously ill. He was emaciated and very tired. Shortly afterwards, I took Wendy to one side. I advised her to phone her brother Simon, get him to cancel his imminent holiday to Turkey and get down to Pennard as soon as possible. Wendy made the phone call. I didn't have a good feeling about this at all. Simon arrived later that evening and the following few days were spent researching nearby rest homes, so that Laurie could be cared for whilst a clearly worn out Val got some respite. When Wendy and Simon told their father of the rest home plan, Laurie was shocked and would have none of it. Simon had been out to buy some walkie talkies so that Laurie could keep one by his side upstairs and still communicate with us downstairs. We all had a good laugh over this, Laurie included, as he couldn't quite get the hang of how it worked, and which button to press when!

I had a stinking cold on Friday 11th August, so I drizzled a load of olbas oil on a tissue, which I put half under my pillow that night. Before I turned in, I took George in to see his Grandfather to say goodnight. I can remember the scene so clearly. Laurie smiled and waved at his grandson and in turn George beamed back at his Grandfather. I then said 'Goodnight' and left Laurie and Val's room, retiring to bed not long afterwards. In the middle of the night, there was a dramatic turn of events. I woke up half groggy from the 'night nurse' capsules I'd popped. It was about 3 in the morning. I looked over to Wendy, the covers had been pulled back and she was up and about. I then heard talking and footsteps moving fast along the upstairs landing, the word 'doctor' was mentioned and then movement downstairs, followed by talking on the phone. Things were serious. Wendy woke me with a panicked look in her eyes. Then came the heart-breaking, "Dad's dying, can you take care of George?" I had that sinking feeling as I quickly dressed and went into George's room. The doctor had arrived and now an ambulance had been called. The ambulance, travelling from the Royal Cornwall Hospital, aka Treliske in Truro, almost thirty miles away, couldn't find the house and never actually made it. It was now around 5am and as I sat keeping an eye on George in his travel cot, with his door half ajar, the quiet, early hours of Saturday 12th August were suddenly punctuated with the sound of crying and intermittent sobs, which was simply awful to hear. A teary-eyed Wendy came in very soon afterwards to announce what I already knew, that her dear father had passed away as a result of pneumonia. He was just seventy.

Ironically, it was the most beautiful late summer's day – blue sky, unbroken sunshine and very warm. I had a sudden thought. Laurie's bedroom window was open. This would attract blowflies, which would be instinctively drawn to Laurie's body. I made my way up to Laurie's room to close his window and stole myself to look at his body lying there in bed. He looked totally peaceful, but despite my crime scene training, it still felt a bit eerie. After all, this was the first time that I had seen the dead body of someone whom I had known in life. You just can't compare this with the hundreds of bodies that I'd photographed and video filmed on scenes of crime and OVS. As Laurie had died unexpectedly at home, by law the police needed to pay a visit before the undertaker, Ron Bray & Son, could take Laurie's body away. The wait for the police seemed like an eternity. When the male officer did arrive, Simon sat with him at the dining room table to answer his questions, following his viewing of the body. Then followed another long wait for the undertaker. Having fed George, I popped my head round the kitchen door leading to the lounge, where Wendy and Simon were comforting their very distraught mother. I fetched the tearful trio cups of tea and coffee and when Ron Bray and his son Dave (a school fried of Wendy's) arrived with the hearse, I told Wendy and Simon that I would deal with the undertakers. The three of them had been through quite enough already.

Later that morning I stole myself to phone Pickles and also to let him know that I'd need more time off for the funeral. I don't recall getting any sympathy. It was just as if he was in job mode. "Yes, yes, fully understood" was all I got. I almost thought he was going to end with, "Affirmative, we are recording!" I just let it wash off me.

In the early evening, we decided to get out of the house and go down to one of our favourite beaches, Trevone, for some sea air. We'd been leaning against this big slab of rock for some time and when we got up and moved away from it, we turned back and noticed the word 'DAD' etched in huge letters. How bizarre, yet how comforting to think that Laurie was with us. The days that followed were very hard for us all, not least Val, who'd lost her dear husband of forty odd years. Val wasn't up to entertaining the idea of a funeral, she was too distraught. Instead, at the time of his cremation at Penmount, in Truro, we all drove out to one of Laurie's favourite spots, picturesque Grogley, located on the Camel Trail en route to Bodmin and one by one, we tossed a different coloured rose from the bridge into the River Camel below. It was deeply moving. We all said a few words, had some silent time and shed tears. Only George was oblivious to it all, in his push chair.

Laurence Arthur Laight (Laurie) was born on 25th November 1924 in London's old East End. The family didn't have much money, and little is known about his schooling, but his impressive working credentials read like a page from 'Who's Who', for Laurie began grafting from a very early age. As a mere lad, he could be found working as a cabin boy on board the famous Woolwich Ferry that links Woolwich with North Woolwich and first mentioned in historical records in 1308 (today, the latter is located in close proximity to London's City Airport). Woolwich itself is located 13.7 kilometres east of Charing Cross on the south bank of the River Thames, in the postal district of SE18. Laurie also worked at his brother Harry's butcher's shop. Aged around seventeen, in early 1942, Laurie joined the Royal Air Force as a radar operator, war time service that included travelling to France. Post war, he carved out a career in sales, working firstly for the 'Singer' sewing machine company, then for 'George S. May Corporation' an American business efficiency company. This was followed by another sales move to 'Derry and Toms' Department store in upmarket Kensington, the 'Gestetner' printing company and then 'Wellington Press' - all London based. Around the late 1940's / early 1950's, Laurie met Valerie Merle Schollick at Friern Barnet Operatic and Dramatic Society. The couple were married on April 2nd 1953, in Whetstone, north London. Their son, Simon, was born on June 27th, 1962 and turned out to be not only a fantastic brother-in-law, Uncle and great friend, but also one of the finest men I have ever had the privilege to meet. In 1968, Val and Laurie began a yearlong move from their London home in Barnet to set up a family home in Cornwall with a three-year-old Wendy and six-year-old brother Simon in tow. It took a year of firstly trawling around Devon to find a suitable home, during which time poor Simon was changing schools, seemingly on a monthly basis – a fact that explains why he looks so sad in all the photographs of him taken back then.

In late December 1969, the Laights moved in to Towan Farmhouse in the pretty little North Cornwall village with the uplifting name of St. Merryn. Here they ran a holiday business with a B&B, 2 holiday flats and 2 caravans. Alongside this, Val worked as school secretary at nearby St Merryn primary school. Laurie also got stuck into market research for the Opinion Research Centre and for the BBC. Additionally, he worked for the Country Landowners Association (CLA) in sales, the Western Union and the Guild of Master Craftsmen. As if there was no stopping him, he was also a North Cornwall District Councillor and a parish councillor whilst the family resided in St Merryn. In the autumn of 1977, Val and Laurie sold the holiday business and moved to the beautiful, Pennard Cottage, which was two cottages knocked into one conversion, in stunning grounds, a couple of miles from the centre of Wadebridge. Val moved schools to join her old headmaster and became school secretary at Trevisker School in St. Eval, just over a nine-mile moped ride away. This school was located on the sprawling RAF St. Mawgan air base and abutting Newquay Airport. Laurie was not only busying himself with councillor duties, but he was vociferous on multiple local and national issues, had plenty of opinions (not all of which were popular) and wasn't afraid of voicing them, in the newspapers, on local BBC Radio Cornwall and on television. Laurie was an ideas man. National ID cards – well that was down to his genius thinking - the brainchild of my dear father-in-law! Then, with a lit cigarette held between pursed lips, he'd be sitting at the kitchen table, bashing out the next hopeful hit on his faithful Olivetti typewriter for such shows as Morecambe and Wise and of course, his

First World War masterpiece 'The Deserter' (subsequently purchased by the BBC).

Coincidentally, Laurie shared his birthday with my Mum, Denise, who was born on that same day exactly twelve years later! Laurie was one of six siblings – Lol (Olive), Lilian (Lil), Harry (a butcher), Winnie (who worked at the prestigious Bank of England briefly), David (who died as a baby when a lump of hot coal jumped out of an open fire and burned him) and of course Laurie. All six siblings slept top to tail in the same bed!

I had known Laurie Laight for only four and a half years, but in that time had come to love that deep, beautifully spoken voice. I used to sit across from him and his typewriter as he regaled me with many stories of years gone by. His command of the English language was second to none. I can see him now in full flow, wine glass of Co-op 'Number One Pale Cream Sherry' in his outstretched right hand, cigarette with half an inch of ash about to fall off in his outstretched left hand, gesticulating as he gently beat the air, punctuating his clever turn of phrase, his use of analogy and metaphor, coupled with many a word I'd secretly have to look up in the dictionary later, with one of his catch phrases, 'so on and so forth'. He was great social company indeed and a superb, erudite raconteur. He was also a talented painter, creative writer and poet. I've already mentioned his short story 'The Deserter' set in World War 1 Cornwall, which was a brilliant undertaking. But his poem 'Ode to a Distant Beauty Spot (On the neck of Sue Lawley)' was also a genius piece of creative writing. Sue Lawley is of course an English broadcaster. She was a BBC newscaster and a presenter on Nationwide. This mid-late '80s poem was selected as the winning entry by then Poet Laureate, Ted Hughes, the judge in the Sunday Independent West Country Poetry Contest and remains one of my all-time favourite poems. Without fail, I'd read this framed, wall-mounted poem on every visit to the Laight family's Cornwall home. I think the poem captures my late Father-in-Law's skill and personality very succinctly. Here it is in full:

Ode to a Distant Beauty Spot
(On the neck of Sue Lawley)
Of all the things for Christmas I'm unlikely to receive,
However rare or costly,
On the whole –
There's nothing you could mention, or imaginings conceive,
I wouldn't swop to kiss that little mole.

Give not your apes, your ivories, your spices from the East,
For – whilst I'd be most grateful –
'Pon my soul,
Mere tusks, or musks, or Simian beasts, aren't up to the feast,
Of one chaste peck, on that neck with a mole.

By all means call it a beauty spot or freckle; to me, though,
Such terms are merely jargon,
Rigmarole;
The point is, it's a tawny jewel that only she could grow,
And damn it, let me kiss it – spot or mole.

Where neckline meets the shoulder, on her dexter side (not left),
Is where you'll find this tiny,
Aureole;
The very place where chokes the rope, on a man with hope bereft,
Of ever laying lips on that dear mole...'

Laurie was witty (most definitely) and opinionated (very often). He could also be stubborn and on occasions irritable, which I put down to the fact that he wasn't very well. For ten years leading up to his death, Laurie had oesophagus constricting episodes, among other problems. Nevertheless, he soldiered on with his plethora of interests that were very dear to him. As I've intimated, he was a frequent contributor to BBC Radio Cornwall and when he wasn't writing or doing phone-ins, Laurie would be in the garden. He'd construct stone walls and paths, or in his workshop he'd mend this and that, having researched extensively how to do something, in a pre-Google world, by ordering library books beforehand, all to save money. Above all, Laurie Laight was one of yesteryear's gentlemen, who was much loved by his family and friends. As my father-in-law, I admired and respected him tremendously and was particularly wrong-footed and stung by his sudden death. I know that if he had been blessed with more years, he would have been a great mentor to both George and Lauren and a wise counsel to us all. Laurie Laight was a real character, a 'one off special', who I feel privileged to have known, albeit for only a very short time. He is of course, so missed and never far from our thoughts.

A few months after Laurie had died, Simon told Wendy and me that, in trying to learn more about whether the human spirit survives after death, he had visited Uxbridge-based spiritualist medium, Bill

Landis, for a psychic reading, which had been recorded onto cassette tape. Today, a Google search defines spiritualism as 'a system of belief or religious practice based on supposed communication with the spirits of the dead, especially through mediums'. During part of what was a very personal reading, apparently Laurie's spirit came through and thanked Simon for the 'roses', which were placed in the coffin. Also, as I've mentioned, at the time of Laurie's cremation, and as a mark of respect and remembrance Val, Simon, Wendy and I (plus eight-month old George in his buggy) had each tossed a different coloured rose off Grogley Bridge into the River Camel below. It was, as you can imagine, a very emotional experience. During the psychic reading, Laurie, through Bill Landis, not only thanked Simon for his roses..... he then went on to name the second bunch of roses in the order of colour that they were thrown into the river! When I heard this, it made what little hair I had, stand up at the back of my neck – there was no way Bill Landis could have known this very private detail! He also made reference to the final words Wendy spoke to her Dad when no-one else had been in the room.

This one event inspired me greatly and saw me joining the SAGB (Spiritualist Association of Great Britain) around mid-1996. Their headquarters used to be in Belgrave Square, but are now in London SW8. At the SAGB I used to attend occasional private psychic readings, group demonstrations and have psychic portraits drawn by the renowned talented psychic artist, the late Coral Polge, who described herself to me once as "being on the wrong side of seventy". Coral drew an incredible likeness of my maternal grandmother, Agnes Mary ('Mama'). She also sketched my North American Indian spirit guide called 'Grey Wolf', as well as Chinese spirit guides and a young lady who Coral said was my unborn sister (my Mum had miscarried), but who had grown up in the Spirit World. I also went to see Arthur Molinari at the London College of Psychic Studies. At the same time, I started reading the books, firstly Coral's, then the most famous medium of all time, Doris Stokes. These were followed closely by Betty Shine and Rita Rogers. Mia Dolan and Lisa Williams would come later. Then came the films and television series. Firstly the 2002 film 'Dragonfly', starring Kevin Costner, then 'Ghost Whisperer', starring Jennifer Love Hewitt and David Conrad. And then came 'Celestine Prophecy' based on the 1993 book by James Redfield, starring Matthew Settle, in which a high school teacher called John Woodson (Settle), on being made redundant from his job, reaches a crossroads in his life. Fate seems to guide him towards Peru, where he becomes embroiled in a search for a missing ninth scroll to a set of eight, ancient parchments, rumoured to reveal 'insights' into the future of mankind. More recently I've been watching the young American medium, Tyler Henry.

So, spiritualism as an interest outside of work had almost developed into a hobby for me, or perhaps I was just keen on finding answers or my path in life. Maybe it had something to do with me working with the dead, I don't know. Either way, when I go for a psychic reading, I tell people 'It's an interest of mine and I keep one foot in their reality and one foot in mine!' What I can't deny is the fact that I feel comforted on every occasion. However, I'd nearly always get snippets of information but usually nothing that would make sense. I tend to visit a medium when I suddenly get a strong urge to see one. There's no other way to explain it. So, I'd been toddling along quite happily for twenty odd years seeing this medium and that, getting the odd 'vibration' here and there and plenty of 'I've got a David with me or a Rose on your Great Grandmother's side of the family – can you take that?'. I'm thinking, well David's a common name and so was Rose a few generations back – I'm scratching my head, willing the medium in question to be a bit more specific, trying in my mind for the jigsaw shapes to gel, but generally getting - well, nothing in particular. Then in November 2017 I went over to my sister Kate's in Huddersfield to have a private reading with 'Psychic Sarah', a Bradford based medium who had come very highly recommended. Kate hadn't told Sarah a thing about the two of us, no family history, no last names, nothing – and I mean absolutely zilch. Kate was completely tight lipped, even going as far as removing family photos from around her house.

As this was Kate's first real reading with a psychic medium, I thought it best to warn her not to get her hopes up too high, for fear that she might be dreadfully disappointed if Mum didn't 'come through'. When Sarah arrived, I found her to be very friendly and amenable and we decided that I'd go first, with Kate listening at the bottom of the stairs, taking any notes if necessary – even though we had a small digital audio recorder in the room. Well, I hadn't been sat down two seconds, when Sarah announced that she had Mum with her, describing her to a tee, but not providing a name. Next Sarah talked about some work aspects, which were all correct. Then came Henry and his link to gardening – my Grandad who had his own allotment! Next, Sarah mentioned Wendy (my wife) and Valerie (my mother-in-law) with everything relating to these people, correct in every way. I was completely blown away by how authentic and powerful my reading was and couldn't wait to play the recording back after Kate had had her reading. Just before the end of my reading I tried to push Sarah to giving Mum's name, but Sarah said that Mum wouldn't give it – which left me hugely disappointed as well as majorly sceptical as it would have meant that there would have been no doubt whatsoever that Mum's spirit was very much alive. Even so, my reading had been powerful and had still yielded the authentic names Valerie, Wendy and Henry. When I popped downstairs, Kate mouthed to me 'Wow', before handing me a notepad and pen and popping up to her spare room to have her reading. Suddenly I heard Sarah say "You're Mum's name is Denise. Your Mum's here with you. Can you tell Paul I'm sorry I didn't give my name to him ...". Bloody hell! Now I was hanging on every word. I'd just had concrete proof that Mum was alive in spirit!

Kate's reading was just as powerful as mine and once we had thanked Sarah and said goodbye, Kate put a brew on and I went to retrieve the voice recorder. When I plugged the device in to Kate's laptop it was registering 0Kb, which I couldn't understand, as the thing had been recording for more than two hours. My brain wasn't computing what I was seeing. I pressed play continually. Nothing. Weird – very weird. I had tested the recording device not once, but three times counting out loud the usual 'one to ten' several times and playing the test recording back, so I knew that it was working. Yet nothing had recorded of either psychic reading. Even more bizarre was when I decided to check the device again with another test record. Sure enough, I heard my own voice play back to me. All I can tell you is that I know the recorder was working before and after the readings. Somehow there had been 'interference' during our readings. That's the only conclusion I could come to. Mum was mischievous in life. Maybe this was her way of being mischievous in the afterlife!. Conversely, our washing machine, which was actually Mum's old machine, had been playing up big time in the lead up to Mum's death. I was so convinced that it to was about to conk out, that I transported Mum's current washing machine to our house, shortly after Mum died. On the very day Mum passed away, however, the old machine started working properly again and carried on working for more than four years after Mum died!

After meeting Psychic Sarah, I'm now a firm believer that the human spirit does survive when we die. In her 2011 insightful book called 'The Survival of the Soul', renowned Anglo-American medium and clairvoyant, Lisa Williams, goes some way to explaining life after death. She addresses the multitude of questions that we all have on the subject, especially when we go through the extremely painful process of grieving for a loved one. Mum always poo-pooed anything that was remotely afterlife connected. A week before she died, I told her that the spirit lives on and as I've stated, I was met with a rolling of her eyes. I like to think that when she passed, Mum got a really nice surprise. Spiritualism is a fascinating subject. I'll leave it to you to make up your own mind about it.

I turned 32 in the September of 1995 and already there were rumblings that OVS was to be dissolved as part of the forthcoming Met Police restructure. Well, that's the line that we were sold anyway. This conveniently played into the hands of Pickles, who saw his chance not just to get rid of me, but also the other boys in OVS. If the truth be known, he had already been plotting and scheming, for it emerged that he was going to continue with operational video and VFI, but attached to South East London, based at Catford Police Station. Bill would still be working with Pete, but more on an ad hoc basis, Liam Tadd would work solo video in North East and Dave would still be working with Matthew John in West and south west London. Technically, all the Photographic Officers (the 'boys') were being returned to scenes of crime under MPS restructuring.

There were to be five areas: North West (2 Area), North East (3 Area), South East (4 Area), South West (5 Area) and Central (One Area). There would be two HPhos per area. I learned that from January 1st, 1996, my new line managers would be Paul Alsford and Dave ('Yeah Mate') Shapland. My outgoing manager, Bob Pickles, would be working with Benjy McPhee on 4 Area, with Benjy in charge of the stills photos and Pickles in charge of.... well, himself. Worse, Derek would also be working out of 4 Area and wasn't looking forward to having Pickles on his area one bit! On hearing the news that OVS was breaking up and seeing Bob rather unnervingly moving boxes of M11 tapes down to Catford and that he would now be operating solo, I came up with a satirical rip take based on the 'Allied Dunbar' television advert at the time, 'Let's face the music and dance'. My parody, sung in a Pickles-esque voice, went something like this:

"Da, da, di, di, di, di, There may be trouble ahead, but whilst I've Benjy and M-Two and South East to hand, (inhales deeply) Let's take the stores....and run, da, da, di, di, di, di, Let's take the stores and run!"

So, at the end of 1995, Operational Video Services ceased to exist. I was both fortunate and unlucky in equal measure, to have had Pickles as a manager. What isn't in dispute is that he was a superb videographer and most of the time he was a thoroughly likeable guy. He taught me so much about crime scene video and video film identification and we got on really well as a team in the early days of OVS. The fact that our working relationship went sour has always irked me – I blame Pickles for mistakenly thinking that my enthusiasm for video – a new and exciting medium for me at the time – was a misinterpreted threat to his position and was not on my radar at all. The fact that Pickles used 'covert bullying' tactics against me, to keep me in my box whilst I was working with him – denying me valuable time on camera and talking about me, was utterly wrong and shameful on his part. I fully accept that by the same token, I could have chosen to leave OVS much earlier (on the basis that if I couldn't stand the heat, I should have buggered off out of the kitchen), but for my part, decided to grin and bear it as to leave would have severely impacted my learning and professional development. I did have some great times in OVS and got on well with everyone else. I forged close friendships with Pete and Derrick, which last to this day and Shirley, who was our admin, not only looked after us, but her cheerful disposition also helped to brighten all our working days.

Christmas 1995 was tinged with sadness as we converged on the Laight family home in Wadebridge – the first Christmas without Laurie. Pennard Cottage was on the market, but houses weren't selling. It was an uncertain time for Val, who couldn't possibly manage in that huge 5-bedroom house on her own. We all looked forward to the time when she could move out and downsize.

CHAPTER 17

Forensic Photographer, MPS 1 Area (Central London) January 1996 – January 1999

New Year. New changes and all that. It was back to taking still photographs of RTAs, assault victims and crime scenes once more and it didn't take long to au fait myself with all the Pentax 6x7cm kit again. Each photographic team had a base station where the photographers would garage their vehicles. Hendon Training School was the base for 2 Area, 3 Area's was Mile End, 4 Area's was Catford, 5 Area's was Earlsfield and 1 Area's was at Canon Row, Westminster, then coded 'CW'. Today my old 1 Area Office is part of the refurbished and altered NSY building with the all too familiar NSY revolving sign outside the main entrance, which of course faces Embankment, the Thames and the London Eye (Millennium Wheel). Back in 1996, I'd get the over ground train from New Malden and then Motspur Park (from February 1997 onwards) to Waterloo each weekday morning, walk via the South Bank, past the Aquarium (no London Eye then), over Westminster Bridge, along embankment to my new office. From there I would pick up my van, travel around the area from job to job and when I wasn't on call, I'd then park back up at CW and walk back to Waterloo. When I was on call, I'd take the van back to VN (New Malden Police Station).

There were photography managers for each area and we fell under the umbrella line management of the Scientific Support Managers (SSMs), who generally hailed from a Fingerprint / Identification Officer background. Photographic fought so hard for so long against this, but looking back, it was going to happen any way (in the words of 'Take That', 'there was more of them than us!'), whether we kicked and screamed or were totally compliant. Historically, the Photogs got on well with the IDO's (the troops on the ground), but disliked and mistrusted the IDO hierarchy. John, our outgoing SSM, had risen up the ladder from the old SOCO (Scenes of Crime Officer) grade and was a very likeable guy indeed. When John retired, his replacement was brought in from outside the Met, which went down like a lead balloon. Standing at least 6' 2" tall in his smelly socks, Devereaux Van-Tate was about as popular as a ring turd in a jacuzzi. I think his whole agenda was to ruffle feathers. None of us liked him, especially me – but more about that a little later. My two line managers, Dave Shapland and Paul Alsford, were both seasoned pros. Dave was an army veteran, a real character with a slight speech impediment and when we first went over to 1 Area, he really ran the scenes of crime department. Dave was very likeable, but wasn't backward about coming forward when critiquing your assignments. Working closely with Dave gave me chance to perfect my impersonation of him, which included a shrugging of the shoulders – "Yeah, mate, whadayou think?", tossing a not so good 10"x8" colour print down on the desk. "Er, flash didn't fire, Dave". You were met with a half-smile and a dismissive "Ha" as a piss take retort. Paul Alsford in contrast, was a surveillance wiz. When Dave retired about a year in to 1 Area, they didn't replace him and instead, Paul took over management of everything photography related - the photogs and the surveillance side of things.

There had been lots of rumours circulating about Paul, that he was mad and unstable, which was utter bollocks. The shit stirrers had been turning that dirty stick big time. Suffice to say I was bricking it quite unnecessarily when I found out that I was going to be working with him. For not the first time in my career, I was forced to eat my words, because I found Paul to be a brilliant tactician, superb leader, a naturally gifted surveillance operative and public order photographer. Everything he did, Paul did for the team – he had no favourites. He'd praise and bollock you in equal measure and so was very fair. Paul was outspoken and not afraid one iota to give his opinions, not all of which, were popular. Nevertheless, he had the courage to get his voice heard, alienating some people along the way (the shit stirrers) and I admired him for that. He got pissed off now and again and occasionally shouted – but then who didn't? Paul was a mover and shaker, highly intelligent, loved the job and all that it entailed, was a bloody hard worker and a unique personality.

I remember Paul relaying one particular job to us that he reconstructed on video. A rape occurred, following a chase, and ended on a roof top with the suspect lying on top of and penetrating this poor young woman. Crucially, the victim remembered seeing particular features including London landmarks from where she was lying. With her help and that from the officer in the case, Paul managed to not only recreate the route, he actually 'fell down' as if being pushed by the suspect onto the ground whilst still filming and assumed the victim's 'rape position'. This audacious footage was so realistic that the victim sobbed in court and the jury gasped in horror. The video was devastatingly effective, sent the defendant to jail for a very long time and I do believe, earned Paul a judge's commendation. It was an impressive piece of work and just one example of how Paul quickly assimilated the details of the investigation, analysed the information he had and thought 'outside the box'. Not many of us would have had the balls to do that. Paul was friendly, assertive, disciplined and possessed a superb sense of humour. He was the wind-up king! I absolutely loved working with him and he was by far the best line manager I ever had. In a different life, I often think that Paul would have been a very close friend of mine. He said it how it was and never set out to court popularity. He always got the job done and he looked after his team. He was also a very modest man. I once praised him for his work on helping to design the Canon XL-1 video camera prototype, which was pure genius and I was met with, "Na, na, na, na, it's not about that, we all had a hand in it".

Paul used to live out in the sticks, somewhere in north west London and among other animals, kept pet ducks. During one particularly memorable on call, I was halfway through having a serious conversation with him on the phone about my next crime assignment, when I suddenly heard what I thought were impromptu duck noises in the background. This was followed by Paul telling me to hang on a minute whilst he put down the phone and went to grab one of his ducks. He returned to the phone and was talking to one of his feathered friends, "Now 'Rosey' (or whatever she was called), say hello to Paul". I was already chuckling on the other end of the phone, but when I heard a loud series of duck quacks down the receiver, I was close to wetting myself as I clutched my sides in uncontrollable laughter. It was pure quality and absolutely hilarious, showing Paul's warmer side as well as displaying his wonderful sense of humour. On another occasion, following my annual PDR (Professional Development Review), I had just finished an on-call job up the road at

Paddington Police Station. I phoned the office and Paul informed me that my printed PDR was now ready for me to read. He was just packing up and would see me the following morning.

Not wanting to wait until the following day, I swung by our office on the way out of town to read the report. I punched the code on the office door. It was obvious that Paul had only just left because I could still detect his presence. The office was L shaped in that you'd open the door and immediately facing you was the duty office board and telephones, then you turned right and looked back on yourself 180 degrees along the expanse of individual photogs' desks. Opposite this was a coat stand. I had a very strong, but bizarre feeling that Paul was somehow, still in the office. I thought I was losing it when I started looking under each desk to see if he was hiding somewhere. God don't be so stupid, I thought to myself. Satisfied that he clearly was not hiding in the office, I began to relax and at that moment looked across to my desk. My eye immediately settled on my printed PDR. I walked over to my table and picked it up.

I was now completely relaxed and fully concentrating on reading my PDR. Suddenly and out of nowhere, a hand clamped itself around my right shin! I leapt back with startled fright and emitted a gargled man scream. At the same moment, Paul emerged from underneath a load of boxes and black sheeting stored under my desk. "You bastard!" I said to him, "You scared the shit out of me", but we were both laughing. He had got me good and proper! Paul knew instinctively that I'd swing by the office to read my PDR that night, not wanting to wait until the morning. Uncannily, Paul knew me better than I knew myself. Some months passed before I found myself in a similar situation of having to pop into the office at the end of an on-call job. This time I was ready. I went in almost guns blazing. "Yep, hi Paul. Know you're in here. You can come out now". This time, I not only looked under every desk, but I also took all the stores and rubbish out from underneath every desk as well, then painstakingly put it all back again. Satisfied, but feeling stupid that Paul wasn't in fact in the room, I relaxed once more as I surveyed the entire office. Sure enough, at that precise moment of total relaxation, a hand reached out and touched my right shoulder. Once more I leapt into the air, as a laughing Paul unwrapped himself from the camouflage of the coat stand in the middle of which he had been hiding! Surveillance ace, wind-up king!

My fellow Photographic Officers were Jules Angel (a seasoned pro who helped teach me when I first started and who is now an eminent Professor working in the States) and Paul Cowley (a six foot two plus West Midlander who was a very popular member of our team). Paul settled in Barnes and still is a keen cyclist. He and I joined at roughly the same time and Paul was definitely one of the lads – always up for a party and a bevvie or two. Behind the often jokey, laddish exterior, which I felt he often liked to portray, lay a fine mind. I caught him more than once with his head buried in 'The Times' reading something that was way beyond me. We enjoyed some great laughs with Paul and he was a bloody good photographer across the board, both on stills and as one of the elite public order photographers. Mick Stevens was a veteran of Photographic and about as laid back as it is possible to be without actually physically being horizontal. Indeed, I think it's true to say that even the proverbial rocket up his backside wouldn't have raised a flicker from one of his eyebrows. He had a very dry wit and would often parody major events with the Met and Met Photographic under the pseudonym of 'Paracetamol'. A very, very funny guy indeed. I warmed to him immediately when I first joined the service in 1990 and was paired up with him in 'AV' (Audio Visual). Needless to say, I was delighted to be teamed up with him once more. I just knew that we were going to be thoroughly entertained. Someone thought it would be a good laugh to put a poster up at Amelia Street, just next to stores, with faces of the old timers when they were considerably younger. The rest of the staff had to guess who was who. Inevitably, there would also be the odd witty caption. I always remember spying a very young Mick Stevens with very straight, shoulder length hair covering his ears. Underneath his photo, someone had written 'no comment', which I always found more amusing than the actual photograph, every time I looked at it.

Chris Lewis, a young, tall, good looking photog in his early 20s, with an enviable mop of blonde, wavy hair, hadn't long joined the Met. Chris was a thoroughly decent bloke, with a great sense of humour. I liked Chris the first day we met and loved working with him. The standing joke was that Chris was always the last person into the office each morning, yet he lived the closest, in Lambeth, but isn't that so often the case? In fact, you could virtually see his flat from our HQ. A good ten minutes into 'Morning Prayers' and Chris would swing the office door open, Paul would bollock him and a slightly ruffled and sheepish but smiling Chris would say, "But I got caught in the bus lane, di'n't I?" Bob, another veteran photographer and keen light aircraft pilot, brought a wealth of stills photography experience to our new team and was also very fond of critiquing all our work, which I found a pain in the rear end, but in fairness, it did keep us on our toes. Simon Meyer, a very friendly and personable guy who joined the MPS a couple of years after me, was our man on surveillance and we tended to see him only very occasionally. In terms of manager and fellow team members, I couldn't have asked for a better bunch of photogs and personalities if I'd tried.

A few memorable jobs come to mind during my time on 1 Area. I was photographing a haul of priceless figurines at West End Central Police Station (then coded Charlie Delta) and requested a room off the custody suite to construct a makeshift studio for the purpose. The custody sergeant had told me to handle these artefacts with kid gloves as they were extremely valuable, prior to them being returned to their owners. Nearing the end of the shoot, I inadvertently picked my heavy camera bag up off the floor, which had been used to prop open the door. I wanted the camera bag to be nearer the camera and tripod. Having dumped the bag down, I turned to look back and to my horror, saw the bottom of the door catch one of the priceless figurines. I think I shouted "NOOOO!" at the same time the figurine keeled over and was unceremoniously decapitated! Simultaneously, the Custody Sergeant and two middle-aged PCs came running over. "What the hell have you just done?", the Custody Sergeant glared at me, as I stood there white as a sheet, pathetically trying to fit the severed head back on to the decapitated porcelain body with a phantom tube of superglue. One of the other PCs stood there looking grim, shaking his head, before saying "Take you a good few years to pay that one off". The other PC stepped a little closer and examined the damaged figurine. "Wouldn't wanna be you when Lord and Lady Northcott-Gresham find out". I just stood there, staring blankly at the three Police Officers, thinking that the end of the world had come. Suddenly the Custody Sergeant grinned, before saying in a broad Cockney twang "Ah, got you Photog, we was only windin' you up!" "Bastards, the lot of you", I said smiling and very much relieved, feeling the colour return to my cheeks. All three coppers had been in on the wind up from the start. The figurine was worthless tat – if it was a porcelain sow's arse, it would have been more valuable!

In January 1996, an eight-bedroom Notting Hill mansion provided the setting for the arrest of the mastermind to a series of off-licence armed robberies. The middle-aged male suspect had been handcuffed, read the riot act and was being led from room to room, whilst plain clothed officers conducted a detailed search of premises, periodically asking the arrested man questions relating to items of property seized. In one bedroom, a sliding, mirrored door revealed a walk-in wardrobe, on the floor of which, a loose piece of patterned, dark red coloured carpet had been peeled back to reveal an under-floor safe containing several hundred thousand pounds in wodges of £50's and £20's. Having already videoed the arrest and several rooms, I was just setting up my practise zoom-in from the bedroom door towards the sliding wardrobe door, when I heard the suspect's son crying out in the hallway behind me – "Daddy, Daddy, I want my Daddy…". It was an emotional moment and I let my guard down as I hit the record button and started filming. I remember trying to keep the video camera rock steady and the zoom smooth, all the while conscious that tears were rolling down my cheeks. In that moment, this particular job really got to me, more than any gruesome dead body had ever done. It was the realisation that this small boy knew that the police were taking his father away and that he might not see him for some considerable time. My heart went out to this little fellow, fated to be born to a miscreant.

It was 21st February 1996 and I hadn't long commenced my stint on 1 Area, when I was asked to go to Braybrook Street, W12, close to Wormwood Scrubs Prison to photograph a new memorial that had recently been unveiled to commemorate the lives of three of the Met's finest: PC Geoffrey Fox, age 41, DC David Wombwell, age 25 and Sergeant Christopher Head, age 30, who were murdered on 12th August 1966. The slaying of these three unarmed police officers in front of children playing out in the street, occurred just after the euphoria of England's world cup victory and caused a public outcry at the time, becoming one of the most infamous murders of the '60s. Thousands lined the streets for the officers' funerals, with many in tears. There was also a memorial stone for David Wombwell at St. Stephens Church, Uxbridge Road, W12 (where the funeral service took place) and a memorial plaque in the front entrance of Shepherds Bush Police Station, to photograph.

It was mid-afternoon on that August day back in 1966 and having committed an armed robbery, Harry Roberts and two accomplices, John Duddy and John Witney, were sitting in a van in Braybrook Street, when the three police officers approached the vehicle to ask questions. Roberts, who was in the front passenger seat, used his Luger pistol to first shoot dead DC Wombwell whilst he was writing in his notebook. Then he shot Sergeant Head, as the latter ran back to their unmarked police car to summon armed officer help. PC Fox was murdered by John Duddy.

All three murderers were handed life sentences and just cheated the hangman because capital punishment had been abolished the previous year. The trial judge described the slaying of these brave officers as "The most heinous crime for a generation or more".

- The famous Russian composer, Boris Tchaikovsky who was born in 1925, died on February 7th 1996
- On 18th February 1996, the satirical puppet show 'Spitting Image' aired its final episode. 'Ballykissangel', 'Silent Witness' and 'Changing Rooms' were also on TV and children's television series 'Teletubbies' premiered on BBC2. Due to their popularity, toy Teletubbies were in short supply, but Wendy eventually managed to order one by stopping off at a phone box on her way to work early one morning to access the order line as it opened. 14-month old George was delighted with 'Po', the red- coloured Teletubby
- March 9th - American entertainer George Burns, famous for his large cigars, died
- March 13th - unemployed Thomas Hamilton opened fire in Dunblane Primary School, killing sixteen little ones and a teacher, before turning the gun on himself
- March 25th - Mel Gibson's 'Braveheart' film won best picture Oscar at the 68th Academy Awards
- May 20th my favourite 'Doctor Who' actor Jon Pertwee, passed away
- In mid-June, the IRA detonated a huge bomb in Manchester, which injured over 200 people and wrecked a vast swathe of the city centre
- July 5th - the first mammal to be successfully cloned from an adult cell, 'Dolly' the sheep, was born at Midlothian's Roslin Institute in Scotland. By late summer, Boris Yeltsin won a second term as Russian President

In August 1996, almost a calendar year after Wendy's Dad passed away, Pennard Cottage finally sold, but not before the price had reduced considerably. The housing market was static, which meant that one lucky middle-aged couple bought Val's sanctuary for a song! It was all hands to the pumps as we cleared the house room by room, vacuuming as we went until Pennard was but a mere shell and ready to be loved anew. As we loaded the last of the knick-knacks into the back of Simon's red Honda Civic, I remember Simon turning to me and saying with a resigned look of sadness, "I can't believe this is happening". We closed the door on Pennard Cottage for the very last time and moved Val in to Guineaport Parc, close to the centre of Wadebridge. Fortunately, Val had acquired the keys to her new three-bed semi-detached house a week earlier, which meant that we were able to get in there, rip up old carpets and undertake some urgent maintenance and painting, before the moving in date. The previous owners had kept numerous pets including several birds, all of whom seemingly had free reign around the house. It was in a shit state. Val looked after George, while Wendy, Simon and I donned white forensic suits, overshoes and masks and started gutting the place. God knows what the neighbours thought! The carpets were alive with creepy crawlies and I remember scraping dried, concrete-like bird droppings from the walls throughout the house. On the day of the move, it was warm and sunny and many items from the old house had been stacked on the lawn. We'd been on the go all day and with decorating, I'd been on the go all week. By 6pm I was flagging and flopped down on the grass. Poor Simon powered by Duracells and adrenalin was still running around and wouldn't stop until he was satisfied that his mother was settled.

Some of the hit films of 1996 included 'The Nutty Professor', 'Matilda', 'The Rock', 'The English patient', 'Jerry Maguire', '101 Dalmatians' and 'Mission Impossible', starring Tom Cruise as Jim Phelps. 1996's pop hits included The Spice Girls' 'Wannabe' and 'Say you'll be there' and George Michael's 'Jesus to a Child'.

1996 had been a memorable year indeed, but 1997 was to prove even more so. George's artistic talent revealed itself at only 2½ years old, when his depiction of the human form – a painting - blew all the staff away at his Kingston nursery 'Kidsenter'. Towards the end of January 1997, William Jefferson Clinton was sworn in for a second term as U.S. President. A few days later, Madeleine Albright became the first female Secretary of State. On May 2nd, Anthony Charles Lynton Blair became the first Labour Prime Minister in eighteen years, following a landslide general election victory. On June 2nd, mass murderer Timothy McVeigh was convicted of fifteen counts of murder and conspiracy for his part in the 1995 Oklahoma City bombing. He was subsequently executed by lethal injection.

On August 31st in the early hours of the morning, came the utterly devastating news that Princess Diana, the 'Peoples' Princess', had been killed together with her boyfriend Dodi Al-Fayed, following a car crash in Paris' Pont de L'Alma road tunnel. The outpouring of grief for Princess Diana is something I'll never forget. I popped into town to view many of the floral tributes that lay metres thick outside Buckingham and Kensington Palaces, days before her State funeral at Westminster Abbey on 6th September 1997. The funeral service was watched by over two billion people worldwide. Diana, Princess of Wales, was the former wife of Prince Charles and mother of Prince William and Prince Harry. She was a celebrated charity worker, especially for her support of the International Campaign to ban Landmines, Great Ormond Street Childrens' Hospital, mental illness, cancer and HIV/AIDS. Princess Diana was stunningly prepossessing, a much-admired fashion icon and was a truly remarkable woman. And now this national iconic figure was suddenly gone leaving a massive void in peoples' lives. It was a truly dreadful time. Princess Diana's brother, the Earl Spencer summed up her role:

"Diana was the very essence of compassion, of duty, of style, of beauty. All over the world she was a symbol of selfless humanity. All over the world, a standard bearer for the rights of the truly downtrodden, a very British girl who transcended nationality…".

Princess Diana is at peace, buried in the grounds of her family home the Althorp estate, Nottinghamshire, on 6th September 1997.

On 1 Area, we were going through a quiet spell and after some political argy- bargy, we ventured into the other areas as and when they needed help. I enjoyed this as it offered me a good variety of assignments and a change of scenery. We'd also acquired a small Panasonic mini-dv video camera and we were able to put this to good use on 'walk throughs' and graffiti jobs. I'd just returned from covering several jobs near Regents Park Zoo, when my arms suddenly broke out in hives. Hundreds of little red dots all over the place. When I opened our office door, Paul was sitting at the duty office desk. When he saw me, he covered his face and all but ordered me out of the room. It was late in the day and so I told him I'd go home and get the doctor to check it out. I wasn't overly concerned as the spots didn't hurt – they weren't even itching. Mick Stevens was also in the office and also bore witness to my spotty state. The following morning, I got checked out, the rash had all but disappeared and it was concluded that I was probably allergic to something I'd ingested. Coincidentally I'd developed man flu and ended up taking the day off. I phoned in sick, only to find Mick manning the duty office and answering the phone in his customary, almost suave "Yeees, Good Morning, Mick Stevens, here". I gave Mick the rundown and heard him chuckling, mischievously. "I think I'll tell Paul that you've got Ellison's disease and that it's extremely contagious!" Mick said. "Just so long as you don't let the wind up go on all day!" I countered. All I heard was "Ha, ha, ha, ha, ha, ha, ha, ha" from the other end of the phone. 'Paracetamol' was one of the best pranksters that Met Police Photographic had ever known and he was about to wind up our line manager, big time. I hadn't heard anything all day and decided to phone Mick at teatime. "You did tell Paul it was a wind up, didn't you Mick?" Again, more chuckling down the phone. "Mick?!!!" "Well, not exactly…ee…. arrrr….ee", Mick retorted. I went into CW the following morning where the full extent of Mick's wind up hit me as Paul blasted me with "You f***ing c***!!!, have you any idea how much time I wasted yesterday?!!" "It was nothing to do with me Paul", I countered, but Paul was having none of it. Mick was grinning and chuckling at my two o'clock. It transpired that Mick had not only told Paul that I was highly contagious, but that I had also contracted Ellison's disease, which was considered very serious indeed and he might want to consider everyone getting medically checked out as well as decontaminating the office. Fortunately, things hadn't reached the decontamination stage, but Paul had been on the phone for hours that previous day, seeking advice and researching the 'disease'. Every time I think of the Ellisons disease incident, I'm reminded of Mick's mischievous grin, his chuckle and the twinkle in his eyes and of the happy times I spent in Mick's company. Quality Mr. Stevens, pure quality!

1997 brought us the births of American model and personality Kylie Jenner, as well as the English actress and 'Game of Thrones' star Maisie Williams. We also lost American actors James Stewart and Robert Mitchum, fashion designer Gianni Versace, as well as the Indian nun, missionary and saint, Mother Teresa.

Among the great 1997 films were: 'Titanic' starring Kate Winslet & Leonardo DiCaprio and directed by James Cameron; 'Face Off' starring John Travolta and Nicholas Cage; 'The Full Monty' with Robert Carlyle, 'L.A Confidential', 'Men in Black', 'Tomorrow Never Dies' with Pierce Brosnan in the role of James Bond, 'Air Force One', 'The Devil's Advocate' with Al Pacino and Keanu Reeves and of course, the comedy film 'Bean' starring Rowan Atkinson. 1997 pop hits included Elton John's 'Candle in the Wind', The Spice Girls' Spice up your Life' and 'Too Much' and one of my all-time favourite songs 'You have been loved', a hauntingly powerful number by George Michael about his late partner Anselmo.

I was also in court a few times during this momentous year. I had photographed a vicious rape scene involving a young lady in a lock up garage in Shepherd's Bush some months previously. The scene was quite small and contained. Exterior views showed the lock up garage from both directions and the view into the garage from opposite. There was a vintage, black-coloured Bentley inside, which you could only just walk around. There were numerous tools hung up on the walls and the garage had that garage-workshop, nuts and bolts/oily smell about it. At the front of the Bentley there was a sturdy metal work bench, on top of which, a thin, minging mattress had been placed. The dirty deed had taken place here. There was also a condom wrapper under the front of the vehicle.

Fast forward to mid-summer and I found myself donned in my best navy-blue suit, white shirt, dark blue tie and polished black brogues, pacing up and down outside Number One court at the Old Bailey (Central Criminal Court), arguably the most famous legal setting in the world. After twenty minutes of anxious waiting, an usher called my name and I was escorted up a flight of stairs and onto the witness stand. I carefully laid a copy of my statement and album of scene photographs out in front of me. I was promptly sworn in and promised 'to tell the truth, the whole truth and nothing but the truth, so help me God', before Prosecution Counsel stood up at my two o'clock. I was asked to verify my name and job title, after which Counsel guided me through a couple of straightforward questions relating to my scene documentation.

Then it was the turn of the Defence Counsel. I was now completely calm, almost revelling in the location I found myself in. The middle-aged senior barrister peered down at his bundle, shuffled some papers, took off his spectacles and peered up at me. I was determined not to make a balls up like I had done at Epsom Magistrates Court over the Dangerous Dogs case and definitely not here in front of all these eminent people. I was on my guard this time and ready for the trap questions. To my surprise, the inquisition that followed centred around whether I had moved anything in the garage, taken any tools off the wall, or touched the car. Defence's questions were all met with a confident "No, Sir", but directed to the judge, as I had been taught in my court training some years before. Then came the key question out of the blue, which started with some unnecessary patronising: "Now this is a very good set of photographs.

Nobody here is disputing that, but did you move the Bentley, Mr. Canning?" The question seemed farcical and I almost laughed out loud, but Defence was deadly serious. The judge had stopped scribbling and was looking straight at me, as were the twelve men and women opposite me, who constituted the jury. I stared studiously at the judge and simply replied, "No Sir, I did not." Defence continued to try and chip away. "Are you sure, Mr. Canning?" and "Not even by a foot in order to get a better viewpoint, perhaps?" The thought of me trying to budge a vintage car that must have weighed well over a ton, was bloody outrageous. The courtroom was deathly silent and all eyes were on me, waiting in expectation for my answer. "No Sir", I told the packed courtroom for what seemed like the umpteenth time. Then, just as quickly, Defence looked at the judge and said the customary "No further questions, M'Lud", before taking his seat once more. The judge looked over at me. "Very well Mr Canning, thank you, you may step down" to which I replied, "Thank you, M'Lud".

Barely a week after this court appearance and I was back in the very same courtroom. This time another rape case, a different judge, jury and lead protagonists. Apparently, the accused wasn't happy with the signature that I had provided on my witness statement, so I had been summoned to produce a specimen signature in court. This would then be shown to the accused and his representatives for scrutiny, cross-referencing it with the original on my statement. Following the official oath and name confirmation, it was M'Lady from the judge's bench who explained what was about to happen. I would be given a sheet of paper and a pen and I was to sign my name accordingly. When the judge had finished speaking, I looked at her and said, "I don't think I'll be able to replicate my signature M'lady as it's slightly different each time". WHOA! Big, big mistake. I had just technically answered the judge back without being invited to speak first. M'lady turned to me frowning over the top of what were in all probability, a very expensive pair of half-moon spectacles, then in stern tones, she retorted, "I'm not asking you to replicate your signature Mr. Canning, merely to provide a specimen signature!" to which I quickly replied, "Yes, M'lady", considering myself well and truly bollocked. A female usher then approached the witness box and in hushed tones said, "Would you like blue ink or black ink, Mr Canning?", holding out her outstretched hand to reveal a pen of each colour described. This seemed farcical. I could have said what I was thinking - "Well, I don't really give a shit", or the kinder "Well I'm not really bothered, you choose", or played 'ip, dip, sky blue...', or even scratched my head in mock bewilderment. If the television quiz show 'Who Wants to be a Millionaire' had been airing (it didn't air until 4th September 1998), I might have been tempted to 'ask the jury (audience)' as I couldn't 'phone a friend'. I did not, however, wish to upset the judge anymore, so I went with black ink, duly provided my signature, whereupon the same usher took the sheet of paper to the defendant's table. After a few moments of whispering and gesticulating the defence team seemed satisfied and I was promptly asked to step down. This particular appearance proved to be an anti-climax because I had been looking into possible questions and rehearsing the answers in my head. As a forensic photographer, I was just another expert witness, but could be asked questions on anything. It was a known fact that usually, when Defence Counsel summoned us to give evidence, it was because they were desperate, not because they wanted to know why your second flash gun hadn't fired! If a photographer stuffed up in the witness box or was accused of lying, discrepancies in time keeping, touching or moving something, or any one of a number of malfeasances, this then introduced an element of doubt into the jury's minds.

For a third time in as many weeks, I was called to the Old Bailey for yet another rape case that had occurred in a childrens' playground near Hammersmith. I had dug out my original album of photos and a copy of my witness statement and had tried to second guess the possible questions I might be asked. I was starting to feel at home at the Central Criminal Court as I carefully laid my papers and album out in front of me on the witness stand for what was to be my 'hat-trick' appearance at number one court. I was quickly sworn in, placed the bible back in its place and rested both of my hands in front of me. An usher then handed me a black and white copy of a map, on which I could see some circled numbers with arrows pointing out from each. Following Prosecution's customary questions, Defence Counsel – a short, rotund, balding man, who bore an uncanny resemblance to the 'Fat Controller' in the 'Thomas the Tank Engine' stories by Reverend Wilbert Awdry - opened with his questions. The exception was that this fat controller wore a wig and gown, not a top hat and morning suit!

"From the map in front of you Mr Canning, I wonder whether you could tell the court where photograph number eight was taken from", the Fat Controller said in an unsurprisingly bumptious tone. I took hold of the map, then turned it this way and that as a hushed court waited for my response. As my brain cells quickly fired into life, it had dawned on me that the map I was looking at was a very small-scale illustration of a very large area including and surrounding the rape scene concerned. I stared at the schematic, rotated it to the right, then to the left, but it was difficult from the scale to decipher what I was actually looking at, never mind where a specific photograph had been taken from. I looked at the judge with exasperated pleading, "I'm sorry M'Lady, I'm finding it very difficult to orientate this map and compare it to my photographs" (basically everything was far too small scale). The judge lowered her glasses and then turned to the Fat Controller. "Yes, yes, I quite agree. Mr Montagu-Davies, this is quite unfair on Mr Canning. Please withdraw this map and continue with your questioning of the witness". I couldn't believe it. Half time score: Yours truly 1, Fat Controller, Nil!

Some easy questions then followed from Defence regarding my coverage of the triangular patch of green and the childrens' play equipment within this green. I had covered everything that comprised the full 360 degrees. There were wide angle, closer intermediate images and re-establishing views, so I was confident that nothing had been missed. The Fat Controller was flicking through my 10"x8" album, periodically scratching his chin. Then came the curveball question. "Mr Canning, during the time you took to photograph this scene, did you notice any portions of aircraft?" Without hesitation, I stared at the judge open-mouthed and with a clearly baffled expression retorted, "Aircraft, M'Lady?" The judge lowered her half-moon spectacles, peered over the top of them and with a mildly berating tone said, "Toy aircraft Mr Canning, toy aircraft!", following which, the entire courtroom fell into raptures of laughter, brought to an abrupt end by two firm taps of M'Lady's gavel. I just stood there staring at the courtroom with a slight smile. The court and all its players had me pegged, once again, as a piss-taker, but my comment was anything but. In forensic photography, we used to cover light airplane crash sites. They were after all a type of serious personal injury accident and often proved to be a fatal accident scene, so this is what immediately came to mind. Furthermore, when a forensic photographer (or any other expert witness) is called to court to give evidence it can often be mid-way through the trial, so unless you've been party to all the facts, know the background to the case inside-out and perhaps have attended court every day, you couldn't possibly know any one detail of the trial. My questioning of the 'aircraft' was completely genuine.

In this particular case, the portion of aircraft that Defence was referring to was part of a plastic toy aeroplane that the victim's child, who bore witness to his mother's rape, had with him at the time of the incident. The question was important because firstly, I didn't remember seeing this light, blue-coloured toy at the scene, which had apparently been stamped on by the defendant. Secondly, and of pivotal importance, even though I had covered the scene in its entirety, none of my images showed any portions of aircraft and I never found out the reason why. It was a sneaky, bastardesque question from Defence, expecting me to be completely familiar with the entire case. For my part, that court appearance stands out as the most memorable. The jury certainly enjoyed a good laugh at my expense anyway. I probably attended court a dozen or so times whilst employed with the MPS and my only disappointment is not facing the distinguished and much revered Defence barrister, Mr Michael Mansfield, Q.C..

I had some good experiences on 1 Area, fun with my colleagues, interesting assignments and a great deal of court experience as well. The first 1 Area Christmas meal in 1996 was a very merry, alcoholic affair, which included having drinks in Kensington with actors from the TV drama series, 'The Bill'. Added to the mix there were also some not so nice experiences. I was attending an on call fatacc in Morden in early October 1996. I'd finished my tea just before 6pm when the call came in, so I cycled up to New Malden Police Station to pick my van up and drove the couple of miles to the scene. I knew the location very well indeed, Hillcross Avenue close to where it becomes Links Avenue. Hillcross Avenue connects Morden at its north east end with, among other roads, Grand Drive at Morden Park, where I was driving from. By the time I arrived at the accident scene half an hour later, the sun had already set and ambient lighting conditions were gloomy. The scene was quite compact involving a brand new, green coloured, Honda Civic 1.4i five-door hatchback that had collided with a pedestrian, who had unfortunately been killed. The direction of travel was approximately north east towards Morden and required three approach views, a reverse angle view, a front three-quarter view of the Honda and finally a close up of the front, nearside vehicle damage. Clad in dark blue denim jeans, trainers, long sleeve thick shirt, MPS navy-coloured scenes of crime coat and hi-vis jacket, I set to work. It was whilst setting up the third approach shot that it happened – I went down on one knee to take the photographs and felt a sharp tingling. It was only when I got up, I noticed the right knee area on my jeans. The jeans were ripped and stained with blood. Shit and derision, major uncool Cans! I'd taken my eye off the ball and hadn't paid attention to health and safety. There was broken glass all over the place and I'd just cut my knee on it. Doh! I had a first aid kit in my van, quickly patched myself up and finished the assignment. The AI was none the wiser as it was getting darker by the second. In post-script, as a paper exercise I decided to put a claim in for damaged clothing. The jeans were only a few weeks old and I still had the receipt. I wasn't holding out much hope, but was pleasantly surprised when the MPS reimbursed me for the cost of a new pair.

There were lots of funny incidents, some of which I've already recalled. My manager Paul had decided to take himself off for a few nights trekking and camping in some remote corner of Scotland. Having returned, he was eager to show us his video diary, so a group of five or six of us gathered round this massive television. The scenery was undeniably stunning. Much of Paul's filming during this trip was of him holding the Palmcorder outstretched in one hand and pointing it back towards himself. On one particular shot, he left the camera on a hill side recording and suddenly Paul walked into shot. At that moment I piped up with an oriental accent, "Do you know who that was, that was Crint Easserwood, yes, Crint Easserwood, very tall", re-enacting the New York subway scene from the 1988 film 'Crocodile Dundee 2'. We all fell about laughing.....except Paul, but I think he was laughing inside!

I'd completed a serious assault scene at a Barber's in Shepherd's Bush during late August 1997 and had just emerged from the premises onto the outside pavement, when I caught the eye of an extremely well-dressed black gentleman. With a twinkle in his eye and a big smile he said to me in a lovely Caribbean twang "Look at you, you dashin' blade". Whether he was taking the piss or extending a compliment mattered not – it really made me smile and made my day, made more humorous by the fact that this guy was immaculate from head to toe and I, in comparison, was positively scruffy.

Shortly after this, I had the 'pleasure' of attending a fatal fire scene during the working day down the road in Hammersmith. The Lab Sergeant was Ron Turnbull, who had worked on hundreds of crime scenes including the 1992 Rachel Nickel Murder scene on Wimbledon Common. Armed with a wealth of experience, this wise, affable Scotsman was a firm favourite amongst us forensic photographers. It was always a great comfort to know he was working a scene with you. The photographers and Lab Sergeants had a mutual respect for one another. Ron had walked me through this current scene in suburban west London. An adult male and an adult female had been taken to hospital, but had subsequently died of smoke inhalation. The seat of fire was a chip pan in the kitchen and with copious amounts of combustible material in the vicinity, the fire had taken hold very quickly and destroyed the place. So, there I was, clad in my green overalls, reinforced wellies and hard hat, methodically working my way through this gutted, five room, ground floor apartment, when Ron popped his head round a charred door into what was the remains of the lounge. "Paul, have you not finished yet?" a clearly narked Ron said glaring at me. "You've been here ages" he continued. I was completely taken aback. I'd never had a cross word with Ron or seen him get angry.

What Ron didn't know was that in the weeks leading up to this scene, I thought I'd been having trouble with my Pentax 45mm wide angle lens. It just didn't appear to be in sharp focus. Had I dropped or knocked it? I didn't think so. I popped into Amelia Street and swapped it as faulty. This second lens didn't appear much sharper. I was getting worried. I just couldn't think for the life of me what the problem was. I then came up with a great idea. I invested in a retractable steel tape measure that I'd check the focus distance with. I mocked up a scene room, set the focus barrel to 12 feet, then measured. Twelve feet exactly – but the image just didn't look sharp. When the negs came back from processing, I carefully examined every image with a magnifier. Pin sharp. As were the prints of course. I continued to use my tape measure in scenes because it was so disconcerting focusing a lens that to me was registering as clearly not sharp.

What Ron Turnbull had picked up on was my cautious way of working, it had dramatically slowed me down almost to 'Brian the snail' proportions. I was upset that I had incurred Ron's chagrin. Then – the breakthrough. A letter popped through the door at home inviting me for an eye test. I hadn't been for at least three years and at my last appointment I had 20/20 vision. When my vision was measured at my local Wimbledon optician's, it transpired that there had been a marked deterioration in my middle distance to far vision. This explained why everything approaching the twelve feet mark on my wide-angle lens looked unsharp, yet my close up vision was fine. An eyesight deterioration just hadn't been on my radar. Once I was fitted with specs, the massive problem I'd been shouldering vanished, crime scene photography returned to normal and my way of working rapidly speeded up. I never did get to tell Ron this story, but I hope one day to set the record straight.

Having just corrected one problem, I went headlong into another. It was now early autumn 1997 and I'd just arrived back at CW, ready to clock off for the day. I opened up the rear van doors, reached in and yanked a bag towards me. At that precise moment I felt a sharp pain in my lower back, which caused me to drop the bag. My walk from the office to Waterloo main line station was uncomfortable and by the time I arrived home, my back was excruciatingly painful. I dropped like a sack of shit onto the lounge floor as my lower back muscles went into spasm, the pain travelling through the sciatic nerve and all the way down my left leg. And there I stayed for the next week, (constipated fortunately) unable to stand up. I peed into a bottle and washed and slept where I lay. After an intensive home physio visit and donned in sexy, white Velcro support corset, I walked for the first time in seven days from the front door all the way through to the kitchen and back again, multiple times. Toddler steps at first until gradually I regained my strength. Three weeks later I was back at work and back to normality.

During 1997, a two-year old George had started at Montessori nursery in Wimbledon dividing the day between there and nearby St Matthew's CE Primary school, located in Cottenham Park Road. The Montessori method of education encourages children to learn concepts by doing and employing all the senses whilst working with materials, rather than receiving direct instruction. Children are developed holistically – physically, socially, emotionally and cognitively. The concept is a good one, but George wasn't over enamoured by Montessori, was extremely finicky with his food to the extent that he developed an eating problem during his time at nursery. Suffice to say that George's time at Montessori nursery was short lived. He later started at Coombe Hill School in Kingston, which he loved.

Volunteering to cover the photography of those arrested on New Year's Eve at Charing Cross Police Station was a necessary evil. I wasn't exactly relishing the prospect of bringing in the new year with a load of drunks, stinking of gip, stale piss and shit, but it was a pretty good money earner. Usually very worse for wear, a variety of colourful people would be brought into the custody suite and charged, usually for being drunk and disorderly, for criminal damage to property, or for an array of assault offences. Once charged, they would be photographed full length against a portable background.

There would be a steady stream of 'customers' throughout the festive evening. The closing stages of 1997 were very memorable as close to midnight, having already photographed around a dozen arrests, the custody suite door burst open and two burly male police officers entered dragging a completely legless middle-aged down and out. The suite at this moment was a hive of activity, with this extremely dishevelled guy, who wreaked of excrement, lying in the recovery position on the charge room floor. I was standing by my tripod-mounted Pentax 6x7, immediately to this guy's right when suddenly amidst the din, I heard a protracted growl. This was followed by a river of vomit that spewed forth from the drunken man's mouth. I grabbed hold of the camera equipment and jumped out of the way just in time. When I looked up, one of the arresting officers was looking at me and with a half sympathetic and half sarcastic smile, he said to me 'Happy New Year', just as Big Ben was chiming midnight!

And as those famous chimes continued, ushering in 1998, I didn't know it then, but I had just started my last ever operational year of scenes of crime duties. The winter and spring were filled with a multitude of crime jobs. In May, Mum popped down to babysit 3½ year old George, whilst Wendy and I enjoyed a much-needed weekend break at one of our favourite haunts, Brighton. Wandering around the famous Lanes, the long promenade walks, a bag of chips on the pier – absolute heaven! Then in August, we had our usual two-week beach holiday down in Cornwall, where Val completely spoiled us. What a love. Wendy's Mum was without a doubt, one of the most unselfish people that I've ever had the privilege to know. You couldn't hope to meet a finer lady if you tried.

1998 also saw me start cookery night classes at New Malden's Coombe Girls' School, under expert instruction from Brazilian tutor Zee Noble. Wendy was very keen to get me booked on the course! It was called 'Cooking Mainly for Men' and it was great fun from that very first evening. In fact, it turned out to be more of a social club with its very own MPS Photographic Derek lookalike, albeit with long hair and minus the resting bitch face. When I walked into the school at the start of term, 'Derek' was on the phone telling one of the regulars 'Hills' not to forget the vat of wine. Hills dutifully obliged, taking a very large box of Sauvignon Blanc from the boot of his immaculate, Windsor blue-coloured Rolls Royce Corniche 11 convertible with its magnolia fine lines, hide trim, dark blue everflex hood, carpets and lambswool rugs. We all chipped in for the wine of course, which we had on the go, as it were, whilst concocting all manner of culinary delights that ranged from thick carrot and coriander soup, vegetable curry, turkey and apricot casserole to mouth-watering desserts such as my then signature prune and Armagnac tart and mascarpone and banana pie. At the end of each term, we would host a family and friends evening held at the school where some of us would cook the starter, another group would prepare the mains and a third group would make a variety of desserts. In our minds we came close to wearing chef whites, but in reality, we donned a chequered apron and toque blanche! The parties at Zee and husband John's house were equally entertaining. Happy days!

Then, it was back to the grindstone and the push from autumn to Christmas. I'd just celebrated my 35th birthday and I had returned to New Malden Police station from an early evening on-call. I popped round to the rear van doors and as I reached in to pull out my rucksack, I felt a sudden, sharp pain in my lower back. Recognising the symptoms, I quickly locked up the Astramax van, returned the keys and logbook to the police station and then cycled the mile back home in great discomfort. I quickly showered as the pain was steadily intensifying and phoned the duty office with the bad news – to take me off on-call duties. What followed was three more weeks off work. For the first few days I slept on the floor as moving was far too painful and I had a physio round to the house as per last time. I was bricking telling my manager, Paul, but he was actually cool about everything and cheered me up by taking the piss. His nickname for me, since my last episode of back pain the previous year was 'Sicknote' (from the TV series 'London's Burning'). Policy dictated that Paul had to do a home visit after a week and I was still on the floor when he called round. It seemed very strange having my manager sitting in my house, but Paul did everything by the book. As I've said before, he was no nonsense, very fair and in my opinion, people should have respected him more. He was also sympathetic to my plight.

Whilst still on sick leave, I booked an appointment to see a Consultant Orthopaedic Surgeon at New Malden's private New Victoria Hospital, located on Coombe Lane West. Through Wendy's work as an Office Manager for Verity, a computer software company based in Epsom, the family were covered on private health insurance. Two weeks after suffering the initial sharp pain, I walked slowly into this cottage hospital and after checking in was called in to see the specialist. Mr. Larry Harker shook hands in a very formal manner and gestured, almost impatiently for me to sit down. The medic was shorter than me at around 5 feet ten, had a receding head of silver hair and I put his age at around 58. My MRI scans, which had been done prior to this meeting, were clipped onto a viewing box.

Mr. Harker, I quickly deduced was all business and no nonsense and had about as much personality as a cardboard scrotum. He picked up his glasses from his ornately carved oak desk and peered at me. After I had offered a quick precis of my job, medical history and back pain, Larry Harker, completely devoid of any compassion whatsoever, stared at me and dropped the bollock. "Well, Mr Canning, I'm afraid your crime scene career is over". This single comment cut me to the quick. My MRI scans showed a bulging of disc material at L4 L5 and L5 S1 areas of the lumbar spine. In short, the diagnosis of degenerative disc disease meant that I could no longer carry on lugging heavy equipment on a regular basis, not unless, of course I wanted to bugger up my back completely. Surgery was suggested, although I was told this was only offered to the most serious cases (of which I was one). I was also informed that surgery would come with a 50:50 chance of being left in a wheelchair. I needed a more sedentary role. I walked out of that hospital thinking the world had come to an end. I was completely shell-shocked. My whole life was scenes of crime. It's what I had trained for. What the hell was I going to do now? The thought of relinquishing all operational commitments and sitting behind a desk for the rest of my days was about as far removed from euphoric as it gets! Strange how fate intervenes though …

I returned back to 1 Area in November on light duties, answering the phones, filling out forms, directing my fellow photogs to assignments, pen-pushing. Whoopy-do. I got involved with various committees and the setting up of the DNA database, but I wasn't happy at all. The spark had gone. I'd lost my joie de vivre. My mo-jo was buggered and I was about as much use to my team as a teat-less condom. I was aware of behind the scenes whispered conversations and rumblings as to what to do with me. Rick Dooley, the 5 Area SW SSM was reported to have said to Charmaine, Head of Photographic Branch at Amelia Street, that he didn't want an 'invalid' on his area. Lovely! Nobody wanted me, but then I didn't blame them for not wanting me, because I wasn't up to the job. Was I to receive my marching orders? Would I be medically retired? I was only 35 for God's sake – too young back then to write my memoirs.

The negative feelings continued in the same vein. One day our 1 Area SSM walked into our office. I'd returned from sick leave and he looked at me and said "Ah, it's the malingerer" and walked out again. I immediately saw red. I calmed myself down and twenty minutes later, I went and knocked on the SSM's door. I went in, sat down and faced this tall, brooding man, challenging him directly over his highly inappropriate behaviour. "I didn't like what you said just now". Van-Tate stared back at me. "Pardon?" was all he said. "You called me a malingerer and I didn't like it" I countered. The SSM seemed perplexed and then to my utter amazement retorted, "I didn't say that, I don't use words like that. No, that wasn't me". I was so angry that not only did he not apologise, but he also just denied it. This man in a position of power had just blatantly lied to my face. I decided to stare him out for about ten seconds before saying, "It must have been someone else who looked a lot like you then". I abruptly got up, left the SSM's office and left it hanging in the air. I had the right hump after that. I didn't like this SSM from day one and now I had proof that Devereaux Van-Tate was a lying, self-righteous bastard!

By mid-December 1998, it was decided to move me back to Photographic HQ at Amelia Street, Elephant and Castle, where I'd be on light duties, printing in the colour room. My outgoing manager, Paul, had been very sympathetic in his summary comments on my PDR. He knew me well. In fact, he knew me better than I knew myself. We shared a similar work ethos – intertwining working damn hard with taking the piss, regularly - and he commented on how devasted that must have made me feel, knowing that I couldn't do the job I had trained for and that I loved. Paul Alsford wasn't just the best manager that I ever had, he was also good company – very clever, very astute, a quick thinker and very witty. I learned much from him, especially about organising and fixed observation post surveillance. I probably had some of my happiest times in the MPS on 1 Area and that was largely down to Paul Alsford's impetus and of course to my fellow 1 Area teammates. When I left 1 Area, Central London, the feeling was totally different compared to when I left Operational Video Services at the end of 1995. I felt a sense of bereavement, of loss. My operational scenes of crime days were done, now consigned to history!

CHAPTER 18

On Light Duties at MPS Photographic HQ, Amelia Street, London, SE17

January – May 1999

It was January 1999, the year the Euro was introduced and the start of the very last year of the twentieth century. I found myself back in the Colour Room at Photographic HQ, affectionately referred to as 'Amelia Street', a reference to the location in which our headquarters was based. Tony was my initial manager until they recruited a guy who was new to the MPS, a middle-aged chap called Peter, who needed moulding a bit into our way of thinking, but a sound guy, nevertheless. As luck would have it, I was also working in a great team – a very friendly bunch of guys and gals including Steve, Kev, Dave, Pete, John, 'Big' John, Kim and Derek. We all got on very well indeed and I quickly readjusted to being 'back inside' again. There were many funny moments, none more so than when I arrived at Amelia Street one morning. I had just walked past the general office when I clocked a strange movement through the door's glass panel in my peripheral vision. I stepped back and peered in through the glass – the rhythmical back and forth movement was an esteemed colleague larking about having simulated sex with the office manager, on her desk...as you do at close to eight on a busy Monday morning! It was even funnier when I stepped inside the office and casually bid the two "Good morning", mid-thrust, smiled and walked out again. Only this particular colleague could get away with pulling a cunning stunt like that. Every time I think of those two it makes me chuckle – of course it would never happen now amidst all the 'snowflakes'! There were frequent trips down the Wally road to 'Mari's' café, breakfast runs and not too infrequent pizza lunches. Crucially, my back felt ok, I was receiving regular physio treatment at the New Victoria Hospital back home and I undertook a series of back exercises daily. Workwise,

I was colour printing hundreds of crime images for court and where I had to be careful was bending down and loading the heavy rolls of printing paper onto the Polly printers.

We were kept busy with frequent calls to come in on Saturdays when necessary. This all meant more, much needed money in overtime.

When 22-year-old British Neo-Nazi militant David Copeland embarked on a two-week nail bombing spree aimed at some of our Black, South Asian and Gay communities over three successive weekends from 17th to 30 April, we had our work cut out for us. Firstly, Copeland targeted Brixton, a suburb with a large black population. On 17th April he placed a holdall packed full of nails and explosives outside an Iceland supermarket in Electric Avenue. The following weekend, another holdall was placed in the East End's Brick Lane, the heart of the Bangladeshi community. On 30th April, Copeland let rip again, placing a similar holdall in Soho's Admiral Duncan Public House, located in Old Compton Street, which just happened to be the centre of London's Gay community. The bombs claimed the lives of three people, one of whom was pregnant and more than 140 others were injured, some seriously.

The London nail bombings stretched resources over an extended period. We were still dealing with material from the Brixton attack, when shocking news came in on 26th April that TV presenter and newscaster Jill Dando had been murdered. She was just 37, successful, attractive, blissfully happy and engaged to be married. It was particularly shocking as Jill was one of the nation's favourites. She had presented the 'Holiday' programme and as well as reading the BBC news, she also fronted BBC's 'Crimewatch' with Nick Ross, whom I had met at my Duke of Edinburgh's Gold Award presentation 16 years earlier. The shooting of this much-loved television personality on her own doorstep in Fulham, shocked and repulsed the nation. Barry George, a local man was arrested, convicted and sentenced to prison. However, he was subsequently acquitted and Jill's murder case remains open. Following the post-mortem, senior management – knowing that I'd exercise discretion, approached me to handle the urgent printing of the post-mortem photographs. I waited until the colour room and adjoining album room were completely empty, when everyone downed tools and scarpered for lunch, before I set to on the grim task. I not only printed the images, but I also made up the albums and sealed them for collection, before everyone else returned (some of whom were young, new starters and could quite possibly have been affected by these photographs). The content and description of Jill Dando's post-mortem photographs will forever remain confidential. Suffice to say they were very upsetting.

Under MPS restructuring, Photographic HQ was to fall under the umbrella of Specialist Operations ('SO'), whereas the five area photographic teams all fell under the command of that area's Scientific Support Manager. In addition to the area photography on call, staffed by an area on call duty officer, there now existed an 'SO' photography on call for staff based at Amelia Street, managed by an 'SO' Photography duty officer on rotation. Over the weekend of 30th April – 2nd May 1999, I was SO duty officer. Due to the fact that the nail bombings were dealt with by SO13 (the Anti-Terrorist Squad), I was inundated with requests. From Friday evening to the early hours of the following Monday morning I made and received a total of 231 calls via land line, mobile and pager. I barely had time to go to the loo, never mind a shower. By early Saturday, I already had my two SO photographers Matt and Paul, fully committed. Matt was back at the Admiral Duncan Pub, having already attended the night before, and Paul was down at the suspect's address in Hampshire. From Hampshire, I then had to send Paul to another SO13 scene at Stonebridge Park LT station. My SO13 liaison photographer, Matt S, was tied up with victim post-mortems, so when two more SO13 scenes were called in (phone boxes in Belgrave Road and The Vegas Hotel in Warwick Way, SW1), I then had to call on volunteers. Simon M cancelled his own social engagements at short notice to make himself available for duty.

I trawled through the list of photographic staff at regular intervals. Nick M very kindly volunteered to come to Amelia Street to print a number of very urgent 'lifts' and I also needed Steve H in at Amelia Street processing and printing. A tad before 11.30am SO13 were on the blower again to me, requesting that the public toilets opposite the MPS owned Trenchard Section House, located in Broadwick Street, W1, be photographed. One of my volunteers, Simon S was duly dispatched, but because of cross contamination, I knew he'd only be allowed to photograph the exterior. To overcome this problem, Nick M once again offered his services, travelling from Amelia Street. Nick then photographed an additional two scenes at Leicester Square and Carnaby Street, before returning to Amelia Street and eventually finishing mid-evening.

At 2.30pm two further requests were made from my colleagues in the Anti-Terrorist squad to photograph the nail bombing suspect at Charing Cross Police Station, if memory serves, and also a small scene at Bermondsey Underground, which back then was a construction site. Due to cross-contamination and having combed the staff list numerous times, I was unable to supply further photographers and was thus forced to turn to 'area' for what was known as 'mutual aid'. With his photographers under severe pressure themselves, it was nothing short of a miracle that my old manager Paul Alsford (inundated with phone calls and jobs himself) was able to undertake the most skilful juggling act in history, by supplying two photographers (half his complement) for the above jobs. I considered it a very lucky coincidence that Paul was area Duty Officer that weekend and for his invaluable help, I was eternally grateful.

Bits and bobs were phoned in during the afternoon. Just after 6pm an armed robbery scene came in, which Nick B volunteered to undertake.

On Sunday 2nd May, my photographers Matt and Paul returned to 'The Admiral Duncan' and to Hampshire, respectively. SO13 liaison photographer Matt S undertook the photography of the suspect at Charing Cross (which had actually been postponed from Saturday 1st May). Simon M gave up a second day, travelling to Amelia Street to print urgent finger marks for 1 Area Major Incident Pool (1 AMIP) involved with the Jill Dando Enquiry and was then dispatched to another SO13 scene at The Airways Hotel, St. George's Drive, SW1.

On Monday 3 May, Paul returned for a third, full, consecutive day to the suspect's address in Hampshire. After an early morning area/mutual aid firearms job at Streatham, Matt returned to Amelia Street to help out David in the colour room.

If it wasn't for all these photographers volunteering, the aid from area, coupled with the shear hard work, determination and professionalism of all the photographic staff over the weekend, the system would have broken down. It would have only taken another device to explode elsewhere or perhaps another armed robbery scene, and we would have been on our knees. It was great to work with such a professional and good-humoured bunch of guys. I ended up writing a report and recommending that a copy be put on each photographer's file.

It was still early May 1999 and it had dawned on me for a while, what on earth was I going to do long term. Would I go for promotion and climb up the managerial ladder, leave photography and get a different job within the police, or leave the MPS entirely? I knew I couldn't go on working light duties in the colour room indefinitely.

My mate Pete, who joined the MPS at the same time as me, had recently been promoted to HPho and had been tasked with setting up forensic photography training at what was Hendon Training School's 'Scientific Support College', later to be known as the 'Crime Academy Forensic Faculty'. Right now, it was the first week of May and Pete had popped into Amelia Street to see Charmaine, Assistant Director and Head of SO3(2) Photographic Services. He then suggested to me that we pop out for a cup of tea at Mari's, as he wanted to discuss an urgent matter with me. I'd worked with Pete in the Colour Room, on scenes of crime and on OVS. Now seated with our teas, he completely wrong-footed me by asking me whether I'd like to join him at Hendon working as an instructor. Wow – what an opportunity! I'd been head-hunted to join the Scientific Support College. I was naturally over the moon.

CHAPTER 19

A Skeleton in the Closet over the water Pre-Christmas 1998

Roisin stiffened as she heard the sound, for it was a familiar sound, not a welcoming sound, but one which pulled at every nerve ending, whipping her up into near panic. The creak on the half-landing spelled despair for the girl, more a deep-rooted unhappiness wrapped up in a childhood full of tears. The stairs creaked again as the sound drew closer. The girl was petrified to the core. She could do nothing but succumb as before. Please dear God, she thought, when would it end? When would she be free? She could scream, but she quickly rebuked herself for the useless thought, for her mother and siblings were totally oblivious - locked in slumber. She sat on her bed in tremulous expectation, hands clasped and when she spied the Bakelite doorknob turn quietly and so very slowly, she jumped like a frightened rabbit, with all hope now bereft.

The face suddenly appeared and he stared at the fifteen-year-old girl through huge spectacles. The man was short, balding and in his mid-50s, a cross between Thomas Hamilton of Dunblane notoriety and John Reginald Halliday Christie, the war-time Notting Hill murderer. The man had always been overweight, his rotund girth indicative of a greedy lifestyle - for too long he had over-indulged. A solicitor by day, he somehow held down a 9-5 job, drifting and devoid of ambition and motivation. He cared only for himself. He was utterly selfish. In public, he appeared respectable, but behind closed domestic doors he was a control freak - a dictatorial, unbearable tyrant, with the manners and respectability of a pig. His wife and childrens' lives were miserable as they endured the pendulum of his awful mood swings. Prone to frequent, violent outbursts, made infinitely worse with alcohol - shouting, swearing and door slamming were inevitably followed with bouts of physical cruelty as his wife and young children were regularly slapped, beaten with sticks or pushed about. The only peace and quiet the family got was when he was out working.

For Roisin however, there was to be no respite from this man who once more had invaded the privacy of her bedroom. He hadn't knocked, but then why should he? It was his house. He owned it and the contents therein. In his warped mind, that also included the girl. 'Come to Daddy' the family patriarch said softly, but sternly - his eyes wide, feral and demonic. She dutifully obeyed him, because he possessed the ultimate power. He had complete control of her. As she was led away from the sanctuary of her bedroom, she tried to blot out the imminent terror that was now so close at hand. Father and daughter entered the clandestine hellhole that was his office. With the door closed and locked, Roisin's nightmare was reawakened as her depraved father sexually abused her again. Powerless to fight, the girl tried to concentrate on the reason why. The very man she once trusted and who had responsibility for her safe keeping, had robbed her of her innocence long ago and was now repeatedly raping her to satisfy his perverted, incestuous lust. Her father was worse than an animal. He belonged in the gutter, no prison would be bad enough. He was a child molester and Roisin longed to be free from this monster and his vice-like spell. The paedophile would always end the sessions with a warning to his daughter, "This is our secret and you're not to dare tell anyone. If you do, I'll have you banished from this house forever, because you'll be responsible for the break-up of our family and you do know how important family unity is, do you not?"

Roisin was so unhappy. She just wanted a way out. Hers was a desperate, seemingly impossible situation, from which there seemed no escape. Although frightened, she longed to tell someone. She longed for it to be over. Who, though, would believe her and besides, if she sicked up the sordid detail, who would want to listen? What would the family, the neighbours and her friends think of her? My God, what would they say? An eternal pariah, they would ignore her with certainty. No, Roisin could never tell - the secret would stay secret, just as Daddy had said.

Sounds like the stuff that terrifying storybooks are made of, doesn't it? Fiction?..... I think not. Fast forward to pre-Christmas 1998, almost two decades after these appalling events occurred. Roisin was my cousin. She invited me to a local hostelry to discuss a family matter of some urgency. Nothing I had seen or heard in forensics, in the murder scenes and mortuaries of London could have prepared me for what I was about to hear. With drinks barely started, Roisin, desperate to offload to a family member she could trust, let me have both barrels. The woeful tale commenced and as the person sitting opposite me shared their heavy burden, my lower jaw sagged and I stared into her sadness in stunned disbelief. I shook my head gravely as I assimilated the detail, sinking back into my chair like a 'here today, gone tomorrow politician' as Sir Robin Day once famously said to John Nott.

I met up with my cousin, a highly successful Lincolns Inn Fields chambers criminal barrister, a couple of times a year (usually for a well-oiled meal and catch up), obviously miles away from the wigs, gowns and court room dramas. She was highly intelligent and well organised. With high speed efficiency, Roisin retrieved the horrible facts from an imaginary court bundle sandwiched within a locked filing cabinet in her mind, for the events had been catalogued, synthesised, shuffled, compartmentalised and presented to me in chronological order. When she had finished, I offered what words of reassurance I could conjure up, for seeing me had indeed been an ordeal for her. Tremendous courage had been shown for the stakes, in Roisin's mind, were high. She risked alienating and possibly losing me, not just as her closest cousin, but as a friend and confidant and a rift could have so easily precipitated. Having thoroughly groomed her, Roisin had been sexually abused by her father 'Seamus McKelwee', over a five-year period from age thirteen to eighteen in the late '70s and early '80s.

As I drove home after that meeting, a range of emotions flooded in as I wrestled with the enormity of the leviathan. What I now knew was anathema to my conscience and the putrid thoughts burned inexorably like a white-hot branding iron on my very soul. I felt acute anger, horror and sadness and was sickened to the very core, for I knew that it would take me a long time to come to terms with the fact that the father of my cousin was capable of such degrading and vile behaviour.

With my cousin's permission I wrote to the abuser McKelwee sparing no emotion. Christ, in years gone by, I had supped alcohol in the company of this paedo swine, completely oblivious as to his despicable criminal activities. By way of flimsy comparison, I could only relate to the trauma by the physical, verbal and mental abuse that my own father had subjected me to as a child. That had culminated in him calling me 'a useless shit' and which, inevitably led to an irreparable rift between us. Now, as my scorching pen chastised, I was all fired up and my dislike for Roisin's depraved father bubbled over like a witch's cauldron. I could only begin to imagine the terror and torture this despicable person had put my poor cousin through. This man had effectively destroyed a significant chunk of Roisin's life, her childhood marred and debauched by the perverted sexual cravings of her paedophiliac father. What brought vomit exploding like a volcano was that in his twisted mind, he and Roisin were 'an item' and he apparently yearned that one day she would carry his child. The fact that Roisin had gone on to carve out a successful career - she was at the top of her game - was a credit to her courage and gut determination as a survivor. And to the day I die, I will always admire her for it.

From the safety of his Cork City sanctuary, and hiding behind his own guilt, the child molester audaciously wrote back to me by return, a dictatorial epistle, a sickening missive, foisting all the blame on to Roisin. Shockingly, through his highly delusional eyes, he had done no wrong. Roisin, he said, was the instigator, she had thrown herself at him and enjoyed every 'session' and that was all there was to it. End of story. Seeing me as a very real threat, all this 'last word merchant' could do by spurning me was to taunt me almost in a child-like way with a disparaging letter containing put-downs a plenty: "I'm surprised that someone in your position, working for the police, would use words like 'paedophile' and 'rape' so liberally when you quite obviously don't know the meaning of the words" and threatening, "You're not welcome to visit me anymore. My housekeeper has instructions to turn you away. Keep out of my City!" And then there was, "You clearly do not possess the capacity to forgive. I only hope that you are never in a position to beg for forgiveness". And "I have apologised to Roisin and her sisters, with sincerity and repentance and remorse", which of course was utter bollocks. He never once apologised – not to Roisin, her siblings, or to any of the wider family. McKelwee remained unrepentant and deluded until the day he died, fuelled by his over inflated hubris.

How can you forgive the unforgivable? This monster's vile deeds are similar to other nefarious offenders and go way beyond a mere severance of trust. The shock waves of repulsion reverberate around generations of an entire family. Experts claim that there are hundreds of thousands of child molesters in the United Kingdom alone. When you add to that the families of victims affected as well, it all adds up to a great deal of anger, distrust and melancholy throughout society. On hearing my cousin's plight, I felt compelled to help Roisin and other abuse victims. I approached a local Wimbledon based charity Kelly-Anne's Survivors of Childhood Sexual Abuse, which was run by Anne and Eugene Kelly. They counselled hundreds of victims and their relatives. They told me all those years ago that the problem of sexual abuse is not only endemic, but is reaching epidemic proportions. The figures they quoted back then were shocking and were a scandalous reflection of the authorities' relative inaction. At the time, the figures showed that one in four boys and one in two girls in this country had been, or were likely to be, abused (be it mental, physical or sexual). I found that hard to digest, but you only have to turn on the news, read the papers, look at social media today, to discover that paedophiliac activity is still very much an ongoing problem. We live in a society, a significant minority of whom are morally diseased.

In the United States, Megan's Law was introduced after seven-year old Megan Kanka was viciously raped and murdered by a paedophile who lived on the little girl's street. Megan's Law, introduced at the end of October 1994, requires convicted abusers to register with police upon their release from prison. Megan's Law helps protect society by providing information on convicted paedophiles to law enforcement agencies and where high-risk abusers are concerned, to the general public.

At the turn of the 21st Century, former Sunday newspaper 'The News of the World' undertook its own campaign to name and shame known paedophiles and called for a 'Sarah's Law'. Among other things, this requested tougher sentences for abusers and giving people the right to know where a paedophile resides. This all came in the wake of the murder of little Sarah Payne in July 2000. Perhaps the real problem lies within the family. It is a known fact that the majority of abuse occurs behind closed doors, 'out of sight, out of mind'. Tragically, my cousin Roisin's case is not unique, mirroring the family paedophile's modus operandi of grooming and keeping secrets. The difficulty arises in getting the victim who, remember, has been controlled, manipulated, terrorised and often threatened with death, to freely open up about their experiences. The victims of these beasts face a lifetime of torment - unable to trust, lacking confidence and frequently depressed. In some cases, the abused, overdosing on despair, turn to suicide as the only offer of hope available to them on the table. More recently, major strides for justice have been made in shining the spotlight on offenders: high profile abuse cases such as Jimmy Saville, Stewart Hall, Rolf Harris, Harvey Weinstein and the '#Metoo' campaign.

The old adage 'our children are our future', has never been as important as it is today. As responsible adults and parents, we should value and respect our precious children more. We have a moral duty to protect our little ones from this scourge and to ensure that these abusers, who prey so indiscriminately and rob our children of their innocence, happiness and well-being, are brought to book.

Wendy and I organised two sponsored walk fundraisers in 1999 and 2000 raising £8,500 for Kelly-Annes. I walked by Roisin's side for both events – her confidence building, in what was to be a long and difficult road. Husband and wife team, Eugene and Anne Kelly, who ran the charity did everything in their power to offer a protective and supportive arm to the many who had their lives devastated by sexual abuse. Anne was abused and tortured as a child by her father and put in a paedophile ring by him when she was six. The chronicle of events that comprised her childhood were shocking, but meeting Anne, her husband Eugene and their daughter Kerri-Anne for the first time, was an awesome experience. Knowing them back then and the valuable work they undertook was truly humbling. They offered a beacon of hope to the dejected and worked closely with victims on rebuilding trust and confidence, so cruelly severed and denied by their perpetrators. Anne's dreadful experiences put her in a unique position to offer expert and appropriate support and counselling to the needy.

As for Seamus Mckelwee, thoughts of that horrible abuser periodically anger and torment me, for I'll never forget the day Roisin told me everything. Her father should have been her protector, he should have worshipped the ground she walked on as his beautiful, precious daughter. Instead he was devoid of love. He was irrevocably a paedophile with no remorse, who left this world in May 2001 in the knowledge that he lost any love and respect from his family long ago.

CHAPTER 20

Forensic Photography Instructor, Metropolitan Police Service Crime Academy Forensic Faculty, Hendon, London

May 1999 – August 2004

My leaving do in the Colour Room came at the end of the second week in May 1999 and involved quite a lot of water! It had become something of a tradition to drench anybody leaving the team and moving on to new pastures. I was fully prepared for my soaking. Clad in a t-shirt and shorts, I entered the C41 colour neg processing room, where black, plazzy sheets had been taped over everything, including the clear bank of small plastic drawers that housed scores of irreplaceable, processed, 120 colour roll film, awaiting collection by different scenes of crime photogs. The 'soakers' took a huge risk – any water on those films could have proved catastrophic. My whole team were in there. Big John and Peter let rip with the hose and I was suitably covered. Needless to say, I'd brought a complete change of clothes with me. Derek videoed the proceedings on mini-dv tape for posterity, after which I gave a little speech at the end, looking like a drowned rat. I had some happy times in the Colour Room and had the privilege of working with another amazing bunch of people. Following a couple of drinks after work, that was that. I had officially left the Colour Room after four and a half months, which had nicely helped to bridge the gap between the termination of operational scenes of crime and what was to become an exciting new career as a Metropolitan Police, Hendon Training School Instructor.

My new weekday commute to Hendon started on the third Monday in May 1999 and involved getting up at 5.15am and leaving the house at 5.55am. I walked to my local railway station, Motspur

Park, from where I'd get a train at 6am to Waterloo, Britain's largest railway station of 24 platforms. When combined with Waterloo East and underground stations, it is the busiest station in Europe. Twenty-five minutes later I would be striding across Waterloo's concourse and underneath its famous four-sided clock, manufactured by 'Gents of Leicester', with my rucksack over one shoulder, a takeaway coffee in one hand and the morning free Metro paper in the other and then take the escalators down to the underground system's Northern Line. From here I'd pick up an Edgware line train which would take me north through the centre of town, via Camden Town and on all the way up to Colindale, the last but two stops on the line. Emerging from Colindale tube station, I'd take a left and walk along Colindale Avenue to the roundabout, hang a right onto Aerodrome Road and then I'd arrive at Peel Centre, aka the MPS Training school. My normal hours were 8am-4pm, but I was always at the Centre for around 7.25am. From front door to office, the journey time (with no hold-ups of course) used to take around 1½ hours.

I don't actually remember my very first day at Hendon except for the fact that I was greeted by my mate Pete, who was now my line manager, and who would be writing my PDRs for the next five years. What was to follow would be one hell of a learning curve. I didn't know it when I started, but I was to stay at Hendon for the rest of my time in the MPS and after 5 years and three months, I'd emerge as a qualified Instructor with a post-grad teaching qualification from Greenwich University. I ended up teaching and mentoring hundreds of students, giving presentations to visiting overseas dignitaries from Bulgaria, Russia, Jamaica, the USA and Greece, writing a book about Diversity and Race Relations, co-authoring a training manual called 'ICEFLO' (The Immediate Capture of Evidence by Front Line Officers) to enable police officers to undertake initial photographs when first arriving at a crime scene, conducting training needs analyses and subsequently co-directing a training course for the Greek Police in Athens…oh and getting promoted!

In its simplest form, my remit was to design, deliver, develop and assess a variety of photography, video (using the Canon XL-1 camera) and non-technical courses such as Health & Safety, Diversity, Human Rights and Courtroom Skills, which I ended up doing aplenty. Playing Prosecution Counsel during mock court cases was quite straightforward. The role of Defence Counsel, however, was not. It was 'scary biscuits', right out of my comfort zone and involved thinking very quickly on my feet, which I just couldn't do when I first started. I found that in time, I became adept at playing Defence, only because I thoroughly prepped - meticulously looking over each student's case notes beforehand, working out an angle of attack and then leading them unwittingly to a great big hole in the ground. For one poor student, his nerves got the better of him as he told the 'court', "Well I suppose I could have moved the knife...". I was already in mid-attack and couldn't believe my luck. With mock incredulity and protracted sarcasm, I stared at the 'witness' before turning to the jury and repeating the last words uttered, very slowly and deliberately, "Well I suppose I could have moved the knife...". I then turned to the judge and said with feigned resignation and a shake of my head in disbelief, "No further questions, M'Lud", following which, I abruptly sat down for dramatic effect, leaving the poor student still standing and red-faced in the witness box!

I also developed a 'night scene' photography course and a 'Crimescope' specialised lighting course for scene searching of marks, based on MPS photography legend Ken Creer's original one. Courses ranged from 1 day to 4 weeks' duration. I assisted in the recruitment and selection of new staff members, undertaking interviews and practical assessments to determine their suitability. I continued to provide a mentor service to students, offering support and advice even after they had left the Scientific Support College / Crime Academy. As an instructor, I quickly got to grips with knowing that the training and development of staff is a prerequisite to building a secure and professional department.

The post of Instructor was on 'level transfer' at the same Photographic Officer grade and required the applicant to:

- be professionally qualified and have at least five years' experience in the photographic discipline;
- have effective team membership skills;
- be creative and innovative;
- have the ability to manage resources, change and customer needs; have good inter-personal and communication skills

I was offered the job, however, although Pete knew I had ability by the bucket load, there was just one slight hurdle to overcome......my confidence in merely standing up just facing more than a handful of people, never mind instructing them, had of course been put through a mincing machine by my father and amounted to the square root of sweet damn all, forcing me to wear a fragile façade as a replacement confident person. I hadn't told Pete about this when I applied and it didn't need a two-year old to tell me that as the bulk of my job would entail being in front of a sea of faces, I would need to seek help for what I viewed at the time, as being a serious handicap – and fast.

Fortunately, the wheels had already been set in motion at the tail end of 1998 when George's Godmother, Renee, mentioned a special programme of transformative learning that she'd attended, run by a leading American company. The intensive three-day initial course provided an awareness of the fundamental structures in which we all know, think and act. Through a combination of individual and group exercises, lectures and participant 'stories' came a shift in awareness – an opening up to what's possible in life for yourself and for others. By sharing experiences with people, powerful connections were made and I found that I was able to think and act beyond the restraints that I'd placed my thinking under i.e. telling myself repeatedly that I had no confidence, I couldn't stand up and talk to a group of people, people would laugh at me, I'd be shit. All negative stuff.

During the first morning, I had a major breakthrough when I crossed the Rubicon and took the microphone for the very first time in my life and shared my experience of my father with 120 people I'd never met before. That single event changed my life forever. To my surprise, I was not only euphoric, but contrary to my hitherto belief, I did have confidence. I just hadn't tapped into it and my negative thoughts were shutting it down, so it was hardly surprising that I'd crap myself at the first whiff of a talk or presentation. Running away as it were, didn't mean that I was thick or was being a coward, it meant that I never allowed conditions to be right and therefore there was never any possibility of moving forward. Following the success of this basic course, I went on to enrol in the 'Advanced Course' and then the 'Self Expression and Leadership Programme' (SELP). The foundation course gave me the courage and confidence to engineer a reconciliation meeting with my father, with me controlling the date, time and place, both the running and outcome of the meeting and crucially, confronting my father over his atrocious, bullying behaviour. The advanced and SELP courses enabled me to stand up, face people, deliver training and opened up the possibility for me to organise two, multi-thousand-pound major fundraisers within a year of each other and speak on a soap box at both events in Hyde Park, London. I was involved with these external self-development courses for six months and got what I needed out of them.

In mid-June Pete and I enrolled on the first week of our mandatory two-week 'Train the Trainers' course. The second 'development' part of the course was held over a week in the November. Our 15-strong group comprised a mixture of serving uniformed police officers, detectives and police civilian staff. Leading the group was Kim, who was in her early 30s and a few years younger than me. Kim was not only an experienced police officer, but she also proved to be friendly, approachable, supportive and a damn good instructor. At the end of week one, we each had to deliver a thirty-minute presentation on a subject of our choice and at the end of week two, a ten-minute presentation on a work-related subject. Feedback would follow each presentation in the form of self-critique, group and then instructor comments. The presentations were all videoed, so that after your feedback session, you'd then go into another room and watch yourself. This was a very useful exercise as it picked up on any annoying habits, like scratching your nose repeatedly, or moving around the room too much, or saying, 'ok' a million times, which could be distracting to the learning experience. We had a very strong group and we bonded quickly. The instruction was intense and included front loading, individual and group exercises, as well as role play – all stuff that would have been way out of my comfort zone and given me the shits just a handful of months before. I talked about organising a sponsored event for my first presentation, which culminated in me showing my fellow students part of my first Hyde Park sponsored walk.

My second presentation was ten minutes' duration, focusing on Health and Safety. The pièce de résistance was a two-minute PPE clothing game, where two teams were shown a photo of a crime scene, for example an arson and each team firstly had to find all the relevant PPE and then secondly, help dress their nominated fellow team member in the correct items of protective clothing, necessary to carry out that assignment. The first team to have their nominated team mate fully dressed was the winner. It was hilarious, got everyone participating and the real beauty was that of course learning was achieved in the process. I gleaned so much from that invaluable course about different teaching and learning styles, of planning and assessing learning and of delivery methods. Most of us stuck to the good old flip chart and wipe board, but one of my fellow course attendees, Dave, was an IT expert and he was using PowerPoint for his presentation. After that, I took the work's laptop home for the weekend and taught myself PowerPoint from scratch, as I'd never used it before. I also noticed Dave periodically looking over our heads during his delivery. It wasn't until the end of his presentation that he showed everyone the back wall behind us. The whole lesson was bullet pointed on four large sheets of A1 paper. I thought this was a great technique and have used the idea off and on since. My presentation also taught me to thoroughly check the functionality of any electrical kit, as my video took a while to start. The main teaching mantras that I learned back then and which have stuck with me through all these subsequent years of instruction are: 'Failing to prepare is preparing to fail' and 'Tell me and I'll forget, show me and I'll remember, involve me and I'll understand.'

For the first year or so, photographic training just consisted of Pete and me running essentially photographic and video courses along with refresher courses for new and existing forensic photography staff within the MPS. It was all film back then, but we did have the 2.7-megapixel sensor Nikon D1, a beaut of a DSLR camera, manufactured on June 15th 1999, as well as the Canon XL-1 for the video courses. Prior to the photography course for new staff, we'd conduct a 'Suitability Assessment' to ensure that the department as well as the MPS was employing the right type of people with the relevant skills, knowledge and attitude to match.

My first ever course run jointly with Pete was a four-week photography course for new MPS photogs, Julie, Dan, Richard and Lyndsey, who were all young, friendly, very intelligent, good humoured and dynamic. The month culminated in a series of practical assessments with a written examination, which saw all four passing and students and instructors going out for a celebration lunch. I have fond memories of my first ever training course and learned so much about me as a person as well as from my four, vibrant and inspiring students.

With only two of us, decision making was vastly easier. Pete was very much the leader, the activist, the 'ideas man' and I was the implementer, which suited me fine. As polar opposites, but sharing much common ground, we worked very well together and often we'd leave the confines of Rowan House and walk around the grounds of the training school bandying around ideas for new courses, or to improve existing ones. I'd always have my notebook with me. By the time we returned back to Rowan, I'd have the skeleton of a course sketched out on paper, the scaffolding on which I'd build the different ideas buzzing around my mind. Pete would leave it to me to then further design and flesh out the detail. I absolutely loved all this.

Many a time, we'd 'shoot the shit' together, solve the problems of the world and end up back in the office, with our spectacles on our desks, holding our sides in uncontrollable laughter. We'd also enjoy great nights out, always on a Friday at the end of a course and usually in Holborn, starting off at 'The Shakespeare's Head' for a decent 'Spoons' meal and moving on to Covent Garden. Following one very alcoholic celebration evening, I recall opting to walk back to Waterloo in a desperate bid to sober up, stopping at the London Eye en route, only to end up giving a group of Japanese tourists a guided tour of central London, as you do! By the time I got back to Motspur Park Station, being so hammered that I almost missed the last train, still too scared with inebriation to face my wife, I sat on my local station at some ungodly hour, watching a group of foxes playing on the railway! I have such fond memories of those quality times.

The whole of training school was spread over many acres and had several buildings. Scientific Support College / Crime Academy Forensic Faculty fronted the parade square where new uniformed police recruits would have their passing out parades. Quite often you'd get to see the MPS Commissioner. Sir Paul (now Lord) Condon visited quite regularly and when he stepped down in 2000, Sir John (now Lord) Stevens took up the baton. Adjacent to one end of Rowan House was the skid pan and close by were a collection of wrecked motor vehicles adjacent to a vehicle examination garage, which were fantastic to use in our Photography of Motor Vehicles course. In addition to the cadet school, the site also housed amongst others, a marked-out road junction for role play, an eight-lane running track with viewing stand, a gym and a decent size swimming pool. For the first year at least, Pete and I were regular gym users and I also swam and ran on average around three times a week. Rowan House itself was set over three floors. On the ground floor was the admin office and reception, student lounge, mock court, photographic office, photographic mini-lab room, studio with equipment storage room, darkroom and fingerprint training suite. On the first floor, were offices and classrooms and the top floor comprised rooms on either side of the corridor that had been converted into crime scenes. Those rooms on the opposite side of the building to the parade square came equipped with CCTV monitoring and VHS recording capability.

It must have been the tail end of 2000 that the SSC suddenly saw an explosion in its workload due in no small part to the fact that the UK was witnessing a massive upturn in 'volume crime' – an exponential increase in burglaries and thefts from motor vehicles, or more precisely according to the Association of Chief Police Officers (ACPO):

"...any crime which, through its sheer volume, has a significant impact on the community and the ability of the local police to tackle it. Volume crime often includes priority crimes such as street robbery, burglary and vehicle-related criminality, but can also apply to criminal damage or assaults".

AS a result, the MPS needed to recruit so called 'Level 1' crime scene examiners to deal with this mushrooming crime. An eight-week training course for eight students was devised. This comprised two weeks each of fingerprints, scenes of crime examination / evidence retrieval and scene photography. There would also be a week of theory and practical exams and a week of mock court training. The SSC had close to several hundred students to train over a rolling, continuing programme that would take about eighteen months to complete, with each course overlapping the next one. Naturally, we needed more staff. Two new photographic instructors joined our ranks at Rowan: Steve Meyler and Cheryl Reynolds, who were both excellent in the classroom. Steve was typically laid back with an infectious sense of humour and used to deliver his courses in his trade-mark flip-flops. He was a very likeable colleague indeed and brought with him a wealth of experience from scenes of crime, public order photography, as well as his professional practice pre-Met and of course, his life experience, which was invaluable. Apart from that he was a really accomplished trainer and was immensely popular with our students. He was also bloody hilarious and I loved co-training with him. Today, like so many of us, he's ex-Met, living in his beloved Ireland (probably still wearing his flip-flops) and amazingly successful. Earlier in 2018 Steve co-produced a high end, coffee-table book with acclaimed author Helena B. Scott, entitled 'Loftus: The Hall of Dreams', depicting the large, ghostly, Loftus Hall country house, which is located on the Hook peninsula, County Wexford, Ireland. Steve Meyler's black and white, evocative, stunning images are nothing short of superb quality and hauntingly beautiful. In 2019, Steve then followed 'Loftus' with another book entitled, '66 Hours', which recalls the February 1914 'Helen Blake', Fethard lifeboat tragedy, off the coast of County Wexford. Congratulations Steve!

Cheryl in contrast, brought to the classroom not only her accrued scenes of crime skills, but she also had a background as a medical photographer. She too had a great sense of humour. Cheryl is such a lovely, kind person, full of positive energy, life force and effervescence. Bubbly, smiling and friendly, Cheryl was superb at delivering, injecting her own brand of professionalism into every course and like Steve, the students warmed to her. Again, similar to Steve, running a course with her was uplifting and inspiring. Cheryl and Steve remain two of the finest colleagues that I've ever had the privilege to work with.

In the build-up to the Level 1 training kicking off, some of the forensic photographers out on area and at Amelia Street perceived this photographic training as a direct threat to their own jobs and were running around like headless chickens. I was labelled a 'turncoat' and a 'brown nose' by my wider photographic colleagues, which was naïve and short sighted of them, as well as being a tad unfair. As history has shown, the writing was on the wall. The training of the Level 1's was destined to happen anyway. Until I had run a couple of Level 1 courses I must admit that I privately had one or two doubts whether I could teach professional photography to former telephonists, chefs and solicitors as the level 1 courses comprised men and women from all walks of life, who were new to the MPS.

A few courses in however and one of my opening pep up lines to a new cohort of students was that I promised each of them, many of whom had never picked up a camera before, that I would get them taking professional quality photographs within three days. It wasn't rocket science, it was a skill which could readily be taught. Because the forensic photographers had ruled the roost for so long, they had become deluded that no-one else was capable of doing their job. What actually transpired short to medium term was a harmonious working situation in which the Level 1 examiners concentrated on volume crime and the pro photographers concentrated on serious, technically more demanding assignments such as murders. However, long term, the plan was to reduce the number of pro photographers to a bare minimum and to have the majority that remained, retrain as scene examiners, whilst simultaneously giving the Level 1's a career path to Level 2 and 3 etc., gradually increasing the responsibilities and degree of photographic difficulty by introducing fire scenes and night scenes photography, for example.

As the workload increased further, we took on Nicola, Patrick and Pete Fawcett, all of whom I'd worked with before on scenes of crime. Pete, a veteran of SO3(2) Photographic had opted to spend his last year with us as an instructor, prior to his retirement in 2002. It was lovely to see that his enthusiasm for forensic photography, for teaching and his craft, never waned.

In the summer of 1999, George was 4½. Our annual Cornwall summer break was special this year for two reasons. Firstly, we spent a couple of amazing days on the Scilly Isles, taking a shuttle flight from Newquay Airport to St. Mary's and exploring, St. Mary's, Tresco and Bryher. Situated off the Cornish Coast in Southwest England, the heathland-covered Scillies comprise an archipelago – some 5 inhabited and a further 140 uninhabited islands. This landscape photographer's paradise is an area of outstanding natural beauty with picture-postcard views and sandy beaches at every turn. The Abbey Garden on Tresco houses an array of subtropical plants, where garden lover, my mother-in-law Val, was in her element and it is also home to the Valhalla Museum, which has an impressive display of old ships' figureheads. Former Prime Minister James Harold Wilson, Baron Wilson of Rievaulx, who was Prime Minister of the UK from 1964 to 1970 and again between 1974 and 1976, loved the Scillies so much that he and his wife kept a holiday home there and when he died aged 79 in May 1995, he was buried in the churchyard of St. Mary's old town. His widow, Baroness Mary Wilson, an English poet, lived to 102 and when she passed away in June 2018, she was also buried in the same churchyard.

Secondly, the UK was gearing up for 'eclipse mania'. The much hyped-up event predicted that some of the best views of the total solar eclipse would occur in western Cornwall and we just happened to be on holiday when the moon passed between the earth and the sun on the morning of 11 August 1999. We had gathered for a champagne breakfast at Mike's (a close friend of Wendy's brother, Simon) Mother's house, a gorgeous bungalow in spacious grounds, overlooking the Camel estuary at Padstow. Unfortunately, conditions were too cloudy and we didn't view the eclipse at all, only witnessed its effects. However, further south from us the clouds at Perranporth, 8 miles south west of Newquay, parted just in time for the hundreds gathered there to get an amazing view. It was very much a case of being in the right place at the right time. Approaching totality around the 11am mark, it was a bizarre sight as the sky darkened by the second, confusing all the birds into thinking that it was roosting time. I remember the cacophony of sea bird screeches reaching a crescendo like an invasion of banshees when totality peaked at around 11.11am and lasted for more than a minute. It was suddenly and very weirdly night-time in the middle of the day! A barrage of camera flashes firing on the opposite hillside signalled the start of the phenomenon, as each device engaged its auto flash firing mechanism in response to the rapidly decreasing light level. Even the late astronomer, Sir Patrick Moore, who was fronting a live television broadcast, didn't manage to get a good view. Simultaneously, the ambient temperature nosedived and we reached for our fleece jackets. Then, just as quickly, the eclipse was over, the light levels increased and everything returned to normal as if nothing had happened. It was also during this 1999 summer break that we bought body boards and George and I surfed for the first time. It was addictive – we didn't want to come out of the water. Wendy and I would take it in turns to watch George whilst the other hit the surf. There's an embarrassing photo in the family albums somewhere of me emerging from the surf.....holding a child's surfboard and exclaiming in a broad Ozzy accent, 'What a ripper'! Hm.... moving swiftly on.

One of the most bizarre, initially highly suspicious death scenes that needed to be visually documented by my former colleagues in MPS Photographic occurred on 22 September 1999. Two Thai women were found deceased, their bodies lying together under a tree in Hyde Park. However, this was no murder scene, or suicide pact. It transpired that the 2 women, who had sought shelter from stormy weather, were killed by a bolt of lightning after their underwired bras melted and acted as a metal conductor. Dr Iain West, who undertook the post-mortems, discovered burns on the deceased which he said were 'typical electrical storm damage'. The force from the atmospheric bolt of electricity also turned a brick, found on the ground between the 2 deceased females, into dust!

We returned to Cornwall just after Christmas to mark the end of the twentieth century and welcome in the new millennium. A late afternoon walk along beautiful Harlyn Bay was followed by champagne and a firework display in Wadebridge, on the banks of the River Camel to usher in what computer speak called 'Y2K'. To mark the new century and second millennium, a huge ferris wheel was constructed on the south bank of the Thames in London, right opposite the MoD building and my old 1 Area office at CW, now the current home to MPS headquarters, New Scotland Yard. The wheel known as the 'Millennium Wheel' or 'London Eye', was opened on New Year's Eve 1999 for ceremonial purposes and to the public in February 2000. At the time, it was the world's tallest ferris wheel standing at 135 metres, with a diameter of 120 metres.

I was involved in a whole range of issues and meetings as an instructor, one of which centred around trauma counselling. I had known of two poor chaps medically retired from the MPS through post-traumatic stress disorder, so my involvement with getting Occupational Health trauma counselling for all relevant photographic staff began with a letter to Charmaine, Head of Photography, back in November 2000.

On the last day of January 2000, mass murderer Dr Harold Shipman was sent down for life, having been found guilty of killing fifteen of his patients in the Greater Manchester area between 1995-1998. A two-year enquiry that followed identified an astonishing 250 victims that Shipman had in all probability killed, making the former GP one of the most prolific mass murderers in modern history. Shipman hanged himself in jail almost four years later. On 10th June 2000, the much-awaited Millennium Bridge opened, but embarrassingly had to close almost immediately after it started swaying, giving rise to its nickname 'wobbly bridge'. On 20th July 2000, the good old British Ford Escort ceased production after 32 years. We were lucky enough to own two of them during the '90s.

Tragedy struck on 25 July 2000, when a chartered Air France (Flight 4590) Concorde crashed into a hotel in Gonesse, two minutes after taking off from Paris. Sadly, all 109 passengers and crew, together with four people in the hotel were killed. It transpired that the Concorde had run over metal debris dropped from another plane during take-off at Charles de Gaulle, which had not only blown a tyre, but had also punctured a fuel tank that caused a catastrophic fire and engine failure. It was to be the only fatal Concorde crash in the aircraft's long history of service. The year 2000 also brought us the first series of 'Big Brother' hosted by Davina Mccall, in which Craig, a happy-go-lucky builder from Liverpool, won the prize of £70K, giving all his winnings to his childhood friend who had Down Syndrome and was in need of an operation. This first series, comprising eleven housemates, was also memorable because of Darren and his friendship with 'Marjorie', one of the chickens and 'Nasty Nick' (*'I've made a mistake'*) who was evicted from the Big Brother house for fibbing and cheating.

2001 started with the inauguration of the 43rd President of the USA, George W. Bush on January 20th. Towards the end of February, the UK was affected by the foot and mouth epidemic. By the time the authorities had wrestled the situation under control, six million cattle and sheep had been destroyed, Cumbria being the worst affected area. By late April Wendy and I received the joyous news that we were expecting another child in January 2002!

For a few years now I had been harbouring angry feelings towards my father over his mistreatment of me (one biproduct of which, was my dislike of male doctors). My GP referred me to the famous Priory clinic at Roehampton for an initial consultation in late 2000. What followed were several sessions of cognitive analytical therapy, held in South Kensington after work and over the first five months of 2001. The treatment sought to identify chains of events, procedural sequences, thoughts, emotions and motivating factors that helped sustain the problematic cycle of anger and blame that I had apportioned to my father – and then change my way of thinking through coping mechanisms. Therapy also revealed that I had not dared entertain the prospect of blaming my mother as well for seemingly just 'standing by and doing nothing' as to lose both parents would just be too much to bear. The reality was that my poor mother, who had been bullied, threatened and ground down so that she was powerless to act, was also very much a victim of abuse herself. The therapy sessions continued over some months, but these deep routed feelings are never fixed quickly.

At work, meetings were afoot to start planning for the Photographic Branch centenary in the November. We had grandiose ideas about a Covent Garden centenary banquet, but in the end a contact of Pete's introduced us to Director and Executive Producer Maggie Fogarty, of former TV company 'BFM Productions'. BFM undertook factual programmes for all the UK's main broadcasters and they were very interested in filming the work of the MPS forensic photographer in what morphed into a three-part November 2001 documentary series called 'Shooting the Crime'. Many colleagues past and present (and of course yours truly) featured in the series in what was a fitting tribute to the tireless work of MPS Photographic Branch. At least we had something to mark the special occasion of the centenary as the Gala dinner, sadly, never got off the ground.

Photographic Branch or simply 'The Section' as it came to be known, was started in 1901 as an experiment. During Queen Victoria's reign, an act of parliament of 1871 stated that all criminals must be photographed. Nine years later there were some 14,000 images of prisoners held on file at Scotland Yard. Following the confiscation of a prisoner's camera, in 1901 the Metropolitan Police took a series of test crime scene images. The Home Office then gave a grant of nineteen shillings and ten pence, which roughly equated to 98p for the purchase of film, processing chemistry and related materials. On the back of the success of this experiment, the first full time police photographer was employed in 1902. With an increased budget of £100, the first photographic room was built three years later at 'The Yard' and again it was stocked with confiscated prisoner equipment. Costing the princely sum of £79, the Section's first Leica 35mm camera was purchased in 1924. Pre-1955, The Section was comprised of solely police officers. Between 1955 and 1981 however, Photographic Branch transitioned into a civilian operation. This freed up vital resources, namely the uniformed bobby, for duties elsewhere. In 1986, Photographic headquarters relocated from New Scotland Yard to a brand new, purpose built, two storey building, in Amelia Street, London, SE17. The department witnessed many changes over the decades and attended a huge number of assignments, with many hitting the news headlines and a small number of which, I have written about within these pages. At the turn of the millennium, The Section comprised more than 80 forensic photographers and technicians. With its responsibility to the Anti-Terrorist branch, The Section also had a remit to support UN war crime investigations, the most notable being the ethnic cleansing atrocities committed in the Kosovo War (early 1998 – June 1999) under the Serbian leader, Slobodan Milošević's regime. Multiple MPS forensic photography teams were dispatched to Kosovo in former Serbia during late 1999 and into 2000 with the unenviable task of documenting the bodies, identifying features and possessions uncovered from mass graves. This also continued at the end of 2004 and into 2005 with photographic teams covering disaster victim identification evidence in the aftermath of the Indian Ocean earthquake and tsunami. The catastrophic destruction was sorely felt in Indonesia, India, Sri Lanka and on the south west coast of southern Thailand and claimed more than a quarter of a million lives.

Sadly, through further restructuring and cutbacks, there are now only a handful of dedicated Professional Photographers left, numbering about sixteen. The Amelia Street site was demolished in 2017 and the small core of specialist photographic staff are now based at Lambeth. Incorporating what was the 'Evidence Recovery Unit', they provide professional photography and video filming at scenes using high spec digital camera equipment, including their own drone. They also provide primary fingerprint evidence from exhibits, using lasers, ultraviolet and other specialist light sources. If I thought that we were overstretched at times back when I first started in the Met in 1990 (when there were close to 100 photographers and technical staff), I can't imagine what the pressure must be like now. In

2017 alone they had a run of large-scale jobs to contend with, seemingly one after the other:

- 22nd March 2017 - terrorist attack on Westminster Bridge and outside London's Palace of Westminster
- 22nd May 2017 - the bombing following the Ariana Grande Concert at the Manchester Arena (in terms of casualties, the deadliest terrorist attack on the UK mainland since the 7th July London bombings in 2005)
- 3rd June 2017 - the hit and run terrorist attack on London Bridge followed by knife attacks in Borough Market
- 14th June 2017 - the Grenfell Tower fire in London's North Kensington claimed 71 lives and injured 70 others

Taking Grenfell alone, the small contingent of highly skilled police photographers (my former colleagues) were at that scene for months until they had completed their full, visual documentation of the scene – an incredible achievement!

Back in 2000, the photographic department processed half a million negatives, produced 1.5 million prints and undertook just shy of 21,000 crime assignments. As film was replaced by digital imagery, research and development was never as important to keep abreast of industry changes and advances and to explore the uses of so called 'new media' within the judicial system. The Home Office Scientific Development Branch's 'Digital Imaging Guidelines' updated in 2007, provide the Standard Operating Procedure (SOP). This was a complete audit trail from gaining permission to take photographs all the way through to destruction of images and gives advice, among others, on taking, saving, copying and storing digital photographs.

Suitable photography qualifications, a good sense of humour, the right attitude, sound professional work ethic, the ability to de-stress and of course, a strong stomach are essential requirements for the job of forensic photographer.

On 23rd July 2001, the forensic world lost a giant, the infamous Glaswegian Home Office pathologist, Dr Iain West, to lung cancer. He was just 57. Iain West headed up the team at Guys Hospital and my colleagues and I had worked with him on a more or less daily basis, although I found that he could be a tad terse on occasions during a post-mortem. I preferred chatting to him over coffee at Westminster Mortuary before a PM, where he'd often regale us of different cases he'd worked on, his anecdotes usually being delivered through a cloud of cigarette smoke! Dr West was highly experienced, not just in suspicious death, murder and explosive injury investigations, but also in the organisation of major disaster enquiries. His huge caseload included:

- The 1984 WPC Yvonne Fletcher shooting outside the Libyan Embassy
- The IRA Hyde Park and Harrods bombings in 1982 and 1983 respectively
- The 1984 IRA bombing of Brighton's Grand Hotel, which narrowly missed killing Prime Minister Thatcher
- The 1988 Clapham and 1999 Paddington rail disasters
- The murder of television presenter Jill Dando (1999)
- The mysterious death of former Buckingham MP and latterly publishing magnate, 68-year-old Robert Maxwell aboard his luxury yacht, the Lady Ghislaine on 5th November 1991

As with the saying of our parents' generation 'Everyone remembers what they were doing when JFK was assassinated', I remember very clearly where I was on the afternoon of 11th September 2001. We had a small course running at Hendon, which coincidentally had almost finished, when one of my students emerged from the student lounge completely shocked saying that a plane had just hit one of the World Trade Centre twin towers in New York. It was horrific. We hastily packed up for the day and about ten of us gathered around the only TV set in Rowan House linked to an aerial in the student lounge. Saudi Arabian born terrorist leader Osama Bin Laden had masterminded a series of co-ordinated Al-Qaeda attacks against the United States of America, using hijacked passenger airliners. Separate aircraft were flown into each of the twin towers. When the South Tower collapsed just before 10.00am local time (3pm BST), less than an hour after being hit by the second passenger jet, there were gasps all around the student lounge. Hijacked airliners had also been crashed into the Pentagon in Arlington County, Virginia and due to passengers fighting to reclaim their plane from terrorists, a fourth airliner crashed into the grass in Shanksville, Pennsylvania.

World Trade Centre's North Tower collapsed about an hour and a half after the South Tower and watching the film footage of the solitary tower standing without its mate, you got this eerie feeling that it would fall too. Seven hours later, World Trade Centre building 7 also collapsed. The news was truly shocking. I'll never forget seeing the fires and plumes of smoke, the ghastly images of people jumping to their deaths and of course the collapse of both towers. 2977 people were killed and many injured, including brave emergency service personnel, in what came to be known simply and poignantly as 9/11. The site of the twin towers massacre became one of the biggest, single crime scenes in modern history. It would be the best part of ten years before Osama Bin Laden was eventually caught and killed by US forces in Abbottabad, Pakistan on 2 May 2011.

Having been transfixed by the horrendous news on the other side of the Atlantic, everyone left the Scientific Support College in stunned silence. There hadn't been many people in the college that day anyway and I returned to my first-floor office still replaying the graphic TV images in my mind. I unlocked my door and went to retrieve my rucksack, but something made me freeze. I stared up at my pin board which hung on the wall above my desk. In the middle of the collage of printed photographs was a dusty, rectangular empty space where an image had once been. Then I looked down and saw my own photograph of the twin towers on the floor and the four drawing pins that had been used to secure it to the felt board were neatly placed on my desk. I'd taken this image years previously during my trip to the States in 1986 and I kept a copy on the wall above my desk. To this day, I cannot explain how that image came to be on the floor as my office had been locked and I had the only key. To search for a spare key would have been highly irregular and though possible, not easy to explain! No-one had been in my office that day, not even the cleaner. My twin towers photograph had symbolically fallen almost in sympathy with, and at the same time, as the actual towers fell in New York. I felt very moved by the horrendous events and sent the Mayor of New York a framed photograph of my twin towers image (one of my personal favourites) taken on my 1986 visit to the USA with my best man, Aly Baines. The image was actually sent to outgoing Mayor Rudi Giuliani towards the end of 2001, but was actually gratefully received and acknowledged by new incumbent Mayor Michael Bloomberg in early January 2002, who wrote to me personally.

Two weeks after 9/11, a very nervous yours truly was sitting in business class on board a jet, bound for Athens from LHR, nervously cradling a snifter of brandy – my second. For it was only after my second double brandy that I began to relax as at the time, the general feeling was that every plane, worldwide was a terrorist target. Work had sent me out to examine the photographic facilities and conduct a training needs analysis for the Hellenic National Police in Athens, in the wake of the 8th June 2000 murder of 52-year-old British military attaché, Brigadier Stephen Saunders. The army general had been gunned down in a case of mistaken identity, by two motorcyclists believing that the Brigadier had been involved in bombing Yugoslavia during the Kosovo war in 1999. The assassination was carried out in early morning rush hour Athens traffic, whilst Brigadier Saunders was travelling to the British Embassy. Long since defunct Marxist terror organisation '17 November' claimed responsibility. New Scotland Yard's Anti-terrorist Squad, among other organisations, offered its help in the subsequent investigation. Reading between the lines, I got the feeling that the crime scene's integrity had been heavily compromised. It just wasn't contained, allowing members of the public to crawl all over it and the Greek authorities were understandably very embarrassed about this. My brief in Athens was to:

- Establish the structure and current operation of the Photographic Department
- Examine available equipment and assess its efficiency
- Observe a Crime Scene photographer working and comment on their method
- Assess the quality of photographs
- Ascertain details of the audit trail: film processing, negative storage, documentation and continuity / integrity of the image
- Establish the customer's training requirements
- Identify key areas for training

I found the photographic set up and processing facilities to be ok, it was their crime scene etiquette that gave cause for concern. A single visit to an armed robbery at a 'Bureau de Change' in suburban Athens told me all I needed to know about the Greek Police forensic approach to crime scenes. On arrival, there was no cordon control, which left the scene unprotected forensically. Six Police Officers, devoid of any PPE, were already milling around the scene, one of whom was seen drinking coffee. Blood spots on the tiled floor appeared to have been trodden on. No notes were taken either before, during or immediately after completion of photography in the equivalent of an 'I.R.B.' (Incident Report Booklet), therefore arrival and departure times were, at the very best, approximate. The camera bag was placed on the floor by the safe and the photographer leant on surfaces, which all contributed to the scene being contaminated.

Furthermore, there was no continuity between the photographs - storytelling, scene linkage and chronology were all poor. The exterior of the premises was photographed last with no attempt made at asking people to get out of shot. This crime scene visit told me immediately that the Hellenic National Police didn't just need forensic photography training, they needed crime scene examination / evidence retrieval and finger print training as well – in short, a full package of measures by our people - and all well before the Greeks hosted the 2004 Olympic Games in Athens!

From late 2001 through most of the 'noughties', the American crime thriller/espionage drama series '24' aired on TV starring Kiefer Sutherland as highly proficient Counter-Terrorist agent Jack Bauer. Each series comprised 24 episodes and covered 24 hours in Jack Bauer's life, using the 'real time' method of narration. They frequently employed split-screen filming to relay multiple events occurring at the same time in the often political, high octane storyline. I found the series gripping, completely addictive and therefore compulsive viewing.

One of my favourite TV programmes of the late '90s through to early summer 2002, was the American made legal comedy drama series created by David E. Kelley 'Ally McBeal', starring Calista Flockhart in the title role. It centred around the lives and loves, eccentricities and dramas of a fictional Boston-based firm of lawyers called Cage and Fish, played by Peter MacNicol and Greg Germann respectively. It was hilariously funny, yet at times poignantly sad. My highlights were Richard Fish's catchphrase 'Bygones', his penchant for ladies' 'under chin turkey wattles' (which he'd insist on touching), John Cage's insistence on a fresh toilet bowl (flushing his toilet by remote), dancing to Barry White in the Gents' toilet, Billy's death in court (Ally's ex), music predominantly by Vonda Shepherd and Ally's completely wacky personality. It was marvellous, pure quality viewing!

Out of all the film genres, with the exception of science fiction and horror, fantasy adventure ranks about my favourite. So, it was with eager anticipation that cinemagoers were blessed with Joanne Rowling's 'Harry Potter and the Philosopher's Stone' and then Peter Jackson's marvellous direction of Tolkien's 'Lord of the Rings: The Fellowship of the Ring' in 2001. This was followed a year later by Lord of the Rings: The Two Towers' and 'Harry Potter and the Chamber of Secrets'; In 2003 we had 'The Lord of the Rings: The Return of the King' and in 2004 'Harry Potter and The Prisoner of

Azkaban'. There were obviously more Harry Potter and of course 'Hobbit' films to follow in the ensuing years and plenty more fantasy adventure films to delight audiences.

January 24th, 2002 was another joyous day in the Canning household. A little sister to George, Lauren Lily Victoria was welcomed into the world at 1.53pm in Kingston Hospital, Surrey, weighing in at 8lb 4oz. After years of hoping, Wendy and I had been blessed with a 'Heaven sent' gorgeous daughter, who has quickly grown up into a beautiful young woman. Intelligent, strong and not one to suffer fools gladly, but yet sensitive, kind, loving, fun-loving, spiritual, homely and caring, Lauren epitomises the role model daughter and is every bit a daddy's girl! Our family was now complete. Life couldn't get any better than this. We were in clover!

When Lauren was only 9 ½ months old, I received an urgent call from a doctor in Slough's Wexham Park Hospital, to inform me that my Great Aunt Norah, younger sister of my beloved Grandfather Harry Meyer, had taken a turn for the worse and could I come as soon as possible? Aunt Norah had fainted and fallen at a bus stop near her Bracknell home on a Friday early in November 2002 and we had been to visit her in hospital over the weekend. It was now Monday morning and I hadn't long arrived at Peel Centre in Hendon. I was executor to my Aunt Norah's estate, with eight cousins standing to benefit from her will, so I carried quite a heavy responsibility. I hot-footed it out of Rowan House and by the time I reached Aunt Norah's bedside in Slough, it was around 10.30am. Six hours later, I needed to pop out as I was desperate for the loo. When I crept back into her room, one look at Aunt Norah's face in repose, eyes open, pupils fixed, dilated and staring into the distance, told me that she had passed away. Bizarrely, Norah's friend Pam, who was sitting next to her with her head bowed and holding Norah's hand, weeping silently, hadn't even noticed. Aunt Norah, together with her late husband Uncle Ron, had been lovely to our family. They were gentle, kind, church-going folk and after Uncle Ron's death in 1997, Aunt Norah had never been the same. They were very much in love and she missed him terribly. I remember how heart-breaking and beautiful it was to hear her sing Abba's 'I have a dream' a few years beforehand in April 2000 at her 90th birthday party and I was lucky enough to get a photograph of a ninety-two-year-old Aunt Norah, holding a six-month-old Lauren during that summer of 2002.

Two prominent members of the Royal family died in 2002, firstly the Queen's younger sister Princess Margaret aged 71 on 9th February and then on 30th March, Queen Elizabeth The Queen Mother, passed away at the grand old age of 101. 2002 also saw the tragic murders of Amanda 'Milly' Dowler from Walton-on-Thames, Surrey by Levi Bellfield and later that year, the ten-year-old Soham girls, Holly Wells and Jessica Chapman by Ian Huntley. John Thaw, The Sweeney's Jack Regan, died on 21st February followed by comedian Spike Milligan on 27th February. Moors murderer Myra Hindley also died in 2002, as did another of my favourite American actors, James Coburn on 18th November. James Coburn starred in many films, but two of my best-loved characters were John Mallory in Sergio Leone's 'A Fistful of Dynamite' and Sedgwick, the 'Manufacturer' in the second world war epic, 'The Great Escape'.

In the autumn of 2002 Pete and I embarked upon our post-grad teaching qualification and the various assignments combined with teaching courses kept us busy until we qualified in June 2003. In January 2003, London experienced two periods of unusually heavy snowfall, previously witnessed in 1991. The first was on January 8th, but it was during the second spell around 30th, that I almost got snowed in after a day's work at the Peel Centre. I set out trudging two miles north along Grahame Park Way through inches of the white stuff to Mill Hill Broadway Station, with fellow instructor Geoff Hewlett and SSC / Forensic Faculty Head, Dave Ince. Unfortunately, the tube network in north London was now at a complete standstill. After a couple of hours waiting in a Mill Hill Broadway café to keep warm, I jumped on a main line train bound for Sutton that had come in from Luton. By the time the train pulled into Wimbledon, everything was running normally in south London and I eventually got home around 9pm, but I had come so close to actually staying the night at Rowan House, such was this bizarre weather. The following day provided a great photo opportunity to document the snow scene at the training school.

Towards the end of February, I had to take Lauren into A&E when she became dehydrated following a virus. I ended up cradling her in my arms for fifteen hours. As soon as they got a drip into her, she was right as rain. It was, however, reminiscent of George who was a tad older when he had a similar condition. Again, we spent a memorable night in Kingston Hospital with him, another extremely busy evening in Kingston A&E. It was around this time too that I suffered an anaphylactic shock. I'd had a stinking cold and took some Sudafed for the first time. I quickly deteriorated and Wendy was very worried. My face swelled up like the elephant man and an ambulance was duly called. Cool as a cucumber, I had time to shower, Wendy got my bag together with water, snacks and taxi money and I made sure I wore shorts and a t-shirt, as I was well aware that it would be roasting down at Kingston Hospital. Whilst in the back of the ambulance I wasn't so good, I could feel my heart rate go through the roof. The paramedic was concerned so the driver pulled over en route to the hospital and I got a quick shot of adrenaline in my backside. It not only made me feel out of this world with the sudden rush, but seemed to cure my flu-like symptoms in an instant and returned my heart rate to normal! Wendy was unable to come with me as we had George and little Lauren at home, so it was a very worrying night for her. Then it was 6 hours in A&E hooked up to a heart monitor and various machines and the inevitable taxi home at 3 in the morning. The postscript to that little adventurette was my follow-up appointment with my GP a week later. She had just prescribed an 'EpiPen' for me to carry with me at all times, just in case, when I asked her perhaps an obvious question. "What would have happened if I had delayed getting to hospital?" The GP fixed me a stare, before saying, "It would have been very serious indeed!" .... Oh, Jeepers, creepers...

Pete and I flew out to Athens in June 2003 to deliver a ten-day bespoke forensic photography course to ten students – police officers from the Hellenic National Police. The course encompassed the following:

- An overview of police photography
- Health and safety
- Documentation (including statement writing)
- Equipment
- The photography of motor vehicles
- Internal and external crime scenes
- Property
- Drugs
- Fire scenes (low light level interiors)
- Shoe, tool and finger marks
- Night scenes
- Post-mortems (using mannequins!)
- Video awareness.

Theory presentations and demonstrations were followed with practical exercises using colour film. We also held regular formative assessment recap Q&A sessions. Films were processed after each practical session and classroom tutorials were held using a negative to positive viewer linked into a large television set. Summative assessments at the end of the instruction took the form of a written theory examination and a practical crime scene and separate motor vehicle assessment – each requiring a thorough visual documentation. At the end of the assessments, time was needed for Pete and me to do the marking and checking, before we could undertake the final module. This included the course recap, Q&A / course feedback, issuing of exam results and certificates and of course, re-visiting the course aim and associated objectives. As it was the middle of summer and outrageously hot in the Mediterranean afternoon sun, reaching searing temperatures of 43 degrees plus, classroom and practical training tended to start early around 7.00am. By noon, teaching was knocked on the head as conditions were not conducive to learning, or teaching for that matter.

Our accommodation in Athens was on the top floor of the President Hotel, which was advantageous because of its proximity to the roof-top pool. My only complaint delivered in Greek (óchi ntous kourtína!) to a somewhat taken aback hotel clerk was that the shower curtain was missing from my bathroom. Ordinarily this wouldn't have been a problem, except that every time I did shower, water satched everything, including the toilet. Otherwise, we really enjoyed our stay. The Hellenic National Police were superb hosts. The students like Panos, Christos, Dimitrios (the giant), Elias and Thanasis were great characters. Pete and I made wonderful friends with the training co-ordinator and lead photographer, Nasos Maroudas and his wife Violetta. I lost count of the number of times we were taken sightseeing to places such as the Parthenon and the Oracle at Delphi and taken out for meals in the evening. On successful completion of the course, which culminated in Pete and me being presented with plaques and certificates, everyone was in very buoyant mood. Our last night was a Greek feast of sumptuous local cuisine, washed down with copious amounts of Raki, Tsipouro and Ouzo! The course had been very challenging due to the language barrier (at times we were forced to teach using NVCs (non-verbal communication) and because of the heat and humidity.

Our family holiday in August 2003 saw us fly out to Geneva. From Geneva (Cointrin) international airport we hired a VW estate to take us south east along the A40 over the Swiss border to our final destination Chamonix-Mont-Blanc, the winter ski resort and site of the first winter olympics in 1924. It was a distance of some 83 kilometres and about an hour 20 driving time. We weren't too sure of the route but fortunately Wendy managed to put her fluent French to use and obtained directions from someone who we followed for part of the way. Chamonix is an elevated town in the Auvergne-Rhône-Alpes region of south-eastern France, but close to the borders of both Switzerland and Italy. Hiring the car was a complete waste of money as once in Chamonix, we didn't use the vehicle at all for the entire week's duration, we should have organised transfers instead. We were booked in at the centrally located Ginabelle Apartments, which turned out to be dire. It was a hot summer in Chamonix and our apartment was under the eaves devoid of air conditioning and cooling fans. I couldn't even stand up in half of it the ceiling was so low. After only a night, we transferred to the Mont Blanc Hotel, which was quite literally a breath of fresh air. There was no shortage of activities and the highlight was the long toboggan run reachable via ski lift, which offered an adrenaline rush, a thrilling downhill speed ride which we enjoyed countless times. The famous red coloured rack and pinion train-tram from Chamonix takes the discerning visitor to the Montenvers site at an altitude of 1913 meters. From here you get a breath-taking panorama of the Mer de Glace glacier, the Drus and the Grands Jorasses.

At circa 7½ kilometres in length and around 200 metres in depth, coupled with all its tributary glaciers, the Mer de Glace is the longest and biggest glacier in France. The tour of the Grotte de Glace, which is re-sculpted annually, takes the visitor deep inside the glacier and was definitely worth seeing. At 8½ years old, George was a typical lad who loved this adventure. Wendy didn't fancy the steep cable car rides – some of the highest in the world - so she looked after an 18 month old Lauren, who had been off colour for a few days, leaving George and me to take the rides of our lives up and down the steep mountain slopes. Firstly, we travelled up the Aiguille du Midi where the views of surrounding snow-capped peaks at an altitude of circa 3842 metres were just stunning. Although digital photography had been around for some years, I was still shooting on film using my trusted Nikon SLRs loaded with Kodachrome 64. I was very pleased with my polarised mountainscape vistas, in particular the views I captured of the 4810-metre peak of Mont Blanc, the highest mountain in the Alps and in Europe. Whilst it might have been warm down in the valley, it was bitterly cold and sub-zero at the top of the Aiguille du Midi. I had to work quickly to get all the shots in the bag as George had fewer layers on than me and was only a slip of a lad. Even so, the penetrating cold reduced George to tears as he retreated under cover to keep warm. I felt very bad about that. A hot chocolate and breakfast in the cosy mountain-top café soon got him warmed up again and provided some consolation. With batteries recharged George and I then rode the cable car up the opposite side of the valley from Chamonix to the viewpoint at Planpraz and then via another cable car to the 2525 metre summit of Le Brévent. George also has fond memories of a particular bakery in Chamonix where he savoured his first ever brioche bun!

2003 had turned out to be another eventful year. Whilst standing on a chair in the playground during school games, George managed to fall off and break his wrist, prompting Wendy to dash out of her job at Kings College Boys School in Wimbledon, to take George to hospital, which fortunately was right on the doorstep. However, it necessitated two visits in one night to Kingston A&E. During the first visit, George's wrist was simply strapped up. Unfortunately, this just exacerbated the pain and the poor soul was in agony. So, Wendy returned to A&E, waiting several hours, when they put the wrist in a plaster cast. This was eventually removed 6 weeks down the line by an extremely hairy, bushy-bearded man. In the interim of course, George couldn't write so he was pleased as punch to be given access to a tablet device to do his schoolwork on.

Pete and I were made up with our teaching post grads. We had put so much work into this crucial qualification and actually heard that we had both passed whilst out in Athens, so it was another cause for celebration. On 3rd August, police used the taser for the first time. On 30th August another legend of an actor passed away, Charles Bronson. Among other roles he had played Bernardo O'Reilly in 'The Magnificent Seven', Danny the 'Tunnel King' in 'The Great Escape' and of course, architect and vigilante Paul Kersey in Michael Winner's 'Death Wish' series of films. If my memory serves, it was also around 2003 that the MPS lost the great Lab Sergeant Bruce Hoskyns, who collapsed suddenly with a heart attack whilst out walking his dog and with whom I'd worked with on a great many occasions. The number of people at Bruce's funeral was very much indicative of the esteem in which this particular Metropolitan Police Service Detective was held.

On 13th September, I reached the landmark age of 40 where life begins! To mark the occasion, Wendy treated me to a survival weekend run by ex-special forces on the South Downs. The highlights of this rewarding experience were building a wigwam shelter with a central fire pit; walking for miles just living off berries and plants in the forest and trapping, killing, skinning and eating a rabbit. On the first of the two nights spent surviving, shelter was a very crude affair indeed – a moderate size tarp slung over an overhanging branch. Together with the other three members of the group, I slept in my sleeping bag on the hard forest floor. I awoke just after three in the morning, busting for a slash and looking to my right, then to my left, and wondered why the guys on either side of me had seemingly upped and gone. I began to get worried, when I thought to look behind me. The other guys, including the leader were all fast asleep….. further uphill! In the night I'd managed to slide unhurt some five metres or so downhill, before coming to a stop. It was a great idea for a present and I loved every minute of the weekend.

On 24th October the Concordes made their last commercial flights. I remember spotting several of the BA Concordes flying over London around this time, coming back from Waterloo after work. It was an awesome sight and to think that this plane looked futuristic compared to the old-fashioned cars and surrounds when it first flew in 1969 – amazingly it still looked out of this world in the 21st century. Just to pitch up at the back of Heathrow to see this majestic aircraft take off and hear the roar of those four, powerful Rolls Royce / Snecma Olympus 593 turbojet engines is a fantastic memory. I, like so many, was very sad to see the demise of this very special aircraft. On 9th December, the UK's first toll motorway, the M6 Toll, aka The Midland Expressway opened, providing a much-needed by-pass through what had become a continually congested section of the M6 through the West Midlands.

At the tail end of the year, on December 29th, 2003, the nation lost one of its favourites to prostate cancer, the much-loved entertainer and comedian, Bob Monkhouse, OBE. He was 75. Bob Monkhouse was also an actor, a comedy writer, a television presenter, an erudite stand-up comedian, renowned for his ability to ad-lib, as well as being the host of television game shows such as 'The Golden Shot', 'Celebrity Squares', 'Family Fortunes' and 'Bob's Full House'. Bob was also an expert on silent cinema history and an avid film collector. During his multi-decade career, Bob meticulously recorded gags, idiosyncrasies, one-liners, ideas and sketches in a series of leather-bound books which accompanied him to every performance. In the summer of 1995, two of these books were stolen and after offering a £15,000 reward the precious books were eventually returned some eighteen months later. Bob's last ever stand-up gig in the summer of 2003, was recorded in front of a select and intimate gathering of fellow comedians in the basement at Great Portland Street's Albany pub in London. The show also included a rare appearance by Bob's friend, the gifted impressionist, Mike Yarwood, whom I greatly admired in my youth. The gig attended by David Walliams and Jon Culshaw among others, was all the more poignant because everyone knew that Bob was dying. Indeed, by the year's close, the irreplaceable, immensely talented Bob Monkhouse would exit the stage for the very last time.

In summer 2003, I was getting what my dear friend Derek once described as 'itchy beard'. I'd been at what was now known as the Crime Academy Forensic Faculty for over 4 years and I felt like it was time to move on, although back then I didn't know what to. The instructor group dynamics had changed for the worse since Pete Fawcett's retirement the previous May. A new guy pitched up who resembled a tall, blonde version of a young Arnold Schwarzenegger. He could be ebullient, sometimes childish and unfortunately his disruptive reputation not only preceded him, but often got the better of him. Conversely, he could be a really nice guy when he put his mind to it. Even so, he and I weren't destined to be BFF's. I felt uneasy when he was around and it started to affect my enjoyment of teaching at Hendon. However, promotion to Forensic Training Development Manager was on the cards and I, like many of my colleagues, applied. My interview with a ten-minute flip chart presentation and twenty minutes of panel questions, was unexpectedly enjoyable and I was delighted to get the job at the end of the process. Shortly after my promotion, Pete was promoted to Senior Instructor level, leaving me to become Head of Photography training. I had been promoted amongst my peers and it ended up being an uncomfortable and difficult situation. There was no manual for promotion and I got little or no help from senior colleagues. It was very much a case of 'the loneliness of the long-distance runner' with me left to get on with it, whilst one or two of my photographers regularly tested my patience.

Patrick was hounding me over surveillance courses, which looking back was probably a good thing, but it was the new guy who really started putting the boot in, answering back and repeatedly turning up late for work that took the biscuit. With a cocky grin and poser's swagger he had the gall to say to me "Paul, you need to start cracking the whip a bit more", when I challenged him for the third time in succession over turning up late. He tried my patience at every turn and was starting not only to piss me off, but worse, he was proving to be unmanageable. A few months after promotion our house in New Malden was put on the market and Wendy and I had a plan for our future. Houses weren't really shifting, so I was completely wrong-footed when in July 2004, we had ourselves a buyer. I think I shocked myself when, at the end of that month, I found myself typing out my letter of resignation to Senior Training Manager, Kim Belcher, who was a fantastic colleague. Pete at the time was on annual leave and was probably just as shocked as I was when I told him on his return. I think my former colleagues had me down as a 'lifer' in the MPS and I'm sure if circumstances had been different, I might have carried on for a few more years. In truth I wasn't happy, I needed a change of scenery and the new photography instructor's antics were really just the final nail in the coffin that helped make a difficult decision easy for me.

Up until then teaching, assessing and mentoring had been stimulating and immensely rewarding, with only a few hiccups. Three trainee photographers proved to be high maintenance – northern lad Troy Mullery was friendly and good humoured enough, but he just didn't cut it as a photographer, frequently mumbling and getting flustered over simple things. His recall of PPE during one memorable formative assessment is forever etched in my mind: "Er, boooots, shiny yellor corrt (he meant hi-vis jacket), tripod condom thingies (he meant plastic tripod feet covers) ...". His co trainee, Scandinavian Agnetha Gustavsson was Troy Mullery's complete opposite. She was very intelligent and a quick thinker and Troy's faltering slow pace very quickly got on her nerves. Agnetha eventually left the MPS with the immortal words, "I will sue you!" .....Really?? Hm. Then there was 'Susan', who's photographic experience was in equestrian photography. Her specialist interest was Gymkhanas. She too proved to be a bit of a handful and when she failed her photography assessment, that was red rag to a bull! Susan all but lost it, screaming at me "But I've never failed anything in my life!" Susan blamed me for failing her and subsequently reported me for, in her view, not conducting a fair set of assessments! It was, of course, rubbish. Thankfully Dave Ince dealt with her and correctly quashed the whole thing within an hour.

Neville was a lovely, friendly ex-copper who was on one of my Level 1 courses. A few years older than me, I warmed to him immediately. He was the oldest student in the group, but was one of the best, if not the wisest and he was extremely switched on, as you might expect coming from a police officer background. I returned early from lunch for the afternoon classroom session one time, only to find Neville sitting in his seat with his head bowed and his arms folded. When I asked, "Are you ok Neville?", he looked up and without warning let rip. "If you don't do anything about those two girls, I will!" Unbeknownst to the instructors, two young, female post graduate members of the group had been incessantly winding Neville up and mimicking him within earshot. I hadn't been aware of this and I was shocked. Once Neville had brought me up to speed, along with some of the others, I'd heard enough. I had zero tolerance when it came to bullying. Sending the rest of the students on an extended lunch break, I separated the girls. Pete interviewed one of them in his office and I interviewed the other girl in mine. Both female students realised that they'd been caught out and both were in tears when faced with the gravity of their offence. They were up in front of Dave Ince and made to apologise to Neville immediately on pain of being immediately chucked off the course and out of the Met. The whole fiasco was dealt with very well and turned around within an hour. The students took their places back in my classroom and from then on behaved themselves.

Barring the last six months, I'd had some truly amazing experiences during my time as an Instructor at the Forensic Faculty – teaching and mentoring hundreds of talented students, who themselves went on to achieve great things including working on major investigations. As an example, at least two of my ex-students attended the Paddington / Ladbroke Grove rail crash on 5th October 1999 in which 31 people were killed and some 500 people were injured.

I had designed, delivered, developed and assessed a great many technical, as well as non-technical, courses. I'd loved being part of a mock air crash investigation using the training facilities at Heathrow Airport, during which, I photographed and filmed both exterior and interior of the aircraft. The crashed aircraft sim was quite realistic, especially considering that volunteer members of the public were hired for the day and made up with equally realistic injuries. They would either play corpses, immobile seriously injured, or walking wounded. Once the 'wounded' had been removed from the aircraft, the bodies and body parts would be tagged and each would be meticulously video filmed and photographed.

Being involved with the Photographic Branch Centenary and subsequent 'Shooting the Crime' Documentary series also comes to mind, as well as researching and writing my Diversity and Race Relations booklet. Then of course there was studying and gaining my teaching qualification, the Training Needs Analysis in Athens, the design and co-delivery of a ten-day forensic photography course for the Greek Police, again in Athens as well as appearing in crime scene photography documentaries and giving presentations to visiting dignitaries. By far my most exasperating achievement was writing a business case, would you believe, for getting a telephone installed in the vehicle examination garage with the capacity for calling the emergency services. The garage was annexed from the rest of the buildings at the training centre and working alone there was a risk. The whole thing took weeks convincing a jobsworth Superintendent that having the capability of summoning help on the hurry up at the touch of a few buttons might just be a good thing. I did, however, enjoy taking on an ambassadorial role when it came to liaising with other forces and external organisations, both nationally and internationally. My strong professional work ethic had been honed over the years and translated into me combining a dedicated, organised, disciplined, meticulous approach, with being relaxed, good humoured and very proactive, coupled with a mature management style - even if I do say so myself! Student feedback supported this and enabled me to constantly keep the bar high, take on board suggestions for ways to improve, all the while constantly fine tuning and striving to improve. Senior Training Manager, Kim Belcher, summed up my work ethic when I applied for Forensic Training and Development Manager:

'The fact that he was chosen for the Scientific Support College / Forensic Faculty, and [the fact that] I have witnessed his skills / experience at first hand, leaves me in no doubt that in Paul the Crime Academy and MPS have an outstanding practitioner, worthy of an immediate middle management / 'V' Band role within the organisation'.

Taking part in Pete's spoof 'X-Files' film with all my colleagues at the Crime Academy, not least of whom was the legend that is 'Doctor Barry Baz' (our wonderful photographic technician), was another highlight of my Hendon years. Pete's brilliantly conceived send up of the X-Files was shot early in 2002, just before Pete Fawcett retired and turned out to be very funny indeed.

My 'all-points bulletin' leaving letter really summed up how I felt back in early August 2004:

'Dear All - My family and I are relocating to Lancashire at the end of the month and I will be leaving the MPS on Monday 16th

August. I plan to concentrate on my photography, teaching and coaching.

I will be having a leaving drink on Friday 13th August - 4-30pm onwards - at the Bierdrome, then the Shakespeare's Head, (close to Holborn tube), so if you can make it, it will be great to see you and say goodbye.

I've had an interesting and very enjoyable fourteen years plus in the MPS. I was engaged in scenes of crime photography and video for a number of years before taking up a position as an instructor at the Scientific Support College (now Crime Academy Forensic Faculty).

Helping to make a difference to the lives of others by teaching a skill, has been immensely rewarding. I feel proud, not only to have taught so many fine students, but also to have had the chance to work with a great bunch of people.

I would like to thank all those whom I have worked with and everyone who has offered advice and help to me over the years.

Very best wishes for the future

Paul Canning'

I was presented with cards and gifts, the most memorable of which, was a caricature drawn by a local artist. It depicted me as the Lord of the Rings Wizard, Gandalf the White on his horse, 'Shadowfax' at a crossroads. A signpost pointed right to Hendon from the direction that I'd just come from and pointed left to Lancashire, my new destination. I was very touched with this as it summed up my situation perfectly.

Having worked with Pete in different departments since we both joined the MPS together in the summer of 1990, I was now saying goodbye to him professionally, for the very last time. By selecting me for the Scientific Support College, Pete had done me 'a solid'. I will always remain indebted to him for seeing that teaching potential in me, believing in me and for giving me a chance, especially coming so soon after my lower back crisis. We shared some happy times together, none more so than in the early days at what was the Scientific Support College. Pete had had some close shaves. I recall an incident where he rolled his car and ended up upside down. Another time, he had a blow-out on the motorway and his car spun through 360 degrees into the path of juggernaut and came to rest, facing the correct way in the direction of travel, on the hard shoulder. A very frightening experience indeed. Way before I started at Hendon though on 12th August 1997, Pete and his first wife were only part way through a trekking / camping holiday in north America with an internationally recognised company and whilst travelling through Navajo Indian country in Arizona they visited a picturesque, dried up Antelope Canyon river bed with its twisting walls of sandstone.

Pete scrambled down a scree slope with his camera to take some photographs with five other members of his party including the Trek leader. However, as soon as Pete sized the first image up, he realised that he'd need his tripod. Humming and hawing about whether he should bother, Pete told me that as he was standing in the middle of that riverbed, he suddenly thought, 'What would Paul do? – well of course, Paul would have used his tripod!' So, decision made, Pete scrambled back up the canyon scree slope to where the trek's mini coach was parked to fetch his tripod and speak to his wife. She was waiting by the vehicle with three other members of their party who had decided not to venture down, when at that very moment a couple of indigenous people came running up to the vehicle waving their arms and shouting frantically "The water is coming, the water is coming!" Seconds later, Pete, his wife and the others heard an almighty roar as a torrent of water from flash floods miles upstream cascaded passed beneath them with the other five members of the trekking party plus the trek leader, Pancho, still photographing and lapping up the scenery on the valley bottom. There were reportedly a further six people from another unrelated tour group also in the canyon. It had been an unfortunate act of nature that had caught the tourists completely off guard. The swirling mass of rocks and boulders collected on the journey downhill towards Lake Powell turned the water at this point into a giant, lethal washing machine. It meant that those down there stood no chance at all.

Eleven people tragically lost their lives that day with Pancho being the sole survivor of the twelve who were in the Canyon the moment the flash flood water hit. When Pete returned to work earlier than expected and relayed his chilling ordeal, we all thanked God that he and his wife had survived. Pete then added, if it wasn't for the fact that he thought of me and scrambled back up from the canyon floor to fetch his tripod, he wouldn't have made it through to tell the tale. To diffuse the seriousness of the situation with an injection of gallows humour, we had a laugh and a hug and Pete turned to me and said, "So thanks to you Pauly – you saved my life!" If we had lost Pete at this stage, besides a cavern full of grief, I would never have become an instructor! Fate had indeed played a good hand.

I'd only left the MPS just over a year, when in the autumn of 2005, Pete collapsed in San Francisco. He was given emergency first aid by his travelling companion, Steve Field, another highly talented and respected MPS forensic photographic colleague and was subsequently diagnosed with a benign (now known to be cancerous) brain tumour. I saw Pete prior to his op in the days when the tumour was pressing down inside his brain, causing him to stutter. I then saw my friend immediately post op in Hampstead's Royal Free Hospital with his skull full of staples and doped up with analgesia. But Pete being Pete bounced back after a long recuperation. More than a decade later, he was struck down again with another fast-growing cancerous sarcoma tumour, which destroyed a sizeable chunk of his pelvis – that was in the summer of 2018, which I refer to again a little later on. True to form, Pete's courage and strength of character and the love and support of his family and many friends is getting him through this new round of recuperation. The 'force' is indeed strong within him!

As stated, I would never have become an instructor without Pete's support. I valued Pete's help, advice and counsel, but above all I value his friendship to this day. As a personal leaving present, Pete drew another of his famous, humorous, caricatures of me, together with a type-written, very moving tribute. It was only relatively recently (September 2018) that I came to look at it again, having not read it since leaving the MPS fourteen years previously and thought, I have to include such a *lovely and touching tribute in this book:*

"Paul and I joined the Met together in 1990. To date his career has spanned operational scenes of crime stills, operational video, running the Area duty office at Cannon Row [now the current MPS HQ, New Scotland Yard], and then in 1999 he joined the Scientific Support College. During the past 14 years we worked together on many occasions, including the first Warrington bombing, the Sussex Arms pub bombing, numerous demonstrations and of course in June 2003, we trained the Greek Police, together in Athens. During all these years, Paul has proved himself to be one of the most professional, loyal, hardworking and steadfast individuals I have ever had the pleasure to work with. His eye for detail and dedication to the task at hand are unsurpassed. His reward for his efforts came in July 2003 when he graduated with his Certificate in Education and this was followed by his long overdue promotion to V band in February 2004.

Yet this career, of which he should be very proud, may have come to an abrupt and premature end, in December 1990 at our Christmas do. Spirits were high and fun was being had by all. Paul thought it would be funny to scare me with a party popper, so crept up behind me to let it off. Unfortunately, just as he did, I turned around to see what was happening, and he fired the popper into my left eye. Needless to say my eye swelled and closed and started watering profusely, yet I will always remember the concerned words of [former Chief Photographer] Ernie Whatmore….." That was silly".

Paul and I have been friends for 14 years. He once asked me why we became friends and I glibly replied…." Out of necessity". This was wrong. We became friends because we wanted to. But 'friend' is so commonly used, that the other day I really tried to pin down what is properly meant by it. Turning to the dictionary: a friend is defined as 'someone whom you are attached to through affection and esteem, who is a favoured companion, a supporter and an ally, and well-rounded and solid.' I concluded from this, that Paul was indeed a true friend!

Alongside being a huge support at work, he has always been there for me in my times of need. He has been my counsellor when I needed to cry and has put up with my roller coaster love life for years. Paul, you will never really understand what a great support and at times…. saviour of my sanity, you have been. I am so very pleased for you and also for Wendy, George and Lauren as you set out on your new adventure, it has been an honour and a pleasure to work with you and a privilege to call you my friend….and long may our friendship last" (4th August 2004).

In leaving the Crime Academy Forensic Faculty, I was also leaving the Metropolitan Police Service at a time when further changes were afoot. The methods for crime scene recording and detection are improving exponentially and it is vital that the modern Forensic Photographer keeps abreast of all developments, both technological and otherwise. When I left the service in late summer 2004, I felt that the 'Section' was as committed as ever to providing a professional service - a dedicated and efficient resource, doing its bit to help fight against crime and in so doing, helping to make our capital city, safer.

When I reminisce over my fourteen plus years as a Metropolitan Police Service Forensic Photographer and Instructor, that period of time was an eye opener at every turn. I quickly learned to take the rough with the smooth. It was one huge roller coaster journey, visually documenting the cesspits of iniquity. Man's inhumanity to man, horrible accident scenes, heart-wrenching deprivation, child abuse and neglect. It was truly awful, but simultaneously fascinating and rewarding. I had a fire in my belly and an enthusiasm for my craft that spurred me on through frequent vicissitudes. I met and worked with some amazing people and I'm so pleased that I was given this propitious opportunity. I wouldn't have missed it for the world!

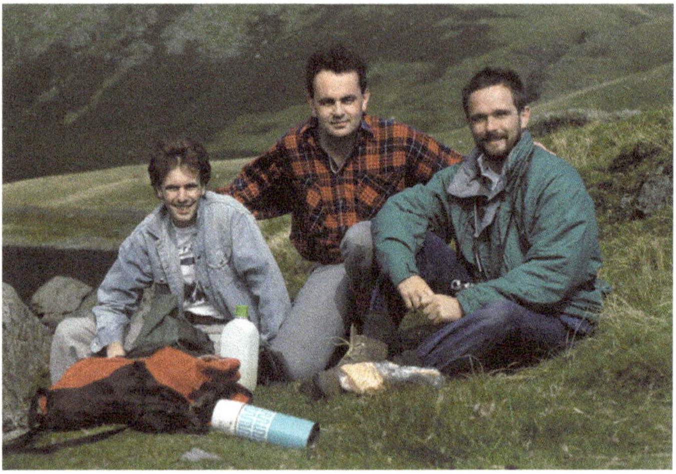

With my two best friends, Aly Baines on the left and Simon Wallis on the right, during a Lake District hike, Langdales, Cumbria, 1990.

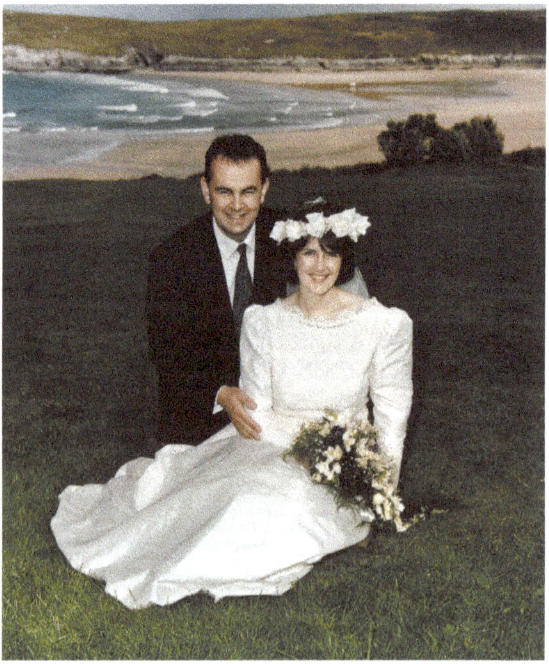

Wendy & me on our wedding day, Crantock Bay Hotel, Newquay, Cornwall, 12th September 1992. Photography, courtesy of Janet Young, Wadebridge, Cornwall.

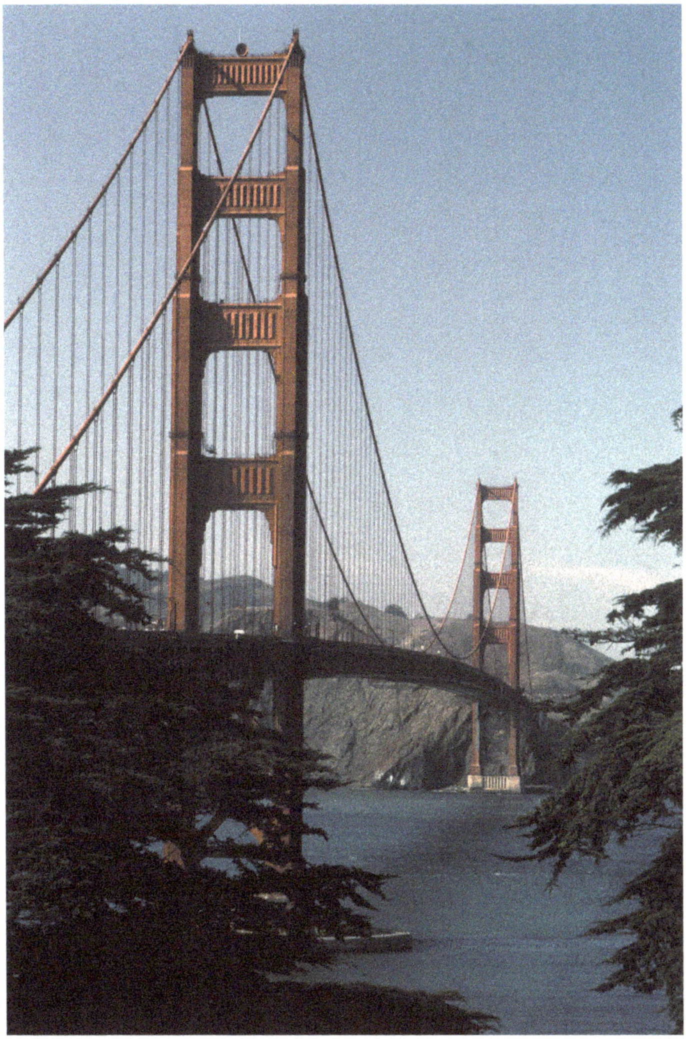

The Golden Gate Bridge, San Francisco, California, during our USA honeymoon in September 1992.

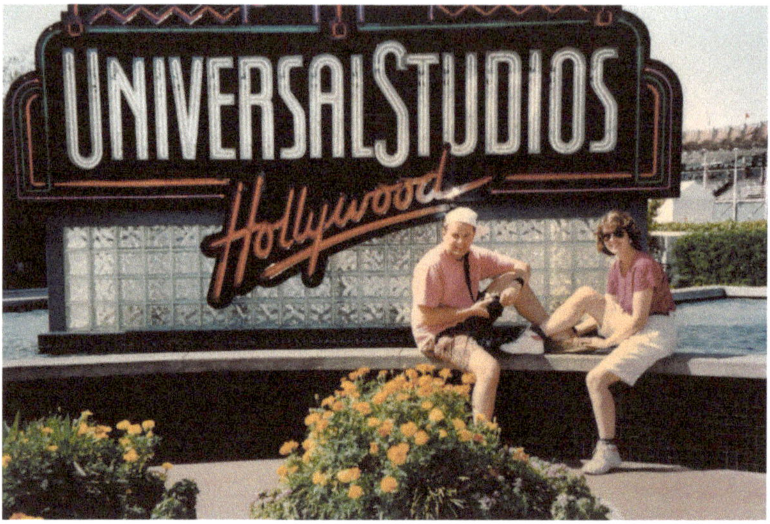

Wendy & me in Hollywood during our USA honeymoon, September 1992.

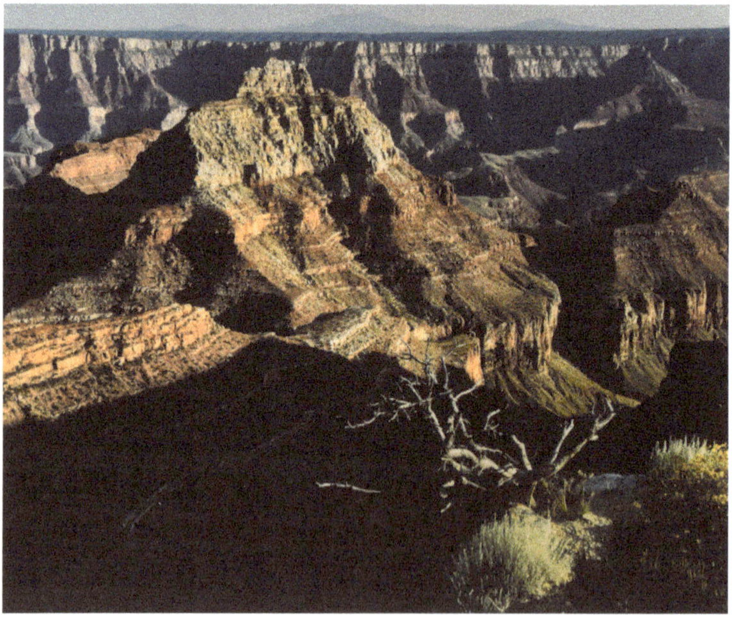

Grand Canyon south rim during our USA honeymoon, September 1992.

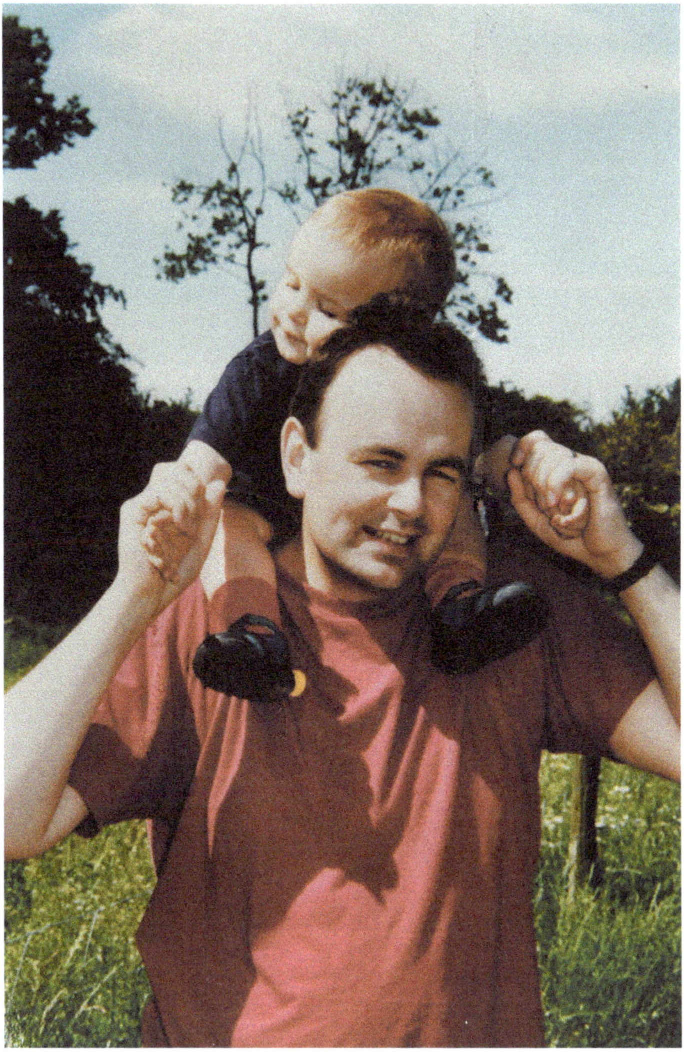

With George, aged 18 months, June 1996.

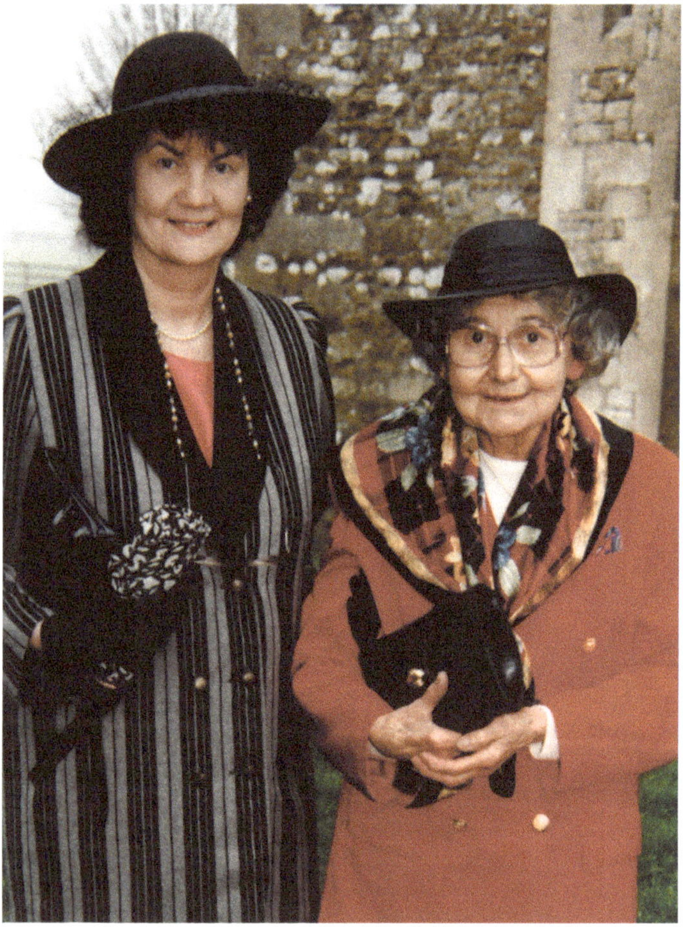

My Mum, Denise and my Grandma, Sylvia, in March 1997.

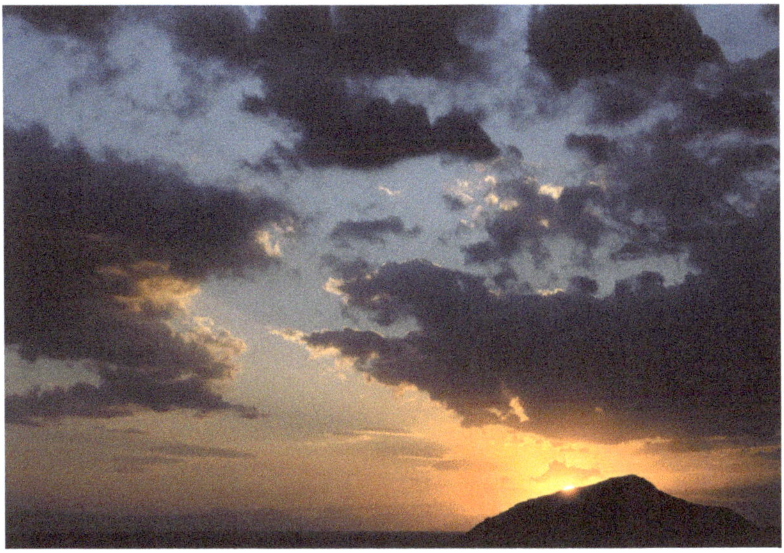

Sunset, Cape Sounion, from the Temple of Poseidon, located approximately 70 km south of Athens, 4th September 2001.

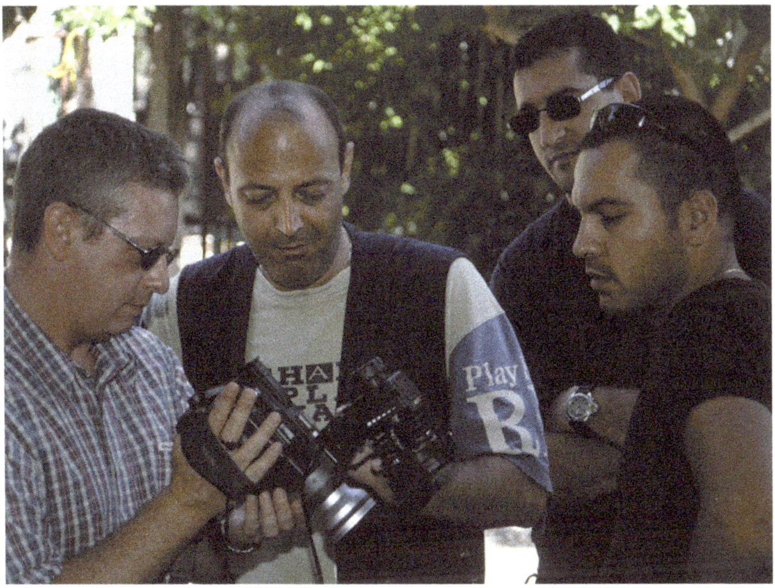

My co-trainer, Peter Goadby-Watt instructing Hellenic National Police Officers in crime scene video, Athens, Greece, June 2003.

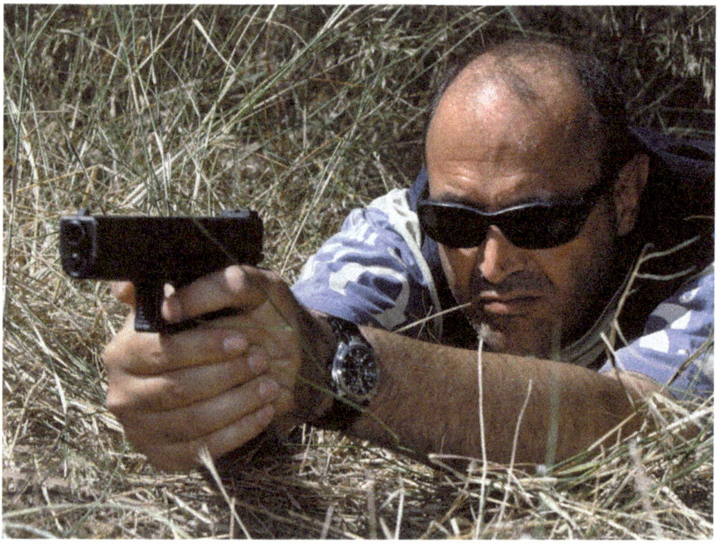

My good friend Nasos Maroudas during our forensic photography training of the Hellenic National Police in Athens, June 2003. My family and I last saw Nasos back in 2012 during a trip to London. Mysteriously, I haven't seen or heard from him since and I've had no luck contacting his family?

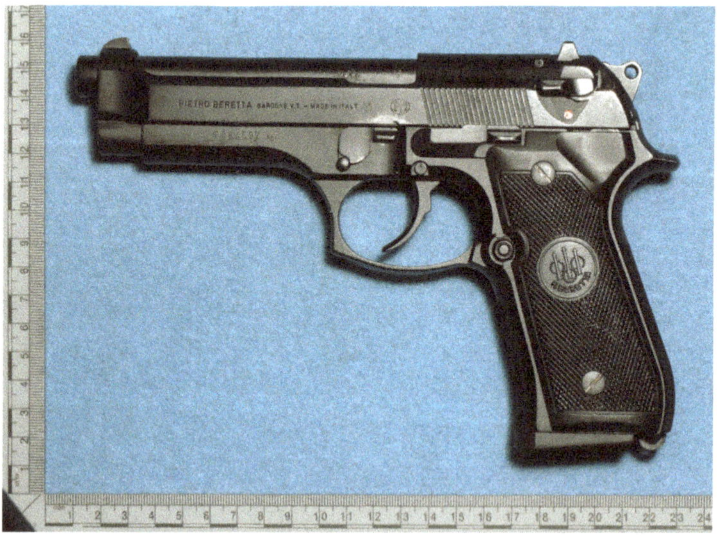

Forensic photography training - setting up a scaled firearm for photography with the identifying label removed.

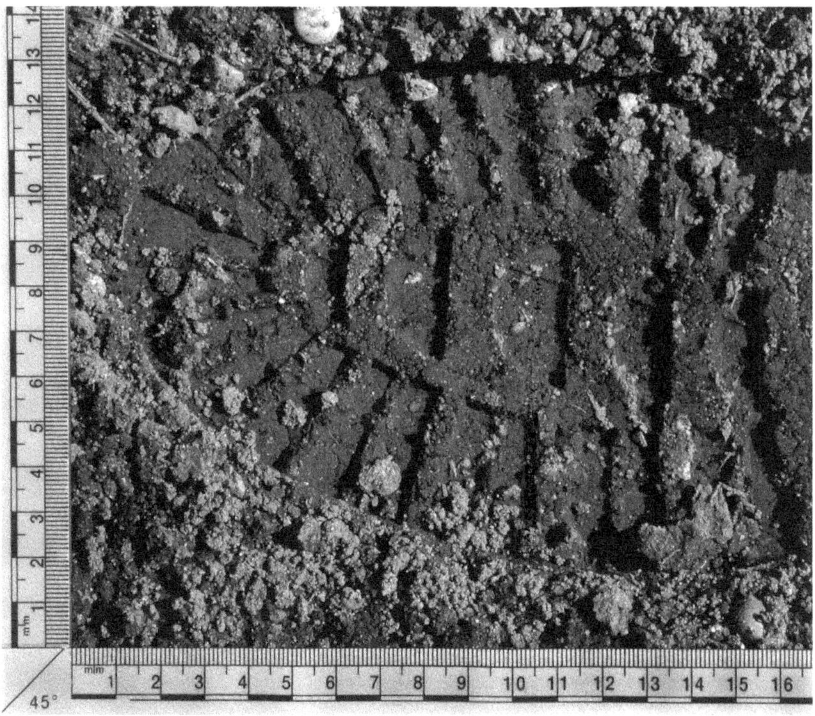

Forensic photography training - setting up a scaled shoe impression with the identifying label removed.

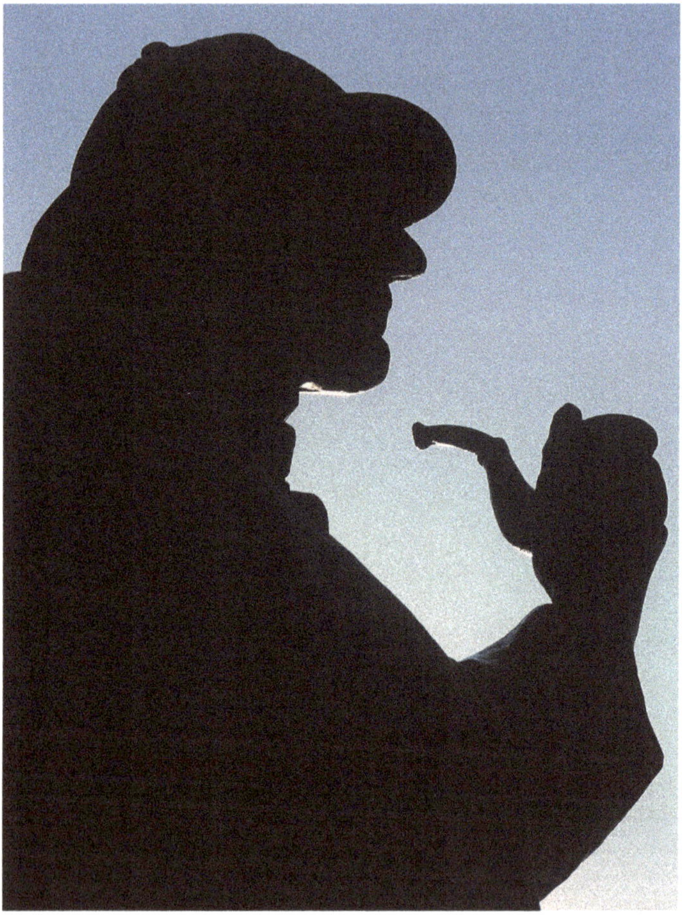

Statue of fictional private detective Sherlock Holmes, sculpted by John Doubleday in 1999, outside Baker Street Tube Station on Marylebone Rd, London, NW1.

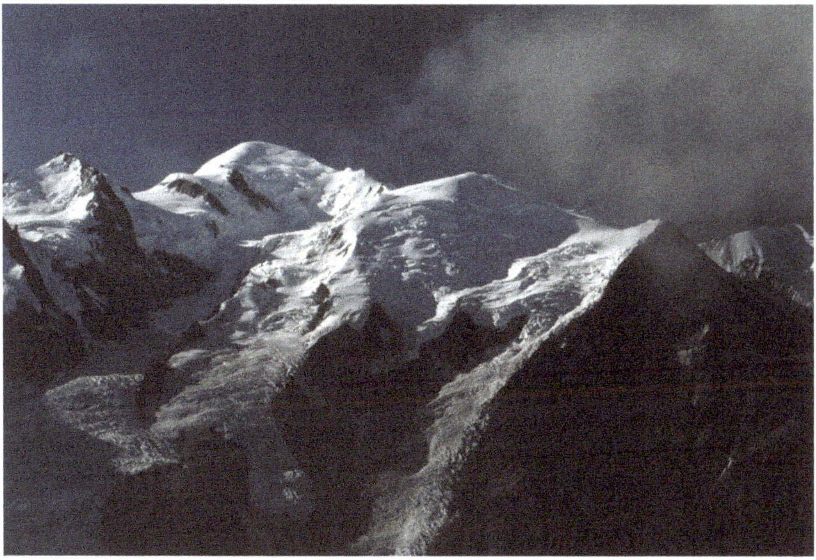

The 4810 metre peak of Mont Blanc, the highest mountain in the Alps and in Europe, July 2003.

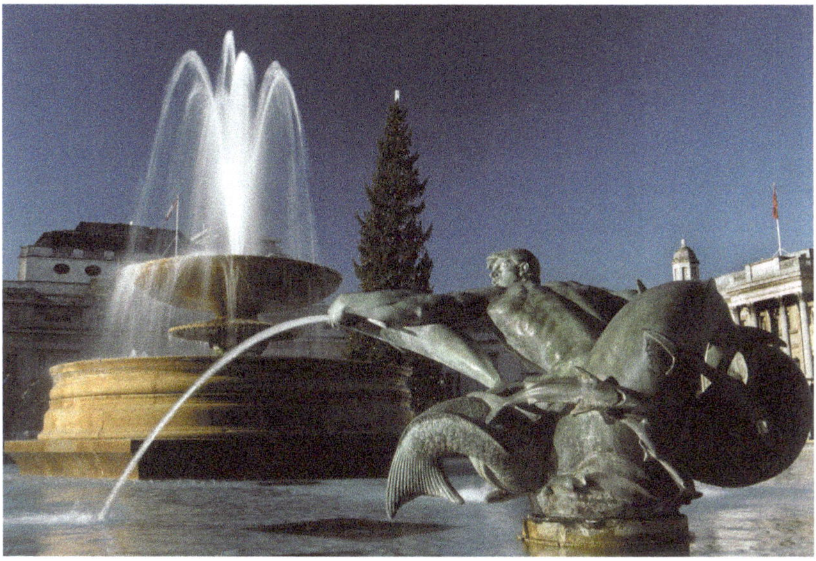

Fountain and Christmas tree in Trafalgar Square, London, December 2003. The gift of a tree has been given each year since 1947 by the people of Norway for Britain's help during the Second World War.

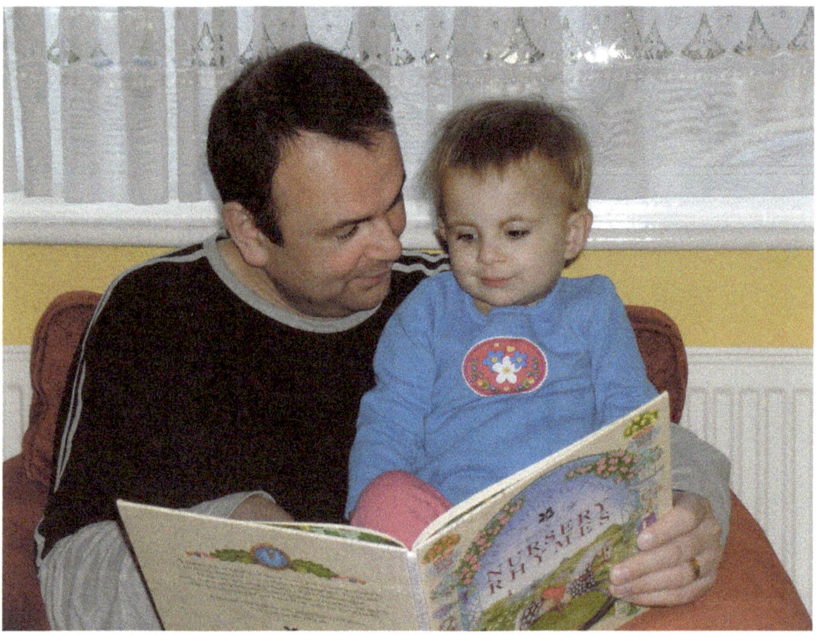

With Lauren, aged 2, at our home in Motspur Park,
Surrey, on 9th April 2004.

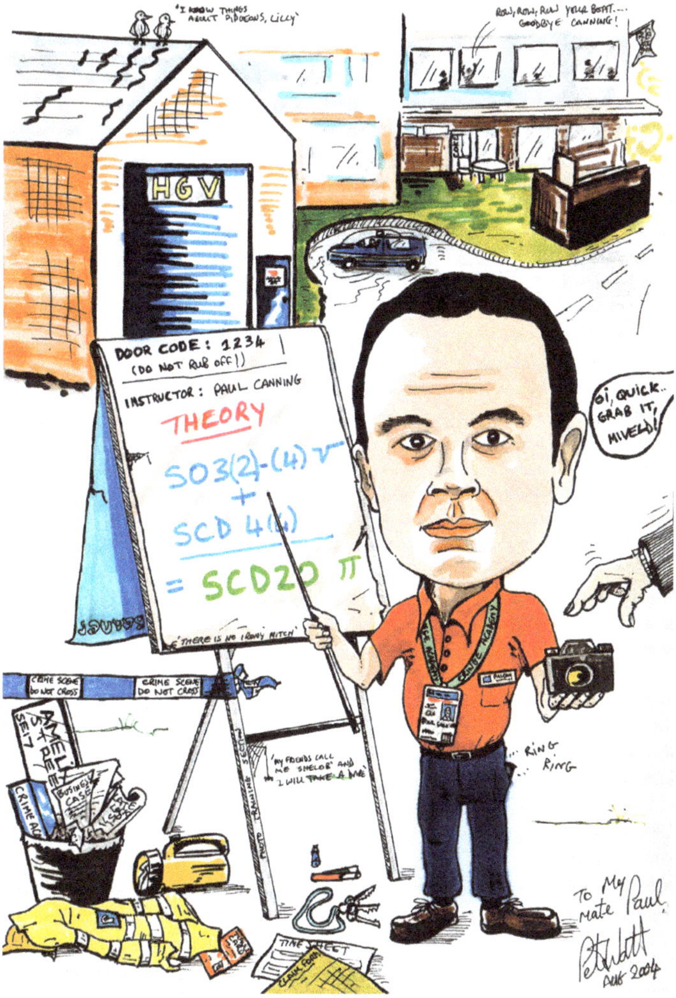

Caricature of me in my teaching attire by my friend and former Met Police colleague Peter Goadby-Watt, on the occasion of me leaving the Metropolitan Police Service for good, August 2004.

PART 4

The Lancashire Journey

CHAPTER 21

South to North: Goodbye London, Hello Lancashire August 2004

With my MPS leaving do completed and what had been our London home for 7½ years (31 Phyllis Avenue in New Malden) now an empty shell, it was off to Cornwall for an extended holiday. George, although excited about the move, had said a reluctant goodbye to his school friends at Kingston's Coombe Hill School. He was nine, Lauren was just 2½ and has no recollection of the move. Wendy and I had been house hunting up on Lancashire's Fylde coast for some months having initially looked at the Lake District. We looked at quite a few different houses in and around Poulton-le-Fylde, near Mum's. When we did finally put an offer in on a semi-detached place up on Highcross Hill, we were gazumped at the last minute. We subsequently found out that the roof later caved in on that property – did someone mention poetic justice?!

We extended our search to the pretty market town of Garstang, but nothing was available, so we turned to 'Over Wyre', where we found a lovely 3-4 bed detached house, with a separate garage and utility block in spacious grounds. We put in an offer and following a bit of agro concerning an undisputed triangular strip of land, which is now our land, the house in Preesall where we still reside was in the bag. We travelled up to the north at the end of August, staying the night at a very nice hotel in Lancaster. Unfortunately, both George and Lauren contracted food poisoning that night and were very ill indeed – not a great start! We moved into our new home the next day on September 1st 2004. A day or so later, George started Year 5 at Carter's Charity School, a mile up the road. Poor fellow had been plucked from a large, London suburban school where he was very happy and had many friends to a small rural West Lancashire school, where he was mocked for his southern accent from day one – we couldn't have got much more of a contrast if we'd tried. He was able to independently catch a school bus from the end of our road to school, very different to the car journey school in London. We were nervous at first that he'd know where to get off that bus on his way home, but he seemed to manage it ok. Sadly, George was not happy at Carters and at first we thought we'd made a big mistake. It would be some years later that he would come to understand our reasons for escaping London and the rat race, in search of a slower paced, better quality of life. Lauren, meanwhile, was oblivious to it all. When she was enrolled in nearby St. Oswald's Church play group, run by Kath P and her staff, Lauren loved it. She quickly formed a bond with a girl who was to become her best friend until the end of High School, Geena.

Wendy started her new job working on the administrative side for Blackpool Teaching Hospitals NHS Foundation Trust and I became a house husband. The plan was for me to start my own photography and tuition business, so when I wasn't ferrying Lauren to nursery or taking her in her pushchair for long walks, I was researching business start-ups and writing to every contact in my address book for private commissions. In my breaks I'd be in the back garden, which initially needed a lot doing to it. Next to the garage there was an old cattery and two small sheds sitting on a sizeable concrete patio. Adjacent to this was a greenhouse with its own power supply, running under the lawn with a pathway leading to it. Behind the greenhouse was a huge fruit and veg patch which was full of weeds and acted as a magnet to flies of different varieties. My vision was to dismantle everything, have the allotment weeded and flattened and so have this cluttered corner of the garden laid to lawn. This project was undertaken throughout September 2004 with the help of two local gardeners at minimal cost. The vision was that in a few years we'd be able to play badminton on that lawn during the summer months - a vision that I'm pleased to say came to pass. As soon as we took possession of the property, we had to call local builders in to give the entire house a thorough re-pointing of all the brickwork, due to previous land movement. This lasted a fortnight and involved dust, mess and noise by the multi-bucket load. The following year, both gable ends required similar attention.

George celebrated his tenth birthday on 21st December 2004. As a treat, I took him for a tour of the GBOAC Concorde at Manchester Airport's viewing park. We both loved it. He sat in HM The Queen and HRH The Duke of Edinburgh's seats up front and felt very important indeed. My initial impression was just how cramped the interior was. When we came to view the cockpit, it took some persuading for George to don the Captain's hat and sit in the pilot's seat to pose for me. I am happy to report that I did get my shot of a smiling George in the Captain's seat – a priceless photo for the album. George was very much into his aircraft and became an expert on the many types taking off and landing at Manchester. In fact, most modes of transport fascinated him. Prior to moving North, he and I would spend hours 'playing' on the trains and trams in London. On a Saturday I'd take him up to Waterloo from Motspur Park and then he'd decide which train we'd get back to Wimbledon. We might do this a couple of times. Whilst he loved the trains, he didn't like the roar of the high-speed trains and as they approached the platform he used to hide behind my legs, clinging on for dear life, stamping his feet up and down, but still looking until the train and the noise had faded into the distance. Come to think of it, George didn't like any loud noise, especially hissing. A kettle boiling, Gran's pressure cooker, street line painters, lawn mowers ... we even had his hearing tested but it was fine, he was just very sensitive to this type of noise! Then we'd cross over the platforms and take a tram ride out to Croydon for a coffee, hot chocolate and a slice of cake! He used to spend the entire journey sitting up looking out of the windows and I used to study his face, which clocked absolutely everything, from the station names, to other trams and the faces of people getting on and off. We enjoyed some fun times together.

Early in 2005, I booked myself onto a 'how to start your own business' course at local Blackpool and the Fylde College, whilst simultaneously doing freelance photography work, much of which involved a bit of bartering. In April 2005 I met Lance Buck, then chef and owner of 'The Minstrel's Gallery' in Lakeland's Hawkshead. He designed my first website, flyer and business cards in return for me photographing an array of dishes from The Minstrel's Gallery for marketing material. By the end of April, I started trading as 'PhotoNotion', a photography consultancy offering forensic, commercial and industrial photography as well as private one-to-one and small group practical photography tuition. The tuition side of things was very sporadic indeed whereas surprisingly, the examination of suspicious death photographs and subsequent report writing for court, kept me busy for months from late summer 2005 and throughout 2006.

24-year-old Petar Sutovic had been found dead at his mother's flat in the Serbian capital Belgrade on 27th January 2004. When questioned, no-one at the block of flats in Belgrade where Petar resided remembered seeing or hearing anything unusual on the night that he died.

Petar's mother Susan Sutovic, an Acton-based, internationally renowned human rights lawyer, grew suspicious after details of her son's death emerged and hired a raft of forensic specialists to investigate, including yours truly. Susan's first instinct was that her son had been murdered in revenge for her representing opponents of the former Serbian Milosevic regime. British and Serbian authorities were insistent that all the evidence was indicative of a narcotics overdose by a young man with a history of ill-health, following a serious accident with a lorry whilst on holiday in Israel. Susan Sutovic is adamant that her son has never been involved with drugs.

Working day and night and employing hundreds of hours studying images, I compiled a report of my findings. In addition to examining seven police scene photos, there were scene photos taken by Mrs Sutovic' housekeeper, clothing and footwear photos taken by Mrs Sutovic herself, scene photos taken by an ex Met Police scene examiner and a scene video and selective stills from this video taken by a private investigator. The initial pages of my report examined copies of the seven police scene photographs. Subsequent pages commented on other scene photographs, the video clip and the clothing and footwear. My report included comments on photographic prints as well as digital files of these prints. I compared the prints with their respective digital files and I was confident that each print was a true representation, in terms of content, of its digital file and that they hadn't been digitally manipulated. I went on to produce a supplementary report, early in the October 2005, several additional smaller reports and a huge 116-slide PowerPoint presentation, produced in both English and Serbian, utilising all the available imagery and combining graphics and animation, for use in court. I'd never compiled anything so big and complex before or since.

Allan Bayle, former Met Police colleague of mine and a highly experienced and globally respected forensic scientist and I, travelled out together to Belgrade with Susan Sutovic in January 2007 to conduct a detailed examination of Petar's flat and surrounds. During this trip, I video filmed and took a huge number of 'still' images of the exterior and interior and also from street level. My reports and detailed PowerPoint presentation (which appeared in court), I believe, speak volumes about Petar Sutovic' untimely death. I was to write:

"In my opinion, these seven police scene photographs do not show how Petar came to meet his premature and alleged unlawful death".

I was of the opinion that Petar's death was stage-managed and that he was violently assaulted, a conclusion that unbeknownst to me, had separately been reached by other forensic investigators. After more than a decade of fighting for justice, on 25th February 2016, Senior Greater London Coroner Andrew Walker ruled that Petar Sutovic had been murdered.

Petar sounded a lovely lad and I wished that I'd had the honour and privilege of meeting him in life. He was good looking, clever and with his whole exciting life ahead of him. Petar had planned to follow his mother into law, but his studies and plans were kiboshed due to a serious vehicle accident in Israel. Undeterred and still recovering from his injuries, Petar travelled to Belgrade in 2003, where he was in the process of starting a property investment company.

I won't forget this assignment in a hurry, nor the hours of intensive examination and amount of work, which kept me busy often well into the early hours. My brain would frequently be hit with multiple facts simultaneously and I'd have to stop immediately and hastily write all the points down and then highlight them all so that I wouldn't forget anything. At the risk of sounding silly, when I was in the midst of my work surrounded by all the photos, scribbled notes and highlighted post-its on my desk, I sensed Petar's presence, a friendly, calm, intelligent force with a keen mind helping to guide me and put together the pieces of what very often felt like such a gigantic jigsaw. The thought of a spiritual Petar watching over me gave me tremendous comfort, which helped spur me on.

On my journey through life I've met some truly remarkable people. I admire Susan Sutovic for her gutsy determination and indefatigable, tireless devotion to working voluminous hours to right a wrong and get justice for her son.

I was still dealing with the Petar Sutovic case, when Allan Bayle rang me in early October 2005 to inform me about another suspicious death of a young man called Jeremiah Duggan. The family of the deceased needed my help examining a considerable number of scene photographs.

Jeremiah, known as Jerry, was a young, vibrant, intelligent, British Jewish student, who was the son of divorced parents, Erica and Hugo Duggan. From 2001 until his death, Jerry was studying French and English in Paris. In the days immediately preceding his death, Jerry had been attending a youth 'cadre' school and conference, hosted by the Schiller Institute, a policy and research centre wing of the far-right group 'LaRouche'. It was run by Lyndon LaRouche, an American political activist, and many claimed it had a dangerous cult status attached to it.

On March 27th, 2003, Jerry was allegedly hit by two vehicles and died on an Autobahn outside the German city of Wiesbaden, just over 45 minutes after telephoning his mother back in England in a highly distressed state and fearing for his life. Jeremiah Joseph Duggan was only 22 and had a promising future ahead of him. The Duggan family believe that Jerry had been sucked into an extremist cult, in effect, finding himself isolated in a hornet's nest of anti-Semites and that he was killed because of it.

Following lengthy legal proceedings by the Duggan family lawyers, a new inquest was ordered into Jerry's death in May 2010 and in Germany two years later, Wiesbaden police reopened their investigation on the orders of the Frankfurt Higher Regional Court. The second UK inquest eventually took place over three days in May 2015 at North London Coroner's Court in Barnet, presided over by Coroner Andrew Walker and attended at separate times by Allan Bayle and me to give our expert testimonies.

Similar to the Petar Sutovic case, I spent many, many hours pouring over a large number of photographs and produced reports of my findings. I also produced a PowerPoint presentation using all the images and graphics with animation for use in court. The presentation was translated so I could produce a version in German.

My brief from the Duggan family was to try to establish whether the photographs provided represented a traffic accident death or a crime scene in which Jeremiah was unlawfully killed.

I therefore studied the photographs for signs of the accident (such as the condition of the road, signs of debris, car parts and broken glass) commensurate with the damage to the vehicles. I also studied the vehicles and the deceased for physical, chemical and biological traces that would point to contact between the deceased and the vehicles. I was to write:

"*In my opinion, the photographs...show an inaccurate, confusing picture of events. I do not believe that they depict how Jerry came to meet his premature death. I believe that it is possible that Jerry lost his life elsewhere and was subsequently placed at this scene*".

Again, unbeknownst to me Allan Bayle and other eminent forensic scientists had already arrived at the same conclusion, i.e. that Jerry's supposed accident scene was stage-managed. Unfortunately, despite all the experts' reports, the Coroner disagreed with this stage-managed scenario. Andrew Walker, found my conclusions completely implausible when I delivered my evidence back in May 2015 to a hushed gathering of Duggan family, legal representatives and members of the press in the first-floor courtroom at Barnet Coroners Court in north London. Coroner Andrew Walker went on to deliver a narrative verdict in "totally rejecting this was a suicide". The outcome at coroner's court wasn't the 'unlawful killing' verdict that the Duggan family had been hoping for, however suicide was ruled out and the narrative verdict (an inquest verdict that records the factual circumstances of a death) left room for further investigation.

Meanwhile Jerry's mother and father, Erica and Hugo and their family keep searching for the truth. They simply want answers, justice for their son and closure. My work on the Jerry Duggan investigation is memorable not only because of the complexity of the case but also due to the large number of images that I had to work with. On top of that, the subsequent long hours spent examining, report writing and designing a presentation in both English and German, in addition to the planning and preparation that I put into delivering my expert testimony at Coroner's Court.

No person should ever have to endure even a tiny fraction of the turmoil that Susan Sutovic, Erica Duggan, their families, or indeed any family losing a loved one – especially under suspicious circumstances, have gone through. As King Théoden said in Tolkien's 'Lord of the Rings: The Two Towers' film (2002), as he nonchalantly tossed the pretty, white flower, simbelmynë on to the grave of Théodred, his son and heir: "No parent should have to bury their child".

Jerry was interred in Highgate Cemetery, Petar is in Gunnersbury Cemetery.

Rest in peace then, Petar Milos Sutovic and Jeremiah Joseph Duggan.

Let justice prevail, lads. Always thinking of you...

CHAPTER 22

Getting into Medical Photography...Eventually

When 2006 was ushered in, I still very much had my hands full with both the Sutovic and Duggan suspicious death cases. These were quickly followed by several similar, smaller cases working for national newspapers, where grieving parents had lost their children under suspicious circumstances abroad. Back in late 2004, my father had been diagnosed with oesophageal cancer at the age of 82 and doctors had given him between twelve and eighteen months to live. I hadn't spoken to him since 1999 (after I found out some hard hitting truths about how he'd lived his life and his treatment of others) – he just didn't exist in my life and visa versa. Now it was early February 2006 and I had just got off the phone with Mum. Dad was feeling very unwell and had called his own ambulance. That was on the morning of Thursday 2nd. Mum, despite everything and as dutiful as ever, went into hospital every day to visit him. Over the weekend, I learned that Dad didn't have long left. His heart was very weak and as is typical of many dying patients, many of his last few hours left on this earth were spent sleeping. Vicky, Kate and I were estranged from Dad because of his diabolical physical, verbal and psychological abuse of all three of us, so we kept our distance and didn't visit him. Nevertheless, we asked Mum to keep us all updated on his end of life journey. On the Monday 6th February, Mum phoned me. "Paul – he's dead", I heard Mum say abruptly. I had been expecting it, so it wasn't a shock at all. Finally, the troublesome old man was out of our lives for good and the sense of relief I felt was immense. Still, out of duty and for Mum's benefit, I travelled immediately to Blackpool Victoria Hospital to what is currently Ward 7 on the first floor. Mum was sitting waiting for me in the visitors' room. I asked nursing staff if I could go in and see Dad. So, there I was, looking at my father now in repose minus his dentures. I approached his enormous right ear and in hushed tones spoke to the now, very much dead, not so nice in life, Doctor Jim Canning.

Bizarrely, I gave him a bollocking for making the family's lives so miserable. Dr Jim, for his part, just lay there and took it, not uttering a sound. When I was finished giving out, I simply turned around, left that little side room and didn't look back. There was nothing more to be said. I needed to get that off my chest. On my way out of the hospital, I dropped the barely untouched, half bottle of Bell's whiskey that Dad had been hiding in his bedside locker into the nearest bin. We had the rest of Dad's belongings in a large bag.

My father was gone. I stopped and thought. My father was gone. He was no more and we were free. I wanted to cry, just out of relief, but there were no tears to be had. I was just hit by the sudden finality of it all and a weighty burden carried for so long, had been lifted from many a shoulder that day. Dad was academically brilliant as a medical doctor and any consultancy or professorship would and should have been a walk in the park for someone of his intellect. But Dad squandered his chances and spent his lifetime making a misery of other peoples' lives. The real pisser is that Dad could have really achieved, made a huge difference in the world and we would have all been so proud of him, but for whatever reason, he chose a different path. My father threw away a precious, God-given life and in the end died a drunkard, engulfed by cancer in a lonely hospital side room, ironically located above what is now my office - spurned and unloved.

Over the next few weeks, in between work on the Sutovic and Duggan jobs, I'd pop round to what was now Mum's house in Victoria Road, Poulton to help clean and tidy the house. For cathartic reasons, I started in the attic, spring cleaning, working my way downwards. Vicky and Kate joined us to plan the funeral, which was to be a quiet affair at Carleton Crematorium. Afterwards, just the four of us went to the Squirrel pub in Bispham for a lovely roast lunch. It was over this meal that Mum mischievously beamed at us and declared, "I'm the merry widow!", which we all thought was priceless. The irony, however, was that Mum's immediate merriment and sense of freedom was to be short lived. Dad's ashes had barely cooled, when I heard Vicky from within Dad's study say, "Oh my God!" We all came running in to see what the matter was. Vicky was holding up a document she'd found among Dad's papers ... "You know what he's gone and done....?" Our bitter and twisted father had seemingly changed his will at the last minute (a month before his death), not only cutting the three siblings out of any inheritance (no real surprises there), but leaving a shed load of money to dear 'Suzanne Nobles', a neighbour who lived opposite! She had apparently been coming in daily to check on 'lonely' Dr Jim, share his whiskey and no doubt sweet talk him especially when she knew that she was coming into money! That blasted woman had a nerve and even turned up to Dad's funeral. Mum and Vicky later invited Nobles over to try and persuade her to back down over the will, but greed got the better of this not-so-nice neighbour and she was having none of it. She wanted her full share and was prepared to fight for it. She wasn't interested in hearing about what the real Jim Canning had been like, the cruel acts he'd forced on his wife and children and that his wife never had the courage to leave him for fear of what he would do ...

Having suffered at the hands of this man for so many years, it was devastating to feel that Mum wasn't even going to benefit financially after his death. As bitter as the pill was to swallow, there was nothing more to be done than to put the unpleasant matter in the hands of the solicitors and let them thrash it out. We all collectively finished tidying Mum's house, but we couldn't sell anything as it was now part of the estate, which of course was being contested. Legal arguments continued for almost three years and went right up to the wire with Mum and her barrister about to walk into court. A last-minute deal was reached early in 2009. Mum was forced to sell 27 Victoria Road to downsize, she had to pay all the legal fees and that repugnant neighbour, Nobles, came away feeling very pleased with herself, netting around '30 bags'! (£30k). Mum was finally released from all the worry and stress and moved to a bungalow at 90 Highcross Road, just up the hill from Baines School in February 2009. Only now, freed from previous horrors, was she able to live out her days in contented happiness. 27 Victoria Road, the house that Vicky, Kate and I grew up in under Dad's authoritarian rule, was sold to a local builder, who largely demolished the pre-war dormer bungalow and built an even bigger version with a huge extension on the same site, whilst keeping the outhouses and garage block. It made for a strange contrast of old and new. In mid-February 2006, Grandma had been admitted to St. George's Hospital, Tooting with heart failure and I was fearing the worst. I'd just booked a mini break for myself, flying out from Heathrow to Athens to see my good friend Nasos and his wife Violetta, but was ready to cancel my Greek visit at a moment's notice. In the event, it wasn't necessary. I went to visit Grandma in hospital and I couldn't believe my eyes when she beamed at me as I walked onto her ward to give her a hug. After a few days, Grandma defied all the doctors by being well enough to go home!

In March 2006, I first met my colleague and friend Mick Gardiner from Gardiner Associates Training and Research at his fire investigation training ground in Wethersfield, Essex. More of my GATR affiliation a little later on. That same month I had concerns for my business. It became worryingly quiet and further, I had neglected the advertising and marketing because I had been deep in work. To bolster the coffers and out of necessity I took a part time job at a local supermarket, working at the very busy fuel station in Thornton-Cleveleys. This not only involved serving customers, but topping up stock and the inevitable cleaning. The manageress was a no nonsense lady with the unusual name of 'Senga', which I'd never heard of. I soon learned that Senga was actually Agnes spelled backwards and woe betide anyone who ever called her Agnes to her face, as she had always hated her real name! I was very tempted by the piss take, but resisted – just, leaving the supermarket with my testicles intact and unable (thankfully) to sing soprano! The fuel station was damn good retail experience and as I've intimated, I needed the work out of necessity.

Remembering back to our holiday to Cornwall in summer the previous year, 2005, I was to experience the first in a series of stings. I was halfway up a ladder at Val's in Wadebridge, trimming the sizeable garden hedge with a set of electric clippers, when I sliced clean through a wasps' nest that was hidden in the depths of the conifer leaves. All hell broke loose as hundreds of seriously pissed off wasps emerged en-mass from the fractured nest and chased yours truly, who didn't need to be told twice, to run! I jumped off the top of the ladder, threw down the clippers and bolted towards the conservatory with the angry insect mob in hot pursuit and who were clearly baying for blood. I just remember that awful sound of incessant buzzing in both ears as at least 5 of the buggers had found their mark just as I had got inside to safety. Val introduced me to the age-old remedy of vinegar. I'd been stung on my face, neck, shoulder and chest, but following liberal application, the acetic acid contained in the vinegar effectively neutralised the wasp stings! I might have effused an odour, strongly resembling the inside of 'Barnys' our local take away chippy, but within 15 minutes the wasp stings were no longer bothering me!

Blow me down, during our summer Cornish break in 2006, I was stung again! Whilst swimming with the family off Hayle Beach,

I suffered the consequences of disturbing a 'lesser Weever fish' with my bare foot. Retribution was immediate and very painful. I had just come out of the sea and was walking in the shallows, when I felt a sharp sting and immediately thought I'd trodden on a piece of glass. My relief was short lived, when I looked down to survey the non-existent damage of jagged cut and blood gushing out, only to see a little red mark on the sole of my right foot. The pain intensified exponentially. The lifeguards had already spotted me, the tell-tale sign of a weever fish victim being a swimmer or surfer hobbling up the beach! By the time I'd reached the lifeguard station I was in agony – they already had the kettle on, but not for a cuppa! Treatment consisted of dunking my foot in a vat of the hottest water bearable for half an hour to draw out the venom. The pain quickly subsided. Karma prevailed when shortly afterwards a fellow beach goer declared they'd found my weever fish…and slotted the bastard!

The venomous weever fish is extremely well camouflaged, lurks in the shallows and typically attacks before and after low tide. This sneaky git had thrust one of its needle-sharp venomous barbs into my foot and the pain and discomfort (which can last up to 24 hours) is not something that I ever wish to repeat. Needless to say, I avoided further contact with this dreaded fish by investing in a pair of wet suit shoes.

Ironically, a few weeks after returning from Cornwall, and with my weever fish experience still very much in my mind, I heard the sad news that world famous naturalist, zoologist, conservationist and TV personality Steve Irwin, had been attacked by a short-tail stingray, whilst filming at Batt Reef, Queensland. Multiple strikes from its poisonous serrated barb at the end of the tail from this flattened, diamond shaped fish, punctured Steve's heart.

Steve was an immensely popular, much admired Australian zookeeper, a charismatic, yet sometimes controversial personality. He gained world-wide fame for the TV series 'The Crocodile Hunter'. Steve was also known for his catchphrase 'crikey!', his high level of exuberance and enthusiasm whilst presenting in his broad Australian accent, donned in his signature khaki shorts and as someone who introduced many to the excitement and wonders of the natural world. Steve Irwin sadly succumbed to his stingray injuries and died on 4th September 2006 aged just 44. His amazing work is continued by his widow Terri and children, Bindi and Robert, Bindi's husband Chandler and Australia Zoo Director and Steve's friend, Wes Mannion and their staff.

In early September, George started secondary school at Saint Aidans, conveniently situated a mile from our house. Then almost immediately, we congregated at the Ritz for afternoon tea in London, all dolled up to the nines to celebrate Wendy and Simon's Mum's 80th birthday on 8th September – a wonderful occasion. Just before my birthday a handful of days later, we lost Des Tweats who had been battling a form of leukaemia for over three years. He was only 65. Des was more than a family friend – he was an inspiration to me. I used to work for him at the newsagents on the Breck in Poulton from age 13 until I was about 19 and latterly, his second wife became very good friends with Mum. Above all, I admired and respected Des so much. He and I used to bear hug in the middle of Poulton, which goes a hell of a long way to explaining what Des embodied - everything that says 'kind, warm-hearted, considerate, friendly, funny, and thoroughly likeable bloke'. His loss affected me deeply and it was sorely felt in the local community. His legacy lives on through his two wonderful grown up children, Mark, Emma and all the grandchildren.

Less than a month later, on 8th October 2006, I was at home when my mobile phone rang. It was Mum's brother, my Uncle Graham. He never phoned me, so I knew instinctively that it was bad news. I'll never forget his words as long as I live: "I'm afraid you've lost your Grandma....." I was devastated and in tears for ages. I'd been lucky enough to reach the age of forty-three and still have both my mother and my Grandmother living. I was also lucky to have flown down to London with George to see Grandma the very day before she died, would you believe. My sister Vicky had visited her in the afternoon and became the last relative to see her alive. We had no indication that Grandma wasn't well. She was quite simply a treasure and she and I shared a close bond. Vicky had driven her up to Poulton in the July for a rest and she stayed with Mum at 27 Victoria Road. Almost immediately, she had a bit of a 'funny turn' with erratic breathing and we had to call the doctor. Yet, she rallied and recovered from that and in the same visit came over to see our house, which she loved.

Grandma's funeral service at London Road Cemetery, Mitcham on 25th October 2006, was followed by interment in my Grandad's plot. I based my eulogy for Grandma on two of my favourite poems of all time by one Harry Harbord Morant, soldier, war poet and convicted criminal! Immortalised in the 1980 film 'Breaker Morant' (starring Edward Woodward, another one of my favourite actors),

Morant was a First Lieutenant with the Bushveldt Carbineers. Dubbed 'Scapegoats of the Empire' the film is a poignant Australian drama concerning the 1902 court Martial of Lieutenants Morant, Handcock and Witton. These three were accused of murdering a captured enemy and an unarmed civilian in the Northern Transvaal during the second Anglo-Boer War, which led to Morant and Handcocks' execution by firing squad!

I recall segments from two of Lieutenant Morant's poems from memory, all the more remarkable as they were allegedly penned the night before his dawn execution!:

"The night's a trifle chilly, and the stars are very bright
A heavy dew is falling, but the fly is rigged alright.
You may rest your bones 'til morning, then if you chance to wake,
Give me a call about the time that daylight starts to break..."

(From 'Westward Ho')

"It really ain't the place nor time to reel off rhyming diction,
But yet we'll write a final rhyme while waiting crucifixion.
For we bequeath a parting tip of sound advice for such men,
Who come across in transport ships to polish off the Dutchmen –
If you encounter any Boers, you really must not loot 'em,
And if you wish to leave these shores, for pity's sake don't shoot 'em!
Let's toss a bumper down our throat before we pass to Heaven,
And toast: The trim-set petticoat we leave behind, in Devon."

(From 'Butchered to make a Dutchman's Holiday')

My eulogy to my beloved Grandma, therefore, based loosely on the above powerful, poignant and often witty poetry ran as follows:

Ode to Grandma (Sylvia Lily Meyer: 18/12/1912 – 8/10/2006)

'It seems a trifle silly to reel off rhyming verse
Yet I'll write these simple lines whilst waiting for the hearse

When the sun is sinking and your mind from cares set free
What a blessing how refreshing is a cup of Grandma's tea

Grandma, Grandma now that you've passed
Resting in peace – free from pain at last

You'd sing at your old piano you used to fondly play
And I'd stand there at the front room door, to hear your music all day
Take your pick……Brahms, Mendelson or Liszt
Ah! You'll be sadly missed
'Fudgy', they used to call her in her salad days gone by
She'd always have a yarn to tell that'd make you laugh or nearly cry

I remember her smile and her lively wit
Reminiscing in her chair by a fire that was always lit
In her Hampshire brogue, she couldn't half jaw
She had me in stitches more than once and falling on the floor
I could listen to her for hours – I always wanted to hear more
You know, she once declared with a saucy grin – and I'll swear it was no sin
That the 1st of May was 'Kick Bum Day'!

Grandma hated mud and dirt – a pinny she would wear
She was always neat and tidy with lovely wavy hair
She'd polish her brass with enviable pride
That you almost felt obliged to pay her, before you stepped inside

I spent many happy times at that Bruce Road flat
A friendly welcome you'd be assured – and that's a matter of fact
An array of homemade fare, baked with loving care
Steak pie, allotment veggies then loganberry tart with custard, tasty meals – nothing lacked

She also adored her M&S – for she'd settle for nothing less

Now Sylvie worried a lot – she had funny old ways
Never bothered me, 'cause she was simply my Grandma – lovely as always

'PG tips' was her favourite brew
But then that's something most of us here, well - knew
Never made in haste
And gladly received for its welcome taste

So when that sun is sinking
And you might just be thinking

Perhaps a cup of tea you're drinking – (ok, or something stronger if you'd prefer!)
Let's knock a bumper down our throats and toast Sylvia Lily who's now in Heaven
That kind and gentle, wonderful, old girl – you know the one at 37

With fond affection, we wave 'Goodbye' in sad farewell
But not too sad, because we can tell
That Sylvie is with Harry now in some other place, much higher
So, let's look back with love and laughs and smiles...... and just thank God, for Sylvie Meyer!'

As I stood by the open grave, the reality of the sombre occasion really hit me. I tossed a handful of earth onto my Grandmother's now lowered coffin, as a glint of a reflection caught my eye – the sheen from the brass name plate. I followed this with a smile as I threw in ... a tea bag, which I know Grandma would have found very funny. Grandma Meyer will always be remembered for her lively wit, smile, warmth, kindness and generosity of spirit. She was held in very high esteem. My 'textbook' Grandma was a one-off and I not only thanked God for her, but I was also fortunate to have her in my life for so long.

Just before the funeral, I went for an interview at Marks and Spencer outlet store in Fleetwood (which has since sadly closed down). Part of the interview process required me to select clothing for a middle-aged woman for an evening formal function and then a young lady for a 21st birthday bash. Having researched beforehand, I did just fine and got offered the job. Like the fuel station, it was part time hours and involved 'Living Our Customer First' – the M&S motto at that time, which I not only fully embraced but relished. I served customers, dealt with stock, cleaned and tidied. It was great experience. I got to work with and meet some fun people and the staff discount helped! With tape measure around my neck and a dozen, little black dresses swishing rhythmically and draped carefully over my arm, I used to purposely mock mince through that store with so much hilarity that sometimes I thought I was on the set of '70's sitcom 'Are You Being Served?' The expert forensic photographer was leading a double life as an out of the closet expert garment folder and knicker and bra packer! I was to work at Marks and Sparks for just over a year until the following October 2007. Again, it was a job taken out of necessity, to bolster the sheckles.

About the most memorable event of 2006 on the UK stage was our monarch, Queen Elizabeth II turning 80 on 21st April. Film releases of 2006 included Daniel Craig's first outing as 007 James Bond in 'Casino Royale', and which also starred Eva Green and Mads Mikkelsen as the main baddy, Le Chiffre. There was also 'Holiday' starring Cameron Diaz, Jude law, Jack Black and Kate Winslet, which was very watchable. Among the pop releases were 'I Don't Feel Like Dancin' by the Scissor Sisters and 'Patience' by Take That. Notable 2006 deaths included the airline entrepreneur, Sir Freddie Laker, scandal-riddled politician John Profumo and cricketer Fred Trueman.

I was doing OK workwise in 2007. In addition to Marks and Sparks, I had quite a few commercial photography jobs coming in. Among them, was an exciting challenge - undertaking all the photography for a local Blackpool school, St. Mary's Catholic College (now Academy), for their new school prospectus. I spent a number of hours over quite a few visits, which stretched into 2008, accumulating some very pleasing imagery indeed. This included two young pupils examining a globe in geography (which made the prospectus front cover), an older female pupil juggling (I was particularly pleased with the degree of motion blur on the coloured juggling balls); chemistry experiments, drama, sports, art, cookery, needlework and a group of GCSE female dancers photographed as a mirror reflection, which worked really well. I also photographed the new college chapel. Happy memories of a great assignment on St. Walburga's Road – and all on the doorstep!

In October 2007, our family flew out to Alicante on the invitation of Wendy's uncle, Nigel Schollick. This was still all part of Val's birthday celebrations with all the family present. Val and Simon flew from London, but back in 2007, Blackpool Airport was very much open to commercial traffic and ran daily flights to and from Alicante. It was a popular tourist destination in itself, but of course you've got Benidorm, another Brit tourist magnet, just up the coast. The idea of driving leisurely to our local airport at Squires Gate, parking in a side street with unlimited free parking and simply walking across the road into departures was very convenient. You used to be able to fly from Blackpool to London Stansted in barely three quarters of an hour – another very handy service. Unfortunately, rather than expand Blackpool Airport the decision was made to close it instead, which was a great shame and in my opinion represented a missed opportunity for some potentially exciting local investment. So, the

Canning family rendezvous was at Alicante airport with Val and Simon, prior to picking up a hire car that would take us the 64 kilometres to Nigel and his wife, Barbara Jane's Calpe villa, aptly named Villa Barbara. Calpe is a beautiful, tranquil South East Spanish haven, where the Alboran and Balearic seas intertwine. To the north east is Valencia, to the east is the island of Ibiza and many kilometres south across the water is the African continent and specifically, Algiers.

Nigel, three years younger than his sister Val, was the epitome of gentlemanly kindness. Nigel had videoed our wedding in 1992 and had made ornately carved shelves for George and Lauren (complete with the children's names on) when they were babies. On the occasion of his 70th birthday, he'd invited the entire family to enjoy a weekend break in a plush Bournemouth hotel – all expenses paid. On the last evening we were all summoned to Nigel and Barbara Jane's suite and treated to the surprise of our lives. As a gift, Nigel gave us each an envelope containing a wodge of monetary notes, the exact sum being your age times ten. This was an unusual, extremely generous gesture – but that was Nigel. Wendy, George and I headed back to our home in New Malden, Surrey uplifted and richer than when we set off. You occasionally read of things like this happening around the world, but to experience it as a recipient was just lovely.

So, you can imagine how crestfallen we suddenly became, when Val told us at Alicante airport the awful news that her brother had been diagnosed with terminal bone cancer and had been given just twelve to eighteen months to live. In addition to celebrating Val's 80th, getting the whole family together now took on a much more poignant meaning. However, far from melancholic depression, we all enjoyed ourselves, including our host – there was swimming, table tennis and badminton matches, walks, meals and sunbathing. We also had a fun excursion to Mundomar marine animal park in Benidorm. Nigel and I had several deep and meaningful conversations over the course of our stay. It was during one of these talks that, without warning, he offered me, point blank, £5000 to pump some life into my business. If I had confidence that the money could pay dividends in mega quick time, I would have accepted what amounted to yet another generous and totally unselfish gesture. But I humbly declined as I couldn't guarantee I'd be able to pay him back and I remember Nigel's face as he was trying to read me. He said I was very brave to turn him down and that not many people would have had the courage to do so. I know that Nigel respected my decision – but again, what a lovely thing to do.

With news of his cancer diagnosis, I knew that my time in Spain wouldn't be all relaxing. I decided to turn the break into a self-imposed busman's holiday. I was almost overcome with a sense of urgency to photograph and video Nigel surrounded by his family, who absolutely adored him. There were posed groups and impromptu shots galore. In my mind, this brief took on the air of a wedding photography assignment as one by one, I mentally check boxed each crucial image. These were the most poignant family photographs that I've ever taken. For Christmas 2007, Nigel's last Christmas, Wendy and I compiled a photo book with all the images that I had garnered on the Spain holiday. As a present, we gave a copy to Nigel and Barbara Jane and one each to their two daughters, Nicola and Diana. Evocative photographs, especially of loved ones, can become invaluable keepsakes and as we all know can gain intrinsic value over time. To have both daughters reduced to tears on the phone over that Christmas is something I'll always remember – and it really got to me. It has been said that a photograph paints a thousand words. The realisation that my album of plates had not only been well received but had touched the hearts of several families, served as a reminder of sometimes how pivotal photography can be as a powerful medium of communication. The kind, wise and highly respected gentleman who was Nigel Schollick quietly exited the stage just a week before the following Christmas in 2008. He was still young at 78. Nigel's memory and invaluable life lessons live on.

Memorable 2007 events in the UK included Tony Blair stepping down as Prime Minister on 27 June and handing the reins over to Gordon Brown. When the latest 'Primus Inter Pares' incumbent announced his new cabinet the following day, Jacqui Smith became the first female Home Secretary. Notable films included 'Sweeney Todd: The Demon Barber of Fleet Street', starring Johnny Depp and Helena Bonham Carter and 'Harry Potter and the Order of the Phoenix', starring Daniel Radcliffe, Emma Watson and Rupert Grint. My favourite television programme by far over 2006-2007 was 'Life on Mars' starring John Simm and Philip Glenister. Among the many famous people we lost during 2007 were: broadcaster and journalist Magnus Magnusson, actors John Inman and Gareth Hunt, author and television presenter Phil Drabble (famous for presenting the sheep dog trials programme 'One Man and his Dog') and comedian, Bernard Manning.

For George's 13th birthday on 21st December 2007, his Godparents John and Renee very kindly treated him to a flying lesson. It was a bitterly cold, but beautifully clear winter's day – sunshine and bright blue sky as Simon and I buckled ourselves up in the rear of the Cessna 172S four-seater at Blackpool's Squires Gate Airport. Wendy, Val and Lauren stayed in the hanger cradling a hot drink whilst we were carried up into the sky. Following a full safety briefing and check list by the pilot, George, a veteran of so many computer flight simulations, was now enacting this for real as he guided our little plane expertly to the end of the runway. His take-off was textbook and he flew in a wide circle over the Fylde coast, which encompassed a view of our house. The visibility was perfect and I managed to take a few photos. It was a thrilling experience and one I won't forget in a hurry, let alone George.

In late November 2007, I went for an interview in Manchester for a permanent, full time post as medical photographer with a biopharmaceutical company specialising in developing drugs to prevent and reduce scarring. The company called 'Renovo' was based in the Manchester Incubator Building, Grafton Street off Oxford Road and was located opposite the Manchester Royal Infirmary. Following a successful interview with the then Head of Medical Photography, Jo and the Principal Photographer, Kevin (who I had worked with in my Met Police days), I was offered the job with an early January 2008 start date. The only downside was the three plus hours travelling to and from. It wasn't so bad in the summer months but in the depths of successive bitterly cold winters, standing on a freezing Poulton-le-Fylde station at six in the morning day after day, was no joke. I joined a predominantly young, vibrant, professional, female team of medical photographers who were mostly in their late 20s or early 30s. In Jo's words, I was "dead old". At 44 I was definitely the 'father of the house'. Until that point, I hadn't considered myself to be old, never mind 'dead old' and the thought of appearing grandadesque quite amused me. I think that Jo would have preferred someone much younger, but to give her her dues, she did hire me. Jo and I were never destined to be best buddies, but I liked her a lot, we got on amicably for the whole duration and I respected her position as team manager. I also got on well with everyone else in the team, particularly Zoe, whose invaluable help and support lifted my photoshop skills to the level required to complete much of the complex graphics required for my uni coursework. Nice one Zoe!

Renovo was set up in 2000 by CEO Professor Mark Ferguson and his wife, Dr Sharon O'Kane, Executive Director of R&D. With the set up came an extensive leveraging of scientific knowledge to help develop multiple product candidates in scar prevention and reduction. The company was floated in 2006 and in June 2007 formalised an agreement with Shire Plc from Ireland to develop & commercialise 'Juvista' (human recombinant transforming growth factor beta-3). Renovo won a European Biotechnica Award early in October 2007. A major criterion in selection of the award winner being marketability, relevance, impact of product & existence of a potentially successful marketing concept & strategy.

UK and European clinical trials at multiple sites looked very promising with signs pointing to significantly reduced scarring in the skin. The financial potential of this one drug alone was enormous with a multi-million-dollar market of unmet medical need. But Renovo wasn't just reliant on Juvista. As a biopharmaceutical company, it was developing a portfolio of drugs to prevent and reduce scarring at multiple body sites that included the skin, eyes, nerves, internal organs, tendons and ligaments and to accelerate wound healing. The company's aim was not only to be world leader but to be the first to market in the United States and Europe with a pharmaceutical drug to prevent and reduce scarring. Renovo's three other lead drugs were 'Juvidex', designed to improve subsequent scarring especially in eye drop form to target prevention and reduction of corneal scarring. 'Prevascar' was designed to modulate inflammatory response resulting in an improvement in subsequent scarring. It was also being investigated for its potential to enhance regeneration of peripheral nerves following injury or trauma. 'Zesteem' was designed to accelerate wound healing in the skin - re-epithelialisation following surgery or wounding.

My day to day job involved taking standardised images of clinical trial patients who would be randomised and 'blinded' (injected at the wound site with either placebo or drug). The images would then be uploaded to a database, archived and entries strictly controlled on multiple spreadsheets. Long before the standardised image taking, the protocol for a particular trial would be created following strict guidelines:

- Formulate an image identification table
- Arrange camera equipment and technical issues, right down to all the relevant camera settings being glued and taped into position
- The relevant camera frame would contain the image label and 'white spot' for correct colour analysis (the size of camera

frame dependant on size, number and spacing of scars being photographed)

- Design the case report file pages
- Undertake training and write standard operating procedures
- Take images at set time points (e.g. day 1, week 1, month 1 etc.) and upload to a secure image management system (IMS) database
- Images processed by the Image Processing team

Independent external panels would then view the processed images and the results of the panel scoring would go to the statisticians. Although the photographic team quality controlled its own images, by providing in effect written feedback on each other's images, as previously aforementioned, a separate imaging team existed to exactly colour manage every image. The eight medical photographers would often travel the length of the UK to visit trial sites on specific time points to take set images. Additionally, clinical trials sites were scattered throughout Europe and the USA and photographs at these sites would invariably be taken by local clinical staff. We conducted photography training at the initiation of every trial and then as required. This was part of our remit - keeping a hawk eye on image quality across all trial sites, frequently visiting sites to give the local clinicians extra training sessions to up the quality, ensure correct standardisation of all imagery and more often than not, beam the most recent images back to Renovo in Manchester via internet dongle. I remember on several occasions – one in Poland, the other in Denmark - leaning out of a hospital tower block hanging on to the company laptop for dear life, just to get a better signal so that the images would send. The combination of audio-visual equipment interference and low signal strength were our biggest bug bears.

As well as travel to Glasgow Royal Infirmary, I got down to East Grinstead Hospital via shuttle flight from Manchester to Gatwick and across to Hull Royal Infirmary. I also went to Bristol and Selly Oak and I was lucky to get a few overseas trips whilst working at Renovo. Sometimes I'd be accompanied by a research nurse or 'CRA' (Clinical Research Associate). More often than not, I'd be on my own. Destinations included: Bochum in Germany; Copenhagen and Odense in Denmark, the Latvian capital, Riga, Posnan in western Poland and Elblag in Northern Poland. Renovo was a huge operation comprising circa 160 employees and over 50 clinical trials sites. It had a fully equipped clinical trials unit (CTU), its own HR department and among others, had doctors, nurses, an army of scientists and statisticians and an equally high number of talented Clinical Research Associates overseeing the entire complex programme. Many of these were leading on individual trials, such as breast reduction, breast augmentation, skin grafting, scar revision, varicose veins, keloid scars and mole excision. The social scene was great as you might expect for Manchester, with regular meals out in the Northern Quarter and ten pin bowling nights, which were always enjoyable. There were also trips to the Institute of Medical Illustrators annual conference at Glasgow and Crewe.

In short, my brief at Renovo was to ensure high quality images were taken internally and externally. I had to ensure that all trial site visits were covered, I had to track visits to ensure that all the images were available, (we used a system of coloured flags on our tracking databases to bring our attention to any problems or pending site image uploads / training etc.). I had to feedback to site within 24 hours, recalling patients if necessary if images were inaccurate. I also provided support to external sites via phone, email and whilst training. I had to ensure that all archiving was accurate and completed before the deadlines and ensure that all relevant logs were completed. Capturing, logging, storing, archiving, tracking and feedback became my day to day working norm. I also undertook a lot of PR photography for the annual report, company leaflets and intranet. This suited me fine as I had cut my teeth on portrait photography even before I had left college back in the mid '80s. I also worked late shifts and Saturdays when required, covering trial patients at our CTU. Some European site initiations would occur over a weekend, necessitating travel out of hours.

As a prerequisite for accepting the Renovo Medical Photography role, I had to undergo a year of study with Staffordshire University to gain the Clinical Certificate in Medical Illustration, rubber stamping me as a bone fide Medical Photographer. I was fortunate and very grateful that Renovo paid for all this at a cost of several thousand pounds. The induction day at Staffs Uni was on January 15th, 2010 and set out the course content and requirements. The twelve months of distance learning theoretical and practical assignments comprised: legal and ethical issues encountered in medical illustration; anatomy and physiology; computer skills for medical illustration; healthcare location photography; patient photography and lighting techniques; ophthalmic photography; dental photography and surgical photography, which included operating theatre etiquette. Every weekend throughout 2010 and into early February 2011 was devoted to study. The course was very testing and certainly no push over. I joined the Institute of Medical Illustrators at the same time and pulled on all their available learning resources and advice. I was relieved to gain a distinction on successful completion of the course, giving me a better understanding of medical photography and leading to my gaining state registration as a Medical Illustration practitioner. My lever arch file of completed coursework was two inches thick and my practical work and training constituted similar, voluminous hours.

I undertook my ophthalmic photography training with Steve and Tim in Medical Illustration at Blackpool's Victoria Hospital, producing the required 'nine positions of gaze' and fundus retinal images that included the macula, optic disc, nasal and temporal views. My dental photography training was with Mandy in Medical Photography at Wythenshawe Hospital, South Manchester and saw me producing the required extra oral, intra oral and cleft palate views. I undertook surgical photography with my friend, Consultant Orthopaedic Surgeon Steve Mannion at Blackpool's Spire Fylde Coast Hospital and for my uni assignment I decided to concentrate on a total knee replacement operation (TKR). I photographed Steve's TKR from start to finish using a Nikon D300s camera and wide angle to tele zoom lens with a special bracket that I'd constructed myself designed to house two Metz 45 flash guns. The visual documentation captured the key moments of 'Femoral Trial', 'Impaction of tibial and femoral prostheses', 'Insertion of definitive spacer', ''capsular closure' and finally stitching and dressing to the 'closed wound'. Whilst Steve was delighted with my images, the examiner was not! He cited that I had disregarded the brief's instructions in opting to study and research such a complex operation. I should have chosen a simpler procedure such as 'dupuytren's contracture', a hand condition in which one or multiple fingers become permanently bent in a flexed position. Usually starting as small, hard nodules lying just under the skin of the palm, the condition grows worse over time until the fingers can no longer be straightened. As a 'punishment' I was marked down on that assignment because of it!

The euphoria over gaining my Clinical Certificate in Medical Illustration with distinction, however, was short lived. It was early February 2011 and rumours were circulating that Renovo was in trouble. The previous year, the company had to shave some of its staff and Medical Photography lost Zoe, a wonderful colleague and a highly valued member of the team, although thankfully she immediately went on to carve out an even better career for herself as a Clinical Research Associate. Now the boss, Mark Ferguson (affectionately known as 'Prof'), had called a company meeting. It was the most extraordinary meeting that I'd ever attended. There was no way to soften the blow. Prof announced to an initially hushed gathering that there had been a catastrophic, late stage failure of Renovo's lead scar reducing drug, Juvista. The first European Phase III trial for Juvista in scar revision surgery failed to meet either its primary or secondary endpoints. The primary endpoint for efficacy was a photographic-based assessment 12 months after surgery, assessed by an independent panel of experts using the 'Global Scar Comparison Scale', while secondary endpoints included an assessment using the same scale by patients and also the clinical trial investigator.

In spite of the end point stats being checked multiple times, the results came back the same. The air was one of disbelief and incredulity. Prof, along with the rest of us in the company, were devastated about the result. Prof was later to tell journalists that the outcome "was a clear miss, not a narrow miss" and that the results were both "strange and perplexing". He was confident, as we all were, that the trial had been conducted correctly and that the result was accurate. The clinical trials had involved tests on the appearance of scars, giving different doses of the drug to over 350 people spread across 56 UK, European and US sites. Overnight £100 million was shaved off Renovo's market value, with shares plummeting from 68p to 17p as investors shrank back and digested the shocking news. Shire had reportedly invested more than 75 million pounds into Renovo on the back of promising earlier results. With no further development taking place, Renovo at that time said that it "regrettably concludes that the efficacy of Juvista is insufficient to demonstrate significant benefit when tested in a broad population of scar revision patients".

Everyone had given their all to Renovo and many in that company meeting had been momentarily reduced to defunct automatons. Some were shaking, others were in tears and visibly shocked. It was bloody awful to be a part of it. This coup de grace meant redundancy and company closure. The only upside was that we had about three and a half months' notice – valuable time to plan and prepare. It was actually decision made, because I was contemplating looking for another post on successful completion of the 'Clin Cert'. The best news was that everyone went on to gain other jobs. Since 2012, Professor Mark Ferguson has been the Director General of the Science Foundation, Ireland – a leading position in the formulation and implementation of Irish Science policy which sees him act as key advisor on science matters to the Irish government. A very amenable and approachable guy, Mark was a pleasure to work for.

The last few months with Renovo were concerned with winding up the company. We were involved with all the asset photography, offering the scientific equipment and machinery up for sale. This included thousands of pounds worth of camera gear and accessories, which was offered at discount second-hand price and for which, we got first dibs. Every day, someone would be leaving, having been snapped up by another biotech or clinical research organisation, as gradually Renovo became a Marie Celeste.

In March 2011 I was shocked to learn of the death from cancer of one of my Arnold school contemporaries, Richard Samson. Richard was one of Lonely Planet's geniuses and was also the 'Lex' on television's 'Countdown' for a while. He died at home in beautiful Melbourne, but a memorial service was also held in London, which I attended. On the day of his funeral, family and friends released balloons into the sky as a touching tribute. Richard, or 'Bammo Boy' as I used to call him at school, was only 47 but by all accounts, managed to pack a lot into his tragically short life.

On 11 March 2011, the world held it's breath as we learned of the Fukushima nuclear accident in Okuma, Fukushima Prefecture, Japan. On the back of a massive 9.1 magnitude earthquake, which occurred 231 miles northeast of Japan's capital, Tokyo and following a 15 metre tsunami, the power supply and cooling system of three Fukushima Daiichi reactors were left disabled with all three cores having melted within a few days. The earthquake, tsunami and nuclear accident collectively cost many thousands of lives.

During the three and a half years spent at Renovo, there were quite a few things happening in the UK. On 28 March 2008, Terminal Five (and home to British Airways), opened amidst prolonged teething problems with its IT. In May Boris Johnston ousted Ken Livingstone to become the new London Mayor. In August, Barry George was acquitted of murdering television presenter Jill Dando. Woolworths store announced that it would be closing all 807 of its UK stores by 5th January 2009, in effect making 27,000 people redundant. In the November, Lewis Hamilton made history when he became Formula One's youngest ever world champion. Robert Napper pleaded guilty to murdering Rachel Nickel on Wimbledon Common on 15th July 1992. Film releases included: 'Mama Mia', 'Quantum of Solace', 'Twilight', 'Gran Torino' and 'Valkyrie'. Pop music hits included: 'Rockstar' by Nickelback, 'Valerie' by Mark Ronson and Amy Winehouse, 'Relax Take it Easy' by Mika, 'Back to Black' by Amy Winehouse and 'Ruby' by the Kaiser Chiefs. My two favourite television series were 'Ashes to Ashes' starring Keeley Hawes and Philip Glenister and 'Merlin' starring Colin Morgan and Bradley James. A number of famous people passed away in 2008, including: 'The Birds' actress, Suzanne Pleshette, actors Charlton Heston, Heath Ledger and Roy Scheider and singer Eartha Kitt. Actors Paul Newman (famous for 'Butch Cassidy and the Sundance Kid' and 'Cool Hand Luke') and also 'Madigan' actor Richard Widmark, also passed away.

Following the November Presidential election, on 20th January 2009 former Illinois Senator Barack Hussein Obama II, at 47, became the first African American to win the Presidency. He became the 44th 'POTUS' and went on to serve two, four-year terms at the White House. President Obama's running mate and Vice President was Joe Biden.

On 6th January 2009, the closure of Woolworths was complete, marking an end to 100 years of the retail giant. April saw the outbreak of the H1N1 swine flu epidemic, which had originated in Mexico and eventually spread to the UK. On 18th July, the world's oldest man and one of the last surviving servicemen of the 1914-18 First World War, Henry Allingham, died at the ripe old age of 113. Only a week later, Harry Patch who was the last British survivor of the first world war trenches, died at a similar 'innings' to Henry at 111. The reality star Jade Goody also passed away in 2009, as did Farrah Fawcett and Michael Jackson on the same day in June. We also lost Tony Hart, Danny La Rue, Wendy Richard, Mollie Sugden, Patrick Swayze and Edward Woodward. New television shows included 'Miranda' and 'Pointless' with film releases including James Cameron's awesome 'Avatar' starring Sam Worthington and Zoe Saldana and 'Harry Potter and the Half Blood Prince'. Pop music hits included: 'Poker Face' by Lady Gaga, 'I Gotta Feeling' by the Black Eyed Peas, 'Halo' by Beyonce and 'Hallelujah' by Alexandra Burke.

July 2009 saw the family holidaying in Brussels and Bruges, which was Wendy's old stomping ground and where she lived and worked in the mid to late '80s. Highlights were the very poignant, but inspiring tour of the World War 1 trenches, war graves and

Menin Gate at Ypres. The Belgian beer and fries dipped in bearnaise sauce were also memorable highlights!

2010 was a UK election year resulting in a hung parliament following voting on 6th May – Conservatives being placed with 20 seats short of a required House of Commons majority. Gordon Brown tendered his resignation to the Queen five days later and the following morning the Liberal Democratic Party formed a coalition government with the Conservatives – David Cameron becoming the new Prime Minister and LibDem leader Nick Clegg becoming Deputy Prime Minister.

On 2nd June, taxi driver Derrick Bird went on the rampage in western Cumbria, shooting and killing 12 people and injuring another 25. Before police could catch him, Bird cheated jail by turning the gun on himself. The resignation of Gordon Brown the previous month forced a Labour Party leadership contest with Ed Miliband, narrowly beating his brother David to become in effect Opposition Leader.

A number of famous people died in 2010 who included from the acting community: Tony Curtis, Corin Redgrave, Lynne Redgrave, Christopher Cazenove, Ingrid Pitt, Simon MacCorkindale and Jean Simmons. We also lost my favourite star of Gilbert and Sullivan operettas, John Reed – known for his nimble performances in the principal comic roles with the D'Oyly Carte Opera Company. "I can tell a woman's age in half a minute...and I do..." from 'Princess Ida', always used to crack me up. Winston Churchill, grandson of Sir Winston also passed away, as did snooker player, Alex 'Hurricane' Higgins, politician Sir Cyril Smith, former Met Police Commissioner Sir Robert Mark, TV comic actor Sir Norman Wisdom, broadcaster and writer Claire Rayner and acclaimed television journalist Brian Hanrahan.

Among the film releases of 2010 were 'Harry Potter and the Deathly Hallows' and 'The King's Speech'. Television brought us the first season of 'The Great British Bake Off' and the last episodes of 'The Bill', which had run since 1984. The pop music hits for 2010 included 'Bad Romance' and 'Alejandro' by Lady Gaga as well as 'Broken Heels' by Alexandra Burke.

CHAPTER 23

Malawi, Huddersfield University, Kurdistan (Northern Iraq) and Libya, June 2011 – November 2012

Following a final Medical Photography team meal out and a few cheeky beers in Manchester's Northern Quarter with wider Renovo colleagues, that was it – my time at Renovo, as everyone else's, was now history. Literally days after leaving, I popped round to Steve Mannion's house for a pre-Malawi visit briefing. Steve had invited me to Malawi to undertake a photographic and video documentation of the inspiring work that he and his medical team undertake for his charity 'Feet First Worldwide'. It was now early June and I had already been given a raft of prophylaxes at my local surgery, which included a course of anti-malaria tablets to take at regular intervals over the coming weeks. I invested in deet sprays and nets to keep the pesky mozzies at bay whilst I was deep in the heart of the African continent. I'll let my article below, published in the 'Lancashire Life' Magazine, summarise my amazing Malawi experience during the last two weeks in June 2011 set the scene:

'Feet First Worldwide is a charity founded in 2004 by Blackpool Orthopaedic Consultant Steve Mannion. The charity's aim is to treat and prevent disabilities in children worldwide.

Steve and his team work in developing countries such as Malawi, Laos, Ethiopia and Papua New Guinea treating children and adults with disabilities. Steve works part-time for the NHS in a job-share post at Blackpool Victoria Hospital in addition to working at Spire Fylde Coast Hospital. This means he can visit poor countries such as Malawi 3 or 4 times a year. Here, he not only operates on disabled children, but also undertakes vital orthopaedic procedures and delivers surgical training for local medics.

One of the most common musculoskeletal conditions Steve and his dedicated team treat is club foot or 'congenital talipes equino-varus'. Around 500 children are born with this condition in Malawi every year and there are approximately 5000 children awaiting this life-changing treatment. As Steve says "children born with club foot should be treated in the first year of life. If this doesn't occur, then the deformity becomes fixed and needs a complex operation to correct it. Untreated, the child cannot walk, cannot wear normal shoes and cannot go to school". Up to the age of 1 treatment is via the Ponseti method, which involves manipulation followed by casting at regular intervals, but which crucially can be undertaken by nurses, medical assistants and physiotherapists rather than surgeons. However, children with this debilitating condition presenting over the age of 1, unfortunately require intricate and complex surgical correction by orthopaedic surgeons such as Steve. The consequence of this is an ever-increasing waiting list because there is currently only 1 orthopaedic surgeon for the whole of Lilongwe, the capital of Malawi. When you bear in mind the total population of Malawi is 14 million, this is obviously of concern!

In June 2011 I travelled to Malawi in central south eastern Africa with Steve and his team to photograph Steve's pioneering club foot work. Alongside Steve were Dr Simon Mills (Consultant Anaesthetist), Bernadette Huyton (Senior Orthopaedic Theatre Sister), Daniella Baldwin (Radiographer) and me (Photographic Consultant). I'd never been to Africa before and my visit proved a real eye-opener.

We started our work in the hospitals of the country's capital Lilongwe. I was shocked to witness the number of children presenting with limb deformities and the number of horrendous burn injuries caused by children wandering into unprotected road-side fires. But as my photographs show, many children still had time to give me a smile despite being in pain whilst awaiting operations. Nevertheless, there were some frightened children in need of a comforting hand of reassurance. Many Malawians are very poor and will walk for hours or even days to get to hospital to see Steve and his team. Once there, they wait patiently, hour after hour, until they are seen and treated. Typically, the patient's family travels with them and they all pitch up in the hospital grounds where everything from cooking, washing, cleaning and sleeping is undertaken. They arrive at hospital frequently exhausted with some just 'crashing out' on the grass outside the hospital entrance until it is their turn to be seen. It all seemed so primitive, but yet how wonderful to be surrounded by your whole family prior to surgery, during recovery and for recuperation. It's all very different to the lonely, elderly patients found on NHS wards in the UK today, with no family around them.

The team found the lack of post-operative pain relief shocking and quite upsetting. Limited analgesia was available and wasn't necessarily administered as we would do in this country which was very frustrating to observe.

We travelled for several hours to the north of the country to Rumphi Hospital. Due to their limited funds, the resident medical teams have been forced to improvise with the equipment available. For example, [...], traction means using an iron weight or even a brick hanging from a string – a far cry from the sophisticated equipment used in the UK! A kettle was used as part of the surgical equipment sterilisation process (surgical tools were actually put inside the kettle and left in the boiling water). The sinks were filthy, they just don't have the time or the facilities to maintain the levels of hygiene that are essential in our country. In the grounds of Nkhata Bay Hospital (also in the north of the country), I spotted another improvisation – an ambulance created from an old motorbike with a dirty tray attached to a sidecar. An example of how much can be achieved from so little. It was heart-warming to see how innovative these people could be and their continual determination to overcome adversity.

A young teenager was wheeled out on a trolley into the recovery area following surgery to repair his broken left ankle. 'Recovery' proved to be a communal corridor, not a designated, fully equipped, supervised enclosed area. Another jaw-dropping realisation, and yet life-changing and life-saving operations were being conducted before my eyes – I felt very humbled.

An elderly lady sat dignified and motionless on the operating table, she neither winced nor uttered a sound as an epidural was administered. Her grotesque leg injury was caused by a dog bite, it had to be cleaned, 'debrided' and then painstakingly skin grafted. The composure these wonderful people show is astounding, they just calmly deal with each situation as it arises.

Back in the capital, we had to wait in our vehicles one evening before leaving the car park at Lilongwe's Dae Yung Luke Hospital as four masked medical personnel slowly carried a covered stretcher bearing a recently deceased person. They passed right in front of the bonnet of our truck. Behind the stretcher followed a dignified procession of grieving family and friends who were accompanying their loved one to the mortuary in a separate building. Apparently, this procession is customary when someone dies in hospital. What a contrast to our society where the death process is very much hidden from view. Nothing in the murder scenes or mortuaries of London as a forensic photographer prepared me for this moment – it was moving, poignant and heart-breaking and I found it hard to hold back the tears. If I could have hugged every grieving person and 'made it all better' I would have, but instead I felt completely helpless – it's a moment I'll never forget.

Malawi has a low life expectancy (circa age 50) and a high infant mortality rate. I lost count of the number of ubiquitous coffin shops in every town and village that we passed through. HIV and AIDS are very prevalent and there is a high risk of diseases such as malaria, rabies, typhoid fever and hepatitis A to name but a few. Malawi is among the least developed and most densely populated countries in the world. Its economy is based on agriculture - farming with cattle and goats and producing tobacco, cotton, sugar cane, tea and potatoes.

Despite the adversity, Malawians are not melancholy people. On the contrary, they are friendly, inquisitive and welcoming, making the most of what they have. As many of them cannot afford cars, they adapt and improvise creating "vehicles" out of wheels and pieces of wood. Bicycles are everywhere you look, piled sky-high with logs or sacks of grain, it gives the saying, 'carrying everything but the kitchen sink' new meaning! In the hospitals, clinics and wards I always got a handshake and a smile. I now know why they call Malawi 'the warm heart of Africa'. To experience Malawi is very special and leaves you with a strong desire to return. We could surely learn a thing or two from the Malawi people about family love and support and their capacity to overcome adversity.

Consultant Orthopaedic and Trauma Surgeon Steve Mannion featured in the BBC documentary 'Super Doctors' with Lord Winston. Steve is supported by Feet First Worldwide's trustees as well as local people. Please support this inspiring, life-changing charity – funds are desperately needed so we can continue to send surgical teams out to places like Malawi. 100% of funds raised are used directly for the purpose of the charity and all work is done by volunteers. All funds raised will ensure that more children are able to grow up leading normal lives, more adults will have life changing surgery and the essential work of Feet First can continue.'

Malawi, formerly known as Nyasaland and officially known as The Republic of Malawi is a beautiful sprawling, developing nation located right down in the southeast of the African continent. Landlocked, it is enveloped by Mozambique on its south, east and west sides, by Zambia to its northwest and Tanzania to its northeast. Lilongwe as stated, is the nation's capital with Blantyre in the south being the second largest city. Malawi, whose population is over 18 million, is dominated by the great African Lake, Lake Malawi. At around 580 kilometres in length and about 75 kilometres at its widest point, Lake Malawi not only occupies around a third of the country, but it is the ninth largest lake in the world and home to a huge variety of fauna and flora and a massive diversity in fish stocks, which has helped sustain indigenous peoples for millennia – the most popular being four different species of chambo, sardine and the large kampango catfish.

Lake Malawi National Park, one of five national parks, is located at the southern end of the lake. There are also four wildlife and game reserves in addition to two other protected areas in the country. I was lucky enough to visit one such wildlife reserve at Nkhotakota, north of Lilongwe and nestling on the western shores of Lake Malawi. In the safe company of an armed ranger and my medical team, I photographed crocodiles and walked, probably too close for comfort, in the path of their tracks! Malawi is also home to elephants, hippos, big cats, monkeys and bats, not to mention a great variety of birds, including birds of prey, waterfowl and parrots. It was no comfort at all that Malawi is also home to a variety of snakes, most of which, are highly venomous. These include the feared Black Mamba, the Eastern Green Mamba, the short, fat, Puff Adder as well as poisonous tree snakes. Without antivenom, a strike from a Black Mamba will guarantee your journey into the afterlife between 7 and 15 hours following a bite! Fortunately, the closest I got to one of these creatures was driving over a dead Black Mamba on the road. With so much mileage to cover, we took it in turns to drive the two Feet First Toyota vehicles. At one point I was driving behind Steve with Sauvier, another English orthopaedic surgeon in the front passenger seat. I'd driven over the dead snake earlier and when darkness hit, I think Steve clipped a bat, which then smacked into the left-hand side of our vehicle's windscreen, one of its wings becoming jammed under the wipers. When we stopped, Sauvier did the honours – mindful of rabies, he carefully used a long stick and disentangled the potentially diseased, now deceased bat from the wiper blades.

The team worked incredibly hard over that two weeks in June 2011. It was great at the end of it all to relax and for us all to enjoy one or two well-earned beers on our last night in Lilongwe. I came away with some great medical images for Steve, a varied portfolio of travel photographs depicting the Malawi people and their country and some special memories. It was an adventure that was to leave a lasting impression on me.

No sooner had I returned from Africa, it was George's graduation from Saint Aidan's, his high school for the last five years. George started there as quite an introverted eleven-year old, often retreating to the library at lunchtimes to avoid the bullying antics of two particularly undesirable girls who had followed George from Junior School. Barely a year later, George had joined local dramatic group 'SODS' (Saint Oswalds' Dramatists), under the direction of stalwarts Anne and Trev Markland. This turned out to be the making of him and, in combination with support and nurturing from Saint Aidan's, George really started to fly. He netted a bevy of GCSEs, became Deputy Head Boy and was held in very high regard by staff and students alike. When George got up on stage to sing at his leaver's assembly, it was a defining, beautiful moment and caught many teachers by surprise. This was the first time he'd had the courage to sing in front of the school. Their gobsmacked expressions were priceless. As a parent, it was lovely to witness and made me so very proud. Wendy and I credit Deputy Headteacher Anthony Lord and his staff for helping to shape George into the man he has become today. I can't speak too highly of Saint Aidan's Church of England High School. This rural Preesall school with its stunning outlook across to the Bowland Fells promotes a powerful Christian sense of inclusivity and community belonging and is strong on its pastoral care. The positive vibes and the vibrant aura that the school exudes are palpable the moment you walk through the main gate.

In preparing young people for adult life in the wider world, Saint Aidan's very much lives up to its John 10:10 motto, "That they may have life, and have it in its fullness". So, back to George's graduation during the first week in July 2011. George had invited his friends to ours for pre-drinks. Some friends of ours lent us a marquee, and everyone assembled in our garden. It was a glorious, warm, blue sky day and I took plenty of photographs to document the occasion. The highlight was seeing an old, red, AEC London double decker 'Routemaster' bus pull up outside our house to take George and his fellow high school graduates to a dinner and party at Blackpool's De

Vere (now The Village) Hotel. Designed by London Transport and built by the Associated Equipment Company and Park Royal Vehicles between 1954 and 1968, the famous front-engined bus exhibited the traditional layout that I remember all too well growing up – front-mounted engine, half a driver's cab, rear 'jump on and jump off' platform and rear stairs. Even the neighbours all came out to look! It was pure nostalgia and another defining moment in the lives of our children that I won't forget in a hurry.

In early January 2011, and after much family discussion, we decided to get a cat. We all went to a local animal sanctuary and picked out a tortoiseshell, a beautiful, young, spayed, female cat, whom we named Finty. Unfortunately, it transpired that Finty had been living rough on the streets for many months and her feral behaviour, continual biting and swiping at us with claws fully extended (not to mention peeing on the curtains and furniture) was getting worse. We had been told we had to keep Finty indoors, which was probably a mistake. When we caved in to her incessant meowing to explore the garden, she bolted out of the kitchen door and shot straight up to the top of our pine tree, taking an eternity to coax her down. The bad behaviour just got worse and peeing on Wendy's handbag was the last straw. Rightly or wrongly we felt that we had no choice but to return Finty to the sanctuary, which I did alone. This single action proved to be one of the most awful and upsetting experiences of my entire life, akin to a bereavement – I had obviously become very fond of our feline friend, for there were times when she was placid and loving and I know we'll all cherish those moments in hoping that Finty received the treatment she deserved and went to a good home. Looking back, we could have done with help from American cat behaviourist expert, Jackson Galaxy (aka Richard Kirschner), host of the television show 'My Cat from Hell'!

Having post processed all the images from my Malawi adventure, we took our annual summer holiday in Cornwall, following which, it was time to put some serious thought into work and my next job. It was now early September and following a call to my friend Pete at the Met Police Crime Academy Forensic Faculty, I took a call from Chris Gregg. Chris was former Chief Superintendent and Head of West Yorkshire's Homicide and Major Enquiry Team. He just happened to be looking for, among other experts, a forensic photographic expert to train a group of Libyan students in forensic photography as part of an MSc programme due to commence at Huddersfield University the following month. Chris was working with ex Met Police

Commissioner Lord Stevens at Axiom International. Lord Stevens was my old MPS boss and a man described as 'The most successful Commissioner of the Metropolitan Police in modern times....'. Axiom International was a major forensic science and law enforcement provider, also founded by Professor Angela Gallop CBE, one of the world's most eminent forensic scientists and cold case investigation specialists, who has worked on a great many publicly prominent cases. Angela published her book 'When the Dogs Don't Bark: A Forensic Scientist's Search for the Truth' in February 2019.

In West Yorkshire, Chris had been the lead on many high-profile investigations, including heading up the Harold Shipman murders enquiry. His reputation as one of the finest police officers and detectives that this country has ever produced preceded him. In 2008, Chris was awarded the Queen's Police Medal (QPM) for his outstanding contribution to police services, which speaks for itself. So it was with some hilarity and embarrassment on my part that I almost dropped the phone when Chris rang, seemingly out of the blue, to invite me to a meeting with Angela and other forensic specialists at Huddersfield University. I was told that I would be liaising with Jake Ireland, a former West Yorkshire police superintendent, who had been put in place at the university by Axiom as their link man and Programme Director. Tracy Alexander, a former MPS, highly experienced Crime Scene Manager, Head of Forensic Intelligence and forensic science whiz was also on hand for ready advice and input. Tracy is currently Director of Forensic Services at City of London Police and visiting Senior Lecturer at Kings College, London.

Following a very fruitful meeting with Professor Gallop, a contract for my teaching provision was duly signed and Jake provided some tips on submitting my hours for salary and expenses. One of the Huddersfield University English lecturers, Dionne Coburn, who was affiliated with the Libyan programme, took charge of my equipment shopping list. I got on with Dionne really well and had a great laugh with her. I found it a breath of fresh air to be dealing with such a young, fun-loving and upbeat person instead of a piddly pen-pushing pillock. Dionne thought that going out and purchasing all the camera equipment for my course was really exciting. She gave me some good advice and naturally, working at the university, knew the place intimately, and she was well placed to help me during my time there. So, there I was, researching the 'Hudders' segment for this book, thinking that I'd look her up, give her a ring, clarify a few uni facts and maybe pop onto campus to say 'Hello' over a coffee, but only to get the shock of my life…to learn only recently that lovely Dionne had sadly passed away at the end of September in 2016 after a long battle with cancer. I mean, she was only 42 for goodness sake. Dionne was popular, well respected, an invaluable part of the Libyan MSc programme and I know her loss is sorely felt. R.I.P. Dionne.

What hadn't been dialled in to my fee, was my time for planning and writing what was to be a fifteen-week course, commencing 3rd October 2011 and running until 27th January 2012. After a bit of a struggle, I eventually managed to negotiate a 2-week fee (!), but at the end of that period I only had a third of the course written and knew that I'd be starting week one in effect, with having to design subsequent weeks following each day's tuition. For peace and quiet I used to do this back in my hotel room. I eventually had the course completely written by the halfway stage. The MSc timetabling meant that in week one I would teach Monday to Thursday inclusive, and in week 2 I would teach Monday to Wednesday inclusive and alternating throughout. My accommodation was split between a central Huddersfield family-run hotel (with a 'big boy's breakfast'!) and the local Premier Inn, both of which were no more than a five-minute walk from campus. Conveniently, we were running two cars at that time. I took the Vauxhall Zafira to Huddersfield and Wendy was quite content to take her canary yellow Nissan Micra to her place of work.

On my first Monday, I left home at the crack of dawn, arriving at my hotel around 7.30am. The owners were very accommodating, allowing me access to my room and offering me breakfast. The first day was an induction day for the students anyway, which gave me time to unpack and unbox all the new photography equipment, put it together, test it out and create an inventory of everything. I'd arranged to meet Dionne at 9am on campus and she got me security cleared, my pass created and then she took me to what would be the crime scene photography classroom for the duration of the course. At the front of the class was a huge, wall-mounted, rectangular wipe board. In the left-hand corner was a multi-media lectern, wired into a ceiling-mounted data projector as standard. From here I could connect up my laptop and also control the room lighting. In the right-hand corner was a brand-new Panasonic 'Vierra' TV. Like the camera equipment, this had been bought especially on my instructions to enable quick group critiquing of practical assignments by attaching a mini HDMI umbilical from each student camera straight into the TV and then reviewing the results.

After exhaustive research for a relatively inexpensive DSLR kit, capable of taking both decent quality stills and video, I plumped for the latest consumer level DX format Nikon D3100, which had been released by Nikon in August 2010. It comprised a CMOS chip, packing 14.2-megapixels, a reasonably quick Nikon 'EXPEED 2' image processor, sensor cleaning, a large three-inch, 230,000 dot resolution fixed LCD screen, a live-view mode, full high definition 1080 progressive scan (1920×1080 pixel) video recording capability with full-time autofocus in movie mode. The camera system came equipped for Nikon F-Mount lenses and you could shoot in JPEG or Nikon electronic file format (RAW). Student work could be saved via SDXC memory cards. For each kit, I chose a Nikkor 18-55mm Vibration Reduction lens fitted with a UV filter, a 60mm macro lens for injuries and close-up work, a Nikon SB900 flash gun with coily cord to connect to the camera, a 'Calumet' tripod with 3-way head, a Nikon 'MC-DC2' remote locking release and a 2-hour AA battery charger with a set of 8 rechargeable (2 sets) batteries. All the kit, with the exception of the tripod of course, fitted snugly into a padded, black, canvas camera bag, which came equipped with a handy shoulder strap. Each pair of students was issued with a 4 Gb memory card for uploading all their practical work and a USB memory stick to store their classroom lectures and theoretical assignments.

I had requested a flip chart with several A1 pads, a pack of coloured marker pens and a high capacity memory stick to store all the students' modular assignments and assessments. Each student was given an A4 folder, an A4 ruled notepad and pens, which would also house my handouts for each module. With ten students in my group working in pairs, they used 5 camera kits. There was an instructor's kit and also one complete kit spare for emergencies. I planned the course down to the n'th degree, being very much an organised Virgo, a dotting the i's and crossing the t's sort of person! Theory sessions would be interspersed with demonstrations and group exercises. Homework following each module would be project based, for example with the crime scenes module, students were given the following brief:

'Using a small exterior location and two interior rooms, in no more than 15 photographs, provide a clear, visual documentation of a 2-location abduction and assault scene, together with a brief, bullet-pointed, type-written account of your main considerations.'

There would be both interior and exterior practicals, regular formative assessments in the shape of Q&A's, quizzes and group discussion. Summative assessment would be during week 15 – a written theory exam and several practical assessments, with marking formulae devised for both. There would be input from many forensic scientists during the fifteen weeks. Similarly, I was asked to provide a forensic photographic input to the scene examiners course during week 8 and to do no end of photographic jobs as I was seen as 'Johnny on the spot with the camera'. One particular module springs to mind – the fire scene investigators. The esteemed scientist Dr Roger Berrett had come up from his Weybridge, Surrey home to deliver his specialism. Back in the '90s, when Roger was based at what was the Met Police's Fire Investigation Unit (FIU) housed at Lambeth, I worked with him on a regular basis at fire scenes all over London. And what a character. Roger would be there with his characteristic generous wavy, silver-white head of hair, donned in his green overalls and reinforced black wellies, dropping fag ash all over the scene, theorising about this and that, whilst simultaneously regaling us with a funny experience and inevitably telling jokes. I always knew that behind that slightly eccentric exterior, lay a highly intelligent and very fine mind. No-one had a bad word to say about Roger. He was held in very high regard indeed. I hadn't realised that he'd be joining us in Huddersfield and when I heard his all too familiar voice emanating from the adjacent classroom, I popped in to see him and renew my acquaintance with this giant of the forensic science world. On more than one occasion, I had to stop teaching whilst in mid flow and nip into Roger's classroom to help him sort out his audio-visual presentation equipment – unfortunately the techno stuff wasn't one of Roger's strengths!

The most impressive demonstration by far, during my four months teaching at Huddersfield University was delivered by Clive Gregory with his accelerant detector dog Trooper. (Fast forward to today, Clive is one of my fire investigation colleagues from Gardiner Associates Training and Research - GATR). To demonstrate Trooper's skills, and with Trooper out of the room, Clive planted a match underneath the side of the lectern in my classroom. With a large group of onlookers situated at the back of the room, he then went to fetch Trooper, who made an immediate bee line for the lectern and located the match within a matter of seconds. Extremely impressive. In recent years, I was to see Clive re-enact a more complex version of this scenario, using a cigarette butt laced with a tiny amount of accelerant and hidden in a huge, overgrown field on GATR's 'Phoenix Heights' Wethersfield fire training ground. Once again, Trooper located the accelerant in less than a minute, proving that in fire investigation, the canine team are by far the quickest, the most accurate and therefore the most efficient method currently available for screening fire scenes and other scenes for accelerant traces.

Clive spent 31 years with the West Midlands Fire Service. 12 of these were spent as a specialist investigator with the Fire Research and Investigation Department, examining a huge number of arson and murder by fire scenes. In 1996, Clive pioneered the use of accelerant detector dogs by UK fire services with his faithful dog 'Star' – the UK's first ever fire investigation dog. Clive then went on to establish his company 'C.P. Gregory and Associates Ltd.' in 2001, which specialises in fire investigation training and in the training of the accelerant detector 'K9' teams. Unfortunately, Clive lost Star in 2008. He then had 'Trooper' and 'Gunner', but sadly lost Trooper in 2018. Like Star, these highly trained detector dogs with their ultra-sensitive sense of smell, can sniff out and locate accelerant substances such as petrol, paraffin, cellulose thinners and methylated spirit, much more quickly than any portable detection equipment. They not only reduce the time scene examiners spend searching for vital evidence that a fire was started deliberately, but it also means there's a massive cost saving implication. I had the privilege of meeting Star back in 2006 when I first became part of the GATR team and Trooper, of course, in recent years. Although these lovely dogs are no longer with us, their memory and legacy live on, not just in Gunner, but in the ever-expanding fire investigation canine teams in use throughout the UK – a phenomenal achievement.

As a professionally qualified instructor, every course that I design must have an overall aim and associated learning outcomes (so called SMART objectives – Specific, Measurable, Achievable, Relevant and Timed / Timely). The aim of my 15-week course for the ten Libyan students was 'to instruct students in the techniques and procedures to competently photograph a variety of crime scene of assignments'. The associated objectives were:

- To be fully conversant with all the equipment to be used
- State what your photographic aim should always be in terms of the final image
- Demonstrate an understanding of basic photographic techniques
- Discuss problems associated with various crime scene assignments
- Demonstrate the ability to adapt techniques to different scenes

- Successfully photograph items of property, assault victims, a post mortem, a motor vehicle assignment, a road traffic accident, shoe, finger, tool and tyre marks, crime scenes (including an interior scene, an exterior scene, a fire scene, a night scene and a scene that has been video recorded)
- Develop the ability to critically assess your own work (which I always regarded as the most important objective) always striving to make the next image better quality than the last.

All my PowerPoints, handouts and reports had to be designed within the Axiom corporate template. My only qualm with this is that I ended up with less room on each slide to insert my information, but like most things in life, I got around the problem. Since my trainee instructor days in the Met Police, I've always been mindful of over doing the front loading, opting instead for one quarter theory and three quarters practical approach. This has been based on the old learning adage 'tell me and I'll forget, show me and I'll remember, involve me and I'll understand'. I obviously had the advantage of teaching a practical subject anyway where learning could be readily checked. Following each theory session, there was plenty of time for practical exercises and critique feedback sessions, then more practical exercises to really help cement the learning.

On the second day I met my ten students, an all-male class ranging in age from mid-20s to early 50s. Dionne, who was also overseeing the Libyan students' English lessons, had suggested the pairings. We placed a student with good written and spoken English with one who was not so good. They were all characters and I got on with them very well. I began with a brief self-introduction, course overview and a laying down of 'domestics and ground rules'. Then we went around the room inviting the students to give me a quick summary of themselves. I introduced myself by my first name, but the students insisted on calling me 'Teacher'! I soon found out it was a cultural thing. My introductory lecture was an overview of crime scene photography. The rest of the course consisted of multiple theory modules and their associated practical elements. This included: photography and camera, documentation, assault victims' injuries, property and drugs, external and internal scenes, fire scenes, post mortems, microscopy, motor vehicles, fatal and serious personal injury road traffic accidents, night scenes, visible marks, latent marks, video, crime scene management, court presentation and statement writing.

I had never used a microscope before, never mind in a laboratory setting. In effect I almost didn't know the arse end from the eyepiece and had to therefore thoroughly research both types in use at Huddersfield University during the latter part of 2011. I had the high-powered Leica ICC50 HD and the low-powered Leica EZ4 HD, both microscopes having integrated 3-megapixel CMOS cameras with high definition output linked to Leica capture and enhancement computer software. Starting with laboratory health and safety and ending with a good few hours of practise and photography of the equipment for my presentation, my research on this one topic alone took hours! I was leaving nothing to chance. If only I had been photographed donned in my white lab coat!

I'd never been to Huddersfield and I warmed immediately to the large West Yorkshire market town and its Victorian architecture. Converted mills punctuate the landscape and hint of Huddersfield's role in the industrial revolution. Situated approximately halfway between Manchester and Leeds in the borough of Kirklees, Huddersfield certainly didn't convey to me the fact that it's actually the eleventh largest town in the UK, with a population of more than 163,000. Huddersfield is famous as the birthplace of actor James Mason and of Labour Prime Minister, James Harold Wilson, the future Baron Wilson of Rievaulx, in 1916. Harold Wilson's statue stands proudly in St. George's Square, outside the main entrance to the Grade 1 listed railway station, described by former Poet Laureate, Sir John Betjeman as, "the most splendid station façade in England", in fact second only to London's St. Pancras. Huddersfield was also the birthplace of rugby league. Coincidentally, My sister Kate lives and works a stone's throw away on the outskirts, so it was handy to be able to meet up occasionally.

In addition to the run of the campus for scene photography practicals, which backs on to the Huddersfield Narrow Canal, there was a mock crime house which I littered with shoe, finger and tool marks. I also set the crime house up complete with mannequin dead body for the scene assessments during week 15. For the motor vehicles module, Jake Ireland provided uni transport to take the students to a local vehicle accident repair specialist for practical experience photographing all the necessary views. There was also a fire station visit for fire scene practise and several invaluable trips to the disused fire training ground in Bradford, which had some realistic burnt out rooms. It was this location that my students competently photographed using the 'timed exposure and painting with light' technique. The realistic mannequin was also delivered to my classroom, which caused quite a stir when the students arrived! This enabled me to improvise the post-mortem photography module as we were denied access to the local mortuary. Similar improvisation was needed for the night scene module. Jake Ireland couldn't get any motor vehicles on to campus for the students to photograph, so we used my Zafira and another staff member's car. We also had to notify security and let them know of our presence on campus out of hours when it was dark, especially considering how much flash was being fired. One evening, an inquisitive Vice Chancellor rocked up and took a keen interest in what I was teaching.

Like any student cohort, I found that my group varied in their abilities both in terms of academia and practical nous, where naturally one or two needed a little more help than the others. Marwan was great on the theory side, but struggled with the common sense, methodical approach needed for the practicals. Conversely, Ahmed sometimes wrestled with the theory, but was a highflyer with the practicals. My job was to recognise those weaknesses early on and endeavour to get everyone up to the same high standard by course close. All the students were characters – some more than others. Juima was the youngest student. Good looking and a hit with the young ladies, he was also the class joker and would often try to get one over on me by claiming that he had this appointment and that and that he needed to leave early, which of course was utter bollocks. He tried it once or twice and I stamped hard on it as I could see the other students watching as he approached me. They had probably put him up to it and were testing the water. I knew that I had to act, so when he was threatened with automatic failure, Juima miraculously started to toe the line! Marwan, the oldest student, had certain endearing qualities. These were balanced by the fact that he only had one eye, which made him appear quite formidable. Marwan's claim to fame was that he was Colonel Gaddafi's personal portrait painter, which quickly gathered credibility when Marwan brought his amazing artwork in to show me. Chris Gregg from Axiom popped into my classroom a few times during the course, the first time being when we were mid flow through the assault victim module, with students practising photographing 'fake injuries' on each other. The classroom walls were adorned with A1 'aide-memoire' sheets containing main points to remember from each module. From what I remember, Chris appeared suitably impressed by what he saw.

Reading between the lines I gathered that a large number of mature Libyan students were brought over from their native country to be trained in the various aspects of crime scene investigation, due to the increased volatility amongst warring factions in Libya. These trained forensic 'experts' would then form part of the rebuilding mechanism to help transition (hopefully) Libya into a peaceful, stable democracy one day. I had barely started week three of the MSc course with the Libyan students when breaking news came in on the morning of 20th October 2011 that the deposed Libyan leader, Colonel Muammar Gaddafi, had been captured by National Transitional Council forces, hiding in a culvert, west of his birthplace, Sirte, located south east of the capital, Tripoli. Gaddafi was killed soon after being captured and jostled by an angry mob, who stabbed and shot him. Understandably, this resulted in tension between some students at Huddersfield University who were loyal to the former leader and those who were vehemently against Gaddafi.

It was during a morning break, shortly after news of the former Libyan leader's death broke, that I had my head down marking project work at the front of the class, when my thoughts were interrupted by a commotion at the back. Another Libyan student from the crime scene investigators cohort had started a fight with one of my students and when I looked up, I couldn't believe what I was seeing – a full blown fisticuffs scrap was well under way! Instinctively, I pushed back my chair, raced to the back of the class and barged in between the two fighters holding them apart. I bellowed at both students, "How dare you do that in my classroom!!", chastising them like kids for their loss of control and inappropriate behaviour. I all but ordered them separately off campus. I then had to report the entire fiasco to Jake and Dionne, whereupon said students were suitably bollocked.

The postscript to that little bit of excitement was that later on the same day I was paid a visit by the guy who'd started the fight. He'd come to apologise! Approaching me slowly and cautiously, clearly humbled, barely being able to make eye contact with me and continually wringing his hands, the student began in a heavily accented, broken English, "Teacher.... I am.. very sorry...for what I have done. It will..not...happen...again...". Good on him for having the guts to come and personally apologise. Part of me felt a little sorry for him and it was also bordering on comical as the poor fellow was not only clearly remorseful, but he was stooped so low that I thought at one point he was going to keel over and head butt the carpet! My own student had already apologised shortly after I had broken up the fight. All the instructors were on their guard at this time, as heightened tension, reflecting the instability back in Libya, manifested itself in little campus skirmishes. We picked up the vibe immediately and dispersed troublemakers before any situation had time to develop.

In general, the fifteen-week course went well, there being very few mishaps. As with all my courses I'd put my absolute all, my heart and soul, into the Libyan MSc programme on the basis of that old adage previously mentioned, 'failing to prepare, is preparing to fail'. On reflection, the setbacks and challenges that I did encounter collectively amounted to little more than a minor inconvenience. Once I'd finished writing the course in my hotel room, I'd generally relax by reading or escaping from the real world by watching the cult, eight season, supernatural television series 'The Vampire Diaries' (TVD), starring Nina Dobrev, Ian Somerhalder and Paul Wesley, which ran from 2009 to 2017.

In January 2012, I rounded off the testing four-month course with a board blast of all the main points raised. Unfortunately, two of my students didn't quite make the grade. Overall, course feedback was favourable and following the success of the Libyan MSc programme, I was invited back to Huddersfield University to guest lecture, which I did alongside lecturing at UCLAN – the University of Central Lancashire and at Kings College, London.

2011 had been another eventful year in the UK, which saw the rate of VAT rising from 17.5% to 20%, the Chilcot enquiry into the Iraq war was in full swing. 2011 was also the year of the UK census and the marriage on 29th April of Prince William and Kate Middleton aka the Duke and Duchess of Cambridge in Westminster Abbey. St. Paul's Cathedral completed a 40 million-pound, fifteen-year, restoration project. In mid-July, the final part of the Harry Potter series of films, 'Harry Potter and the Deathly Hallows Part 2', which saw the demise of Harry's long-standing arch nemesis, Tom Riddle aka Lord Voldemort, released in the UK. In early August thousands of people started rioting and looting in towns and cities all over the UK, which initially started as protests in Tottenham following the police shooting of local man, Mark Duggan. Later in August, Red Arrows pilot Jon Egging tragically died at the Bournemouth Air Festival following a display. In September, energy firm 'Cuadrilla' announced controversially that it had located huge shale gas resources underground in parts of Lancashire. Among the famous faces who passed away during 2011 were Elisabeth Sladen who starred in 'Doctor Who' and the 'Sarah Jane Adventures', boxer Sir Henry Cooper, composer John Barry, CEO of Apple and Pixar, Steve Jobs, posthumously disgraced radio DJ, television presenter and abuser Jimmy Savile and talented singer songwriter Amy Winehouse who was so young at only 27. We also lost Pete Postlethwaite, Susannah York, Michael Gough, Anna Massey and Elizabeth Taylor from the acting community.

In July 2012, Axiom International invited me to join a small group of scientists headed by Professor Angela Gallop to examine the forensic science facilities in Erbil (the capital of Kurdistan) and most populous city in Northern Iraq. Out of all the places on my bucket list, I never thought that I'd be going to the very heart of the Middle East and to be honest, it made me feel nervous. Imagine how I would have felt, if I had been making the journey in the wake of General Qasem Soleimani's assassination on 3rd January 2020 and the subsequent retaliatory Iranian missile strike on the US military base in Erbil! Back in 2012, it was still very tense following years of unrest, but to my surprise as soon as I was in the country, I felt relaxed. We were treated like Gods and before we even arrived at the forensic science lab in baking heat, we had a meeting and took tea with one of the ministers. We were a team of seven – Angela, Rachael, Tony, Ian, David, Luke and me and our expertise included toxicology, drugs, forensic science, fingerprinting, crime scene examination and of course forensic photography. We had three full days in Kurdistan, with two full days examining the forensic science laboratory (FSL). Following a guided tour of the facilities, we split into our various specialisms to visit particular areas and in effect go on a fact-finding mission. We had complete free reign over the entire site and I set about firstly interviewing the photographic personnel, then photographing all the equipment and facilities to help all the team members compile their own reports. This was very intensive, hot, exhausting work, but I was pleased with the complete visual documentation, especially as it helped everyone out. My written report highlighted the need for some initial training encompassing: an overview of crime scene photography; principles of photography; scenes of crime photography; post mortem photography; night scene photography; Digital Imaging Guidelines and the photography of motor vehicles. I went on to completely cost out new camera kits as well as equipment such as printers that needed to be updated along with additional specialised kit that needed to be purchased such as microscopes.

I was inspired by what I saw at the FSL in Erbil and I particularly liked the enthusiasm and courteous disposition exhibited by the staff. They had clearly made a start as the basics were already in place and they did have systems that worked, albeit not yet interlinked. From the photographic perspective I had quite a few recommendations and I know that my fellow team members did too. I came away thinking that if FSL took on board our advice and underwent the necessary infrastructure modifications, implementation of procedures, equipment changes and training, then FSL Erbil would become a true centre of excellence – a model for the rest of the country to follow.

We were invited to the Minister's hilltop residence one evening to dine with him. This was very lavish, served out in the open and consisted of both fish and meat courses. It was delicious. I also remember several cats wondering around our table – the smell of fish and meat driving them bonkers. In between meetings at our plush hotel, the Erbil International, we had time to immerse ourselves in local culture. We visited the old city with its beautiful wall paintings and the nearby market, which sold literally everything. We were also driven into the eastern Taurus mountains close to the border with Iran, which was breath-taking. Kurdistan comprises to the north, south-eastern Turkey and to the south northern Iraq. To the east is north-western Iran and to the west (known as Rojava) is northern Syria. So technically, we were visiting Southern Kurdistan, which is confusing as we were in Northern Iraq (with the Iraqi capital, Baghdad, located approximately 350 kilometres to the south of Erbil)!

One of my abiding memories is having a chat over dinner with Kamal, who was Kurdistan military in charge of our security and our liaison man in Erbil. He was talking about how his country had suffered under Saddam Hussein's brutal dictatorship, which was characterised by invasion, economic sanctions and wide-scale death. Saddam Hussein Abd al-Majid al-Tikriti ruled Iraq from 16 July 1979 until 9 April 2003. He was executed by judicial hanging for crimes against humanity on 30 December 2006 at the age of 69. Saddam authorised the Halabja chemical attack, known as Bloody Friday, against the Kurdish people on March 16th, 1988 in the final days of the Iran-Iraq war. Mustard gas and unidentified nerve agents were used, which killed between 3000 and 5000 people and injured between 7000 and 10000 more. Kamal lost members of his family and friends during the genocide and he played a key role in the capture of Saddam Hussein. It was at that moment, sitting next to and chatting with him, that I put two and two together and realised that Kamal was of course, Peshmerga. He was born a fighter and fiercely proud of his homeland. When I asked him what he'd do if he came face to face with those responsible for killing his family and friends, he looked me in the eye courageously and defiantly and said, "I would hang them of course!" After I'd heard Kamal's heart-breaking story, it was difficult not to disagree.

My trip to Iraqi Kurdistan had been successful, but the team encountered a few problems on the way home. We flew in and out via Frankfurt and on arrival back at Heathrow, where I had to spend the night prior to taking the morning shuttle back to Manchester airport, I learned that my luggage had been left in Frankfurt and would be delivered to my home address some days later. This forced me to buy essentials such as toothbrush, paste and deodorant. Fortunately, I had packed underpants, socks and shirt in my hand luggage. Also, the whole team travelled back with a tummy bug. Terrified at the thought of hogging one of the toilets for the duration of the four+ hour flight from Erbil to Frankfurt, I bunged myself up with Diocalm. The anti-diarrhoea pills weaved their magic, but I could hear and feel my stomach innards breakdancing for the whole duration. I just about made it to the privacy of my hotel room at Heathrow where I violently vacated my bowels! Yes, a memorable overseas trip indeed.

In the summer of 2012, George's involvement with the scouting movement had come to an end. A decade earlier, he started off with his first pack, the 2nd Malden Cambridge based in New Malden, Surrey. I remember it as if it was yesterday, this small lad, standing with his fellow cubs, having fallen in for pack circle with Akela and having to say his Promise:

I promise that I will do my best
To do my duty to God and to the Queen
To help other people and to keep the Cub Scout Law

The Leader, Gary, then asked George to say the Cub Scout Law:

Cub Scouts always do their best, think of others before themselves, and do a good turn every day.

Gary then welcomed George into the Pack, whilst simultaneously putting the Group neckerchief around his neck and fastening it with a woggle. As a new cub, George was then presented with his Investiture Certificate and badges. He saluted the leader and duly fell back in to his position within the Pack circle, as a fully-fledged Cub Scout. I was a very proud father. What followed was ten years' shear enjoyment and adventure of scouting affiliation. A love of the outdoor life and a strong sense of belonging and being part of something really great. This continued as we moved up North and involved hiking in the Lake District, camping, learning campcraft skills, adventures in the Lake District, Yorkshire and at Waddecar Scout camp, along with kayaking tuition on the boating lake at Fleetwood, leadership skills and confidence building. 'Akela, we will do our best! Be prepared!'

Teaching in Libya was planned for October 2012. Jake Ireland, the link man for Axiom's Huddersfield Libyan Students had already experienced several trips to Tripoli in 2012 to set up security, paving the way for forensic experts to visit, and had encountered no problems. Jake informed me by email that, whilst there was no doubt that security pan Libya was to some extent fragmented and subject to sudden change, he was of the opinion that the situation in Tripoli was generally safe. Counter measures had already been set up to ensure our safety whilst in Libya. These included travelling with security, setting up a place of safety to head to, should it all kick off and planned escape routes out of the country. For this trip we would be staying at the Dar Tellile beach front hotel, approximately 80 kilometres west of Tripoli in Sabratha, which had been the scene of fierce civil war fighting only the previous year! In an emergency, if things got noisy, our escape from Dar Tellile would be by road, approximately 100 kilometres west to the Tunisian border. Alternatively, if we had time, via the airport with a convenient route pegged out straight from the hotel which would bypass Tripoli. In a dire emergency, escape and evasion would be via speed boat to Malta – a sod of a long journey (hopefully with lots of fuel and supplies on board)! Either way, I always slept with my passport nearby, a grab bag packed with essentials and valuables and my clothes and shoes neatly laid out, in the event things went pear shaped and I needed to get out fast! For the November trip, I was advised we would be staying at a boutique hotel, The Bustan, much closer to the centre of Tripoli. It was just a twenty-minute drive to Tripoli International airport, itself situated circa 28 kilometres to the south of Tripoli. The Bustan Hotel was in a secure compound with armed guards. There were several Libyan agents also in play, one based in Tripoli and the other staying at our hotel to do the driving. Both would be part of our security detail and closely monitoring the situation. Jake had walked around the streets of the capital, which included the Souk, on many occasions and felt perfectly safe. Trips out to any active crime scenes would be in police vehicles. Jake assured me that the situation in Libya was being constantly monitored and he was in personal contact with embassy staff who would inform him immediately of any deterioration in security.

Armed with this knowledge, I made the decision to go on both trips. First, I needed to purchase high risk travel insurance to cover me. After an exhaustive internet search, I couldn't seem to find the right package that would cover me for everything including being kidnapped, injured or killed by acts of war and terrorism and medical evacuation. Jake, who had already made multiple trips to Tripoli was of the opinion that I didn't need all this, but I begged to differ. Even the British Embassy's advice was not to travel. Securing insurance therefore was a challenge. Suddenly, one morning completely out of the blue, I received a snotty email from Jake saying that I had been dropped from this part of the MSc programme and that my services were no longer required! Bloody hell – I didn't see that one coming. Reading between the lines, Jake thought that I was going over the top with my insistence on high level insurance cover and he obviously perceived me as a thorn in his side, which he could do without. To me Jake's behaviour just came across as 'throwing his teddies out of his pram', he was being unprofessional to say the least. I emailed Angela at Axiom straight away and by the middle of the afternoon I had been miraculously re-instated! Looking back the situation was ludicrous and quite comical – the only time in my life that I've been hired, fired and re-hired by the same organisation all on the same day and with breakneck speed! Although I would still have to deal with Jake on the trip, I made a mental note to keep him at arms' length. I never did receive an apology from him, which told me everything I needed to know about that particular person!

I did eventually find a company specialising in high risk insurance and went for the top all singing all dancing level of cover. The reason for my insistence on getting this kind of insurance was that in the event of me being prematurely catapulted into the afterlife, I needed to be satisfied that my family would be looked after. The cost of getting medevaced from a conflict zone costs considerably more than loose change in your pocket. Standard travel insurance policies don't usually cover acts of war and terror and come with an FCO Travel Advice exclusion. The best value I found included a pay-out should I er…not be 'around' … full medical & evacuation coverage and repatriation back to the UK including ongoing coverage of medical and rehabilitation costs. My equipment, belongings and valuables were covered as standard.

So, I got the green light and flew out to Tripoli on 12th October 2012 for just under two weeks. I braced myself for a confrontation and bad words on arrival at Tripoli airport as I saw Jake Ireland walking towards me. Jake was perfectly civil, bordering on being charming, as though nothing had happened. No mention of his inappropriate, truculent behaviour whatsoever. Our driver took us to our hotel, Dar Tellil, which was stunning. It made an immediate impression on me, from the sweeping driveway and decadence of the marble interior to the massive outdoor swimming pool and array of sun loungers at the rear. All of this backed straight onto a deserted, picturesque beach and the gentle sway of the huge expanse of warm, south west Mediterranean waters. My en-suite room was spacious and clean, although the décor and furniture conveyed a tired appearance. My own balcony looked out onto the swimming pool, beach and Mediterranean. It was idyllic. Indeed, I was to come away from that trip with some amazing sunrise photographs over the swimming pool. However, it was heart-breaking to see the many bombed out and shell-ridden buildings nearby, standing as an eerie testament to Libya's ongoing volatility.

The oil rich country of Libya, encompassing an area approaching 1.8 million square kilometres, is the fourth largest country in Africa and the sixteenth largest in the world. The country is a sovereign state in Africa, being located in the far north of the continent, fronting the south west Mediterranean Sea. Tunisia borders Libya to the west, Egypt lies to the east, with Sudan to the south and Chad and Niger to Libya's south west. Tripoli is the nation's capital and largest city, located in north-west Libya. Benghazi is Libya's second largest city and is located just over 1000 kilometres (or an eleven-hour drive) east along the coast. The population of Libya stands at circa six million. The country was formerly a kingdom from 1951 until Muammar Gaddafi instigated a military coup in 1969, toppling King Idris. Colonel Gaddafi, the despotic leader, ruled Libya through dictatorship until he was overthrown during the 2011 war and killed following his capture later the same year in October 2011.

The long car journey from our hotel at Sabratha was punctuated with checkpoints. One of these consisted of two giant, metal shipping containers, propped up on concrete slabs to make a crude bridge over the main road. The heavily armed guards didn't put me off. Nor did I get the willies when I noticed the trucks littered either side of these checkpoints, sporting heavy calibre machine guns and canon mounted on the rear. What did cause me to turn my head to the right - not once but three times in a 'triple take' kind of action - was a dead body lying on the pavement just forward of one of these checkpoints, covered in a crude, cloth shroud. The giveaway was the shape of the deceased under the shroud and a pair of feet protruding out! I did get a little edgy and my mind was working overtime wondering how the deceased came to meet his fate. Was he a Gaddafi loyalist who was challenged at the checkpoint and was he under duress, or did he attack the checkpoint and was then shot by guards? I never did find out, but that dead body lying by the roadside left a lasting impression and gave me a reality check that I was definitely residing, albeit temporarily, in an unstable country thousands of miles away from home.

When I arrived at the CID building, enveloped by a large perimeter wall, I naively expected to waltz into a classroom and see my ten students sitting there eagerly awaiting 'Teacher's' return. These were the same students I'd taught when they were over in England after all. What I actually found was only two of my students who were chatting in a larger group, smoking on the stairwell. They did smile and came over to shake hands, but they didn't stop what they were doing and come into class. In fact, my entire visit was characterised by a 'couldn't care less' attitude – students drifting in and out of lessons seemingly on a whim, with no clear focus.

I was quite depressed with this state of play, but resolved to formulate a top-notch Billy Bollocks game plan setting out my proposed aim and goals for the second November trip in a report of my findings for Axiom penned at the end of my first trip to Libya.

What I found was that more than four decades of dictatorship had taken its toll. In fact, 42 years of suppression and control under Muammar Gaddafi's regime, a 2011 revolution culminating in Gaddafi's death and one year on coincidental fighting in the former leader's bastion, Bani Waled to quell Gaddafi Loyalist remnants and you had a country still desperate for freedom, but not yet fully liberated.

As the saying goes, 'when you've a revolution – you've confusion', such was my strong initial impression when I first walked into CID Tripoli. People standing or sitting around smoking and chatting in this NATO bombed building. They were receiving a salary, but not working because there was not yet the incentive, focus and professional work ethic in place. The country's fractured infrastructure needed to be rebuilt. Strategies needed to be devised and implemented. Among others, there needed to be a clear management structure, quality assurance and control, administrative support, inter and cross-departmental co-operation and an efficient and harmonious working environment. At that particular moment there was discord and further, people needed to be constantly told what to do and pointed in the right direction. Against this backdrop of inefficiency and uncertainty, from what I'd seen, I believed that things were fundamentally not happening as they should because the Libyan people did not yet feel safe.

Not one of the 10 essential Scenes of Crime Photography SOPs had been written when I arrived. This gave me a steer on what the students would achieve for the rest of the SOPs if left entirely to their own devices! On leaving Tripoli at the end of the October 2012 visit, I was forced to write the first four SOPs with instructions for the students to work together translating these 4 SOPS and also to write the remaining 6 SOPs in English and again in Arabic by the time I returned to Libya during the second week in November!

So, the purpose of my 2nd trip to Libya from 10th – 27th November 2012 was to ensure all 10 Photography SOPs were written satisfactorily. In addition, the photographers who had been to Huddersfield were required to undertake practise photography sessions in the following four areas:

- Scene photography
- Motor vehicle photography
- Visible marks photography
- Photography of injuries

They would then be competency tested against the corresponding SOPs. If no live scenes, including fire scenes, were available then competency testing would be undertaken with mock-up scenes. Initial post-mortem photography competency testing would be undertaken using a mock-up. It was hoped that in the future, with better working practices in place, the photography of night scenes, RTAs and post-mortems could be competency tested. Health and Safety SOP and Digital Imaging Guidelines SOP were competency tested by means of a scene scenario dynamic risk assessment and Q&A respectively. Post Libya visit, I reported on my findings and competency testing of the former Huddersfield University Photographers.

I drafted a letter about the photographers' poor attendance and winged it to Jake, which he then incorporated into a strongly worded letter to the Colonel in charge:

"Paul has come to Tripoli from the UK especially to deliver 'in-country' support and mentoring to all former Libyan students who attended his photography course at Huddersfield University as part of the forensic science programme.

With the exception of Sunday 14th October, not one photographer has stayed with Paul from 9 am until 2pm each day to practise the photography skills taught in the UK. We are very disappointed at your consistency in either turning up for 10 minutes when you feel like it and then leaving or as happened on Thursday 18th October – not turning up at all. If nothing else – this is unprofessional and disrespectful.

Paul will be returning to Tripoli CID on 11th November and his last day in CID will be 26th November. During these dates Paul expects all former Huddersfield University photography students to attend the practise scene photography, vehicle photography and photography of injuries sessions.

All former photography students will then be practically tested against the following Standard Operating Procedures (SOPs): Scene Photography SOP, Motor Vehicle Photography SOP and Photography of Injuries SOP.

Failure to attend the practise photography sessions (which may include live scenes) and the practical tests may well result in Colonel A not allowing you to continue in paid employment as photographers.

It is hoped that students will attend every day and make use of Paul's expertise. He looks forward to seeing you all on Sunday 11th November at 9am for the first practise photography session".

And that very much told them!

My day usually finished by 4pm at the latest and as soon as I got back to Dar Tellil, I hit the pool, swimming a hundred lengths daily. On one occasion I was lying on a sun lounger, poolside, engrossed in a Chris Ryan novel when I got the fright of my life. A fighter jet buzzed very low over the hotel and moments later, I heard the distinctive double thud of distant bombing as the aircraft had jettisoned its lethal cargo!

I had a very strange experience with a pair of black shoes that I wore daily to work at CID in Tripoli. I'd had them resoled and re-heeled at an exorbitant cost of twelve pounds before I flew out to Libya, but the heat caused these new soles and heels to not just unstick but completely come off! Jake had spotted a street-side cobbler in the small town of Sabratha, near to where we were staying. I dropped the shoes off with this little old man who looked to be pushing eighty. When I picked them up later that day, they were as good as new. And the cost? A mere 2 Dinar – then the equivalent of just one British pound. Not just cheap, but a pucker job and quality service to boot (no pun intended).

Staying at Dar Tellile meant that we were ideally placed to visit the awe-inspiring Roman ruins at Sabratha in Libya's Zawiya District, a UNESCO World Heritage Site. The ruins look out over the Mediterranean and are located approximately 70 kilometres west of Tripoli. I spent a couple of hours on the site and came away with some great shots of the famous theatre, bas relief carvings on the bottom of the stage and remains of arches and columns all set against a rich, cloudless, blue sky. I also have photos of some of Sabratha's old buildings riddled with high calibre rounds and machine gun holes – remnants of the civil war the previous year. I took quite a few photos during my tour of Tripoli's thriving Souk and the crumbling alleyways backing on to the famous market. On one side street I came across a pile of discarded rubbish, twenty or thirty bags dumped in a heap, then I spied at least six alley cats combing through the remains of rotting food, for any scraps to devour. My dusk photo taken of a mother and child walking towards me in a very atmospheric Souk back street, remains one of my favourites taken from the first Libya trip. Having smudged the Souk, I joined Jake and other visiting forensic specialists in an open-air, sit-down, evening meal at a restaurant very near the Souk at the Marcus Aurelius Arch. The local speciality was stewed baby camel cooked with vegetables in an earthenware pot. The top of this pot was hacked off in front of you, the food plated up and brought straight to your table with a side of couscous. It sounded good, smelled delicious and tasted even better and all washed down with a few glasses of red wine. Well, I thought 'When in Libya….'

The October trip had been a fact-finding mission and a setting out of what I needed to achieve by the end of the November visit, never mind that it constituted a complete let down. The students had really just drifted in and out with a disinterested attitude. That would all change come the November trip! The day before I was due to fly back out to Tripoli, I had an interview for a permanent job as a medical photographer at Blackpool's Victoria Hospital. The interview went well, which included a PowerPoint presentation of my work portfolio to date. I clocked the lady who went in before me as well as the lady who was waiting to go in after me. I immediately pegged them both as very experienced professional medical photographers and as a result, I wrote the job off in my head as I thought I didn't stand a chance. The following morning, I had passed check in and security at Manchester airport and had a window seat in Departures. I was just waiting for my gate to be announced, idly watching the planes take off and land whilst sipping a piping hot Costas skinny latte, when my phone suddenly rang. It was Steve, Head of Medical Photography at Victoria Hospital, Blackpool to say I'd got the job! Wow – I wasn't expecting that at all as competition was very tough indeed. I was really chuffed, all the more so as it meant that I had the security of a permanent job to look forward to in the new year after I had completed my November training with the Libyan students.

I was back in Libya on 10th November 2012. I had a strict agenda and was operating a zero-tolerance policy for piss takers and lazy bastards. I was ready to kick arse with the students if they didn't play ball. We were staying at the Bustan Hotel, a secure compound with armed guards and a mere twenty minutes-drive from CID just on the outskirts of Tripoli. My en suite room was clean and spacious, with a very comfortable bed, wide desk to do all my work and from which, I could skype home via my laptop. The paths leading to the single storey accommodation blocks were lined with colourful flowers and ubiquitous fig trees. The hotel had a great restaurant, games area and a fully equipped multi-gym that looked out onto an infinity pool, which was lit up at night. Like Dar Tellile, I used the pool daily. I also made use of the cardio-vascular machines in the gym as part of my daily workout.

Stalwart Forensic Scientist Dr. Roger Berrett, who had a special interest in fire reconstruction and whom I had last seen at Huddersfield University earlier that year, travelled out to Tripoli and stayed with us for a week. He wasn't in the best of health then, but nevertheless was still on top form with his lovely blend of serious, animated conversation, punctuated with quick-witted repartee. Shortly after this trip, I think Roger was diagnosed with cancer which he battled for quite a while. It was with immense sadness that I learned of his passing on 25th March 2016 at the age of 76. I felt privileged to have known and worked with Roger Berrett in a number of different locations over the years. He was a giant of a man in forensic science circles, having qualified in inorganic chemistry. Roger began his working life in the Drugs section at the MPS Forensic Science Laboratory, gradually working his way up to the top of the ladder and then becoming an operational member of the MPS Fire Investigation Unit. A former Vice President of the Forensic Science Society and latterly independent forensic consultant, Roger was a gifted scientist and great communicator. He was engaging and enthusiastic, reliable, clever, funny, friendly and above all, a thoroughly likeable man. I have very fond memories of Roger Berrett, typically telling a funny story with cigarette in hand, he left a lasting, positive impression on me. He is missed by all who knew him.

By the end of my November visit to Libya, I had really put all the students through their paces with different practical scenarios. My strategy was to keep the students busy, keep testing them, keep them on their toes all the time and don't give them even a second to think about being lazy and not turning up. Fortunately, my plan worked. Most of the students passed their assessments, but unfortunately one chap just couldn't get to grips with the practical side. He was a personable, friendly guy, but he had zero common sense and no crime scene logic. One of my abiding memories of this student is seeing him trampling all the way through a mock crime scene without thinking, complete with fully extended tripod on his shoulder, like a rocket launcher! Totally FUBAR!

It was a very busy stay as I also had marking to do, never mind the module SOPs to write, check and have translated into Arabic, as previously stated. Finally, I had my closing report and recommendations to write for Axiom.

Before departing Libya, I visited the Souk in Tripoli several more times and on the way back to the hotel asked the taxi driver whether he could take me through Gaddafi's bombed out compound, so I could photograph it. I took some unforgettable images of burnt out cars sitting on top of giant slabs of concrete that had been brought crashing down by NATO air strikes. I also took photographs of some amazing wall graffiti depicting the liberation of Libya and the demise of its dictator. In one particular satirical image, on the left-hand side, is a caricature of Gaddafi stumbling over next to an open prison cell door, with his 'crown' falling off and his teeth dropping to the ground. In contrast, the dead former leader is depicted on the right-hand side of the artwork as a confident looking despot shaking hands with Hitler, whilst a smug looking Mussolini and Stalin look on, together with a grinning Saddam Hussein. In the middle of this artwork were the words 'Libya free'.

When I left Libya towards the end of November 2012, the country was fractured and unstable, but desperate to find its feet again. The bombed-out buildings, some riddled with holes from high calibre rounds, scenes of destruction everywhere you looked, were stark reminders of a very much on-going struggle. There are more than 1000 kilometres of beautiful, untapped Mediterranean coastline along Libya's northern edge, just waiting for peace and prosperity to usher in investors and a string of boutique hotels. One day Libya, a country with masses of potential, will be truly free and a thriving holiday mecca. One day I hope to return to Libya to see it all!

Approaching Christmas in the autumn academic term in 2012, hot on the heels of his electrifying performance as Tony in SODs' adaptation of 'West Side Story', George was a recognised Blackpool Sixth Ambassador and Student Governor. He was already performing around Lancashire as the male vocalist for the prestigious LYJO (the Lancashire Youth Jazz Orchestra). He then masterminded the first ever joint concert between Blackpool Sixth Performing Arts, Music and Media and LYJO, then under the skilful direction of Stuart Grylls. And what an amazing, uplifting evening it turned out to be. We were very proud to be sitting in the audience. 2012 culminated in George's milestone 18th birthday. Wendy and I even handed over our house so that George could have a party. Quite a brave thing to do as parents! I must admit I did half expect to see the place a wreck on the inside with booze bottles littering every room and graffiti adorning every wall, but no, the house was immaculate. George and his friends had tidied and cleaned throughout. When we arrived home the next day, I popped outside to our utility room to put some washing on and noticed a pile of dirty clothes on the floor, waiting to be washed. As I knelt down to pick them up, I slightly lost my footing and put my left hand out onto the pile of dirty washing to steady myself. I felt the sticky mess and smelled it all at once … the disgusting stench of human vomit. George had completely forgotten about his friend's soiled garment – oops and yuck!

2012 was an Olympic year. In the January after almost two decades, Gary Dobson and David Norris were given life sentences for the 1992 murder of Stephen Lawrence. On 6th February Her Majesty The Queen celebrated her Diamond Jubilee with 60 years on the throne. Mid-April marked the centenary of the sinking of RMS Titanic. The month of April turned out to be the wettest on record in the UK. On 18th May, the Olympic flame arrived in Cornwall all set for the torch relay, prior to London hosting the 2012 summer Olympic games. When the Olympic torch made its way to Lancashire, we saw it on the streets of Blackburn and we also managed to borrow it from one of Wendy's work colleagues – and of course it was duly photographed! On 22nd July Sir Bradley Wiggins became the first British cyclist to win the Tour de France. On 27th July the Olympic games commenced with the opening ceremony in London. By the games' close Team GB finished third in the medal table, netting 29 gold medals and 65 medals in total. The 29th August saw the opening ceremony of the 2012 summer Paralympic Games which ended on 9th September. Wendy's brother Simon managed to get me a ticket and I enjoyed a brilliant afternoon and evening in the company of Simon and two of his friends at the Olympic Park near Stratford. On 22nd October, surgeons undertook the first robotic open-heart operation in Britain at Wolverhampton's New Cross Hospital. London's Royal Albert Hall premiered the James Bond film, 'Skyfall'. At the end of October, the first mobile 4G network was launched in eleven cities, which offered high speed mobile data services.

We lost quite a few famous faces in 2012, including comedian Frank Carson, Ken Goodwin (one of my favourite comedians from my youth), journalists and broadcasters Sir Alastair Burnet and Derek Jameson, hairdresser Vidal Sassoon, Bee Gees legend Robin Gibb, darts player Jocky Wilson, singer and variety performer Max Bygraves, physicist and radio astronomer Sir Bernard Lovell, politicians Sir Rhodes Boyson and Jack Ashley, TV broadcaster Kenneth Kendall, astronomer Sir Patrick Moore and Thunderbirds creator Gerry Anderson. From the acting world we lost Clive Dunn of 'Dad's Army' fame, Philip Madoc, Eric Sykes and Simon Ward.

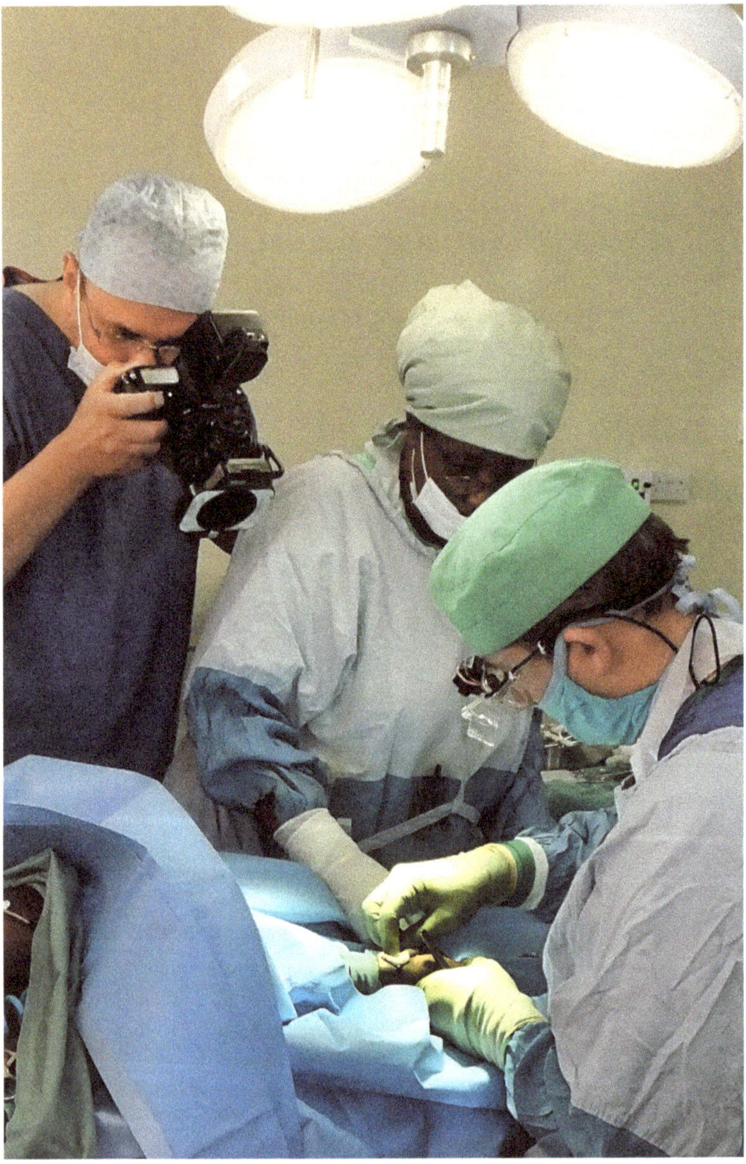

Photographing one of Consultant Orthopaedic Surgeon Steve Mannion's operations at Lilongwe's DaeYang Luke Hospital, Malawi, June 2011.

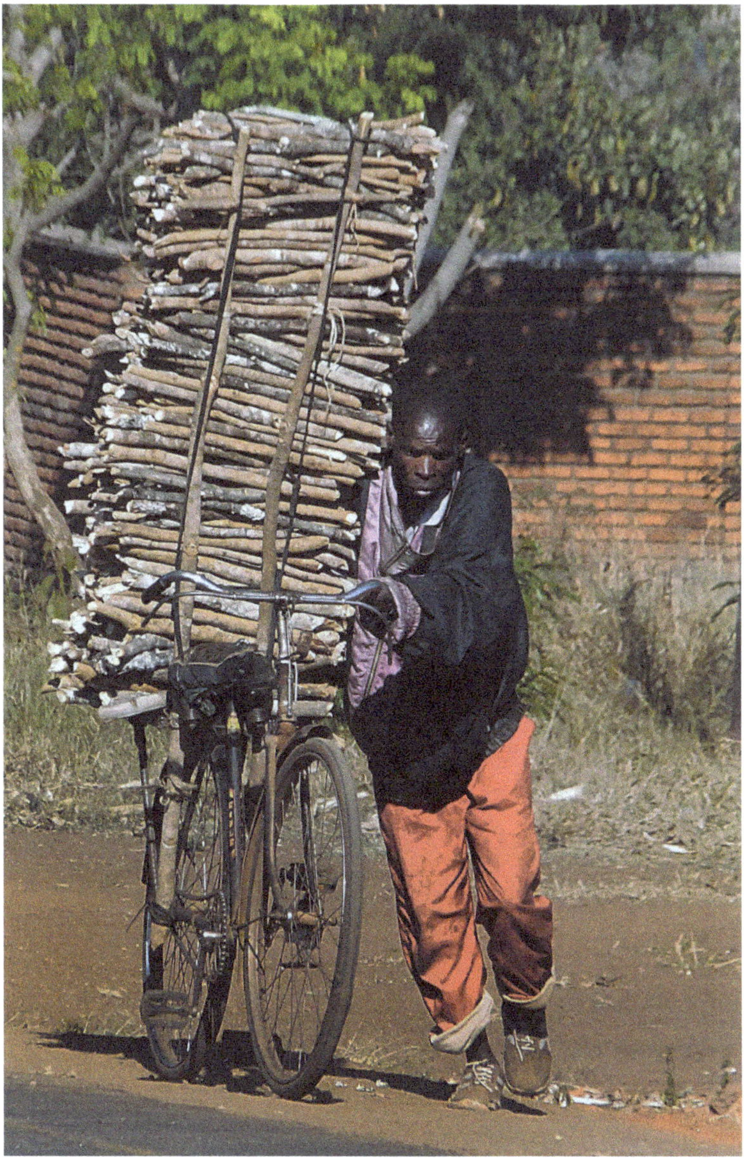

'Everything but the kitchen sink', bicycle load, Malawi, Africa, June 2011.

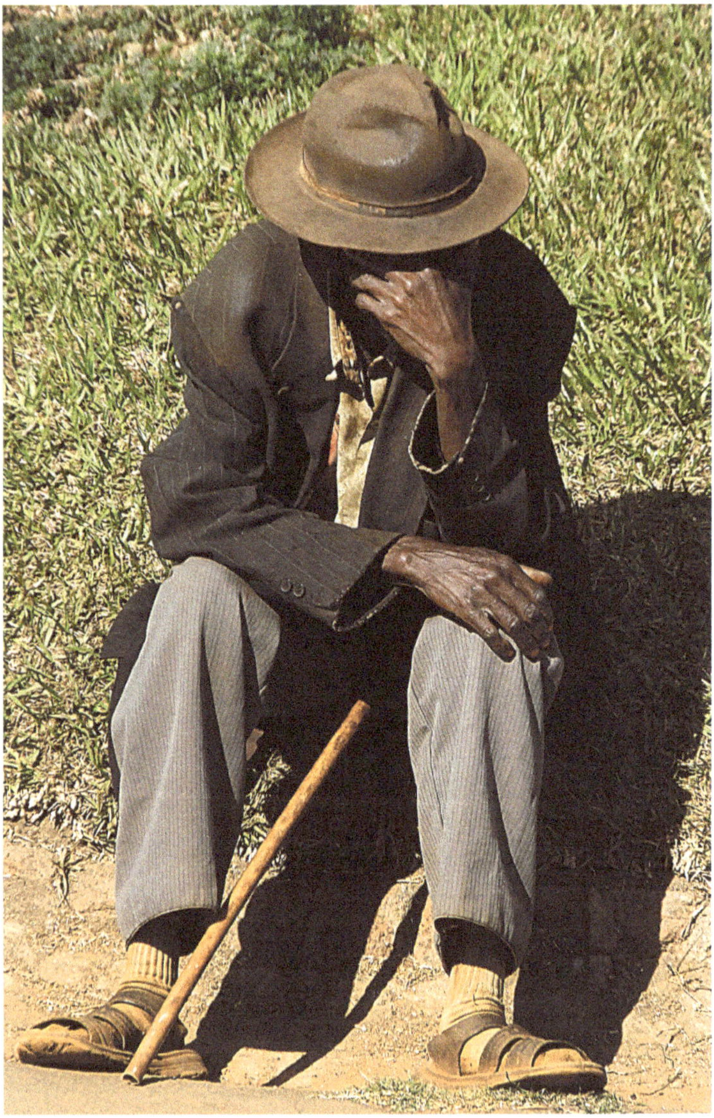

Awaiting his turn to be seen by doctors, this man rests outside DaeYang Luke hospital, Lilongwe, Malawi, having walked miles, June 2011.

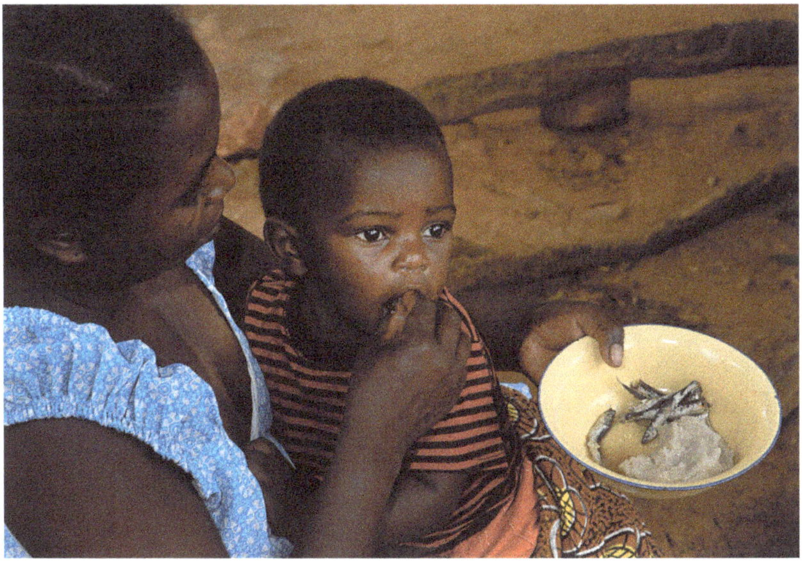

A Patient's relative feeding a child in the grounds of Nkhata Bay District Hospital on the western shores of central Lake Malawi, June 2011.

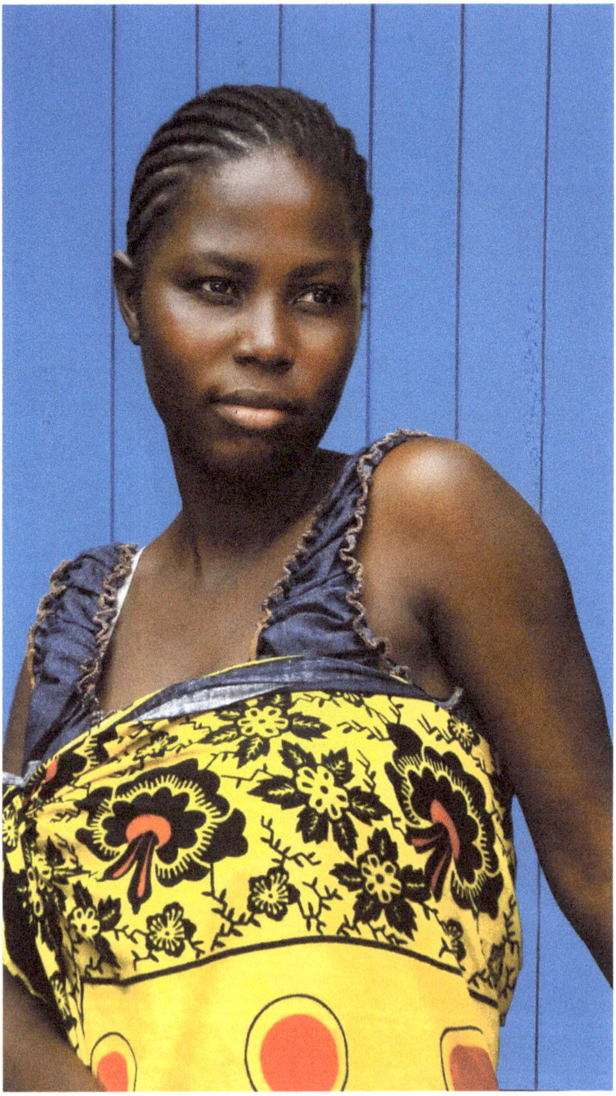

A young Malawi girl in vibrant colours, June 2011.

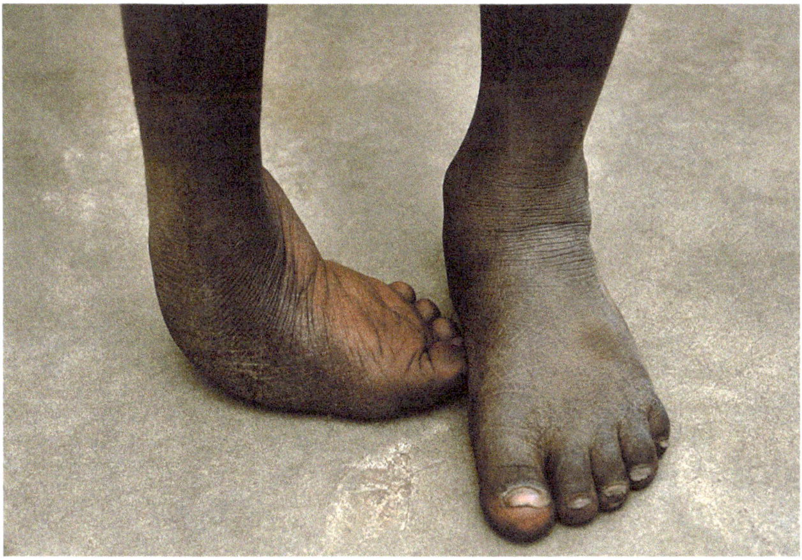

A young patient presenting with right congenital talipes equino-varus or club foot, Map Clinic, Lilongwe, Malawi, June 2011.

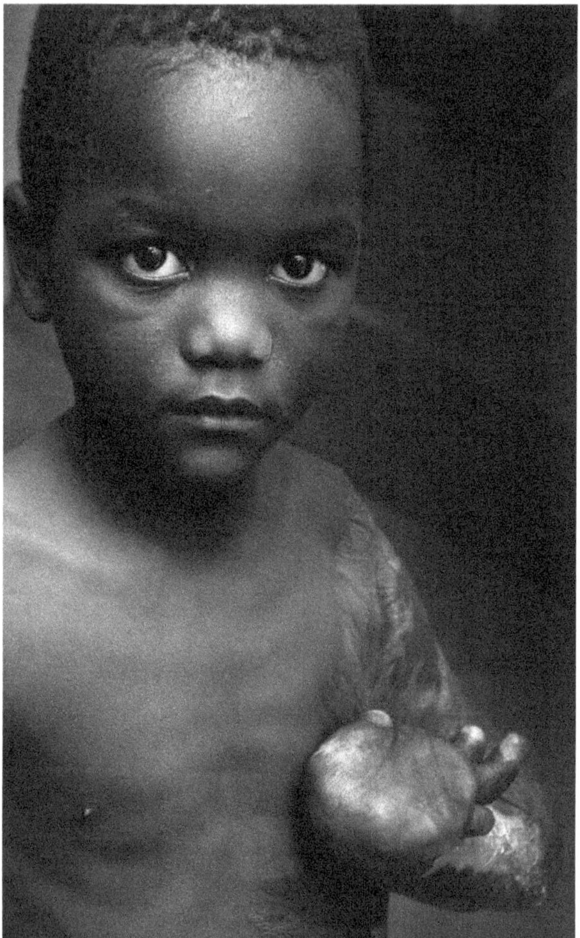

A young boy with left arm and hand burns injuries, Map Clinic, Lilongwe, Malawi, June 2011.

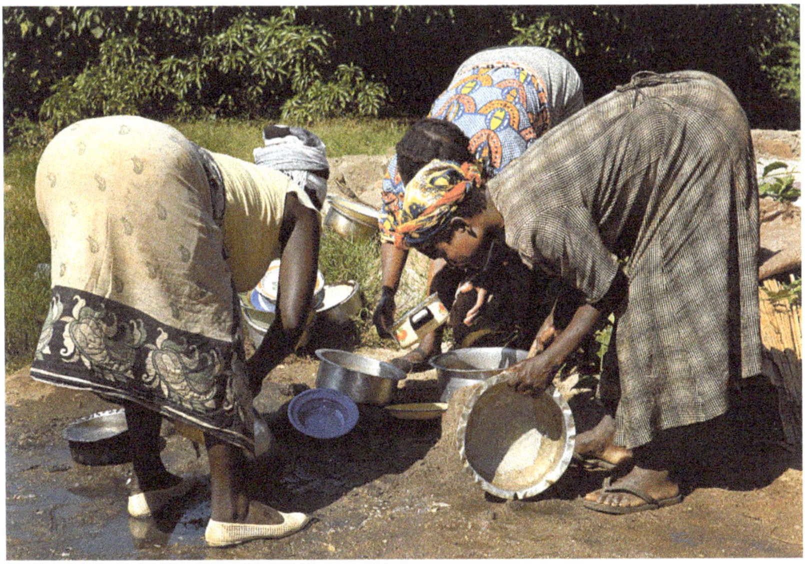

Women washing pots in the family waiting area, grounds of Nkhata Bay District Hospital on the western shores of central Lake Malawi, June 2011.

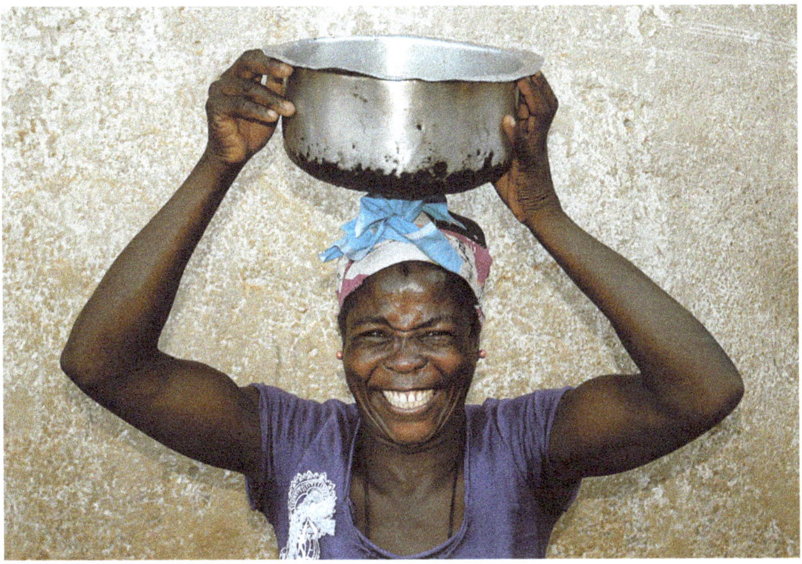

A woman carrying a bowl on her head in the grounds of Nkhata Bay District Hospital, Malawi, June 2011.

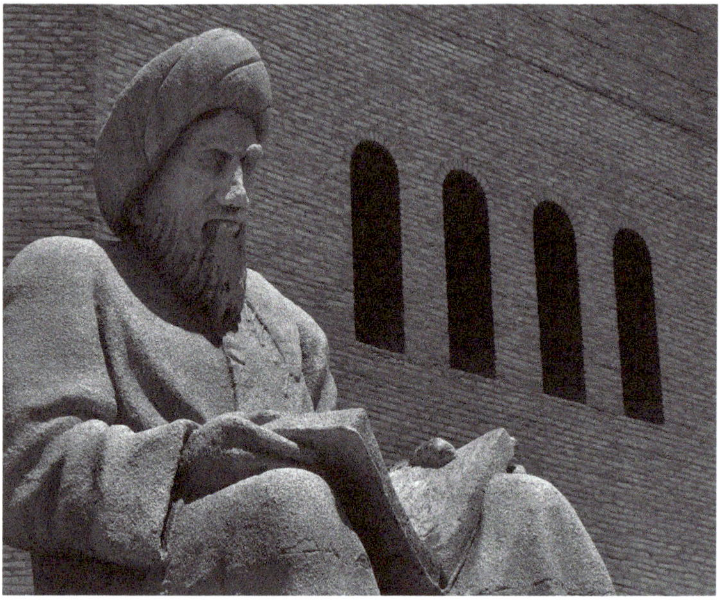

Old City, Erbil, Kurdistan, Northern Iraq, July 2012.

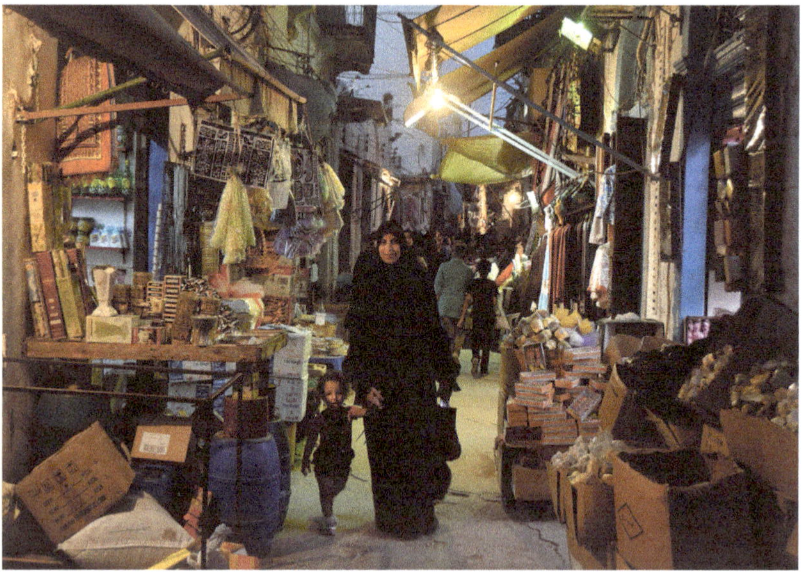

Tripoli Souk, Libya, North Africa, October 2012.

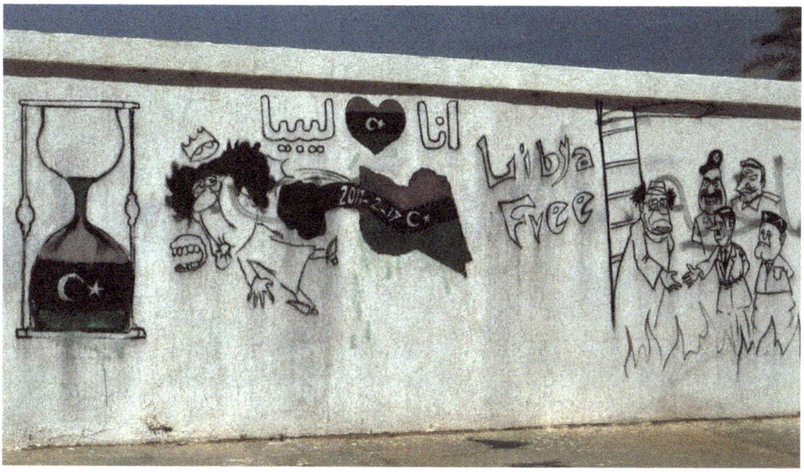

Wall graffiti photographed one year after the downfall of former leader Colonel Muammar Gaddafi, Tripoli, Libya, North Africa, October 2012.

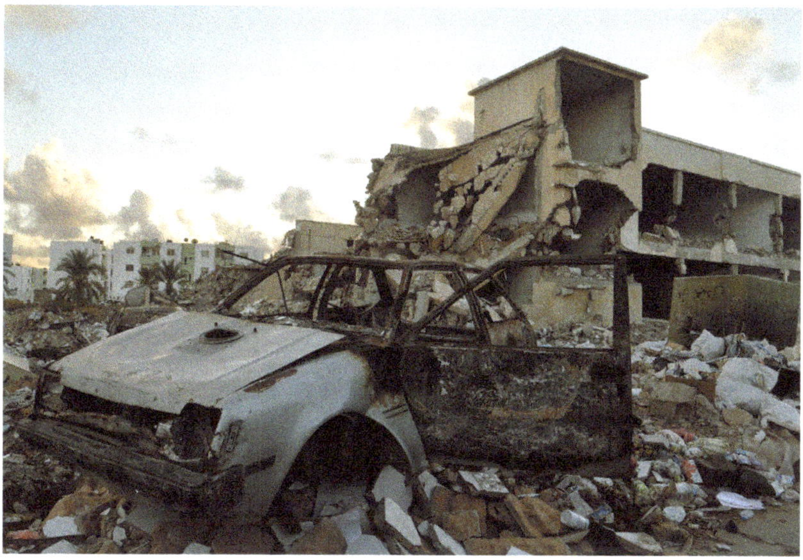

Colonel Gaddafi's bombed out compound in Tripoli, Libya, November 2012.

CHAPTER 24

NHS Medical Photographer (February 2013 to date) and Gardiner Associates Training and Research (GATR) – Training the UK's Fire Investigators in Forensic Fire Scene Photography (2006 to date)

On February 4th, 2013, I took up my new post as one of two, full-time, staff medical photographers at Blackpool Victoria Hospital, known as 'The Vic', for short or by its full title 'Blackpool Teaching Hospitals NHS Foundation Trust'. Working with the manager Steve, a twenty year plus veteran of the department, has indeed been an education. In February 2020 we recruited a new member to our small team, Chimane, who is professional, a highly respected and valued colleague, hard-working, friendly, good-humoured, a joy to work with and quite frankly, a welcome breath of fresh air.

The hours are 8.30am to 4.30pm Monday to Friday, which suit me fine. On top of this is on-call, which is about as different to scenes of crime on call as it gets. In the police, on-call was mandatory and you were guaranteed to be working out of hours and for long periods. At Blackpool Vic, Medical Photography operate a voluntary on-call and I average 2-4 call-outs, including at weekends per month. We were using the 12.3 Mp, DX sensor, Nikon D300s DSLR camera system and lenses, brought to the marketplace in late summer 2009, for ages. This equipment has recently (early spring 2020) been replaced and updated with the Nikon D780 kit. The old 300S cameras were hammered over the years and were quite literally falling apart. The Nikons are used in conjunction with Sigma and Kenro ring flash for even illumination of subject matter, especially useful when photographing into recesses and orifices, to prevent hard shadows. I find myself photographing sacral, bottom and anal pressure ulcers on a daily basis and they particularly lend themselves to ring flash-lighting (no funny intended!). The beauty of the ring flash, apart from the consistency of emitted illumination, is that I can operate the camera one-handed if I have to. This allows me to unclip the ring flash and use it to side light a wound, the often bulbous, diabetic charcot foot, or simply bounce the damn thing – if direct light casts too strong a shadow, for example. We also carry Nikon SB flash guns.

Until the end of 2019, we used 'Topcon' for eye scanning and fundus photography, after which, fundus imaging and scanning was undertaken by an all singing, all dancing superior resolution 'Heidelberg Spectralis' system, complemented by the Optos ultra-wide field retinal imager, which have made all our lives (and more importantly the patients' lives) vastly easier.

Wendy, who has worked for the NHS since we moved up here, is an Improvement and Development Manager in Occupational Health. She's now also based at Blackpool Victoria Hospital, so the two of us travel into the Vic together. My role involves the accurate recording of injuries, surgical procedures, wounds, pressure ulcers, medical conditions and diseases – generally to document as visual evidence and for charting the progression of conditions and resulting treatment, to aid the clinician. We also cover a lot of specialist ophthalmic work, in additional to technically demanding surgery (particularly in unusual cases) as well as specialised clinics. Each patient referral requires an appropriate level of consent (medical record only, teaching or medical publication consent). The job, as I've intimated, is essentially documentary and evidential in nature, is largely reactionary, responding to photographic requests as they arise, which are then fitted around the daily morning and afternoon ophthalmology clinics.

Ophthalmology assignments comprise conventional studio photography of the outer eye and eyelids, 'slit-lamp' photography of the outer eye and layers of the eyeball and specialised imaging and 'ocular coherence tomography' (OCT) light wave scanning of the retina located at the back of the eye. Ocular coherence tomography is a pivotal tool used in ophthalmology for primarily viewing retinal pathology as well as the eye's anterior segment, for improving referral accuracy and to monitor onset and progression of disease. All manner of eye conditions and diseases are covered that include ptosis (droopy eyelids), ectropion (a condition where the lower eyelids droop and curl outwards, exposing the reddened surface of the inner eyelids), pterygium (a pinkish, triangular tissue / blood vessel growth on the cornea of the eye, typically originating on the cornea near the nose), iris naevi (moles), AMD (age related macular degeneration - an eye disease which typically presents after the age of 50 that can progressively destroy the retina's macula (located at the back of the eye) and is responsible for our sharp, central vision when we view objects straight in front of us and CNV (Choroidal Neovascularisation. CNV is the creation of new blood vessels in the choroid or vascular layer of the eye (between the retina at the back and the white coloured sclera at the front of the eye). CNV is a major cause of visual acuity loss). Conditions such as AMD and CNV are photographed using the specialised fundus retinal camera (Heidelberg), as part of a 'fundus fluorescein angiography' or 'FFA', in addition to being scanned.

An FFA is a very common ocular procedure that is undertaken, usually by a nurse working together with a medical photographer, to give the requesting ophthalmic doctor more information about a suspected condition in the choroid and retina at the back of one or both eyes. A small volume of yellow-coloured, sodium fluorescein dye is injected via a cannula into a vein in the patient's arm or hand. Depending on the patient's circulation, the dye then quickly travels (in a matter of seconds) to the retina at the back of the eye. Here the fluorescing dye highlights the blood vessels and is particularly useful as it pinpoints any leaking blood vessels and also where the retinal blood supply is weak within the retina's vascular profusion. A video, followed immediately by timed photographs are taken with the fundus camera from the moment the dye is injected and will show the pivotal moment the dye floods through the back of the eye. The time between dye injection and when it appears at the back of the eye, provides an objective rate of blood flow measurement through the blood vessels being photographed. FFA's can detect many conditions and diseases from tumours to artery and vein occlusions (blockages).

Other photographic requests come in from all over the hospital, from Accident and Emergency, Intensive care, High Dependency, Acute Medical Unit, wards, clinics, theatres and cardiac theatres. A photographic request can cover literally everything from a colour image depicting the optic nerve head, to plastics, orthopaedics, Ear, Nose and Throat (ENT), Diabetic Foot Clinic, mole mapping for dermatology, gastroenterology, urology, neurology, orthodontics, microbiology, pathology and surgery.

Images taken before, during and after a particular treatment or procedure can provide valuable evidence to the health professional.

As a teaching hospital, we're also able to provide photographs and videos of wounds and complex surgical procedures for medical staff to incorporate into their teaching and training, sometimes showcasing new equipment or techniques.

Unfortunately, I do get to see the results of Blackpool's less attractive side – the alcoholism, the drugs and the homelessness. Only recently, I arrived at the department about to swipe in when I was almost overwhelmed by the stench of faeces and body odour. It transpired that a poor homeless man, covered in his own filfth and excrement, had snuck into a little used under stairs washroom and had in effect been living rough there, undiscovered for a few days. Once disturbed, the unfortunate down and out simply upped and shuffled away. A thorough deep clean of the area was undertaken by two cleaners donned in white, disposable suits, masks, gloves and overshoes. The forensically suited duo approached the fetid room cautiously and looked for all the world like they were about to embark on a detailed murder scene examination.

As a medical photographer, I am frequently called upon to take images for evidence in safeguarding incidents – innocent and defenceless kiddies who have been sexually and physically abused – slapped, whipped, kicked, punched and neglected, in some cases with matted and unwashed hair riddled with lice. In another very sad case, a small girl presented with burn marks having been tortured with a lit cigarette. I was called to photograph a heart wrenching neglect occurrence, a baby was so emaciated you could see its bones. That particular little one, and the look of horror on the Consultant Paediatrician's face, won't be forgotten in a hurry.

Occasionally, we have to record deceased babies, which can be very upsetting, particularly when relatives are present. On one occasion, I thought I was just going to take a couple of images of a still born in its crib, in a quiet room. So, when the midwife opened a door for me to walk through, I was instead greeted with the grieving couple who both looked about seventeen, propped up in bed cradling their dead child and surrounded on both sides by no fewer than twenty, ashen faced relatives. They all stared firstly at me, then at my camera and flash as if I was an obtrusive, unwanted paparazzi! The scene to any onlooker must have been bizarre and I was absolutely mortified that I had been put in this position without warning. The poor parents. What I wanted to do was turn around and run. What I actually did, was call on all my years of experience and diplomatic communication skills to take half a dozen, very discreet bereavement photos. When

I left that room, I had tears in my eyes and headed straight to the hospital chapel for a few minutes of quiet reflection. Both safeguarding and infant death can be a harrowing experience, but it is important to remain professional, as an accurate visual record can be crucial in court cases.

My qualifications in photography, Medical Illustration and teaching, coupled with my work and life experience over the years, working in technically and emotionally challenging arenas, has equipped me to deal with most situations that the hospital throws at me. However, just as I was beginning to think that there's not much now that I haven't seen, I visited a lady in her mid-90s late in 2019. Before photography had even started, the patient started crying and moaning, exclaiming to the nurse who was with me "I just want to go to sleep…I just want to die". It was so sad to witness. Equally poignant, was the occasion when I entered one of our wards to photograph an elderly gentleman's sacral sore only to be told in hushed tones that my patient had died just half an hour beforehand – a sobering thought indeed! Then there was the retired chap who limped into the Medical Retina Unit to have an eye scan recently. On leaving, he turned to me and said, "Forty years ago I was as fit as a fiddle and milking a hundred cows a day". Similarly, the sprightly 95-year old gentleman, who, also following his eye scan, shook hands with me (pre-Covid) and with a twinkle in his eye and a wry smile said, "Aye, thanking you Sonny, I thought I'd come in here for a quick MoT". Come to think of it there was another eye scanning patient several years before – I wondered why I couldn't scan the gentleman's right eye. It took twenty minutes of buggering about and not even a flicker of a signal was visible. Then the man piped up to tell me in no uncertain terms that the eye in question was prosthetic…doh! Even when finished work, waiting in the main hospital reception for Wendy to take me home, there's no escaping 'things' - you see and hear so much, like the irate, obese, middle-aged lady who turned to her other half to enquire whether he'd got her tablets in the shopping bag he was carrying. "No I haven't", he replied, "Do you want me to go back?" The lady half turned, mid shuffle to the entrance, snorted and said, "Na, I'm not bothered, you can sue 'em when I die!"

And I'll never forget the little old lady brought in from a care home following a fall, covered from head to toe in bruises and being cuddled by the ward manager and also the gentle touches and softly spoken words of our local hospice nurses, as they assisted me with my sensitive photographic documentation of a shrunken body peppered with pressure ulcers. The wounds belonged to someone, a man, not much older than me, whom I was destined never to know and who right now, was all but out of time – the compassion shown at these special moments were the photographs I took in my mind, but was forbidden to take in reality. As a medical photographer, it's imperative to have a good rapport with everyone you meet. I feel very strongly about making the patient's experience the best it can possibly be. Patients don't expect to be photographed in hospital and quite often they're understandably nervous, put out and frightened, so it means a lot to me to get it right and to always take time to explain what I'm doing and why. Those few extra moments to build that trust and respect and to put the patient at ease can make all the difference.

Since joining Blackpool Victoria Hospital in 2013, I've been involved with a variety of projects. One of the more recent and rewarding involves working on 'Patient Diaries' in ITU and HDU – the brainchild of the talented former Sister (now Advanced Practitioner) Cat. Here the patient is generally unconscious and is photographed showing all the equipment surrounding them. The idea is that the images are shown to the patient and their families as they recover, which can significantly help with their emotional rehabilitation. In October 2019 we started a Saturday pilot tele-dermatology clinic, for the fast track visual documentation, subsequent diagnoses, consultation and health care management of suspect cancerous skin moles and tumours, which is proving to be very successful. Up and coming projects include 3D imaging for diabetic foot ulcers and equipping the hospital wards and district nurses in the community setting with a mobile device and app to better aid the reporting and documentation of pressure ulcers (it was whilst being part of a working group for this mobile app that I first heard one of the team talk about how many 'Goats' and 'Cows' there were, which perplexed me. I thought the Met Police had loads of abbreviations, well the NHS is no different. Goat stands for 'gadget on a trolley' and a cow is a 'computer on wheels').

At the end of August 2019, I spent a morning with one of our District Nurses in Fleetwood and saw first-hand, the problem of not having a photographic capability to visually document and / or refer pressure ulcers and wounds to senior clinicians. One visit to a middle aged, obese, male patient with swollen legs, poor mobility and an ungradable bottom ulcer that had turned necrotic in the three days since the last district nurse visit, convinced me that equipping all our district nurses with a good quality photographic device, had to be seen as a prerequisite.

The job is extremely busy, challenging and not for the faint hearted as you do need a strong stomach and sometimes even an imaginary peg on your nose. This is especially useful on some of the wards with the ever-present smell of stale urine, faeces, sweaty bottom odour, vomit and necrotic wounds, which I find even worse than a gutted corpse! You also have to be prepared for the unexpected, such as the patient in tears, angry, asleep, or unresponsive. On peeling back the bedclothes, you can even be faced with your patient having had a massive seepage, defecating everywhere, or you go to photograph a sacral pressure ulcer only to discover that the patient has no legs – as can happen on a not too infrequent basis. Seeing the array of ulcers with accompanying missing toe, foot or leg amputations on a Tuesday afternoon's diabetic foot clinic, is about as stark a reminder as one can get of the devastating effects of diabetes. I'd put it on a par with the inevitable daily sight of the blue, canvas covered trolleys on the main ground floor corridor being wheeled by the pale blue shirted, rubber-gloved porters, delivering their recently deceased cargo to the hospital mortuary's fridge room. Only very recently, I turned around on the ground floor corridor to see one such blue canvas covered trolley 'chasing me'. Everyone and everything passes along the old ground floor corridor, which is so long it seems to stretch to infinity. Whether jovial, grieving, smiling or pensive, we all travel the same road. It's the only place I know that brings all of the following together in the same place: people dressed in their pyjamas, the Chief Exec, clinical and clerical staff, a police officer, a pregnant lady, a chaplain, a resus team rushing to an emergency, a cleaner, a maintenance man, a painter, an anxious patient's relative, a wheelchair user ... in fact Uncle Tom Cobley and all can share the same roadway as a corpse!

Fortunately, most visitors are oblivious of the deceased being wheeled up to the mortuary. Equally unpalatable are the sounds of patients throwing up, retching, shouting, groaning and the yelps of patients who are clearly suffering and in distress, or the rare times patients or their relatives 'kick off'. In my utopian NHS, every hospital inpatient would have their own dedicated Florence Nightingale and St. Camillus de Lellis – one of each for both daytime and night-time. Sadly, the reality is that many patients, especially the very elderly, have infrequent visitors, or worse – no visitors at all. It's heart-breaking seeing the look of despair on their faces, when all they want is for someone to sit by their bedside, hold their hand and keep them company.

With access to virtually all areas of the hospital I get to clamp my eyes on myriad weird and wonderful sights that most people will never see. To attend cardiac theatre when the name of the game is open heart surgery, to set eyes on a beating heart right there in front of you, to see one of our highly skilled cardiothoracic surgeons performing a 'CABG', is an incredible privilege. A CABG is referred to as a 'cabbage', a coronary artery bypass operation to restore normal blood flow to a blocked coronary artery. Another day it might be a heart valve replacement or an 'elephant's trunk' procedure (used to treat aortic aneurysms involving both the ascending aorta or aortic arch and the descending thoracic or thoracoabdominal aorta), which again, is a rare privilege. All too often I'll pick up the office phone and talk to a Consultant or some other senior clinical bod, who wants me to drop what I'm doing and come right now to photograph their patient. On this occasion it's a male consultant and he's talking to me as if I'm a fellow doctor, in medical language with protracted terminology and all very quickly. I pick up on half a word, 'glut', before I hear two words I understand: 'thank' and 'you' and then the line goes dead. I haven't got a bloody clue what I'm about to photograph, so I turn to trusty Google. Bingo. Got it. It's the gluteal region – the buttocks, which turn out to be huge and belonging to a very obese gentleman indeed. Said derrière was red, sore and peppered with crusty lesions! Turning to Google for help reminds me of a story my father told me years ago. As a young, qualified medical doctor on the night shift at Mitcham's Wilson Hospital some time back in the late 1940's, Dad had to carry out an emergency procedure on a patient and found himself right in at the deep end. He was the only doctor and had to quickly read up on what to do immediately beforehand as he was unsure. The op, apparently, was a complete success!

I use our fully equipped studio with its ceiling track-mounted electronic flash heads, to photograph mobile patients referred to us from clinics such as ENT, plastics, ophthalmology and breast care. When photographing intimate injuries, protocol dictates that we have to have a chaperone who is the same sex as the patient present. I photographed an obs and gynae ward patient quite recently who had a severe labial lesion. When I arrived to document this lesion, I somehow got it into my head that I would be photographing a 1 to

2cm cut in the nether region, however I shockingly discovered that the wound was so severe that the poor patient was now devoid of her vagina and surrounding tissue. Similarly, a Urology theatre request saw me photograph a set of testicles...from the inside of their casing! Necrotising fasciitis had eaten away at the scrotal tissue and following debridement, this had unfortunately left this particular patient with no scrotum. Another sensitive case days later and I found myself photographing a 'de-gloved' penis following an alleged biting incident. Equally unpalatable was witnessing first-hand the destructive nature of penile cancer, which robbed a middle-aged gent of his manhood. There are not too infrequent visits to any one of a number of operating theatres, which always provide cases of interest, be they a large, 'pulsating aneurysm' for vascular surgeons or the removal of an entire leg at the hip, by Orthopaedic surgeons. A very recent ophthalmology case saw me photographing a patient's eye socket. Witnessing a patient remove their prosthetic leg is one thing, but removing a false eye is quite another!

Once a week we visit one of our satellite rehabilitation facilities, Clifton Hospital, located in Lytham St Annes, to photograph any patient pressure ulcers, wounds or injuries.

The Vic has its own communications department who undertake the bulk of the PR photography for the Trust's intranet, internal promotion and press releases. Sometimes 'Comms' will ask us to help out or refer a particular job and visa versa. I tend to cover portraits of all the board members and directors as well as individual department portraits such as Cardiology, Childrens' ward and Haematology ward, to make it easier for patients and relatives to put a name to a face. Early in 2020 I completed all the imagery for the Trust's Dermatology intranet site, which was a thoroughly enjoyable project.

Bizarre experiences include recently photographing an elderly male patient's leg ulcers and having to give the nurse a hand when she moved the patient from his chair to the bed. The unfortunate patient got stuck half on and half off the bed and was in danger of slipping off. We had to shout for additional help. Again, very recently, I was called to photograph a massive abdominal cyst in theatre. As I stepped out on to the theatre floor from the scrub anteroom I exclaimed "Wow!" when I first saw it. This prompted the surgical team to reply "Yeah, that's exactly what we said". Then there was the studio appointment, where an elderly lady presented with a cancerous eight-inch cheek tumour, which unfortunately resembled a bulbous, crusty, detumescent penis! It begged the question, why on earth wait for so long to have it taken off? On another occasion, I was in one of the Clifton Hospital wards just about to take a photograph of a male patient's sacral pressure ulcer. So, imagine the scene, 'Danny' the HCA (Health Care Assistant) had turned the patient on his left side, exposing his bare bottom to the camera. Danny's left hand was steadying the patient and his right hand was slightly raising the patient's uppermost (right) buttock. Just as I was about to press the camera's shutter release, the patient farted loudly and immediately followed through with a cascade of runny and extremely malodorous faeces. The patient shouted out in a strong Lancashire accent for all to hear, "Aye – that was a bit naughty!" Danny and I exchanged a smile and quickly looked away from each other to stifle our laughter. A very recent trip to our orthopaedic ward to photograph a middle-aged female patient saw me go through my initial spiel explaining the taking of consent. Half-way through my patter and a shocked patient jabbed at me, "You what? You wanna whip my knickers down?" The partially deaf patient had misheard 'take consent' for 'take knickers down'. Fortunately, everyone fell about laughing...thank God! Similar to my work in forensic photography, it's important to see the funny side of things. A short time ago, I was loading some images from my encrypted memory stick onto one of our secretary's computers for a consultant to view, when the screen prompted me to input my password. I looked down at the keyboard, stared and just started to giggle. The keyboard had seen so much use from this secretary's fingers that the letters pertaining to the keys had been erased. Not being a trained typist, I didn't know where each key was. About all I could manage was 'QWERTY', a fat lot of good if that's not your password! Dina, the secretary was very sympathetic saying "I'm on my third keyboard!". I just found the whole situation very comical.

My background in forensics and as an instructor certainly helps with my role! After many decades in the photography profession, I still get a buzz every day as I never know what I'm going to be faced with – be it a snake bite in AMU – eye scanning 72+ patients on a brain-frazzled Thursday in the Medical Retina Unit - photographing a petri dish in microbiology - a squamous cell carcinoma (SCC) on a patient's cheek - training a team in the use of 'stills' and video on an iPad - revamping the department's medical photography policy - mentoring student nurses whilst on attachment to the Ophthalmic Surgical Unit (where Medical Photography is based) - sourcing new camera equipment for our department, or research work for my own continuing professional development.

In 2018 I chose to visit other Trusts (in my own time) to see how we can improve our working practises. It would be nice to eventually shelve all printing and go fully electronic, a project that I'm currently working on. Clinicians should be able to call up an image of their patient at the touch of a button from anywhere on site, or off site via remote encrypted access. I'm always in search of new ideas, alternative, smarter ways of undertaking tasks if it means simplifying processes and increasing efficiency.

Typical examples of regular jobs are:

- any number and manner of pressure ulcers on the wards
- a PR job (that's public relations, not a per rectum examination, as Adam Kay would say!)
- foot and ankle surgery
- a child's bat ears
- safeguarding
- a deformed set of teeth in orthodontics
- an unusual birthmark on a new-born in the neo-natal unit
- a complicated leg fracture in A&E prior to operation in theatre
- training images for physiotherapy
- radiology
- a cancerous tumour specimen in pathology
- a penile lesion
- a pair of swollen testicles the size of monkey bollocks or indeed, on photographing a sacral pressure ulcer, also photographing what appeared to be a sizeable pair of testicles, which only turned out to be a large prolapse, deformed female genitalia!

The daily workload keeps me on my toes and the mileage around the hospital and up and down the stairs shaves a few inches off the old belly. I must be doing something right as in 2018 Steve and I were nominated for 'Non-Clinical Team' of the year, no mean feat. All this, and I still have to find time to undertake my annual mandatory training, which includes basic life-saving skills, health and safety, fire safety, data access and diversity.

One of my abiding memories of working as a medical photographer has been consoling colleagues when they've lost loved ones. Conversely, shortly after Mum died at the Vic, towards the end of 2015, I spotted Sister Debbie (one of the ward nursing staff who helped look after Mum in her final days and hours) enjoying a solitary Costa coffee in her break. I had just finished work and ordered mine before quickly slipping out. I went to sit up on the mezzanine to discreetly avoid her, not because I didn't want to speak her, far from it, but because I didn't want to disturb this hard-working nurse on her much needed break. A minute later, I looked up and Debbie was right there, she'd come to sit next to me, picking me up and sharing my pain for twenty whole minutes. Debbie gave up her entire break just to console me! What a magical, unselfish thing to do. Sister Debbie epitomises compassion, loveliness, warmth, and sincerity and I'll never forget the strength she gave me on that lonely, bleak day. She is very much a modern-day Florence Nightingale and a heaven-sent blessing for our Trust.

On one particular occasion I sat in intensive care and comforted a critically ill patient's parents earlier in 2017, having had to gain their trust in photographing their daughter for her Patient Diary. The patient, an only child, died of sepsis shortly after my chat with them. *Sepsis* is a life-threatening condition if not treated urgently and arises when the body's response to infection causes injury to its own tissues and organs. As a coincidence, I spotted a poignant floral tribute to this very patient just around the corner in my local church yard whilst out walking. I made the connection immediately and just as circumstance completely wrong-footed me, it caught me off guard and saw me fumbling for a tissue to wipe away my tears.

In the spring of 2020, the UK was of course in the grip of the coronavirus pandemic and Medical Photography saw its workload around the Victoria Hospital temporarily reduced. We stopped visiting the wards and just took on ophthalmology, safeguarding and emergencies. Rotating working from home never materialised, so us three medical photographers stayed at the hospital during the health crisis to plough through a huge backlog of job data entries, get to grips with a shed load of new equipment and generally have a damn good clean, tidy and sort out – jobs that kind of fell by the wayside pre-Covid, with no time to do anything but consistently work your backside off, firefighting in top gear, constantly yawning, feeling knackered and I guess at times, a heartbeat away from being completely fubar. In such situations I know some people turn to smoking, regular drinking, anti-depressants or a mixture of all three. In my case it was comfort eating. When Steve and I worked our rear ends off for 3½ years, prior to Chimane joining us, I turned to the food cupboard for late night 'snacks' seven days a week. My weight rocketed, I started wheezing again and I found that I was reaching for my inhaler almost daily. I knew I had to turn things around otherwise I risked a premature journey - wheeled under a blue tarp along the ground floor corridor to the mortuary's fridge room!

Fortunately, there are a hell of a lot more ups than downs. With the exception of a single abomination, I've had the privilege of knowing and working closely with some lovely, wonderful staff. One or two senior doctors, deluded with self-importance and 'consultantitis', need to take a reality check. They like to talk down to you and look past you as if you're donned from head to toe in Harry Potter's invisibility cloak. However, most of them thankfully treat you as an equal and with respect. Dr Sheila, who retired earlier in 2018, was simply the most wonderful ophthalmic doctor. She was always kind and courteous and took time to explain everything. She went above and beyond. We loved her and I know her patients did. Sheila's bedside manner was exemplary and should have been used in doctors' training manuals for them to emulate. What a great loss to the Trust and of course to the patients.

I find myself working harder now in my late 50s than I was in my mid-20s, or maybe that's just my perception?! The reward I get at the end of the working day is knowing that I've helped both medical staff and patients alike.

In the summer of 2013, Lauren completed Year 6 and left Hambleton Primary School and in the September, she started at St Aidans Church of England High School, located only a mile from our house. After her first day, she came home and said, 'please don't make me go back to that place'! Of course, she did go back the next day and ended up doing really well. Just before George left Blackpool Sixth that same summer, he travelled with the music department to Italy in July, giving well received performances to locals and tourists alike, firstly at Lake Garda, then in Venice and finally in Verona. Almost as soon as George had returned from Italy, already with a tan, we flew to the Greek island of Santorini for a rare family holiday abroad.

Santorini is located in the southern Aegean Sea approximately 200 kilometres south east of the Greek mainland. It is the largest island in a cluster of islands and is essentially the residue of a massive eruption of thousands of years ago, precipitating a volcanic caldera. Santorini's capital is Fira, located on the cliff top, looking down onto the caldera's lagoon. The airport is east of the centre of the island with the quiet, pretty, traditional village of Oia, famed for its sunsets located in the north west, about 11 kilometres from Fira. Typically, when we visited, we all agreed that we'd seen far better sunsets near our home, from the sea wall at Preesall!

Oia, like Fira, has a cliff top location and is famous worldwide for its quaint houses lining narrow streets and for its blue domed churches. Oia also commands breath-taking views of the islands of Thirassia and the volcanoes, Palia Kameni and Nea Kameni. We stayed at Perissa, about 13 kilometres / 25 minutes' drive from the airport. Perissa is famed for its volcanic, black sandy beach and is located on the south east side of Santorini. With no shortage of shops, tavernas and restaurants, sunbathing followed by eating out was a great experience. We took a boat / excursion from the old port of Fira to the harbour of Erinia and hiked to the top to see the sulphur-smelling, smoking craters and great views. Then it was back down to the harbour again, where our boat took us to Palea Kameni to sample the delights of the hot springs – the famous mud baths, a volcanic eruption remnant. George and I jumped off the boat in the small bay of Agios Nikolaos and swam the short distance to the hot springs. To have a therapeutic mud bath was one of the highlights of our Santorini visit. The other, was finding that the soles of an expensive pair of flip-flop sandals had disintegrated in the heat just by walking on hot sand! We all came away from the week-long vacation, wishing it had been for two weeks. Ah well – there's always next time! Then, hot on the heels of Santorini, George was off again to the August Leeds festival. I have a photograph of him somewhere, donned in bandana and wellies, looking very tanned and covered in mud!

September 13th, 2013 saw my milestone 50th birthday, during which I was thoroughly spoiled. Apart from wonderful presents, the cake made locally in Poulton-le-Fylde was undoubtedly one of the many highlights. It was in the shape of the Lake District fells, containing many film quotes and a Nikon camera made of sponge, chocolate and dusted with cocoa powder – yummy! I wanted to take some time out to reflect on some extraordinary experiences that have helped make and shape me, by finishing writing this book, then. Somehow, things were predictably busy and the book continued and of course, so did the experiences!

In the autumn of 2013 George commenced a three-year BA acting degree at University of Wales Trinity Saint David (UOWTSD). Trinity was a long old drive, some 5 ½ hours firstly to Chester and then picking up the A483 through picturesque Welsh countryside via Wrexham, Oswestry, Welshpool, Llandrindod Wells, Builth Wells and then on to the A40 at Llandovery following the River Towy to Trinity in Carmarthen. I have many fond memories of doing that drive, firstly in snow with the Vauxhall Zafira for George's audition and interview, then with the Kia Sportage and also hire van. I stayed in cheap B&B accommodation above pubs, or kipped in George's bed with him on the floor. When we all visited and as a treat, we'd stay with Fiona and Caron at their charming five-star country house 'Llwyn Helyg' set amidst picture postcard surrounds and located in Llanarthney, a stone's throw from and east of Carmarthen. This friendly, hospitable couple made us feel very welcome, with piping hot tea and home-made biscuits on arrival. Nothing was too much trouble. Caron got the maps out and recommended places to visit (and there's plenty to do just within a couple of miles radius, never mind exploring the stunning Pembrokeshire coastline) and even suggested venues for dinner. If we thought the house was grand from the outside, the interior was certainly 'en flique' and quite extraordinary, reflecting an inherent love, care and attention to detail of our perfect hosts. The décor, with its woodwork, use of stone, marble and art, is stunning throughout. The ensuite bedrooms are immaculate with very comfortable beds, stylish linens and luxury bathrooms, complete with huge jacuzzi bathtubs and state of the art showers that you climb steps to get to. Fiona is a talented cook, second only to Wendy, and her Welsh breakfasts are to die for. Caron has a vast audio collection within his music room, which is more akin to a grand concert room. The acoustics are stunning. I've stayed at many guest houses over the years and Llwyn Helyg is superior in every sense of the word. Wales is a magical, beautiful place and when time and circumstance permit, we will return.

In early 2006, following another call to Pete at Hendon's Crime Academy Forensic Faculty, I was put in touch with Mick Gardiner from Gardiner Associates Training and Development. I wanted to see whether his team of experts were in need of any photography help and it turned out that my timing was fortuitous. After a very fruitful telephone conversation, Mick invited me down to see one of their famous 'burns days', during which I'd take photographs of fires set in a range of specially designed and constructed compartments from ignition to extinguishing and then fire damage following damping down. These burnt compartments create a controlled but authentic environment for fire and arson scene examiners to hone their investigative skills. GATR's former base, prior to 2010, was situated adjacent to a disused runway at MoD Police Headquarters, Wethersfield in Essex. In 2010, the GATR 'field' operation, 'Phoenix Heights' was reborn and relocated to outside the MoD airbase perimeter, where theoretical and practical fire / crime investigation training, testing and research facilities were constructed.

The team, all highly experienced, retired fire fighters, fire investigators and forensic practitioners are a great bunch of people with an engaging sense of humour. Mick Gardiner is the leader of the team of associates and his impressive credentials speak for themselves - some 27 years spent in the fire service, eleven of which have been as a fire investigator, coupled with the huge amount of work that Mick, supported by his loyal team, Alan Munford, Mick Cloonan, Paul England (who left GATR in September 2020), Chris Ward, Dave Stokes ('Stokesy'), John Hubble, Clive Gregory, Malcolm Jenkins and 'Techy' Nick Stuart et al have all undertaken since the setting up of GATR in 1995 to improve fire investigation through the provision of fire and arson investigation training programmes. That story is worthy of a book in its own right.

Mick Gardiner is the author of FM Global's Guide to Fire and Arson Investigation. He is also a contributor to design and development of the UK National Occupational Standards (NOS) and many other national and international initiatives. Mick is the former Lead Assessor for the Council for the Registration of Forensic Practitioners (CRFP) and European representative on the International Association of Arson Investigators (IAAI) Training & Education working group. Mick was also an advisor to the hugely popular television drama series 'London's Burning' which ran from February 1988 (following the success of the 1986 film) to August 2002 over 14 series and 172 episodes! With a busy schedule of business planning, meetings and lectures at home and abroad, it's a wonder that Mick gets the time to go on holiday! Mick's partner Jill Warwick, a former Met Police Skipper with 28 years' service, is a pivotal part of GATR operations. With a special interest in Equality and Diversity and communication and interview skills, she is not only the MD, but also helps to keep Mick ... and the rest of us ... in check!

As the GATR website states, it:

'... *is the UK's major provider of inter-agency fire investigation training to police and fire authorities. The company ethos is that training should be delivered by people who possess and practice intrinsic skills in the subject areas that they teach. To that end, from its launch in 1996, Gardiner Associates has assembled a multi-disciplined team of practitioners.*

Gardiner Associates Training and Research (GATR) is an Institution of Fire Engineers (IFE) 'recognised' training course provider and our core theory and practical courses are approved under the Continuing Professional Development scheme by the Forensic Science Society, providing an assurance of quality and content relevance.

The GATR team has long fostered the inter-agency team approach to fire investigation and organises its training courses and other events accordingly.

Our courses are challenging, enjoyable and rewarding.'

Following that first visit to GATR back in 2006, I liked it so much that I decided to stick around! At the time of writing this section, I've now been part of Mick Gardiner's team for more than fourteen years and during this time, have taught hundreds of students, working closely with GATR in delivering the photography theoretical and practical modules as part of the highly successful Practical Development Refresher (PDR) courses. I'm also the lead on Fire Scene Photography training for GATR and have supplied training at the customer site as well as supporting material for the photography of fire scenes as part of the Skills for Justice Awards (SFJA) Level 5 (L5c) Certificate in Fire Investigation. In addition to teaching fire investigators all they need to know about fire scene photography, including tips on how to competently present their visual documentation in court, I photograph all the burnt scene rooms as well as the obligatory student, staff and visitor group shots, so that GATR keeps a stock of fire related images for marketing and publicity purposes. To that end, I have also covered the photography for the impressive burns days, which, on occasions, have had invaluable training input from American fire experts John DeHaan and Jack Malooly. Both gentlemen were formerly with the ATF (Bureau of Alcohol, Tobacco, Firearms and Explosives) and have many years of service. John is currently an independent fire investigator and author of Kirk's Fire Investigation and Forensic Fire Investigation. Former Senior Special Agent Jack Malooly is currently a Consulting Fire and Explosion Investigator.

With Gardiners, my teaching role on the Practical Development Refresher first gives a theoretical overview of photography and the camera, including concepts such as lighting – exposure - depth of field - image composition - audit trail - written documentation - camera /

equipment functionality - storage of images and court presentation. I follow this with covering scene analysis and photographic story-telling, starting from the exterior and working methodically towards the interior using a combination of wide angle, intermediate and close up shots, image enhancement versus image manipulation, digital imaging guidelines, scene photographic problems such as contrast, flare, reflections, flash fall off and white balance and recommended image capturing systems from digital SLR to drones.

It has been said several times throughout this book that 'a picture paints a thousand words' and the underlying importance of this idiom in terms of accurately recording the fire scene, can't be overstated, for:

"Photographs may be the most persuasive factor in the acceptance of the fire investigator's theory of the fire's evolution".

"The goal in documenting any fire or explosion investigation is to accurately record the investigation through media that will allow investigators to recall and communicate their observations at a later date [utilising for example] photographs, video, diagrams, maps, overlays, audio recordings, notes and reports" (National Fire Protection Association 921 Chapter 16).

As with any skill, if you don't practise it regularly, you'll get rusty. As part of my continuing professional development, I use my own time for my GATR fire work, to keep my hand in and my training skills current. Since my Met Police crime scene days, I've always had a very strong affinity with the fire service and my work with Gardiner Associates keeps me close to my fire service colleagues. I always look forward to my trips down to Phoenix Heights not just for the teaching, but for the social interaction with like-minded professionals!

2014 saw my mother-in-law, Val's health starting to decline. It had come on the back of a broken shoulder and gradual weight loss. Val had been almost a life-long smoker, but all credit to her, she kicked the habit years previously. However, she harboured a smoker's cough, which I noticed when I first met her in Cornwall early in 1991, not long after Wendy and I had first met.

Born in Whetstone to Frank and Lily Schollick in September 1927, Val and her brother Nigel grew up as teenagers during the second world war and through north London amateur dramatics (Friern Barnet Operatic Society) Val met her future husband, Laurie, a sales and advertising executive. They eventually tied the knot in April 1953. Their son, Simon was born in 1962 and three years later, Wendy entered stage left. In 1969, the same year that we moved from Carshalton to Poulton-le-Fylde, Val, Laurie and the children upped sticks from their Barnett home in search of a better life, which they were to find in all its splendour in Cornwall. Shortly after I came on the scene (early in 1991), Wendy took me down to the country sanctuary that was Pennard Cottage, the Laight's idyllic Wadebridge family home, to meet the two, charming people who were destined to become my parents-in-law.

Val was lovely, kind, considerate, caring and totally unselfish. She had a wonderful sense of humour and we'd frequently be in stitches laughing with her. Year after year on our Cornwall holidays, we turned her house upside down each time we stayed with her. She wasn't in the least bit bothered, she was just happy to see us. Val wasn't just kind, she was also very generous like her brother Nigel – always giving us money, buying George and Lauren this and that and even helping us out financially when times were tough. Part of her legacy exists to this day – Val bought Wendy and me life membership of the National Trust. What a fantastic, original and thoughtful present. Throughout Val's declining health in 2014, Wendy was driving down to Cornwall every other weekend to be with her Mum, alternating weekends with her brother Simon, who travelled from London. After prolonged periods in Treliske Royal Cornwall Hospital and a number of community hospitals, Val was discharged back home over late summer. She had support from nurses and therapists who visited every day to try and help her regain her strength and confidence. Unfortunately, she deteriorated slightly and was readmitted to Treliske, before being discharged to a local Wadebridge care home for respite, which she didn't like at all. Wendy and Simon eventually found much nicer facilities at Windmill Court Care Home in St. Minver, near Polzeath. It was intended to be a temporary measure, but Val sadly passed away there on 21st November 2014. She was 87.

Val's funeral was held on 1st December 2014 at Penmount Crematorium, set in beautiful grounds on the outskirts of Truro. We had just left for the funeral, following behind the hearse, when just up from the Betjeman Centre in Wadebridge, we spied an old man on the opposite side of the road. As he spotted the black-coloured car, he bowed and doffed his cap – which was poignant and so lovely to see. The Crem chapel was packed to overflowing with standing room only – a measure of the love and esteem in which Val was held. The wake was held at the Betjeman Centre, where Val was so much an integral part. Wendy and Simon had laid on a mini coach to take Val's Betjeman Centre friends to and from Wadebridge, which I thought was a nice touch as many of them didn't drive. I feel blessed to have had such a wonderful mother-in-law and I'll let my eulogy describe to you the sort of person she was:

"I'd just like to say a very few words about Val. She was a devoted and proud Wife, Mum, Gran, Sister, Mother-in-Law, Sister-in-Law, Aunt, Great-Aunt, cousin and special friend to many people.

A Betjeman Centre stalwart, Val also loved her garden, which was always filled with an enviable array of colours. If you needed a lesson in correct punctuation, English grammar and social etiquette – Val was the person to turn to and look up to.

She had a most endearing personality – and a joie de vivre. She was warm and welcoming and lit up the room with her lovely smile, distinctive laugh and engaging sense of humour. Val would frequently have us all in hysterics.... when more often than not, the joke was on her. She was indeed a great sport.

Like her brother, Nigel, Val possessed a tremendous generosity of spirit - greatly enriching the lives of those who knew her.

Val, showed great courage, resilience and determination during the protracted illness which gripped her during the last year of her life, characteristically underplaying how dire at times she really felt, none more so than in her final weeks – when uppermost in her mind was caring for those she loved.

Valerie Laight was thoroughly decent, wise, funny, adorable, a constant, irreplaceable, a huge support and just fantastic to be around – she was all of this and a lot more besides. But above all, she was kind, unselfish and quite simply, a lovely person to have known.

Let us take some comfort from the cherished memories we have and our love and respect for this wonderful lady to help soothe the burden of our mutual grief.

Val - May you dance with angels and shine forever amongst the brightest of stars. Farewell then. Sleep Well. Thank God for Valerie Laight!"

In Lauren's words:

"My Gran was a very special person, she always cheered you up when you were down. She was the best Gran ever and I always used to tell her that. Gran used to call me many things but the best was, 'my angel' – that made me feel very special. When she died I felt a bit of my heart had gone. But I know now that she is in a very special

place and that place is Heaven. She will be with all her family and friends who have passed away and she won't be ill anymore. It makes me happy in a way that I know she will be with her loved ones and I am sure that she is here with us and smiling at how many people are her friends.

I love you very much Gran. You will always be in my heart and one day I will see you again and that day will be very special!"

George also gave a touching, faultless tribute to his Gran and last to speak was Simon, who gave a very personal and poignant eulogy to his late mother and all without notes.

The passing of Valerie Laight, a much-loved family matriarch, towards the close of 2014 was the end of an era for us all. The void in our lives was huge and our grief lasts to this day. Val's memory lives on.

The most beautiful black and white photograph of my parents-in-law, Val and Laurie Laight, adorns our bedroom dresser. Taken in their salad days circa early 1950's, a bespectacled, confident, smiling and clearly happy Laurie, his left arm leaning on Val's shoulder – the two, looking radiant, the image speaking volumes about a young couple so obviously in love and with their whole lives ahead of them. This is my favourite image of two people who showed me nothing but warmth and kindness – lovely, decent, down to earth and utterly selfless, it was a privilege to have known them.

At the same time that Wendy was travelling down to Cornwall every other weekend, another desperate situation was unravelling. 45-year-old Kendelle Provan was an outwardly happy-go-lucky person, but who suffered much in life. Inwardly she was a private person wrestling with her demons. Scottish born, she lived on her own in St Annes with several dogs, cats and guinea pigs for company. In late summer 2014 Kendelle was working closely with Wendy at the NHS offices housed on the first floor of Blackpool Football Stadium. It was quite simply a joy to be on the receiving end of Kendelle's cheery disposition. Whenever I phoned for Wendy and Kendelle picked up the phone, she was always so warm and friendly, despite never having met me. I was to say later that her telephone manner alone should have been bottled and used as an example for others to follow. Unfortunately, despite a very confident exterior, Kendelle suffered a huge lack of confidence. She had privately sought advice from HR about the behaviour of one colleague towards her, she hadn't told anyone else about it though and only told Wendy when she was very poorly.

It was now mid-September and Kendelle had become unwell, Wendy and other colleagues encouraged her to see the doctor. Being scared of medics and hospitals, Kendelle was reluctant. She did eventually go off sick with a doctor's note, but Wendy had become concerned over the nature of some conversations and texts she received. Then Kendelle stopped answering text messages and Wendy intuitively knew that something was wrong. Kendelle was exceptionally private and never socialised with anyone outside of work, but Wendy decided to make her a meal and drive to her home. She asked me to go with her. Wendy knocked on her front door and was quickly joined by one of Kendelle's neighbours who lived opposite. The neighbour had been helping Kendelle while she'd been ill. It was some time before the front door was opened for Wendy and the neighbour to step inside. The place had been completely neglected and it became immediately obvious that Kendelle was struggling. When Kendelle eventually emerged holding on to Wendy's arm, she was stooped over, her hair was bedraggled, she was limping, and she was only wearing one shoe. She was clearly in a terrible state. The three of us went into the neighbour's house for a cuppa. Kendelle looked and sounded awful. She was slurring her words, presented with slight ptosis and the left side of her mouth was drooping. I thought she'd had a stroke. We were so concerned that an ambulance was called to take Kendelle to Victoria Hospital. At the Vic, medics thought that she'd been drinking – this was about as far removed from the eventual diagnosis as was possible.

My wife once again went into hyper efficient mode and, with a small group of Kendelle's friends, helped arrange for Kendelle's animals to be looked after (with help from social services and the RSPCA) and they made regular visits to hospital to visit her. Kendelle, it transpired, had no immediate family for support. She had one distant Aunt and some cousins, but she had given specific instructions for them not to be contacted as she'd previously fallen out with them. Wendy as ever proved to be the modern-day Florence Nightingale. Exhaustive tests were carried out and alarmingly poor Kendelle was diagnosed on 1st October 2014 with CJD (Creutzfeldt-Jakob Disease) the human form of Mad Cow Disease. This is a rare, degenerative brain disorder that leads firstly to dementia and then death. It affects only about one person in every million worldwide. The tell-tale signs of CJD are a rapid mental deterioration, memory loss, anxiety, depression, personality changes, impaired thinking, difficulty speaking, dysphagia, insomnia, blurry vision or blindness and sudden, jerky movements.

It was arranged to have Kendelle looked after in a specialist Kirkham care home. By now, and against Kendelle's express wishes, someone unknown (but probably the previously mentioned colleague who Kendelle found intimidating) had made contact with Kendelle's cousins. At this time Wendy was also travelling to Cornwall on alternate weekends, to be with her very sick Mother, who had but two months to live. Somehow, she simultaneously balanced caring for her Mum, who was more than 350 miles away, with equivalent compassionate care for her once bubbly work colleague – God knows how she did it. This was especially difficult, when we found out that Kendelle was dying. With CJD, death usually occurs within twelve months. In Kendelle's case she was diagnosed at the start of October and died, tragically, within sixteen days. The end for this upbeat Scot, who smiled in the face of adversity, was very quick, but extremely peaceful. She died at the care home, surrounded by Wendy and two friends.

Wendy's unselfish actions didn't go unnoticed. She was nominated for a 'Going the Extra Mile' Trust award amidst very stiff competition and was unanimously selected as the winner. The award comprised an engraved paperweight, £80 of Argos vouchers and £400 to spend on equipment for her team. This thoroughly deserved prize was presented at a special awards evening at Blackpool Sixth, by the inspiring parents of Jane Clough, one of BVH's staff nurses who was brutally stabbed to death in a planned, frenzied attack by her former partner in the hospital grounds back on the evening of July 25th 2010.

As for Wendy, she rebounded from Kendelle's funeral straight into bracing herself for her own Mother's death 4 weeks later and ensuing funeral. I always knew my wife was strong but keeping a cool head whilst simultaneously caring for two dying people, who are hundreds of miles apart, holding down a hectic job and looking after her own immediate family, in my book, takes the biscuit. Amazing person the wife! She's one in a million, which is one of the reasons why we all love her, why she is so cherished and why I married her.

We also lost many from the world of entertainment in 2014 including Robin Williams, Philip Seymour Hoffman, Rik Mayall, Lauren Bacall, Mickey Rooney, Shirley Temple, Ralph Waite, Kate O'Mara, Bob Hoskins, Eli Wallach, James Garner, Dora Bryan, Elaine Stritch, Sir Richard Attenborough, Mike Smith, Richard Kiel, Joan Rivers, Lynda Bellingham, Alvin Stardust, Lynsey de Paul, Acker Bilk, PD James, Warren Clarke, Joe Cocker and Billie Whitelaw.

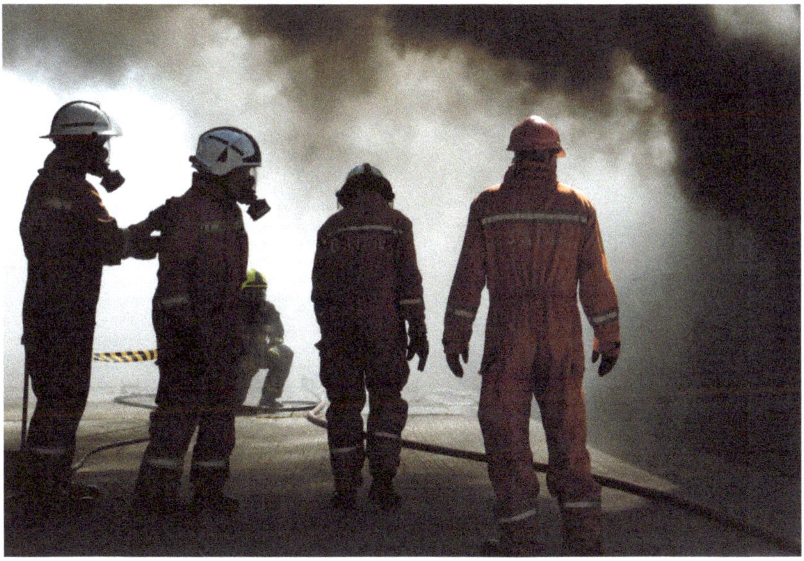

During 'burns day' with Gardiner Associates Training & Research (GATR), (specialists in fire investigation training), Phoenix Heights, Wethersfield, Essex, Sept 2016.

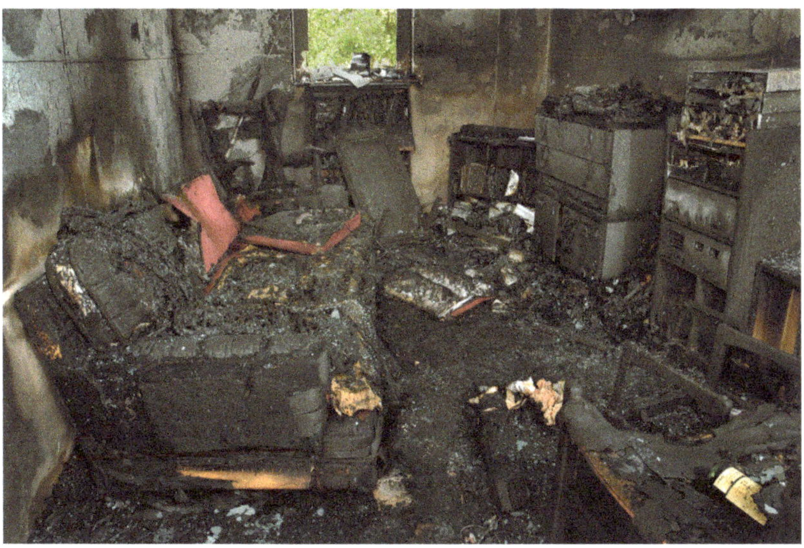

Fire-damaged scene compartment at GATR, May 2007.

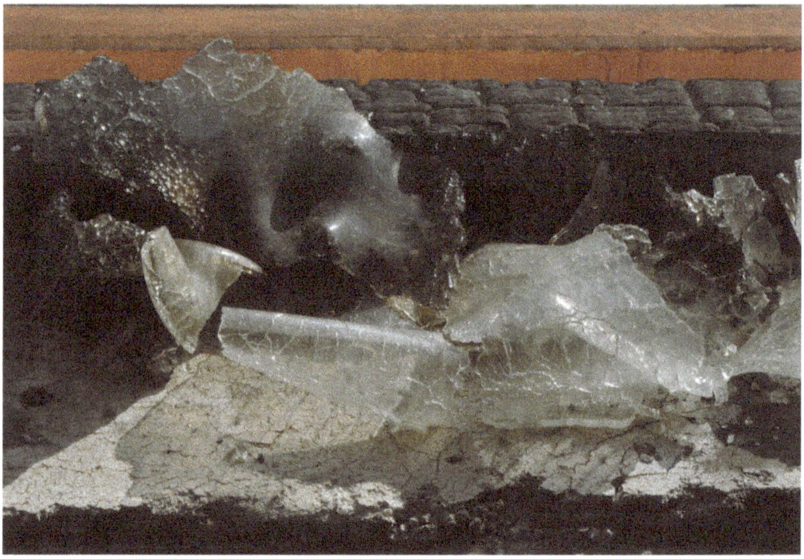

Fire scene compartment 'folded glass', post fire, having been subjected to extremely high temperatures, GATR, April 2014.

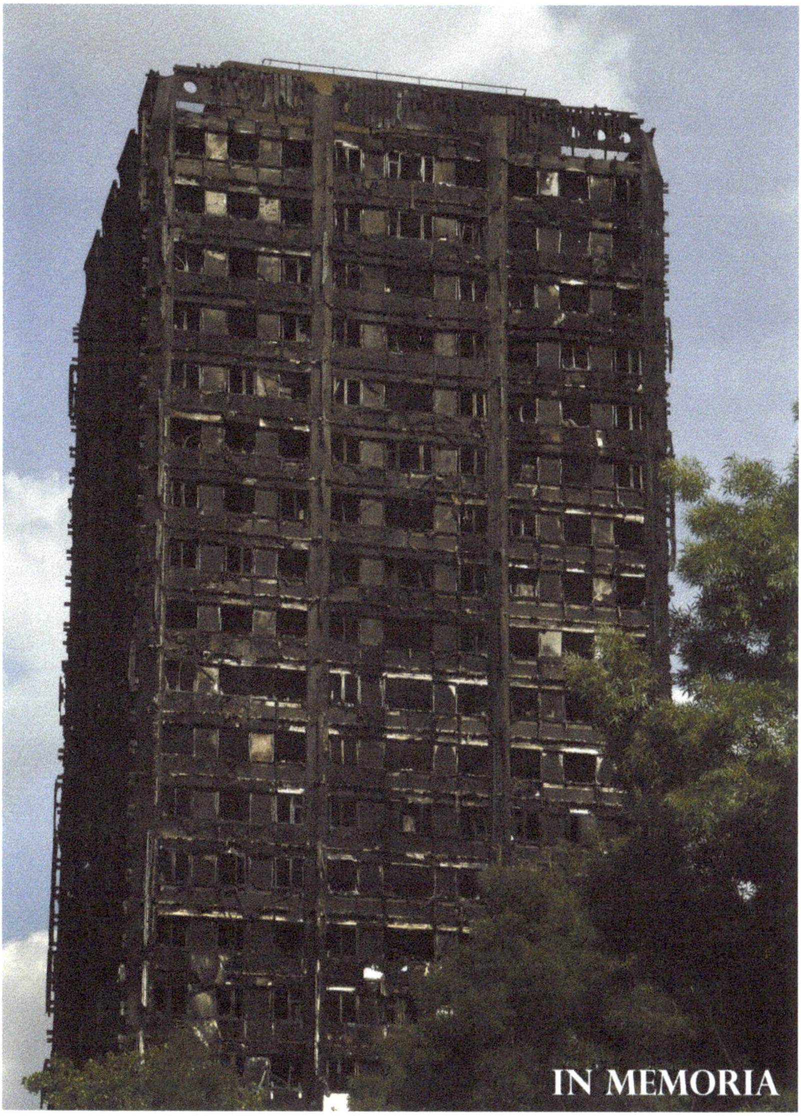

Grenfell Tower, North Kensington, London, June, 2017 In Memoria. My closing slide when teaching fire scene photography to the UK's fire investigators. I dedicate my fire scene photography lectures to all the victims and victims' families of fire disasters worldwide.

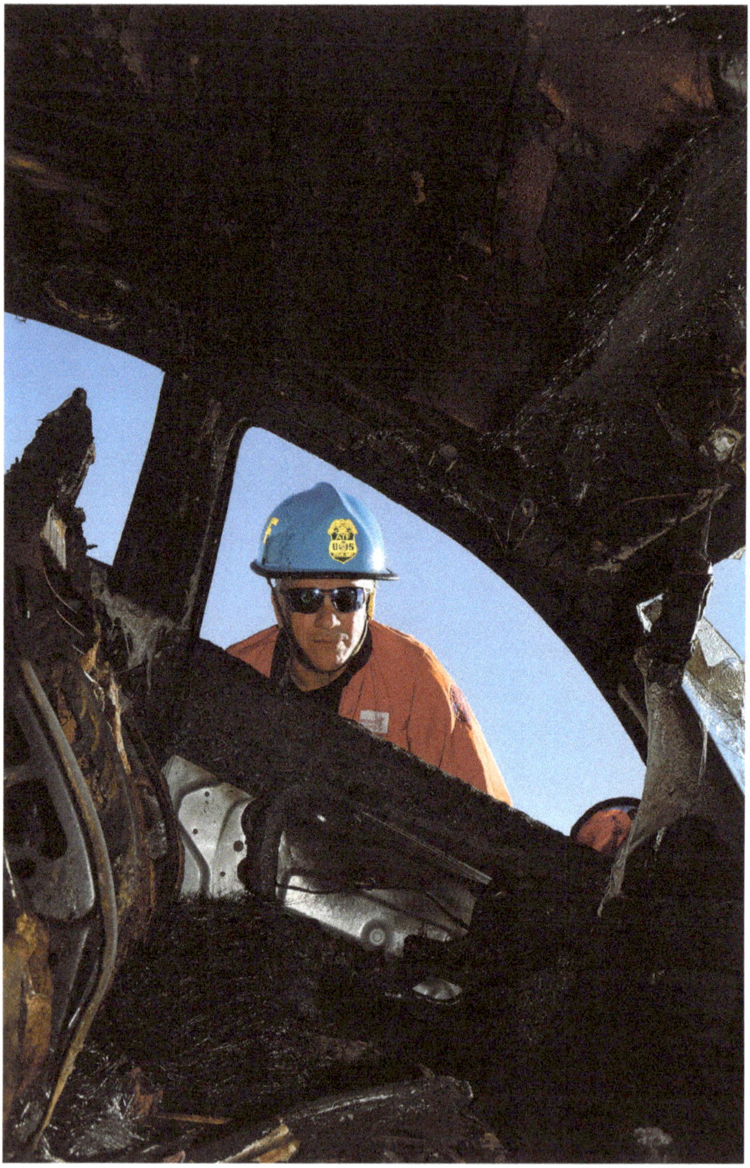

The 'Daddy' of UK fire investigation, Mick Gardiner of Gardiner Associates Training & Research at Phoenix Heights, Wethersfield, Essex, September 2018.

CHAPTER 25

When a Mother Dies

Our family were still reeling from the death of Valerie Laight when 2015 was welcomed in. The last thing Wendy and I felt like doing was celebrating. To get me through this enormously stressful period, I turned to comfort eating. Our food bill went through the roof and I started to wheeze, one of the bi products of my weight gain. On January 1st, 2015, I had reached an obscene weight of 16 stone 10 pounds – a record high. I had become the archetypal fat bastard and needed to do something – and fast. By the time my diet finished five months later, I had shed 33 pounds and on June 1st I weighed in at 14 stone 5 pounds, which incredibly still put me in the overweight category. Miraculously my wheezing vanished and I felt and looked much healthier. Work was busy-busy for both Wendy and me. George spent the summer following the end of his second year at uni working at 'PGL' Boreatton Park in Shropshire – hard graft but damn good experience.

Mum's childhood friend Daphne visited her at the end of June with her husband Tony from Australia and on 8th August we had an American themed leaving party for George in our garden, who was about to study Stateside. Naturally I took the obligatory photos and what I didn't know then was that I had just photographed a healthy-looking Mum for the very last time. We had booked to see the musical 'Cats' at Blackpool Opera House on 2 August 2015, which was superb and this was followed by our annual Cornwall summer holiday – our first without Val. In early September, to celebrate my birthday and our anniversary, my sisters treated Wendy and me to an overnight, luxury Grasmere spa break in the Lake District. This was a lovely idea to help us fully relax after difficult, recent months. It was very kind and much needed.

Mum was simply great, a fabulous, engaging person who endeared herself to others. She was a laugh a minute, could talk the hind legs off a donkey, but conversely, she was also a good listener…

and she loved her family. Mum had the best parents in the world (Grandma and Grandad were thoroughly decent people and I loved them dearly) and by all accounts she had a first-class childhood – save for a little hiccup which turned out to be wartime evacuation. Oh and then an even bigger hiccup at barely eighteen, when she was still really just a girl, Mum met the not so good Doctor James Michael Canning at his GP practice in Mitcham ... and so began more than 50 years of a turbulent and unhappy relationship. When Dad died on February 6th, 2006, Mum was finally rid of this evil bully. After the fiasco of Dad's changed will, which took more than 2 years to sort out, Mum eventually lived out her retirement enjoying her new-found freedom. And live it out she did! Always a classical music buff, Mum had long been an admirer of the Spanish opera tenor Placido Domingo. She developed a passion for Placido's work, bought the CDs and DVDs and inevitably travelled Europe to see her hero perform. This was partly my 'fault' as I was always reminding Mum of the 'John and Connie Day philosophy'. The Days were a likeable retired couple who hailed not a million miles from the sound of Bow Bells - old next-door neighbours of ours from the late 70's / early 80's, who, no sooner had they returned from one holiday, would start planning and looking forward to the next trip away. Having something to look forward to obviously proved a great tonic, but when a friend of Connie's pointedly asked, "All these holidays are a lovely idea, Con, but what are you gonna do if, you know, er something happens to one of you?" Connie, relaying the story to Mum, came back at her friend with a classic retort in her sauciest cockney twang, "Well, if somefink 'appens, we won't be going, will we?" I reminded Mum about the Days' dictum and it always made her laugh, but she also knew that the Days were far from stupid and that it made perfect sense. Come back from one trip abroad and start planning your next one – that way, you've always got something to look forward to – and should the grim reaper come calling in between trips, at least hopefully you could die happy, knowing you had a trip to look forward to!

And so it was that Mum lived out her retirement doing exactly as she pleased. For once in her life, she was her own boss, making her own decisions and enjoying life to the full. Mum was always happy to see us and when she wasn't off galivanting around Europe in pursuit of Placido, she'd be holding daily 'court', doing the crossword and catching up with her friends in Poulton's New Penny Grill cafe – after of course, her obligatory work out at the local YMCA gym.

I was pleased for Mum, she was free of Dad's talons. She was her own boss and living her life exactly how she wanted to live it – enjoyably.

Mum's mortality had crossed my mind several times over the years, mainly because she had heart palpitations and type 2 diabetes, but both conditions were controlled with medication. If she felt palpitations starting, so called supraventricular tachycardia, she'd press on the carotid artery for a few seconds until her heart rate returned to normal. If she was out walking, Mum would often find a bench or garden wall and sit out, what she brushed aside as a mild inconvenience. Mistakenly thinking that because Grandma reached almost 94 and Grandad (a life-long smoker) had passed away at 81, we somehow thought that Mum would just go on until her late 80s or early 90s.

So save for the controlled diabetes and occasional heart palpitations, Mum seemed fit and healthy. Here was someone who went to the gym five times a week minimum and walked everywhere. She was always careful to eat the correct number of vegetables each day and to drink the appropriate amount of water. Mum seemed to be the epitome of the fit, healthy and active retiree. There was no cause to think otherwise.

Having painted Lauren's bedroom, our spare room and then George's bedroom, it was now late September 2015. In decorating mode, we thought it would be a good idea to finish the season painting and decorating our lounge, having just had a wood burning stove, hearth and surrounds installed a few weeks previously. I was up to my eyeballs in work, both at Victoria Hospital where of course I was working as a Medical Photographer and then grafting at home dealing with the lounge into the evenings. Weirdly I hadn't spoken to Mum or seen her for a few weeks, so I resolved to give her a call on my mobile. It was now week commencing Monday 12th October and I'd just finished work at Clifton Hospital, waiting for a taxi to take me back to base, with the phone ringing. After a few seconds, Mum picked up and after apologising for not being in contact for a while I asked her how she was. Expecting to hear the usual "Fine, thank you", I was completely wrong-footed when Mum told me that she hadn't been feeling well for the last few weeks - really from 4th October during Sunday lunch at the New Penny, when she hadn't been able to finish her meal. "I mean I had a scone and flora, ate a little bit and had to bring the rest home for the birds (garden birds)", I remember Mum lamenting. In this single conversation, alarm bells were sounding, ricocheting around my head louder than Big Ben – something was dreadfully wrong, but I tried to dismiss it. She's fine. She's Mum. She's ok. But the Mother who never got ill, who hadn't been ill for forty years, who'd never complained of being ill, had just told me that she wasn't well. So now I was very concerned!

My mind returned to the previous month ... on 24th September, Wendy and I took Lauren to Blackpool's Grand Theatre to see 'Dreamboats and Miniskirts', which was fantastic. This was followed by a day trip to Edinburgh on Saturday 26th and Wendy being presented with a work award 'for going the extra mile' at Blackpool Sixth Form on Monday 28th September, a ceremony which meant leaving Lauren at Mum's for tea – nothing out of the ordinary there. I had, however, noticed Mum scratching her arm during September. Then during early October, she came out in hives of spots all over her body, including her head. What the hell was that all about?

We thought Mum may have had an infection of some kind. I desperately wanted to see her, but we both decided that it would be better if I stayed away for the moment, in case she was actually infectious. I told her to see the doctor, but characteristically and typical of many of her generation - she didn't want to go. I kept on badgering her to get an appointment and Mum in turn voiced her reluctance. She didn't want a fuss made. A few months previously, Mum fell on her back step, bashing the right side of her face and in the process, gave herself a nasty looking black eye, which took about two weeks to fully clear up. I remember thinking, I wonder whether that was due to a clumsy fall or whether she felt faint because of palpitations or was it due to something else? Was this connected?

On Thursday 15th October, Mum had seen a locum doctor who had prescribed antihistamines for the hives and after an even stronger course of medication, the rashes – diagnosed as 'chronic urticaria', suddenly disappeared. But Mum still looked very, very unwell and there was growing concern for her health. Kate and I knew that we had to get Mum back to the Doctor's. Kate made the call to get Mum the urgent appointment that she so badly needed. By this time, however, Mum was feeling weak, lethargic, had diarrhoea, God knows what else and crucially had been 2½ weeks off her food. Alarmingly, the feeling of going off her food was getting worse with each day that passed.

On Saturday 17th October, I was waiting in the car while Wendy finished some shopping. I turned on Radio 2 and the announcer introduced the next song, a beautiful number sung in a rich baritone voice, by none other than Alexander Armstrong, television's 'Pointless' quiz show host and one half of the comedy duo, Armstrong and Miller. The track was from Alexander's soon to be released album 'A year of Songs'. The track that I was now listening to was called 'On Days Like These'. As I sat there waiting for Wendy, listening to these beautifully sung lyrics, '…it's on days like these that I remember…', that I suddenly felt an air of poignancy and a deep-rooted fear for Mum's future. 'On Days Like These' would become synonymous with the period surrounding Mum's illness. I tried to dismiss it of course but the nagging feeling about Mum wouldn't go away. My feelings were exacerbated when Kate voiced similar concerns to me. I dropped Wendy off at home but returned to Poulton to see Mum briefly and to pick the morning paper up from her (a ritual that had been going on for years). Ironically the New Penny Grill was crowded and so I just saw Mum opposite St. Chad's Church for a quick 5-minute chat.

I was shocked when I eventually saw her. She was still managing a smile, but walking slowly and deliberately towards me. I looked down at Mum's tummy, which was clearly bloated. I was looking at my 78-year old mother who appeared to be 8 ½ months pregnant! Simultaneously, I noticed that Mum had sunken cheeks with similar weight loss from her neck, which was quite alarming to see. At this stage Kate and I were thinking the worst with bowel cancer or a cancerous bowel obstruction as the possible cause. We were by now extremely worried, especially as we felt that Mum hadn't mentioned all her symptoms to the Doctor. I left Mum on that Saturday 17th October, feeling dreadfully worried. She was due to see Margaret, the practice nurse at Poulton's Lockwood Avenue surgery on the following Wednesday afternoon at 3pm (21st October) for her flu jab, but in the event, Kate managed to jack up an early morning urgent appointment with the senior practice medic.

Kate spoke to the doctor following Mum's appointment with him and he was sufficiently troubled to urgently refer Mum to a Consultant Colorectal Surgeon, who in turn was so concerned, he had Mum admitted to hospital that same day (Tuesday 27th October 2015).

Three days later, Mum received the diagnosis that we were all dreading, terminal, metastasised ovarian cancer. Before Mum's hospital admission I recall asking her, "Cards on the table Mum, what do you think is wrong with you?" Mum's casual, almost throw away reply will be etched in my mind forever. She looked me in the eye and replied, "Cancer, the end of course", in a matter of fact way, shrugging her shoulders as if she was casting aside some banal, irrelevant fact. I was really shocked by this and tried not to show it, offering up something like "You can't say that Mum, let's wait until you've seen the Consultant". But Mum was right…she knew! Mum's demise was very rapid indeed. A week from diagnosis to death – not even time to be transferred to the local hospice. My two sisters and I held a 24-hour vigil in the days leading up to Mum's passing. The end when it came was very peaceful, with Vicky, Kate and me holding Mum's hands along with Staff Nurse (now Sister) Tracy also in attendance. It was 10.35 p.m. on Friday 6th November 2015.

I thought back to late September / early October and Mum's urticaria. The hives she was covered in and couldn't stop scratching, I surmised, were the outward manifestation of her cancer. Mum was riddled with this bastard disease and the hives were a way of telling the world, in effect, how ill she really was inside.

Dealing with Mum's death was one thing, having to tell my own mother in hospital that she was about to die was quite another! A gaunt, weary Mum, now presenting with prominent facial and neck weight loss studied me thoughtfully, in an inquisitive way for a few moments before turning to Kate and saying, 'Switzerland'?, a macabre humorous reference to my wicked joke of months before threatening, if ever she got terminally ill, we'd cart her off to the renowned euthanasia clinic, Dignitas? It was difficult to read Mum's expression, which was if anything, completely blank. If Mum was frightened inside, it certainly didn't show on her face. She remained dignified and stoical to the last. Our family were so, so grateful for the hospital care that Mum received and we were particularly grateful to the lovely Graham, Victoria Hospital's then lead chaplain for his support and comforting words. My abiding memory of Graham is of a softly spoken, kindly man, with a warm and welcoming smile and of his catchphrase, 'Blessings' – which will stay with me always. Thank you Graham. Your reassuring words helped me to come to terms with my overwhelming grief. You are truly blessed.

Immediately following Mum's death, I popped out of her hospital side room to give Wendy the bad news. When I came back into the room, for some weird reason I half expected to see Mum sitting up in bed with a mug of coffee, talking and laughing, but there she was, quiet and still. It wasn't horrible or macabre like you see on telly or read in books. She just lay there peacefully, free from pain at last. But I resigned myself to the fact that it wasn't really Mum there, it was just her body, which was a mere shell. I believed that her spirit was very much alive and well in the Spirit World. In spite of all this, events had unfolded so fast that part of me didn't accept what had just happened. I think we were all stunned and very much on auto pilot. Vicky, Kate and I stayed inside room 19 for about an hour, during which time I decided that we needed to collect all Mum's things that night and take them back to her house. I left Vicky and Kate with Mum's body whilst I made a first trip down to Kate's car with some of Mum's belongings. We collected the last of Mum's stuff and all met back at Mum's house, just before midnight, totally shattered.

And so started the grief process. In the days that followed raw grief for me was characterised by frequent bouts of sobbing – I just couldn't help it, it felt like it was beyond my control. It didn't need to be a thought or piece of music that set me off. I would be fine one minute and then suddenly from nowhere the tears would start and I'd have a little weep. What undoubtedly kept the three of us going was the fact that Mum's house needed sorting and we had a funeral to arrange. Vicky went into organised mode and suggested that we all had individual tasks – an excellent idea. As executor to Mum's estate, Vicky would sort out the finance and the paperwork. Vicky also wanted to inform relatives and friends of Mum's passing. Kate wanted to tidy and clean the house with our help. It was my job to sort the garage out, register the death at the hospital and with Kate's help start planning Mum's funeral. We all had our respective jobs to do and because we were busy, we had focus, the three of us united in common purpose. Yet there was still time to stop and ponder, still time to ache and still time to cry. The immediate grief was just awful, akin to your stomach being strangled into a tight knot, coupled with a wraparound headache. Sometimes I was able to get several tasks completed in quick succession, other times I'd want to hide in a wardrobe, curl up into a ball and shut out the world whilst a wave of grief completely overwhelmed me, which, translated, meant that at these moments I was about as useful as an ashtray on a motorbike! At such times I'd regress in a millisecond into a 5 year old child pining for his Mummy! I was reminded of the fact that no matter how old you are, when you lose a parent, grief can overwhelm you and reduce you to tears, as was witnessed during the closing lines of the extremely moving, poignant eulogy given by former President George W. Bush at the Washington funeral of his late father, former President George H.W. Bush on December 5th 2018.

I wanted it so much just to talk to Mum again, to see her, to hear her voice, to see her smile and to hear her laugh. I'd give anything just to have her back with us – the healthy Mum just as she always was. But reality struck again and the 'hit home' was as hard as ice-cold stone. Mum was gone and there was no buffer. Nine years previously, Grandma was alive and I had two generations in front of me. Now those two tiers had vanished, and it was my generation who were jockeying up for position! Mum had lived her life and now that life had ended. Once the church, crematorium and wake venue had been booked, relatives and friends were informed of the funeral date, which was 24th November 2015 at St. Chad's Church, Poulton-le-Fylde, a day before what would have been Mum's 79th birthday. Kate and I also designed the funeral order of service. There were several draft versions produced and by the time I made the fifth call to the printers I was still fine tweaking, as we wanted this to be error free and a fitting tribute to a wonderful mother. For the front cover of the order of service, I selected a recent colour photograph of Mum taken in June when her childhood friend, Daphne and husband Tony visited her from Australia. We decided that an old black and white image of Mum in air hostess uniform taken in her salad days would adorn the back cover. Mum had chosen 'Xerxes: Ombra mai fu (Largo) by George Frederic Handel as the entrance aria as performed by Placido Domingo. Carolyn, the Curate, would then read some opening words of scripture and following the opening prayer, the initial hymn would be 'He Who Would Valiant Be' (original words by John Bunyan, Pilgrim's Progress, dated 1684). My eulogy was next in the order of service, which I set about writing over three evenings, a week before Mum's funeral. I timed it at 11½ minutes, which Wendy thought was far too long. I begged to differ. This was my one chance to talk about Mum, her life, what she had done, and what she meant to all of us. I just wasn't prepared to cut this once in a lifetime speech down to a couple of minutes, so I went against my wife's advice (for the first time in my life!) and went with the full version of what I had penned in tribute. Kate had booked her friend, Jane, a classically trained opera singer to perform Mum's favourite soprano aria 'Tosca: Vissi d'Arte' (I live for Art) by Giacomo Puccini. This performance would follow my eulogy. Once Jane had finished singing, an audio tribute would be played, pre-recorded by George, who was studying at the California State University. It was Mum's express wish that George shouldn't interrupt his studies and fly back to the UK for her funeral. I felt that history was repeating itself as years earlier when Grandad had passed away in April 1988, it was Mum who was insistent that I should not interrupt my new job and fly back from Miami for Grandad's funeral – I felt gutted, but respected Mum's wishes at the time. So, I knew exactly what George must have been feeling and going through. I felt very upset for him.

Following George's audio tribute, Vicky's son Alex (my nephew) would read out two famous poems from 'Pippa Passes', by Robert Browning, which would be followed by the very apt, 'Dust if you must', by Rose Milligan. 'All Things Bright and Beautiful' (words by Cecil Frances Alexander, 1848) was to come next, an all-time favourite hymn, which would be followed by Carolyn's 1. Corinthians 13:1-13 bible reading. Carolyn's address, prayers (including the Lord's Prayer) and notices would precede the final hymn 'I Vow To Thee My Country' (with words by Sir Cecil Spring Rice, 1908). The final poem 'She is Gone', by David Harkins would be read by family friend, Dr Elizabeth Haslett. The 'Commendation' and 'Blessing' would precede the Exit Aria 'Tosca: E Lucevan le Stelle' (The Stars are shining brightly), by Giacomo Puccini and performed by Placido Domingo. This would complete the St. Chad's Church funeral order of service. The funeral cars would then take us to the Committal at Carleton Crematorium for a 15-minute service. This would comprise entrance music 'Ave Maria' by Johann Sebastian Bach and Charles Gounod, performed by Placido Domingo; words from scripture; Psalm 23 (The Lord is my Shepherd); The Committal, Final Prayers and Blessing. The exit music would be 'Fireworks Suite Minuet' by George Frideric Handel. Mum had chosen the majority of the order of service herself, which Vicky and Kate checked with her in her final days. We think she would have been pleased with the service, especially with Kate's added touches of Jane's singing and Liz's poetry reading. On the back cover of the order of service, we invited people to make a donation in memory of Mum to her chosen charity 'Diabetes UK'.

In the days approaching the funeral, Kate set about deep cleaning Mum's house and simultaneously I came up with the crazy notion of weeding Mum's front garden, because it would look nice when Mum's hearse pulled up outside! (who said I'm mad?!) Kate did a superb job on the house and I like to think that I did ok on the garden, although it was a bitterly cold experience.

Carolyn the Curate undertook Mum's funeral, which was seamless. The only hiccup was that Uncle Graham (Mum's brother) and his wife, Auntie Janice and their daughter (our cousin) Claire, missed their train from London and half of the funeral service! I was so focused on holding it together that although I was aware of Mum's hearse pulling up outside her house, my mind was elsewhere. Likewise, Mum's photograph and flowers adorned the top of her coffin in the church, but I could only periodically bring myself to look that way and only a fleeting glance at that. I do recall midway through my eulogy that a shaft of sunlight burst through the church windows and fell upon the end of the coffin, which I thought was a marvellous sight. As the service had really been contained within the church bit, the crematorium service that followed was quite short – just a formality. The wake at Mum's favourite local café, The New Penny Grill, gave us a chance to thank relatives and friends for coming and to relax a little. Café owner Stephen, had kindly adorned Mum's favourite table with a copy of that day's crossword, partly completed. We propped Mum's photograph up in her usual seat and placed a copy of the order of service on that quiet table, devoid of people. It was very poignant and I found that I couldn't linger there too long, for it was like a scene from Les Misérables, 'Empty Chairs at Empty Tables'.

My eulogy delivered in church on that very cold late November day in 2015 was my tribute to Mum and I feel that it really sums up Mum's life, the sort of person she was and the esteem in which she was held:

MUM / Denise / Granny: 25/11/1936 – 06/11/2015

'Denise Canning, our Mum, was born on 25th November 1936 to Harry and Sylvia Meyer (our textbook grandparents) in Colliers Wood, formerly Surrey - now London SW19.

Mum was raised with her brother Graham (our uncle) in a small Mitcham flat, number 37 Bruce Road, which Grandma lived in until her death 9 years ago.

Mum went to Gorringe Park Juniors and Links Road Secondary School in Mitcham and also Senior school in Rowan Road, Streatham.

During World War 2, Mum was evacuated to Rhyl in Wales.

She left school at 15 with no qualifications and for the next 6 years during the 1950's worked at the prestigious outfitters, hosiers and gloves store, 'Swears and Wells', 192 Regent Street, London. During her time at Swears and Wells, the management often asked Mum to model some of the designs.

Mum then became an air hostess with former RAF pilot Gerry Freeman's 'Transair' between 1957 and 1959. As one of the original

'Trolley Dollies', Mum flew Douglas DC3 Dakotas and latterly Vickers Viscount 800 turboprops out of Croydon airport (which used to be London's main airport pre-war) and then from the rapidly expanding Gatwick.

Her Transair years saw Mum travelling extensively throughout Europe and Africa and until recently Mum attended the annual Transair reunion at Gatwick airport, which she absolutely loved.

On 19 August 1959, a Transair Dakota returning from Barcelona crashed into Mount Montseny in the Catalan Pre-Coastal Range after entering cloud, killing all 29 passengers and 3 crew. With only a small, intimate number of crew on rotation, the possibility that Mum could have been flying that dreadful day was very high indeed. Fate played a hand and Vicky, Kate and I were thus destined to be born.

Mum met our late father, a medical doctor when she was only 18. She left Transair in 1959 to devote the rest of her married life to becoming a housewife and mother.

When our father gained a new posting, our family upped sticks and moved from Carshalton in Surrey to Poulton in August 1969. So began our connection with this lovely church of St. Chad's through our schooling at Sheaf Street under the awesome headmaster, William Clarkson and church worship under Rev TJ Stretch and Rev Paul Goodson.

As we were growing up, Mum felt that she wanted to make up for her lack of qualifications and showed determination, focus and a strong desire to succeed, when she went to night school to achieve a great many 'O' and 'A' levels during the '70s and '80s.

Mum was well travelled – a love that was nurtured during the Transair years of the late '50s and in recent decades, saw her visit Australia and multiple trips to the USA and Europe.

Mum loved wildlife and nature, the garden birds and of course our 4 pedigree Siamese cats that were a massive part of our family from the early 1960s right up until 2006.

After our father died in 2006, Mum's love of classical music really blossomed and her interest, nay fascination with the great tenor Placido Domingo started in earnest. Mum has stalked.... I mean followed Placido Domingo all over Europe and across to the USA. Her home became a shrine to her idol with his images vastly outnumbering those of her family! Mum was in the line-up recently to shake Placido Domingo's hand. Once she'd shaken hands, she ran to the other end of the line to do it all over again! We teased her mercilessly about this and other antics. But this was Mum's passion in later life and with a focus and love of Placido Domingo and his singing and conducting – Mum found happiness in these last years being her own boss and doing exactly what she wanted to do. This interest led to new friendships with people from all over Europe. Indeed, Mum's friend Judy from her Manchester 'Placido Teas' group told me "how happy, even euphoric, the 'Placido experience' made her; the wonderful music, meeting him afterwards, enjoying cafe life and 'sightings' around the opera houses. Denise was 'up for everything' with great stamina, great love for life and adventure". And this was as recently as July!

Mum loved quiz programmes, the daily crossword, historical dramas and romances. She was an avid reader. Mum was very patriotic, admired the Royal Family and was very knowledgeable about Royal Family history. She loved walking and keeping fit and going to the gym religiously, at least five times a week until mid-October when cancer showed its ugly face and stopped her in her tracks.

Mum was very proud of us her children and of her wonderful grandchildren, Alex, George & Lauren. Denise was a devoted Mother, Granny, Sister, Mother-in-Law, Sister-in-Law, Aunt, Great-Aunt, cousin and friend to many people, past and present. She retained her cultured London accent all through her life and was a real lady!

Mum loved the beauty and colour of the outdoors, but hated housework and gardening with a passion. It was fact that Mum would prefer to spend money jetting off to see Placido Domingo than getting work done on the home.

Seriously though - Mum's philosophy was that life is for living and you should enjoy it. She had far more important things to be doing than cleaning and cooking. For this reason, Mum was absolutely adamant that her grandson – our son George should not interrupt his studies in the United States and come back for her funeral.

Mum always made a positive impression on people. She was a kindly soul who endeared herself to others. She loved a giggle and a joke and would hold daily 'court' at Stephen and Lucy's New Penny, having a naughty cake or piece of warm apple pie with ginger ice cream, or putting the world to rights with her friend Sue. Of course, Mum was most in her element when she was 'in the bosom of her family' as she used to say. Mum had a great personality and was very warm-spirited. She had a lovely smile and a wonderful sense of humour. With her failing hearing we'd often have a laugh at her expense, only to be caught out because she'd heard every word.

Poor Mum was so brave and showed great courage and dignity, trying to come to terms with this dreadful cancerous disease, which got a strangle hold in the last few weeks, but that we now know, developed suddenly and completely undetected over many months. When told the news that her illness was terminal, Mum was cross for only about ten seconds and then her expression changed to one of disappointment for some of the things she still wanted to do (all of them Placido Domingo related) but then characteristically she returned instantly to her mothering role, fussing over this and that and proving that uppermost in her mind was caring for those she loved.

The following is based on one of my favorite poems by Rudyard Kipling

Have you heard about our Mum Denise?
Not this tide.
When d'you think that she'll come back? – with this autumn chill or
with a summer breeze
Not with this wind blowing, and this tide.

Has anyone else had word of her?
Not this tide.
For what is sunk will hardly swim,
Not with this wind blowing, and this tide.

Oh, dear, what comfort can we find?
None this tide,
Nor any tide,
Except she did not shame her kind—
Not even with that wind blowing, and that tide.

Then hold our heads up all the more,
This tide,
And every tide;
Because our lovely Mum has slipped through that magical door,
And gave to that wind blowing and that tide!

Our Mum had a real strength of character. She was wise, intelligent, a good listener, but who could also talk for England (a trait I seem to have inherited!), a good counsel, adorable, huggable, kind, warm-hearted, generous, a constant, a one off, irreplaceable, a massive support and simply lovely to be around. Mum was very funny, sometimes exhibiting a girlish sense of humour which could be quite mischievous. On our discovery of a life insurance policy recently, on the outside of the envelope was written, "You can only get this when I die, Ha Ha!" Similarly, on me breaking the awful news to Mum that she had terminal cancer just a week before she died, Mum turned to Kate and said, "Switzerland!".

Also, we were teasing Mum that we would play pop music at her funeral, to which she retorted, "If you dare do that, I'll open the coffin lid and sit up!" - Yes – Mum was definitely up for a laugh. What a character!

Mum's was indeed a life to be celebrated. Mum was a thoroughly decent person. She was all of this and much, much more. We'll all miss her terribly but let us take some collective comfort from the cherished memories we have and our love and respect for this wonderful lady to help assuage our mutual grief.

To take from the immortal words of Ronnie Barker: 'WHAT LUCK'

WHAT LUCK – that Mum wasn't on board the Dakota that crashed back in 1959, for we her children and grandchildren would not be here today

WHAT LUCK – that Mum found a dear friend in Sue and in her extended family - Lucy, Stephen and their many lovely customers at the New Penny

WHAT LUCK – that Mum found an interest and passion in the winter of her life that made her burst with joy

WHAT LUCK – that we had so much quality time with and have so many happy memories of our wonderful Mum and to tell Mum just how much we love her and how much she was loved and appreciated by so many people

And finally, WHAT LUCK, WHAT WONDERFUL LUCK - that God gave us all Denise Canning

Mum may the angels cherish you and may you shine for all eternity. God bless you'.

November gave way to a mild December and Christmas beckoned with the promise of a little family cheer, albeit the happiness derived from watching George and Lauren excitedly opening their presents. The four of us and Simon gathered around the dining table for Christmas lunch and it struck me again that within a calendar year we had lost both Mothers, for there would normally have been seven of us gathered around the table. Once everyone had helped themselves to vegetables and relishes aplenty, I proposed a short toast to absent Mothers and loved ones. I took a sip of bubbly and remembered sitting around the same dining table only four and a bit months before, when we sat outside with a seemingly healthy Mum on a beautiful, early August afternoon, enjoying the American themed leaving party as a send-off for George, who would be flying off to Los Angeles to study the following week. We were joined at that mini gathering by two large, turquoise-green dragonflies, which circled round and round for quite a few minutes. I even photographed one of them when it came to land on a bush behind the pond. Now, I'd never seen these majestic insects in our garden before and we'd already seen ten summers 'Over Wyre'. This got me thinking. The sudden appearance of dragonflies apparently, is strongly indicative of spiritual presence, the significance of which hadn't gone unnoticed that late summer's day. I thought at the time that it was Val and Laurie coming to join the party and wave off their Grandson but looking back I now feel that it was a sign from Spirit to say that Mum didn't have long with us on earth. Indeed, less than four months later, Mum was gone!

Christmas 2015 was as difficult as 2014 – two successive years to deal with two Mums passing. A time of celebration, when the last thing you want to do is celebrate anything, but somehow I got through it, we all got through it. God knows how.

We also lost some famous faces in 2015. Among the actors to pass away were Sir Christopher Lee (one of my all time favourites), Rod Taylor, Star Trek's Leonard Nimoy, Omar Sharif, Maureen O'Hara, Patrick Macnee and Geoffrey Lewis. We also lost English singer, television presenter, actress and author, Cilla Black, OBE, who was 72. Born Priscilla Maria Veronica White, Cilla had a string of top ten hits, including, 'Anyone Who Had a Heart' and 'You're My World'. On television Cilla will be remembered for hosting her own variety show, Cilla and the hugely popular Blind Date, The Moment of Truth and Surprise Surprise. Cilla Black was a national treasure who is sorely missed.

The 2016 new year festivities passed me by. My immediate focus was the four separate ceremonies required to scatter Mum's ashes (Mitcham, Grasmere, St Chad's Churchyard in Poulton and Mdina in Malta). The first of these was attended by Vicky and me and we ended up burying a small pot of ashes in Grandma and Grandad Meyer's grave in London Road Cemetery, Mitcham, early in January and prior to meeting up with Mum's brother, Graham and his wife Janice and daughter Claire for lunch. The bulk of Mum's ashes were interred in St. Chad's Churchyard, Poulton-le-Fylde, following a short ceremony, presided over by the Reverend Carolyn on 21st January 2016. I followed my sisters and Carolyn out of church, so that I could wipe away my tears, undetected. Carolyn carefully poured the ashes into a pre-dug hole, a spot that we had chosen just before the service. A small cloud of dust rose from this pit and was gently carried away on the cold breeze. We found this strangely, quite comforting. I was much more upset at this service, far more so than Mum's actual funeral, I guess because I wasn't concentrating on standing up and speaking for ten minutes or so.

Mum's house was placed on the market in early February and thereafter followed sporadic viewings, most of whom we deemed to be time wasters. I was probably at my lowest ebb, but thankfully realised that I needed professional help. I sought solace in grief counselling through work, which turned out to be a tremendous support.

By mid-February a cluster of snowdrops and saffron coloured crocuses adorned the piece of turf that covered Mum's ashes. Mum would have approved as she was always admiring the flowers in St. Chad's. On Saturday 9th April 2016, Vicky, Kate and I travelled to Grasmere to scatter the second pot of Mum's ashes overlooking the beautiful lake. We found a lovely spot at the Rydal end of Grasmere lake, slightly elevated on the lower slopes of Loughrigg Fell and in front of a small tree where several clusters of daffodils nodded in the breeze. This, we all agreed would be perfect. Mum loved to look at things, she was inherently inquisitive, especially when it came to nature and she loved coming to Grasmere. Whilst Kate duly sprinkled the ashes, Vicky and I looked on, whilst the tears rolled down my cheeks, amidst serenity. It was all very moving. Kate then read the poem that her friend Liz had read to us at Mum's funeral, 'She is Gone'. It was lovely. The spot we chose was tranquil, the view idyllic and the weather couldn't have been better.

And so with three ashes ceremonies done and dusted (pardon, yet again for the terrible pun), it was left to me to fly out to Malta, the first place that Mum said she ever really felt happy and where she wanted some of her ashes to be scattered. My flight was on Saturday 30th April 2016, with the fourth, and final, scattering planned for Sunday Morning, 1st May 2016. Six years previously, Mum and I had a wonderful five days together visiting the picturesque island of

Malta and it was whilst wandering around the ancient walled city of Mdina that Mum turned to me and said, completely out of the blue, "Now listen carefully, this is where I want a sprinkling of my ashes to be scattered when I'm dead!" I just stared at Mum inanely, but my protestations fell on stony ground. "Over here", she jabbed with an outstretched hand, pointing over the wall to the fields beyond. I recall at the time quickly changing the subject and Mum, once she had repeated the request, never raised the issue again, but somehow I knew just by looking at her, how much this meant to her. It also dawned on me the enormity of the responsibility that she was entrusting me with.

I couldn't picture it at all back then, knowing that at some time in the future I would return to the very spot where Mum and I stood in May 2010 and almost surreptitiously, lob a load of my Mother's incinerated remains over an old, city wall in some far away Mediterranean country. It just seemed absurd, somewhat comedic. But now almost sixth months after Mum's passing, I was preparing to fly out to this lovely country with, among other things, a precious cargo of ashes in my rucksack! The funeral directors, used to such requests, had already supplied me with a 'To whom it may concern' letter and this, together with a copy of Mum's death certificate, I would duly show to security and check in at Manchester Airport to verify that the ashes were legitimate. Bob, the taxi driver, was chatty from the moment he picked me up from home at the ungodly hour of 3am. Barely an hour and ten minutes later, I found myself walking into departures at Manchester Airport's terminal 1. I thought I was wide awake, but whilst going through security I set the alarm off because I'd forgotten to take my watch off.... doh! This resulted in me being given the 'full monty' in terms of being frisked. Then to cap it all, a mini panic moment set in when all my belongings failed to materialise through the x-ray machine. I waited patiently at the receiving end of the numerous trays of possessions that were spewing out of the screener like a sausage machine. There was no sign of my bag! I was vaguely aware of an official holding up a black rucksack saying, "Who's bag is this?" Suddenly the penny dropped. I was looking for a dark red suitcase and not a black rucksack – er – the suitcase that I had already checked in! I quickly reclaimed my rucksack, put on my belt and shoes and put my wallet and other valuables away. I definitely put that one down to lack of sleep. The 6.30am flight out was on time and uneventful. Even the pre-warning of turbulence was nothing to write home about. Three hours later we were touching down at Luqa airport. I cleared security quicker than a fart dispersing in a gale and was met by a smart, casually dressed taxi driver holding my name up in the arrivals hall. Twenty minutes later we arrived at my accommodation for the next two nights, the Grand Hotel Excelsior.

The Republic of Malta is an idyllic, southern Mediterranean archipelago, situated about 207 miles north of Libya and about 50 miles south of Sicily. This beautiful gem comprises seven islands, but only Malta, Gozo and Comino, the three largest islands, are actually inhabited. In the Maltese capital Valletta, a plaque on the wall of the Grand Master's Palace fronting St. George's Square (just above and beyond the further of two sentry boxes) commemorates King George V1 awarding the George Cross in 1942 for the country's resilience and bravery during World War 2. Malta is steeped in history and over time, has had many multicultural influences. Valletta itself was founded by the Knights of St. John. The country has multiple fortresses and temples, churches and chapels, but is perhaps more well known for the Hal Saflieni Hypogeum, an underground web of ancient halls and burial chambers. Malta's Roman Catholic faith can be traced back to 60AD, when St. Paul was shipwrecked here. Unsurprisingly, religion and religious festivals play an important part in the Maltese calendar with village feasts or 'festas', complete with obligatory procession, fireworks and luminous street decorations, being a must see. Malta is also famed for its long tradition of beekeeping and corresponding harvest of honey and beeswax. It gained independence in 1964 and became a Republic ten years later. In 2004, Malta joined the European Union.

Having freshened up in my hotel room, I decided to take off and just walk Valletta's grid system of streets. It took a while to acclimatise as the local temperature was already nudging 26 degrees centigrade. It was also more than a tad humid. I hadn't gone two paces before I could feel the beads of sweat start to form on my brow. I had forgotten that Malta's humidity can be well in excess of 65%. However, the shade countered by offering up a cool, refreshing breeze and I felt instantly at home. I had come here just on the cusp of the summer temperature rise. Exhibiting a characteristic central Mediterranean climate, the mercury climbs to an average of 32 degrees centigrade between May and October. The blue-sky days are typically hot, dry and sunny. In contrast, the winter months are cool and can be rainy. As I walked up hill towards Valletta's bus terminal, camera stored safely in my rucksack, I rounded a left corner and to my surprise there was the Phoenicia Hotel, where Mum and I stayed on our May 2010 trip. The Phoenicia, a five-star haven of decadent luxury was, as I stared at its front entrance façade, now a mere shell. It had been completely gutted. Any thoughts of a quiet afternoon tea in Mum's honour, were immediately quashed by the fact that you could gaze through one side of the building right through to blue sky on the opposite side. This lovely hotel, gardens and vicinity, were a building site. I continued on walking, treading in the steps that Mum and I had trodden years before.

The traditional, rickety, old, yellow buses that had served the island well for donkeys' years had now been replaced with a modern, sleek, green and white fleet. Memories of the 2010 trip kept crowding in. It had only been six years, but in the interim, I had forgotten most of our previous trip. It was all coming back with every stride, a photograph here and a laugh and giggle there. As I walked down Republic Street, Valletta's main thoroughfare, passed St. John's Cathedral – famed for Caravaggio's masterpiece 'The beheading of St. John the Baptist' - I was momentarily overwhelmed with sadness, but strangely at the same time comforted. I pulled out a tissue to wipe the tears from reddened eyes which, fortunately, were hidden from public stares by my sunglasses. Suddenly I happened upon the famous Café Cordina, Valletta's oldest café, famed for its array of beautifully presented, delicious cakes and pastries. I stopped for a few seconds to drink the atmosphere – locals chatting, tourists consulting their maps and pocket guides, lovers canoodling. I was enveloped in happiness - people from different countries in this same spot, enjoying being in the moment. I clocked the upbeat mood but felt none for myself. It was very reminiscent of my time on the Norway cruise liner, when I sought solace up on deck after learning the news that my Grandfather had died back in April 1988. It was the same sort of empty, shitty feeling, somewhat greatly magnified. Mum had insisted we sample the café's delights and treated us to a coffee and 'naughty' cake. I made a mental note to have that coffee and cake in Mum's memory, later that afternoon. The remainder of that warm Saturday however, I was quite content to just wander and photograph. I wasn't in the least bit worried about getting lost. I had been here before and as the minutes ticked by, so my familiarity with this place grew.

After an hour or so I wandered back to the Café Cordina and found an empty table, a few parasol rows back from the main thoroughfare. A busker was playing classical music as I pondered the menu for a few minutes and chose lemon cheesecake, with a fresh orange juice and café latte. It was time to reflect again whilst people watching. Close by sat two coquettish girls in their early 20s, busy talking whilst simultaneously checking their iPhones and typing messages with well-manicured fingernails, seemingly traversing their respective mini keyboards at breakneck speed like accomplished concert pianists! The people at my '12 o'clock' had their backs to me. Those at my 1 through to 4 o'clock were busy talking, laughing and like me savouring the Café Cordina's many delights. Then sitting at my '11', I noticed a lovely, old, distinguished looking gentleman with a huge handlebar moustache and an equally generous head of wavy, silver-grey hair. But it was the unravelled, black leather pouch, resting on the table top that suddenly caught my attention. It contained around four different coloured pipes with a bottom zipped section to house one's tobacco of choice. The old gentleman had selected an ornately carved, sepiolite meerschaum and after ritually loading his pipe with tobacco and carefully lighting it, sat back slowly and inhaled the cool, dry, aromatic smoke whilst joining the rest of us gathered, savouring the pleasant Maltese atmosphere. A waft of pipe smoke blew my way and the satisfying aroma took me right back as it was not dissimilar to my Grandfather's Boars Head roll ups that I was so used to smelling in my youth.

Following refreshments, I walked some more over several hours and cursed myself for not clocking the mileage on my mobile phone app. When I grew tired of walking, dinner beckoned at a local hostelry, washed down with a refreshing, cold pint of the local beer called Cisk.

Following a really good night's sleep, I awoke early on Sunday 1st May and after a cup of coffee in my room, which served as a quickie breakfast, my rucksack was soon packed and I was out of the hotel, faster than a rat up a drainpipe and walking towards the bus station. I soon found stand 'C', where a bus bound for Rabat and Mdina was waiting. No sooner had I paid my one euro and fifty cents, my bus departed out of Valletta. First to the suburb of Floriana and then onwards to smaller suburbs, all the time heading westwards. It was the most enjoyable bus journey and all the while, I kept recognising places. After barely twenty-five minutes, my bus had arrived in Rabat where I got off. I wanted to walk the last few hundred meters uphill towards the walled city of Mdina, because this is what Mum and I did in 2010, so I thought it was only right that I should do the same. It was only just gone 9am and the place was devoid of tourists – exactly as I had hoped.

I soon found myself at Mdina's main gate and after a couple of photographs, I commenced my slow walk into the old city along Villegaignon Street. I found that I was stopping every few meters to take photographs, such is the beauty and quaintness of Malta's original capital city, which lies 13.8km west of Valletta. Mdina is very atmospheric – evidence of its time served as a defensive fortification abounds and it is a maze of winding alleys. It houses old palaces, museums and squares and the five-star Qwara Palace Hotel, where Mum and I had afternoon tea six years previously. Mdina has been inhabited since the Bronze age. Indeed, Malta's well to do families have their ancestral homes here. It's so charming, it's easy to get side-tracked and wander off the main drag, down one of the myriad winding alley ways. My priority was to scatter Mum's ashes without being detected. This meant saving any more sightseeing and inevitable photography until later. So, I continued along Villegaignon Street, passed the baroque style late 17th century / early 18th century St. Paul's cathedral and onwards to Bastion Square.

Suddenly I was there – when nobody else was. I felt like a criminal about to pull a job off as I scanned the area. I walked quickly to the raised battlements and before mounting the steps, picked a few leaves to toss into the air to check the wind direction. After all, I did not want the embarrassment of being covered in my Mother's ashes! I stood on top of the battlement walkway and looked out. The wall was horrendously thick. Worse – it was so thick, there was no way I could gently scatter Mum's ashes over it because I just couldn't reach over. Then I found the ideal spot, just to the right of the wall-mounted viewing binoculars. I spied a protective grill in the wall where you could look out over the fields to the coast. Crucially it also meant that I could scatter Mum's last remains, which would easily clear the wall that was narrow at this point. Further, there were bushes behind me, which would shield me from any onlookers in the dwellings that fronted Bastion Square. I popped my rucksack down on the walkway and threw the leaves in the air and watched the breeze take them along and over the wall – not ideal, but it would have to do. I then reached into my rucksack and gently removed the top from the last pot of Mum's ashes. Another glance around. Phew, all clear. I was good to go. I leant over the grill in the wall and shook the tube several times, watching in wonderment as several small clouds of grey dust drifted out, up and then parallel with the wall that fronted Bastion Square. I shook the pot again and took aim, but simultaneously the wind must have changed direction, for instead of clearing the wall, the dust blew back in my face, in fact I was covered in my mother's ashes. I spent the next few minutes rectifying this awful cock-up by patting myself down and 'de-ashing' myself! Mum would have found this hilariously funny, no doubt, after giving me a bollocking! I checked the pot. One final shake and it was empty. Replacing the lid, I carefully popped the pot back in my rucksack and pulled out a copy of Mum's funeral order of service in its place. I then turned to find the poem 'She is Gone' by David Harkins and read aloud the verses, just as Kate had done at the Grasmere ashes scattering ceremony that all three siblings had attended a month previously. When I had finished reading, the tears came, as a powerful wave of emotion washed over me – another stark reminder that Mum was in fact no longer with us. I stood and gazed out over the view that Mum had led me to in 2010. OK, as views go, we've all seen better. Even Knott End and Fleetwood at sunset were higher up the wow factor ladder. But this was Mdina in Malta – the first place that Mum truly felt happy and it was this view to the Maltese coast that she so loved, which put it Himalayan peaks above perhaps visually more aesthetic vistas – that added power to what I was now looking at.

And so, Bastion Square, Mdina in Malta took its place with the other three ashes scattering venues: St. Chad's Church yard in Poulton-le-Fylde, Grandma and Grandads' grave in Mitcham and the lower slopes of Loughrigg Fell, overlooking Grasmere, Lake District, Cumbria. Each to become known affectionately and simply as 'Mum's spot', where family members could journey to for quiet reflection of a Mother so missed and so loved.

Just as I wiped the last of many tears away from my eyes, so I became aware of movement to my right. The first of many tourists had arrived. Cue sunglasses back on (I felt like Horatio Cane at the start of the hit television series 'CSI Miami'). Having only had a cup of coffee at my hotel for breakfast, I was quite hungry, but disciplined myself to walk the alleyways of Mdina first and then stop for brunch at Fiorelli's, which, coincidentally, just happened to be a stone's throw away from Mum's spot! It was now 12.30pm and incredibly I had been at Mdina for over three hours. I brought a few gifts for the family and walked back along Villegaignon Street towards the main gate. I felt that it was time to leave and waited under the shade of a tree close to where a bus would take me back into Valletta. I didn't have long to wait. I had my euro fifty at the ready and climbed aboard. Perfect timing, as the tourist buses were now thronging and in my mind's eye, Mdina would be overrun with visitors. Job done,

I relaxed a little taking in all the scenery as the bus started to put distance between itself and Mdina. But we hadn't even left Rabat when another memory came back to me as I looked out of the bus window towards the Ta' Qali crafts village. On our visit in 2010 a barefoot Mum had absent-mindedly kicked her bed post on the morning of our visit to Mdina and unbeknown to us, had actually broken her toe! We didn't know the extent of her injury until we returned home from Malta. What was incredible is that we walked for miles around Mdina, then on through Rabat suburb and down to Ta' Qali, before walking back out the way we had come in, which was some considerable distance to re-join the main road and getting a bus back to Valletta. I recall that Mum only mentioned that her toe felt bruised once – the whole time we were away and I never saw her limping or wincing in pain – what a remarkable woman!

After a quick trip back to the hotel to freshen up over a cup of tea on my balcony, I planned out how I would spend the remainder of my last day. I would first go for a swim in the not so warm outdoor pool (ah, that's why nobody else was in the pool!) followed by a ferry trip over to Sliema for early evening shots looking back over the picture postcard Valletta skyline, with the infamous dome of St. Paul's Church very much taking centre stage. Then I would get the ferry back to Valletta and have a last wander through the streets of the Maltese capital, grab a bite to eat and the equivalent of a pint, before heading back to my hotel room for a shower, bag pack and rest. I decided that it would be too much to try and cram in another bus ride to the pretty fishing village of Marsaxlokk, situated to the south east of Valletta. Mum and I had visited Marsaxlokk on the 2010 trip – but then we had five days compared to my 1½! In addition to the Marsaxlokk harbour side Sunday market, I trawled the inevitable souvenir stalls selling among other things, fish and in contrast, Maltese tablecloths with crochet finishing! I had also spent quality time photographing some of the many colourful luzzus, the traditional, sturdy and stable wooden fishing boats, vibrantly painted in reds, yellows, greens and blues. Adorning port and starboard sides of these vessels' bows, the 'eye of osiris' can be seen which, according to legend, exists to protect fishermen whilst out at sea. The luzzu design is said to date back to when the Phoenicians first came to Malta in 800 BC.

I didn't feel a great yearning to visit Marsaxlokk on this trip, nor did I really have time to visit the national war museum again at Fort St. Elmo, housing the island's George Cross. So, following my swim, I headed once more out of the Grand Hotel Excelsior – north east and downwards along the Great Siege Road to pick up the ferry that would take me across Marsamxett harbour to Sliema. Marsamxett is located on Valletta's west side and is one of three natural harbours on the island of Malta. On the east side of Valletta is the Grand Harbour, which houses a cruise liner terminal. A port has existed here since Roman times. Malta's third port is the deep-water facility located beyond Marsaxlokk fishing village in the south east. Marsamxett, that I now found myself crossing by ferry, lends itself to the yachting fraternity. The early evening light over the Maltese capital was perfect and I got the shots that I had previsualised. After a quick walk along Sliema promenade there was nothing left than to board the return ferry, disembark and walk the Maltese capital one last time. After half an hour or so I found a local taverna and fancied a pizza washed down with a cold Cisk.

My return flight from Luqa back to Manchester took off at a more sociable hour, late the following morning, during which I had plenty of time to reflect on a very successful trip. I had packed masses into 1½ days – walking, sightseeing, swimming, photography and as the reader now knows, the ashes scattering…not all of which, cleared the walled city! As I previously intimated, I think that following a mild bollocking and piss take, Mum would have been pleased. I feel that I did her proud by returning a part of her to Malta and in doing so, upholding one of her dying wishes. At the outset, I had a strong feeling that somehow this trip to Malta would be my last – a closing of a chapter so to speak, but I was pleasantly surprised to find that I came away with a powerful affinity for this beautiful island and an even stronger sense of wanting to return again soon – Mum's spiritual influence perhaps?

And now it begins – a new chapter in my life, our lives – life without Mum. Of course, I feel different. The grief isn't as raw, but nevertheless it's there and palpable. A big part of me died on November 6th 2015 and I guess since that terrible event, I lost some of my zest for life and that's what I've got to get to grips with - life doesn't stop just because someone else's has. Life for everyone else affected must continue and it would be wrong to be in a permanent state of limbo, of Queen Victoria-esque grieving. Life is for living, for enjoyment, for having many different experiences, good and bad and then learning from them and then progressing onwards - and of course it's about helping others. I've thought about Mum every single day since her passing and will continue to do so as long as I live. It's been far from an easy ride. But the positives are that I am blessed with a loving and supportive wife and two fantastic children, George and Lauren. Both are blessed with good looks and have a strong and determined approach to life. Both are fun-loving. I have every confidence that they will be successful. I feel lucky that my 'inner circle' have, in their own way, steered me through the heartbreak of loss. If I think about it rationally, we all lose somebody at some stage, I'm just 'selfishly' pissed off that with me, it's now! Mum was kind, funny, supportive and a constant in our lives. She definitely left her mark. She's now gone and we must pick ourselves up, hold our heads high, take a deep breath and carry on – just as Mum would have done and would want us to do. Thank you for everything Mum. Just like Grandma and Grandad, you're the best, so I guess now all that's left to say on the subject of Mum is, "Farewell then, I'll be seeing you...", but in the immortal words of Vincent Price playing Dr. Phibes, "Not for some considerable time, I trust!".

George had by now returned from LA to his uni in Wales. For the main house production of the second term of his third and final year, George and his Uni contemporaries put on Shakespeare's 'Macbeth'. George performed as King Duncan and also the doctor in full beard, giving an electrifying performance. I'll never forget a brooding King Duncan seen under an angled stage spotlight, an image that had been skillfully captured by one of George's Uni colleagues. He thoughtfully worked out and then reserved me the best seat in the house, centrally located, a few rows back from the stage. My only regret was not attending the matinee in addition to the evening show. I loved every minute and in my biased opinion, everyone was brilliant!

On 16th June 2016, the MP for West Yorkshire constituency, Batley and Spen, Helen Joanne Cox (Jo Cox) was murdered. Jo was sickeningly shot and stabbed by a far-right nutcase, Thomas Mair, multiple times in Birstall, where she was about to hold a constituency surgery. She was only 41, days away from her 42nd birthday. Jo Cox was an inspirational, vivacious, down to earth, hardworking wife, Mum, rising star of the Labour Party and in my opinion, the nation was robbed of a Prime Minister in the making. This heinous crime shocked us all and Jo's loss is sorely felt.

George graduated from the University of Trinity Saint David in the summer of 2016 with a first-class BA honours degree in acting – a very fine achievement indeed. Once again, George had surpassed himself and our pride knew no bounds. As a bonus we were blessed with very warm weather for the July graduation ceremony, which was uplifting, inspiring and thoroughly enjoyable. In next to no time, George landed a job as an usher at Lord Andrew Lloyd Webber's prestigious Grade 1 listed Theatre Royal Drury Lane in London's Covent Garden, with the purpose of learning the mechanics of a working theatre from front of house rather than just from an on stage, or back stage perspective. The job suited George well and I lost count of the number of famous faces George had seen. In October 2016 he very kindly treated us (and his Uncle Simon) to an evening performance of 'Charlie and the Chocolate Factory', complete with Royal Box seating, pre-drinks and refreshments during the interval. 'Charlie' was another runaway success and we all agreed that it had been a night to remember.

The 21st October 2016 marked the 50th anniversary of the terrible tragedy that was the Aberfan disaster in South Wales. At approximately 9.15 on the morning of 21st October 1966 when I was but an oblivious three-year-old, a huge mound of coal waste that had for many years been continually dumped on a mountainside from a nearby colliery, located above the Welsh village of Aberfan, suddenly became unstable following a period of heavy rainfall. What had constituted Tip number seven, slid down as an avalanche into the village, the resultant slurry engulfing Pantglas Junior School, where lessons had begun, as well as houses and other buildings. The adjacent secondary school also incurred some damage. 144 people were killed in Aberfan just south of Merthyr Tydfil on that fateful morning. Of the 144, 116 were children. 109 children and 5 teachers perished at Pantglas Junior School. 6 adults and a further 29 children were injured. R.I.P..

Throughout George's time working in London, Wendy's brother, Simon, generously and unselfishly put George up rent-free at his house in Ruislip and all seemed to be going swimmingly until disaster struck.

Early in November 2016, George was out for a meal with Simon when he had difficulty in swallowing (dysphagia) with partial paralysis of the face. Simon rang us from the hospital. Wendy and I thought that George had either suffered a stroke or that he had 'Bell's Palsy'. After a worrying night in the Acute Medical Unit with Simon in West London's Hillingdon Hospital under the watchful eye of Dr Paresh Mistry and his team, the Doctors took tests and suggested he went home, to return the following week to see them. I took the train down to get him and brought him back home to us for the week. It was a week of terrible worry as alarmingly he deteriorated further as the week went on. The paralysis prevented him from eating and drinking properly, we even had to wipe out his mouth with tissue to remove the saliva he couldn't swallow. Wendy drove him back down to London a week later for his appointment with Consultant Neurologist Dr Stuart Viegas at Hillingdon Hospital.

Dr Viegas took one look at George and admitted him there and then to AMU for urgent tests. Dr Viegas' preliminary diagnosis was 'Myasthenia Gravis' (MG), a rare chronic autoimmune condition that affects many of the body's muscle groups, but particularly the muscles that control breathing, the facial and swallowing muscles and those of the arms and legs. With MG, George's own antibodies that would normally fight infection couldn't function correctly and started attacking the communications system between his brain and some of his muscles – (the signal that sends nerve impulses to the muscles to make them move). This can damage the neuromuscular junction (where the nerve meets the muscle).

George presented with typical symptoms – unable to talk, problems swallowing, chronic fatigue, weakness, facial paralysis and ptosis (droopy eye lid) all served to confirm Dr Viegas' MG diagnosis. It was serious. We hadn't realised it then, but coincidentally on his entering Hillingdon Hospital, George had gone into 'myasthenic crisis' and we came within a gnat's whisker of losing him. Dr Viegas immediately put George on intravenous immunoglobulin (IVIg), plasma enriched with antibodies purified from donor blood. George was also given 'pyridostigmine' to help enhance communication between nerves and muscles and 'prednisone' to inhibit his immune system, limiting his own antibody production. Wendy observed a seemingly miraculous, albeit minute, improvement within 20 minutes of him taking this life saving medication. Thankfully, George responded well to treatment, but spent a few weeks in hospital with ITU on continual standby should events change. Wendy and I took it in turns to go down to Hillingdon Hospital to be by his bedside. On discharge, he came home to us for further recuperation. For the first year following diagnosis, George was on a high dosage combo of drugs to treat his MG, which saw him go into remission and heralded a massive reduction in his intake of MG drugs.

Myasthenia Gravis is quite rare as it normally affects older people. The condition is even more rare in (young) 21-year old males and made George something of a celebrity patient amongst the medical staff and medical students at the Hillingdon Hospitals NHS Foundation Trust. On 7th December, I accompanied George to his outpatient's appointment at Hillingdon Hospital's AMU and after Stuart Viegas had gone through all the usual tests for MG muscle weakness, including the famous 'chicken wings' test with George's arms beating up and down, number one son was declared 'pharmacologically in remission'! He was nevertheless to remain on medication and his care was transferred to a Neurologist at Blackpool Victoria Hospital. Such was George's medical success story, that doctors from both Paresh Mistry's team (the Acute Medical Unit (AMU) where George was first admitted and initially diagnosed) and Stuart Viegas' team came in to say hello and marvel at George's return to good health. This was the first time they'd seen him well and the first time they'd heard his normal voice! It was like a family reunion or an actor's curtain call. It was so good to shake every one of those doctors' hands and thank them for effectively saving George's life. I came away from Hillingdon Hospital elated, indebted to the AMU and Neuro teams for the five-star NHS treatment given to George and I will never forget the massive sense of relief and perfect joy Wendy and I experienced and just how wonderful life felt at that moment – to have our precious son back, alive, cured and well!

Less than two weeks later, on 18th December 2016, Mum's brother, Uncle Graham Meyer sadly died aged 76, ironically on what would have been his own mother's (my Grandma's) birthday. Coming so soon on the back of Mum's passing (and Wendy's Mum, and George's illness), this was a huge blow which almost knocked me off my feet. Vicky, Kate and I were to get another shock at the funeral when we saw the likeness of Graham to our mother on the order of service – it was like staring at Mum! At work there was no time for grieving as unfortunately, I couldn't just down tools - we were short staffed and I was holding the fort. I didn't see much of Graham and his wife Janice (Jan) and their two children, Andrew (born in June 1970) and Claire (born in January 1973), when I was growing up. Geographical distance was bandied about as a lame excuse for not meeting up more frequently – it was more my father's wrong-doing (what a surprise!) and probably because he was jealous of the warmth and happiness they exuded. Undoubtedly, my father's negative vibes and shit stirring had made their mark and so the Meyers never came to visit. Graham and Jan were a lovely couple. Graham was very much into his cricket and football and in latter years his grandchildren and of course, his beloved Jag (a car he cherished), were his pride and joy. Graham reminded me so much of my Grandad Harry – placid and amiable and together with Andrew and Claire, all three had inherited the Meyer wit and joie de vivre. With the funeral not until early January 2017, Christmas was once again a subdued affair full of mixed emotions. 2014, 2015 and 2016 had constituted 'the Canning family's annus horribilis hat trick'.

Among the famous faces who left us in 2016 were English rock singer David Bowie, English theatre and screen actor Alan Rickman, English record producer George Martin, American author Harper Lee, former actress and First Lady of the USA, Nancy Reagan, American musician Prince, American boxer Muhammad Ali, American actor and writer Gene Wilder, Canadian singer-songwriter Leonard Cohen, Hungarian-American actress Zsa Zsa Gabor, English pop star and singer songwriter George Michael, American actress and writer Carrie Fisher and American actress, dancer and singer, Debbie Reynolds.

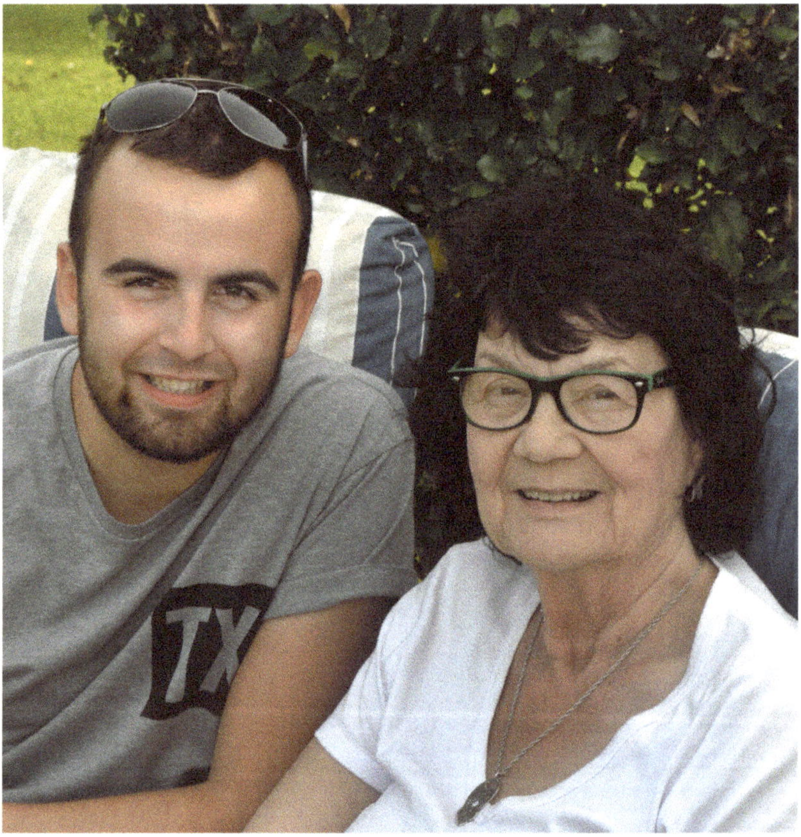

Last photo of a well-looking Mum with George in our back garden, 15 August 2015. Sadly, less than 3 months later, she was gone.

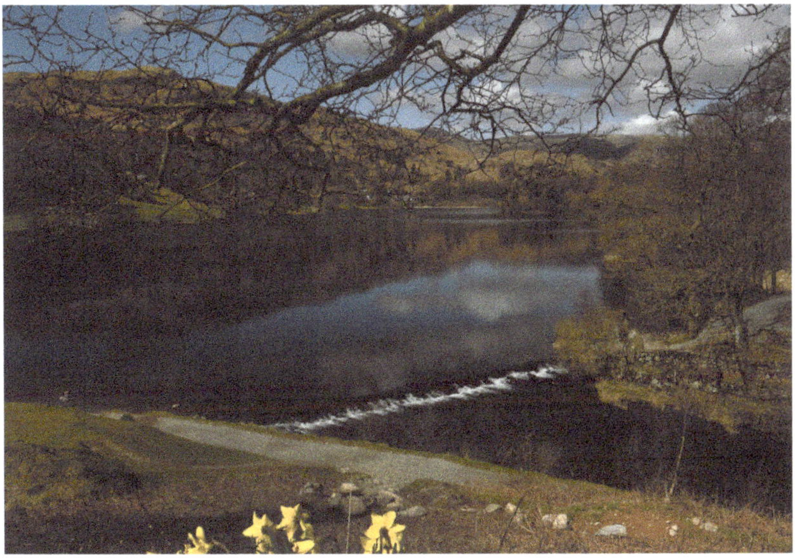

Overlooking Grasmere Lake (Rydal Water end), Cumbria, from where some of Mum's ashes were scattered on 9th April 2016.

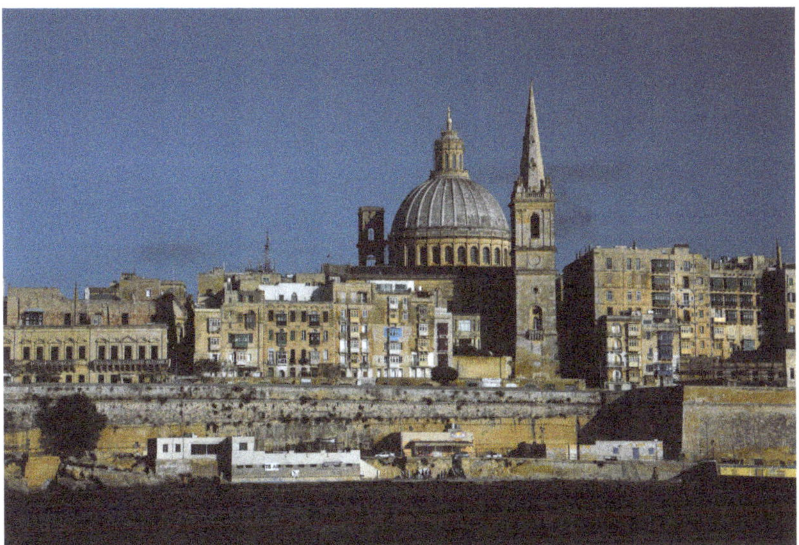

Beautiful Valletta, on the occasion of my trip to Malta to scatter some of Mum's ashes, 1st May 2016.

CHAPTER 26

Australia Family Holiday - Summer 2017

Once Mum's estate had been settled, the money was shared three ways between Vicky, Kate and me. I put a significant chunk of it into the house, but knowing that Mum wouldn't have spent a penny on her own home if she could have helped it, opting to go abroad instead, I decided to cash out on the holiday of a lifetime and take the family to Australia during the summer of 2017. We'd had a tough few years and Mum always said to me that we should go to Oz. She'd been herself and was very keen for us to go – it's what she would have wanted. I had no qualms therefore in funding this expensive adventure - and what a journey it turned out to be. George was still in recovery from his myasthenia gravis and no-one really knew how the year would pan out for him, so we had to secretly get clearance from his Consultant that it would be safe for him to travel. Once that was sorted, our mornings travelling to work together were spent working out how we would tell George and Lauren our plan! We chose a random evening when we were all together and decided to give them a number of cryptic clues as to a forthcoming 'treat'. This culminated in the final giveaway clue – a boomerang - hidden in the garden! Given that we rarely went on holiday (other than to Cornwall), they couldn't quite believe it. George was in shock and Lauren cried! Suffice to say, we were all really excited about the prospect of visiting 'down under', not least because we would be reunited with Julie Little, our lovely bridesmaid and good friend, who we hadn't seen for thirteen years, as well as her brother Pete and the rest of the 'Little' clan.

A month before we ventured to Oz, we all travelled to London for Simon's birthday to see the amazing Jeff Lynn's ELO in concert at Wembley, which was out of this world. Old favourites like 'Turn to stone' and 'Sweet Talkin' Woman' were interspersed with recent creations such as, 'When I Was a Boy' from the 2015 album 'Alone in the Universe'. However, when old favourite, 'Mr Blue Sky' boomed out from a multitude of speakers, everyone was in raptures. I think we were on our feet at this stage. Supporting acts were the brilliant Tom Chaplin, lead singer from one of my favourite bands 'Keane' and British country and western duo, Ben Earle and Crissie Rhodes, 'The Shires'. Crissie courageously sang the hauntingly beautiful 2016 release 'Daddy's Little Girl', as a tribute to her father who had passed away only a short time before the concert.

July 25th, 2017 was my last day of work prior to the big holiday. It was the culmination of months of hard work and had seen me coming into the office on two consecutive weekends to clear my backlog. All that was left now was to say goodbye to esteemed work colleagues such as Podiatrist Debbie, who had recently returned from maternity leave. She showed me a photo of her beautiful baby girl, which filled me with positivity. Then I bumped into Tissue Viability Nurse Emma, another cheerful, effervescent, friendly soul, who had not long returned from Oz on her honeymoon and was able to give me the lowdown on what to see and what to avoid. Then I picked up my regular Costas skinny latte takeaway and sat in the main reception of Blackpool Victoria Hospital to wait for my chauffeur, Wendy, to pick me up and take us home. I sat there watching the faces – some happy, some sad, some vacant and unreadable. Occasionally I zoned out and just let my mind wander. At long last I was on holiday. I couldn't wait. When we drove away from work, I didn't look back. Following a chippy tea, that evening was spent last minute packing and house tidying.

The following morning, the 26th, we drove into Poulton for breakfast at Mum's favourite café the New Penny as a treat. Once back at home and waiting for the taxi to take us to the airport, George lined us up for the departure selfie, on the drive, complete with new, matching suitcases! Our driver Bob arrived with his seven-seater to take us to Manchester Airport for around 4pm, only to discover that the Emirates check-in desk didn't open until 5.15pm. So, with 1¼ hours to kill, we became the front of what would become a very long Emirates queue, along with a retired Kiwi couple and a band of other extremely excitable people. Check-in was a breeze. Sadly, this was not the case for security. I'm sure we all had that sinking feeling when we hit the mile-long snaking queue, which took ages and included the new body scanners, in which you have to hold your hands up over your head. I had visions of my beltless trousers suddenly falling down. Fortunately, this didn't happen, but I did leave a mini toothpaste and deodorant in my hand luggage by accident, prompting a hand search of said luggage.... doh! Suddenly, we found ourselves in duty free and the girls disappeared to eye up the offers, after which it was time for a pasty, wedges and a slow saunter to our Gate 12, where we waited a further hour to board our airbus A380. Beyond excited! Once boarding had commenced, we were in our seats by 9.00pm

The A380-800 is an experience and a half, complete with a main deck and an upper deck for first and business class users. We were sat with the rabble – three seats together behind the wing, port side and an aisle seat opposite, which is where I parked my posterior. The back of the seat in front had a good size television screen for accessing films, documentaries, music and wi-fi. We were each provided with earphones, a cushion and a blanket, which did come in handy as the cabin temperature dropped later on in the flight. Pulling my red flight socks on proved to be an undignified, awkward undertaking, much to the amusement of the family and surrounding passengers.

At a cost of just under $446 million, this massive, wide bodied, double decker jet (currently at the time of writing, the world's largest passenger airliner manufactured by Airbus) is fitted with four powerful engines – either 'Rolls Royce' Trent's or 'Engine Alliance' Turbofans. Entering commercial service with Singapore Airlines in October 2007, the Emirates economy class, where the humble Canning family were seated, has a '3-4-3' seating configuration with two aisles. Similar to all advancements, it won't be long before the upgrade 'plus' version becomes available. Unlike the old, traditional Jumbo Jet 747 'bubble', the upper deck of the A380-800 extends the entire length of the aircraft. Depending on the configuration of the class system, the A380-800 can seat between 525 and 853 people. The Airbus A380-800 has a cruising speed of 560 miles per hour and can fly non-stop for a phenomenal range of circa 8,500 nautical miles.

This was to be the first long-haul flight as a family since Wendy and I set out on honeymoon twenty-five years before, bound for San Francisco, enjoying a glass of champers or two up in business class on North West Airline's 747 bubble. As I glanced over at my family prior to take off, I felt enormous pride for our two lovely children, now young adults, and of course pride for my rock, my gorgeous wife, Wendy, who herself had worked damn hard both in her day job and at home to bring us to where we are now. Then I noticed that Lauren was crying. Wendy was already there with hugs and cuddles. Lauren was just nervous of the initial take-off. She was just fine for the subsequent flights. I spent most of the flight to Dubai listening to classical music and then my iPod. The meal, when it came, consisted of chicken and pasta, cheese, crackers and fruit crumble. A friendly stewardess came around with juice and coffee. I rated the meal good, but not exceptional as the chicken was a tad chewy! With a top up of juice and coffee it set us up thus far.

This, our first Emirates A380-800 flight, touched down in Dubai just after 7am local time (4am BST) on Thursday July 27th, after a 6½ hour flight. The number of stewards and stewardesses disembarking our aircraft served as a reminder of just how big the A380 Airbus is. It must have taken a good twenty-five minutes for us to leave the plane. The moment we finally walked out and down the stairs to a waiting bus that would take us to security for transfers, the local 104-degree Fahrenheit heat hit us ... and what a shock to the system. Security at Dubai compared with Manchester was a breeze. Then it was a driverless train to take us to our gate 'A5' and the inevitable toilet stop, before boarding our next Emirates A380 for the next leg of our trip – the 9.25am to Singapore. We had similar seating arrangements as per the first flight, but on the opposite (right side) and over the wing. We were all pretty tired at this stage, having travelled through the night with little or no sleep. I found that I was nodding after I'd barely sat down for two minutes, with no interest in watching a film or listening to music. Due to the tight transfer time we forgot to pick up more supplies before boarding. Flight EK404 eventually took off 35 minutes later than scheduled at around 10.00am. The meal and drinks took ages to come and the chicken was even tougher than on the previous flight. Lauren was probably glad to have missed this meal as she slept all the way through delivery and clear up. As for each flight, I got up several times and walked up and down the aisles, amazed at the sheer number of people and marvelling at just how this huge aircraft actually manages to lift off the runway at all. I thought I'd got away with not spilling any lunch or drink down me when a stewardess accidentally knocked my elbow as my coffee cup was about to touch my lips. I had a millisecond to brace myself for a scorching in the genitalia, which miraculously didn't happen. I escaped with a few stains to my trousers and polo shirt. The poor stewardess, to her credit, was most apologetic and rushed to get me extra napkins for the mop up job. As well as films, music and wi-fi, you were constantly updated with the flight's progress. With an eta in Singapore of 9.05pm, this A380-800 was now cruising at 576 mph at an altitude of 36,987 feet on a 116-degree heading. Oh, and it was a bit cold outside – minus 46 degrees centigrade. I found it quite difficult keeping up with the time difference, doing lots of calculations all at once. After I felt brain ache coming on, simplification was the order of the evening. There is a plus three-hour time difference between the UK and Dubai and a further plus four-hour difference between Dubai and Singapore – er – making the total difference between the UK and Singapore plus seven hours.

This trip of a lifetime coincided with the year of our silver wedding anniversary (September 12th, 2017). I know Mum would have been absolutely thrilled and excited by this Oz holiday and had fate played Mum a different hand, she would have undoubtedly come with us. I texted Vicky and Kate just before departure from Manchester on our Antipodean adventure to let them know that I was carrying a photo of Mum with me throughout this trip. The photo was of Mum just as she was about to take a photo of Placido Domingo with the Nikon digital camera we all bought her – in July 2015 before she fell ill.

At 9pm exactly our Airbus A380 touched down on Singapore tarmac, but not before we all had to fill in a registration card. Unlike the previous flight, there was only ten minutes until we disembarked and we filed past a bunch of masked clad officials who were screening for flu. Wendy had a thermometer pushed against her temple – she must have looked hot and bothered – but she passed! Then it was straight through passport control to pick up our four suitcases. 'Dragon', the name of our taxi transfer chap, met us holding up a sign with the name 'Canning' correctly spelled. This air-conditioned mini coach was a welcome relief to the wall of heat and humidity that whacked us in the face when we put one foot out of the airport. It was a thirty-minute run to our hotel, during which, our driver proved to be quite the tour guide. The views of Singapore at night were very memorable. Following a smooth hotel check in, I showered, changed and ordered room service. The room was OK, it wasn't the Ritz, but it was a welcome respite from the heat outside.

The next morning, Friday 28th July, we were up before 6am and quickly hit the breakfast room. The food itself proved sumptuous, providing for an array of cultures. There was everything from cold meats to cooked meals, pastries, different rolls of bread for toasting, to an array of yoghurts, cereals and juices. My cup of Americano coffee though was too strong, so I quickly reverted to tea. Wendy, George and Lauren were feeling tired, possibly due to a combination of jet lag, temperature and humidity. At 9am we met Walter Tan in the hotel lobby for a four-hour tour of Singapore and non-stop talking! I had booked this bespoke tour over the internet before we left home, had read up on Walter and knew that he would be the man for us. I put Walter in his early 60s and he didn't disappoint. He was very personable, kind, accommodating, very witty, very friendly and extremely knowledgeable. Above all he was passionate about his birthplace and the ideal person to show us around.

We travelled first by air-conditioned coach to Merlion Park, located in the central business district at One Fullerton. The statue of the 8.6-metre-tall Merlion, a Singapore mascot, is a mythical creature comprising a lion's head and a fish's tail and has a fountain of water spouting from its mouth, making for an impressive sight overlooking the waterfront. The statue completed in 1972 used to be located near the mouth of the Singapore River and was relocated to its current position in April 2002. We posed for the obligatory photos that Walter obligingly took, before a boat trip that would take us under Fullerton Road / Esplanade Drive Bridge. We got great views of Singapore from the waterway that included the Raffles landing site, Parliament House and the famous upmarket Clarke Quay. Named after Sir Andrew Clarke, the second Governor, the Quay is situated upstream from the mouth of the Singapore River. Sir Andrew played a pivotal role in the early 1870's in helping to establish Singapore as a major Malay port.

It was so hot and humid that Walter lent Lauren his fan to try and keep cool. With humidity at 95 % I was continually dripping sweat. As soon as I took my Nikon D810 out of my camera bag, it steamed up and I couldn't use it for several minutes until it had warmed up. The kit had been in a cool air-conditioned hotel room all night and I'd completely forgotten about condensation! From Carke Quay, our tour boat retraced its steps back to the Merlion statue and cruised around the marina taking in the panorama of skyscrapers and the weirdly designed Artscience Museum, opened in 2011.

Shaped like multiple fingers of a hand, this impressive sculpture was designed by Moshe Sadie and is known as 'The Welcoming Hand of Singapore'. It was the world's first ArtScience building. Behind it stands the equally impressive structure that is the Marina Bay Sands Hotel, which comprises three skyscrapers with what looks to the layman like a boat / surfboard / ironing board perched on top! This unique, breath-taking structure opened in 2010 and actually houses a massive casino, hotel, shops restaurants and theatres. The three towers are somewhat wider at the base and start to narrow with increased elevation. Each of the three towers comprises two asymmetrical legs, one of which, is curved and leans against its partner leg. What I rather flippantly described as a surfboard, is actually a work of architectural and structural engineering genius – the 340 metre 'Skypark' sits on a cantilevered base which not only straddles all three towers, but actually overhangs the north tower. The Skypark is also home to a 150-metre infinity swimming pool, jogging tracks and gardens. I'd never seen anything like Marina Bay Sands and spent many minutes just staring at it in wonderment.

From Marina Bay, it was back into the air-conditioned minibus and onwards for a very interesting walk along Smith Street in Chinatown, located centrally in the Outram district. Among others, Walter showed us an unusual store that catered for the deceased person's journey to the afterlife, selling everything from burial suits to mobile phones made from easily combustible paper and card. Steeped in heritage, there are museums and Chinese, Buddhist and Hindu temples at every turn. One of the oldest shrines in Singapore being the 1827 Sri Mariamman Temple, a pivotal place of worship for the country's Tamil Hindus. Constructed around 1820, Thian Hock Keng, (meaning the Temple of Heavenly Happiness), with its elaborately painted doors, gold leaf panelling and beautifully decorated beams, is the oldest Chinese temple in Singapore.

Amidst all the haggling, hustle and bustle of busy street life, the aroma of cooking is very prevalent. Café's and street carts by the dozen sell an array of food and drink from duck to stingray and crab. Old shophouses and vibrant coloured buildings bursting with red and gold tones line the streets and ubiquitous decorations and lanterns dance like fireflies above your head.

We then headed north to the Malay Heritage Centre, situated in the restored and refurbished Kampong Glam, or Muslim Quarter of the city, located north of the Singapore River in the area known as Rochor. As soon as we exited the minibus, we could hear the familiar call to prayer emanating from the loudspeakers mounted on the Sultan mosque, which I had last heard in Tripoli back in 2012. Walter told us all about the variety of spices that are grown here that include lemon grass, nutmeg and basil. We continued our amazing journey of Singapore wandering through the markets selling exotic fruit such as the extremely smelly 'durian' that tastes like a savory, sweet and creamy combo, but because it absolutely stinks it's actually banned on the Singapore Rapid Mass Transit! We were driven north, back through Little India, whose location in the area of Rochor is east of the Singapore River, passing the main thoroughfare of Serangoon Road, but didn't have time to stop and get out. The area looked incredibly run down, but undoubtedly a photographer's paradise!

Following an extremely informative tour, we arrived back at our hotel, the 'Royal Plazza on Scotts' around 1.15pm. Back in the hotel room, I think it was showers all round before we totally zonked out for an afternoon siesta. Around 6.30pm we were back out-front climbing into a taxi to take us to the Gardens by the Bay and the famous glass trees. I'd read about these trees and had seen photographs on-line, but being up close and personal in reality, took the biscuit, as seeing them lit up at night exuding an array of vibrant colour, was truly awe-inspiring. The waterfront Gardens are set in 250 acres of reclaimed land that have been turned into a nature park, located in the centre of Singapore. There are three gardens stocked with myriad flora: Bay South, Bay Central and Bay East and the plan is to transform Singapore into the world's botanical capital. Designed to envelope the city in greenery, I estimated that there was a half an hour queuing time for the lift which took you up the centre of one of the glass tree's giant concrete and steel trunks and then out onto a wobbly walkway, known as the 'OCBC Skyway' (Overseas Chinese Banking Corporation Limited). Although it was dark, I still got a sense of being considerably high off the ground and at 22 metres I didn't blame the rest of the family for not traversing the walkway. They took one step out of the lift and immediately descended by the emergency stairs! I was a tad nervous myself, but I was absolutely determined to cross to the other side and get some images as well. Once I'd got over my vertigo, I could focus on the reason I was there in the first place – to admire this Supertree Grove and gardens and to look up still and marvel in its creation – and of course to endeavour to take some images. Cranking the D810's sensor sensitivity rating up into the multi-thousands ISO, I somehow produced a sharp photograph looking across to the Marina Bay Sands Hotel. Photographic conditions were far from ideal up there due to the risk of blur from people constantly traversing and bouncing the 128-metre walkway. And to cap it all, an official told me off for using my tripod! Save for a couple of images from the far end of the walkway, I resolved to take all the remaining 'timed exposure' images from ground level, at a lower ISO and with the camera tripod-mounted at a typical exposure of ISO 800, one second at f10.

The unusual design of these glass trees, coupled with the vibrancy of colour exhibited during the 'Garden Rhapsody Light and Sound Display', made for some eye catching and rewarding imagery. We had just ordered an array of spicy treats for dinner at an Indian restaurant overlooking the glass trees, when I realised that the sound and light display was just starting. Within a minute flat, I raced outside, mounted the camera on top of my Hama travel tripod, composed, focused and took a light meter reading – a dozen images later, the job was in the bag. The branches of these so called 'super trees', which tower some 50 metres into the sky, are constructed from thousands of thick wire rods, bent and moulded into realistic tree shapes. They're also fitted with solar panels, hanging gardens and receptacles to capture the rainwater. When I got back inside the restaurant, my meal had only just arrived – perfect timing. Unfortunately, all the gift shops on site were closed, which disappointed the others somewhat. We made our way to the park entrance to wait only a few minutes for a taxi to take us back to our hotel, arriving back around 10.15pm. I spent half an hour mucking about trying to sort check-in for our Singapore Changi to Melbourne flight the following teatime, eventually giving up and resolving to check in manually at the airport.

We'd packed a massive amount into our first day in Singapore. In contrast, our second and last day (Saturday 29th July) was a lazy affair. Following a long lie in and morning coffee / brunch, we ventured out of the Royal Plazza on Scotts only to find the humidity zapping our strength, so we returned to the comfort of the hotel's air conditioning and treated ourselves to a full-on Malaysian afternoon tea. Similar to the breakfast menu, there was a huge array of fish dishes – not good, if most of your family don't eat fish – and delicious cooked pork, beef and noodles, loads of yummy desserts and of course juice, tea and coffee. The restaurant was extremely busy and completely taken over to the afternoon tea – it was a popular place to be and we seemed to be the only westerners! We'd already checked out of our respective rooms, so following tea, we chilled out in the main foyer until our early evening taxi transfer to Changi airport arrived at 5.45pm. Airport security was a breeze and following immigration checks, where you were required to place your thumb onto a scanner, it was on and through to a massive airport lounge, which for all intents and purposes was more like an upmarket shopping mall. With over five hours until take off, the family were in their element perusing the shops of every designer brand. The entire mall was light, spacious and clean. Even the toilets were immaculate – the urinals being nicknamed the 'long drop'! Everything about this airport lounge oozed sophistication and sucked you into a warm and welcoming space that catered to the discerning passenger's every whim. They even had an automatic foot massager. Unfortunately, during our 2-day visit to Singapore we didn't get to visit the famous Long Bar at Raffles Hotel as the building was being refurbished so instead, at George's suggestion, we opted for a Singapore Sling in the airport lounge.

The famous drink was developed by a Hainanese bar tender working at the Long bar circa 1915, when it was originally called a 'gin sling'. Over the decades the recipes have changed and today differ depending on where in Singapore you order one. As a rule of thumb, the suggested ingredients include gin, cherry liqueur, Cointreau, Bénédictine, Grenadine, pineapple juice, fresh lime juice and Angostura bitters. Once measured, all the ingredients are emptied into a cocktail shaker together with some ice cubes and given a damn good shake. The mixture is then strained and poured into a 'hurricane glass' and garnished with a maraschino cherry and a segment of pineapple as standard – delicious! The downside is that this cocktail is heavy on the wallet.

After a quick tea, we arrived at our gate 'C23' ahead of the crowds and breezed through security with no hassle. On this A380-800, our seating allocation was similar to the previous outward flights and was scheduled to depart at 10.40pm local time. We were eventually airborne close to 11.30pm, after which it took an hour and a half to be served. During this time, I reflected on our brief sojourn to Singapore and everything that we'd managed to pack into this whirlwind stopover. George summed up our Singaporean adventure in a Facebook post based on information that our tour guide, Walter had imparted to us:

"A nation once described by former Indonesian President B J Habibie as 'a little red dot on a map', Singapore has truly flourished into a prosperous state, punching above its weight and cementing its place as an Asian Tiger. Sir Thomas Stamford Raffles and Lee Kuan Yew would be proud of their country today. Majulah Singapura!"

When our meal did arrive, it came with a smile and in the form of a very welcome chicken dish with chocolate mousse dessert. I guess that if you're seated over the wing, you must expect to be the last to be served. I had been writing up my notes from our Singapore visit for some time when I glanced at my watch followed by the flight path on the screen in front of me, to realise that not only was it the early hours of Sunday morning 30th July, but we were actually flying over Western Australia. We were finally 'Down under'. G'day!

Our flight EK404 was due to land at 07.51 and I'd not slept a wink. At least we were served some good tucker. Simultaneously, I put my watch forward by two hours, so we were now nine hours ahead of British Summer Time. We flew through what was described as severe turbulence, which Lauren and Wendy did not like at all. I had visions of the aircraft dropping like a stone, the overhead storage lockers opening, luggage flying around the cabin and people screaming like the disaster films. Fortunately, as quickly as it started, the turbulence subsided. At long last, it was wheels down on Australian soil at exactly 7.50am local time where the weather in Melbourne was a sunny, but chilly 10 degrees centigrade. We had flown 3,840 miles from Singapore.

Once through security, baggage reclaim and immigration, we took a 'maxicab' from Australia's second biggest airport, Tullamarine (opened in 1970) to our accommodation for the next few nights in downtown Melbourne. Our bridesmaid and dear friend Julie Little had generously treated us to her William Street based 'Wyndham Apartment', which boasted two bathrooms, two bedrooms, a lounge / dining room and kitchenette. It was clean, cosy, extremely comfortable and just perfect ... and the beds were heaven. This gesture was extremely kind and generous of Julie and speaks volumes about her personality. Whilst waiting for the apartment to be ready, although we were very tired, we decided to take the free circular tram around Melbourne to get our bearings and start to familiarise ourselves with this charming South East Australian state of Victoria's capital.

We alighted at Federation Square opposite Flinders Street Station and made a bee line for the information centre. I think we all instantly fell in love with Australia's 'cultural capital' Melbourne, which had been built on Port Philip, a large natural bay, by free settlers in 1835. Sir Richard Bourke, the then Governor of what was the colony of New South Wales, named this metropolis 'Melbourne' after the British Prime Minister William Lamb, the second Viscount Melbourne – Queen Victoria's close advisor. Melbourne officially received city status in 1847 and then in 1851 the city became the capital of the new Victoria colony. The 1850's Victorian gold rush helped cement its place as one of the largest and richest cities on the planet. Today, the population of Melbourne is just over 4.75 million. The locals are referred to as Melburnians! The city has a temperate oceanic climate which means it can be chilly in winter and very warm in the summer months, with extremes of weather added into the mix.

We savoured every second of our time in this beautiful city. We all decided to walk back to the apartment following the map and drinking in the sights as we went. We enjoyed a leisurely swim in the rooftop pool before dining on cheese, crackers and a complimentary bottle of chardonnay, which was delivered to the apartment by a young, friendly and smiling female host. All this and the whole family were in bed before 6pm!

The next day, Monday 31st July, we decided on breakfast in the apartment before a very pleasant walk via Little Bourke Street, Queen Street and then over the bridge spanning the River Yarra, and along Southbank Promenade. We were due to meet a childhood friend of Wendy's brother Simon - Mike and his partner Kim - for 10am at the circa 297 metre-tall 'Eureka Skydeck 88'. This is Australia's second tallest building behind 'Q1' in Queensland, which was opened in October 2006, with construction commencing in 2002 at a cost of 415 million US dollars. It is renowned for having most of its space available for residential occupancy – some 84 floors. Including the underground space, there are 92 floors in total. This impressive structure, designed by local architects 'Fender Katsalidis' was named after an 1854 rebellion during the Victorian gold rush, known as the 'Eureka Stockade'. Elements of this event have been incorporated into the design and blue, white and red colour scheme for the building. When I set eyes on it in July 2017, Eureka Skydeck was the tallest building in Melbourne. Towards the bottom of the tower, an ingenious art formation can be seen - a white box that looks like a beehive containing a number of gold-coloured bees inside. There are also bees outside the box and a queen bee perched on top. Having already photographed the skyscraper exterior with my Nikon D810 and 18-35mm polarised wide-angle zoom, I set to on photographing the bees artwork. It would have been photogenic on its own, but I noticed a team of men clipped on to harnesses, cleaning the bees and this added additional interest to the photographs that I was taking.

The compact 'Hoddle Grid' forms the centre of the metropolis' CBD. The city centre has a reputation for its historic and prominent lanes and arcades, most famously, Royal Arcade, Block Place and Degraves Street, where myriad cafes and shops abound. It was great to see Mike again, who had moved to Melbourne a number of years previously, and to meet Kim. Wendy and Lauren declined the opportunity to go to the top of the Skydeck (!) so whilst they explored the famous Lanes, Mike, Kim, George and I paid our twenty dollars to be catapulted skywards to the 88th floor's observation deck in seconds. It was a crisp morning, not unlike a UK sunny day in late October or early November and the stunning views of Melbourne were clear and breath-taking. The external viewing platform with meshed barrier, known as 'The Edge' (closed in high winds), enabled me to poke the Panasonic Lumix' Leica lens through one of the apertures, which meant that I wasn't photographing through glass and getting hideous reflections. This glass cube actually extends itself by three metres to hang over the edge of the tower. For those who dare, on entry the glass is opaque, but when the cube is fully extended it becomes clear. Needless to say, we dared! On the electronic doorway to this outside viewing facility is the wording 'The Southern Hemisphere's highest viewing platform with the world's only edge experience'. Having spent a good hour up there and with a memorable bird's eye view of the city and images in the bag, we all journeyed back to terra firma and left Eureka Skydeck at Number 7, Riverside Quay, Southbank behind as another great holiday memory.

We all then took a ferry to the quaint suburb of Williamstown, a one-hour cruise, 9 km south west of Melbourne. Located in the local government area of the City of Hobson's Bay, Williamstown has a population of circa 13,200 and buildings include BAE Systems Australia Marine Division! Williamstown, named in honour of William 1V, is also home to the 'Timeball Tower', a lighthouse built in 1849-50. A timeball is an obsolete time-signalling device, consisting of a large painted wooden or metal ball that is dropped at a predetermined time, principally to enable navigators aboard ships offshore to verify the setting of their marine chronometers – now replaced by electronic time signals. Today there are over sixty time balls around the world. We enjoyed a saunter around this sleepy backwater for a few hours that included lunch, before jumping on board the return 3.30pm ferry. We were rewarded with some lovely views of Melbourne bathed in rich, low angled sun. At the end of our trip, the ferry passed Eureka Skydeck and under the St. Kilda Road Bridge, where we disembarked, walked up a flight of steps to emerge in Federation Square. We had a quick look in St. Paul's Cathedral, where I took a few photographs and then arranged to return the following morning with my tripod to take more detailed, timed exposure images. We said our goodbyes to Mike and Kim and crossed the road to a lovely old pub called the Prince's Bridge Hotel serving an array of delicious, cooked food, beers, coffees and teas. The family then wandered back to the apartment via Swainston Street's many shops, turning left at the junction with Little Bourke Street. With clothes washing and drying all done, our evening snack consisted of cheese, crackers and doughnuts washed down with a complimentary bottle of Morgan's Bay Victoria Chardonay. I then popped up to take some night shots of the roof top swimming pool.

The next morning, Tuesday 1st August, Wendy and I set off promptly at 8.25am from the apartment and made our way to St. Paul's Cathedral, leaving George and Lauren to do their own thing. Wendy and I had come to St. Paul's specifically for me to take detailed photographs of a mid-nineteenth century, ornate sideboard and carved screen. This substantial piece of furniture used to be housed in Aldingham Hall, a very grand historic home located opposite St. Cuthbert's Church, six miles south of Ulverston and circa eight miles east of Barrow-in-Furness on the east coast of the Furness Peninsula, facing Morecambe Bay in South Lakeland, Cumbria. Aldingham, a magnificent structure (and now a care home), was built in 1846 over four years by the parish rector, Dr. John Stonard, who died in 1849 before the hall was completed. Dr. Stonard bequeathed the hall to his manservant, one Edward Jones Schollick, who was reported to have saved his master's life on the treacherous Morecambe Bay sands. Even so, apparently 'EJ', who was a philanthropist, having interests in shipbuilding and iron ore, wasn't that popular and ended up emigrating to Australia in 1876, specifically to Melbourne, taking several pieces of Aldingham Hall furniture with him, which of course included the 'Melbourne cathedral' sideboard. EJ Schollick just happened to be a distant relative of Wendy and her brother, Simon, on their Mother's side. The early Victorian sideboard, which Wendy and Simon tracked down, has a carved panel depicting mediaeval English Kings and is based on the York Minster choir screen. It was presented to Melbourne's St. Paul's Cathedral by EJ's son, H.S. Schollick, together with two chairs in the sanctuary, in 1940.

I'd just completed my photography of the nave, stained glass and of course, the Schollick sideboard (having first asked for the metal guards to be removed), when one of my tripod leg fasteners broke! We'd seen what we needed to see, so Wendy went off wandering and I took myself on a photographic tour of Melbourne's CBD, but not before I'd bought a replacement tripod from 'Michael's Camera store' in Elizabeth Street. The shop assistant, a young

Yugoslavian guy, tried to smudge me with the all-singing all dancing carbon fibre affair – a 'bad boy', four sections per leg, twist and lock tripod, which retailed at 450 Aussie dollars – cheap at twice the price! On seeing my horrified expression, he then changed tack showing me the less expensive 270-dollar version. I eventually settled for a bog standard 'does the job' tripod costing 69.95 ozzy dollars – which saw me through the rest of the holiday and is still going strong. I decided to put my new acquisition through its paces by photographing the famous graffiti art in Hosier Lane, knowing that if my new tripod wasn't up to the job, I could replace it before leaving Melbourne.

The graffiti artwork was something to behold. It was literally ubiquitous, covering large swathes of brickwork, doorways, awnings and recesses. Even the pavement bollards and large recycling wheelie bins hadn't escaped the brush or spray can. A couple of giggling, fun-loving, young ladies sat in an arched recess, which framed my sneaky shot perfectly. A welder crouched down on the pavement and I spied yet another photo opportunity – sparks flying, welder concentrating and all against a backdrop of a graffitied wall. The designs were varied and almost out of this world – an all seeing eye with curled fingers growing out of the top; a multi-coloured face of a beautiful, young woman with huge emerald green, staring eyes, black eyebrows and pouting, but smiling, red-lipsticked mouth; two pairs of black and white 'Nike' trainers tied to a street light with their respective laces and with a graffitied walled background and individual facial works of art, wall-painted and blending into adjacent similar artwork all skilfully crafted in a broad spectrum of eye-catching colours. Even the graffiti artists' tags were themselves works of art. I was able to fully appreciate the Hosier Lane graffiti and wanted to capture its essence with my camera in all its fullness. To ensure that the tripod held the D810 securely, I then set up an eight minute 'time-lapse' image in Federation Square, that captured the movement of trams, buses, cars, taxis and pedestrian traffic. The shot worked out well and I had no further qualms about my new tripod. I had lunch at the Prince's Bridge Hotel on the corner of Swainston and Flinders, where after about twenty minutes the rest of the family joined me. I followed this with more photography whilst the family shopped. We all met back at Wyndham Apartments and Lauren and I decided on a swim in the rooftop pool. Room service from Little Billy's café next door was the unanimous decision, during which we reflected on another great day in this gorgeous city.

For our final day in Melbourne, Wednesday 2nd August, we all did our own thing. Wendy was meeting up with a distant relative, Cousin Raymond (descendent of EJ), and I decided to walk up to Melbourne Central, a large, trendy shopping precinct that George had visited the day before. I wanted to photograph the famous domed glass roof and clock with birds that sing 'Waltzing Matilda' at 11am. I then continued my walk down to Federation Square again, stopping to photograph – well anything that caught my eye, including the ubiquitous tourist information officers, clad in red baseball caps or woolly hats and red jackets displaying a blue 'I' on the back. I hopped on a circular tram back to William Street and then walked back to the apartment for a quick cuppa, following which, Lauren and I went on a four-mile walk. We crossed over the Yarra and wended our way along Southbank, before stopping in Federation Square for the last time and savouring the local vibe over raspberry lemonades. We all topped off our stay in Melbourne with pizzas at 'Max on Hardware'.

Having cleared and cleaned Julie's apartment and with packing all but completed, we turned in around 10.30pm, but I didn't sleep at all well, waking up firstly at midnight and again at 3.40am. I had weird dreams where Wendy was driving a new Mini Clubman, which was out of control. We crashed and had to kick out the windscreen to get out. Then I was at the front of a queue with Cheryl, one of my old Met Police colleagues, about to collect a massive plate containing different cakes and gateaux. I spied an anniversary edition of Cadbury's Cream Egg – a huge creation, which I grabbed from a shelf behind the counter. The ladies serving and everyone else in the queue behind gasped and finger-pointed in mutual chastisement ... then I woke up! I popped down to see 'Long', a very helpful young chap on reception who printed out our boarding passes for the next two legs of our onward travel – firstly from Melbourne to Uluru and then from Uluru to Sydney. Long also phoned the Uluru resort to confirm our bookings for both the sunset and sunrise tours.

It was now Thursday 3rd August and at 6.20am a Maxi Taxi took us and all our luggage to Tullamarine airport – a forty-minute journey. Following self-check in for the four large suitcases, security was very efficient with just Wendy being tested for explosives! We had time for mushroom and cheese croissants before walking quite a distance to our gate 49 at about 9am. George remarked that a travellator or two wouldn't have hurt! I noticed quite a few Jetstar A320's and also a Singapore Airlines A320. Finally, when it was time to cross the tarmac to board in what was quite a fresh morning, I whipped my Panasonic compact camera out and shouted to the rest of the clan who were walking ahead. As they turned around, I clicked off two frames before getting a bollocking from airside staff to whom I mouthed a sheepish apology. Our Jetstar A320 took off from Melbourne Tullamarine 23 minutes late at 9.53am., although the first officer was later to announce that we'd be arriving at our desert destination on time.

Goodbye Melbourne, we loved you!

The meals, snacks and drinks on board this Uluru bound aircraft were all at a price, so it was a good job we brought snacks on board with us. When the stewardess arrived at our seats with egg-lettuce sandwiches and a cup of tea for 'Canning Family', I promptly refused, thinking that we'd have to pay, only to then realise that apparently we'd pre-paid for this food, which we hung onto for later! There was a little turbulence mid-flight, which lasted for about five minutes, but nothing too untoward. Our first sighting of Uluru from the windows of the A320 was awesome – a huge rocky outcrop surrounded by red sand. We touched down just after noon. Walking across the tarmac into the tiny Arrivals area reminded me of Newquay airport in Cornwall. There was just one carousel and there weren't thousands of people like major international airports – just the way I like it. There were air-conditioned coaches out front – all dropping off at our hotel, the Desert Gardens, Uluru resort. The journey time from airport to hotel was just eight minutes and twenty-two seconds! (I know.... I need to get out more). Once we had checked in at reception and wheeled our suitcases through leafy grounds, we found our two adjacent, spacious rooms. The only downside was swatting about twenty flies in each room first, before we could unpack! We then had a quick bite to eat, explored the Uluru resort grounds and shops and chilled before our 5pm sunset tour to Uluru itself.

Nathan, our coach driver, took us the short hop into the national park itself and told us to be back at the coaches by 6.30pm, when a different coach would take us deeper into the park for our evening barbeque. As soon as we arrived, I was filled with excitement at the prospect of capturing Uluru bathed in the warm hues of the setting sun. George and I marched on ahead of the girls (and other tourists) to the viewing area, where I quickly claimed my pitch and erected my tripod. With the D810 securely mounted, I took frequent shots as the colour of the lighting and the shadows were changing almost by the second. All the while, I was conscious of the entire landscape bathed in a terracotta red dust. It was a landscape photographer's dream – I got some very pleasing shots as the sun was setting lighting up the west face of Uluru.

Then we were driven a mile or two further into the National Park, where in the middle of nowhere tables were laid, places were set and a barbeque fit for a king, queen and their entourage, had already been started. We were alongside Uluru, under a star-lit sky and we dined on a feast of beef, chicken, lamb and kangaroo. We all sampled kangaroo – a culinary first, which tasted a bit like beef, but not as nice. The meat and vegetables were washed down with a couple of glasses of Shiraz, my red wine of choice. Following coconut cake and cups of tea, a local guide gave us a really informative astronomy talk with a clear star-studded sky, whilst I set up a few timed exposure shots on my tripod mounted Nikon D810. They say that there's a first time for everything. Well the first shot I took of the southern hemisphere night sky, it was so clear and the moon so bright that I ended up getting flare on that first image…from the moon! Watching Uluru's changing colours as the sun set and dining out in the open beneath the stars was an awesome experience. In George's words:

"We watched the sun set over Uluru and watched the rock turn from red to purple, before dining on kangaroo steak and a spot of stargazing in the southern hemisphere – wonderful company with another English family and another from Guadeloupe. Magical. Uluru, known to the west as Ayers Rock, is situated in the Uluru-Kata Tjuta National Park and is sacred to the Pitjantjatjara Anangu aboriginal peoples of Central Australia. Every feature of it has meaning in Tjukurpa or Dreamtime – the Anangu law that explains how the world was created. It is over 600 million years old. It is such a privilege to see it once in a lifetime".

The vast sandstone 'inselberg', known as Uluru to the indigenous aboriginals and Ayers Rock to the rest of the world, one of the most instantly identifiable features on the planet, is a UNESCO World Heritage site. Standing at 348 meters in height and rising some 863 meters above sea level, Uluru is located approximately 335 kilometres to the south west of Alice Springs and is situated in the southern part of Australia's Northern Territory. To walk the 9.4 km circumference takes several hours, something that Mum thankfully got to undertake. Uluru and Kata Tjuta, located 25 kilometres to the west, together form the Uluru-Kata Tjuta National Park.

Early next day, we all awoke at 5am to board coaches to take us back to Uluru to view the changing colours of the rising sun striking the red rock. There were probably in excess of a hundred tourists assembled on and around an observation platform three quarters of an hour beforehand, braving the bitter cold, to witness and capture on camera, this amazing spectacle of sunrise. People were bundled up in fleeces, blankets, hats and gloves...it was freezing. Then it was back to the minibus to drive around to the west corner to take some more photographs, where Uluru was completely in shadow. I resolved to return early the next morning to take close-up detail of this leviathan rock. We were back at the Desert Gardens Hotel by 8.30am, where we all enjoyed a hearty cooked breakfast. We had a chilled day, looking around the hotel complex and just relaxing. I took the opportunity to sort all the camera kit out for the following morning's big shoot, after which, it was time for late morning cocktails. After an early evening meal, I thought I'd turn in at around 8pm., having booked a morning hop-on-hop-off 49 Ozzy dollar ticket to take me to the east corner of Uluru, where I'd walk along the perimeter path getting detailed shots and actually touching this magical rock (but only at specific places where you had permission) that we'd travelled the other side of the world to see.

I fell asleep dreaming of red desert, craggy outcrops, smiling, indigenous aboriginal peoples and the excitement of breath-taking vistas that I planned to capture in the morning, only to wake up at 11.40pm with what felt like terrible indigestion. The tummy ache just wouldn't abate and left me restless and unable to settle. The two 'Day Nurse' capsules I popped didn't touch the pain and so it went on all through the night and into Saturday morning 5th August. I could barely move. Wendy had to call the equivalent of the 111 service and the advice was to see a doctor within 1-3 days if the pain hadn't subsided. Very helpful! I had to cancel my walk around the perimeter of Uluru and was mightily disappointed I can tell you. The previsualised images of Uluru rock features, Uluru itself with perhaps a Walawuru wedge-tailed eagle soaring overhead, thousand-year-old plus rock paintings, springs, waterholes and an abundance of fauna and flora, would have to wait until next time. On the subject of fauna, I wanted so much to photograph the Ngiyari (Thorny Devil), the Malu (Red Kangaroo), Dingoes and the Liru – Uluru's extremely venomous Mulga snake - but it wasn't to be. Wendy as ever was a love and managed not only to secure me a full refund, but also had the check out time of the rooms extended until 11.30am. I managed to crawl out of bed at 10.40am for a shower, finding that the hot water at least provided temporary relief to help dull the pain.

Somehow, I just about got dressed and with everyone's help, managed to clear the room and walk to reception, leaving Wendy to check us out. Also, in my favour was the fact that Uluru airport was less than 10 minutes away and being a small facility, baggage drop and security were somewhat simplified. Our outward Jetstar flight was slightly late arriving, but ground staff managed to turn things around very quickly. Wendy had a quiet word with one of the staff and let on that I wasn't very well and could we possibly board first as a queue was now forming? It then almost went pear shaped when said member of staff came over to assess me and asked whether I'd had diarrhoea and sickness (I hadn't) – she was reluctant for me to board at all! Eventually they let me through. If I'd been struck with D&V we would have had to stay put! There were no medical facilities to write home about at the Uluru resort and it dawned on me that we'd come very close to me being flown to Alice Springs hospital, for treatment – a 45-minute flight. The only other alternative, which was a non-starter anyway, was a 444 km / 5½ hour drive via Lasseter highway / State Route 4 and the National Highway 87. What we didn't know at the time was that I had big problems with my gall bladder ... more of that later.

Having been given the green light, we were quickly ushered across the warm tarmac and to our waiting plane. I felt a tad embarrassed, but nevertheless very grateful for this gesture and dared not make eye contact with the other passengers for fear of rebuke. We sat in row 4 near the front on the plane's right-hand side and take off was at 2.44pm 'Co-ordinated Universal Time' (UTC), with a flight duration estimated to be 2 hours and thirty-seven minutes. The good news was that at 4.35pm, some 16 hours after it had rudely awakened me from blissful sleep, my stomach had finally settled somewhat, but I felt completely washed out due to the lack of shut eye and having not eaten for 24 hours. I was very fortunate to have a good team in my family, who rallied around me fetching and carrying, when I must have appeared to all and sundry like the archetypal moaning Victor Meldrew!

5.50pm heralded wheels down at Sydney's Kingsford-Smith airport and following a shared pick up and drop off service (not recommended – it took forever), we finally arrived at our accommodation, the Grace Hotel at 77 York Street around 8pm. I still didn't feel great, so I sat down and left Wendy to check us in. Unfortunately, she discovered that there had been a mix up with the room booking and the mess seemed to take an eternity to unravel.

Once sorted, our rooms on the 10th floor were lovely, clean and spacious. By the time I'd had a hot shower, I was seriously flagging and in a shit state, bordering on semi-fubar. I fell asleep almost before my head touched the pillow, to the pleasant aroma of hot chips, cooked, spicy food and the arrival of a sumptuous room service that I was destined never to taste. Just how close I came to being hospitalised, ruining the climax of our trip down under for the entire family and therefore cutting this dream holiday short, wouldn't be realised until I had a worse, recurring episode in February 2018 and then hospitalisation a few months later in the April!

When I woke up the following morning on Sunday 6th August, I felt considerably better, in fact back to normal health. After a very leisurely breakfast at 7.30am, we were all assembled in the enormous reception area of the Grace Hotel excitedly awaiting the arrival of Julie (Oolie) Little, our close friend, who we hadn't seen for thirteen years. I'll never forget the moment that Oolie walked into reception just before 9am, it was magical long hugs all round. It was so good to see her after such a long passage of time. We walked with her from our hotel down to the famous Rocks area for a pre-booked Harley Davidson trike tour of Sydney from 10.30am until 11am.

The previous evening I'd been too out of it to appreciate even an iota of Sydney's magical magnetism. Now though, as we stepped out on to York Street on a glorious morning, the full wonder of this Antipodean jewel opened up before our eyes. Located on Australia's east coast, the ocean-side metropolis of Sydney is the oldest and largest city as well as being the state capital of New South Wales. Captain Arthur Phillip sailed into Botany Bay in 1788 with a ship full of convicts to establish a penal colony. This he named 'Sydney' after the Home Secretary of the day, Thomas Townshend (1st Viscount Sydney). Of course, Sydney as an area has been inhabited by indigenous Australian peoples for more than 30,000 years. As soon as gold was discovered in 1851, Sydney's prosperity was secured. Today, this vast city has a population approaching 5.2 million and geographically envelopes Port Jackson, sprawling around 70 km towards the famous Blue Mountains to the west, Macarthur to the south and Hawkesbury, located to the north. Georges and Cooks Rivers are to the south and the Nepean and Parramatta Rivers are located to the west.

Sydney's inner city is spread over about ten square kilometres. For the tourist, there is so much to see – the harbour and bridge, the opera house, the Royal National Park and the Royal Botanic Garden,

Donal Crone's golden topped Sydney Tower Eye, completed in 1981 and standing 309 metres above Sydney's central business district and rising above Centrepoint shopping mall. There is also Taronga Park Zoo, ubiquitous Aboriginal rock art, and some seventy Beaches, to name but a few attractions. Sydney's climate is classed as 'humid subtropical'. The area has very warm to hot summers, cool to pleasantly warm winters and an even distribution of rainfall over a twelve-month cycle.

The Rocks, one of Sydney's oldest areas, is located on the southern shore of Sydney Harbour, north west of the CBD and derives its name from the rocky outcrops on the western side of Sydney Cove, the original site of the first convict settlement. The Rocks area, simply a great place to hang out, is characterised by narrow alleyways packed with numerous heritage sites, Georgian sandstone buildings, covered market stalls, souvenir shops, trendy restaurants offering an array of culinary excellence, cafes and bars, art galleries, oldy-worldy pubs and warehouse transformations. You can spend a day just immersing yourself in the cobbled streets that are Nurses Walk, Playfair Street and Mill Lane.

So, at 10.30am we all donned helmets and black bikers' leather jackets. Wendy, George and Lauren sat in the rear of the lead Harley and Oolie and I sat in the rear of the second Harley. Mistakenly, I thought that we would be trundling along taking in all of Sydney's sights at an octogenarian's sedate pace. Instead, as a 53-year old motorcycling virgin - I was in for a thrilling, awe inspiring ride, which saw a somewhat nervous yours truly initially hanging on for dear life as our Harley rider accelerated effortlessly away from The Rocks. As I rapidly got used to this beast's speed, I found myself settling in as our two Harley Davidsons catapulted us north over the famous Harbour Bridge to Milsons Point, where our photos were taken for posterity. Then, our riders fired up their characteristically deep-throated machines and transported us back over the bridge with the wind in our faces. Right then, riding over one of the most famous bridges in the world, we were all living the dream – it was a truly awesome experience!

Leaving the Harleys, leathers and helmets behind, we then walked around Circular Quay to the basement Opera House car park, where Oolie drove us a short way out to meet two of her close friends Glen and Jo Jo. They treated us to a full-on tour of Sydney Harbour on their boat along with a hot dog lunch and plenty of vino, moored up on the west side of the Harbour Bridge. It was simply the most joyous experience. Glen and his husband Jo Jo are two of the nicest, kindest, fun-loving guys I've ever met and it was generous of them to give up so much time to show and treat us to their Sydney. I for one enjoyed our boat trip so much, I almost felt bereft when we stepped back on terra-firma again. Having been in the naval section of the Combined Cadet Force at my old school Arnold, and then of course working aboard cruise liners worldwide, my second home was on the water and when I was on it, the only problem I had, like an 'old sea dog', was that I couldn't get enough of it.

Then it was back to the Grace Hotel to freshen up and change, before being treated to a grand 'Little Family' reunion held in our honour on the veranda of Sydney's Glenmore pub, in the shadow of the harbour bridge. The open topped balcony bar had been booked just for us and the views of the opera house and the bridge were stunning. We were joined by Oolie's amazing brother, Pete, his wife Keryn and two of their children, Angus and Ryan. Also, there was Oolie's sister Anne and her husband Dave with their two children, Grace and Anthony. Glen and Jo Jo also joined the party. Over a sumptuous, well-oiled meal, I was in the moment – enjoying what I enjoy the most – the company of family and wonderful friends, flitting from group to group and being left elated from inspiring, authentic conversation. After that day I was in seventh heaven.

Breakfast on Monday morning 7th August was another chilled affair at The Grace, following which, we took a leisurely stroll to the opera house to meet Oolie for a 10am group tour. Approaching this famous icon from Circular Quay and standing beneath its shadow looking out to the harbour bridge was a truly awesome experience. White tiled and shaped to look like the sails of a yacht, this multi-venue performing arts centre – this masterpiece of architecture and structural engineering, is unsurprisingly a UNESCO world heritage site and is located on Bennelong Point, Sydney Harbour, between Sydney Cove and Farm Cove and was designed by Danish architect Jorn Utzon. It took fifteen years of on-off construction work and overruns and was opened by Her Majesty Queen Elizabeth 11 in 1973. Once everyone in our group had been fitted with headphones and a receiver pack, our informative and very humorous guide took us on an exploration of the concert halls and studios. I loved every minute of the tour, which was interspersed with historic film clips that charted the timeline from initial concept to completion. We enjoyed light refreshments at one of the opera house cafes and soaked up the chilled Ozzy atmosphere by the bucket load.

We then strolled back to convict-built Circular Quay to book a Blue Mountains and Featherdale Wildlife Park Tour for Wednesday. After that we took a fast 15-minute ferry to Manly. With its beachfront promenade, Manly is popular with both locals and tourists and is packed with shops, cafes and restaurants. We enjoyed a stroll around the town, took photos on the beach and found a great café on a side street serving a delicious tomato and basil soup. Then it was fast ferry back to Circular Quay for around 3pm and onwards to our hotel for a freshen up and a cup of tea. At 5 pm we walked to the opera house for 'Badu Gili' – meaning the 'water light' show in Gadigal language. This free, daily show at around sunset in early August (circa 5.45pm) and again at 7pm explores the ancient stories in an inspiring, amazing, contemporary seven-minute presentation, which is projected along the eastern Bennelong sail of the Opera House. Once I'd secured my pitch, photographically, the biggest challenge was the prevailing wind and using a flimsy tripod designed for light weight travel use. What I needed was my faithful crime scene Manfrotto – a weighty 'bad boy' which would easily have kept the camera steady. Instead, I was forced to crank up the ISO into the multi thousands and open up the aperture, so that the shutter speed wouldn't be too slow as to risk camera shake due to wind movements. The tripod only just held the heavy D810 steady. Fortunately, these mental exposure calculations paid off and I got firstly, some lovely dusk images and then a great sequence of shots as the projected presentation progressed. One of these images we used on the cover of a collection of Australian holiday images that we gave to George and Lauren as presents for Chistmas 2017. With the shots firmly in the bag, Oolie, who had parked her car conveniently in the Opera House's underground car park, drove us to The Rocks. There we went to 'The Wharf' (an eatery run by Oolie's company Fresh Catering), where Oolie treated us to shared entrees and mains, which was the equivalent of culinary heaven. Leaving the girls to chat over their G&T's, George and I attended the 7.30pm performance of Disapol Savetsila's 'Australian Graffiti' produced by the Sydney Theatre Company.

I have always loved live theatre, regardless of whether the production is musical, Shakespeare, or something completely different and Savetsila's play didn't fail to disappoint. It is a humorous and touching exploration of the migrant experience and signified the debut of a talented, young playwright. I was left with the haunting impression of one of the play's poignant lines, "You can't stay away from this place. It's your home". Since we'd touched down in Melbourne, I was beginning to feel this way about Oz – I didn't want to leave. The girls were still deep in chat when we filed out and meandered our way back to the bar seating area, where we then enjoyed a leisurely coffee and shared dessert. Having had the most wonderful evening already, Oolie then drove us out to Mrs. Macquarie's Point, part of the domain near the Royal Botanic Gardens. Mrs. Macquarie was the wife of Major general Lachlan Macquarie, Governor of New South Wales from 1810 to 1821. Beautiful and peaceful even at night and under a stiff wind, the Royal Botanic Gardens laid out in 1816 and located at Farm Cove, sprawl over 30 delightful hectares of trees, gardens and palm groves. Trying to take photographs of the Opera House, Harbour Bridge and northern suburbs at night proved more problematic than my earlier shots of Badu Gili on the Bennelong sail. It was cold, dark and windy - everyone stayed in the car whilst I grappled with my flimsy tripod trying with not much luck, to keep the camera steady during each timed exposure. It was no use, the wind was just too strong and most of my shots exhibited a degree of blur with one just about being passable. Needless to say, I made a mental note to shoot this scene again on my return to Sydney – whenever that may be!

Following breakfast on the morning of Tuesday 8th August, Oolie picked us up at 'The Grace' and drove us out first to the suburb of Vaucluse and then onwards to the eastern suburbs to one of the most famous surfing beaches in the world, Bondi, located approximately 7 kilometres from Sydney's CBD.

Lauren and I walked the circa 1km length of Bondi and I couldn't pass up this golden opportunity to secure one or two cool surfing images at the southern end of the beach. Surfers here have to be mindful of a notorious and hazardous rip current known as the 'Backpackers' Rip' (so called due to its proximity to the bus stop). We then all enjoyed a relaxed coffee and cake at the Bondi café, before Oolie dropped George off in town and me, close to the Harbour Bridge, whilst the girls went shopping.

Nicknamed 'the coathanger' and held together with six million Melbourne crafted, hand-driven rivets, Harbour Bridge, the famous British designed, steel 'through arch bridge' (where the base of the arch lies below the deck and the top of the arch rises above it) spans Sydney harbour and was opened in 1932. Standing 134 metres above sea level, the arch span measures an impressive 504 metres. The structure constitutes the world's tallest steel arch bridge and it is also the world's sixth longest spanning-arch bridge.

The deck carries vehicular, rail, bicycle and pedestrian traffic with the circa 2.4 km road across the bridge, called the Bradfield Highway. Its iconic design was influenced by New York City's Hell Gate Bridge.

I didn't fancy doing the Harbour Bridge climb – I'm fine with heights if you're enclosed but climbing a high structure, albeit clipped on with a harness, but in an almost carefree 'John Noakes of Blue Peter fame' – Nelson's column sort of style, in the open – forget it. I chose to do the next best thing – I took to the pedestrian walkway on the eastern side of the bridge (the cycle lane is on the western side and the rail tracks lie between the 8-lane road and the cycle lane) to saunter across the length of the bridge from Dawes Point at the southern Rocks end to Milsons Point in the lower North Shore area. I then walked all the way back again, opting for a fifteen-dollar payment to climb the 202 steps up one of the Harbour Bridge's 89 metre, concrete faced with granite, look-out pylons. Designed by Scottish architect Thomas S. Tait, there are two pairs of pylons – one pair at each end of the bridge. The top of the south side / eastern pylon not only offered breath-taking 360 degree views of Sydney, the harbour and the expanse of water, but I was so close to the top of the bridge itself, height wise, I could see the faces of people climbing to and coming down from the 'summit'. This left me with a slight pang of disappointment that perhaps I'd wimped out! Nevertheless, I was very pleased with the dramatic vista photos I got from this particularly high vantage point. I left this iconic landmark behind and made my way back to the Grace Hotel to shower, change and freshen up, before leaving with Wendy and Lauren to join Oolie for another fantastic evening meal at 'The Governors Table' in Sydney Museum, on Bridge and Phillip Streets. George wanted time to himself to chill out and didn't join us this time. Since his MG diagnosis, he was more prone to tiredness, so we left him to rest.

It was now Wednesday 9th August – our penultimate day in Sydney. Following a very early morning breakfast in our room, we left the Grace and walked a good few blocks to the Hotel Sheraton on the Park to meet Ian from 'Andersons Tours'. He was to be our coach driver and tour guide for the day trip that we had booked to the rugged, dramatic, awe-inspiring and utterly vast Blue Mountains and Featherdale Wildlife Park. Joining the five of us (including Oolie), there were four other Brits, one girl from Singapore, one girl from the

USA and two Hawaiian girls. We'd deliberately chosen a more intimate, more personalised tour over the large coach trips, preferring to travel with a small group. Following Ian's commentary through the CBD and out to the suburbs, it was then 80 miles (130 km) northwest / a two-hour non-stop drive to one of Australia's most famous natural wonders, the Blue Mountains, a UNESCO world heritage site.

The photos I'd seen on the internet didn't do this area of outstanding natural beauty, justice – the huge expanse of seemingly infinite, blue-hazed bushland landscape encompassing steep cliffs, waterfalls and eucalyptus forests is just so breath-taking and the mountain air was pure oxygen! We were treated to a very high cable car ride known as the 'Scenic Skyway' at Katoomba's Scenic World. During the 72-person ride, and while traversing the gorge 270m above the valley floor, a section of liquid crystal glass turns part of the floor transparent mid-way through the ride, offering superb views of Katoomba Waterfalls below. This was followed with a cable railway descent via the 'Scenic Cableway' to an informative walk through the forests, surrounded by tree overhangs and the ubiquitous, super strong vines. We then experienced a ride on the Katoomba Scenic Railway, being pulled backwards up a 52-degree incline. This railway was originally part of the Katoomba mining tramways constructed between 1878 and 1900 to transport coal and oil shale. The operation eventually closed in 1945 and was turned into a tourist attraction. We were given an insight into mining and fauna and flora and took photos of 'The Three Sisters', a well-known, unusual sandstone rock formation located on the northern escarpment of the Jamison Valley.

We then had coffee and pastries, bought souvenirs and listened to a thoroughly absorbing Aboriginal Culture talk, before taking more photos at the Three Sisters observation area at 'Echo Point', overlooking the Jamison Valley and Wentworth Falls. Ian then drove us a few miles further to Wentworth Golf Club for lunch – a relaxed country club, with fish, chicken and salad, sponge with custard, tea, coffee and juice, on the menu. Back on board the mini-coach, Ian then drove us to another look out point, which took in miles of Eucalyptus trees and offered yet more photographic opportunities to encompass the vistas with the back of the Three Sisters.

At Featherdale Wildlife Park, located about 73 km (an hour's drive) to the east of Katoomba, we fed kangaroos (one of which had a cute joey in its pouch) and photographed koalas. We left Featherdale around 4.20pm and Ian then drove us to the Olympic park, where we caught the ferry back along the river to Circular Quay. We arrived back to a Sydney in darkness at 6.20pm where Oolie had booked us a circular restaurant table in the 'Contemporary Arts Centre' where her office is based. It was amazing and offered the most fantastic night-time view of the Harbour Bridge and Opera House. We were treated to more sumptuous culinary delights with a choice of Korean chicken, chicken and pesto salad, potato and spaghetti. We were so full we skipped dessert and simply had coffees. Our lovely waiter, Leo, then took photos out on the veranda with the Harbour Bridge and Opera House behind. We walked back to our hotel for 9pm and were in mutual agreement that it had been a thoroughly interesting and most enjoyable day.

The date we were all dreading – Thursday 10th August, our last day - had finally arrived. Following breakfast, packing and a room tidy, we checked out at 11.30am and a kindly concierge printed our flight boarding passes for us. We walked down once more to the 'Contemporary Arts Centre', a museum housed in an Art Deco building, displaying modern and often controversial exhibitions, and took the lift up to the fourth floor to meet up with Oolie for the last time. Oolie had brought her Mum along to join us for drinks – such a lovely elderly lady, a real character and great company. Over drinks, I took the obligatory photos and we swapped stories, before walking round to the Opera House for the last time to say our goodbyes. Oolie had excelled herself. She had rolled out the red carpet for us and her kindness and generosity seemingly knew no bounds. The Little family are quite simply lovely, decent, warm, inspiring folk and to be on the receiving end of their hospitality, nay, to have them as close friends, is to be blessed. With a final round of the gift shops, a last saunter along Sydney's oldest street, George Street and a final, lingering look at the picture postcard Harbour Bridge and Opera House, we treated ourselves to a taxi back to the Grace Hotel to pick up our luggage and then at 5pm, a station waggon to take us via Darling harbour, to Kingsford Smith, Sydney's international airport, for 6pm.

The Emirates bag check in proved a doddle with not a single person waiting. Security was almost as easy. We had a very expensive meal that wasn't all that, following which, we made our way to our gate 57 for a boarding of 8.40pm. With a take-off scheduled for 9.10pm, we eventually pushed off the stand at 9.15pm and were airborne at 9.35pm. This was a 13-hour, circa 12,040-mile flight to

Dubai, which took us north west over The Northern Territory, then leaving Oz, over Indonesia, then Malaysia, the Bay of Bengal, India and the Arabian Sea – it all seemed to pass very quickly. Our A380-800 cruised at an altitude of 37,985 feet and at a speed of 561 mph. The outside temperature at this height was minus 51 degrees centigrade. An hour out of Dubai at 4.30 in the morning, stewardesses came round with champagne and chocolates for our 25th wedding anniversary and took Polaroid photographs of Wendy and me – something I think George and Lauren had a hand in! At 5.30am on the nose, we touched down in Dubai. At the airport there was time for a loo stop, a freshen up, a whistle stop tour of duty free and then a hassle-free boarding of 'EK017' – our final Airbus A380-800 for the 5,661-kilometre (3704 miles) flight back to Manchester. We pushed off the stand at 7.30am and take off was at 7.47am local time. We had breakfast and a well-oiled lunch on board, arriving back at Ringway at 11.48am BST. It was a cool 16 degrees centigrade at Manchester airport, cloudy and threatening rain…of course. Bob picked us up and all that was now left was the hour and a bit journey home via the M60, M61, M6 and M55.

In Australia 2017, I achieved what I set out to do, namely, to give the family a holiday of a lifetime and it was exactly that – one hell of a thrilling experience enjoyed by all, but which George and Lauren will remember hopefully long after they dress me in a 'mushroom suit' and I'm potting compost. I think Lauren summed up the holiday experience. There were initial tears leaving Manchester – I think that we were all a tad nervous of flying, which were replaced with tears coming home – we were all sad to leave Australia. None of us wanted to come back home from the 'Dreamtime'. We saw some amazing sights, I took loads of photographs and we were in the company of some awesome, inspiring people!

2017 turned out to be another eventful year during which, many famous faces passed away. Cressida Dick became, at long last, the first female Metropolitan Police Commissioner in the force's 188-year history. On 2nd March 2017, four people lost their lives and more than forty others were injured in the terrorist attack on Westminster Bridge. Following this attack, PC Keith Palmer was then stabbed to death outside the Palace of Westminster. On 22 May a suicide bomber attacked the Manchester Arena following a pop concert by American singer Ariana Grande. There were a great many casualties and the attack was the deadliest since the 7/7 London bombings in 2005. On 3rd June there was further outrage, when a hit and run vehicle on London Bridge driven by Islamist extremists killed seven people and injured 48. This was followed by knife attacks at Borough Market. On 14th June, an inferno destroyed Grenfell Tower in West London killing 72 and injuring more than 70 others. The paper five-pound notes ceased to be legal tender and by the same token, the old, round, one-pound coins also went out of circulation. On 21st August 2017, the world's most famous clock, Big Ben fell silent as a four-year repair and renovation project commenced on the building. On 20th November, Her Majesty the Queen and Prince Philip celebrated their 70th wedding anniversary.

Among those who left us were: Sir Peter Hall (Founder of the Royal Shakespeare Company and former National Theatre director); television presenter Keith Chegwin; television presenter Brian Cant from Childrens' 'Play School' and 'Play Away'; television producer and director William G Stewart who fronted Channel 4's '15 to 1' quiz show for many years; Radio 2's Desmond Carrington; socialite and former 'It girl' Tara Palmer-Tomkinson; 'Playboy' magazine founder Hugh Hefner; Colin Dexter (author of the 'Inspector Morse' books); 'Paddington Bear' creator Michael Bond; the scientist Heinz Wolff who hosted the television series 'The Great Egg Race' from 1977 to 1986; Clare Hollingworth, the veteran war and Daily Telegraph correspondent who broke the news that Germany was about to invade Poland in September 1939, signifying the start of the second world war and the former model Christine Keeler, who in 1963 became mixed up in the John Profumo affair, which spelled the death knell for the Harold Macmillan government. Moors murderer Ian Brady also died, as did disgraced publicist Max Clifford, cult leader Charles Manson, former England, Watford and Aston Villa football manager Graham Taylor, former Irish Republican Army member and latterly politician and peace negotiator, Martin McGuiness, Cormac Murphy O'Connor the former Archbishop of Westminster and leader of the Roman Catholic Church in England and Wales and photographer, film-maker and former husband of Princess Margaret from 1960 to 1978, Lord Snowdon (Antony Armstrong-Jones) and film critic, Barry Norman. From the political world, former Labour MP Tam Dalyell and former Labour MP and Father of the House Sir Gerald Kaufman, also passed away as did country music star Glen Campbell, Rock 'n' Roll legend Chuck Berry, actor and singer David Cassidy (from 'The Partridge Family) and legendary rock'n'roll performer Fats Domino best known for his songs 'Ain't That A Shame' and 'Blueberry Hill'.

My favourite Country and Western singer of all time, Don Williams, also passed away at the age of 78. His hits included, 'You're My Best Friend', 'I Believe in You', 'Lord, I Hope This Day Is Good', 'Gypsy Woman' and 'Tulsa Time'. I grew up listening to the deep, velvet tones of this gentle giant and have fond memories of his performance at the Royal Albert Hall in the early '90s. "You're my bread when I'm hungry, You're my shelter from troubled winds, You're my anchor in life's ocean, But most of all you're my best friend". R.I.P. Don Williams.

Legendary entertainer, Sir Bruce Forsyth, famed for catch phrases such as, 'Didn't he do well', 'Nice to see you, to see you nice' and 'Good game, good game', also passed away. The BBC Director General Tony Hall said of Sir Bruce, "He invented, and then reinvented, Saturday night entertainment across the decades with shows from 'The Generation Game' to 'Strictly Come Dancing'. And, of course, his catchphrases were part of the national conversation".

From the acting world we lost, Robert Hardy, Tim Pigott-Smith, Martin Landau of 'Mission Impossible' and 'Space 1999' fame, Bill Paxton, Gordon Kaye (Rene Artois in 'Allo-'Allo), Liz Dawn (Vera Duckworth in Corrie), Roy Barraclough, Peter Sallis (Last of the Summer Wine), Geoffrey Bayldon (Catweazle), Rodney Bews (The Likely Lads / What ever happened to the Likely Lads?), Keith Barron, Roy Dotrice and of course Sir Roger Moore, who Wendy and I were lucky to see in conversation at Leeds theatre, a few years before. Actor, Sir John Hurt also passed away early in 2017 and I recalled recently a 'Facebook' tribute that I posted at the time: 'RIP Sir John Hurt – from the characters of Richard Rich in A Man for All Seasons and the doomed Timothy Evans in 10 Rillington Place, to the Elephant Man Joseph Merrick, the voice of the great dragon in Merlin and the War Doctor in Doctor Who – he was so wonderfully versatile and of course that distinctive voice, which was instantly recognisable. Another of my favourites gone to tread those great boards in the sky!'.

Of all the famous people who died in 2017, by far the person, whose loss had the most impact on me was television's longest serving 'Blue Peter' presenter (from 1965-1978), Halifax born, John Noakes, who was 83. He was an absolute daredevil and a legend. I remember as a lad watching him in 1977 effortlessly and fearlessly climb up Nelson's Column with no harness or rope – a feat that would give today's health and safety bods, kittens. John became the first civilian in Europe to freefall from a height of five miles when, with the help of the RAF, he jumped out of a plane back in 1973. I also recall John's famous, high speed bobsleigh ride down the Cresta Run in Switzerland, which saw him crash out. After this unfortunate event, John showed the television audience the bruises that he had accumulated on his thigh by dropping his trousers! However, he was probably most famous for his relationship with his faithful border collie canine companion, Shep, a partnership which sported the catch phrase 'Get down Shep!'. Nine years after John left Blue Peter, he sadly lost Shep and in an emotional return to the BBC, announced Shep's death to the nation. John Noakes for me will always be remembered with affection. He was the archetypal Blue Peter presenter, a firm favourite and a huge part of my childhood.

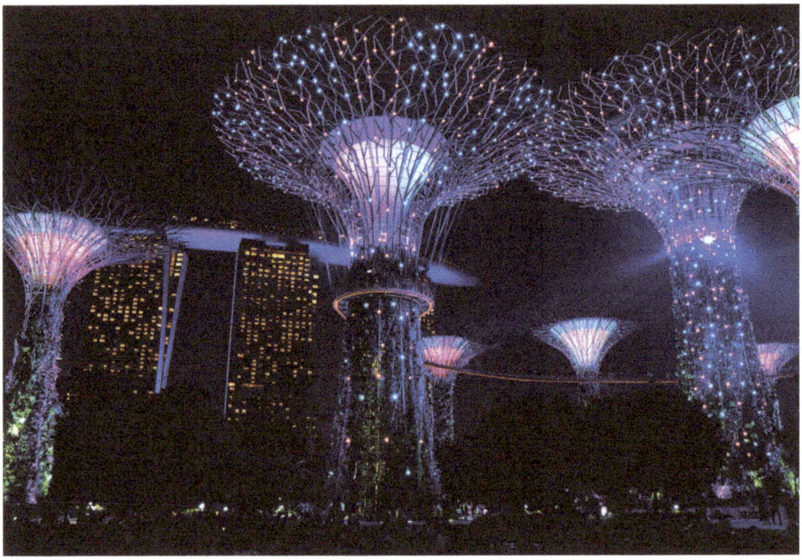

Singapore light show, Supertrees, Gardens by the Bay, 28th July 2017.

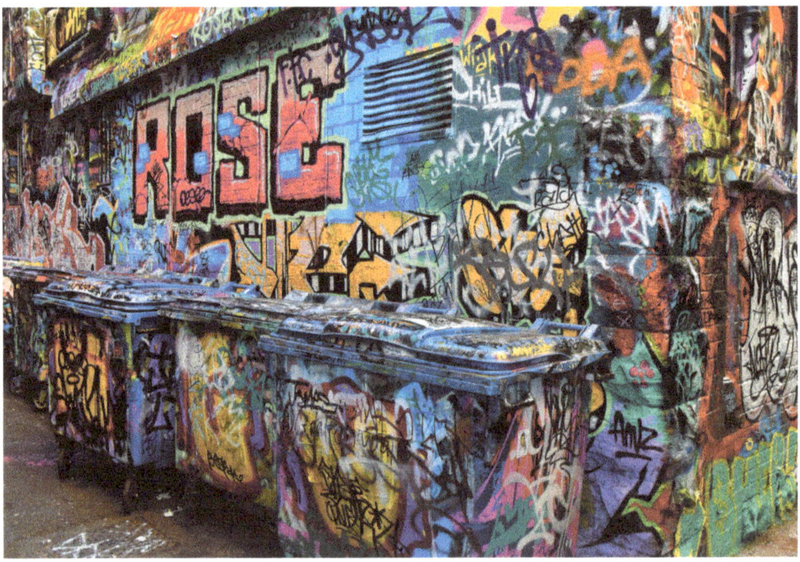

Graffiti art, Hosier Lane, Melbourne, Australia, 1st August 2017.

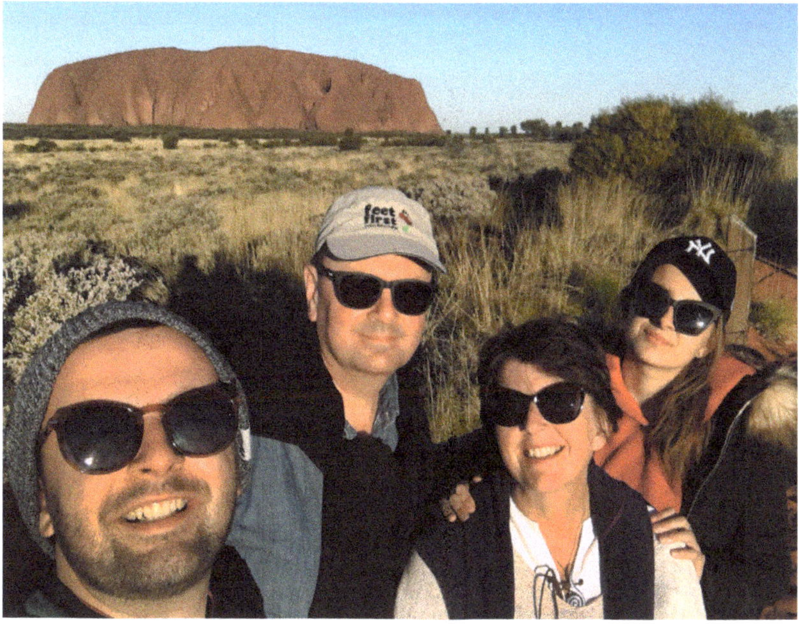

The Cannings at Uluru (Ayers Rock), Northern Territory, Australia, 3rd August 2017, photography by George Canning.

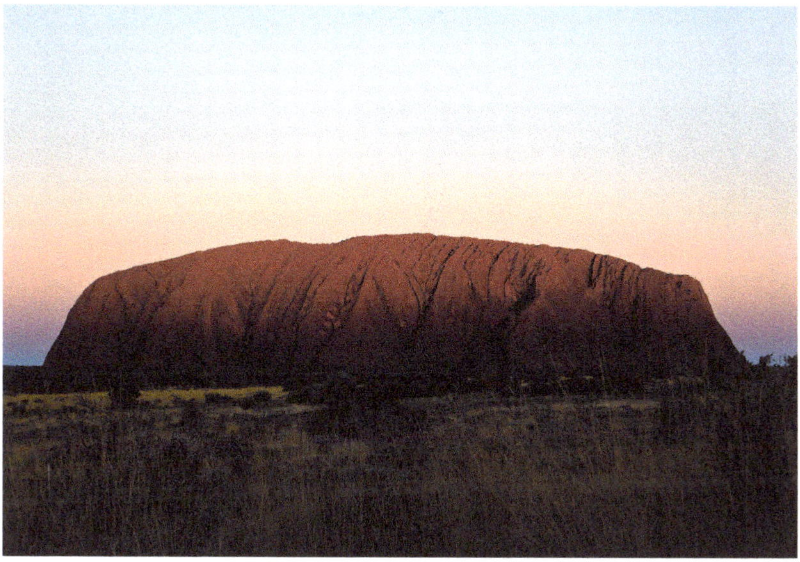

Uluru (Ayers Rock), Northern Territory, Australia, at sunset, 3rd August 2017.

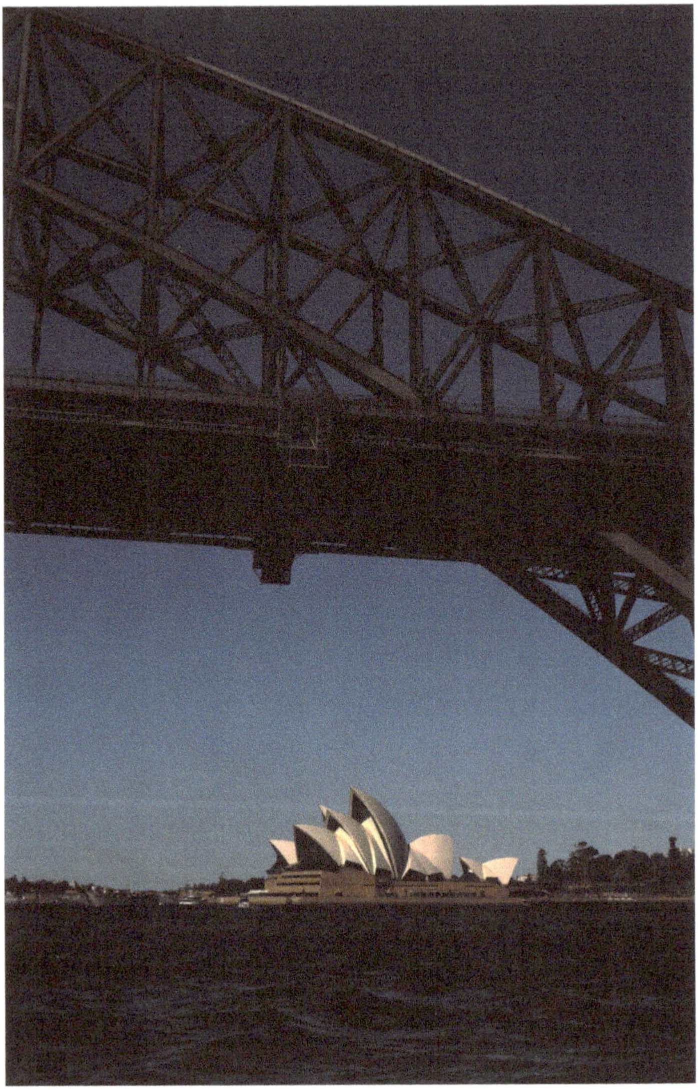

Sydney Harbour Bridge and Opera House, 6th August 2017.

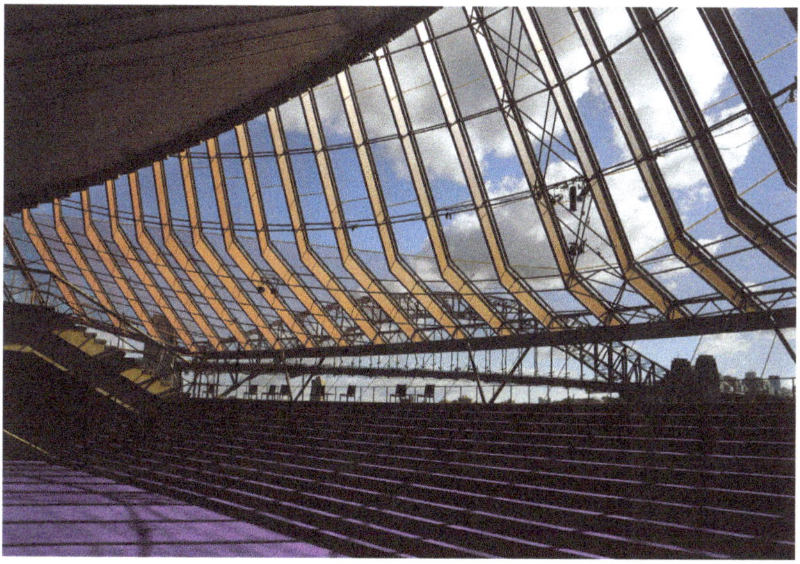

Sydney Opera House, 7th August 2017.

CHAPTER 27

Sudden Hospital Admission: 21 April 2018

Still high on the memories of Oz, it was now late 2017. On the television front I'd just worked my way through favourite horror / supernatural genre 'Vampire Diaries' spin off multi series 'The Originals' starring a whole bunch of talented actors who included Joseph Morgan, Daniel Gillies, Phoebe Tonkin, Charles Michael Davis, Claire Holt, Danielle Campbell, Riley Voelkel, Leah Pipes, Yusuf Gatewood, Nathaniel Buzolic, Steven Krueger, Rebecca Breeds, Sebastian Roché, Nathan Parsons, et al. There was also dystopian action genre 'The Divergent' series of films by Veronica Roth (Divergent, Insurgent and Allegiant) starring Shailene Woodley and Theo James. My next series of choice was Netflix' Salem (2014-2017). Roughly based around the 17th century Salem witch trials, this American supernatural horror stars Janet Montgomery, Shane West, Seth Gabel, Tamzin Merchant and the brilliant Stephen Lang as 'Increase Mather'. Game of Thrones, aka 'A Song of Ice and Fire', which kicked off with its first series in April 2011, is set in the fictional Seven Kingdoms of Westeros and the continent of Essos. The fantasy drama charts the brutal power struggles among the realm's noble families and their fight to clinch the Iron Throne, while simultaneously, other families struggle for independence. The eight series is characterised by violence, executions, coarse language, sex, nudity and a culling of a series main character, when the viewer least expects it. Game of Thrones, which stars Peter Dinklage, Kit Harrington, Lena Headey, Emilia Clarke, Sophie Turner, Maisie Williams, Nikolaj Coster-Waldau et al, concluded with its eagerly awaited and mixed reviewed eighth series in 2019. Remember, 'Winter is coming', 'You know nothing Jon Snow', 'You're a Crow Jon Snow', 'Nothing fucks you harder than time', 'A Lannister always pays his debts!' and of course, "There is only one thing we say to death: Not today" ...

Post flu jab in early December 2017, I noticed that I was lacking in energy. This carried on into 2018. I just wasn't firing on all four cylinders. I'd been working flat out at the hospital, in fact – overworking. We were on a break in Cornwall during February 2018 half term when I suddenly fell sick with a mild fever and actually threw up. This was preceded by severe abdominal pain, which took about six hours to subside. I'd arranged to visit my counterpart medical photography set up at Treliske Hospital in Truro on this trip. I felt bloody awful, but I'd pre-arranged to meet them and I was determined to keep the appointment. The next day I flew from Newquay to London to visit Medical Photography at Chelsea and Westminster Hospital. It was at Chelsea and Westminster that one of the senior photographers took one look at me and told me to my face that I looked knackered and ought to consider ways of slowing down and getting a better work-life balance. Cheeky bastard. Ordinarily I would have taken umbridge over such a comment from someone whom I'd never met before – but I hate to admit it, he was right, I was in a shit state! A fact confirmed when I was diagnosed with a mutant strain of Ozzy flu the day after I got back from London. With very little energy, all I could do was sit, flop and sleep. It took two weeks to recover and the last thing I wanted to do was go back to a busy hospital – but back I went.

I'd experienced five 'episodes' from mid-2014 of acute abdominal pain, which would present as typically emanating from the whole tummy area and be long-lasting, growing ever more intense and causing me to lie down, roll around, get up, walk around, get down on all fours and then repeat the whole restless process over and over again. No matter what I did, the pain was persistent and clung on limpet like for between four and six hours, with seemingly nothing to do than to let the wretched thing take its course. After this time, the pain gradually dissipated. Each episode was worse than the last.

The first time this stomach pain came on, the experience was quite frightening. I was up the ladder washing Val's conservatory roof down in Wadebridge in early 2014. I managed to get my entire t-shirt saturated with torrents of cold water emanating from the hose and ricocheting from the brick wall above the conservatory. This cleaning process took a couple of hours and I was vaguely aware of a tummy ache brewing. A night in pain followed. Then months later, it happened at home with similar symptoms. On our last night at Ayers Rock it occurred again and lasted pretty much until we got to Sydney.

In February 2018, overnight the tummy pain presented once more with the same pattern of symptoms, but the pain was worse. I remember Wendy asking me at the time whether I wanted her to call an ambulance. I declined, knowing that the pain would eventually subside. I ended up on the bathroom floor 'bending the knee' to an imaginary Game of Thrones' Jon Snow, when in reality I was down on both knees 'hugging the porcelain chariot' and vomiting big time. After a day in bed I was back to normal and even regained my appetite in super quick time later that evening, which I considered unusual following a bout of nausea.

2 months later, at 3.40am on Saturday 21st April 2018, I was woken from a deep sleep by that now, all too familiar feeling of severe pain in my gut. The symptoms were exactly the same – the mild fever, not being able to get comfortable, vomiting. Wendy asked me twice whether I wanted her to call an ambulance, but each time I declined. When I couldn't stand the pain any longer, she called an ambulance. The operator suggested someone stand outside the property to wave them down. Half an hour later, I was getting worse and Wendy rang again to find out how long the paramedics would be. Incredibly she was told that an ambulance had not been dispatched, but instead my case had been triaged to an on-call doctor and we were to wait for a call back. Wendy had a 'firm' conversation with them saying an ambulance was required but their response was 'not everyone who rings 999 gets an ambulance you know'!!! Nice one – good job we rang then! In the middle of this latest telephone conversation, I was busy heaving and throwing up bile. Wendy had to try and get me down the stairs and in the car and drive me herself. We explained to Lauren what was happening. Wendy gathered some essentials into my rucksack, then drove me to Blackpool's Victoria Hospital. It was a 30-minute nightmare of a journey, during which, every pothole we went over felt like salt being poured into a gaping wound – it was agony and I squealed like a pig each time in objection. We arrived around 8.30am and checked in at the Urgent Care Centre reception. By this time, I was in a shit state and totally fubar, doubled over in pain, breathing quickly in short bursts and moaning pathetically. Fortunately, they could see I needed urgent attention and there was no delay getting me checked in. I was whisked straight into an A&E holding bay for about 5-10 minutes, before being wheeled into a wider observation bay. I looked out onto the main A&E reception desk, behind which, sat consultants in their green scrubs, a couple of sisters in their navy-blue dresses and a staff nurse in her light blue dress, all busy chatting about this case

and that. Health Care Assistants in their white tunics were rushing around from cubicle to cubicle and it wasn't long before a staff nurse came in to see me to carry out 'obs' (observations) – blood pressure, temperature and heart rate and to check my heels and bottom for pressure ulcers. I was also declared 'nil by mouth' in case I needed to be rushed to theatre. A cannula was inserted into my right arm to deliver medication intravenously. A sodium chloride and water mix (saline fluid) drip was connected immediately to this cannular as my stats showed that whatever gastro problem I was about to be diagnosed with, I was somewhat dehydrated. Constant updates to A&E's status were coming in as doctors and nursing staff pointed at a bank of large computer screens and I was even there to witness a staff hand-over as the night staff clocked off and briefed the incoming day shift.

The decision was made to give me some morphine and an anti-emetic to stop me throwing up again (also a possible side-effect of being given morphine). I was babbling incoherently and actually crying with the pain. I also noticed that my whole body was involuntarily trembling. The morphine dose must have been quite low I surmised as I would need to be reasonably coherent for ongoing medical staff 'interrogation' throughout what was fast becoming a protracted day. When the morphine was administered, I was half expecting to go to sleep straight away but was surprised when nothing seemed to be happening. I was, however, very tired and my mouth and lips were dry – a side effect from the morphine shot. I was very much aware of the pain, which was still sitting at around a seven / eight out of ten on the 'ouch' scale. I guess the small dose was designed to just take the edge off my pain for the hours that I lay in A&E.

Later that day Larry, an HCA whom I recognised, came and wheeled me into the x-ray room. On arrival, I was informed that I would need to be sitting up for twenty minutes prior to having the x-ray taken, so I was duly wheeled back and left to sit up for the designated time, which was very uncomfortable. Although the morphine had dulled the pain, it was still palpable and further, it felt as if I'd been kicked in the stomach multiple times. When I was eventually wheeled into x-ray for a second time, I managed to transfer beds, but was shocked at how unsteady I was. I was aware of medical staff by my side, ready to break my fall in the event I collapsed. When a female nurse came into my bay to do further obs mid-afternoon she commented, "That's better than when you first came in", with a tone that confirmed I was in a bad way earlier. By about 5.30pm it was decided to admit me to Ward 19 on the first floor, back then this was the hospital's Surgical Assessment Unit. By now my pain was more like a dull ache. Wendy stayed with me until around 8.30pm, during which time I was drifting in and out of consciousness. I was still woozy from the morphine shot. The four hourly obs comprising blood pressure, heart rate and temperature were all fine and fortunately tied in with two, decent four-hour pockets of kip. I needed to drink loads, which of course meant that I was desperate for the loo.

Around 7.45am on Sunday 23rd April, I was brought a hot, steaming mug of tea, my first since that Friday evening and by God it tasted good. This was quickly followed by Weetabix with milk and two wholemeal slices of toast and butter. Delicious! I had regained my appetite.

Breakfast was followed by Consultant's ward round. I heard my name being mentioned, together with my bed number and a smiling, young middle-aged gentleman of oriental descent, offered his hand. I liked Mr. Thu Linn immediately. This amenable Consultant Colorectal Surgeon had an entourage of a trio of junior doctors, all of whom had folders and were listening and observing me intently.

In the middle of Mr Linn's visit, I suddenly had a funny thought of the 'Carry On' films with one of my old favourites, Kenneth Williams ("Stop messin' about"), announcing to the ward in that characteristic nasal tone: "There's nothing basically wrong with you. I want a barium test, saliva, blood and urine analyses and whilst you're about it, syringe his ears out!". Fortunately, Mr Linn didn't say that. He ordered a CT (computed tomography) scan – a sophisticated type of x-ray, designed to show anatomical information of internal organs and which would show detailed imagery of any soft tissue damage that the x-rays could not reveal. He said the scan would hopefully be later that day or failing that, tomorrow, after which, I'd need to be seen again for a colonoscopy and check-up as an outpatient. Following Mr. Linn's visit, I felt reassured. On this male bay in ward 19, I was by far the youngest man in residence. I wasn't being big-headed, this was a fact. The other five gents all looked to be in their early 80s. At that moment I was thankful that I was the 'boy' of the bay. Nothing was secret. Everyone heard everyone else - "Yes, love, they've just got my bowels working nicely", a cheerful voice resounded from two beds along. The nice man next to me in number eight, was talking slowly and quietly behind a closed curtain to his wife, but of course, I heard every word. "Sweetheart, I knew you'd be upset...Yes, darling, I know, I know... Alright, I'll let you go back to what you were doing.... Love you Sweet...". I found all this very touching and very moving.

At 10.50 am, Adam, the porter came to take me down to 'X-Ray Central' on the ground floor for my CT scan. It was Sunday and fortunately it was very quiet. 'Julie' the radiographer introduced herself and checked my date of birth. The moveable table on which I was now lying took me under the CT machine where I was instructed via a small loudspeaker to hold my breath for approximately ten seconds, then breath out and finally, to breath normally. A dye was then injected into my cannula so that any obstructions or abnormalities would show up. Julie warned me that it would produce a sensation of me wanting to wee! When the dye was injected, I first felt a warm sensation in both ears, which was quickly followed by a warm sensation in my 'crown jewels'.

At 12.15pm Mr. Linn suddenly reappeared by himself. He had the result of my latest scan. It showed a slight inflammation of my gall bladder, which would be treatable with a change in diet to one of the low-fat variety and rest, plenty of water and increased exercise. The discharge summary letter would go on to state "Gallbladder is slightly thick wall which suggests acalculous cholecystitis. No gallstones seen. Otherwise normal". That was at least good news - that there were no gallstones present, which can serve to block the flow of bile from the bile ducts and so interrupt the digestive process. Mr Linn arranged for me to have a precautionary colonoscopy three weeks hence, in May, together with an abdominal examination and then be seen in outpatient's clinic after about six weeks. His surgical team also took care of my sick note, as I would need time to recover at home. Then it hit me like a sledgehammer. This had been a serious health warning. No more chocolate, pizza or cheese for me for quite a while – in fact I needed a massive reduction in fatty foods straight away.

During this time, George was at Manchester Met Uni completing a Teacher Training Degree. Wendy had told him about my hospital visit and he made a surprise visit back to see me. To put a slight downer on things, I arrived home only to find George had developed swollen glands and a raging high fever, prompting us to call 111 overnight for specialist medical advice, prior to him seeing the local GP the following morning (not so great!). Wendy looked after us both and thankfully, George, like his old man, recovered.

Meanwhile, I still had further tests to undergo. On the morning of the colonoscopy examination (8th May), our friend Cindy very kindly drove me in and dropped me off at the door to Gastro. Having only waited about five minutes, due to a 'DNA', I was suddenly called through ahead of schedule to one of several examination rooms, where I was instructed to get changed behind a small screen and then lie firstly on my back, then on my left side. There were four clinicians in the room – a young doctor, a senior colorectal nurse and two gastro nurses, who were all very nice. My examination would be performed by the junior doctor under the watchful eye of the senior colorectal nurse. I was also told that "it's fine to pass wind – we're used to it, it's our wind, not yours!" I was given permission to fart in public! I couldn't believe it! I was able to watch the entire procedure on a colour monitor, as first the colonoscope negotiated the large bowel, followed by the small bowel, which I found fascinating. Thankfully there were no signs of cancer, just a bit of wear and tear of the large bowel. Just as quickly as it started, it was all over. Wendy collected me at 4.15pm, 2½ hours from walking in the front entrance of Gastro. Once again, I'd experienced NHS treatment at its finest. Good on you Blackpool Victoria Hospital staff!

On my sister Kate's birthday, May 18th, I had an appointment at Fleetwood Medical Centre for an ultrasound examination of my gallbladder, together with all the major organs. With the other organs looking fine, the radiographer pointed to a definite problem with my gallbladder. Mr Linn's MDT X-ray meeting on 23rd May was to confirm a porcelain gallbladder, which is the calcification of the gallbladder wall – in my case, small gallstones (which hadn't shown up previously) on the gallbladder wall coupled with multiple episodes of gallbladder wall inflammation and subsequent scarring of the gallbladder wall. I saw Mr Linn for my follow-up outpatient appointment at 1.40pm on June 11th. He drew a sketch of the liver and gallbladder and explained that you can have a gallbladder full of gallstones and have a lifetime free of pain, never in fact having a problem. However, my episodes of acute pain were due to periodic inflammation triggered by calcification of the gallbladder wall. The only way forward Mr Linn tendered, was removal of my gallbladder or cholecystectomy. In Mr Linn's words, "It has to come out!" I was listed for a provisional date of August 15th, 2018, which was subsequently confirmed. It was to be my first ever surgical operation.

Just before the end of Lauren's GCSEs, I hired a van locally and George and I drove to Stockport to clear out his flat in sweltering heat, signifying the very end of his PGCE year and another year of hard graft studying and teacher training at firstly Saint Aidans School, Preesall and then at Stockport Academy.

Meanwhile, back on the domestic front, after two years and hundreds of hours of dedicated, painstaking hard work, Lauren finished her GCSE examinations – 24 papers in total, on Thursday 21st June 2018. We'd walked by her side throughout the headache and sometimes trauma of assignments, assessments, mock exams, tests, past papers and revision exercises and spurred her on to keep her focus, which to her credit, she did amazingly well. I'd been out photographing with Lauren for her Art projects, we helped with printing, trimming and sticking and we all helped with design and presentation ideas. Wendy, George and I sat with Lauren to keep her motivated, inspired and fired up. I'll always remember our chats, sometimes late at night and of course, our hugs ... and a hug from Lauren is always special! The sense of jubilation throughout the Canning household on the evening of Lauren's last examination, German writing, was palpable, euphoric even and I'll never forget the sheer joy Lauren exuded at that perfect moment in her life. She had quite rightly earned her long summer break of rest, parties, holiday in Cornwall and time with her friends to 'chillax'. The following day, Friday 22nd June, Wendy and I attended her leavers' assembly, which at times was quite emotional. As outgoing Deputy Head Girl, Lauren gave an excellent speech, which was peppered with funny anecdotes and very well received. I was left thinking 'my girl's a born natural!' I am immensely proud of her. The following week Lauren and the rest of her Year 11 cohort had their end of School Prom. This special occasion involved a trip to the local spa for spray tan, the hairdressers, the beauty parlour for nails and make-up tips. There was a dress to buy, together with shoes, bag and jewellery and when they all came together, the end result was class. Lauren looked even more stunning than she normally does – if that's possible and in my biased opinion, was the belle of the ball. We'd hired a navy-blue Bentley saloon to whisk her in style to the local venue, the Devere Hotel (now The Village) on the outskirts of Blackpool. George and I raced ahead to film and photograph her arrival and to see all her contemporaries pulling up in their respective vehicles, which ranged from top end Beemers and Porsches to Ferraris, Lamborghinis and Maserati's. However, one young lady outdid everyone else by arriving on her horse, which I thought was a really original idea.

We'd already enjoyed a very warm early summer, measured by the number of evenings after work we were able to sit out in the garden supping a glass or two of wine and by the number of evenings we had to sleep with the fan on in our bedroom (almost constantly). 2018 was of course not only a world cup year, but was memorable for the England team's fine performance in reaching the semi-finals. Simultaneously we had Wimbledon tennis and a plethora of other sports going on around us. The UK basked in glorious sunshine and we chose the second week in July for our Cornwall holiday, sadly without George, who had other commitments. Every day in Cornwall was utter bliss – beach walks, cycling, barbeques, lie-ins and long blue-sky days. Wendy and I also completed another four 'challenges' given to us for our Silver Wedding anniversary – a tandem ride from Wadebridge to Padstow, building 25 sandcastles on Trevone Beach, taking up playing squash again (which almost killed me after a thirty-five year lapse) and feeding each other Maltesers using only a straw! Other silver wedding anniversary challenges included: from my sister Vicky, visiting all sixteen lakes plus nine tarns in the Lake District; visiting six places in Cornwall, each beginning with the letters that make up the word 'silver'; collecting 25 leaves from the Lake District, drying them out and creating a montage keepsake; go segwaying; complete 'Go-Ape'; climb the 1085 metre peak, Snowdon; go camping; go vegetarian for a month; row across Lake Windermere; take dancing lessons (Hm!); go on a Norwegian cruise, walk or cycle around Richmond Park and then visit friends Sarah and Dave, visit wallabies in Battersea Park and from my sister Kate, make 25 different chutneys and jams! Needless to say, with so many to fit in the challenges are still ongoing!

Cornwall was a much-needed break, but not nearly long enough. When we returned home following an arduous drive up the M5 and M6, we found the lawns were tinder dry due to lack of rain and we had two seagull chicks being reared on our roof, one of which, had flown down into the back garden and couldn't fly back up again. We had to run the daily gauntlet of being dive bombed by the overprotective parent gulls, incessant seagull chatter and screeching and the endless round of constant, ubiquitous gull poop – a real annoyance! Nevertheless, George had the barbeque fired up and tea prepared for us, which was a lovely surprise.

Unbeknownst to the rest of the world, a virtually unheard-of area of northern Thailand was about to be put on the map permanently. On Saturday 23rd June 2018, a dozen boys aged between eleven and sixteen – the 'Wild Boars' Football Club players, together with their 25-year-old coach entered the locally famous Tham Luang cave system at Masai, Chiang Rai Province after their football practice and became trapped three miles deep into the cave system. Monsoon rains partly flooded some of the numerous caverns, in effect blocking any escape for the thirteen. The alarm was raised when the boys failed to return home that night and local officials discovered the boys' bicycles locked to a fence, together with shoes and football boots close to the mouth of the cave. Having already spent more than a week trapped in the cold and darkness without food, what followed was a gutsy, three-day international, British-led rescue operation, comprising among others, five elite Thai Navy Seals and more than one hundred Thai, British, Danish and Australian caving and diving experts together with a massive backup in the form of a whole army of volunteers – the boys and their coach having all been found alive huddled together on a muddy ledge, incredibly some 800 meters underground by a British cave diving team on July 2nd. Many other volunteer divers from around the world helped out by delivering oxygen cylinder refill tanks to strategic points and tightening the life-line guide rope along the treacherous rescue route. Initially food, water, foil blankets and medicines were brought in to prepare for the fact that the thirteen might be trapped for some length of time. Meanwhile, water pumps were working overtime endeavouring to drain the rising, flood waters.

On July 6th tragedy struck when 37-year old Thai Navy Seal diver, Sergeant Major Saman Gunan passed out and died whilst helping to establish an airline to the thirteen. An original plan was to leave the team underground until the monsoon floodwaters had receded – but this could have meant for weeks on end. However in the end, with waters rising inexorably, the rescue team were left with no alternative but to chaperone the boys and their coach out through the dangerous labyrinth of tunnels, which included ten 'choke points' – areas of the mud-clogged cavern where the tunnel system became scarily narrow. Donned in full face masks, the boys and their coach either swam or were pulled along, each with two diver chaperones – one in front and one behind. At the choke points, one diver carried each boy's oxygen cylinder. This was a daring and incredible feat, bearing in mind that some of the boys couldn't swim! Some of the rescued boys were carried out of the cave on stretchers to ambulances parked nearby.

In hospital, the boys' parents had to don surgical attire and masks and were prevented from embracing their sons due to the high risk of infection. The first eight boys were immediately inoculated against rabies and tetanus and given antibiotics as it was thought that they might have been bitten by bats deep inside the cave system. Two of the lads suffered with pneumonia and the whole team had hypothermia. The story of the twelve Wild Boar Football Club players and their coach becoming trapped in Chiang Rai's Tham Luang Cave will go down in history. It is one of the most inspirational stories of danger and rescue that I've ever followed, was probably the most discussed story around the world during 2018 and demonstrated the courage of the boys, their coach and all those involved in the hazardous rescue, not least of whom Thai Navy Seal Saman, who tragically and selflessly gave his life. The Thai Navy Seals confirmed the success of the rescue operation on social media via their official 'Facebook' page: "12 Wild Boars and coach out of the cave. Everyone is safe. Now just waiting to pick up four frogs (Navy Seals). Hooyah". As a lasting and fitting tribute to all those involved in the successful rescue, a large mural, entitled 'The Heroes' was created in Chiang Rai, with hero Saman taking centre stage.

On 18th July, the whole family, including Wendy's brother Simon, attended George's PGCE Graduation ceremony at Manchester Metropolitan University. It was another proud, milestone occasion in all our lives and represented the culmination of a very challenging academic year for him. I took loads of photographs of this memorable day. The ceremony was followed by a canapes and drinks reception at the university and to round off the day, we all enjoyed an evening meal dining out at Salford Quays.

Following my 'pre-op' appointment on Monday 30th July to check that I was fit and well for surgery, George travelled down to London in jubilant mood on Sunday 5th August, to check out suitable properties for rent – flat shares with like-minded professionals, prior to him starting his new job in a south east London secondary school. All seemed well. However, on the Tuesday evening 7th August it all went to ratshit, George failed to ring in as he promised and all his activity on social media became stagnant. Wendy feared the worst, whilst I said that George had undoubtedly run into friends, was out having a few cheeky 'lemonades' and didn't want to be contacted (although that was out of character). When he failed to materialise at Wendy's brother Simon's house after the last tube home, circa 1.30am, we were forced to file a missing person's report with local police.

After an agonising night, Wendy immediately travelled down to London by train first thing in the morning. I had to work unfortunately, as my Manager Steve had just lost his mother and was off on bereavement leave. Not only had I been up all night with no sleep whatsoever, I then had to do a hectic day's work, pretend that nothing was wrong, sympathise with work colleagues over Steve's Mum and all the while liaise with the ever-shifting family crisis unfolding in London. It turned out to be the longest and most stressful day of my life, as well as Wendy's. Any thoughts of pre-operation nerves at that point went completely out of the window!

It transpired only later that day that George had been the victim of a horrendous crime – the details of which will forever remain confidential. It is George's story to tell, should he choose to tell it. In the process of the initial stages of the police investigation, George suffered severe mental anguish, akin to a breakdown, which saw him resign from his new teaching position before he'd even started it and he became reduced to a shell of his former self. It was utterly shocking to witness as he sat cocooned for days on end enveloped in a protective duvet, unable to string a sentence together, sleeping/living in a downstairs spare room. We immediately engaged the services of a counsellor to help heal the mind and a top Manchester law firm to handle all legal aspects of George's case. For the next year and a half, while investigations continued at an agonisingly slow pace, we all went through absolute hell. Finally, On 4th March 2020, George received the joyous news from the police that it was finally all over – the sword of Damocles had been lifted. He could, at last, live his life in all its fullness. George's ordeal, indeed, my family's ordeal, had lasted 19 extremely long months. Again, the immortal words of Martin Luther King, Jr come to mind: "Free at last, Free at last, Thank God almighty, we are free at last…".

So it was that in the middle of a very serious family crisis, I wandered into 'Surgical admissions' at Blackpool's Victoria Hospital at 11 am on the morning of Wednesday 15th August 2018, surprisingly in a pretty calm and relaxed state for my planned surgery. I had cleared all my backlog of work during the preceding two weeks by coming in at weekends and was fully up to date with nothing outstanding – a good place to be, so at least I didn't have to worry about work. Once I'd checked in with reception, I took a seat for what I knew would be a few hours of waiting, during which I had plenty of time to reflect. Pre-operatively things couldn't have been better. I'd lost a stone and a half through cycling, walking and a low fat / high fibre diet, following my last A&E admission back in April, although incredibly for my age and height I was still apparently borderline overweight / obese. All my medical 'obs' were normal. I had showered, put a load of washing on, had a light breakfast of porridge made with water, mixed with sultanas and a light sprinkling of sugar, a mug of tea and a tumbler of good old Adam's ale.

I hadn't been waiting long before a lovely Health Care Advisor (HCA) Christine called me through to a small interview room, where she meticulously went through all my medical particulars (apparently I've shrunk an inch in my middle age – no longer standing tall at six foot, but standing tall, none the less!). I was also issued with my hospital gowns – the first one, you put your arms into at the front and it does up at the back, the second, you put on the normal way over the top, wearing it like a dressing gown. Once Christine had completed her questions on my medical form, I then walked back into Surgical Admissions reception for yet more reflection. Then suddenly I got a bit sentimental and emotional and thought, what if something happens and I don't make it through the op – ought I to write something on my phone for my family to find and read after I've, er, well, you know…'gone'? I chastised myself for being a silly old fart, but nevertheless went ahead and bashed out a few small lines:

'To Wendy, George and Lauren, if I don't make it back from this operation and have 'gone on ahead' I want you all to know I love you very much and I'm very proud of all you've achieved. Go on and do loads more. Love life and don't waste a second. I'll always be with you. Big bear hugs and lots of love. Paul / Dad xxxx.'

Then I was called through for a second time to see Mr Linn's Registrar, a lovely, jokey, amenable guy in his mid-30s, who talked me through the whole operation and got me to sign the all-important consent form as standard. Then it was back to the waiting room again for about ten minutes before Jessica, a young, friendly anaesthetist on Dr Sharma's team, called me through to explain what she, predominantly, would be doing on the anaesthetic side of things. Around 1.50pm in walked a buoyant Mr Linn, who went through his entire plan for my operation, including drawing a sketch of the liver and gallbladder and offering full explanations. Just before he left the room, Mr Linn did warn me that I would be in pain afterwards. "It is painful surgery", he said. "It is a common misconception that if you have keyhole surgery for gallbladder removal, there is no pain. There will be a lot of pain afterwards, but we give you painkillers".

In fairness, I had read up in depth on gall bladder post op aftereffects and I figured that this would be the case, so it didn't faze me. I'd be a brave boy!

After surgery I was taken to Ward 15b. Once Wendy had made sure that I was settled, she left me at 8pm to sleep it off. The operation had turned out to be more complex than originally thought, but nevertheless a resounding success. Fortunately, you can lead a perfectly normal life without a gallbladder.

To fight any infection, I was given liquid antibiotics – a powerful amoxycillin / metronidazole combo fed intravenously. I was dosed up to the hilt with the painkillers codeine, paracetamol and oramorph oral solution. Every two hours or so either Nicola or Angela (staff nurses) would pop in and do my obs. It was now dark outside and from the clock on the wall to my right, I could see that it was approaching 11pm.

Around 7am on what was now the morning after my op, Thursday 16th August, it was changeover time. The night staff clocked off and 'Ross', an experienced staff nurse popped in to do my obs. 'Debbie', 15b's friendly housekeeper popped round with breakfast at about 7.40am. This welcome nourishment comprised two Weetabix with milk, two slices of buttered wholemeal toast and a mug of steaming hot tea. No sooner had breakfast cleared, in walked Thu Linn – my life saver - with a cheery smile and outstretched hand, which I shook in gratitude. Ross was by Mr. Linn's side. Thu inspected all the operation wounds and seemed very pleased that there were no signs of infection, or redness. The abdominal drain had collected no bile, a further indication that all seemed well and I was on the slow road to recovery. Mr Linn told Ross that the drain could be removed and I was duly given a sick note signing me off work for four weeks. I also learned that they'd keep me in until after lunch and then I would be discharged. I asked Thu if he was pleased with the way my op had gone and he reiterated that it was a tad more complex as my gallbladder was well and truly attached to my liver and required to be carefully prized off, but yes, he was pleased.

Once lunch had been consumed – vegetable soup, brown roll, chicken pasta, vanilla ice cream and a mug of tea, Ross brought in my discharge meds that had arrived from pharmacy – co-amoxyclav 500/125mg (antibiotics to prevent post-op infection), codeine phosphate 30mg and paracetamol 500mg painkillers – all to be taken at the dosage one, 3 times a day.

I was under no illusions as I'd been forwarned, that the immediate aftermath of the op would be very uncomfortable indeed. My wounds were very sore and for three days pain in my right shoulder became acute - an irritation akin to a nasty athlete's stitch, caused by trapped operation gas to inflate my abdomen and which collectively made me pull a face every time I put undue pressure on the wounds. I also felt chronically fatigued. Getting in and out of bed and up from a sitting position was a challenge, so much so that I was very nearly salivating for my next round of painkillers before it was a safe time to take them. Amazingly and God only knows how - I held off taking the oramorph. Someone muttered something about high pain threshold. Bugger it, I should have taken the Oramorph – forget trying to do the macho thing.

Each day that passed, I noticed slow signs of recovery. There would be trips to the local GP surgery to check on the status of my slightly swollen, bruised and painful abdominal wounds, (which were all fine), but there would be no driving for three weeks or cycling for a month. Walking would start so very slowly, with an elderly man's shuffle around my garden's perimeter and the promise of a low-fat lolly at the end as a reward!

A few weeks before my op, Pete, my old friend from my Met Police days was in Stanmore's Royal National Orthopaedic Hospital having a cancerous pelvic tumour and part of his pelvis removed – a very serious op during which, Pete lost a huge volume of blood – very nearly his entire body's worth! His herculean ordeal made my operation look like I was being admitted simply to have a graze on my hand tended to by the school matron! In life I've learned just as there's always someone who's done it bigger and better than you, there's always someone who's worse off than you. Pete is another one of life's incredible people – a survivor most definitely, a 'Mister Positive' built with a cast iron constitution, strong as an ox and lover of life – an ideas man and a 'doer', he is not only a naturally gifted lensman and 'Star Wars' fan, but a wonderful inspiration, dear friend and unquestionably, a role model for others to follow. So, I was quite humbled to receive a message from Pete wishing me well in my recuperation after everything he had gone through and continues to endure saying, "...heal well. The force is strong in you".

Following successful removal of all of Pete's pelvic sarcoma in summer 2018, which had in effect wrapped itself around his sciatic nerve and right hip joint - what followed for my old friend, was an intense, multi-week hit of recuperation, physiotherapy and then radiotherapy. The unpleasant after effects of this oncology treatment, Pete's wife Nicki described to me as akin to internal sunburn, which didn't present until some four weeks after radiotherapy had ended. This unfortunately coincided with my planned November 2018 visit, which Pete just wasn't up to – so we postponed until early February 2019.

So it was that I journeyed down to London on a crisp winter's morning on the back of a spate of snow and bitterly cold sub-zero temperatures, which at one stage put a question mark over this trip as well. Nevertheless, I was absolutely determined to see my old friend of nearly 30 years. The excitement mounted as I walked to Kings Cross from Euston and hopped on a Peterborough-bound train. It was now a very pleasant, bright and fresh Saturday morning. Thirty-five minutes later, having shot past rolling fields adorned with melting snow, I arrived in the lovely Hertfordshire town of Hitchin, where a taxi took me to Pete and Nicki's wonderful, century-old house with its cosy living space, light, atmospheric rooms, beautiful, spacious kitchen and equally appealing rear garden.

Not really having the remotest clue, what state of wellbeing or mobility I'd find my friend, imagine my surprise and joy, when Pete himself opened the door, wearing a huge smile – and quite mobile on his crutches. Even Pebbles, an adorable, extremely friendly feline, came to greet me. Not only that, but it had also been two years since I last saw Pete and there he was, fresh faced, cancer free and looking healthy and years younger. We talked for ages and at length and of course touched on his operation. Reading between what was spoken and what was left unsaid, I deduced that Pete had come very close to dying. In talking about the subject that most of us are too shit scared to address, Pete told me that he isn't afraid to die – after all, death is the one thing that's certain in life, as LOTR's Lord Elrond, warning his daughter Arwen over her intended, Aragorn, "…[He] will come to death, whether by the sword, or the slow decay of time…", which explains why Pete has emerged so positive – it's as though his brush with death has given him a renewed sense of purpose and being. Pete is undoubtedly the most focused guy I know. However, although he was smiling and jovial, I could tell that this most recent near-death encounter, subsequent oncology treatment, physiotherapy, countless trips toing and froing from home to hospital and goodness knows what else, had taken its toll emotionally. And then there is Pete's wife Nicki – his 'rock' – I cannot even begin to imagine what this incredible, courageous woman has been through. 'Tough times' undoubtedly doesn't even come close. There were moments when my friend was in tears and we just hugged, which kind of gave me a snapshot of the rocky journey that had been travelled thus far and that Pete is still very much coming to terms with his ordeal.

Against Wendy's advice, I thought that it would be great to bring all my photographic gear with me and with Pete's help, photograph my friend. It proved to be just the tonic as instantly I was transported back to our Met Police days, the two of us bouncing around ideas, talking shop and building up the shots – like the couple of pros we are! It's as though we'd time travelled back twenty years, planning out a new course, whilst walking around the vast grounds that constituted Met Police Training School, Hendon. I came away with some very pleasing images, first using available light and then employing a couple of wireless flash units, controlled from camera. We were both in the zone, in our element and I know it did us both a world of good. Pete then reciprocated by photographing me with his own Nikon D810 and portrait lens, seemingly with effortless speed and efficiency, proving that he was quickly learning to work around his disability and further – that he's lost none of his magic touch.

Six months after cancer had forced Pete to temporarily put down his cameras, like a rising phoenix, my friend was back in the game, taking his amazing style of eye-catching, beautifully lit portraits, sometimes from a wheelchair, occasionally standing.

I came away from Hitchin bouncing off the rail carriage sides, on a real high, feeling elated, uplifted and inspired, but also with a strong realisation of just how dysfunctional I had in fact been living my own life of late. My visit to Pete and Nicki filled me with aspiration for what's possible in life. Pete has photo shoots galore lined up with people chomping at the bit for his services, all for when he's good and ready. Pete has a wonderful, optimistic outlook on life and I'm so, so pleased for him. I left Hertfordshire with a massive smile on my face. Good on you Matey!

During the time of my op and recuperation, the world lost the 'Queen of Soul' music, the legend, Aretha Franklin, who died at the age of 76 in Detroit, Michigan on 16th August. She had many memorable hits that included, '(You Make Me Feel Like) A Natural Woman' and 'I Say a Little Prayer'. Then, two days later, the world lost Nobel Peace Prize winner and seventh Secretary-General of the United Nations (from January 1997 to December 2006), Kofi Atta Annan, who died at the age of 80 in Bern, Switzerland. At the time of writing this section (late summer 2018) the current United Nations

Secretary-General, Antonio Guterres said, "Kofi Annan was a champion for peace and a guiding force for good". Kofi Annan was a man of peace and a man of principle and I admired him greatly. The following quote by Kofi remains one of my favourite: "To live is to choose. But to choose well, you must know who you are and what you stand for, where you want to go and why you want to get there". Former President of the USA Barack Obama said of Kofi Anan, "His integrity, persistence, optimism, and sense of our common humanity always informed his outreach to the community of nations. Long after he had broken barriers, Kofi never stopped his pursuit of a better world, and made time to motivate and inspire the next generation of leaders".

The day before I went into hospital for my op, shortly before midday on Tuesday 14th August 2018, disaster hit the port city of Genoa in North-west Italy's Liguria region when a 200-metre section of the Morandi motorway bridge broke off and fell, along with many vehicles. Forty-three people died and dozens more were injured. The route over the bridge is the main road in and out of Genoa, which links to the A10 Motorway and the route to France.

During the first few weeks of August, torrential rain hit the southern Indian State of Kerala, an area renowned for its tropical backwaters and picturesque beaches, precipitating the worst flooding in a century. The death toll exceeded 400 with in excess of 800,000 inhabitants being left homeless and being cared for across 4000 relief camps. Rivers burst their banks, homes and infrastructure collapsed with around 10,000 kilometres of road network destroyed or badly damaged. Continuous flooding triggered landslides which engulfed entire villages, drowning communities in a deadly, sludgy mess.

Then, on Thursday 23rd August 2018 during my recuperation following painful gallbladder surgery, some brilliant news. Lauren popped up to her old school, Saint Aidan's, to receive her GCSE results. The clever girl had done brilliantly, achieving incredible passes in nine subjects. I felt so proud of her. Lauren rightly deserved this success for the hundreds of hours that she had slogged away during years 10 and 11. It was also no mean feat as a new grading structure had come into force for Lauren's academic year, which initially confused the hell out of everybody. Out went the easy to understand A to C grades, which were passes when I did my O Levels back in 1980. In came the new system of grades 1-9, where grades 9 to 4 are passes – grade 9 being an A star, star down to grade 4 being a low pass, but a pass, nevertheless. At the time of writing, the general populous were still trying to get their heads around the new system. I guess it's the same balls-up mega confusion whenever there's any major change. Dare I mention Brexit or further back in history, decimalisation? No, that really dates me!

CHAPTER 28

Tom Ray, Sepsis Survivor, Autumn 2018

Suddenly it was September and almost as if on cue, the long, warm summer drew to an inevitable close. Lauren started at Blackpool Sixth and was excited from day 1. She chose English Language, Media Studies and Psychology and really enjoyed the lessons. Lauren enjoyed being treated like a young adult. Gone are the uniforms – you wear casual clothes and also out are addressing the teachers as 'Sir' or 'Miss'. Blackpool Sixth is a clean, modern, fully equipped environment, fully geared to facilitate modern learning.

Then on September 5th came the dreadful news, not even two days after 'tweeting' that she had a matter of days to live, BBC 'Five Live' talented presenter and breast cancer sufferer and campaigner, Rachel Bland, died. She was only 40. Rachel's story was inspiring, uplifting, yet poignant and deeply moving as she showed tenacious courage during adversity, battling the bastard disease that eventually claimed her life. She won praise and the hearts of many for co-hosting with fellow cancer sufferers Lauren Mahon and Deborah James, a podcast addressing all the taboos surrounding cancer, called 'You, Me and the Big C'. She also ran a blog. Rachel Bland left behind, fellow journalist and husband Steve and son, Freddie. She had a positive impact on so many people and was indeed a shining example to us all.

Then to lighten the mood, in mid-September 2018 Wendy and I went to the cinema to see 'Mamma Mia! Here We Go Again' (sequel to the 2008 romantic musical comedy 'Mamma Mia!'). It was packed once more with great Abba songs, all brilliantly remastered by the geniuses who are Björn Ulvaeus and Benny Andersson. The story yo-yos between 1979 and present day. The film stars Amanda Seyfried, Lily James, Meryl Streep, Pierce Brosnan, Colin Firth, Stellan Skarsgärd, Julie Walters, Christine Baranski, Andy Garcia,

Dominic Cooper, Cher, et al. It provided the perfect escape tonic from my slightly shitty reality. I was catapulted back to my flares and wedge shoe-wearing, shoulder length wavy hair tossing, spotty-faced teenaged, late '70s years. Mamma Mia 2 was feel good from the start. With a strong cast, the angelic voices of Amanda Seyfried and Lily James were refreshing to hear – the latter, outstanding as the young Donna and Julie Walters, bloody hilarious as usual. The film was both funny and powerfully poignant in equal measure. The church of Agios Ioannis Kastri on Skopelos, provided the setting for Sophie's baby boy's christening ceremony towards the film's climax, all played out with the hauntingly beautiful 'My Love, My Life' sung as a duet between Sophie and Donna's spirit, which proved a sudden and unexpected tear jerker! The only downer of the film was having to step back into my reality once it was over. 'Mamma Mia! Here We Go Again', released at London's Hammersmith Apollo in July 2018 was brilliantly crafted and a joy to watch.

On September 28th, 2018, a massive earthquake measuring 7.5 on the Richter scale hit the Indonesian island of Sulawesi, triggering a tsunami and a volcanic eruption of Mount Soputan. Six-metre high waves battered the capital of the province of Central Sulawesi, the city of Palu, located about 1,650 kilometres from the Indonesian capital, Jakarta, causing utter devastation. The city was all but destroyed, covered in mud and debris and strewn with dead bodies. Very quickly the death toll had reached more than 1,950 with thousands still missing and unaccounted for, amidst powerful aftershocks. Bali's neighbouring island of Lombok was still trying to recover from the series of earthquakes in July and August that claimed almost 500 lives. Roads were blocked, many buildings – homes and businesses had collapsed and together with vehicles had simply been washed away. The earthquake also precipitated severe instances of liquefaction, where the soil is turned into liquid as a result of earthquake forces, making large swathes of ground highly unstable. Tens of thousands of people had been displaced, as the government called on the international community for aid and assistance. Meanwhile mass burials commenced amidst fears that the spread of disease could claim more lives.

In early October, Wendy forwarded on to me an email at work advertising a special 'Grand Round' with guest speakers Tom and Nicola Ray. Tom is a sepsis survivor and he and his wife Nicola are sepsis champions. Grand Rounds were often organised at work to enable guest speakers to talk to staff on a variety of interesting topics over a lunchtime period. Anyone who was available could attend, but with only two Medical Photographers for the entire Trust, it was usually extremely difficult for one of us to get there. However, I'd photographed a lot of sepsis patients in the past and this was one talk I was determined to attend. I put the time and date in our work diary.

Back in December 1999, Tom had just given up his job (working with his wife, Nicola in their video production business) to become a house husband – something I did when we moved up from London to Lancashire in 2004. Then, from being a completely healthy man in his late 30s, Tom suddenly became very ill with stomach pains, violent nausea and acute headaches. He had mottled skin and became confused. With Nicola nine months pregnant with their second child, Tom was rushed to A&E with his very alarmed wife. In hospital tests were run to try and explain Tom's seriously low blood pressure. Sepsis caused by a dental visit when his mouth was nicked, coupled with a chest infection, was eventually diagnosed.

Sepsis is a life-threatening condition caused by the body's immune system overreacting and going haywire during an infection and in effect, attacking itself and the body. It will eventually lead to multiple organ failure and death. Around 150,000 people in the UK are affected by sepsis every year and almost a third will die. However, Sepsis is treatable with prompt medical intervention – fluids and antibiotics.

Due to the resulting poor circulatory problems, both of Tom's forearms were amputated, along with both his lower legs, Surgeons ended up scraping most of Tom's face away, leaving plastic surgeons to rebuild his nose, chin and cheeks and endeavouring to salvage something of his mouth. Tom spent a 'pregnancy term' in hospital and emerged from his enforced incarceration, a quadruple amputee with additional facial amputations and a legacy of facial disfigurement. The couple's son was born with Tom still in a coma and Tom didn't set eyes on his little boy until two months later when he spied him through his facial bandages. Daughter Grace, who was three at the time fled the room when she saw Tom in recovery, not believing he was her father. Nicola was left with no option but to give up work to become Tom's full-time carer and so money soon became tight. With mediocre state help, Tom and Nicola were forced to sell their house and move in with Nicola's mother, which was far from ideal. In recovery, Tom wrote about his horrendous ordeal and subsequent survival journey in his book, 'Starfish', which was turned into a film in 2016, starring Tom Riley and Joanne Froggatt.

Due to the difficulty in finding suitable work, Tom has been working in a call centre for a number of years and is also a motivational speaker. He refuses to use a wheelchair. He has adjusted to life using his prostheses and walks and drives with the aid of a specially adapted car.

Having photographed several patients with sepsis at Blackpool Victoria Hospital, I know that cases can start with a relatively minor infection, a small cut or bite and because of this, sepsis can often be misdiagnosed in the crucial early stages. Signs not to ignore, especially when accompanied by an infection are a high or low body temperature, shivering and a raised heartbeat. The skin may well be cold and clammy. The patient may feel dizzy, nauseous and be vomiting. They may have slurred speech, chronic muscle pain and severe breathlessness. In addition, they might not have passed urine for a day. We are all susceptible but the very young and very old are especially vulnerable. So too are people with weakened immune systems, those who have had recent surgery and those being treated for a serious illness in hospital.

Meeting Tom and Nicola for the first time was a powerful, amazing experience. I was struck with how brutally candid they both are and fiercely resilient and positive, staying strong for their family's sake, throughout a very difficult journey, when seemingly everything was stacked against them. I found the couple's story of sepsis survival very inspiring, deeply moving, yet simultaneously uplifting. They are without a doubt two of the most courageous people I've ever had the privilege to meet. I got the chance to pose one of many questions I had which was, 'Has Tom ever suffered severe harassment as a result of disfigurement?' I was stunned by his answer. He hadn't. Yes, people, especially children will stare from time to time, but Tom and Nicola get out into the community spreading the word about the dangers of sepsis, so they are in effect being looked at all the time. I suppose Tom feels that if the family have survived such a horrendous ordeal, they can more than cope with the odd stare. I told Tom in an email that I do get to photograph patients with sepsis now and again and without disclosing names or identities, I told him of two particular cases that I had been involved with – a similar quadruple amputee, who emerged from their ordeal a determined fighter and embracer of life. The other was a young lady whose parents I sat and chatted with one lonely afternoon, they just wanted someone to talk to, but sadly their daughter didn't make it. I then found out that this patient lived virtually on my doorstep and was doubly shocked to see her name as a floral tribute staring back at me as I walked past my local churchyard, not even a stone's throw away from my house.

Tom and Nicola's poignant and emotional presentation had a profound effect on me. It helped restore my faith in mankind and human kindness. Tom emailed me saying, "It is difficult reliving our painful story, but we do it for those who can no longer speak for themselves...Speaking from the heart we're kind of trying to celebrate something about the value of human life deep down. And that unites us with our audiences because that's what all their [medical staff] work is for. A virtuous circle". What an inspiring bloke and you couldn't hope to meet a nicer couple!

Around mid–October, I popped down to London on a Nikon camera course, before flying from Gatwick to Newquay and then by taxi to Wadebridge, for what I affectionately call my 'Cornwall sabbatical' – time to recharge my batteries, forget about work and reflect on life. On 22nd October, I met my surgeon, Mr Thu Linn, during an outpatient appointment. He gave me a visual check of my operation scars and enquired about my health, post op, which I was pleased to report, was good, with the exception of feeling a tad tired, which was to be expected. He signed me off with that characteristic smile, humble bow and warm handshake. If only there were more like him!

On 29th October 2018, 189 people lost their lives when a Boeing 737 Max 8 'Lion Air' jet plummeted into the Java sea, just 13 minutes after take-off from Jakarta en route north to Pangkal Pinang on the island of Bangka. Two days prior to this dreadful incident, came the simply awful news that a helicopter carrying the hugely respected Leicester City football club chairman, Vichai Srivaddhanaprabha, his assistant, Kaveporn Punpare, Nursara Suknamai, a former Thai beauty queen, also employed by the Chairman, the pilot Eric Swaffer and his co-pilot girlfriend, Izabela Lechowicz, had crashed, moments after taking off from Leicester's King Power Stadium. The helicopter took off from the middle of the football stadium shortly after the match conclusion that saw Leicester City equalise 1-1 with visiting side, West Ham. Following a near vertical climb and short hover, the tail rotor from the Chairman's Agusta Westland AW169 became detached, sending the strickened helicopter into a 'dead man's curve' spin, precipitating the loss of all five on board. Miraculously the courageous pilots somehow steered the doomed aircraft to a deserted car park, 200 yards outside the stadium and away from hundreds of fans, so as not to endanger the lives of those on the ground and in the knowledge that their impending crash wasn't survivable. On impact the AgustaWestland erupted in a fireball, which hampered any rescue attempt. Vichai, a much loved, respected and hugely admired family man and Thai billionaire, bought the 'Foxes' in 2010 and saw his team promoted from the championship four years later to become the unlikeliest Premier League champions in 2016.

CHAPTER 29

Armistice Day Centenary, November 11th 2018

November 11th, 2018 marked the centenary of Armistice day – the end of the Great war, the First World War, at the eleventh hour of the eleventh day in the eleventh month, 1918. Millions of people gathered not just in the UK, but around the world to mark this poignant and sobering occasion. Her Majesty The Queen and members of the Royal Family, together with senior politicians and dignitaries attended the annual London Cenotaph service in Whitehall, with renovations at the Palace of Westminster temporarily being halted so that Big Ben's bell could chime before and following the two minutes silence. Of course, there were a multitude of remembrance services across the UK including at Westminster Abbey, Glasgow Cathedral, Belfast's St Anne's Cathedral and at Llandaff Cathedral in the Welsh capital. The Royal Albert Hall played host to the Queen, senior royal family members and Prime Minister May and her husband on the eve of the Armistice centenary, for a grand remembrance concert. Following the Last Post, poppies were dropped from the ceiling of the iconic building. The National Memorial Arboretum in Staffordshire also kept a candlelit vigil on the Saturday evening. Then at 7pm on the evening of the Armistice centenary and beginning with Westminster Abbey, over a thousand beacons were lit the length and breadth of the United Kingdom – the fires symbolising the end of the dark days of war and a return to the lightness of peacetime. Seventy world leaders, who included Chancellor Merkel and Presidents Macron and Trump, gathered in France, where of course many of the battles of the Western Front were fought.

At Blackpool's Victoria Hospital, a scale model of the Menin Gate at Ypres was erected inside the main entrance with the sides cloaked in poppies. It was a wonderful idea and fitting tribute to the Great War's armed service personnel. I spent an enjoyable early

Saturday 10th November morning photographing this memorial with invaluable help from George. Then there were all the 'shadow soldiers' and other-worldly cut-outs; the restored and coloured World War 1 documentary film, 'They Shall Not Grow Old', by highly acclaimed 'Lord of the Rings' and 'The Hobbit' trilogies director, Peter Jackson. The black and white silent film footage utilised original cine film from Imperial War Museums' archive and employing modern production techniques, was painstakingly and carefully hand-coloured one frame at a time, the speed of the film was corrected to iron out the 'jittering' we associate with very old silent film and then the combined footage, 3-D digitised to enable us to see and hear the soldiers as we imagined them to be. Peter Jackson also used forensic lip readers to decipher the troops' conversations and then he used actors to voice their words. The original, now coloured film was interspersed with old interviews with Great War survivors. Seeing the film in colour gave the footage a chilling clarity and immediacy - an edge that made the horror of what happened all the more real, creating a snapshot of army life in the trenches and on the battlefield as it was and almost bringing those young first world war heroes back to life. These courageous lads look like anyone you'd see today on the street. Peter Jackson, in my opinion, is a genius and 'They Shall Not Grow Old' on its own proves why.

The hand-crafted poppies – a poignant and ubiquitous sight, many of which, had been meticulously and lovingly knitted, in addition to those made by the Royal British Legion – symbolised the blood spilled and the first flower to grow in the battle-scarred fields. The huge sand portraits entitled, 'Pages of the Sea' in tribute to the fallen soldiers, an ingenious idea inspired by film-maker Danny Boyle, were crafted at low tide early morning on 11th November by large teams using stencils and rakes on 32 beaches from Cornwall to the Shetland Isles, and Pembrokeshire to Donegal. Folkestone depicted war poet Wilfred Owen and in Blackpool, it was Lance Corporal John Edward Arkwright, who, on 23 August 1914 landed in France with the 1st Battalion, King's Own Royal Lancaster Regiment. And then like ghosts, they faded and disappeared when the incoming tide took them.

The war poetry is particularly sobering and hauntingly beautiful. Laurence Binyon's, 'For the Fallen' (1914) penned in North Cornwall, contains the famous 'Ode of Remembrance' lines:

"They shall grow not old, as we that are left grow old:

Age shall not weary them, nor the years condemn.
At the going down of the sun and in the morning, We will remember them".

And the equally powerful lines by John Maxwell Edmunds written in 1916:

"When you go Home, tell them of us and say, For your Tomorrow, we gave our Today".

'Dulce et Decorum Est' by Wilfred Owen is powerful and deeply moving in equal measure:

'Bent double, like old beggars under sacks,
Men marched asleep. Many had lost their boots,
Gas! GAS! Quick, boys! - An ecstasy of fumbling
My friend, you would not tell with such high zest
To children ardent for some desperate glory,
The old Lie: Dulce et decorum est
Pro patria mori' (meaning *'It is sweet and honourable to die for one's country').*

In May 1915, Canadian poet, surgeon, author, artist and soldier, Lieutenant Colonel John McCrae wrote the now infamous war memorial lines that we hear every Remembrance Sunday entitled 'In Flanders Fields':

'In Flanders fields the poppies blow
Between the crosses, row on row,
We are the Dead. Short days ago
We lived, felt dawn, saw sunset glow,
Loved and were loved, and now we lie,
In Flanders fields.

We shall not sleep, though poppies grow
In Flanders fields'.

Siegfried Sassoon's 'Aftermath', written after the end of the war in March 1919, urges us never to lose sight of the awfulness of what happened:

'Look down and swear by the slain of the War that you'll never forget...and the stench: Of corpses rotting in front of the front-line

trench? Have you forgotten yet?...Look up, and swear by the green of the spring that you'll never forget'.

Then, of course, there's the haunting, moving notes of remembrance music such as Elgar's 'Nimrod' from the 'Enigma Variations', hymns such as 'O God, Our Help in Ages Past' and 'Abide With Me' and 'Battle O'er' – the traditional, heart-breaking Scottish lament played by a lonesome piper at the end of battle.

By far the most powerful act of Remembrance I witnessed on this most memorable of reflective days – 100 years to the day from when the guns fell silent, was a matinee and evening production at Preston's Guild Hall entitled 'Armistice, The Great War Remembered', written, produced and directed by my oldest and dearest friend, Simon Wallis, Headteacher of Barnacre Road Primary School in Longridge. Simon's initial interest in WW1 can be linked to his paternal grandfather, Eliot Wallis, who, as a young infantry officer, fought in and survived the Great War. The production involved hundreds of school children from the now legendary, 15-strong, Longridge Cluster Schools. The incredible hard work from Simon and his team, and their drive and passion for more than 18 months, culminated in the production of an awe-inspiring, thought-provoking, emotionally powerful collection of set pieces that depicted the unfolding story of the First World War. It showed how uncompromising, horrific and destructive battle was, how war favoured no class and impacted everyone, yet also demonstrated the bravery of a distant generation who gave so much. It was quite simply a huge undertaking, a masterpiece and a fitting tribute to those who gave their all.

In Simon's words, "I wanted to bring to life the story of the First World War for children, so that they would be interested and keen to learn about this historic event that touched the lives of millions of people". Indeed, there was a staggering estimate of 37.5 million casualties. It was a very grim story of course and although there were light-hearted moments, Simon made no attempt to "sugar the pill". 'Armistice' covered topics such as how the war started with the assassination of Archduke Ferdinand of Austria; mobilisation, recruitment and enlistment into Lord ('Your Country needs you') Kitchener's army; the types of weapons used that included the Lee Enfield bolt action rifle, the dreaded zeppelins, the use of poisonous gas such as chlorine, the early tank and the Maxim machine gun; rat-infested, trench-foot inducing trench warfare and 'going over the top' into 'no-man's land' directly into the line of fire like cannon fodder; disfigurement and shell-shock (PTSD); Charlie Chaplin; The

Christmas Truce; The home front – rationing and families receiving the feared telegram; the role of women working for the war effort, not just in the home, on land, or in the factories but also the British nurses ('The Roses of No Man's Land') who in Simon's words "… endured shelling and male-chauvinism, they witnessed the true horror of war, watching men bleed slowly to death or choke on poison gas"; the use of horses and dogs in the war; the great battles fought on land, air and sea that included, The Somme, Passchendaele (Ypres), Jutland and those fought in the skies that also involved the 'Aces' – pilots credited with downing five or more enemy aircraft, the most famous being Germany's Manfred Von Richthofen (The Red Baron).

So massive congratulations to all who took part and who were involved in the production of 'Armistice - The Great War Remembered'. There were great performances, beautiful singing, recitals, comic elements and poignant moments, none more so than during the finale, when the 19,240 knitted display of poppies was laid out. Each poppy depicted a soldier fallen, the total reflecting the number of lives lost on the first morning of the Battle of the Somme, July 1st 1916. The children involved in the production will remember this for the rest of their lives…and of course, tell their children! Simon was rightly awarded a High Sheriff of Lancashire's award for the way in which he depicted succinctly the horror and futility of war – so many lives wasted needlessly. In the paradoxical words of Thomas Hardy taken from one of my favourite poems of his, 'The Man He Killed':

'Yes quaint and curious war is. You shoot a fellow down you'd treat if met where any bar is, or help to half a crown'.

Bravo Simon old friend, Bravo!

CHAPTER 30

2018: The Quickest Year So Far

Christmas 2018 was a very relaxed, enjoyable event with just the four of us, Wendy's brother, Simon and my sister, Kate. To walk off the excesses, we took a trip out to Ingleton falls, a very scenic round trip of just over four miles. It encompassed plenty of picturesque waterfalls and steps and proved to be the perfect inspirational tonic.

For one of my Christmas presents, George gave me the 'Maze Runner' trilogy on DVD, a series of dystopian, science-fiction action adventure films that are based on the James Dashner novels and star Dylan O'Brien and Kaya Scodelario et al. The first film, 'The Maze Runner' was released in September 2014. This was followed by 'Maze Runner: The Scorch Trials' in September 2015 with the concluding film and in my opinion, the best of the three films, 'Maze Runner: The Death Cure', released in January 2018. The Death Cure is breath-taking, edge of your seat action all the way and constitutes one of the most entertaining films that I've seen in a long time.

A number of significant events occurred in 2018:

June 24th - moorland fires attributed to the work of arsonists broke out in Lancashire and Greater Manchester. The first of these was started on Saddleworth Moor, located barely fifteen miles north east from the centre of Manchester. Then more fires broke out 35 miles away from Saddleworth Moor to the north west, at Winter Hill, followed by Scout Road (a few miles south east of Winter Hill) near Bolton and then a further fire to the north west of Winter Hill at Healy Nab near Chorley. Involving around 120 brave firefighters from five different fire services, crews battled for days to dampen down and painstakingly manually beat down fires, successfully keeping flames and smoke away from buildings and communication masts. The smoke from the combined fires morphed to produce a huge plume, which we could see more than forty miles away from Lytham Saint Annes.

July 22nd - the longest total lunar eclipse of the 21st century occurred

October 23rd - the longest (34 miles) sea crossing bridge-tunnel system and the longest fixed link on the entire planet was opened by Xi Jinping, the President of China. The Hong Kong-Zhuhai-Macau Bridge cost $18.75 billion to build, work started in December 2009 and finished in February 2018.

November 8th - Western USA suffered a huge, destructive wildfire in Butte County, California, which claimed 88 lives, injured 17 firefighters and civilians and destroyed thousands of buildings. The fire was investigated and found to be caused by a faulty power line.

November 14th - Prince Charles celebrated his 70th birthday.

December 12th - Prime Minister Theresa May's leadership was called into question over her handling of 'Brexit', specifically over calling off the vote in Parliament on her Brexit withdrawal agreement with the European Union, which precipitated a vote of confidence being called. Mrs May won this by 200 votes (63%) to 117 against, leaving Mrs May immune from such a vote for another year, but seeing her almost under daily attack from all sides of the House of Commons.

December 22nd - coming only three months after a massive earthquake struck off the central Indonesian island of Sulawesi, triggering a tsunami that flattened the coastal city of Palu and claimed more than 2,000 lives, poor old Indonesia was hit again with a giant tsunami caused by the eruption of Anak Krakatau, west of Java. Several hundred people lost their lives and close to a thousand were injured.

We lost a whole load of immensely talented people in 2018, not least of whom was the revered scientist and best-selling author of among others, 'A Brief History of Time', Stephen Hawking, who passed away aged 76. Professor Hawking suffered from a form of motor neuron disease known as 'ALS'. He was a wheelchair user and as his degenerative symptoms persisted, he needed a voice simulator to talk.

On 24th July at the age of 101, aviator Mary Ellis died. During World War 2, she was a member of the Air Transport Auxiliary from 1941, delivering planes from factory to airfield. Mary flew about 1,000 aircraft during the war and the 76 different types included Spitfires and Wellington bombers. Mary had several near misses, being shot at whilst flying over Bournemouth, landing in fog at the same time as another Spitfire was coming towards her and also when she crash-landed when her Supermarine Spitfire's undercarriage jammed, causing the Rolls Royce Merlin engine to overheat. After the war she flew jets, becoming one of the first women to fly the 'Gloster Meteor', Britain's first jet fighter. In the '50s and '60s, Mary became manager of Sandown Airport on the Isle of Wight. At 101 She was still driving every day to her local shops. She recalled, "Up in the air on your own. And you can do whatever you like. I flew 400 Spitfires. And occasionally I would take one up and go and play with the clouds. I would like to do it all over again…".

On the very last day of November, the great Statesman and 41st POTUS, George Herbert Walker Bush died at the age of 94. He was married to Barbara, former First Lady, for 73 years until her death in April 2018, having had the longest marriage for any president in the history of the United States of America. The former Second World War aviator, Texas oil tycoon, CIA head and family patriarch of the Bush dynasty, was hugely admired around the world, Prime Minister May saying that George Bush's "ethos of public service was the guiding thread of his life and an example to us all". Former Vice President Al Gore stated that George Bush, "served our nation with extraordinary integrity and grace". President Bush was in office at the end of the Cold War, using all his diplomatic skills and his humility to end the global stand-off peacefully and in the process, seeing a collapse of the old Soviet Union in 1991. One of George Bush's grandsons, George P. Bush, summed up the late, former president: "He was more than a great man; he was a good man. His courage was matched by his compassion; and his dedication to country was equalled only by his devotion to his family".

The funeral of President HW Bush with its touching eulogies was without a doubt, one of the most moving and poignant events that I've watched these many years. As is American custom for former Presidents, sitting Presidents, Presidents-elect and those who have given distinguished service to the nation, George Bush was given a state funeral service, which for the former President was held at the National Cathedral in the nation's capital, Washington DC on an overcast, cold Wednesday 5th December. The service was attended by his son and former President, George W Bush and family, serving President Trump and past Presidents, Barack Obama, Bill Clinton and Jimmy Carter and their wives. Historian and Bush biographer, Jon Meacham eulogised the late President George HW Bush as, "America's last great soldier Statesman", and referring to when he was a young US navy pilot after his plane was shot down during

World War 2, “His life was a perennial effort to prove himself worthy of his salvation on that distant morning”.

Former Canadian Prime Minister Brian Mulroney said of the late President, “When George Bush was President of the United States of America, every single head of government in the world knew that they were dealing with a gentleman, a genuine leader - one who was distinguished, resolute and brave…I believe it will be said that…no occupant of the Oval Office was more courageous, more principled and more honourable than George Herbert Walker Bush”. Following a meeting with George HW Bush at his summer home in Walker’s Point, Kennebunkport, Maine on September 2nd 2001, Brian Mulroney told the funeral service that he was reminded of the “simple and true [lines] that speak to the nature of George Bush and his love of family and precious surroundings:

There are wooden ships, There are sailing ships, There are ships that sail the sea, But the best ships are friendships, And may they always be”.

CHAPTER 31

The 'No Brexit' year - 2019

2018 seemed to be a volatile, discordant year for politicians trading insults with one another in the run up to what we all thought was going to be 'Brexit' in March 2019, the palpable feeling of malaise seemingly exacerbated by the spontaneity of social media. Even Her Majesty The Queen appeared to be appealing for calm and "peace on earth and goodwill towards all", when during her Christmas Day broadcast to the nation she talked about the power of 'faith, family and friendship' being a "constant" and "a source of comfort and reassurance". Speaking of the Commonwealth she said "Its strength lies in the bonds of affection it promotes and a common desire to live in a better, more peaceful world. Even with the most deeply held differences, treating the other person with respect and as a fellow human being, is always a good first step to greater understanding". Then in late January 2019 at a Sandringham-based event, the Queen talked of coming together to seek the "common ground", 'respecting others' points of view' and remembering to 'always keep the bigger picture in mind', in searching for a way forward through a more harmonious public discourse - remarks widely seen as an appeal for unity, a veiled reference to this undercurrent of toxicity and deep divisions within the nation over Brexit. Society could do a lot worse than to heed the sound advice from our wise, learned and much-loved Monarch.

2018 for me, proved another action-packed year and the quickest twelve months on record. It's almost as if some unseen force pushed the accelerator down on my life and I was anxious to counter by slamming the anchors on. Having undergone a major operation in 2018 and had time to reflect, I was and still am preoccupied with an overwhelming desire to do something completely different...whilst still taking photographs of course! Maybe it's because I've overstayed my welcome in the 'death, dying and suffering business' for far too long. I seem to be working harder now than when I first qualified, or maybe that's my perception, or just an age thing? Perhaps it's simply that I need a change of scenery, a change of direction, or that sometimes I get a nagging feeling that I'm not the least bit valued by an establishment that has become too large and too focused on bigger things, to care about the individual. Even former junior doctor, now comedian, Adam Kay said as much in his 2017 book, 'This is Going to Hurt', "I'm pretty unshockable, but I'll never cease to be amazed by hospitals' wilful ineptitude when it comes to caring for their own staff". However, as an inpatient during my 2 recent episodes in hospital, I was treated like a king and experienced NHS treatment at its very best.

All too quickly, Jools Holland's excellent, star-studded, annual 'Hootenanny' was over and 2019 was ushered in, albeit to a rocky start. For example, the Brexit debate, failure to leave the EU as planned on 29th March, Brexit extension (or debacle – depending on your point of view) and even the Duke of Edinburgh crashing and rolling his Land Rover on the edge of the Sandringham Estate on January 17th. He miraculously and thankfully emerged unscathed, but two women in another vehicle were slightly injured. Then on January 25th, disaster struck in south-eastern Brazil when a dam collapsed at an iron ore mine near the town of Brumadinho, flooding another dam below and claiming 34 lives with a further 300 people missing.

In February 2019 I got into another Netflix TV series, recommended by George. It was CBS/Warner Bros' (CW's) American teen drama, 'Riverdale', based on the 'Archie' comics, airing initially in January 2017 and which stars a host of talented young actors who include: KJ Apa as Archie Andrews, Lili Reinhart as Betty Cooper, Cole Sprouse as Jughead Jones, the series narrator and Camila Mendes as Veronica Lodge. I was a tad sceptical at first, but after a few episodes I soon got hooked on the drama, which almost 'gives a nod' towards the 1990-1 cult series, 'Twin Peaks'. There are certain uncanny similarities: the murder of a central high school character and subsequent bizarre deaths, the show's eerie visuals, the oddball characters, the dream sequences and the strong undercurrent that leaves you feeling that almost nothing is as it seems. Even the design for the town's sign reminds me of Twin Peaks. Riverdale had me gripped and is definitely worth a viewing. I was halfway through watching this series when the tragic news emerged that Luke Perry, who played Archie's Dad Fred Andrews, passed away on 4th March 2019 following a massive stroke. He was only 52.

Following Riverdale and again on Netflix I stumbled across the US political thriller TV drama series, 'Designated Survivor', starring Kiefer Sutherland, Natascha McElhone, Italia Ricci, Maggie Q, Adan Canto, Kal Penn et al. The show's executive producer Kiefer Sutherland plays the US Secretary of Housing and Urban Development, who, following an explosion that kills everyone in government ahead of him in the line of presidential succession, finds himself suddenly catapulted to POTUS as the named designated survivor for the State of the Union address. Sutherland as the hastily sworn in new President Thomas Kirkman rapidly comes to grips with his inexperience as the most powerful leader of the free world, while seeking answers to those behind the devastating Washington terrorist attack. Gripping, tense, frightening, entertaining and thoroughly recommended!

On 6th May 2019 Buckingham Palace announced the birth of a son, Archie Harrison Mounbatten-Windsor to Prince Harry and Megan (the Duke and Duchess of Sussex). Archie, born at 05.26 BST, weighed in at 7lbs 3oz.

The next day, the acclaimed HBO / Sky UK television miniseries 'Chernobyl' premiered in the UK. The award winning historical drama, starring Jared Harris, Emily Watson and Stellan Skarsgård, focuses on the April 1986 Chernobyl nuclear disaster near Pripyat, in the old Soviet Union and the ensuing, marathon clean-up operation.

On 13 May 2019 the American actress, singer and animal welfare activist, Doris Day passed away. She was 97. Then, a week later one of the giants and heroes from the world of Formula One motor racing, Niki Lauda, died at the age of 70. Born, Andreas Nikolaus Lauda in Austria's capital Vienna, Niki was a three-time F1 winner in 1975, 1977 and 1984. He was also the only champion in the history of the sport to have won for the two most successful constructors, Ferrari and McLaren. Niki was also a successful businessman and pilot, but undoubtedly more famous for his amazing courage, resilience and recovery after crashing at the Nürburgring during the 1976 German Grand Prix in which he suffered horrific head and facial burns together with lung damage from inhaling toxic gases. Unbelievably Niki Lauda was back in the cockpit a mere forty days later!

A series of commemorative events marked the 75th anniversary of Operation Neptune known as D Day (6th June1944). D-Day signified the largest air, land and seaborne invasion the world has ever seen and the beginning of the offensive to free Nazi-occupied north west Europe. A number of dignitaries joined the Queen and HRH The Prince of Wales at an initial event in Portsmouth (one of the key D Day embarkation points) on 5th June 2019. These included outgoing British Prime Minister Theresa May, American President Donald Trump, Canadian Prime Minister Justin Trudeau, French President Emmanuel Macron, German Chancellor Angela Merkel and poignantly, some of the last surviving D Day veterans, all of whom were well into their nineties with shiny medals proudly on display. The Queen stood up twice to applaud the veterans – I don't think I've ever seen that before.

On 7th June 2019, in the wake of the Brexit Debacle, Theresa May resigned but remained as Prime Minister until newly elected Tory Party favourite, 55-year-old Boris Johnson took over the reins of government on 24th July 2019.

At this time Lauren was researching different universities to see which one might offer her the best course for studying a BA in TV Production. Following an interesting and very informative tour of the School of Film and Television at Cornwall's Falmouth University, on 9th June 2019 Lauren and I then visited Gloucestershire University's, Cheltenham Campus, focusing on their BA (Hons) course in Television Production. We liked both sites, but Falmouth seemed to be the favourite. Then on 3rd July 2019, George and Lauren visited Leeds Trinity University, they also offered a BA (Hons) course in Television Production. They both came away buzzing, Lauren was convinced that Leeds was where she'd like to be based for her degree course. With the chance of a life-changing semester studying abroad and plenty of work experience opportunities, the course equips students with a variety of skills from camera operator, directing, presenting and editing, to vision mixing and floor managing. On graduating, through a now established network of contacts, the University gears the student up to be 'industry ready' and with an eye-catching portfolio of professional television work tucked under their arm to show prospective employers, student are helped to springboard to their first job in the profession. Geographically, it's near perfect. 90 miles / 2 hours by road or a tad over 2 hours by rail, east of home – far enough for Lauren to be independent, but close enough for her to come home for a weekend or for us to visit her in a day. Leeds itself is 25 minutes by rail to York, 3 hours by rail to Edinburgh and 2¼ hours by rail to London's Kings Cross. The university is a mere 3 miles to Leeds Bradford Airport and within striking distance of Channel 4 Television. Exciting stuff.

On 5th July, the legendary sporting journalist and horse racing pundit, John McCririck, died aged 79. At times controversial, John McCririck was famed for his signature deerstalker, side whiskers, arm waving and loud, booming, eccentric deliveries.

On 14th July, England beat New Zealand in the final at Lord's to win the ICC Cricket World Cup

Throughout the latter end of 2018 and during 2019, a phenomenal medical achievement was being masterminded and put into practice – the high risk, surgical separation of conjoined identical twins, sisters Safa and Marwa. The girls, joined end to end at the crown of their heads ('craniopagus'), were born by caesarean section in Hayatabad hospital, Peshawar, Pakistan, on 7th January 2017. The successful series of delicate operations to 'unfuse' the girls' heads, untangle a network of shared blood vessels and rebuild their misshapen brains and distorted, tubular shaped skulls, were carried out over many months at London's Great Ormond Street Hospital by Paediatric neurosurgeon Owase Jeelani and plastic surgeon Professor David Dunaway and their respective teams – a brilliant result!

On 19th July 2019, Dutch actor, writer and environmentalist, Rutger Hauer passed away. He was 75. Rutger Hauer was probably best known for his portrayal of Roy Batty, the self-aware android in the 1982 film, Blade Runner. However, I will forever remember Rutger Hauer's electrifying performance as the suicidal homicidal maniac in the chilling 1986 American road action horror movie, The Hitcher, which I recall vividly as a tense, frightening, edge of your seat experience.

As the long month of July drew to a close and all of us at Blackpool Teaching Hospitals eagerly awaited pay day on 31st, great swathes of the UK were hit with storms bringing torrential rain and pockets of flooding. Amidst severe weather warnings and as a bi-product of this unprecedented incessant rain, a bridge located on the Grinton Moor Road, near Grinton collapsed as flash flooding and a month's worth of rainfall in a handful of hours descended on part of North Yorkshire. It also saw the fire station in Leyburn as well as many homes, under water. Then, around 1,500 residents of Whaley Bridge in Derbyshire were evacuated to a nearby school, pubs, offices and local businesses, taking initially only their pets and medication with them, following the partial collapse of a nearby dam spillway. A large section of concrete slabs constituting part of the apron wall holding back a phenomenal 283 million gallons of water in Toddbrook Reservoir was damaged. The earth dam, which has a puddle clay core, was constructed in 1831.

Firefighters, engineers who included members of the Canal and River Trust who own the reservoir, the Environment Agency, mountain rescue and volunteers worked around the clock, initially employing ten, high voltage pumps (more pumps were brought in) to drain water from the full reservoir, so lowering the pressure on the dam wall to help with assessing the damage, reduce the risk of further erosion to the clay underneath the damaged concrete slabs and repair the gaping hole with some initial 400 tonnes of aggregate put in place by an RAF Chinook helicopter on Friday 2nd August 2019. A further 70 tonnes were deposited by the Chinook the following day with another 55 of the one tonne bags being dropped on Sunday 4th. Roads and parks around the affected reservoir were closed due to the flooding risk and associated threat to life from a sudden, catastrophic failure of a burst dam and also a possible breaching of the River Goyt, lower down. A week after being evacuated, the dam was declared safe and the residents of Whaley Bridge were allowed back into their homes. Questions, however, still remain. How safe are the nation's dams and with climate change ushering in more extreme weather conditions, are we likely to see more damage to our infrastructure in the future?

For much of spring and summer 2019, Wendy, George, Lauren and Simon were busy getting the house in Cornwall ready for holiday letting. This involved hundreds of hours, sometimes working well beyond midnight, clearing, tidying, painting, cleaning and organising workmen to bring the house up to the high standard expected by the letting industry, which all cost a small fortune. Val's lovely house that we'd stayed in for years, aptly named 'Little Sidings', is a cosy, three-bed semi and lies on what was the Bodmin to Padstow railway line in Wadebridge, North Cornwall. It's a stone's throw from the John Betjeman Centre (the old railway station) and town centre shops. The long since disappeared railway is now 'The Camel Trail', which runs from Bodmin to Padstow (via Wadebridge) and is enjoyed by holiday makers and locals alike, from walkers and joggers to horse riders and cyclists. Wadebridge is a beautiful part of the country – I should know, I've been going there for almost 30 years. The holiday home stands on the banks of the River Camel and is very close to the 'Challenge Bridge', which links Wadebridge on the west bank to Egloshayle on the east side.

Seeing TV personality, Anneka Rice back on our screens, partnering up with reigning champion Kevin Clifton in the seventeenth series of 'Strictly Come Dancing' in the autumn of 2019 was very nostalgic as it took Wendy and me back to when we first met. The hugely successful television series, 'Challenge Anneka' was on our screens at the end of the eighties and in to the early nineties. Each programme consisted of Anneka Rice being given a task to try and complete within a set period of time – usually a few days. Anneka would have no idea initially of what each task would entail and she would have to persuade companies and people to contribute their time and resources for free, but it was always for an extremely good cause. The team would roll up in a huge, blue-coloured, logoed lorry and Anneka would be donned in a blue jump suit and would be seen driving a similar coloured buggy, together with her film crew that included legendary soundman, Dave Chapman.

One such challenge kicked off well into November 1991, when Anneka was set the '180 Foot Bridge' challenge – build a footbridge over the River Camel and hold a party – all within 3 days! At the time Anneka said, "We asked the construction people how long the project would take and they said 6 months and we said ok we'll do it in 6 days". The footbridge, which still stands firm to this day is affectionately known locally as 'Anneka's Bridge'. At the time, many local people pitched in, working tirelessly through the night to complete the project.

On Saturday 3rd August the 64-year-old singer and entertainer, Joe Longthorne MBE, who had battled against cancer for decades, sadly passed away at his home in Blackpool, surrounded by his husband and family.

On 15th August, one of 'our finest' was murdered whilst investigating a burglary. Thames Valley police officer, 28-year-old PC Andrew Harper was sickeningly dragged along the road by a vehicle in the west Berkshire village of Sulhamstead. The popular PC had only been married to his wife for four weeks.

Also on 15th August 2019, a Russian Ural Airlines Airbus 321 made an emergency 'belly flop' landing (with its landing gear retracted and its engines off) in a corn field near Moscow shortly after taking off, having had its engines disrupted by a flock of gulls. The plane, carrying more than 230 passengers and crew, was flying to Simferopol in Crimea from Zhukovsky International Airport. More than 74 people were injured, but miraculously, everyone survived, with the pilots being hailed as heroes and the incident being compared to Captain Chesley 'Sully' Sullenberger's emergency landing, shortly after take-off on January 15, 2009. Sully put the US Airways Flight 1549 down in the Hudson River off Manhattan, when both engines were taken out of action by a bird strike. All 155 people on board survived.

The following day on 16th August, 79-year-old American actor, director and screenwriter, Peter Fonda died. Nominated for the 1969 Academy Award for Best Original Screenplay for the film, 'Easy Rider', Peter Fonda was the son of Henry Fonda, the younger brother of Jane Fonda and the father of Bridget Fonda.

On the last day of August 2019, Lauren became the proud owner of her first car - a 2008, black-coloured Nissan Micra, which she found locally after an exhaustive internet search. The eleven-year-old vehicle was in very good condition with an incredibly low mileage of only 45,500. Lauren then progressed to passing her practical driving test first time on 17th September 2019 (having already passed the driving theory test). Hopefully, this car will see our daughter through her university years and well into her first job! We drove the Micra home in secret and tied it up in a big red bow. Lauren, who wasn't expecting her car to be ready just yet, was made up and her face was a picture. It's special moments such as these that as a parent, the mind treasures forever.

Seemingly, Autumn was upon us once more in super quick time, which also heralded the start of hurricane season in the North Atlantic. At the end of August/start of September, hurricane Dorian (an extremely dangerous Category 5) led the charge in advance of further powerful storms brewing. With winds of 180 mph they battered and decimated the north-western Bahamas, claiming more than forty lives, destroying property, infrastructure and uprooting trees, before moving on to buffet the Florida coastline and the US eastern seaboard. Dorian then wreaked havoc in the Canadian province of Nova Scotia with 100 mph winds and heavy rainfall bringing down trees and cutting the power to nearly half a million homes.

Although the television series premiered on BBC 2 back in September 2013, I caught up with 'Peaky Blinders', a British crime drama, on Netflix in late summer 2019. The May 2018 Bafta winning series, starring Cillian Murphy as Gang leader Tommy Shelby, is mainly set in Birmingham, England and charts the Shelby crime family's exploits, following the end of the First World War. The Peaky Blinders, active in the late 19th to early 20th century, were a Birmingham-based criminal youth gang, whose name is derived from the weapons the group made and employed. In addition to their distinctive haircuts, this criminal gang wore jackets with brass buttons, bell-bottom trousers, cravats and a peaked cap, thought to house small-bladed weapons.

September 1st 2019 was the 80th anniversary of the outbreak of the Second World War in Poland, the occasion marked throughout the UK, with a variety of historical themed events and re-enactments.

The week commencing 2nd September bore witness to some bizarre House of Commons goings on. On 3rd September the Government was left with no working majority following Phillip Lee's defection to the Liberal Democrats. Later that day, 21 Conservative MPs were punished, when they had the party whip withdrawn for going against Tory party orders and giving their support to an opposition motion. That evening, in a packed lower chamber amidst scenes of volatile unparliamentary behaviour, Prime Minister Johnson lost a crucial vote of keeping the option of an exit from the EU without a deal – not that he was ever going to win in the face of a Parliamentary majority dead against that idea! The following day, the MPs against a 'no deal Brexit' took over Commons business to debate their 'Brexit delay bill' that would effectively force the Prime Minister to ask Brussels for a further delay to Brexit instead. The bill received Royal ascent and the PM sought to call a mid-October general election, which failed to get the backing of MPs. Boris Johnson was then forced to ask the European Union for a delay to Brexit to prevent a no deal situation by the 31 October deadline. Mr Johnson also came under fire for his decision to suspend or 'prorogue' Parliament on 10th September ahead of the 31 October deadline.

Whilst prorogation (ending a parliamentary session ahead of tabling a new Queen's speech) is completely normal, in this case there weren't many parliamentary days left until the UK exited the EU and many MPs had expected to use the limited time left to cast a hawk eye over the new Johnson government's Brexit policy, which included this intention to leave the European Union on 31 October 2019 'come what may', which increased the chances of leaving the EU with no deal. Proroguing parliament early drastically reduced the time available to MPs to scrutinise the workings of government and for the MPs to endeavour to pass laws that sought to amend the Johnson government's Brexit plans.

On 5th September the Prime Minister's brother Jo Johnson resigned from the government saying that he was "torn between family and national interest". Then two days later, Secretary of State for Work and Pensions, Amber Rudd, also resigned from the Tory

Party, describing the withdrawal of the party whip from 21 Conservative MPs as an "assault on decency and democracy". Boris Johnson's decision to prorogue Parliament was found by the Supreme Court to be unlawful in late September. Judges declared that it was wrong to prevent MPs undertaking their duties in the run up to what was supposed to be Brexit on 31st October, with Supreme Court president Baroness Hale of Richmond (Lady Brenda Hale) pointing out that "the effect on the fundamentals of democracy was extreme". On hearing the news Labour leader Jeremy Corbyn declared to cheering party conference delegates in Brighton, "...The government will be held to account for what it has done. Boris Johnson has been found to have misled the country. This unelected prime minister should now resign!" OMG – politically and constitutionally unprecedented, explosive stuff indeed...told you the year started and has continued with an uneasy feeling about it!

Then on 9th September and after a tenure lasting more than a decade (one of the longest in the history of the office, which dates back to 1377) Speaker John Bercow, the 'Backbencher's backstop' (allowing MPs to hold ministers to account) announced his resignation. Speaker Berkow shouted the immortal words, 'order, order' for the very last time at 5.30 p.m. on 31 October 2019. The presiding officer of the lower chamber is elected by the Commons at the start of each parliament upon a vacancy. Speaker Bercow was elected to the chair on 22 June 2009, following the resignation of Michael Martin.

On 6th September 2019, Robert Gabriel Mugabe, the former Zimbabwean revolutionary, Prime Minister of Zimbabwe from 1980 to 1987 and President from 1987 to 2017, died aged 95.

On Monday 23rd September 2019, the beleaguered, debt-ridden travel giant Thomas Cook was plunged into liquidation after last ditch talks to raise new funding failed. The travel firm had asked the government for a £250 million bailout, which was not forthcoming. What followed was the largest repatriation in peacetime. Coordinated by the Civil Aviation Authority and costing the taxpayer in the region of £100 million, 'Operation Matterhorn', mobilised scores of charter jets to fly customers home from myriad destinations. It was estimated that 150,000 Britons alone were affected by the company's collapse – my colleague Steve and his wife being among those flown home from Orlando in Florida after a 'slightly extended' stay.

The next day at noon I wandered in to our very own Day Surgery Unit at Blackpool Victoria Hospital to book in for a minor ankle operation. Having had my blood pressure taken and all the other pre-op checks, Consultant Vascular Surgeon Mr Iraj Zeynali talked me through the operation to remove a bulging vein, located at the inner aspect of my right ankle. Having changed into hospital gowns I casually walked into day theatre and popped myself up on to the theatre trolley. The operation was fascinating – bizarrely I watched it all, from initial knife to skin contact through to wound closure with dissolvable stitches and steri-strips. I even studied the offending piece of vein, now detached and very much out of my body – weird, I know. A sight that would no doubt cause many to puke or faint, I was just mesmerized by it all. Nursing staff kept me on the ward for a good hour after the op, during which time I enjoyed my tea and bikkies. The wound healed very quickly. The biggest hassle was taping my lower leg up in a plastic bag prior to showering in the days immediately post op to protect the special anti-deep vein thrombosis stocking I had to wear.

On 2nd October 2019, former BBC and ITN stalwart newscaster and Question Time host, Peter Sissons, died aged 77. When I was growing up, Peter Sissons was a part of our lives, delivering news into the nation's living rooms, nightly. Tony Hall, the BBC director general described him as "One of the great television figures of his time". BBC News presenter Huw Edwards, himself an icon of news reporting, described Peter Sissons as "…a gold standard broadcaster".

Over the weekend of 5th October I flew to Belfast for the annual Institute of Medical Illustrators' Conference, where illuminating presentations covered such interesting topics as: keeping our digital heritage; forensic collaboration and major incident planning during the Manchester Ariana Grande concert bombing; utilising photography in the production of an artificial eye; fungal toe nail photography (delivered by my former Renovo colleague Kevin) and introducing debrief sessions – providing emotional support to Medical Photography staff. Additionally, within the 'New Voices' section there were some equally talented photographers covering topics that included donation; standardising a photographic protocol for hair loss; creating movement within an orbital prosthesis; endometriosis and the role of tele-derm photography in diagnosing skin cancers. The trip to Belfast all went without a hitch right up until I stepped off the plane on my return to Manchester. A young lady decided to do an about turn mid-way through an electronic door and tried to come back airside. This caused the door to jam and a wait for the rest of us passengers of around 15 minutes. Doh!

On 9th October I took a day off from hospital life and treated myself to a location portraiture workshop at Cheshire's stunning Peckforton Castle, run by the highly acclaimed photographer and European Ambassador for Sony Imaging, Hannah Couzens. The day, run in conjunction with world renowned light company, Profoto, was devoted to all things light creating and light shaping, using male and female models in beautiful upbeat surroundings and blending daylight and studio flash to create evocative, eye-catching portraits. Hannah's enthusiasm for photography coupled with her relaxed, down to earth, friendly approach to teaching ensured that I left Cheshire inspired and upbeat and of course, with some very pleasing imagery!

On 11th October, five people were injured as a result of a 40-year old man running amok with a knife in the Arndale Centre in Manchester.

Over the weekend of 12th and 13th October Japan was hit by Typhoon Hagibis, one of the strongest storms to affect the country in years. Amidst severe flooding, landslides and widespread power loss at least 23 people were killed as a result.

On 17th October a revised Brexit deal was agreed by both the UK and the EU. It was a deal similar to that negotiated by former Prime Minister May, but it removed the controversial Irish backstop plan, which opponents argued could have tied the UK to EU customs rules indefinitely. On Saturday 19th October Parliament sat in session for the first time in 37 years to debate the new deal. MPs didn't say no to the revised deal, they voted to delay giving their verdict. Ultimately, Prime Minister Johnson was obliged by law to ask the EU for yet another delay to Brexit. Towards the end of October the EU granted a further extension to Brexit until the end of January 2020. A general election to break the Brexit impasse and get the mess sorted out was set for 12th December 2019.

Amidst all the Brexit 'Yea, but no, but' (the papers' hilarious slant on MP's refusal to hurry through the Brexit legislation), we decided to take some much needed time out from our hectic work life. A week may be a long time in politics, but it proved ludicrously short for our very late summer holiday to Cornwall. Staying in Val's old house at Little Sidings, given a makeover by Wendy, Simon, George and Lauren proved just the tonic. The seven days was a lovely mix of relaxation, walking, cycling, beach and cliff walks, shopping, seeing friends and trips out to picture postcard St. Ives, Fowey and Padstow. There was even time for lunch at 'the Blue Tomato' café in Rock, followed by a saunter along the beach in the direction of Daymer Bay. We were blessed with an Indian summer and fortunately the only rain was on the penultimate and last days. Before journeying home, we drove to Falmouth University's open day on Saturday 26th October, specifically to view the facilities again and for us to learn more about the School of Film and Television - all to help Lauren make an informed choice in her University study location.

Whilst we were on holiday, on 23rd October 2019 a grim discovery was made inside a lorry at Purfleet, Essex. In what appeared to be a people smuggling operation, 39 bodies of Vietnamese nationals were found after the lorry and its refrigerated container arrived from Zeebrugge in Belgium.

On Tuesday 5th November baby goods giant, Mothercare, called in the administrators after succumbing to increased cost pressures, making losses for a number of years and changes in consumer spending patterns - the move immediately putting 2,500 UK jobs in jeopardy.

On the other side of the world, thousands of people were displaced and at least three people lost their lives in more than a hundred bush fires across Australia's New South Wales and Queensland where a state of emergency was declared.

On the evening of 13th November Wendy and I drove to Kendal to see the much loved television presenter, author, mountaineer and adventurer, Ben Fogle. Ben's 'Tales from the Wilderness' as part of his UK tour was riveting, funny and at times poignant. Listening to Ben Fogle live was thoroughly inspiring. As a bonus, I met Ben at the end of the night, got him to sign his latest book called 'Up' and came away with some pleasing photographs of the TV personality. I found Ben to be just as nice in person as he is on the telly. Top bloke!

On the television front, up next for me on Netflix came the critically acclaimed American supernatural horror TV series, 'The Haunting of Hill House', starring Michiel Huisman, Elizabeth Reaser, Oliver Jackson-Cohen, Kate Siegel, Victoria Pedretti, Carla Gugino, Henry Thomas and Timothy Hutton. The story follows a family of five siblings - three sisters and two brothers who are haunted by their paranormal experiences of living in Hill House - fictionally the most haunted house in America, the plot see-sawing between the present day and flashbacks of each sibling to when they were children. The series documented the events leading up to the family fleeing the haunted mansion in 1992. This gripping ghost story had me so spell-bound, I had to watch it through for a second time. "Silence lay steadily against the wood and stone of Hill House. And those who walk there, walk together". Suffice to say, if this is the genre for you, this Netflix series is definitely worth a viewing.

Season 2 was released in the autumn of 2020 and is entitled, 'The Haunting of Bly Manor'. Although some of the original Hill House cast return in this second outing playing new characters, the narrative of Bly Manor is completely different. Victoria Pedretti stars as an American governess, hired by an English aristocrat to look after his young niece and nephew after they fall into his care. All is not what it seems in this gothic romance / supernatural horror drama series as the moment the new, young governess arrives at Bly Manor, she begins to see ghostly figures that haunt the old house. Bly Manor is a bittersweet haunting tale. It's about love, desire, guilt, obsession and tragedy – brilliantly conceived, beautifully filmed and like Hill House, definitely worth a viewing. "It's you, it's me, it's us." Thoroughly watchable, very entertaining and "It's perfectly splendid".

Although first released in 2012, Jed Mercurio's Line of Duty, focusing on the fictional Central Police Force and starring Martin Compston, Vicky McClure, Adrian Dunbar and Craig Parkinson, is a police anti-corruption series for BBC. It's tense, gripping and heart-stopping in equal measure. Brilliant television, but not for those of a nervous disposition! The quality of modern television productions and the myriad techniques involved that include writing, scripting, acting, filming, lighting and sound through to editing and post production, just seems to get better and better – the bar seemingly being raised even higher with each production. Awe inspiring!

On 20th November, real life at Buckingham Palace was plunged into crisis following a BBC interview with Prince Andrew about his association with American financier and sex offender, the late Jeffrey Epstein. The Duke of York announced that he was stepping down from all his royal engagements with immediate effect as the scandal had become a "major disruption" to the Royal Family. One cannot help but feel sorry for, yet admire Her Majesty The Queen for remaining characteristically stoic and dignified throughout what has undoubtedly become another 'annus horribilis'.

On 24th November Sydney-born writer, critic, poet and broadcaster, Clive James passed away aged 80, having been diagnosed with leukaemia in 2010. Famous for his very dry wit and shows such as 'Clive James on Television', the Australian died in Cambridge 'surrounded by his family and his books'.

Then on Tuesday 26th November celebrity chef and culinary great Gary Rhodes OBE died aged just 59. Known for his gelled spiky hair, love of British food and the television series Rhodes Around Britain as well as appearances on such programmes as Masterchef.

In the closing days of November, London witnessed yet another terrorist attack when two innocent members of the public, Cambridge University graduates 23- year-old Saskia Jones and 25-year-old Jack Merritt were fatally stabbed at London Bridge. Three other people were also injured. The suspect, Usman Khan, who unbelievably was known to the authorities and who already had a prior terrorism conviction to his name had been released from prison early. Khan was wearing a hoax explosives vest and was shot dead by armed police at the scene following brave members of the public apprehending and holding down the suspect.

An early 18th birthday present for Lauren was 2 tickets to see Michael Bublé at the Liverpool M&S Bank Arena on Tuesday 3rd December. She took George with her, and we made a weekend of it by staying for a couple of nights in Liverpool. The immensely popular Canadian crooner, by all accounts was on top form, performing popular numbers such as Feeling Good, Haven't Met You Yet and Cold December Night. Needless to say, both George and Lauren were made up and what a great way to welcome in the festive season.

On Friday 6th December I travelled again to Falmouth University with number one daughter for her interview on Penryn Campus with the School of Film and Television. Lauren felt it went well, in fact it went so well that they gave her an unconditional offer! She was delighted. To have an offer in the bag, before Christmas, took a lot of pressure off for her.

On 7th December Virgin Trains' rail franchise expired. It was the longest running and for more than 22 years Virgin operated the West Coast Main line route. Virgin's last train, the 21.42 to Wolverhampton left London Euston on Saturday evening to be replaced early on Sunday morning 8th December with Avanti West Coast (owned by First Trenitalia, a partnership between First Group based in Aberdeen and Italian business Trenitalia), the new franchise operators. George, who was visiting close friends in London over this particular weekend, travelled down to Euston from Lancaster on one of the final Virgin Pendolino services and returned back to the north west of England on a new Avanti service.

Forty three people sadly lost their lives in India in the early hours (local time) of Sunday 8th December, when an inferno ripped through a four storey bag factory located in Azad Market in the capital Delhi's busy, old quarter. When the fire broke out many workers were asleep on the factory's third floor.

Fires raged in near 40 degree heat, barely an hour's drive north of beautiful Sydney, which over the weekend of 7th December, was pictured with the famous Harbour Bridge shrouded in a hazardous, orange-coloured, smokey haze. Fast forward to the end of December and amidst a continuing heatwave across Australia, many fires still burned out of control, temperatures exceeded a scorching 40 degrees centigrade (104 degrees Fahrenheit) in every state and thousands were forced to flee to beaches to escape the bushfires racing with breakneck speed to the coast.

On Monday 9th December New Zealand experienced an eruption of its White island volcano. Alarmingly, tourists were seen walking inside the volcano's crater moments before it exploded. At least 16 people were killed and about twenty suffered serious burns. Located off the coast of the country's North Island, White Island or Whakaari is a highly active volcano and last erupted in 2016.

On the same day, one of the last surviving RAF Battle of Britain pilots from WW2, Flight Lieutenant Maurice Mounsdon died aged101. Maurice Mounsdon was a member of what Sir Winston Churchill called 'The Few', a group of around 3,000 pilots who bravely fought in the skies above southern England to fend off higher enemy numbers in the German Luftwaffe.

Thursday 12th December was of course a General Election day and I along with millions of others cast my vote. The following day the Conservative party under Boris Johnson was returned to power, having run a campaign with the main thrust being 'Get Brexit Done' after they won 365 seats to Labour's 203. For the Tories, with a 'thumping' Commons majority of 80, it was their largest majority since 1987 and meant that the UK would now be able to leave the European Union by the end of January 2020.

On 18 December singer, songwriter, actor and entertainer, Kenny Lynch sadly passed away, aged 81. His hits, Up on the Roof and You Can Never Stop Me Loving You, reached number 10 in 1962 and 1963 respectively. Kenny Lynch also used to tour with the Beatles in the good old days. Again on 18th December Donald Trump became the third POTUS in history to be impeached by the House of Representatives. A trial in the Senate was then set up to decide whether the President remained in office. Senators voted on February 1st 2020, against calling witnesses or admitting new evidence, which paved the way for an acquittal four days later. The two charges were that President Trump abused his power and that he obstructed Congress.

On 20th December, the nation's MPs voted by 358 to 234 in favour of the EU (Withdrawal Agreement) Bill, effectively backing Prime Minister Johnson's plan for the UK to leave the European Union on 31 January 2020.

21st December heralded George's 25th birthday as well as being about as close as you could get to the shortest day and the winter solstice that year. Following his favourite cooked breakfast, a walk in the Trough of Bowland was followed by present opening and an evening spent in the company of his close friends – very fine friends indeed.

On Christmas Eve, Prince Philip, aged 98, returned to Sandringham from hospital just in time for Christmas. The Duke of Edinburgh had been in London's King Edward V11's hospital since Friday 20th December on the advice of his doctor, as a precaution for a pre-existing condition.

Christmas Day heralded the start of a much needed two-week rest from a relentlessly busy working environment for Wendy and me and much needed family time for all. It was a very relaxed affair for the four of us and Wendy's brother, Simon – the first time there had been so few of us around the dinner table for Christmas. Her Majesty The Queen's Christmas Day message acknowledged that 2019 had been "quite bumpy" and that life's path is never "smooth". In the wake of quite a volatile Brexit debate and The Duke of York withdrawing from public life following a BBC interview about his friendship with the late sex offender, Jeffrey Epstein and The Duke of Edinburgh's car crash in January, among other incidents, The Queen advised that taking "small steps" can help heal divisions.

On Boxing Day we headed south in two cars via the M6, M5 and A30 to our holiday home in Wadebridge, Cornwall for more rest and crucially to bring in the next decade, as we did twenty years before for the new millennium.

CHAPTER 32

2020: A New Decade Beckons

New Year's Eve 2019 finally arrived. It was the day in England and Wales when heterosexual civil partnerships were enshrined in law. This had followed lengthy legal wranglings against the law, which had hitherto only allowed same sex couples to enter into civil partnership since 2005. The new law means that heterosexual civil partners will enjoy the same property, inheritance and tax entitlements as married couples and same sex civil partners.

Whilst Lauren ploughed her way through a mound of college homework, Wendy and Simon went around Little Sidings, our holiday home, room by room with notebook and pen, meticulously detailing the jobs still to be done prior to the 2020 letting season kicking off in earnest. Although, right then, no-one could have foreseen the damage that Atlantic Storm Brendan would bring to the UK in mid-January 2020. Unfortunately, severe wind gusts toppled most of the garden wall and fencing, fronting Guineaport Road at Little Sidings, necessitating a complete rebuild and repair at great cost.

Meanwhile, George was back home in the north entertaining his friends and preparing like the rest of us, for the late evening festivities. In the afternoon, I took the mountain bike out on the Camel Trail, Padstow bound, to clear my head, collect my thoughts and shave a bit off the old belly.

And then suddenly the moment had arrived – it was the end of the year and a wrap on an eventful ten years, known as the twenty-tens. Lauren was staying over in Polzeath and celebrating with one of her best friends, Zoe. Around ten to midnight Wendy, Simon and I headed out of Little Sidings, donned in winter coats with a bottle of champers and three glasses in hand and walked along the River Camel a short way and then on to Anneka's bridge where other locals had already gathered.

Prosit Neujahr! as the Germans say. On the stroke of midnight it was out with the old and in with the new as Wadebridge treated us to a 5 minute spectacular firework display. Everyone cheered and I popped the cork on the fizz and got pouring during what constituted the first few seconds of 2020. And thanks to one of George's best mates Johnny – in 2020 we were also introduced to some really cool music by American dream pop duo Victoria Legrand and Alex Scally, aka 'Beach House', who formed in Baltimore in 2004.

Late morning on New Year's Day the three of us drove over to the surfing mecca that is Polzeath, to meet up with Lauren, Zoe and her parents Deanna and Dave (Deanna and Wendy have been friends since early school days). Following coffee, beach walk (where one chap sauntered passed me donned in turquoise swimming shorts and precious little else, looking for all the world like he was out in the midday summer sun) and obligatory surfing photos, taken in the direction of Hayle Bay and the mouth of the Camel, we were treated to bacon butties, tea and Christmas cake on Deanna and Dave's balcony, which offers an enviable view of Polzeath beach and the bay.

Little did we realise that the new year would kick off with an international crisis that would bring the USA and Iran almost to the brink of war. America affected a drone strike assassination of Iran's second in command, leader of the Quds force, Major General Qasem Soleimani in the Iraqi capital of Baghdad, on 3rd January. On 7th January, 50 people were killed and more than 200 injured in a stampede as crowds of Iranians gathered for the burial of Qasem Soleimani in the city of Kerman, South East Iran.

Back in the UK, Her Majesty The Queen, summoned senior royals to Norfolk on 13th January for the 'Sandringham Summit' to discuss the future roles of Prince Harry and his wife Meghan, the Duke and Duchess of Sussex, following the Sussex' surprise announcement that they planned to step back as senior members of 'the firm' and 'transition' to work to become financially independent ("...[they] have made clear that they do not want to be reliant on public funds in their new lives") with a plan to split their time between the UK and Canada. Following the discussions at the Queen's Norfolk home, an historic and unprecedented statement was released by our Monarch, who stated that whilst she would have preferred Harry and Meghan "to remain full-time working members of the Royal Family", the Queen understood, supported and respected the couple's "wish to live a more independent life as a family while remaining a valued part of my family". On 18th January Buckingham Palace announced that Prince

Harry and his wife Meghan would no longer use their HRH titles and would not receive public money for royal duties. Further, the couple would cease representing The Queen. Her Majesty stated that, "It is my whole family's hope that today's agreement allows them to start building a happy and peaceful new life".

On 21st January 77-year old 'Python' – actor, director, author, screenwriter, comedian and historian, Terry Jones passed away. He was most famous for his work with Michael Palin, Eric Idle, John Cleese, Graham Chapman and Terry Gilliam in the 1970's surreal comedy sketch series Monty Python's Flying Circus and subsequent Python films such as Monty Python and the Holy Grail. Fellow Pythons paid tribute with Sir Michael Palin calling Terry Jones, "One of the funniest writer-performers of his generation" and John Cleese tweeted, "[he was] a man of so many talents and such endless enthusiasm". "Spam, Spam, Spam, Spam!...Lovely Spam! Wonderful Spam!"

On 24th January 2020, Lauren turned 18, which was such a joyous occasion and we marked it by opening presents whilst sipping champagne. There was the obligatory birthday photograph by yours truly, followed by a family meal at a renowned, stylish Italian restaurant and then the special day culminated at home watching a thoroughly entertaining video of Lauren's 18 years, painstakingly collated, created and edited by George – who also spent around 18 months creating a beautiful album of photos and memorabilia for his sister. An heirloom to be treasured.

On 26th January, the tragic news emerged from the United States of a helicopter crash in the city of Calabasas, California. American pro basketball icon, Kobe Bryant, his 13-year-old daughter and seven others all sadly lost their lives when their Sikorsky S-76B went down in fog and burst into flames. 41-year-old Kobe, described by former POTUS Barack Obama as "a legend on the court", was considered to be one of the greatest players of all time. A five time National Basketball Association champion and double Olympic gold medallist, Kobe, fresh out of high school, played his entire 20-season career in the NBA with the infamous Los Angeles Lakers.

On 28th January, the nation lost another favourite, broadcaster Nicholas Parsons, who was 96. I have fond memories of watching him front the ITV game show Sale of the Century in the seventies and early eighties. Wendy and I remember bumping into him a few decades ago at a charity, celebrity cricket match in Motspur Park, Surrey, close to where we used to live.

Then of course, at 11.00 p.m. on 31st January 2020 and after 47 years of membership and more than 3 ½ years after a referendum was held on 23rd June 2016 by the outgoing Cameron Government to ask the UK electorate whether we should stay a member of or leave the European Union, we historically left the EU and entered an 11-month transition period. A commemorative 50 pence coin, one of three million to enter circulation at the end of January bears the date '31 January' and the inscription, 'Peace, prosperity and friendship with all nations'. So now the UK looks ahead with bated breath to what life will be like in the ensuing years, post Brexit.

On 5th February 2020 Hollywood giant Issur Danielovitch aka Kirk Douglas, passed away at the incredible age of 103. He was an absolute legend of an actor, whom I grew up with as a kid watching him in many an American western film, typically as a tough guy gunslinger. The son of Jewish Russian immigrants, Kirk Douglas grafted all the way to the top. Known for his rugged good looks and commanding screen presence, Kirk Douglas was one of the last surviving actors from Hollywood's golden age.

The father of acclaimed actor Michael, Joel, Peter and the late Eric and the father-in-law of Michael's wife, actress Catherine Zeta Jones, Kirk Douglas enjoyed an enviable career that spanned more than seven decades. He was an actor, a producer, a director, a writer and a philanthropist, who, in film director Steven Spielberg's words, made a "breath-taking body of work" – in fact some 90 films, including Gunfight at the O.K. Corral (1957), Tough Guys (1986), Lonely are the Brave (1962), 20,000 Leagues Under the Sea (1954), the Heroes of Telemark (1965) and of course his role as the famous earless Dutch painter Vincent van Gogh in Lust for Life (1956). However, his most infamous role was undoubtedly as the Roman slave Spartacus in the 1960 Stanley Kubrick epic of the same name.

Michael Douglas said of his father, "Kirk's life was well lived, and he leaves a legacy in film that will endure for generations to come, and a history as a renowned philanthropist [he left his entire £61 million fortune to charity] who worked to aid the public and bring peace to the planet". Kirk Douglas was indeed Spartacus! R.I.P.

Storm Ciara created havoc on Sunday 9th February. An amber weather warning saw severe gales and heavy rain sweep over the UK, claiming several lives, causing widespread flooding, felling trees and bringing with it, travel chaos. In some areas people were without power and there were 90 mph gusts of wind. More than 100mm of rain fell in a very short time in parts of northern England and northern Wales. Many flights were cancelled, vehicles were overturned and in East Yorkshire the Humber Bridge was closed for only the second time since its construction. The Dartford Crossing in Kent was also closed to traffic and all ferry services from the port of Dover were suspended due to strong winds.

A few days later, Prime Minister Boris Johnson confirmed that the controversial High Speed 2 (HS2) rail link phase 1 (due to be completed 2028-2031) between London and Birmingham and phase 2 from Birmingham to Leeds and from Birmingham to Manchester (due to be completed 2035-2040) would be built.

The coronavirus world pandemic also accelerated during March – more on that later.

On Saturday 4th April 2020, following a three month campaign, the London MP for Holborn and St Pancras and former Director of Public Prosecutions and head of the Crown Prosecution Service, 57-year-old Sir Keir Starmer, the odds-on favourite, was elected as the new Leader of the Labour Party, with 40-year-old Angela Rayner being chosen as Deputy leader.

On 6th April, the acting world lost the legendary British thespian Honor Blackman, who was 94. Famed for her talent, unique voice and beauty and with a career spanning eight decades, I remember Honor Blackman as Cathy Gale, when I was growing up, in re-runs of the popular 1960's series, The Avengers alongside Patrick Macnee's 'John Steed'. But the East London born actress will forever be best remembered as Pussy Galore alongside Sean Connery as 007 in the 1964 Bond classic, Goldfinger.

On 22nd April, Elon Musk's SpaceX programme launched its partially reusable Falcon Heavy (Falcon 9) rocket into space, deploying a seventh batch of some 60 Starlink broadband satellites, bringing the total number deployed into space to 422. The final operating altitude of the satellites was expected to be in the region of 341 miles (550 kilometres) above Earth.

On the penultimate day in April, Prime Minister Boris Johnson and his then fiancée Carrie Symonds, announced the arrival of a baby son, whom they named Wilfred Lawrie Nicholas Johnson. Wilfred and Lawrie were the couples' grandfathers and Nicholas was a tribute to Dr Nick Price and Dr Nick Hart, both of whom saved the prime minister's life from coronavirus.

The end of May and early part of June 2020 also saw violence, unrest, mass protests and anti-racism demonstrations erupt in cities across the USA and in other nations, including the UK, following the horrendous killing on 25th May in the town of Powderhorn, Minneapolis, Minnesota, of 46-year-old African-American George Floyd, whilst in police custody. Video footage depicting the arrest outside a shop, sickeningly shows white police officer Derek Chauvin, kneeling on George Floyd's neck whilst the poor man was pinned down. The police officer was subsequently charged with the killing and understandably this case served to reignite people's anger, Stateside, over police killings of black Americans. In London, defying social distancing rules, masked and gloved protesters came together in an unlawful and risky gathering during coronavirus and knelt and held a minute's silence, followed by chants of "no justice, no peace" and "black lives matter". And in Bristol over the weekend of 6th June 2020, protesters pulled down a statue of 17th Century slave trader Edward Colston and dumped it in the harbour. Barely a week later, ahead of more protests, statues such as that of Sir Winston Churchill were boarded up due to fears they could be vandalised – Prime Minister Johnson calling the situation "absurd and shameful" that the statue of our wartime leader could be vandalised because he had expressed opinions then which were "unacceptable to us today", but Sir Winston remained a hero for his steadfast and unflinching leadership in saving the nation from "fascist and racist tyranny". The Cenotaph in Whitehall, the bust of Nelson Mandela and other key statues were also unusually covered up in early June 2020. In the US President Trump said that Mr Floyd's death had "filled Americans with horror, anger and grief". R.I.P. George Floyd.

30th May in the space flight calendar was a monumental day. Following the end of the space shuttle programme in 2011, nine years later at 8.22 p.m. British Summer Time, (3.22 p.m. Florida, Stateside, Eastern Standard Time) Elon Musk's private company SpaceX catapulted astronauts Doug Hurley and Bob Behnken from Kennedy's world famous 39A launch pad into orbit aboard the Dragon capsule, sitting on top of the Falcon-9 rocket on a 19-hour journey to dock with the International Space Station. The Dragon capsule had been named 'Capsule Endeavour', after the combined endeavour of NASA, SpaceX and the USA following the retirement of the shuttle programme in 2011 and also for sentimental reasons – the two astronauts both had their maiden flights on board the shuttle Endeavour and it meant so much, keeping the name alive. The two-man crew were expected to stay on board the ISS for between one and four months. The iconic, landmark launch set against a background of a modern day tragedy – the Covid-19 pandemic and all that this crisis entailed from screening to social distancing and of course not to mention weather problems, saw the American crew successfully taking off from US soil for the first time in almost a decade.

Immediately following take-off, the Falcon headed out to the Atlantic in a north-easterly direction. At the 2½ minute mark the lower, re-usable, first stage of the Falcon rocket separated and made its way back to SpaceX' autonomous (robot-controlled) spaceport drone ship for retrieval out at sea, called 'Of Course I still Love You'. Approximately 8½ minutes after lift-off, Doug and Bob were safely through the earth's atmosphere and tearing through orbit. The new space capsule was being trialled by the astronauts, so en route to the ISS they tested out new equipment and procedures and took control of the capsule themselves during manual flying exercises in a craft that had touch screen commands and no control stick. In the future, it is hoped to send at least four astronauts up into space at a time. To keep the costs down, NASA will no longer own the space vehicles – it will purchase this 'taxi' service offered initially by Elon Musk's company and later, by other business giants like Boeing and Sir Richard Branson's Virgin. NASA's relationship with private space travel companies also means it can channel billions of saved dollars into the more challenging undertaking – that of landing men and women on the moon once more and interplanetary travel to Mars. The lunar programme called 'Artemis' aims to land astronauts on the moon again by 2024.

At 3.30 p.m. BST on Sunday 31st May, in what was a fully automated procedure, SpaceX' Dragon capsule successfully manoeuvred underneath and docked to a port on the ISS' bow. The initial 'soft capture' docking, slightly ahead of schedule, occurred at 3.16 p.m. BST right over the border of China and Mongolia as the sun was setting. The hard capture involving 12 seals or hooks, occurred at 3.30 pm – the air-tight seal completing the docking process. What followed was almost two hours of vestibule pressurisation, leak, temperature and equipment checks, followed by the hatch opening at 6.02 p.m. BST. In a historic and euphoric moment, astronauts Doug Hurley and Bob Behnken 'floated' into the ISS and were welcomed aboard to join the rest of the space station crew – fellow NASA astronaut Chris Cassidy and Russian cosmonauts Anatoly Ivanishin and Ivan Vagner to handshakes and hugs all round. This SpaceX vehicle was the first mission to the ISS carrying humans.

Doug and Bob's brief was to test all the onboard scientific and maintenance systems and to provide feedback to the NASA and SpaceX engineers and analysts. The space-travelling duo could now claim a Stars and Stripes flag placed on the ISS by astronauts from the last space shuttle flight back in 2011. As an incentive to the astronauts that were to follow, the Atlantis shuttle crew left the American flag behind once they left the ISS. This particular US flag is highly symbolic as it flew with astronauts John W. Young and Robert Crippen aboard Columbia, on the first orbital shuttle flight on 12th April 1981. The flag was subsequently returned to Earth ready for the next space crew to journey into orbit.

On 31st May 2020, my all-time favourite actor and action hero, director, producer, multi-Oscar award winner and nominee, movie legend, male masculinity icon, Clint Eastwood, celebrated his 90th birthday.

On 10th June, Prince Philip, the Duke of Edinburgh celebrated his milestone 99th birthday with Her Majesty The Queen. To mark the occasion, the Queen and the Duke who have been married for 73 years, were photographed together standing side-by-side in the quadrangle at Windsor Castle, where they had been isolating due to coronavirus.

On 18th June, Forces' Sweetheart and one of the nation's best loved entertainers, Dame Vera Lynn, sadly passed away at the grand old age of 103. Dame Vera's songs such as 'We'll Meet Again', 'The White Cliffs of Dover', 'I'll Be Seeing You' and 'If Only I Had Wings', helped to bring a little cheer and raise the morale of the troops during the second world war. Six weeks before she died, in the midst of the Covid-19 pandemic and ahead of VE Day 75, Dame Vera, reflecting on the heroism of World War 2, said that simple acts of bravery and sacrifice still define our nation. Labour leader Sir Keir Starmer said of Dame Vera, "Her songs still speak to the nation in 2020 just as they did in 1940", while Defence Secretary Ben Wallace said that Dame Vera Lynn "lifted our nation and its Armed Forces in their moment of maximum peril". During Dame Vera Lynn's funeral on 10th July 2020, as a mark of respect, two Spitfires made three, midday passes over the funeral procession as it made its way through Ditchling in East Sussex, home of the famous singer for fifty years.

Then on 6th July, the world lost another great, Italian composer Ennio Morricone, who died in Rome, aged 91. Morricone was also a trumpet player and conductor who composed hundreds of scores for film and television. He is perhaps most famous for his collaboration with Italian film director Sergio Leone and particularly for his powerful scoring of the so called 'Spaghetti westerns' in the 1960's.

On 10th July 2020, the soccer world lost Jack Charlton (AKA John Charlton OBE DL). He was 85. Along with his younger brother Bobby, Jack Charlton was part of the winning England 1966 World Cup squad. Jack's playing career was spent entirely with Leeds United from 1950 to 1973 as a defender and he later became a football manager at Sheffield Wednesday, Middlesbrough, Newcastle and of course he coached the Republic of Ireland national side for a decade from 1986 to 1996, during which time, the Irish side achieved unprecedented success.

On 17th July 2020, the Queen's granddaughter Princess Beatrice married Edoardo Mapelli Mozzi in a secret ceremony at Windsor Castle, attended by the Queen, the Duke of Edinburgh and close family members.

The 4th August 2020 marked the 150th anniversary of an organisation that was originally called 'The British Society for Aid to the Sick and Wounded in War'. This famous society became known as the British Red Cross in 1905, becoming an integral part of an umbrella of global humanitarian organisations, wrapping its angel wings around and supplying aid during and in the aftermath of disasters and health crises, world-wide.

Also on 4th August, after a two month visit to the International Space Station, astronauts Doug Hurley and Bob Behnken plummeted through a fiery atmosphere and returned to Earth...or rather, water, with a historic, quadruple parachute-aided splashdown of their SpaceX Dragon Capsule called 'Endeavour' – just off Florida's Gulf coast and south of Pensacola. Splashdown was at 14.48 Eastern Daylight Time / 19.48 British Summer Time.

On 13th August, our beautiful daughter Lauren received her A-Level results just after 8 a.m. via email, achieving fantastic grades in all three of her subjects: English, Media Studies and Psychology. This brilliant news came on the back of Lauren gaining an unconditional offer to study television production at Leeds Trinity University in September 2020, for three years. Due to the Covid crisis and amidst controversy and what was described as a "huge mess" as the exams appeal guidance was hastily withdrawn, hours after publishing it, Lauren's year made history as her actual A level summer exams were cancelled due to lockdown and her final marks were estimated - supposed to be based on her mock exam results, course work, assessments and predicted grades, although whether predicted grades were actually taken into account, remains to be seen.

Then shortly afterwards amidst calls for the Education Secretary Gavin Williamson to resign, the government u-turned and it was announced that A-level and GCSE students in England were to be awarded the grades estimated by their teacher alone, rather than hitherto, by an algorithm – a formula which took into account an estimated grade, a ranking compared with every other pupil in a particular class and then together with schools' previous years' performance in each subject (previous years' summer grades), the figures were crunched and spat out to give a final grade. The idea behind the algorithm or mathematical formula method was that in each school, pupils would receive similar grades compared with those awarded to their school in previous years. Teachers' rankings would then decide those students receiving the top grades in their particular schools. The dramatic U-turn by the Tory government came on the back of a huge uproar after a whopping 40% of students saw their result downgraded by the exams regulator, Ofqual. Days later and at the eleventh hour, exam board Pearson held back many BTec results just prior to release and regraded them to bring them in line with A-levels and GCSEs. Heads said the last minute changes were unacceptable and unfair on students who had already suffered so much disruption to their education during Covid. The Education Secretary was subsequently urged to review the handling of both A-level and GCSE results in the wake of both sets of exams being cancelled due to the coronavirus pandemic.

Head teachers warned of "volatility" in the 2020 A-level results and further that some grades – lower than expected appeared to be "unfair and unfathomable". Indeed, in England more than a third – some 36% of A-level entrants received a lower grade than teachers predicted. Prime Minister Boris Johnson was subsequently to blame the 2020 summer exam results cock-up on a "mutant algorithm". It was somewhat telling that Labour leader Sir Keir Starmer described the eleventh hour changes as "shambolic" and that the system "smacks of incompetence".

August 15th 2020 marked the 75th anniversary of VJ Day, or Victory over Japan Day (also known as Victory in the Pacific Day, or V-P Day), which signified the end of the Second World War as Imperial Japan officially surrendered. Here in the UK, the Royal Family led our nation's commemorations of the 75th anniversary with Her Majesty The Queen thanking those "who fought so valiantly".

The Queen added, "Those of us who remember the conclusion of the Far East campaign, whether on active service overseas, or waiting for news at home, will never forget the jubilant scenes and overwhelming sense of relief".

On 17th August, the highest temperature on Earth was officially recorded in California's Death Valley National Park, when the mercury reached 130 degrees Fahrenheit (54.4 degrees Celsius).

On the television front, I became mesmerised by Allan Cubitt's 3-series, Irish-British crime drama 'The Fall', brought to Netflix in August 2020. Starring Gillian Anderson, Jamie Dornan and John Lynch, the series centres around a Met Police Superintendent (Anderson) brought in by the Police Service of Northern Ireland (PSNI) to review an ongoing murder investigation. This tense series, which was first screened between May 2013 and September 2016, is gripping, psychologically disturbing, shocking, horrific and an amazing piece of television.

On 10th September actress Dame Diana Rigg passed away aged 82. In a long and very distinguished career Dame Diana, a star of both stage and screen had many memorable roles. I remember as a lad watching her play Emma Peel in the '60's television series The Avengers and as the only 'Mrs James Bond', as Tracy in 'On Her Majesty's Secret Service' where she married George Lazenby's 007 character. More recently Dame Diana played Olenna, Head of House Tyrell in the cult television series Game of Thrones, from 2013 to 2017.

In late August Steve, our Medical Photography manager, aka work's 'Mr. Fix-it', beer lover and connoisseur, barbeque king, Volkswagen enthusiast, Mr nice guy and my close colleague for the last 7½ years at Blackpool's Victoria Hospital, was shockingly diagnosed with Stage 4 metastasised cancer. With a positive mindset, buoyed up by all the messages of support and love from his family, many friends and work colleagues, Steve reluctantly stepped away from the job he loved so much on Friday 11th September 2020, to undergo vital chemotherapy. Poor fellow celebrated his landmark 50th birthday the following month under the double whammy of having cancer during Covid-19 (just before Christmas 2020 Steve also contracted Coronavirus). All our thoughts are with him for his treatment and recuperation journey. This all marked a time of change at work as well as a period of uncertainty I suppose. Now down to just Chimane and me as the only two medical photographers covering a large, very busy west Lancashire hospital, we got the go ahead to advertise for two new medical photographers on a 12 month contract. A senior colleague and I interviewed for these posts during the third week in October and selected the two best candidates. Short term, we required help with our daily ophthalmology and Saturday tele-dermatology clinics. All I'll say is, thank God for Jane Gray from the Manchester Royal Eye Hospital and her wonderful team, who came to our rescue! Simultaneously, we were informed that we needed to vacate our office at some stage to relocate to one end of our photographic studio, which first needed to be gutted to accommodate the growing medical photography team (the move took place at the end of January 2021).

On 12th September, Wendy and I celebrated our 28th wedding anniversary, during which, I reflected on almost three decades of wonderful married life. My birthday, the following day coincided with the 80th anniversary of the Battle of Britain, with a memorial service held in Westminster Abbey, followed with a flypast by four iconic WW2 planes – three Supermarine Spitfires and a Hawker Hurricane.

On Sunday 20th September, after much waiting and anticipation, Wendy and I took Lauren to Leeds Trinity University to begin her three-year degree course in television production. With a packed car full of her belongings, we successfully moved Lauren into her cosy first floor campus flat, complete with small, but functional ensuite. Due to Covid social distancing measures, we were only given a two hour time-slot and shortly after 1 o'clock we hugged our precious daughter goodbye and quietly left her to embark on her new adventure. Understandably there were a few initial nerves and collywobbles – not surprising because the poor girl had been stuck at home for the previous 6 months due to Covid, had her A levels cancelled and had largely been deprived of large scale social interaction. However Lauren is a strong girl and she's totally got this. As I put on my 'Facebook' post, to misquote LOTR's Gandalf, "Now come your Uni days…may they be blessed". My beautiful daughter has achieved much already and I have no doubt whatsoever that she will achieve many more successes throughout her life's journey. I'm proud of you beyond words, Lauren and you are so loved!

On 31st October 2020, the acting world lost the amazing Sean Connery (aka Sir Thomas Sean Connery), who was 90. For me Oscar-winning Scottish actor Sean Connery was the archetypal James Bond, the first actor to play Ian Fleming's 007 character. His body of work included seven Bond films between 1962 and 1983 as well as great motion pictures such as The Hill, A Bridge Too Far, Highlander, Indiana Jones and the Last Crusade, The Hunt for Red October and The Rock. Some of my favourite Connery film quotes are from A Bridge Too Far, as Major General Urquhart on being presented with a cup of tea from Corporal Hancock:

"Hancock, I've lunatics laughing at me from the woods. My original plan has been scuppered now that the jeeps haven't arrived. My communications are completely broken down. Do you really believe any of that can be helped by a cup of tea?" (Corporal Hancock) *"Couldn't hurt, sir"*.

From The Rock as John Patrick Mason:

"Womack! Why am I not surprised you piece of shit!"

From Diamonds are Forever:

(Plenty O'Toole) *"Hi, I'm Plenty…Plenty O'Toole"*.

(James Bond)" *…Named after your father perhaps?"*

From Goldfinger:

(Pussy Galore) *"My name is Pussy Galore"*.

(James Bond) *"I must be dreaming"*.

On Saturday 7th November, following an agonising, nail-biting wait since election night on 3rd, which could have seen the result go either way, news broke that Democrat Joseph Robinette Biden Jr (Joe Biden) had won the state of Pennsylvania to take him over the crucial 270 electoral college seats required to win him the 2020 USA presidential election. Pending any legal challenges from an unhappy, outgoing President Trump, who was not at all of the mind to concede too quickly, if at all, Joe Biden was set to become the 46th POTUS on 20th January 2021. He previously served for two terms as the 47th American Vice-President from 2009 to 2017 under President Barack Obama. President elect Biden gained more than 74 million votes, more than any other president elect in history. He will also be the oldest president. Joe Biden's running mate, Kamala Harris will become the first female, the first black and the first Asian-American vice-president.

Due to Covid, Remembrance Sunday on 8th November led by the Queen, was a somewhat toned down, socially distanced service at the Cenotaph in London's Whitehall, with less than 30 veterans in attendance and the public banned for the first time. Following the customary two-minute silence at 11.00 a.m., Prince Charles, the Prince of Wales laid a wreath on behalf of the Queen, who looked on from the Foreign, Commonwealth and Development Office building.

On 14th November the sad news emerged that legendary English television presenter, chat show and game show host, comedian and singer, Des O'Connor (aka Desmond Bernard O'Connor, CBE) had passed away, aged 88. Over the years, the popular crooner had notched up 36 albums, had four singles in the top ten and a number one hit called, 'I Pretend'. For many years, Des O'Connor, who also performed more than a thousand one man shows at the London Palladium, was part of our lives especially on Saturday evening television. The following day, legendary former Liverpool, Tottenham and England international football goalkeeper, Ray Clemence, MBE, sadly died aged 72. Among his accolades Ray Clemence was capped for England 61 times.

Following a successful demo flight back in May 2020, at 00.27 GMT on Monday 16th November, American astronauts Commander Michael Hopkins, Shannon Walker and Victor Glover, together with Japanese astronaut Soichi Noguchi (known as Crew-1), who would spend the next six months in space, blasted off from Florida's Kennedy Space Centre aboard SpaceX' Dragon capsule perched atop a Falcon-9 rocket bound for the International Space Station (ISS). The launch was conducted by the United States space agency Nasa using the transport hardware in effect as a taxi (astronaut capsule and rocket) provided by private space transportation services company SpaceX. The dragon capsule docked just as the 410 km high ISS was flying over the American state of Idaho. Many microgravity experiments were planned, together with at least four space walks, one of which, was to fit MDA UK's Colka communications terminal that would enable astronauts to link with family and scientists on Earth, utilising home broadband speeds via radio equipment. Crew-1 made history on this the first completely certified, commercial space 'taxi' system designed for crew / crew rotational transport. Crew-1 were also the very first international crew of four to take off into space on an American commercial Dragon capsule.

On 18th November, as part of what Prime Minister Johnson called a 'green industrial revolution' to help tackle climate change, the government announced that from 2030 there would be a ban on all new petrol and diesel cars in the UK, although some hybrid vehicles would still be allowed.

On 22nd November, the mountaineering world lost "the father of modern mountain rescue in Scotland", the legendary mountaineer, search and rescuer and author, Dr Hamish MacInnes OBE, FRSGS, who was 90.

Also in November 2020 I watched the remarkable fourth series of 'The Crown' starring Olivia Colman, Tobias Menzies, Helena Bonham-Carter, Gillian Anderson, Emma Corrin, Erin Doherty et al. The Crown charts the life of Queen Elizabeth 11 from her marriage to Prince Philip, Duke of Edinburgh in 1947 through to the present day. Having just caught up with Season 3, which covers Huddersfield's Harold Wilson being elected Prime Minister in 1964 through to the Queen's Silver Jubilee in 1977, the 10-episode, Series 4 introduced the characters of former prime minister Margaret Thatcher and Princess Diana. We binge-watched the entire series!

Meanwhile after three weeks of quality entertainment, the final of 'I'm a Celebrity Get Me Out of Here!' 2020 culminated in author and podcaster Giovanna Fletcher winning and being crowned the first ever Queen of the Castle, with Radio 1 DJ Jordan North coming second and television host Vernon Kay landing third place. Due to coronavirus travel restrictions this year's series hosted by Ant McPartlin and Declan Donnelly and normally filmed in Australia, took place at Gwrych Castle in Abergele, North Wales. Giovanna, wife of McFly's Tom Fletcher, exclaimed after her win, "I can't believe it, this has been the most amazing experience".

On 7th December the mountaineering world lost Douglas Keith Scott CBE to cancer at the age of 79. In his long mountaineering career, Doug Scott climbed many of the highest peaks on Earth, which included some 30 first ascents, but none more so than being the first person to summit the world's number one, Mount Everest, via the notoriously difficult south-west face route, together with Dougal Haston on 24th September 1975 – the famous expedition led by Sir Chris Bonington. Mount Everest had a then height of 29,028 ft / 8,848m (from December 2020 the new height including the snow cap on the summit, is officially recognised by Nepal and China as being 8,848.86m / 29,032 ft). I'm so glad that I got to see Doug Scott at the Royal Geographical Society in Kensington back in November 2018, lecturing alongside fellow renowned climbers, Sir Chris Bonington and Paul Braithwaite. R.I.P. Doug Scott.

On 10th December, actress Dame Barbara Windsor sadly succumbed to Alzheimer's at the age of 83. The much loved star of stage and screen and latterly ambassador for the Alzheimer's Society since 2014, was perhaps best remembered for her roles in the Carry On comedy films and as landlady of the Queen Vic, Peggy Mitchell in the popular soap EastEnders.

On Saturday 12th December Sir Richard Branson's Virgin Galactic company undertook an historic, first crewed test flight of its rocket propelled space tourist plane - the reusable Unity vehicle taking off from a commercial spaceport located in New Mexico, USA that has been specifically designed and built to cater for the exciting prospect of space tourist flights, due to commence in 2021.

On 20th December, Formula 1 motor racing ace, Lewis Hamilton won the BBC Sports Personality of the Year 2020 – his second time winning the award. Lewis Hamilton equalled Michael Schumacher's record of seven world titles with four championships on the trot in 2020 and he also exceeded Schumacher's total of 91 Grand Prix wins. Lewis Hamilton was knighted in the New Year's Honours list.

With EU and UK negotiators talking through the night and almost at the eleventh hour on Christmas Eve 2020 the European Union and the UK reached a post-Brexit trade deal, Prime Minister Boris Johnson declaring that "We have taken back control of our laws and our destiny". In the aftermath the PM promised to concentrate on "levelling up the country" and "spreading opportunity", to "deliver for people who felt left behind". The UK exited EU trading rules on New Year's Eve 2020, eleven months after officially leaving the 27-member European Union on 31st January 2020. During this time leaders on both sides needed this period to negotiate a deal for life afterwards. From 1st January 2021, the EU and the UK formed two separate markets. The UK government went on to say that "We have taken back control of our money, borders, laws, trade and our fishing waters". European Commission President Ursula Von der Leyen described the deal as, "good, fair and balanced". British businesses were collectively holding their breath as they had already suffered so much with the Covid-19 pandemic and were not looking forward to tariffs on their exports or taxes on imports being introduced and indeed possible further disruption at the port of Dover and elsewhere with border checks and stops – should a Brexit deal not have been reached.

Over the Christmas weekend many parts of the UK were battered by heavy rain and high winds from Storm Bella, with gusts of more than 100 mph recorded.

The theme of the Queen's 2020 Christmas Day message was one of reassurance following a terrible year with the ongoing coronavirus pandemic, with Her Majesty saying that for those having to cope without friends and family that they "are not alone" and that all people really wanted for Christmas "was a simple hug or a squeeze of the hand". The Queen said that in spite of all the social distancing measures the health crisis had actually brought us all closer. "Even in the darkest nights there is hope in the new dawn". The Queen praised the many acts of kindness and said that the Royal Family had been greatly inspired by the large numbers volunteering to do their part to help.

"In the United Kingdom and around the world, people have risen magnificently to the challenges of the year, and I am so proud and moved by this quiet, indomitable spirit."

On 9th April 2021, flags around the nation flew at half mast to mark the passing of Her Majesty The Queen's 'liege man of life and limb' and 'strength and stay all these years', Prince Philip, Duke of Edinburgh, who was 99. The Duke was highly respected around the world as a devoted consort and huge support to the Queen for the best part of 70 years. Indeed he was the longest serving consort in British history. Prince Philip, who was two months and one day shy of his 100th birthday, passed away peacefully at Windsor Castle. He had been married to the Queen for more than 73 years since 20th November 1947. The royal couple had four children, eight grandchildren and ten great-grandchildren.

The former polo player, carriage driver and Royal Navy officer who saw active service during World War 2, retired from public life in August 2017, having undertaken some 22,219 solo engagements since 1952, in addition to the many thousands carried out with the Queen. In January 2019, the Duke emerged unharmed from a serious accident in which he rolled his Land Rover on the edge of the Sandringham estate. Two women in another car were injured.

Prince Philip was renowned for his strong views, strength of character and the occasional gaffe. Throughout his life he was involved with a plethora of interests, from wildlife and the environment to industry. Prince Philip was the architect of the Duke of Edinburgh's Award and since its inception on 1st September 1956, the scheme has been phenomenally successful in the development of young people through involvement in myriad outdoor activities. I was one of many thousands of people lucky enough to benefit from undertaking the award scheme and had the privilege of meeting His Royal Highness for my gold award presentation at St. James's Palace in March 1983.

HRH was truly 'an extraordinary man' who had 'an extraordinary life'.

Prince Philip, Duke of Edinburgh 1921-2021.

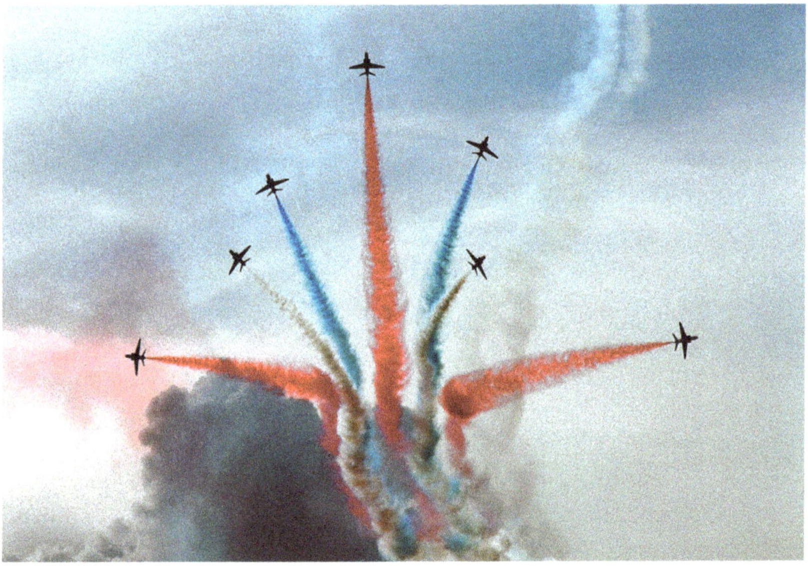

RAF Red Arrows display performing at Windermere, Cumbria, July 2006.

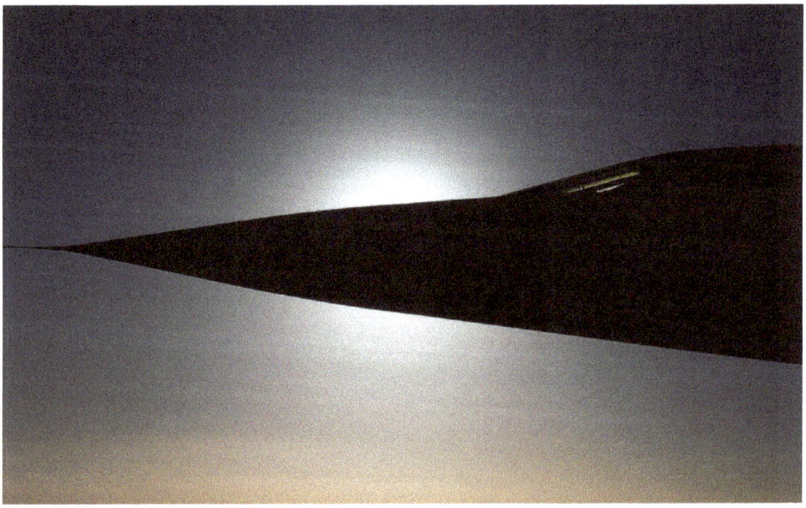

Flagship Concorde G-BOAC, Manchester, George's 10th birthday, December 2004.

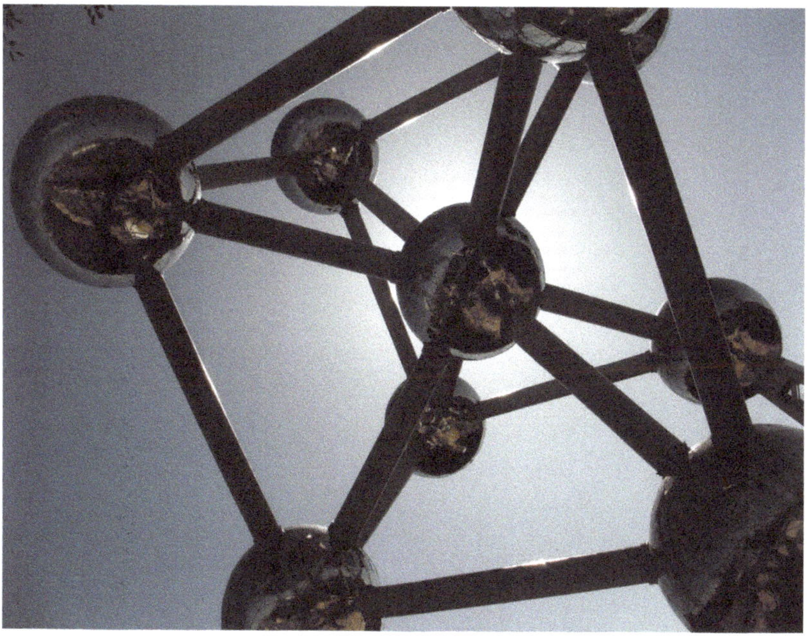

The 1957 constructed, 102 metre-high Atomium, Heysel Plateau, North Brussels, Belgium, 15th August 2009.

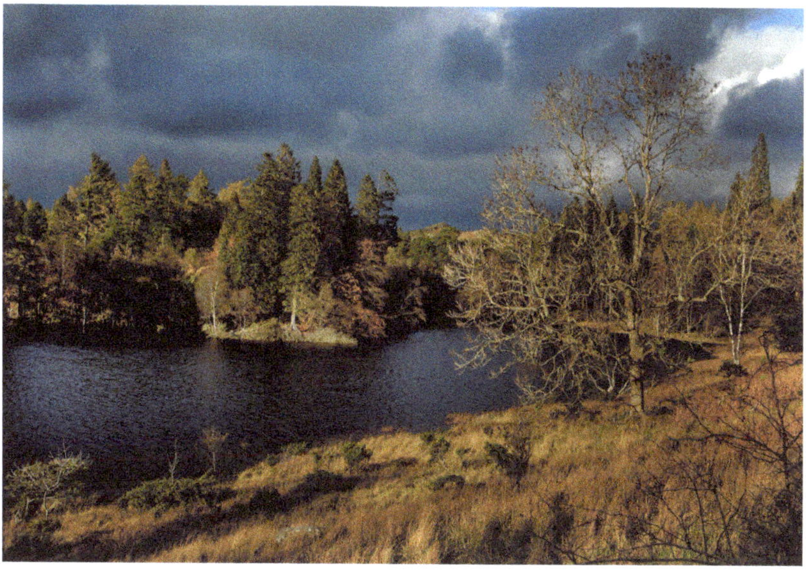

Tarn Hows, Lake District, Cumbria, February 2012.

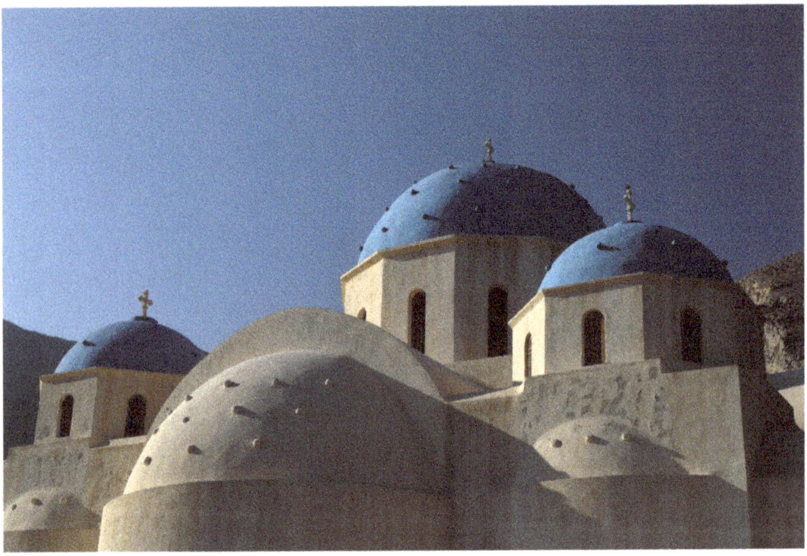

Santorini family holiday, end of July 2013.

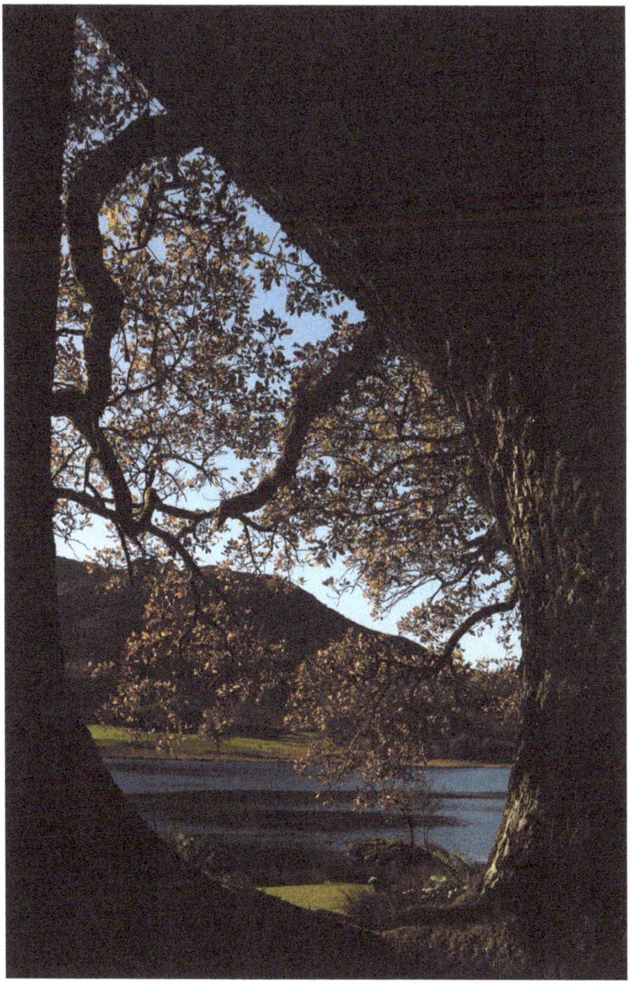

Rydal Water, Lake District, Cumbria, October 2017.

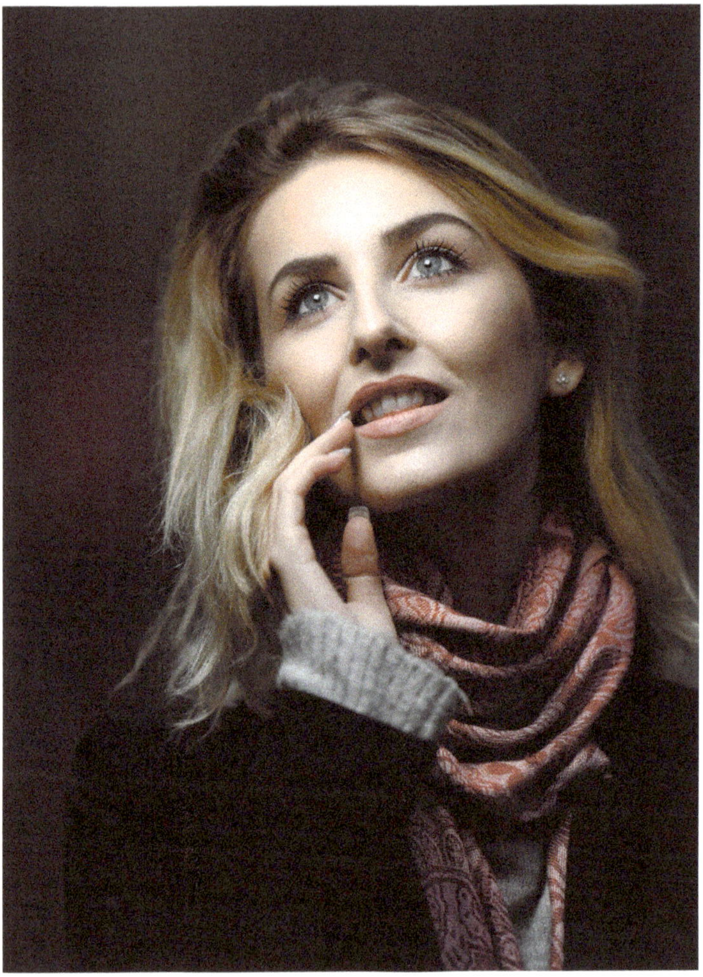

Professional model Amber Tutton, Nikon portraiture masterclass, London, November 2017.

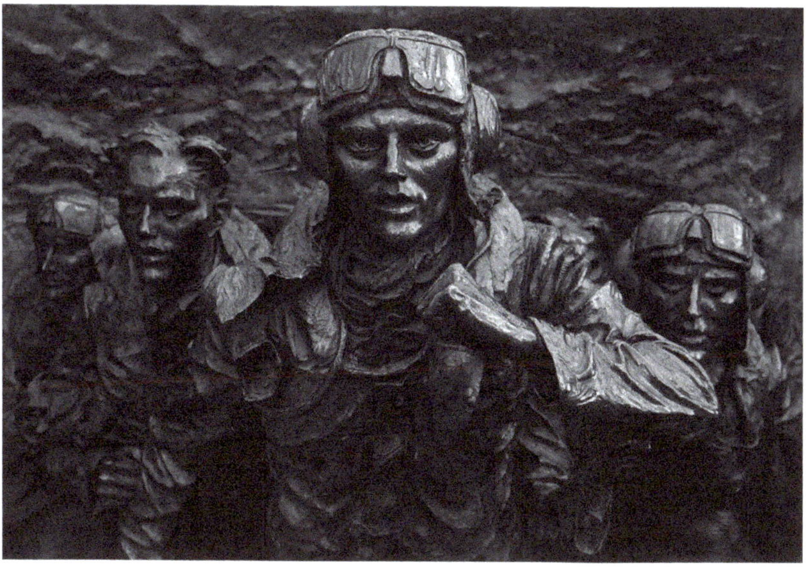

Per Ardua Ad Astra, RAF Memorial, Victoria Embankment,
London, February 2018.

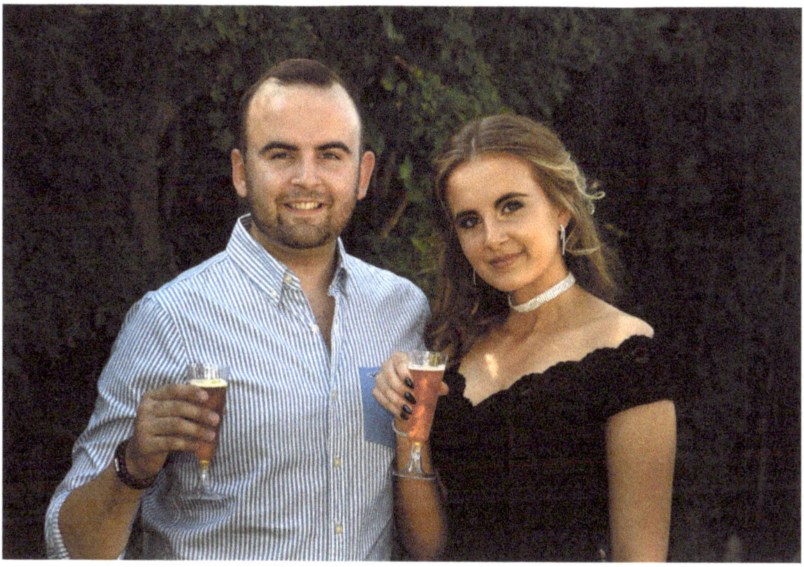

George and Lauren on the evening of Lauren's
High School Prom, 26th June 2018.

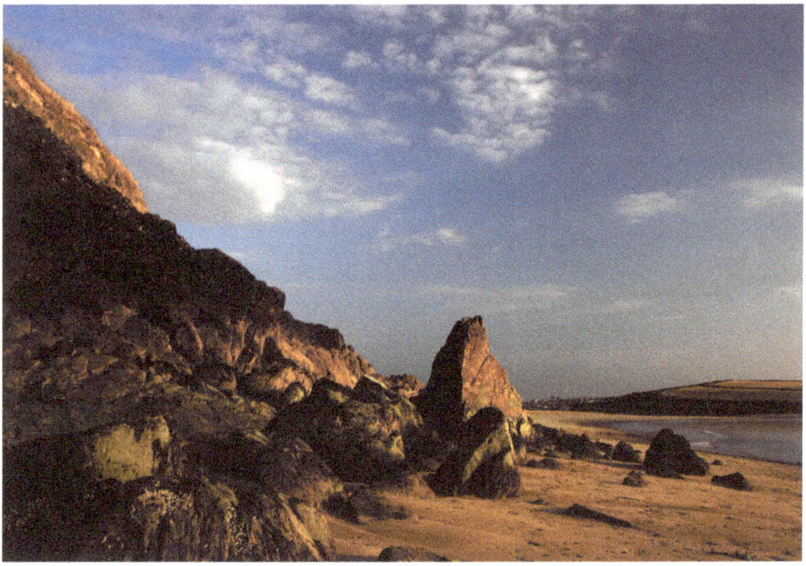

Daymer Bay, Cornwall, July, 2018.

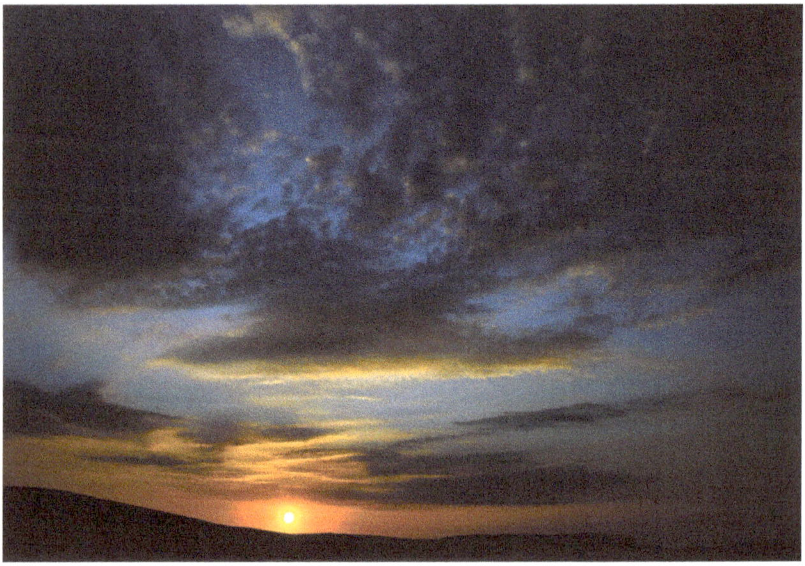

The Camel Estuary from Rock, Cornwall, July 2018.

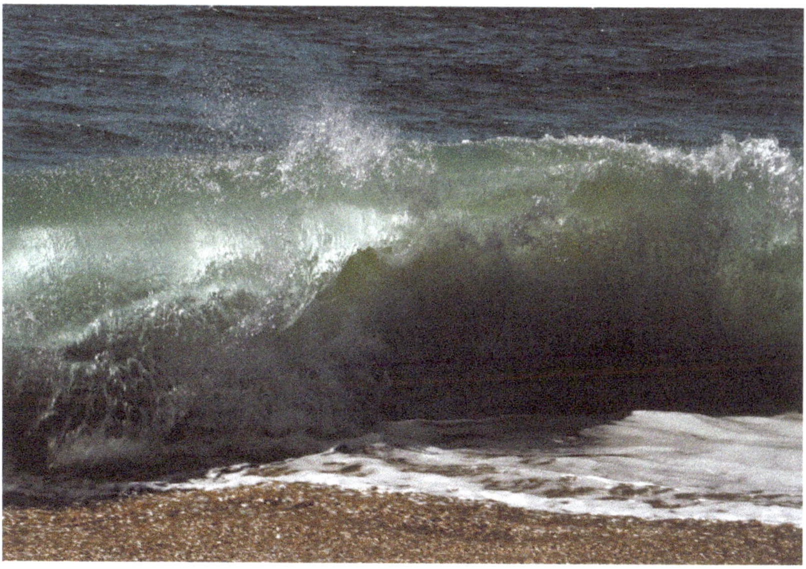

Waves crashing on Constantine Bay Beach, Cornwall, July 2018.

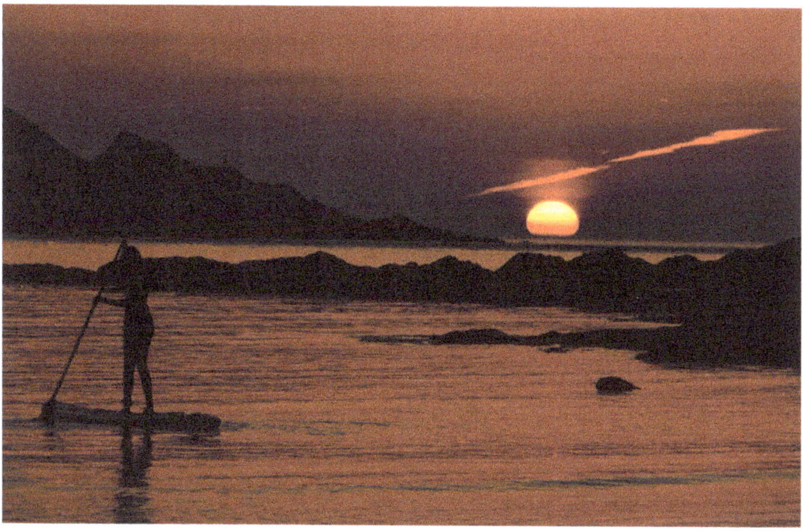

Daymer Bay Sunset, Cornwall, July 2018.

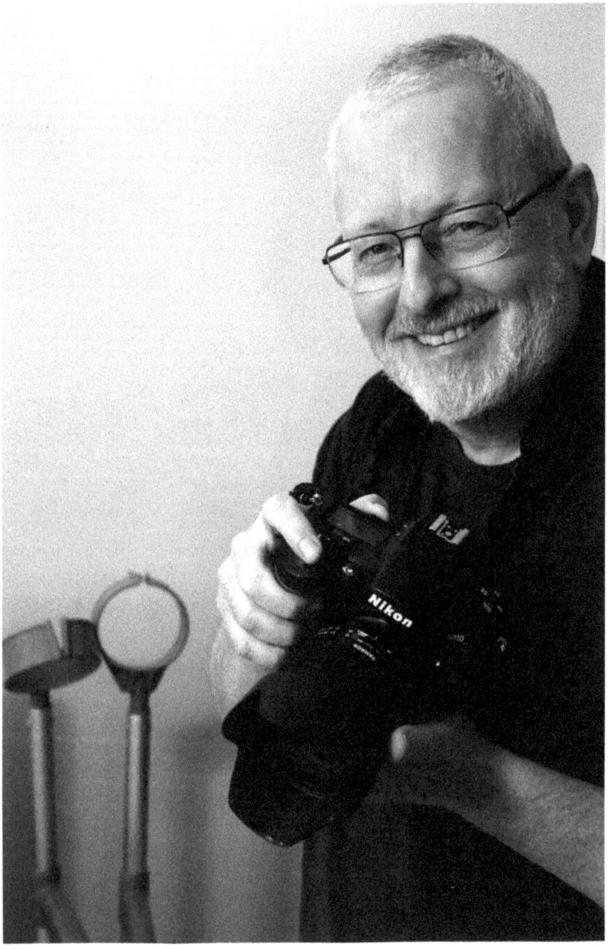

My mate Pete (Peter Goadby-Watt), Hitchin, Hertfordshire,
2nd February 2019.

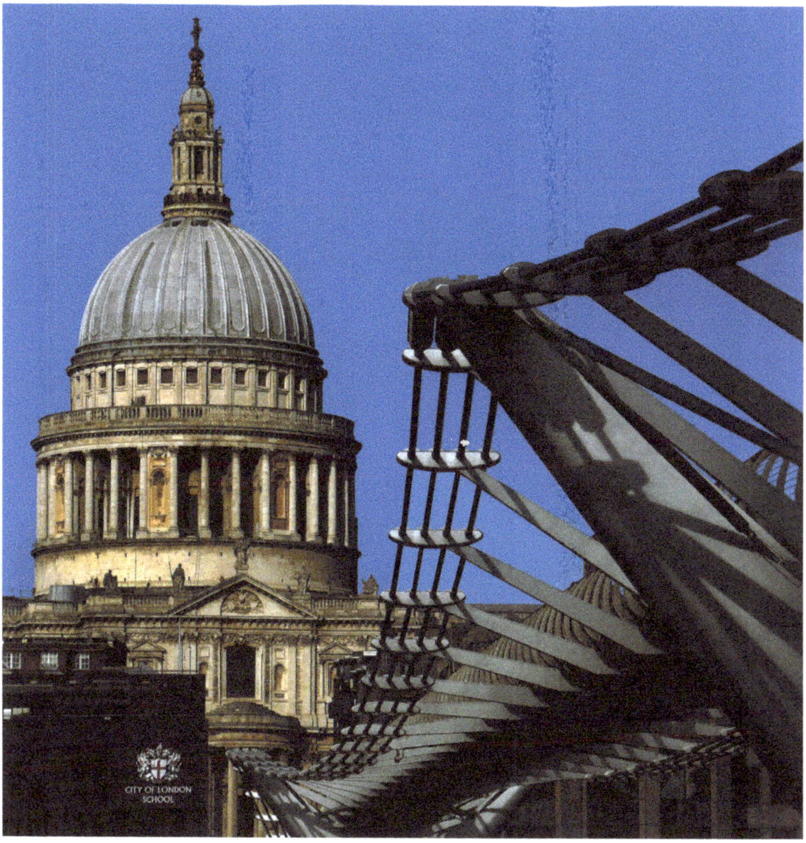

St. Paul's Cathedral from the Tate Modern, end of February 2020, three weeks before the first Covid-19 national lockdown.

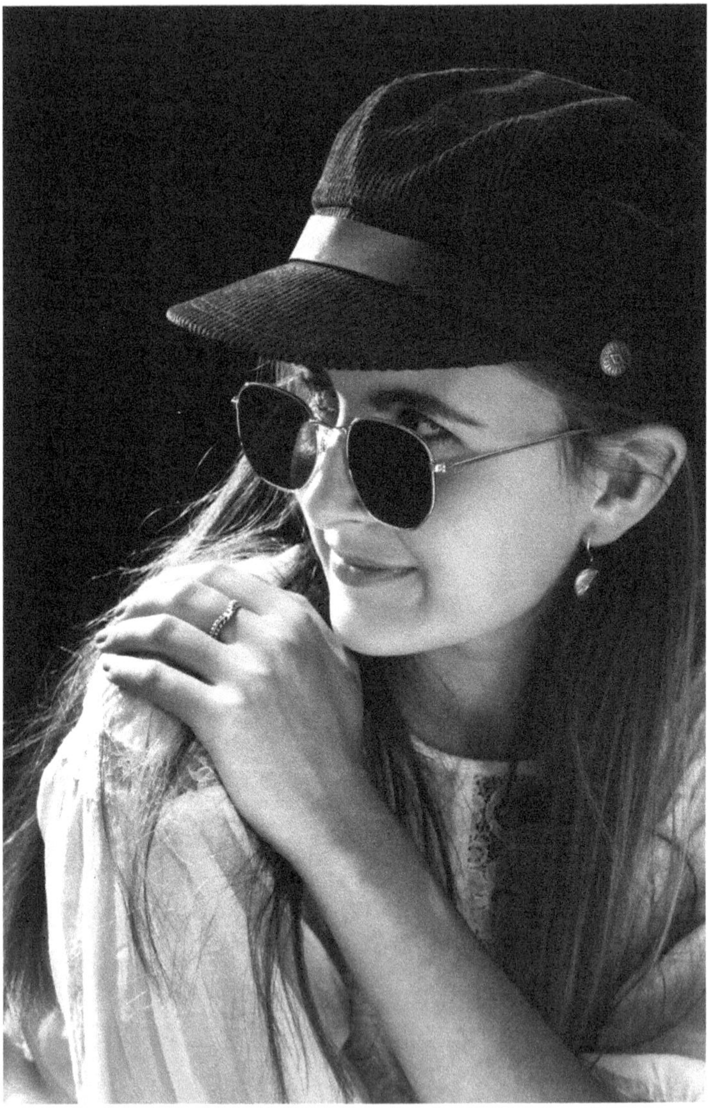

Lauren, July 2020.

CHAPTER 33

The Covid Crisis

As for the Canning family, well, January 2020 saw us returning to the red rose county of Lancashire a good few days into the new year, just as a picture postcard sun was setting on the beautiful Fylde Coast – our home. For us, our new year Cornwall break had been idyllic and simply the most perfect way to start 2020, a leap year, with the promise of Euro 2020, Wimbledon, an exciting Tokyo Olympic and Paralympic Summer of games, not to mention a whole variety of other sporting events to look forward to, to usher in a brand new decade ...or so we all thought.

That is, until Coronavirus (officially called 'Sars-Cov-2' / Covid-19) let rip and created havoc, terror, upset and death across the world. By Spring, the nation would witness initial, wide scale, selfish, panic buying of essential items (especially toilet rolls and hand sanitiser) followed by mass dumping of products by the side of bins because the excess items had gone out of date.

The world grappled with the coronavirus Covid-19 respiratory virus outbreak that was declared a world-wide pandemic on 11th March 2020. We suddenly had new daily vocabulary and in-phrases such as:

Stay at Home - Protect the NHS - Save Lives - Stay Alert - Control the Virus - Hands, Face, Space - Social Distancing - 2 metres - Self-Isolate – Lockdown - Circuit-Breaker – Work from Home - Patient Zero - Covid-Secure - Flatten the Curve - R number – Covidiot - Maskne (mask-related acne) – PPE – Shielding - Social Bubble - New Normal – Furlough - Rule of Six - Covid-secure marshals - Silent Spreaders - Long Covid – Moonshot - Herd Immunity.

The most vulnerable, the over 70s with underlying conditions, were urged to effectively cut themselves off from community life for weeks and stay put, although some insisted on going out for their morning paper as per usual. In what was known as 'shielding', the NHS contacted the most at risk groups, urging them to stay in their homes for 12 weeks. Many countries closed their borders, whilst air, sea and rail travel were all severely affected, as were many peoples' incomes.

The sporting calendar was decimated. The Olympics and Paralympics were postponed. Wimbledon was cancelled for the first time since World War 2 and Euro 2020 was put back for a year. Many established businesses crashed such as Laura Ashley, Flybe, Cath Kidson, Debenhams, Victoria's Secret, Edinburgh Woollen Mill, Ponden Home, Peacocks, Jaeger and Bonmarché. Arcadia, the owner of Topshop, Burton and Dorothy Perkins filed for administration at the end of November 2020. Companies managing ground operations at UK airports stated that they were close to collapse, which threatened thousands of jobs. Plant, tree and shrub growers were also worried for the future in the wake of around 2,000 garden centres and nurseries closing.

Many more people lost their jobs or were 'furloughed' as a result of businesses being ordered to close during the pandemic.

Mass public gatherings were stopped and we all had to wash our hands regularly with soap and water for as long as it took to sing 'Happy Birthday' twice, or disinfect with alcohol / hand gel. More people were seen out in public wearing face masks to try and shield themselves from the virus, whose main symptoms were a fever / high temperature, a continuous dry cough and shortness of breath. (Loss of taste and smell were later added to the list of symptoms). We were all asked to observe social distancing rules and keep at least 2 meters away from each other. During my Saturday 21st March tele-dermatology moles clinic, to prevent possible infection I 'elbow-bumped', instead of shaking hands with a patient for the very first time. Home working was also advised. We were reminded to regularly disinfect surfaces that are frequently touched such as door handles, taps and handrails. As the pandemic escalated, we even disinfected grocery items, delivered to our home. At the Victoria Hospital in Blackpool, instructions were issued on how to correctly don and doff items of PPE. Returning home from the hospital each day, before we entered the house, we would first wash our hands in the utility room, then disinfect the car – handles, steering wheel, gear lever, etc.. and enact the same strict routine throughout the virus outbreak. Then we changed out of the clothes we had been wearing to leave work, put on clean, casual clothes and immediately put the 'contaminated' washing on a 60 degree hot wash to kill any suspected germs.

Following the first reported death in China on January 11th 2020, the WHO subsequently declared a global emergency. By mid-March there were 250,000 infected people and more than 10,000 deaths worldwide. In March the UK introduced a national lockdown under the banner of 'Stay at Home, Protect the NHS, Save lives'. Under lockdown we were only allowed to venture out to the shops for basic necessities, daily exercise, a medical need, caring, or travelling to and from essential work. Further, we were warned that these measures could continue for another six months. Shops selling non-essential products were told to close and gatherings in public of more than two people who were not living together were immediately banned. Shops, restaurants, cafes, pubs, clubs, theatres, cinemas, gyms, leisure centres and in fact any venue where people gather, were asked to close on 20th March. John Lewis was forced to close all 50 of its stores for the first time in the company's 155-year history.

The coronavirus crisis simultaneously brought out the worst and the best in people. Awful, selfish, behaviour such as panic buying, hoarding, fighting over products in supermarkets and nurses and emergency staff being spat at, threatened and even targeted to steal their ID badges with the aim of trying to get free perks. On the other hand, the warmth of the human spirit still shining as brightly as any star in the many acts of kindness witnessed, people watching out for each other and just being, well, nice. At Blackpool's Victoria Hospital, gifts that included biscuits, chocolates and sweets were delivered from the public by the cart load and divvied up to teams by our lovely, hard-working, dedicated 'Blue Skies' fundraising team. Businesses brought in a variety of treats and free bottled water and items were distributed fairly to departments in recognition for continued hard work. Food takeaway businesses offered discounts for the NHS. On one particular day, locally acclaimed fish and chip chain, Seniors, delivered a massive volume of assorted, tasty dishes to hospital staff, completely free. Champion!

When I walked in to my local Costas on Friday 20th March 2020 feeling spent after another intensive, exhausting day at the hospital, fully expecting to see little change from the fiver that was about to be debited from my visa, Wendy's cappuccino and my skinny latte were offered to me with the cost waived. I was utterly gobsmacked and humbled and right then at that moment, I felt so appreciated! That single, wonderful act did much to rekindle my spirits. Our hospital also introduced free, daily, hot, meals until the middle of July and free on-site parking during the crisis.

The most poignant story of kindness that I read was that of the unselfish bravery of 72-year-old Italian priest Father Giuseppe Berardelli, who died in hospital of coronavirus in Lovere, Bergamo Province, Lombardy, in northern Italy – but not before he gave his respirator (that his parishioners had bought for him) to a younger Covid-19 patient. I hope they erect a shrine to him, so he'll not be forgotten.

On Monday 23rd March 2020, as stated, to further prevent the spread of Covid-19 – "the biggest threat this country has faced for decades", Prime Minister Johnson announced unprecedented, draconian and tough new controls on peoples' lives in the UK. The nation was effectively locked down.

At 8 p.m. on Thursday 26th March the nation showed its appreciation for those of us who work tirelessly for the NHS, by standing on their doorsteps and applauding, cheering and banging saucepans. This 'clap for carers campaign', which started online, was very emotional. There were even firework displays to round off a lovely evening. At the same time, major venues all over the UK turned NHS blue, prompting the hashtag #Makeitblue across social media platforms – but the outpouring of thanks and love was really a shout out to all those from carers to shelf-stackers, who were doing their bit for the nation to help in the fight against coronavirus. A second clap for carers was held at 8 p.m. exactly a week later and recognised everyone from teachers to bin men, cleaners and delivery drivers who were working hard to keep the nation going during the challenging and unsettling health crisis – social media promoting the hashtag, #ClapForOurCarers. The applause then continued every Thursday during the weeks to follow.

The end of March 2020 saw the construction of the first temporary hospital - the 4,000 patient Nightingale in east London's Excel centre (erected in just under 10 days, staffed by NHS medics and the military and opened via video link by Prince Charles on 3rd April, who declared that "In this dark time, this place will be a shining light"). Nightingale hospitals were subsequently built in Manchester, Birmingham, Cardiff, Glasgow, Bristol and Harrogate.

I write this section on the coronavirus pandemic whilst on annual leave away from my job at Blackpool Victoria Hospital. Right now, I'm sitting in a reclining chair, typing away, now and then pausing to look out of my conservatory window at the birdfeeder, to watch the myriad pretty goldfinches with their red caps, flock to devour an abundance of sunflower seeds. The weather outside is a mild 9 degrees

C and periodically the sun peeks out and also periodically, I'll munch on a custard cream and take a sip of refreshing tea. All very satisfying – idyllic even. You'd be forgiven if you thought that life was hunky-dory. Oh, if only that were the case. But we live in extraordinary times and this, the last of my days off before the end of the NHS leave year on 31st March – is no ordinary leave. I'd already cancelled a cycle ride with my close friend Simon and fire scene photography training in Essex was also postponed under government restrictions. I was also hoping to drive up to the Lake District for a hill walk or two, perhaps visit Mum's spot, (where some of her ashes were sprinkled) overlooking Grasmere, for some quiet reflection amidst the daffodils. But like the rest of us, I'm under virtual house arrest and find myself having to 'redefine my sense of time', as one of our national treasures Stephen Fry stated. Nevertheless, I'm using the time wisely and having a daily schedule, whilst trying to ignore the pings on my phone carrying regular updates from work – designed to be helpful by keeping me in touch, but actually proving to be an embuggerance in their obtrusiveness. There's no shortage of domestic jobs, there's films and TV, not to mention all the funny videos, memes and gifs posted on social media – all designed to keep everyone positive – and there's reading, resting, playing board games and working out. I have an exercise bike in the conservatory and then there's badminton in the garden with the family. It wasn't windy and we ended up rackets in hand, enjoying a marathon for over two hours until the pesky midges came out to play. Fantastic, well, that is until we all woke the following day with achy limbs!

However, tired limbs pale into insignificance when in every county people are getting sick and some are dying. Reading the daily, gloomy mortality figures, forms part of the news at the moment. Front line staff are being infected, falling due to a lack of correct PPE – hardworking, highly thought of, caring doctors and nurses, sometimes leaving behind young children. I am reminded again of some poignant lines from the 1835 William Wordsworth poem entitled, 'Extempore Effusion Upon the Death of James Hogg':

'How fast has brother followed brother,
From sunshine to the sunless land!
A timid voice that asks in whispers,
"Who next will drop and disappear?"'

When I returned to work on April fool's day, the atmosphere was eerily different. No longer allowed to wear our department-labelled black scrubs, which clearly marked us out as medical photographers, we were now required to don clean, blue scrubs (later down the line the rule changed to allow either green or blue scrubs) every day. Five people had died of Covid-19 at Blackpool Victoria Hospital (sadly, as elsewhere, that figure increased daily) and things had ramped up a notch on the PPE side of things – the wearing of plastic aprons, gloves and masks when photographing and eye scanning patients had become mandatory. We needed visors too, but due to a shortage we ended up hole-punching a piece of acetate and threading the mask ties through the holes, before tying everything at the back, for added aerosol protection.

Around the start of April, ubiquitous rainbow pictures, predominantly drawn by children urging everyone to keep positive, were placed in myriad windows and on noticeboards. The idea was to cheer people up during the lockdown, the message being that with rainbows, the sun would eventually shine following heavy rainfall.

Amidst the Coronavirus pandemic on Sunday 5th April 2020, in a pre-recorded rallying speech from Windsor Castle, Her Majesty The Queen spoke with calm determination to the nation about the value of self-discipline and of "quiet good-humoured resolve" still characterising the country. "We should take comfort that while we may have more still to endure, better days will return: we will be with our friends again; we will be with our families again; we will meet again."

The Queen's speech had barely started, when dramatically Prime Minister Johnson was whisked from self-isolation in Downing Street to the nearest hospital, St. Thomas'. There, the PM was treated for "persistent symptoms" of the coronavirus and alarmingly moved into ICU the following day. Fortunately he recovered and on 12th April Mr Johnson left hospital to recuperate at Chequers. Expressing his relief at this good news, the PM's father, Stanley Johnson declared that Boris "almost took one for the team". On the same day came the shocking, sobering news that the UK hospital death toll from the coronavirus had exceeded 10,000, which prompted Health Secretary Matt Hancock to declare, "today marks a sombre day in the impact of this disease...".

On Easter Saturday 11th April the heart-breaking news came in that the USA had just become the first country in the world to record a death toll of more than 2,000 in a single day. This was followed quickly with more horrific information that the US had clocked up more than 20,000 deaths and surpassed Italy for the nation with the highest number of fatalities from Coronavirus in the world. Alas, the US death toll would go on to climb, much, much higher. Covid-19 hit New York State the hardest, prompting New York State Governor Andrew Cuomo to describe the coronavirus outbreak as a "silent explosion that ripples through society with the same randomness, the same evil that we saw on 9/11".

I felt so sorry for Andrew Cuomo and the dire situation that he was faced with as grim scenes emerged from the Big Apple - outside hospitals, of body bags being forklifted into huge, refrigerated mortuary trucks, ambulances constantly tearing along eerily empty, Mary Celeste-esque streets and the most upsetting of all, drone footage depicting hazmat-clad workers undertaking mass burials on Hart's Island – a renowned area of New York City, located in north-eastern Bronx, that's been used for interment for the last 150 years. Reachable only by boat, this desolate, little island is historically associated with melancholy. Hart or Hart's Island is a strip of land no bigger than a mile in length and barely a third of a mile wide, located immediately east of City Island and part of the archipelagic Pelham group of islands. Devoid of headstones, it's a potter's field awash with mass graves, stacked edge-full with the coffins of the dejected - paupers and those deceased leaving behind no known next of kin. How heart-wrenchingly sad. Those poor souls. R.I.P..

In the Queen's traditional Easter message, she used the theme of lighting candles to mark events and uniting people and with light overcoming darkness, to highlight this pivotal occasion, "As dark as death can be – particularly for those suffering with grief – light and life are greater". The Queen stated that, "May the living flame of the Easter hope be a steady guide as we face the future".

Hospital staff were beginning to feel the strain, others had gone well beyond that point. Almost daily, you'd learn of a colleague who'd become symptomatic and was forced into self-isolation. Elsewhere in the UK horror stories were emerging of some hospitals on the brink with a lack of critical care beds, staff, antibiotics and CPAP masks and of having to improvise, fashioning head and body protection out of plastic dustbin liners and utilising eye protection donated from school science labs, or even using skiing goggles. Unconfirmed reports also came in of respiratory protection face masks arriving at hospitals bearing new expiry dates adjacent to previous expiry dates, rendering the piece of kit out of date and a liability. Unnerving reports also emerged that in some cases doctors were having to examine patients suspected of having Covid-19, from a distance of just 20 cm away – well within aerosol range, without the correct PPE and with possible fatal consequences!

Disinfecting all equipment, surfaces and self were undertaken numerous times a day. If I wasn't washing my hands with soap and water, I was washing them with alcohol-based hand sanitiser. And the office door handles would also be alcohol cleaned along with keyboard, desk, mouse and telephone. This went on relentlessly and became incorporated into our daily routine, just like brushing your teeth. The downside to this daily drenching in sanitiser was that my hands resembled those of a withered Egyptian mummy and continually moulted dead skin before they were nourished back to life with moisturising cream. Meanwhile, Wendy was working very long days with the NHS Community Nursing teams based at Blackpool Football Stadium. She'd set up the Blackpool drive through coronavirus swab testing site for NHS staff – the first of its kind in the area. So much work was put into that one project alone, a team effort with a core group of dedicated colleagues – much of it done as additional hours in the evenings and at weekends!

On Tuesday 21st April, The Queen turned 94 and for the first time in her long reign, cancelled her birthday gun salute, as it wasn't appropriate during the coronavirus crisis (The Queen's official birthday marked by 'Trooping the Colour', is traditionally held on Horse Guards Parade in London on the second Saturday in June, but this was also cancelled in 2020 (only for the second time during the Queen's reign. It was previously cancelled in 1955 due to a national rail strike), but a smaller, much lower-key, socially distanced ceremony on Saturday 13th June 2020 with some of the soldiers who were deployed throughout the UK to help in the fightback against coronavirus - the Welsh Guards, together with other members of the Household Division, was held in the quadrangle at Windsor Castle to mark this special occasion.

On 23rd April Oxford was the location for the first human trial in Europe of a Covid-19 vaccine with two trial participants being injected, of more than 800 volunteers recruited for the study. That evening, the BBC screened a three-hour Comic Relief / Children in Need combo charity fundraiser, which raised almost £27½ million and attracted an audience of 8½ million viewers. Participants included the cast of EastEnders, David Walliams and Matt Lucas reprising their iconic, hilarious Little Britain roles, the Dr Who stars, comedians Peter Kay, Catherine Tate, Miranda Hart and Dawn French. Even Prince William, the Duke of Cambridge appeared in a surprise sketch with the much loved Stephen Fry. In addition to funny sketches, all the stars of the very welcome extravaganza entitled 'The Big Night In' sent messages of hope and support during the pandemic. With the government promising to double the total amount of money raised on the evening, the grand total of £55 million went to all those vulnerable people around the UK affected by coronavirus.

Saturday 25th April saw another grim milestone. The total number of people who had died from Covid-19 in UK hospitals passed 20,000. It took just 51 days (less than two months) from the announcement of the first UK death from coronavirus to reach the 20,000 mark.

Also on 25th April, Wendy had a very kind offer from a local Poulton-le-Fylde lady equipped with her own 3-D printer, to supply much needed aerosol-trapping visors for front-line staff to use whilst undertaking the crucial, daily, drive-through virus swab-testing at Blackpool Football Stadium. People then got their 'thinking caps' on during the health crisis and came up with more ingenious ideas, for example, 'ear savers' would take a mask's elastic away from the back of the ears and place this tension more evenly at the back of the head, which proved more comfortable. There were even ear savers with a hole in the middle to accommodate a pony tail! As masks became compulsory, different colours and designs emerged, which included cartoon character face coverings for children and see through designs to better enable lip reading and to see one's facial expressions.

On the last day of April, the NHS in setting out its combat plans for the second phase of the Covid-19 pandemic, stated that non-coronavirus urgent cases should be stepped up, together with urgent outpatient appointments and the restarting of routine elective surgery, cancer surgery and appointments, heart attack and stroke care over the next six weeks.

Despite the problems caused by coronavirus, the public were determined to do their bit, helping those in need in any way they could, from voluntary work to donations and fundraising. The most notable fundraiser was Captain Tom Moore, a 'near Centenarian' and second world war veteran of the British army, who raised just shy of £33 million to help the NHS in the ongoing fight against coronavirus with an on-line fundraiser, which saw 'Captain Tom' complete 100 laps of the 25-metre loop around his garden where he lived in the Bedfordshire village of Marston Moretaine, with the aid of his walking frame. Indeed 100 laps were completed before his

100th birthday on 30th April 2020, which was the original aim. Captain Tom was subsequently knighted by the Queen, using her father, King George V1's sword, on 17th July 2020. It was a prestigious award, so richly deserved. The PM declared that Captain Tom had given the nation "a beacon of light through the fog of coronavirus". Sadly, Captain Tom passed away in his 101st year on 2nd February 2021 and out of respect and in memoriam, the nation took to their doorsteps the following evening and clapped for him. An awe-inspiring story and a remarkable gentleman. R.I.P. Captain Tom.

On 1st May 2020, the UK death toll (from hospitals and the community) stood at 27,510. The 6th May marked an awful milestone. The UK death toll from coronavirus passed 30,000, having overtaken Italy for our nation to become the first country in Europe to reach this horrendous statistic. Sickeningly, the UK also had the second highest coronavirus mortality in the world, standing behind the USA, whose death toll stood at more than 70,000.

On a brighter note an incredibly uplifting piece of artwork by the elusive artist Banksy, which shows a young boy in t-shirt and dungarees kneeling down by a waste paper basket, was put on display at Southampton General Hospital. In the mainly black and white painting, Banksy's tribute to NHS workers, the little boy has thrown his toy spiderman and batman figures away and instead is playing with his new action superhero of choice, an NHS nurse who, with arm outstretched and pointing forwards in typical Superman style, is donned in hat, facemask, dress, cape and an apron bearing the iconic Red Cross emblem – which is depicted as the only area of colour – small, subtle and desaturated, within the expanse of this monochromatic creation. It nevertheless serves to draw the viewer's eye to this powerful image, with all the significance that it effuses. This genius painting, called 'Game Changer' is believed to have been a collaboration between NHS hospital managers and the famous artist.

On a very special Bank Holiday Friday 8th May and with an equally special, pre-recorded televised address to the nation by HM The Queen, there were a series of events commemorating the 75th anniversary of cessation of hostilities on the continent at the end of World War 2, AKA Victory in Europe (VE Day). In thanking the second world war generation the Queen said, "They risked all so our families and neighbourhoods could be safe". And comparing with virus lockdown restrictions 75 years on…nevertheless, "our streets are not empty, they are filled with the love and the care that we have for each other". WW2 forces sweetheart, the late Dame Vera Lynn said, "I hope that VE Day will remind us all that hope remains even in the most difficult of times and that simple acts of bravery and sacrifice still define our nation as the NHS works so hard to care for us. Most of all, I hope today serves as a reminder that however hard things get, we will meet again." Although the nation were unable to commemorate publicly Labour leader Sir Keir Starmer said, "We can still remember together" and referring to the Covid-19 pandemic, "We owe so much to the generation of VE Day. We must do everything we can to care for and support them through the current crisis".

Meanwhile at Victoria Hospital in Blackpool, our medical photography attendance at wards had tailed off dramatically since the government's strict lockdown rules were announced on 23rd March. This, coupled with a blanket halt on all clinics initially, followed by a huge reduction in patients attending our ophthalmology clinics, who mainly comprised older 'shielded' patients, meant that we only attended safeguarding, urgent jobs and what few ophthalmology patients actually turned up for clinic. Patients were fearful and kept away from the hospital in droves– even our tele-dermatology clinics (for photographing potential cancerous moles) stopped. This unprecedented temporary downturn in work took a few days of adjustment. I'd been working flat out – just the two medical photographers – for more than 3 years, so it was rather like bowling along in top gear one day and the next, suddenly slowing it down to first gear. Massive change. However, this was actually a blessing because there was a backlog of jobs to sort out and data to input, the office was in a very untidy state, smelled of decay and the new Nikon D780 equipment needed testing and sorting out. All this took hours, but we had ample time to get done what we needed to get done. As the pandemic wore on, the hospital was noticeably quieter. Every morning, I'd call into 'Scrub Hub' on the main ground floor corridor to either be issued with a set of regulation blue or green scrubs, such was the new rule during the pandemic. At the end of each working day, I'd doff my scrubs and change back into my own clothes. Ward jobs, clinic and theatre work began to pick up again during week commencing 11th May and coincided with the NHS drive, post coronavirus peak, to get people into hospital for their outpatient appointments and operations as soon as it was safe to do so.

During early May I underwent 'FIT' testing to ascertain the appropriate mask that I was required to wear whilst undertaking patient photography during the pandemic. To test my sensitivity, having initially worn a huge, mainly plastic-type head shield that if you can imagine it, vaguely resembled an overstretched bee-keeper's hat with plastic replacing fabric mesh, Julia, one of our Trust's senior nurses who was conducting proceedings, then sprayed the visor and after about thirty seconds, I could taste a metallic, hair-spray-like substance at the back of my throat. Having washed my mouth out with water, I then waited for the metallic taste to dissipate. Ten minutes later I was ushered back into the testing room, instructed how to correctly don and doff my mask and then once securely fitted, I popped the oversized plastic 'beekeeper's hat' over my head once more and Julia went through a range of tests that included me looking up and down, to the side, bending down a few times and then reading continuously. In effect, I was recreating all the actions that one might do at the patient's bedside, and all the while spraying the hairspray-like substance at the visor. I couldn't detect the metallic taste at all, which meant that thankfully, I was good to go with that particular mask. The FIT test, therefore, is designed to ensure that the mask you can wear 'fits' correctly and forms a good seal around your nose and mouth and crucially, inhibits the transmission of aerosols, such as Covid-19 and you are only allowed to wear the type of mask that you have been FIT tested for, for obvious reasons.

Every day the 'Head Shed' would issue a 'Covid-19' update to all staff detailing the numbers of virus positive patients that the surrounding Fylde Coast community had seen, the number of people currently being seen as inpatients, the total number of hospital deaths and the number of patients successfully treated and discharged. The update would also carry PPE updates, medical advice, health and wellbeing advice, in addition to any other advice for staff, as well as news items. Having ridden the virus storm at the Victoria Hospital during late March and April, May started with some very sad news indeed – the loss of the Vic's first member of staff to coronavirus. 68-year-old Eleuterio 'Boy' Gibela was taken by Covid-19 on May 2nd. He was a much loved, highly respected and valued member of the hospital's domestic staff, who had worked at the Trust for nearly 20 years. As a mark of respect, Steve, Chimane and I joined hundreds of other staff who formed part of a guard of honour, a collection of NHS key workers who wrapped themselves around the entire Blackpool Victoria Hospital site, prior to Eleuterio's funeral on

Monday 18th May 2020. The cortege passed us by a few minutes after 2.30 p.m. and we all broke into spontaneous applause at the site of the hearse. In what was a very emotional experience, Eleuterio's family filmed us on their mobile phones through open car windows as they passed us by, but it was the clearly distraught face of Eleuterio's widow, racked with pain, that left a haunting impression on me, such that I'll not forget it in a hurry. Eleuterio's death was a heart-breakingly, stark reminder of the challenging times and daily situation faced by us all. R.I.P. Eleuterio.

But then, in contrast a few days later, a good news story emerged from Blackpool's Victoria Hospital. Ruby Dawson, one of only a handful of babies in the world to be born with coronavirus, left the Vic fully recovered with her Mum and Dad through an NHS staff guard of honour. Back in March, Mum Kathrine, who was 32 weeks pregnant had been admitted to A&E with what she believed was a chest infection. However, following confirmation that she was Covid-19 positive, a decision was made to deliver her baby to give mother and daughter the best chance of survival. Kathrine's condition subsequently worsened. She was left fighting for her life and required sedation and ventilator support following her baby's early delivery on April 1st via caesarean section. Worse still, because both Mum and daughter had the virus, the baby's Dad was not allowed to visit them. Thankfully, after quite a few nerve-racking weeks, Mum and baby Ruby made a full recovery. This amazing success story was down to the dedicated, gold star care of my Trust's wonderful clinical team. Bravo Guys!

Having been FIT tested for my protective 'anti-Covid' mask during early May 2020, I got a rare chance to experience what the guys and girls at the sharp end of Covid-19 hospital treatment, were having to endure day in and day out – donning the full coronavirus PPE. I got called by Consultant Cardiothoracic Surgeon Professor Nidal Bittar to cardiac theatres, who at the time were using our ophthalmic operating areas. I was already wearing my 'FFP3 1863' FIT-tested mask when I stepped into the prep room, to be greeted by two friendly ODPs (Operating Department Practitioners), who in operating a buddy system to keep me safe, helped me don the rest of my PPE. This consisted of full head and neck surgical hood, tied at the back of my neck quite tightly, a visor, a long-sleeved surgical gown that you put your arms into at the front and which is then tied by yourself to the front left hand side and long-sleeved surgeon's gloves marked up to denote right and left hand. In typical operating fashion, the gloves went over the sleeves of my gown and formed a seal at my wrists. Under instructions to leave my camera bag in the prep room, I had taken the liberty of pre-setting and testing the camera and ring flash prior to donning my PPE.

Clog-stepping on to the operating theatre floor in full Covid PPE was a bizarre experience. One must be ever cognisant of operating theatre etiquette, watching for tubes and wires and being especially careful not to touch any blue-coloured sterile drapes. Intra-operative photography following a patient's excised, metastasized thyroid carcinoma, was quick and straightforward and I made a mental note to visit the patient the next day in HDU recovery to gain their informed, signed publication consent for images taken. I then proceeded to take some images of the surgeons and theatre personnel in full PPE for our hospital's communications team, by way of documenting Coronavirus-related subject matter to accompany news articles and for historical purposes. I had only worn this protective equipment for about 20 minutes and felt hot and claustrophobic with it on.

During May 2020 my colleague Chimane and I had already set about the herculean task of documenting PPE-clad Victoria Hospital staff from a variety of departments, working hard during the Covid crisis. This marathon assignment, which I nicknamed 'The Covid Photography Project' was made possible by the fact that when the pandemic was worsening, all our clinical work, save for emergencies and some ophthalmic clinics, ceased (outpatients appointments, elective surgery, clinics and ward visits stopped for a time to keep as many people away from hospitals as possible for fear that they'd spread the virus), freeing up our time. Areas covered included cardiac surgery, haematology and oncology, Blackpool football stadium drive-through swab team, urology, catering, ward nurses, A&E, ward rounds and pathology. We also photographed much of the new safety and social distancing signage around the hospital. I came up with the idea of photographing an entire Covid-19 ICU PPE donning and doffing sequence for future infection control training purposes. To this end, I enlisted the help of one of our ICU nurses, Aimee, who walked me through the entire procedure. This on its own was a huge task, even without the hours of multi-image post-processing, but thanks to this dedicated nurse's time, not to mention patience, I was rewarded with a crop of very pleasing photographs.

It has to be remembered that staff treating Covid-positive patients in hospital ICUs and designated Covid wards are literally wearing this kit for hours on end, during which time they are very uncomfortable - constantly hot and sweating profusely in their scrubs worn underneath and alarmingly, progressively dehydrating in the process. Some of our ICU nurses and ward nursing staff also suffered skin reactions (so called 'maskne' – mask-related acne), bruises and pressure ulcers to their noses, faces and under their chins from the constant, tight wearing and chaffing of masks. I got to wear the entire Covid PPE for a handful of minutes in Cardiac theatre during Professor Bittar's operation. Following careful doffing of soiled PPE that included disinfecting my theatre clogs and camera gear, I found that I was red-faced, hot and perspiring.

Then, during the Covid Photography Project, Chimane and I got the green light to photograph clinicians caring for the most seriously ill coronavirus patients – we photographed inside the danger zone - Covid-19 ICU itself. This initially involved completely donning the required PPE. First came the long-sleeved, washable, full length, dark-blue coloured gown. Then came the FFP3 mask pulled under the chin and pressed down either side of the bridge of the nose for a tight fit. Next up was a disposable theatre hat and once we'd fitted those to just over the tops of our ears, we both donned our respective 'direct splash protection' face shields. These visors are elasticated to fit on to your head and cushioned on the inside with foam, which sits comfortably against the forehead. And we still weren't done! Next came the disposable, long, cream-coloured, surgical gloves, which surprisingly are very easy to get on, unlike their shorter, blue-coloured counterparts, which often rip if you commit the cardinal sin of daring to offer them up to even a hint of a sweaty hand. Invariably, an embuggerance at the best of times! The long, cream-coloured gloves are designed to be pulled over the cuffs of the gown, to form a seal. Last, but not least, Chimane and I each donned a pair of disposable, blue-coloured, stretchy, overshoes, which took me right back to my early days on scenes of crime in the Met Police.

At last, we were ready to step into the 'hazard zone', but in the knowledge that we were PPE'd up to the hilt and protected to the max. On the entrance doors to what is normally cardiac intensive care, were all the warning signs that told us not to go any further without first donning the required gamut of PPE. An ominous, yellow-coloured sign that bore a skull and crossbones, also hammered home the grim reality of what potentially lay beyond.

After 45 minutes in Covid-19 ICU, Chimane and I had taken a fair number of images, including the obligatory photos of each other clad in all the PPE. My photographs included a nursing sister having a perfectly normal conversation on the phone, whilst wearing a grey-coloured respirator mask, another respirator-clad sister typing at a laptop, wearing the long, cream-coloured gloves and doctors and nursing staff discussing a Covid-positive patient's observations. I noticed that two of the Covid patients being treated were 'barrier nursed', i.e. additional precautions were being implemented to prevent the spread of the contagion. Attending nurses wore disposable, yellow, blue, or green-coloured plastic aprons over their blue-coloured gowns and disposable blue gloves over their long, cream-coloured gloves (cream-coloured gloves effectively became the nurse's skin), with the addition of disposable plastic, long-sleeved, arm coverings.

By the time we came to doff all our PPE, I for one was drenched in sweat, hot and in need of water and, as I've said, I was only wearing all the PPE for less than an hour. I needed a wash, a clean pair of scrubs and a lot of liquid refreshment after what constituted one hell of an experience. But all this was nowhere near as frightening and adrenaline charged as the daily gauntlet of fear that all the front-line clinical as well as myriad support staff have had to run throughout the Covid crisis in the hospital. In Covid-19 ICU where the most serious coronavirus patients have been treated, doctors and nurses amidst exhaustion and dehydration, have been in tears, continually wrestling with their own feelings of terror, simultaneously having to park those fears whilst with grit and determination, battling an unseen evil to save the critically ill. Many front line clinical staff opted to live away from their families during Covid for weeks on end, for fear of infecting their loved ones at home. Due to the highly infectious nature of Covid, it became particularly difficult and acutely painful trying to explain to family members why they were not allowed in to the hospital to see their sick relatives. At Blackpool Victoria Hospital, since the beginning of the pandemic, (and pre-second wave) 94 Covid-infected patients deteriorated sufficiently to require intensive care, which for some patients meant ventilation.

In my former life in the police and now currently in my role as hospital medical photographer, I've set eyes on God awful, I mean bloody (quite literally) horrible things that nobody should expect to see, never mind hear. But one thing's for certain, the teams of expert clinicians in all our hospitals fighting on the front line are united in a common focus, hell bent on doing the very best for all the patients in need of care. And what's more, not only have I seen it, I've seen it up close and personal. I've seen the nurse cuddling a patient, I've seen the tender holding of hands, I've been there with sobbing, bereaved relatives when a loved one has passed away and it's acutely humbling – it gets me every time, creating pictures in my mind that will be with me forever. I've come within touching distance of the angst, the determination and compassion in their eyes. And it's brought tears to my own eyes. I've witnessed the tiredness and the sweaty brows and I'm fiercely in awe of every one of them. They're like tight-knit families and their resilience, nay, absolute resolve – their indefatigable, unbreakable ethos and professional work ethic are what will see those who work in our magnificent, our truly amazing NHS, through a crisis such as the Covid-19 pandemic. We've a great team at Blackpool Victoria Hospital and I'm proud to work amongst such talent and dedication. In George's words, "For all our woes and troubles in today's society we are ever blessed and thankful for the United Kingdom National Health Service".

Recapping on the spread of Covid-19 in the UK – On 31 December 2019, China first informed the World Health Organisation of "pneumonia of unknown cause". On 31 January 2020 the first coronavirus positive cases were made public. On 2nd March 2020 the first Covid-19 death occurred in the UK according to NHS England. On 23 March 2020 Prime Minister Johnson's government imposed a blanket lockdown across the nation. On 10th April 2020 the highest daily UK death toll in hospitals (not including care homes and the community) of 980 from confirmed Covid, was recorded. On 30th May 2020 the total number of coronavirus deaths across all settings stood at 38,489.

The 5th June marked another awful landmark statistic – the number of UK Covid positive deaths in all settings passed the 40,000 mark to reach 40,261 – the second country after the USA to pass this grim milestone.

Mid-June, the 15th marked the re-opening of all 'non-essential' businesses, alongside zoos, safari parks and drive-in cinemas. On this day, masks and face coverings on public transport and for hospital staff, outpatients and visitors, became a mandatory requirement. This was in line with World Health Organisation guidelines that said that non-medical face coverings should be worn in public places where it was not possible to socially distance. So started an 'even newer normal' for me with a brand new routine at work – the compulsory wearing of a surgical face mask for the whole of the working day. I'll never forget joining that long queue to get in the main entrance at Blackpool Victoria Hospital to first rub my hands with alcohol sanitiser, then don my first mask of the day (up to a change of four masks per day). The initial problem was my glasses would mist up (until a kindly urology consultant passed on the tip of the folded tissue placed inside the top of the mask to absorb warm air and push your exhaled breath downwards), so I took them off on my journey to 'Scrub Hub' to pick up my scrubs for that day. The second was the heat and claustrophobia. The only times that I removed my mask whilst in the hospital, was when I was working in the office alone, whilst eating lunch and whilst taking regular gulps of water.

Circa mid-June, reflecting the national picture, all staff at Blackpool Teaching Hospitals NHS Foundation Trust were required to undergo an antibody test by having a blood sample taken, to ascertain whether we'd already had the Covid-19 virus. Results were then either emailed or texted to the individual. This would then help researchers map out staff infection rates. Wendy and I both had the test, but sadly neither of us had the antibodies.

On 16th June, some exciting news. Dexamethasone, a cheap and widely available steroid, was found to help save the lives of patients stricken with coronavirus. In what was described as a major pandemic breakthrough, the low dose steroid treatment was found to cut the risk of death by one third for ventilated patients and for patients on oxygen, deaths were cut by a fifth - those in the high risk category. The drug only appears to help the more serious cases – those struggling with their breathing. It is not for mild coronavirus symptoms. Dexamethasone appears to stop some of the damage to the body when the immune system goes into a cytokine storm, or immune system over-reaction. As it is a low cost drug, dexamethasone could also be used in poorer countries, wrestling with high numbers of coronavirus patients.

On the day that saw social distancing guidelines change from the hitherto set 2 metres in England to "one metre plus", Wendy, George and I enjoyed a post-lockdown haircut in safety, wearing face coverings (courtesy of our visor-clad hairdresser Janet who lives next door!), but I hadn't yet been for a post-lockdown pint. I more favoured an unopened bottle of Yellowtail Shiraz that George and Lauren bought me for Father's Day. Smooth, rich and packed with berries and spice – it's a damn good Aussie red.

On the NHS' 72nd birthday on Sunday 5th July 2020 many landmarks across the nation were lit up blue on the Saturday evening to mark the occasion – my own Blackpool Victoria Hospital and Blackpool Tower being two of those looking suitably resplendent.

During the third week in July, it became a mandatory requirement for us medical photography staff to join our clinical colleagues and undertake a weekly nose and throat swab to test for coronavirus. The over-arching aim of this weekly swab test was to minimise the risk to patients during a time of increased elective activity, to allow for identification of any staff-related Covid-positive cases (including asymptomatic cases). For the record, I duly undertook my first self-swab on Thursday 16th July 2020 at 10.15a.m., having carefully read through the instructions.

On 20th July, we learned that a coronavirus vaccine, known as 'chAdOx1nCov-19' had been developed by Oxford University. The vaccine, made from a genetically engineered virus which gives chimpanzees the common cold, appears to be safe and crucially it triggers an immune response. On receiving injections of the vaccine, trial participants were found to have made antibodies and so called T-cells or 'Thymus cell lymphocytes' (types of white blood cells originating from the Thymus, which are able to identify which of the body's cells have been targeted and infected by Covid-19). These then actively seek out foreign bodies and fight them off. This in effect means that the vaccine resembles the coronavirus and the body's immune system is learning how to attack it. As side effects, nearly three quarters of trial participants developed either a fever or a headache. The trial study is still on-going and it is not yet known how effective the vaccine will be in the long term, i.e. how long the antibody and T-cell immune response will last. The USA and China have undergone their own tests and have produced similar, promising results.

On 29th July at Blackpool Victoria Hospital, the last Covid-19 patient from the first wave of coronavirus to leave the intensive care unit, 47-year-old Roehl Ribaya, left ICU to continue his rehabilitation on a general ward. Staff lined the way to say goodbye. Roehl, an aerospace engineer had been in ICU for 2 months, following his admission to hospital at the end of May, with almost seven weeks spent on a ventilator. Sadly, Roehl succumbed to the effects of 'Long Covid' (lasting symptoms of Covid-19) and passed away in mid-October 2020.

At the end of July, together with 249 fellow Trust employees engaged in regular close patient contact as part of their job, I enrolled on to Public Health England's 'Siren Study', or to give it the full title and description, 'Siren-Sars-Cov2 immunity and reinfection evaluation – the impact of detectable anti Sars-Cov2 antibody on the incidence of Covid-19 in healthcare workers'. This was quite a commitment for everyone, as the study, which set out to get a better understanding of whether prior infection of Covid-19 actually protects against future infection with the same virus, i.e. whether antibody responses are sustained, was based over a 12 month period. It involved having blood (for antibodies), nose and throat swabs being taken fortnightly, with regular assessment questionnaires in between the tests.

Specifically, the Siren study will give a useful and important steer as to the number of healthcare workers infected with Covid in the preceding months and whether factors such as differences in age, ethnicity, family history, genetic make-up of the individual, or indeed, any other factors reveal any crucial pointers. With regular swab and blood samples extracted, the study team will be able to measure the proportion of frontline NHS staff that are exposed to Covid-19 and obtain a clearer picture of the speed of transmission. Blood samples taken at different time points will show how the body's defence mechanism antibody levels change over time and also the different types of antibodies that may be present in each timepoint blood sample. Viruses from different people will be compared to see how they relate to each other, through examination and comparison of each virus' genetic composition.

On Sunday 30th August, the 'Thank U NHS' World War 2 spitfire, piloted by owner John Romain, flew over Lancashire hospitals and we were lucky enough to see the flypast – a tribute to NHS workers, outside the main entrance to Blackpool Victoria Hospital – an awesome sight! Just to view this iconic fighter plane, which had been emblazoned with the names of thousands of key workers, with its distinctive wing shape and powered by the deep throated Rolls Royce Merlin engine, was a truly awe-inspiring sight. It reminded me just how proud I am to work for the NHS and of course, proud to be British. The BBC were there and interviewed Wendy and me, resulting in a brief appearance on the local news later that day!

Towards the end of August 2020 around 25 million coronavirus cases were officially confirmed with some 846,000 deaths across the world. In the UK the death toll from Covid stood at 41,501 on 31st August. Of course these figures were likely to be much higher as many people who'd contracted the virus and did not show symptoms, hadn't been tested.

At the end of the summer UK universities were being urged to bin plans for face to face tuition until Christmas to prevent a second wave of Covid-19. In spite of university bosses working hard to plan for a safe return to all areas affecting student life, it was feared that more than a million students travelling around the nation was "a recipe for disaster".

Then, outbreaks of Covid occurred at universities and reports emerged of campus lockdowns and self-isolation across the nation from Scottish universities to Manchester Metropolitan University where around 1,700 students had to self-isolate after 127 tested positive for Covid-19. Even Lauren, barely three weeks into her first semester at Leeds Trinity, learned that she too was about to be locked down amidst an increase in student positive cases and a steep rise in coronavirus infections in and around Leeds itself. Fast forward to the end of the first week in October, Wendy took time out of work to drive over to Leeds and bring Lauren back home to continue her studies there, on-line, for the rest of her first semester of her first year. Poor Lauren was forced to self-isolate on her return home for two weeks and all because one of her flatmates had ignored the rules, acted irresponsibly and selfishly, resulting in her becoming Covid positive.

The news and media reported that thousands of 'incarcerated' students were complaining that they'd only just started university, that much of their initial coursework was undertaken on-line and that they would have been better off at home, with universities starting at Christmas or later. There was a pessimistic feeling amongst many students that university bosses perhaps knew that a lockdown was coming, but just wanted 'bums on seats' - students starting anyway because it meant losing accommodation and course fees if they did not. Cardiff and Swansea went into lockdown on Sunday evening 27th September, whilst London mayor Sadiq Khan warned that the metropolis was at a "very worrying tipping point" following a marked rise in the contagion.

On 26th September, shortly after it went live, Wendy and I downloaded the NHS Covid-19 Test and Trace app to our iPhones. Using contact tracing technology, the app clocks other app users who are in the vicinity. Should any of those users later test positive for Covid-19, Wendy and I would then be alerted via the app on our phones, together with advice of what to do next. The NHS app also allows us to report any coronavirus symptoms as well as finding out whether a test is required. The app can also be used to scan official

NHS QR (quick response matrix barcode) codes to check in to places we visit – the data on places visited held on the app for 21 days. However, the app hasn't been devoid of teething problems.

The 29th September brought us the sad and sobering news that the number of deaths from Covid-19 worldwide had topped the one million mark, although the figure was expected to be much higher as testing rates in many countries were still low, coupled with the fact that coronavirus deaths were not being recorded.

The UK death toll from Covid-19 stood at 42,143 on 30th September 2020. Sadly, with the second wave of the contagion already on the march, this figure was set to rise even further.

For me, the 28th October kicked off early and in the same vein as any other day – busy. I'd just completed a set of retinal scans on an ophthalmic patient in our Medical Retina Unit, when I found myself coughing for about the fourth time in an hour. Just as I was dismissing it as a touch of catarrh, Amanda one of our ophthalmic nurses popped her head around the door of the OCT (eye scanner) room and with a concerned look, all but ordered me off the unit, out of the hospital and back home pending the results of a Covid mouth and nose swab test. Nobody was taking any chances.

I duly attended the hospital drive through swab centre and after a tense wait and a few phone calls, fortunately the result came back negative and I returned to work. But it could have so easily gone the other way. Phew. My 'rejoicing' was very short-lived, however, when a concerned Chimane texted me to say that she had Covid-like symptoms and had been feeling unwell. I immediately told Chimane to stay at home and self-isolate, to recall her partner who was already at work and get him to also stay at home and arranged for her to get a test. On Halloween night Chimane texted me again to say that she had unfortunately tested positive for Covid-19 and would have to stay away from work for a minimum of ten days. After wishing her well for a speedy recovery, I turned my attention to the fact that out of the three of us I was the only Medical Photographer fit enough to work. Steve had cancer, Chimane had Covid and I was, er, well.... still coughing, albeit with catarrh. Nevertheless I could still work and fortunately I had the help of Jane Gray's talented team from the Manchester Royal Eye Hospital to assist with the daily ophthalmology clinics. I managed a half smile to myself as I thought of an old song I first heard as a kid by Burt Bacharach and Bob Hilliard, which became a hit for The New Christy Minstrels in 1962, 'Three Wheels on my Wagon'. For me at Blackpool Victoria Hospital, starting

November 2020, it was now a case of, 'One wheel on my wagon, I'm still rolling along, them Cherokees after me, I'm all in flames at the reins, but I'm singing a happy song'.

Well that one wheel on my wagon finally came off too when amidst a tense American Presidential election I came home from work on 4th November with a raging fever and a worrying, scarlet / maroon-coloured leg rash. Following a fast tracked Covid swab test, which fortunately came back negative, we were suspecting cellulitis, which our doctor subsequently confirmed through photos sent to the surgery. The 5th November, Bonfire Night, I continued to do battle with an all-consuming fever. It would take me a good three weeks to get over what constituted a very nasty case of cellulitis, which at its most virulent, saw me hobbling, unable to walk and in severe pain!

As more depressing news rolled in that the number of worldwide coronavirus infections had more than surpassed the 50 million mark, precipitating more than 1¼ million deaths, simultaneous breaking news on my sister Vicky's milestone 60th birthday, Monday 9th November, informed us that American pharmaceutical giant Pfizer together with its German biotech partner, BioNTech, had just declared that their Covid vaccine, could prevent more than 90% of people from catching Coronavirus, with initial results suggesting that their vaccine protected 94% of adults over the age of 65 - those most at risk from Covid-19.

On 20th November it was announced that the NHS was setting up vaccination centres across the UK in readiness for a mass inoculation programme to be undertaken by hospitals and GPs in the community, the moment the first Covid-19 vaccine had been approved by the MHRA (Medicines and Healthcare Products Regulatory Agency). As part of her new role as an Improvement and Development Manager with Occupational Health, Wendy played a pivotal role in masterminding Blackpool Victoria Hospital's vaccination centre, a challenging project, which took weeks of planning, coordination and setting up.

The moment the planned month-long lockdown ended on 2nd December, a tougher three-tiered system of regional restrictions was introduced, with some tiers strengthened and many more were set to move into higher tiers to safeguard and build on lockdown progress already achieved and in order for families, where possible, to see different households at Christmas. Weddings and collective worship were set to resume. Gyms, leisure facilities, hairdressers and non-essential shops in England were expected to reopen, together with a relaxing of the 10 pm closing time for pubs and restaurants (last orders would now be at 10 pm with an additional hour for drinking up time) in those regions allowing opening, post 2nd December.

Then the good news - no – the bloody fantastic news. On 2nd December, the day second lockdown ended and the new, tougher, three-tier system of restrictions was ushered in, it was announced that the MHRA – the British regulator had approved the American-made Pfizer / BioNtech Covid vaccine, declaring it safe for mass inoculation use and in so doing, making the UK the first nation on the planet to approve this coronavirus vaccine, which offers up to 95 % protection against the contagion. Further Covid vaccines were to follow, most notably from the Oxford University / AstraZeneca partnership (given the green light for use on 30th December 2020) in the UK and the Moderna vaccine from the USA.

Tuesday 8th December 2020 marked 'V-Day', the historic rolling out of the Covid vaccination programme, UK-wide. Some 70 hospitals (including Blackpool Victoria) acted as hubs for administering the two-part jab, with doses of the American / German-made Pfizer / BioNTech vaccine given three weeks (subsequently changed to twelve weeks) apart for each person. On the same morning, Blackpool Victoria Hospital's vaccination hub opened. Wendy and her colleague Paul Shaw had spent voluminous hours over many days planning and preparing for this moment, under impossible time pressures, with too many pre-dawn starts with accompanying late evening finishes for me to even dare count up. This day saw their incredible hard work come to fruition, witnessing the Fylde Coast's first Covid-19 vaccine. A truly awesome achievement – congratulations both! The vaccination programme couldn't have come fast enough as pre-Christmas saw at least one new mutant strain of coronavirus, which seemed to transmit at an alarmingly faster rate - a fact born out in the exponential rise in Covid-19 infections and hospital admissions from Christmas onwards.

Restrictions at the time meant that Wendy's brother Simon, a NW London resident and therefore under the toughest of restrictions in the newly created Tier 4, could not travel up to be with us in Tier 3 for the festive period. Christmas 2020 would prove to be the first Christmas that Simon hadn't spent with us in 25 years! As a small consolation, we were still able to have Simon with us, momentarily, via 'WhatsApp' video call.

On Christmas Day the total number of deaths in the UK within 28 days of a positive test for Covid-19 surpassed 70,000, another dreadful milestone – the total standing at 70,195. On Boxing Day the

London Ambulance Service (LAS) received 8,000 call-outs in what was described as one of the LAS' busiest days in its history. Simultaneously, hospitals in the south and south east of England reported that they had seen a "real rise in pressure" reflecting an increase in the number of coronavirus patients requiring treatment. Many more areas were placed under Tier 4 restrictions, including Fylde and Wyre in West Lancashire, as the nation witnessed an explosion in Covid-19 infections.

The total number of UK deaths due to Covid increased to 73,512 on 31st December – a truly awful statistic and a very sad end to 2020. Shockingly, the death rate accelerated in early 2021 and by 26th January more than 100,000 people had succumbed to Covid-19 in the UK, with the mortality rate continuing to rise further. On the first day of spring (20th March 2021), the UK death toll from Covid stood in excess of 126,000 and by 1st April 2021 it had already climbed higher than 127,000.

On Wednesday 3rd February 2021 it was finally my turn to become part of history and to receive the first dose of the Oxford University-AstraZeneca vaccine at my place of work, Blackpool Victoria Hospital.

We all look forward to when this disease nightmare becomes history, when we're free once more and no longer restricted, when perhaps, the country has finally made it to what Prime Minister Boris Johnson called his 'New Jerusalem', and we send this bastard Covid packing (perhaps long after we've all been vaccinated) and the epidemiologists and the politicians have analysed all the stats and crunched the figures and the millions of questions have been answered and an inquiry held. However, for all those who have lost loved ones, the ripple effect of grief within family and friends, will be unimaginably painful and long-lasting. Many more have suffered terribly – wracked with pain and discomfort. I think we're all glad to see the back of 2020, which will perhaps go down in history as many peoples' annus horribilis!

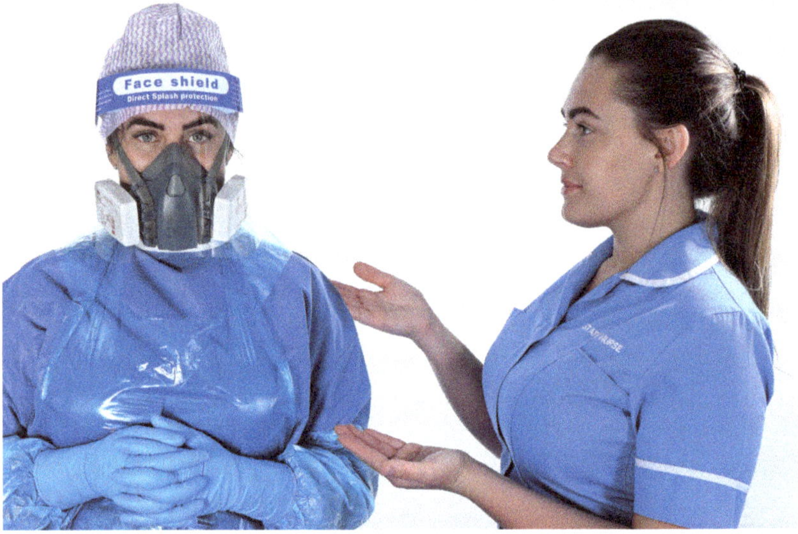

Intensive Care Unit (ICU) Staff Nurse Aimee Wade looking towards the nurse whom she has had to become - seen here donned in full barrier nurse Covid-19 PPE.

The photographs of ICU Staff Nurse Aimee Wade were taken as part of a PPE donning & doffing sequence for training use during and post Covid at Blackpool Victoria Hospital, July 2020. Photography by Paul Canning; Copyright: Blackpool Teaching Hospitals NHS Foundation Trust

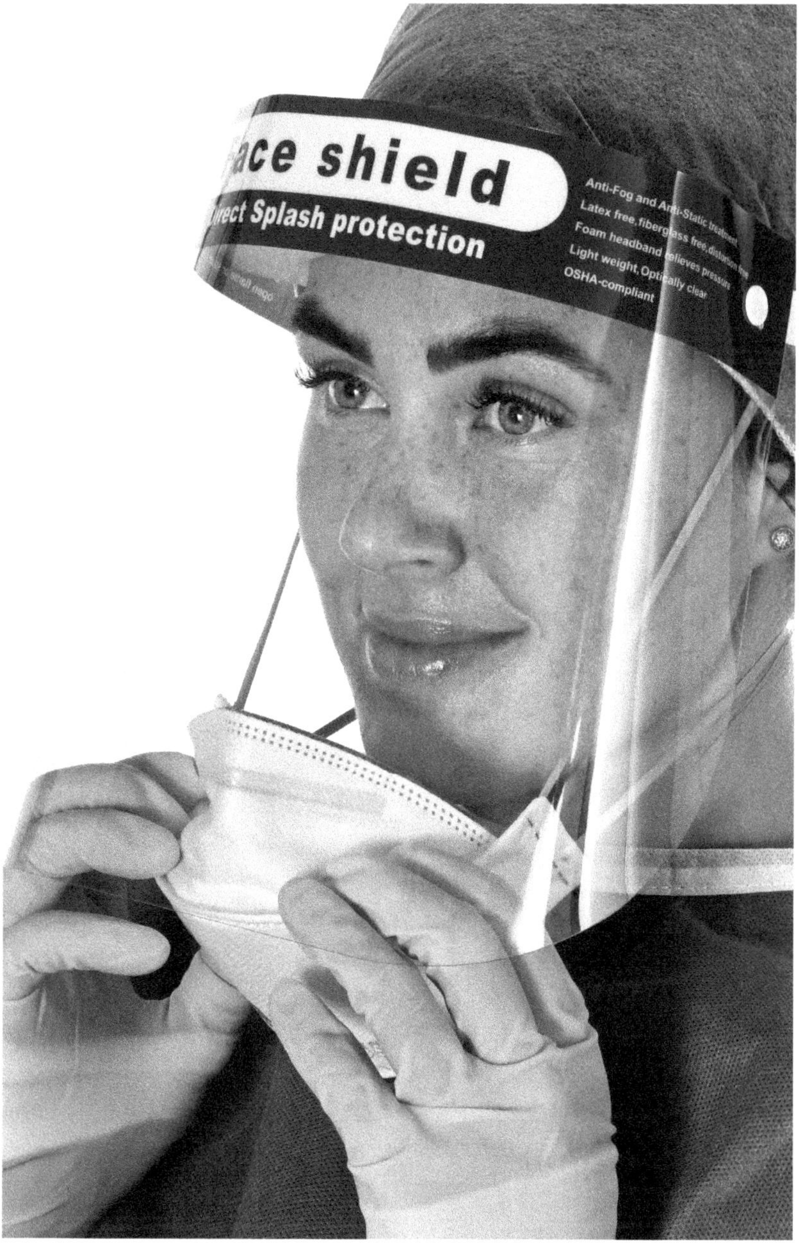

Staff Nurse Aimee Wade. Photography by Paul Canning;
Copyright: Blackpool Teaching Hospitals NHS Foundation Trust

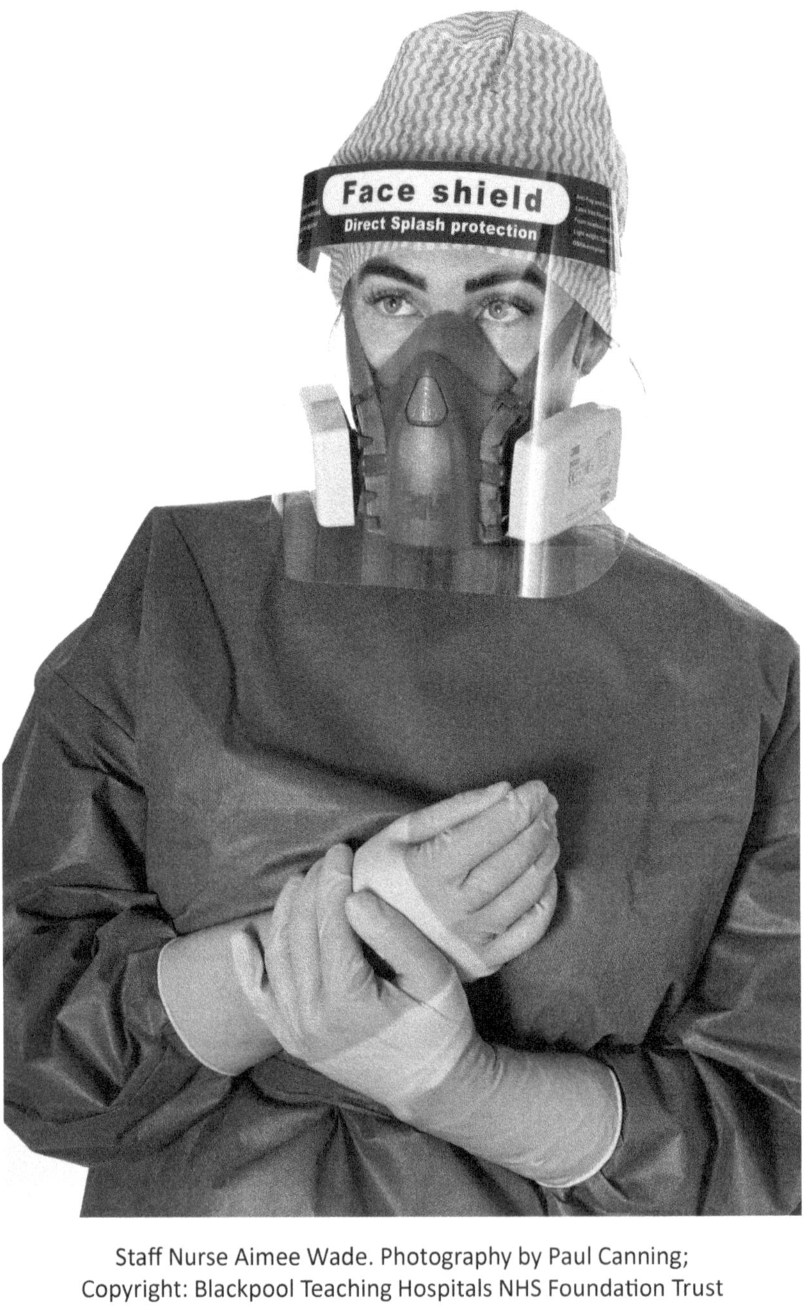

Staff Nurse Aimee Wade. Photography by Paul Canning;
Copyright: Blackpool Teaching Hospitals NHS Foundation Trust

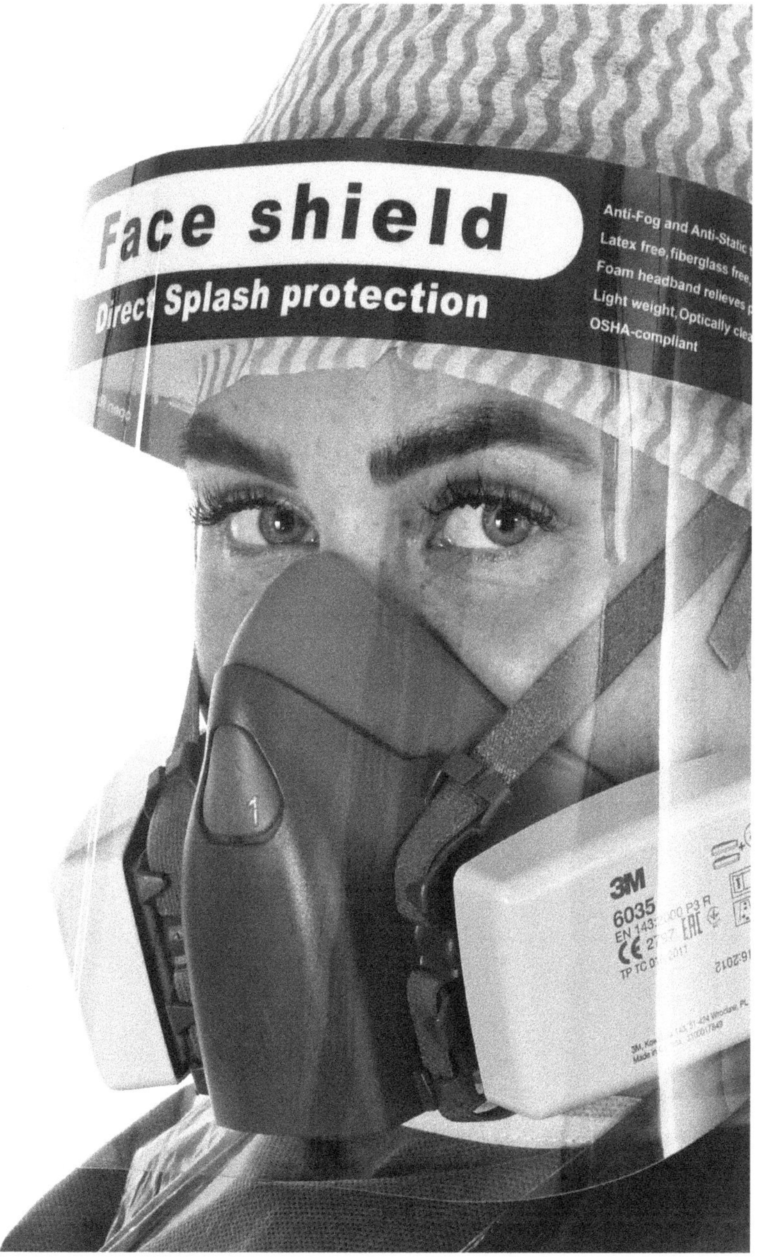

Staff Nurse Aimee Wade. Photography by Paul Canning;
Copyright: Blackpool Teaching Hospitals NHS Foundation Trust

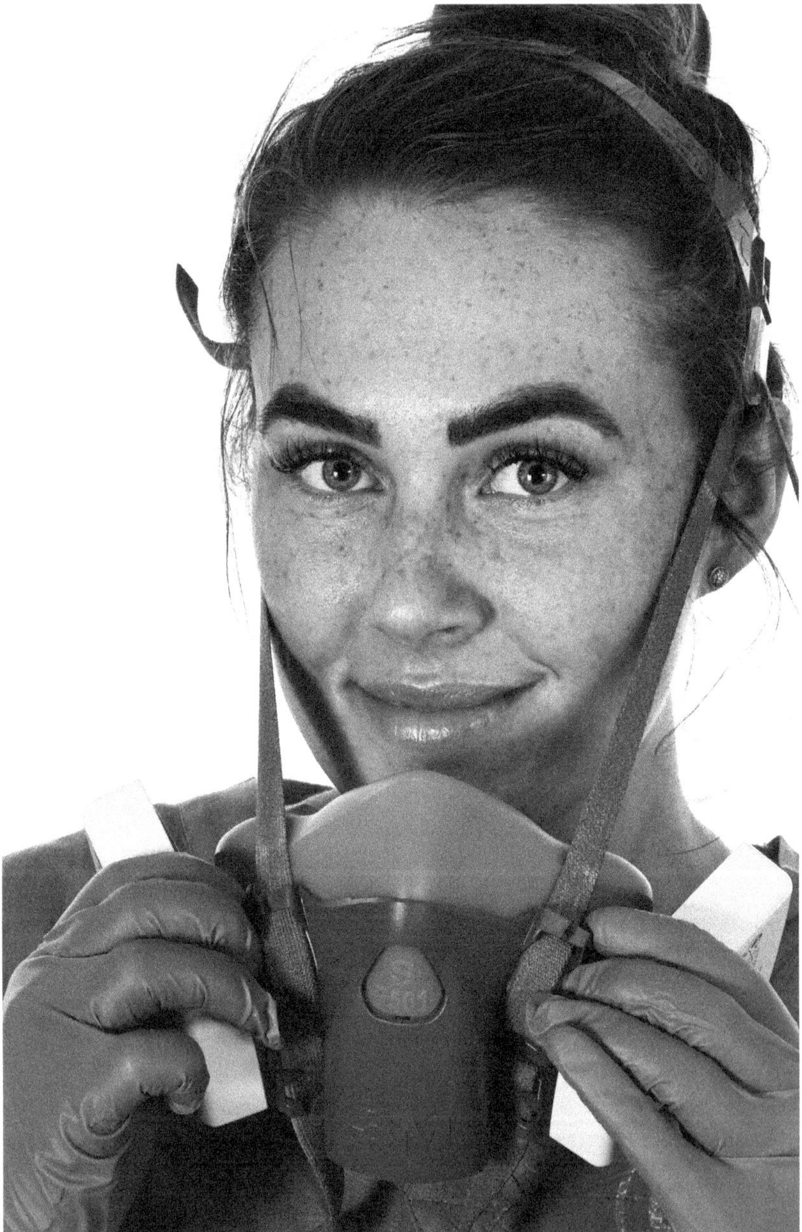

Staff Nurse Aimee Wade. Photography by Paul Canning;
Copyright: Blackpool Teaching Hospitals NHS Foundation Trust

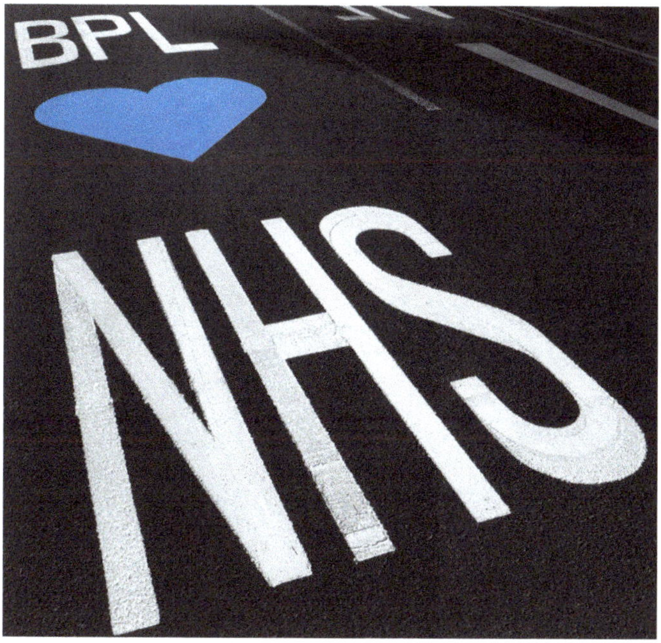

Blackpool (BPL) loves NHS road sign, located outside A&E,
Blackpool Victoria Hospital, May 2020. Photography by Paul Canning;
Copyright: Blackpool Teaching Hospitals NHS Foundation Trust

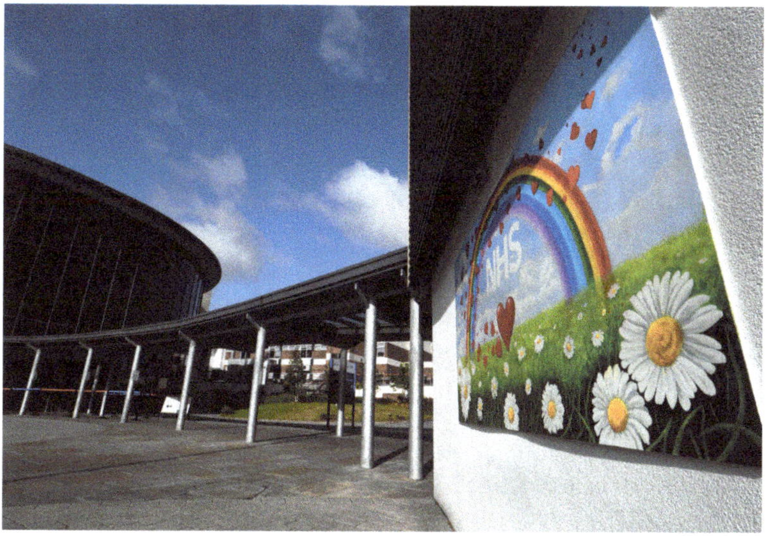

Mural and front entrance, Blackpool Victoria Hospital, May 2020.
Photography by Paul Canning; Copyright: Blackpool Teaching
Hospitals NHS Foundation Trust

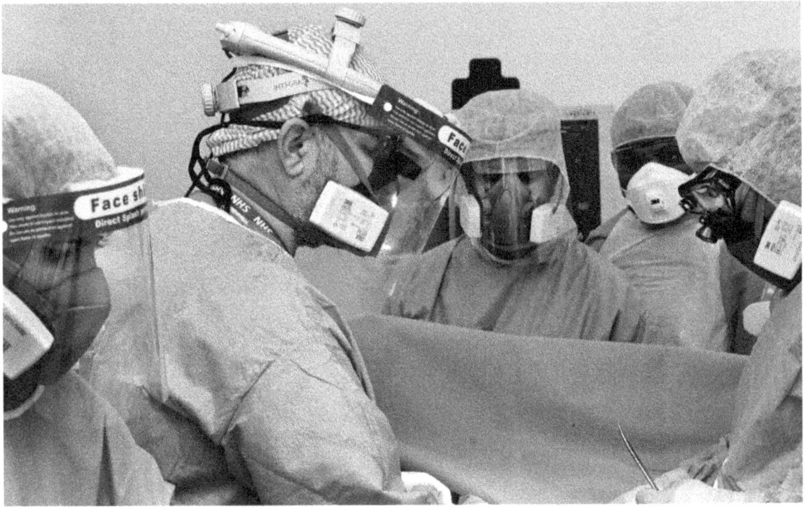

Consultant Cardiothoracic Surgeon Professor Nidal Bittar operating in temporary Cardiac Theatre, Ophthalmic Surgical Unit theatres, Blackpool Victoria Hospital, May 2020. Photography by Paul Canning; Copyright: Blackpool Teaching Hospitals NHS Foundation Trust

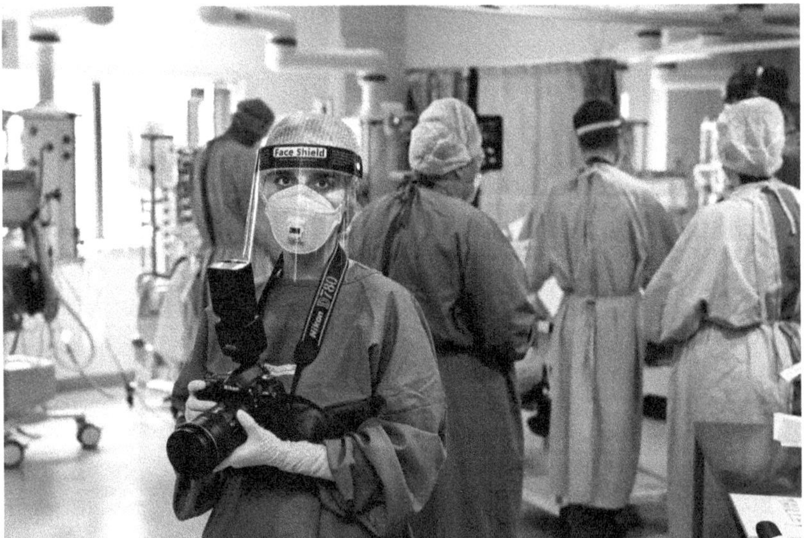

My colleague, medical photographer Chimane Moore donned in full PPE, Covid-19 Intensive Care Unit (ICU), Blackpool Victoria Hospital, June 2020. Photography by Paul Canning; Copyright: Blackpool Teaching Hospitals NHS Foundation Trust

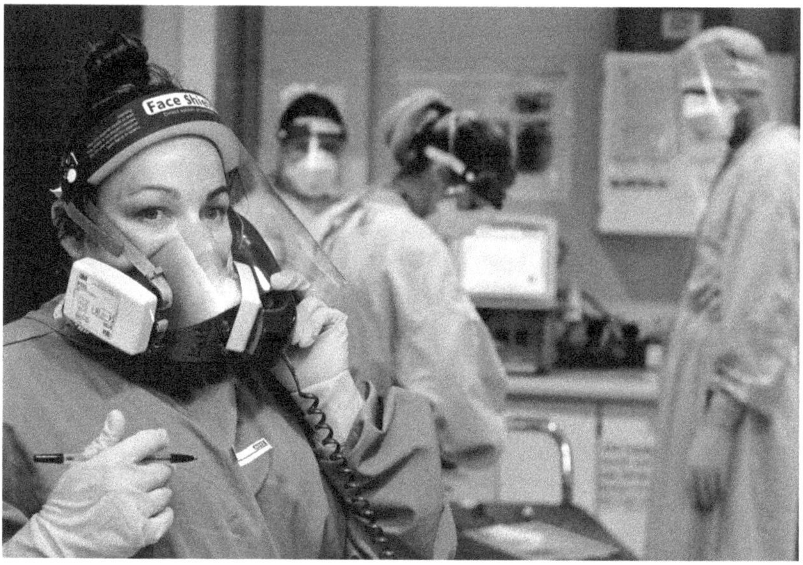

Sister Katie Clarke trying to hold a normal telephone conversation donned in full PPE, Covid-19 ICU, Blackpool Victoria Hospital, June 2020. Photography by Paul Canning; Copyright: Blackpool Teaching Hospitals NHS Foundation Trust

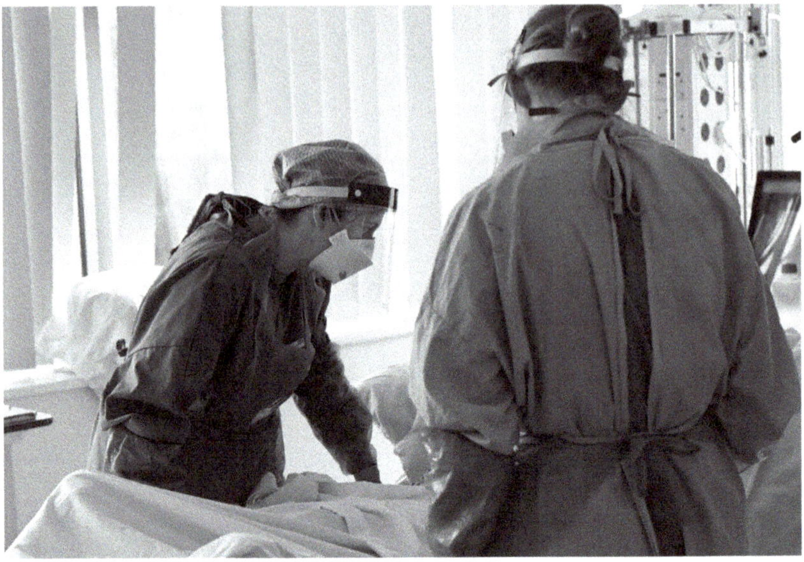

Tending to a 'barrier nursed' coronavirus patient in Covid-19 ICU, June 2020. Photography by Paul Canning; Copyright: Blackpool Teaching Hospitals NHS Foundation Trust

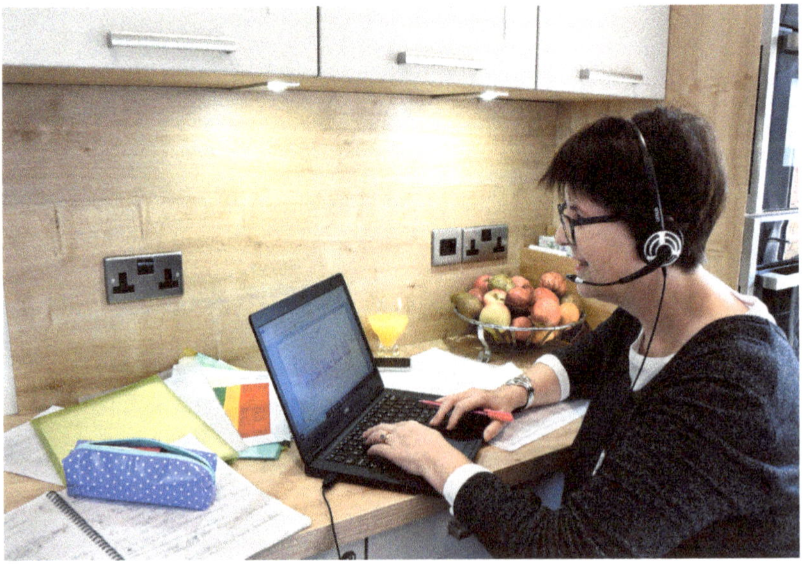

Wendy working from home in her previous role as Project Support Manager, Quality Improvement, August 2020.

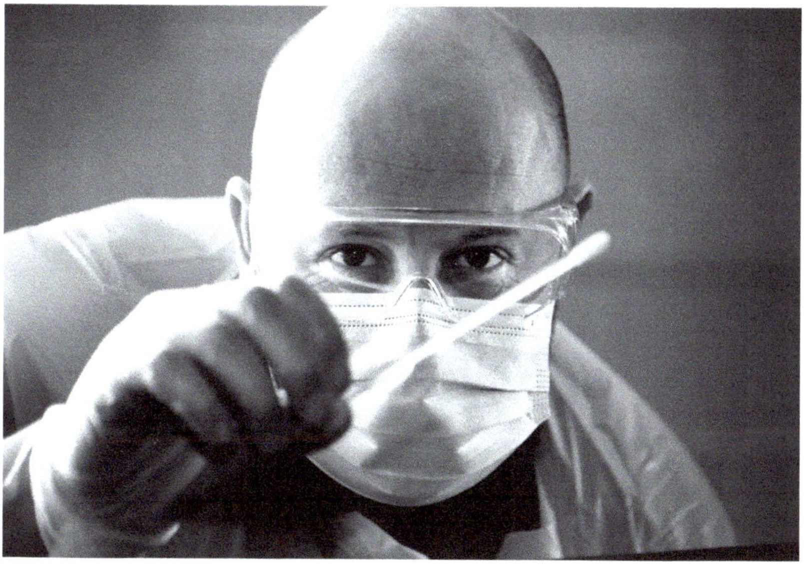

Paul Shaw helping to ensure the smooth running of Blackpool Teaching Hospitals' drive-through swab site, May 2020. Photography by Paul Canning; Copyright: Blackpool Teaching Hospitals NHS Foundation Trust

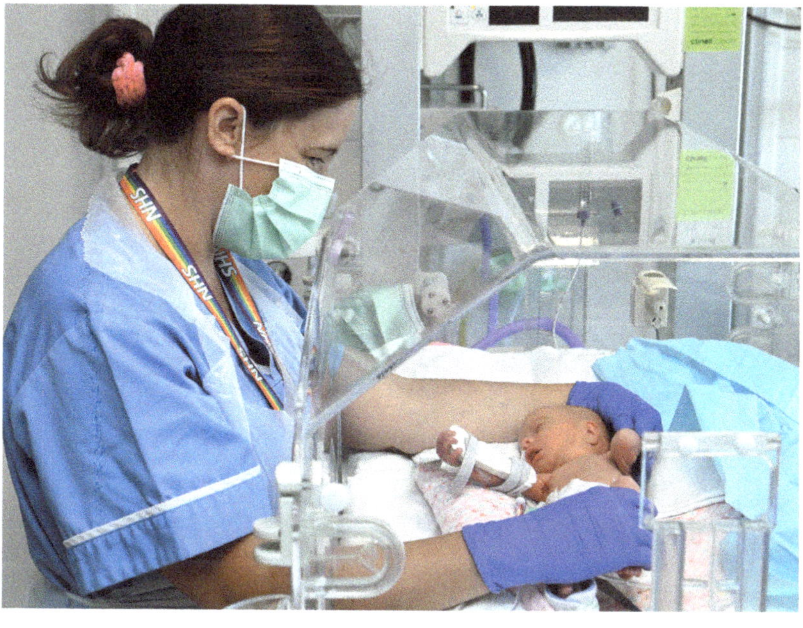

Neo Natal Unit, Blackpool Victoria Hospital, May 2020. Photography by Paul Canning; Copyright: Blackpool Teaching Hospitals NHS Foundation Trust

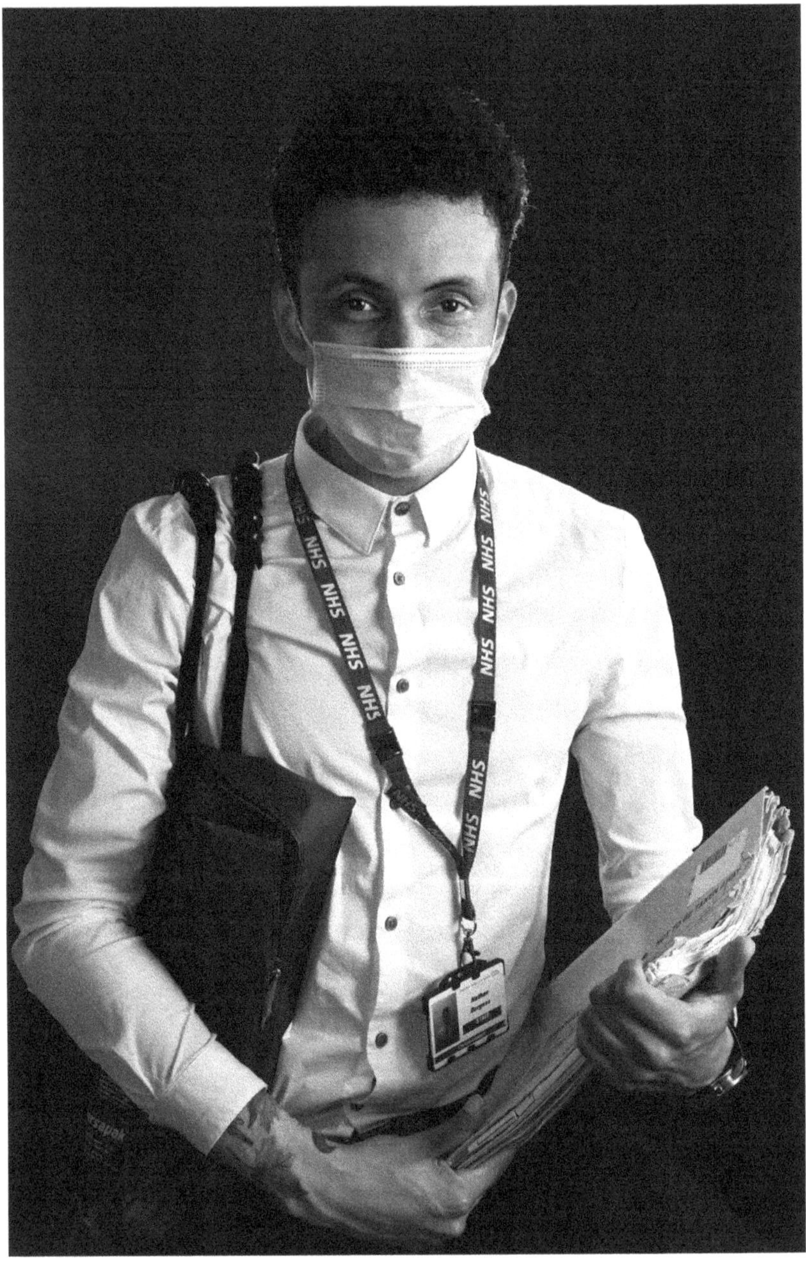

Nathan, one of Blackpool Victoria Hospital's vital administrative support personnel, July 2020. Photography by Paul Canning; Copyright: Blackpool Teaching Hospitals NHS Foundation Trust

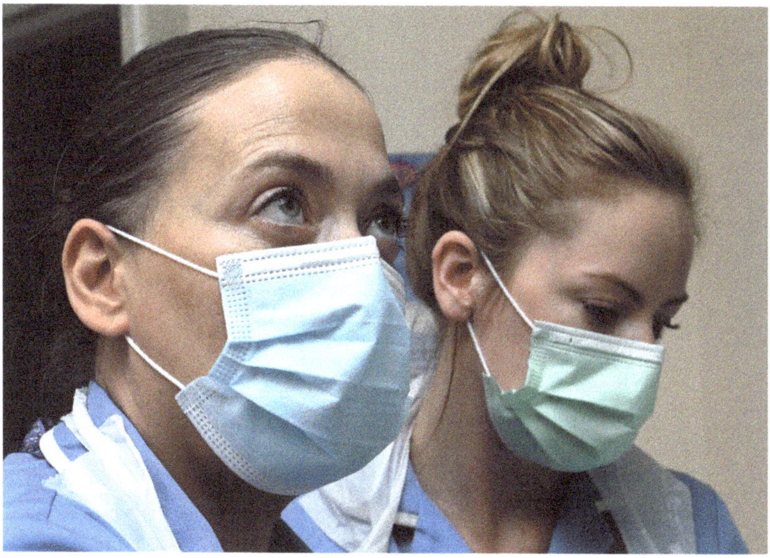

Staff Nurses administering patient medication on the ward, Blackpool Victoria Hospital, May 2020. Photography by Paul Canning; Copyright: Blackpool Teaching Hospitals NHS Foundation Trust

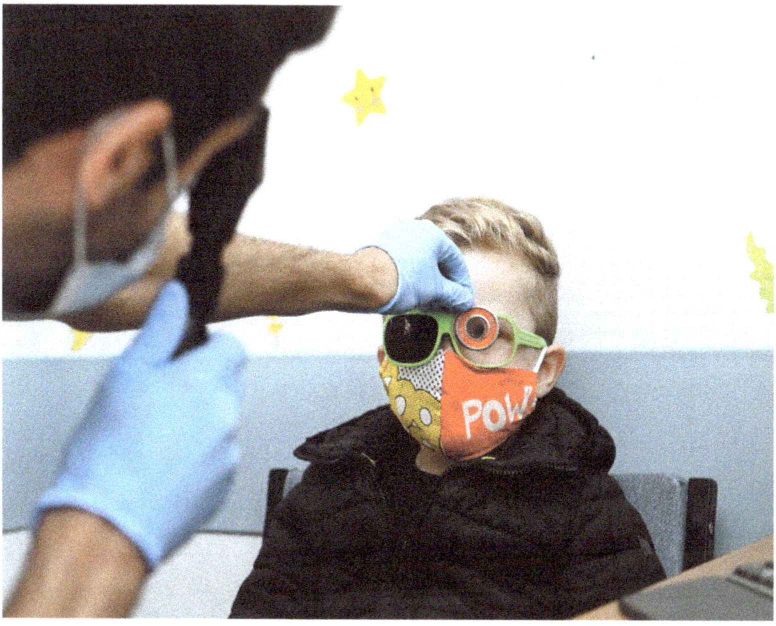

Orthoptics Children's Clinic, Blackpool Victoria Hospital, July 2020. Photography by Paul Canning; Copyright: Blackpool Teaching Hospitals NHS Foundation Trust

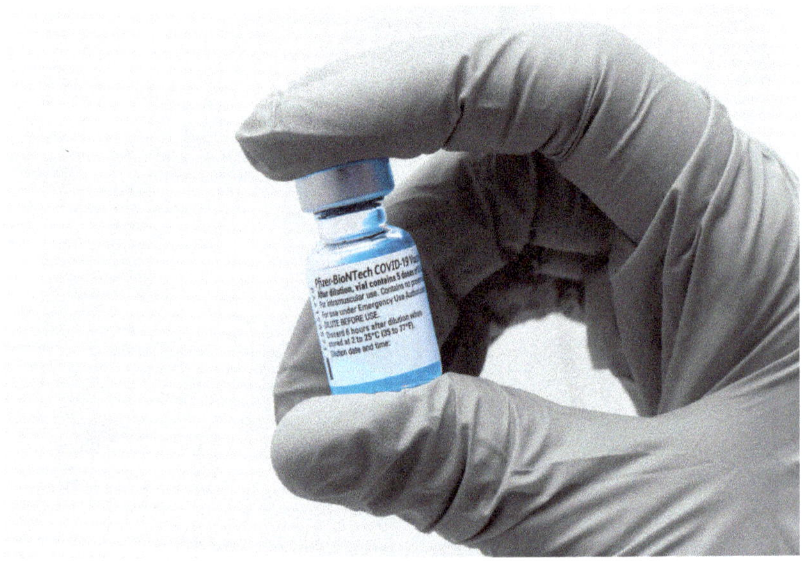

The great hope – a way out of lockdown and back to freedom? Pfizer-BioNtech's Covid-19 Vaccine. January 2021. Photography by Paul Canning; Copyright: Blackpool Teaching Hospitals NHS Foundation Trust

CHAPTER 34

Epilogue: What's Next?

Similar to the character John Woodson in the film, 'Celestine Prophecy', 2021 saw me arrive at a major crossroads once more, wondering which fork in the road fate was going to lure me.

In the words of the 35th POTUS, John Fitzgerald Kennedy, "...I find myself at what might be called the awkward age – too old to begin a new career and too young to write my memoirs", yet a life story to date is what this manuscript in the preceding chapters has unfolded to be.

I have been shaped by diverse experiences and influenced by a great many people. As a kid, I grew up in an era that was pre-home computer, pre-internet and pre-mobile, I cycled and walked everywhere and when I wasn't out gallivanting, I'd be hovering and pestering outside the bread and cake factory located at the bottom of Park Road in Poulton, waiting with my tongue hanging out for any free, misshapen, discarded confectionery tossed my way. I climbed trees, (I nicked apples from some of them), I enjoyed regular Sekiden plastic pellet gun battles with my friends and constructing all manner of vehicles out of Lego. I remember painting Airfix model aeroplane kits, racing my matchbox cars on a looped track set out in our long hallway, or pulling the cord on my action man commander, which by the way issued eight different orders depending on how far out you pulled the cord: 'This is your commander speaking' - 'Enemy in sight: range 1000' - 'Volunteer needed for a special mission' - 'Action Man patrol, fall in' - 'Enemy aircraft, action stations' - 'Mortar attack, dig in' - 'Commander to base, request support fire' - 'Hold your fire until I give the order'. I loved the water and anything boat-related and I was obsessed with exploring (trespassing on) the railway.

I listened to a wide selection of music genres that included rock, heavy metal, punk rock, pop, jazz, classical, country and western, Irish and Scottish dance music and even Gilbert and Sullivan operettas. I used my father's cassette recorder and then my 'Walkman' and like everyone else, I recorded the top 40 pop charts on a Sunday. My pop music collection knows no bounds, but my favourite bands from the last 25 years are Keane and Coldplay and from further back, Genesis, R.E.M. and Dire Straits. I have a love of traditional Irish folk and country music – the beautiful, uplifting, often haunting sounds of the accordion, fiddle and tin whistle are ingrained in my soul as much as photography.

I might have had an abusive and unhappy childhood, with life not always being a bundle of laughs, but I've also been blessed. I have had quite a few lucky breaks to temper the bad times and I've had pivotal people who've been there for me and have influenced and helped me along the way – as Melissa advised her sister Dana Scully in the 1997 Season 5, Episode 6 airing of The X Files called 'Christmas Carol':

"Life is just a path ... what's really important in life ... [is] the people you're going to meet along the way ... you don't know who you're going to meet or how your life is going to change ... or, how you're going to change the lives of others."

It has been my family above all who have and continue to believe in me wholeheartedly – my fantastic wife, Wendy and two great (now grown up) children, George and Lauren along with my two wonderful sisters Vicky and Kate and not forgetting Simon, Wendy's brother, who is simply an amazing brother-in-law and friend. I've cherished every stage of George and Lauren growing up, from their first words and steps through to the many academic successes. George using me as a climbing frame when he was a tiny fellow, the games of 'big tickle' and 'the darkness game', George's coaster-spinning as a toddler, the Beatrix Potter stories and videos which humanised the animal characters like Peter Rabbit, Jemima Puddle-Duck and Samuel Whiskers and singing along to Australian Band 'The Wiggles' many hits. I do recall on occasion driving back from Cornwall, bombing along the M5 somewhere in north Devon and singing along to Winnie the Pooh's 'Rumbly in My Tumbly' ... only to glance in the rear view mirror to see that George had fallen asleep ... probably as a result of my dulcet tones! Oh and then there was Lauren's fascination with critters – on one occasion I'd buckled her in to the car seat, was about to set off, when I got the shock of my life as I checked the rear view mirror – she was examining a huge worm, which she'd somehow smuggled into the car and had hoisted it up between forefinger and thumb, millimetres away from her face, I thought she was going to eat it. She must have only been about three at the time. There was also the famous occasion when we were about to set off from home and realised that we'd left poor Lauren fastened in her car seat, which we'd left in the middle of the lounge floor!

Also, very memorable were Lauren's numerous junior school hair styles and of course her famous, maniacal laughter, which she reproduced aged ten, amidst hilarity when she met former Blue Peter Presenter, Barney Harwood (who recorded her laugh on his mobile phone). Reports from Mrs. Hobhouse, now retired headteacher at Coombe Hill Infants School in Kingston, that a very young George would make a point of seeing Mrs. Hobhouse every morning and wishing her a very cheery, 'Good Morning', which undoubtedly made her day. The nightly thud we'd hear coming from George's room as he fell asleep, dropping the Encyclopaedia Britannica to the floor, such was his thirst and fascination for the world about him. Then there were George's consummate stage performances over the years: as Eddie in Willy Russell's 'Blood Brothers' (summer 2008); Sweeney Todd in 'Sweeney' (summer 2010) – a breath-taking delivery; Prospero in 'The Tempest' at Nuffield Theatre, Lancaster University for Shakespeare Schools festival in October 2010, which completely blew me away for his faultless delivery of so many complex lines; and as Lumiere in 'Beauty and the Beast' (Easter 2011). I remember too, the great occasion that Wendy took a call from Alfie Boe at home – she almost dropped the iron on her foot. I subsequently took George to meet Alfie backstage at Blackpool's Opera House, where he gave number one son some invaluable singing tips. George went on to have some favourite tracks recorded onto CD, which included 'Bring him home' from 'Les Mis', which Alfie Boe kindly critiqued. I have a photo somewhere of a teenage George, just a few days shy of his seventeenth birthday in December 2011 with Alfie Boe, having presented Alfie with a thank-you present – a basket of traditional sweets that included 'Fisherman's Friend' lozenges, which are of course made locally, in Fleetwood, Alfie's home town.

Then there was Lauren tearing around the house and garden on her roller skates like an American diner girl and teaching both to ride bicycles, George's lengthy, well written and very welcome blogs during his California State Uni studies and his penchant for labelling his pen drives and hard drive after the American orbiter shuttles, (Enterprise (only flown within the Earth's atmosphere), Columbia, Challenger, Discovery, Atlantis, and Endeavour). But above all it's George and Lauren's wise counsel, unconditional love and warmth and happiness that they exude that means the world to me. I was reminded of this on Midsummer's day, 21st June 2020, with the world having been through and lost so much in the coronavirus pandemic, I reflected on just how powerful the bond of family is. The day in question, as well as being the longest day, was of course Father's Day. I not only received two, great cards from George and Lauren, but an array of wonderful presents which were inscribed on cards set inside envelopes, which I had to open, every hour throughout the day. So much thought and ingenuity had been put into this, I felt humbled, but so appreciated. God forbid, if I kicked the bucket tomorrow, at least I can leave this world in the knowledge that I was fortunate enough to love and to have been loved.

With Wendy, I have walked by my childrens' side through troubles, triumphs, sickness, sadness, but mostly good and happy times, filled with fun and laughter, as Dr. Frank Reeves said in the film, 'A Matter of Life and Death', "...nothing is stronger than the law in the universe, but on Earth, nothing is stronger than love". And on the subject of love I have to confess that I agree wholeheartedly with Sir Winston Churchill's sentiment, "My most brilliant achievement was my ability to be able to persuade my wife to marry me!"

Well – I don't feel quite like Frodo Baggins about to leave Middle-Earth on a ship bound for the Undying Lands, but I do feel it's nearing the end of one monumental chapter. Whatever I do, it would perhaps be wise as Kennedy once said to, "... use time as a tool, not as a couch". I entered this world with people still reeling from the aftermath of the Cuban missile crisis and today the world is still a volatile place. JFK also once said, "The supreme reality of our time is the vulnerability of this planet". Collectively there are huge issues to tackle, not least our carbon footprint and climate change.

It's pretty obvious that I didn't get on at all with my father – I've kind of given that strong impression, right? There are many awful events that have taken place connected to him over the years. Some I've deliberately 'forgotten' because I've tried so hard to bury them and some I have purposely omitted from these pages out of respect for those involved. Suffice to say that if some of his 'shenanigans' had been made known to the police at the time, I am under no illusion that my father would have been imprisoned years ago – and for a very long time. With the hindsight of an adult mind I can see that when my father suddenly started cycling to work in the late '70s, this was unlikely to be born out of a desire to keep fit as he claimed and more likely as a result of him probably having been disqualified for drink driving. Likewise, I can't help but wonder if our sudden move from London to Lancashire back in 1969 was perhaps due to some wrongdoing of his, where he was removed from office to a far flung place on the Fylde Coast, and then not quite at the tail end of his career, suddenly announcing his retirement...these events all have hidden meanings I'm sure.

From that fateful, God awful day when my dad crossed a line destined never to return, when he called me a useless shit, and when it dawned on me with absolute jaw-dropping clarity that he cared not one iota for me, huge chunks of my life...correction...my entire life has been, "a perennial effort to prove myself worthy... [since] that distant morning", to take from Jon Meacham's eulogy of the gentleman statesman, the late POTUS George HW Bush. My father's inappropriate behaviour went way beyond unacceptable and many suffered greatly (and are still suffering) because of it. Although I was initially dealt a shitty hand of cards, as I have shown, I also count myself fortunate to have been blessed along the way. As a photographer I always like to keep things in focus and if ever I veer off point and allow myself to get just a tiny bit down, letting my mind wander back to such negative events as one of Dad's many unwelcome diatribes, I remind myself of some favourite lines that I heard on a 1980 episode of 'The Professionals' entitled, 'Discovered in a Graveyard' - excerpts from 'Desiderata' by Max Ehrmann:

"Go placidly amid the noise and the haste and remember what peace there may be in silence. .... do not distress yourself with dark imaginings. Many fears are born of fatigue and loneliness. ...be gentle with yourself. You are a child of the universe no less than the trees and the stars; you have a right to be here. ...be at peace with God, whatever you conceive Him to be. And whatever your labors and aspirations, in the noisy confusion of life, keep peace in your soul. With all its sham, drudgery and broken dreams, it is still a beautiful world..."

Never mind "winter is coming", winter / early 2021 is upon us. 2020 has been a very bumpy year indeed and the world has suffered greatly, not least with the Covid-19 coronavirus pandemic, which is still a dominant, worrying and annoying part of our lives in the form of a third wave of the contagion - a fast-transmitting, variant strain. George is in a flat share locally and because of Covid, Lauren's BA three year television production degree at Leeds Trinity Uni moved its lectures and tutoring on line, so for the remainder of this first year (all three semesters), Lauren studied at home. 2020 will certainly be a year to remember as it has been full of changes – and as I've intimated, I feel that change is still very much in the air.

So - whoever you are, wherever you are, whoever you're with and whatever you're doing - be happy, smile, laugh lots, be kind to people (#bekind) and remember as Ben Fogle said when he stood on top of the world in the summer of 2018, "... go and climb your Everest". A sound, thought-provoking piece of advice indeed, which has got me thinking about the question, 'What's next?'

Two final, prophetic quotes to leave you with:

"Those who have a good heart usually help too much, trust too much, give too much, love too much and sadly always seem to hurt the most...if you're one of those people, never stop being you."

And for someone like me, whose confidence was torn to shreds and nearly destroyed, who was terrified of public speaking but yet, who rallied and overcame so much to win through – this one by Joseph Campbell particularly resonates:

"The very cave you are afraid to enter, turns out to be the very source of what you are looking for".

Thank you, MP, Central Two Zero Seven Nine, Out.

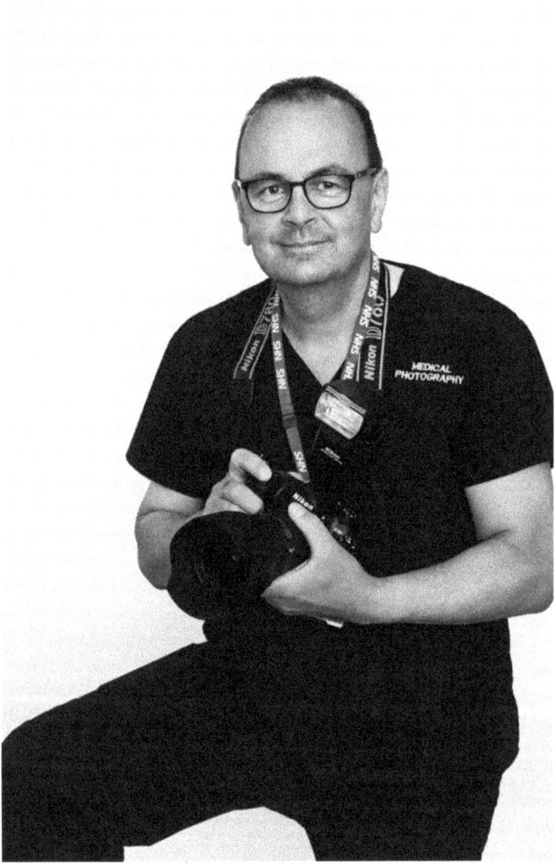

Me in my day to day medical photography scrubs, photographed by my colleague Chimane Moore, September 2020.

Paul Canning – About

Paul Canning was born in Croydon in 1963 and educated in Blackpool and Greenwich and Staffordshire Universities. He grew up in a pre-internet and mobile phone era, handwriting many letters to secure him his first job as a South-East London-based wedding and portrait photographer during early summer 1986.

He then travelled half way around the world as a cruise ship photographer before landing his dream job in 1990 as a crime scene forensic photographer with the Metropolitan Police Service (MPS) in London. Paul then qualified as an instructor and was later promoted to Forensic Training and Development Manager and Head of Photography Training. In late Summer 2004 Paul and his young family left London for a less hectic life in Lancashire.

In 2011 Paul qualified as a medical photographer, having first worked for a Manchester-based biopharmaceutical company. He then took up a post with Blackpool Teaching Hospitals NHS Foundation Trust in 2013, where he is currently a senior medical photographer.

In his spare time, through his strong affiliation with Gardiner Associates Training and Research (GATR), Paul is the lead on photography training, instructing the UK's fire investigators in forensic fire scene photography.

Paul has been married to Wendy since 1992 and they have two grown up children, George and Lauren. They live in Preesall, Poulton-le-Fylde on Lancashire's beautiful Fylde Coast.

www.ingramcontent.com/pod-product-compliance
Ingram Content Group UK Ltd.
Pitfield, Milton Keynes, MK11 3LW, UK
UKHW051458260225
4770UKWH00005B/12

9 781839 755071